PAGE 40 ON THE ROAD

and insider tips

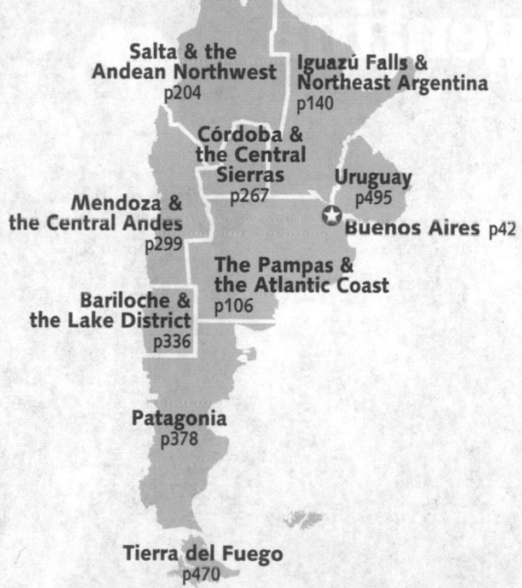

PAGE 587 SURVIVAL GUIDE

VITAL PRACTICAL INFORMATION TO HELP YOU HAVE A SMOOTH TRIP

THIS EDITION WRITTEN AND RESEARCHED BY

Sandra Bao,

Gregor Clark, Carolyn McCarthy,

Andy Symington, Lucas Vidgen

welcome to Argentina

City Life

Just wait till you get here. Arriving in Buenos Aires is like jumping aboard a moving train. Outside the taxi window, a blurred mosaic of drab apartment blocks and haphazard architecture whizzes by as you shoot along the freeway toward the center of the city. The driver – probably driving *way* too fast while chain-smoking and talking incessantly about government corruption – finally merges off the freeway. Then the street life appears – the cafes, the purple jacaranda flowers draped over the sidewalks and *porteños* (residents of Buenos Aires) in stylish clothing walking purposefully past the newspaper stands, candy kiosks and handsome early-20th-century stone facades. And it's not just BA that's a stunner – Córdoba, Mendoza and Bariloche each have their unique personalities and attractions, and are all worthy of your visit.

Natural Wonders

While Argentina's big cities have a lot of urban pleasures to offer, their real purpose is to springboard travelers into the country's greatest attraction: the natural world. From mighty Iguazú Falls in the subtropical north to the thunderous, crackling advance of the Perito Moreno Glacier in the south, Argentina is a vast natural wonderland. The country boasts some of the Andes' highest peaks, several of which top 6000m near Mendoza and San Juan. It's home to rich wetlands

Start free associating on the word 'Argentina,' and it's quickly apparent why the country has long held travelers in awe: tango, beef, gauchos, fútbol, Patagonia, the Andes. The classics alone make a formidable wanderlust cocktail.

(left) Día de la Tradición (p113), San Antonio de Areco
(below) Caminito (p55), La Boca

that rival Brazil's famous Pantanal, mountains painted in rustic colors, deserts dotted with cacti, massive ice fields and arid steppes in Patagonia, cool lichen-clad Valdivian forests, glacial lakes, Andean salt flats, a spectacular Lake District, penguins, flamingos, caimans, capybaras and more. All unforgettable sights and adventures waiting for you to experience and be amazed by – and you will be, bet on that!

Argentine Culture

Tango is possibly Argentina's greatest contribution to the outside world, a steamy dance that's been described as 'making love in the vertical position.' In Buenos Aires especially, you'll find endless venues for perfecting your tango moves, from dance salons to *milongas* (dance events) to atmospheric cafes. Satisfying that carnal craving for juicy steaks isn't hard to do in the land that has perfected grilling those wonderfully flavorful sides of beef. *Parrillas* (steak houses) are on practically every corner and will offer up any cut you can imagine. Add an exhilarating passion for *fútbol* – Argentines are truly devoted to this sport and experiencing a live match should be on your itinerary – and you have a rich edgy culture, part Latin American and part European, that you can't help but fall in love with.

Argentina & Uruguay

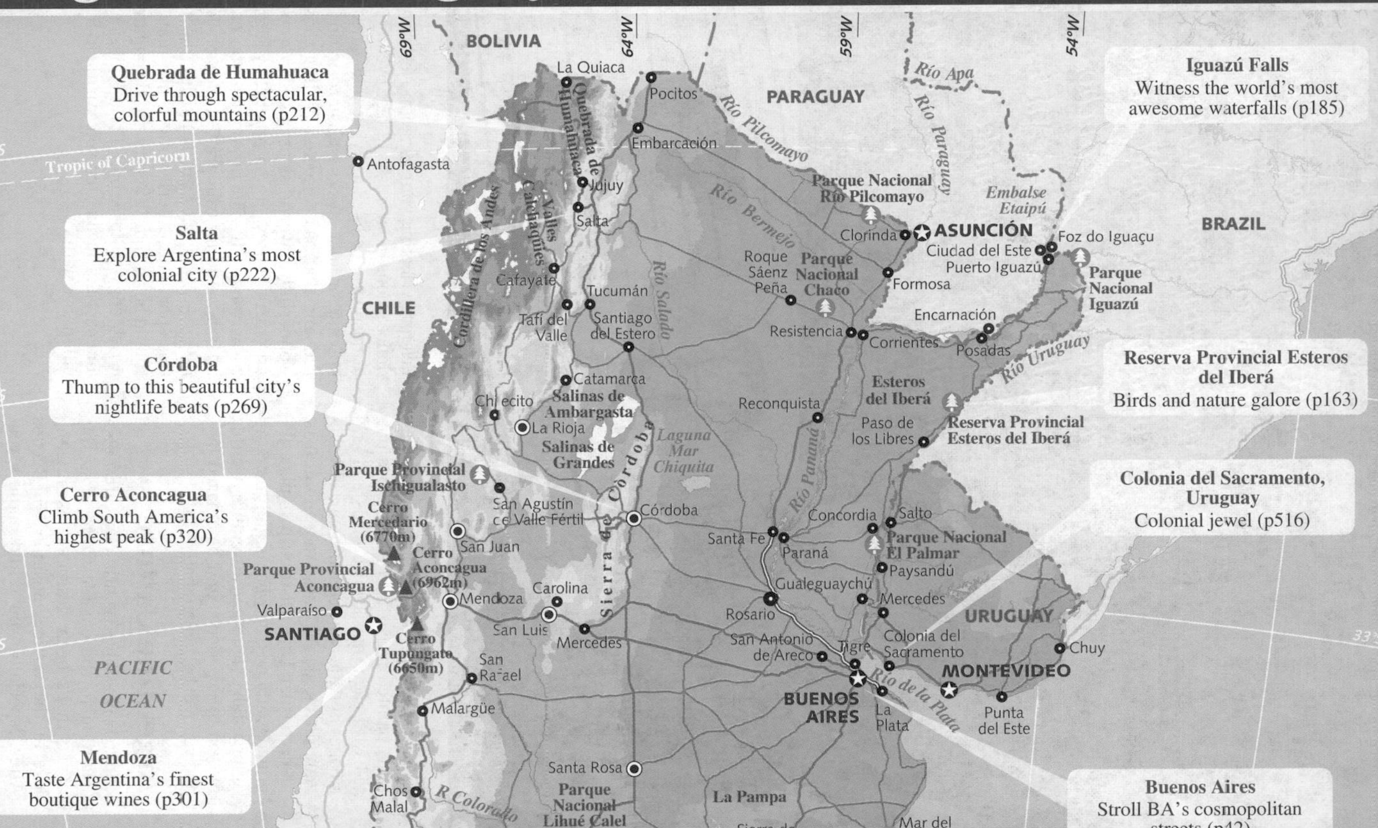
Quebrada de Humahuaca
Drive through spectacular, colorful mountains (p212)
Salta
Explore Argentina's most colonial city (p222)
Córdoba
Thump to this beautiful city's nightlife beats (p269)
Cerro Aconcagua
Climb South America's highest peak (p320)
Mendoza
Taste Argentina's finest boutique wines (p301)
Iguazú Falls
Witness the world's most awesome waterfalls (p185)
Reserva Provincial Esteros del Iberá
Birds and nature galore (p163)
Colonia del Sacramento, Uruguay
Colonial jewel (p516)
Buenos Aires
Stroll BA's cosmopolitan
69°W
64°W
59°W
54°W
23°S
28°S
33°S
Tropic of Capricorn
BOLIVIA
PARAGUAY
BRAZIL
CHILE
URUGUAY
PACIFIC
OCEAN
ASUNCIÓN
SANTIAGO
BUENOS AIRES
MONTEVIDEO
La Quiaca
Pocitos
Embarcación
Antofagasta
Jujuy
Salta
Cafayate
Tucumán
Tafí del Valle
Santiago del Estero
Catamarca
Chilecito
La Rioja
Salinas de Ambargasta
Salinas de Grandes
Laguna Mar Chiquita
Sierra de Córdoba
Parque Provincial Ischigualasto
San Agustín de Valle Fértil
Cerro Mercedario (6770m)
Cerro Aconcagua (6962m)
Parque Provincial Aconcagua
Cerro Tupungato (6650m)
San Juan
Mendoza
Carolina
San Luis
Mercedes
Valparaíso
San Rafael
Malargüe
Chos Malal
R Colorado
Santa Rosa
Parque Nacional Lihué Calel
La Pampa
Río Pilcomayo
Río Bermejo
Río Salado
Río Paraguay
Río Apa
Parque Nacional Río Pilcomayo
Clorinda
Formosa
Roque Sáenz Peña
Parque Nacional Chaco
Resistencia
Corrientes
Reconquista
Río Paraná
Esteros del Iberá
Paso de los Libres
Reserva Provincial Esteros del Iberá
Embalse Etaipú
Ciudad del Este
Foz do Iguaçu
Puerto Iguazú
Parque Nacional Iguazú
Encarnación
Posadas
Río Uruguay
Concordia
Salto
Parque Nacional El Palmar
Paysandú
Santa Fe
Paraná
Gualeguaychú
Mercedes
Rosario
San Antonio de Areco
Tigre
Colonia del Sacramento
Río de la Plata
La Plata
Chuy
Punta del Este
Mar del

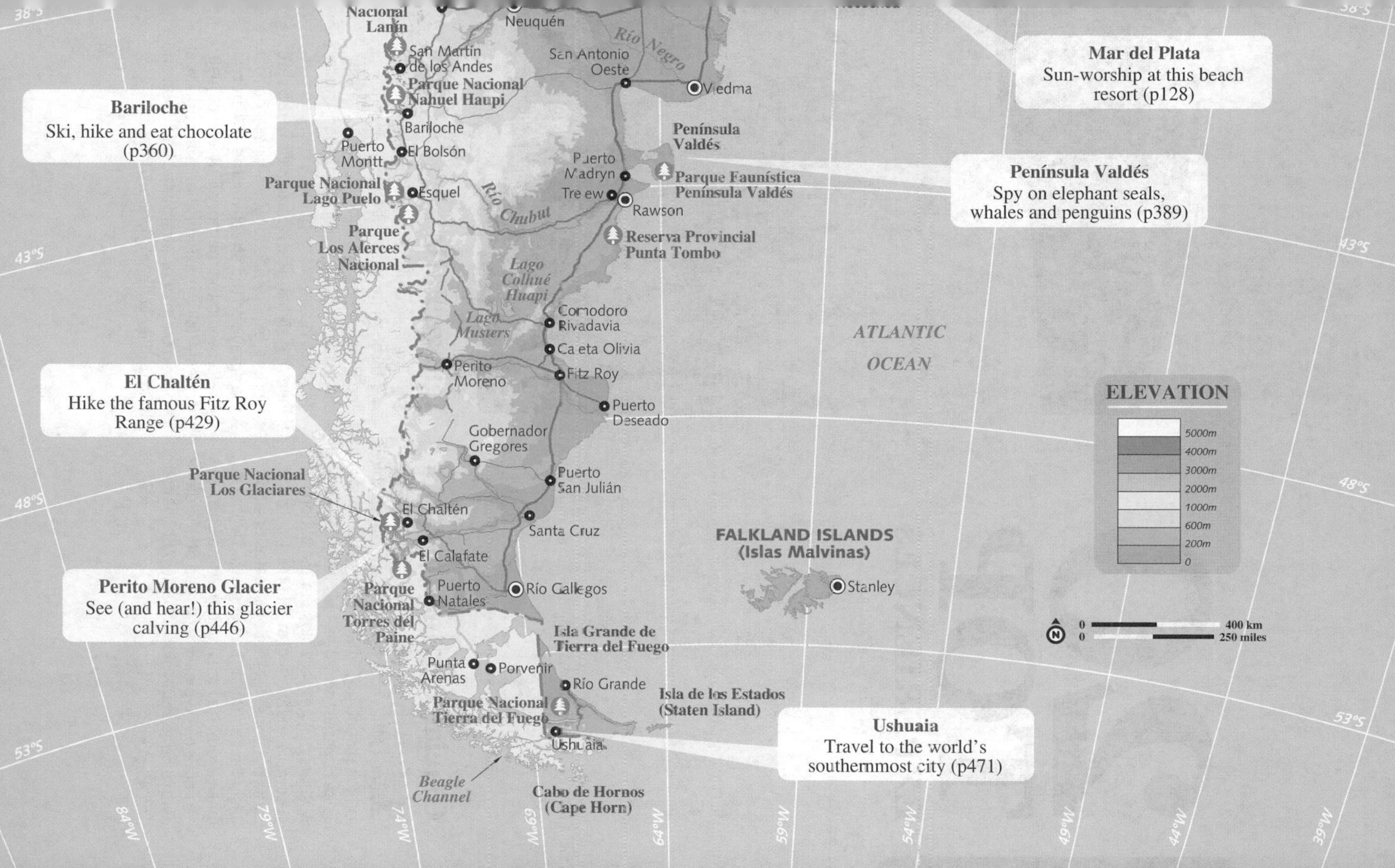

Bariloche
Ski, hike and eat chocolate (p360)
Mar del Plata
Sun-worship at this beach resort (p128)
Península Valdés
Spy on elephant seals, whales and penguins (p389)
El Chaltén
Hike the famous Fitz Roy Range (p429)
Perito Moreno Glacier
See (and hear!) this glacier calving (p446)
Ushuaia
Travel to the world's southernmost city (p471)
Parque Nacional Lanín
Neuquén
San Martín de los Andes
Parque Nacional Nahuel Haupi
Bariloche
Puerto Montt
El Bolsón
Parque Nacional Lago Puelo
Esquel
Parque Los Alerces Nacional
San Antonio Oeste
Río Negro
Viedma
Península Valdés
Puerto Madryn
Trelew
Rawson
Parque Faunística Península Valdés
Reserva Provincial Punta Tombo
Río Chubut
Lago Colhué Huapi
Lago Musters
Comodoro Rivadavia
Caleta Olivia
Fitz Roy
Perito Moreno
Puerto Deseado
Gobernador Gregores
Puerto San Julián
Parque Nacional Los Glaciares
El Chaltén
Santa Cruz
El Calafate
Parque Nacional Torres del Paine
Puerto Natales
Río Gallegos
Isla Grande de Tierra del Fuego
Punta Arenas
Porvenir
Río Grande
Parque Nacional Tierra del Fuego
Isla de los Estados (Staten Island)
Ushuaia
Beagle Channel
Cabo de Hornos (Cape Horn)
ATLANTIC OCEAN
FALKLAND ISLANDS (Islas Malvinas)
Stanley
ELEVATION
5000m
4000m
3000m
2000m
1000m
600m
200m
0
0 400 km
0 250 miles
38°S
43°S
48°S
53°S
84°W
79°W
74°W
69°W
64°W
59°W
54°W
49°W
44°W
39°W

20 TOP EXPERIENCES

Glaciar Perito Moreno

1 As glaciers go, Perito Moreno (p448) is one of the most dynamic and accessible on the planet, but what makes it exceptional is its constant advance – up to 2m per day. Visitors can get very close to the action via a complex network of steel boardwalks. Its slow but constant motion creates an audio-visual sensation as building-sized icebergs calve from the face and crash into Lago Argentino. A typical way to cap off the day is with a huge steak dinner back in El Calafate.

Iguazú Falls

2 The peaceful Iguazú river, flowing through the jungle between Argentina and Brazil, plunges suddenly over a basalt cliff in a spectacular display of sound and fury that is one of the planet's most awe-inspiring sights. The Iguazú Falls (p185) are a primal experience for the senses: the roar, the spray and the sheer volume of water live forever in the memory. But it's not just the waterfalls; the jungly national parks that contain them offer a romantic backdrop and fine wildlife-watching opportunities.

1

Quebrada de Humahuaca

3 You're a long way from Buenos Aires up here in Argentina's northwestern corner (p212), and it feels a whole world away. This spectacular valley of scoured rock in Jujuy province impresses visually with its tortured formations and artist's palette of mineral colors, but is also of great cultural interest. The Quebrada's settlements are traditional and indigenous in character, with typical Andean dishes supplanting steaks on the restaurant menus, and llamas, not herds of cattle, grazing the sparse highland grass.

Cementerio de la Recoleta

4 A veritable city of the dead, Buenos Aires' top tourist attraction (p59) is not to be missed. Lined up along small 'streets' are hundreds of old crypts, each uniquely carved from marble, granite and concrete, and decorated with stained glass, stone angels and religious icons. Small plants and trees grow in fissures while feral cats slink between tombs, some of which lie in various stages of decay. It's a photogenic wonderland, and if there's strange beauty in death you'll find it in spades here.

3

HEMIS/ALAMY ©

4

5

GARETH MCCORMACK / LONELY PLANET IMAGES ©

6

EDUARDO LONGONI/CORBIS ©

Hiking the Fitz Roy Range

5 With rugged wilderness and shark-tooth summits, the Fitz Roy Range (p434) is the trekking capital of Argentina. Climbers may suffer on its windswept, world-class routes, but hiking trails are surprisingly easy and accessible. Park rangers help orient every traveler who comes into El Chaltén. Once on the trail, the most stunning views are just a day hike from town. Not bad for those who want to reward their sweat equity with a craft beer at the brewery.

Wine Tasting Around Mendoza

6 With so much fantastic wine on offer, it's tempting just to pull up a bar stool and work your way through it, but getting out there and seeing how the grapes are grown and processed is almost as enjoyable as sampling the finished product. The best news is that wine tasting in Argentina isn't just for wine snobs – there's a tour to meet every budget (p306), from DIY bike tours for backpackers to tasting-and-accommodation packages at exclusive wineries.

DANITA DELIMONT/GETTY IMAGES ©

Gaucho Culture

7 One of Argentina's most-enduring icons is the intrepid gaucho, whose tradition began when Spaniards let loose their cattle on the grassy pampas so many centuries ago. These nomadic cowboys lived by breaking in horses (also left by the Spaniards), hunting cows and drinking *mate*. Today the best place to experience gaucho culture is during November's Día de la Tradición (p23) in San Antonio de Areco. Otherwise check out folkloric shows at *estancias* (ranches) or at the Feria de Mataderos (p98) in Buenos Aires. Gaucho, San Antonio de Areco (p113)

Ruta de los Siete Lagos

8 A journey of extraordinary beauty, the Seven Lakes Route is a don't-miss road trip. The road winds through lush forests, past waterfalls and dramatic moutain scenery and skirts the various crystal-blue lakes that give it its name. You can bus it in a couple of hours, but taking your time – either in a rental car or on a bike – is a decision you won't regret. Lago Falkner

Nightlife in Córdoba

9 Boasting seven universities (and counting), it's no surprise that Argentina's second city (p269) is one of the best places for night owls in the entire country. The wide variety of cute sidewalk bars, thumping mega-discos and live music venues (all more or less within walking distance) could keep you occupied for months. While you're in town, try to catch a *cuarteto* show – popular all over the country, the style was invented in Córdoba and all the best acts regularly play here.

Ushuaia

10 Location, location, location. Shimmed between the Beagle Channel and the snow-capped Martial Range, this bustling port (p471) is the final scrap of civilization seen by Antarctica-bound boats. But more than the end of the earth, Ushuaia is a crossroads for big commerce and adventure. Snow sports brighten the frozen winters and long summer days mean hiking and biking until the wee hours. Happening restaurants, the boisterous bars and welcoming B&Bs mean you'll want to tuck in and call this port home for a few days.

Colonia del Sacramento

11 Uruguay's historic window on the Río de la Plata, this photogenic 17th-century town (p516) was contested by the Spanish and Portuguese for nearly 100 years. Traces of the tumultuous past are everywhere, from the competing Spanish and Portuguese drainage patterns of Colonia's cobblestone streets to the small cluster of historical museums ringing its colonial plazas. Directly across the river from Buenos Aires, Colonia is Uruguay's only Unesco World Heritage site and a popular weekend destination, thanks to atmospheric restaurants and river views at sunset.

10

MICHAEL S. NOLAN/ROBERT HARDING SPECIALIST STOCK/CORBIS ©

11

ASUNCION MORENO

Skiing at Las Leñas

12 Hitting the slopes at Las Leñas (p326) isn't just about making the scene – although there is that. This mountain has the most varied terrain, the most days of powder per year and some of the fastest and most modern lift equipment in the country. Splash out for some on-mountain accommodation or choose from a variety of more reasonably priced options just down the road, but whatever you do, if you're a snow bunny and you're here in season, mark this one on your itinerary in big red letters.

Colonial Salta

13 Argentina's northwest holds its most venerable colonial settlements, and none is more lovely than Salta (p222), set in a fertile valley but a gateway to the impressive Andean cordillera not far beyond. Postcard-pretty churches, a sociable plaza and a wealth of noble buildings give it a laid-back historic ambience that endears it to all who visit. Add in great museums, a lively folkloric music scene, some of the country's most appealing lodging options and a fistful of attractions within easy reach in the province: that's one impressive place. Iglesia San Francisco (p226)

12

13

TRAVELSTOCK44 / ALAMY ©

ANDREW PEACOCK/LONELY PLANET IMAGES ©

TOM BOYDEN/LONELY PLANET IMAGES ©

San Telmo

14 One of Buenos Aires' most charming and interesting neighborhoods is San Telmo (p54), lined with cobblestone streets, colonial buildings and a classic atmosphere that will transport you back to the mid-19th century. Be sure to take in the Sunday *feria* (street fair), where dozens of booths sell antiques and knickknacks, while buskers perform for loose change. Tango is big here, and you can watch a fancy, spectacular show or catch a casual street performance – both will wow you with amazing feats of athleticism. Market, Plaza Dorrego (p54)

Bariloche

15 A gorgeous lakeside setting, adjacent to one of the country's more spectacular and accessible national parks, makes Bariloche (p360) a winning destination year-round. During winter you can strap on the skis and take in the magnificent panoramas from on top of Cerro Catedral. Once the snow melts, get your hiking boots out and hit the trails in the Parque Nacional Nahuel Huapi where a well-organized network of mountain refuges means you can keep walking as long as your legs will take it. Parque Nacional Nahuel Huapi (p368)

Península Valdés

16 Once a tawny, dusty peninsula with remote sheep ranches, today Península Valdés (p389) is a hub for some of the best wildlife watching on the continent. The main attraction is seeing endangered southern right whales get acrobatic and up-close; whale-watching tours actually attract these huge mammals. But the cast of wild characters also includes killer whales, Magellanic penguins, sea lions, elephant seals, rheas, guanaco and numerous sea birds. There's a ton to be seen on shore walks, but diving and kayak tours take you even deeper into the ambience. Southern elephant seal

GM PHOTO IMAGES/ALAMY ©

Jesuit Estancias

17 The Jesuits brought some fine things to Argentina – wine making and universities to name just two. They also constructed some gorgeous *estancias* (ranches). Many are wonderfully preserved, listed as Unesco World Heritage sites and open to the public, often featuring fascinating museums. The crowds can't detract from the palpable sense of history in Alta Gracia (p286), but if you'd like to have one to yourself (and maybe even sleep in the old slave quarters), head for Santa Catalina (p287). San Ignacio Miní (p179)

Los Esteros del Iberá

18 These protected wetlands (p163) offer astonishing wildlife-watching opportunities around shallow vegetation-rich lagoons. Head out in a boat and you'll spot numerous alligators, exotic bird species, monkeys, swamp deer, and possibly the world's cutest rodent, the capybara – but no you can't take one home. It's an out-of-the-way location, and a wealth of stylish, comfortable lodges make this a top spot to book yourself in for a few days of relaxation amid an abundance of flora and fauna. Laguna Iberá (p166)

Aconcagua

19 The tallest peak in the western hemisphere (p320) is an awe-inspiring sight, even if you're not planning on climbing it. People come from all over the world to do so, though – it's not a task to be taken lightly, but if you can take the time to train and acclimatize and you're good enough to reach the top, you'll be granted with bragging rights as one of a select group who have touched the 'roof of the Americas.'

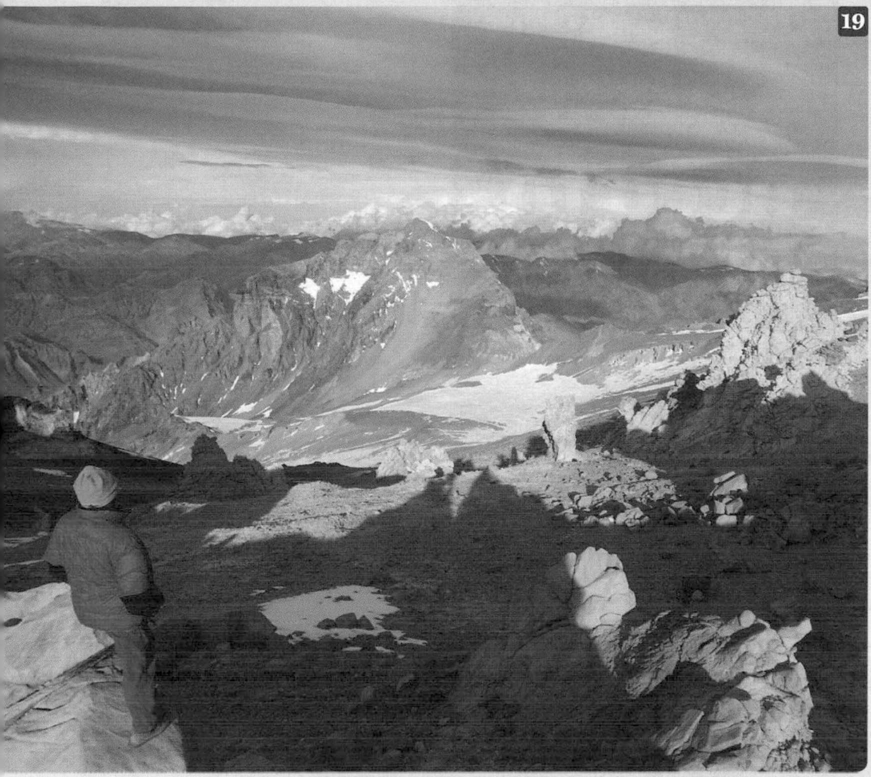

19

Mar del Plata

20 Argentina's premier beach resort (p128) is a heaving zoo in summer – but that's what makes it such fun. Compete with *porteños* (Buenos Aires residents) for a patch of open sand, then lay back and enjoy watching thousands of near-naked bodies worship the sun, play sand games or splash around in the surf. Outdoor activities such as surfing, fishing, horseback riding and even skydiving are also on offer. When the sun goes down it's time for steak or seafood dinners, followed by late-night entertainment from theater shows and nightclubs.

need to know

Currency
» Argentine peso (AR$)

Language
» Spanish

When to Go

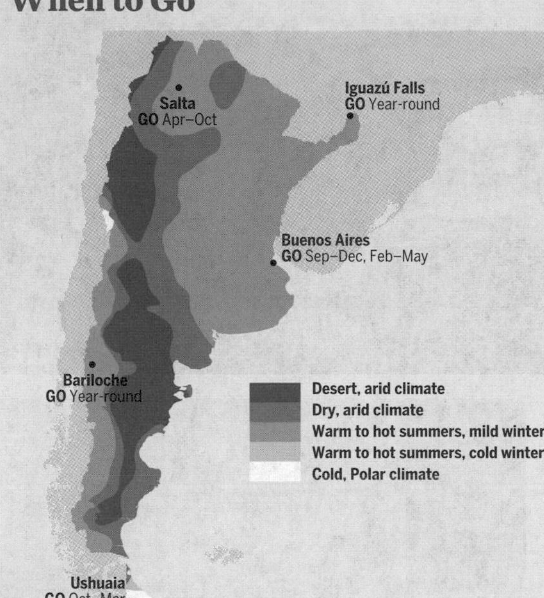

High Season
(Nov–Feb)

» Patagonia is best (and most expensive) December to February.

» Crowds throng to the beaches from late December through January.

» For ski resorts, busiest times are June to August.

Shoulder
(Sep–Nov & Mar–May)

» Temperature-wise the best times to visit Buenos Aires.

» The Lake District is pleasant; leaves are spectacular in March.

» The Mendoza region has its grape harvests and wine festival.

Low Season
(Jun–Aug)

» Good time to visit the North.

» Many services close at beach resorts, and mountain passes can be blocked by snow.

» July is a winter vacation month, so things get busy.

Your Daily Budget

Budget up to

AR$250

» Double room in budget hotel: AR$100–250, dorm bed: AR$50–70

» Budget restaurant dinner main: AR$30–45

» Get set lunches or supermarket takeout; some sights have free admission days

Midrange

AR$250–400

» Double room in midrange hotel: AR$250–500

» Midrange restaurant dinner main: AR$45–65

Top End over

AR$400

» Double room in top-end hotel: AR$500+

» Fine restaurant dinner main: AR$65+

Money

» ATMs widely available. Credit cards accepted at most midrange to top-end hotels, restaurants and shops, and some budget places. Traveler's checks *not* widely used.

Visas

» Generally not required for stays of up to 90 days. Americans, Australians and Canadians must pay a 'reciprocity fee' when arriving by air (see p602).

Cell Phones

» Local SIM cards (and top-up credits) are cheap and widely available, and can be used on unlocked GSM 850/1900 compatible phones.

Driving

» Drive on the right; steering wheel is on the left side of the car.

Websites

» **Argentina Independent** (www.theargentinaindependent.com) Wide-ranging topics.

» **Argentine Post** (www.argentinepost.com) Covering Buenos Aires and Argentina.

» **Buenos Aires Herald** (www.buenosairesherald.com) An international view of the country.

» **Bloggers in Argentina** (www.bloggersinargentina.blogspot.com) Argentine bloggers.

» **Lonely Planet** (www.lonelyplanet.com/argentina) Destination info, hotel bookings, forums and more.

Exchange Rates

Australia	A$1	AR$4.65
Brazil	R$1	AR$2.51
Canada	C$1	AR$4.35
Chile	CH$100	AR$0.90
Euro	€1	AR$5.68
Japan	¥100	AR$5.54
New Zealand	NZ$1	AR$3.62
UK	UK£1	AR$6.82
Uruguay	UR$1	AR$0.22
USA	US$1	AR$4.35

For current exchange rates see www.xe.com.

Important Numbers

Argentina Country Code	☎54
Directory Assistance	☎110
International Access Code	☎00
National Tourist Information (in Buenos Aires)	☎11-4312-2232
Police	☎101; ☎911 in some large cities

Arriving in Argentina

» **Aeropuerto Internacional Ministro Pistarini** ('Ezeiza'; p100)
Shuttle Bus – frequent to downtown BA in 40 to 60 minutes; AR$60–70
Local Bus – two hours to downtown; AR$2
Taxi – use official city taxi services only (avoid touts); AR$180

» **Aeroparque Jorge Newberry** ('Aeroparque', airport with domestic flights; p100)
Shuttle Bus – frequent, 10 to 15 minutes to downtown; AR$24
Local Bus – take 33 or 45, AR$2.50
Taxis – around AR$35 to downtown or Palermo

Rates on the Rise

Lonely Planet aims to give its readers as precise an idea as possible of what things cost. Rather than slapping hotels or restaurants into vague budget categories, we publish the actual rates and prices that businesses quote to us during research. The problem is that prices change, especially in Argentina, where inflation runs rampant. But we've found that readers prefer to have real numbers in their hands so they can make the calculations once they're on the road, then apply them across the board. This is still more precise than price ranges.

Argentina remains a decent-value destination. Although we anticipate prices will continue to rise, we've still opted to provide the prices given to us at the time of research. Our advice: call or check a few hotel or tour-operator websites before budgeting your trip, just to make sure you're savvy about going rates.

if you like...

Cities

Argentina is famous for its delightful natural wonders, but also lays claim to some big cities worthy of your presence. Gourmet restaurants, world-class museums, fine shopping, cutting-edge music, rocking nightlife and so much more – all contribute towards satisfying your needed dose of big-city culture. Just remember to spruce up your threads and pack fancy shoes.

Buenos Aires The mother of all Argentine cities. Plan to spend several days exploring the world-class offerings of this unique and astounding metropolis (p42)

Córdoba From Jesuit ruins to modern art to *cuarteto* music (Córdoba's claim to fame), you'll experience it all in this historic city (p269)

Bariloche Ski, hike or go white-water rafting during the day, then munch on chocolate and Patagonian lamb at night (p360)

Ushuaia Stunningly located at the foothills of the Andes' southernmost reaches, Ushuaia is the world's main departure point for Antarctica (p471)

Hiking & Mountaineering

Lining Argentina's western edge like a bumpy spine, the glorious Andes rise to nearly 7000m at Aconcagua's peak and offer some of the continent's finest hiking and mountaineering. Head south to El Chaltén for the epic ascents of Cerros Torre and Fitz Roy, or settle in at Bariloche to take in scenic day hikes. Up north, Mendoza is your best base for conquering Aconcagua. Meanwhile, the network of national parks offers everything from forest to mountain to desert and even subtropical tromps.

Bariloche Set on the shores of Lago Nahuel Huapi, Bariloche is surrounded by snowy peaks that beckon climbers (p360)

El Bolsón Drawing in hippies like patchouli is this laid-back town with nearby hikes to forests, waterfalls and scenic ridges (p371)

El Chaltén Argentina's ground zero for premier hiking, boasting gorgeous glaciers, pristine lakes and unparalleled mountain landscapes (p429)

Mendoza Mountaineers flock here to summit Cerro Aconcagua, South America's highest peak (p320)

Beaches

Ah, those waves lapping on the shore, salty wind on your face and warm sand between your toes. What says 'vacation' more than a day at the beach? Head to Argentina's best sandy destinations, all lined up like soldiers along the Atlantic edge of Buenos Aires. There's a beach for every taste, whether you're looking for a party, adventure sport or isolation. It's worth mentioning one of South America's premier beach destinations, where Argentina's rich and famous head when they want classy sun and surf – Uruguay's Punta del Este (p532).

Mar del Plata Popular with Argentina's middle class, 'Mardel' turns into the country's biggest summertime party (p128)

Necochea Miles of beachcombing, decent surf breakers and even a pine forest to explore (p136)

Pinamar Very popular destination with variety nearby – from affordable neighborhoods to one of Argentina's most exclusive beach resorts – Cariló (p125)

Puerto Madryn Whether you like windsurfing, whale-watching or diving, Puerto Madryn caters to your desires (p383)

DOUGLAS STEAKLEY/LONELY PLANET IMAGES ©

» Parque Nacional Los Glaciares (p434)

Food

It's no secret – Argentina is known for its steak, steak and more steak. But in Buenos Aires, ethnic restaurants are everywhere, and around the country tasty regional cuisines offer your taste buds a special treat. Vegetarians and vegans will have a hard time outside the big cities, though pasta, pizza and salads are common choices everywhere.

Andean Northwest If you make it up north, be sure to try *locro* (a hearty meat stew), *humitas* (sweet tamales) and *empanadas* (meat or vegetable turnovers)

Atlantic Coast Despite a huge coastline, Argentina isn't known for its seafood. If you're near the sea, however, be sure to try some fish, shrimp, oysters and king crab

Lake District The area around Bariloche is known for its wild boar, venison and trout – plus locally made chocolates

Patagonia If you like lamb, you'll be in heaven while in Patagonia. Here, *cordero* is on every menu and sheep ranches reign supreme

Memorable Landscapes

Argentina is pretty much made up of amazing landscapes, from its cactus filled deserts up north to its lofty Andean peaks in the west to its scenic, deep-blue lakes and piercing verdant forests down south. Throw in the wonders of Iguazú Falls and the bleak expanses of Patagonia, and the word 'unforgettable' is sure to come up.

Andean Northwest Undulating desert landscapes are punctuated by sentinel-like cacti, alien rock formations and whole mountainsides sporting palettes of colors (p204)

Iguazú Falls Spanning over 2.5km, these are the most incredible waterfalls you will ever see on earth, bar none (p185)

Lake District Argentina's 'little Switzerland' is just that – snow-dusted mountains looming over lakes edged by forest (p336)

The Andes Mountains Strung along the whole of South America, this spectacular mountain range is stunningly beautiful (p429)

Patagonia Not many regions in the world can evoke the mysticism, wonderment and yearning of Argentina's last frontier – even if most of it is barren, windy nothingness (p378)

Wildlife

Argentina's environments translate into homes for many creatures, from the flightless, grasslands-loving *ñandú* (rheas) to the majestic Andean condors and pumas to the desert-dwelling camelids such as llamas, guanacos and vicuñas. But certain concentrated areas are popular destinations for wildlife.

Península Valdés This bleak, oddly shaped peninsula attracts a plethora of wildlife such as southern right whales, elephant seals, Magellanic penguins and orcas (see p392)

Esteros del Iberá Rich and amazing wetlands that harbor a wide range of interesting critters, from comical capybaras, black caimans and howler monkeys to countless bird species (p163)

Iguazú Falls These spectacular falls are located in tropical rainforest that is also home to several kinds of monkeys, lizards and birds (including toucans!). Also watch for begging coatis (p186)

Ushuaia The southernmost city in the world has a few colonies of cormorants, sea lions and even penguins (p477). It's also the stepping-off point to Antarctica, a fantastic wildlife wonderland (p487)

If you like... glaciers, Perito Moreno in Patagonia will fascinate with its constant and thunderous calving

Wine Tasting

By now you've heard – Argentine wines are world-class. Most famous is malbec, that dark, robust plum-flavored wine that has solidly stamped the region of Mendoza on every oenophile's map. But Argentina has other fine varietals worthy of a sip or two – fresh torrontés, fruity bonarda and earthy pinot noir. Try them all; you'll be tipping your glass in agreement.

Mendoza Argentina's powerhouse wine region, producing the majority of the country's grapes (p301)

San Juan Much less famous than its Mendoza cousin, but well known for its syrah and bonarda (p332)

Cafayate Just south of Salta, this smaller town is famed for the torrontés grape, among others (p240)

Patagonia You don't think of wine when you think of Patagonia, but this bleak desert region is establishing a reputation for pinot noir. Maybe it's the wind (p378).

Colonial Architecture

While Argentina isn't world-renowned for its unique buildings, its status as an ex-Spanish colony means there are some fine examples of colonial architecture to be found around the country. Up north, the cities of Córdoba, Salta and Tucumán are worth a visit for their pretty colonial centers (among other things). In Buenos Aires head to San Telmo, with its historical buildings and atmosphere. And across the Río de la Plata, in Uruguay, lies the lovely colonial town of...wait for it...Colonia.

Córdoba Argentina's second-largest city boasts a beautiful center dotted with colonial buildings (p269)

Salta & Tucumán These northern cities have more than their share of beautiful old architecture (p222 and p245)

Buenos Aires It's mostly French- or Italian-styled buildings downtown, but head south to San Telmo for a simpler colonial feel (p42)

Colonia del Sacramento An easy boat ride away from BA lies Uruguay's architectural gem of a town (p516)

Adventure Sports

As the 8th-largest country in the world, Argentina covers a lot of ground and offers plenty of adventurous sports. Wild rivers boast great rafting and kayaking, while bare mountainsides are primed for rock climbing. High thermals mean lofty paragliding, while skiers and snowboarders roar down world-class slopes. If you're looking for adrenaline, you've found it. For a more extensive list of activities and destinations, see Argentina Outdoors (p29).

Skiing & Snowboarding The best ski resorts are Mendoza's Las Leñas (p326), Bariloche's Cerro Catedral (p361) and San Martín de los Andes' Cerro Chapelco (p357)

Rock Climbing Try Cerro Catedral just outside Bariloche (p361), the rocky walls around El Chaltén (p440) and the granite boulders of Los Gigantes (p293), 80km west of Córdoba

Paragliding Some of the best spots are La Cumbre (p284), Bariloche (p364) and Tucumán (p246)

Rafting & Kayaking Hit the white water around Mendoza (p305), Bariloche (p363) and Esquel (p416)

month by month

Top Events

1 **Fiesta Nacional de la Vendimia**, March

2 **Festival y Mundial de Tango**, August

3 **Carnaval**, February

4 **Día de la Tradición**, November

5 **Vinos y Bodegas**, September

January

January is peak summer in Argentina. *Porteños* (Buenos Aires citizens) who can afford it leave their sweltering city and head to the beach resorts, which are very crowded and expensive. It's also high season in Patagonia, so expect top prices there too.

Festival Nacional del Folklore

Near the city of Córdoba, the town of Cosquín hosts the National Festival of Folk Music (www.aquicosquin.org, in Spanish; p281) during the last week of January. It's the country's largest and best known *folklórico* (folk music) festival.

February

It's still summertime, but crowds at the beaches and in Patagonia start to thin later in the month. The Andean deserts and the Iguazú region continue to be very hot, but it's a great time to visit the Lake District. Mendoza's grape harvest begins.

Carnaval

Though not as rockin' as it is in Brazil, this celebration is very rowdy in the northeast, especially in Gualeguaychú (p170) and Corrientes (p159). Montevideo, the capital of Uruguay, is another party spot (see p506). Dates vary depending on the city.

March

Autumn is starting in Argentina, and temperatures are more pleasant in Buenos Aires (though it's rainy). Prices fall at the beaches and in Patagonia, but the weather remains warm. The north starts to cool, and Iguazú Falls isn't quite so hot and humid.

Fiesta Nacional de la Vendimia

Mendoza city's nearly week-long National Wine Harvest Festival (www.vendimia.mendoza.gov.ar, in Spanish; p306) kicks off with parades, folkloric events and a royal coronation – all in honor of Mendoza's intoxicating beverage.

April

The forests of the Lake District start changing from verdant green to fiery reds, yellows and oranges. Patagonia is clearing out but you might get lucky with decent hiking weather. BA heads into low season, with still-pleasant temperatures.

Festival Internacional de Cine Independiente

Independent film buffs shouldn't miss this festival (www.bafici.gov.ar) in BA, which screens more than 100 films from Argentina and Uruguay. Awards are given out in separate categories; guest directors and actors are invited.

May

It's late autumn and BA is cool as the rains die back. It's a good time to visit Iguazú Falls, and the crowds leave Mendoza – though the vineyards are still a gorgeous red from autumn leaves.

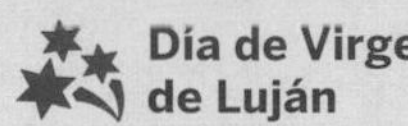

Día de Virgen de Luján

On May 8, thousands of devout believers make a 65km pilgrimage to the pampas town of Luján (p110) in honor of the Virgin Mary. Other pilgrimages take place in early October, early August, late September and December 8.

June

Winter begins in Argentina. Services at the beach resorts and Patagonia begin to dwindle, but it's an ideal time to visit the deserts of the Andean Northwest and the Iguazú Falls, which have fewer rains and less heat at this time of year.

Anniversary of Carlos Gardel's death

On June 24, 1935, tango legend Carlos Gardel died in a plane crash in Colombia. Head to BA's Chacarita cemetery to see fans pay their respects at his grave and statue, leaving a lit cigarette between his fingers. There are also tango events around the city.

July

Ski season is at its peak, so make sure your wallet is packed full and head off to the resorts around Bariloche, San Martín de los Andes and Mendoza. Whale-watching season starts heating up in the Península Valdés area.

Semana de Artesanía Aborígen

In the Lake District's Junín de los Andes, up to 20 surrounding native Mapuche communities get together to show off and sell their traditional arts and crafts.

August

Beach resort towns are dead and Patagonia is desolate and cold. BA is still cool, but it's a great time to explore the theaters, museums and art galleries.

Festival y Mundial de Tango

World-class national and international tango dancers perform throughout BA during this two-week festival (www.tangobuenosaires.gob.ar). There's a competition where couples compete fiercely for the title of 'world's best tango dancers.' Plenty of classes and workshops are also held.

Toreo de la Vincha

In a remote northern adobe village is a festival that pits a garlanded bull against young men who try to rob it of its crown. Interested? For more see p219.

September

Spring has sprung, and it's peak season for whale watching (both southern right whales and orcas) around Península Valdés. Polo season begins in BA, and the ski slopes wind down.

Vinos y Bodegas

Lovers of the grape shouldn't miss this huge BA event (www.expovinosybodegas.com.ar, in Spanish), which highlights vintages from dozens of bodegas (wineries) all over Argentina. Mix with thousands of sommeliers, restaurateurs, journalists and just plain wine aficionados.

October

It's a fine time to visit BA and Central Argentina. The season is just starting in Patagonia, but the crowds haven't quite descended. Flowers are blooming in the Lake District.

Fiesta Nacional de la Cerveza/ Oktoberfest

Join the swillers and oompah bands at Argentina's National Beer Festival, Villa General Belgrano's Oktoberfest (www.elsitiodelavilla.com/oktoberfest, in Spanish; p283) in the Central Sierras.

Eisteddfod

This lively Welsh festival, featuring plentiful grub and choral singing, takes place in the Patagonian towns of Trelew (p397) and Trevelin (p420). It's great for inducing one of those wait-am-I-really-in-South-America? moments.

November

In BA, the weather is perfect and the jacaranda trees show off their gorgeous purple blooms. It's a good time to visit the beach resorts and

Patagonia, since the crowds and high prices are still a month or so away.

Día de la Tradición

This festival salutes the gaucho and is especially significant in San Antonio de Areco (p113), the most classically gaucho of towns. However, it is also important (and much less touristy) in the mountain town of San José de Jáchal (p333).

December

Summer begins and it's excellent beach weather at the resorts (just before the January peak). It's also ideal weather for outdoor activities in the Lake District, and penguin (and hiking) season starts in Patagonia.

Buenos Aires Jazz Festival Internacional

BA's big jazz festival (www.buenosairesjazz.gob.ar) takes place over five days in venues all over the city, attracting 30,000 spectators. Jazz musicians of all kinds are featured – emerging and established, avant-garde and traditional, national and international.

El Tinkunaco

On December 31 a curious ceremony takes place in the northern city of La Rioja, symbolizing the resolution of a cultural clash between colonizing Spaniards and the Diaguita (an indigenous people). For more see p261.

(above) Festival y Mundial de Tango
(below) Día de la Tradición, San Antonio de Areco

itineraries

Whether you've got six days or 60, these itineraries provide a starting point for the trip of a lifetime. Want more inspiration? Head online to lonelyplanet.com/thorntree to chat with other travelers.

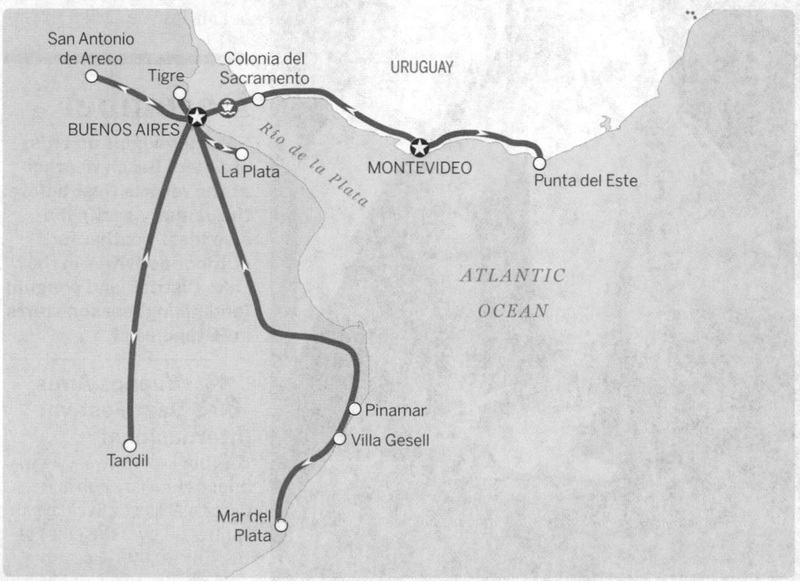

One Week

A Week Around Buenos Aires

Seen the capital city from top to bottom and wondering what else to do? Well, if you like water, **Tigre** is a great nearby choice – a bustling delta and popular *porteño* (resident of Buenos Aires) getaway. And not far away is peaceful **San Antonio de Areco** with a history of gaucho culture and surrounded by *estancias* – or tidy **La Plata**, with its huge cathedral.

Perhaps you'd prefer the beach? **Pinamar** and **Villa Gesell** make a great summer weekend trip, as does **Mar del Plata** – the biggest Argentine beach destination of them all. Or head inland to **Tandil**, a pretty town near scenic hills and a large recreational reservoir.

And then there's Uruguay – just a (relatively) short boat ride away. **Colonia del Sacramento** is truly charming, filled with cobbled streets and atmospheric colonial buildings. **Montevideo** is kind of like BA's little sister – smaller and less frantic, but still offering big city delights like a beautiful theater, historic downtown and eclectic architecture. And if you really want to party, take your bikini to **Punta del Este** – a magnet for celebrities, rich *porteños* and whoever else just wants to have a good time.

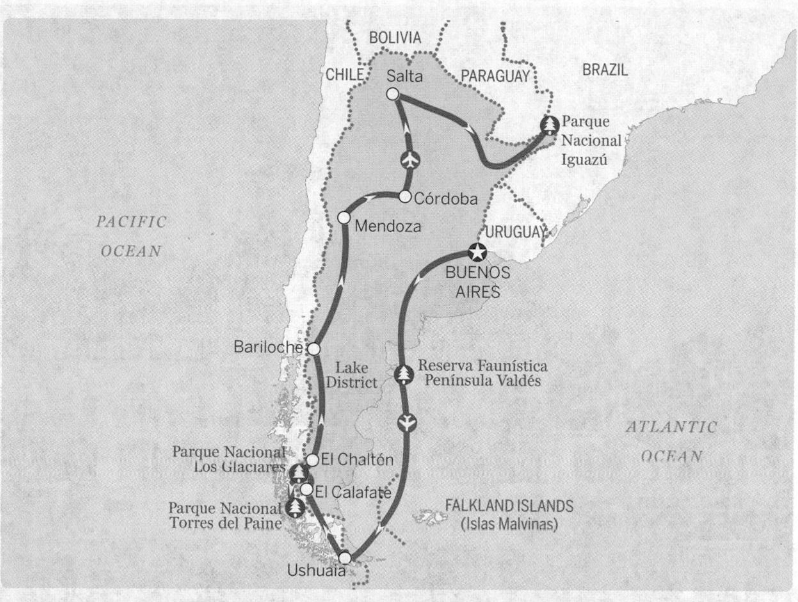

One Month

Unmissable Argentina

Argentina is a huge country – the world's eighth largest – and experiencing all its highlights thoroughly will require at least a month, plus a lot of airplane flights. If you want to see both the north and south, plan your trip accordingly: Patagonia is best in January and February, but this is when the northern deserts are at their hottest (doing both might be best in spring or fall). Tailor the following destinations to your tastes, spending more or less time where you want it.

Take a few days to explore the wonders of **Buenos Aires**, with its fascinating neighborhoods and big-city sights. If it's the right season, head south for wildlife viewing at **Reserva Faunística Península Valdés** – the whales, elephant seals and penguins are especially popular. From here hop a flight to **Ushuaia**, the southernmost city in the world and prime jumping-off point to Antarctica (add another two weeks and *minimum* US$5000 for this trip!).

Now you'll head north (your only choice) to **El Calafate**, where the stunning **Perito Moreno Glacier** (in Parque Nacional Los Glaciares) is one of the world's most unique sights. If you love the outdoors, cross the border to Chile's **Parque Nacional Torres del Paine**, an awe-inspiring cluster of mountains boasting some of earth's most beautiful landscapes. Back in Argentina is **El Chaltén**, another world-class climbing, trekking and camping destination.

Further up the spine of the Andes is Argentina's **Lake District**, where a chocolate stop in **Bariloche** is a must. Gorgeous scenery, outdoor activities and lovely nearby towns can easily add days to your itinerary. Your next destination is now **Mendoza**, Argentina's wine mecca, which also offers great outdoor adventures and mind-blowing Andean scenery. A 10-hour bus ride lands you in **Córdoba**, the country's second-largest city with amazing colonial architecture and cutting-edge culture. From here it's a flight north to pretty **Salta**, where you can explore colorful canyons, charming villages and cacti-dotted desert panoramas.

Pack up your bags again and head east to **Parque Nacional Iguazú**, where the world's most massive falls will simply astound you – they're nearly 3km long and made up of 200 separate waterfalls. Now fly back to Buenos Aires, do what you missed doing the first time around (or do the stuff you loved again) and party till your plane leaves.

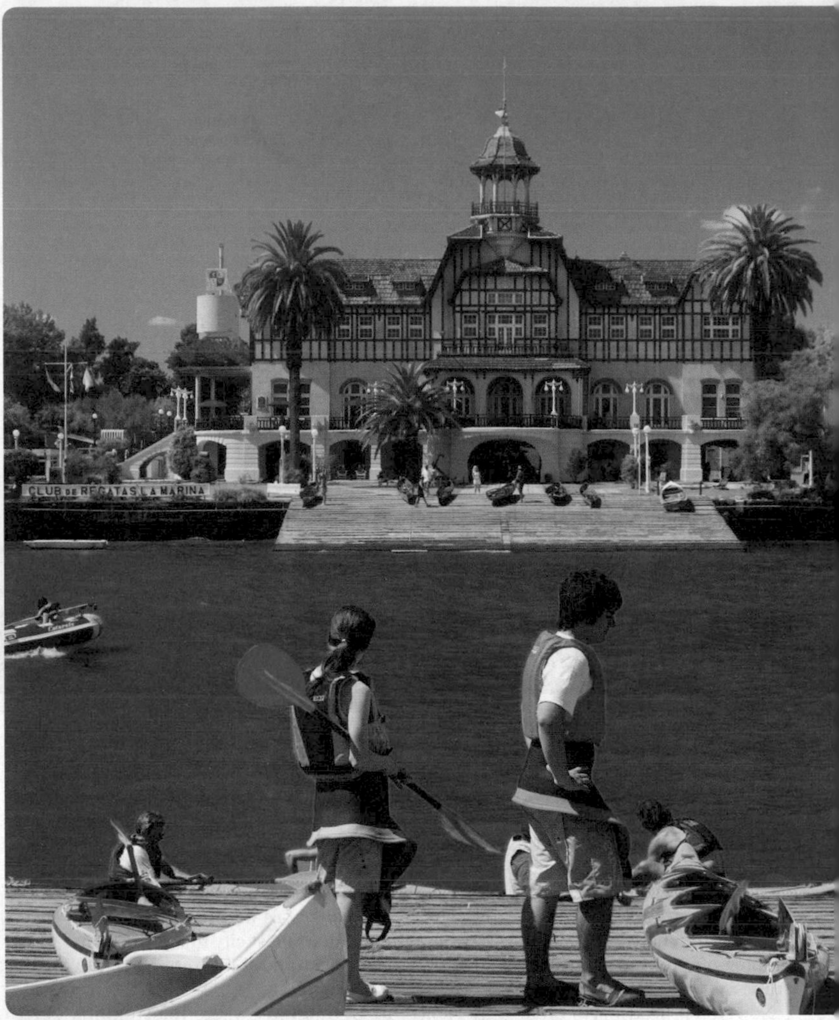

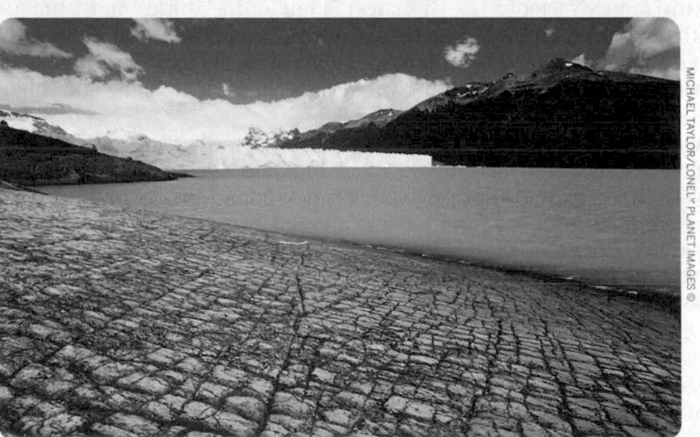

» (above) Tigre (p103)
» (left) Glaciar Perito Moreno (p446)

MICHAEL TAYLOR/LONELY PLANET IMAGES ©

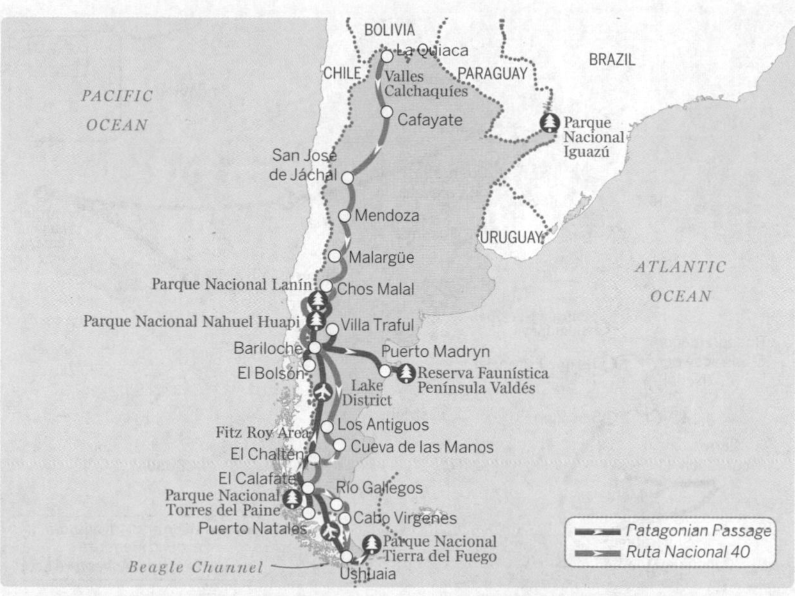

One Month

Ruta Nacional 40

Argentina's quintessential road trip, RN 40 travels the length of Argentina (more than 5000km) and through some of the country's remotest regions.

Start in **La Quiaca**, at the border with Bolivia. Heading south, you'll pass through the wildly scenic villages of **Valles Calchaquíes**. Then it's a pause at lovely **Cafayate**, before passing traditional **San José de Jáchal**. Take a breather in **Mendoza** to drink wine, then explore the volcanic landscapes around **Malargüe**.

Continue south, stopping to check out the lagoons and hot springs around **Chos Malal**. Detour to the national parks of **Lanín** and **Nahuel Huapi** for epic hiking before hitting **Bariloche**. Further on, consider sidetracking to **Los Antiguos** if it's cherry season, and stop at **Cueva de las Manos** for indigenous art.

Take a side trip to **El Chaltén** for hiking, then drive to **El Calafate** and see the Perito Moreno Glacier. Cross the border to Chile and explore stunning **Parque Nacional Torres del Paine** before doglegging west to **Río Gallegos**, where RN 40 ends nearby at **Cabo Virgenes**. Now consider continuing to **Ushuaia** on RN 3; it's as far south as any highway in the world goes.

Two to Three Weeks

Patagonian Passage

Begin in **Ushuaia**, in Tierra del Fuego, where you can kayak or hop on a boat to cruise around the Beagle Channel. Nearby **Parque Nacional Tierra del Fuego** offers a few end-of-the-world hikes (literally).

Now fly to **El Calafate**, in Patagonia, and lay your eyes on the spectacular and unforgettable Perito Moreno Glacier in **Parque Nacional Los Glaciares**. You'll also want to bus down to **Puerto Natales** and hike in the famous **Parque Nacional Torres del Paine** – you'll need at least four to six days here to appreciate it fully. Head north again to **El Chaltén** for world-class hiking and camping in the **Fitz Roy Range**.

With an extra week, fly to the **Lake District** and **Bariloche**, where you can hike (or fish, or raft, or bike) for days on end in the gorgeous national parks of **Nahuel Huapi** and **Lanín**. If you have an extra day or two, take a day trip to the hippie enclave of **El Bolsón**, or to the cute village of **Villa Traful**.

Finally, stop in **Puerto Madryn** to see the whales, elephant seals and penguins at **Reserva Faunística Península Valdés** – just make sure they're in season.

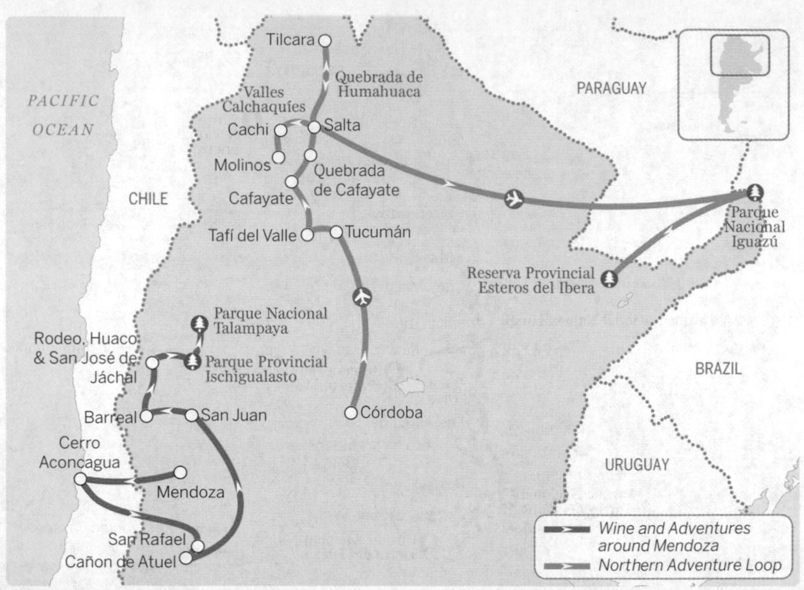

Three Weeks
Northern Adventure Loop

Start in **Córdoba**, Argentina's second-largest city, to explore one of the finest colonial centers.

Now fly north to historic **Tucumán** for some eclectic architecture and a lively street scene. Over to the west is pretty **Tafí del Valle**, and getting there via a gorgeous mountain road is half the fun. A bit further north is beautiful **Cafayate**, the place to knock back some aromatic torrontés wine. Sober up and travel through the epic **Quebrada de Cafayate** to **Salta**, whose central plaza is one of Argentina's best preserved; this is also where the famous 'Train to the Clouds' begins.

From Salta, head back south to the otherworldly region of **Valles Calchaquíes**, and the adobe villages of **Cachi** and **Molinos**. After this peaceful interlude, journey back north through the magnificently eroded valley of **Quebrada de Humahuaca**, where you can overnight in lively little **Tilcara**.

Return to Salta and fly to the incredible **Parque Nacional Iguazú**, home to nearly unbelievable waterfalls. And if you like animals, another worthy destination is **Reserva Provincial Esteros del Iberá**, an amazing wetlands preserve full of capybaras, caimans and countless bird species.

Two Weeks
Mendoza Wine & Adventures

Uncork your trip in beautiful **Mendoza**, located on the flanks of the Andes. Not only are there world-class vineyards surrounding the city, but outdoor enthusiasts will be in heaven. White-water rafting and skiing are awesome in the area, and **Cerro Aconcagua** (the western hemisphere's highest peak) isn't too far away.

Now take a crack-of-dawn bus to **San Rafael**, where you can rent a bike and ride out to the city's wineries – some of which specialize in sparkling wine. The area is also home to scenic **Cañon de Atuel**, a colorful, mini Grand Canyon. Then backtrack up north to **San Juan** to try the excellent syrah and other regional whites produced near this leafy provincial capital. You can also rent a car and head west to ethereal **Barreal** for rafting, mountaineering and land sailing, then go further north to explore the remote and traditional villages of **San José de Jáchal**, **Rodeo** and **Huaco**. Finally, be sure to visit the amazing landscapes of **Parque Provincial Ischigualasto** and **Parque Nacional Talampaya**, both boasting spectacular rock formations – along with petroglyphs and dinosaur fossils.

Argentina Outdoors

Best Bases for Thrill Seekers

Bariloche (p360) One of Argentina's premier outdoor cities, with fine hiking, skiing, biking, fishing, rafting and even paragliding

Mendoza (p301) One word: Aconcagua. Plus great skiing, rafting, rock climbing and more

El Chaltén (p429) World-class hiking, trekking, rock climbing, kayaking and fishing

Puerto Madryn (p383) Dive with sea lions, or go windsurfing and kayaking

Junín de los Andes (p346) Gorgeous rivers offer some of the world's best fly-fishing (for huge trout!)

Córdoba (p293) The closest city to Los Gigantes, Argentina's rock-climbing mecca (80km away)

Barreal (p330) Tops for trekking, rafting, windsurfing and – hold on to your hats – land sailing

La Cumbre (p284) *The* place in Argentina for paragliding, and there's skydiving too

From the rugged wilderness of Patagonia to the massive peaks of the Andes, Argentina has long bewitched the world's most adventurous souls. For anyone with a little grit and a love of the great outdoors, it's more than just a magnet – it's a mecca. Mountaineering, hiking and skiing have long been Argentina's classic outdoor pursuits, but these days locals and visitors alike are doing much more. They're kite surfing in the Andes, paragliding in the Central Sierras, diving along the Atlantic coast and pulling out huge trout in the Lake District. And they're always having fun.

Hiking & Trekking

Argentina is home to some seriously superb stomping. The Lake District is probably the country's most popular hiking destination, with outstanding day and multiday hikes in several national parks, including Nahuel Huapi (p368) and Lanín (p349). Bariloche is the best base for exploring the former, San Martín de los Andes the latter.

Patagonia, needless to say, has out-of-this-world hiking. South of Bariloche, El Bolsón (p371) is an excellent base for hiking both in the forests outside of town and in nearby Parque Nacional Lago Puelo (p377). Parque Nacional Los Glaciares offers wonderful hiking in and around the Fitz Roy Range; base yourself in El Chaltén (p429) and wait out the storms (in the brewery, of course).

Head to Parque Nacional Torres del Paine (p462), in Chile, for epic hiking. Tierra del Fuego also has good walks, conveniently in Parque Nacional Tierra del Fuego (p482).

MUSH!

You can't say you've done it all until you've tried dog sledding. Argentina's a great place to start. Operators near Caviahue (p342) offer dog sledding, as do operators in San Martín de los Andes (p351). And how about dog sledding at the end of the world, in Ushuaia (p476)? Obviously, this activity is possible only when there's snow, during the winter months of June to October (though in Ushuaia the season might be longer).

Then there are the high Andean peaks west of Mendoza. Although these areas are more popular for mountaineering, there's some great trekking here as well. The northern Andes around Quebrada de Humahuaca (p217) are also good.

Most sizeable towns in the Lake District and Patagonia have a hiking and mountaineering club called Club Andino. These are good places to get information, maps and current conditions. We've listed the clubs in Information sections throughout this book (Bariloche, Junín de los Andes, El Bolsón and Ushuaia all have one).

Lonely Planet's *Trekking in the Patagonian Andes* is a great resource to have if you're planning some serious trekking. And for camping information, see p588.

Mountaineering

The Andes are a mountaineer's dream, especially in San Juan and Mendoza provinces, where some of the highest peaks in the western hemisphere are found. While the most famous climb is Aconcagua (p320), the highest peak in the Americas, there are plenty of others in the Andes – many of them more interesting and far more technical. Near Barreal (p330), the Cordón de la Ramada boasts five peaks more than 6000m, including the mammoth Cerro Mercedario, which tops out at 6770m. The region is less congested than Aconcagua, offers more technical climbs and is preferred by many climbers. Also near here is the majestic Cordillera de Ansilta (p330), with seven peaks scraping the sky at between 5130m and 5885m.

The magnificent and challenging Fitz Roy Range (p434), in southern Patagonia, is one of the world's top mountaineering destinations, while the mountains of Parque Nacional Nahuel Huapi (p368) offer fun for all levels.

Rock Climbing

Patagonia's Parque Nacional Los Glaciares (p434), home to Cerro Torre and Cerro Fitz Roy, is one of the world's most important rock-climbing destinations. Cerro Torre is considered one of the five toughest climbs on the planet. The nearby town of El Chaltén is a climber's haven, and several shops offer lessons and rent equipment. If you don't have the time or talent for climbs of the Cerro Torre magnitude, there are plenty of other options.

Los Gigantes (p293), in the Central Sierras, is fast becoming the country's de facto rock-climbing capital, with lots of high-quality granite. Operators in Córdoba offer lessons and transportation. There's also climbing around Carolina (p296).

In Mendoza province, Los Molles (p326) is a small, friendly hub for rock climbing, and there's more nearby at Chigüido (near Malargüe). Around Mendoza city are the draws of Los Arenales and El Salto.

Cerro Otto, in Parque Nacional Nahuel Huapi (p368), has popular climbing routes. Finally, in the Pampas, there's some climbing in Tandil (p115) and Mar del Plata (p132).

Fishing

Where to Fish

Together, Patagonia and the Lake District constitute one of the world's premier fly-fishing destinations, where introduced trout species (brown, brook, lake and rainbow) and landlocked Atlantic salmon reach massive sizes in cold rivers surrounded by spectacular scenery. It's an angler's paradise.

In the Lake District, Junín de los Andes is the self-proclaimed trout capital of Argentina, and lining up a guide to take you to Parque Nacional Lanín's superb trout streams is easy. Nearby Aluminé (p345) sits on the banks of Río Aluminé, one of the country's most highly regarded trout streams. Bariloche is another excellent base.

Further south, Parque Nacional Los Alerces (p422) has outstanding lakes and rivers, and you can do day trips to El Chaltén's Lago del Desierto or Laguna Larga (p439). Río Gallegos (p446) is a superb fly-fishing destination. Other important Patagonian rivers include Río Negro and Río Santa Cruz.

» (above) El Bolsón (p371)
» (left) Río Atuel, near San Rafael (p322)

The city of Río Grande (p490), on Tierra del Fuego, is world-famous for fly-fishing. Its Río Grande river holds some of the largest sea-running brown trout in the world. For more about fishing in Tierra del Fuego, see p492.

Deep-sea fishing is possible in Camarones (p401) and Puerto Deseado (p405).

In subtropical northeast Argentina, the wide Río Paraná (p141) attracts fly-fishers, spin fishers and trollers from around the world, who pull in massive river species, such as surubí (a massive catfish) and dorado (a troutlike freshwater game fish). The dorado, not to be confused with the saltwater mahi-mahi, is a powerful swimmer and is one of the most exciting fish to catch on a fly.

There's also good fishing in Mendoza (p306), Uspallata (p317) and Barreal (p330).

Guides & Services

In smaller towns such as Junín de los Andes, you can usually go to the local tourist office and request a list of local fishing guides or operators. Another good option for independent anglers heading to the Lake District is the **Asociación de Guías Profesionales de Pesca Parque Nacional Nahuel Huapi y Patagonia Norte** (www.guiaspatagonicos.com.ar, in Spanish), which maintains a list and contact details of licensed guides for northern Patagonia and the Lake District.

In northern Argentina, which doesn't have tourist infrastructure as accommodating as the Lake District's, it's virtually impossible to fish without a guide – and usually a boat.

For more info about fly-fishing, contact **Asociación Argentina de Pesca con Mosca** (☎in Buenos Aires 011-4773-0821; www.aapm.org.ar, in Spanish).

Rules & Regulations

In the Lake District and Patagonia, the season runs November to between mid- and late April. In the northeast the season runs February to October. Certain lakes and streams on private land may stay open longer.

Trout fishing is almost always mandatory catch and release. Throughout Patagonia (including the Lake District), native species should *always* be thrown back. These are usually smaller than trout and include perca (perch), puyen (common galaxias, a narrow fish native to the southern hemisphere), Patagonian pejerrey and the rare peladilla.

Fishing licenses are required and available at tackle shops, *clubs de caza y pesca* (hunting and fishing clubs), and sometimes at tourist offices and YPF gas stations.

SAILING: NO WATER NECESSARY

In San Juan province's Parque Nacional El Leoncito, the lake bed of Pampa El Leoncito has become the epicenter of *carrovelismo* (land sailing). Here, people zip across the dry lake bed beneath Andean peaks in so-called sail cars. If you're interested, head straight to Barreal (p330).

Skiing & Snowboarding

Argentina's mountains have outstanding skiing, offering superb powder and plenty of sunny days. Many resorts have large ski schools with instructors from all over the world, so language is not a problem. At some of the older resorts equipment can be a little antiquated, but in general the quality of skiing more than compensates.

There are three main snow-sport areas: Mendoza, the Lake District and Ushuaia. Mendoza is home to Argentina's premier resort, Las Leñas (p326), which has the best snow and longest runs. The Lake District is home to several low-key resorts, including Cerro Catedral (p370), near Bariloche, and Cerro Chapelco (p357), near San Martín de los Andes. Although the snow doesn't get as powdery here, the views are superior to Las Leñas. And Esquel, further south in Patagonia, *does* have great powder at La Hoya.

The world's most southerly commercial skiing is near Ushuaia (p476). The ski season everywhere generally runs mid-June to mid-October.

Cycling

Cycling is a popular activity among Argentines, and spandex-clad cyclists are a common site along many roads (despite a decided lack of bike lanes in the country). There are some outstanding paved routes, especially in the Lake District and, to a lesser extent, in the Andean northwest.

In the northwest, there are several excellent road routes, including the highway from Tucumán to Tafí del Valle; the direct road from Salta to Jujuy; and – arguably most spectacular of all – Quebrada de Cafayate (p244). The Central Sierras (p267) are also great candidates for cycling, and the mostly paved network of roads rolls past a countryside that is, at times, reminiscent of Scotland. Mendoza boasts some epic routes through the Andes, but most are doable only for the seasoned cyclist – those lacking thighs of glory can entertain themselves pedaling between wineries in Maipú (p318).

In the Lake District's Parque Nacional Nahuel Huapi (p368) there are several excellent loops (including the Circuito Chico) that skirt gorgeous lakes and take in some of Patagonia's most epic scenery. Cyclists often take their bikes on the Cruce de Lagos (p371), a famous two-day boat/bus journey across the Andes to Chile. Instead of busing the road stretches, they ride.

Patagonia is a popular and mythical destination, with its desolate, beautiful landscapes and wide-open skies. Be ready for fierce, multi-directional winds and rough gravel roads, however, and take four-season gear even in summer – when long days and relatively warm weather make for the best touring. Ruta 40 (p417) is the classic road down here, but thru-cycling is tough because of the winds and lack of water; most cyclists alternate sections with Chile's Carretera Austral.

In recent years Buenos Aires (p63) has become a slightly more bike-friendly destination. And for more info on the logistics of getting around Argentina on bike, see p602.

Mountain Biking

Mountain biking is fairly undeveloped in Argentina and you'll find few places that have true single tracks for mountain bikers. However, at most outdoor hubs (such as Bariloche) you can rent a mountain bike for a day of independent pedaling or for guided mountain-bike rides – a fantastic way to see parts of an area you otherwise wouldn't.

Good places with mountain-bike rentals include San Martín de los Andes (p351), Villa la Angostura (p358), Bariloche (p361) and El Bolsón (p372) in the Lake District; Esquel (p416) in Patagonia; Mendoza (p305) and Uspallata (p317) in Mendoza province; Barreal (p330) in San Juan province; Tilcara (p216) in the Andean Northwest and Tandil (p118) in La Pampa province.

White-Water Rafting & Kayaking

Currently, Río Mendoza and Río Diamante, in Mendoza province (see p305), are the reigning white-water destinations, while Río Juramento near Salta (p227) is an exciting possibility.

If you want great scenery, however, it's all about Patagonia. The Río Hua Hum and Río Meliquina, near San Martín de los Andes (p351), and Río Limay and Río Manso, near Bariloche (p363) are both spectacular. So is Río Aluminé, near wee Aluminé (p345). From the Patagonian town of Esquel (p416) you can join a rafting trip on the incredibly scenic, glacial-fed Río Corcovado. A relatively unknown rafting destination is Barreal (p330), but it's more about the epic Andean scenery than the rapids. Scenic class II to III floats are possible on most of these rivers, while class IV runs are possible on the Ríos Mendoza, Diamante, Meliquina, Hua Hum and Corcovado. Experience is generally unnecessary for guided runs.

Kayaking is possible on many of the rivers mentioned, and also around Ushuaia (round Cape Horn! see p477), El Chaltén (p440), Viedma (p379), Puerto Madryn (p385), Paraná (p155), Rosario (p146) and Salta (p227).

> **SLOPE OF THE WIND**
>
> From around the world, windsurfing and kite-surfing fanatics drag an insane amount of gear to an isolated spot in the central Andes: Dique Cuesta del Viento, literally 'slope of the wind reservoir' (p333). The reservoir, near the wee village of Rodeo, in San Juan province, is one of the best windsurfing and kite-surfing destinations on the planet. Its consistent and extremely powerful wind blows every afternoon – without fail – from October to early May. We checked it out, and it blew us away!

Paragliding & Skydiving

Paragliding is popular in Argentina and it's a great place to take tandem flights or classes. Why? Because it's affordable and there are outstanding places to do it. Many agencies in Bariloche (p364) offer paragliding. Tucumán (p246), Salta (p227) and La Rioja (p260) have options in the Andean Northwest. Perhaps the best place is La Cumbre (p284), in Córdoba's Central Sierras – it's also a thrilling place to try skydiving.

Travel with Children

Best Regions for Kids

Buenos Aires

Argentina's biggest city holds plenty of museums, parks and shopping malls – many with fun areas for kids

Atlantic Coast

Beaches, beaches and more beaches – bring swimsuits and sun protection and start building castles

Mendoza

Wine tasting is off-limits for the kids, but you can also go skiing, dog-sledding and white-water rafting

Iguazú

Waterfalls and wildlife galore, plus thrilling boat rides that guarantee a fun soaking

Península Valdés

Rich with charming wildlife, such as splashy whales, smelly elephant seals and super cute penguins

Bariloche

Outdoor activities are the draw here – go hiking, rock climbing, horseback riding and rafting

While Argentina is best known for its steak, gauchos and tango – not your top kid-friendly themes – there is plenty this country has to offer your little ones. There are dinosaur museums to wow at, beach resorts to splash around in and plenty of outdoor activities to use up all that extra energy. You'll find Argentina makes a good, interesting and, yes, at times challenging but fun family destination.

For more general information, see Lonely Planet's *Travel with Children*.

Argentina for Kids

Argentina is remarkably child-friendly in terms of general travel safety and people's attitudes towards families. This is a country where family comes first.

Once children are old enough to cross the street safely and find their way back home, Argentine parents will often send unaccompanied pre-adolescents on errands or neighborly visits. While you're not likely to do this, you can usually count on your children's safety in public (be aware of crazy Argentine drivers, however!).

Argentina's numerous plazas and public parks, many with playgrounds, are popular gathering spots for families. This is a country where people frequently touch each other, so your children may be patted on the head by friendly strangers. Kids are a great icebreaker and certainly make it easier for you to meet the locals.

And remember that families stay out very late in this country – it's common to see young kids and babies out past midnight with their parents. There's no early curfew and everyone's out having fun, so consider doing the same!

Children's Highlights

Watching Wildlife

» Visit Güirá Oga zoo and Parque das Aves in the Iguazú Falls area

» Esteros del Iberá is full of marsh deer, black caimans and adorable capybaras

» Southern right whales, elephant seals and penguins on Península Valdés

» Parque Temaikén, just outside Buenos Aires, an excellent zoo with only the most photogenic animals

Energy Burners

» Parque de la Costa, in Tigre, offers roller coasters and other theme-park fun

» Complejo Termal Cacheuta, outside Mendoza, is a thermal-baths complex with wave pool and waterslides

» The Andes mountains offer great skiing around Bariloche and Mendoza

Rainy Days

» The Glaciarium, El Calafate's slick new museum, highlights the wonders of glaciers

» Kids can overnight in their pyjamas at Museo Paleontológico Egidio Feruglio, Trelew's dinosaur museum

» Museo de La Plata is Argentina's best natural history museum – the taxidermy and skeletons are especially awesome

» Shopping centers have kid-centric amusements, such as playgrounds, video arcades, toy stores and ice-cream shops

Outdoor Fun

» Super-active Glaciar Perito Moreno and jagged icebergs in Parque Nacional Los Glaciares

» Horseback rides and folkloric shows are highlights during your stay on an *estancia*

» The petrified forests of Patagonia aren't all that petrifying – unless you're a tree

Planning

Outdoor activities, such as swimming or visiting parks, are best outside June through August (with the exception of skiing, of course). Small kids often get discounts on such things as motel stays, museum admissions and restaurant meals. Supermarkets in most of Argentina offer a decent selection of baby food (expensive), infant formulas, disposable diapers, wet wipes and other necessities. Big pharmacies like Farmacity also stock some of these items.

Strollers on crowded and uneven sidewalks can be a liability, so consider bringing a baby carrier. Public bathrooms are often poorly maintained, and baby changing tables are not common.

Au pairs and babysitters are available (mostly in BA); check www.aupairinargentina.com or do a search at the expat website www.baexpats.org.

In this guidebook, very child-friendly destinations have been marked with a 👪.

Sweet Dreams

The great majority of hotels accept children without any problems; the most upscale may even offer babysitting services. The only places with minimum age restrictions might be small boutique hotels or guesthouses. Hostels are usually not the best environment for kids, but some welcome them.

During the summer reserving a hotel with a pool might be a good idea. Also look for places with kitchenettes. Apartments are available, especially in Buenos Aires; in less urban holiday destinations you can look for *cabañas* with full kitchens. Larger camp sites often have *cabañas*, common cooking facilities and sometimes play structures.

Dining

Most restaurants offer a selection of food suitable for children (vegetables, pasta, pizza, meat and chicken).

Empanadas (meat, vegetable or egg turnovers) make good healthy snacks, and don't forget to take the kids out for ice cream – it's a real Argentine treat!

Breast-feeding in public is not uncommon, though most women are discreet and cover themselves.

Transportation

Children under 18 traveling with only one parent theoretically need a notarized document certifying that both parents agree to the child's travel. Parents may also wish to bring a copy of the custody form; however, there's a good chance they won't be asked for either document.

When it comes to public transport, Argentines are usually very helpful. It's common for someone sitting to give up a seat for a parent and small child.

regions at a glance

As the eighth-largest country in the world, Argentina boasts nearly every kind of environment, from glaciated mountain peaks to cacti-dotted deserts to animal-rich swamplands and shrubby arid steppes. Outdoor fun-seekers will find their blissful adventures, beachcombers their warm stretches of sand and wine lovers their luscious vineyards.

The bigger cities, such as Buenos Aires or Córdoba, boast endless nightlife, entertainment, shopping and restaurants, along with a dose of culture, such as excellent museums, tango dance halls and colonial history. Argentina offers pretty much everything you might be looking for in a destination, so choose your desires, give yourself enough time to experience them all and just take off!

Buenos Aires

Food ✓✓✓
Nightlife ✓✓✓
Tango ✓✓✓

Steaks & More

There are plenty of fine steak houses in Buenos Aires. But you'll also find dozens of ethnic restaurants covering cuisines from France, Sweden, Greece, Mexico, Brazil, India, China, Thailand, the Middle East… and practically anywhere else.

Burn the Midnight Oil

BA is indeed the city that never sleeps. After dinner (often ending after midnight) *porteños* head out for a drink, then hit the nightclubs around 3am. Other events happen at a more 'reasonable' hours, but you get the idea – this city loves staying up late.

Sultry Dancing

Ah, the tango. There's no denying the attraction of this sexy dance. And BA boasts countless dance venues and classes, along with world-class competitions. Put on your dancing shoes and get ready to fall in love – you're in the heart of tango land here.

p42

The Pampas & the Atlantic Coast

Beaches ✓✓
Gaucho Culture ✓✓
Hiking ✓

Life's a Beach

Buenos Aires in January can seem nearly abandoned (that's because everyone's at the beach). Coastal cities, such as Mar del Plata, Pinamar and Necochea become heaving hubs full of sun-bronzed Argentines lying on hot sands during the day and partying all night long.

Gaucho Culture

This quintessential icon's heyday was centuries ago, but today their culture is kept alive in San Antonio de Areco, where an annual festival celebrates the gaucho's life. You can also visit an *estancia* (ranch), where horseback riding, gaucho demonstrations and *asados* (barbecues) are highlights.

Hiking

The ancient, worn-down mountain ranges of the Pampas aren't as spectacular as the youthful Andes. But around Sierra de la Ventana are some hikes offering dramatic views of surrounding landscapes – including one where you peek through a rock 'window'.

p106

Iguazú Falls & the Northeast

Water Features ✓✓✓
Wildlife ✓✓
Festivals ✓✓

Wide Rivers, Mighty Iguazú

Towns and cities along the region's two major rivers are focused on great waterside strips for boating, strolling, eating and partying, while large fish attract anglers and gourmets alike. Up north, the world's most impressive waterfalls, Iguazú, will leave you in awe.

Cute Capybaras

The Esteros del Iberá wetlands hold an astonishing wealth of creatures, including snapping caimans and roly-poly capybaras. There's a cornucopia of birdlife easily viewed among the low grasses. A long hop north brings you to Iguazú's national park and jungle ecosystem, equally rich in distinct wildlife species.

Carnaval

Brazil's proximity to this zone has left a legacy in the exuberant Carnaval celebrations. The most famous is in little Gualeguaychú, a short trip from Buenos Aires, but Corrientes and Posadas lose nothing by comparison.

p140

Salta & the Andean Northwest

Indigenous Culture ✓✓✓
Colonial Cities ✓✓
Activities ✓✓

Before Columbus

The northwestern peoples saw the Inca, then the Spanish arrive. Centuries later, the ruins of cities remain, but the food, daily life and handcrafts speak of a persisting, living, changing culture that you can get to know a little in the region's settlements.

Historic Towns

The northwestern cities are Argentina's oldest, and there's an unmistakable time-honored feel to them. Venerable churches, stately facades, and handsome plazas planted with lofty trees, together with the relaxed pace of life, give these places an ambience unlike any other.

Out & About

The Andes dominate the geography here, and offer excellent climbing, walking, and 4WD excursions. But subtropical national parks replete with bird and animal life show a different side. Elsewhere, top-notch hang-gliding and paragliding give the chance to see how things look from topsides.

p204

Córdoba & the Central Sierras

Historic Buildings ✓✓✓
Nightlife ✓✓
Paragliding ✓✓

Oldies But Goodies

The Jesuit legacy in Córdoba extends beyond wine making and higher education – they also constructed some fabulous buildings. Córdoba city boasts an entire block of well-preserved Jesuit architecture and there are further examples scattered around the province.

Bring on the Night

Catch an independent movie or a play, dance the night away or grab a few quiet drinks in a cozy bar – whatever you're looking for, Córdoba's young population and vibrant cultural scene make finding it a snap.

Take to the Skies

If you've ever even been vaguely tempted to try paragliding, this is the place to do it – the world-famous launch sites of La Cumbre and Merlo are home to scores of instructors (some world champions in the sport) offering tandem flights that will have you soaring with the condors.

p267

Mendoza & the Central Andes

Wine Tours ✓✓✓
Mountains ✓✓
Rafting ✓✓✓

Hear It on the Grapevine

Get to the heart of Argentina's magnificent wine culture by visiting the vineyards, talking to the winemakers and seeing how it all comes together, from planting the vine to tasting the final, delicious product.

Lofty Ambitions

Snow-capped year-round and dominating the horizon, the Andes are one of Argentina's iconic images. Get up close and personal with them by climbing Aconcagua, the Americas' highest peak, or hitting the slopes in Mendoza's world-class ski resorts.

Wet & Wild

All that snowmelt from the Andes does more than just irrigate the grapevines. It also feeds a couple of rivers that gush down from the mountains, giving rafters the ride of their lives.

p299

Bariloche & the Lake District

Activities ✓✓✓
Village Life ✓
Paleontology ✓✓

Get Out There

A true year-round destination, there's always something to do in the Lake District. Powder hounds hit the slopes in season at the province's top-notch ski resorts while the rest of the year the mountain trails, hikers' refuges and expansive vistas make it a trekker's paradise.

Kicking Back

One of the joys of traveling through this region is discovering small alpine villages nestled in the forest, surrounded by breathtaking mountain scenery – the perfect remedy for big-city blues.

Jurassic Parks

Some truly huge animals used to roam these parts – including the world's largest dinosaur and the world's largest carnivore. The sites where they were discovered are open to the public to teach a humbling lesson in size.

p336

Patagonia

Hiking ✓✓✓
Wildlife Watching ✓✓✓
Adventure ✓✓✓

Wild Hiking

Iconic hikes around Fitz Roy and Torres del Paine bring deserved fame to the trails of Patagonia. But if you have time, check out the millennial forests of Parque Nacional Los Alerces and the electric turquoise lakes of ultra-remote Parque Nacional Perito Moreno.

Creature Feature

Abundant marine life makes the coast, and Península Valdés in particular, the hub for watching wildlife, but there's also the subtle allure of Patagonia's guanaco herds, soaring condors and ñandús that sprint across the steppe.

Real Adventure

Riding on an *estancia*, driving Ruta 40, glacier chasing or just getting deep into the Andean wilderness, Patagonia is all about unfettered freedom and the allure of the unexpected.

p378

Tierra del Fuego

Hiking ✓✓
Sea Travel ✓✓✓
Winter Sports ✓✓

Hoof It

Austral summer's long days make for backpacking bliss. Dientes de Navarino is the iconic Fuegian trek but the enchanted forests of Parque Nacional Tierra del Fuego also give a quick dose of big nature.

Set Sail

You don't have to round Cape Horn to find magic in these southern seas. Sail the Beagle Channel in search of marine life and indigenous ruins, boat through the Chilean fjords or paddle a sea kayak.

Winter Wonderland

Brave a winter journey to the frozen ends of the earth. From June to October, snow makes Ushuaia adventure central. Shush down the slopes of Cerro Castor, ski cross-country or boom over the snowdrifts driven by sled dogs. Crackling bonfires, sushi dens and comfy lodges cap the day.

p470

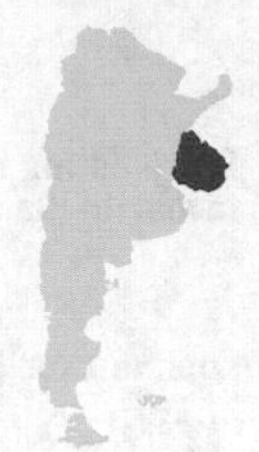

Uruguay

Beaches ✓✓✓
Estancias ✓✓✓
Food & Wine ✓✓

A Beach for Every Taste

Beachside bliss wears many faces on Uruguay's Atlantic coast: chasing the perfect surf break at La Pedrera, getting friendly with sea lions at Cabo Polonio or scanning the sands for international celebrities at Punta del Este.

Wide Open Skies

Uruguay's gaucho soul lies in its vast interior landscapes. For a taste of traditional ranch life, spend a few nights on an *estancia*, riding horseback into an endless horizon by day, savoring the warmth of the fire and the brilliance of the stars by night.

Carnivore Paradise

Something's always grilling in Uruguay. The classic *parrillada* of steak, pork chops, chorizo and *morcilla* (blood sausage) is enough to make any carnivore swoon, especially when accompanied by a glass of Tannat from one of the country's up-and-coming wineries.

p495

Every listing is recommended by our authors, and their favourite places are listed first

Look out for these icons:

 Our author's top recommendation  A green or sustainable option  No payment required

See the Index for a full list of destinations covered in this book.

On the Road

Buenos Aires

Includes »

Best Places to Eat

- Oviedo (p81)
- Café San Juan (p80)
- Sarkis (p82)
- Chan Chan (p79)
- Siamo nel Forno (p83)

Best Places to Stay

- Poetry Building (p75)
- Home Hotel (p76)
- Miravida Soho (p76)
- 1890 Hotel Boutique (p74)
- Chill House Hostel (p76)

Why Go?

Whip together a beautiful metropolis with gourmet cuisine, awesome shopping and frenzied nightlife – and you get Buenos Aires. It's a rough-hewn mix of Paris' architecture, Rome's traffic and Madrid's late-night hours, all spiked with Latin American flavor. Buenos Aires is cosmopolitan, seductive, emotional, frustrating and chock full of attitude, and there's no other place like it in the world. Seek out classic BA: the old-world cafes, colonial architecture, curious markets and diverse communities. Rub shoulders with Evita at Recoleta's famous cemetery, fill your belly with luscious steaks, dance the sultry tango and take in a crazy *fútbol* (soccer) match. Unforgettable adventures? You'd better believe it.

Everyone knows someone who has been here and raved about it. You've put it off long enough. Come to Buenos Aires and you'll understand why so many people have fallen in love with this amazing city. There's a good chance you'll be one of them.

When to Go

Buenos Aires

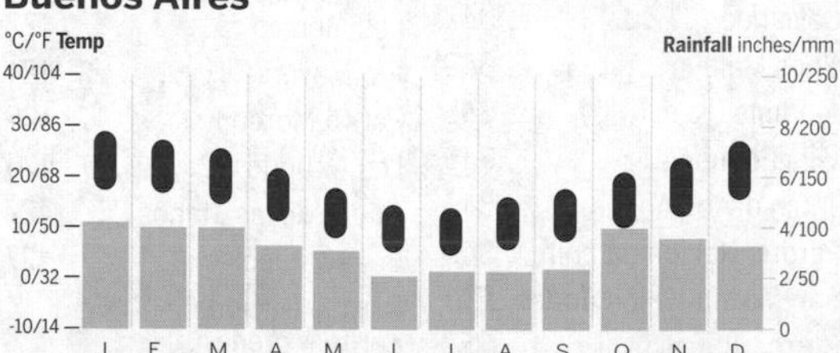

Oct–Dec Spring means warm days to drink cocktails outdoors and admire blooming jacarandas.

Aug Winter's peak brings BA's tango festival; or visit museums, art galleries and cultural centers.

Mar–May Explore Buenos Aires in fall and catch the city's Independent Film Festival in April.

Supper Clubs

A hot Buenos Aires trend these days are *puertas cerradas* (closed-door restaurants). These prix-fixe restaurants are usually only open on weekends and are great for meeting fellow diners, since the limited tables are often communal and the atmosphere's intimate. Most won't tell you the address until you make reservations (mandatory, of course). But if you want that feeling of being somewhere 'secret' – and eating special food – these places are highly appealing. For our favorite ones, see p79.

BUENOS AIRES 101

BA is a huge metropolis, but most places of interest are in just a few easily accessible neighborhoods.

The heart of the city is **Microcentro**; it's small enough to walk around fairly easily. Just east is **Puerto Madero**, with scenic docklands and a large ecological park. Further south is **San Telmo**, known for its lovely colonial architecture and Sunday fair. South of here is **La Boca**, famed for colorful houses clad in corrugated metal.

West of the Microcentro sits **Congreso**, BA's seat of politics, boasting some stately buildings. To the north is upscale **Retiro**, home to the city's main train and bus station. And just northwest lie **Recoleta** and **Barrio Norte**, boasting some of BA's most expensive real estate and dotted with art museums, fancy shops and luxurious mansions.

Further north is **Palermo**, an upper-middle-class suburb with spacious parks, plenty of shopping and heaps of restaurants; it's subdivided into the trendy neighborhoods of Palermo Soho, Palermo Hollywood and Las Cañitas, among others. And edging Palermo's borders are **Belgrano** and **Once**, both home to concentrations of ethnic Chinese, Korean, Peruvian and Jewish people.

BA's Ezeiza airport is about 35km south of the center; see p100 for tips on arriving there.

Top Five BA Splurges

» Hit the lovely spa at the five-star Four Seasons Hotel (p75)

» Reserve a seat or two at the closed-door restaurant Casa Mun (p79)

» Find that perfect Victrola in a San Telmo antiques shop (p97)

» Set aside a day, head to the countryside and go horseback riding (p66)

» End your adventures by being driven to the airport in a luxury car (p101)

PESKY INFLATION

Be warned: while accurate at print time, prices in this chapter (and book) are likely to rise rapidly. Unofficial inflation rates hover around 25% (officially it's 10%). Check before booking.

Fast Facts

» Population: 2.8 million

» Area: 202 sq km

» Telephone code: 011

» Per capita meat consumption: 60kg (132lb)

Must-try Foods

» *Bife de chorizo* – sirloin steak

» *Dulce de leche* – milk caramel sauce

» *Empanadas* – baked, savory turnovers

» *Mate* – a bitter ritual tea

» *Helado* – the best ice cream in the world

Resources

» Local journalism: www.goodairs.com

» Alternative articles and tips: www.landingpadba.com

» Popular expat website: www.baexpats.org

» Apartments, jobs, lovers: http://buenosaires.craigslist.org

Buenos Aires Highlights

1. Commune with BA's rich and famous dead at **Cementerio de la Recoleta** (p59)
2. Absorb some history and see the presidential offices at **Plaza de Mayo** (p47)
3. Check out the very popular Sunday **antiques fair** at Plaza Dorrego (p54) in San Telmo
4. Feast on tasty steaks or more exotic cuisine in Palermo's **Las Cañitas** (p82)
5. Marvel at amazingly high leg kicks and sexy moves at a **tango show** (p87)
6. Shop in the fun and stylish designer boutiques of **Palermo Viejo** (p96)
7. Party all night long in BA's chic and super-happening **nightclubs** (p93) in Palermo
8. Attend a loud, exciting and always passionate **fútbol game** (p96)
9. Strolling, shopping and people-watching on always-bustling **Av Florida** (p46)
10. Wander **Caminito** and watching weekend buskers in La Boca (p55)

0 2 km
0 1 miles

Río de la Plata

Av Costanera R Obligado
Pier
Aliscafos (Hydrofoils)
Parque 3 de Febrero
Estación Saldías
Av Figueroa Alcorta
Av del Libertador
PALERMO CHICO
Estación Maritima
Floralis Genérica
Quiroga
Av General Las Heras
See Retiro, Recoleta & Barrio Norte Map (p60)
RECOLETA
Dársena A
Bulnes
Austria
1 Cementerio de la Recoleta
Av Callao
Av del Libertador
Estación Retiro
Retiro
Agüero
BARRIO NORTE
RETIRO
San Martín
Av Eduardo Madero
Gallo
Pueyrredón
Av Santa Fe
Florida
Dársena Norte
Av Córdoba
Facultad de Medicina
Callao
Av Córdoba
Lavalle 9
ALMAGRO
Av Florida
Dique No 4
Reserva Ecológica Costanera Sur
Carlos Gardel
Pueyrredón
TRIBUNALES
Florida
LN Alem
Carlos Pellegrini
Plaza de Mayo
Lago de las Gaviolas
Pasteur
ONCE
MICROCENTRO
LA CITY
2
Alberti
Pasco
Congreso
Av de Mayo
Av 9 de Julio
Perú
Plaza de Mayo
Dique No 3
Av Tristán Achaval Rodríguez
Plaza Miserere
Lago de los Patos
BALVANERA
CONGRESO
Belgrano
Paseo Colón
Av Ing Huergo
See The Center, Congreso & San Telmo Map (p48)
Av Belgrano
MONTSERRAT
Independencia
PUERTO MADERO
San Telmo
CONSTITUCIÓN
3
Dique No 1
Pichincha
San José
San Juan
General Urquiza
Jujuy
See La Boca Map (p58)
Av Brasil
Av Juan de Garay
Bernardo de Irigoyen
Dársena Sur
Av Almirante Brown
Av Martín García
Canal Sur
Av Entre Ríos
BARRACAS
Av Chiclana
Av Jujuy
Defensa
LA BOCA
Av Caseros
Av Amancio Alcorta
Brandsen
Caminito 10

History

Buenos Aires was settled in 1536 by Pedro de Mendoza, an adventurous and aristocratic Spaniard who financed his own expedition to South America. Food shortages and attacks by indigenous groups prompted Mendoza's hasty departure in 1537; to add insult to injury, he died at sea on the way home. Meanwhile, other expedition members left the settlement, sailed 1600km upriver and founded Asunción (now capital of Paraguay).

By 1541 the original settlement was completely abandoned. In 1580 a new group of settlers moved downriver from Asunción under Juan de Garay's command and repopulated Mendoza's abandoned outpost.

For the next 196 years Buenos Aires was a backwater and smuggler's paradise due to trade restrictions imposed by mother Spain. All the same, its population had grown to around 20,000 by 1776, the year Spain decreed the city as capital of the new viceroyalty of Río de la Plata.

After repelling British invasions in 1806 and 1807, the settlers reckoned they could handle themselves without Spain's help. Napoleon's 1808 conquest of Spain led to Buenos Aires' *cabildo* (town council) cutting ties with its mother country in May 1810. Decades of power struggles between BA and the other former viceregal provinces ensued, escalating more than once into civil war.

Finally, in 1880 the city was declared the federal territory of Buenos Aires and the nation's capital forevermore. Agricultural exports soared for the next few decades, which resulted in great wealth accumulating in the city. Well-heeled *porteños* (BA citizens) built opulent French-style mansions, and the government spent lavishly on public works, including parks, ornate offices and a subway. Much of BA's unique look dates from this period.

But the boom times didn't last forever. Immigration burgeoned and export prices began to drop. The 1929 Wall Street crash dealt a final blow to the country's markets, and soon the first of many military coups took over. It was the end of Argentina's Golden Age.

Pollution, poverty, unemployment and decaying infrastructure became constant problems in the following decades. Shantytowns popped up as social problems grew and the city failed to absorb its increasing population; even today, greater Buenos Aires holds an astounding one-third of Argentina's population. Extreme governments and a roller-coaster economy have been constant plagues, and though the late 20th century saw a turnaround in the country's economy, the recent global financial crisis has had an impact. For more on Argentina's tumultuous history, see p558.

Sights

MICROCENTRO

BA's Microcentro is where the big city hustles: here you'll see endless crowds of business suits and power skirts yelling into cell phones as they hasten about the narrow streets in the shadows of skyscrapers and old European buildings.

BUENOS AIRES IN...

Two Days

Start with a stroll in **San Telmo** and duck into some antiques stores. Walk north to **Plaza de Mayo** for a historical perspective, then wander the **Microcentro**, perhaps veering east to **Puerto Madero** – a great spot for a break.

Keep heading northward into **Retiro** and **Recoleta**, stopping off at the **Museo Nacional de Bellas Artes** to admire some impressionism. Be sure to visit the **Cementerio de la Recoleta** to commune with BA's bygone elite. For dinner and nightlife, **Palermo Viejo** is hard to beat.

On day two take in the **Congreso** neighborhood or head to **La Boca**. Shop in **Palermo Viejo** and at night catch a **tango show** or a performance at the **Teatro Colón**.

Four Days

On your third day consider taking a daytrip to **Tigre**, or **Colonia** in Uruguay. On the fourth day you can go on a unique **tour**, take a **tango lesson**, check out **Palermo's parks** or head to the **Mataderos fair** (if it's a weekend). Be sure to find yourself a good steak restaurant for your last meal.

Florida, a long pedestrian street, is the main artery of this neighborhood. It's always jammed during the day with businesspeople, shoppers and tourists seeking vehicle-free access from north to south without the ubiquitous bus fumes and honking taxis. Buskers, beggars and street vendors thrive here as well, adding color and noise. Renovated old buildings, such as beautiful Galerías Pacífico, add elegance to the area.

Further south is BA's busy financial district, where there are several museums to investigate. After that comes Plaza de Mayo, often filled with people resting on benches or taking photos of the surrounding historic sites.

TOP CHOICE Plaza de Mayo PLAZA
(Map p48) Planted between the Casa Rosada, the Cabildo and the city's main cathedral, grassy Plaza de Mayo is BA's ground zero for the city's most vehement protests. In the plaza's center is the **Pirámide de Mayo**, a small obelisk built to mark the first anniversary of BA's independence from Spain. Looming on the plaza's north side is the impressive **Banco de la Nación** (1939), the work of famed architect Alejandro Bustillo.

Today the plaza attracts camera-toting tourists, the occasional camera thief, and activists. And if you happen to be here on Thursdays at 3:30pm, you'll see the Madres de la Plaza de Mayo; these 'mothers of the disappeared' continue to march for social justice causes.

Casa Rosada BUILDING
(Pink House; Map p48) Taking up the whole east side of the Plaza de Mayo is the unmistakable pink facade of the Casa Rosada. Though the offices of 'La Presidenta' Cristina Kirchner are here, the presidential residence is in the calm suburb of Olivos, north of the center.

The side of the palace facing Plaza de Mayo is actually the back of the building. It's from these balconies, however, that Juan and Eva Perón, General Leopoldo Galtieri, Raúl Alfonsín and other politicians have preached to throngs of impassioned Argentines. Pop celebrity Madonna also crooned from here for her movie *Evita*.

The salmon-pink color of the Casa Rosada, which positively glows at sunset, could have come from President Sarmiento's attempt to make peace during his 1868–74 term (blending the red of the Federalists with the white of the Unitarists). Another theory is that the color comes from painting the palace with bovine blood, which was a common practice in the late 19th century.

There are free **tours** (☎4344-3600) available on Saturday and Sunday from 10am to 6pm; just walk in and join the next group waiting for a tour.

FREE Museo del Bicentennario MUSEUM
(Map p48; ☎4344-3802; Avs Paseo Colón & Hipólito Yrigoyen; ⏰11am-7pm Wed-Sun) Behind the Casa Rosada you'll notice a glassy wedge marking this sparkling new museum, housed within the brick vaults of the old *aduana* (customs house). Head down into the open space, which has over a dozen side rooms – each dedicated to a different era of Argentina's tumultuous political history. There are mostly videos and a few artifacts to see, along with a cafe, temporary art exhibitions and an impressive restored mural by Mexican artist David Alfaro Siqueiros.

Catedral Metropolitana CATHEDRAL
(Map p48; ☎4331-2845; www.catedralbuenosaires.org.ar; cnr Av Rivadavia & San Martín; ⏰7:30am-6:30pm Mon-Fri, 9am-7pm Sat & Sun) BA's baroque cathedral is a significant religious and architectural landmark, but more importantly it contains the tomb of General José de San Martín, Argentina's most revered hero. Outside the cathedral you'll see a flame keeping his spirit alive. Tours in Spanish of the church and crypt are available; call or check the website.

FREE Cabildo BUILDING
(Map p48; ☎4342-6729; Bolívar 65; ⏰10:30am-5pm Wed-Fri, 11:30am-6pm Sat & Sun) This mid-18th-century town hall building is now a museum. It used to have colonnades that spanned Plaza de Mayo, but the building of surrounding avenues unfortunately destroyed these. The museum inside offers scanty exhibits, but a lively crafts market sets up in the patio on Thursday and Friday – and the cafe is a great place to relax.

Galerías Pacífico LANDMARK
(Map p48; ☎5555-5110; Avs Florida & Córdoba; ⏰10am-9pm) Covering an entire city block, this beautiful French-style shopping center dates from 1889 and boasts vaulted ceilings with paintings done in 1954 by muralists Antonio Berni, Juan Carlos Castagnino, Manuel Colmeiro, Lino Spilimbergo and Demetrio Urruchúa. All were adherents of the *nuevo realismo* (new realism) school of Argentine art. For many years the building

The Center, Congreso & San Telmo

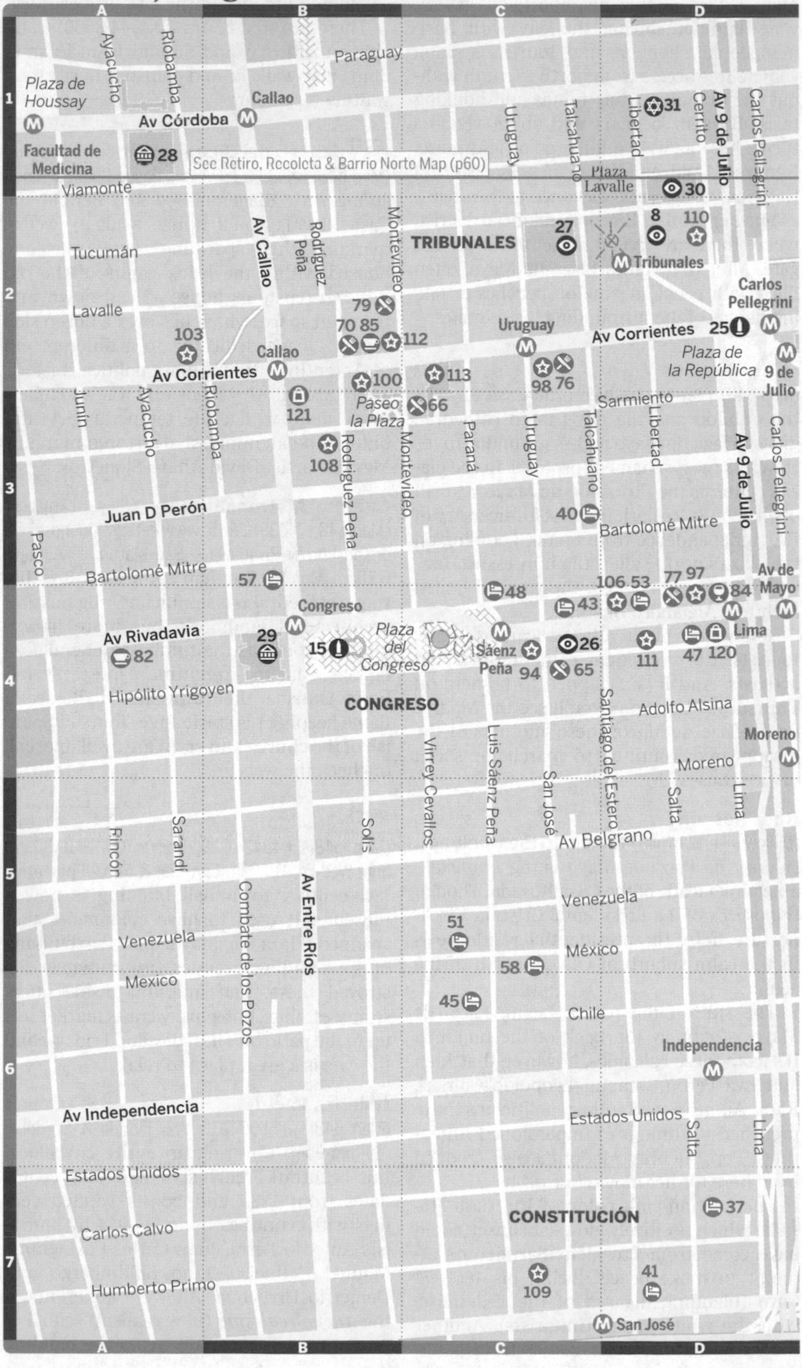

See Retiro, Recoleta & Barrio Norte Map (p60)

0 400 m
0 0.2 miles
Av Córdoba
Grierson
Suipacha
Esmeralda
Maipú
Florida
San Martín
Reconquista
Bouchard
Viamonte
Puerto Madero tourist kiosk
Olga Cossettini
Av de los Italianos
Plaza Roma
Tucumán
Lavalle
Dique No 4
Leandro N. Alem
Florida
Av Corrientes
Av Leandro N Alem
Av Eduardo Madero
Av Alicia Moreau de Justo
Juana Manso
Sarmiento
Diagonal Norte
MICROCENTRO
Juan D Perón
Diagonal Roque Sáenz Peña
25 de Mayo
Av Rosales
PUERTO MADERO
Dealessi
Diagonal Roque Sáenz Peña tourist kiosk
Catedral
Plaza de Mayo
LA CITY
Parque Colón
Puente de la Mujer
Dique No 3
Av Rivadavia
Av de Mayo
Av de la Rábida
Perú
Bolívar
Piedras
Chacabuco
Tacuarí
Av Julio Roca
Plaza AP Justo
Belgrano
MONTSERRAT
5 de Julio
Balcarce
Av Paseo Colón
Av Ing Huergo
Venezuela
Mexico
Defensa
Bernardo de Irigoyen
Dique No 2
To Reserva Ecológica Costanera Sur (southern entrance) (600m)
Plazoleta Olazábal
Av Independencia
Independencia
R Vera Peñaloza
Estados Unidos
Paseo Colón
Azopardo
Carlos Calvo
Humberto Primo
Plaza Dorrego
SAN TELMO
Dique No 1
South American Explorers
Av San Juan
San Juan
See La Boca Map (p58)
E
F
G
H
1
2
3
4
5
6
7

The Center, Congreso & San Telmo

Top Sights

Plaza de Mayo F3
Plaza Dorrego F7

Sights

1 Academia Nacionel del Tango E3
2 Basilica Nuestra Señora del Rosario F5
3 Cabildo F4
4 Casa Rosada G3
5 Catedral Metropolitana F3
6 Centro Cultural Borges F1
7 El Zanjón de Granados F6
8 Escuela Presidente Roca D2
9 Ex-Correo Central G2
Farmacia de la Estrella .... (see 18)
10 Fragata Sarmiento H4
11 Galerías Pacífico F1
12 Iglesia Nuestra Señora de Belén G7
13 Manzana de las Luces F4
14 Mercado San Telmo F6
15 Monumento a los Dos Congresos B4
16 Museo Argentino del Títere E6
17 Museo de Arte Moderno de Buenos Aires (Mamba) G7
18 Museo de la Ciudad F4
19 Museo de la Policía Federal F2
20 Museo del Bicentennario G3
Museo del Patrimonio .... (see 28)
21 Museo Etnográfico Juan B Ambrosetti G4
22 Museo Fortabat H1
23 Museo Mitre F2
Museo Mundial del Tango .... (see 1)
24 Museo Penitenciario G7
25 Obelisco D2
26 Palacio Barolo C4
27 Palacio de Justicia C2
28 Palacio de las Aguas Corrientes A1
29 Palacio del Congreso B4
30 Teatro Colón D1
31 Templo de la Congregación Israelita D1

Activities, Courses & Tours

32 Expanish E3
33 Say Hueque F5
34 Say Hueque E1
35 Tangol F6
36 University de Buenos Aires (UBA) G2

Sleeping

37 1890 Hotel Boutique D7
38 Art Factory E5
39 Brisas del Mar E7
40 Fiamingo Apart Hotel C3
41 Garden House D7
42 HI Obelisco Suites E2
43 Hostel Estoril-Terrazas Estoril C4
44 Hotel Alcázar E3
45 Hotel Bonito C6
46 Hotel Frossard E2
47 Hotel Reina D4
48 Hotel Sportsman C4
49 Hotel Suipacha Inn E2
50 Ideal Hostel E2
51 Kilca Hostel C5
52 Mansion Dandi Royale E6
53 Milhouse Annex D4
54 Milhouse Youth Hostel E4
55 Moreno Hotel F4
56 Portal del Sur E4
57 Residencial Universitaria Azul B3
58 Sabatico Hostel C5

was semi-abandoned, but a joint Argentine-Mexican team repaired and restored the murals in 1992.

Inside you'll find upscale stores and a large food court. The occasional tourist-oriented tango show happens in front on pedestrian Florida (especially on Sundays), while the excellent Centro Cultural Borges takes up the top floor.

Centro Cultural Borges CULTURAL CENTER
(Map p48; ☎5555-5359; www.ccborges.org.ar; cnr Viamonte & San Martín) One of BA's best cultural centers, located in the beautiful Galerías Pacífico building. Affordable offerings include classes, workshops, cinema, music concerts, dance shows, art exhibitions and stage productions.

Manzana de las Luces BUILDINGS
(Map p48) The Manzana de las Luces (Block of Enlightenment) includes the city's oldest colonial church, the Jesuit **Iglesia San Ignacio**. During colonial times this was BA's center of learning, and it still symbolizes high culture in the capital. The first to occupy this block were the Jesuits, and two of the five original buildings of the Jesuit

Eating

- Aldo's Vinoteca ... (see 55)
- 59 Amici Miei ... G7
- 60 Bar El Federal ... F6
- 61 Bar Plaza Dorrego ... G7
- 62 Broccolino ... E1
- 63 Café San Juan ... F7
- 64 Casal de Catalunya ... E6
- 65 Chan Chan ... C4
- 66 Chiquilín ... C3
- 67 Dylan ... F7
- 68 Gran Parrilla del Plata ... F6
- 69 Granix ... F3
- 70 Heladería Cadore ... B2
- 71 i Central Market ... H2
- 72 i Fresh Market ... H4
- 73 La Parolaccia Trattoria ... H4
- 74 Mash ... F5
- 75 Parrilla al Carbón ... E2
- 76 Pizzería Güerrín ... C2
- 77 Plaza Asturias ... D4
- 78 Pura Vida ... F2
- 79 Saatva ... B2
- 80 Siga la Vaca ... H6
- 81 Vía Flamina ... F3

Drinking

- 82 Café de los Angelitos ... A4
- 83 Café Tortoni ... E3
- 84 Debar ... D4
- 85 El Gato Negro ... B2
- 86 Gibraltar ... F6
- 87 Indie Bar ... G6
- 88 La Cigale ... G1
- 89 La Puerta Roja ... E6
- 90 La Puerto Rico ... F4
- 91 London City ... F3
- 92 Los del Barco ... F5
- 93 Pride Café ... G6

Entertainment

- 94 Ávila Bar ... C4
- 95 Bahrein ... F2
- 96 Boutique ... F5
- Café Tortoni ... (see 83)
- 97 Cantares ... D4
- 98 Cartelera Baires ... C2
- 99 Cartelera Espectáculos ... E2
- 100 Cartelera Vea Más ... B2
- 101 Confitería Ideal ... E2
- 102 El Balcón & Todomundo ... F7
- 103 El Beso ... A2
- 104 La Marshall ... F6
- La Puerto Rico ... (see 90)
- 105 La Trastienda ... G5
- 106 Los 36 Billares ... D4
- 107 Luna Park ... G2
- 108 Maluco Beleza ... B3
- Mitos Argentinos ... (see 102)
- 109 Niño Bien ... C7
- Piazzolla Tango ... (see 69)
- 110 Tango Porteño ... D2
- 111 Teatro Avenida ... D4
- Teatro Colón ... (see 30)
- 112 Teatro Presidente Alvear ... B2
- 113 Teatro San Martín ... C2

Shopping

- 114 Arte y Esperanza ... G4
- 115 Cualquier Verdura ... F7
- 116 En Buen Orden ... G6
- 117 Feria de San Telmo ... F7
- 118 Gil Antigüedades ... F7
- 119 Walrus Books ... F6
- 120 Wildlife ... D4
- 121 Zival's ... B3

Procuraduría still remain. Dating from 1730, these buildings include defensive tunnels discovered in 1912. The Universidad de Buenos Aires has occupied the site since independence in 1810. **Tours** (☎4331-9534; Perú 272; AR$12) in Spanish are available; drop by for a schedule.

Ex-Correo Central BUILDING

(Map p48) This massive beaux arts building, filling an entire city block, used to house BA's main post office. It took 20 years to complete and was originally modeled on New York City's main post office. The structure is currently being remodeled into a museum, offices and exhibition spaces, which might be finished in late 2012.

Museo de la Ciudad MUSEUM

(Map p48; ☎4331-9855; Defensa 219; admission AR$1, Mon & Wed free; ⊙11am-7pm) Upstairs, wander among the permanent and temporary exhibitions on old *porteño* life – toys and other everyday artifacts, plus whole period rooms. Downstairs (in the next-door annex) are salvaged doors and ancient hardware. Nearby, at the corner of Defensa, is the **Farmacia de la Estrella**, a functioning pharmacy with gorgeous woodwork and elaborate late-19th-century ceiling murals.

Museo Etnográfico Juan B Ambrosetti MUSEUM

(Map p48; ☎4345-8196; Moreno 350; admission AR$3; ⏰1-7pm Tue-Fri, 3-7pm Sat & Sun) This small but attractive anthropological museum displays collections from the Andean northwest, Patagonia and elsewhere in South America. Beautiful indigenous artifacts are presented, including intricate jewelry and Mapuche ponchos, while an African and Asian room showcases priceless items. Tours are available in English and Spanish (call for hours).

Basílica Nuestra Señora del Rosario NOTABLE BUILDING

(Map p48; cnr Defensa & Av Belgrano) Further south, this 18th-century Dominican basilica has a colorful history. On its left tower are the replicated scars of shrapnel from fire against British troops who holed up here during the 1806 invasion. Tours in Spanish are available (☎4331-1668; admission by appointment only Mon-Fri, at 3:30pm & 4:30pm Sun) displays the flags that were captured from the British.

FREE **Museo de la Policía Federal** MUSEUM

(Map p48; ☎4394-6857; San Martín 353, 7th fl; ⏰2-6pm Tue-Thu) In the heart of the financial district, this museum proudly displays a whole slew of uniforms, medals, guns, drug paraphernalia and gambling exhibits. Avoid taking your kids into the room way in back – grisly forensic photos and dummies of murder victims are disturbing.

Museo Mitre MUSEUM

(Map p48; ☎4394-8240; San Martín 336; admission AR$5; ⏰1-5:15pm Mon-Fri) Bartolomé Mitre, who became Argentina's president in 1862, resided at this colonial house, now a museum. After leaving office, he founded the influential daily *La Nación,* still a *porteño* institution. The museum reflection 19th-century upper-class life well. It's full of Mitre's personal effects, such as home decorations and furniture.

Museo Mundial del Tango MUSEUM

(Map p48; ☎4345-6967; Av de Mayo 833, 1st fl; admission AR$15; ⏰2:30-7:30pm Mon-Fri) Located below the Academia Nacional del Tango is this tango museum – for fans of the dance only. Two large rooms are filled with tango memorabilia, from old records and photos to historic literature and posters. Tango shoes are also featured, but the highlight has to be one of Carlos Gardel's famous fedora hats.

PUERTO MADERO

The newest and least conventional of the capital's 48 official barrios is Puerto Madero, located east of the Microcentro. Once an old waterfront, it's now a wonderful place to stroll, boasting cobbled paths and a long line of attractive brick warehouses that have been converted into ritzy lofts, business offices and upscale restaurants. Today this neighborhood holds some of BA's most expensive real estate.

In the mid-19th century the city's mudflats were transformed into a modernized port for Argentina's burgeoning international commerce. Puerto Madero was completed in 1898, but it had exceeded its budget – and by 1910 the amount of cargo was already too great for the new port. Only the 1926 completion of Retiro's Puerto Nuevo solved these problems.

TOP CHOICE **Museo Fortabat** MUSEUM

(Map p48; ☎4310-6600; www.coleccionfortabat.org.ar; Olga Cossettini 141; admission AR$20; ⏰noon-9pm Tue-Sun) Rivaling Palermo's Malba museum for cutting-edge looks is this fancy art museum. It shows off the collection of multi-millionaire Amalia Lacroze de Fortabat, Argentina's wealthiest woman. The museum's airy salons exhibit works by famous Argentine and international artists – look for Warhol's take on Fortabat herself. Movable aluminum panels above the roof open and close, keeping sun off the glassy ceiling. Call ahead for tours in English.

Fragata Sarmiento MUSEUM

(Map p48; ☎4334-9386; Dique No 3; admission AR$2; ⏰10am-7pm) Over 23,000 Argentine naval cadets and officers have trained aboard this 85m ship, which sailed around the world nearly 40 times between 1897 and 1938 but never participated in combat. On board are the records of its voyages, nautical items and even the stuffed remains of Lampazo (the ship's pet dog).

Reserva Ecológica Costanera Sur NATURE RESERVE

(off Map p48; ☎4893-1640; Av Tristán Achával Rodríguez 1550; ⏰8am-7pm Tue-Sun) The beautifully marshy land of this nature preserve makes it a popular site for weekend outings, when hundreds of picnickers, cyclists and families come for fresh air and natural views. If you're lucky you may spot a river turtle or a coypu; bird watchers will adore the 200-plus bird species that pause to rest here. Tours in Spanish are available on weekends at 10:30am and 3:30pm, when you can also rent bikes just outside the park's northern and southern entrances. Full-moon tours are also available; call to reserve.

CONGRESO

Congreso is an interesting mix of old-time cinemas and theaters, bustling commerce and hard-core politics. The buildings still hold that European aura, but there's more grittiness here than in the Microcentro: it has a more local city feel, with an atmosphere of faded elegance and fewer fancy crowds.

Separating Congreso from the Microcentro is Av 9 de Julio, 'the widest street in the world!', as proud *porteños* love to boast. While this may be true – it's 16 lanes at its widest – the nearby side streets Cerrito and Carlos Pellegrini make it look even broader.

TOP CHOICE **Teatro Colón** NOTABLE BUILDING

(Map p48; ☎4378-7127 www.teatrocolon.org.ar; Cerrito 628) Started in 1880 and finished in 1908, the Teatro Colón is a major landmark and gorgeous world-class facility for opera, ballet and classical music. It was the southern hemisphere's largest theater until the Sydney Opera House was built in 1973. Opening night featured Verdi's *Aïda*, and visitors have been wowed ever since. Even at times of economic hardship, the elaborate Colón remains a high national priority.

Newly renovated in 2010 for Argentina's bicentennial celebrations, the Teatro Colón offers popular and worthwhile daily **tours** (English/Spanish tour AR$60/AR$20; ⏲English 11am, noon, 1pm & 2pm, Spanish every 15min 9am-3.45pm).

Palacio del Congreso NOTABLE BUILDING

(Map p48; ☎4010-3000, ext 2410; Hipólito Yrigoyen 1849) Colossal and topped with a green dome, the Palacio del Congreso cost more than twice its projected budget and set a precedent for contemporary Argentine public-works projects. It was modeled on

BUENOS AIRES FOR CHILDREN

Palermo's **Parque 3 de Febrero** (Map p64) is a huge park where on weekends traffic isn't allowed on the ring road (and you can rent bikes, boats and in-line skates nearby). Other good stops here include a planetarium, a zoo and a Japanese garden. If you're downtown and need a nature break, there's **Reserva Ecológica Costanera Sur** (Map p48), a large nature preserve with good bird-watching and no vehicular traffic.

Shopping malls make safe destinations for families – one of the best is **Abasto** (Map p64), which boasts a full-blown children's museum (actually a fancy playground) and a mini-amusement park.

In San Telmo, check out the puppet museum, **Museo Argentino del Títere** (Map p48; ☎4307-6917; www.museoargdeltitere.com.ar; Estados Unidos 802; admission free; ⏲9:30am-12:30pm & 3-6pm Tue, Wed & Fri, 3-6pm Thu, Sat & Sun), which has inexpensive weekend shows.

Recoleta's **Museo Participativo de Ciencias** (Map p60; ☎4806-3456; www.mpc.org.ar; Junín 1930; admission AR$20; ⏲vary widely, see website) is a hands-on science museum with interactive learning displays. In Caballito is the good **Museo Argentino de Ciencias Naturales** (Natural Science Museum; p63).

Tigre (p103), north of the city, makes a great day excursion. Get there via the Tren de la Costa; it ends right at Parque de la Costa, a typical amusement park with fun rides and activities. Take a boat trip on the delta or wander the market for fruit and house wares.

Outside the city is the exceptional zoo, **Parque Temaikén** (☎03488-436-900; www.temaiken.com.ar; RP 25, Km 1, Escobar; adult/child 3-10 AR$106/82; ⏲10am-7pm Tue-Sun Dec–mid-Mar, to 6pm mid–Mar-Dec). Only the most charming animal species are on display (think meerkats, pygmy hippos and white tigers), roaming freely around natural enclosures. An excellent aquarium comes with touch pools, and plenty of interactive areas provide mental stimulation.

To help calm down temper tantrums, visit one of BA's dozens of ice-cream shops; see p82 for suggestions.

the Capitol Building in Washington, DC, and was completed in 1906. Across the way, the **Monumento a los Dos Congresos** honors the congresses of 1810 in BA and 1816 in Tucumán, both of which led to Argentine independence.

Inside the Congreso, free guided tours are given of the Senado at 11am and 4pm every weekday except Wednesday; tours of the Congreso are given at 11am and 5pm on the same days. Go to the entrance on Hipólito Yrigoyen and bring photo ID.

Palacio Barolo BUILDING

(Map p48; ☎4381-1885; www.pbarolo.com.ar; Av de Mayo 1370) This striking, 22-story building was commissioned by cotton tycoon Luis Barolo, designed by Italian architect Mario Palanti and finished in 1923. The building's design reflects Dante's *Divine Comedy;* its height (100m) is a reference to each *canto* (song), the number of its floors to verses per song (22), and its divided structure to hell, purgatory and heaven. At the top is a lighthouse with amazing 360° city views.

There are **tours** (AR$40; on the hr 4-7pm Mon & Thu) in English and Spanish. Special evening tours also available; see website.

FREE **Palacio de las Aguas Corrientes** BUILDING, MUSEUM

About six blocks west of Plaza Lavalle, this gorgeous and eclectic Swedish-designed waterworks building (1894) is topped by French-style mansard roofs and covered in 170,000 glazed tiles and 130,000 enameled bricks. If you like quirky museums, check out the small **Museo del Patrimonio** (Map p48; ☎6319-1104; cnr Córdoba & Riobamba; admission free; ⌚9am-1pm Mon-Fri) on the 2nd floor; it's full of pipe fittings, a few beautiful tiles and odd toilets. Guided **tours** (⌚11am Mon, Wed & Fri) offer a backstage glimpse of the building's inner workings. Bring photo ID and enter via Riobamba.

Obelisco MONUMENT

(Map p48) At Avs 9 de Julio and Corrientes lies the city's famous Obelisco, 67m high and built in 1936; it's the destination of *porteño* sports fans when they have a big win to celebrate.

Plaza Lavalle PLAZA

(Map p48) The plaza is surrounded by the austere neoclassical **Escuela Presidente Roca** (1902), the French-style **Palacio de Justicia** (1904) and the landmark Teatro Colón. Nearby is the **Templo de la Congregación Israelita**, Argentina's largest synagogue.

SAN TELMO

Full of charm and personality, San Telmo is one of BA's most attractive and historically rich barrios. Narrow cobbled streets and low-story colonial housing retain an old-time feel, though the tourist dollar continues to bring about changes.

Historically, San Telmo is famous for the violent street fighting that took place when British troops, at war with Spain, invaded the city in 1806. British forces advanced up narrow Defensa, but an impromptu militia drove the British back to their ships. The victory gave *porteños* confidence in their ability to stand apart from Spain, even though the city's independence had to wait another three years.

After this San Telmo became a fashionable, classy neighborhood, until, in the late 19th century, a yellow-fever epidemic hit, driving the rich north into present-day Recoleta. Many older mansions were subdivided and became *conventillos* (tenements) to house poor families. Years ago these *conventillos* attracted artists and bohemians looking for cheap rent, but these days they're likelier to be filled with fancy shops, cheap hostels or rich expats.

Plaza Dorrego PLAZA

The heart of San Telmo is Plaza Dorrego. It hosts a famous and hugely popular antiques market on Sundays, when nearby streets are closed off to vehicular traffic. Hundreds of street stalls sell both antiques and modern knickknacks while buskers work the crowds. There are also good donation tango shows, but watch your bag.

Plaza Dorrego is much calmer on other days, when tables are set up for peaceful dining.

TOP CHOICE **El Zanjón de Granados** MUSEUM

(Map p48; ☎4361-3002; www.elzanjon.com.ar; Defensa 755; ⌚tours on the hour 11am-3pm Mon-Fri, every ½hr 1-6pm Sun) This amazing architectural site is one of the more unusual places in Buenos Aires. Below the remains of a mansion, a series of old tunnels, sewers and water wells going back to 1730 were discovered. All have been meticulously reconstructed, brick by brick, and attractively lit, offering a fascinating glimpse of the city's architectural past. Choose between hour-long tours during the week (AR$60 in both Spanish and English) or half-hour tours on Sundays (AR$30 in Spanish, AR$40 in English).

Museo de Arte Moderno de Buenos Aires (Mamba) MUSEUM
(Map p48; ☎4342-3001; www.museodeartemoderno.buenosaires.gob.ar; Av San Juan 350; admission AR$1, Tue free; ⏲noon-7pm Mon-Fri, 11am-8pm Sat & Sun) Housed in a former tobacco warehouse, this spacious and newly remodeled museum shows off the works of both national and international contemporary artists. Expect temporary exhibitions showcasing everything from photography to industrial design, and from figurative to conceptual art. There are plans to integrate the old cinema museum next door, too.

FREE **Museo Penitenciario** MUSEUM
(Map p48; ☎4361-0917; Humberto Primo 378; ⏲2-6pm Thu-Sun) Just off Plaza Dorrego, this prison museum occupies a building that was first a convent, then a women's prison. Don't miss the homemade playing cards and shivs, plus the tennis balls used to hide drugs. Old jail cells and an infirmary are also exhibited.

FREE **Museo Histórico Nacional** MUSEUM
(Map p58; ☎4307-1182; Defensa 1600; ⏲11am-6pm Wed-Sun) This national historical museum is located at the supposed site of Pedro de Mendoza's original founding of the city in 1536. Major figures of Argentine historical periods, such as San Martín, Rosas and Sarmiento, are represented, along with a few artifacts and paintings. Exhibits are a bit sparse, but the security is great – be prepared to hand over your bag while you look around.

Iglesia Nuestra Señora de Belén CHURCH
(Humberto Primo 340) Near Plaza Dorrego, this baroque, neocolonial building was a Jesuit school until 1767, when the Bethlemite order took it over.

Mercado San Telmo BUILDING
An old fruit-and-vegetable market that still functions today, it's worth a peek for its architecture. It's located in the center of the block bordered by Estados Unidos, Bolívar, Carlos Calvo and Defensa.

LA BOCA

Blue collar and raffish to the core, La Boca is very much a locals' neighborhood. In the mid-19th century, La Boca became home to Spanish and Italian immigrants who settled along the Riachuelo, the sinuous river that divides the city from the surrounding province of Buenos Aires. Many came during the booming 1880s and ended up working in the many meat-packing plants and warehouses here, processing and shipping out much of Argentina's vital beef exports. After sprucing up the shipping barges, the port dwellers splashed leftover paint on the corrugated-metal sidings of their own houses – unwittingly giving La Boca what would become one of its claims to fame. Unfortunately, some of the neighborhood's color also comes from the rainbow slick of industrial wastes on the river.

Caminito, near the southern edge of La Boca, is the barrio's most famous street, and on weekends busloads of camera-laden tourists come here for photographs and to browse the small crafts fair while watching tango dancers perform for spare change. A riverside pedestrian walkway offers a close-up sniff of the Riachuelo, while a few museums provide mental stimulation.

Four blocks inland is **La Bombonera stadium** (Brandsen), home of the Boca Juniors football team – the former club of disgraced superstar Diego Armando Maradona.

Fundación Proa MUSEUM
(Map p58; ☎4104-1000; www.proa.org; Av Don Pedro de Mendoza 1929; admission AR$12; ⏲11am-7pm Tue-Sun) This elegant art foundation exhibits works by only the most cutting-edge national and international contemporary artists in both traditional and more unusual mediums. Visit the rooftop terrace (no need to pay entry for this) – the views are excellent, and you can grab a meal or drink in the fancy restaurant.

Museo de Bellas Artes de La Boca Benito Quinquela Martín MUSEUM
(Map p58; ☎4301-1080; Av Don Pedro de Mendoza 1835; suggested donation AR$8; ⏲10am-6pm Tue-Fri, 11am-6pm Sat & Sun) On display at this

> **BOCA WARNING**
>
> La Boca is not the kind of neighborhood for casual strolls – it can be downright rough in spots. Don't stray far from the riverside walk, El Caminito or La Bombonera stadium, especially while toting expensive cameras. And certainly don't cross the bridge over the Riachuelo. There's nothing you'd really want to see outside the touristy areas, anyway. Buses 29, 64 and 152 go from Palermo or the city center to La Boca. Taxis are best after dark.

Going to a Fútbol Game

In a land where Maradona is God, going to see a *fútbol* (soccer) game can be a religious experience. The *superclásico* between the Boca Juniors and River Plate has been called the number one sporting event to see before you die, but even the less-celebrated games will give you insight into Argentina's national passion.

Attending a regular match isn't too difficult. Keep an eye on the clubs' websites, which inform when and where tickets will be sold; often they're sold at the stadium before the game. The price for *popular* (bleachers) tickets run AR$40 to AR$70, while *platea* (seats) are usually from AR$60 to AR$150.

If you want to see a *clásico* – a match between two major teams – getting a ticket will be much harder. Plus Boca doesn't even put tickets for its key matches on sale; all tickets go to *socios* (members). Instead, you're better off going with an agency such as Tangol (see p69). Expect to pay around AR$400 to AR$600 for a *clásico*, and AR$1200 for a *superclásico* (River-Boca). Not cheap, but it's much easier (and safer) getting a ticket this way; fake tickets are common.

If you want to chance getting your own *clásico* or *superclásico* ticket, however, you can always look online at www.buenosaires.craigslist.org or www.mercadolibre.com.ar. And if you're confident in your bargaining skills, scalpers will always exist.

Dress down, and try to look inconspicuous when you go. Take only minimum cash and keep your camera close. You probably won't get in with water bottles, and food and drink in the stadium is meager and expensive. Arrive early to enjoy the insane build-up to the game. Most importantly – don't wear the opposing team's colors.

Clockwise from top left

1. Spectators, La Bombonera Stadium (p55)
2. Maradona mural, Caminito (p55) **3.** *Superclásico* (p557), La Bombonera stadium

TEAMS

Buenos Aires has two-dozen professional football teams – the most of any city in the world. Here are some of them:

» **Boca Juniors** (☎4362-2260; www.bocajuniors.com.ar)

» **River Plate** (☎4789-1200; www.cariverplate.com.ar)

» **Racing** (☎4229-8389; www.racingclub.com)

» **Independiente** (☎4201-7634; www.caindependiente.com)

» **San Lorenzo de Almagro** (☎4016-2600; www.clubsanlorenzo.com.ar)

TERRY CARTER/LONELY PLANET IMAGES ©

2

JESUS OCHOA/LONELY PLANET IMAGES ©

3

TERRY CARTER/LONELY PLANET IMAGES ©

La Boca

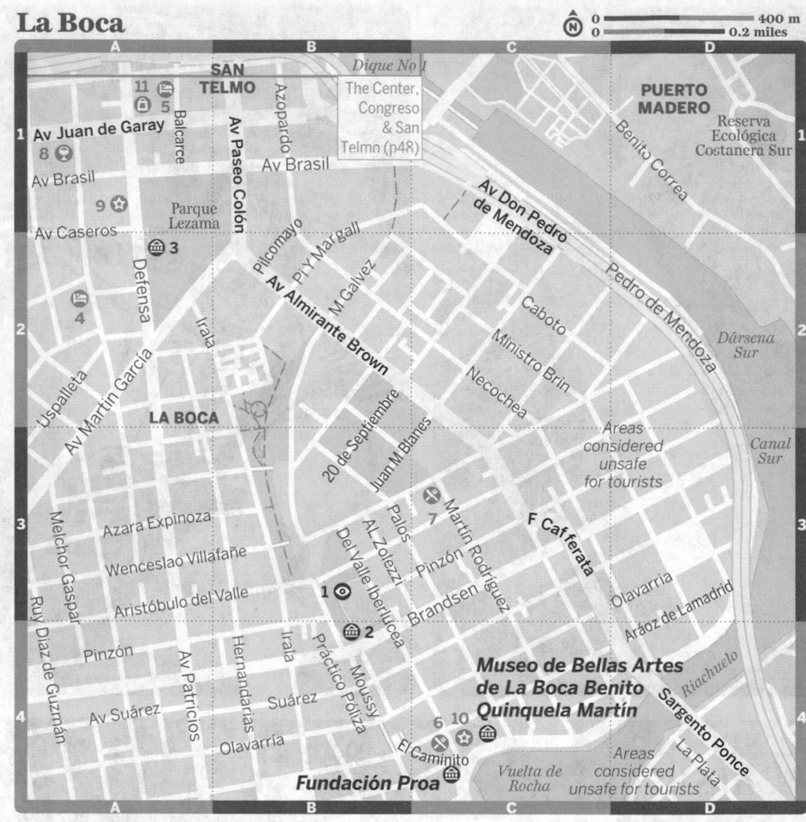

modern museum are the works of Benito Quinquela Martín, which center on La Boca's port history. There are also paintings by more contemporary Argentine artists, along with a small but excellent collection of painted wood figureheads (carved statues decorating the bows of ships).

Museo de la Pasión Boquense MUSEUM
(Map above; ☎4362-1100; www.museoboquense.com; Brandsen 805; admission AR$35; ⏰10am-5:30pm) High-tech and spiffy, this museum chronicles La Bombonera stadium, some soccer idols' histories, past highlights (on many videos), the championships, the trophies and, of course, the goooooals. It's located right under the stadium; peek at the pitch for a few extra pesos.

RETIRO

Well-located Retiro is one of the ritziest neighborhoods in BA – but it hasn't always been this way. The area was the site of a monastery during the 17th century and later became the *retiro* (country retreat) of Agustín de Robles, a Spanish governor. Since then, Retiro's current **Plaza San Martín** – which sits on a bluff – has played host to a slave market, a military fort and even a bullring. Things are more quiet and exclusive these days.

Plaza San Martín PLAZA
(Map p60) French landscape architect Carlos Thays designed the leafy Plaza San Martín, whose prominent monument is the obligatory equestrian statue of José de San Martín. Surrounding the plaza are several landmark public buildings, such as the **Palacio San Martín**, an art-nouveau mansion originally built for the elite Anchorena family and sometimes open to the public; the huge and beautiful Palacio Paz; and the 120m-high **Edificio Kavanagh** (1935), once South America's tallest building.

La Boca

Top Sights
Fundación Proa.................................C4
Museo de Bellas Artes de La Boca Benito Quinquela Martín...C4

Sights
1 La Bombonera Stadium....................B3
2 Museo de la Pasión Boquense...........B4
3 Museo Histórico Nacional.................A2

Sleeping
4 Casa Bolivar.......................................A2
5 Sandanzas Hostel.............................A1

Eating
6 El Samovar de Rasputín.....................C4
7 Il Matterello.......................................C3

Drinking
8 Doppelgänger A1

Entertainment
9 Centro Cultural Torquato Tasso A1
10 El Samovar de Rasputín....................C4

Shopping
11 Moebius...A1

The 76m **Torre de los Ingleses**, across Av del Libertador from Plaza San Martín, was a donation by the city's British community in 1916. Opposite the plaza is the impressive and busy **Estación Retiro** (Retiro train station), built in 1915 when the British controlled the country's railroads. Don't wander behind the station – it's a shantytown.

Palacio Paz BUILDING
(Map p60; ☎4311-1071, ext 147; www.palaciopaz.com.ar; Santa Fe 750; tours in English/Spanish AR$50/35; ⏰English 3:30pm Wed & Thu, Spanish 11am & 3pm Wed-Fri, 11am Sat) This gorgeous palace, also called the Círculo Militar, was once the private residence of José C Paz, founder of the still-running newspaper *La Prensa*. Inside are ornate rooms, salons and halls with wood-tiled floors, marble walls and gilded details. Nearly everything was ordered from Europe and assembled here.

Museo de Arte Hispanoamericano Isaac Fernández Blanco MUSEUM
(Map p60; ☎4327-0228; Suipacha 1422; admission AR$1, free Thu; ⏰2-7pm Tue-Fri, 11am-7pm Sat & Sun) This neocolonial-era mansion turned museum holds some gorgeous pieces of silverwork, religious paintings, Jesuit statuary and antiques. There's been no effort to place items in any historical context, but everything is in great condition, and an attractive garden provides a peaceful sanctuary. Call ahead for tours in English, German or French.

Museo de Armas MUSEUM
(Map p60; ☎4311-1071, ext 179; Santa Fe 702; admission AR$10; ⏰1-7pm Mon-Fri) If you're big on weaponry, don't miss this extravagant museum showcasing over 2000 bazookas, grenade launchers, machine guns, muskets, pistols, lances and swords – even the gas mask for a combat horse is on display. Don't miss the Japanese suits of armor.

Teatro Nacional Cervantes BUILDING, MUSEUM
(Map p60; ☎4815-8883; www.teatrocervantes.gov.ar; Av Córdoba 1155) This ornamented building dates from 1921 and is home to a historical theater with grand tiled lobby and plush red-velvet chairs. Enjoy the elegance – however faded – with a tour (call for the schedule).

On the corner, and attached to the theater is the tiny, low-key **Museo Nacional del Teatro** (☎4815-8883, ext 156; cnr Córdoba & Libertad; admission free; ⏰10am-6pm Mon-Fri). Check out the gaucho suit worn by Carlos Gardel and the *bandoneón* that once belonged to Paquita Bernardo, Argentina's first musician to play this accordionlike instrument.

RECOLETA & BARRIO NORTE

BA's wealthiest citizens live and breathe in Recoleta, the city's most exclusive and fashionable neighborhood. In the 1870s many upper-class *porteños* relocated here from San Telmo during a yellow-fever epidemic. Today you can best see the wealth of this sumptuous quarter on **Av Alvear**, where many of the old mansions (and newer international boutiques) are located.

Full of lush parks, classy museums and French architecture, Recoleta is best known for its Cementerio de la Recoleta. The **Plaza Intendente Alvear** hosts the city's most popular crafts fair. A little further north is the sinuous sculptural flower **Floralis Genérica**, whose giant metal petals close up at night – if all the gears are working, that is.

Barrio Norte is a subneighborhood southwest of Recoleta, but the lines are blurred.

TOP CHOICE **Cementerio de la Recoleta** CEMETERY
(Map p60; ☎4803-1594; cnr Junín & Guido; admission free; ⏰7am-5:30pm) Wander for hours in this amazing cemetery where 'streets' are

Retiro, Recoleta & Barrio Norte

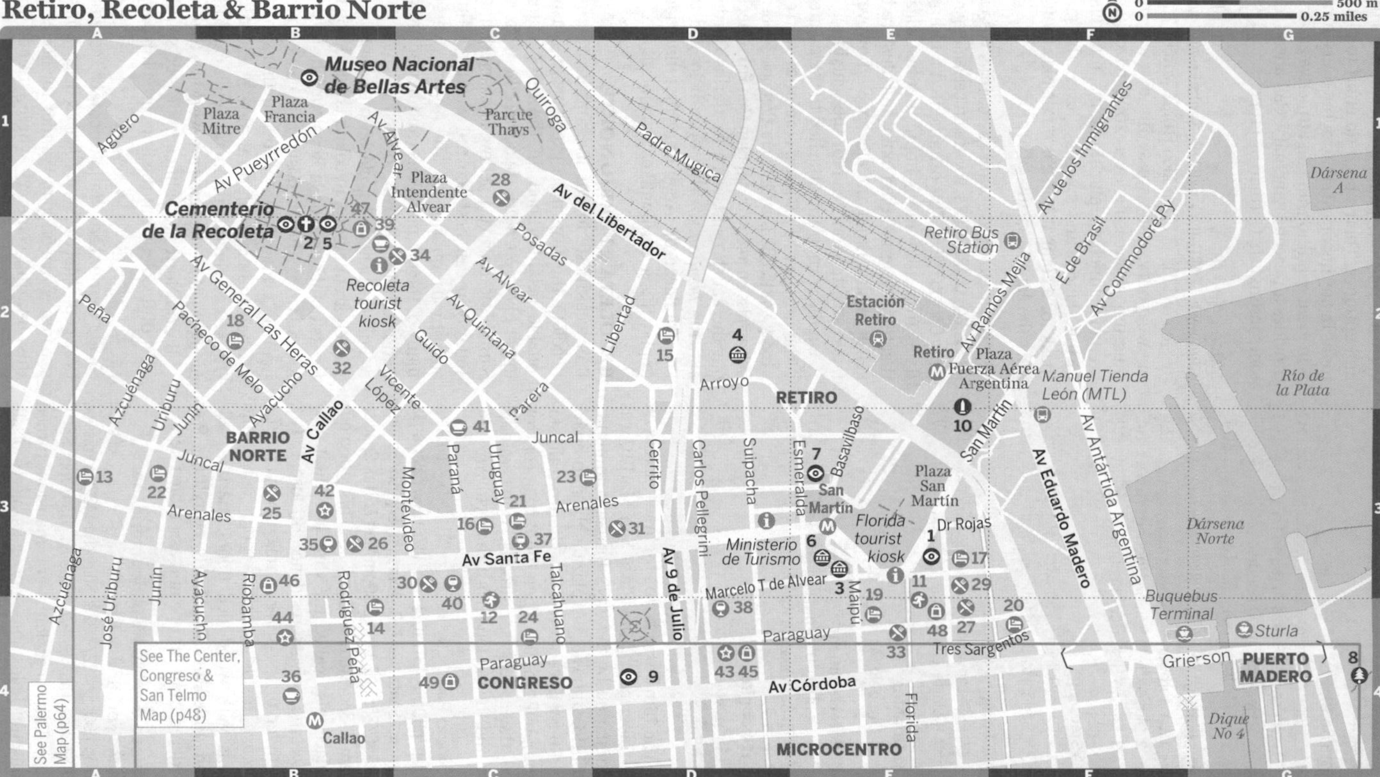

Retiro, Recoleta & Barrio Norte

Top Sights
Cementerio de la Recoleta B2
Museo Nacional de Bellas Artes B1

Sights
1 Edificio Kavanagh E3
2 Iglesia Nuestra Señora del Pilar B2
3 Museo de Armas E3
4 Museo de Arte Hispanoamericano Isaac Fernández Blanco D2
Museo Nacional del Teatro .... (see 9)
5 Museo Participativo de Ciencias B2
6 Palacio Paz E3
7 Palacio San Martín E3
8 Reserva Ecológica Costanera Sur (northern entrance) G4
9 Teatro Nacional Cervantes D4
10 Torre de los Ingleses E2

Activities, Courses & Tours
11 Tangol E4
12 VOS C4

Sleeping
13 A Hotel A3
14 Design Suites B4
15 Four Seasons D2
16 Hotel Bel Air C3
17 Hotel Central Córdoba E3
18 Hotel Lion D'Or B2
19 Hotel Pulitzer E4
20 Hotel Tres Sargentos F4
21 Marseille des Anges C3
22 Poetry Building A3
23 Recoleta Hostel C3
24 Yira Yira Guesthouse C4

Eating
25 Como en Casa B3
26 Cumaná B3
27 Dadá E4
28 El Sanjuanino C1
29 Filo E3
30 Freddo C3
31 Gran Bar Danzón D3
32 Rodi Bar B2
33 Sipan E4
34 Una Altra Volta C2

Drinking
35 Casa Bar B3
36 Clásica y Moderna B4
37 El Alamo C3
38 Flux D4
39 La Biela B2
40 Milión C3
41 Nucha C3

Entertainment
42 Basement Club B3
43 ND/Ateneo D4
44 Notorious B4

Shopping
45 Arte y Esperanza D4
46 El Ateneo B3
47 Feria Artesanal B2
48 Kelly's Regionales E4
49 Portobello Vintage Boutique C4

lined with impressive statues and marble sarcophagi. Crypts hold the remains of the city's elite: past presidents, military heroes, influential politicians and the rich and famous. Hunt down Evita's grave, and bring your camera – there are some great photo ops here. Tours in English are available at 11am on Tuesday and Thursday (call to confirm). For a great map and information, order Robert Wright's PDF guide (www.recoletacemetery.com).

TOP CHOICE Museo Nacional de Bellas Artes
MUSEUM

(Map p60; ☎5288-9900; www.mnba.org.ar; Av del Libertador 1473; admission free; ⏰12:30-8:30pm Tue-Fri, 9:30am-8:30pm Sat & Sun) Arguably Argentina's top fine-arts museum, this destination is a must-see for art lovers. It showcases works by Renoir, Monet, Gauguin, Cézanne and Picasso, along with many classic Argentine artists such as Xul Solar and Edwardo Sívori. There are also temporary exhibits and a small gift shop.

Iglesia Nuestra Señora del Pilar
CHURCH, MUSEUM

(Map p60) Next door to the cemetery, this 1732 baroque colonial church has a small **museum** (historic cloisters; donation AR$5; ⏰10:30am-6:15pm Mon-Sat, 2:30-6:15pm Sun) to the left and upstairs.

PALERMO

Palermo is heaven on Earth for BA's middle class. Its large, grassy parks – regally punctuated with grand monuments – are popular

DON'T MISS

EVITA'S GRAVE

She's Recoleta's biggest star, and everyone who visits the cemetery wants to see her final resting place. Here's how to find it: Go up to the first major 'intersection' from the entrance, where there's a statue. Turn left, continue until a mausoleum blocks your way, go around it to the right and turn right at the wide 'street.' After three blocks look to the left and you'll likely see people at her site, along with bunches of flowers.

destinations on weekends, when families fill the shady lanes, cycle the bike paths and paddle on the peaceful lakes. Many important museums and elegant embassies are also located here, and certain subneighborhoods of Palermo have become some of the city's hottest destinations for shopping and nightlife.

Palermo's green spaces haven't always been for the masses. The area around **Parque 3 de Febrero** was originally the 19th-century dictator Juan Manuel de Rosas' private retreat and became public parkland after his fall from power. Within these green spaces you'll now find a zoo and planetarium. Just south of the zoo is **Plaza Italia**, Palermo's main transport hub.

One of the capital's most trendsetting areas is **Palermo Viejo**, a scenic neighborhood with colonial buildings and plenty of fine shopping, dining and nightlife; it's further subdivided into Palermo Soho and Palermo Hollywood. The heart of this neighborhood is **Plaza Serrano**, a small but very popular plaza surrounded by bars and restaurants, and host to a small weekend arts fair. Another popular but much smaller neighborhood to the north is **Las Cañitas**; many restaurants and other nightspots here attract hordes of hipsters at night, when Av Báez clogs with traffic.

TOP CHOICE Museo de Arte Latinoamericano de Buenos Aires (Malba) — MUSEUM

(Map p64; ☎4808-6511; www.malba.org.ar; Av Figueroa Alcorta 3415; admission AR$22, Wed AR$10; ⊙noon-8pm Thu-Mon, to 9pm Wed) Sparkling inside its glass walls, this airy modern arts museum is BA's fanciest. Art patron Eduardo Costantini displays his limited but fine collection, which includes work by Argentines Xul Solar and Antonio Berni, plus some pieces by Mexicans Diego Rivera and Frida Kahlo. A cinema screens art-house films, and there's an excellent cafe for watching the beautiful people.

TOP CHOICE Museo Nacional de Arte Decorativo — MUSEUM

(Map p64; ☎4802-6606; www.mnad.org; Av del Libertador 1902; admission from AR$5; ⊙2-7pm Tue-Sun) Located in the stunning beaux-arts mansion called Palacio Errázuriz (1911), this museum displays the posh belongings of the Errázuri-Alvear family. Everything from Renaissance religious paintings and porcelain dishes to Italian sculptures and artwork by El Greco and Rodin can be admired; call for tours in English or French. The outside cafe in front is a fine place to refresh yourself on a sunny day.

Jardín Zoológico — ZOO

(Map p64; ☎ 4011-9900; www.zoobuenosaires.com.ar; cnr Avs Las Heras & Sarmiento; admission AR$23-34; ⊙10am-6pm Tue-Sun Oct-Mar, to 5pm Apr-Sep) Artificial lakes, pleasant walking paths and over 350 species of animal entertain the crowds at this relatively good zoo. Most of the enclosures offer decent space and some buildings are impressive in themselves – check out the elephant house. An aquarium, a monkey island, a petting zoo and a large aviary are other highlights.

Jardín Japonés — GARDENS

(Map p64; ☎4804-4922; www.jardinjapones.org.ar; cnr Avs Casares & Berro; admission AR$8; ⊙10am-6pm) This peaceful paradise is one of the capital's best-kept gardens, where you can enjoy lovely ponds filled with koi and spanned by pretty bridges. The teahouse and restaurant make for good breaks, and Japanese culture can be experienced through occasional exhibitions and workshops.

Museo Evita — MUSEUM

(Map p64; ☎4807-0306; www.museoevita.org; Lafinur 2988; local/foreigner AR$5/15; ⊙11am-7pm Tue-Sun) Everybody who is anybody in Argentina has their own museum, and Eva Perón is no exception. You can see her immortalized in Museo Evita through videos, historical photos, books, old posters and newspaper headlines – even her fingerprints are recorded. The prize memorabilia, however, would have to be her wardrobe: dresses, shoes, handbags, hats and blouses stand proudly behind shining glass, forever pressed and pristine.

Museo de Arte Popular José Hernández MUSEUM

(Map p64; ☎4803-2384; www.museohernandez.buenosaires.gob.ar; Av del Libertador 2373; admission AR$1, Sun free; ⏲1-7pm Wed-Fri, 10am-8pm Sat & Sun) This modest-sized museum showcases a beautiful permanent exhibition of silverwork (gaucho knives, horse spurs, *mate* gourds), along with some religious artifacts and diverse changing exhibitions ranging from folk crafts to modern toys.

Museo Xul Solar MUSEUM

(Map p64; ☎4824-3302; www.xulsolar.org.ar; Laprida 1212; admission AR$10, Thu free; ⏲noon-8pm Tue-Fri, to 7pm Sat, closed Feb) Xul Solar was a painter, inventor and poet, and this museum highlights over 80 of his bizarre, surreal and even cartoonish paintings; the guy was in a class of his own.

Tierra Santa THEME PARK

(☎4784-9551; www.tierrasanta-bsas.com.ar; Av Costanera R Obligado 5790; admission AR$40; ⏲call for hours) Even respectful, devout Catholics will find this – the 'world's first religious theme park' – a very tacky place. It boasts animatronic dioramas of Adam and Eve and the Last Supper, but its *pièce de résistance* is a giant Jesus rising from a fake mountain – aka the resurrection – every half hour. It's just north of Palermo, near the water.

Planetario Galileo Galilei PLANETARIUM

(Map p64; ☎4771-9393; www.planetario.gov.ar; cnr Avs Sarmiento & Belisario Roldán) This planetarium has shows and celestial viewings.

Centro Islámico Rey Fahd MOSQUE

(Map p64; ☎4899-0201; www.ccislamicoreyfahd.org.ar; Av Int Bullrich 55) This landmark mosque, built by Saudis on land donated by former president Carlos Menem, is southeast of Las Cañitas. Free tours in Spanish are offered on Tuesday, Thursday and Saturday at noon (bring your passport and dress conservatively).

BELGRANO

Bustling Av Cabildo, the racing heartbeat of Belgrano, is an overwhelming jumble of noise and neon; it's a two-way street of clothing, shoe and houseware shops that does its part to support the mass consumerism of *porteños*.

Only a block east of Av Cabildo, **Plaza Belgrano** is the site of a modest but fun weekend crafts fair (see p98).

Near the plaza stands the Italianate **Iglesia de la Inmaculada Concepción**, a church popularly known as 'La Redonda' because of its impressive dome. Four blocks northeast of Plaza Belgrano is **Barrancas de Belgrano**, an attractive park on one of the few natural hillocks in the city. And nearby, just across the train tracks, Belgrano's small **Chinatown** offers decent Chinese restaurants and cheap goods.

Museo de Arte Español Enrique Larreta MUSEUM

(☎4784-4040; Juramento 2291; admission AR$1; ⏲1-7pm Mon -Fri, 10am-8pm Sat & Sun). This is the best of Belgrano's several museums. It's on the plaza and displays the Argentine novelist's gorgeous art collection.

ONCE & AROUND

BA's most ethnically colorful neighborhood is Once, with sizable groups of Jews, Peruvians and Koreans. The cheap market around Once train station always bustles, with vendors selling their goods on sidewalks and crowds everywhere.

Museo Argentino de Ciencias Naturales MUSEUM

(off Map p64; ☎4982-6595; Ángel Gallardo 490; admission AR$5; ⏲2-7pm) West of Once is Caballito, a calm residential neighborhood. Here, in the large round park called Parque del Centenario, you'll find this good natural-science museum. It's definitely worth a peek for its musty taxidermy and cool skeleton room.

Museo Casa Carlos Gardel MUSEUM

(Map p64; ☎4964-2071; Jean Jaurés 735; admission AR$1; ⏲11am-6pm Mon & Wed-Fri, 10am-7pm Sat & Sun) This museum offers tango fans some insight into the dance's most famous singer.

Activities

The extensive greenery in Palermo provides good areas for recreation, especially on weekends when the ring road around the rose garden is closed to motor vehicles. Recoleta has grassy parks also, if you can avoid the dog piles. Best of all is the Reserva Ecológica Costanera Sur (p52), an ecological paradise just east of Puerto Madero; it's excellent for walks, runs, bike rides and even a bit of wildlife viewing.

Cycling

Buenos Aires' new bike lanes are making cycling in the city a safer proposition, but there greener places to spin your wheels.

Palermo

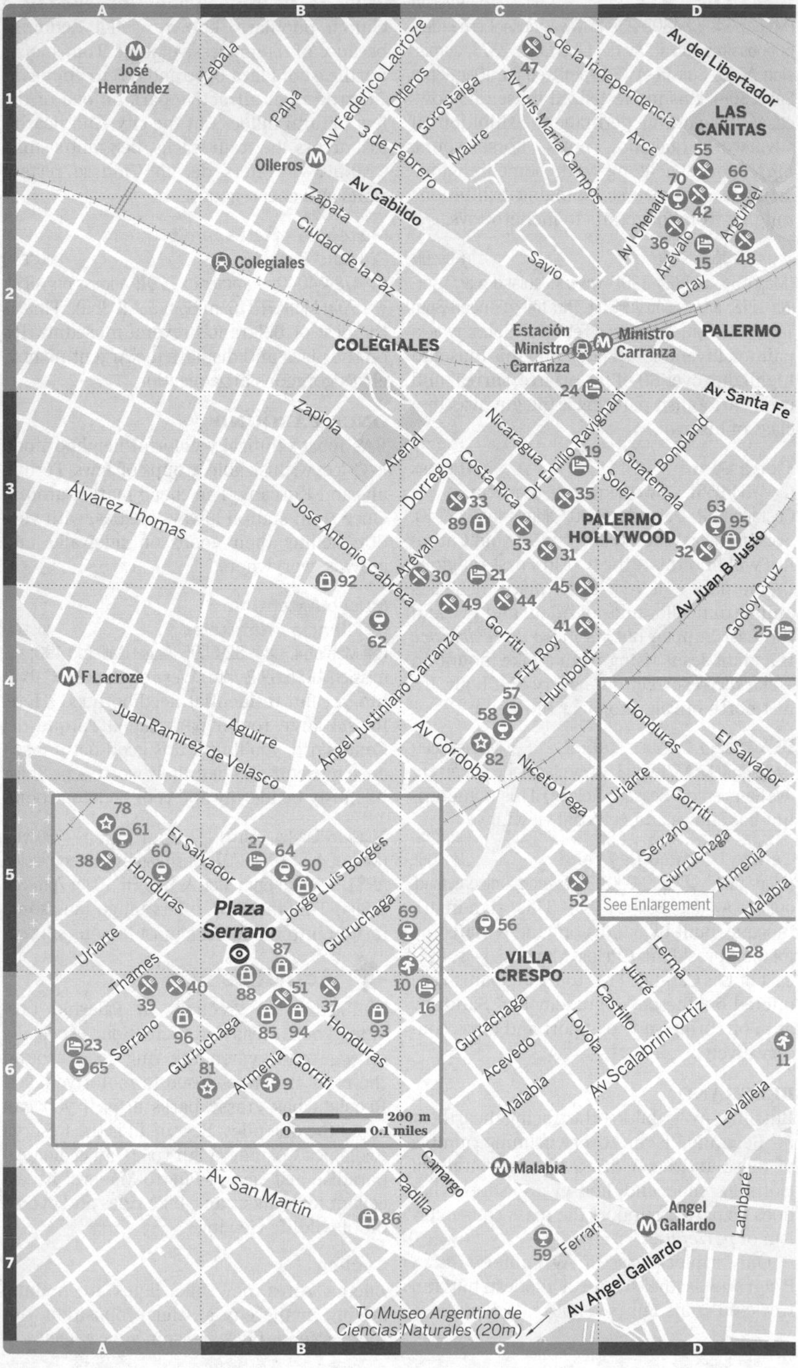

A B C D

1 2 3 4 5 6 7

José Hernández
Olleros
Colegiales
COLEGIALES
Estación Ministro Carranza
Ministro Carranza
LAS CAÑITAS
PALERMO
PALERMO HOLLYWOOD
F Lacroze
Plaza Serrano
VILLA CRESPO
Malabia
Angel Gallardo

Zebala
Palpa
Av Federico Lacroze
Olleros
3 de Febrero
Gorostiaga
Maure
Av Luis María Campos
S de la Independencia
Av del Libertador
Arce
Av Cabildo
Zapata
Ciudad de la Paz
Savio
Av I Chenaut
Arévalo
Argüibel
Clay
Av Santa Fe
Zapiola
Arenal
Dorrego
Nicaragua
Costa Rica
Dr Emilio Ravignani
Soler
Guatemala
Bonpland
Álvarez Thomas
José Antonio Cabrera
Arévalo
Av Juan B Justo
Godoy Cruz
Gorriti
Fitz Roy
Humboldt
Ángel Justiniano Carranza
Juan Ramirez de Velasco
Aguirre
Av Córdoba
Niceto Vega
Honduras
El Salvador
Uriarte
Gorriti
Serrano
Gurruchaga
Armenia
Malabia
See Enlargement
El Salvador
Honduras
Jorge Luis Borges
Gurruchaga
Uriarte
Thames
Serrano
Gurruchaga
Armenia
Gorriti
Honduras
Lerma
Jufré
Castillo
Loyola
Gurrachaga
Acevedo
Malabia
Av Scalabrini Ortiz
Lavalleja
Camargo
Padilla
Av San Martín
Ferrari
Lambaré
Av Angel Gallardo

47 55 66 70 42 36 15 48 24 19 35 33 89 53 31 63 95 32 92 30 21 45 49 44 41 62 25 57 58 82 78 61 38 60 27 64 90 69 87 88 51 37 40 39 96 85 94 93 10 16 23 65 81 9 52 56 28 11 86 59

0 200 m
0 0.1 miles

To Museo Argentino de Ciencias Naturales (20m)

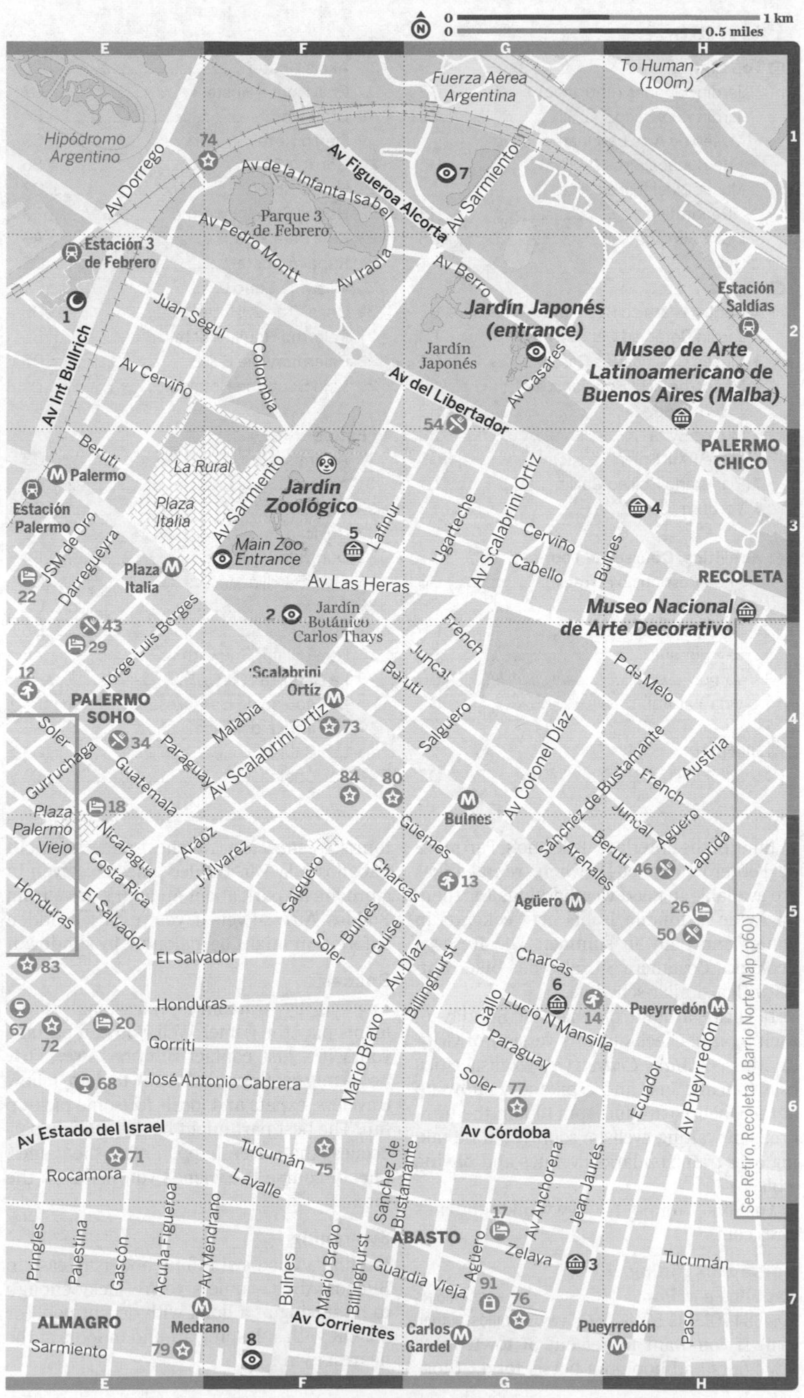

Fuerza Aérea Argentina
To Human (100m)
Hipódromo Argentino
Av Dorrego
Av de la Infanta Isabel
Av Figueroa Alcorta
Av Sarmiento
Parque 3 de Febrero
Av Pedro Montt
Av Iraola
Av Berro
Estación 3 de Febrero
Jardín Japonés (entrance)
Jardín Japonés
Estación Saldías
Museo de Arte Latinoamericano de Buenos Aires (Malba)
Juan Seguí
Colombia
Av Int Bullrich
Av Cerviño
Av del Libertador
Av Casares
PALERMO CHICO
Beruti
La Rural
Palermo
Estación Palermo
Plaza Italia
Jardín Zoológico
Av Sarmiento
Lafinur
Ugarteche
Av Scalabrini Ortiz
Cerviño
Cabello
Bulnes
JSM de Oro
Darregueyra
Main Zoo Entrance
Plaza Italia
Av Las Heras
RECOLETA
Museo Nacional de Arte Decorativo
Jardín Botánico Carlos Thays
Jorge Luis Borges
French
Juncal
Beruti
P de Melo
Scalabrini Ortíz
PALERMO SOHO
Soler
Gurruchaga
Guatemala
Paraguay
Malabia
Av Scalabrini Ortíz
Salguero
Av Coronel Díaz
Sánchez de Bustamante
French
Austria
Plaza Palermo Viejo
Nicaragua
Costa Rica
Honduras
El Salvador
Aráoz
J Álvarez
Güemes
Bulnes
Charcas
Juncal
Agüero
Laprida
Arenales
Beruti
Salguero
Bulnes
Soler
Guise
Av Díaz
Billinghurst
Agüero
El Salvador
Charcas
Honduras
Gorriti
José Antonio Cabrera
Gallo
Lucio N Mansilla
Paraguay
Pueyrredón
Mario Bravo
Soler
Ecuador
Av Pueyrredón
Av Estado del Israel
Av Córdoba
Tucumán
Rocamora
Lavalle
Sanchez de Bustamante
Av Anchorena
Jean Jaurés
ABASTO
Zelaya
Tucumán
Pringles
Palestina
Gascón
Acuña Figueroa
Av Medrano
Bulnes
Mario Bravo
Billinghurst
Guardia Vieja
Agüero
ALMAGRO
Medrano
Av Corrientes
Carlos Gardel
Pueyrredón
Paso
Sarmiento
See Retiro, Recoleta & Barrio Norte Map (p60)
0 1 km
0 0.5 miles

Palermo

Top Sights

Jardín Japonés (entrance)....G2
Jardín Zoológico....F3
Museo de Arte Latinoamericano de Buenos Aires (Malba)....H2
Museo Nacional de Arte Decorativo....H3
Plaza Serrano....B5

Sights

1 Centro Islàmico Rey Fahd....E2
2 Jardín Botánico Carlos Thays....F3
3 Museo Casa Carlos Gardel....G7
4 Museo de Arte Popular José Hernández....H3
5 Museo Evita....F3
6 Museo Xul Solar....G5
7 Planetario Galileo Galilei....G1
8 Verbum....F7

Activities, Courses & Tours

9 Anda Responsible Travel....B6
10 Centro Valletierra....C5
11 DWS....D6
12 Say Hueque....E4
13 Vamos....G5
14 Vida Natural....G5

Sleeping

15 248 Finisterra....D2
16 Akais Hostel....C6
17 Chill House Hostel....G7
18 Craft Hotel....E4
19 Fierro Hotel....C3
20 Gorriti 4290....E6
21 Home Hotel....C3
22 Hostel Suites Palermo....E3
23 Kala Petit Hotel....A6
24 Kapaké Hostel....C2
25 Miravida Soho....D4
26 Onze Trendy Hotel....H5
27 Palermo House Hostel....B5
28 Palermo Viejo B & B....D5
29 Vain Boutique Hotel....E4

Eating

30 Artemisia....C3
31 Azema....C3
32 Bio....D3
33 Cusic....C3
34 Don Julio....E4
35 El 22 Parrilla....C3
36 El Primo....D2
37 Freddo....B6
38 Hola! Siniór Shawarma....A5
39 La Cabrera....A6
La Esquina de las Flores....(see 87)
40 La Fabrica del Taco....A6
41 Las Cabras....C4
42 Las Cholas....D1

Bike paths interlace Palermo's Parque 3 de Febrero (Map p64), where rental bikes are available in good weather; look for them on Av de la Infanta Isabel on weekends in winter and daily in summer. The Reserva Ecológica Costanera Sur also has bike rentals with a similar schedule.

If you're around on the first Sunday of each month, check out BA's version of Critical Mass, or *Masa Critica* (www.masacriticabsas.com.ar). Just find a bike and show up at the Obelisco around 4pm to join the hundreds of waiting cyclists; soon you'll be taking over traffic on large avenues and having a blast.

For bike tours, try www.bikingbuenosaires.com.

Horseback Riding

Caballos a la Par HORSE RIDING
(4384-7013; 15-5248-3592; www.caballos-alapar.com) If you want to get out of town for a few hours and hop on a horse, forget those touristy *estancias* (ranches) and check out Caballos a la Par. Guided rides are given in a provincial park about an hour's drive from Buenos Aires. Even if you've never ridden before, you might be galloping by sundown.

Soccer

Inspired by watching professional *fútbol* teams play the game? Well, you can partake yourself – just contact **Buenos Aires Fútbol Amigos** (www.fcbafa.com) to join fellow travelers, expats and locals for some pick-up fun. The best part might be the *asados* (barbecues) that often happen after the games, plus of course the friends you make on the pitch.

Swimming

Finding a good swimming hole isn't easy in Buenos Aires – unless you're lucky enough to be staying at a hotel with decent pool (or are OK with splashing around indoors at the nearest gym).

43 Las Pizarras ... E4
44 Meraviglia ... C4
45 Miranda ... C4
46 Natural Deli ... H5
47 Natural Deli ... C1
48 Novecento ... D2
49 Olsen ... C4
50 Oviedo ... H5
51 Persicco ... B6
52 Sarkis ... C5
53 Siamo nel Forno ... C3
54 Un Altra Volta ... G2
55 Veikko ... D1

Drinking

56 878 ... C5
57 Bangalore ... C4
58 Carnal ... C4
59 Casa Brandon ... C7
60 Casa Cruz ... A5
61 Congo ... A5
62 Frank's Bar ... B4
63 Geno's Beer Bar ... D3
64 Magdalena's Party ... B5
65 Mundo Bizarro ... A6
66 Office ... D1
67 Shanghai Dragon ... E5
68 Sitges ... E6
69 Sugar ... C5
70 Van Koning ... D2

Entertainment

71 Amerika ... E6
72 Bach Bar ... E6
73 Club Aráoz ... F4
74 Crobar ... F1
75 El Camarín de las Musas ... F6
76 Esquina Carlos Gardel ... G7
77 Glam ... G6
78 Kika ... A5
79 La Catedral ... E7
80 La Peña del Colorado ... F4
81 La Viruta ... B6
82 Niceto Club ... C4
83 Salon Canning ... E5
84 Thelonious Bar ... F4

Shopping

85 Bolivia ... B6
86 Calle Murillo (600 block) ... B7
87 Calma Chicha ... B5
88 Feria Plaza Serrano ... B6
89 Hermanos Estebecorena ... C3
90 Lo de Joaquin Alberdi ... B5
91 Mercado de Abasto ... G7
92 Mercado de las Pulgas ... B3
93 Nadine Zlotogora ... B6
94 Rapsodia ... B6
95 Sugar & Spice ... D3
96 Zival's ... A6

Parque Norte SWIMMING
(☎4787-1382; www.parquenorte.com; Avs Cantilo & Guiraldes; AR$50 admission Mon-Fri, AR$65 Sat & Sun; ⏲ 9am-8pm Mon-Fri, 8am-8pm Sat & Sun) When the temperatures and humidity skyrocket, head north to the neighborhood of Nuñez. where Parque Norte offers several huge shallow pools (up to four feet deep) plus a water slide and plenty of grassy areas to lounge about. Bring a towel.

Yoga

Most gyms and some cultural centers schedule yoga classes. Even some health-oriented restaurants, such as Natural Deli (p81) offer yoga, tai chi and/or meditation. There are significant discounts for weekly or monthly class packages.

Buena Onda Yoga YOGA
(☎15-5423-7103; www.buenaondayoga.com) Classes taught by women expats at several locations around BA.

Happy Sun Yoga YOGA
(☎15-6093-3462; www.happysunyoga.com) More women-expat-run yoga classes, held in a Recoleta studio.

Vida Natural YOGA
(Map p64; ☎4826-1695; www.vidanatural.com.ar; Charcas 2852) This natural-therapy center in Palermo offers Ashtanga, Hatha and Iyengar yoga. Therapeutic massage and harmonizing Tibetan bowls also available.

Centro Valletierra YOGA
(Map p64; ☎4833-6724; www.valletierra.com; Costa Rica 4562) This slick Palermo Viejo studio has Hatha, Kundalini and Ashtanga yoga classes.

Courses

Visitors have many opportunities to study almost anything in BA. Most cultural centers offer a wide variety of classes at affordable rates. For tango classes, see p90.

Language

BA is a major destination for students of Spanish, and good institutes are opening up all the time. Nearly all organize social activities and home-stay programs, and all have private classes.

For something different, try **Spanglish** (www.spanglishexchange.com). It's set up like speed dating; you'll speak five minutes in English and five in Spanish, then switch partners.

University de Buenos Aires LANGUAGE COURSE
(UBA; Map p48; ☎4343-2733; www.idiomas.filo.uba.ar; 25 de Mayo 221) The university offers regular and intensive, long-term Spanish classes (these last for one to four months between March and December, or four to eight weeks in January and February). Italian, German, French, Portuguese and Japanese also taught. It's cheap, but classrooms are run down.

Below are just a few institutes; it's always best to ask around for current recommendations.

DWS (Map p64; ☎4777-6515; www.danielawasser.com.ar; Av Córdoba 4382)

Expanish (Map p48; ☎5252-3040; www.expanish.com; Juan Perón 700)

Vamos (Map p64; ☎5352-0001; www.vamospanish.com; Coronel Díaz 1736)

Verbum (Map p64; ☎4861-7571; www.verbum.biz; Salguero 553)

VOS (Map p60; ☎4812-1140; www.vosbuenosaires.com; Marcelo T de Alvear 1459)

Cooking

Taking cooking classes in a small group or privately are probably the best options for short-term visitors who don't speak Spanish. There are several options in BA, a few with expat chefs who have their own 'closed door' restaurant (see p79).

Casa Mun COOKING COURSE
(www.casamun.com/sushi-making-classes) Chef Mun instructs on the history and intricacies of making sushi.

Cooking with Teresita COOKING COURSE
(☎4293-5992; www.try2cook.com) Learn to cook empanadas and *asado* (barbecue grill), or go on a culinary shopping expedition.

Dan Perlman COOKING COURSE
(www.saltshaker.net/class-schedule) Ex-New Yorker Dan Perlman teaches Italian, Mediterranean, Asian and vegetarian classes.

Kala Cooking COOKING COURSE
(☎4773-1331) Make typical dishes such as *empanadas, milanesas* (breaded cutlets), *locro* and *asado*; taught by Gladys and her daughter Florencia, out of their guesthouse.

Those proficient in Spanish and seeking long-term cooking classes can try **Instituto Argentino de Gastronomía** (IAG; ☎5032-1414; www.iag.com.ar; Montevideo 968), **Mausi Sebess** (☎5218-4031; www.mausisebess.com; Av Maipú 594, Vicente López) or **Escuela Alicia Berger** (☎4784-8502; www.escuelaaliciaberger.com; Ciudad de la Paz 1242).

Photography

Get to know Buenos Aires through the lens of a camera.

Foto Ruta COURSE
(☎6030-8881; www.foto-ruta.com; per person AR$100) This workshop is run by two expat women who send folks out into neighborhoods with a few 'themes' to photograph – then everyone watches the slide show.

Tours

There are plenty of organized tours, from the large tourist-bus variety to guided bike rides to straight-up walks. Most travel agencies broker tours or offer their own.

The City of Buenos Aires organizes **free thematic tours** (☎4114-5791; www.bue.gov.ar); check the website or stop by a tourist office for a schedule.

If you have an MP3 player and are self-sufficient, check out www.mptours.com. You can download self-guided tours and maps of BA neighborhoods for US$4.99 each, walking, stopping and listening at your leisure. You can also try the city's audio tours for free (www.bue.gov.ar).

All companies listed below offer tours in English and possibly other languages; some companies listed under 'Group Tours' also do private tours.

Group Tours

Biking Buenos Aires CYCLING TOUR
(☎15-6208-2176; www.bikingBuenosAires.com; per person from AR$190) Friendly American guys take you pedaling around various neighborhoods, often utilizing the city's new bike lanes. Bike rentals available.

Graffitimundo ART TOUR
(☎15-3683-3219; www.graffitimundo.com; per person AR$90) Expat-run tours of BA's best graffiti and stencil art, with some proceeds

going to the artists themselves. Graffiti bike tours also available (AR$120).

Cultour WALKING TOUR
(☎15-6365-6892; www.cultour.com.ar; per person from AR$85) Good tours run by academics and students from UBA (University of Buenos Aires), with an emphasis on the historical and cultural facets of Buenos Aires.

BA Walking Tours WALKING TOUR
(☎15-5773-1001; www.ba-walking-tours.com; per person from AR$150) Explore Buenos Aires through these neighborhood-specific walking tours. Also offers a six-hour comprehensive tour and a tango night tour.

BA Free Tour WALKING TOUR
(☎15-6395-3000; www.bafreetour.com; free/donation) Free (well, donation) walking tour given by enthusiastic young guides from Monday to Saturday.

Buenos Aires Bus BUS TOUR
(☎5239-5160; www.buenosairesbus.com; ticket AR$70) Hop-on, hop-off topless bus with around 20 stops. Runs every 20 minutes at designated stops (see website).

Say Hueque ADVENTURE TOUR
(www.sayhueque.com) Microcentro (Map p48; ☎5199-2517; Viamonte 749, 6th fl); Palermo (Map p64; Thames 2062); San Telmo (Map p48; Chile 557). Friendly company that offers 'independent' and adventure packages around BA and Argentina.

Seriema Nature Tours NATURE TOUR
(☎5867-7000; www.seriematours.com) Does mostly multiday nature and bird-watching tours around Argentina, but also has half- and full-day tours relatively near Buenos Aires.

Tangol TOUR
(www.tangol.com); Retiro (Map p60; ☎4312-7276; Florida 971, Suite 31); San Telmo (Map p48; Defensa 831) Travel and tour agency that offers a little bit of everything: city tours, tango shows, guides to *fútbol* games, air tickets, hotel reservations and countrywide packages – plus much more.

Private Tours

Man Tour MALE TOUR
(☎15-6963-7259; www.landingpadba.com/the-man-tour-buenos-aires; per person from AR$580) Attention, men: get a straight-razor shave, visit a custom hat shop and smoke a stogie at a cigar bar. Seriously, it's a guided tour.

Anda Responsible Travel CULTURAL TOUR
(Map p64; ☎3221-0833; www.andatravel.com.ar; Agüero 1050, 4A; tours from AR$270) Organizes tours around BA and Argentina with sustainability in mind, by introducing travelers to local communities, fair-trade organizations and social projects. Most notable for its La Boca tour, which gets travelers involved with local organizations working towards improving the lives of its citizens.

BA Local CUSTOM TOUR
(☎15-6908-9100; www.balocal.com; tours from AR$500) Three expats guide personal shopping tours, art tours and off-the-beaten-path (or regular city) tours.

Buenos Tours WALKING TOUR
(☎3221-1048; www.buenostours.com; tours for 1-3 people from AR$400) Arranges walking tours guided by friendly, knowledgeable and responsible local expats.

Festivals & Events

Check with tourist offices for other happenings and for exact dates, as some vary from year to year. For more festivals and events in BA and around the country, see p21.

Chinese New Year CULTURAL
Head to Belgrano's tiny Chinatown for food, firecrackers and festivities. (Usually January: date depends on the lunar calendar.)

Feria del Libro BOOKS
(www.el-libro.org.ar; La Rural) The largest book festival in Latin America, attracting over a million book lovers for three weeks, April to May.

arteBA ART
(www.arteba.com; La Rural) Popular event in May, highlighting contemporary art, introducing exciting new young artists, and showing off top gallery works.

Fashion BA FASHION
(www.bafweek.com.ar) This August event shows off the latest designer threads, both nationally and internationally. A fall collection happens in February or March.

Casa Foa DESIGN
(www.casafoa.com) Top-notch architecture, design and decoration fair, located at a different renovated (and usually historical) building each year. Runs September to October.

Pepsi Music MUSIC
(www.pepsimusic.com.ar) September's 10-day music festival showcases some very famous

bands, both from Argentina and abroad; in 2011 the headliner was Red Hot Chili Peppers.

Creamfields MUSIC
(www.creamfieldsba.com) BA's answer to the UK's outdoor, all-night, cutting-edge electronic-music and dance party, with dozens of international DJs and bands; held in November.

Marcha del Orgullo Gay GAY & LESBIAN
(www.marchadelorgullo.org.ar) In November, thousands of BA's gay, lesbian and transgender citizens proudly march from Plaza de Mayo to the Congreso.

Campeonato Abierto de Polo SPORTS
(www.aapolo.com) Watch the world's best polo players and their gorgeous horses thunder up and down Palermo's polo fields in December.

Sleeping

Over the last few years Buenos Aires has seen its accommodation options increase exponentially. Boutique hotels and guesthouses, especially, have mushroomed in neighborhoods such as San Telmo and Palermo, and hostels are a dime a dozen. You shouldn't have trouble finding the type of place you're looking for, but it's still a good idea to make a reservation beforehand – especially during any holidays or the busy summer months of November through January.

Many places will help you with transportation to and from the airport if you reserve ahead of time. The most expensive hotels will take credit cards but cheaper places might not (or may include a surcharge for credit-card payment). Some kind of breakfast, whether it be continental or buffet, is included nearly everywhere; the same goes for wi-fi and air-con.

At Hostelling International (HI) hostels, buying a membership card gives a discount off listed prices. Another hostel club is www.minihostels.com. Prices at top-end hotels often vary depending on occupancy levels. As a general rule we've listed rack rates; calling ahead or reserving via websites usually results in better pricing.

Prices below are for high season (roughly November to February). Rates can skyrocket during peak seasons (Christmas and Easter) or drop during slow seasons.

For a list of apartment-rental websites, see p77.

MICROCENTRO

As well as being very central, the Microcentro has the best range and the largest number of accommodations in the city. Towards the north you'll be close to the popular pedestrian streets of Florida and Lavalle, as well as the neighborhoods of upmarket Retiro and Recoleta. The Plaza de Mayo area contains the bustling banking district and many historical buildings, and is within walking distance of San Telmo. During the day the whole area is very busy, but nights are much calmer as businesspeople flee the center after work. Don't expect creative cuisine in this area – for that you'll have to head to Palermo.

TOP CHOICE **Portal del Sur** HOSTEL $
(Map p48; ☎4342-8788; www.portaldelsurba.com.ar; Hipólito Yrigoyen 855; dm AR$55-65, s/d AR$240/300; ❄@📶) Located in a charming old building, this is one of the city's best hostels. Beautiful dorms and sumptuous, hotel-quality private rooms surround a central common area, which is rather dark but open. The highlight is the lovely rooftop deck with views and attached bar and lounge. Has free tango lessons, Spanish lessons and walking tour; plenty of other activities available.

Moreno Hotel HOTEL $$$
(Map p48; ☎6091-2000; www.morenobuenosaires.com; Moreno 376; r AR$700; ❄@📶) Housed in an atmospheric historical building is this modern, minimalist hotel. Don't be put off by its edgy location or the living-room-like lobby on the 2nd floor; the six categories of rooms are all beautiful, and some are huge and come with Jacuzzi. The best part is the rooftop terrace; there's also a fine wine-bar restaurant.

Hotel Alcázar HOTEL $$
(Map p48; ☎4345-0926; www.hotelalcazar.com.ar; Av de Mayo 935; s AR$190-210, d AR$240-270; ❄📶) One of BA's better budget deals, the Alcázar has simple remodeled rooms (get one with an outside window) that are mostly small, but clean and good value. It's centrally located and just steps away from the famous Café Tortoni, which is handy since breakfast isn't included. There are also some nice interior tiled patios. Reserve ahead.

Hotel Suipacha Inn HOTEL $$
(Map p48; ☎4322-0099; www.hotelsuipacha.com.ar; Suipacha 515; s AR$280, d AR$320-400; ❄📶) This well-located hotel is a good deal in the Microcentro – it's only a couple of blocks from the Obelisco and on a pedestrian street. It could use a facelift, but you do get small, basic and tidy rooms, most with a

fridge, safe box and a tiny bathroom. Treat yourself and upgrade to a more spacious 'superior' room.

Milhouse Youth Hostel HOSTEL $
(Map p48; ☎4345-9604; www.milhousehostel.com; Hipólito Yrigoyen 959; dm/d AR$70/290; ❄@📶) Best known as BA's premiere party hostel, this popular HI spot offers a plethora of activities and services. Dorms are good and private rooms can be very pleasant; most surround a pleasant open patio. Common spaces include a bar-cafe (with pool table) on the ground floor, a TV lounge on the mezzanine and a rooftop terrace above. A gorgeous annex building nearby offers similar services.

Hotel Frossard HOTEL $$
(Map p48; ☎4322-1811; www.hotelfrossard.com.ar; Tucumán 686; s/d AR$300/320; ❄@📶) This intimate hotel has 24 high-ceilinged older rooms of different sizes in a charming building. Singles are tiny and doubles are small, but triples have more breathing room. The location is excellent; the pedestrian streets of Florida and Lavalle are just a block away.

HI Obelisco Suites HOSTEL $
(Map p48; ☎4328-4040; www.hostelsuites.com; Av Corrientes 830; dm AR$80-90, s/d AR$200/300; ❄@📶) This sizeable, apartmentlike HI hostel features large dorms (four to eight beds) and pleasant private rooms; every three rooms share a bathroom. Common areas include a trendy bar-lounge with a pool table, and separate small rooms for Spanish classes and watching TV. The single kitchen is tiny, however. Lots of activities are on offer and it's very central.

Ideal Hostel HOSTEL $
(Map p48; ☎6091-1565; www.idealsocialhostel.com; Suipacha 362; dm AR$42-59, r AR$195-230; ❄@📶) Pretty much in the dead center of Buenos Aires is this decent, cheap hostel. It's in an atmospheric older building with wood and tile floors, though unfortunately the spaces are somewhat mazelike and the dorms (bedding four to 12 people) can be tight. At least the balcony overlooking pedestrian Suipacha is nice, and right next door is Confitería Ideal, a tango hotspot.

CONGRESO

Congreso contains many of the city's older theaters, cinemas and cultural centers. Lively Av Corrientes has many modest shops, services and bookstores. The Plaza de Congreso area is always moving, sometimes with mostly peaceful public demonstrations. Generally, this area is not quite as packed as the Microcentro and has a less business and touristy flavor, but still bustles day and night.

TOP CHOICE **Hotel Bonito** BOUTIQUE HOTEL $$
(Map p48; ☎4381-2162; www.bonitobuenosaires.com; Chile 1507, 3rd fl; r AR$400-640; ❄@📶) Lovely boutique hotel with just five artsy, gorgeous rooms mixing the traditional and contemporary. Some have a loft, cupola sitting area or Jacuzzi; floors can be wood or acid-finished concrete. Warm atmosphere, with small bar area and good breakfast.

Hostel Estoril-Terrazas Estoril HOSTEL $
(Map p48; ☎4382-9684; www.hostelestoril.com.ar; Av de Mayo 1385, 1st fl; dm AR$60, r AR$200-250; ❄@📶) Tasteful, colorful hostel in a 100-year-old building, with pleasant rooms, nice kitchen and common areas and even an internal patio. You can also access the rooftop terrace on the 6th floor, which has amazing views of Av de Mayo and Palacio Barolo; more dorms are available up here.

Fiamingo Apart Hotel HOTEL $$
(Map p48; ☎4374-4400; www.fiamingoapart.com.ar; Talcahuano 120; r AR$400; ❄📶👪) Great for families, the Fiamingo features huge suites that lean more toward comfortable and convenient than fancy. All come with attached kitchenettes (no stoves, just microwaves and sinks) and some have balconies. Staff are friendly and windows are double-paned for peace and quiet. Reserve ahead.

Hotel Reina HOTEL $
(Map p48; ☎4381-2496; www.hotelreina.com.ar; Av de Mayo 1120; s AR$200-230, d AR$220-250; ❄📶) This charming old building still has a subdued elegance that's apparent in the grand halls, the classic elevator and the original light fixtures. Some rooms are simple, while others are lovely – with high ceilings, wood floors and balconies (try for the 2nd floor). Tango classes can be given in the airy salon.

Sabatico Hostel HOSTEL $
(Map p48; ☎4381-1138; www.sabaticohostel.com.ar; Mexico 1410; dm AR$60, r AR$200-250; @📶) This exceptional, well-maintained hostel is located off the tourist-beaten path in an atmospheric neighborhood. Rooms are small but pleasant and the great common areas include a nice kitchen, airy patio hall and nice rooftop terrace with tiny soaking pool. There's occasional live music on weekends, plus bike rentals.

ANDREW BAIN/LONELY PLANET IMAGES ©

4

MARCOS BRINDICCI/REUTERS/CORBIS ©

MICHAEL TAYLOR/LONELY PLANET IMAGES ©

TERRY CARTER/LONELY PLANET IMAGES ©

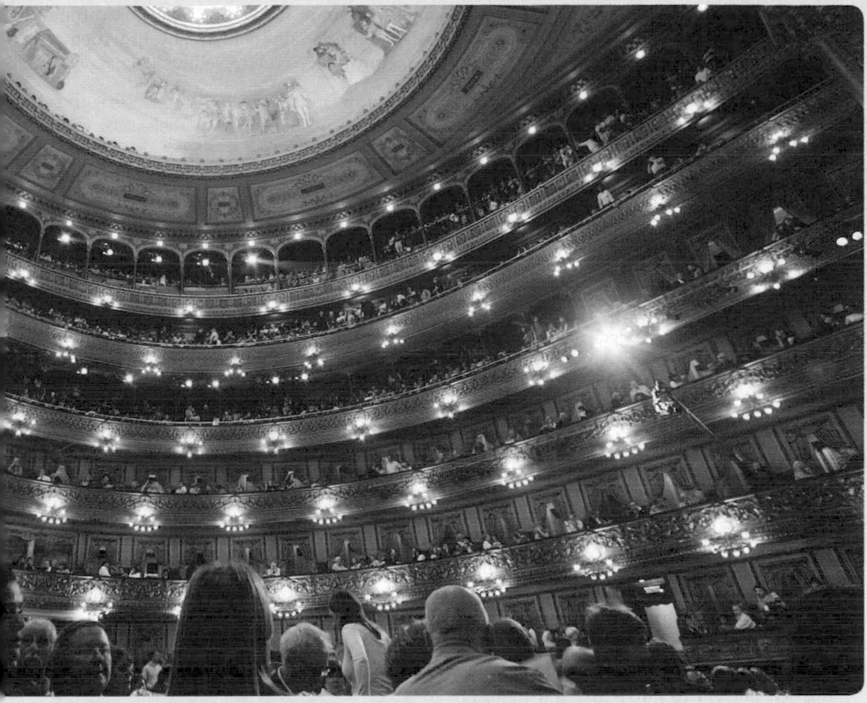

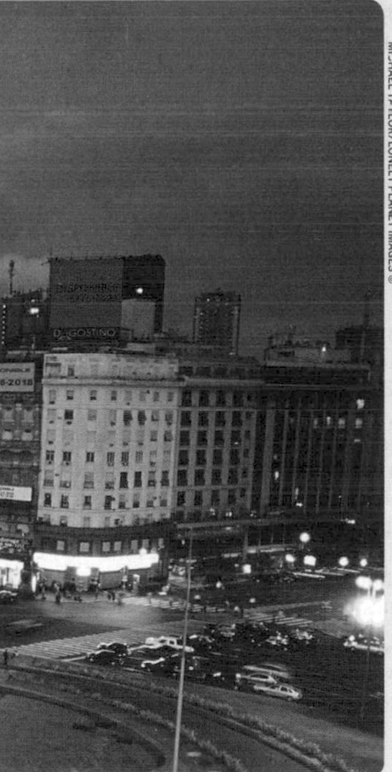

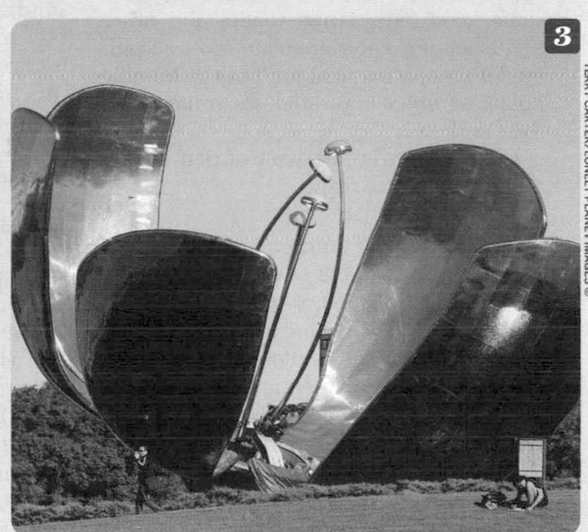

1. Caminito (p55)
La Boca's most famous street contains buildings with colorful facades.

2. Teatro Colón (p95)
Buenos Aires' much loved theater regularly hosts performances by prominent figures.

3. Floralis Genérica (p59)
This giant sculptural flower, built in 2002 by Eduardo Catalano, has petals that close up at night.

4. Obelisco (p54)
This 67m-high monument keeps a watchful eye over Av 9 de Julio.

Kilca Hostel HOSTEL $
(Map p48; ☎4381-1966; www.kilcabackpacker.com; Mexico 1545; dm AR$55, r AR$140-160; @📶) The slightly artsy Kilca is in the offbeat Montserrat neighborhood – great if you want fewer tourists and more local activity. It's definitely funky, sporting very laid-back atmosphere and no luxuries, and is located in an early-1900s house with large six- to nine-bed dorms. The highlight is the leafy courtyard. Dog and cat on premises.

Hotel Sportsman HOTEL $
(Map p48; ☎4381-8021; www.hotelsportsman.com.ar; Av Rivadavia 1425; s AR$85-132, d AR$130-185) This ancient, rundown and dark hotel has creaky wood staircase and mazelike hallways. Basic but decent budget rooms have either shared or private bathrooms. Character abounds, and there's a very rustic kitchen. No breakfast, but it's still a cheap deal.

SAN TELMO & CONSTITUCIÓN

South of the Microcentro, San Telmo has some of the most traditional atmosphere in Buenos Aires. Buildings are more charming and historical than those in the center, and tend to be only a few stories high. Many restaurants and fancy boutique stores have opened here in recent years, and there are some good bars, tango venues and other nightspots for entertainment. Most accommodation options here are hostels, humble hotels or upscale guesthouses rather than five-star hotels.

Constitución is just west of San Telmo, and much less touristy.

TOP CHOICE **1890 Hotel Boutique** BOUTIQUE HOTEL $$
(Map p48; ☎4304-8798; www.1890hotel.com.ar; Salta 1074; r AR$435-760; ❄@📶) A bit off the beaten path, but still close to San Telmo, this beautiful hotel has outdoor covered hallways with grassy garden areas that offer a little respite from Buenos Aires' streets; and while each the six lovely rooms are different, all boast high ceilings and wood floors. There's also a nice large common area with breakfast table.

Casa Bolivar BOUTIQUE HOTEL $$
(Map p58; ☎4300-3619; www.casabolivar.com; Bolívar 1701; r from AR$435; ❄📶) Fourteen spacious studios and loft apartments have been lovingly renovated into attractive and modern spaces at this amazing mansion, some with original details such as carved doorways or painted ceilings. Separate entrances join with common hallways connecting through the complex, and there are lovely garden patios in which to relax. No breakfast.

Mansion Dandi Royal BOUTIQUE HOTEL $$$
(Map p48; ☎4307-7623; www.hotelmansiondandiroyal.com; Piedras 922; s AR$368, d AR$506-620; ❄@📶🏊) Catering to tango fanatics, this 1903 family mansion has been renovated into a luxurious themed hotel complete with murals, glass chandeliers and a curved wooden staircase. The 29 rooms are gorgeous; most come with antique furniture, claw-foot tubs and high ceilings. There's a small but lovely rooftop pool and sunny patio, while tango classes take place in the salons.

Art Factory HOSTEL $
(Map p48; ☎4343-1463; www.artfactoryba.com.ar; Piedras 545; dm AR$60, s AR$190-210, d AR$210-250; ❄@📶) Friendly and uniquely art-themed, this fine hostel offers more private rooms than most – and all feature huge murals, painted and decorated by different international artists. Even the hallways and water tanks have colorful cartoonish themes, and the 1850s mansion adds some elegant atmosphere. Large rooftop terrace and separate bar-lounge area with pool table.

Sandanzas Hostel HOSTEL $
(Map p58; ☎4300-7375; www.sandanzas.com.ar; Balcarce 1351; dm AR$60-70, d AR$220-250;@📶) This friendly hostel has just 28 beds and is enthusiastically run by its five young owners, all artists or social workers. It's a colorful place with good-sized dorms, six doubles (three with bathroom) and occasional cultural events. The location is in a gritty blue-collar neighborhood near Plaza Lezama. Free bike rentals.

Garden House HOSTEL $
(Map p48; ☎4305-0517; www.gardenhouseba.com.ar; San Juan 1271; dm AR$53-60, s AR$203-220, d AR$220-260; @📶) A bit off the beaten tourist path, this friendly hostel has two dorms (four and eight beds), seven doubles (a couple with pretty patios) and some casual but cozy common spaces. Most rooms share bathrooms. It's a bit far from the center and on a busy avenue, but the vibes are good. Cheap but excellent Friday-night *asados* (barbecues) take place on the terrace.

Brisas del Mar HOTEL $
(Map p48; ☎4300-0040; www.hotelbrisasdelmar.com.ar; Humberto Primo 826; s AR$70-80, d AR$80-90; 📶) Long-running old cheapie hotel with

no luxuries – except for cable TV. Has basic but decent budget rooms, the cheapest ones with shared bathrooms – try for an upstairs one as they are brighter. All face tiled hallways lined with plants, and there's a very rustic, unstocked kitchen.

RETIRO

Retiro is a great, central place to be, *if* you can afford it – many of BA's most expensive hotels, along with some of its richest inhabitants, are settled here. Close by are leafy Plaza San Martín, the Retiro bus and train stations and many upscale stores and business services. Recoleta and the Microcentro are just a short stroll away.

Hotel Pulitzer BOUTIQUE HOTEL $$$

(Map p60; ☎4316-0800; www.hotelpulitzer.com.ar; Maipú 907; s/d AR$500/540;) Very well located, this large new boutique hotel has a black-and-white lobby and minimalist decor. Rooms are spacious and stylish, boasting flat-screen TVs and elegant bathrooms; some have a balcony. The highlight, however, is the beautiful rooftop terrace with attached bar, offering great views over the city. There's also a restaurant, cocktail bar and even a swimming pool.

Four Seasons HOTEL $$$

(Map p60; ☎4321-1200; www.fourseasons.com/buenosaires; Posadas 1086; d from AR$2500;) No surprise here – the Four Seasons offers all the perks that define a five-star hotel, such as great service and white terry-cloth robes. Rooms are large and beautiful, with contemporary furnishings and decorations, and the finest suites (AR$3700 to AR$39,000!) are located in an old luxurious mansion next door. There's also a gorgeous spa and an outdoor heated swimming pool.

Hotel Bel Air HOTEL $$$

(Map p60; ☎4816-0016; www.hotelbelair.com.ar; Arenales 1462; r AR$680-850;) Upscale travelers and businesspeople especially will love the sinuous bar-lounge, located next to reception. Upstairs, rooms are nicely designed in earthy colors and have modern furnishings, though they're not super luxurious. Great location between the Retiro and Recoleta; wi-fi costs an extra AR$45 per day(!).

Hotel Tres Sargentos HOTEL $

(Map p60; ☎4312-6082; tresargentos@hotmail.com; Tres Sargentos 345; s/d AR$230-290;) A great deal for the location, this simple budget hotel is located on a pedestrian street. Rooms are plain but clean, carpeted and comfortable. Some even offer a bit of a view – ask for a floor up high.

Hotel Central Córdoba HOTEL $

(Map p60; ☎4311-1175; www.hotelcentralcordoba.com.ar; San Martín 1021; s/d AR$200/220;) Here is one of Retiro's most affordable hotels, with simple neat rooms featuring desk areas and tiled floors. Sizes vary, so have a look around; ask for an inside room if you want quiet. The location is spot on and it's very popular, so book ahead.

RECOLETA & BARRIO NORTE

Most of the accommodations in Recoleta are expensive, and what cheap hotels there are tend to be full much of the time. Buildings here are grand and beautiful, befitting the city's richest barrio, and you'll be close to Recoleta's famous cemetery, along with its lovely parks, museums and boutiques.

TOP CHOICE Poetry Building APARTMENT $$$

(Map p60; ☎4827-2772; www.poetrybuilding.com; Junín 1280; r AR$520-760;) These gorgeous studios and one- or two-bedroom apartments are perfect for families or small groups. Each one is different, eclectically decorated with 'modernized' antique furniture, and all come with fully stocked kitchens. Some boast an outdoor balcony or patio, but if you don't get one simply hang out on the beautiful common terrace with soaking pool. Weekly discount.

A Hotel BOUTIQUE HOTEL $$

(Ex-Art Hotel; Map p60; ☎4821-4744; www.ahotel.com.ar; Azcuénaga 1268; r AR$380-620;) Stunningly beautiful, this boutique hotel features a small covered patio with an interesting wall of mirrors and a wonderful rooftop terrace with a Jacuzzi and wood deck. Tasteful rooms (some small) have a contemporary mix of decor – think concrete floors, plasma TVs, ironwork details and original high doors. The biggest have romantic canopied beds and balconies.

Yira Yira Guesthouse GUESTHOUSE $

(Map p60; ☎4812-4077; www.yirayiraba.com.ar; Uruguay 911 1B; s/d/tr AR$140/200/240;) This intimate apartment is run by the helpful Paz, who lives on-site. With four large rooms (all with shared bathrooms) facing the central living area, it's a good place to meet other travelers and very well located, smack in the center of the downtown neighborhoods. Two-night minimum stay and RSVP required.

Hotel Lion D'or HOTEL **$$**
(Map p60; ☎4803-8992; www.hotel-liondor.com.ar; Pacheco de Melo 2019; s AR$200-240, d AR$250-330; ❄📶) These digs have their charm (it's an old embassy), but rooms vary widely – some are small, basic and dark, while others are absolutely grand and may include a (nonworking) fireplace. All are good value and, while a few are a bit rough around the edges, most have been modernized for comfort. There's a great old marble staircase and nice rooftop area and the elevator is just fabulous. Cheap breakfast option; some rooms share bathrooms.

Marseille des Anges HOTEL **$$$**
(Map p60; ☎5219-2526; www.marseilledesanges.com; Arenales 1392; r from AR$615; ❄@📶) A good choice, well located in snazzy Recoleta. Rooms are large and comfortable, and the best come with balcony or front-facing window. All have great bathrooms with cutting-edge multispray showers. The overall feel here is friendly and intimate, the atmosphere traditional with modern comforts.

Design Suites HOTEL **$$$**
(Map p60; ☎4814-8700; www.designsuites.com; MT de Alvear 1683; r AR$630-965; ❄@📶) Futuristically elegant, with that minimalist style so trendy in BA hotels these days, Design Suites offers a great location and exclusive atmosphere. All suites have flat-panel TVs, attractive decor, small kitchenettes and a wall-bank of windows bringing in plenty of light. Some balconies available.

Onze Trendy Hotel BOUTIQUE HOTEL **$$**
(Map p64; ☎4821-2873; www.onzeboutiquehotel.com; Ecuador 1644; d AR$400-600; ❄@📶) Gorgeous from the get-go, this boutique hotel offers 11 different rooms with unique touches such as dressing rooms and traditional *mantas* (hand-woven blankets) for decoration. Try for the upstairs rooms; they're more interesting, and some have balconies. It's a lovely place with an exclusive feel.

Recoleta Hostel HOSTEL **$**
(Map p60; ☎4812-4419; www.hirecoleta.com.ar; Libertad 1216; dm AR$60-70, r AR$190-230; ❄@📶) Long-running hostel in an awesome location. Hardly intimate, though, and a bit rough around the edges despite being an HI hostel. On offer are segregated dorms (four to eight beds), eight private rooms – half with a private bathroom – a decent kitchen and sunny rooftop terrace. There are lots of stairs, so be in shape.

PALERMO

About a 10-minute taxi ride from the center (and also well connected by bus and Subte lines), Palermo is the top choice for many travelers. Not only is it full of extensive parklands – which are great for weekend jaunts and sporting activities – but you'll have heaps of cutting-edge restaurants, designer boutiques and hip dance clubs at your fingertips. Most of these places are located in the extensive subneighborhood of Palermo Viejo, which is further divided into Palermo Soho and Palermo Hollywood.

TOP CHOICE **Home Hotel** BOUTIQUE HOTEL **$$$**
(Map p64; ☎4778-1008; www.homebuenosaires.com; Honduras 5860; r from AR$700; ❄@📶🏊) Sleek, friendly and very stylish boutique hotel with paradisial garden and pool, great intimate bar-restaurant, plus spa.

TOP CHOICE **Miravida Soho** GUESTHOUSE **$$$**
(Map p64; ☎4774-6433; www.miravidasoho.com; Darregueyra 2050; r AR$660-865; ❄@📶) Run by a helpful German couple, this lovely guesthouse comes with six beautifully remodeled, elegant rooms. All are very comfortable and one has a private terrace. There's a wine cellar, table-and-bar area for evening wine tastings, a small relaxing patio and even an elevator. It serves good, full breakfasts; reserve ahead.

TOP CHOICE **Chill House Hostel** HOSTEL **$**
(Map p64; ☎4861-6175; www.chillhouse.com.ar; Agüero 781; dm/s AR$70/170, d AR$210-255; @📶) One of the coolest-vibe hostels in BA is at this remodeled old house, boasting high ceilings and a rustic artsy style. There are two dorms, eight private rooms with bath (No 6 is especially nice) and an awesome rooftop terrace where weekly *asados* take place. Run by a French and Argentine team; free bike rentals too.

Fierro Hotel BOUTIQUE HOTEL **$$$**
(Map p64; ☎3220-6800; www.fierrohotel.com; Soler 5862; r AR$920-1100; ❄@📶🏊) Resplendent in its red, black and white color scheme, this is a beautifully elegant boutique hotel. The rooms are spacious, with luxurious touches such as Egyptian-cotton bedsheets, large flat-screen TVs and bathroom towel warmers. The rooftop wood deck and pool come with excellent Palermo views and the on-site restaurant is renowned. There's also a sauna and a pleasant grassy garden.

SHORT- & LONG-TERM RENTALS

Any hotel, hostel or guesthouse should significantly discount a long-term stay, so negotiate a deal in advance. There are also many guesthouses that specialize in weekly or monthly stays and these offer a more intimate experience. If you're interested in spending time with a host family, see www.coret.com.ar. To rent a room in a house, check out www.sparerooms.com.ar. And for other options try www.buenosaires.craigslist.org and www.couchsurfing.com.

Traditionally you need a local's lien to help you cover rent for an apartment, but so many long-term foreigners have poured into BA that a plethora of rental agencies and websites have popped up to help them find housing without this requirement. Expect to pay a much higher monthly rate for this service, however; locals usually commit to at least one year when obtaining a lease for unfurnished apartments, and consequently pay less. Sites to check:

» www.adelsur.com
» www.alojargentina.com.ar
» www.apartmentsba.com
» www.barts.com.ar
» www.buenosaireshabitat.com
» www.friendlyapartments.com (gay oriented)
» www.oasisba.com
» www.roomargentina.com
» www.santelmoloft.com
» www.stayinbuenosaires.com
» www.tucasargentina.com
» www.yourhomeinargentina.com.ar

Students especially should check out **Residencia Universitaria Azul** (Map p48; ☎5353-9433; www.azul-residencia-universitaria.com; Av Callao 86; ❄@☜), located in a lovely 1905 building. A one-time fee encourages longer-term stays; all rooms share bathrooms, kitchens and common areas.

And if you'd like someone to check out an apartment before you rent it, **Madi Lang** (www.baculturalconcierge.com) can make sure the place isn't on a busy street, in an outlying neighborhood or near a construction site.

Craft Hotel BOUTIQUE HOTEL $$$
(Map p64; ☎4833-0060; www.crafthotel.com; Nicaragua 4583; r AR$630-840; ❄@☜) Contemporary hotel with clean lines and artsy recycled touches; the stairs are made from old colorful wood panels. Rooms have Scandinavian aesthetics and come with flat-screen TVs, MP3 docks, cement floors, showers (yes – often *in* the room!) and sometimes balconies. This hotel's best feature, however, has to be the rooftop lounge area. Bike rental available.

248 Finisterra BOUTIQUE HOTEL $$$
(Map p64; ☎4773-0901; www.248finisterra.com; Av Báez 248; s AR$690, d AR$720-960; ❄@☜) Smack in the middle of Las Cañitas' nightlife lies this elegant, Zenlike boutique hotel. There are four classes of minimalist rooms, all beautifully contemporary and most a good size. Best of all is the rooftop terrace, with wood lounges and a Jacuzzi, though there's also a small grassy garden in back.

Vain Boutique Hotel BOUTIQUE HOTEL $$$
(Map p64; ☎4774-8246; www.vainuniverse.com; Thames 2226; r AR$750-1200; ❄@☜) Fifteen elegant rooms, all with high ceilings and wood floors, in a lovely renovated building. Excellent outdoor terrace with living room area, and small bar-restaurant in the lobby.

Palermo Viejo B&B GUESTHOUSE $$
(Map p64; ☎4773-6012; www.palermoviejobb.com; Niceto Vega 4629; s AR$300, d AR$340-460; ❄@☜) This small and intimate B&B is located in a remodeled *casa chorizo* – a long,

narrow house. The six rooms all front a leafy outdoor patio hallway and are simple but quite comfortable; two have lofts. All come with fridge and a good breakfast.

Kala Petit Hotel GUESTHOUSE **$$**
(Map p64; ☎4773-1331; www.kalapetithotel.com; Thames 1263; d from AR$320; ❄@📶≋) This family-run place is a great midrange deal in Palermo, especially because there's a garden with small pool and *asado* area in back – plus a nice kitchen available for guests. The six rooms are simple but pleasant, and three share bathrooms. Located in an older house.

Gorriti 4290 GUESTHOUSE **$$**
(Map p64; ☎4862-8300; www.gorriti4290.com.ar; Gorriti 4290; d AR$240-360; ❄@📶) For an intimate stay, seek out this small, friendly spot. There are only four rooms (three with shared bathrooms) and all are simple yet comfortable, with quality beds and linens. The common area is interesting – there's a catwalk above the dining room and a tiny rooftop patio. The owners live on site.

Akais Hostel HOSTEL **$$**
(Map p64; ☎4833-9518; www.akaishostel.tk; Costa Rica 4520; dm/r AR$110/320; ❄📶) The Akais is more like a tiny hotel. There are only two private rooms – one with private bathroom and the other with balcony – and two dorm rooms with six beds each. There isn't really any indoor common area, but the awesome rooftop terrace with wood deck, bar area and views over Plaza Palermo Viejo make up for this. Great location; kitchen available.

Hostel Suites Palermo HOSTEL **$**
(Map p64; ☎4773-0806; www.hostelsuites.com; Charcas 4752; dm AR$70-80, r AR$220-300; ❄@📶) Good large hostel in a old mansion, best for quieter types. Nice rooftop terrace and lots of events offered, plus bike rental.

Kapaké Hostel HOSTEL **$**
(Map p64; ☎4773-1150; www.kapake.com.ar; Paraguay 5570; dm AR$60, s/d AR$180/280; ❄@📶) Small, slightly upscale hostel with modern common spaces and pleasant patio/rooftop terrace. Intimate, quiet and secure.

Palermo House Hostel HOSTEL **$**
(Map p64; ☎4832-1815; www.palermohouse.com.ar; Thames 1754; dm AR$50-60, r AR$200-250; ❄@📶) Hike upstairs to the 3rd floor, where everybody is hanging out in the reception-bar-kitchen-dining area. A bank of windows makes it bright, graffiti wall art makes it colorful and the metal deck offers fresh air. It's a very casual, funky, dingy party-style hostel with four- to nine-bed dorms (some tight with three-tier bunks) and private rooms with high ceilings.

Eating

Eating out in Buenos Aires is a gastronomical highlight. Not only are the typical *parrillas* (steak houses) a dime a dozen, but the city's Palermo Viejo neighborhood boasts the most varied ethnic cuisine in the country. You can find Armenian, Brazilian, Mexican, Indian, Japanese, Southeast Asian and Middle Eastern cuisines – and even fusions of several. Most are acceptable and some are exceptional.

Microcentro eateries tend to cater to the business crowd, while nearby Puerto Madero is full of elegant and pricey restaurants. Congreso is pretty traditional cuisine-wise, except for its 'Little Spain' neighborhood. Recoleta is another expensive neighborhood with touristy but fun dining options on Roberto M Ortiz (near the cemetery). San Telmo keeps attracting more and more worthwhile restaurants.

Reservations are usually unnecessary except at the most popular restaurants – or if it's the weekend. Except at five-star restaurants, wait staff provide simply adequate service – nothing fancy. Upscale restaurants charge a *cubierto,* a small cover charge for utensil use and bread. This doesn't include the tip, which should be around 10%.

A thorough online review website for BA restaurants is www.guiaoleo.com (in Spanish); for good blogs in English there are www.saltshaker.net, www.thelostasian.com and www.pickupthefork.com.

If you just don't feel like going out, check out www.buenosairesdelivery.com – food will be delivered straight to your hostel, hotel or home from one of dozens of restaurants, at no extra cost.

MICROCENTRO

Aldo's Vinoteca ARGENTINE **$$**
(Map p48; ☎5291-2380; Moreno 372; mains AR$40-70; ⏲breakfast, lunch & dinner) Located just under the Moreno Hotel, this restaurant/wine shop is an upscale eatery serving a small but tasty menu of meat and pasta dishes, all amidst walls lined with wine. What makes this place unique, however, is that the wine is sold at *retail* prices. This means you're not getting a restaurant markup, thus making it easier to drink up the close-to-500 labels available.

Broccolino ITALIAN $$$

(Map p48; ☎4322-7754; Esmeralda 776; mains AR$40-100; ⊙lunch & dinner) Pick from over 20 sauces (including squid ink!) for your pasta, with a choice of rigatoni, fusilli, pappardelle and all sorts of stuffed varieties. If you can't decide on your topper, try the delicious Sicilian sauce (spicy red peppers, tomato and garlic) or the pesto with mushrooms and garlic. Portions are large and the bread homemade.

Granix VEGETARIAN $$

(Map p48; ☎4343-4020; Florida 165, 1st fl; all-you-can-eat AR$57; ⊙lunch Mon-Fri; ☑) Stepping into this large, modern lacto-ovo-vegetarian eatery will make you wonder if *porteños* have had enough steak already. Pick from the many hot appetizers and mains; there's also a great salad bar and plenty of desserts. It's only open for weekday lunches, and located in a shopping mall. Take-out is available.

Parrilla al Carbón PARRILLA $

(Map p48; ☎4328-0824; Lavalle 663; mains AR$20-50; ⊙lunch & dinner) Cheap *parrilla* at a small, discreet eatery on pedestrain Lavalle; it's next to Balcarce cafe. Go for a quick *choripan* (sausage sandwich; AR$9) at the counter or, for more comfort and a better view of the TV, snag one of the few crowded tables and order a half-portion of the *vacío* (a chewy but tasty flank cut).

PUERTO MADERO

i Fresh Market INTERNATIONAL $$

(Map p48; ☎5775-0335; cnr Villaflor & Olga Cossettini; mains AR$40-50; ⊙breakfast, lunch & dinner) It's not on the water, but a sidewalk table does just fine at this upscale cafe-restaurant. Choose a gourmet sandwich or salad, and be sure to peek at the luscious dessert case. Its sister restaurant, **i Central Market**, is a few blocks away and much fancier.

La Parolaccia Trattoria ITALIAN $$

(Map p48; ☎4343-1679; Av Alicia Moreau de Justo 1052; mains AR$50-76; ⊙lunch & dinner) This popular Italian eatery specializes in homemade pastas. Reserve one of the few tables with a water view, then enjoy penne with salmon, gorgonzola ravioli or *cappelletti* (a small stuffed pasta) in four cheeses. A nearby branch, **La Parolaccia del Mare** (Av Alicia Moreau de Justo 1170), specializes in seafood.

Siga la Vaca BUFFET $$$

(Map p48; ☎4315-6801; Av Alicia Moreau de Justo 1714; lunch AR$85-110, dinner AR$98-110; ⊙lunch & dinner) Only the truly hungry should set foot in this excellent all-you-can-stuff-in *parrilla*. Work your way from the appetizer salad bar to the grill, where the meat hangs out. Eat slowly and pace yourself, and you'll only need to eat once that day. One drink and a dessert are included in the price, which varies depending on the meal and day.

DON'T MISS

TOP FOUR CLOSED-DOOR RESTAURANTS

Puertas Cerradas, or closed-door restaurants, offer an exclusive atmosphere as they're located in the chef's own homes. Expect communal tables, but don't worry – your fellow diners are usually interesting. You'll get the address after booking.

Casa Saltshaker (www.casasaltshaker.com) Sample the eclectic Mediterranean creations of chef Dan Perlman.

Casa Felix (www.colectivofelix.com) Diego Felix and Sanra Ritten serve up a gourmet, fish-based menu, with vegetarian or vegan dishes upon request.

Cocina Sunae (www.cocinasunae.com) Chef Christina Sunae cooks up delicious – and at times spicy – Southeast Asian food.

Casa Mun (www.casamun.com) Very tasty Asian fusion dishes by Chef Mun, blending Japanese, Korean, Chinese and California styles.

CONGRESO

TOP CHOICE **Chan Chan** PERUVIAN $

(Map p48; ☎4382-8492; Hipólito Yrigoyen 1390; mains AR$30-45; ⊙lunch & dinner Tue-Sun) A welcome newcomer to Congreso's dining scene is this very popular and artsy Peruvian joint. Dishes range from duck to rabbit to lamb (don't worry – no guinea pig), plus of course their delicious mixed ceviches and plenty of seafood choices. Try the *chicha morada* (a tasty corn-based fruity drink), or go for a pisco sour. Such reasonable prices mean there's often a wait.

Chiquilín PARRILLA $$

(Map p48; ☎4373-5163; Sarmiento 1599; mains AR$43-70; ⊙lunch & dinner) Going strong for 85 years, Chiquilín is a large and comfortable restaurant with a classic atmosphere that adds a bit of personality (think ham legs hanging from the ceiling). The best food here is the *parrilla* and the pasta, though you'll also find seafood, omelets and specialty salads, along with plenty of desserts. Open late.

Pizzería Güerrín PIZZERIA **$**
(Map p48; ☎4371-8141; Av Corrientes 1368; slices AR$3.50-5, whole pizzas AR$36-50; ⏰11am-1am Sun-Thu, till 2am Fri-Sat) Just point at a prebaked slice behind the glass counter and eat standing up with the rest of the guys. To be more civilized, sit down and order your pizza freshly baked – this way you'll choose from a greater variety of toppings. *Empanadas* and plenty of desserts also available.

Plaza Asturias SPANISH **$$**
(Map p48; ☎4382-7334; Av de Mayo 1199; mains AR$30-80; ⏰lunch & dinner) For authentic – or at least as authentic as you can get in Argentina – Spanish cuisine, this traditional and busy corner restaurant is your Mecca. Seafood casserole, Spanish-style octopus and paella Valenciana are popular choices, or try the roasted lamb or thick steak. Hanging hams and loud wait staff round out your experience; for a better deal, come at midday and order the set lunch.

SAN TELMO & CONSTITUCIÓN

TOP CHOICE **Café San Juan** INTERNATIONAL **$$**
(Map p48; ☎4300-1112; Av San Juan 450; mains AR$50-75; ⏰lunch & dinner Tue-Sun) Some of San Telmo's best international cuisine can be found at this fine bistro, run by the now-famous but still-humble chef Leandro Cristobal. Meat lovers should order the spectacular *ojo de bife* (ribeye), but this is also a great spot to try seafood – it's flown in daily from Patagonia. Reservations essential for dinner.

Amici Miei ITALIAN **$$**
(Map p48; ☎4362-5562; Defensa 1072; mains AR$44-75; ⏰lunch & dinner Tue-Sat, lunch Sun) Try to get here early to snag one of the few two-person balcony tables overlooking Plaza Dorrego. Even if you don't, the pappardelle with pork ragout or squash tortellini with almonds will still be a treat. Nonpasta specialties include fish and polenta dishes, all delicious.

Gran Parrilla del Plata PARRILLA **$$**
(Map p48; ☎4300-8858; Chile 594; mains AR$43-65; ⏰lunch & dinner) There's nothing too fancy at this traditional corner *parrilla* – just old-time atmosphere and generous portions of good grilled meats at decent prices. There are also pastas for that vegetarian who gets dragged along. Divided into two sections but they're right next to each other.

Casal de Catalunya SPANISH **$$$**
(Map p48; ☎4361-0191; Chacabuco 863; mains AR$65-90; ⏰lunch Tue-Sat, dinner daily) Unsurprisingly big on seafood, this excellent Catalan restaurant offers treats such as shrimp wrapped in bacon, seafood paella and rabbit with garlic mayonnaise. Try the house specialty, *cochinillo* (roasted pork), and don't miss the luscious *crema Catalana* for dessert. Reserve on weekends.

Bar Plaza Dorrego ARGENTINE **$$**
(Map p48; ☎4361-0141; Defensa 1098; mains AR$30-64; ⏰8am-2am Sun-Thu, to 4am Fri & Sat) You can't beat the atmosphere at this traditional joint; sip your *cortado* (coffee with milk) by a picture window or sidewalk table and watch the world pass by. Meanwhile, traditionally suited waiters, tango music and scribbled graffiti on the counters take you back in time – *if* you can ignore the new Starbucks across the street.

Bar El Federal ARGENTINE **$$**
(Map p48; ☎4300-4313; cnr Perú & Carlos Calvo; snacks AR$25-55; ⏰8am-2am Sun-Thu, till 4am Fri & Sat) This historic, classic bar dates from 1864; check out the amazing counter area. The specialties here are sandwiches (especially turkey breast) and *picadas* (shared appetizer plates), but there are also burgers, pastas, omelets and desserts. Sidewalk tables are the perfect perch for you to watch San Telmo go by.

Mash INTERNATIONAL **$$**
(Map p48; ☎015-6829-6829; Mexico 518; mains AR$42-60; ⏰dinner Tue-Sat) Run by a rather eccentric gay Brit and his Argentine partner (who both ran eateries across Europe), this cozy restaurant-bar in San Telmo has a small menu but the dishes are exotic and tasty, ranging from Tandoori chicken to fajitas to Thai green curry to lamb rogan josh.

LA BOCA

TOP CHOICE **Il Matterello** ITALIAN **$$**
(Map p58; ☎4307-0529; Martín Rodríguez 517; mains AR$40-65; ⏰lunch Tue-Sun, dinner Tue-Sat) The food is sublime at this Genovese trattoria. Old family recipes include lasagne bolognese and *tagliatelle alla rucola* (tagliatelle with arugula). For a special treat, the house *tortelli verde* (small pasta pillows stuffed with cheese and garlic) is hard to beat – and the carbonara sauce is renowned.

El Samovar de Rasputín ARGENTINE $

(Map p58; ☎4302-3190; De Valle Iberlucea 1251; mains AR$25-45; ⏰10am-8pm Wed-Sun) On a warm summer day choose the street seating at this atmospheric old joint, which offers great people-watching opportunities. The food is nothing new – basic pasta, sandwiches, *milanesas* and *parrilla* – but on weekends there's tango dancing and *candombe* (Latin American style of rhythmical drum music with African influences) drumming nearby.

RETIRO

Filo ITALIAN $$

(Map p60; ☎4311-0312; San Martín 975; mains AR$50-70, pizzas AR$40-60; ⏰lunch & dinner) Your choice is likely to be excellent at this artsy restaurant, as it does a great job on its 20 varieties of pizza and 10 kinds of salads (try the smoked salmon). Other tasty choices include panini, pasta and meats, along with a whirlwind of desserts.

Dadá INTERNATIONAL $$

(Map p60; ☎4814-4787; San Martín 941; mains AR$39-64; ⏰noon-3am Mon-Sat) Tiny bohemian Dadá feels like a local neighborhood bar in Paris. Get cozy in a corner seat and order something savory off the menu, which offers creative meat, fish and pasta dishes. And don't forget your cocktail; the bartenders at Dadá know how to mix a drink.

Gran Bar Danzón INTERNATIONAL $$$

(Map p60; ☎4811-1108; Libertad 1161; mains AR$65-95; ⏰dinner) It's hard to be hipper than this popular lounge bar-restaurant. A cool-looking conservation system makes it possible for many wines to be offered by the glass, one of which should go well with the pork ribs, duck *confit* or veal osso bucco. Lots of sushi options as well.

Sipan PERUVIAN $$$

(Map p60; ☎4315-0763; Paraguay 624; mains AR$70-130; ⏰lunch & dinner Mon-Sat) Split the plates with a friend at this attractive Japanese-Peruvian restaurant – they're meant to be shared. Both traditional and Asian-influenced creative dishes are available; try the popular 'Sipan roll' (with shrimp, crab, avocado and cream cheese) and one of the well-spiced ceviches.

RECOLETA & BARRIO NORTE

TOP CHOICE **Oviedo** MEDITERRANEAN $$$

(Map p64; ☎4822-5415; Beruti 2602; mains AR$70-110; ⏰lunch & dinner) Chef Martin Rabaudino oversees one of the best kitchens in the city. This is a truly elegant place, with professional service and a classy atmosphere. Fish and meat dishes are the specialty; choose from tempting dishes such as the Kobe beef flank with French beans, trout fillet with mushrooms terrine, or Patagonian lamb. The wine list is excellent.

Natural Deli CAFE-DELI $

(Map p64; ☎4822-1228; Laprida 1672; mains AR$40-48; ⏰8am-midnight Mon-Sat, 9am-midnight Sun; 🖉) Modern, organic deli offering delicious natural foods. Choose from creative gourmet sandwiches and wraps, fresh salads or vegetarian tarts. You can add echinacea and ginseng to the healthy juices and *licuados* (blended fruit smoothie), and there's even a small health food section. Another **branch** (Map p64; Gorostiaga 1776) has a yoga and acupuncture studio.

Cumaná ARGENTINE $

(Map p60; ☎4813-9207; Rodriguez Peña 1149; mains AR$27-32; ⏰lunch & dinner) Cumaná specializes in deliciously homey, stick-to-your-ribs *cazuelas* (pot stews), which are baked with squash, corn, potatoes and/or meats, among other tidbits. Also popular are the pizzas, *empanadas,* pastas and calzones. Come early if you want a table.

Rodi Bar ARGENTINE $$

(Map p60; ☎4801-5230; Vicente López 1900; mains AR$35-88; ⏰7am-2am Mon-Sat) A great option for well-priced, unpretentious food in upscale Recoleta. This traditional restaurant with fine old-world atmosphere and extensive menu offers something for everyone, from inexpensive combo plates to relatively unusual dishes such as marinated beef tongue.

Como en Casa ARGENTINE $

(Map p60; ☎4816-5507; Riobamba 1239; mains AR$35-48; ⏰8am-midnight Tue-Sat, 8am-8:30pm Sun & Mon) This gorgeous cafe-restaurant has an elegant atmosphere. It's best feature is the shady patio, complete with large fountain and surrounded by grand buildings – a must on a warm day. A few dinner options available.

El Sanjuanino ARGENTINE $

(Map p60; ☎4805-2683; Posadas 1515; mains AR$30-50; ⏰lunch & dinner) Some of the cheapest food in Recoleta, attracting both penny-pinching locals and thrifty tourists. Sit on the main floor or in the basement and order spicy *empanadas,* tamales or *locro* (a spicy stew), or take your food to go – Recoleta's lovely parks are just a couple of blocks away.

LICKING YOUR WAY THROUGH BA

Because of Argentina's Italian heritage, Argentine *helado* is comparable to the best ice cream in the world. Amble into a *heladería* (ice-cream shop), order up a cone (pay first) and the creamy concoction will be artistically swept up into a mountainous peak. Important: *granizado* means with chocolate flakes.

Here are some of the tastiest *heladerías* in town:

Dylan (Map p48; Perú 1086, San Telmo)

Freddo Barrio Norte (Map p60; Av Santa Fe 1600); Palermo (Map p64; Armenia 1618) Many branches; check www.freddo.com.ar

Heladería Cadore (Map p48; Av Corrientes 1695, Congreso)

Persicco Las Cañitas (Map p64; Migueletes 886); Palermo (Map p64; cnr Honduras & Gurruchaga); Palermo (Map p64; Salguero 2591)

Una Altra Volta Palermo (Map p64; Av del Libertador 3060); Recoleta (Map p60; cnr Quintana & Ayacucho)

Vía Flaminia (Map p48; Av Florida 121, Microcentro)

Veikko (Map p64; Chenaut 1790, Las Cañitas)

PALERMO

TOP CHOICE Sarkis MIDDLE EASTERN $$
(Map p64; ☎4772-4911; Thames 1101; mains AR$28-58; ⏰lunch & dinner) There's a reason this longstanding Middle Eastern restaurant is still around: the food is awesome. For appetizers, don't miss the *boquerones* (marinated sardines) or *hojas de repollo rellenas* (stuffed vine leaves). Follow up with lamb in yogurt sauce. At night from Sunday to Thursday, a fortune teller reads diners' coffee grounds.

TOP CHOICE Olsen SCANDINAVIAN $$$
(Map p64; ☎4776-7677; Gorriti 5870; mains AR$70-80; ⏰lunch & dinner Tue-Sat, 10:30am-8pm Sun) Olsen is famous for its Sunday brunch, but dinner isn't bad either; order organic chicken with goat cheese, or white fish *ñoquis* (gnocci). Lunches are prix fixe (AR$60 to AR$70), and on a warm day you can sit in the gorgeous front garden. The popular bar serves more than 60 kinds of vodka, assiduously kept at -18°C.

Las Pizarras INTERNATIONAL $$
(Map p64; ☎4775-0625; Thames 2296; mains AR$55-68; ⏰dinner Sun-Tue) At this simple and unpretentious restaurant, Chef Rodrigo Castilla cooks up a changing rainbow of eclectic dishes such as grilled venison or rabbit stuffed with cherries and pistachios. Those with meeker stomachs can choose the asparagus and mushroom risotto or any of the homemade pastas. The chalkboard menu on the wall adds to the casual atmosphere.

Don Julio PARRILLA $$
(Map p64; ☎ 4832-6058; Guatemala 4699; mains AR$40-90; ⏰lunch & dinner) A *parrilla* highly recommended for its exceptional meat dishes – it's as good as its fancier neighbors, but with a much more traditional feel. Nice corner location with sidewalk tables, and the wine list is also better than average.

Miranda PARRILLA $$$
(Map p64; ☎4771-4255; Costa Rica 5602; mains AR$60-80; ⏰lunch & dinner) Popular for its luscious steaks, Miranda is a fashionable, modern *parrilla* with concrete walls and high ceilings – but the food is the main attraction here. The meat is good quality and grilled to perfection. If you score a sidewalk table on a warm day, life for a carnivore just doesn't get much better.

Bio VEGETARIAN $$
(Map p64; ☎4774-3880; Humboldt 2192; mains AR$50-55; ⏰lunch daily, dinner Tue-Sun; 🖉) The health-conscious should make a beeline to this casual corner joint, which specializes in healthy, organic and vegetarian fare. Feed your body and soul quinoa risotto, seitan curry, mushroom stir-fries and mustard tofu with yamani rice.

Novecento INTERNATIONAL $$
(Map p64; ☎4778-1900; Av Báez 199; mains AR$40-77; ⏰lunch & dinner) Full weekend brunches are served at this elegant corner restaurant; go for the French toast, eggs Benedict or waffles with fig syrup. Or choose the all-you-can-eat option: dishes are brought to you (AR$154

for two people). Dinner means dishes such as Patagonian lamb and salmon farfalle.

Azema INTERNATIONAL **$$$**
(Map p64; ☎4774-4191; AJ Carranza 1875; mains AR$65-80; ⏰dinner Mon-Sat) Run by eccentric chef Paul Jean Azema (who has cooked for Kurt Cobain, among others), this restaurant serves up 'French colony cuisine' – an interesting array of Asian, French and Argentine fusions. Dishes run the gamut from Vietnamese spring rolls to Tandoori chicken salad to rabbit in Dijon mustard and Chardonnay. Seafood dishes are great and the kitchen isn't afraid of using its spices.

La Fábrica del Taco MEXICAN **$**
(Map p64; ☎4832-0815; Gorriti 5062; tacos AR$10-14; ⏰lunch & dinner Tue-Sun) You might just feel you're in a Mexican beach town at this very casual, colorful taco joint. Authentic Mexican cooks hover at the front grill, slapping together tasty and familiar tacos *(al pastor, carne asada, pollo con queso, vegetariano)*. There is even *aguas frescas de tamarindo* (fresh tamarind juice). The *Chimichurri* (sauce made of olive oil, garlic and parsley) on the menu, however, brings you back to BA.

El 22 Parrilla PARRILLA **$**
(Map p64; ☎4778-1095; Carranza 1950; mains AR$30-50; ⏰lunch & dinner) A cheap unpretentious *parrilla* isn't that easy to find in upscale Palermo Viejo. This casual family-style joint is an exception, serving up huge portions for great prices. The lunch specials are an even better deal, especially if you score a sidewalk table.

El Primo PARRILLA **$$**
(Map p64; ☎4772-8441; Baéz 302; mains AR$30-70; ⏰lunch Tue-Sun, dinner daily) Popular and classic corner *parrilla* in happenin' Las Cañitas. Try the *vacío* (preferably *jugoso* – it'll come medium rare); it's a tasty, chewy cut and the half-portion is enough for most people. The *brochettes* (shish kebabs) are house specialties.

Las Cholas ARGENTINE **$$**
(Map p64; ☎4899-0094; Arce 306; mains AR$35-60; ⏰lunch & dinner) Las Cholas has found the golden rule of many successful restaurants: good food, trendy design and decent prices. Traditional Argentine foods such as *locro* and *cazuelas* stews are worth a shot, but the *parrilla* is also excellent. Expect a wait and so-so service.

Meraviglia INTERNATIONAL **$**
(Map p64; ☎4775-7949; cnr Gorriti & Angel J Carranza; mains AR$35-40; ⏰9am-7pm Mon & Wed, till midnight Thu & Fri, 10:30am-7pm Sat & Sun; ✎) Wonderful airy and bright vegetarian cafe with small but high-quality menu. Choose homemade granola and yogurt for breakfast or well-prepared salads, tarts and sandwiches for lunch or a late-afternoon snack. Everything is freshly made with mostly organic ingredients, and a few healthy products are available for purchase.

TOP CHOICE **Siamo nel Forno** PIZZERIA **$$**
(Map p64; ☎5290-9529; Costa Rica 5886; small pizzas AR$50-60; ⏰dinner Tue-Sun) Possibly the city's best Naples-style pizzas, made with

MEATLESS IN BUENOS AIRES

Argentine cuisine is internationally famous for its succulent grilled meats, but this doesn't mean vegetarians – or even vegans – are completely out of luck.

Most restaurants, including *parrillas*, serve a few items acceptable to most vegetarians, such as green salads, omelets, pizza and pasta. Key words to beware of include *carne* (beef), *pollo* (chicken), *cerdo* (pork) and *cordero* (lamb). *Sin carne* means 'without meat' and the phrase *soy vegetariano/a* (I'm a vegetarian) will come in handy when explaining to an Argentine why in the world you don't eat their delicious steaks.

Close to the Microcentro there's **Granix** (p79) and **Saatva** (Map p48; ☎4374-5125; Montevideo 446; ⏰lunch Tue-Sun, dinner Sat & Sun). **Pura Vida** (p85) has nutritious juice combinations plus a few veggie snacks, while **Broccolino** (p79) specializes in pasta – it's not meat-free, but there are many vegetarian choices.

The Palermo Viejo area has more upscale options, including **Bio** (p82), **Meraviglia** (above) and **Artemesia** (Map p64; ☎4776-5484; Gorriti 5996; ⏰lunch & dinner). **La Esquina de las Flores** (Map p64; ☎4832-8528; Gurruchaga 1630; ⏰8:30am-8pm Mon-Fri, till 8:30pm Sat, 10am-6pm Sun) is a long-running veggie cafeteria/health shop.

Even raw foodists have an option: gourmet, vegan, raw-live food, organic when possible, delivered to your door. Check out www.cocinaverde.com.

quality ingredients and finished in a hot wood-fired oven so their thin crusts char beautifully.

La Cabrera PARRILLA $$$
(Map p64; ☎4831-7002; Cabrera 5099 & 5127; mains AR$70-100; ⊙lunch & dinner) Hugely popular for grilling up BA's most sublime meats. Expensive, but main dishes come with heaps of little complimentary side dishes. The two locations are half a block apart.

Cusic INTERNATIONAL $
(Map p64; ☎4139-9173; El Salvador 6016; mains AR$33-40; ⊙10am-8pm Wed-Sun) Super-cute bistro with healthy and absolutely delicious gourmet sandwiches, salads and breakfasts. Pull the spoon to ring in.

Las Cabras ARGENTINE $$
(Map p64; ☎5197-5303; Fitz Roy 1795; mains AR$42-55; ⊙lunch & dinner) Good-value Northern Argentine specialties and *parrilla,* all wrapped up in a casual, trendy atmosphere. Good-sized portions and popular, so come early or wait.

Hola! Siniór Shawarma MIDDLE EASTERN $
(Map p64; ☎4834-6118; Honduras 5328; shawarmas AR$22-27; ⊙lunch & dinner Mon-Sat) Cheap, good shawarmas that are the rage in BA right now – like giant burritos, filled with meat, veggies and salsas. Limited seating.

Drinking

Cafes are an integral part of *porteño* life, and you shouldn't miss popping into one of these beloved hangouts to sip dainty cups of coffee and nibble biscuits with the locals. There are plenty of cafes in the city, and while you're walking around seeing the sights you're bound to run across one and find an excuse for a break. Some cafes are old classics and guaranteed to take you back in time.

Most cafes serve all meals and everything in between: breakfast, brunch, lunch, afternoon tea, dinner and late-night snacks. Generally they open early in the morning and late into the evening.

In a city that never sleeps, finding a good drink is as easy as walking down the street. Whether you're into trendy lounges, Irish pubs, traditional cafes or sports bars, you'll find them all within the borders of BA.

Argentines aren't huge drinkers and you'll be lucky to see one rip-roaring drunk. One thing they *do* do, however, is stay up late. Most bars and cafes are open until two or three in the morning, and often until 5am on weekends – or until the last customer stumbles out the door.

And if you like to party with young, heavy-drinking crowds, check out **Buenos Aires Pub Crawl** (☎15-5464-1886; www.pubcrawlba.com).

CONGRESO

Café de los Angelitos TRADITIONAL CAFE
(Map p48; ☎4952-2320; Av Rivadavia 2100) Originally called Bar Rivadavia, this spot was once the haunt of poets, musicians…even criminals. Restored to its former glory, this historic cafe is now an atmospheric hangout, with elegant surroundings and fancy dressed waiters. At night there are fancy, expensive tango shows on offer (reserve ahead).

Clásica y Moderna TRADITIONAL CAFE
(Map p60; ☎4812-8707; Av Callao 892) Catering to the literary masses since 1938, this cozy and intimate bookstore-cafe continues to ooze history from its atmospheric brick walls. It's nicely lit, offers plenty of reading material and serves upscale meals. There are also regular live performances of folk music, jazz and tango.

El Gato Negro TEAHOUSE, CAFE
(Map p48; ☎4374-1730; Av Corrientes 1669) Tea-lined wooden cabinets and a spicy aroma welcome you to this pleasant little sipping paradise. Enjoy cups of imported coffee or tea along with breakfast and dainty *sandwiches de miga* (thinly sliced white-bread sandwiches). Tea is sold by weight, and exotic herbs and spices are also on offer.

Debar BAR
(Map p48; ☎4381-6876; Av Rivadavia 1132) A popular bar in an area not known for its nightlife, Debar is big on international music and has theme music nights (eg British pop). Businesspeople come for an after-work *trago* (drink), while travelers and expats hit it later in the evening. If you like sweet things try the *postrecito,* a house drink made with Kahlua and Bailey's.

RECOLETA

La Biela TRADITIONAL CAFE
(Map p60; ☎4804-0449; Av Quintana 600) A Recoleta institution, this landmark has been serving the *porteño* elite since the 1950s, when racing-car champions came here for their java jolts. The outdoor front terrace is unbeatable on a sunny day, especially when the nearby weekend *feria* (street market) is in full swing – but it'll cost you 20% more.

Milión COCKTAIL BAR
(Map p60; ☎4815-9925; Paraná 1048) This elegant and sexy bar is in a renovated mansion. The garden out back is a leafy paradise, overlooked by a solid balcony that holds the best seats in the house. There is an elegant tapas selection to accompany the wide range of cocktails (pay first, then catch the bartender's eye!), while downstairs a restaurant serves international dishes.

Casa Bar SPORTS BAR
(Map p60; ☎4816-2712; Rodríguez Peña 1150) The American expat who runs it spent years rebuilding an old house into this atmospheric bar. Attractions include dozens of beers to choose from, US football and baseball on TV, BA's best spicy chicken wings and occasional brunch on Sundays. Good mix of locals and foreigners; popular with pilots.

El Alamo SPORTS BAR
(Map p60; ☎4813-7324; Uruguay 1175) El Alamo draws expats with US sports on TV, though it also shows plenty of soccer games. The music's rock, there's pub food for the hungry and – most importantly – beer-pong games happen on Tuesday evenings. Women drink beer free from 4pm to early evening, and pitchers are discounted during happy hour.

Nucha MODERN CAFE
(Map p60; ☎4813-9507; Paraná 1343) There *must* be something in the tempting pastry counter – perhaps cheesecake, *medialunas* (croissants) or lightly layered afternoon cake – to go with your imported tea, iced coffee or *mate* (tea-like beverage) at this cute cafe. Crowds flood in for afternoon tea and tasty lunch sandwiches, but breakfast is also served.

MICROCENTRO

La Cigale BAR
(Map p48; ☎4893-2332; 25 de Mayo 597) Sultry downtown lounge popular with mixed crowds of all ages and nationalities. The curvy downstairs bar serves tasty cocktails; try the mojito or Latin lover. Happy hour runs until 10pm, and there are 10 kinds of burgers on the menu. Upstairs live music and DJs frequently entertain; on weekends there's dancing into the wee morning hours. Popular on Tuesday for its DJs and 'French night.'

Café Tortoni TRADITIONAL CAFE
(Map p48; ☎4342-4328; Av de Mayo 825) Buenos Aires' most notoriously touristy cafe – on busy days there's a line just to get inside. Famous for its stuffy, almost rude service personnel and overpriced menu. It's a tourist trap for sure, but retains a beautiful, classic atmosphere and one of the city's landmarks. Also offers relatively affordable tango shows in the evenings (see p87).

London City TRADITIONAL CAFE
(Map p48; ☎4343-0328; Av de Mayo 599) This classy cafe has been serving java addicts for over 55 years, and claims to have been the spot where Julio Cortázar wrote his first novel. Your hardest work here, however, will most likely be choosing which luscious pastry to have with your freshly brewed coffee.

La Puerto Rico TRADITIONAL CAFE
(Map p48; ☎4331-2215; Adolfo Alsina 416) One of the city's historic cafes, going strong since 1887 – and not too touristy. Located a block south of Plaza de Mayo, it serves great coffee and pastries, the latter baked on the premises. Old photos on the walls hint at a rich past and the Spanish movies that have been filmed here.

Pura Vida JUICE BAR
(Map p48; ☎4393-0093; Reconquista 516; juices AR$18-25, snacks AR$26-35; ⏲9am-5pm Mon-Fri) Step into this healthy juice bar for fruit blends and smoothies. The Green Monster (celery, cucumber and apple) is especially refreshing,

WINE TASTING 101

Big on wine? There are a few ways to find out what Argentina's best grapes have to offer. Try a wine tasting!

Casa Coupage (☎4833-6354; www.casacoupage.com.ar) is run by a friendly Argentine couple, both sommeliers, in their beautiful Palermo Soho apartment. Includes light tables for the wine and a food-pairing meal.

US native Daniel Karlin organizes wine tastings of boutique vintages with food pairings in his lovely Palermo bar/loft, **Anuva Wines** (☎15-5768-8589; www.anuvawines.com). Best of all, he'll send your wines to the USA – BA's most affordable wine-shipping service.

Private wine tastings are run by enthusiastic Brit **Nigel Tollerman** (☎4966-2500; www.0800-vino.com) in his atmospheric basement cellar. He'll also deliver fine-quality Argentine wines to your hotel, and has a premium-wine storage service.

and you can add wheatgrass, yogurt, spirulina or bee pollen to your selection. Sandwiches, wraps and salads are also available.

SAN TELMO

La Puerta Roja BAR

(Map p48; ☎4362-5649; Chacabuco 733) There's no sign and you have to ring the bell, but once inside there's hot music and cool vibes, with low lounge furniture in the main room and a pool table tucked behind. Come early for a good seat and to munch on the excellent and cheap food options – there's little space to eat later. Adventurous? Try the 'chili bomb' cocktail.

Gibraltar PUB

(Map p48; ☎4362-5310; Perú 895) One of BA's classic expat pubs, with a cozy atmosphere and a good bar counter for those traveling alone. Good exotic food includes Thai, Indian or English dishes, or the sushi on Sunday. There's a pool table in back along with a smoking patio – and upstairs is an exclusive-feel cigar bar serving cocktails.

Los del Barco BAR

(Map p48; ☎4331-3004; Bolívar 684) A great option for late-nighters in San Telmo, this funky watering hole is open till 5am Tuesday to Saturday, offering a wonderfully local atmosphere without pretension. The pizza, sandwiches and burgers are cheap and go well with the house mojito, while the music is an eclectic mix of rock, soul, funk, '70s, '80s and ska.

Doppelgänger COCKTAIL BAR

(Map p58; ☎4300-0201; Av Juan de Garay 500) Some of BA's best and creative cocktails are the highlight of this upscale bar; choose from dozens. Food is also available.

Indie Bar BAR

(Map p48; ☎4307-0997; Av Paseo Colón 843) Friendly bar staff make it easy for solo drinkers to feel comfortable, as do the creative cocktails. Weekend DJs plus basement space for dance parties.

PALERMO

Magdalena's Party BAR

(Map p64; ☎4833-9127; Thames 1795) Popular bar with an international mix of owners. A bit upscale but still laid-back, with good service and *buena onda* (good vibes). DJs spin from Thursday to Saturday nights, with cheap drinks making this a good pre-club bar; try the vodka lemonade by the pitcher. Happy hour runs from 8pm to midnight daily, and tasty expat-friendly food is served, such as freshly ground hamburgers, fish burritos and organic coffee. Weekend brunch too.

Sugar BAR

(Map p64; ☎4831-3276; Costa Rica 4619) Palermo Soho bar that's super popular for its happy hour, which runs from 7pm to midnight – pints, glasses of wine or mixed drinks are AR$12 each. Attracts foreign students and expats (it's partially expat-run); all servers speak some English. Great eclectic mix of music, from James Brown to the Killers. Thursday to Saturday there's a minimum drink purchase.

Congo COCKTAIL BAR

(Map p64; ☎4833-5857; Honduras 5329) The highlight at this beautiful and trendy bar is the back patio – *the* place to be seen on hot summer nights. The music is tops too, with DJs spinning almost every night, and inside are elegant low lounges in creative spaces. Full food menu available, along with some tasty, stiff cocktails.

878 BAR

(Map p64; ☎4773-1098; Thames 878) Enter a wonderland of elegant, low lounge furniture and red brick walls. If you're a whiskey lover, there are over 100 kinds to try. Tasty classic and original cocktails also lubricate the crowds, happy to revel in the jazz, bossa nova and good old rock music playing on the speakers.

Office BAR

(Map p64; ☎2050-3942; Avévalo 3031) Best for its small, open-air rooftop. US-comfort food: hamburgers, chicken wings and quesadillas.

Frank's Bar COCKTAIL BAR

(Map p64; ☎4777-6541; Arévalo 1445) Plush, elegant speakeasy bar that 'requires' a password (via telephone booth) to get in. Curious, aren't you?

Geno's Beer Bar BEER BAR

(Map p64; ☎4771-7593; Guatemala 5499) Like beer? Come here and try the over 40 kinds, then. If you're hungry, there's beer soup and beer ice cream(!).

El Carnal BAR

(Map p64; ☎4772-7582; Niceto Vega 5511) The open-air roof terrace, with its bamboo lounges and billowy curtains, can't be beat for a cool chill-out on a warm summer night. Wednesday there's raggae and Saturday is dominated by pop and '80s beats – but Thursday is big for Niceto Club drinks (the popular nightclub is just across the street).

Shanghai Dragon PUB
(Map p64; ☎4778-1053; Aráoz 1199) Newest entry by the owners of highly successful Gibraltar and Bangalore pubs, but with cheap Chinese food instead of Indian.

Mundo Bizarro BAR
(Map p64; ☎4773-1967; Serrano 1222) This futuristically retro and stylishly slick lounge bar is open all night on weekends, when everything from old-time American music to hip DJs and jazz stir up the airwaves. Monday is sushi night and Wednesdays means 20% off drinks until midnight, but you can hop on the dancing pole at any time if you need some attention.

Van Koning PUB
(Map p64; ☎4772-9909; Av Báez 325) Great rustic spaces make this intimate Las Cañitas pub feel like the inside of a boat; after all, it has a 17th-century-style seafaring theme complete with dark-wood beams, flickering candles and blocky furniture. Filled with Dutch expats on the first Wednesday of the month.

Many hotels and restaurants in Palermo have great bars; try **Home Hotel** (p76), **Casa Cruz** (Map p64; ☎4833-1112; Uriarte 1658) or **Bangalore** (Map p64; ☎4779-2621; Humboldt 1416). For the hippest scene in town, head to Plaza Serrano (in Palermo Viejo) and settle in at one of the many trendy bars surrounding the plaza.

☆ Entertainment

Nonstop Buenos Aires has endless possibilities for entertainment. Dozens of venues offer first-rate theatrical productions, independent or contemporary movies, sultry tango shows, raging dance parties and exciting sports matches.

Most newspapers publish entertainment pages; the *Buenos Aires Herald* has one in English called 'Get Out.' Also check www.vuenosairez.com (in Spanish) and www.argentinaindependent.com (in English).

Major entertainment venues often require booking through **Ticketek** (☎5237-7200; www.ticketek.com.ar), which incurs a service charge. At *carteleras* (discount ticket offices), you can buy tickets at 30% to 50% discount for many events like tango shows, theater, movies, concerts and even restaurants. Here are three:

Cartelera Baires (Map p48; www.carteleraaires.com; Av Corrientes 1382) In Galería Apolo.

Cartelera Espectáculos (Map p48; ☎4322-1559; www.123info.com.ar; Lavalle 742) Right on pedestrian Lavalle.

Cartelera Vea Más (Map p48; ☎6320-5319; www.veamasdigital.com.ar; Av Corrientes 1660, local 2)

Tango Shows

Sensationalized tango shows aimed at tourists are common and 'purists' don't consider them authentic – though this doesn't necessarily make them bad. Modest shows are more intimate and cost far less, but you won't get the theatrics, the costume changes or the overall visual punch. For discount tickets to some shows, check the *carteleras*.

The website www.tangotix.com has some tango show reviews and can help you choose the right show depending on your needs; it also sells discounted tickets.

Some *milongas* (tango academies) occasionally put on affordable tango shows; check out **Confitería Ideal** (p93) and **La Viruta** (p93) or **Academia Nacional del Tango** (☎4345-6967; www.anacdeltango.org.ar; Av de Mayo 833).

For free (that is, donation) tango, head to Galerías Pacífico, where there are performances on the pedestrian street (especially Sundays). In San Telmo on Sundays, dancers perform in Plaza Dorrego. Another good bet is weekends on Caminito in La Boca.

Café Tortoni TANGO SHOW
(Map p48; ☎4384-1095; www.cafetortoni.com.ar; Av de Mayo 829; show AR$100-120) Buenos Aires' landmark and very touristy cafe offers three or four shows per day. Performers change nightly so it's a crapshoot whether you get good ones or not, but usually the shows are decent enough for most people and relatively affordable. The more expensive show has more dancers and musicians; reserve a day or two ahead in person for all shows.

Tango Porteño TANGO SHOW
(Map p48; ☎4124-9400; www.tangoporteno.com.ar; Cerrito 570; show with/without dinner AR$500/180) One of the city's best shows takes place in this renovated and historical art deco theater (1100-seat capacity), right in the center. Snippets of old footage are interspersed with plenty of athletic (and sensual) tango dancing. Juan Carlos Copes – a famous Argentine

(Continued on page 92)

The Tango

History of Tango

The air hangs heavy, smoky and dark. A lone woman, dressed in slit skirt and high heels, sits at one of the small tables surrounding a wooden dance floor. She casually looks around, in search of the subtle signal. Her gaze sweeps over several tables and suddenly locks onto a stranger's eyes, and there it is: the *cabeceo* a quick tilt of his head. She briefly considers the offer, then nods with a slight smile. The man approaches her and she rises to meet him, and the new pair head out toward the dance floor.

The tango hasn't always been quite so mysterious, but it does have a long and somewhat complex history. Though the exact origins can't be pinpointed, the dance is thought to have started in Buenos Aires in the 1880s. Legions of European immigrants, mostly lower-class men, arrived in the great village of Buenos Aires to seek their fortunes. Missing their motherlands and the women they left behind, they sought out cafes and bordellos to ease the loneliness. Here the men cavorted with waitresses and prostitutes, creating a dance blending machismo, passion and longing, with an almost fighting edge to it.

Small musical ensembles were soon brought in to accompany early tangos, playing tunes influenced by pampas *milonga* verse, Spanish and Italian melodies and African *candombe* drums. (The *bandoneón,* a small accordion, was brought into these sessions and has since become an inextricable part of the tango orchestra.) Here the tango song was also born. It summarized the new urban experience for the immigrants and was permeated with nostalgia for a disappearing way of life. Themes ranged from profound feelings about changing neighborhoods to the figure of the mother, male friendship and betrayal by women. Sometimes, raunchy lyrics were added.

The perceived vulgarity of the dance was deeply frowned upon by the reigning elites but it did manage to influence some brash young members of the upper classes, who took the novelty to Paris and created a craze – a dance that became an acceptable outlet for human desires, expressed on the dance floors of elegant cabarets. The trend spread around Europe and even to the USA, and 1913 was considered by some 'the year of the tango.' When the evolved dance returned to Buenos Aires, now refined and famous, the tango finally earned the respectability it deserved. The golden years of tango were just beginning.

Clockwise from top left
1. Café Tortoni (p87) **2.** Museo Casa Carlos Gardel (p63) **3.** Dancing the tango

KRZYSZTOF DYDYNSKI/LONELY PLANET IMAGES ©

2
En tu muerte y por tu nombre
lloraron hasta los hombres
que lloran solo una vez !!

DANITA DELIMONT/GETTY ©

3

TIPS IMAGES/TIPS ITALIA SRL A SOCIO UNICO /ALAMY ©

Tango at a Milonga Today

Buenos Aires is full of *milongas* (tango halls), from classic venues with old-time atmosphere to hip warehouse spaces where dancers wear jeans – in other words, there's something for everyone.

At an established *milonga*, finding a good, comparable partner involves many levels of hidden codes, rules and signals that dancers must follow. In fact, some men will only proposition an unknown woman after the second song, so as not to be stuck with a bad dancer. After all, it's considered polite to dance at least to the end of a set (four songs) with any partner; if you are given a curt *'gracias'* after just one song, consider yourself excused.

Your position in the area surrounding the dance floor can be critical. Ideally, you should sit where you have easy access to the floor and to other dancers' line of sight. You may notice singles sitting in front, while couples sit further back. Generally couples are considered 'untouchable' – for them to dance with others, they either enter the room separately, or the man may signal his intent by asking another woman to the floor. Now 'his' woman becomes available to others.

The *cabeceo* – the quick tilt of the head, eye contact and uplifted eyebrows – can happen from way across the room. The woman to whom the *cabeceo* is directed either nods yes and smiles, or pretends not to have noticed. If she says yes, the man gets up and escorts her to the floor. If you're at a *milonga* and don't want to dance with anyone, don't look around too much – you could be breaking some hearts.

Don't be surprised to see different *milongas* put on at a single venue, depending on the time or day. Each *milonga* can be run by a different promoter, so each will have its own vibe, style, music and table arrangement, as well as age levels and experiences.

For a long list of *milongas* and instructors, see www.caseronporteno.com/tangomap.php. Or get a copy of Sally Blake's practical guide *Happy Tango: Sallycat's Guide to Dancing in Buenos Aires* (www.sallycatway.com/happytango), which has information on *milongas* – how to dress for them and act in them – plus the inside scoop on the city's tango scene.

Tango classes are often available in the same venue as *milongas*, in the hours before they start. But you can find them everywhere from youth hostels to cultural centers – some are even included free when you book a fancy tango show. Tourist-oriented classes are often taught in English.

So what is the appeal of the tango? Experienced dancers will say that the rush from a blissful tango-connection with a stranger can lift you to exhilarating heights. But the dance can also become addictive – once you have fallen for the passion and beauty of the tango's movements, you can spend your life trying to attain a physical perfection that can never be fully realized. The true *tanguero* simply attempts to make the journey as graceful as possible.

MILONGAS

- Salon Canning
- Niño Bien
- Gricel
- Confitería Ideal

For reviews on these *milongas* and more, see p92.

Clockwise from top left

1. Learning to dance the tango **2.** Tango dancing at a *milonga* (p92)

1

JAVIER PIERINI/GETTY ©

2

ALISON WRIGHT/CORBIS ©

(Continued from page 87)

dancer in his time – usually makes a cameo. Free tango class offered beforehand with dinner show.

Esquina Carlos Gardel TANGO SHOW
(Map p64; ☎4867-6363; Carlos Gardel 3200; show with/without dinner AR$560/380) One of the fanciest tango shows in town plays at this impressive 400-seat theater. The Abasto neighborhood was once Carlos Gardel's old stomping ground, and he even hung out at this locale. The memorable show starts with a good film about the area, then goes on to highlight top-notch musicians and performers. Most tables are communal and you sit sideways to the stage, so upgrade if you care.

Piazzolla Tango TANGO SHOW
(Map p48; ☎4344-8201; www.piazzollatango.com; Florida 165; show with/without dinner AR$480/280) This beautiful art-nouveau theater used to be a red-light cabaret venue. The show here is based on the music of Ástor Piazzolla, a *bandoneón* player who revolutionized tango music by fusing in elements from jazz and classical music. Be aware most tables are communal and you'll be facing sideways to watch the show. Free tango lesson with dinner show.

Esquina Homero Manzi TANGO SHOW
(☎4957-8488; www.esquinahomeromanzi.com.ar; Av San Juan 3601; show with/without dinner AR$410/140) An impressively refurbished old cafe, Esquina Homero Manzi was named after one of Argentina's most famous tango lyricists. Today you can take tango lessons here from 6pm to 9pm, then sit back and watch the traditional show – which highlights Manzi's music – in the 300-seat venue.

Los 36 Billares TANGO SHOW
(Map p48; ☎4381-5696; www.los36billares.com.ar; Av de Mayo 1265; shows AR$20-50) A combination restaurant-cafe-bar-billiards hall, this atmospheric old place has been around for nearly 100 years. It offers affordable shows; tango on Tuesdays and tango plus flamenco on Thursdays. Call for other nights as show times can vary; minimum purchase of food and drinks may be required.

La Puerto Rico TANGO SHOW
(Map p48; ☎4331-4178; www.lapuertoricocafe.com.ar; Alsina 416; Sat show AR$150, dinner show AR$250) This historic cafe puts on casual tango shows on Sunday at 2pm (free with food/drink purchase). On Saturday nights there's a fancier theatrical performance that includes tango and flamenco dancers, with singers and live music; reserve ahead for the best table.

El Balcón & Todomundo TANGO SHOW
(Map p48; ☎4362-2354; Humberto Primo 461, 1st fl) Located above Plaza Dorrego, the upstairs restaurant puts on free shows – but you have to order some food to see them. Shows run on Friday and Saturday nights, and on Sundays throughout the day. The ground floor restaurant below, Todomundo, has shows on Monday and Thursday evenings (also free with purchase).

Centro Cultural Torquato Tasso TANGO MUSIC
(Map p58; ☎4307-6506; www.torquatotasso.com.ar; Defensa 1575; shows AR$40-120) One of BA's best live-music venues, with top-name tango *music* performances. Attracts bands that mix genres together, such as fusing tango or *folklórico* (folk music) with rock; keep an eye out for Orchestra Típica Leopoldo Federico, Sexteto Mayor and La Chicana.

Milongas

Milongas are dance events where people strut their tango skills. The atmosphere at these events can be modern or historical, casual or traditional. Most have tango DJs that determine musical selections, but a few utilize live orchestras.

Milongas either start in the afternoon and run until 11pm, or start at around midnight and run until the early-morning light (arrive late for the best action). Classes are often offered beforehand.

A unique casual and outdoor *milonga* takes place in the bandstand at the Barrancas de Belgrano park in Belgrano, around 6pm from Friday to Sunday evenings.

For more on *milongas*, see p90.

Salon Canning MILONGA
(Map p64; ☎4832-6753; Av Scalabrini Ortiz 1331) Some of BA's finest dancers grace this famous venue, which offers a great dance floor and live orchestras. Well-known tango company **Parakultural** (www.parakultural.com.ar) often stages good events here, attracting the crowds.

Niño Bien MILONGA
(Map p48; ☎4147-8687; Humberto Primo 1462, 1st fl) Takes place on Thursday in Centro Región Leonesa and attracts a wide range of aficionados – and tourists. It has a beautiful atmosphere, a large ballroom and spacious wood dance floor, but it still gets very crowded (come early and dress well).

Club Gricel MILONGA
(☎4957-7157; www.clubgriceltango.com.ar; La Rioja 1180) This old classic (far from the center: take a taxi) attracts an older, well-dressed crowd, along with plenty of tourists. Wonderful aging wood dance floor and authentic vibe.

Confitería Ideal MILONGA
(Map p48; ☎5265-8069; www.confiteriaideal.com; Suipacha 384, 1st fl) The mother of all historic tango halls, with many classes and *milongas* offered pretty much continuously. Live orchestras often accompany dancers; shows almost nightly. Good for beginners.

La Catedral MILONGA
(Map p64; ☎15-5325-1630; www.lacateralclub.com; Sarmiento 4006, 1st fl) If tango can be trendy and hip, this is where you'll find it. The grungy warehouse space is very casual, with funky art on the walls and jeans on the dancers. A great place to come to learn tango, especially if you're young. Located 1½ blocks south of the Medrano Subte stop.

La Viruta MILONGA
(Map p64; ☎4774-6357; www.lavirutatango.com; Armenia 1366, basement) Beginner classes are given before the *milongas*, translating into many inexperienced dancers earlier on – so if you're an expert get here late (after 3:30am). Best for 'nuevo tango' – mixed dance styles, with rock, salsa and folk music thrown in. Informal vibe, with lots of live orchestras and dance exhibitions.

El Beso MILONGA
(Map p48; ☎4953-2794; Riobamba 416, 1st fl) Another traditional and popular place that attracts very good dancers. Located upstairs, with an intimate feel (ie tables are crowded together) and a convenient bar as you enter.

La Marshall MILONGA
(Map p48; ☎4300-3487; www.lamarshall.com.ar; Av Independencia 572) Held on Wednesday and everyone's welcome, but La Marshall is best known for being a gay-friendly *milonga*. A good opportunity to dance with either sex, either leading or following. Also at El Beso on Fridays.

Nightclubs

BA's *boliches* (nightclub) are the throbbing heart of its world-famous nightlife. To be cool, don't arrive before 2am (or even 3am) and dress as stylishly as you can. Taking a nap before dinner helps keep you up all night. Admission sometimes includes a drink; women often pay less than men. Payment for admission and drinks is nearly always in cash only. Some clubs offer dinners and shows before the dancing starts.

Check out the website www.vuenosairez.com for current happenings.

For one of BA's biggest and most unique parties, check out **La Bomba de Tiempo** (www.labombadetiempo.com); it's at 7pm every Monday at Ciudad Cultural Konex (p96).

Kika NIGHTCLUB
(Map p64; www.kikaclub.com.ar; Honduras 5339; ⏲Tue-Sat) Being supremely well located near the heart of Palermo Viejo's bar scene makes Kika's Tuesday-night popular 'Hype' party (www.hype-ba.com) easily accessible for the trendy crowds. It's a mix of electro, rock, hip hop, drum'n'bass and dubstep, all spun by both local and international DJs. Other nights see electronica, raggaeton, Latin beats and live bands ruling the roost.

Niceto Club NIGHTCLUB
(Map p64; www.nicetoclub.com; Niceto Vega 5510; ⏲Thu-Sat) One of the city's biggest and long-running crowd-pullers on Thursday nights, **Club 69** (www.club69.com.ar) draws in locals and foreigners looking for a raunchy good time. Expect everything from gorgeous showgirls to subversive performance art to large drag queens in elaborate costumes; not surprisingly, very popular with the gay crowd. DJs and live music entertain, with edgy international acts an occasional treat.

Bahrein NIGHTCLUB
(Map p48; ☎4314-2403; www.bahreinba.com; Lavalle 345; ⏲Tue-Wed & Fri-Sat) Bahrein is hugely popular for its Tuesday night drum 'n' bass parties – highlighted with fast, aggressive electronic rhythms by resident DJ Bad Boy Orange. Trance, house and popular tunes round out the music menu, while an elegant upstairs restaurant provides much-needed energy.

Basement Club NIGHTCLUB
(Map p60; Rodriguez Peña 1220; ⏲Thu-Sat) This cool but unpretentious subterranean club is known for first-rate DJ line-ups spinning electronica and tech/minimal/funky house beats to a diverse young crowd. Thanks to the Shamrock, the ever-popular Irish pub upstairs, the place sees plenty of traffic throughout the night; just descend the stairs after enjoying a few pints at ground level.

Crobar NIGHTCLUB
(Map p64; www.crobar.com.ar; cnr Paseo de la Infanta Isabel & Freyre; ⏲Fri & Sat) This large, pricey

and perennially popular club dishes up some of BA's best electronic music. Both resident and international guest DJs mash up the latest beats, but there's also a back room for those who prefer classic rock, '80s remixes and occasional live bands. Meanwhile, the main levels are strewn with mezzanines and walkways for perfect viewpoints of the beautiful crowds.

Club Aráoz NIGHTCLUB

(Map p64; www.clubaraoz.com.ar; Aráoz 2424; ⏲Thu-Sat) Also known as 'Lost,' this small club's finest hour is on Thursday, when hip-hop rules the roost and the regulars start break dancing around 2am. It's popular with local youths especially, and there's no dress code – a good thing, since it gets hot and sweaty.

Boutique NIGHTCLUB

(Map p48; www.boutiqueba.com; Perú 535; ⏲Wed) This cavernous disco is infamous for its Wednesday night 'after-office' party (read: meat market), which starts at the normally ungodly-early-for-a-nightclub hour of 7pm. It's a huge space with multiple balconies and a great sound system; note the amazing building, an old factory designed by Eiffel – who also did that peculiar Parisian landmark.

Maluco Beleza NIGHTCLUB

(Map p48; www.malucobeleza.com.ar; Sarmiento 1728; ⏲Wed & Fri-Sun) Located in an old mansion is this popular Brazilian *boliche*. It gets really packed with crowds happily grinding to samba fusion music and watching lithe, half-naked dancers swinging on the stage; there's plenty of fun to be had. Upstairs it's darker and more laid-back. If you're craving Brazilian cuisine, sign up for the Wednesday night dinner-show.

Clubland NIGHTCLUB

(www.clublandba.com; Av Costanera R Obligado 6151; ⏲Fri & Sat) Famous international DJs spin tunes for the youthful, spruced-up and snobby crowds at this huge electronica club (past its peak heyday but still plenty of fun). Laser lightshows and a great sound system keep the blissed-out masses entranced. Saturday nights are best, but don't come until after 4am – giving you time to party while watching the sunrise on the terrace (bring your shades). Pricey drinks.

Live Music

Smaller venues showcase mostly local groups; international stars tend to play at large venues such as soccer stadiums or Luna Park. Clásica y Moderna cafe (p96) occasionally hosts jazz groups.

With so many *porteños* boasting Spanish ancestry, it's not surprising that there are a few flamenco venues in town. Most are located in Congreso's Spanish neighborhood, near the intersection of Salta and Av de Mayo.

Música folklórica also has its place in BA. There are several *peñas* (folk-music clubs) in the city, but other venues occasionally host folk music – keep your eyes peeled.

Luna Park STADIUM

(Map p48; ☎5279-5279; www.lunapark.com.ar; cnr Bouchard & Av Corrientes) Originally a boxing stadium, this huge stadium has a capacity of 15,000 and is the fateful location where Juan Perón met Eva Duarte (aka Evita), and where Maradona got married.

Mitos Argentinos ROCK

(Map p48; ☎4362-7810; www.mitosargentinos.com.ar; Humberto Primo 489; ⏲Fri & Sat) This cozy old brick house in San Telmo has lots of tables, a perfectly sized stage and a small balcony above. Known for its tributes to *rock nacional* (Argentine rock) bands; good for scouting out upcoming new talent.

ND/Ateneo ROCK, BLUES

(Map p60; ☎4328-2888; www.ndateneo.com.ar; Paraguay 918) Theater with good acoustics and quality concerts, especially rock, jazz and folk. Also puts on theater and other artsy shows.

La Trastienda ROCK, REGGAE

(Map p48; ☎5533-5533; www.latrastienda.com; Balcarce 460) The large theater in the back of the restaurant can entertain over 700 people, and showcases all sorts of live music – but mostly rock and reggae. Look for headliners such as Charlie Garcia, Los Divididos, Marilyn Manson and the Wailers.

El Samovar de Rasputín ROCK, BLUES

(Map p58; ☎4302-3190; Del Valle Iberlucea 1232) Eighty-seat venue located opposite its original location (where there are photos of Napo, the hippie-ish owner, with Keith Richards, Eric Clapton and Pavarotti). Argentine bands entertain on Saturday nights.

Notorious JAZZ

(Map p60; ☎4813-6888; www.notorious.com.ar; Av Callao 966) Slick and intimate, this is one of BA's premier jazz venues. Up front is a CD store; in back, the restaurant-cafe (overlooking a verdant garden) hosts live jazz every night. Tango and Brazilian beats also play.

GAY & LESBIAN BA

In July 2010 Argentina became the first Latin American country to legalize same-sex marriage and Buenos Aires has become a huge gay destination, lending momentum to local events such as November's **Marcha del Orgullo Gay** (Gay Pride Parade; www.marchadelorgullo.org.ar) and the **Queer Tango Festival** (www.festivaltangoqueer.com.ar). And let's not forget that the 2007 Gay World Cup took place here.

A good starting point for information is the gay welcome center **Pink Point** (☎4328-6559; www.pinkpointbuenosaires.com/wordpress; Lavalle 669, local 24), which can help you get oriented in BA. There's also lots of gay literature, such as *La Otra Guía* (www.laotraguiaweb.com.ar), *Gay Maps* (www.gmaps360.com) and *The Ronda* (www.theronda.com.ar), available free at many businesses. Heftier magazines such as *Imperio* can be bought at some newsstands.

For all sorts of gay travel information in Buenos Aires, from tours to restaurants to where to take a steam, see www.thegayguide.com.ar.

Especially gay-friendly accommodations include the **Axel Hotel** (www.axelhotels.com/buenosaires) and **Lugar Gay** (www.lugargay.com.ar), which is a casual B&B but also acts as an information center. For apartments, check out www.friendlyapartments.com.

Popular bars include the loud **Sitges** (Map p64; ☎4861-3763; www.sitgesonline.com.ar; Av Córdoba 4119) and casual **Flux** (Map p60; ☎5252-0258; MT de Alvear 980). The coffee shop **Pride Café** (Map p48; ☎4300-6435; Balcarce 869) attracts mixed crowds, while **Casa Brandon** (Map p64; ☎4858-0610; www.brandongayday.com.ar; LM Drago 236; ⏲8pm-late Wed-Sun) is a restaurant-bar-art gallery-cultural center. And for a fun night of guided drinking and partying, there's **Out & About Pub Crawl** (www.outandaboutpubcrawl.com).

The best nightclubs are hot-and-bothered **Human** (off Map p64; www.humanclub.com.ar; Av Costanera R Obligado & Av Sarmiento), rough-and-tumble **Amerika** (Map p64; ☎4865-4416; www.ameri-k.com.ar; Gascón 1040) and sexy-beautiful **Glam** (Map p64; ☎4963-2521; www.glambsas.com.ar; José Antonio Cabrera 3046). Current hot parties include Friday night's **Fiesta Plop** (www.plop-web.com.ar) and the monthly **Fiesta Dorothy** (www.fiestadorothy.com).

There aren't many places catering exclusively to lesbians. Try long-running and intimate **Bach Bar** (Map p64; ☎15-5184-0137; www.bach-bar.com.ar; JA Cabrera 4390), but otherwise there are the gay spots listed above. **La Fulana** (www.lafulana.org.ar) is a lesbian cultural center.

Finally, gay classes and *milongas* are given at **La Marshall** (www.lamarshall.com.ar) and **Tango Queer** (www.tangoqueer.com).

Thelonious Bar JAZZ
(Map p64; ☎4829-1562; www.theloniousclub.com.ar; Salguero 1884, 1st fl; ⏲Wed-Sat) Cozily ensconced on the 1st floor of an old mansion, this intimate, dimly lit and artsy jazz bar has high brick ceilings and a good sound system. Great line-ups entertain into the early morning hours, but you can also come early for dinner and good seats.

Ávila Bar FLAMENCO
(Map p48; ☎4383-6974; Av de Mayo 1384; ⏲Thu-Sat) Long-running and cozy Spanish restaurant with pricey shows (AR$140), but tasty Spanish-style meals are thrown in. Occasional Sunday shows; reservations mandatory.

Cantares FLAMENCO
(Map p48; ☎4381-6965; www.cantarestablao.com.ar; Av Rivadavia 1180; ⏲Fri & Sat) This intimate flamenco venue once hosted the Spanish poet Federico García Lorca. Dances are highly authentic, as the musicians and dancers have gypsy ancestry. Lessons available.

La Peña del Colorado FOLK
(Map p64; ☎4822-1038; www.lapeniadelcolorado.com; Güemes 3657) Near-nightly *folklórico* shows are awesome at this rustic, brick-and-stucco restaurant-bar, and afterwards (on Friday and Saturday nights) audience members pick up guitars to 'compete.' Monday night means tango singers. Tasty northern Argentine food available.

Teatro Colón CLASSICAL MUSIC
(Map p48; ☎4378-7100; www.teatrocolon.org.ar; Cerrito 628) BA's premier venue for the arts, Teatro Colón has hosted prominent figures such as Placido Domingo and Luciano Pavarotti. There's also ballet and opera. See also p53.

Teatro Avenida CLASSICAL MUSIC
(Map p48; ☎4812-6369; www.balirica.org.ar; Av de Mayo 1222) This beautiful 1906 venue highlights mostly classical music, ballet and flamenco – but its biggest strength is opera.

Teatro San Martín CLASSICAL MUSIC
(Map p48; ☎4371-0111; www.teatrosanmartin.com.ar; Av Corrientes 1530) Along with art exhibitions, ballet, photography, cinema and theater, this large complex also hosts classical ensembles.

Theater

Av Corrientes, between Avs 9 de Julio and Callao, has traditionally been the capital's center for theater, but there are now dozens of venues throughout the city. The following venues include both the traditional and the alternative.

See also Teatro Colón (p53) and Teatro San Martín (above).

Ciudad Cultural Konex PERFORMING ARTS
(Map p64; ☎4864-3200; www.ciudadculturalkonex.org; Sarmiento 3131) Has multidisciplinary performances that often fuse art, culture and technology; also hosts an amazing Monday-night percussion show called La Bomba de Tiempo.

El Camarín de las Musas ALTERNATIVE THEATER
(Map p64; ☎4862-0655; www.elcamarindelasmusas.com.ar; Mario Bravo 960) Trendy venue offering contemporary dance, films, plays and theatrical workshops. There's a good cafe-restaurant in front.

Teatro Nacional Cervantes THEATER
(Map p60; ☎4816-4224; www.teatrocervantes.gov.ar; Libertad 815) Architecturally gorgeous theater featuring three halls, a grand lobby and red-velvet chairs. Has good productions at affordable prices. See also p59.

Teatro Presidente Alvear THEATER
(Map p48; ☎4373-4245; www.teatrosanmartin.com.ar; Av Corrientes 1659) Inaugurated in 1942 and named after an Argentine president whose wife sang opera, this theater holds over 700 and shows many musical productions, including tango.

Cinemas

BA is full of cinemas, both historical neon classics and slick modern multiplexes. The traditional cinema districts are along pedestrian Lavalle (west of Florida) and on Av Corrientes, but newer cineplexes are spread throughout the city; most large shopping malls have one.

Check out the *Buenos Aires Herald* for original titles of English-language films. Except for kids' films, most movies are in their original language (with Spanish subtitles).

Sports

Fútbol is a national obsession, and witnessing a live game part of the Buenos Aires experience. Argentina is no amateur league; the country's national team won the World Cup in 1978 and 1986 (one of only eight countries ever to have won the cup). The men's team also walked away with gold at the 2004 and 2008 summer Olympics. And Lionel Messi, currently Argentina's most famous *fútbol* player, won FIFA's World Player of the Year award in 2009 and its new Ballon d'Or award in 2010 and 2011.

For details on going to a *fútbol* game, see p56.

Other popular spectator sports include rugby, basketball, polo and field hockey. *Pato* (like rugby on horseback) deserves an honorable mention for being the most 'traditional.'

Shopping

Shopping is practically a sport for many Buenos Aires' citizens, who despite steeply rising inflation continue to shop as if there's no tomorrow. As the saying goes, 'An Argentine will make one peso and spend two.'

In the Microcentro, Florida is a multipurpose pedestrian strip that buzzes with shoppers, while Av Santa Fe is a bit less pedestrian-friendly but equally prominent as the city's main shopping artery. San Telmo is ground zero for antiques, and Av Pueyrredón near Once train station is *the* place for cheap (and low-quality) clothing. Jewelry shops are found on Libertad south of Corrientes. Leather jackets and bags are cheapest on Calle Murillo (500–600 block, Map p64), in Villa Crespo.

For both brand-name and avant garde fashions, Palermo Viejo is the place to be. This neighborhood, split by railroad tracks into Palermo Soho and Palermo Hollywood, has the most concentrated number of clothing boutiques between Plaza Serrano and Plaza Palermo Viejo. You'll find housewares and plenty of knickknack shops here too.

As in other Western countries, bargaining is not acceptable in most stores. High-price items such as jewelry and leather jackets can be exceptions, especially if you buy several. At street markets you can try negotiating for better prices – just keep in mind you may be talking to the artists themselves, who generally don't make much money. San Telmo's antiques fair is an exception; prices here are often inflated for tourists.

CONGRESO

Portobello Vintage Boutique CLOTHING
(Map p60; Paraguay 1554; ⏲10am-7pm Mon-Fri, to 5pm Sat) Excellent vintage clothing boutique run by a British-Argentine couple. Expect jackets, dresses, shirts and bottoms from the 1940s on up, in great condition and sold at affordable prices. A few records, jewelry and other accessories too.

Zival's MUSIC
(Map p48; www.zivals.com; Av Callao 395; ⏲9:30am-9:30pm Mon-Sat) One of the better music stores in town, especially when it comes to tango, jazz and classical. Listening stations are a plus. Also in **Palermo** (Map p64; Serrano 1445).

Wildlife OUTDOOR EQUIPMENT
(Map p48; Hipólito Yrigoyen 1133; ⏲10am-8pm Mon-Fri, 10am-1pm Sat) Crampons, knives, tents, backpacks, climbing ropes, foul-weather clothing and military gear can be found at this somewhat musty-smelling place. Sell your stuff here, too.

MICROCENTRO

Arte y Esperanza CRAFTS
City (Map p48; Balcarce 234; ⏲8.30am-6pm Mon-Fri); Retiro (Map p60; Suipacha 892) This store sells fair-trade, handmade products that include many from Argentina's indigenous craftspeople. Shop for jewelry, pottery, textiles, *mate* gourds, baskets, woven bags and animal masks.

Kelly's Regionales SOUVENIRS
(Map p60; Paraguay 547; ⏲10am-8pm Mon-Fri, to 3pm Sat) The cowboy hats, Mapuche ponchos, animal masks, alpaca knives and *mate* gourds are all good 'made-in-Argentina' buys at this large shop, but plenty of cheap knickknacks also line the shelves.

RECOLETA

El Ateneo BOOKS
(Map p60; Av Santa Fe 1860; ⏲9am-10pm Mon-Thu, till midnight Fri & Sat, noon-10pm Sun) Buenos Aires' landmark bookseller stocks a limited number of books in English, including Lonely Planet guides. There are several branches within the city, but this one – the Gran Splendid – is in a gorgeous old renovated cinema.

SAN TELMO

Walrus Books BOOKS
(Map p48; Estados Unidos 617; ⏲noon-8pm Tue-Sun) The best English-language bookstore for quality (mostly used) literature and non-fiction. Buys or exchanges certain books too.

Cualquier Verdura ECLECTIC
(Map p48; Humberto Primo 517; ⏲noon-8pm Thu-Sun) Located in a lovely, refurbished old house, this fun store sells eclectic items from vintage clothing and entertaining soaps to kitchen gadgets and novelty toys. Note the *mate*-drinking Buddha above the fountain in the patio.

Moebius CLOTHING
(Map p58; Defensa 1356; ⏲1:30-8:30pm Mon, 11am-8:30pm Tue-Sat, noon-8:30pm Sun) Highly original bags, retro knickknacks, handmade jewelry and ingeniously designed women's clothes are highlights here, but you'll never know exactly what you'll find. The recycled-material items are always the most fun.

En Buen Orden ANTIQUES
(Map p48; Defensa 894; ⏲11am-6pm) If you like sorting through endless shelves full of knickknacks such as old jewelry, little medals, old lace, musty shoes and antique figurines, then this place is for you.

Gil Antiguedades ANTIQUES
(Map p48; Humberto Primo 412; ⏲11am-1pm & 3-7pm Tue-Sun) Find antiques galore here, including baby dolls, china plates, old lamps, feather fans, Jesus figures and huge glass bottles. Best of all is the basement – it's stuffed with some amazing vintage clothing and accessories, some of which is in their annex.

PALERMO

Nadine Zlotogora CLOTHING
(Map p64; El Salvador 4638; ⏲11am-8pm Mon-Sat) Nadine's gorgeous dresses and tops combine feminine styles with nearly magical fabrics, creating fantastically romantic wearables. Thick and billowy base textiles are layered with lacy tulle and silky edging – a feast for the eyes as well as the skin.

Bolivia CLOTHING
(Map p64; Gurruchaga 1581; ⏲11am-8pm Mon-Sat, 3-8pm Sun) There's almost nothing here that your young, hip and metrosexual brother wouldn't love, from the skinny jeans to the latest-style shirts. It's a paradise for the man who isn't afraid of patterns, plaid or pastels.

BUENOS AIRES STREET MARKETS

Some of BA's best crafts and souvenirs are sold at its many street markets, often by the artists themselves. You may have to sort through some tacky kitsch, but you'll also find creative and original art. Often there is also 'free' (ie donation) entertainment from casual performers.

Locals and tourists alike come to the wonderful **Feria de San Telmo** (Map p48; Plaza Dorrego; ⏲10am-5pm Sun); you'll find antique seltzer bottles, jewelry, artwork, vintage clothing, collectibles and donation tango shows. Lots of fun, but keep an eye on your wallet. Some vendors hang around on Saturdays also.

Recoleta's hugely popular **Feria Artesanal** (Map p60; Plaza Intendente Alvear; ⏲10am-7pm) has dozens of booths and a range of creative goods. Hippies, mimes and tourists mingle; nearby restaurants provide refreshment. It runs on weekends and is located just outside the cemetery.

Costume jewelry, hand-knit tops, mate gourds, leather accessories and a whole lot of junk fill the crafts booths at the lively **Feria Plaza Serrano** (Map p64; Plaza Serrano; ⏲10am-8pm Fri-Sun) on fashionable Plaza Serrano in Palermo.

Belgrano's pleasant **Feria Plaza Belgrano** (cnr Juramento & Cuba; ⏲10am-8pm Sat & Sun) market is great on a sunny weekend. You'll find high-quality imaginative crafts, as well as some kitschy stuff. It's calmer and less touristy than the more central *ferias*.

The unique **Feria de Mataderos** (☎Mon-Fri 4342-9629; Sat 4687-5602; www.feriademataderos.com.ar; cnr Avs Lisandro de la Torre & de los Corrales; ⏲11am-8pm Sun Apr to mid-Dec, 6pm-midnight Sat late Jan to mid-Mar) is far off in the barrio of Mataderos, but it's worth hiking out here for the shows of horsemanship, folk dancing and cheap authentic treats. From downtown, take bus 155, 180 or 126 (one hour). Confirm hours beforehand; it closes for a couple weeks 'between' seasons.

Hermanos Estebecorena CLOTHING
(Map p64; El Salvador 5960; ⏲11am-8pm Mon-Sat) The Estebecorena brothers apply their highly creative skills to original, highly stylish, very functional men's clothing that makes the artsy types swoon. Selection is limited, but what's there really counts.

Calma Chicha HOMEWARES
(Map p64; Honduras 4909; ⏲10am-8pm Mon-Fri, 11am-8pm Sat, 1-8pm Sun) Big on leather, this fun household spot has a variety of butterfly chair styles and brightly colored cowhide rugs. Penguin pitchers, stylish handbags and thick sheepskins are other must-haves.

Rapsodia CLOTHING
(Map p64; Honduras 4872; ⏲10am-9pm) With fabrics from linen to leather, street casual to sequins, this larger boutique shop is a must for fashion mavens. There are cutting-edge jeans, cowboy-style shirts and other frilly, lacey, exotic things. Several branches in town.

Sugar & Spice FOOD
(Map p64; www.sugarandspice.com.ar; Guatemala 5419; ⏲10am-1:30pm, 2:30-7pm Mon-Fri, 9am-1pm Sat) Nibble the exotic (for Argentines at least) creations of Frank Almeida, a long-time American expat. Herb cookies, almond biscotti, hazelnut panettone and peanut-butter brownies soothe homesick taste buds, and you can try samples at the store.

Lo de Joaquin Alberdi WINE
(Map p64; www.lodejoaquinalberdi.com.ar; JL Borges 1772; ⏲11am-9:30pm) Excellent wine shop that carries only Argentine brands. Wine tastings with food pairings happen on Thursdays at 7pm (AR$60). See p85 for other wine-tasting options.

Mercado de las Pulgas MARKET
(Map p64; cnr Álvarez Thomas & Dorrego; ⏲11am-7pm Tue-Sun) This covered market sells eclectic items such as antique and modern furniture, vintage glassware, paintings, lamps, bird cages, elegant mirrors and unique chandeliers. Prices aren't cheap, so bargain.

Mercado de Abasto MALL
(Map p64) For high-class shopping, wander through the gorgeous shopping mall; it has especially good kids' entertainment. Located in the neighborhood of Once, right near the subte stop Carlos Gardel.

Information

Concierge Services

BA Cultural Concierge (☎15-5457-2035; www.baculturalconcierge.com) Madi Lang's concierge service helps you plan itineraries, arrange airport transportation, run errands, reserve theater tickets and do a thousand other things for your trip to run smoothly.

Emergency

Ambulance (☎107)

Police (☎101, ☎911)

Tourist police (Comisaría del Turista; ☎4346-5748, 0800-999-5000; Av Corrientes 436; ⏲24hr) Provides interpreters and helps victims of robberies and rip-offs.

Internet Access & Telephone Offices

Internet cafes and *locutorios* (telephone offices) with internet access are very common in the center; you can often find one by just walking a couple of blocks in any direction. Rates are cheap and connections are fast. Most cafes and restaurants have free wi-fi.

You can rent a desk, cubicle, office or meeting room via **Areatres** (Map p64; ☎5353-0333; www.areatresworkplace.com; Malabia 1720) There are fax and copy services, complete internet connections, networking social events – even a zenlike patio. Also at Humboldt 2036.

Media

BA's most popular newspapers are the entertaining, tabloid-like *Clarín* and the more moderate and upper-class *La Nación*. *Página 12* provides a leftist perspective and often breaks important stories. *Ámbito Financiero* is the voice of the business sector, but it also provides good cultural coverage.

Medical Services

Dental Argentina (☎4828-0821; www.dental-argentina.com.ar; Laprida 1621, 2B) Dental services with English-speaking professionals.

Hospital Británico (☎4304-1081; www.hospitalbritanico.org.ar; Perdriel 74)

Hospital Italiano (☎4959-0200; www.hospitalitaliano.org.ar; Gascón 450)

Money

Banks and *cambios* (money-exchange offices) are common in the city center; banks have longer lines and more limited opening hours but may offer better rates. Avoid the shady figures on Av Florida, offering *'cambio, cambio, cambio'* to passing pedestrians. Using these unofficial street changers is not recommended; there are quite a few fake bills floating about (see boxed text, below).

American Express (☎4310-3000; Arenales 707) Changes traveler's checks 10am to 4pm Monday to Friday.

TRAVELING SAFELY IN BUENOS AIRES

While crime does exist in BA (as it does in any big city) and you'll notice that *porteños* are very security conscious, in general BA is fairly safe. In many places you can comfortably walk around at all hours of the night, even as a lone woman, as people generally stay out very late. However, be careful at night in some neighborhoods, including Constitución (around the train station), the eastern border of San Telmo, and La Boca (where, outside tourist streets, you should be careful even during the day).

Crime against tourists is almost always of the petty sort, such as pickpocketing in crowded markets or buses, or bag snatches when you're not looking – things smart travelers can certainly guard themselves against. Be wary of the old 'mustard trick' – someone pointing out some bird droppings or whatever on your clothing, placed there by an accomplice, and offering to clean it up (while your valuables go off with the accomplice).

Other things to watch out for are fake bills. Most people get them in dark environments like taxis or nightclubs, but even Ezeiza's *cambios* (exchange houses) have been known to pass them. Get to know your bills; check www.santelmoloft.com/2011/07/22/fake-money-in-argentina for good tips.

Minor nuisances include the lack of respect shown by vehicles toward pedestrians, lax pollution controls and high noise levels. For dealing with taxis, see p102.

If you've been robbed in some way, contact the tourist police to file a claim. **Defensoría del Turista** (www.www.defensoriadelturista.org); San Telmo (☎15-4046-9682; Defensa 1250); La Boca (☎4302-7816; Pedro de Mendoza 1835); Calle Florida tourist kiosk (Map p60; ☎15-3856-1943; Diagonal Norte & Perú) Puerto Madero tourist kiosk (Map p48; ☎15-4078-8654; Dique 4) is an ombudsman that helps tourists who have been ripped off or 'abused' by businesses (hotels, transportation services, travel agencies etc). It has offices around the city, including those listed here.

For more safety tips, see the Directory (p595).

MasterCard (☎4340-5700; Perú 143)

Visa (☎4379-3300; Corrientes 1437, basement)

Post

The post office has branches located all over the city.

Correo Internacional (☎4316-1777; Av Antártida Argentina; ⏲10am-5pm Mon-Fri) Only for shipping international parcels over 2kg.

DHL Internacional (☎0810-122-3345; www.dhl.com.ar; Av Córdoba 783) Many branches around town.

Federal Express (☎0810-333-3339; www.fedex.com; Maipú 753)

OCA (☎4311-5305; www.oca.com.ar; Viamonte 526) For domestic packages.

Tourist Information

There are several small government tourist offices or kiosks in BA; hours vary throughout the year. The official tourism site of Buenos Aires is www.bue.gov.ar and the government site is www.buenosaires.gov.ar.

Florida tourist kiosk (Map p60; Florida & Marcelo T de Alvear)

Puerto Madero tourist kiosk (Map p48; ☎4315-4265; Dique 4)

Diagonal Roque Saénz Peña tourist kiosk (Map p48; ☎4114-5791; Florida & Diagonal Roque Saénz Peña)

Recoleta tourist kiosk (Map p60; Quintana 596)

Retiro tourist office (Map p60; ⏲7:30am-2:30pm Mon-Fri) In Retiro bus terminal, across from bus slot 36.

Ministerio de Turismo (Map p60; ☎4312-5550; www.turismo.gov.ar; Av Santa Fe 883; ⏲9am-5pm Mon-Fri) Dispenses information on Buenos Aires, but focuses on Argentina as a whole.

South American Explorers (Map p48; www.saexplorers.org; Piedras 1178; ⏲2-6pm Mon-Fri) Good information and services for the independent traveler, but requires annual membership.

Travel Agencies

Anda Responsible Travel, Say Hueque and Tangol (p68) all sell airplane tickets and arrange tours in BA and Argentina; staff speak English.

Getting There & Away

Air

Buenos Aires is Argentina's international gateway and easily accessible from North America, Europe and Australasia, as well as other capital cities in South America.

Almost all international flights arrive at BA's **Ezeiza airport**, about 35km south of the center. This a modern airport has good services such as ATMs, restaurants and duty-free shops, an internet cafe and wi-fi (in some restaurants).

For more important tips on arriving in Ezeiza, see the boxed text, p602. For information on getting to and from Ezeiza once you're in Argentina, see p101.

Most domestic flights use **Aeroparque Jorge Newbery airport**, a short distance north of downtown BA. Flight information for both airports, in English and Spanish, is available at ☎5480-6111 or www.aa2000.com.ar.

Boat

BA has a regular ferry service to and from Colonia and Montevideo, both in Uruguay. Ferries leave from **Buquebus terminal** (Map p60;

BUSES FROM BUENOS AIRES

DESTINATION	COST (AR$)	DURATION (HR)
Bariloche	520	20-22
Comodoro Rivadavia	535	24
Córdoba	250	10
Foz do Iguaçu (Brazil)	540	19
Mar del Plata	155	6
Mendoza	425	14
Montevideo (Uruguay)	160	9
Puerto Iguazú	400	19
Puerto Madryn	435	18
Punta del Este (Uruguay)	250	12
Rosario	90	4
Santiago (Chile)	380	20

TRAINS FROM BUENOS AIRES

DESTINATION(S)	STATION	CONTACT
Bahía Blanca/Carmen de Patagones	Constitución	www.ferrobaires.gba.gov.ar
Concordia/Posadas	Federico Lacroze	www.trenesdellitoral.com.ar
La Plata	Constitución	☎0800-362-7622
Luján	Once	www.tbanet.com.ar
Mar del Plata or Tandil or Pinamar	Constitución	www.ferrobaires.gba.gov.ar
San Isidro/Tigre/Rosario/ Córdoba or Tucumán	Retiro	www.tbanet.com.ar, www.ferrocentralsa.com.ar

☎4316-6500; www.buquebus.com; cnr Av Antártida Argentina 821). There are many more launches in the warmer months of September to April.

Bus

BA's modern **Retiro bus terminal** (Map p60; www.tebasa.com.ar; Av Antártida Argentina) is 400m long, three floors high and has slots for 75 buses. The bottom floor is for cargo shipments and luggage storage, the top for purchasing tickets and the middle for everything else. The **Information booth** (☎4310-0700; ⏲6am-10pm) will help you find the right long-distance bus (or check the terminal's website); it's located near the escalators at the southern end of the terminal. Other services include a **tourist office** (⏲7:30am-2:30pm Mon-Fri) on the main floor across from bus slot 36, ATMs, telephone offices (some with internet), cafes and many small stores.

You can buy a ticket to practically anywhere in Argentina and departures are fairly frequent to the most popular destinations. Reservations are not necessary except during peak seasons (January, February and July). And remember to keep an eye on your bags!

The table, p100, shows some sample destinations; be aware that ticket prices vary widely according to bus company, class, season and inflation.

Retiro bus terminal is connected to the local bus system, but it's a giant snarl and hard to figure out. There's a nearby Subte station and Retiro train station. Street taxis are numerous, though *remises* (call taxis) are generally more secure – there are several *remise* booths near the bus slots; all are open 24 hours.

Train

Privately run trains connect Buenos Aires' center to its suburbs and nearby provinces. The three main central stations are served by Subte. Some destinations outside BA are shown in the table above.

Getting Around

To & From the Airport

SHUTTLE If you're traveling solo, the best way to and from Ezeiza is to take a shuttle with transfer companies such as **Manuel Tienda León** (MTL; Map p60; ☎4315-5115; www.tiendaleon.com; cnr Av Eduardo Madero & San Martín). You'll see its stand immediately as you exit airport customs. Shuttles (AR$60 to AR$70 one way, 40 minutes) run every half hour, 6am to midnight and will deposit you either at MTL's office (from where you can take a taxi) or at some central hotels. Avoid its taxi service at the airport, which is overpriced at AR$235.

Shuttles to Aeroparque (domestic airport) cost AR$60; from Aeroparque to the center AR$24.

TAXI At Ezeizas airport, go past the transportation 'lobby' area, through the doors to the reception area and – avoiding *all* touts – find the freestanding stand of **Taxi Ezeiza** (☎5480-0066; www.taxiezeiza.com.ar; ⏲24hr), which charges AR$180 to the center and has a blue sign. For a cheaper deal (AR$165), head outside the airport doors to another **taxi stand** (GCBA; ☎15-6987-0183; ⏲24hr) with a yellow 'Taxi Authorized Cars' sign. Taxis to Aeroparque cost about AR$210 and from there to the city around AR$35.

For tips on how to avoid getting ripped off in a taxi, see p102. And for more Ezieza Arrival Tips, see p602).

BUS Real shoestringers can take public bus 8 (AR$2) from Ezeiza, which can take up to two hours to reach the Plaza de Mayo area. Catch it outside the Aerolíneas Argentinas terminal B, a short walk (200m) from the international terminal. You'll need change for the bus; there's a Banco de la Nación just outside customs. To get from Aeroparque to the city center, take public bus 33 or 45 (don't cross the street; take them going south).

CAR US expat Fred (or another English-speaking driver) at **Silver Star Transport** (☎in the USA 214-502-1605, in Argentina 011-15-6826-8876; www.silverstarcar.com) will pick you up at Ezeiza

SUBE CARD

If you're planning on staying in BA for a while, the **SUBE card** (www.sube.gob.ar) is a free, rechargeable card that you can use for the Subte (subway), local buses and (in the future) some trains. It saves you time in line, and you don't have to spend those precious coins. Get it at some of the larger Subte stations, post offices or OCA offices around the city (check the website); you'll need your passport. Charging the card itself is easy, and can be done at many kioskos or Subte stations.

in a luxury car and deliver you to your hotel for AR$530. Fred also does city tours. There are car-rental agencies at Ezeiza, but we don't recommend driving in Buenos Aires.

Bicycle

Vehicular traffic in BA is dangerous and hardly respectful toward bicycles but things are improving, with bike lanes around the center and a bike share program (mainly for residents). Some areas call out for two-wheeled exploration, such as Palermo's parks and the Reserva Ecológica Costanera Sur. On weekends and some weekdays you can rent bikes at these places.

For more information see p63. You can also join a city bike tour (p68).

Bus

To understand BA's huge, complex bus system buy a *Guia T* (bus guide); they're sold at any newsstand, but try to find the handy pocket version (AR$10) or check www.omnilineas.com and click on 'city buses.' Most routes run 24 hours.

Local buses (*colectivos*) take either coins or a magnetic bus card called SUBE (see above), but won't take bills. Bus ticket machines on board give small change from coins. Most rides around town cost AR$2.50. Offer your seat to the elderly, pregnant and women with young children.

Car

Most local drivers are reckless, aggressive and even willfully dangerous. They ignore speed limits, signs, lines and signals, tailgate, and honk even before signals turn green. Buses are a nightmare to reckon with, potholes are everywhere, and congestion and parking are a pain. Pedestrians seem to beg to be run over.

Public transport is great and taxis are cheap and plentiful but if you still insist on renting a car, you'll need to be at least 21 years of age and have a valid driver's license, credit card and passport; an international driver's license isn't crucial.

Avis (☎0810-9991-2847; www.avis.com.ar; Cerrito 1527)

Hertz (☎4816-8001; www.milletrentacar.com.ar; Paraguay 1138)

New Way (☎4515-0331; www.newwayrentacar.com; Marcelo T de Alvear 773)

Subte (Subway)

BA's **Subte** (www.subte.com.ar) is the quickest way to get around the city, though it can get mighty hot and crowded during rush hour. It consists of Líneas (Lines) A, B, C, D, E and H. Four parallel lines run from downtown to the capital's western and northern outskirts, while Línea C runs north-south and connects the two major train stations of Retiro and Constitución. Línea H runs from Av Corrientes to the south, running through Once.

One-ride magnetic cards for the Subte cost AR$2.50. To avoid queues and hassle buy several rides or get a SUBE card (see boxed text).

At some stations platforms are on opposite sides, so make sure of your direction *before* passing through the turnstiles.

Subte trains operate from 5am to (around) 10:30pm Monday to Saturday and 8am to (around) 10pm on Sunday and holidays. Service is frequent on weekdays; on weekends you'll wait longer.

Taxi & Remise

Buenos Aires' numerous taxis are conspicuous by their black-and-yellow paint jobs. The meter should always be used and the fare ticks upwards about every two blocks when the vehicle is moving (you'll pay for waiting in stuck traffic, too). Taxis looking for passengers will have a red light lit on the upper right corner of their windshield.

Most taxi drivers are honest but there are a few bad apples. Do not give the driver large bills relative to the fare; they will not want to give you change and it has been known for drivers to deftly replace a larger bill with a smaller (or fake) one. One solution is to state how much you are giving them and ask if they have change (*'¿Tiene usted cambio de un cincuenta?'* – Do you have any change for a 50?).

Be especially wary of receiving counterfeit bills (look for a watermark); at night have the driver *prender la luz* (turn on the light) so you can carefully count and check your change. If you're worried about receiving a fake bill, repeat to him the last few numbers of the bill you give him to make sure he doesn't switch it.

Pretend to have an idea of where you're going; a few taxis offer the 'scenic' route (though also be aware there are many one-way streets in BA). A good way to do this is to give the taxi driver an intersection rather than a specific address. Also, if you are obviously a tourist going to or from a touristy spot, don't ask how much the fare is beforehand; this makes it tempting to quote a higher price rather than using the meter.

Try to snag an 'official' taxi, usually marked by a roof light and license number printed on the doors. Official drivers must display their license on the back of their seat or dashboard; write down the details in case of problems or forgotten items.

Most *porteños* recommend you call a *remise* instead of hailing street cabs. *Remises* look like regular cars and don't have meters. They cost a bit more than street taxis but are more secure, since an established company sends them out. Any hotel or restaurant will call a *remise* for you.

AROUND BUENOS AIRES

So you've spent days tramping on noisy and busy streets, visiting all the sights and smells of BA; you're ready to get away from the capital and experience something different and more peaceful. Where do you go?

San Isidro

About 22km north of Buenos Aires is peaceful and residential San Isidro, a charming suburb of cobblestone streets lined with some luxurious mansions, as well as more-modest houses. The historic center is at Plaza Mitre with its beautiful neo-Gothic cathedral; on weekends the area buzzes with a crafts fair. There's a **tourist office** (☎4512-3209; Libertador 16362; ⏰8am-5pm Mon-Fri, 10am-6pm Sat & Sun) near the plaza.

Once owned by Argentine icon, General Pueyrredón, the **Museo Histórico Municipal General Pueyrredón** (☎4512-3129; Rivera Indarte 48; admission free; ⏰10am-6pm Tue & Thu, 2-6pm Sat & Sun) is an old colonial villa set on spacious grounds with faraway views of the Río de la Plata. Note the algarrobo tree under which Pueyrredón and San Martín planned strategies against the Spanish. To get here from the cathedral, follow Av Libertador south five blocks, turn left on Peña and after two blocks turn right onto Rivera Indarte.

Even more glamorous is the Unesco site **Villa Ocampo** (☎4732-4988; Elortondo 1837; admission Thu & Fri/Sat & Sun AR$12/$18; ⏰12:30-6pm Thu-Sun), a wonderfully restored mansion. Victoria Ocampo was a writer, publisher and intellectual who dallied with the literary likes of Borges, Cortázar, Sabato and Camus. The gardens are lovely here; tours in English and a cafe are also available.

Also worth a visit is **Quinta Los Ombues** (☎4575-4038; Varela 774; admission free; ⏰10am-6pm Tue & Thu, 3-7pm Sat & Sun), a historical house with some period items once owned by prominent local figures. It's located one block behind the cathedral.

Getting There & Away

The nicest way to reach San Isidro is via the **Tren de la Costa** (www.trendelacosta.com.ar), whose southernmost station (Maipú) is in the suburb of Olivos. Get to Maipú on bus 59 or 152; some 60s buses also go (ask the driver). The Mitre train from Retiro train station also reaches Maipú (get off at Mitre station and cross the pedestrian bridge). You can also go directly to San Isidro with buses 60 (again, ask the driver) and 168.

Tigre & the Delta

The city of Tigre (35km north of BA) and the surrounding delta region is one of the most popular weekend getaways for weary *porteños*. Latte-colored waters – rich with iron from the jungle streams flowing from inland South America – will hardly remind you of a blue paradise, but there are hidden gems in this marshy region. Boat rides into the delta offer peeks at local stilt houses and colonial mansions, and you can explore along some peaceful trails. Many lodgings are located throughout the region, making getaways complete. All along the shorelines are signs of water-related activity, from kayaking to wakeboarding, canoeing to sculling.

Sights & Activities

Tigre itself is very walkable and holds some attractions.

Puerto de Frutos HARBOR

(Sarmiento 160; ⏰10am-6pm) Be sure to check out this popular dock area where vendors sell housewares, furniture, wicker baskets, toys, souvenirs and knickknacks; weekends are busiest.

Museo de Arte Tigre MUSEUM

(☎4512-4093; Paseo Victorica 972; admission AR$10; ⏰9am-7pm Wed-Fri, noon-7pm Sat & Sun) Tigre's fanciest museum is located in an old (1912) social club. This beautiful art museum showcases famous Argentine artists from the 19th and 20th centuries. The building itself is worth a visit.

Museo Naval MUSEUM
(Naval Museum; ☎4749-0608; Paseo Victorica 602; admission AR$3; ⌚8:30am-5:30pm Mon-Fri, 10:30am-6:30pm Sat & Sun) This worthwhile museum traces the history of the Argentine navy with an eclectic mix of historical photos, model boats and airplanes, artillery displays and pickled sea critters.

Museo del Mate MUSEUM
(☎4506-9594; www.elmuseodelmate.com; Lavalle 289; admission AR$10; ⌚11am-6pm Wed-Sun) For something special, visit this museum with over 2000 items dedicated to the national drink. There's a small outdoor *mate* 'bar' as well.

Parque de la Costa AMUSEMENT PARK
(☎4002-6000; www.parquedelacosta.com.ar; admission AR$60-150) Near to Puerto de Frutos is Tigre's amusement park. Call for current hours.

Tours

The waterways of the delta offer a glimpse into how locals live along the peaceful canals, with boats as their only transportation. Frequent commuter launches depart from Estación Fluvial (located behind the tourist office) for various destinations in the delta (AR$26 to AR$40 roundtrip). A popular destination is the Tres Bocas neighborhood, a half-hour boat ride from Tigre, where you can take residential walks on thin paths connected by bridges over narrow channels. There are several restaurants and accommodations here. The Rama Negra area has a quieter and more natural setting with fewer services, but is an hour's boat ride away.

Several companies offer inexpensive boat tours (AR$35 to AR$70, 1½ hours), but commuter launches give you flexibility if you want to go for a stroll or stop for lunch at one of the delta's restaurants.

Bonanza Deltaventura ADVENTURE TOUR
(☎4409-6967; www.deltaventura.com) Adventures include walks, canoe trips, bike rides, horseback rides and *asados*.

Tangol's Tigre Tour GUIDED TOUR
(☎4312-7276; www.tangol.com) Full-day tour that includes transport from BA's center to Tigre (via train) and back (via boat).

El Dorado Kayak KAYAKING
(☎15-4039-5858; www.eldoradokayak.com) Kayaking tours deep inside the delta; all equipment and lunch included.

Selknam Canoas BOAT TOUR
(☎4731-4325; www.selknamcanoas.com.ar) Off-the-beaten-path watery tours in wooden Canadian-style canoes, including moonlight and custom outings.

Sleeping & Eating

The huge delta is dotted with dozens of accommodation possibilities, from camping to B&Bs, fromo *cabañas* to beach resorts and activity-oriented places. The further out you are, the more peace and quiet you'll experience (but bring mosquito repellent). Since places are relatively hard to reach – you generally arrive by boat – the majority also provide meals.

The **Tigre tourist office** (www.vivitigre.com.ar) has photos of and information on all accommodation places, and many are listed on its website. The following places are in Tigre itself. Prices listed are for Saturday night, when you should always book ahead; on weekdays, rates can plummet by up to 30%.

Hotel Villa Victoria GUESTHOUSE $$$
(☎4731-2281; www.hotelvillavictoria.com; Liniers 566; AR$500-780; ❄@≈) Run by an Argentine-Swedish family, this boutique hotel is more like a fancy guesthouse. Only six simple yet elegant rooms are available, and there's a clay tennis court and pool in the large grassy garden. Swedish, French and English are spoken.

Casona La Ruchi GUESTHOUSE $$
(☎4749-2499; www.casonalaruchi.com.ar; Lavalle 557; s/d AR$190/280; @☜≈) This family-run guesthouse is in a beautiful old mansion (built in 1893). Most of the four romantic bedrooms have balconies; all have shared bathrooms with original tiled floors. There's a pool and large garden out back.

Tigre Hostel HOSTEL $
(☎4749-4034; www.tigrehostel.com.ar; Av Libertador 190; dm AR$80, r AR$250-350; ❄@☜) This odd hostel is divided into two buildings. The first is the original mansion with eight en-suite private rooms and large garden boasting great hangout decks; the second is a nearby mazelike building with little atmosphere, and with dorms and private rooms that all share bathrooms.

As far as food goes, Tigre's cuisine is not cutting-edge, but dining can be atmospheric. Stroll Paseo Victorica, the city's pleasant riverside avenue. For an upscale meal, try **Maria Luján** (☎4731-9613; mains AR$50-80; Paseo

Victorica 611; ⊙breakfast, lunch & dinner), which also has a great patio boasting river views. Another good eatery is bohemian **Boulevard Saenz Peña** (☎5197-4776; mains AR$45-65; Blvd Saenz Peña 1400; 10:30am-7pm Wed-Sat), where you can nibble healthy breakfasts and gourmet sandwiches and salads.

Information

Tourist Office (☎4512-4497; www.tigre.gov.ar; ⊙8am-6pm) Located behind McDonald's; will help you sort out the complex delta region. There's a smaller booth (☎4512-4547) at the train station and another at the entrance to Puerto de Frutos.

Getting There & Away

BUS Take bus 60 (marked 'Panam') straight to Tigre (1½ hours).

BOAT The commuter boat **Sturla** (Map p60; ☎4731-1300; www.sturlaviajes.com.ar; Grierson 400) goes straight to Tigre from Puerto Madero (AR$20, one hour, 6:30pm Monday to Friday) but there's only one per day. Their tour boat goes from Puerto Madero to Tigre and around the Delta (AR$130 to AR$145, 10am daily).

TRAIN The nicest way to reach Tigre is via the **Tren de la Costa** (www.trendelacosta.com.ar), a pleasant electric train that starts in the suburb of Olivos (local/foreigner AR$10/16, every half hour). To get there, take a train from Retiro station (Mitre Line) and get off at the Mitre station, then cross the bridge to the Tren de la Costa. Buses 59, 60 and 152 also go to the Tren de la Costa.

Alternatively, from Retiro train station take a train line called 'Ramal Tigre' straight to Tigre (one hour).

The Pampas & the Atlantic Coast

Includes »

Why Go?

The seemingly endless fertile grasslands that make up the pampas financed Argentina's golden years over a century ago, and the area is still the nation's economic and political powerhouse. Not only does most of Argentina's juicy beef come from here, but the region is also home to 40% of Argentina's voters.

These humble pampas are often overlooked by travelers, but there are hidden gems here and there. A visit to lovely San Antonio de Areco offers a taste of living gaucho culture, while the picturesque hills around Tandil and Sierra de la Ventana offer plenty of opportunities for hiking. And the Atlantic coast's bustling beaches make a great escape from Buenos Aires' summer heat.

You can also spend a few days in one of the region's many historic *estancias* (ranches), where the huge sky and faded elegance of Argentina's past can all be experienced first-hand.

Best Places to Eat

- Acqua & Farina (p126)
- Taberna Baska (p134)
- L'Eau Vive (p112)
- Cervecería Modelo (p110)
- Epoca de Quesos (p119)

Best Places to Stay

- Villa Nuccia (p133)
- Paradores Draghi (p113)
- El Aleph Hotel Boutique (p133)
- Antigua Casona (p114)
- Lo de Titi (p118)

When to Go

Mar del Plata

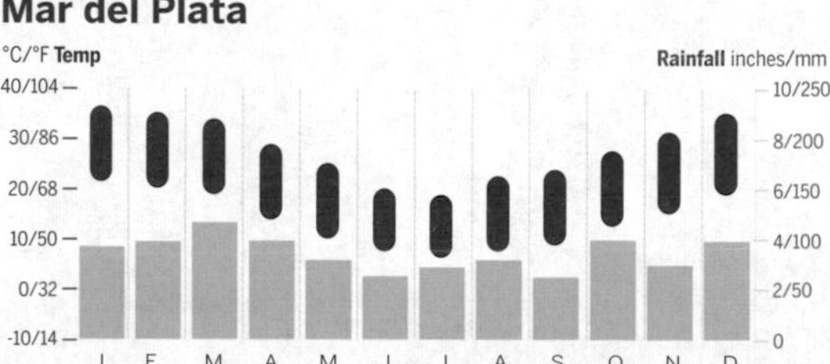

Jan–Feb Summer means great weather for the beach resorts, though prices and crowds skyrocket.

Oct–Nov & Mar–Apr Spring and fall are fine times to explore Tandil and Sierra de la Ventana.

Early Nov Día de la Tradición – the gaucho celebration – begins in San Antonio de Areco.

NORTHERN PAMPAS

The pampas is both a general term for a large geographic region of fertile plains and the name of the province that lies to the west of Buenos Aires. The pampas grasslands roll southwards from the Río de la Plata to the banks of the Río Negro, stretching west towards the Andes and all the way up to the southern parts of Córdoba and Santa Fe provinces, taking in the entire Buenos Aires and La Pampa provinces.

The rich soil and lush natural grasses of the northern pampas make it Argentina's best cattle-raising country. The region yields plentiful hides, beef, wool and wheat for global markets, stamping Argentina on the world's economic map.

The Pampas & the Atlantic Coast Highlights

1 Soak up the sun and crowds in the Atlantic Coast's largest city, **Mar del Plata** (p128)

2 Peek through a natural rock 'window' atop the mountain **Cerro de la Ventana** (p121)

3 Go gaucho in **San Antonio de Areco** (p112), the prettiest town in the pampas

4 Sample some country life – and deli meats and cheese – in pleasant **Tandil** (p115)

5 Go windsurfing, kiteboarding or cycling in the beach resort of **Pinamar** (p125)

6 Explore the lagoon, spot flamingos or just chill out in **Mar Chiquita** (p129)

7 Join the masses on their holy pilgrimage to **Luján** (p110)

From the mid-19th century, the province of Buenos Aires was the undisputed political and economic center of the country. When the city of Buenos Aires became Argentina's capital, the province submitted to national authority but didn't lose its influence. By the 1880s, after a brief but contentious civil war, the province responded by creating its own provincial capital in the model city of La Plata.

La Plata

☎0221 / POP 650,000

Just over an hour from Buenos Aires, this bustling university town has the same belle époque architecture, gracious municipal buildings, leafy parks and nightlife as BA, but on a smaller scale. The big tourist draws are its natural history museum, one of Argentina's best, and the imposing neo-Gothic cathedral.

When Buenos Aires became Argentina's new capital, Governor Dardo Rocha founded La Plata in 1882 to give the province of Buenos Aires its own top city. Rocha chose engineer Pedro Benoit's elaborate city plan, based upon balance and logic, with diagonal avenues crossing the regular 5km-square grid pattern to connect the major plazas, creating a distinctive star design. Elegant on paper, this blueprint creates confusion at many intersections, with up to eight streets going off in all directions. However, it probably made La Plata South America's first completely planned city.

Sights

La Plata's main sights are all within walking distance. Near Plaza Moreno is the neo-Gothic **cathedral** (☎423-3931; www.catedraldelaplata.com; ⏰10am-7pm), which was begun in 1885 but not inaugurated until 1932. The cathedral was inspired by medieval predecessors in Cologne and Amiens, and has fine stained glass and polished granite floors; tours (daily at 11am, 2:30pm and 4pm, reservations necessary) are AR$10 and include a museum and elevator ride to the top. There's also a gift shop and cafe.

Opposite the cathedral is the **Palacio Municipal**, designed in German Renaissance style by Hanoverian architect Hubert Stiers. On the west side of the plaza, the **Museo y Archivo Dardo Rocha** (☎427-5591; Calle 50, No 935; admission free; ⏰9am-5pm Mon-Fri, 3-6pm Sat & Sun) was the vacation house of the city's creator and contains period furniture and many of his personal knickknacks.

Two blocks northeast, the **Teatro Argentino** (Av 51, btwn Calle 9 & Calle 10) is a fantastically ugly concrete monolith, but boasts great acoustics and quality performances:

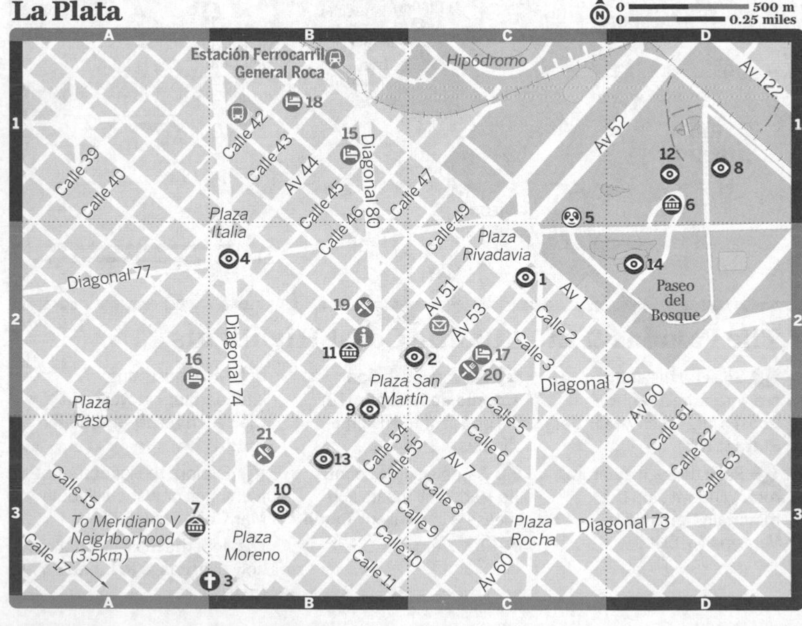

ballet, symphony orchestras and opera. Two blocks further northeast, in front of Plaza San Martín, is the ornate **Palacio de la Legislatura**, also in German Renaissance style. Nearby, catch the French Classic **Pasaje Dardo Rocha**, once La Plata's main railroad station and now the city's major cultural center, containing two museums. Also close by is the Flemish Renaissance **Casa de Gobierno**, housing the provincial governor and his retinue. On Sundays, check out the lively **feria artesanal** (crafts fair) on Plaza Italia.

Plantations of eucalyptus, gingko, palm and subtropical hardwoods cover **Paseo del Bosque**, parkland expropriated from an *estancia* at the time of the city's founding. It attracts a collection of strolling families, smooching lovers and sweaty joggers. Various interesting sights are strewn within, such as a small lake with paddleboats for rent; the open-air **Teatro Martín Fierro**, that hosts music and drama performances; the **Observatorio Astronómico** (☎423-6593; www.fcaglp.unlp.edu.ar); the modest **Jardín Zoológico** (☎427-3925; admission AR$5; ⊙10am-6pm Tue-Sun); and the **Museo de La Plata** (☎425-7744; www.fcnym.unlp.edu.ar/abamuse.html; admission AR$6, free Tuesdays; ⊙10am-6pm Tue-Sun). This excellent museum has paleontological, zoological, archaeological and anthropological collections of famous Patagonian explorer Francisco P Moreno. Countless display rooms offer something for everyone: Egyptian tomb relics, Jesuit art, amusing taxidermy, amazing skeletons, mummies, fossils, rocks and minerals, scary insects and reconstructed dinosaurs. There's also a cafe. Arrange English tours in advance; it's worth going to on weekends when school groups aren't around.

One of Argentina's most famous homes is **Casa Curutchet** (☎482-2631; www.capba.org.ar; Av 53 No 320; admission local/foreigner AR$10/40; ⊙10am-2pm Tue-Fri, closed Jan), designed by French-Swiss architect Le Corbusier for Pedro Curutchet, an Argentine surgeon. It's a beautiful piece of modern architecture and was featured in the award-winning movie *El hombre de al lado* (2009). Reserve in advance for tours.

If you just want to catch La Plata's main sights, hop on the **Bus Turístico** (www.buenosaires.tur.ar/busturistico; admission free) – it's a open-roofed tourist bus that runs from Friday to Sunday only, four times per day. Loops take one hour.

La Plata

Sights

1	Casa Curutchet	C2
2	Casa de Gobierno	C2
3	Cathedral	B3
4	Feria Artesanal	B2
5	Jardin Zoológico	C1
6	Museo de La Plata	D1
7	Museo y Archivo Dardo Rocha	A3
8	Observatorio Astronómico	D1
9	Palacio de la Legislatura	B2
10	Palacio Municipal	B3
11	Pasaje Dardo Rocha	B2
12	Paseo del Bosque	D1
13	Teatro Argentino	B3
14	Teatro Martín Fierro	D2

Sleeping

15	Benevento Hotel	B1
16	Frankville Hostel	A2
17	Hostel del Bosque	C2
18	Hotel García	B1

Eating

19	Carnes Don Pedro	B2
20	Cervecería Modelo	C2
21	Wilkenny	B3

Sleeping

Benevento Hotel HOTEL $$
(☎423-7721; www.hotelbenevento.com.ar; Calle 2, No 645; s AR$288-360, d AR$420-530; ❄@📶) This charmingly renovated hotel offers beautiful rooms with high ceilings and cable TV. Most have wood floors, plus balconies overlooking the busy street; top-floor rooms are the most modern and sport views.

Frankville Hostel HOSTEL $
(☎482-3100; www.frankville.com.ar; Calle 46, No 781; dm AR$55-65, d AR$150; @📶) La Plata's first hostel and still its best one. Dorms are small with shared bathrooms outside but they're clean and have lockers. Back patio for socializing; there are plans for rooms with private bathrooms. HI (Hostelling International) card discount.

Hostel del Bosque HOSTEL $
(☎489-0236; www.hosteldelbosque.com.ar; Calle 54, No 460; dm AR$55-75, r AR$160; @📶) Located in a modern building block with little *onda* (good vibes), but the back patio garden is great. Dorms are tight and there's one ensuite private room. Rooftop terrace and one secure parking spot available; well-located.

BUSES FROM LA PLATA

DESTINATION	COST (AR$)	DURATION (HR)
Bahía Blanca	240-270	8-10
Bariloche	520-590	24
Córdoba	250-290	10
Mar del Plata	140	5
Mendoza	400	15

Hotel García HOTEL **$**
(Calle 2, No 525; s AR$100, d AR$150) Friendly and clean, this budget place 200m from the bus terminal offers 20 small, basic rooms. Showers are open – so everything in the bathroom gets wet – but the cable TV makes up for it.

Eating & Drinking

TOP CHOICE **Cervecería Modelo** ARGENTINE **$$**
(cnr Calles 5 & 54; mains AR$35-60; breakfast, lunch & dinner;) Dating from 1894, its ceiling hung with hams and peanut shells strewn on the floor, this classic place serves ice-cold ales to a happy crowd. There are great sidewalk tables, and it's not too old to boast a big-screen TV and wi-fi.

Wilkenny ARGENTINE **$$**
(cnr Calle 11 & 50; mains AR$35-60; breakfast, lunch & dinner) Popular place with a traditional Irish-pub feel and a decent range of food such as salads, sandwiches and pastas. On Thursday and Friday nights you might catch some live music.

Carnes Don Pedro ARGENTINE **$**
(Diagonal Norte 1005; per kilo AR$49; lunch & dinner Mon-Sat) Great cheap takeout-only option; just pile up your choices and head to nearby Plaza San Martín for a picnic. There's plenty of food, from fresh salads to *parrilla* (mixed grill) to many cooked meat and vegetable dishes.

A 10-minute taxi ride from the center, in the historic bohemian neighborhood Meridiano V, you'll find **Bar Imperio** (Calle 17, btwn Calles 70 & 71), **Mirapampa** (cnr Calles 17 & 71) and **Ciudád Vieja** (cnr Calles 17 & 71), all restaurant-bars offering live music from Thursday to Sunday nights. There's also a weekend crafts fair, plus theater, cinema and cultural centers – no wonder it's popular with students.

Information

Municipal tourist office (427-1535; www.laplata.gov.ar; 10am-5:30pm Mon-Fri, 11am-4pm Sat & Sun) Just off Plaza San Martín.

Post office (cnr Calle 4 & Av 51)

Getting There & Away

Plaza bus 129 connects Buenos Aires with La Plata every 20 minutes (AR$10, 1¼ hours). It leaves from the side street Martín Zuvería, located almost directly in front of Buenos Aires' Retiro train station, making stops along Ave 9 Julio and at Constitución train station.

La Plata's bus terminal has plenty of connections to other parts of Argentina.

La Plata is also served by Buenos Aires' Roca suburban train line, with regular services from the Constitución station.

Luján

02323 / POP 106,000

Luján is a pleasant, compact riverside town that several times per year overflows with pilgrims making their way to Argentina's most important shrine. It boasts a huge Spanish-style plaza with imposing neo-Gothic cathedral, as well as a couple of interesting museums. The riverside area is lined with restaurants and barbecue stands selling *choripan* (a spicy pork sausage in a crunchy roll). You can rent boats for a paddle, while a chairlift carries sightseers over the grubby river – an oddly charming touch.

On the first Saturday in October thousands of Catholics start a 65km pilgrimage walk from Buenos Aires to Luján (see boxed text, p111). Other large gatherings occur on May 8 (**Virgin's Day**), the first weekend in August (the colorful **Peregrinación Boliviana**), the last weekend in September (the **'gaucho' pilgrimage** – watch for horses) and December 8 (**Immaculate Conception Day**).

Sights

Basílica Nuestra Señora de Luján CATHEDRAL
Every year over five million pilgrims from throughout Argentina visit Luján to honor the Virgin for her intercession in affairs of peace, health, forgiveness and consolation. The terminus of their journey is this imposing basilica, built from 1887 to 1935. The neo-Gothic church is made from a lovely rose-colored stone that glows in the setting sun. The statue of the Virgin, which dates from 1630, sits in the high chamber behind

the main altar. Under the basilica you can tour a **crypt** (admission AR$4; ⏱frequent between 10am-5pm) that's inhabited by Virgin statues from all over the world. Masses take place in the basilica several times a day.

Complejo Museográfico Enrique Udaondo MUSEUM
(admission AR$1; ⏱2:30-5pm Wed, 11:30am-5pm Thu & Fri, 10:30am-6pm Sat, Sun & holidays) This gorgeous colonial-era museum complex rambles with several display rooms, pretty patios and gardens. The Sala General José de San Martín showcases Argentina's battles for independence, while the Sala de Gaucho contains some beautiful *mate* (a tea-like beverage) ware, horse gear and other gaucho paraphernalia.

The nearby **Museo de Transporte** (same details as above) has a remarkable collection of horse-drawn carriages from the late 1800s. Also on display is the first steam locomotive to serve the city from Buenos Aires and a monster of a hydroplane that crossed the Atlantic in 1926. The most offbeat exhibits, however, are the stuffed and scruffy remains of Gato and Mancha, the hardy Argentine criollo horses ridden by adventurer AF Tschiffely from Buenos Aires to New York. This trip took 2½ years, from 1925 to 1928.

Sleeping

Luján can easily be done on a day trip from Buenos Aires. If you decide to overnight on a weekend, however, be sure to reserve ahead.

Hotel Hoxón HOTEL $$
(☎429970; www.hotelhoxon.com.ar; 9 de Julio 760; s AR$215-330, d AR$345-525; ❄@🛜🏊) The best and biggest in town, with modern, clean and comfortable rooms. Superiors are carpeted and come with fridge and air-con. The swimming pool comes with raised sun deck.

Hotel del Virrey HOTEL $$
(☎420797; www.hoteldelvirreylujan.com.ar; San Martín 129; r AR$280; ❄🛜) Right near the basilica is this modern hotel offering small but good rooms.

Hostel Estación Luján HOSTEL $
(☎429101; www.estacionlujanhostel.com.ar; 9 de Julio 978; dm AR$80, s/d AR$110/190; ❄@🛜) This small, modern hostel is just steps from the basilica. There are just four clean rooms (including two six-bed dorms), some with balcony, plus kitchen use and a large common area.

Eating

Pilgrims won't go hungry in Luján – the central parts of San Martín, 9 de Julio and the riverfront are all lined with restaurants.

LA VIRGENCITA

Argentina's patron saint is a ubiquitous presence – you can spot her poster on butcher-shop walls, her statue in churches throughout the country and her image on the dashboards of taxis. She wears a triangular blue dress, stands on a half moon and radiates streams of glory from her crowned head.

In 1630 a Portuguese settler in Tucumán asked a friend in Brazil to send him an image of the Virgin for his new chapel. Unsure what style of Virgin was required, the friend sent two – including one of the Immaculate Conception. After setting out from the port of Buenos Aires, the cart bearing the statues got bogged near the river of Luján and only moved when the Immaculate Conception was taken off. Its owner took it as a sign, and left the statue in Luján so that a shrine could be built there. The other statue continued its journey to the northwest.

Since then the Virgin of Luján has been credited with a number of miracles – from curing tumors and sending a fog to hide early settlers from warring Indians, to protecting the province from a cholera epidemic. She was rewarded for her trouble in 1886 when Pope Leo XIII crowned her with a golden coronet set with almost 500 pearls and gems.

The massive pilgrimage to her basilica, where the original statue is still venerated, starts on the first Saturday in October. Throngs of the faithful walk the 65km from the Buenos Aires neighborhood of Liniers to Luján – a journey of up to 18 hours. If you arrive on the first Sunday in October (for Día de Virgen de Luján), you'll spot families of exhausted pilgrims snoozing in the square, enjoying barbecues by the river and filling plastic bottles with holy water from the fountain.

TOP CHOICE L'Eau Vive FRENCH $$
(☎421774; Constitución 2112; 3-course menu AR$60; ⊙lunch & dinner Tue-Sat, lunch only Sun) Just 2km from the town center you'll find this friendly French restaurant run by Carmelite nuns from around the world. Taxis here cost about AR$15, or take bus 501 from the center.

Cervecería Berlin ARGENTINE $
(San Martín 151; mains AR$20-45; ⊙lunch & dinner) With tables on its small front deck, this is a good choice on a warm day. Food isn't fancy – burgers, sandwiches and waffles – but there are plenty of drinks.

Café La Basilica ARGENTINE $$
(San Martín 101; mains AR$30-60; ⊙8am-8pm Mon-Thu, 7am-2am Fri & Sat, 8am-7pm Sun) This classic corner bar offers satisfying meals of homemade pastas and grilled meats. There's English translation on the menu.

Information

Post office (Mitre 575)

Tourist office (☎427082; ⊙8am-5pm) Near the river at the west end of Lavalle, in the domed, yellow building.

Getting There & Away

Lujan's **bus terminal** (Av de Nuestra Señora de Luján & Almirante Brown) is just three blocks north of the basilica. From Buenos Aires, take Transportes Atlántida's bus 57 from outside the Plaza Italia or Once train stations, which leaves every half-hour (AR$15, two hours). There are also daily train departures from Estación Once in Buenos Aires, but you need to change trains in Moreno.

San Antonio de Areco

☎02326 / POP 23,000

Nestled among lush farmlands, San Antonio de Areco is one of the prettiest town in the pampas. About 115km northwest of Buenos Aires, it welcomes many day-tripping *porteños* who come for the peaceful atmosphere and picturesque colonial streets. The town dates from the early 18th century and preserves a great deal of criollo and gaucho traditions, especially among its artisans, who produce very fine silverwork and saddlery. Gauchos from all over the pampas show up for November's Día de la Tradición, where you can catch them and their horses strutting the cobbled streets in all their finery.

San Antonio de Areco's compact town center and quiet streets are very walkable. Around the Plaza Ruiz de Arellano, named in honor of the town's founding *estanciero* (*estancia* owner), are several historic buildings, including the **iglesia parroquial** (parish church).

The **puente viejo** (old bridge; 1857), across the Río Areco, follows the original cart road to northern Argentina. Once a toll crossing, it's now a pedestrian bridge leading to San Antonio de Areco's main attraction, the Museo Gauchesco Ricardo Güiraldes.

Areco shuts down during siesta time in the afternoon.

Sights

Museo Gauchesco Ricardo Güiraldes MUSEUM
(cnr R Güiraldes & Sosa; admission AR$10; ⊙11am-5pm Thu-Mon) Inaugurated by the provincial government in 1938, a decade after the death of Ricardo Güiraldes, author of the gaucho novel *Don Segundo Sombra* (see the boxed text, p114), this museum in Parque Criollo is a sort of gaucholand of restored or fabricated buildings, including an old flour mill, a re-created *pulpería* (tavern) and a colonial-style chapel. The main deal is a 20th-century reproduction of an 18th-century *casco* (ranch house), which holds a wooden bed belonging to Juan Manuel de Rosas (a famous Argentine *caudillo*, or warlord), lots of gorgeous horse gear and various works of gauchesco art. Two rooms are dedicated to Güiraldes himself.

Museo y Taller Draghi MUSEUM, WORKSHOP
(Lavalle 387; admission AR$10; ⊙10:30am-1pm & 4-7pm Mon-Sat, 10:30am-1pm Sun) This small museum and silversmith workshop highlights an exceptional collection of silver *facónes* (gaucho knives), beautiful horse gear and intricate *mate* paraphernalia. There's also some jewelry and leather bags; everything is for sale.

Museo Las Lilas MUSEUM
(www.museolaslilas.org; Moreno 279; admission AR$30; ⊙10am-8pm Fri-Sun) Florencio Molina Campos is to Argentines what Norman Rockwell is to Americans – a folk artist with wide-ranging appeal whose themes are based on comical caricatures. This pretty courtyard museum displays his famous works; entry includes coffee and a *medialuna* (croissant) in the cafe. Hours are shorter late May to late September.

San Antonio de Areco

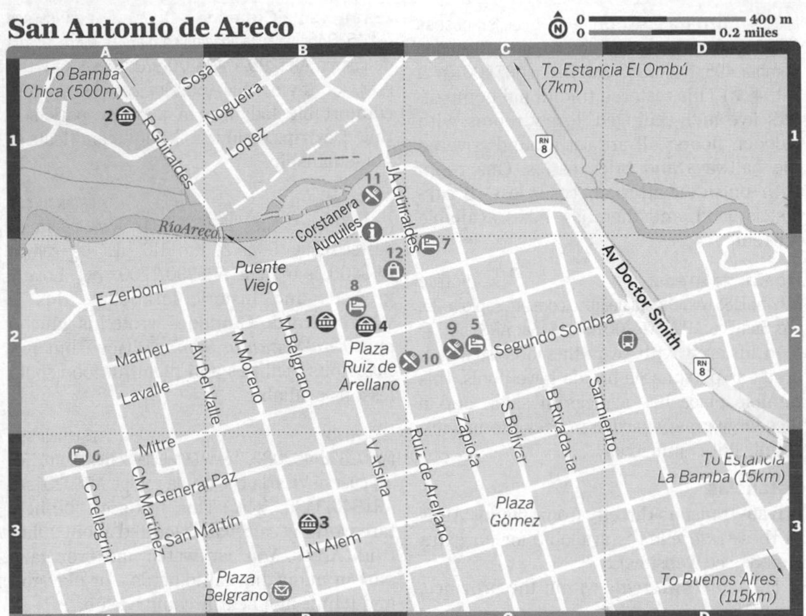

Centro Cultural Usina Vieja MUSEUM
(V Alsina 66; admission AR$3; ⏲11am-5pm Tue-Sun) Set in an old power plant dating from 1901, the Centro Cultural Usina Vieja is an eclectic museum with a funky collection of ancient radios, sewing machines and record players. Farm equipment, sculptures, an old-time grocery store and even a small airplane are also on display.

Festivals & Events

San Antonio de Areco is the symbolic center of Argentina's vestigial cowboy culture, and puts on the country's biggest gaucho celebration for **Día de la Tradición** (a week-long event in early to mid-November; call the tourist office for exact dates). If you're in the area, don't miss it; attractions include a horseback procession through the town, displays of horsemanship, folk dancing and craft exhibitions. Main events take place at Parque Criollo.

Sleeping

While San Antonio is a popular destination for day trips out of Buenos Aires, it's worth hanging around as there are some lovely places to stay. Book on weekends, when prices go up.

San Antonio de Areco

Sights

1 Centro Cultural Usina Vieja B2
2 Museo Gauchesco Ricardo Güiraldes A1
3 Museo Las Lilas B3
4 Museo y Taller Draghi B2

Sleeping

5 Antigua Casona C2
6 Estancia La Cinacina A3
7 Hostal de Areco C2
8 Paradores Draghi B2

Eating

9 Almacén Ramos Generales C2
10 La Esquina de Merti C2
11 Puesto La Lechuza B1

Shopping

12 La Olla de Cobre B2

TOP CHOICE **Paradores Draghi** GUESTHOUSE $$
(☎455583; www.paradoresdraghi.com.ar; Matheu 380; s Sun-Thu only AR$300, d AR$400; ❄@📶🏊) Large, gorgeous rooms (two with kitchenette) are available at this tranquil place. There's a grassy garden with beautiful pool, greenhouse breakfast room and two patios in which to relax.

TOP CHOICE **Antigua Casona** GUESTHOUSE **$$**
(☎456600; www.antiguacasona.com; Segundo Sombra 495; r AR$380 Sun-Thu, r AR$400 Fri & Sat; ❄📶) This restored traditional home offers five high-ceilinged, lovely rooms with wooden floors; all are set around covered tile hallways and brick patios. One room with outside bathroom costs less. Breakfast is good, and there are bikes available for rent.

Hostal de Areco HOTEL **$**
(☎456118; www.hostaldeareco.com.ar; Zapiola 25; s/d Sun-Thu AR$130/200, r Fri & Sat AR$250; ❄📶) Clustered with two other hotels, which aren't as personable but do have pools, this humble place has a pleasant salon and a nice large grassy garden in back. Rooms are simple but comfortable.

Estancias

Private transfers directly from Buenos Aires to these *estancias* is available for an extra charge (see websites).

For more *estancias* within the province, see p116.

Estancia La Cinacina ESTANCIA **$$$**
(☎452045; www.lacinacina.com.ar; B Mitre 9; día de campo AR$290, r AR$870-970; ❄🏊) On the edge of town, this touristy *estancia* offers comfortable lodgings in a pretty park setting. Daytrips include folk shows and feats of horsemanship.

La Porteña ESTANCIA **$$$**
(☎in Buenos Aires 15-5626-7347; www.laportenia deareco.com; Ruta 8, Km 110; día de campo AR$400, s/d from AR$900/1200; 🏊) Lovely grounds and historic location – this is where Ricardo Güiraldes wrote his gaucho epic *Don Segunda Sombra*. Good but not luxurious facilities and plentiful food; polo lessons available.

El Ombú ESTANCIA **$$$**
(☎02326-492080; www.estanciaelombu.com; RP 31, cuartel VI, Villa Lía; día de campo AR$320, s/d AR$940/1480; ❄🏊) This historic, 300-hectare working *estancia* is located about 20km from Areco. You can watch and even take part in managing cattle herds – or play golf and tennis at a nearby country club.

THE GLORIOUS GAUCHO

If the melancholy *tanguero* (tango dancer) is the essence of the *porteño* (resident of Buenos Aires), then the gaucho represents the pampa: a lone cowboy-like figure, pitted against the elements, with only his horse for a friend.

In the early years of the colony, the fringe-dwelling gauchos lived entirely beyond the laws and customs of Buenos Aires, eking out an independent and often violent existence in the countryside. They slaughtered cattle roaming free and unsupervised on the fertile pampas and drank *mate*, the caffeine-rich herbal tea.

As the colony grew, cattle became too valuable to leave unprotected. Foreign demand for hides increased and investors moved into the pampas to take control of the market, establishing the *estancia* system where large landholdings were handed out to a privileged few. Many free-wheeling gauchos became exploited farmhands, while those who resisted domestication were threatened with prison or the draft.

By the late 19th century, those in charge felt the gaucho had no place in modern Argentina. President Sarmiento (who governed 1868–74) declared that 'fertilizing the soil with their blood is the only thing gauchos are good for' – and already much gaucho blood had been spilled, their horsemanship making them excellent infantrymen for Argentina's civil war and the brutal campaigns against the Indians.

Like so many heroes, the gaucho only won love and admiration after his demise. His physical bravery, honor and lust for freedom are celebrated in José Hernández's 1872 epic poem *Martin Fierro* and Ricardo Güiraldes' novel *Don Segundo Sombra*. His rustic traditions form part of Argentina's sophisticated folk art, with skilled craftspeople producing intricate silver gaucho knives and woven ponchos, while his image is endlessly reproduced – most amusingly in Florencio Molina Campos' caricatures.

These days, the gaucho-for-export is much easier to spot than the real deal, especially in folkloric shows at many *estancias*. But the gaucho's ancestors can be found on cattle farms throughout the pampas, riding over the plains in their dusty *boinas* (a kind of beret) and *bombachas* (riding pants). And on special occasions, such as the Día de la Tradición (see p113) they sport their best horse gear and show off their riding skills.

Eating

Almacén Ramos Generales ARGENTINE $$
(Zapiola 143; mains AR$25-60; ⏲lunch & dinner) Come to this traditional, local mainstay if you want an old-time atmosphere in which to eat fish, meat or pasta dishes.

La Esquina de Merti ARGENTINE $
(Ruiz de Arellano 147; mains AR$30-46; ⏲breakfast, lunch & dinner) Right on the plaza is this cafe-restaurant with great old feel. Typical *parrilla* (mixed grill) is on offer, but there are also *milanesas* (breaded cutlets), pasta and some finer dishes too. Cash discount.

Puesto La Lechuza PARRILLA $$
(Costanera Aquiles; mains AR$30-60; ⏲lunch & dinner Sat, lunch Sun) Best on a warm day, when you can enjoy a lunch of empanadas or barbecued beef under the trees near the river. Live guitar music on Saturday nights; open weekends only.

Shopping

San Antonio de Areco's artisans are known throughout the country. *Mate* paraphernalia, *rastras* (silver-studded belts) and *facónes* (gaucho long-bladed knives), produced by skilled silversmiths, are the most typical items. The tourist office has an extensive list of artists and their trades.

If you're looking for a gift of artisanal chocolates or *alfajores* (cookie-type sandwiches), try **La Olla de Cobre** (☎453105; Matheu 433; ⏲10am-1pm & 3-7:30pm Wed-Mon). You can sit down for a coffee or drinking chocolate as well.

Information

There are a few banks with ATMs along Alsina.

Post office (cnr Alvear & Av Del Valle)

Tourist office (☎453165; cnr E Zerboni & Ruiz de Arellano; ⏲9:30am-7pm Mon-Fri, 8am-8pm Sat & Sun)

Getting There & Away

General Belgrano and Chevallier run frequent buses from Buenos Aires to Areco (AR$35-40, two hours). A few long-distance services are available.

SOUTHERN PAMPAS

Spreading out from the capital, the pampas region extends south beyond the borders of Buenos Aires province and west into the province of La Pampa.

In the southern part of Buenos Aires province, the endlessly flat plain is punctuated by sierras, or hills. The Sierras de Tandil are ancient mountain ranges, worn to soft, low summits with heights that barely reach 500m. A little to the west, Sierra de la Ventana's jagged peaks rise to 1300m, attracting hikers and climbers.

Further west again, in the province of La Pampa, are the modest granite boulders of Parque Nacional Lihué Calel.

The hillside towns of Tandil and Sierra de la Ventana offer outdoor activities and a relaxing country atmosphere, while La Pampa's provincial capital of Santa Rosa is a decent resting point for overland travelers on their way west or south.

Tandil

☎0249 / POP 124,000

Pretty Tandil sits at the northern edge of the Sierras de Tandil, a 2.5-million-year-old mountain range worn down to gentle, grassy peaks and rocky outcroppings – perfect for rock climbing and mountain biking. It exudes a rare combination of laid-back country charm with the energy of a thriving regional city. The town center is leafy and relaxed, with many places observing the afternoon siesta. Later in the evening, however, locals crowd the squares and streets, shopping and partaking in the city's cultural offerings. On a side note, Tandil is known for nurturing a disproportionate number of Argentina's tennis stars – the latest of whom is Juan Martín del Potro.

The town arose from Fuerte Independencia, a military outpost established in 1823. In the early 1870s, it was the scene of one of the province's most remarkable battles, when renegade gauchos gathered in the hills before going on a murderous rampage against landowners and recent immigrants. Eventually the immigrants prevailed, and the culinary skills they brought from Europe have made the area an important producer of specialty foods. Today, Tandil is famous for its cheeses and cured meats, which can be sampled in eateries and stores throughout town.

Sights

Tandil's museums include the historical **Museo Tradicionalista Fuerte Independencia** (☎4435573; 4 de Abril 845; admission AR$10; ⏲2:30-6:30pm Tue-Sun Mar-Nov, 4-8pm Tue-Sun Dec-Feb), which exhibits collections on the

Staying on an Estancia

One of the best ways to enjoy the open spaces of the pampas is to visit an *estancia* (ranch). Argentina's late 19th century belle epoque saw wealthy families adorn their ranches with lavish homes and gardens.

Those glorious days being long gone, many of these establishments are now open to tourists. The *día de campo* – or 'day in the country' – usually includes a huge *asado* (barbecue grill) with drinks, a tour of the historic home and use of the property's horses, bicycles and swimming pool. Some places offer a *show gauchesco* (gaucho show), featuring folk dances and feats of horsemanship, while others host polo matches. *Estancias* are a sustainable tourism option, helping to preserve part of the country's past while providing an impressive guest-to-tree ratio. Most offer overnight stays, which include meals and activities.

ESTANCIA OPTIONS

All within a few hours of Buenos Aires:

» **Los Dos Hermanos** (☎ 4723-2880; www.estancialosdoshermanos.com) Best for horseback riding.

» **Juan Gerónimo** (☎ 02221-481414; www.juangeronimo.com.ar) The place for nature-lovers.

» **La Oriental** (☎ 02362-15-640866; www.estancia-laoriental.com) Lovely house and setting.

» **La Candelaria** (☎ 02227-424404; www.estanciacandelaria.com) Extravagant French-style castle.

» **La Margarita** (☎ 4951-0638; www.estancialamargarita.com) Unique, 'self-catering' option.

» **Guapa Polo** (☎ 15-5111-8214; www.guapapolo.com.ar) Learn to play polo.

For other areas, see p114, p428 and p284.

Clockwise from top left

1. *Asado* (barbecue grill) **2.** Gaucho **3.** Musicians playing tango **4.** Drinking *mate*

2

3

AREA CODE CHANGE

Tandil is due to get a new area code, which would change from 02293 to 249. A '4' will also be added to the beginning of every telephone number. For example:

old number 02293-123456

new number 249-412-3456

town's history. Photographs commemorate major events, and the place is filled with relics – from carriages to ladies' gloves. The **Museo de Bellas Artes** (4432067; Chacabuco 353; admission by donation; 8:30am-12:30pm & 4-8pm Tue-Fri, 4-8pm Sat & Sun) has temporary exhibits of Argentine and international artists.

The walk to **Parque Independencia** from the southwestern edge of downtown offers good views of the city, particularly at night, while the central **Plaza de Independencia**, surrounded by the typical municipal buildings and a church, is where the townspeople stroll in the evenings.

Calvario, a hill ostensibly resembling the site of Christ's crucifixion, attracts masses of visitors at Easter, when a passion play is held.

At the north edge of town the Piedra Movediza (a 300-ton 'rocking stone') teetered precariously atop **Cerro La Movediza** for many years before finally falling in 1912. A 'replica' nonmoving stone was built in 2007. Take bus 503 (blue).

For more good views, head 4.5km west of town to **Cerro El Centinela** (admission AR$30; 11am-5pm Mon-Fri, 10:30am-6:30pm Sat & Sun), a hilltop with two restaurants plus a ski-lift-type ride. Open only weekends outside warm months; a taxi here costs AR$20.

The **Reserva Natural Sierra del Tigre** (admission AR$14; 9am-7pm in summer, till 5:30pm in winter, closed Wed & rainy days) is 6km south of town, at the end of Calle Suiz, off Av Don Bosco. The rocky hills are fun to climb, and in spring the reserve is filled with fragrant wild flowers. The peaks offer views of the town and local farms. A somewhat incongruous collection of animals – llamas and donkeys among them – have free run of the park, while their natural predator, the puma, is sadly caged. Taxis here cost around AR$25 one way; arrange pickup for a return ride.

Activities

The **Dique del Fuerte**, only 12 blocks south of Plaza Independencia, is a huge reservoir that you can easily walk around in a couple of hours. In summer, the Balneario Municipal runs several **swimming pools** and you can rent **canoes** and **kayaks**. There are also a few restaurants nestled along its shoreline.

To go horseback riding in the Reserva Natural Sierra del Tigre or other surrounding areas, call **Gabriel Barletta** (442-47725, 02293-15-4509609; cabalgatasbarletta@yahoo.com.ar). For bike rentals, contact **Sergio** (445-2454, 02293-15-4647234).

Several tour agencies offer a range of activities around the town and the sierras. **Chao Tandil** (443-2542; www.chaotandil.com.ar) has trekking, canoeing, rappelling, mountain biking and rock climbing.

Sleeping

Reservations are a must during summer, Easter week and holiday weekends. If you have your own transport, the many cabañas along Av Don Bosco are a good option – the tourist office provides lists of fully equipped cabins, many of which have pools.

TOP CHOICE **Lo de Titi** GUESTHOUSE **$$**
(442-0926; www.lodetiti.com.ar; Lobería 1050; s/d AR$370/490;) Just four fine, big rooms are available at this awesome place. There's a huge grassy garden, colorful eclectic decor and great common room with kitchen use. Prices drop outside summer.

Belgrano 39 B&B B&B **$$**
(442-6989, 02293-15-607076; hutton@speedy.com.ar; Belgrano 39; s/d AR$200/300;) There are just two rooms at this peaceful B&B, both comfortable doubles, plus a large lovely garden with pool. Run by a one-of-a-kind British woman; reservations necessary.

Las Acacias GUESTHOUSE **$$**
(442-3373; www.posadalasacacias.com.ar; Brasil 642; s/d AR$380/440; @) Located in an old dairy, this wonderful place has nine elegant rooms set around covered hallways and gardens. Rustic atmosphere and tasteful decor; prices drop outside summer.

Estancia Ave Maria ESTANCIA **$$**
(442-2843; www.avemariatandil.com.ar; s/d AR$735/905 Mon-Thu, AR$935/1025 Fri-Sun; @) This historic and beautiful 300-hectare *estancia* offers big rooms with views of the hills, and comfortable common areas.

Prices include breakfast and dinner, plus activities such as horseback rides. It's located 9km west of town.

Hotel Cristal HOTEL $
(☎444-3970; hotelcristal_tandil@yahoo.com.ar; Gral Rodríguez 871; s/d AR$145/205; @📶) A basic budget hotel, with a sunny garden where guests can enjoy breakfast.

Casa Chango HOSTEL $
(☎442-2260; www.casa-chango.com.ar; 25 de Mayo 451; dm AR$75, r AR$210-300; @📶) Passable hostel in a rambling old building with old tiles, crumbling patios and a nice back garden. Most dorms are six to eight beds; avoid the one with 18. Private rooms are tiny, but there's one good-sized room with private bathroom.

Eating

TOP CHOICE **Epoca de Quesos** ARGENTINE $$
(cnr San Martín & 14 de Julio; mains AR$30-60; ⏲9am-11pm) Stuffed with tourists on a busy weekend, Epoca de Quesos sells over 40 local cheeses and dozens of cured meats, which you can sample. Or snag a table in the pleasant garden out back and order a sampler plate with specialty beer to match. Regular main dishes too.

Tierra de Azafranes INTERNATIONAL $$
(☎443-6800; cnr San Martín & Av Santamarina; mains AR$35-85; ⏲lunch & dinner Wed-Mon) This hip and smartly decorated restaurant is known for its fish, pastas, risottos and paella. Get the seafood stew on Wednesday night.

Benevento ITALIAN $
(cnr San Martín & L N Alem; pasta AR$31-45; ⏲lunch & dinner Tue-Sun) This restaurant does only pasta, and does it very well – it's all homemade and deliciously fresh. Try the *tallarines* (fettucine) with smoked ham, asparagus and vodka cream. Discount on takeout.

Carajo PARRILLA $$
(cnr Saavedra Lamas & García; mains AR$50-70; ⏲lunch & dinner Tue-Sun) With a great outdoor terrace overlooking the Dique del Fuerte, this *parrilla* is unbeatable on a warm sunny day. Closed Sunday night outside the warm months.

Also recommeded:

Q'Tupé INTERNATIONAL $$
(Av Brasil 184; mains AR$30-65; ⏲lunch & dinner) Delicious gourmet salads, sandwiches and specialty dishes.

Aquí No Es INTERNATIONAL $$
(Chile 735; mains AR$40-70; ⏲breakfast, lunch & dinner) Bohemian food, artsy vibe, casual garden.

Drinking

For a small town, Tandil has several good bars.

Antares BAR
(9 de Julio 758; ⏲6pm-late) One of Antares many branches, it sports the typical Antares look – an attractive, modern restaurant-bar with just-for-looks copper tap cylinders behind the bar. Live music Thursday to Sunday; closed Monday.

Bar Tolomé BAR
(cnr Gral Rodríguez & Bmé Mitre; ⏲7pm-late) Dead midweek and lively on weekends (when there's occasional live music), this relaxed bar serves pizzas and sandwiches when a beer's not enough.

Antique Bistro BAR
(Gral Rodríguez 687; ⏲8am-late) A sophisticated mood prevails at this tiny old-fashioned piano bar, where live folk and tango bands perform from Wednesday to Saturday nights.

Shopping

Talabartería Carlos A Berruti SOUVENIRS
(Gral Rodríguez 787; ⏲9:15am-1pm & 4:30-8:30pm Mon-Sat) Especially good for leather, this store also stocks an assortment of *mates*, knives, silverwork and ponchos.

Almacen Serrano FOOD
(☎444-8102; cnr Av Avellaneda & Gral Rodríguez; ⏲9am-1pm & 4:30-9pm Mon-Thu, 9am-9pm Fri & Sat, 10am-9pm Sun) Sells cheese, salamis and hams from the region, as well as locally made beers and sweets.

Information

There are plenty of banks with ATMs in the center.

Post office (Gral Pinto 621)

Tourist office (☎444-8698; Rodríguez 445; ⏲9am-8pm Mon-Sat, 9am-1pm Sun)

Tourist office (☎443-2225; www.tandil.gov.ar; Av Com Espora 1120; ⏲9am-6pm Mon-Sat, 9am-1pm Sun) On the northern edge of town. There's another **tourist office** at the bus terminal.

Getting There & Away

Tandil's bus terminal is within walking distance of its town center, if you don't mind walking 12 blocks. Otherwise taxis will cost about AR$12.

BUSES FROM TANDIL

DESTINATION	COST (AR$)	DURATION (HR)
Buenos Aires	120-140	5½
Córdoba	310-350	16
Mar del Plata	55	3
Mendoza	375-450	16
Necochea	45	3

Trains from Buenos Aires' Constitución station arrive in Tandil on Friday and head back on Sunday, but double check as service can be suspended.

Getting Around

Tandil's excellent public transportation system reaches every important sight. Bus 500 (yellow) goes to Dique del Fuerte, bus 501 (red) goes to the bus terminal, and bus 503 (blue) goes to Cerro La Movediza, the university and the bus terminal.

Sierra de la Ventana

0291 / POP 5000

Sierra de la Ventana's main attraction is the wealth of outdoor activity it offers: hiking up nearby peaks, trout fishing and bathing in the streams and pools, riding on horse or bicycle through the hills, and climbing or rappelling among the rocks. Weekends fill with families from around the province coming to enjoy the picturesque hills.

The town is divided into two sections by Río Sauce Grande; Villa Tivoli has most of the services, while Villa Arcadia is residential. There's only one main street, and afternoons tend to be quiet as folks take a siesta break.

Activities

Lots of outdoor pursuits are on offer in this region, and you can tackle most on your own. For hiking guides try **Luan & Ventur** (0291-15-416-0931; luan_ventur@hotmail.com), which goes to Garganta del Diablo (see p121), the only way to explore that gorge. It also organizes rappelling, horseback riding and other tours.

Sergio Rodriguez (491-5355; www.sergiorodrigueztur.com.ar; cnr Av San Martín & Iguazú), also known as GeoTur, does tours to a nearby winery and an *estancia*.

For bike rentals head to **El Tornillo** (0291-15-431-1812; Roca 142; 10am-7pm, closed in afternoons during hot weather). The river area behind Hotel Aihuen is popular for splashing about, and beyond is a hill to climb.

Sleeping

Book ahead in summer and during long weekends. The tourist office has a list of *cabañas* (cabins).

La Casa de Juani HOSTEL $
(0291-15-416-0931; hostellacasadejuani@hotmail.com; Camino de las Carretas s/n; dm AR$70, r AR$160;) Next to fields on the edge of town is this tiny but beautiful hostel with just one private room and one four-bed dorm (camping and *cabañas* coming). Bike rentals available; it's a 10-minute dusty walk from the YPF gas station.

Hotel Atero HOTEL $$
(491-5002; cnr Av San Martín & Güemes; s/d AR$300;) Comfortable and homey rooms, some with balconies overlooking the street, make this a good midrange choice. It's right in the middle of town, and has a restaurant.

Aihuen Hotel HOTEL $
(491-5074; www.com-tur.com.ar/alihuen; cnr Tornquist & Frontini; s/d AR$100/200;) About four blocks from the main drag, near the river, is this charmingly old-style hotel on grassy grounds. It's hardly luxurious, with creaky wood floors and simple furnishings, but there's certainly some atmosphere. A nearby building has more modern rooms.

Hostería Maiten HOSPEDAJE $
(491-5073; hosteriamaiten@yahoo.com.ar; Iguazú 93; r AR$220;) Sixteen very basic but clean rooms with open-shower bathrooms cluster around a leafy garden patio at this central, friendly and family-run place. Prices drop outside January/Februay.

Camping El Paraíso CAMPGROUND $
(0291-15-407-4530; camping_elparaiso@yahoo.com.ar; Los Tilos 150; campsites per person AR$22, cabañas from AR$80) This decent campground is pretty central, with dusty shady sites and various services. Small *cabañas* with bunks and outside baths are available. It's 2½ blocks from the main street.

Eating

Some restaurants close one or more days per week outside the December to March summer months.

El Ceibo ARGENTINE **$$**
(☎491-5173; Calle Sauce Grande; mains AR$40-70; ⊙lunch & dinner Wed-Mon) Upscale restaurant specializing in regional dishes such as rabbit, venison, trout and boar. Find it across the river towards Villa Arcadia; it's at the Hotel El Ceibo. From May to mid-December the restaurant is only open Thursday to Sunday.

Sol y Luna ARGENTINE **$$**
(☎491-5316; Av San Martín 658; mains AR$35-60; ⊙lunch & dinner) An attractive place serving everything from homemade pastas and pizzas to *parrilla* and fresh trout. Open in high season only.

Parrilla Rali-Hué PARRILLA **$$**
(☎491-5220; San Martín 307; mains AR$30-50; ⊙lunch & dinner) It's beef only at this casual joint, where locals flock to dine on the *parrillada* for two – good value at AR$90.

Information

Banco Provincia (San Martín 260) The town's only bank; it has ATMs.

Post office (cnr Av Roca & Alberdi)

Tourist office (☎491-5303; ⊙8am-8pm) Across the tracks from the train station.

Getting There & Around

Condor Estrella (☎491-5091) buses to Buenos Aires (AR$180, eight hours, six times weekly) and Bahía Blanca (AR$35, two hours, twice daily) leave from a small office on Av San Martín, a block from the YPF gas station. There are more services to Bahía Blanca with local *combi* (long-distance van) companies such as **Expreso Cabildo** (☎491-5247; cnr San Martín & Iguazú in remise office) and **Norte Bus** (☎0291-15-468-5101, San Martín 155). Norte Bus provides door-to-door service and costs AR$45.

There are several trains per week from Buenos Aires (AR$37-60); some arrive at Tornquist, 48km away.

Transporte Silver (☎491-5383; Av San Martín 156) runs a door-to-door service between Sierra de la Ventana and Tornquist (AR$16.50, one hour), stopping at Villa Ventana (AR$10, 25 minutes) and Parque Provincial Ernesto Tornquist (AR$14, 40 minutes). The minibuses run two or three times daily (more in summer, December to March).

Parque Provincial Ernesto Tornquist

This 67-sq-km **park** (☎491-0039; admission AR$10; ⊙8am-5pm Dec-Mar, 9am-5pm Apr-Nov), 22km from Sierra de la Ventana, draws visitors from throughout the province. There are two entrances. The first is 5km west of Villa Ventana and home to the **Centro de Visitantes**, which has a small display on local ecology. The main hike here is **Cerro Bahía Blanca** (three hours roundtrip), offering great views. There are also **Cuevas con Pinturas Repustres**, or cave paintings, but you can only visit these with a guided tour by Luan & Ventur (p120).

The park's highlight, however, is at its other entrance, 3km further west. The five-hour (round-trip) hike to 1150m **Cerro de la Ventana** leads to a window-shaped rock formation near its peak. The climb offers dramatic views of surrounding hills and the distant pampas. Register with rangers before 11am at the trailhead, and take plenty of water and sun protection.

If you don't have the energy, there are shorter destinations such as **Piletones** (2½ hours round-trip) and **Garganta Olvidada** (one hour round-trip). To visit the gorge and waterfall pool at **Garganta del Diablo** (six hours round-trip), you must go with a tour company, (p120).

Transportes Silver minibuses from Sierra de la Ventana (AR$14, 40 minutes) and Villa Ventana (AR$8, 15 minutes) head to the park two or three times daily (more in summer). For better timing to catch the park opening, you can also check Condor Estrella's morning bus schedule to Bahía Blanca. Remises to the park cost AR$75 to AR$85.

For accommodation options near the park, see the boxed text p122 or check with Sierra de la Ventana's tourist office.

Santa Rosa

☎02954 / POP 120,000

About 600km from Buenos Aires – and a long way from pretty much anywhere else – Santa Rosa is unlikely to be of interest unless you find yourself traveling overland, in which case it's a convenient stopping point and transport hub. It's a pleasant enough place, however, with a small-town feel, friendly people and busy plaza area.

WORTH A TRIP

VILLA VENTANA

Just 17km northwest of Sierra de la Ventana is the peaceful village of Villa Ventana. There's nothing much to do here except wander the dusty streets, which meander through pretty residential neighborhoods full of pine trees, and investigate the ruins of South America's first casino (by guided tour only; see the tourist office). Villa Ventana is also a closer base than Sierra de la Ventana from which to visit Parque Provincial Ernesto Tornquist.

There are several places to stay, though none are budget. **Cabañas La Ponderosa** (☎491-5491; www.laponderosacabanias.com.ar; cnr Cruz del Sur & Hornero; *cabañas* from AR$240) near the entrance to town, has good-sized, homey and comfortable wood cabañas, some with loft and all with kitchenette. And for something special there's **Posada Agua Pampas** (☎491-0210; www.aguapampas.com.ar; cnr Calle Las Piedras btw Hornero & Canario; r from AR$470; ❄@📶≋), with gorgeous rooms built from local stone and recycled wood, right down to the hollow-log bathtubs. Prices fall during weekdays and from April to mid-December; cash discount.

Get to Villa Ventana with Transportes Silver minibuses (AR$10, 20 minutes), which leave from Sierra de la Ventana three to five times daily (depending on the season); remises cost AR$45. Bahía Blanca buses can also stop near the entrance to town. The **Tourist office** (☎491-0095) is located at the town's entrance.

Sights & Activities

FREE **Museo Provincial de Historia Natural** (Quintana 116; admission free; ⏰variable) was being remodelled at research time, but will likely include a bird taxidermy collection, local dinosaur fossil discoveries and even live snakes.

Art lovers can visit **Museo Provincial de Artes** (☎427332; cnr 9 de Julio & Villegas; admission free; ⏰8am-8pm Mon-Fri, 6-9:30pm Sat & Sun), which features several rooms showcasing temporary exhibitions; check out the tree growing inside.

Laguna Don Tomás, 1km west of the city center, is the place for locals to sail, swim, play sports or just stroll.

Sleeping & Eating

Hotel Calfucurá HOTEL **$$**
(☎433303; www.hotelcalfucura.com; San Martín 695; s/d AR$285/450; ❄📶≋) Santa Rosa's best hotel, with modern atmosphere, handy location near the bus terminal and very comfortable carpeted rooms. In summer, worth it for the pool.

Residencial Atuel HOTEL **$**
(☎422597; www.atuel.aehglp.org.ar; Luro 356; s/d AR$100/170; ❄) Just steps from the bus terminal, this friendly place has worn but tidy rooms with cable TV. It's certainly good enough for one night.

Camping Municipal Don Tomás CAMPGROUND **$**
(☎434568; Av Uruguay; campsites per person AR$10, with car AR$18) Basic, grassy sites with picnic tables and little privacy. From the bus terminal, take the 'circular' bus (taxis AR$25). It's at the west end of Av Uruguay. Summer only.

La Recova ARGENTINE **$$**
(cnr Yrigoyen & Avellaneda; meals AR$30-70; ⏰7am-1:30am) Good for breakfast, this modern place right on Plaza San Martín does the whole *confitería* (cafe) thing to perfection. Also sandwiches, pizzas and meats.

Information

You'll find several ATMs in the city center.

Municipal tourist office (☎436555; Luro 365; ⏰7:30am-8pm Mon-Fri, 10am-1pm & 4-8pm Sat & Sun) At the bus terminal; don't confuse it with the nearby (and more visible) 24-hour bus information office.

Post office (Hilario Lagos 258)

Provincial tourist office (☎424404; www.turismola pampa.gov.ar; cnr Luro & San Martín; ⏰7am-9pm Mon-Fri, 9am-1pm, 5-9pm Sat & Sun) Across from the bus terminal; longer hours in January/February.

Getting There & Away

Aerolíneas (☎427588, Pico 267) flies to Buenos Aires. The airport is 3km from downtown.

The **bus terminal** (Luro 365) is seven blocks from the plaza. Long-distance buses include Bahía Blanca (AR$98, five hours), Neuquén (AR$167, 7½ hours), Buenos Aires (AR$215 to AR$290, eight hours), Puerto Madryn (AR$220, 10 hours), Mendoza (AR$270 to AR$320, 12 hours) and Bariloche (AR$360 to AR$410, 12 hours).

For car rentals there's **H&C Rent a Car** (☎02954-15-697755, cnr Independencia & San Marzo).

Reserva Provincial Parque Luro

☎02954

Home to a mix of introduced and native species, as well as over 150 species of birds, this 76-sq-km **reserve** (www.parqueluro.gov.ar; admission AR$4; ⏰9am-8pm) is a peaceful place to spend time away from the city. Avoid Sundays if you don't like crowds, however, and bring water and sun protection in the baking summer.

At the turn of the 20th century a wealthy local, Doctor Pedro Luro, created Argentina's first hunting preserve here, importing exotic game species such as Red deer and European boar. He also built an enormous French-style mansion to accommodate his European guests. As sport hunting fell out of vogue and the European aristocracy suffered the upheavals of WWI and the Great Depression, Luro went broke. The reserve was sold, then neglected, its animals escaping through the fence or falling victim to poachers.

Since its acquisition by the province in 1965, Parque Luro has served as a refuge for native species such puma and wild fox, along with exotic migratory birds including flamingo. One of the park's biggest draws, however, is during the fall mating season of the Red deer. In March and April the males bellow loudly (called 'la Brama') to attract female harems, while scuffling amongst themselves. There are guided visits to witness this spectacle.

Hourly tours of the **Castillo** (per person AR$8), Luro's mansion, offer insight into the luxurious eccentricities that Argentine landowners could indulge. As the story goes, Luro was only able to obtain the gorgeous walnut fireplace by purchasing an entire Parisian restaurant. Besides the museum, there's a **Sala de Carruajes** – a collection of turn-of-the-century carriages.

HOME, HOME ON THE...FEEDLOT?

They've always been one of Argentina's biggest tourist attractions – those juicy, grass-fed steaks full of seriously beefy taste. But these days, this type of beef has nearly disappeared. Stuffing cattle into pens and feeding them grain is becoming a standard way of finishing them off. Today, over 80% of Argentina's cows slaughtered each year experience their last few months in a feedlot.

Carnivorism was not always mass produced in Argentina. The country's agriculturally rich and vast pampas plains were ideal grounds for raising beef. Up until 2001, around 90% of cattle ate only their natural food: grass. But in the last ten years, several developments have changed this. The price of agricultural crops such as soybeans, of which Argentina is one of the world's top producers, has skyrocketed, making it more lucrative to grow the legume than dedicate space to cattle. A severe drought in recent years dealt another blow to the beef industry – there just wasn't enough grass to feed the herds.

But perhaps the biggest factor detrimental to the grass-fed cattle has been government subsidies for feedlot development, with the intention of producing beef more quickly than before. It's less profitable to raise a fully grass-fed cow – which takes much longer to reach maturity – than a grain-fed one. And the Argentine government also passed legislation keeping beef prices artificially low within its borders, while at the same time using taxes to discourage cattle ranchers from making profits by exporting beef. So even more ranchers have turned pastureland into soy or corn rows to stay alive.

Very soon, practically all Argentine cattle will live out their last few months in dirt-floor corrals, limiting their movements and eating an un-cow-like diet of grains. They'll be shot full of immunizations and antibiotics, which are crucial to treating ailments brought on by these unnatural conditions. Their beef will be slightly less tasteful and nutritious, yet more tender – due to the lower percentage of muscle, plus higher fat. And the modern world of commercial beef production will finally have caught up to Argentina, wiping away a part of its history, reputation...and that famous Argentine pride.

The park's sights are all located around a 6km ring road; reach the **Centro de Interpretación** by following the road 2.2km from the entrance. The basic **restaurant** and **campsites** (☎415649; per person AR$30) are 500m beyond that (take food, though there's a small store). And 300m further up the road are nice **cabañas** (☎415649; from AR$220) that sleep up to five. A few short nature walks veer off the ring road.

Parque Luro is 35km south of Santa Rosa. From the bus terminal, catch the Dumascat bus to General Acha (AR$8, 25 minutes, four daily) and ask to be dropped off at the park entrance. Find out when a bus returns to Santa Rosa. Taxis cost AR$100 each way (negotiate your return time), or you can rent a car in Santa Rosa.

Parque Nacional Lihué Calel

☎02952

In the local indigenous language of Pehuenche, Lihué Calel means Sierra de la Vida (Range of Life), and describes a series of small, isolated mountain ranges and valleys that create unique microclimates in a nearly featureless pampean landscape.

This desert-like **park** (☎436595; www.lihuecalel.com.ar; admission free) is a haven for native cats such as puma and yagouaroundi. You can spot armadillo, guanaco, mara (Patagonian hare) and vizcacha, while birdlife includes the rhea-like ñandú and many birds of prey such as thc carancho (crested caracara).

Lihué Calel receives only about 400mm of rainfall per year, but sudden storms can create brief waterfalls over granite boulders near the visitors center. Even when the sky is cloudless, the subterranean streams in the valleys nourish the *monte* (a scrub forest with a surprising variety of plant species). Within the park's 10 sq km exist 345 species of plants, nearly half the total found in the entire province.

There are a few walks in the area, including the hour-long hike to the 589m peak **Cerro de la Sociedad Científica Argentina**; watch for flowering cacti such as *Trichocereus candicans* between boulders. From the summit, there are outstanding views of the entire sierra and surrounding marshes and salt lakes.

About 8km from the visitors center is **Viejo Casco**, the ruins of the old house of former Estancia Santa María. It's also possible to make a 9km walking circuit via the **Valle de las Pinturas**, where there are some petroglyphs.

More information is available at the **visitors center**, where there's a small museum. Spring is the best time to visit the park, when flowers are blooming and the temperatures aren't too hot.

Sleeping

Near the visitors center is a comfortable and free campground with shade trees, firepits (bring wood), picnic tables, toilets and showers. Stock up on food before arriving; the nearest decent supplies are at the town of Puelches, 32km south.

The closest hotel is **ACA** (☎436101; r AR$140), on the highway 3km from the park (or 1.5km via a trail), with a handful of OK rooms and a restaurant. Otherwise you can try a *hospedaje* (family home) in Puelches; the provincial tourist office in Santa Rosa can arrange a stay.

Getting There & Away

Parque Nacional Lihué Calel is 220km southwest of Santa Rosa, and there are no direct buses to the park. Most south-bound buses (ie to Neuquén or Bariloche) can drop you off on the highway near the entrance, or snag the daily minibus that heads to Puelches (AR$60, three hours). Check with the provincial tourist office for details.

Driving (rent a car in Santa Rosa) is the best way to visit the park.

ATLANTIC COAST

Argentines can justly claim Latin America's highest peak (Cerro Aconcagua), its widest avenue (Buenos Aires' 9 de Julio) and perhaps its prettiest capital, but its beaches aren't tropical paradises strewn with palm trees. There's no white sand here, the winds can be fierce and the water is cloudy rather than turquoise. Despite all this Argentina's beaches are hardly unpleasant places in summcr, and cach January and February they reliably attract tens of thousands of well-heeled *porteños* (residents of Buenos Aires) escaping the capital's unrelenting heat. In fact, so many people flock to the shore that at times you might have a hard time finding a free spot to spread your towel.

So if you don't mind the lively summer crowds, the Atlantic Coast offers a wonderful escape. And if you want to avoid the summer crowds, simply visit in the shoulder months of December and March, when the weather is still warm enough to enjoy the beaches and their activities. In the dead of winter, however, coastal towns here take on an abandoned feel and the foul weather can become downright depressing. Mar de Plata is an exception – the coast's largest city offers something to do all year round.

Accommodation prices vary widely along the coast, depending on the season. They rise sharply from mid-December through February, when reservations are crucial (and a few places require minimum-nights stays). Prices then start declining in March but rise again during Easter, after which most places close down until November. At the places that do stay open, bargains can be found during these cooler months.

Prices and opening hours noted in this chapter are for the January to February high season. In other months, opening hours (especially at tourist offices and restaurants) are much shorter.

San Clemente del Tuyú

02252 / POP 13,000

With absolutely none of the glitz or glamour of the resorts down the coast, family-oriented San Clemente is a favorite for low-key beachgoers. The **tourist information office** (☎423249; cnr Avs Costanera & 63; ⏰8am-midnight) is across from the beach; there are plenty of restaurants on the main drag, Calle 1.

A few kilometers north of San Clemente del Tuyú are several protected areas, including **Reserva Natural Municipal Punta Rasa** (whose beach is popular with kiteboarders) and **Parque Nacional Campos del Tuyú** (home of the rare pampas deer).

For tamer wildlife there's **Mundo Marino** (www.mundomarino.com.ar; admission AR$119; ⏰10am-8pm), South America's largest marine park. Another attraction is the popular recreation center **Termas Marinas** (www.termasmarinas.com.ar; admission AR$57; ⏰10am-8pm), featuring mineral-rich thermal baths.

Sleeping

Brisas Marinas HOTEL $$
(☎522219; www.brisas-marinas.com.ar; Calle 13, No 50; r AR$280-350; wi-fi) A reasonably attractive choice just steps from the beach, with simple, nice and clean rooms, some with balcony.

Hotel Top HOTEL $
(☎522005; www.hoteltopsanclemente.com.ar; Av Costanera 1657; s/d AR$120/240) Almost too good of a deal, with 23 small but tidy rooms with cable TV, and right on the beach.

Hotel 5 Avenue HOTEL $
(☎421035; Calle 5, No 1561; s/d AR$130/180) Just a block and a half from the beach, this friendly place offers worn budget rooms with tiny bathrooms.

Getting There & Away

The **bus terminal** (cnr Avs Talas and Naval) is about 25 blocks from the town center. There are local buses and taxis to the center. Frequent buses connect San Clemente to Buenos Aires (AR$130, 4½ hours), Pinamar (AR$30, 2½ hours) and also Mar del Plata (AR$67, four hours).

Pinamar

☎02254 / POP 25,000

Located about 120km northeast of Mar del Plata, Pinamar's warm waters make a very popular destination for middle-class *porteños*. It's a busy place in summer, so if you're seeking a bit of tranquillity, head to its southern and more residential neighborhoods of Ostende and Valeria, which are less conveniently located but offer more affordable sleeping options. Even further south is woodsy Cariló, Argentina's most exclusive resort and home to expensive houses, fashionable restaurants and sandy side roads.

Pinamar was founded and designed in 1944 by architect Jorge Bunge, who figured out how to stabilize the shifting dunes by planting pines, acacias and pampas grass. It was once the refuge for the country's upper echelons, but is now somewhat less exclusive and more laid-back.

Pinamar's film festival, **Pantalla Pinamar** (www.pantallapinamar.com), takes place in March and there are concerts and parties on the beach around New Year.

Activities

The main activity in Pinamar is simply relaxing and socializing on the beach, which stretches all the way from north of the town down to Cariló. But the area also offers a wealth of outdoor activities, from windsurfing and waterskiing to horseback riding and fishing. You can also ride bicycles in the wooded areas near the golf course, or through the leafy streets of nearby Cariló.

For bike rentals, try **Leo** (☎488855; Av Bunge 1111; ⌚9am-8pm). If you want to learn how to kiteboard, go to Sport Beach, the last *balneario* located about 5km north of Av Bunge. There are many more options for activities – ask at the tourist office.

Sleeping

Reservations are a must in January, when some places have a week minimum stay.

PINAMAR

Hotel Las Calas HOTEL $$$
(☎405999; www.lascalashotel.com.ar; Av Bunge 560; r AR$700; ❄📶) This boutique-style hotel has tasteful rooms with king-size beds – the bigger ones with a loft. There's also a small but great wood sundeck and games room. It's right on the main drag, in the middle of the bustle.

Hotel Mojomar HOTEL $$$
(☎407300; www.hotelmojomar.com.ar; Burriquetas 247; d from AR$550; ❄📶) This upscale but not luxurious hotel is nicely located three blocks off Av Bunge, but a block from the beach. There's a beautiful lobby and small, comfortable rooms, some with sea view; go for a suite if you need more space.

Hotel Trinidad HOTEL $$
(☎488983; hoteltrinidad@telpin.com.ar; Del Cangrejo 1370; r AR$300;📶) Right near Hospedaje Acacia and a good budget option in Pinamar, this hotel has 26 pleasant rooms with small bathrooms and cable TV.

Hotel La Gaviota HOTEL $$
(☎482079; Del Cangrejo 1332; d AR$300) Twenty tidy, almost pretty rooms are available at this slightly unusual hotel. Many rooms surround a cute back patio dotted with flowers; no breakfast.

Hospedaje Acacia HOSPEDAJE $
(☎485175; Del Cangrejo 1358; d AR$200) Good basic cheapie with old mattresses, a few blocks from Pinamar's tourist office and about a 15-minute walk to the beach. There's a little garden patio in back; no breakfast.

OSTENDE & VALERIA

Pinamar has little budget accommodation – it might be worth heading to Ostende and Valeria, a few kilometers away, where you'll find low-key lodgings close to the beach.

To get here from Pinamar's bus station you can always taxi, but you can also take the 'Montemar' bus for AR$3; it stops a block away from Hostería Candela (at Valeria's roundabout) and passes right by Camping Saint Tropez, which is a block from Albergue Bruno Valente.

Hosteria Candela HOSTERÍA $$
(☎486788; Jorge 434, Valeria; r AR$300; 📶) Just two blocks from the beach at Valeria is this good family-run place with eight clean, spacious rooms and a nice grassy garden.

Camping Saint Tropez CAMPGROUND $
(☎482498; www.sainttropezpinamar.com.ar; Quintana 178, Ostende; campsite for 2 persons with tent AR$90; ⌚Oct-Apr) Due to its location near the beach, this small site fills up in summer. Apartments also available (from AR$300).

Albergue Bruno Valente HOSTEL $
(☎402783; info@aaaj.org.ar; cnr Mitre & Nuestras Malvinas, Ostende; dm AR$70) In Ostende, about 10 blocks south of Pinamar's center, is this seriously ugly hostel – but perhaps the remodel will change this. It's just steps from the beach; look for it behind Hotel Soleado. Could be closed outside summer.

Eating

The beach is lined with restaurants serving beach grub like fried calamari and burgers.

TOP CHOICE **Acqua & Farina** PIZZERIA $$
(cnr Cerezo & Boyero, Cariló; mains AR$27-50; ⌚lunch & dinner) Head to Cariló for the best thin-crust pizza around, as well as fresh salads and homemade pastas. Located in Cariló plaza, the last stop for the local 'Montemar' bus.

Cantina Tulumei SEAFOOD $$
(Bunge 64; mains AR$40-80; ⌚lunch & dinner) A good place for reasonably priced, quality seafood. Fish is prepared in at least a dozen different sauces, or go for the shrimp omelette and octopus salad. Homemade pastas also available.

Tante INTERNATIONAL $$$
(De las Artes 35; mains AR$60-80; ⌚breakfast, lunch & dinner) This classy restaurant, bar and tea room was the home of a well-known soprano who wowed the crowds in the '50s. Now it specializes in gourmet meat dishes and European specialties such as fondue, though it also serves homemade pasta and fish.

Information

Municipal tourist office (☎491680; cnr Av Bunge & Shaw; ⌚8am-9pm)
Post office (Jasón 524)

Getting There & Away

Pinamar's bus terminal is about eight blocks north of the town center, just off Av Bunge. Destinations include Buenos Aires (AR$130, six hours), Mar del Plata (AR$50, 2½ hours) and San Clemente del Tuyú (AR$30, 2½ hours). There are frequent buses to nearby Villa Gesell (AR$12, 30 to 45 minutes).

Trains may or may not be running from Buenos Aires Constitución train station to Pinamar's Estación Divisadero, about 2km north of town.

Villa Gesell

02255 / POP 32,000

Smaller and less flashy than its neighbors Pinamar and Mar del Plata, laid-back Villa Gesell is still a hit with the younger crowd. Uniquely for the coastal towns, it offers a wood-planked beach boardwalk, making walks along the sands much easier. It's also known for summer choral performances and rock and folk concerts, and there are plenty of outdoor activities to enjoy. The town is compact, with most services located on its main drag, Av 3, three blocks from the beach.

In the 1930s, merchant, inventor and nature lover Carlos Gesell designed this resort of zigzag streets, planting acacias, poplars, oaks and pines to stabilize the shifting dunes. Though he envisioned a town merging with the forest he had created, it wasn't long before high-rise vacation shares began their malignant growth and the trees started to disappear.

Sights & Activities

The **Muelle de Pesca** (Playa & Paseo 129), Gesell's 15m fishing pier, offers year-round fishing for mackerel, rays, shark and other marine species.

You can rent surf gear from **Windy** (474626; www.windyplayabar.com.ar; Paseo 104), down on the beachfront. For bicycle rentals try **Casa Macca** (468013; Av Buenos Aires btw Paseo 101 & Av 5). Surfing and horseback riding are other popular activities.

Aventura Faro Querandí (468989; cnr Av 3 & Paseo 132) runs four-hour tours in 4WD jeeps to a local lighthouse.

For a totally different atmosphere visit **Mar de las Pampas**, an exclusive woodsy neighborhood that's a 15-minute bus ride south from Villa Gesell's bus terminal. It has sandy streets, expensive lodging (rented only by the week in summer) and upscale services – all dropped into a pine forest. The beach here is less crowded, too. Beyond Mar de las Pampas is **Mar Azul**, another (less exclusive) beach town.

There's a nightly **feria artesanal** (crafts fair; Av 3 btwn Paseos 112 & 113) from mid-December to mid-March. Expect lots of handmade jewelry, carved wood, paintings and the usual souvenirs.

Sleeping

Campgrounds charge around AR$60 to AR$80 per person per night. Most close at the end of March, but two at the southern end of town on Av 3 (at the beach) are open all year: **Autocamping Casablanca** (470771; www.autocampingcasablanca.com) and **Camping Monte Bubi** (470732; www.montebubi.com.ar). Both have lots of services and *cabaña*-style accommodations. The Mar Azul bus from the terminal goes right by.

Costa Bonita HOSPEDAJE **$$**
(462457; www.gesellcostabonita.com.ar; Av 4, No 648; r AR$390; wi-fi) Twenty-two tastefully decorated rooms with high ceilings are available at this small, family-run guesthouse in a residential neighborhood near the center. Upstairs rooms have more light. There's also a tiny gravel patio area to hang out in.

Hotel Tamanacos HOTEL **$$$**
(468753; tamanacos@gesell.com.ar; cnr Paseo 103 & Av 1; s/d AR$250/450; wi-fi) One block from the beach, this cute hotel has some nice common areas, particularly the front deck. The 21 small, homey rooms have tiny baths, but with beach umbrellas provided you won't be in them most of the time.

Hotel Merimar HOTEL **$$**
(462243; www.gesell.com.ar/hotelmerimar; cnr Paseo 107 & Playa; r AR$460; wi-fi) Rooms here have old carpets and outdated furniture, but if you score a beachfront room with balcony (reserve ahead, they're the same price!), the views are worth it. If you can't get a view, at least the breakfast salon has them, and you're still near the beach.

Residencial Viya HOSPEDAJE **$$**
(462757; www.gesell.com.ar/viya; Av 5, No 582, btwn Paseos 105 & 106; d AR$350) Rooms are simple, with open-shower bathrooms, but they're comfortable enough at this family-run *residencial* (budget hotel) on a quiet street. The best rooms open to the central leafy garden.

La Deseada Hostel HOSTEL **$$**
(473276; www.ladeseadahostel.com.ar; cnr Av 6 & Paseo 119; dm AR$150; @ wi-fi) Good-looking hostel

tucked away six blocks from the beach and a 15-minute walk from the center. Good common areas and grassy garden; dorms have eight beds. Much quieter outside summer, when prices fall and private rooms are available. Dog on premises.

Hospedaje Villa Gesell HOSPEDAJE $
(☎466368; www.hospedajevillagesell.com.ar; Av 3, No 812; r AR$300) You can't get more cheap or central than this family-run spot with 10 budget rooms, most around a little patio area. There's also a garden in back.

Eating

Las Margaritas ITALIAN $$
(☎456377; Av 2, No 484, btwn Paseos 104 & 105; mains AR$40-60; ⊙dinner) Charmingly cozy and quiet, this place serves excellent homemade pasta, including a shrimp and squid ink ravioli. The tiramisú is excellent. Reserve in summer.

La Delfina PARRILLA $$
(cnr Paseo 104 & Av 2; mains AR$35-60; ⊙lunch & dinner) A huge menu means there's something for everyone at this popular *parrilla*. If you need some extra protein, try the 'El Supremo' *bife de chorizo* – a steak that comes with two eggs and bacon. There's also a low-calorie section and everything in-between.

Sutton 212 ARGENTINE $$
(cnr Paseo 105 & Ave 2; mains AR$40-60; ⊙breakfast, lunch & dinner) This lively restaurant-bar serves dishes ranging from Mediterranean to Asian fusion, along with gourmet crepes, sushi and sandwiches. There's live bossa nova and jazz at dinner, then a DJ later in the evening, when the place becomes a happening bar.

La Pachamama ARGENTINE $
(Av 2, No 411; empanadas AR$4.50, pizzas AR$22-30; ⊙lunch & dinner) This casual eatery bakes up delicious Salta-style empanadas and fresh pizzas – perfect for a quick budget meal. Covered wood booths in front.

Information

Post office (cnr Av 3 & Paseo 108)

Tourist office (☎478042; Paseo 107 btwn Avs 2 & 3; ⊙8am-8pm) Conveniently located in the center. Also at the bus terminal.

Getting There & Away

The **bus terminal** (cnr Av 3 & Paseo 140) is 30 blocks south of the town center; a local bus ride to the center takes 20 minutes.

Destinations include Buenos Aires (AR$150, six hours), Mar del Plata (AR$32, two hours) and Pinamar (AR$8, 30 to 45 minutes). You can buy bus tickets in the town center at **Central de Pasajes** (☎472480; cnr Av 3 & Paseo 107), saving you a trip to the terminal.

Mar del Plata

☎0223 / POP 650,000

Four hundred kilometers from Buenos Aires lies Mar del Plata ('Mardel'), the premier Argentine beach destination for *porteños*. If you end up here on a summer weekend, you'll be guaranteed to say 'Wow, this beach is crowded.' There might a couple of places where you could get in a few swimming strokes without taking somebody's eye out, but mostly it's shoulder-to-shoulder, sun-frazzled bodies. After spending a few days on its comically packed sands, watching street performers on the beachside Plaza Colón or exploring the wonders of the port, however, you might get the sense of adoration that the country feels for this place.

During the week, and especially outside of summer, the crowds disperse, hotel prices drop and the place takes on a more relaxed feel. And if summer crowds don't appeal, visit in spring or autumn, when prices are lower and the area's natural attractions are easier to enjoy. After all, Mardel is a large city and has attractions other than its beach.

Rivadavia becomes a pedestrian street only during the summer months; San Martín is always pedestrian.

History

Europeans were slow to occupy this stretch of the coast, so Mardel was a late bloomer. Not until 1747 did Jesuit missionaries try to evangelize the southern pampas indigenous people; the only reminder of their efforts is a chapel replica near Laguna de los Padres.

More than a century later, Portuguese investors established El Puerto de Laguna de los Padres. Beset by economic problems in the 1860s, they sold out to Patricio Peralta Ramos, who founded Mar del Plata proper in 1874. Peralta Ramos helped develop the area as a commercial and industrial center, and later as a beach resort. By the turn of the century, many wealthy *porteño* families owned summer houses, some of which still grace Barrio Los Troncos.

Since the 1960s the 'Pearl of the Atlantic' has lost some of its exclusivity with the Argentine elite seeking refuge in resorts such as nearby Pinamar or Punta del Este (Uruguay). Still, Mar del Plata remains the most thriving Argentine beach town.

Sights

Beaches BEACHES

Mar del Plata's beaches are mostly safe and swimmable. Downtown fronts onto the most central beach, **Playa Bristol**, with its wharf and restaurant; the boardwalk here, next to the casino area, is always packed with activity. The next beach to the north is **Playa La Perla**, favored by a younger crowd and filled with *balnearios* (bathing resorts, or section of beach with services such as beach chairs and parasols). To the south of Punta Piedras (Torreón) are **Playa Varese** and **Cabo Corrientes**, a pair of small beaches that are protected by small rocky headlands.

South of these beaches, at the more fashionable end of town, lies **Playa Grande**, also crowded with *balnearios*. About 11km south of center, just past the port, you'll find the huge **Punta Mogotes** complex – slightly more relaxed and favored by families, who fill the *balnearios* to overflowing in January. This is also the location of **Playa Waikiki**, a popular spot for surfing.

Beyond the lighthouse is a less urbanized area. Though the beaches here are still filled with yet more *balnearios* in the summer, they're a quieter option. And for the adventurous, there's **Playa Escondida** (www.playaescondida.com.ar), some 25km south of Mardel and possibly Argentina's only legal nude beach. Bus 221 gets you there.

Museums

Built in 1909 as the summer residence of a prominent Argentine family, the Villa Ortiz Basualdo is now the **Museo Municipal de Arte Juan Carlos Castagnino** (Av Colón 1189; admission AR$8, Wed free; ⌚5-10pm). Resembling a Loire Valley castle, its Belgian interior exhibits paintings, photographs and sculptures by Argentine artists.

In the Villa Emilio Mitre (1930), another former summer residence of the Argentine oligarchy, lies the **Museo Archivo Histórico Municipal Roberto T Barili** (Lamadrid 3870; admission AR$5; ⌚8am-5pm Mon-Fri, 5-9pm Sat & Sun). Inside is a small but good museum of Mardel's history, told through well-displayed relics such as 1800s clothing and photographs. Check out the view from the 3rd-floor tower.

Housing the most extensive seashell collection you're ever likely to see, the **Museo del Mar** (Av Colón 1114; admission AR$30; ⌚10am-11pm) exhibits more than 30,000 shells, representing 6000 species from around the world. The museum also contains a small tide pool and aquarium.

Kids and science fans might enjoy the **Museo Municipal de Ciencias Naturales** (Av Libertad 3099; admission AR$5, Wed free; ⌚10am-5:30pm), a small science museum with aquarium and dinosaur bones. In summer special exhibitions can skyrocket the admission fee and they're only open in the evenings.

WORTH A TRIP

MAR CHIQUITA

A humble and windy little gem, the beach-side village of Mar Chiquita is home to **Albúfera Mar Chiquita**, a 35km-long lagoon with huge biodiversity – over 220 bird and 55 fish species live within its waters. There's good fishing in the area, and the beach is popular for windsurfing and kiteboarders – or just hanging out for a bit.

A good and homey place to stay is **Hostería Bariloche** (☎469-1254; mchpao@hotmail.com; cnr Beltran & Echeverría; s/d from AR$180/200; @) a friendly, family-run place with 10 rooms and apartments. They also rent-wind sports equipment and give lessons. Campers can head to **Camping Santa Rosa** (☎469-1300; cnr Rivera del Sol & playa; campsites for four people AR$100).

The **visitors center** (☎469-1288; cnr Belgrano & Rivera del Sol; ⌚8am-8pm) is at the beach; if it's not open, call nearby Santa Clara's **tourist office** (☎460-2433). It organizes tours around the lagoon (reserve ahead). Bring money – the closest ATM is 4km away in Mar de Cabo.

Mar Chiquita is 34km north of Mar del Plata. Rápido del Sud runs frequent buses that can drop you at the highway 2.5km outside Mar Chiquita (they don't enter town). Most No 221 local buses do enter town (double check with the driver) and run every two hours in summer to/from Mar del Plata.

Mar del Plata

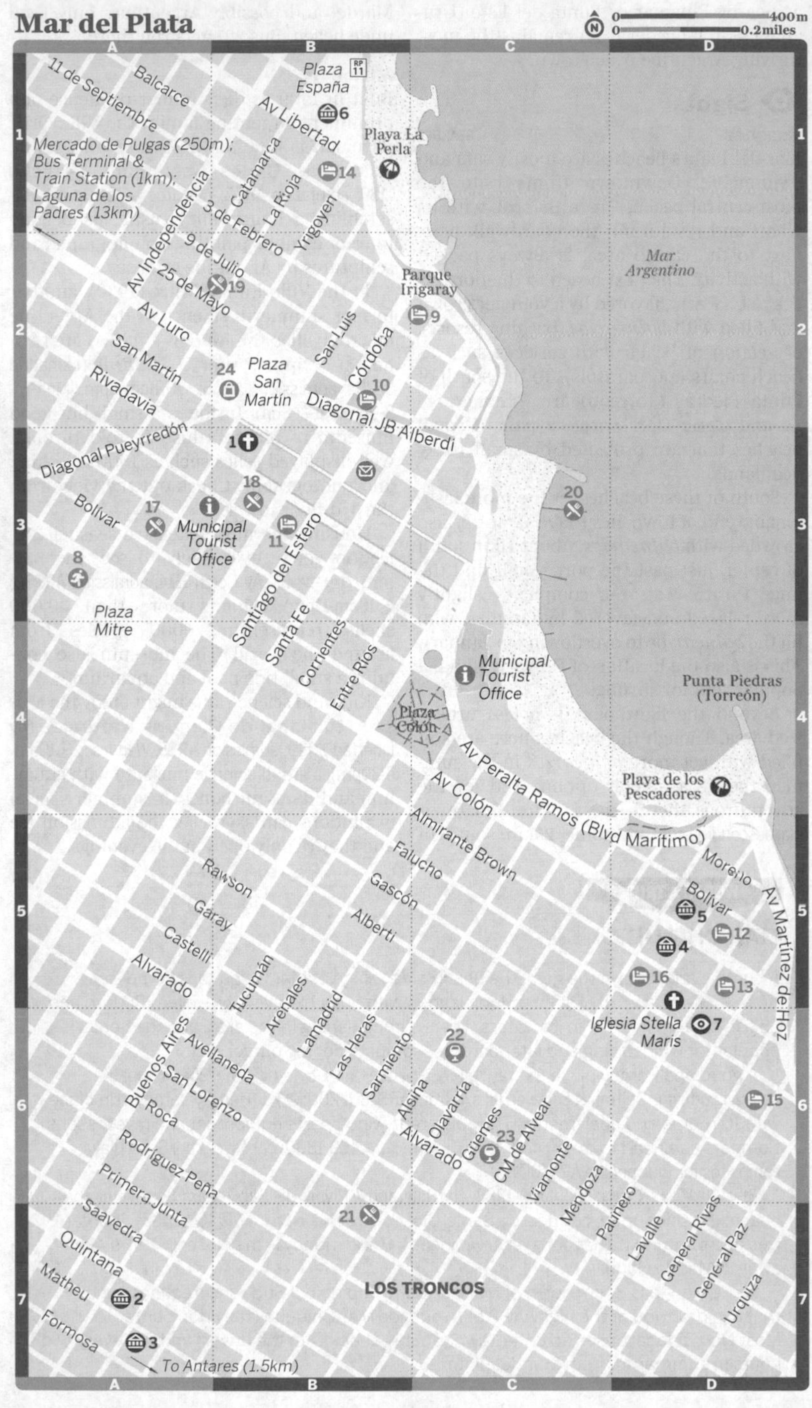
0 400m
0 0.2miles
Plaza España
Playa La Perla
Mercado de Pulgas (250m); Bus Terminal & Train Station (1km); Laguna de los Padres (13km)
Mar Argentino
Parque Irigaray
Plaza San Martín
Municipal Tourist Office
Plaza Mitre
Municipal Tourist Office
Plaza Colón
Punta Piedras (Torreón)
Playa de los Pescadores
Iglesia Stella Maris
LOS TRONCOS
To Antares (1.5km)
11 de Septiembre
Balcarce
Av Libertad
Catamarca
La Rioja
Yrigoyen
Av Independencia
3 de Febrero
9 de Julio
25 de Mayo
Av Luro
San Martín
Rivadavia
San Luis
Córdoba
Diagonal JB Alberdi
Diagonal Pueyrredón
Bolívar
Santiago del Estero
Santa Fe
Corrientes
Entre Ríos
Av Peralta Ramos (Blvd Marítimo)
Av Colón
Almirante Brown
Falucho
Gascón
Alberti
Moreno
Bolívar
Av Martínez de Hoz
Rawson
Garay
Castelli
Alvarado
Tucumán
Arenales
Lamadrid
Las Heras
Sarmiento
Buenos Aires
Avellaneda
San Lorenzo
Roca
Rodríguez Peña
Primera Junta
Saavedra
Quintana
Matheu
Formosa
Alsina
Olavarría
Alvarado
Güemes
CM de Alvear
Viamonte
Mendoza
Paunero
Lavalle
General Rivas
General Paz
Urquiza

Mar del Plata

Puerto Mar del Plata PORT

Mar del Plata is one of the country's most important fishing locations and seafood-processing centers, and its port area – located 8km south of the city center – is worth a visit.

At the entrance to the port, just off Av Martínez de Hoz, you'll see a large cluster of seafood restaurants surrounding a parking lot. This is the **Centro Comercial del Puerto**, and it's a good place to grab a bite to eat; just pick a place that looks busy.

You can also take your bus (see following) directly to the port's scenic and slightly touristy wharf, called the **Banquina de Pescadores**, which lies beyond the restaurant cluster – this saves you a 10-minute walk through an ugly industrial area. This picturesque wharf is home to dozens of orange fishing boats and the fisherfolk who follow their routine here. You might see a sea lion's head poking out of the water; these animals have established a large colony – all male – nearby on the *escollera sur* (southern jetty).

To get to this jetty, tromp south of the wharf about a block or so (there is no real path) and go past the port's security entrance, then turn left onto the road. This is another ugly industrial area, but eventually becomes the more pleasant jetty that leads 2km out to sea. On the way you'll pass a graveyard of **ruined ships**, half-sunken and rusting in the sun, and are likely see the colony of male sea lions lazing on a beach or behind a section of chain link fence. And at the tip of the windy *escollera sur* is a restaurant, which offers nourishment, along with panoramic views of the city.

Local bus 511 goes all the way to the wharf from downtown; you'll need a magnetic card to board (see later under 'Getting Around'). Bus 221 only reaches the seafood restaurants at the port's entrance. A taxi costs AR$50.

Centro Cultural Villa Victoria CULTURAL CENTER

(☎492-0569; Matheu 1851; admission AR$8; ⏲10am-1pm, 5-9pm in Jan & Feb, 2-8pm Wed-Mon from Mar-Dec) Victoria Ocampo, founder of the literary journal *Sur*, hosted literary salons with prominent intellectuals from around the world at this, her summer chalet. It's now a cultural center that features changing art and cultural exhibitions.

Catedral de los Santos Pedro y Cecilia CATHEDRAL

Facing the leafy Plaza San Martín, this neo-Gothic building features gorgeous stained glass, an impressive central chandelier from France, English tiled floors and occasional choral concerts.

FREE **Torre Tanque** WATER TOWER

(☎451-4681; Falucho 995; admission free; ⏲8am-4pm Mon-Fri) This interesting medieval water storage tower, atop Stella Maris hill, was finished in 1943 and is still functioning. It offers awesome views over Mar del Plata and further out to sea.

Aquarium Mar del Plata AQUARIUM

(☎467-0700; www.aquariummardelplata.com; Av Martínez de Hoz 5600; adult/child 3-10yr AR$98/70; ⏲10am-8pm) Located 14km south of the center, near the lighthouse, is Mar del Plata's aquarium. Animals on display include penguins, flamingos, crocodiles and lots of fish. There are sea-lion, dolphin and waterskiing shows, along with a cinema. You can also swim with sharks (among other watery creatures) and sit on the beach. Get here on bus 221 or 511.

Laguna de los Padres LAKE

A popular weekend destination for *marplatenses,* this lake offers a bucolic setting and a range of activities, including bird-watching, fishing, water sports, biking, hiking and rock climbing. The area was first settled in 1746 as a Jesuit Mission aimed at rounding up the nomadic tribes of the area – there's a replica of the original chapel by the lake's shore. You can camp near the lake, and there are good places to eat in the pleasant nearby town of Sierra de los Padres.

The lake is just 13km out of Mardel along RN 226; the town is 4km further. Bus 717 (from Av Luro in Mardel; buy a magnetic card first, see p135) goes to Sierra de los Padres, but it doesn't take the side road to the lake – you'll have to get off at the highway and walk a kilometer just to reach the shore, or double back from Sierra de los Padres in a *remise.*

Activities

Mar del Plata and its surrounds offer plenty of opportunity to enjoy outdoor activities and adventure sports.

Biking is a good, green way to get around town. The streets of Los Troncos are relatively calm and pleasant for cycling. Bicycles can be rented from **Bicicletería Madrid** (☎494-1932; Yrigoyen 2249).

Surf is best in March or April. **Kikiwai Surf School** (☎485-0669; www.kikiwaisurfclub.com.ar; Av Martínez de Hoz 4100), run by surf pioneer Daniel Gil, offers surfing classes and rents boards; find it at Waikiki beach (about 11km south of center).

As the sea lions attest, Mar del Plata is one of the best spots for fishing in Argentina. The rocky outcrop at **Cabo Corrientes**, just north of Playa Grande, is a good spot to try, as are the two breakwaters – **Escollera Norte** and **Escollera Sur** – at the port. Freshwater fishing is popular at Laguna de los Padres (see opposite), while **Mako Team** (☎493-5338; www.makoteam.com.ar) offers ocean fishing excursions.

The rocky cliffs by the sea and the hills of Sierra de los Padres make for excellent climbing and rappelling. **Acción Directa** (☎474-4520; www.acciondirecta.com.ar) runs a school – it also offers mountain biking, canoeing and overnight active camping trips.

Horseback riding and skydiving are possibilities – contact the tourist office for details.

Tours

Crucero Anamora CRUISE

(☎489-0310; www.cruceroanamora.com.ar) This 30m boat offers harbor tours several times daily in summer (AR$79) and twice daily on weekends in winter from Dársena B at the port.

Municipal Tourist Office WALKING TOUR

(Blvd Marítimo) Conducts free organized tours (called 'Paseos Para Gente Inquieta')

LITERARY LADY OF LA PLATA

She was 'the most beautiful cow in the pampas' according to French novelist Pierre Drieu, and Jorge Luis Borges called her 'the most Argentine of women.' In the 1920s and 1930s, Victoria Ocampo gathered writers and intellectuals from around the globe to her home, Villa Victoria (p131), creating a formidable literary and artistic salon.

Ocampo never went to university, but her voracious appetite for knowledge and love of literature led her to become Argentina's leading lady of letters. She founded the literary magazine *Sur,* which introduced writers such as Virginia Woolf and TS Eliot to Argentine readers. She was also an inexhaustible traveler and a pioneering feminist, and was loathed for her lack of convention. A ferocious opponent of Peronism, chiefly because of Perón's interference with intellectual freedom, Ocampo was arrested at Villa Victoria at the age of 63. She entertained her fellow inmates by reading aloud and acting out scenes from novels and cinema.

If Victoria is remembered as a lively essayist and great patroness of writers, her younger sister, Silvina, was the literary talent, writing both short stories and poetry. Silvina won several literary prizes for her works, and in 1940 married Adolfo Bioy Casares, a famous Argentine writer and friend of Jorge Luis Borges.

of unusual city sights, such as an alfajor or textile factory – though they also go to the port and museums. Reserve ahead at the main tourist office (p135).

Festivals & Events

The city's **International Film Festival** (www.mardelplatafilmfest.com) takes place in November. Launched in 1950, it's South America's most important film festival.

In January Mar del Plata also celebrates **Fiesta Nacional del los Pescadores** (Fisherman's Festival), which sees locals cooking up seafood feasts, along with a traditional procession.

Another large celebration is February's **Fiesta Nacional del Mar** (National Sea Festival), which includes the election and coronation of a 'Sea Queen.'

Sleeping

Prices start climbing in November and December, are highest in January and February, then drop off in March. Reserve ahead during peak times. In the off-season some of Mar del Plata's accommodations close their doors.

Mar del Plata's crowded campgrounds are mostly south of town; the tourist office prints out information about their facilities.

TOP CHOICE El Aleph Hotel Boutique BOUTIQUE GUESTHOUSE $$$
(451-4380; www.elalephmdq.com.ar; LN Alem 2542; r AR$480-640) Most of the lovely rooms are set around covered wood walkways and a grassy garden with small pool, offering an upscale paradise. The feel is exclusive but relaxed, with afternoon tea and wine tastings on tap, and kitchen use available. Reservations necessary; no children under 12; cash payment only. Located a couple blocks south of Playa Varese.

TOP CHOICE Villa Nuccia GUESTHOUSE $$$
(451-6593; www.villanuccia.com.ar; Almirante Brown 1134; d AR$690) This beautiful guesthouse is in a renovated house, and offers eight simple yet elegant and spacious rooms – a couple have balconies and most come with whirlpool tubs. There's a large green lawn out back with a swimming pool and Jacuzzi; afternoon tea service is offered. Run by a young, traveling Argentine couple.

Playa Varese Inn HOSTERÍA $$
(451-1813; www.playavareseinn.com.ar; Gascón 715; r AR$250) Fifteen simple, comfortable and good-sized rooms with concrete floors are on offer at this nice little *hostería*. It's just 1½ blocks from the beach and has cable TV. Reserve ahead; it's popular.

Hotel Sirenuse HOTEL $$
(451-9580; www.hotelsirenuse.com.ar; Mendoza 2240; d AR$330-430) A good choice just a few blocks from Playa Varese is this friendly, family-run place. All rooms have a warm and homey feel, with a European touch – not a surprise given that the owners are French-German-Argentine. Various languages spoken.

City Hotel HOTEL $$
(495-3018; www.cityhotelmardelplata.com; Diagonal JB Alberdi 2561; d AR$360-450) This large, worker-owned cooperative hotel has an old-school feel and delightful back garden. It's worth paying a bit extra for the 'superior' rooms – they're larger and their bathrooms come with bathtubs; the front ones have balconies. Two-room 'apartments' (no kitchen) available.

Etoile HOTEL $$
(493-4968; www.hoteletoilemdq.com.ar; Santiago del Estero 1869; d AR$400) Its central location, plus spacious carpeted rooms (some with long 'entry' space and sofa), make this place good value. Get a quieter room in back – they're still bright. Buffet breakfast.

Alta Esperanza Hostel HOSTEL $
(495-8650; www.altaesperanzahostel.com.ar; Av Peralta Ramos 1361; dm AR$85-125, r AR$320-350) Proud to be Mardel's first waterfront hostel, and located in an historic, Normandy-style building. Offers six- to 12-bed dorms and a few private rooms, and best for non-party types – this is a place to relax. Try to reserve a sea-view room. Occasional art shows or cultural events are hosted here.

La Pergola Hostel HOSTEL $
(493-3695; www.lapergolahostel.com.ar; Yrigoyen 1093; dm AR$70) A decent hostel in a cool old Tudor-like building. Some of the four- and eight-bed wood-floor dorms have balcony and partial sea views, and there's a great terrace with pergola. The dining/communal/games area is in the cold basement, though. One private room in high season (AR$250); dog on premises.

Hostel del Mar HOSTEL $
(☎486-3112; www.hosteldelmar.com.ar; Av Colón 1051; dm AR$80-100; @) Here's a very casual, small hostel just 1½ blocks from the beach, with nice grassy back garden. Bathrooms can get tight when it's full. It's big on surfing, offering board rentals and lessons; bike rentals also available.

Eating

Mar del Plata's numerous restaurants, pizzerias and snack bars often struggle to keep up with impatient crowds between December and March, and there are always long lines. For fresh seafood head south of town to the port, which has several restaurants cooking up the catch of the day.

TOP CHOICE **Taberna Baska** BASQUE $$
(☎480-0209; 12 de Octubre 3301; mains AR$35-90; ⏲lunch & dinner) Just a few blocks inland from the port is this renowned Basque restaurant, running for over 50 years. It has old-school atmosphere and serves up delicious dishes like garlic shrimp, mixed seafood stews, fish in seven kinds of sauce, and *bacalao* (dried, salted cod).

Tisiano ITALIAN $$
(San Lorenzo 1332; mains AR$50-70; ⏲lunch & dinner) Locally recommended, fine Italian restaurant – start with the salmon carpaccio and follow up with the chicken and spinach crepes, squash *sorrentinos* (large, round filled pastas) or linguini with shrimp. Seven kinds of gourmet salads as well.

El Palacio del Bife PARRILLA $$$
(Córdoba 1857; mains AR$60-80; ⏲lunch & dinner) A recommended, classy *parrilla* with a massive menu. Come hungry and come wanting meat, although the homemade pastas are also worth a try. There's also seafood, *milanesas* (breaded cutlets) and rice dishes. Not cheap, but portions are large. Takeout food 20% off.

Viento en Popa SEAFOOD $$
(☎489-0220; Martínez de Hoz 257; mains AR$35-80; ⏲lunch & dinner) A very popular restaurant, Viento en Popa cooks up beef, chicken and pasta dishes – but seafood is its specialty. Only the freshest ingredients are used for the fried calamari, seafood stew and various sautéed fish plates. Look for it a couple blocks short of port's restaurants, just north of the YPF gas station.

Montecatini ARGENTINE $$
(☎492-4299; cnr La Rioja & 25 de Mayo; mains AR$40-70; ⏲lunch & dinner,) For solid, good-value dishes, make like the locals and head to this large, modern and popular restaurant. There's something for everyone on the menu – meat, fish, pasta, *milanesas*, stirfrys, sandwiches – and portions are generous. Good for families and large groups; several branches around town.

Pescadores SEAFOOD $$
(☎493-1713; Blvd Marítimo & Av Luro; AR$40-70; ⏲lunch & dinner) Located out on the fishing pier, this seafood restaurant offers great water views – especially from its 2nd floor (open in summer only). The menu runs through typical Mardel offerings of meat, pasta and seafood, but you're here for the views.

El Jamón INTERNATIONAL $
(☎493-7447; Bolívar 2801; mains AR$30-45; ⏲lunch Mon-Sat, dinner Wed-Sat) There's little atmosphere at this neighborhood favorite, with plastic plants swinging from the beams. It's still full of locals, however, all enjoying the roasted *vacio* (flank steak), shrimp kebab or mussels provencal (menu choices change daily).

Drinking

At the Playa Grande end of town, the areas along Irigoyen and LN Alem, between Almafuerte and Rodríguez Peña, are popular nightlife magnets.

Antares BAR
(Córdoba 3025; ⏲8pm-late) The eight homebrews on tap at Mar del Plata's only microbrewery include imperial stout, pale ale and barley wine – excellent cures for the Quilmes blues. Food is available and there is live music most weekends.

Almacén Condal BAR
(cnr Alsina & Garay; ⏲9am-late) For traditional old atmosphere (the building is over 100 years old), you can't beat this funky corner bar. Talk to the locals at the long bar while munching the pub grub – it's sure to take you back in time.

La Bodeguita del Medio CUBAN BAR
(Castelli 1252; ⏲7pm-late) Named after one of Hemingway's favorite haunts, the mojitos at this atmospheric joint do him proud and are two-for-one between 7pm and 9pm. The Cuban dishes and bar snacks go down well, and there's occasional live music.

Shopping

Calle Güemes is lined with upscale stores.

Diagonal de los Artesanos CRAFTS FAIR
(Plaza San Martín; 6pm-late) Vendors set up their stalls every summer evening on Plaza San Martín to sell everything from *mate* gourds and knives to sweaters and silverwork. Open Friday and Saturday afternoons outside summer.

Mercado de Pulgas FLEA MARKET
(Plaza Rocha; 10am-8pm Fri-Sun) This relaxed flea market, selling everything including the kitchen sink, is at 20 de Septiembre between San Martín and Av Luro, seven blocks northwest of Plaza San Martín.

Information

Money

There are several money exchanges along San Martín and Rivadavia.

Jonestur (San Martín 2574)

La Moneta (Rivadavia 2623)

Post

Post office (Av Luro 2460 & Santiago del Estero)

Tourist Information

Municipal tourist office (495-1777; www.turismomardelplata.gov.ar; Blvd Marítimo 2270, in edificio casino; 8am-10pm) Exceptionally helpful. A smaller office is at Belgrano 2740.

Getting There & Away

Air

Aerolíneas Argentinas (496-0101; Moreno 2442) has several daily flights to Buenos Aires.

LADE (491-1484; Corrientes 1537) is cheaper but flies much less frequently.

Bus

Mar del Plata's sparkling bus terminal is next to its the train station, about 2km northwest of the beach. To get to the center, take local bus Nos 511, 512 or 513; taxis cost AR$25.

At the corner of San Martín and Corrientes, in the city center, are a couple of travel offices that sell long-distance bus tickets – saving you a possible trip to the bus terminal.

Train

The **train station** (475-6076; Av Luro 4500) is 2km from the beach. There are regular overnight trains from Buenos Aires' Constitución train station (AR$60-80, six hours), along with the fancier *Marplatense* and *Talgo* trains (AR$100-200, six hours, day and evening departures). Reserve tickets well ahead in summer.

Getting Around

The **airport** (478-0744) is 10km north of the city. To get there by bus, take bus No 542 (marked 'aeropuerto') from the corner of Blvd Marítimo and Belgrano.

Despite Mar del Plata's sprawl, frequent buses reach just about every place in town. However, most buses take magnetic cards ('tarjetas de aproximación') that must be bought ahead of time at *kioskos* and charged up. Popular bus 221 is an exception: it takes coins. The tourist office is a great resource for more transport details.

Car rentals are available at **Budget** (495-2935; Córdoba 2270).

BUSES FROM MAR DEL PLATA

DESTINATION	COST (AR$)	DURATION (HR)
Bahía Blanca	145	7
Bariloche	525	18-20
Buenos Aires	145-165	5½
Córdoba	415	16-18
Mendoza	470	18-20
Necochea	45	2¼
Pinamar	45	2½
Puerto Madryn	365	17
Tandil	55	3
Villa Gesell	32	2

Necochea

02262 / POP 92,000

Totally pumping in summer and near dead in winter, Necochea's beach-town feel is undisturbed by the highrises that keep springing up. With nearly 70km of beachfront, it's fairly certain that you'll be able to find a spot to lay your towel. Windy Necochea also has the best waves on the coast, attracting surfers throughout the year. The foresty Parque Municipal Miguel Lillo is a great bonus here, as are the walking and horseback riding opportunities out to the west of town. Another plus is that Necochea offers some of the best-value lodging on the coast.

Most of Necochea's services, such as the post office, banks and bus terminal, are inland about 3km from the beach.

Sights & Activities

The dense pine woods of **Parque Provincial Miguel Lillo**, a large greenbelt along the beach, are widely used for cycling, horseback riding, walking and picnicking. Horses and bikes can both be rented inside the park.

The Río Quequén Grande, rich in rainbow trout and mackerel, also allows for easy rafting, particularly around the falls at **Saltos del Quequén**. At the village of **Quequén** at the river's mouth, several stranded shipwrecks offer good opportunities for exploration and photography below sculpted cliffs. The **faro** (lighthouse) is another local attraction.

With some of the best waves along the Atlantic coast, Necochea is a hit with surfers. One surf school is **Monte Pasubio Surf Camp** (451482; www.montepasubio.com.ar; Av 502, No 1160), across the river in Quequén, where you can arrange classes and rent boards in summer.

Sleeping

Note that some accommodations are only open December to March.

The following are all within four blocks of the beach.

Hostería del Bosque HOTEL **$$**
(420002; www.hosteria-delbosque.com.ar; Calle 89, No 350; r AR$390-460;) This *hostería* is by far the most atmospheric place to stay in town. Rooms are large and comfortable, and some have views of Parque Lillo across the street. Nice grassy garden in back.

Belle Maison B&B **$$**
(462335; www.bellemaison.com.ar; Calle 4, btwn Paseos 106 & 107; r from AR$330;) Just five lovely rooms are available at this boutique hotel, actually a large house in a residential neighborhood near the center. Common spaces include a small garden, and there's even a bar counter inside.

Tres Reyes HOTEL **$$**
(522011; www.hotel-tresreyes.com.ar; Calle 4, No 4123; r from AR$360;) With an excellent location right on the square, this hotel has comfortable rooms and suites, some with park view. Next door is the budget **Hotel Mirasol** (www.mirasolhotel.com.ar).

Jamming Hostel HOSTEL **$**
(02262-15-407508; www.jamminghostel.com.ar; Calle 502, No 1685; dm AR$80) This mediterranean-style hostel is near the beach in nearby Quequén, 6km from Necochea's bus terminal (a taxi costs AR$25). It's big on skateboarding and surfing culture. A restaurant and one private room available (AR$180).

Hospedaje La Casona HOSPEDAJE **$**
(423345; Calle 6, No 4356; d AR$200, apt AR$250) This rustic, family-run place offers guests basic rooms along with a spacious garden with a *parrilla*. There are also apartments with kitchenettes.

Eating & Drinking

There are several dining options around Plaza San Martín. Many of the *balnearios* have eateries where you can grab a bite beachside. In low season many restaurants are only open on weekends.

Taberna Española SPANISH **$$$**
(520539; cnr Calle 83 & 80; mains AR$60-90; lunch & dinner) If you're looking for fine seafood, Spanish-style, head to this well-regarded restaurant. The 'special' menu includes a starter, main dish and dessert (AR$70). There's another location next to Hostería del Bosque, Calle 89 No 360. Reserve in summer.

Chimichurri Asador PARRILLA **$$**
(Calle 83, No 345; mains AR$50-70; lunch & dinner) Only carnivores are welcome at this *parrilla*, favored by locals for its delicious meats.

Antares ARGENTINE **$$**
(Calle 4, No 4266; AR$40-70; dinner Tue-Sun) This is yet another branch of the beautiful bar-restaurant chain. There's a decent selection of pub-style food, along with several

WORTH A TRIP

MIRAMAR

If you've got kids consider a side trip to Miramar, a family-friendly destination with long, wide beach and gentle waves (surfable in spots). Compared to Mar del Plata, 45km to the north, Miramar fairly low-key – but like any other Argentine resort it does get crowded in summer.

Get information at the **tourist office** (☎02291-420190; cnr Calle 21 & Costanera; ⏰8am-10pm), located at the beach. Ask about the various activities possible in town, such as horseback riding, golfing or fishing. Miramar is known for its surf, more easily accessible at the north end of town where there are a few surf schools.

For accommodations, consider **Aventureiro Hostel** (☎02291-430981; Calle 16 No 1067; www.aventureiro.com.ar; dm AR$125, r AR$250; @📶), an average hostel but just a couple blocks from the beach; or the pleasant-enough **Hotel Danieli** (☎02291-432366; Calle 24 No 1114; www.hoteldanielimiramar.com.ar; s/d from AR$400/530; 📶). The bus terminal is at Av 40 and Calle 15, within six blocks of the center.

Those looking for downright isolation can head to **Mar de Sud**, a small town 16km south of Miramar. It's known for its rustic atmosphere, black-rock beach and fishing waters – and claims some hotel ruins as a main tourist attraction. There are no tall buildings here and much fewer services than its neighbor, so if you're looking to get away from the crowds this should be your stop.

craft-style beers (actually brewed in Mar del Plata).

If you need a drink, check out the bars on Calle 87 between Calles 4 and 6.

Information

Municipal hospital (☎422405; Av 59, btwn Calles 100 & 104)

Municipal tourist office (☎438333; cnr Avs 2 & 79; ⏰8am-10pm) On the beach; also at the bus terminal from mid-December to March.

Post office (Calle 6, No 4065)

Getting There & Away

The **bus terminal** (Av 58, btw Calle 47 & Av 45) is 3.5km from the beach (taxis cost AR$15, or take local bus 513, marked 'playa'). Destinations include Buenos Aires (AR$176, seven hours), Mar del Plata (AR$45, 2¼ hours), Tandil (AR$45, three hours) and Bahía Blanca (AR$105, five hours).

Bahía Blanca

☎0291 / POP 302,000

Grandiose buildings, an attractive plaza and boulevards lined with shade trees and palms lend oft-overlooked Bahía Blanca the feel of a cosmopolitan city in miniature. Its chief advantage is as a resting point during overland trips from Buenos Aires to Patagonia, but it's not entirely without interest.

The hordes of sailors who dock here, at what is now South America's largest naval base, attest to Bahía Blanca's militaristic beginnings. In an early effort to establish military control on the periphery of the pampas, Colonel Ramón Estomba situated the pompously named Fortaleza Protectora Argentina at the natural harbor of Bahía Blanca in 1828.

Sights & Activities

On the outskirts of town – in a former customs building that's hardly noticeable among the massive grain elevators and fortress-like power plant of Puerto Ingeniero White – the **Museo del Puerto** (☎457-3006; cnr Guillermo Torres & Cárrega; admission by donation; ⏰8am-noon Mon-Fri, 4-8pm Sat & Sun) is a tribute to the region's immigrants, and includes an archive with documents, photographs and recorded oral histories. The best time to visit is for a weekend afternoon tea, when local groups prepare regional delicacies, each week representing a different immigrant group. Take bus 500 from the plaza.

The neoclassical **Teatro Municipal** (Alsina 425) is the performing-arts center. In the same building is **Museo Histórico** (☎456-3117; admission free; ⏰9am-12:30pm Tue-Fri, 4-8pm Wed-Sun). Displays include indigenous artifacts and collections that represent episodes in the life of the region, such as its founding as a military base and the arrival of the railways. Worth checking is **Museo de Arte Contemporáneo** (☎459-4006; Sarmiento 450; admission free; ⏰2-8pm Tue-Fri, 5-8pm Sat & Sun), showcasing local and national artists.

On weekends an afternoon **artisans market** takes over Plaza Rivadavia, opposite the Municipalidad.

Sleeping

Catering mainly to the business set, accommodations in Bahía Blanca are generally more expensive than in other Argentine towns its size; however, good deals can be found.

Rio Oja Apart Hotel HOTEL **$$**
(☎481-9922; www.aparthotelrio-oja.com.ar; Estados Unidos 65; s/d AR$240/300;) If you're just passing through, this modern hotel is a good choice – it's near the bus terminal. The eight rooms are different sizes but efficient and stocked with a tiny closet kitchenette.

Hotel Muñiz HOTEL **$$**
(☎456-0060; www.hotelmuniz.com.ar; O'Higgins 23; s AR$195-315, d AR$290-420; @) Centrally located and in a beautiful old building, the Muñiz offers four levels of decent but unmemorable rooms, and hallways that are cold and tiled. The lobby, however, has great old atmosphere.

Firenze Hotel HOTEL **$**
(☎455-7746; Rondeau 39; s/d AR$130-180;) A good deal for what you get, this small hotel has 17 simple rooms – most with wood floors – in a remodeled old building. Bathrooms have open showers.

Hotel Victoria HOTEL **$**
(☎452-0522; www.hotelvictoriabb.com.ar; General Paz 84; s/d AR$180/290;) This well-kept old building has good, comfortable rooms with cable TV, set around a central courtyard.

Bahía Blanca Hostel HOSTEL **$**
(☎452-6802; www.hostelbahiablanca.com; Soler 701; dm AR$42, s AR$50-70, d AR$100; @) Located in an ancient hotel, this hostel isn't exactly cozy – but staff are friendly. Basic private rooms are set around an old patio; the cheapest share bathrooms. Many transient male workers stay here, so it doesn't have that usual 'international' flavor. Pickup from bus terminal if car is available.

Eating

Piazza ARGENTINE **$$**
(cnr O'Higgins & Chiclana; mains AR$40-55; breakfast, lunch & dinner) A popular cafe on the plaza, with an extensive menu that includes pizza, pasta, meats and gourmet salads and sandwiches. Also 'lite' choices such as soy milanesas. Popular sidewalk tables and a fully stocked bar too.

Bambú BUFFET **$$**
(Chiclana 298; buffet AR$47-56; lunch & dinner) The best deal in town for the hungry is this *tenedor libre* (all-you-can-eat restaurant) efficiently run by a Chinese family. Choose from heaps of cooked dishes (many with Asian flavor), along with Argentine *asado* (barbecue grill); drinks are extra. Very popular, and there's takeout too.

El Mundo de la Parrilla PARRILLA **$$**
(Av Colón 379; mains AR$40-75; lunch Tue-Sun, dinner nightly) It can get busy at this buzzing *parrilla,* which locals agree is the best in town. The *tenedor libre* (AR$75) sees an endless procession of succulent grilled meats brought to your table. Salad bar and drinks are extra.

Gambrinus ARGENTINE **$$**
(Arribeños 174; mains AR$35-80; lunch & dinner) Located behind the Hotel Italia is this traditional, old-time restaurant that dates from the 19th century. The menu is typically Argentine but there's lots of choice, and it's popular with the locals.

BUSES FROM BAHÍA BLANCA

DESTINATION	COST (AR$)	DURATION (HR)
Bariloche	310	12-14
Buenos Aires	245	9
Córdoba	285	13-15
Mar del Plata	145	7
Mendoza	370	16
Neuquén	170	7½
Sierra de la Ventana	32	2
Trelew	255	10-12

Information

Post office (Moreno 34)

Tourist kiosk (cnr Drago & Av Colón; ⌚9am-1pm, 3-7pm Mon-Sat, 9am-1pm Sun) The bus terminal also has a tourist office.

Getting There & Away

Air

Bahía Blanca's airport is 15km east of town; taxis there cost AR$70 (there are no buses). Airlines include **Aerolíneas Argentinas** (☎456-0561; San Martín 298), **LAN** (☎0810-999-9526; Chiclana 370) and **LADE** (☎452-1063; Darragueira 21).

Bus

Bahía Blanca's **bus terminal** (☎481-9615; Brown 1700) is about 2km southeast of Plaza Rivadavia. Taxis to the city enter cost AR$20-25; there are local buses also, but you'll have to buy a magnetic card at a *kiosco* to use them (and there's no *kiosco* selling them at the terminal).

There are several businesses – including *locutorios* (private telephone offices) and the travel agent **Dakar** (☎456-2030; Chiclana 102) – right at the south end of Plaza Rivadavia that sell bus tickets, saving you a trip to the bus terminal for information. These different businesses sell different bus company's tickets, so ask around if you want a particular schedule, company or price.

Condor Estrella and Expreso Cabildo (buy ticket at platform 1) each offer two or three daily services to Sierra de la Ventana.

Train

Trains leave from the **Estación Ferrocarril Roca** (☎452-9196; www.ferrobaires.gba.gov.ar; Av Cerri 750) for Buenos Aires every day except Monday and Saturday, at around 7pm (AR$44 to $AR73, 12 to 15 hours). There's also a service to Sierra de la Ventana on Wednesday and Friday (AR$11, three hours), and once a week a very slow service heads south to Carmen de Patagones (though it tends to get cancelled from time to time).

Iguazú Falls & the Northeast

Includes »

Best Places to Eat

- Enófilos (p161)
- Bocamora (p192)
- La Cosquilla del Ángel (p171)
- Lo Mejor del Centro (p148)

Best Places to Stay

- Los Silos (p152)
- La Alondra (p159)
- Posada de la Laguna (p167)
- La Cantera Iguazú (p191)
- Atrium Gualok (p202)
- Esplendor Savoy Rosario (p146)

Why Go?

Northeast Argentina is defined by water. Muscular rivers roll through flat pastureland that they flood at will, while fragile wetlands support myriad birdlife, snapping caimans and cuddly capybaras. The peaceful Río Iguazú, meandering through the tropical forest between Brazil and Argentina, dissolves in fury and power in the planet's most awe-inspiring waterfalls.

The river then flows into the Paraná, one of the world's mightiest watercourses, which surges southward, eventually forming the Río de la Plata near Buenos Aires. Along it are some of the country's most interesting cities: elegant Corrientes, colonial Santa Fe and booming Rosario, as well as Posadas, gateway to the ruined splendor of the Jesuit missions.

Dotted throughout the region are excellent reserves and national parks, representative of the biological diversity of this region. The shallow freshwater lakes of the Esteros del Iberá harbor an astonishing richness of wildlife that's easily seen among the aquatic plants.

When to Go

Puerto Iguazú

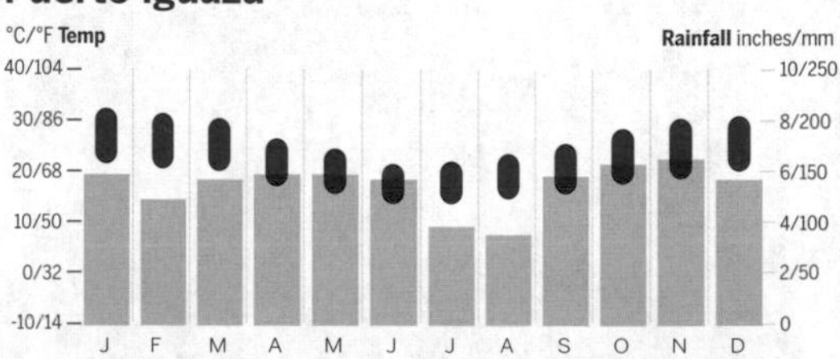

Feb Hot weather and flashy Carnaval celebrations in Gualeguaychú, Corrientes and Posadas.

Aug Cool and dry; spot animals in the Esteros del Iberá gathered around scarce water sources.

Sep–Oct Not too cold, hot or crowded. Iguazú flowing well but flooding and rain less likely.

National Parks & Reserves

There are some excellent national parks within the region, varying from the dry savannas of the Chaco to the rainforests of Misiones.

In the far northeast, Parque Nacional do Iguaçu (p188) and Parque Nacional Iguazú (p186) are the access points for viewing the incredible Iguazú Falls, and also provide a habitat for orchids, big cats, birdlife and other flora and fauna.

Nowhere will you see quite as much wildlife as in the wetlands of Reserva Provincial Esteros del Iberá (p163), while it's the haunting elegance of yatay palm trees that makes Parque Nacional El Palmar (p171) so very special.

Deforestation has denuded much of the Chaco area, so the scrub forests and marshes of Parque Nacional Chaco (p201) and Parque Nacional Río Pilcomayo (p202) are especially valuable, as are the natural reserves that are located further west in the region (see the boxed text, p203).

ALONG THE RÍO PARANÁ

The mighty Río Paraná, the continent's second-longest river at 4000km (after the Amazon at 6405km), dominates the geography of Northeast Argentina. Several of the nation's more interesting cities lie along it; all have their town centers a sensible distance above the shorelines of this flood-prone monster, but have a *costanera* (riverbank) that's the focus of much social life. The river is still important for trade, and large oceangoing vessels ply it to and beyond Rosario, a city whose friendly inhabitants and optimistic outlook make it a great destination.

Santa Fe and Paraná have a relaxing sleepy feel – who can blame them, with the humidity the Paraná generates? – and attractive traditional architecture, while beautiful Corrientes is the home of *chamamé* music (a local musical style derived from polka) and launch pad for the wonderful Esteros del Iberá wetlands.

The Paraná is the demesne of enormous river fish – surubí, dorado and pacú among others – that attract sports fishers from around the world. Their distinctive flavors enliven the menus of the region's restaurants; make sure you try them.

Rosario

☎0341 / POP 1.19 MILLION

The boom times are back for Rosario, birthplace of both the Argentine flag and 'Che' Guevara, and an important river port. The derelict buildings of the long *costanera* have been converted into galleries, restaurants and skate parks, and the river beaches and islands buzz with life in summer. The center – a curious mishmash of stunning early-20th-century buildings overshadowed by ugly apartments – has a comfortable, lived-in feel, and the down-to-earth *rosarinos* (people from Rosario) are a delight. All are very proud of the city's current claim to fame: Lionel Messi, a golden boy of world soccer (football), is Rosario born and bred.

Though it's a private home and you can't enter, you may want to check out the apartment building at Entre Ríos 480, where the newborn Ernesto 'Che' Guevara had his first home.

History

Rosario's first European inhabitants settled here informally around 1720 without sanction from the Spanish crown. After independence Rosario quickly superseded Santa Fe as the province's economic powerhouse, though, to the irritation of *rosarinos,* the provincial capital retained political primacy.

The Central Argentine Land Company, an adjunct of the railroad, was responsible for bringing in agricultural colonists from Europe, for whom Rosario was a port of entry. From 1869 to 1914 Rosario's population grew nearly tenfold.

Though the decline of economic and shipping activity during the 1960s led to a drop in Rosario's population and power, its importance as a port was rivaled only by Buenos Aires. Its title as Argentina's second city, however, was later usurped by Córdoba – a status still hotly contested by *rosarinos*.

Nationalistic Argentines cherish Rosario, which is home to a monument to the nation's flag, as Cuna de la Bandera (Cradle of the Flag).

Sights & Activities

La Costanera NEIGHBORHOOD, BEACH

Rosario's most attractive feature is its waterfront, where what was once home to derelict warehouses and train tracks has largely been reclaimed for the fun of the people. It stretches some 15km from its southern end at Parque Urquiza to the city's northern

Iguazú Falls & the Northeast Highlights

1. Drop your jaw in stunned amazement at the beauty and power of the **Iguazú Falls** (p185)
2. Get personal with the mighty Paraná in livable, lovable **Rosario** (p141)
3. Coo at the cute capybaras of the **Reserva Provincial Esteros del Iberá** (p163)
4. Munch delicious freshwater fish by the Río Uruguay in pretty **Colón** (p170)
5. Ponder a unique experiment in humanity at the ruined **Jesuit missions** (p174)

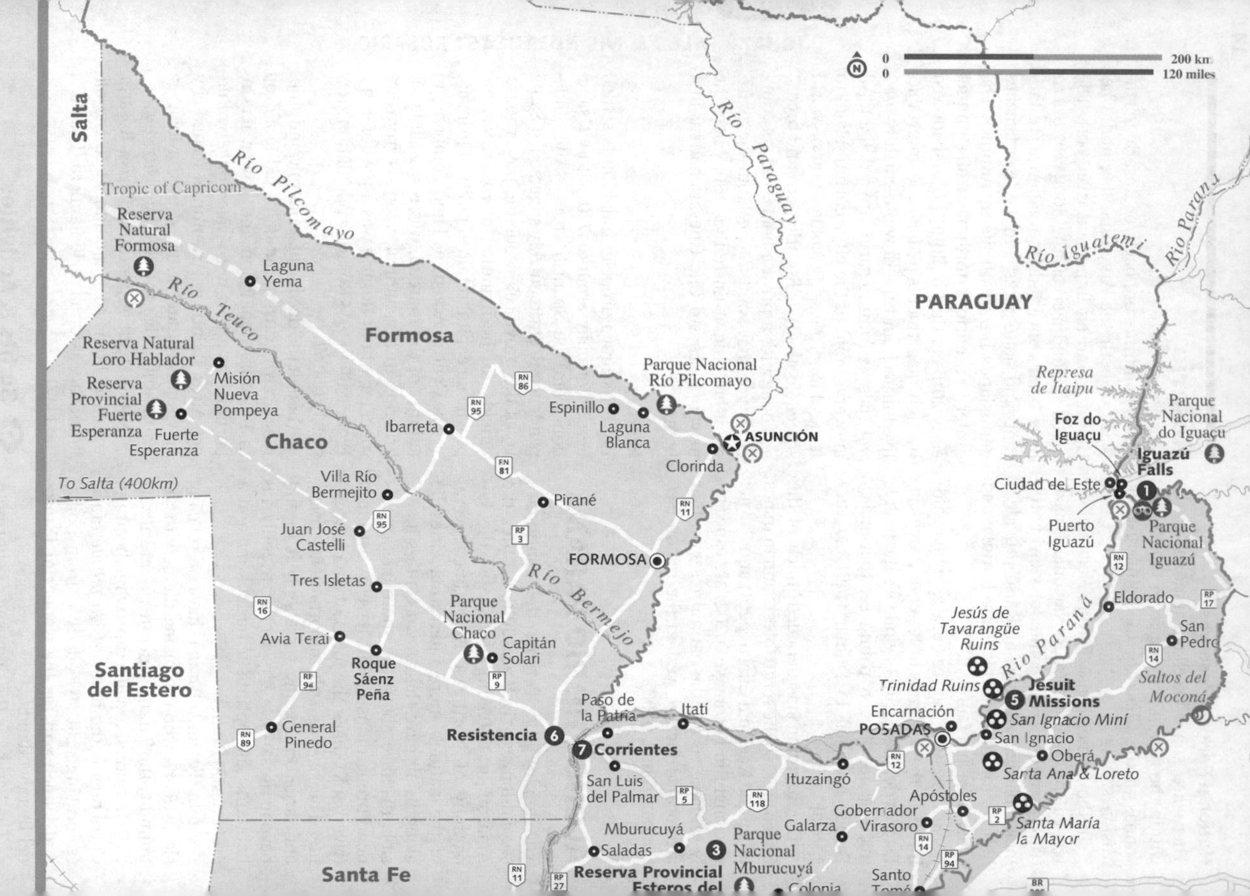

6 Admire the sculptures in **Resistencia** (p197) and plotting a trip to the 'impenetrable' Chaco, a bastion of traditional indigenous culture

7 Live it up at one of the region's classic **Carnaval** celebrations in Gualeguaychú (p170) or Corrientes (p159)

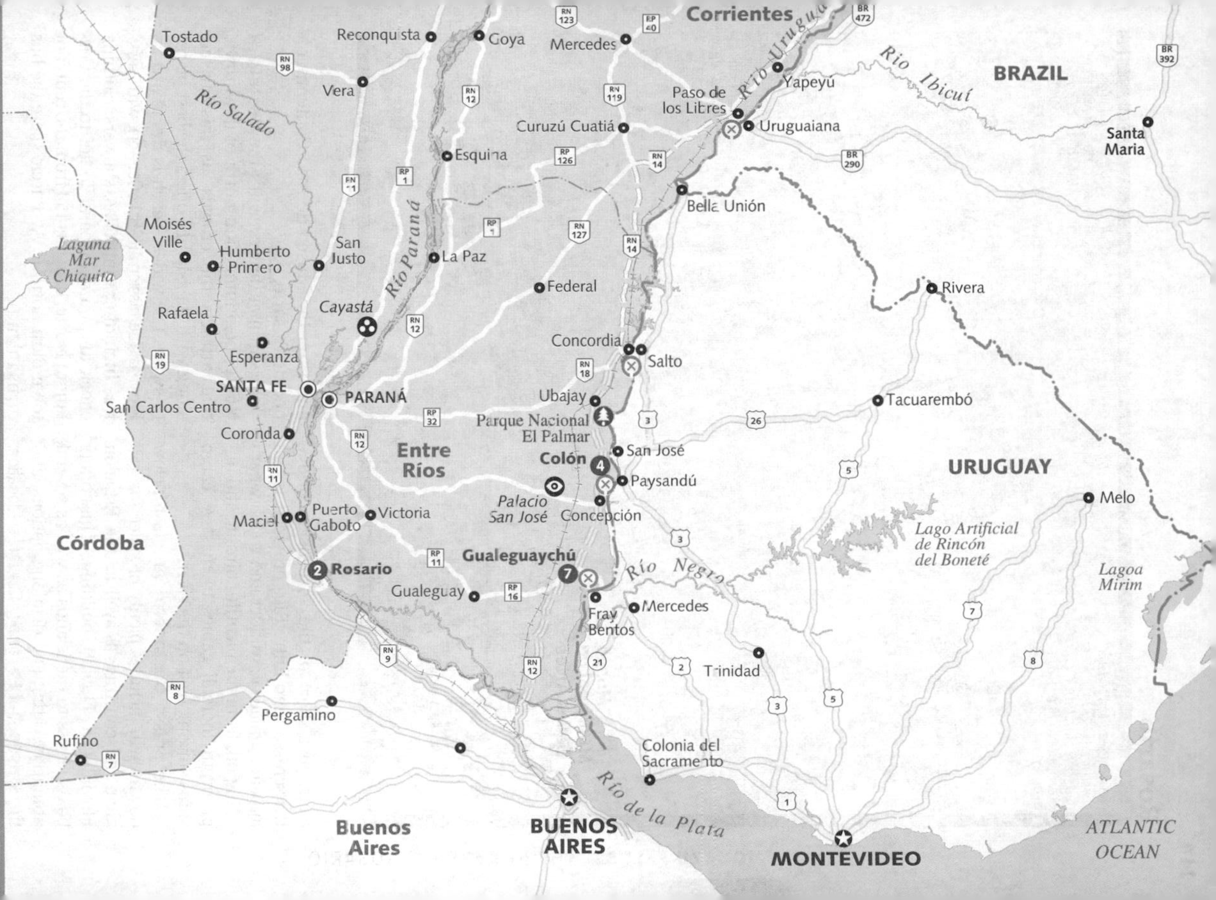

Rosario

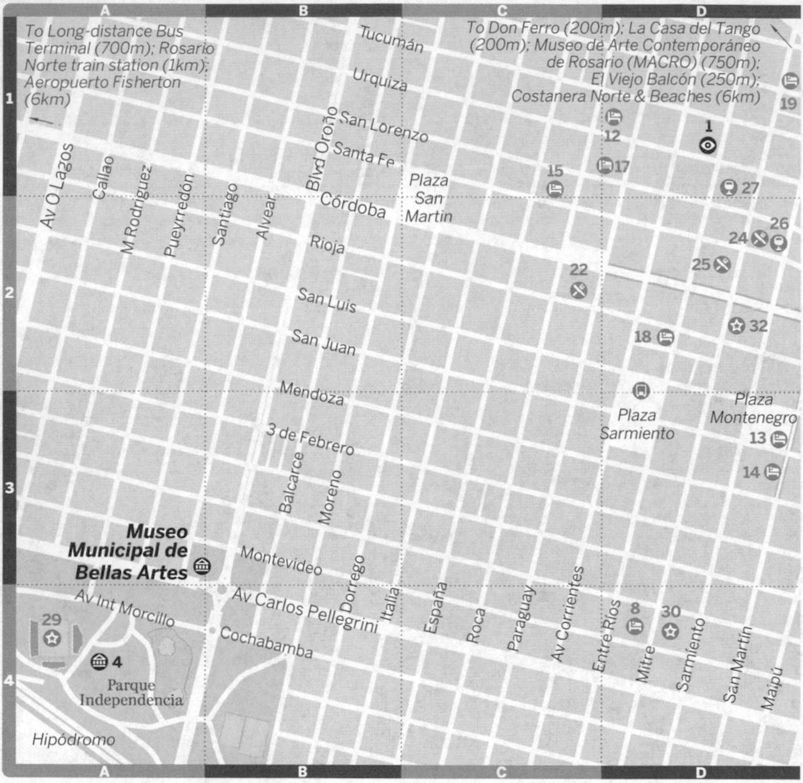

edge, just short of the suspension bridge that crosses into Entre Ríos province. It's an appealing place to wander and watch what's going on, from the plentiful birdlife and impromptu football games to massive cargo ships surging past on the river.

The grassy **Costanera Sur**, just below downtown, includes plenty of space for jogging and courting, as well as the Estación Fluvial (La Fluvial) building. This offers boats across to the islands as well as several upmarket eating and drinking options, and the **Museo Del Paraná y las Islas** (donation; ⌚4-8pm Sat & Sun). This is a labor of love by local painter Raúl Domínguez, documenting life on the river islands with photos, murals and artifacts.

Heading further north, you pass various cultural venues before reaching the **Parque de España** and its mausoleumlike edifice. Beyond here is a zone of bars and restaurants that gets lively at weekends, and then the Museo de Arte Contemporáneo de Rosario.

In summer, however, it's the **Costanera Norte**, beginning 5km north of downtown, that attracts the crowds, as this stretch, along with the islands, offers the best places to swim. The widest beach is **Balneario La Florida** (admission AR$8; ⌚Oct-Apr), with services including umbrellas, showers, clothing check and outdoor bars. To get to the Costanera Norte, take bus 153 from the center of town 6km north to Av Puccio (here the bus turns inland).

FREE Monumento Nacional a La Bandera MONUMENT

(www.monumentoalabandera.gov.ar; Santa Fe 581; ⌚9am-6pm Tue-Sun, 2-6pm Mon Apr-Sep, to 7pm daily Oct-Mar) Manuel Belgrano, who designed the Argentine flag, rests in a crypt beneath this colossal stone obelisk built where the blue-and-white stripes were

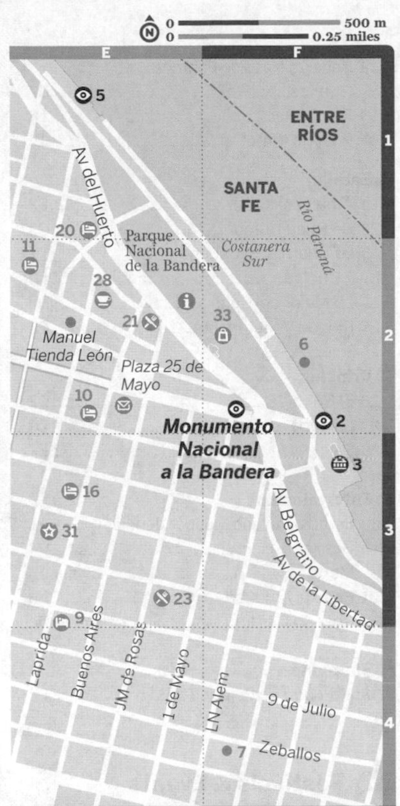

first raised. If rampant nationalism isn't your thing, there's plenty here to look at, but it's worth taking the elevator to the top (AR$3, closes an hour for lunch at 1pm) for the great views over the waterfront, river Paraná and its islands. The attractive colonnade houses an eternal flame commemorating those who died for the fatherland.

Museo Municipal de Bellas Artes GALLERY

(www.museocastagnino.org.ar; cnr Av Carlos Pellegrini & Blvd Oroño; admission AR$4; ⏲2-8pm Mon & Wed-Fri, 1-7pm Sat & Sun) This museum is worth a visit for its brilliantly inventive juxtapositions of fine art – and there are a couple of exceptional European paintings here – with contemporary artworks from the MACRO (Museo De Arte Contemporáneo De Rosario) collection. A *St Andrew* by Ribera, for example, is beautifully matched with a haunting photo portrait by Pierre Gonnord.

Museo de Arte Contemporáneo de Rosario (MACRO) GALLERY

(www.macromuseo.org.ar; Av de la Costa at Blvd Oroño; donation AR$3; ⏲2-8pm Thu-Tue Mar-Aug, 3-9pm Thu-Tue Sep-Feb) Housed in a brightly painted grain silo on the waterfront, this gallery is part of Rosario's impressive riverbank renewal. It features temporary exhibitions, mostly by young local artists, of varying quality, housed in small galleries spread over eight floors. There's a good view of the river islands from the *mirador* (viewpoint) at the top and an attractive cafe-bar by the river.

Museo Histórico Provincial MUSEUM

(www.santafe.gov.ar; Parque Independencia; admission AR$2; ⏲9am-5pm Tue-Fri, 2-6pm Sat & Sun) The well-presented collection of this museum features plenty of postindependence exhibits plus excellent displays on indigenous cultures from all over Latin America. Particularly interesting is the collection of baroque religious art from the southern Andes. Information in Spanish only. From November to April weekend opening is an hour later. It's closed when football is on in the adjacent stadium.

Paraná Delta ISLANDS

Rosario sits on the banks of the Río Paraná upper delta, a 60km-wide area of mostly uninhabited, subtropical islands and winding *riachos* (streams). It's an area rich in bird and animal life, and even the closest islands feel miles away from anywhere, though you can see the city's buildings looming less than a kilometer or two away. Various boat services can be used to reach the islands. From the **Estación Fluvial** (☎447-3838; www.lafluvialrosario.com.ar) there are hourly boats at weekends from mid-September to May, and daily in summer (AR$30 roundtrip) to the southern *balnearios* (river beaches) of Vladimir and Deja Vu. Boats to the northern *balnearios* leave regularly in summer from Embarcadero Costa Alta on the Costanera Norte.

The best way to get a feel for the delta ecosystem is to take a tour in a boat.

Courses

Spanish in Rosario LANGUAGE

(☎437-2860; www.spanishinrosario.com; Catamarca 3095) Rosario's a great place to hang out for a while, and this set-up offers enjoyable language programs to help you put that time to good use. They can arrange family stays and volunteer work placements.

Rosario

Top Sights

- Monumento Nacional a la Bandera ... F2
- Museo Municipal de Bellas Artes ... A3

Sights

1 'Che' Guevara's First Home ... D1
2 Estación Fluvial ... F2
3 Museo del Paraná y las Islas ... F3
4 Museo Histórico Provincial ... A4
5 Parque de España ... E1

Activities, Courses & Tours

6 Ciudad de Rosario ... F2
7 Rosario Bike, Kayak & Motor Boat Tours ... F4

Sleeping

8 Anamundana ... D4
9 Barisit House Hotel ... E3
10 Che Pampa's ... E2
11 Esplendor Savoy Rosario ... E2
12 Hostel La Comunidad ... D1
13 Hotel La Paz ... D3
14 Hotel Plaza del Sol ... D3
15 Hotel Plaza Real ... C1
16 Hotel Romijor ... E3
17 La Casona de Don Jaime II ... D1
18 Roberta Rosa de Fontana Suites ... D2
19 Ros Tower ... D1
20 Rosario Inn ... E1

Eating

21 Amarra ... E2
22 De Buen Humor ... C2
23 La Chernia, El Chucho y La Cholga ... E3
24 Lo Mejor del Centro ... D2
25 Rincón Vegetariano ... D2

Drinking

26 El Cairo ... D2
27 La Sede ... D1
28 Pasaporte ... E2

Entertainment

29 Estadio Parque Independencia ... A4
30 Gotika ... D4
Moore ... (see 2)
31 Peña la Amistad ... E3
32 Rosario Central ... D2

Shopping

33 Mercado de Pulgas del Bajo ... F2

Tours

TOP CHOICE Rosario Bike, Kayak & Motor Boat Tours BOAT, CYCLING TOURS
(☎0341-15-571-3812; www.bikerosario.com.ar, www.kayaktoursrosario.com.ar; Zeballos 327) A professional set-up with boat trips around the Paraná delta (AR$100, 2½ hours) with bird watching and city views. You can also explore the islands by kayak (AR$140, 3½ hours) or combine the two. Good bike tours of the city (AR$100, 3½ hours) are available.

Ciudad de Rosario BOAT TOUR
(☎449-8688; www.barcocr1.com) Near the Estación Fluvial, this converted barge offers two-hour cruises on the Paraná for AR$31; it leaves on weekends and holidays at 2:30pm and 5pm, or 5pm and 7:30pm in summer.

Island Explorer BOAT TOUR
(☎0341-15-628-9287; rosariosail@hotmail.com) Offers trips around the Paraná islands in a speedy inflatable. Trips run on Saturdays and Sundays, last 90 minutes and cost AR$80. Can also arrange trips in a yacht.

Festivals & Events

TOP CHOICE Encuentro de Colectividades MULTICULTURAL
(www.encuentrodecolectividades.com) In November on the riverbank at the intersection with Dorrego, this 10-day party is divided into dozens of areas representing the countries of origin that make up the nation. National food, dress, music and dance performances make for a family-friendly atmosphere.

Semana de la Bandera FIESTA
Climaxing in ceremonies on June 20, the anniversary of the death of Manuel Belgrano, Flag Week is Rosario's major fiesta.

Sleeping

Booming Rosario has a huge number of places to stay. There are over 40 hostels (ask the tourist office for a list) and an ever-increasing herd of midrange hotels.

TOP CHOICE Esplendor Savoy Rosario HOTEL $$
(☎429-6000; www.esplendorsavoyrosario.com; San Lorenzo 1022; r/superior/ste AR$446/532/666;

) Even among Rosario's many elegant early-20th-century buildings, this art nouveau gem is a standout and has recently reopened after a complete renovation. Rooms feature modern conveniences that seem to blend well with the centenarian features. An indoor pool, elegant cafe-bar and roof garden are among the attractions.

TOP CHOICE Che Pampa's HOSTEL $
(424-5202; www.chepampas.com; Rioja 812; dm AR$45-60, tw/d AR$136/180;) Designed with verve and panache, this is one of the best-looking hostels we've ever seen. Plush colors and stylish touches characterize the comfortable dorms, which have a bit of road noise. There are also private rooms available, as well as almost any facility (DVDs, excellent kitchen, barbecue area, patio) you care to mention. The enthusiastic staff caps off an excellent place to stay.

Barisit House Hotel HOTEL $$
(447-6464; www.barisit.com.ar; Laprida 1311; s/d AR$280/320;) Go for one of the upstairs front rooms in this converted historic house if you'll enjoy the romance of original floorboards, high ceilings, windows and balconies. The modern rooms are similarly attractively decorated, and quieter. The personal small-hotel atmosphere is a real drawcard.

Hotel Plaza del Sol HOTEL $$
(421-9899; www.hotelesplaza.com; San Juan 1055; s/d AR$340/370;) Recent renovation has left the rooms here feeling new and looking good; most are very spacious indeed, and the beds are comfortable. It's the best of the clutch of hotels on Plaza Montenegro; there's a gym, sundeck and heated indoor pool on the 11th floor, as well as helpful service. It's pretty decent value, especially if you grab a discount by shopping around online.

La Casona de Don Jaime II HOSTEL $
(530-2020; www.youthhostelrosario.com.ar; San Lorenzo 1530; dm/d AR$60/210;) There's plenty of punch for your peso at this friendly hostel. It's quiet and clean, with a climbing wall in the patio. Dorm beds have plenty of headroom and air-con is available for a little extra. Upstairs are rather smart themed private rooms. Discounts midweek and for HI (Hostelling International) members.

Hostel La Comunidad HOSTEL $
(424-5302; www.lacomunidadhostel.com; Roca 453; dm/d AR$50/140;) Occupying a gorgeous old Rosario building, this spot has lofty ceilings and a light, airy feel. The dorms have handsome wooden bunks and floorboards; a cute private room is also available. There's a bar, lounge area and peaceful vibe.

Hotel La Paz HOTEL $
(421-0905; www.hotellapazrosario.com.ar; Barón de Maua 36; s/d AR$180/220;) Well positioned on Plaza Montenegro, and still looking good after 60 years in operation, this welcoming hotel offers value for money. Family rooms at the front have balconies overlooking Plaza Montenegro. If it's a little faded for your tastes, the same folks run a more modern place, the **Baron del Mil**, next door.

Roberta Rosa de Fontana Suites APARTMENT HOTEL $$
(449-6767; www.rrdfsuites.com.ar; Entre Ríos 914; r AR$350;) Situated very centrally above a colorful cafe, these rooms are modern and commodious, with brushed concrete ceiling, black floors and a small kitchenette. They come in various sizes, making it a good family option.

Rosario Inn HOSTEL $
(421-0358; www.rosarioinnhostel.com.ar; Sargento Cabral 54; dm/d AR$50/140;) Right opposite the massive customs building near the river, this colorful hostel makes up in location and laid-back atmosphere what it lacks in facilities. Set around patios, it offers a helpful welcome, good social scene and activities. The six-bed dorms are comfortable enough; bathrooms are just adequate.

Anamundana HOSTEL $
(424-3077; www.anamundanahostel.com; Montevideo 1248; dm/d AR$70/250;) A block from the Pellegrini eat-street strip, this wins points for comfortable mattresses, warm personal service and an appealing private double. Breakfast is above average, and it's cheaper midweek.

Hotel Romijor HOTEL $
(421-7276; Laprida 1050;) Spacious rooms and warm personal service are the features of this old-fashioned and handily central budget hotel. It was closed for renovations at last visit but should be open again by the time you read this.

Ros Tower HOTEL $$$
(529-9000; www.rostower.com.ar; Mitre 295; r from AR$620;) Great service and facilities in this sleek business-spa hotel with top river views from many rooms.

Hotel Plaza Real HOTEL **$$**
(☎440-8800; www.plazarealhotel.com; Santa Fe 1632; r standard/superior/luxury AR$451/532/949;) Luxurious rooms, apartments and suites in business hotel with rooftop pool. Fine facilities, a cracking breakfast and polite friendly service.

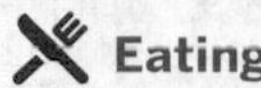

Eating

Central Rosario seems empty come suppertime. That's because half the city is out on Av Carlos Pellegrini. Between Buenos Aires and Moreno there's a vast number of family-friendly eateries, including several barnlike *parrillas* (steak restaurants), dozens of pizza places, several all-you-can-eat buffet joints, bars and excellent ice-creameries. Just stroll along and take your pick. Most places have terraces on the street.

TOP CHOICE **Lo Mejor del Centro** PARRILLA **$**
(Santa Fe 1171; mains AR$28-55) When this *parrilla* went bust, the staff were left high and dry, but the local government let them reopen it as a cooperative, and what a great job they've done. The meat's as good as you'll taste in Rosario, but you can also enjoy homemade pasta, creative salads and a warm, convivial buzz at the tightly packed tables.

Amarra ARGENTINE **$$**
(☎447-7550; www.amarrarestaurante.com.ar; cnr Buenos Aires & Av Belgrano; mains AR$35-70; lunch daily, dinner Mon-Sat;) Smart but relaxed, this restaurant opposite the tourist office has a stylish split-level interior and serves up some very imaginative dishes, beautifully presented and prepared. Its specialty is fish, but the meat is also delicious.

El Viejo Balcón PARRILLA **$$**
(cnr Italia & Wheelwright; mains AR$50-70) Be prepared to wait for a table at this long-time Rosario favorite in a *parrilla*-rich zone by the river. The meat is generously proportioned and of excellent quality: staff even listen to how you want it cooked. But there's enough on the menu here – crêpes, pastas – to cater for all tastes.

La Chernia, El Chucho y La Cholga SEAFOOD **$$**
(www.rubenmolinengo.com; cnr JM de Rosas & Mendoza; mains AR$45-80) Step back a century in time as you walk into this beautifully-decorated romantic corner restaurant. The long menu is all fish, from local river varieties to stews and soups bursting with tasty seafood. Shared platters for two are an enjoyable and good-value way to go here.

Los Jardines de Hildegarda CAFE **$**
(www.losjardinesrestobar.com.ar; riverbank near España; dishes AR$20-40; noon-late Tue-Sun;) Right by the river, this offbeat spot serves a short menu of pasta, mussels, pizza and potato dishes, as well as tasty *licuados* (blended fruit drinks) and plenty of relaxation. The setting is delightful – some may say better than the food. Take the lift down from next to Don Ferro restaurant.

De Buen Humor ICE CREAM **$**
(www.debuenhumorhelados.com.ar; Rioja 1560; cones AR$10-15;) Ice cream here comes from happy cows, they say. We can't vouch for that, but anyone with a sweet tooth will be mooing contentedly at the optimism-filled decor, patio seating and tasty cones, concoctions and fruit salads.

Don Ferro PARRILLA **$$**
(www.puertoespana.com.ar; mains AR$30-85;) A very good-looking *parrilla* in what was once Rosario's train station, with a delightful terrace on the platform, excellent service and seriously delicious meat. It's on the riverbank near España.

Rincón Vegetariano VEGETARIAN **$**
(turinconvegetariano.blogspot.com; Mitre 720; dishes AR$15-22; lunch & dinner Mon-Sat;) This mostly vegetarian place offers a huge range of meat-free hot and cold dishes to eat in or take out. There are always all sorts of deals going.

Drinking

Rosario has a great number of *restobares,* which function as hybrid cafes and bars and generally serve a fairly standard selection of snacks and plates. Many are good for either a morning coffee or an evening glass of wine – or anything in between.

Pasaporte CAFE, BAR
(cnr Maipú & Urquiza; 8am-late Mon-Sat;) A sublimely cozy spot with a pretty terrace and timeworn wooden furniture, including little window booths, the Pasaporte is a favorite for morning coffee with workers from the customs department opposite. But it also has a great evening atmosphere, particularly when the rain's pouring down outside.

El Cairo CAFE, BAR
(www.barelcairo.com; cnr Sarmiento & Santa Fe; 7am-1am Mon-Thu, 7am-3am Fri & Sat, 4pm-1am

Sun;) High ceilinged and elegant, with huge panes of glass for people-watching (and vice versa), this classic Rosario cafe is good at any time of day, but especially in the evening, when it mixes a decent cocktail and puts on good Argentine pub grub. If you've been hankering to try the national beverage, this is also one of the rare places that serve *mate*.

La Sede CAFE
(Entre Ríos 599;) In a striking modernist building, this is a very Argentine cafe with a literary feel. Come here to read a book, enjoy the cakes and quiches or, at weekends, catch an offbeat live performance of something or other.

Fenicia BREWPUB
(www.cervecerlafenicia.com; Francia 168) You can smell the malt at this brewpub, where the delicious ales are produced right beneath your feet. It's a fine place to start exploring this bar-rich nightlife zone, and it also does a handy line in quesadillas, burgers and salads. The roof terrace is good on a warm evening. It's northwest of the center, near the train station.

Entertainment

There are lots of tango places in Rosario; grab the monthly listings booklet *Rosario de Tango* from the tourist office.

La Casa del Tango TANGO
(www.lacasadeltangorosario.com; riverbank at España) This tango center has info on performances around town, offers fun, very cheap evening lessons, and stages various events. There's also a good cafe and restaurant.

Peña la Amistad TRADITIONAL MUSIC
(www.folklorerosario.com; Maipú 1111; 10pm-late Fri & Sat) For a different night out, head down to this folksy spot, where a harp and guitar duo bang out traditional music accompanied by the smell of roasting meat, stamping feet and corks being popped.

Gotika GAY
(www.gotikacityclub.com.ar; Mitre 1539; Fri-Sun) Set behind the imposing facade of a former church, this mainly gay place kicks off at weekends with a variety of music from drum 'n' bass to house.

Moore CLUB
(Estación Fluvial; admission AR$25; Thu-Sat Mar-Nov) One of the few central nightclubs (admission AR$25), this is atmospherically located in the Estación Fluvial building with an outdoor deck and packed upstairs dance floor.

Madame CLUB
(www.mdmdisco.com; cnr Brown & Francia; 11pm-5:30am Fri-Sat) Claiming to be Latin America's biggest club, this massive, stylish former factory complex draws people from Buenos Aires at weekends.

Sports

Rosario has two rival soccer teams with several league titles between them. **Newell's Old Boys** (421-1180; www.nob.com.ar) plays in red and black at **Estadio Parque Independencia**, where the club is based, and has a long, proud history of producing great Argentine footballers. **Rosario Central** (421-0000; www.rosariocentral.com; Mitre 857) plays in blue and yellow stripes at **Estadio 'El Gigante de Arroyito'** (438-9595; cnr Blvd Avellaneda & Génova). Buy tickets from the stadiums or Rosario Central's club office.

Shopping

Mercado de Pulgas del Bajo MARKET
(Av Belgrano; 2-9pm Sat & Sun) A small handcrafts market by the tourist office, where dealers sell everything from silverwork to leather goods. There are several other weekend markets around the city.

Information

There are numerous places to get online, and plenty of spots offer free wi-fi, including the plane-shaded Plaza 25 de Mayo (network: mr_gratuita).

Several 24-hour pharmacies are in the center of town, including one at the corner of San Lorenzo and Entre Ríos.

Banks and ATMs are all over, with a cluster along Santa Fe near Plaza 25 de Mayo. Exchanges along San Martín and Córdoba change traveler's checks (with commission) and cash.

There are many *locutorios* (private telephone offices) around the center.

Hospital Clemente Alvarez (480-8111; Rueda 1110) Southwest of the city center.

Post office (Córdoba 721)

Red Urbana (Av Corrientes 563; per hr AR$3; 24hr) Internet access.

Tourist office (480-2230; www.rosarioturismo.com; Av del Huerto; 9am-7pm Mon-Sat, 9am-6pm Sun) Near the waterfront. There's another office at the long-distance bus terminal.

Getting There & Away

Air

Austral (☎0810-222-86527; www.austral.com.ar) Goes to Buenos Aires.

Gol (www.voegol.com) Serves Porto Alegre and Brasilia in Brazil.

Sol (☎0810-444-4765; www.sol.com.ar) Flies daily to Buenos Aires and also services Mendoza, Córdoba, Montevideo and Tucumán.

Bus

The **long-distance bus terminal** (☎437-3030; www.terminalrosario.com.ar, in Spanish; Cafferata & Santa Fe) is 25 blocks west of the city center. From downtown, any bus along Santa Fe will do the trick.

Rosario is a major transport hub and there are direct daily services to nearly all major destinations, including international services.

Manuel Tienda León (☎0810-888-5366; www.tiendaleon.com.ar; San Lorenzo 935) offers a direct service to or from Buenos Aires' international airport for AR$250. It does pickups from hotel.

Train

From **Rosario Norte train station** (Av del Valle 2750; www.tbanet.com.ar), unreliable services to Buenos Aires (AR$50, six to eight hours) leave at 10:50pm Monday to Friday, returning at 2:30pm. There are four other weekly trains run by **Ferrocentral** (www.ferrocentralsa.com.ar, tickets AR$21-54) that stop here en route between Buenos Aires and Córdoba, and Buenos Aires and Tucumán (see p249), a more interesting trip.

Take bus 138 from San Juan and Mitre to the station.

BUSES FROM ROSARIO

DESTINATION	COST (AR$)	DURATION (HR)
Buenos Aires	122	4
Córdoba	132	7
Corrientes	238	11
Mendoza	265	11
Paraná	56	2
Posadas	322	16
Resistencia	245	10
Salta	296	16
Santa Fe	50	2
Santiago del Estero	196	10
Tucumán	239	12

Getting Around

To/from the Airport

To get to the airport, 8km west of town, take a *remise* (taxi), which costs around AR$50 or AR$60. One operator is **Primera Clase** (☎454-5454).

Bicycle

To rent a bike, head to Rosario Bike, Kayak & Motor Boat Tours (p146), which has well-equipped town bikes for AR$50/60 per half-day/day or AR$220 per week. You'll need your passport and an AR$150 deposit.

Bus

From the local bus terminal on Plaza Sarmiento, bus services run virtually everywhere (see www.rosariobus.com.ar). Have the AR$2 fare in exact change; otherwise buy a *tarjeta magnética* (magnetic bus card) from any kiosk (AR$3.80/10.80 for two/six trips). To get to the city center from the long-distance terminal, take a bus marked 'Centro' or 'Plaza Sarmiento'. It's about AR$15 to AR$20 in a taxi.

Santa Fe

☎0342 / POP 525,093

There's quite a contrast between Santa Fe's relaxed center, where colonial buildings age gracefully in the humid heat and nobody seems to get beyond an amble, and a Friday night in the Recoleta district where university students in dozens of bars show the night no mercy. Capital of its province, but with a small-town feel, Santa Fe is an excellent place to visit for a day or two.

Santa Fe de la Veracruz (its full title) was moved here in 1651 from its original location at Cayastá, 75km to the north. The first Santa Fe was founded in 1573 by Juan de Garay, but by the mid-17th century the location proved intolerable for the original Spanish settlers. Wearied by constant raids by indigenous people, floods and isolation, they packed up the place and moved it to its current location on a tributary of the Río Paraná. Several picturesque colonial buildings remain.

In 1853 Argentina's first constitution was ratified by an assembly that met here, which is a source of great pride to the city. These days Santa Fe's ambitious new riverfront rehabilitation has added extra appeal to this historic city.

Santa Fe's remaining colonial buildings are within a short walk of Plaza 25 de Mayo, the town's functional center. Av San Martín, north of the plaza, is the major commercial street and part of it forms an attractive *peatonal* (pedestrian district) with palm trees and terraces.

To the east, a bridge crosses the river, then a tunnel beneath the Paraná connects Santa Fe with its twin city of Paraná in Entre Ríos.

Sights

Convento y Museo de San Francisco MONASTERY

(Amenábar 2257; admission by donation; ⏲8am-noon & 4-7pm Oct-Feb, 3:30-6:30pm Mar-Sep, closed Sun except for church) The principal historical landmark is this Franciscan monastery and museum, built in 1680. The walls, which are more than 1m thick, support a roof made from Paraguayan cedar and hardwood beams held together by fittings and wooden spikes, rather than by nails. While the museum section is mediocre, the church is beautiful, with an exquisite wooden ceiling and a fine polychrome Christ by the grumpy Spanish master Alonso Cano – it was sent as a sympathy gift to Santa Fe by

Santa Fe

Top Sights

- Convento y Museo de San Francisco A7
- Museo Etnográfico y Colonial Provincial A7
- Museo Histórico Provincial A7

Sights

1 Casa de Gobierno A7
2 Catedral A6
3 Iglesia de la Compañía A6

Activities, Courses & Tours

4 Costa Litoral B4

Sleeping

5 Hostal Santa Fe de la Veracruz A3
6 Hostel Santa Fe B1
7 Hotel Conquistador B3
8 Hotel Constituyentes B3
9 Hotel Emperatriz B3
10 Hotel España A3
11 Hotel Galeón B3
12 Hotel Royal B3
13 Hotel Zavaleta B3
14 Los Silos B4

Eating

15 Círculo Italiano B3
16 Club Social Sirio Libanés B3
17 El Brigadier A6
18 Las Delicias A3
19 Merengo A6
Restaurante España .... (see 10)

the Queen of Spain when the town moved in 1649. Note also the tomb of Padre Magallanes, a priest who was killed by a jaguar that took refuge in the church when it was driven from the shores of the Paraná during the floods of 1825. The cloister has a carved wooden balustrade and is redolent with the perfume of flowers. The monastery is still home to one monk, who is helped out by a trio of priests.

Museo Histórico Provincial MUSEUM
(www.museohistorico-sfe.gov.ar; Av San Martín 1490; admission AR$2; ⌚8:30am-noon & 3-7:30pm Tue-Fri, 4:30-7:30pm Sat & Sun) In a lovable 17th-century building, this museum has a variety of possessions and mementos of various provincial governors and caudillos (provincial strongmen), as well as some religious art and fine period furnishings, including a sedan chair once used to carry around the Viceroy of Río de la Plata.

Museo Etnográfico y Colonial Provincial MUSEUM
(25 de Mayo 1470; admission AR$2; ⌚8:30am-noon & 2-7pm Tue-Fri, 4-7pm Sat & Sun) Run with heartwarming enthusiasm, this museum has a chronological display of stone tools, Guaraní ceramics, jewelry, carved bricks and colonial objects. Highlights include a set of *tablas* – a colonial game similar to backgammon – and a scale model of the original Santa Fe.

Plaza 25 de Mayo SQUARE
The center of colonial Santa Fe is a peaceful square framed by many fine buildings. The vast **Casa de Gobierno** (government house) was built in 1909 and replaced the demolished colonial *cabildo* (town council building), seat of the 1852 constitutional assembly. On the square's east side, the exterior simplicity of the Jesuit **Iglesia de la Compañía** masks an ornate interior. Dating from 1696, it's the province's best-preserved colonial church. On the square's north side the city's **catedral** (cathedral) is a little underwhelming by comparison, and dates from the mid-18th century.

Tours

Costa Litoral BOAT TOURS
(☎456-4381; www.costalitoral.net; Dique 1) From the redeveloped harbor area, a large catamaran runs weekend trips around the river islands (adult/child AR$46/28, two hours, 11am Saturday and Sunday) or to Paraná (Sat & Sun; adult/child AR$75/40, 5½ hours, 2pm Saturday and Sunday) and back, with a couple of hours to explore the city. Book tickets in the bar opposite the dock.

Sleeping

The area around the bus terminal is the budget hotel zone. Many hotels offer a discount for cash payment.

TOP CHOICE **Los Silos** HOTEL $$$
(☎450-2800; www.hotellossilos.com.ar; Dique 1; s/d AR$479/536; ❄@🛜🏊👪) Santa Fe's decaying waterfront has been significantly smartened up in the last few years, and this excellent hotel is the star. Brilliantly converted from grain silos, it features original, rounded rooms with marvelous views and plenty of modern comfort. The vistas from the rooftop pool, spa and sundeck are even better, and service is excellent throughout. A handsome cafe and play area for kids, with console games and minigolf, are other highlights; there's also an attached casino.

Hotel Galeón HOTEL $$
(☎454-1788; www.hotelgaleon.com.ar; Belgrano 2759; s/d AR$245/300; ❄@🛜) Bright, unusual, and all curved surfaces and weird angles, this cheery place is a breath of fresh air. There's a variety of room types, none of which is a conventional shape; the beds are seriously comfortable and the bathrooms pleasant. It's handy for the bus, too.

Hotel Emperatriz HOTEL $
(☎453-0061; emperatrizhotel.wordpress.com; Irigoyen Freyre 2440; s/d AR$150/200; ❄🛜) With a decayed but noble façade and other-era fittings, this hotel seems to have slipped under the radar of the 21st century. The rooms are small and not luxurious – there are various sizes and prices – but they're clean and comfortable enough for this price. It's a slice of old-time Argentina that won't be around in a few years' time.

Hotel Conquistador HOTEL $$$
(☎400-1195; www.lineaverdedehoteles.com.ar; 25 de Mayo 2676; s/d AR$440/510; ❄@🛜🏊) The Conquistador lays on the charm, with sauna, hydromassage, fluffy bathrobes, gymnasium and a huge buffet breakfast. The beds in the twins and singles are happily queen-sized. The pool is outdoor, so only open in summer. Slightly cheaper rooms at the **Hotel España** across the road give you access to the same facilities.

Hostal Santa Fe de la Veracruz HOTEL $$
(☎455-1740; www.hostalsf.com; Av San Martín 2954; s/d AR$286/370;) Decorated with indigenous motifs, this hotel offers spacious superior rooms and decent standards. It'll soon be time for redecorating though – those dozen shades of beige are looking a little dated. Siesta fans will love the 6pm checkout.

Hostel Santa Fe HOSTEL $
(☎455-4000; www.santafe-hostel.com; Blvd Gálvez 2173; dm/d AR$55/180;) Tucked behind a tour agency called Latitud Sur, this hostel has two airless but not-too-crowded dorms with lockers, and a private double. There's also a small pool and it's very handy for the Recoleta nightlife.

Hotel Constituyentes HOTEL $
(☎452-1586; www.hotelconstituyentes.com.ar; San Luis 2862; s/d with bathroom AR$180/250, without bathroom AR$100/160;) Spacious rooms and proximity to the bus terminal are the main drawcards of this relaxed place. Rooms at the front suffer from street noise. Breakfast is a few pesos extra.

Hotel Zavaleta HOTEL $$
(☎455-1841; www.zavaletahotel.com.ar; Hipólito Yrigoyen 2349; s/d standard AR$250/340, superior AR$310/380;) A welcoming plaza-side hotel near the bus terminal. Standard rooms are small.

Hotel Royal HOTEL $
(☎452-7359; Irigoyen Freyre 2256; r without bathroom AR$100) Basic but clean. Many mattresses have given up the ghost, so ask to see a few rooms. Cheap and near the bus terminal...it'll do for a night.

Eating

The best zones for cheap eats are across from the bus terminal, and the nightlife zone of La Recoleta (see Drinking).

El Quincho de Chiquito FISH $$
(cnr Brown & Obispo Vieytes; set menu AR$63) This legendary place is a local institution, and *the* place to go to eat river fish. It's on the *costanera* some 6km north of downtown. There are few frills to the service, and no choice about the menu: four or five courses of delicious surubí, sábalo or pacú are brought out to you. You won't leave hungry. Drinks are extra but cheap. It's around AR$25 each way in a taxi (staff will call you one to take you back) or catch bus 16 from any point on the waterfront road.

Club Social Sirio Libanés MIDDLE EASTERN $$
(25 de Mayo 2740; meals AR$22-55; Tue-Sun) In a rather aristocratic dining room, attentive waiters serve well-prepared Middle Eastern-style dishes; it's a pleasingly unusual place to eat. You enter down the end of a passageway.

Círculo Italiano ITALIAN $$
(Hipólito Yrigoyen 2457; mains AR$35-55) Part of the Italian social club, Círculo Italiano prepares good, moderately priced lunch specials (AR$41 to AR$50 Monday to Friday) and tasty pasta. Come for the ritzy atmosphere, the waiters in linen jackets, the complimentary pâté or the extensive wine list.

Las Delicias CAFE, BAKERY $
(Av San Martín 2882; cakes & pastries from AR$4; 8am-midnight) Delightfully old-fashioned and elegant, with a great shady terrace, this bakery offers some of the most sinful pastries and cakes imaginable; it also does breakfast, afternoon tea and sandwiches. Service is traditional and correct.

Restaurante España ARGENTINE $$
(Av San Martín 2644; mains AR$35-80;) This hotel restaurant has a huge menu that covers the range of fish (both locally caught and from the sea), steaks, pasta, chicken and crepes, with a few Spanish dishes thrown in to justify the name. The wine list is a winner, too.

El Brigadier ARGENTINE $$
(Av San Martín 1670; mains AR$28-64) Half a block from Plaza 25 de Mayo, this refurbished restaurant offers an elegant interior and tasty cuts of meat and river fish that win out, despite a few strange quirks in the service department.

Merengo BAKERY $
(Av General López 2634; alfajores from AR$3) In 1851 Merengo stuck two biscuits together with *dulce de leche* (milk caramel) and invented the *alfajor*, now Argentina's favorite snack. They're still going strong: delicious.

Drinking & Entertainment

Santa Fe's nightlife centers on the intersection of 25 de Mayo and Santiago del Estero, the heart of the area known as La Recoleta, which goes wild on weekend nights – a crazy contrast to the sedate pace of life downtown. Places change name and popularity rapidly, so just head to the zone and take a look around the dozens of bars and clubs. Many have a cover charge redeemable for a drink.

The city's best football team, **Colón** (☎459-8025; www.clubcolon.com.ar), is in the top division. It plays at the **Brigadier Estanislao López stadium** (cnr Dr Zavalla & Pietranera), where you can also pick up tickets.

Information

Telephone and internet shops are all over, including in the bus terminal. Several banks with ATMs can be found along the *peatonal*.

Hospital Provincial José María Cullen (☎457-3340; Av Freyre 2150)

Municipal tourist office (☎457-4124; www.santafeturismo.gov.ar; Belgrano 2910; 7am-8pm) In the bus terminal.

Provincial tourist office (☎458-9476; www.turismo-santafe.org.ar; cnr Amenábar & Av San Martín; 7am-6pm Mon & Wed-Thu, 7am-1pm Tue & Fri) Helpful office for provincial exploration.

Getting There & Away

Aerolíneas Argentinas (☎0810-222-86527; 25 de Mayo 2287) has five weekly flights to Buenos Aires (AR$430). **Sol** (☎0810-444-4765; www.sol.com.ar) flies the same route Monday to Saturday (AR$348) and also services Rosario. The airport is 7km south of town on RN 11. A *remise* will cost about AR$35.

From the **bus terminal** (☎457-4124; www.terminalsantafe.com; Belgrano 2910) there are bus services throughout the country.

BUSES FROM SANTA FE

DESTINATION	COST (AR$)	DURATION (HR)
Buenos Aires	168	6
Córdoba	105	5
Corrientes	189	9
Mendoza	320	13
Paraná	4	40min
Paso de los Libres	110	9
Posadas	295	14
Resistencia	180	9
Rosario	50	2
Salta	406	16
Tucumán	256	11

Cayastá

A fascinating day trip from Santa Fe takes you to that city's original location, the **Cayastá ruins** (Santa Fe la Vieja; admission AR$2; 9am-1pm & 3-7pm Tue-Fri, 10am-1pm & 4-7pm Sat & Sun), picturesquely set beside the Río San Javier, which has actually eroded away a good portion of them.

There's ongoing archaeological excavation and conservation here (and a campaign for Unesco status underway), but the most fascinating find by far has been the **Iglesia de San Francisco**. The Spanish and mestizo inhabitants of old Santa Fe were buried directly beneath the earth-floored church, and nearly 100 graves have been excavated, including those of Hernando Arias de Saavedra (known as 'Hernandarias'), the first locally born governor of Río de la Plata province, and his wife, Gerónima de Contrera, daughter of Juan de Garay, who founded Santa Fe and Buenos Aires.

You can also see the remains of two other churches and the *cabildo* (town council), as well as a reconstructed period house. Near the entrance to the site is an attractive and excellent **museum** housing the finds from the site, including some fine indigenous pottery with parrot and human motifs.

Last entry is strictly one hour before closing.

There's a mediocre restaurant at the site and a couple of decent *parrillas* in town. Several spots offer simple lodgings and boat trips on the river. **Cabañas Cayastá** (☎03405-493300; www.cayasta.com; cabin for 2/4 people AR$450/570; ❄≋) is a riverside resort offering cabin accommodation and a spa.

Cayastá is 76km northeast of Santa Fe on RP 1. Paraná Medio bus company departs regularly from Santa Fe's bus terminal (AR$16, 1½ hours). Ask the driver to drop you at *'las ruinas'*, 1km short of Cayastá itself.

Paraná

☎0343 / POP 270,968

Unpretentious Paraná seems surprised at its own status as capital of Entre Ríos province. Perched on the hilly banks of its eponymous river, it's a sleepy, slow-paced city. The nicest part of town is the riverside where a pretty park slopes down to the *costanera*, where there are beaches, bars, boat trips and hundreds of strollers and joggers. After the defeat of Rosas at the battle of Caseros, Paraná was the capital of the Argentine Confederation (which didn't include Buenos Aires) from 1853 to 1861.

A tunnel beneath the main channel of the Paraná connects the city to Santa Fe.

Sights & Activities

Museo Histórico de Entre Ríos MUSEUM
(Buenos Aires 286; admission AR$2; 8am-12:30pm & 3-8pm Tue-Fri, 9am-noon & 5-7pm Sat, 9am-noon Sun) Flaunting local pride, this modern museum on Plaza Alvear contains information on the short-lived Republic of Entre Ríos and the battle of Monte Caseros, as well as *mate* paraphernalia and numerous solid wooden desks and portraits of Urquiza. Much of it was the collection of a local poet.

FREE **Museo y Mercado Provincial de Artesanías** HANDICRAFTS
(Av Urquiza 1239; 8am-1pm & 4-7pm Mon-Fri, 8am-1pm Sat, 9am-noon Sun) Promoting handicrafts from throughout the province, this is a likable little place. Ask the curator to explain things to you; you'll be amazed at the intricacy of some of the work, like the hats made from tightly woven palm fibers.

Similar traditional *artesanías* (handicrafts) are on display and sale at the **Centro de Artesanos** (cnr Av 9 de Julio & Carbó), under renovation at time of research.

Costanera RIVER BEACH
From the northern edge of downtown, Parque Urquiza slopes steeply downward to the banks of the Río Paraná. During the summer months the waterfront fills with people strolling, fishing and swimming.

There's a stretch of beach west of the **Paraná Rowing Club** (431-2048; www.paranarowingclub.com.ar) at which, for AR$50 per day, you can access facilities, including a private beach and showers (AR$80 including swimming pool). There's also a cafe-restaurant on the water.

A better beach, **Playas de Thompson**, is 1km further east, beyond the port.

Museo de Bellas Artes GALLERY
(Buenos Aires 355; admission variable; 9am-noon & 3-8pm Tue-Fri, 10am-noon & 4-7pm Sat, 10am-noon Sun) A small permanent collection of oils, illustrations and sculptures by provincial artists is complemented by temporary exhibitions in this gallery on Plaza Alvear.

Tours

Costa Litoral BOAT TOURS
(423-4385; www.costalitoral.net; Buenos Aires 212) At weekends, runs afternoon trips to Santa Fe and one-hour cruises on the river (AR$35) in a large catamaran.

Paraná en Kayak KAYAK
(422-7143; www.paranaenkayak.com.ar) Offers easy kayak trips on the river as well as longer routes.

Sleeping

TOP CHOICE **Las Mañanitas** HOTEL $
(421-8324; www.lasmanianitas.com.ar; Carbó 62; s/d AR$140/210;) There's a summerhouse feel about this delightfully relaxed little place, which has nine rooms alongside a courtyard and garden with pool. The rooms are unremarkable though well priced, but it's the light style and grace of the whole ensemble that makes this a winner.

Maran Suites HOTEL $$$
(423-5444; www.maran.com.ar; cnr Alameda de la Federación & Mitre; s AR$430, d AR$575-610;) Towering over the western end of Parque Urquiza, this sleek modern hotel has a rare combination of style and warmhearted personal service. Try to get a room as high up as possible, for city or river views. All the rooms are very spacious and decorated with flair; the 'presidential' suites (AR$1423) are big enough to get lost in and boast a Jacuzzi with memorable vistas over the water.

Paraná Hotel Plaza Jardín HOTEL $$
(423-1700; www.hotelesparana.com.ar; Av 9 de Julio 60; s/d standard AR$199/255, superior AR$298/358;) Set in a lovely old colonial building, this hotel has a peaceful patio that's great for a break from the midday heat. The superior rooms are much more spacious and stylish: worth the upgrade. It's significantly cheaper outside of summer.

Paraná Hostel HOSTEL $
(422-8233; www.paranahostel.com.ar; Pazos 159; dm/d/q AR$60/130/250;) Right in the mix in central Paraná, this hostel has good security, a tree-shaded back patio and garden as well as smart furnishings, decent facilities and comfy dorms. Upstairs are attractive, airy private rooms that share a bathroom.

Gran Hotel Paraná HOTEL $$
(422-3900; www.hotelesparana.com.ar; Av Urquiza 976; s AR$270-415, d AR$390-515;) Fine

Paraná

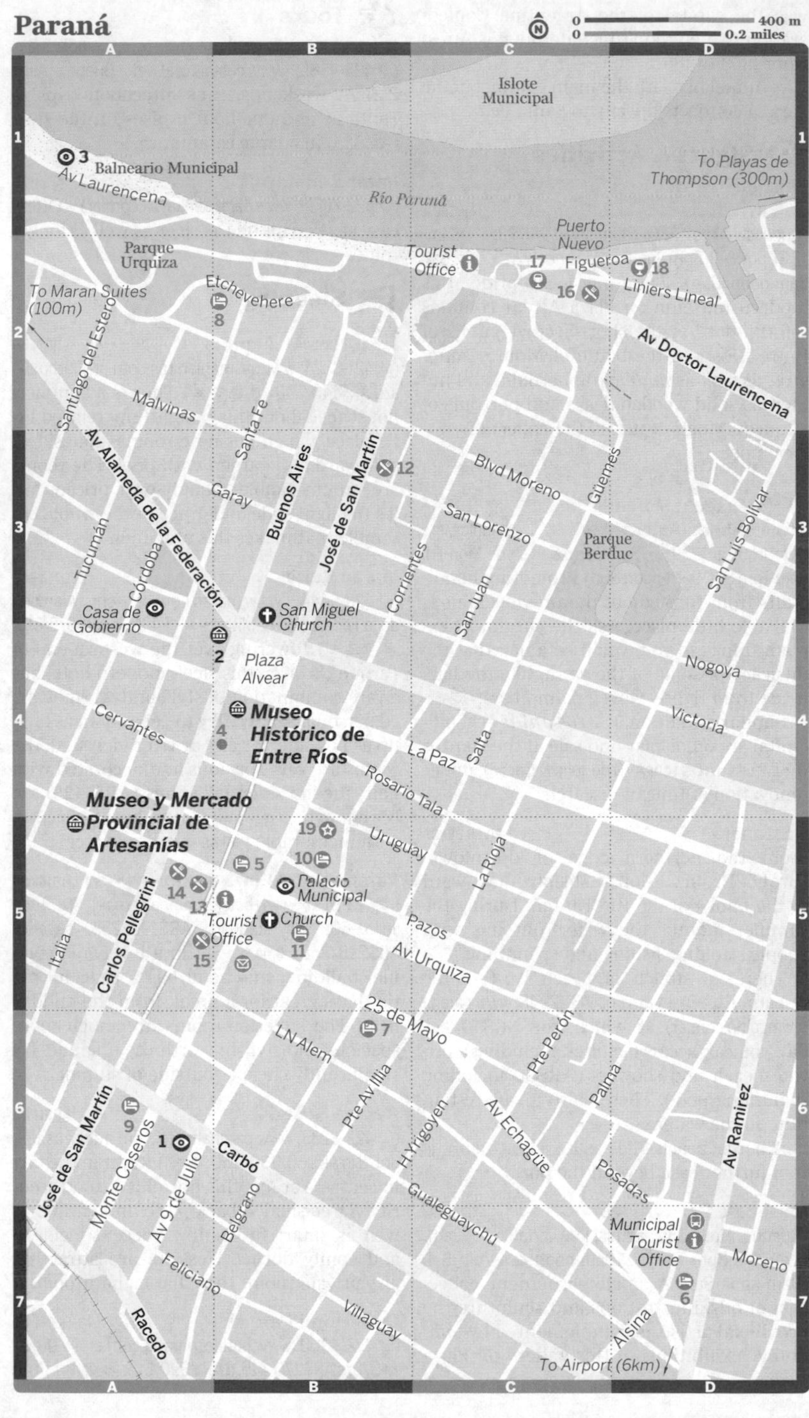

0 400 m
0 0.2 miles
Islote Municipal
Balneario Municipal
Av Laurencena
Río Paraná
To Playas de Thompson (300m)
Puerto Nuevo
Tourist Office
Figueroa
Liniers Lineal
Parque Urquiza
To Maran Suites (100m)
Etchevehere
Av Doctor Laurencena
Santiago del Estero
Malvinas
Santa Fe
Buenos Aires
José de San Martín
Blvd Moreno
Garay
Av Alameda de la Federación
San Lorenzo
Güemes
Parque Berduc
Tucumán
Córdoba
Corrientes
San Juan
San Luis Bolívar
Casa de Gobierno
San Miguel Church
Plaza Alvear
Nogoya
Cervantes
Museo Histórico de Entre Ríos
Victoria
La Paz
Salta
Rosario Tala
Museo y Mercado Provincial de Artesanías
Uruguay
La Rioja
Palacio Municipal
Tourist Office
Church
Carlos Pellegrini
Italia
Pazos
Av Urquiza
25 de Mayo
LN Alem
Pte Perón
Pte Av Illia
Palma
H Yrigoyen
Av Echagüe
José de San Martín
Monte Caseros
Av 9 de Julio
Carbó
Posadas
Av Ramirez
Gualeguaychú
Belgrano
Municipal Tourist Office
Moreno
Feliciano
Villaguay
Racedo
Alsina
To Airport (6km)

service is a major plus at this large hotel on the main square. There are two grades of room, all recently refurbished and spacious. If you don't mind a bit of traffic noise, try for a balcony on the square. There's a health spa and a high-quality restaurant. Good breakfast buffet.

Hotel Itatí HOTEL $
(☎423-1500; hoteles_itati@hotmail.com; Belgrano 135; s/d AR$80/160; ❄@) Welcoming management makes up for the worn carpets and aging sheets at this curiously designed budget hotel. Heating costs a little extra, as does internet use. The dark rooms are fine for the price, with tiny bathrooms.

Howard Johnson Mayorazgo HOTEL $$$
(☎420-6800; www.hjmayorazgo.com.ar; Etcheverry s/n; r AR$630-710; ❄@🛜≋) The long curved facade of this remodeled five-star dominates the waterfront from above. It has great views from large windows and a casino.

Hotel Bristol HOTEL $
(☎431-3961; bristolparana@yahoo.com.ar; Alsina 221; s/d with bathroom AR$100/140, without bathroom AR$70/90; ❄) Right by the bus terminal. Well kept and quiet.

Toma Vieja CAMPGROUND $
(☎433-1721; Av Blas Parera; camp sites AR$20) Scenic site of the old waterworks overlooking the river. Take bus 5 from the bus terminal or bus 1 from the plaza.

Eating

Don Charras PARRILLA $$
(☎422-5972; www,doncharras.com; cnr José de San Martín & San Lorenzo; mains AR$35-60; ⏱Tue-Sun) Thatched and atmospheric, this *parrilla* is a popular Paraná choice. Fridays and Saturdays see special fire-roasted options, but you can enjoy the usual chargrilled selection and solicitous service otherwise. There's also a decent salad bar.

Giovani ARGENTINE $$
(☎423-0527; Av Urquiza 1045; mains AR$33-70; 🛜) With as-it-should-be service and thoughtful touches such as free coffee, this stylish restaurant in the center of town serves excellent meats from the *parrilla* and delectable pasta. Fish isn't such a strong point.

Flamingo Grand Bar CAFE $
(cnr Urquiza & José de San Martín; light meals AR$15-35; ⏱8am-10pm; 🛜) Smart seats and a plaza-side location make this a favorite throughout the day, from morning croissants and juices through to *lomitos* (steak sandwiches) and lunch specials to decent à la carte plates and *picadas* (shared appetizer plates).

Petra BUFFET $
(25 de Mayo 32; buffet AR$42) With a huge range of mostly Chinese food on offer, this redoubtable all-you-can-eat joint sits on the square. Open for both lunch and dinner, with *parrilla* options complementing the hot and cold buffet. Drinks extra.

Quincho del Puerto FISH $$
(Av Doctor Laurencena 350, fish AR$35-51; ⏱lunch & dinner Tue-Sat, lunch Sun) Popular spot for river fish just back from the *costanera*. There are various options, including the tasty (but bony) pacú and surubí.

Paraná

Top Sights
Museo Histórico de Entre Ríos ... B4
Museo y Mercado Provincial de Artesanías ... A5

Sights
1 Centro de Artesanos ... A6
2 Museo de Bellas Artes ... B4
3 Paraná Rowing Club ... A1

Activities, Courses & Tours
4 Costa Litoral ... B4

Sleeping
5 Gran Hotel Paraná ... B5
6 Hotel Bristol ... D7
7 Hotel Itatí ... B6
8 Howard Johnson Mayorazgo ... B2
9 Las Mañanitas ... A6
10 Paraná Hostel ... B5
11 Paraná Hotel Plaza Jardín ... B5

Eating
12 Don Charras ... B3
13 Flamingo Grand Bar ... A5
14 Giovani ... A5
15 Petra ... A5
16 Quincho del Puerto ... C2

Drinking
17 Fish ... C2
18 Ku-va ... D2

Entertainment
19 Cream ... B5

Drinking & Entertainment

Paraná is quiet midweek, but gets busier on Friday and Saturday nights. Most of the action is at the eastern end of the riverfront.

Fish BAR, NIGHTCLUB
(Figueroa s/n; Fri & Sat) Plays the usual mix of mainstream *marcha,* house and salsa.

Ku-va BAR
(www.ku-vaparana.com.ar; cnr Güemes & Liniers Lineal; Fri & Sat) This place offers plenty of atmosphere in an attractive old post office building.

Cream NIGHTCLUB
(www.creamparana.com.ar; Uruguay 190; Thu-Sat) Here you'll feel ancient if you're over 30.

Information

There are several banks with ATMs within a couple of blocks of Plaza 1 de Mayo. Dozens of places offer internet access and phone calls.

Hospital San Martín (423-4545; www.hospitalsanmartin.org.ar; Presidente Perón 450)

Tourist office (423-0183; www.turismoenparana.gov.ar; Pl 1 de Mayo s/n; 8am-8pm) Helpful, with good brochures. There's another branch by the river, and a desk in the bus station.

Getting There & Around

The airport is 6km south of town, accessible only by *remise* (AR$35). **LAER** (0810-777-5237; www.laersa.com.ar) flies to BA on weekdays.

The **bus terminal** (422-1282; Av Ramírez) is opposite Plaza Martín Fierro. Buses 1, 4, 5 and 9 run between the terminal and the town center. Paraná is a hub for provincial bus services, but Santa Fe is more convenient for long-distance trips. Buses leave every 30 minutes for Santa Fe (AR$4, 40 minutes).

BUSES FROM PARANÁ

DESTINATION	COST (AR$)	DURATION (HR)
Buenos Aires	145	6½
Colón	46	4-5
Concordia	50	4-5
Córdoba	110	6
Corrientes	195	10
Gualeguaychú	52	4-5
Paso de los Libres	114	6
Rosario	56	3

Corrientes

0379 / POP 358,223

Stately Corrientes sits below the confluence of the Paraná and Paraguay rivers just across the water from its twin city, Resistencia. One of the nation's most venerable cities, it has elegant balconied buildings dating from the turn of the 20th century that lend a time-worn appeal to its colorful streets. Like many such cities, the *costanera* is everybody's destination of choice for strolling, licking ice creams or sipping *mate* with friends.

Corrientes is a magnet for regional indigenous crafts; Guaraní culture has a strong presence. The city is famous for both its Carnaval and for being the setting of Graham Greene's novel *The Honorary Consul.*

Corrientes was originally called Vera de los Siete Corrientes, after its founder Juan Torres de Vera y Aragón and the shifting *corrientes* (currents) of the Paraná. During colonial times Corrientes suffered repeated indigenous uprisings before establishing itself as the first Spanish settlement in the region.

Sights & Activities

Various operators run boat trips on the Paraná; the tourist office has a list.

FREE **Museo de Artesanías Tradicionales Folclóricas** MUSEUM
(Quintana 905; 8am-9pm Mon-Sat) This intriguing museum is set in a converted colonial house with an interior courtyard. There are two small displays of finc traditional *artesanía* (handicrafts) as well as a good shop selling craft products, but the highlight is watching students being taught to work leather, silver, bone and wood by master craftspeople. Other rooms around the courtyard are occupied by working artisans who will sell to you directly. The museum guides are enthusiastic and friendly.

FREE **Museo Histórico de Corrientes** MUSEUM
(9 de Julio 1044; 8am-noon & 2-8pm Tue-Fri, 9am-noon Sat) This museum is set around an attractive patio and exhibits weapons, antique furniture, coins and items dealing with religious and civil history. It's a little bit higgledy-piggledy, but staff are proud of the exhibition and keen to chat. The room on the War of the Triple Alliance is the most interesting.

CHAMAMÉ

Tango? What's that? Up here it's all about *chamamé,* one of the country's most intoxicating musical forms. Rooted in the polka, which was introduced by European immigrants, it is also heavily influenced by the music and language of the indigenous Guaraní. Its definitive sound is the accordion, which is traditionally accompanied by the guitar, the *guitarrón* (an oversized guitar used for playing bass lines), the larger *bandoneón* (accordion) and the *contrabajo* (double bass). Of course, a *conjunto* (band) is hardly complete without a singer or two.

Chamamé is as much a dance as it is a musical genre, and it's a lively one. It is a dance for a couple, except when the man takes his solo *zapateo* (tap dance). Corrientes province is the heart of *chamamé* and is therefore the easiest place to find a live performance. Sitting in on an evening of music and dancing – or taking to the floor if you're brave – is one of the joys unique to the province.

Check out the Spanish-only website www.corrienteschamame.com.ar for details of performances, and online tunes to introduce you to the genre.

Convento de San Francisco MONASTERY
(Mendoza 450) This colonial monastery dates from the city's founding, and was beautifully restored in 1939. The small colonnade is modeled on Bernini's at St Peter's in Rome, and the monastery has its own **museum** (admission free; ⏲8am-noon & 5-9pm Mon-Fri), with religious art and artifacts.

FREE **Teatro Juan de Vera** THEATRE
(San Juan 637) A striking belle epoque building; ask at the ticket office if you can have a peek inside to see the beautiful treble-galleried theater and its painted ceiling. The cupola retracts when management fancies a starlit performance.

Festivals & Events

Corrientes' traditionally riotous **Carnaval Correntino** competes with Gualeguaychú's for the title of the country's best. Celebrated Friday through Sunday on the last three weekends in February and the first weekend of March, Carnaval's parades along the *costanera* attract participants from neighboring provinces and countries, with huge crowds.

Sleeping

Corrientes has some great places to stay. During Carnaval, the provincial tourist office can help out with lodging in family homes. Many Corrientes hotels offer a 10% discount for paying cash.

TOP CHOICE **La Alondra** BOUTIQUE HOTEL $$$
(☎443-0555; www.laalondra.com.ar; Av 3 de Abril 827; tw/ste AR$490/550; ❄📶🏊) Sumptuously furnished with dark-wood antiques, this wonderfully renovated house is an oasis of relaxation from the unappealing main road. Most of the seven rooms that surround a small finger-shaped pool are suites boasting plush king-sized beds and characterful bathrooms fitted with claw-foot tubs. Wonderfully handsome public areas and classy service add up to a most impressive package. There are often deals below the prices quoted here.

TOP CHOICE **Bienvenida Golondrina** HOSTEL $
(☎443-5316; www.bienvenidagolondrina.com; La Rioja 455; dm AR$65-70; ❄@📶) Occupying a marvelous centenarian building, all high ceilings, stained glass, and artistic flourishes, this hostel makes a great base a few steps from the *costanera.* Comfortable wide-berthed dorm beds have headroom, facilities are great, and the warmly welcoming management couldn't be more helpful.

Turismo Hotel Casino HOTEL $$$
(☎446-2244; www.turismohotelcasino.com.ar; Entre Ríos 650; r AR$506, ste AR$612-1118; ❄@📶🏊👪) By the casino on the riverfront, this stately old place has had a complete refit. It's now an excellent hotel, with modern rooms that are huge, elegantly and artistically furnished, but cozy and quiet. It doesn't cost much to upgrade to a sizeable suite; other drawcards include the big pool with plenty of chaise longues and spa facilities.

La Rozada BOUTIQUE HOTEL $$
(☎443-3001; www.larozada.com; Plácido Martínez 1223; r AR$440-575; ❄@📶) An excellent option near the riverfront, this has commodious apartments and suites set in the tower in the courtyard of an appealing 19th-century,

battleship-gray historic building. Fine views are on offer from most rooms – a balcony room is slightly more expensive – and there's an attractive bar-restaurant. Guests can use the pool at the nearby rowing club.

Astro Apart Hotel HOTEL **$$**
(☎446-6112; www.astroapart.com; Bolívar 1285; s/d AR$260/320; ❄@📶) Top value is to be had at this new place, which features sizeable, handsome white rooms with great beds and large windows. They come with a simple kitchen and offer plenty of handy facilities as reasonably priced extras.

Corrientes Plaza Hotel HOTEL **$$**
(☎446-6500; www.hotel-corrientes.com.ar; Junín 1549; s/d AR$230/310; ❄@📶🏊) A good deal on the square in the heart of modern Corrientes, the Plaza has spacious, faultless modern rooms with LCD television and most with minibar. Staff are friendly and there's a good breakfast spread.

Orly Hotel HOTEL **$$**
(☎442-0280; www.hotelorlycorrientes.com.ar; San Juan 867; standard s/d AR$226/289, superior r AR$480; ❄@📶) Spruce and spotless, this professional and attractive three-star job overlooks a small plaza. It's divided in two; the older standard rooms are fine but smallish, and wi-fi doesn't reach all of them. The superiors are great, with huge beds, modish couches and good bathrooms.

Hotel Victoria HOTEL **$**
(☎443-5547; hotelvictoria1@hotmail.com; Av España 1050; s/d AR$155/200; ❄@📶) This is one of two decent adjacent budget choices near Plaza JB Cabral. The doubles are far better than the twins or poky singles.

Eating

Look out for *mbaipú*, a traditional *correntino* dish of fried beef and onions topped with toasted flour and cheese.

Corrientes

TOP CHOICE **Enófilos** ARGENTINE **$$**
(☎443-9271; Junín 1260; mains AR$50-75; ⏲lunch & dinner Mon-Sat; 📶) An *enófilo* is a wine-lover, so the cellar gets plenty of attention at this attentive upstairs restaurant on the *peatonal*. The wine 'list' is displayed in a small temple at the room's center; traditional *correntino* ingredients such as succulent surubí river fish are given creative flair, and fine cuts of meat are showcased to great advantage with exquisite sauces and fresh vegetables. It's a great place to get off the pizza, pasta and *parrilla* treadmill. There's a set menu available on weekdays for AR$68.

Martha de Bianchetti CAFE, BAKERY **$**
(cnr 9 de Julio & Mendoza; pastries from AR$5; ⏲8am-1pm & 4-11pm Mon-Sat) This old-fashioned Italian-style bakery and cafe serves mind-altering pastries and excellent coffee; each cup comes with *chipacitos* (small cheese pastries). All the yummy treats are warm when the doors open.

La Costa ARGENTINE **$$**
(cnr Costanera & 9 de Julio; mains AR$30-60; ⏲Tue-Sun) On the *costanera* – walk a block beyond the casino to find it – this two-level modern place has a buzzy atmosphere, and serves a wide variety of Argentine dishes, including great *parrillada*. It's popular in the evenings, but you'll appreciate the river views from the floor-to-ceiling windows more over lunch.

Corrientes

Top Sights
Museo de Artesanías Tradicionales Folclóricas B1

Sights
1 Convento de San Francisco C1
2 Museo Histórico de Corrientes B2
3 Teatro Juan de Vera C2

Sleeping
4 Astro Apart Hotel C3
5 Bienvenida Golondrina B1
6 Corrientes Plaza Hotel D2
7 Hotel Victoria D3
8 La Alondra B4
9 La Rozada C1
10 Orly Hotel C2
11 Turismo Hotel Casino A1

Eating
12 Enófilos C2
13 Martha de Bianchetti C2

Shopping
14 La Casa de Chamamé D2
15 Museo de Artesanías Tradicionales Folclóricas B1

El Quincho PARRILLA **$$**
(cnr Pujol & Roca; parrillada for 2 AR$98-119) Rustic and welcoming, this Corrientes classic sits on a roundabout a short walk east of the center. El Quincho is more about Argentine grill classics such as chorizo and *morcilla* (blood sausage) than fancy cuts of steak; there's always a deal on *parrilla* including drinks and dessert that comes out cheaper than the price we've listed here.

Drinking & Entertainment

The area near the intersection of Junín and Buenos Aires contains several bars and clubs pumping along at weekends. The *costanera* also receives some action, with several bars and *boliches* (nightclubs) in the Costanera Sur zone south of the bridge to Resistencia.

Parrilla Puente Pexoa TRADITIONAL MUSIC
(☎445-1687; RN 12 at Virgen de Itatí roundabout; ⏲from 8:30pm Fri & Sat) Corrientes is the heartland of the lively music and dance known as *chamamé* (p159), and seeing a live performance is memorable. This relaxed restaurant features *chamamé* dances every weekend and it can be outrageous fun when the dancing starts. Men and women show up in full gaucho regalia, and up to four *conjuntos* (bands) may play each night, usually starting around 11pm. You can get here via a taxi (around AR$30) or grab bus 102. Make sure you specify it's the *parrilla* you're going to, as Puente Pexoa itself is a place further away.

Shopping

Museo de Artesanías Tradicionales Folclóricas HANDICRAFTS
(Quintana 905; ⏲8am-noon & 4-9pm Mon-Sat) The shop, which is attached to this museum sells a wide variety of traditional handicrafts.

La Casa de Chamamé MUSIC
(Pellegrini 1790) This CD shop specializes in Corrientes' roots music, plus you can listen before you buy.

BUSES FROM CORRIENTES

DESTINATION	COST (AR$)	DURATION (HR)
Buenos Aires	298	13
Córdoba	289	12
Mercedes	59	3
Paraná	195	10
Paso de los Libres	90	6
Posadas	101	4
Puerto Iguazú	198	9
Rosario	238	11
Salta	268	14
Santa Fe	189	9

Information

Locutorios (private telephone offices) and internet places are easy to find. There are many banks with ATMs on 9 de Julio between La Rioja and Córdoba.

Municipal tourist office (☎447-4733; www.ciudad decorrientes.gov.ar; bus terminal; ⏲7am-10pm) Other branch on the Costanera at the end of 9 de Julio.

Provincial tourist office (☎442-7200; www.turismocorrientes.gov.ar; 25 de Mayo 1330; ⏲8am-2pm, 3-9pm) The most helpful.

Getting There & Away

Aerolíneas Argentinas (☎442-3918; Junín 1301) flies from Corrientes airport to Buenos Aires daily, and three times weekly to Asunción, Paraguay. It also flies to both destinations from nearby Resistencia.

The **long-distance bus terminal** (☎441-4839; Av Maipú 2400) is 3km east of the center. Nearby Resistencia has better long-distance bus connections to the west and northwest. Buses to Resistencia (AR$2.50, 40 minutes) leave frequently from the **local bus terminal** (cnr Av Costanera General San Martín & La Rioja). Faster are the shared taxis that zip you into Resistencia for AR$7. They leave from the same intersection, and also from the corner of Av 3 de Abril and Santa Fe.

Getting Around

Local bus 105 (AR$2) goes to the **airport** (☎445-8684), about 10km east of town on RN 12. Bus 6 runs between the local bus terminal and the long-distance bus terminal on Av Maipú. Bus 103 connects the long-distance bus terminal with downtown; a taxi will cost AR$15 to AR$18.

Mercedes

☎03773 / POP 40,667

The main access point for the spectacular Esteros del Iberá wetlands, Mercedes is a rather handsome gaucho town with a mightily easy pace to life. Its claim to fame is the nearby – and completely surreal – roadside shrine to the gaucho Antonio Gil (p163), an enormously popular religious phenomenon.

Manos Correntinas (San Martín 499; ⏲Mon-Sat) is a friendly handcrafts gallery and shop that displays the work of a cooperative of local craftspeople.

Sleeping & Eating

Hotel Sol HOTEL $

(☎420283; San Martín 519; s/d AR$120/200; ❄📶) Situated two blocks down from the plaza, this welcoming spot is built around a stunning patio: a riot of plants, birdsong and gleaming chessboard tiles. The high-ceilinged old rooms opening off it are good for the price; there are also very attractive modern rooms (double AR$260) up at the back.

Hotel Itá Pucú HOTEL $

(☎421015; Batalla de Salta 645; r per person AR$75; ❄📶@) Round the corner from Hotel Sol, this friendly low-roofed hotel has a sort of spaghetti-western feel, and OK rooms that open onto a grassy garden. Breakfast is an extra cost.

Hotel Horizontes HOTEL $

(☎420489; Gómez 734; s/d AR$108/164; ❄📶) A block from the bus station, this bare but very clean hotel offers good value for comfy rooms with compact bathrooms.

Sabor Único ARGENTINE $

(San Martín 518; mains AR$25-50) Moving to these new premises opposite the Hotel Sol at the time of research, this is the town's best eating option, with usual favorites as well as a couple of more typical *correntino* dishes.

Information

There's an irregularly attended **tourist information office** at the bus terminal. There's also a helpful independent **information booth** (⏲9-11am & 4-7pm Mon-Sat) there, run by the town's HI hostel. If it's closed, head to the hostel itself.

Most services are along San Martín, which links the bus terminal with the plaza.

Getting There & Away

The **bus terminal** (☎420165; cnr San Martín & Perreyra) is six blocks west of the plaza. Buses run regularly both ways. Destinations include Buenos Aires (AR$270, 12 hours), Paso de los Libres (AR$25, three hours), and Corrientes (AR$60, 3½ hours).

For information about transport to Colonia Pellegrini and the Esteros del Iberá, see p168.

Reserva Provincial Esteros del Iberá

This stunning wetland reserve is home to an abundance of bird and animal life, and is one of the finest places to see wildlife in South America. Although tourism has been increasing substantially in recent years, Esteros del Iberá remains comparatively unspoiled. The main base for visiting the park is the sleepy village of **Colonia Pellegrini**, 120km northeast of Mercedes; it offers a variety of excellent accommodations and trips to the reserve. Rural *estancias* (ranches) in the larger area also make excellent bases.

The lakes and *esteros* (estuary) are shallow, fed only by rainwater, and thick with vegetation. Water plants and other vegetation accumulate to form *embalsados* (dense floating islands), and this fertile habitat is home to a stunning array of life. Sinister black caimans bask in the sun while capybaras feed around them. Other mammals include the beautiful orange-colored marsh deer, howler monkeys (officially the world's noisiest animal), the rare maned wolf, coypu, otters and several species of bat.

There are some 350 species of bird present in the reserve, including colorful kingfishers, delicate hummingbirds, parrots, spoonbills, kites, vultures, several species of egret and heron, cormorants, ducks, cardinals and the enormous southern screamer, which would really light up Big Uncle Bob's eyes at a Christmas roast. *Ibera: Vida y Color* (AR$40 to AR$60), on sale at various places around town, is a useful wildlife guide with beautiful photos of most of the birds, plants and animals you may see.

GAUCHITO GIL

Spend time on the road anywhere in Argentina and you're bound to see at least one roadside shrine surrounded by red flags and votive offerings. These shrines pay homage to Antonio Gil, a Robin Hood–like figure whose shrine and burial place 9km west of Mercedes attracts hundreds of thousands of pilgrims every year.

Little is known for sure about 'El Gauchito,' as he is affectionately known, but many romantic tales have sprung up to fill the gaps. What is known is that he was born in 1847 and joined the army – some versions say to escape the wrath of a local policeman whose fiancée had fallen in love with him – to fight in the War of the Triple Alliance.

Once the war ended, Gil was called up to join the Federalist Army, but went on the run with a couple of other deserters. The trio roamed the countryside, stealing cattle from rich landowners and sharing it with poor villagers, who in turn gave them shelter and protection. The law finally caught up with the gang, and Gil was hung by the feet from the espinillo tree that still stands near his grave, and beheaded.

So how did this freeloading, cattle-rustling deserter attain saintlike status? Moments before his death, Gil informed his executioner that the executioner's son was gravely ill. He told the soldier that if he were buried – not the custom with deserters – the man's son would recover.

After lopping off Gil's head, the executioner carried it back to the town of Goya where – of course – a judicial pardon awaited Gil. On finding that his son was indeed seriously ill, the soldier returned to the site and buried the body. His son recovered quickly, word spread and a legend was born.

'Gauchito' Gil's last resting place is now the site of numerous chapels and storehouses holding thousands of votive offerings – including T-shirts, bicycles, pistols, knives, license plates, photographs, cigarettes, hair clippings and entire racks of wedding gowns – brought by those who believe in the gaucho's miracles. January 8, the date of Gil's death, attracts the most pilgrims. If you are driving past, the story goes that you must sound your horn or suffer long delays on the road – or, more ominously, never arrive at all.

1
2
4

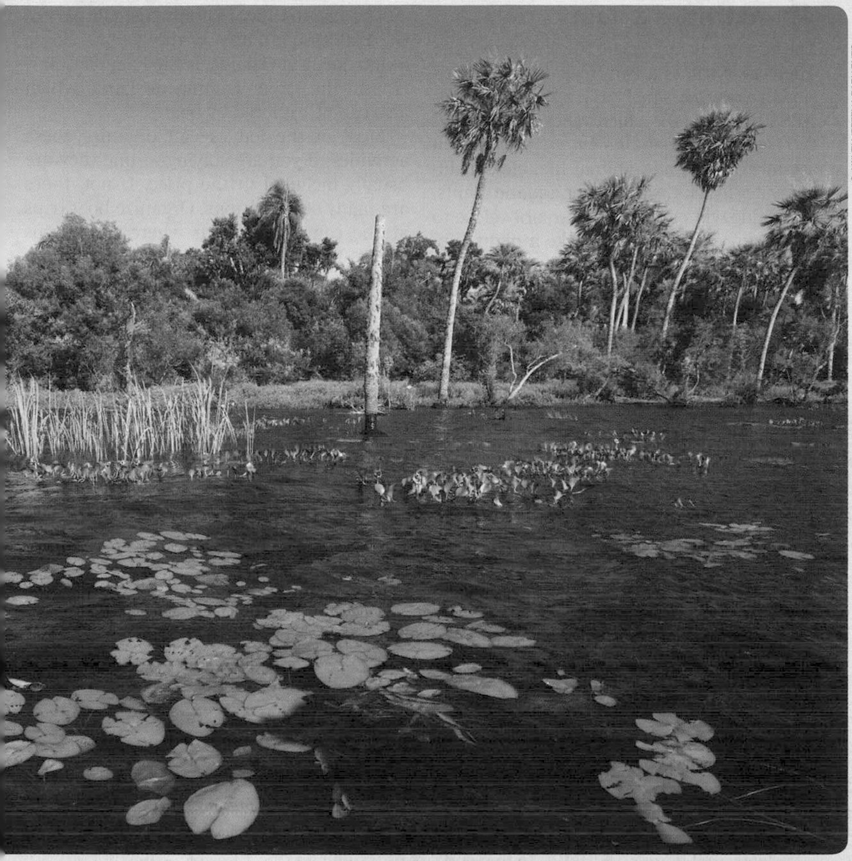

ɪguazú Falls (p185)
ɪwing this jaw-dropping sight is one of the :hlights of a visit to Argentina.

Esteros del Iberá (p163)
ınning wetlands that contain an abundant ay of wildlife and aquatic plants.

Toucan
ɪs colorful bird can be easily seen at ɾque Nacional Iguazú.

San Ignacio Miní (p179)
e best preserved mission ruins in all of ɡentina.

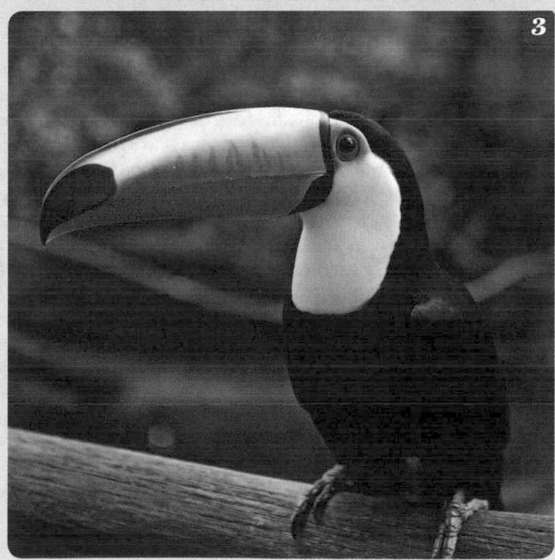

3

Activities & Tours

The best way to appreciate the area is by boat. The classic trip is a two- to 2½-hour excursion in a *lancha* (small passenger motorboat; AR$80 to AR$90), which takes you around the Laguna Iberá and its *embalsados*. You'll see myriad bird and animal life, elegant lilies, water hyacinths and other aquatic plants. The guide will punt you remarkably close to the creatures. You can also take a night trip; go prepared with plenty of insect repellent!

The short path opposite the visitors center gives you a sporting chance of seeing howler monkeys up close, and their other paths here introduce you to the different plants and habitats of the area. You can take guided night walks on one of the paths. Longer guided walks are also available, as are horseback rides (AR$70), although these are more for the ride's sake than for wildlife spotting. Several of the lodges offer a *día del campo* – a day's excursion to a ranch that incorporates horseback riding, an *asado* (barbecue) and other gaucho pursuits.

The Laguna Iberá is only a small part of the 13,000-sq-km area of the Esteros. Some 80km north, at Galarza, is the Laguna Galarza and the larger Laguna de Luna, which also can be explored by boat.

Most of the lodges can organize these activities; if you are staying at one they are usually included in the price. If not, there are many other options. Organize boat trips at the camp site (from where most trips leave). There are several local, independent guides in town; the tourist office has a list. Note that few guides speak English; if you want an English-speaking guide, it's best to go through one of the lodges.

Sleeping

COLONIA PELLEGRINI

Colonia Pellegrini's accommodations are mushrooming, with more than 20 at last count. They are divided between *hospedajes*, usually simple rooms behind a family home, and posadas (inns) or *hosterías*, comfortable lodges that offer full-board rates and excursions. Multiday packages are usually the

ECOLOGICAL ISSUES IN THE IBERÁ

With increasingly unpredictable weather systems assailing Argentina's pasturelands, the wildlife-rich wetlands of the Esteros del Iberá are under threat from a variety of sources, including traditional agricultural practices such as illegal pumping and burning-off to provide cattle-grazing land; local rice-growing interests have agitated for a dam to be built in the area to guarantee water for their crops.

The ecosystem of the Esteros is delicate and environmentalists are understandably anxious that it not be harmed. To this end, US entrepreneur Doug Tompkins has bought large tracts of land around the reserve and proposes to donate them to the Corrientes government, if it guarantees to put them and the existing Iberá wildlife reserve under the control of the Argentine government as a national park.

But many locals – who have named one of the donkeys roaming Colonia Pellegrini's streets after the millionaire – are far from thrilled by Tompkins' purchases, which mean the loss of their longstanding access and irrigation rights and the eviction of people who have lived on the land for generations (though never owned it).

Above all, some suspect that this foreign interest has a more sinister purpose. Beneath this part of northern Argentina – and extending into Brazil, Uruguay and Paraguay – is the Guaraní Aquifer, an immense body of underground fresh water which, as drinking water becomes an increasingly valuable global resource, is taking on major political importance. Nationalistic Argentines (and there are plenty) feel that this aquifer may eventually help put the nation back in a significant position on the global stage and (understandably, given South America's deplorable history of outside exploitation) view Tompkins' involvement with deep suspicion. What seemed like a straightforward act of ecological philanthropy has now become a political hot potato, pitting landowners, agribusiness and local, regional and national politicians against each other. Meanwhile the capybaras and caimans go about their business, oblivious that their fate is being decided at board meetings.

Check out www.theconservationlandtrust.org and www.proyectoibera.org for Tompkins' position and www.salvemosalibera.org (in Spanish) for water issues.

best value here. All the following can book a transfer from Mercedes or Posadas for you.

Posada de La Laguna LODGE $$$
(03773-499413; www.posadadelalaguna.com; Guazú Virá s/n; s/d with full board and activities AR$970/1645;) Simple and elegant, in wide grounds by a lake, it has bright white rooms with great beds and paintings by the owner. The emphasis is on relaxation (ie no TV), and staff pull it off, with friendly service, guided trips and good meals.

Hostería Ñandé Retá LODGE $$
(03773-499411; www.nandereta.com; s/d AR$250/500, 3 days & 2 nights incl full board & excursions s/d AR$1760/2660;) This place has been around longer than any, and is still one of the most pleasing. Surrounded by pines and eucalypts, it's got a peaceful, hidden-away feel that is highly seductive. It's very family friendly, the rooms are colorful, service excellent and the pool is a decent size. Good value.

Posada Rancho Jabirú GUESTHOUSE $
(03773-15-413750; www.posadaranchojabiru.com.ar; Yaguareté s/n; s/d AR$80/160) The best of the options in this price category. Set in a carefully tended garden, it has spotless rooms sleeping up to five in a pretty adobe bungalow. It's run by the friendly folk of Yacarú Porá restaurant next door.

Camping Iberá CAMPGROUND $
(03773-15-629656; www.ibera.gov.ar; Mbiguá s/n; per person 1st/subsequent days AR$45/35, vehicle AR$15) This municipal campground by the lake is a great place with grassy pitches, nearly all with their own *quincho* (thatched-roof building). This is where to go for boat trips; it's also worth checking out the view as the sun sets. Book ahead as it's not huge.

Aguapé Lodge LODGE $$$
(03773-499412; www.iberaesteros.com.ar; Yacaré s/n; small/large r incl full board s AR$628/758, d AR$1040/1343;) This luxurious colonial-style posada is in a beautiful setting above the lake. It has attractive, high-ceilinged rooms along a veranda looking over the lawn to the water, and a wide variety of excursions. Service is multilingual and professional.

Irupé Lodge LODGE $$
(0376-443-8312; www.ibera-argentina.com; Yacaré s/n; s/d standard AR$300/455, superior AR$760;) On the lake near the causeway, this rustic lodge makes you feel very welcome. While the rooms are satisfactory, artistic wooden furniture, a pool and views across the water are the highlights. Superiors are a lot better, more attractive and sizeable with more privacy, air-con and private verandas.

Hospedaje San Cayetano GUESTHOUSE $
(03773-15-400929; www.iberasancayetano.com.ar; cnr Guazú Virá & Aguapé; s/d AR$120/160;) This friendly choice with plunge pool, kitchen and *parrilla* offers a variety of rooms, from simple flop-downs with shared bathroom to twins, doubles and family rooms with good beds and showers. Rooms can be private or shared, and prices are negotiable. The boss runs good boat trips and transfers.

Posada Ypa Sapukai LODGE $$$
(03773-15-514212; www.iberaturismo.com.ar; Mburucuyá s/n; s/d AR$490/580;) Secluded and rustic, this lodge has grounds (with hammocks and chairs for lounging) that stretch down to the lake and small dark rooms. It wins points for the name, which means 'The Cry of the Lake'. Daily excursion included.

Hospedaje Los Amigos GUESTHOUSE $
(03773-15-493753; hospedajelosamigos@gmail.com; cnr Guazú Virá & Aguapé; r per person AR$50-60) An excellent budget choice, with a kindly owner, this offers spotless rooms with big beds and decent bathrooms for a pittance. You can also eat simply but well here.

Hospedaje Iberá GUESTHOUSE $
(03773-15-627261; cnr Guazú Virá & Ysypó; r per person AR$60) Clean rooms with fan and hot water. Bathroom behind a shop.

La Antigua Posada GUESTHOUSE $
(03773-15-401111; iberalaantiguaposada@hotmail.com; s/d AR$195/240;) Cool, high-ceilinged rooms along a veranda. It has a cafe and very helpful owners.

AROUND RESERVE PROVINCIAL ESTEROS DEL IBERÁ

Estancia Rincón del Socorro LODGE $$$
(03782-497073; www.rincondelsocorro.com; s/d incl full board & excursions AR$1560/2080;) Off the Mercedes road, 31km south of Pellegrini, this ranch, owned by ecocampaigner Doug Tompkins, is a place in which to come to terms with the big sky and abundant wildlife. It's substantial country comfort rather than luxury; the pretty rooms interconnect, making them great for family stays, while freestanding cabins sleep two. Around the complex, vast lawns blend into pastureland and contemplation. If this isn't remote enough, head over to **San Alonso**, its sister *estancia*, only reachable by plane.

Estancia San Lorenzo LODGE $$$
(☎03756-481292; www.estanciasanlorenzo.com; d per person incl full board & excursions AR$1240; ⏰Mar-Nov) This divine little four-room *estancia* in Galarza is run by its exceptionally friendly owners who cook, talk, guide you on horseback and buzz you around the nearby lagoons to spy on caimans and capybaras. The food, all of it homemade, is superb (and seemingly endless). It can be tough to get there without a 4WD, but they'll pick you up (AR$500 return) from Gobernador Virasoro (80km away), which is easily reached by bus or car from Posadas.

Hotel Puerto Valle LODGE $$$
(☎03786-425700; www.hotelpuertovalle.com; RN 12, Km 1282; d incl full board AR$1733; ❄📶🏊) This luxurious option is on the bank of the Paraná near the northeastern tip of the Esteros. It boasts five impeccable rooms in spacious grounds that include a caiman farm. Meals are excellent.

Eating

All of the midrange and top-end accommodations options put meals on for their guests. If you ask nicely in advance, and they have space, most of them will let nonguests eat. There are other simple options in town.

Yacarú Porá ARGENTINE $
(cnr Caraguatá & Yaguareté; mains AR$25-45) Run with charm and enthusiasm, this bungalow guarantees a warm welcome. The food is prepared to order and features generous portions of meat, chicken dishes, pasta, omelets and *milanesas* (breaded cutlets).

Don Marcos ARGENTINE $
(cnr Ruta 40 & Guazú Virá; mains AR$20-40; ⏰lunch) On the main road, this offers simple, tasty home cooking. Sometimes opens for dinner at busy times.

Information

The enthusiastic **municipal tourist office** (info.turismo@ibera.gov.ar; ⏰8am-7pm) is at the entrance to the village, after crossing the causeway en route from Mercedes, and it's the best source of general information. The reserve's **visitors center** (⏰7:30am-noon & 2-6pm), on the Mercedes side of the causeway, has an exhibition, audiovisual presentation and short paths.

Note that as yet there is no bank or ATM in Colonia Pellegrini, so take plenty of cash. Internet access is limited; there's unreliable public access at a house on the corner of Guazú Virá and Timbó (AR$6 per hour).

Getting There & Away

The road from Mercedes to Colonia Pellegrini (120km) isn't as bad as everyone says it is, and is gradually getting better, with the first 80km slowly being sealed. Except after heavy rain it's easily drivable in a normal car.

Bus services (AR$35, three to four hours) are basic and unreliable; check at the bus terminal information office. The most reliable departure is at 12:30pm Monday through Friday, and 9:30am Saturday, returning from Pellegrini at 5am.

A faster and more comfortable way to get there is by combi or 4WD. This costs AR$100 per person if there are enough people, more if not. Arrange this through the information booth at the Mercedes bus terminal or contact **Hugo** (☎03773-1541-9092; cnr Guazú Virá & Timbó) in Colonia Pellegrini. If it hasn't been raining, you could also get a *remise* from Mercedes if there's a group of you.

The road from Posadas is much worse (take the turning between Gobernador Virasoro and Santo Tomé if you're in a normal car). Drivers charge AR$800 to AR$1000 for a charter to Posadas, or AR$600 to Gobernador Virasoro, from where frequent buses head the 80km on to Posadas.

There's no gas station in Pellegrini; the closest are in Mercedes and at the main road junction near Santo Tomé. Fill up before you head in. A couple of places in Pellegrini can sell you petrol and diesel.

Be aware that car hire companies in Posadas may refuse you service if you mention that the Iberá is one of your destinations.

ALONG THE RÍO URUGUAY

The second of the two great rivers that converge above Buenos Aires to form the Río de la Plata, the Río Uruguay divides the country of the same name from Argentina, and also forms part of the border with Brazil. Bridges provide access to these neighbors, whose influences have blended with those of indigenous and immigrant groups in the area. The riverside towns on the Argentine side offer plenty and are popular summer destinations for *porteños* (people from Buenos Aires).

Concepción

☎03442 / POP 73,824

Set around a stately plaza, Concepción del Uruguay (its full name) is a typical riverside town, wondering what to do with itself now that trade on the Río Uruguay has died off. It makes a decent stopover on the way north, has a couple of excellent places to stay and boasts the Palacio San José outside town.

Sights

The principal sights in the town itself are around the noble main plaza, where the earthy-pink colored basilica, Palacio San José, holds the remains of Justo José de Urquiza.

Palacio San José PALACE
(www.palaciosanjose.com.ar; RP 39, Km30; adult/child AR$5/1; ⏲8am-7pm Mon-Fri, 9am-6pm Sat & Sun) Topped by twin towers and surrounded by elegant gardens, Justo José de Urquiza's ostentatious pink palace is 33km west of Concepción via RP 39. Set around an arched patio, with a walled garden out the back, it was built partly to show up Urquiza's arch rival in Buenos Aires, Juan Manuel de Rosas, and partly to show the power and wealth of Entre Ríos province. Local *caudillo* (provincial strongman) Urquiza was largely responsible for Rosas' downfall in 1852 and the eventual adoption of Argentina's modern constitution.

Sometime allies such as Domingo Sarmiento and Bartolomé Mitre supped at Urquiza's 8.5m dining-room table and slept in the palatial bedrooms. The bedroom in which Urquiza was murdered by a mob sent by Ricardo López Jordán is a permanent shrine, created by Urquiza's wife.

If you don't mind walking the final 3km to the palace, you can get a Caseros-bound bus from Concepción and get the driver to drop you at the turnoff, but an easier option is to take a *remise* direct from Concepción. **Sarbimas** (☎427777) will take up to four people there and back, including a two-hour wait, for AR$115. Another option is a tour – **Turismo Pioneros** (☎433914; www.turismopioneros.com.ar) will take two people for AR$100, including guided visit. There's a mediocre restaurant at the palace and picturesque grounds for picnicking.

Sleeping

TOP CHOICE Antigua Posta del Torreón BOUTIQUE HOTEL $$
(☎432618; www.postadeltorreon.com.ar; Almafuerte 799; s/d AR$280/320; ❄@📶🏊) This intimate and classy hotel a block west and four south of the plaza offers a real haven for a relaxing stay. It's an elegantly refurbished 19th-century mansion, with rooms surrounding a postcard-pretty courtyard complete with fountain and small swimming pool.

Antigua Fonda HOTEL $
(☎433734; www.antiguafonda.com.ar; España 172; s/d AR$140/200; ❄📶) Likable owners have created this from part of what was once an historic Concepción hotel (though you wouldn't know). Pleasing rooms in shades of cream surround a small grassy garden, with artistic touches and a relaxing vibe. No breakfast, but there's a kitchen you can use. It's a block west and three south of the plaza.

Residencial Centro GUESTHOUSE $
(☎427429; www.nuevorescentro.com.ar; Moreno 130; d AR$140; ❄📶) The best budget deal in town has a variety of rooms around a courtyard. They vary slightly in price depending on size and if they have air-con; there's more light in the ones upstairs. A block down the street is a simpler place, **La Posada** (per person AR$80), that's a better deal for solo travelers.

Eating

El Conventillo de Baco ARGENTINE $$
(☎433809; España 193; dishes AR$35-55) Near the Antigua Posta del Torreón hotel, this handsome place has both indoor and outdoor dining in an attractive patio space and specializes in well-prepared river fish and seafood, with dishes like calamari stew and glazed pork as specialties. Good value.

Café de la Plaza CAFE $
(www.cafedelaplazabar.com.ar; cnr Urquiza & Galarza; light meals AR$20-40; ⏲8am-2pm & 4pm-late) On the northwest corner of the plaza, this offbeat place has a bit of everything, with a terrace, chessboard tiles, tasty coffee, wooden bench-booths, food and regular live music.

Information

Telecentro Uruguay (3 de Febrero 63; internet per hr AR$3) Internet and phone calls just off the plaza.

Tourist office (☎425820; www.concepcionturismo.gov.ar; 9 de Julio 844; ⏲7am-8pm Mon-Fri, 7am-10pm Sat & Sun) Helpful, but not clearly marked, it's two blocks west of the plaza.

BUSES FROM CONCEPCIÓN

DESTINATION	COST (AR$)	DURATION (HR)
Buenos Aires	115	4½
Colón	9	¾
Concordia	26	3
Gualeguaychú	14	1¼
Paraná	40	5

Getting There & Around

The **bus terminal** (☎422352; cnr Galarza & Chiloteguy) is 10 blocks west of the plaza. Bus 1 (AR$1.75) runs between them; a *remise* costs AR$5 to AR$8.

Colón

☎03447 / POP 26,375

The most appealing destination for riverside relaxation in Entre Ríos, Colón is a very popular summer getaway for Argentine holidaymakers. Its population almost doubles in January, but the pretty town takes it all in its stride. With numerous places to stay, a thriving handicrafts scene and worthwhile, out-of-the-ordinary restaurants, it's a great place to be. It's also a base for visiting the Parque Nacional El Palmar.

One of three main Entre Ríos border crossings, Colón is connected to the Uruguayan city of Paysandú by the Puente Internacional General Artigas. The center of the action is Plaza San Martín, a block back from the river, and the street 12 de Abril running up to it.

Sights & Activities

Strolling around the riverbank and quiet leafy streets is the highlight here.

La Casona (www.artesanoslacasona.com.ar; 12 de Abril 106; ⏲9am-noon & 5-8pm), on the corner of the plaza, is a cooperative selling a wide range of handmade goods. There are numerous *artesanía* shops selling everything from *mate* gourds to pickled coypu.

In February the city hosts the **Fiesta Nacional de la Artesanía**, a crafts fair held in Parque Quirós that features high-standard live folkloric entertainment.

There are various boat trips available to explore the river and the Islas Vírgenes. Expect to pay AR$35 to AR$50 for a one- to two-hour excursion. **Itaicora Aventura** (☎423360; www.itaicora.com; San Martín 97) speak English.

Sleeping

There are numerous summer campgrounds, cabins, bungalows and apartments available for rental. The tourist office can supply you with a list.

TOP CHOICE **Hostería 'Restaurant del Puerto'** HOTEL **$**

(☎422698; www.hosteriadecolon.com.ar; Alejo Peyret 158; s/d AR$175/220; ❄@🛜≋♿) In what has a strong claim to be Colón's loveliest house (on its prettiest street), this has cracking, characterful rooms decorated faithfully in keeping with the 1880 building, with enormous windows, plenty of wood and noble rustic furniture. The family duplexes (AR$315 to AR$350) are a good deal, as are midweek discounts. There's a restaurant serving good dinners, and a heated pool and Jacuzzi out back.

Hotel Plaza HOTEL **$$**

(☎421043; www.hotel-plaza.com.ar; cnr 12 de Abril & Belgrano; d standard/superior AR$420/625; ❄@🛜≋) This Colón staple has been around for a while, but it certainly never looked like this before. A sleek refit has left it looking modern and glistening. The rooms aren't quite as posh; the superiors are the new ones, with quality bathrooms. But the combination of plaza-side location (some rooms in each category have balconies) and decent-sized heated pool out the back make it a winner.

WORTH A TRIP

GUALEGUAYCHÚ CARNAVAL

A mellow riverside town, Gualeguaychú (www.gualeguaychu.info) is quiet out of season but kicks off in summer, with the country's longest and flashiest Carnaval celebration. Make a stop here any weekend from mid-January to late February and you'll find things in full swing. The main venue is the Corsódromo, where admission is AR$60 to AR$70 most nights.

There's a string of decent budget hotels along Bolívar between Bartolomé Mitre and Monseñor Chalup, and three hostels in town.

The town is easily reached by bus from Buenos Aires (3½ hours), Paraná and other towns along the Río Uruguay.

Gualeguaychú is also a crossing point to Uruguay: the town of Fray Bentos lies just across the bridge.

Isla Formosa APARTMENTS $$
(☎421146; www.islaformosa.com.ar; 12 de Abril 442; d/f AR$240/320;) On the main street – head straight down Sourigues from the bus station to reach it – this complex offers large, comfortable apartments with decent kitchen that are a good deal for anybody and great for families. Prices are much lower off-season.

Eating & Drinking

There are numerous places to eat. Hit Urquiza for traditional Argentine options.

TOP CHOICE **La Cosquilla del Ángel** ARGENTINE $$
(☎423711; cnr San Martín & Balcarce; mains AR$45-80; Wed-Mon) Colón's best restaurant combines elegant decor, a big welcome and service with a whimsical and unpretentious approach, particularly in the curiously named dishes and the intriguing restaurant name, which translates as 'The Angel's Tickle.' Many dishes combine sweet and savory flavors; try the *mollejitas* (or *mollejas;* sweetbreads). The pasta is recommended and the wine list is above average.

El Viejo Almacén ARGENTINE $$
(☎422216; cnr Urquiza & Paso; mains AR$30-55) A block from the plaza and offering a quiet, brick-walled interior decorated with old-time photos, this has a wide-ranging menu including great homemade pasta, delicious *empanadas,* river fish, and *parrilla* options. Portions aren't as big as in some places,.

El Sótano de los Quesos CHEESE $
(cnr Chacabuco & Av Costanera; mixed plates for 1/2 persons AR$32/58; 4-9pm Tue-Fri, 11:30am-9:30pm Sat & Sun;) Near the tourist office, this intriguing spot serves a wide variety of artisanal cheeses and other delicacies at pretty thatched tables on a lawn looking over the port. There's also locally made wine and beer on hand, and a cellar shop whose aromas will almost compel you to buy.

Information

Tourist office (☎421996; www.colon.gov.ar; cnr Gouchón & Av Costanera; 7am-8pm Sun-Thu, 7am-9pm Fri & Sat) Occupies the former customs building, built by Urquiza. There is also an office in the bus terminal, open 8am to 1pm and 2pm to 8pm daily.

Getting There & Around

Colón's **bus terminal** (☎421716; cnr Rocamora & 9 de Julio) is seven blocks inland (roughly west) of the river and eight blocks north of the main shopping and entertainment street, 12 de Abril. A *remise* into the center costs AR$5 to AR$6.

Destinations include Buenos Aires (AR$115, five hours), Gualeguaychú (AR$20, two hours) via Concepción (AR$9, 40 minutes), Concordia (AR$18, 2½ hours) via Ubajay (AR$9, 1½ hours) and Paysandú, Uruguay (AR$16, 45 minutes).

For details about crossing into Uruguay, see the boxed text, above.

ENTERING URUGUAY

There are three main crossings linking Argentina with its eastern neighbor Uruguay. From south to north these are Gualeguaychú–Fray Bentos, Colón–Paysandú and Concordia–Salto. All three are open 24 hours. See p552, for Uruguayan entry requirements.

Parque Nacional El Palmar

☎03447

On the west bank of the Río Uruguay, midway between Colón and Concordia, the 8500 sq km **Parque Nacional El Palmar** (☎493049; www.elpalmarapn.com.ar; RN 14, Km199; Argentine/foreigner AR$20/40) preserves the last extensive stands of yatay palm on the Argentine littoral. In the 19th century the native yatay covered large parts of Entre Ríos, Uruguay and southern Brazil, but the intensification of agriculture, ranching and forestry throughout the region destroyed much of the palm savanna.

Reaching a maximum height of about 18m, with a trunk diameter of 40cm, the larger specimens clustered throughout the park accentuate a striking and soothing subtropical landscape that lends itself to photography. The grasslands and the gallery forests along the river and creeks shelter much wildlife.

Park admission (valid for 48 hours) is collected at the entrance on RN 14 from 7am to 7pm, but the gate is open 24 hours.

Sights & Activities

All the park's main facilities are 12km down a good dirt road leading from the entrance. Here, the **visitors center** (8am-7pm) has displays on natural history. You can organize canoeing, cycling and horseback-riding trips around the park here. Decent dirt roads lead off the main access road to three viewpoints.

Arroyo Los Loros, a short distance north of the campground by gravel road, is a good place to observe wildlife. South of the visitors center is Arroyo El Palmar, a pleasant stream accessed at two viewpoints, **La Glorieta** and **El Palmar**. These have short marked trails, and the latter has a hide for bird watching. There are three other short trails near the visitors center, and another bird watching hide near the Río Uruguay. Guided walks are available by prior arrangement.

There is excellent access to the river for swimming and boating from the campground.

Sleeping & Eating

In Ubajay there are basic rooms in the bus terminal complex as well as other cheap lodgings.

Camping El Palmar CAMPGROUND **$**
(☎423378; camp sites per person/tent AR$20/15) This sociable campground across the parking lot from the visitors center is the only place to stay that's in the park. It has shady, level camp sites, hot showers and electricity. The shop here sells snacks and food, including slabs of beef for the barbecues; opposite, there's a restaurant.

La Aurora del Palmar LODGE, CAMPGROUND **$$**
(☎421549; www.auroradelpalmar.com.ar; RN 14, Km 202; camp sites AR$20 plus AR$20 per adult; s/d without shower AR$110/200, d/q from AR$250/310;) Between Ubajay and the park entrance, this property, as well as being a cattle ranch and citrus farm, has a protected palm forest at least as spectacular as those in the national park itself. It's an original, well-run place with shady camp sites, family duplex rooms in a pretty bungalow, and rustic wooden rooms in renovated railway carriages. There's a good swimming pool and a restaurant. Canoeing, horseback riding, and palm safaris (AR$55) are available.

DON'T MISS

THERMAL SPAS ALONG THE URUGUAY

Most of the towns along the Río Uruguay – Gualeguaychú, Colón and Concordia for starters – have tapped the region's abundant geothermal aquifers to create appealing thermal spa complexes: a major focus of domestic tourism in these parts. They are well-equipped places with several indoor and outdoor pools of various temperatures. Entry to most of them is around AR$30 to AR$40. Check out www.termasdeentrerios.gov.ar for a complete list.

Getting There & Away

El Palmar is on RN 14, a major national highway, so there are frequent north–south bus services. Any bus running north towards Concordia will drop you at the park entrance, 12km from the visitors center. You could walk or hitchhike from here or else stay on the bus a further 6km to Ubajay, from where a *remise* will cost you AR$50 to AR$60 to the visitors center. Ask the callshop alongside the bus terminal to call you one.

There's also a school bus that heads into the park on weekdays at noon and in the afternoon from Ubajay that will take you for free if it has space.

Several agencies in Colón offer half-day trips to the park, which include a guided walk. **LHL** (☎422222; www.lhlturismo.com.ar; 12 de Abril 119) near the plaza is one: the trip costs AR$60 to AR$90 depending on numbers, plus the park entry fee.

Concordia

☎0345 / POP 170,033

This pleasant agricultural service town on the Río Uruguay won't keep you spellbound for weeks at a time, but makes a convenient stop for a night. It's a citrus town – you can smell the tang in the air at times – and has a fine central plaza, riverside beaches and fishing. It also offers a border crossing, via the Represa Salto Grande hydroelectric project, to the Uruguayan city of Salto.

Sights & Activities

FREE **Museo Regional de Concordia** MUSEUM
(cnr Entre Ríos & Ramírez; 9am-1pm & 2-7pm Mon-Fri, 9am-6pm Sat & Sun) This down-at-heel museum covers Italian immigration and also has some fine old furniture. The main interest is the fabulous building, which blends French neo-renaissance architecture with art nouveau touches. It's badly in need of restoration.

Museo Judío de Entre Ríos MUSEUM
(www.museojudioer.org.ar; Entre Ríos 476; admission AR$20; 8:30am-12:30pm) Three rooms detailing the arrival and struggles of the Jewish gauchos (see p174), their way of life and the Holocaust seen through the eyes of one who experienced it. Also temporary exhibitions.

FREE **Castillo San Carlos** RUIN

In the riverside Parque Rivadavia, at the northeastern edge of town, this ruined castle was built in 1888 by a French industrialist who mysteriously abandoned the property years later. French writer Antoine de Saint-Exupéry briefly lived in the building; there's a monument to his novella *The Little Prince* nearby. There's no charge for wandering around the ruins, but watch the kids.

Sleeping

Hotel Salto Grande HOTEL **$$**

(421-0034; www.hotelsaltogrande.net; Urquiza 581; s/d AR$278/350;) Just south of the main plaza, this polished, modern hotel offers excellent service and fair prices. There are several grades of room; the higher ones have better views and a minibar, but aren't a great deal better than the standards.

Hotel Pellegrini HOTEL **$**

(422-7137; hotelpellegrini@gmail.com; Pellegrini 443; s/d AR$100/190;) By far the best budget choice, this friendly family-run spot offers spotless rooms with TV and bathroom three blocks south of the plaza. Book ahead, as it's popular.

Hotel Concordia HOTEL **$**

(421-6869; La Rioja 518; s/d AR$120/220;) This cheap and cheerful choice occupies a cavernous building. Rooms vary in light, size and mattress quality. Bathrooms, some accessed via in-room stairs, are decent.

Eating

El Reloj PIZZA **$**

(Pellegrini 580; pizza AR$20-35) This spacious brick-walled pizzeria has good ambience and a staggering selection of options. A haven for the indecisive as staff don't grumble about doing half-and-halfs. It also does *parrilla*.

Malaika ARGENTINE **$$**

(422-4867; 1 de Mayo 59; mains AR$46-58; 8am-2am;) Trendy eating has arrived in Concordia in the form of this relaxed and handsome cafe-bar on the plaza. It serves a variety of tasty meals, with salads, pizza, pasta, snacks and more elaborate fare, including plenty of vegetarian options and daily specials. Decent wines, caring service and a romantic mood seal the deal. Also lunches for AR$44.

BUSES FROM CONCORDIA

DESTINATION	COST (AR$)	DURATION (HR)
Buenos Aires	158	6½
Colón	18	2½
Concepción	22	3
Corrientes	197	7
Paraná	83	4½
Paso de los Libres	74	4
Posadas	185	8

Information

Tourist office (421-3905; www.concordia.gov.ar/turismo; cnr Pellegrini & Mitre; 8am-7pm) On the square. The information desk at the bus terminal also has tourist info.

Getting There & Away

There are flights to Buenos Aires with **LAER** (0810-777-5237; www.laersa.com.ar). The **bus terminal** (421-7235; cnr Justo & Hipólito Yrigoyen) is 13 blocks north of Plaza 25 de Mayo. Four daily buses (none on Sunday) go to Salto, Uruguay (AR$20, 1¼ hours).

From the port beyond the east end of Carriego, launches cross the river to Salto (AR$15, 15 minutes) four times between 8:30am and 6:30pm Monday to Saturday.

The Buenos Aires-Posadas train line runs through Concordia. For details about crossing into Uruguay, see p171.

Getting Around

Bus 2 (AR$2) takes Yrigoyen south from the bus terminal to the center. On its northward run catch it on Pellegrini in front of Banco de la Nación. A taxi to the bus terminal from the center should cost about AR$10.

Paso de los Libres

03772 / POP 48,642

The name (meaning 'Crossing of the Free') is the most romantic thing about this border town on the banks of the Río Uruguay. It faces the larger Brazilian city of Uruguaiana on the opposite bank, and is connected to it by a well-used bridge. There's little to detain the traveler, but the town has plenty of cross-border life, a picturesque central plaza and decent sleeping and eating options.

Sleeping & Eating

Hotel Alejandro Primero HOTEL $$
(☎424100; www.alejandroprimero.com.ar; Coronel López 502; s/d AR$275/440;) A surprisingly good hotel, this has a swish lobby and restaurant area and slightly less impressive but very spacious rooms. Ask for one with views over the river and Uruguaiana in Brazil on the other side.

Hotel Las Vegas HOTEL $
(☎423490; Sarmiento 554; s/d AR$140/210;) Despite the burgundy carpets and '70s feel, this is a newish place in the center of town. The rooms are dark but comfortable and have bathrooms with good showers. The rooms up the back have more light and space.

El Nuevo Mesón ARGENTINE $$
(Colón 587; mains AR$30-50) Smartly turned out in black and white – the waiters seem to be camouflaged – this offers really well-prepared dishes. There's pizza, *parrilla* and more elaborate creations, but it's all fairly priced and very tasty indeed. Grab a table outside if the weather's fine.

Information

There's no tourist office, but there are maps of town all over the center. ATMs are on the plaza and along Avenida Colón.

Libres Cambio (Av Colón 901) Changes money.

Getting There & Away

The **bus terminal** (☎425600) is 1km from the center. There are several daily services to Buenos Aires (AR$240, 10 hours) and Posadas (AR$110, five hours), via towns in between. There are also services to Corrientes (AR$90, six hours) via Mercedes (AR$25, three hours). More buses bypass the town, but can drop you off on RN 14, where you can get a taxi the last 16km to downtown.

Buses to Uruguaiana, Brazil (AR$2), leave frequently from 7am onwards, stopping on Av San Martín at Av Colón and across from the bus terminal (by the castlelike building).

For information about visa requirements for crossing into Brazil, see p189. The frontier is open 24 hours. Travelers report that you can transit to Uruguay without requiring a Brazilian visa here.

Getting Around

The area between the bus terminal and downtown is a little dodgy at night. Minibuses (AR$1.50) run from the corner below the bus terminal into town. A taxi to the town center is AR$15.

POSADAS & THE JESUIT MISSIONS

The narrow northeastern province of Misiones juts out like an Argentine finger between Brazilian and Paraguayan territory and is named for the Jesuit missions (see the boxed text, p184) that were established in

THE GAUCHO JUDÍO

The gaucho is one of Argentina's archetypal images, but it's a little-known fact that many a gaucho was of Jewish origin. The first recorded instance of mass Jewish immigration to Argentina was in the late 19th century, when 800 Russian Jews arrived in Buenos Aires, fleeing persecution from Czar Alexander III.

The Jewish Colonization Association, funded by a wealthy German philanthropist, began to distribute 100-hectare parcels of land to immigrant families in the provinces of Entre Ríos, Santa Fe, Santiago del Estero, La Pampa and Buenos Aires.

The first major colony was in **Moisés Ville** in Santa Fe province, which became known at the time as Jerusalem Argentina. Today there are only about 300 Jewish residents left in town (15% of the population), but many Jewish traditions prevail: the tiny town boasts four synagogues, the bakery sells Sabbath bread, and kids in the street use Yiddish slang words like 'schlep' and 'schlock.'

These rural Jews readily assimilated into Argentine society, mixing their own traditions with those of their adopted country, so that it was not unusual to see a figure on horseback in baggy pants, canvas shoes and skullcap on his way to throw a lump of cow on the *asado* (barbecue). Many of their descendants have since left the land in search of education and opportunities in the cities. Argentina's Jews number about 200,000, making them Latin America's largest Jewish community.

To learn more about the *gauchos judíos*, visit the Museo Judío de Entre Ríos at Concordia.

the region and whose ruins are a major attraction. Today San Ignacio Miní is the best restored; it and other ruins (including those across the border in Paraguay; see p177) are easily accessed from the provincial capital, Posadas. Buses churn through Misiones en route to the Iguazú Falls in the north of the province, but a detour will take you to another stunning cascade – the Saltos del Moconá on the Río Uruguay (see the boxed text, p180).

The landscape here is an attraction. Approaching Misiones from the south you will see a change to gently rolling low hills, stands of bamboo, and papaya and manioc plantations. The highway passes tea and *mate* plantations growing from the region's trademark red soil – the province is the main producer of *mate*, Argentina's staple drink.

Posadas

☎0376 / POP 324,756

Capital of Misiones, and a base for visiting the ruins of the Jesuit missions after which the province is named, Posadas is a modern city that gazes across the wide Río Paraná to Encarnación in Paraguay. Brightly colored street signs vie for attention on the bustling, humid streets, and shady trees stand guard in the several parks and plazas. Posadas is a stopover for travelers on their way north to Paraguay or Iguazú, but has plenty of charm of its own, if little in the way of sights.

Posadas

0 — 200 m
0 — 0.1 miles

Sights

The Jesuit missions are the area's big attraction. In town, the mighty Paraná itself is the main sight of Posadas.

Palacio del Mate GALLERY

(Rivadavia 1846; 8am-12:30pm, 4-8pm Mon-Fri, 5-8pm Sat) Better than Posada's couple of desultory museums, this art gallery has temporary exhibitions and some displays on the *mate*-growing process.

Fundación Artesanías Misioneras GALLERY

(cnr Alvarez & Arrechea; 9am-12:30pm & 5-8pm Mon-Sat) Guaraní culture is strong in this part of Argentina, and you'll see Guaraní artists selling their wares throughout the center. Particularly fine pieces are displayed and sold here.

Tours

Many operators around town offer tours to the Iguazú Falls, the Jesuit missions and the Esteros del Iberá.

Guayrá TOURS

(☎443-3415; www.guayra.com.ar; San Lorenzo 2208) Very helpful tour agency offering half-day tours to the Jesuit missions (AR$315 to AR$375), the Paraguayan missions, Saltos del Moconá and more.

Posadas

Sights

1 Fundación Artesanías Misioneras B1
2 Palacio del Mate B2

Sleeping

3 City Hotel B2
4 Hotel Julio César B2
5 Hotel Posadas Urbano A2
6 Le Petit Hotel B3
7 Posadeña Linda B2
8 Residencial Misiones B2
9 Vuela El Pez Hostel B1

Eating

10 El Rayo A2
11 La Querencia B2

Drinking

12 Café La Nouvelle Vitrage B2

Festivals & Events

Posadas celebrates **Carnaval** (in February or March, depending on the year) with great gusto.

Sleeping

Hotel Posadas Urbano HOTEL $$$

(☎444-3800; www.hahotcles.com; Bolívar 2176; s/d/ste AR$452/525/713; ❄@📶🏊) The new kid on the Posadas block has rapidly become top dog with its wide array of facilities and great central location. The bright, large carpeted chambers all have great bathrooms, balconies and big windows with views over town. Suites add space but little else. The atrium pool space, art exhibitions, gym and spa facilities, and appealing lounge area add points.

Posadeña Linda HOSTEL $

(☎0376-15-452-3909; posadenalindahostel@hotmail.com; Bolívar 1439; dm AR$55-65, d AR$150; 📶🏊) Run with a caring attitude, this excellent narrow hostel a short walk from the square offers a genuine welcome, comfortable bunks and a patio with tiny plunge pool. It's colorful and relaxing; there should be air-con and a computer available by the time you read this.

La Aventura HOSTEL, CABINS $

(☎446-5555; www.complejolaaventura.com; cnr Avs Urquiza & Zapiola; dm AR$65, cabins from AR$310; ❄@📶🏊👪) This is a sort of HI-affiliated holiday camp, 4km from the center (bus 3 or 13 from Ayacucho, or a AR$20 taxi ride). Cabins sleep up to four; there are also dorm beds and hotel rooms. In the large, leafy grounds are a river beach, a good restaurant, a pool, tennis court, minigolf and more.

City Hotel HOTEL $

(☎443-9401; www.misionescityhotel.com.ar; Colón 1754; s/d AR$133/224; ❄@📶) Bang on the plaza, the City has just about the biggest sign in a big-sign town. Rooms vary; some are rather uninspiring with lino floors, but others, right up on the 10th and 11th floors, are nicer, with plenty of air and picturesque views from what's just about the city's highest point. The hotel is cheaper during the low season.

Le Petit Hotel HOTEL $$

(☎443-6031; www.hotellepetit.com.ar; Santiago del Estero 1630; s/d AR$200/250; ❄@📶) Peaceful and simple, this is run by a kindly, helpful couple and features dark, clean, adequate rooms with big bathrooms around a leafy patio. You can park easily in this quiet residential zone.

Residencial Misiones GUESTHOUSE $

(☎443-0133; Av Azara 1960; s/d AR$60/100) Offering seriously cheap rooms in a characterful central building, this is a budget option for those who aren't hygiene freaks. The mattresses are in reverse gear, but it gains points for the low prices and the staff's caring attitude. Rooms vary in quality, so have a look at a few.

WORTH A TRIP

YAPEYÚ

It would be untruthful to call this delightfully peaceful place a one-horse town: there are many horses, and the sound of their hooves thumping the reddish earth in the evening is one of the nicest things about it. Yapeyú is a great spot to relax; the sort of place where locals will greet you on the street.

An hour north of Paso de los Libres by bus, this was founded in 1626 as the southernmost of the Jesuit missions. It's also famous for being the birthplace of the great Argentine 'Liberator', José de San Martín.

You can examine the Jesuit ruins – the **museum** (admission free; ⌚8am-noon & 3-6pm Tue-Sun) here has a comprehensive overview of all the missions – and admire the ornate building that now shelters the ruins of the house where San Martín was born in 1778.

Right on the plaza between these two major sights, **Hotel San Martín** (☎03772-493120; Sargento Cabral 712; s/d AR$130/190; ❄) is a simple, welcoming place set around an echoey inner courtyard. For something more upmarket, head to the modern riverside bungalows at **El Paraíso Yapeyú** (☎03772-493056; www.paraisoyapeyu.com.ar; cnr Paso de los Patos & San Martín; bungalow for 2/4 people AR$185/305; ❄🏊), where you can also camp.

There are four to five daily buses (AR$9, one hour) to Paso de los Libres, some going further, and daily services to Posadas in the other direction. More buses stop on the highway at the edge of the town.

VISITING THE PARAGUAYAN MISSIONS

From Posadas there's a tempting and very rewarding day trip to two of the Jesuit missions in Paraguay. The ruined but majestic churches at Trinidad and Jesús de Tavarangüe have been carefully restored and preserve some fabulous stonework.

From Posadas, cross by bus to Encarnación (see p178) and get off at the bus terminal. From here, there are buses (most marked Ciudad del Este) every half-hour or so to Trinidad (G5000, 50 to 60 minutes). Get the driver to let you off at the turnoff to the ruins; it's then a 700m walk.

The **Trinidad ruins** (⏲7am-7pm, to 5:30pm Apr-Sep) are spectacular, with the red-brown stone of the church contrasting strongly with the flower-studded green grass and surrounding hillscapes. Unlike at the Argentine missions, there is much decoration preserved here: the scalloped niches still hold timeworn sculptures, and the font and elaborate baroque pulpit are impressive. The doorways are capped with fine, carved decoration. You can climb to the top of one of the walls, but careful with the kids – there's no guardrail up there. An earlier church and bell tower have also been restored here. There's a hotel and restaurant by the ruins.

For **Jesús de Tavarangüe**, walk back to the main road and turn right. At the gas station 200m away is the turnoff to Jesús, 12km away. Shared taxis (G7000) wait here to fill, and buses (G5000) pass every two hours. You can get a taxi to take you to Jesús de Tavarangüe, wait for you and bring you back to the turnoff for about G20,000.

The restored **church** (⏲7am-7pm, to 5:30pm in winter) at Jesús de Tavarangüe was never finished. The spectacular trefoil arches (a nod to Spain's Moorish past) and carved motifs of crossed swords and keys make it perhaps the most picturesque of all the Jesuit ruins. The treble-naved church, with green grass underfoot, is on a similarly monumental scale as Trinidad. You can climb the tower for views of the surrounding countryside.

Head back to the main road by bus or taxi; buses back to Encarnación stop by the gas station. Last stop is at or by the bus terminal; buses back to Posadas leave from the bus stop outside the bus terminal, opposite the school.

A joint ticket for the ruins at Trinidad, Jesús, and San Cosme (southwest of Encarnación) is G25,000; it's valid for three days.

Note: you may need a visa to enter Paraguay. Currently, Americans, Canadians, Australians and New Zealanders do; Israelis, Brits and other EU citizens don't. A single-entry visa costs US$65 from the Paraguayan consulate in Posadas and can be ready in about an hour. You'll need passport photos, a copy of your passport, proof of an onward ticket and possibly proof of sufficient funds (a credit card may do). You can risk going through without getting your passport stamped, but the fine is US$100 if you get caught.

Hotel Julio César HOTEL $$
(☎442-7930; www.juliocesarhotel.com.ar; Entre Ríos 1951; s/d AR$365/425; ❄@🛜🏊) This four-star job in the city center has light, spacious, summery rooms with fridge and pleasing bathrooms. The slightly pricier superior rooms are identical but on higher floors.

Vuela El Pez Hostel HOSTEL $
(☎443-8706; www.vuelaelpez.com.ar; 25 de Mayo 1216; dm/d AR$49/170, tw without bathroom AR$130; ❄@🛜🏊) Atop a bluff near the *costanera,* this unsigned building contains a very laid-back hostel indeed.

Eating

TOP CHOICE **La Rueda La Tradicional** PARRILLA $$
(☎442-5620; Arrechea & Costanera; mains AR$40-60) Stylish and traditional in feel, with uniformed waiters and sturdy wooden seats, this two-level grill restaurant is in a prime riverside position: look for the wooden wheel outside. There is excellent service, quality meats and a nice line in salads and river fish put this a class above most *parrilla* places.

Itakua FUSION $$
(Costanera s/n; mains AR$40-70;) The in-place in Posadas in recent times, this spacious and stylish bar-restaurant is in the heart of the riverside strip. Traditional Argentine ingredients are given a bit of zip with eclectic European influences: brie, basil pesto and sauerkraut are all seen accompanying local meats here. The quality is reliable, as is the buzzy atmosphere.

La Querencia PARRILLA $$
(443-7117; Bolívar 322; mains AR$33-75;) On the plaza, this upmarket *parrilla* specializes in delicious *galeto* (marinated chicken pieces). Also memorable are the brochettes (giant spikes with various delicious meats impaled upon them). The salads are also unusually well prepared.

El Rayo CAFETERIA $
(Bolívar 2089; light meals AR$17-33) No-frills and effective, this joint is thronged at lunchtime for its delicious *empanadas, lomitos* and good-value pizza. Service comes with a smile, too. Thumbs up.

Drinking & Entertainment

Most of the weekend action is down at the *costanera,* where a knot of eateries, bars and nightclubs go loud and late. Head north up Buenos Aires and its continuation for some nine blocks from the city center.

Café La Nouvelle Vitrage CAFE
(Bolívar 1899;) With a vaguely French feel, this amiable cafe on the plaza has a comfy interior and a terrace perfect for watching everyday life in Posadas go by.

Information

There are several ATMs around the plaza, and call centers and internet places nearby.

Cambios Mazza (Bolívar) Changes traveler's checks.

Hospital General R Madariaga (444-7775; Av López Torres 1177) About 1km south of downtown.

Tourist office (444-7539; www.turismo.misiones.gov.ar; Colón 1985; 8am-8pm Mon-Fri, 8am-noon, 4-8pm Sat & Sun) Has well-informed staff. There's another office at the bus terminal, open the same hours.

Getting There & Away

Air

Aerolíneas Argentinas (442-2036; Ayacucho 1724) flies five times weekly to Buenos Aires.

Bus

Buses to Encarnación, Paraguay (AR$5), leave every 20 minutes from the corner of San Lorenzo and Entre Ríos. With border formalities, the trip can take more than an hour, but is usually quicker.

Everyone gets out to clear Argentine emigration. The bus may leave without you; hang onto your ticket to catch the next one. The same happens on the Paraguayan side. There's a handy tourist office right by Paraguayan immigration, and official moneychangers hanging around. Make sure you get small denominations: a 100,000 guaraní note is hell to change.

Posadas' **bus terminal** (442-5800; RN 12 & Av Santa Catalina) can be reached from downtown by buses 8, 15, 21 or 24 (AR$1.75). It's around AR$30 in a taxi.

Bus services to San Ignacio (AR$14, one hour) depart roughly half-hourly.

Train

The Posadas–Buenos Aires **train service** (443-6076; www.trenesdellitoral.com.ar) is cheap but an exercise in patience. The battered old *Gran Capitán* runs to Buenos Aires' Federico Lacroze train station at 11pm on Wednesday and 3pm on Sunday, leaving from Buenos Aires at 10:50am on Tuesday and 10:05pm on Friday. It theoretically takes 30 hours, but usually takes many more. Tickets in tourist/1st class costs AR$118/180. At time of research a railbus was running from Garupá station, 10km south of Posadas, to meet the train at Apóstoles.

Getting Around

Bus 28 (AR$1.75) goes to the airport from San Lorenzo (between La Rioja and Entre Ríos). A *remise* costs about AR$40. **Avis** (459-6660; www.avis.com.ar; Azará 1908) is a recommended car-rental agency.

BUSES FROM POSADAS

DESTINATION	COST (AR$)	DURATION (HR)
Buenos Aires	362	14
Corrientes	102	4
Paso de los Libres	110	6
Puerto Iguazú	102	5
Resistencia	106	5
Rosario	322	16
Santa Fe	295	14
Tucumán	408	17

Around Posadas

SANTA ANA & LORETO

Atmospherically decaying in the humid forest, these two Jesuit missions are both off RN 12 between Posadas and San Ignacio, the site of another (better restored) mission.

At **Santa Ana** (⌚8am-6pm), which was founded in 1633 but moved here in 1660, dense forest has been partially removed to reveal a settlement that had over 7000 Guaraní inhabitants at its peak. The enormous plaza, 140m square, attests to the importance of the settlement.

The muscular church's thick walls have been propped up with interior scaffolding; a few photogenic strangler figs grow atop them, lending a dramatic effect to what must have been a magnificent building, though none of its decorative embellishments remain. The church was designed by the Italian architect Brasanelli, who also worked on the San Ignacio church.

To the right side of the church is the cemetery, which was used by villagers into the later half of the 20th century but is now neglected. Crypts with doors agape reveal coffins that have fallen from their shelves and burst open; if this place doesn't give you the willies, you haven't watched enough horror movies.

Behind the church, a channel and reservoir remain from what was a sophisticated irrigation system.

Loreto (⌚8am-6pm), founded in 1632, has even fewer visible remains than Santa Ana, and you may feel it's not worth the effort to visit via public transportation. The old adobe latrine and a chapel are partially restored, but the jungle is king here again and it's difficult to interpret the tumbled mossy stones among the trees. It's undeniably atmospheric, though. It was one of the more important missions; a printing press was built here – the first in the southern part of the continent.

Admission for both Loreto and Santa Ana is via a **joint ticket** (Argentines/other Latin Americans/other nationalities AR$30/40/50) that includes San Ignacio Miní and Santa María la Mayor. Both Santa Ana and Loreto are staffed by knowledgeable students, who give recommended tours, included in the admission price. The missions have small museums and kiosks at their entrances.

ℹ Getting There & Away

Buses heading north from Posadas stop at the turnoffs on RN 12 for both sites. Santa Ana's is at Km 43, from where it's a 1km walk to the ruins. Loreto's is at Km 48, with a 3km walk. It can be intensely hot, so take plenty of water. You may be able to hitch a lift on the school bus on your way back; ask at Loreto mission. You can get a *remise* from San Ignacio to take you to both, including waiting time, for about AR$150 to AR$200.

SANTA MARÍA LA MAYOR

Further afield, this is the fourth mission on the joint admission ticket for San Ignacio, Santa Ana and Loreto. A sizable plaza is the main feature, with the church very ruinous. The settlement was a large one, with printing press and prison; the chapel is a 20th-century addition. It's a relaxing place surrounded by jungle that's great for bird watching, with toucans and trogons easily spotted. The visitors center has a good bird-identification pamphlet.

The ruins are right on the RP 2 road between Concepción de la Sierra and San Javier, 110km southeast of Posadas. To get there, take a bus from Posadas to Concepción de la Sierra. There, change to a San Javier-bound service and ask the driver to let you off at the ruins, which are some 25km down the road. You can get a San Javier-bound bus direct from Posadas, but make sure it runs via the ruins – some go a different way.

San Ignacio

☎0376 / POP 6312

The best preserved of the Argentine missions, San Ignacio Miní is the central attraction of this small town north of Posadas. You could visit from Posadas or on your way to Iguazú, but a better idea is to stay the night. The hotels are comfortable, and you'll have a chance to check out the sound-and-light show at the ruins as well as Quiroga's house; both are worthwhile.

San Ignacio is 56km northeast of Posadas via RN 12. From the highway junction Av Sarmiento leads 1km to the center, where Rivadavia leads six blocks north to the ruins.

Sights

San Ignacio Miní RUINS
(www.misiones-jesuiticas.com.ar; entrance Calle Alberdi s/n; Argentines/Latin Americans/other nationalities AR$30/40/50; ⌚7am-7pm) These mission ruins are the most complete of those in Argentina and impressive for the quantity of carved ornamentation still visible and for the amount of restoration done. No roofs remain, but many of the living quarters and workshops have been re-erected.

First founded in 1610 in Brazil, but abandoned after repeated attacks by slavers, San Ignacio was established at its present site in 1696 and functioned until the Jesuits finally gave in to the order of expulsion in 1768. The ruins, rediscovered in 1897 and restored between 1940 and 1948, are a great example of 'Guaraní baroque.' At its peak, the settlement had a Guaraní population of nearly 4000.

The entrance is on the north side on Calle Alberdi, where the first stop is the **interpretation center**. It's an impressive display with plenty of unbiased information (in Spanish and English) about the missions from both the Jesuit and Guaraní perspectives. You can listen to Guaraní music, including some religious pieces composed at the missions, and inspect a virtual model of San Ignacio as it would have been.

The ruins themselves feature interactive panels that provide multilingual information, or you can join an informative free

WORTH A TRIP

THE OTHER FALLS

Iguazú's aren't the only spectacular falls in Misiones province: the remote and unusual **Saltos del Moconá** also live long in the memory. A geological fault in the bed of the Río Uruguay divides the river lengthwise and water spills over the shelf between the two sections, creating a waterfall some 3km long and up to 15m high, depending on the water level.

The falls are at the eastern edge of Misiones province, roughly equidistant from Posadas and Puerto Iguazú. From Posadas, several daily buses leave for El Soberbio (four hours); from here it's 75km to the falls, mostly paved. From the end of the road, if the river is low, you can pick your way along to the falls, but you'll see them much better by taking a boat trip.

Lodges organize trips to the falls and the various parks and reserves that protect the zone, as does friendly **Yabotí Jungle** (☎03755-495266, 03755-15-652853; mocona4x4@yahoo.com.ar; Av Corrientes 481, El Soberbio), which charges AR$130 for a four-hour trip to the falls (AR$390 minimum); the speedboat trip, with Brazilian and Argentine jungle reserves on each side, is an attraction in itself. Operators in Posadas and Puerto Iguazú also arrange trips. The same operators also run trips to remote Guaraní *aldeas* (villages) for AR$80.

Most important: the falls aren't always visible; if the river is high, then you're out of luck. Ring ahead to find out. December to March is normally the best time.

El Soberbio itself is an interesting place, a service center for a lush agricultural area growing tobacco, citronella and manioc. There's a ferry crossing to Brazil, and blond heads are everywhere, a legacy of German and Eastern European immigrants joining the native Guaraní population.

There are several places to stay, including **Hostal Del Centro** (☎03755-495133; www.elsoberbioportaldelmocona.com; cnr Rivadavia & San Martín; r per person AR$80; ❄), right in the center of town but built around a grassy courtyard; rooms are good for this price and there's a kitchen you can use.

Hilltop **Hostería Puesta del Sol** (☎03755-495161; www.h-puestadelsol.com.ar; Suipacha s/n; s/d AR$135/250; ❄) offers decent rooms in a relaxing complex with spectacular views and a huge (summertime) pool. Half-board rates are available, and there are bungalows for groups.

Several jungly lodges are closer to the falls. Accommodations in these places are generally in elegant rustic cabins with great views. Rates (except for Aldea Yaboty) include some or all meals.

Aldea Yaboty LODGE **$$**
(☎03755-15-553069; www.aldeayaboty.com; r/cabin AR$280/400)

Don Enrique Lodge LODGE **$$$**
(☎011-4732-3502; www.donenriquelodge.com.ar; s/d AR$800/1280)

Posada La Misión LODGE **$$$**
(☎011-5654-8388; www.lodgelamision.com.ar; d AR$540)

Tacuapí Lodge LODGE **$$$**
(☎03743-422484; www.tacuapi.com.ar; s/d AR$780/1256)

tour; guides speak English and some also speak French and German. You first pass between rows of Guaraní houses before arriving at the plaza, on one side of which is the enormous red sandstone church. Impressive in its dimensions, it is the focal point of the settlement. While the red-brown stone is very picturesque, the buildings were originally white. Before lime was widely available, it was obtained by burning snail shells.

By the church, the cloisters preserve some ornately carved balustrades and the original flooring of some of the rooms off it. Just before the exit is another museum containing some excellent carved paving stones.

In summer it's worth trying to avoid visiting between 10am and 1pm, as the site gets particularly busy with tour groups at these times.

There is a *Luz y Sonido* (sound-and-light show) at the ruins every night from mid-September to March, and sporadically at other times. It's included in the price of the ticket and the time varies slightly between 7pm and 8pm.

The admission ticket is valid for 15 days, and includes entry to the nearby ruins at Santa Ana and Loreto and also to Santa María la Mayor, a little further afield.

Casa de Horacio Quiroga HOUSE
(Av Quiroga s/n; admission AR$10; 8am-6:45pm) The Uruguayan novelist and poet Horacio Quiroga was a get-back-to-nature type who found his muse in the rough-and-ready Misiones backwoods lifestyle. His house at the southern end of town (a 20- to 30-minute walk) is a simple affair, which he built himself out of stone.

To reach it, you walk a trail through the sugarcane, where panels (in English, too) detail the events of a deeply tragic life so full of shotgun accidents and doses of cyanide it's almost funny.

Grand views of the Paraná (which you'll have to crane to see if the vegetation is high) inspired Quiroga to write his regionally based stories that transcend time and place without abandoning their setting. Some of his short fiction is available in English translation in *The Exiles and Other Stories*.

Next to the stone house is a replica of his initial wooden house, built for the 1996 biographical film *Historias de Amor, de Locura y de Muerte* (Stories of Love, Madness and Death).

Sleeping & Eating

Various simple eating options – serving burgers, pizzas and milanesas – crowd the streets around the ruins; most are open during the day only.

TOP CHOICE **Hotel La Toscana** HOTEL $
(447-0777; www.hotellatoscana.com.ar; cnr H.Irigoyen & Uruguay; s/d AR$110/170;) In a quiet location a couple of blocks back from the highway, this welcoming Italian-run place is a relaxing retreat indeed. Cool, spacious rooms surround a great pool, deck and garden area. It's a top spot to unwind for a few days.

Hotel San Ignacio HOTEL $
(447-0047; www.hotelsanignacio.com.ar; cnr Sarmiento & San Martín; s/d AR$100/160, 4-person cabana AR$250; @) Located bang in the town center, this is an excellent choice for its clean, quiet, comfortable rooms, great bathrooms, benevolent owners and an attached bar and internet cafe. The A-frame cabins out the back are great value for groups. The bar does simple tasty food. You may never find it easier to be the best pool player in town, but the table football is a different story.

Adventure Hostel HOSTEL $
(447-0955; www.sihostel.com; Independencia 469; dm/d AR$56/196; @) Next to the plaza two blocks south of the church, this hostel has darkish and slightly institutional (whitewashed brick) but comfortable dorms and private rooms, and excellent facilities. There's everything from ping-pong and DVDs to seesaws in the spacious grounds, and HI discount.

Itároga ARGENTINE $
(cnr Rivadavia & Lanusse; mains AR$30-45) This sweet little place a block from the central plaza area has a cute terrace, artworks on the walls and friendly service. Pizzas, snacks and tender meat dishes are complemented by river fish and some pretty good mixed drinks.

Information

Tourist office (8am-8pm) Helpful. At the highway junction.

Getting There & Away

The bus terminal is on the main road near the arch that marks the entrance to town. Services between Posadas (AR$14, one hour) and Puerto Iguazú (AR$61 to AR$80, four to five hours) are frequent.

1

3

MARGIE POLITZER/LONELY PLANET IMAGES ©

WALTER BIBIKOW/AMANAIMAGES/CORBIS ©

2

MARK NEWMAN/LONELY PLANET IMAGES ©

The Iguazú Falls

There are few more impressive sights on the planet than this majestic array of cascades on the border of Argentina and Brazil. Set in luxurious tropical jungle, the falls are accessible, but provide a primal thrill that will never be forgotten.

Brazilian Side

1 Hit the Brazilian side first to appreciate the wide panorama from its short viewing path within a birdlife-rich national park. Cascade after cascade is revealed, picturesquely framed by tropical vegetation before you end up below the impressive Salto Floriano (p188).

Garganta del Diablo

2 The highlight of the falls is the 'Devil's Throat.' Stroll out over the placid Iguazú river before gazing in awe as it drops away beneath you in a display of primitive sound and fury that leaves you breathless (p186).

Argentine Side

3 Two spectacular walkways, one high, one low, get you in close to torrents of water of extraordinary power. Expect awesome photos, expect to get wet, and expect to be exhilarated (p186).

Boat Trips

4 Not wet enough yet? Then prepare to be absolutely drenched. Zippy motorboats take thrillseekers right in under one of the biggest waterfalls on the Argentine side. More sedate canoeing and rafting excursions are also available on the Brazilian side (p187 and p188).

Jungle Trails

5 The waterfalls aren't the only thing on offer. National parks on both sides of the river offer various easy-to-medium trails through the jungle that give great wildlife-watching opportunities (p187 and p188).

Clockwise from top left

1. Foz do Iguaçu (p194) **2.** Garganta del Diablo (p187) **3.** Iguazú Falls (p185)

A TRIUMPH OF HUMANITY

For a century and a half from 1609, one of the world's great social experiments was carried out in the jungles of South America by the Society of Jesus (the Jesuits). Locating themselves in incredibly remote areas, priests set up *reducciones* (missions), where they established communities of Guaraní whom they evangelized and educated, while at the same time protecting them from slavery and the evil influences of colonial society. It was a utopian ideal that flourished and led Voltaire to describe it as 'a triumph of humanity which seems to expiate the cruelties of the first conquerors.'

For the Guaraní who were invited to begin a new life in the missions, there were many tangible benefits, including security, nourishment and prosperity. Mortality declined immediately and the mission populations grew rapidly. At their peak the 30 Jesuit *reducciones* that were spread across what's now Argentina, Brazil and Paraguay were populated by more than 100,000 Guaraní. Each mission had a minimum of Europeans: two priests was the norm, and the Guaraní governed themselves under the Jesuits' spiritual authority. The Jesuits made no attempt to force the Guaraní to speak Spanish and only sought to change those aspects of Guaraní culture – polygamy and occasional cannibalism – that clashed with Catholic teaching. Each Guaraní family was given a house and children were schooled.

The typical *reducción* consisted of a large central plaza, dominated by the church and *colegio*, which housed the priests and also contained art workshops and storerooms. The houses of the Guaraní occupied the rest of the settlement in neat rows; other buildings might include a hospital, a *cotiguazú* (big house) that housed widows and abandoned wives, and a *cabildo* (town council) where the Guaraní's chosen leader lived.

The settlements were self-sufficient; the Guaraní were taught agriculture and food was distributed equally. As time went on and the missions grew, the original wooden buildings were replaced by stone ones and the churches, designed by master architects with grandiose utopian dreams, were stunning edifices with intricate baroque stonework and sculpture comparable with the finest churches being built in Europe at the time.

Indeed, the missions' most enduring achievement was perhaps artistic. The Guaraní embraced the art and music they were introduced to and, interweaving European styles with their own, produced beautiful music, sculpture, dance and painting in the so-called Guaraní baroque style. It was perhaps the Jesuits' religious music that most attracted the Guaraní to Catholicism.

However, mission life necessarily had a martial side. Raiding parties of *bandeirantes* (armed bands) from Brazil regularly sought slaves for sugar plantations, and the Jesuits were resented by both Spanish and Portuguese colonial authorities. There were regular skirmishes and battles until a notable victory over an army of 3000 slavers at Mbororó in 1641 ushered in a period of comparative security.

The mission period came to an abrupt end. Various factors, including envy from the colonial authority and settlers, and a feeling that the Jesuits were more loyal to their own ideas than those of the Crown, prompted Carlos III of Spain to ban them from his dominions in 1767, following the lead of Portugal and France. With the priests gone, the communities were vulnerable and the Guaraní gradually dispersed. The decaying missions were then ruined in the wars of the early 19th century.

The 1986 film *The Mission* is about the last days of the Jesuit missions. Most intriguing is the casting of a Colombian tribe, the Waunana (who had had almost no contact with white people) as the Guaraní.

Almost nothing remains of several of Argentina's 15 missions, but those well worth visiting include San Ignacio Miní in San Ignacio, Loreto and Santa Ana; Yapeyú; and Santa María la Mayor. The fabulous Paraguayan missions at Jesús de Tavarangüe and Trinidad can be easily visited on a day trip from Posadas (see p177). There are others to visit not too far away in southern Brazil.

IGUAZÚ FALLS

One of the planet's most awe-inspiring sights, the Iguazú Falls are simply astounding. A visit is a jaw-dropping, visceral experience, and the power and noise of the cascades live forever in the memory. An added benefit is the setting: the falls lie split between Brazil and Argentina in a large expanse of national park, much of it rainforest teeming with unique flora and fauna.

The falls are easily reached from either side of the Argentine-Brazilian border, as well as from nearby Paraguay. Most visitors choose either to stay in Foz do Iguaçu, on the Brazilian side, or in Argentina's Puerto Iguazú. Both have a wide choice of accommodations.

History & Environment

Álvar Núñez Cabeza de Vaca and his expedition in 1542 were the first Europeans to view the falls. According to Guaraní tradition the falls originated when an Indian warrior named Caroba incurred the wrath of a forest god by escaping downriver in a canoe with a young girl, Naipur, with whom the god was infatuated. Enraged, the god caused the riverbed to collapse in front of the lovers, producing a line of precipitous falls over which Naipur fell and, at their base, turned into a rock. Caroba survived as a tree overlooking it.

Geologists have a more prosaic explanation. The Río Iguaçú's course takes it over a basaltic plateau that ends abruptly just short of the confluence with the Paraná. Where the lava flow stopped, thousands of cubic meters of water per second now plunge down as much as 80m into sedimentary terrain below. Before reaching the falls, the river divides into many channels with hidden reefs, rocks and islands separating the many visually distinctive cascades that together form the famous *cataratas* (waterfalls). In total, the falls stretch around 2.7km.

Iguazú Falls

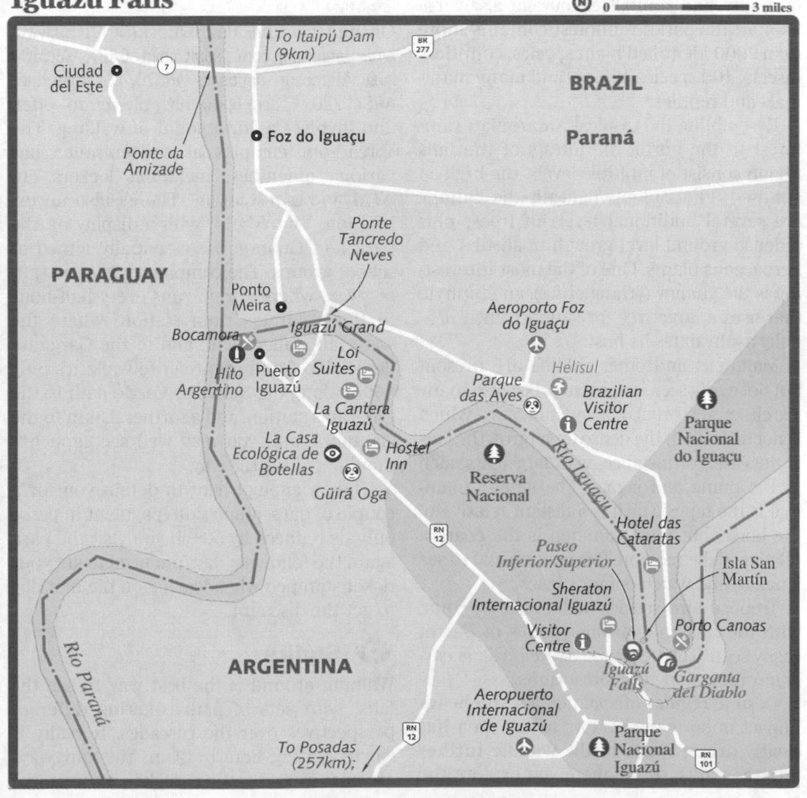

Seeing the Falls

The Brazilian and Argentine sides offer different views and experiences of the falls. Go to both (perhaps to the Brazilian first) and hope for sun. The difference between a clear and an overcast day at the falls is vast, only in part because of the rainbows and butterflies that emerge when the sun is shining. Ideally you should allow for a multiple-day stay to have a better shot at optimal conditions.

While the Argentine side – with its variety of trails and boat rides – offers many more opportunities to see individual falls close up, the Brazilian side yields the more panoramic views. You can easily make day trips to both sides of the falls, no matter which side of the border you choose to base yourself (but see p189 for border-crossing information).

National Parks

The Brazilian and Argentine sides of the falls are both designated national parks: Parque Nacional do Iguaçu and Parque Nacional Iguazú, respectively. High temperatures, humidity and rainfall encourage a diverse habitat: the parks' rainforest contains more than 2000 identified plant species, countless insects, 400 species of birds and many mammals and reptiles.

Resembling the tropical Amazonian rainforest to the north, the forests of the falls region consist of multiple levels, the highest a closed 30m canopy. Beneath the canopy are several additional levels of trees, plus a dense ground-level growth of shrubs and herbaceous plants. One of the most interesting is the guapoy (strangler fig), an epiphyte that uses a large tree for support until it finally asphyxiates its host.

Mammals and other wildlife are present but not easily seen in the parks, because many are either nocturnal or avoid humans – which is not difficult in the dense undergrowth. This is the case, for instance, with large cats such as the puma and jaguar. The largest mammal is the tapir, which is a distant relative of the horse, but most common is the coati, a relative of the raccoon. It is not unusual to see iguanas, and watch out for snakes.

Tropical bird species add a dash of color, with toucans and various species of parrot easily seen. The best time to see birds is early morning along the forest trails.

Despite regular official denials, the heavy impact of so many visitors to the area has clearly driven much of the wildlife further into the parks, so the more you explore the region away from the falls themselves, the more you'll see.

Dangers & Annoyances

The Río Iguaçu's currents are strong and swift; tourists have been swept downriver and drowned in the area of Isla San Martín. Of course, don't get too close to the falls proper.

The heat and humidity are often intense around the falls and there's plenty of hungry insect life.

On both sides, you're almost certain to encounter coatis. Don't feed them; though these clownish omnivores seem tame, they become aggressive around food and will bite and scratch. Both parks have a medical point in case of coati attack.

You are likely to get soaked, or at least very damp, from the spray at the falls, so keep your documents and camera protected in plastic bags. You can buy plastic ponchos at the visitors centers on both sides.

Parque Nacional Iguazú

☎03757

On the Argentine side, this **park** (☎491469; www.iguazuargentina.com; adult/child 6-12yr AR$100/70, Mercosur nationals AR$70/40, Argentines AR$40/20; ⏰8am-6pm) has plenty to offer, and involves a fair amount of walking. The spread-out complex at the entrance has various amenities, including lockers, an ATM and a restaurant. There's also an exhibition, **Ybyrá-retá**, with a display on the park and Guaraní life essentially aimed at school groups. The complex ends at a **train station**, where a train runs every half-hour to the Cataratas train station, where the waterfall walks begin, and to the Garganta del Diablo. You may prefer to walk: it's only 650m along the **Sendero Verde** path to the Cataratas station, and a further 2.3km to the Garganta, and you may well see capuchin monkeys along the way.

There's enough here to detain you for a couple of days; admission (payment in pesos only) is reduced by 50% if you visit the park again the following day. You need to get your ticket stamped when leaving on the first day to get the discount.

Sights

Walking around is the best way to see the falls, with sets of paths offering different perspectives over the cascades. It really is worth getting here by 9am: the gangways are narrow and getting stuck in a conga line of tour groups in searing heat and humidity takes the edge off the experience.

Two circuits, the **Paseo Superior** (650m) and **Paseo Inferior** (1400m), provide most of the viewing opportunities via a series of trails, bridges and *pasarelas* (catwalks). The Paseo Superior is entirely level and gives good views of the tops of several cascades and across to more. The Paseo Inferior descends to the river (no wheelchair access), passing delightfully close to more falls on the way. At the bottom of the path, a free launch makes the short crossing to **Isla San Martín**, an island with a trail of its own that gives the closest look at several falls, including **Salto San Martín**, a huge, furious cauldron of water. It's possible to picnic and swim on the lee side of the island, but don't venture too far off the beach. When the water is high, island access is shut off.

From Cataratas train station, train it or walk the 2300m to the Garganta del Diablo stop, where an 1100m walkway across the placid Río Iguazú leads to one of the planet's most spectacular sights, the **Garganta del Diablo** (Devil's Throat). The lookout platform is perched right over this amazingly powerful and concentrated torrent of water, a deafening cascade plunging to murky destination; the vapors soaking the viewer blur the base of the falls and rise in a smokelike plume that can often be seen several kilometers away. It's a place of majesty and awe, and should be left until the end of your visit. The last train to the Garganta leaves at 4pm, and we recommend taking it, as it'll be a far less crowded experience. If you walk, you'll see quite a lot of wildlife around this time of day, too.

Activities

Relatively few visitors venture beyond the immediate area of the falls to appreciate the park's forest scenery and wildlife, but it's well worth doing. On the falls trails you'll see large lizards, coatis and several species of birds, but you'll see much more on one of the few trails through the dense forest.

Sendero Macuco WALKING

Along the road past the visitors center (you can also access it via a path from the Estación Central trailhead) is the entrance to this nature trail, which leads through dense forest to a nearly hidden waterfall, **Salto Arrechea**. The first 3km of the trail to the top of the waterfall is almost completely level, but there is a steep lateral drop to the base of the falls and beyond to the Río Iguaçu, about 650m in all. This part of the trail is muddy and slippery – watch your step and figure about 1¼ hours each way from the trailhead. You can swim at the waterfall. Early morning is best, with better opportunities to see wildlife, including toucans and bands of caí monkeys. Take insect repellent.

Explorador Expediciones JUNGLE TOURS

(☎421632; www.rainforestevt.com.ar) Using knowledgeable guides, this is the best option for appreciating the national park's flora and fauna. It offers combined driving-walking excursions: the Safara a la Cascada takes you to the Arrechea waterfall (AR$180, 90 minutes, 2pm daily); better is the Safari en la Selva (AR$220, two hours, 10:30am and 4pm daily), a trip in an untouristed part of the park that includes explanations of Guaraní culture. It doesn't require you to buy the falls admission ticket; the afternoon departure includes a transfer back to Puerto Iguazú. Best to book a day or more in advance by phone or at their information booths at the falls.

Iguazú Jungle BOAT TOURS

(☎421696; www.iguazujungle.com) This setup offers the following three excursions: a speedboat ride to the bottom of several of the waterfalls, including an exhilarating drenching under the San Martín torrent (AR$125, 15 minutes); a quiet dinghy ride down the upper Iguazú (AR$50, 30 minutes); and a one-hour trip combining a descent to the river in flatbed trucks along the Sendero Yacaratiá with a trip upriver through rapids to the falls (AR$260, one hour). Discounts are offered for combining any of these tours and you may be able to negotiate cheaper prices at quiet times or late in the day. Book excursions at their booths at the falls; most hotels in Puerto Iguazú can also do this for you.

Full Moon Walks WALKING TOURS

(☎491469; www.iguazuargentina.com; AR$200) For five consecutive nights per month, these guided walks visit the Garganta del Diablo. There are three departures nightly. The first, at 8pm, offers the spectacle of the inflated rising moon; the last, at 9:30pm, sees the falls better illuminated. Don't expect to see wildlife. The price includes admission; a cocktail and dinner afterwards is an extra 70 pesos. Extra bus departures from Puerto Iguazú cater for moonwalkers. Book in advance by phone as numbers are limited. Most hotels in Puerto Iguazú can book this for you.

Sleeping & Eating

There's one hotel within the park. The numerous snack bars offer predictably overpriced snacks and drinks. The food is awful; bring a picnic, eat at one of the two buffet restaurants or lunch at the Sheraton.

Sheraton Iguazú HOTEL $$$
(☎491800; www.sheraton.com/iguazu; standard r with forest/falls view AR$1494/1810, superior r AR$1650/1966; ❄@🛜≋) With a privileged position in the park itself and looking right up the river to the most spectacular section of the falls, the Sheraton backs it up with professional service and spacious rooms with balconies: the superiors are similar to the standards but a lot newer. The jungle-side view is pretty too. There's a good outdoor pool area, as well as a heated pool and spa indoors. Rooms are usually substantially cheaper if booking online. The restaurant has a limited selection (mains AR$95 to AR$125).

La Selva BUFFET $$$
(www.iguazuargentina.com; all-you-can-eat AR$97; ⏲11am-3:30pm) During your visit, this restaurant, which is close to the main entrance, will get talked up so much you'll fear the worst, but it's actually OK, with a buffet of hot and cold dishes, and all-you-can-eat *parrillada*. It's well overpriced but information kiosks dotted around the complex give out vouchers offering a substantial discount so head there first.

Fortín BUFFET $$$
(all-you-can-eat AR$120; ⏲10am-4pm) Well located near the falls walkways, this offers a buffet spread with fairly mediocre *parrilla* choices. It's close to the falls walkways but doesn't appear on park maps. Overpriced; try to bargain.

Getting There & Away

The park is 20km southeast of Puerto Iguazú. From Puerto Iguazú's bus terminal, buses leave half-hourly for the park (AR$10, 40 minutes) between 7:20am and 7pm, with return trips between 7:20am and 8pm. The buses make flag stops at points along the highway. A taxi from town to the park entrance is AR$100.

Parque Nacional Do Iguaçu (Brazil)

On the Brazilian side, this **park** (☎3521-4400; www.cataratasdoiguacu.com.br; 12yr & older/under 12yr/Mercosur nationals/Brazilians R$40.80/6.70/32.55/24.30; ⏲tickets 9am-5pm) is entered via an enormous visitors center, which has a snack bar, ATMs and big lockers (R$8), among other amenities. Parking here costs R$12, but it's free at the Parque das Aves opposite.

Tickets can be purchased using Brazilian, Argentine, Paraguayan and US currency. After buying tickets, you pass through to an exhibition giving information (in Portuguese, English and Spanish) about the geology, history and biodiversity of the falls region. Behind the building, double-decker buses await to take you into the park proper. Keep your eyes peeled for animals. The last bus back from the falls is at 6:30pm.

Sights & Activities

Trilha do Poço Preto GUIDED WALK
(☎3529-9627; www.macucoecoaventura.com.br; per person R$135) The first stop is this 9km guided hike through the jungle on foot, by bike or on a trailer. The trail ends at Taquara Island, where you can kayak or take a boat cruise to Porto Canoas. You can also return via the Bananeiras Trail.

Macuco Safari WALKING, BOAT TOUR
(☎3574-4244; www.macucosafari.com.br; per person R$140) The second stop is for this two-hour safari, which includes a 3km trailer ride through the jungle, a 600m walk to a small waterfall and then a boat ride up towards the falls. Don't confuse it with the Macuco trail on the Argentine side. Alight here, too, for the **Bananeiras Trail** (☎3529-9627; www.macucoecoaventura.com.br; per person R$105), a 2km walk passing lagoons and observing aquatic wildlife, which ends at a jetty where you can take boat rides or silent 'floating' excursions in kayaks down to Porto Canoas. If you plan to do any of these, chat with one of the agents touting them around the park visitors center; they can get you a discount.

Waterfall Observation Trail WALKING, ADVENTURE SPORTS
The third, and principal, stop is at the Hotel das Cataratas. This is where the main waterfall observation trail starts. At the beginning of the trail is also **Cânion Iguaçu** (☎3529-6040; www.campodedesafios.com.br), an activity center offering rafting (R$80), abseiling (R$70), rock climbing (R$50) and a canopy tour (R$70).

From here you walk 1.5km down a paved trail with brilliant views of the falls on the Argentine side, the jungle and the river below.

Every twist of the path reveals a more splendid view until the trail ends right under the majestic Salto Floriano, which will give you a healthy sprinkling of water via the wind it generates. A catwalk leads out to a platform with majestic vistas, with the Garganta del Diablo close at hand, and a perspective down the river in the other direction. If the water's high, it's unforgettable; a rainbow is visible in the spray on clear afternoons.

An elevator heads up to a viewing platform at the top of the falls at Porto Canoas, the last stop of the double-decker buses. Porto Canoas has a gift shop, a couple of snack bars and an excellent buffet restaurant.

The park is open for evening visits once a month on the night of the full moon.

Helisul SCENIC FLIGHTS
(☎3529-7474; www.helisul.com) By the visitors center, this set-up runs 10-minute chopper jaunts at 450m over the Brazilian side of the falls. The environmental impact is debatable (the Argentines suspended their service for this reason), but it's undeniably exhilarating. There are open panels in the windows for photography. The ride costs R$195 per person; it's best done after you've visited the falls themselves. You can also book a 35-minute trip that takes in the Itaipú dam and triple frontier.

Parque das Aves ZOO
(www.parquedasaves.com.br; admission R$25; ⏲8:30am-5:30pm) Near the park entrance is this large bird park. It has a huge assortment of our feathered friends, mostly Brazilian, with good information in English and Spanish. The highlight is the walk-through aviaries, where you can get up-close and personal with toucans, macaws and hummingbirds.

Sleeping & Eating

Hotel das Cataratas HOTEL $$$
(☎2102-7000; www.hoteldascataratas.com; standard r R$938-1074; ❄@🛜🏊) Right in the park near the falls, this excellent pinkish hotel has had a major facelift and is looking all the better for it. It appeals enormously for its location, but only a handful of rooms have falls views, and they are only partial. It's decorated throughout in understated, elegant Portuguese colonial style, with attractive tiles in the bathrooms and dark wood furnishings in the bedrooms. Public areas have cozy appeal, and there's a fine pool area surrounded by the calls of nesting birds. Service is excellent. Don't miss climbing the belvedere for the view of the falls.

Porto Canoas BUFFET $
(buffet R$43; ⏲noon-4pm) After the falls, you (and your camera trigger finger) deserve a break. This spot has a long pleasant terrace overlooking the river just before it descends into maelstrom – a great spot for a beer – and an OK buffet lunch with plenty of salads and hot dishes.

Getting There & Around

'Parque Nacional' buses run from Foz do Iguaçu's urban bus terminal (you pay the fare entering the terminal) to the park entrance (R$2.65, 45 minutes) every 22 minutes between 6am and 7pm, and then every hour until midnight, making stops along Av Juscelino Kubitschek and Av das Cataratas.

A taxi from Foz to the park entrance costs around R$40.

ENTERING BRAZIL

At time of writing, many nationalities required visas to enter Brazil. These included the USA, Australia, Canada and Japan. EU citizens did not. Download the application form at https://scedv.serpro.gov.br and take it to your local Brazilian consulate before you leave home. You can also use the one in **Puerto Iguazú** (Córdoba 264; ⏲8am-noon Mon-Fri), which is likely cheaper (Australia/USA AR$161/644) than in your home country. You'll need a return ticket leaving Brazil, a photo and possibly a bank statement. If you get there early, it can usually be ready by the next working day.

That said, it is often – *but not always* – possible to take a day-trip by bus to the Brazilian falls without a visa. Argentine officials will stamp you out; stay on the bus when it passes Brazilian immigration and don't blame us if you're out of luck that day and get sent back.

Argentina doesn't charge an entry tax at land borders, so you won't be hit for pesos on your return to the country.

To access the Brazilian park from Puerto Iguazú, take the bus to Foz do Iguaçu but get off a couple of stops after crossing the international bridge (the driver will announce it). Here, cross the road, and wait for the Parque Nacional bus at the bus stop opposite. Repeat the process at the same stop on the way back. See p189 for information about entering Brazil.

Puerto Iguazú

03757 / POP 82,227

Little Puerto Iguazú sits at the confluence of the Ríos Paraná and Iguazú and looks across to Brazil and Paraguay. It doesn't really feel like Argentina any more. There's no center and little feeling of community – everyone is here to see the falls or to make a buck out of them. Still, it's quiet, safe and has good transportation connections, and there are also many excellent places to stay and eat.

Sights

There's little to see in the town itself, but 1km west of the town center along Av Tres Fronteras is the **Hito Argentino**, a small obelisk at the impressive confluence of the Ríos Paraná and Iguazú. From here you can see Brazil and Paraguay, with similar markers on their sides. A fairly desultory *artesanía* market is also here.

Güirá Oga ZOO

(www.guiraoga.com.ar; RN 12, Km 5; admission AR$40; 9am-6pm, last entry 4:30pm) Five kilometers out of town on the way to the national park, this is an animal hospital and center for rehabilitation of injured wildlife. It also carries out valuable research into the Iguazú forest environment and has a breeding program for endangered species. You get walked around the park by one of the biologists and get to meet the creatures. The visit takes about 80 minutes.

Puerto Iguazú

0 400 m
0 0.2 miles

La Casa Ecológica de Botellas HOUSE

(RN 12, Km 5; http://lacasadebotellas.googlepages.com; admission AR$20; ⏲8:30am-7pm) About 200m down a side road just before Güirá Oga, this fascinating place is well worth a visit. The owners have taken used packaging materials – plastic bottles, juice cartons and the like – to build not only an impressive house, but furnishings and a bunch of original handicrafts that make unusual gifts. The guided visit will talk you through their techniques.

Tours

Numerous local operators offer day tours to the Brazilian side of the falls (AR$100 to AR$250 depending on what's included), some taking in the Itaipú dam as well. Many have offices at the bus terminal.

Sleeping

There are numerous sleeping options for all budgets, including a string of resort-type hotels between town and the national park. In the streets around the bus station are many hostels – competition means you can find a bed for around AR$35 at some of them. See also the Sheraton at the falls themselves.

Puerto Iguazú

Sleeping

1	Che Lagarto	B3
2	Hostel Irupé	C3
3	Hotel La Sorgente	C2
4	Hotel Lilian	D3
5	Hotel Saint George	C3
6	Jasy	D2
7	Marco Polo Inn	C3
8	Residencial Lola	C3

Eating

9	Aqua	C3
10	Color	C3
11	El Quincho de Tío Querido	B3
12	Feria	B1
13	La Misionera	B3
14	La Rueda	C4
15	La Vitrina	C4
16	Lemongrass	B2
17	María Preta	B2
18	Plaza Pueblo	B3
19	Terra	C3

Drinking

20	Cuba Libre	B2
21	Jackie Brown Bar	B2
22	La Tribu	B2

TOP CHOICE **La Cantera Iguazú** LODGE $$$

(☎427220; www.iguazulodgelacantera.com; Selva Iryapú s/n; d lower/upper AR$684/862; ❄@📶🏊) Nestled in deep forest 1.5km off the falls road, this enchanting, intimate lodge has appealing rooms with balcony in wooden buildings that in some cases still have trees growing through them. The upper-level rooms are the same size but offer better jungle views and have a hammock to appreciate them from. Activities such as biking, guided walks and visits to the nearby Guaraní hamlets are included.

Jasy HOTEL $$

(Los Troncos; ☎424337; www.jasy.com.ar; San Lorenzo 154; d AR$440; ❄@📶🏊) Original and peaceful, these 10 two-level apartments climb a hill like a forest staircase and are all equipped with a balcony gazing over plentiful greenery. Artful use of wood is the signature; you'll fall in love with the bar and deck area. Prepare to stay longer than planned.

Loi Suites RESORT $$$

(☎498300; www.loisuites.com.ar; Selva Iryapú s/n; r AR$1390-1628; ❄📶@🏊) In the jungle yet just a few kilometers from town, this complex has several buildings connected by walkways and is so sizeable it feels more resort than lodge. It's decorated in relaxed country style and features a huge pool area surrounded by trees as its highlight. Rooms are spacious and comfortable; you might as well upgrade to one with a balcony for the bird-watching opportunities. Charging extra for spa use and wi-fi in the rooms seems a bit mean at these rates.

Boutique Hotel de la Fonte HOTEL $$$

(☎420625; www.bhfboutiquehotel.com; cnr Corrientes & 1 de Mayo; r AR$693-866; ❄@📶🏊) This unusual place features characterful individual rooms and suites around a tree-filled courtyard garden romantically lit at night. It's enthusiastically run by a couple who'll make you feel most welcome and part of the family. Numerous small decorative touches make this more than the sum of its parts. There's a classy Italian-influenced restaurant, and a saltwater pool and hot tub among the palms.

Hotel La Sorgente HOTEL $$

(☎424252; www.lasorgentehotel.com; Av Córdoba 454; s/d AR$385/480; ❄@📶🏊) Book ahead for a real treat at this stylish but homey posada. Set around a verdant garden, life couldn't be easier here – if you can't face the long walk around the pool, take the bridge across it. Twin rooms have queen-sized beds; cozy upstairs doubles overlook the pool and banana plants. Breakfast, served in the authentic Italian restaurant, gets the seal of approval, too.

Iguazú Grand HOTEL $$$

(☎498050; www.casinoiguazu.com; RN 12, Km 1640; r from AR$1316;) Don't let the tacky ads for the attached casino put you off this classy place, just short of the bridge across to Brazil. It's comfortably the most upmarket hotel on either side of the falls, with excellent service, pretty grounds, a great pool area and the town's best restaurant. Facilities are top-notch, it's had a recent facelift and children are made very welcome.

Residencial Lola GUESTHOUSE $

(☎423954; residenciallola@hotmail.com; Av Córdoba 255; s/d AR$80/120;) Plenty of price gouging goes on in Puerto Iguazú, but it stops at Lola's front door. This cheap, cheerily run spot is very close to the bus terminal and features compact, clean rooms with bathroom for a pittance.

Hostel Inn HOSTEL $

(☎421823; www.hostel-inn.com; RN 12, Km5; dm/r AR$70/280;) This is more resort than hostel, and you get a lot for your pesos, as the spotless place is set in expansive grounds and has a big pool and all the backpacker-friendly facilities you can imagine. The dorms are commodious and air-conditioned; the ones in separate buildings in the garden tend to be a little quieter. Most readers love it to bits, though some complain about CHS (Cool Hostel Syndrome): you'll know whether it's for you or not. It's 5km into town, but the falls buses (AR$2 to the town center) will stop right outside. HI discount applies.

Hotel Lilian HOTEL $

(☎420968; hotellilian@yahoo.com.ar; Fray Luis Beltrán 183; s/d AR$170/210;) Run by a hospitable family, this friendly place offers plenty of value, with bright and cheerful rooms around a patio. The superior rooms only cost around AR$25 more but have a balcony and heaps of natural light. All the bathrooms are spacious and spotless.

Marco Polo Inn HOSTEL $

(☎425559; www.marcopoloinniguazu.com; Av Córdoba 158; dm/d AR$65/250;) Built motel-style, this friendly hostel is opposite the bus terminal. The dorms are darkish but come with lockers and bathroom, and there's a host of other facilities. It's popular, so book. Substantial HI discount.

Hotel Saint George HOTEL $$$

(☎420633; www.hotelsaintgeorge.com; Av Córdoba 148; s/d standard AR$531/589, s/d superior AR$606/664;) The Saint George has been around for years and is reliable for comfort, service and organization. It's right across from the bus terminal and offers excellent facilities, including a garden and spa complex. Superior rooms are significantly larger, with two big double beds. Ninety pesos more gets you a buffet dinner.

Che Lagarto HOSTEL $

(☎422206; www.chelagarto.com; Av Brasil 24; dm AR$40-80, d AR$310;) The Iguazú version of this popular hostel chain appeals mostly for its excellent public spaces – pool, big deck, plenty of lounging room – and atmosphere. The private rooms are quiet and usually cheaper than we list here; dorms are simple, with bathroom and no lockers.

Hostel Irupé GUESTHOUSE, HOSTEL $

(☎420711; irupeiguazu@yahoo.com.ar; Av Misiones 80; dm/s/d AR$35/80/110;) Good value for private rooms. Tight but cheap ensuite dorms with beds not bunks. Go for rooms at the back, which have more light.

Eating

Restaurants in Puerto Iguazú are pricey but generally of good quality, and open early for dinner to cater for tourists. There are frequently problems with paying with plastic, so ask beforehand or carry cash.

TOP CHOICE **Bocamora** ARGENTINE $$$

(☎420550; www.bocamora.com; Av Costanera s/n; mains AR$60-110;) A superbly romantic location overlooking three nations is reason enough to come to this place just down the hill from the Argentine border marker. It specializes in grilled meats and well-prepared plates of river fish; you're paying a premium for the view here, but it's a great view. Arrive early to bag an outdoor table.

La Rueda ARGENTINE $$$

(☎422531; www.larueda1975.com; Av Córdoba 28; mains AR$58-75) A mainstay of upmarket eating in Puerto Iguazú, this culinary heavyweight still packs a punch. The salads are imaginative and delicious, as are the river fish (dorado, pacú and surubí) creations. The homemade pasta is cheaper but doesn't disappoint. Service is good but slow.

Aqua ARGENTINE $$$
(☎422064; www.aqvarestaurant.com; cnr Av Córdoba & Thays; mains AR$55-80; 📶) Solicitous service and plenty of flavor keep this split-level corner spot filled with the buzz of contented diners. The quality of the meat is excellent, and this is also a recommended spot to get to know some of the region's river fish.

María Preta ARGENTINE $$
(☎420441; Brasil 39; mains AR$48-68; 🍸) The indoor-outdoor eating area and evening guitarist make this a popular dinner choice, whether it's for steaks that are actually cooked the way you want them, for a wide range of typical Argentine-Spanish dishes, or for something a little snappier: caiman fillet.

Feria MARKET $
(cnr Brasil & Félix de Azara) A really nice place to eat is this market in the north of town. It's full of stalls selling Argentine wines, sausages, olives and cheese to visiting Brazilians, and several of them put out mixed deli platters, other simple regional dishes and cold beer for very few pesos. Readers have recommended Ramona's *barraca* (hut), but there are plenty of good ones to choose from.

Color PARRILLA, PIZZA $$
(☎420206; www.parrillapizzacolor.com; Av Córdoba 135; mains AR$35-78) This remodeled pizza 'n' *parrilla* packs them into its tightly spaced tables, so don't discuss state secrets. But the prices are fair for this strip, and the meat comes out redolent of wood smoke; try the *picaña,* a tender rump cut.

El Quincho de Tío Querido PARRILLA $$$
(☎420151; www.eltioquerido.com; Bompland 110; mains AR$45-80; ⏱dinner; 📶) Lively with the buzz of both tourists and locals, this popular *parrilla* has the usual grill favorites as well as giant 'baby beef' steaks and a range of interesting specials. It opens to cater for early-dining gringos. The wine list is pricey.

Terra ASIAN $$
(Av Misiones 125; stir-fries AR$40-60; ⏱Mon-Sat; 🍸) Chalked signatures of myriad satisfied customers mark the walls of this chilled bar-restaurant that specializes in well-prepared wok dishes, with pasta and salads as other options. The streetside terrace fills fast.

Plaza Pueblo FAST FOOD $
(Av Victoria Aguirre s/n; light meals AR$20-40; ⏱10am-10pm) This courtyard terrace is bang in the heart of town but set back from the road, so feels peaceful. It serves beer, pizza and excellent burgers and *lomitos*, all with a smile. Fridays to Sundays there's worthwhile live music from 8:30pm.

Lemongrass CAFE $
(Bompland 231; snacks AR$5-15; ⏱7:30am-midnight) There's something very likable about this artistic little cafe with orchids on the tables. Good fresh juices, decent coffee, delicious sweet temptations and tasty savory tarts are the way to go. We're not sure that, nice as they are, scones and jam constitute an 'English Breakfast' though...

La Vitrina PARRILLA $
(Aguirre 773; mains AR$30-55) This homey barn of a place is the place to come for great *asado de tira* (ribs) among other *parrilla* delicacies. It's less touristy than some and has enticing outdoor seating. There's live music at weekends.

La Misionera BAKERY $
(P Moreno 207; empanadas AR$4; ⏱10am-midnight) Excellent *empanadas* with a variety of fillings, and decent pizza from this well-regarded central bakery.

Drinking & Entertainment

Thanks to ever-increasing tourism and Brazilians from Foz looking for a cheap night out on the weakened peso, Puerto Iguazú's nightlife is lively. The action centers on Av Brasil, where at La Tribu the drinks are expensive but the terrace appealing. Opposite, Jackie Brown Bar pulls in the weekend punters, while the unsubtle Cuba Libre around the corner gets the cross-border Brazilian crowd living it up on the dance floor.

Information

Argecam (Av Victoria Aguirre 1164) Changes money.

Banco de la Nación (Av Victoria Aguirre s/n) ATM.

Hospital (☎420288; cnr Av Victoria Aguirre & Ushuaia)

Macro (cnr Av Misiones & Bompland) ATMs.

Tourist office (☎420800; www.iguazuargentina.com; Av Victoria Aguirre 396; ⏱7am-9pm) There's another office at the airport.

Getting There & Away

Aerolíneas Argentinas (☎420168; Av Victoria Aguirre 316) flies from Iguazú six times daily to Buenos Aires, once to Salta and once to Rio de Janeiro. **LAN** (☎0810-999-9526) flies the BA route three times daily and somewhat more reliably.

BUSES FROM PUERTO IGUAZÚ

DESTINATION	COST (AR$)	DURATION (HR)
Buenos Aires	369-415	19
Córdoba	480	22
Corrientes	198	9
Mendoza	665-800	35
Posadas	102	5
Resistencia	205	10
San Ignacio	60-80	4

The **bus terminal** (☎442-3006; cnr Avs Córdoba & Misiones) has departures for all over the country.

There are international services, as well as Brazilian domestic services, across the border in Foz do Iguaçu (p197). Some buses to Brazilian destinations such as Curitiba or São Paulo leave from the Puerto Iguazú bus terminal, too.

Getting Around

Four Tourist Travel (☎422681; M Moreno 58) runs an airport shuttle for AR$25 per person that meets incoming flights; from town, it needs to be booked in advance. A *remise* costs AR$100. The airport is 25km from town.

Frequent buses cross to Foz do Iguaçu, Brazil (AR$8/R$4, 35 minutes), and to Ciudad del Este, Paraguay (AR$10, one hour), from 7am to 7pm from the local side of the bus terminal. All will stop near the roundabout at the edge of town.

A taxi to Foz do Iguaçu costs around AR$100; to the Brazilian falls it's AR$120.

For information on entering Brazil, see p189.

Foz do Iguaçu (Brazil)

☎045 / POP 308,900

Hilly Foz is the main base for the Brazilian side of the falls, and also gives you a good chance to get a feel for a Brazilian town. It's much bigger and more cosmopolitan than Puerto Iguazú, and has a keep-it-real feel that its Argentine counterpart lacks. On the downside, it's noisier, more chaotic and has more crime. It's not a particularly pretty place, but there's something appealing about it nonetheless.

Foz do Iguaçu is at the confluence of Río Iguaçu and Río Paraná; the Ponte Tancredo Neves links the city to Puerto Iguazú, Argentina, across the Río Iguaçu, while the Ponte da Amizade connects it to Ciudad del Este, Paraguay, across the Paraná. Fifteen kilometers upstream is Itaipú, the world's largest operating hydroelectric project.

Av das Cataratas leads 20km to the falls, passing the turnoff for the Argentine border on the way.

Sights

Itaipú DAM

(☎0800-645-4645; www.itaipu.gov.br; Tancredo Neves 6702; ⏲8am-6pm Sun-Thu, 8am-9pm Fri-Sat) With a capacity of 14 million kilowatts, this binational dam (Usina Hidrelétrica Itaipú) is the second largest hydroelectric power station in the world, and the one that produces most electricity per year. A controversial project, it plunged Brazil way into debt and necessitated large-scale destruction of rainforest and the displacement of 10,000 people. But it cleanly supplies nearly all of Paraguay's energy needs, and 20% of Brazil's.

The structure is impressive; at some 8km long and 200m high, it is a memorable sight, especially when the river is high and a vast torrent of overflow water cascades down the spillway. The **visitors center** is 10km north of Foz. From here, regular tours (*visita panorâmica;* R$20.10) run daily on the hour (8am to 4pm inclusive); more detailed ones (*circuito especial;* R$51, minimum age 14), which take you into the power plant itself, leave eight times daily. There's a night visit on Friday and Saturday at 8pm. A variety of other attractions within the complex include a museum, wildlife park and river beaches.

Across Av Juscelino Kubitschek from Foz's downtown local bus terminal, Conjunto C Norte buses (R$2.65) run north every 10 minutes. It's better to catch the bus on the street rather than from inside the terminal, as it makes a circuit of the city after leaving the terminal before passing by it again.

Tours

There are numerous travel agencies in Foz, and most hotels also have a tour desk. All can book you trips to either side of the falls, visits to Itaipú dam, walks and boat rides.

Sleeping

We've listed rack rates here, but normally you'll get a rate up to 40% lower. Don't be afraid to ask for a discount.

Foz do Iguaçu (Brazil)

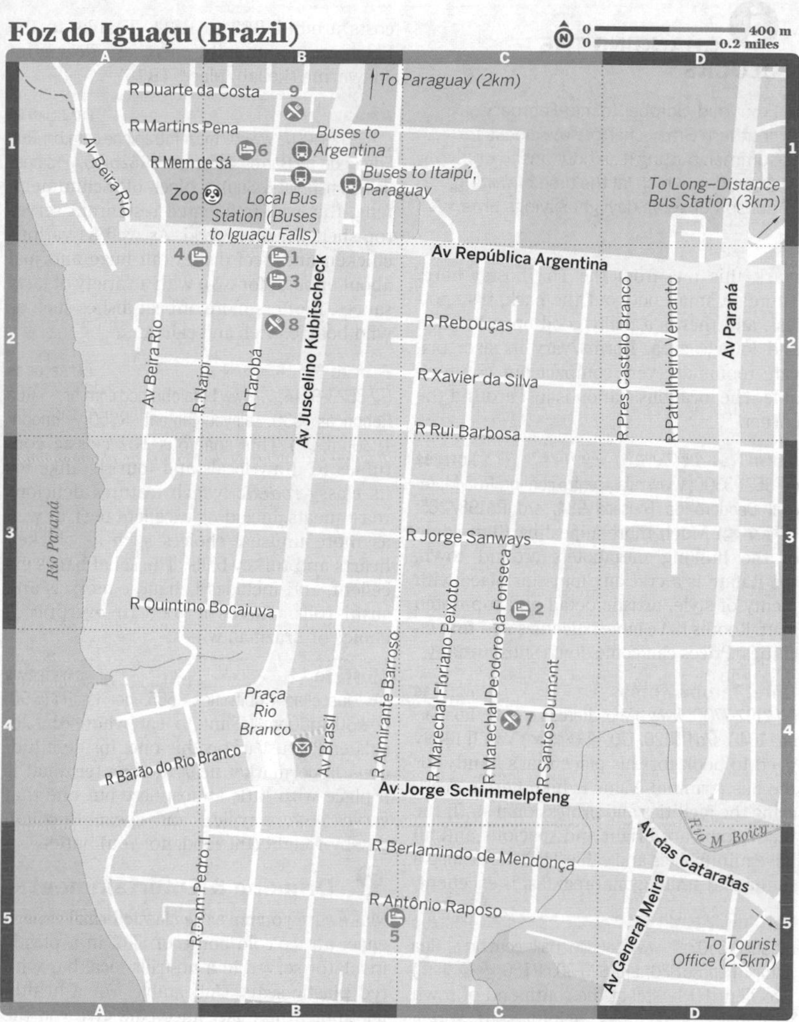

TOP CHOICE **Pousada Sonho Meu** GUESTHOUSE $
(☎3573-5764; www.pousadasonhomeufoz.com.br; Rua Mem de Sá 262; s/d R$130/200; ❄@☎≋) What from the outside looks like an administrative building becomes a delightful oasis barely 50m from the local bus terminal. Guests have use of a kitchen and pool table, and are made to feel very welcome. Rooms are artistically decorated with bamboo.

Iguassu Guest House HOSTEL $
(☎3029-0242; www.iguassuguesthouse.com.br; Rua Naipi 1019; dm R$30-40, d R$90-100; ❄@☎≋) Great facilities and welcoming management

Foz do Iguaçu (Brazil)

Sleeping

1 Hotel del Rey B2
2 Hotel Rafain Centro C3
3 Hotel Tarobá Express B2
4 Iguassu Guest House A2
5 Paudimar Falls Hostel B5
6 Pousada Sonho Meu B1

Eating

7 Armazém C4
8 Búfalo Branco B2
9 Muffato B1

CHANGING THE CLOCKS

From mid-October to mid-February, southern Brazil changes the clocks for summer, putting it an hour ahead of Argentina, which, at the time of writing, doesn't observe daylight savings time.

mark this out from the Foz hostel herd. There's a small pool out the back, it's spotless, and there's a really good open kitchen and lounge area. Dorms vary in size; private rooms are very compact but comfortable. The local bus station is just around the corner.

Hotel Rafain Centro HOTEL **$$**
(3521-3500; www.rafaincentro.com.br; Rua Marechal Deodoro da Fonseca 984; s/d R$198/265;) Much more appealing than some of the hulking megahotels around town, the Rafain is a cracking four-star place with plenty of style, artistic detail and top-notch staff. Rooms have large balconies and fine facilities. Prices can come down substantially.

Hotel Tarobá Xpress HOTEL **$$**
(2102-7700; www.bwhoteltaroba.com.br; Rua Tarobá 1048; s/d R$120/170;) You'll likely need to book for this place that's handy for the bus terminal. Value is high here considering the facilities and professional staff; the tiled rooms are bright and spacious and all have minifridges and cable TV. There's also a sauna and small gym. Breakfast is excellent.

Paudimar Falls Hostel HOSTEL **$**
(3028-5503; www.paudimarfalls.com.br; Rua Antônio Raposo 820; dm R$25-30, r R$80;) Excellent HI hostel at the south end of town with bags of facilities, helpful staff and a lively atmosphere. You can also camp here. There's another branch in big grounds off the road to the falls, 13km from town.

Hotel Del Rey HOTEL **$$**
(2105-7500; www.hoteldelreyfoz.com.br; Rua Tarobá 1020; s/d R$180/255;) Friendly, spotless and convenient hotel. The rooms are spacious and comfortable, facilities are excellent and the breakfast buffet is huge.

Eating

It's easy to eat cheaply here. Many places will do you a soft drink and *salgado* (baked or fried snack) for as little as R$3, and there are cheap local places where a buffet lunch costs around R$8 to R$14. Thanks to the Lebanese community, there are dozens of shawarma (kebab) places (R$6).

Armazém BRAZILIAN **$$**
(3572-0007; www.armazemtrapiche.com.br; Rua Edmundo de Barros 446; mains R$25-50; dinner daily, lunch Sat & Sun) A block off Schimmelpfeng, this well-frequented restaurant serves top-shelf Brazilian food. As well as various chicken and beef dishes (all huge and just about enough for two) with a variety of tasty sauces, it offers more offbeat dishes such as wild boar, ostrich and caiman.

Búfalo Branco BARBECUE **$$**
(3523-9744; www.bufalobranco.com.br; Rua Rebouças 530; all-you-can-eat R$50; noon-11:30pm;) This spacious Foz classic continues to draw locals and tourists alike for its classy *rodízio,* which features delicious roast meats, including excellent beef, as well as more unusual choices such as chicken hearts and turkey balls. The salad bar is excellent, and includes Lebanese morsels and sushi rolls. There's a good (if overpriced) choice of Brazilian wines.

Muffato CAFETERIA **$**
(Av Juscelino Kubitschek 1565; per kg R$16.90; 8:30am-10pm) Want to eat where the locals eat? Trust us on this one. Inside a hideous hypermarket near the bus terminal is a place with little atmosphere but one that serves a very typical and cheap Brazilian pay-by-weight (the food, not you) buffet.

Drinking & Entertainment

Make sure you have the classic Brazil experience: an ice-cold bottle of Skol in a plastic insulator served in a no-frills local bar with red plastic seats. Unbeatable. For a healthier tipple, the many juice bars give you the chance to try exotic fruits such as *acerola, açaí* or *cupuaçu.*

Nightlife in the city centers on Av Jorge Schimmelpfeng. The bars here all specialize in *chopp* (draft beer) and do food.

Information

Hotels and restaurants (and just about everything else including buses) in town accept US dollars, Paraguayan guaraníes and Argentine pesos, but it's always cheaper to pay in Brazilian reais. There are useful foreign-card ATMs in the Muffato supermarket a block past the local bus terminal. Internet places are plentiful.

HSBC (Av Brasil 1131) One of several banks with an ATM around this area.

Paraguayan Consulate (☎3523-2898; Rua Marechal Deodoro da Fonseca 901; ⌚8:30am-12:30pm & 1:30-3:30pm Mon-Fri)

Post office (cnr Juscelino Kubitschek & Rua Barão do Rio Branco)

Safira Turismo (Av Brasil 567; ⌚8:30am-6pm Mon-Fri, 8:30am-12:30pm Sat) Changes traveler's checks and cash.

Teletur (☎0800-451516; ⌚7am-11pm) Toll-free tourist information service with English-speaking operators.

Tourist office (www.iguassu.tur.br; Av Cataratas 2330; ⌚7am-10pm) Unhelpfully located out of town on the way to the falls. Handier are the booths at both local and long-distance bus terminals and at the airport. Also see Teletur above.

Getting There & Away

There are daily flights to Rio de Janeiro, Curitiba and São Paulo among other cities in Brazil, operated by **Gol** (www.voegol.com.br), **TAM** (www.tam.com.br) and more.

Long-distance bus destinations served daily from Foz include Curitiba (10 hours), São Paulo (16 hours) and Rio de Janeiro (22 hours). You can buy tickets with a small surcharge at many central travel agencies, including **Central de Passagens** (☎3523-4700; www.centraldepassagens.com; Av Juscelino Kubitschek 526).

Getting Around

For the airport or falls, catch the 'Aeropuerto/Parque Nacional' bus from the local bus terminal or one of the stops along Av Juscelino Kubitschek; the trip takes 30 to 40 minutes and costs R$2.65, paid as you enter the terminal. A taxi costs about R$35.

The **long-distance bus terminal** (rodoviária; ☎3522-3336; Costa e Silva) is 5km northeast of downtown. To get downtown, taxi it for R$15 or walk downhill to the bus stop and catch any 'Centro' bus (R$2.65).

Buses to Puerto Iguazú (R$4/AR$8) run along Rua Mem de Sá alongside the local bus terminal half-hourly from 8am until 8pm; they stop along Juscelino Kubitschek. Buses for Ciudad del Este, Paraguay (R$4), run every 15 minutes (half-hourly on Sundays); catch them on JK opposite the local bus terminal.

THE GRAN CHACO

The Gran Chaco is a vast alluvial lowland, stretching north from the northern edges of Santa Fe and Córdoba provinces, across the entire provinces of Chaco and Formosa, and into Paraguay, Bolivia and Brazil. It reaches west through most of Santiago del Estero province, drying up as it goes, and skirts the southeastern edge of Salta province. The western side, known as the Chaco Seco (Dry Chaco), has been dubbed the Impenetrable, due to its severe lack of water across an endless plain of nearly impassable thorn scrub.

Crossing the Gran Chaco from Formosa to Salta along the northern RN 81 is brutal and can take nearly two days; RN 16 from Resistencia is much faster.

Deforestation continues apace in the Chaco, with vast areas being cleared to plant soya, of which Argentina is now one of the world's major producers. This has seriously affected Toba tribes, whose traditional environment is being destroyed.

Resistencia

☎0362 / POP 390,874

This provincial capital is perched on the edge of the barely populated wilderness of the Chaco. It isn't the most likely candidate for the garland of artistic center of northern Argentina, yet baking-hot Resistencia has strong claims to that title – its streets are studded with sculpture (500 or more) and there's a strong boho-cultural streak that represents a complete contrast to the tough cattle-and-dust solitudes that characterize the province.

Sights

FREE Museo del Hombre Chaqueño MUSEUM

(JB Justo 280; ⌚8am-noon & 3-8pm Mon-Fri) This small but excellent museum is run by enthusiastic staff (some English spoken) who will talk you through the displays covering the three main pillars of Chaco population: the indigenous inhabitants (there are some excellent ceramics and Toba musical instruments here); the criollos who resulted from interbreeding between the European arrivals and the local populations; and the 'gringos' – the wave of mostly European immigration that arrived from the late 19th century onwards. Best of all is the mythology room upstairs, where you'll get to meet various quirky characters from Chaco popular religion.

FREE Sculptures SCULPTURE

At last count, there were more than 500 sculptures around the city, a number that is set to increase with every Bienal (p198). The streets are packed with them, especially around the plaza and north up Av Sarmiento. Calle Perón/Arturo Illia, a block south of the plaza, is also well endowed. Every Bienal, a brochure is printed with a sculpture walking tour around the city. The most likely place to get hold of the latest one is at the **MusEUM** (www.bienaldelchaco.com; admission free; ⏲8am-noon & 3-8pm Mon-Sat), an open-air workshop on the north side of Parque 2 de Febrero. Several of the most impressive pieces are on display here, and this is where (during the Bienal and quite frequently at other times) you can catch sculptors hard at work.

El Fogón de los Arrieros CULTURAL CENTER, MUSEUM
(Brown 350; admission AR$5; ⏲museum 8-11:40am Mon-Sat) Founded in 1943, this is a cultural center, art gallery and bar that for decades has been the driving force behind Resistencia's artistic commitment and progressive displays of public art. Still the keystone of the region's art community, it is now famous for its eclectic collection of art objects from around the Chaco and Argentina. The museum also features the wood carvings of local artist and cultural activist Juan de Dios Mena. Check out the irreverent epitaphs to dead patrons in the memorial garden; it's called 'Colonia Sálsipuedes' (leave if you can).

Festivals & Events

During the third week of July in even years, the **Bienal de Escultura** (www.bienaldelchaco.com) brings 10 renowned Argentine and international sculptors to Resistencia. Arranging themselves around the fountain at the open-air museum in Parque 2 de Febrero, they have seven days to complete a sculpture under the public gaze. The medium changes every time.

Sleeping

Niyat Urban Hotel HOTEL $$
(☎444-8451; www.niyaturban.com.ar; Yrigoyen 83; s/d AR$285/330; ❄@🛜) Shiny and confident,

Resistencia

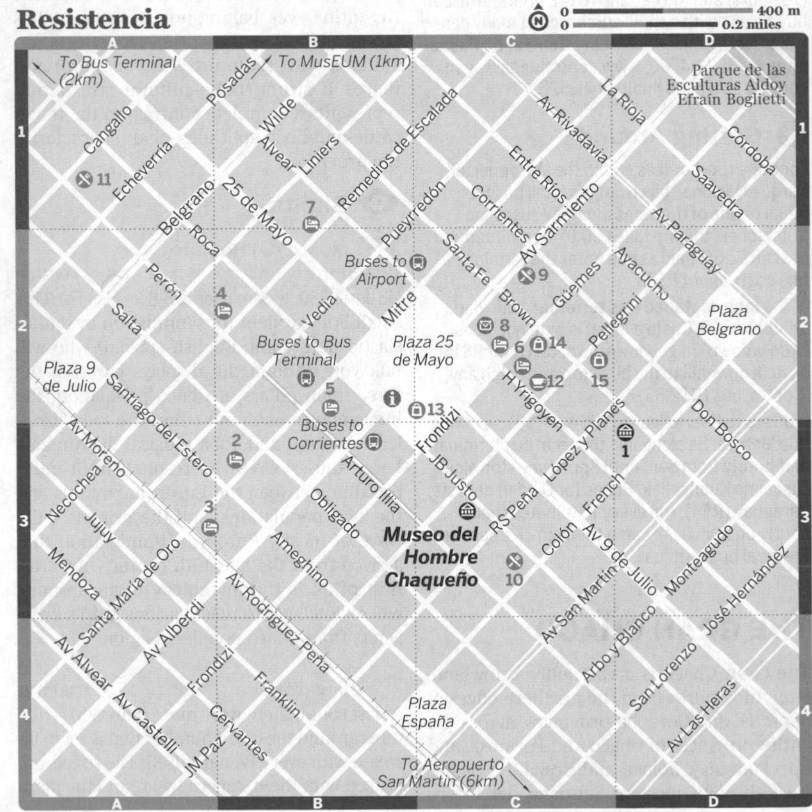

this plaza-side hotel offers excellent service and plenty of value for its gleaming modern rooms, which boast great bathrooms, comfy beds and big flat-screen TVs. Some look over the square. There's also a gym and small spa complex with Jacuzzi.

Hotel Covadonga HOTEL **$$**
(☎444-4444; www.hotelcovadonga.com.ar; Güemes 200; s/d AR$315/340; ❄@📶🏊) With an excellent location close to the plaza and restaurants, this upmarket hotel has fine facilities, including a pool, sauna and Jacuzzi, and personable staff. The public areas are slickly furnished, and the recently renovated rooms feature streetside balconies and attractive wooden floors. While they still exist, unrenovated rooms are significantly cheaper.

Hotel Amerian HOTEL **$$**
(☎445-2400; www.hotelcasinogala.com.ar; Perón 330; s/d AR$387/429; ❄@📶🏊) This swish casino-hotel is the city's smartest choice, with various grades of room and slick service. As well as the slot machines, there's a sauna, gym and self-contained spa complex.

Resistencia

Top Sights
Museo del Hombre Chaqueño C3

Sights
1 El Fogón de los Arrieros D3

Sleeping
2 Casa Mía B3
3 Hotel Alfil A3
4 Hotel Amerian B2
5 Hotel Colón B2
6 Hotel Covadonga C2
7 Hotel Luxor B1
8 Niyat Urban Hotel C2

Eating
9 Coco's Resto C2
10 La Bianca C3
11 Parrillada Don Abel A1

Drinking
El Fogón de los Arrieros ....(see 1)
12 El Viejo Café C2

Shopping
13 Artesanía Stalls C2
14 Chac Cueros C2
15 Fundación Chaco Artesanal C2

Hotel Colón HOTEL **$$**
(☎442-2861; www.colonhotelyapart.com; Santa María de Oro 143; s/d/apt AR$195/284/345; ❄@📶) Art deco fans mustn't miss this 1920s classic, a few steps south of the plaza. It's an amazingly large and characterful building with some enticingly curious period features. Rooms show their age but the refurbished apartments are very spick and span.

Hotel Alfil HOTEL **$**
(☎442-0882; Santa María de Oro 495; s/d AR$90/130;❄📶) A few blocks south of the plaza, the old-fashioned Alfil is a reasonable budget choice. The interior rooms are dark but worthwhile if the significant street noise in the exterior rooms (with their strangely inaccessible balconies) will bother you. Air-con is AR$10 extra, but it's a decent deal despite the lack of breakfast.

Casa Mía HOTEL **$$**
(☎457-0430; www.casamiahotel.com.ar; Santa María de Oro 368; s/d AR$209/297; ❄@📶) Neat, fairly unadorned but modern rooms with good bathrooms. Nice touches such as some art and plants about the place and helpful service.

Hotel Luxor HOTEL **$**
(☎444-7252; camorsluxor@hotmail.com; Remedios de Escalada 19; s/d AR$80/120;❄📶) Central and decent enough place that caters for traveling salespeople, the odd backpacker and local couples looking for a few hours away from disapproving parents' eyes. Breakfast, TV and air-con all cost extra.

Eating

La Bianca ARGENTINE **$**
(Colón 102; dishes AR$25-50; ⏰lunch & dinner Wed-Mon) Busy and bustling, this long-time local split-level favorite keeps 'em coming for its well-priced pasta, pizza and soufflés. There's also meat and salad dishes in generous quantities. A cheap and cheerful option.

Parrillada Don Abel PARRILLA **$$**
(Perón 698; mains AR$30-60; ⏰lunch & dinner, closed dinner Sun) This homey *parrilla* is decorated with photos of satisfied customers and serves substantial portions of pasta and grilled surubí, in addition to the usual grilled beef. It has a convivial family buzz to it at the weekend.

Coco's Resto ARGENTINE **$$**
(☎442-3321; Av Sarmiento 266; mains AR$40-60; 📶) Stylishly occupying two front rooms of

a house, this intimate, well-decorated restaurant is popular with suited diners from the nearby state parliament. A wide-ranging menu of pastas, meats soused in various sauces and long wine list make this a pleasant Chaco choice.

Drinking & Entertainment

El Fogón de los Arrieros BAR, LIVE MUSIC

(Brown 350; ⏲9:30pm-1am) Stopping into El Fogón's friendly bar – a local institution for decades – is almost mandatory. The attached cultural center presents occasional live music and small-scale theatrical events, including Thursday night tango.

El Viejo Café CAFE

(Pellegrini 109; ⏲7am-late Sun-Thu, 1pm-late Fri & Sat) In an elegant old edifice, with an eclectically decorated interior, this is a fine choice at any time of day. Its terrace is a sweet spot for a sundowner, and it gets lively later on weekends.

Shopping

There's a selection of **artesanía stalls** on the southern side of the plaza.

Chac Cueros LEATHER

(www.chaccueros.com.ar; Güemes 186) Specializes in quality goods made from the hide of

INDIGENOUS GROUPS OF THE GRAN CHACO

With some 50,000 members, the **Toba** of the Gran Chaco are one of Argentina's largest indigenous groups, but their existence is nonetheless frequently ignored. Toba protests in 2009 highlighted the stark reality that many communities suffer from abandoned government facilities and, in some, people actually die of starvation. Few Argentines had any idea about the struggles of this *pueblo olvidado* (forgotten people).

As a traveler, it's easy to zip through the sun-scorched Chaco without ever noticing the presence of indigenous people, except, perhaps, for the crafts sold at government-sponsored stores or along the roadside. In Resistencia the Toba live in *barrios* (neighborhoods) that are separated from the rest of the city. And those who don't live in the city either live in towns that travelers rarely visit (such as Juan José Castelli or Quitilipi) or deep within the Argentine Impenetrable, in settlements reached only by dirt roads that are impossible to navigate if you don't know the way. If you do know the way (or you go with someone who does), you'll find Toba *asentamientos* (settlements) that are unlike anything else in Argentina. People live in extreme poverty (although there's always a church) and, except for the occasional government-built health center, nearly all buildings are made of adobe, with dirt floors and thatched roofs.

The Toba refer to themselves as Komlek (or Qom-lik) and speak a dialect of the Guaycurú linguistic group, known locally as Qom. They have a rich musical tradition (the Coro Toba Chelaalapi, a Toba choir founded in 1962, has Unesco World Heritage designation). Along with basket weaving and ceramics, the Toba are known for their version of the fiddle, which they make out of a gas can.

The region's most numerous indigenous group is the **Wichí**, with a population of over 60,000. Because the Wichí remain extremely isolated (they live nearly 700km from Resistencia, in the far northwest of Chaco province and in Formosa and Salta provinces) they are the most traditional of its groups. They still obtain much of their food through hunting, gathering and fishing. The Wichí are known for their wild honey and their beautiful *yica* bags, which they weave with fibers from the chaguar plant, a bromeliad native to the arid regions of the Chaco. Like the Toba, most Wichí live in simple adobe huts.

The **Mocoví** are the Gran Chaco's third-largest indigenous group, with a population of 17,000, concentrated primarily in southern Chaco province and northern Santa Fe. Like the Toba, the Mocoví speak a dialect of the Guaycurú linguistic group. Until the arrival of Europeans the Mocoví sustained themselves primarily through hunting and gathering, but today they rely mostly on farming and seasonal work. They are famous for their burnished pottery, which is the most developed of the Chaco's indigenous pottery.

For more information on the Toba, Wichí or Mocoví, stop by Resistencia's **Centro Cultural Leopoldo Marechal** (☎445-2738; Pellegrini 272; ⏲9am-noon & 4-8pm Mon-Sat) which has crafts exhibits and a shop sponsored by the Fundación Chaco Artesanal, and the Museo del Hombre Chaqueño also in Resistencia. To journey into the Argentine Impenetrable to visit the Toba or Wichí, see p203.

capybaras, valued for the suede produced from their tan, naturally dimpled skin.

Fundación Chaco Artesanal HANDICRAFTS
(fundacionchacoartesanal@gmail.com; Pellegrini 272) Selection of indigenous crafts as well as CDs from the Toba choir (see the boxed text, p200).

Information

There are several ATMs around Plaza 25 de Mayo and lots of internet places around the central streets.

Hospital Perrando (445-2583; Av 9 de Julio 1099)

Tourist office (445-8289; www.mr.gov.ar; Plaza 25 de Mayo; 8am-12:30pm & 2-8pm Mon-Fri, 8am-noon & 3-7pm Sat, 6-9pm Sun) In a kiosk on the southern side of the plaza. Good bilingual city information.

Getting There & Away

From Aeropuerto San Martin, **Aerolíneas Argentinas** (444-5551; JB Justo 184) flies to Buenos Aires' Aeroparque almost daily. **Aerochaco** (0810-444-2376; www.aerochaco.com.ar; Av Sarmiento 715) services Córdoba three times a week.

Resistencia's **bus terminal** (446-1098; cnr MacLean & Islas Malvinas) serves destinations in all directions. Buses make the rounds between Corrientes and Resistencia (AR$7, 40 minutes) at frequent intervals throughout the day. You can also catch a bus (AR$2.50) to Corrientes from the city center, on Av Alberdi just south of the plaza. Faster are the shared taxis (AR$7, 20 minutes) that congregate on Frondizi near Plaza 25 de Mayo.

BUSES FROM RESISTENCIA

DESTINATION	COST (AR$)	DURATION (HR)
Asunción (Paraguay)	70	5
Buenos Aires	298	13
Córdoba	267	14
Mendoza	525	24
Posadas	109	5½
Puerto Iguazú	205	10
Roque Sáenz Peña	45	2
Rosario	255	10
Salta	285	10
Santa Fe	189	7
Santiago del Estero	207	8
Tucumán	247	11

Getting Around

Aeropuerto San Martín is 6km south of town on RN 11; take bus 2 from the northwest corner of the plaza. The bus terminal is a AR$25 taxi ride from the city center, or you can take bus 3 or 10 from opposite the Hotel Colón.

Parque Nacional Chaco

Preserving several diverse ecosystems that reflect subtle differences in relief, soils and rainfall, this very accessible **park** (03725-499161; www.parquesnacionales.gov.ar; admission free; visitors center 9am-7pm) protects 150 sq km of the humid eastern Chaco. It is 120km northwest of Resistencia via RN 16 and RP 9.

Activities

Hiking and **bird watching** are the principal activities here. From the main camp site, there are two short trails, one leading to viewpoints over lakes. A longer 12km road, suitable for cars, bikes, and horses, heads south to the Panza de Cabra lake. You can arrange guides, bikes, and horses in **Capitán Solari**, 6km east of the park.

Sleeping & Eating

The park's main campground is equipped, with power, toilets and drinking water. Though vendors sometimes appear at weekends, you should bring all your own food. In Capitán Solari ask at the *municipalidad* (city hall) for locals who rent rooms to travelers at a fair price.

Getting There & Away

Capitán Solari is 2½ hours from Resistencia by bus. La Estrella runs five buses daily (AR$26).

From Capitán Solari, the park information may be able to organize transportation for you; otherwise you can walk, hitchhike or take a *remise* (AR$25) the 5km to the park. The road may be impassable for motor vehicles in wet weather.

Roque Sáenz Peña

0364 / POP 96,944

Something of a frontier town, Presidencia Roque Sáenz Peña is well out in the Chaco, and is a gateway to the 'Impenetrable' beyond. It's known for its thermal baths, fortuitously discovered by drillers seeking potable water in 1937, and makes an appealing stop, with a rugged, friendly feel to the place.

Sights & Activities

Parque Zoológico ZOO

(adult/child AR$6/1; 9am-6pm Mon-Fri, 8am-6pm Sat & Sun) At the junction of RN 16 and RN 95, 4km east of downtown, the town's spacious zoo and botanical garden emphasizes birds and mammals found in the Chaco region, alongside a few lions, tigers and bears. Featured species are tapir and jaguar, but there are also crocodiles, llamas, monkeys, a bafflingly large chicken pen, snakes, condors and vultures.

Complejo Termal Municipal SPA

(www.elchacotermal.com.ar; Brown 545; 6:30-11:30am & 2:30-8pm) Roque's famous thermal baths draw their saline water from 150m below ground. The center, around since the 1930s, is now a top-class facility, offering thermal baths (AR$10), saunas and Turkish baths (AR$12). Treatments on offer include kinesiology, massage and aromatherapy. On Wednesdays it opens at 8am and at 4pm.

Sleeping

TOP CHOICE Atrium Gualok HOTEL $$

(442-0500; www.atriumgualok.com.ar; San Martín 1198; s/d AR$270/340;) Right next to the spa complex, this fine modern hotel gives a feeling of space throughout. Rooms are indeed set around a lofty central atrium and are sleek, minimalist and great value for this standard of place. There's an enticing pool area and the hotel has its own spa complex and casino. Substantial discount for paying cash.

Hotel Presidente HOTEL $

(442-4498; San Martín 771; s/d AR$130/180;) With plush red carpet and mirrors everywhere, including on the doors of the rooms, this looks like a cross between a Colombian narco-trafficker's mansion and a top-of-the-market 1970s brothel. It's a very pleasing place right in the heart of town, with friendly staff and, for this price, excellent rooms with minibar and comfortable beds.

Eating

The restaurant at Atrium Gualok is Roque's best.

Bien, José! PARRILLA $

(25 de Mayo 531; mains AR$20-45; dinner) Warm personal service melds with delicious meat *empanadas* and decent *parrilla* choices at this good-value restaurant. Every generation is called José here, so ask one of them what the daily special is and enjoy. **Rovetti**, 20m up the road, does enormous *milanesas* (breaded cutlets) for AR$25.

Giuseppe PIZZA $

(Moreno 680; small pizzas AR$20-35) This place has slightly staid decor but is extremely popular in the evening for its tasty pizza and interesting pasta combinations. Try not to sit down the side – the kitchen belts out so much heat you expect brimstone and horned waiters.

Ama Nalec ICE CREAM $

(Moreno 601; ice creams from AR$5; 10am-1pm & 5pm-late) This busy corner place does tempt-

NORTH TOWARDS PARAGUAY

There are daily buses from Resistencia to Asunción, Paraguay's capital, making the crossing in Argentina's far north at **Clorinda**, a chaotic border town with little of interest beyond its bustling markets.

To stop somewhere more interesting en route, try baking-hot **Formosa**, a medium-sized city and provincial capital two hours north of Resistencia on the bus. Hotels, restaurants and services can be found along Avenida 25 de Mayo, which links the sleepy plaza with the waterfront on the Río Paraguay – the best place to stroll once the temperatures drop.

About 6km out of town, **Laguna Oca** offers good bird watching. For more, hit **Parque Nacional Río Pilcomayo**. This lies 126km northwest of Formosa and 55km west of Clorinda. Daily buses connect these towns with **Laguna Blanca**, an easy-paced citrus town, where you'll find inexpensive lodgings – **Residencial Guaraní** (cnr San Martín & Sargento Cabral) is the standout – and *remises* that will take you into the national park. In the park itself, the main feature is **Laguna Blanca**, where rangers can take you out in boats to spot caiman.

WORTH A TRIP

PENETRATING THE IMPENETRABLE

If you have a yen to get off the beaten track, the more remote areas of the Chaco are for you. The key access point for the Impenetrable is the town of **Juan José Castelli**, 115km north of Roque Sáenz Peña, and served by two daily buses from Resistencia (AR$77, five hours) via Roque. From Juan José Castelli, you can head west along *ripio* (gravel) roads to remote Fuerte Esperanza (shared *remises* run this route), which has two nature reserves in its vicinity – **Reserva Provincial Fuerte Esperanza** and **Reserva Natural Loro Hablador**. Both conserve typical dry Chaco environments, with algarrobo and quebracho trees, armadillos, peccaries and many bird species. **Loro Hablador**, 40km from Fuerte Esperanza, has a good campground and short walking trails with ranger guides. Fuerte Esperanza has two simple *hospedajes* (family homes). Further north, **Misión Nueva Pompeya** was founded in 1899 by Franciscans who established a mission station for Matacos in tough conditions. The main building, with its square-towered church, is a surprising sight in such a remote location.

Various operators offer excursions and packages, which include visits to the reserves, Misión Nueva Pompeya and indigenous communities in the area. **Carlos Aníbal Schumann** (☎0364-427-1073; www.ecoturchaco.com.ar; Av San Marín 500, Juan José Castelli) comes recommended and also runs a campground and lodge in Villa Río Bermejito, a riverside settlement 67km northeast of Juan José Castelli. **Tantanacuy** (☎0364-449-7621; www.chacoagreste.com.ar) is a *hostería* (lodging house) between Castelli and Fuerte Esperanza that offers packages with accommodations, transfers and excursions.

ing little pastries and very tasty ice cream, a godsend in Roque's paralyzing heat. It has some unusual flavors – figs in cognac is worth a lick.

Information

Av San Martín has several banks with ATMs and numerous internet/telephone places. There's tourist information available in the thermal baths complex.

Getting There & Away

The **bus terminal** (☎420280; Petris, btwn Avellaneda & López) is seven blocks east of downtown; take bus 1 from Mitre. There are regular buses to Resistencia (AR$45, two hours), and services running west to Tucumán, Santiago del Estero Mendoza and Salta also stop here.

Salta & the Andean Northwest

Includes »

Best Places to Eat

» Casa de las Empanadas (p243)

» Mi Nueva Estancia (p248)

» La Vieja Casona (p262)

» José Balcarce (p232)

Best Places to Stay

» Estancia los Cuartos (p250)

» Killa (p241)

» La Merced del Alto (p237)

» Posada El Arribo (p209)

» Con los Ángeles (p217)

» Carpe Diem (p227)

Why Go?

Argentina's northwest sits lofty, dry and tough beneath the mighty Andes. Nature works magic here with stone: weird, wonderful, tortured rockscapes are visible throughout.

There's a definite Andean feel with traditional handicrafts, Quechua-speaking pockets, coca leaves, llamas, indigenous heritage, Inca ruins, and the high, arid puna (Andean highlands) stretching west to Chile and north to Bolivia. The region's cities were Argentina's first colonial settlements and have a special appeal.

Several popular routes await. From travelers' favorite Salta, head through a national park studded with cactus sentinels on your way to gorgeous Cachi, then down through traditional weaving communities in the Valles Calchaquíes to Cafayate, home of some of Argentina's best wines. Another route from Salta soars upwards to the puna mining settlement of San Antonio de los Cobres, heads north to the spectacular salt plains of the Salinas Grandes, and then down to the visually wondrous and history-filled Quebrada de Humahuaca.

When to Go

Salta

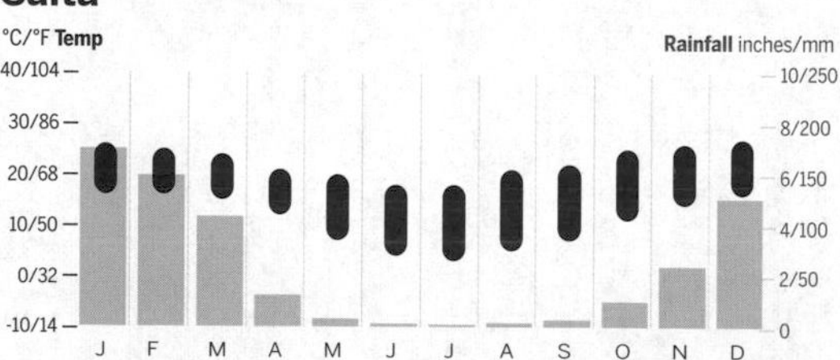

Feb–Mar Temperatures high but Carnaval celebrations are worth seeing.

Jul–Aug Chilly up on the puna, but it is the most pleasant time to visit.

Sep–Oct A good compromise, with fewer tourists in Salta and acceptable spring temperatures.

National Parks

This region holds some important national parks, mostly in Jujuy and Salta provinces. **Parque Nacional Calilegua** (p216) preserves subtropical cloud forest and is home to an array of birdlife, as well as pumas and jaguars. Far-flung **Parque Nacional Baritú** (p216) contains subtropical montane forest and is home to monkeys, big cats, otters and forest squirrels. **Parque Nacional El Rey** (p205) is the most biologically diverse park in the country and teems with birdlife, including toucans. Between Salta and Cachi, **Parque Nacional Los Cardones** (p236) is full of cactus-studded photo opportunities. Much further south, **Parque Nacional Talampaya** (p266) has aboriginal petroglyphs, photogenic rock formations and local flora and fauna.

JUJUY & SALTA PROVINCES

Intertwined like yin and yang, Argentina's two northwestern provinces harbor an inspiring wealth of natural beauty and traditional culture. Bounded by Bolivia to the north and Chile to the west, the zone climbs from the sweaty cloud forests of Las Yungas westward to the puna and some of the most majestic peaks of the Cordillera de los Andes.

The two capitals – comfortable Jujuy and colonial, beloved-of-travelers Salta – are launch pads for exploration of the jagged chromatic ravines of the Quebrada de Cafayate and Quebrada de Humahuaca; for the villages of the Valles Calchaquíes, rich in artisanal handicrafts; for the stark puna scenery; for nosing of the aromatic Cafayate torrontés whites; or for rough exploration in the remote national parks of El Rey or Baritú.

Jujuy

☎0388 / POP 278,336 / ELEV 1201M

Of the trinity of northwestern cities, Jujuy lacks the colonial sophistication of Salta or urban vibe of Tucumán, but nevertheless shines for its livable feel, enticing restaurants and gregarious, good-looking locals. It's got the most indigenous feel of any of Argentina's cities.

San Salvador de Jujuy (commonly called simply Jujuy) was founded in 1593 at the third attempt, after the previous two incarnations had been razed by miffed indigenous groups who hadn't given planning permission.

The province of Jujuy bore the brunt of conflict during the wars of independence, with Spain launching repeated invasions down the Quebrada de Humahuaca from Bolivia; Jujuy was famously evacuated in what is known as the *éxodo jujeño.*

The city's name is roughly pronounced *hoo-hooey;* if it sounds like an arch exclamation of surprise, you're doing well.

Sights

FREE **Culturarte** GALLERY

(cnr San Martín & Sarmiento; ⌚8:30am-midnight Mon-Fri, 8:30am-1pm & 4:30pm-midnight Sat & Sun) An attractive modern space, the Culturarte showcases exhibitions by well-established Argentine contemporary artists. There's also a cafe-bar with a great little balcony elevated over the street.

Museo Arqueológico Provincial MUSEUM

(Lavalle 434; admission AR$2; ⌚8am-8pm Mon-Fri, 9am-1pm & 3-7pm Sat & Sun) The standout exhibit is a vivid 3000-year-old fertility goddess figure, depicted with snakes for hair and in the act of giving birth. She's a product of the advanced San Francisco culture, which existed in Las Yungas from about 1400 BC to 800 BC. There's also a selection of skulls with cranial deformities (practiced for cosmetic reasons) and mummified bodies.

Museo Histórico Franciscano MUSEUM

(Belgrano s/n; admission AR$5; ⌚9am-1pm & 5-9pm Mon-Sat) Alongside the San Francisco church and convent, this retains a strong selection of colonial art from the Cuzco school,

COCA CHEWING

Once you get seriously north, you see signs outside shops advertising *coca* and *bica*. The former refers to the leaves, mainly grown in Peru and Bolivia, which are used to produce cocaine. *Bica* refers to bicarbonate of soda, an alkaline that, when chewed along with the leaves (as is customary among Andean peoples), releases their mild stimulant effect and combats fatigue and hunger. Chewing coca and possessing small amounts for personal use is legal, but only in the northern provinces of Salta and Jujuy. Taking them into other provinces or into Chile is illegal, and there are plenty of searches.

Salta & the Andean Northwest Highlights

1. Wonder at nature's palette in the **Quebrada de Humahuaca** (p212)
2. Observe weavers at work in the memorable **Valles Calchaquíes** (p236)
3. Cleanse your lungs in the crisp mountain air of **Tafí del Valle** (p250)
4. Hit Wild West **Chilecito** (p264), the base for uplifting mountain excursions
5. Soak up the colonial ambience and relax in the enticing boutique hotels of sophisticated **Salta** (p222)
6. Taste your way through the torrontés at northern Argentina's wine capital of **Cafayate** (p240)

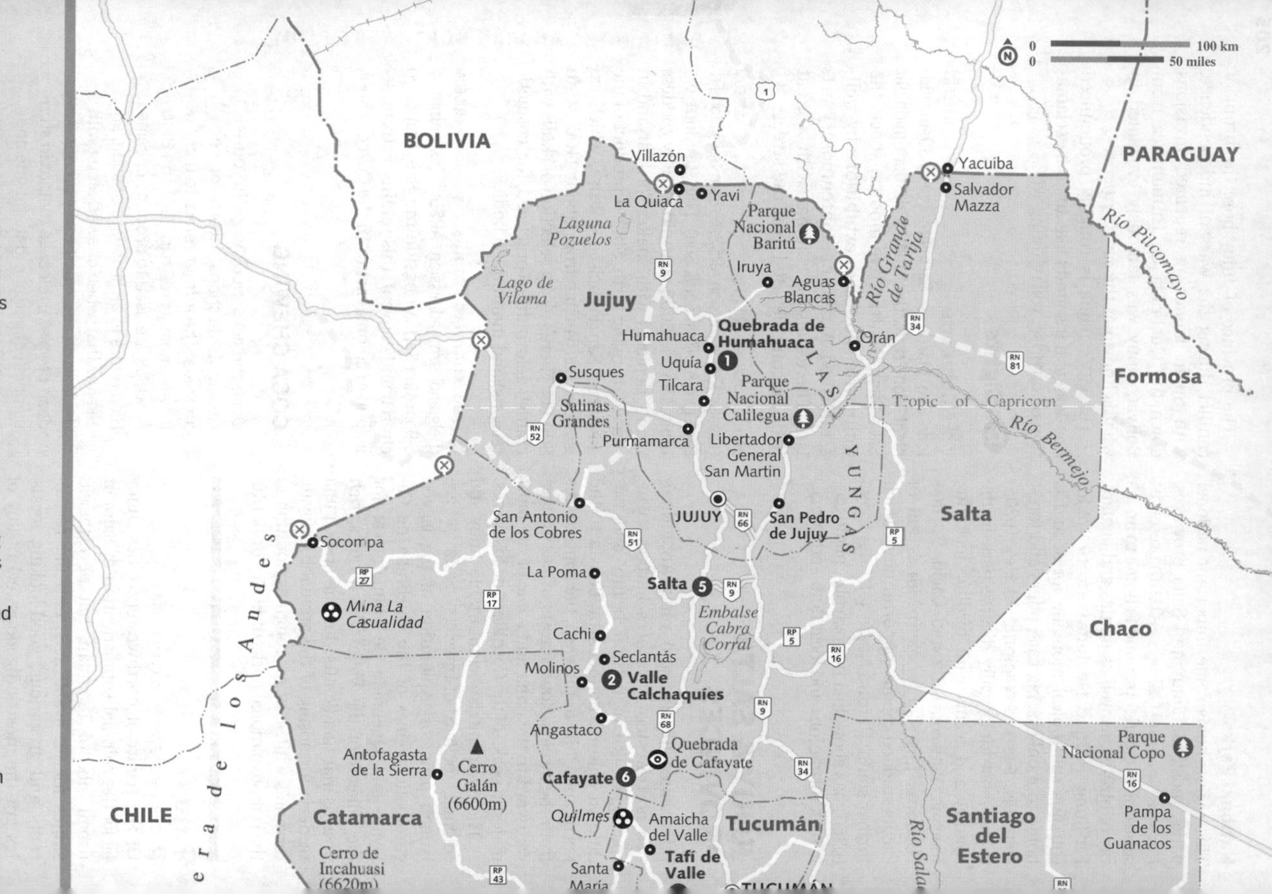

❼ Try the regional **cuisine** of the far northwest, where llama meat and quinoa replace beef and pasta on the menu.

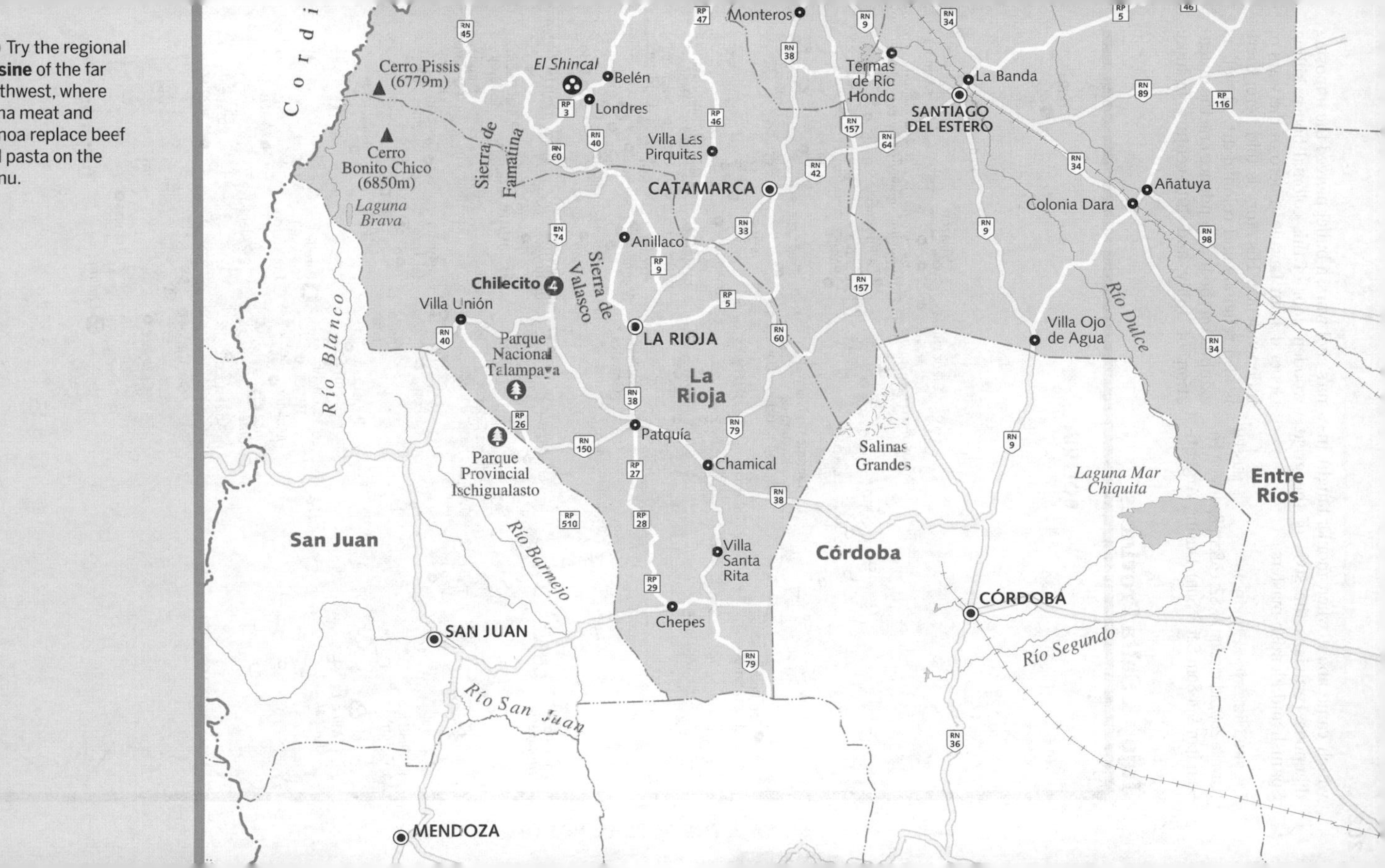

which came about when monks taught indigenous Peruvians the style of the great Spanish and Flemish masters.

Museo Histórico Provincial MUSEUM
(Lavalle 256; admission AR$2; ⌚8am-8pm Mon-Fri, 9am-1pm & 4-8pm Sat & Sun) During Argentina's civil wars, a bullet pierced the imposing wooden door of this colonial house, killing General Juan Lavalle, a hero of the wars of independence. His story is told here; there is also religious and colonial art, as well as exhibits on the independence era, the evacuation of Jujuy and 19th-century fashion.

Jujuy & Salta Provinces

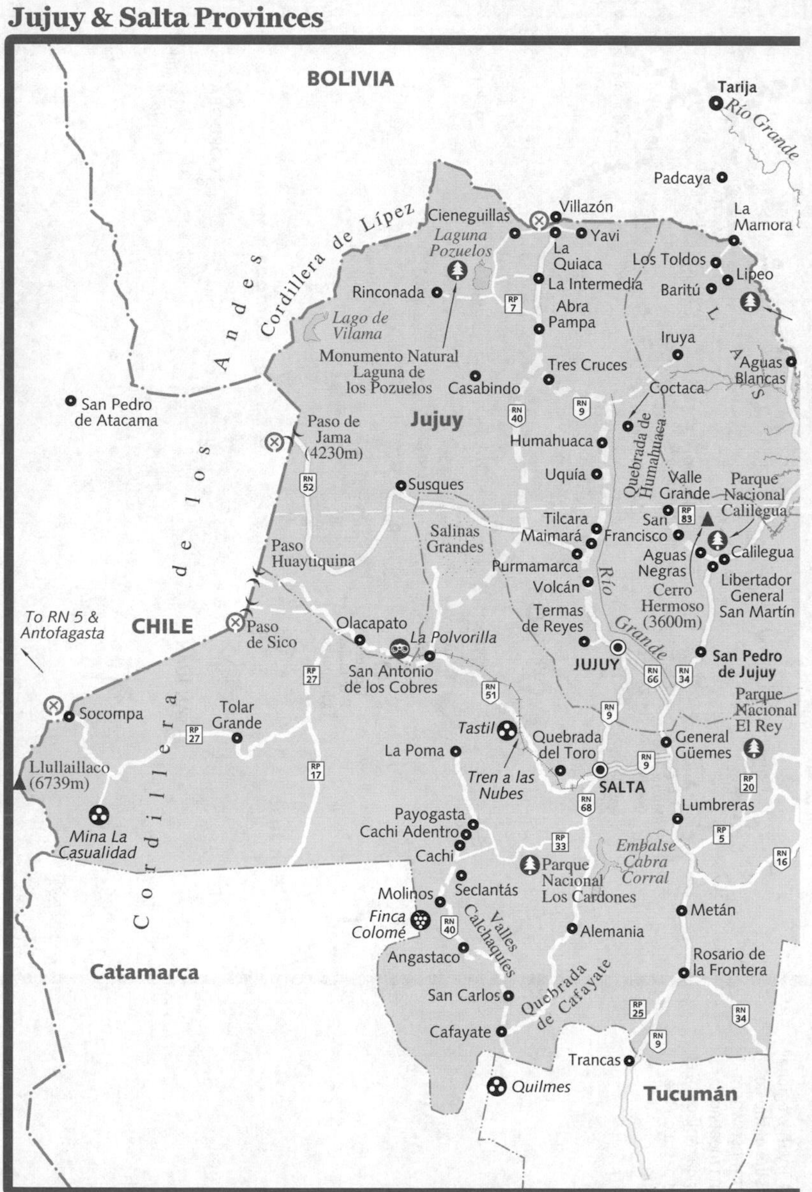

There are some English labels, and guides on hand to answer questions.

FREE **Cabildo & Museo Policial** MUSEUM
(Pl Belgrano s/n; ⌚8am-1pm & 4-9pm Mon-Fri, 9am-noon & 6-8pm Sat & Sun) On the plaza, the attractively colonnaded *cabildo* (colonial town hall) houses the Museo Policial. Police museums in Argentina are funny things, with grisly crime photos, indiscriminate homage to authority and the odd quirky gem – in this case the discovery that in 1876 you could expect a five peso fine if you wanted carnal knowledge of a llama.

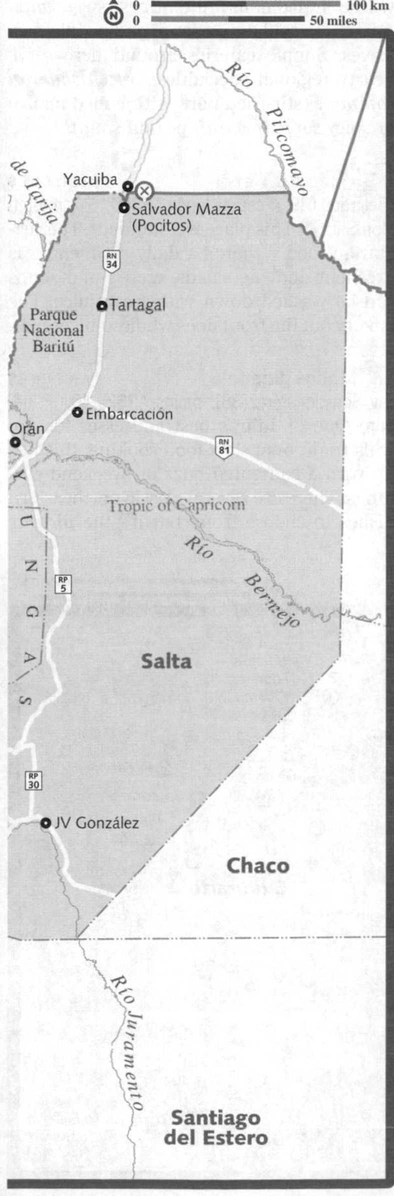

Tours

Several Jujuy operators offer trips to the Quebrada de Humahuaca, Salinas Grandes, Parque Nacional Calilegua and other provincial destinations. The Provincial Tourist Office can give you a full listing.

Noroeste TOURS
(☎423-7565; www.noroestevirtual.com.ar; San Martín 136) Based at Club Hostel, it hits the Quebrada de Humahuaca area, Salinas Grandes and more.

Festivals & Events

In August, Jujuy's biggest event, the week-long **Semana de Jujuy**, commemorates Belgrano's evacuation of the city during the wars of independence. The next-largest gathering is the religious pilgrimage known as the **Peregrinaje a la Virgen del Río Blanco** on October 7.

Sleeping

There are lots of cheap *residenciales* in the chaotic streets around the bus terminal.

TOP CHOICE **Posada El Arribo** BOUTIQUE HOTEL $$
(☎422-2539; www.elarribo.com; Belgrano 1263; s/d AR$250/380; ❄@🛜🏊) An oasis in the heart of Jujuy, this highly impressive family-run place is a real visual feast. The renovated 19th-century mansion is wonderful, with high ceilings and wooden floors; there's patio space galore and a huge garden. The modern annex behind doesn't lose much by comparison, but go for an older room if you can.

Ohasis Jujuy HOTEL $$
(☎424-1017; www.ohasishoteljujuy.com; Ramírez de Velasco 244; s/d AR$348/468; ❄@🛜🏊) Smart, welcoming, modern and efficient, this is a recent arrival with comfortable rooms, an outdoor heated pool and an above-average breakfast. Spa facilities and a gym are other enticing features.

Club Hostel HOSTEL $
(☎423-7565; www.clubhosteljujuy.com.ar; San Martín 134; dm/d AR$60/180; @🛜) Busy and buzzy, this hostel has good dark dorms that have

lockers, bathrooms and only four berths per room. The private rooms with bathrooms are also decent, and there's a kitchen and tiny Jacuzzi out the back. HI discount applies. Friendly staff also operate a tour agency.

Hostal Casa de Barro HOSTEL $
(☎422-9578; www.casadebarro.com.ar; Otero 294; dm/d without bathroom AR$65/120; 📶) With a light-hearted and genuinely welcoming feel, this original and enjoyable place has rooms that are bright and chirpy, and shared bathrooms that are very clean. The place is decorated throughout with rock-art motifs. There's a comfy lounge and a kitchen, and breakfast is included.

Hotel Internacional HOTEL $$
(☎423-1599; www.hinternacionaljujuy.com.ar; Belgrano 501; s/d AR$250/310; ❄@📶) Perched on a corner of the plaza, this high-rise has smallish but bright cream-colored rooms with good-looking clean bathrooms. Some have spectacular views out over the plaza, and nice touches include a morning paper put under your door. Good value.

Residencial Alvear GUESTHOUSE $
(☎422-2982; aurora627@wirenet.com.ar; Alvear 627; s/d with bathroom AR$105/165, without bathroom AR$55/110) A variety of rooms is tucked away behind the Chung King restaurant. They're OK for the price, but select carefully (upstairs) as some of those with shared bathroom are a little poky. The further back, the quieter it gets.

Eating

Jujuy's lively **Mercado del Sur**, opposite the bus terminal, is a genuine trading post where indigenous Argentines swig *mazamorra* (a cold maize soup) and peddle coca leaves. Simple eateries around here serve hearty regional specialties; try *chicharrón con mote* (stir-fried pork with boiled maize) or spicy *sopa de maní* (peanut soup).

TOP CHOICE **Madre Tierra** BAKERY, CAFE $
(Belgrano 619; 4-course lunch AR$50; ⏱7am-6pm Mon-Sat; ✎) This place is a standout. The vegetarian food – there's a daily set menu – is excellent and the salads, crepes and soups can be washed down with fresh juice. The bakery out the front does wholesome breads.

Manos Jujeñas ARGENTINE $
(Av Senador Pérez 381; mains AR$25-40; ⏱Tue-Sun) One of Jujuy's best addresses for no-frills traditional slow-food cooking, this fills up with a contented buzz on weekend evenings. There are several classic northeastern dishes to choose from, but it's the *picante*

Jujuy

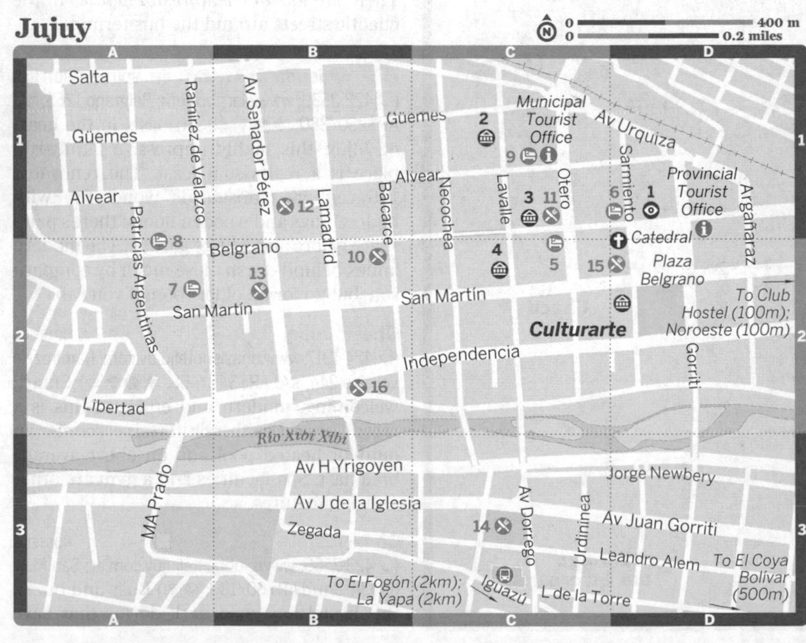

– marinated chicken or tongue or both with onion, tomato, rice and Andean potatoes – that's the pride of the house.

Krysys PARRILLA $$
(☎423-1126; Balcarce 272; mains AR$35-55; ⊙Mon-Sat; 📶) The best *parrilla* (steak restaurant) option is this central, upscale place offering all your barbecued favorites in a relaxed atmosphere. But there's plenty more on the menu, with a range of tasty sauces to go with the chicken, pork or beef, and various appetizing starters. Prices are fair, and you'll get the meat the way you want it cooked.

Chung King ARGENTINE, PIZZA $$
(Alvear 627; mains AR$32-52; 📶) This is a popular, worthwhile restaurant with an extensive Argentine menu including good-value daily specials; it has an even more popular attached pizzeria. In fact, despite the name, about the only chow you can't get here is Chinese.

Marazaga ARGENTINE $$
(☎424-3427; Av Senador Pérez 222; mains AR$40-55; ⊙dinner; 📶) Offering traditional Andean plates alongside trendy new creations. The vegetarian crepe starter is tasty; but the pork with honey-mustard sauce could have a more dignified bed than crinkle-cut chips.

Jujuy

Top Sights

	Culturarte	D2

Sights

1	Cabildo	D1
2	Museo Arqueológico Provincial	C1
3	Museo Histórico Franciscano	C1
4	Museo Histórico Provincial	C2
	Museo Policial	(see 1)

Sleeping

5	Hostal Casa de Barro	C2
6	Hotel Internacional	D1
7	Ohasis Jujuy	A2
8	Posada El Arribo	A2
9	Residencial Alvear	C1

Eating

	Chung King	(see 9)
10	Krysys	B2
11	Madre Tierra	C1
12	Manos Jujeñas	B1
13	Marazaga	B2
14	Mercado del Sur	C3
15	Miralejos	D2
16	Viracocha	B2

But, as in Russian roulette, there are more positive than negative outcomes.

Miralejos ARGENTINE $$
(Sarmiento 368; meals AR$25-45; ⊙8am-midnight) This is plaza-side dining at its finest. Miralejos offers the full gamut of steak and pasta (with a wide choice of interesting sauces), with a few local trout dishes thrown in. The outside tables are a great place for breakfast and the eclectic music selection is interesting, to say the least.

Viracocha ARGENTINE $
(cnr Independencia & Lamadrid; mains AR$24-38; ⊙lunch Wed-Mon, dinner Wed-Sat & Mon) Atmospheric vaulted restaurant serving excellent traditional dishes like *picantes* of any meat you can think of, pickled llama, and warming peanut soup.

Drinking & Entertainment

Jujuy's folkloric *peñas* (folk music clubs) serve food every night but only tend to have live music at weekends. **El Coya Bolívar** (☎0388-15-472-5311; Lisandro de la Torre 634; ⊙music Thu & Fri) is a short walk from the bus station, while **El Fogón** (☎0388-15-588-2040; RN9; ⊙8pm-late Sat) and **La Yapa** (☎402-0637; Mejías 426, Barrio Malvinas; ⊙8pm-late Fri & Sat) are a cab ride away. The big *boliches* (nightclubs) are out on RN9 south of town.

Information

There are many central banks with ATMs. Call centers and internet places abound.

Hospital Pablo Soria (☎422-1228; cnr Patricias Argentinas & Av Córdoba)

Municipal tourist office (☎402-0054; turismo@municipiodejujuy.gov.ar; cnr Otero & Alvear; ⊙7am-10pm) Friendy and helpful.

Provincial tourist office (☎422-1343; www.turismo.jujuy.gov.ar; Gorriti 295; ⊙7am-10pm Mon-Fri, 9am-9pm Sat & Sun) Excellent office with good brochures and staff.

Getting There & Away

Air

Andes (☎431-0279; www.andesonline.com; San Martín 1283) flies six times weekly to Buenos Aires via Salta. **Aerolíneas Argentinas** (☎422-7198; Av Senador Pérez 355) services Buenos Aires' Aeroparque Jorge Newbery daily.

Bus

The old-school **bus terminal** (☎422-1375; cnr Av Dorrego & Iguazú) has provincial and long-distance services, but Salta has more choice.

BUSES FROM JUJUY

DESTINATION	COST (AR$)	DURATION (HR)
Buenos Aires	498	19-22
Córdoba	300	14
Humahuaca	25	3
La Quiaca	58	4-5
Mendoza	440	20
Purmamarca	17	1¼
Salta	42	2
Salvador Mazza	146	6-7
Susques	42	4-5
Tilcara	18	1¾
Tucumán	113	5

Buses going from Salta to San Pedro de Atacama in Chile (AR$200) stop here around 8:30am.

Getting Around

Jujuy's El Cadillal airport is 33km east of the center. A shuttle service leaves from the cathedral an hour and a half before Aerolineas flights, but check it's running. Otherwise it's AR$100 in a *remise* (radio taxi).

If you're after a rental car, **Avis** (☎424-9800; www.avis.com; Güemes 864) or **Hertz** (☎422-9582; www.hertz.com; Belgrano 715), in Hotel Augustus, are central choices; there are also branches at the airport.

Quebrada de Humahuaca

North of Jujuy, the memorable Quebrada de Humahuaca snakes its way upward toward Bolivia. It's a harsh but vivid landscape, a dry yet river-scoured canyon overlooked by mountainsides whose sedimentary strata have been eroded into spectacular scalloped formations that reveal a spectrum of colors in undulating waves. The palette of this Unesco World Heritage–listed valley changes constantly, from shades of creamy white to rich, deep reds; the rock formations in places recall a necklace of sharks' teeth, in others the knobbly backbone of some unspeakable beast.

Dotting the valley are dusty, picturesque, indigenous towns that have a fine variety of places to stay, plus historic adobe churches, and homey restaurants serving warming *locro* (a stew of maize, beans, beef, pork and sausage) and llama fillets. The region has experienced a tourism boom in recent years and gets very full in summer, when accommodation prices soar.

There are many interesting stops along this colonial post route between Potosí (Bolivia) and Buenos Aires; buses run every 40 minutes or so, so it's quite easy to jump off and on as required. The closest place to hire a car is Jujuy. The Quebrada shows its best side early in the morning, when colors are more vivid and the wind hasn't got up.

PURMAMARCA

☎0388 / POP 510 / ELEV 2192M

Little Purmamarca, 3km west of the highway, sits under the celebrated Cerro de los Siete Colores (Hill of Seven Colors), a spectacular and jagged formation resembling the marzipan fantasy of a megalomaniac pastry chef. The village is postcard pretty, with ochre adobe houses and ancient algarrobo trees by the bijou 17th-century church. This, and its proximity to Jujuy, has made it perhaps the northwest's most over-touristed spot; if you're looking for an authentic Andean village, move on. Nevertheless, Purmamarca is an excellent place to shop for woven goods; a flourishing poncho market sets up on the plaza every day.

Apart from shopping for handicrafts, make sure you take the easy but spectacular 3km walk around the *cerro* (hill), whose striking colors are best appreciated in the morning or evening sunlight.

Sleeping & Eating

Huaira Huasi HOTEL $$

(☎490-8070; www.huairahuasi.com.ar; Ruta 52, Km 5; d/apt for four AR$399/679; ❄@📶) One of a handful of characterful hotels on the main road above town, this stands out for its valley views and handsome terracotta-colored adobe buildings. There are two apartments that sleep five and are just beautifully decorated with local fabrics and cardón wood; rooms are obviously smaller but still lovely. Good value.

Los Colorados APARTMENTS $$

(☎490-8182; www.loscoloradosjujuy.com.ar; Chapacal s/n; s/d/q AR$340/500/720; 📶❄) Looking straight out of a science-fiction movie, these strange but inviting apartments are tucked right into the *cerro,* and blend in with it. They are stylish and cozy; fine places to hole up for a while.

El Pequeño Inti GUESTHOUSE $
(☎490-8089; elintidepurmamarca@hotmail.com; Florida s/n; s/d AR$140/170) Small and enticing, this is a fine little choice just off the plaza. Offering value (for two), it has unadorned rooms with comfortable beds and marine-schemed bathrooms.

Hostería Bebo Vilte HOSTEL, CAMPGROUND $
(☎490-8038; Salta s/n; camping per person AR$20, dm/d without bathroom AR$40/120, s/d with bathroom AR$150/200; 📶) A useful all-round option behind the church, this has good motel-style rooms with bathroom, simpler interior rooms, dorms, and a camping area with barbecues. Prices are somewhat negotiable.

Terrazas de la Posta HOTEL $$
(☎490-8053; www.terrazasdelaposta.com.ar; d AR$390-480; ❄📶) Handsome rooms with spacious bathrooms share a veranda with great sierra views. Superiors are newer and larger.

El Churqui de Altura ARGENTINE $$
(Salta s/n; mains AR$36-65) Substantially overpriced, but dishes of local trout, goat or llama stews and oven-cooked empanadas are pretty tasty.

El Rincón de Claudia Vilte ARGENTINE $
(Libertad s/n; admission AR$10, mains AR$22-45) Balladeers serenade diners in nearly every eating establishment, but if you want the whole local music deal over your meal, this is the best *folklore* (folk music) option.

Information

There's an ATM on the plaza.

Tourist office (Florida s/n; 7am-7pm Mon-Fri; 8am-8pm Sat & Sun) Just off the plaza.

Getting There & Away

Buses to Jujuy (AR$17, 1¼ hours) run every one to two hours; others go to Tilcara (AR$4, 30 minutes) and Humahuaca (AR$13 , 1¼ hours). There's at least one bus every day to Susques (AR$30, three to four hours) via Salinas Grandes.

Purmamarca has no gas station; the closest can be found 25km north, at Tilcara, or south, at Volcán. Westward, the nearest is in Susques, a 130km steep climb away.

TILCARA

☎0388 / POP 4358 / ELEV 2461M

Picturesque Tilcara, 23km further up the valley from the Purmamarca turnoff, is many people's choice as their Quebrada de Humahuaca base and offers a huge range of accommodation from luxury boutique retreats to hostels. The mixture of local farmers getting on with a centuries-old way of life and arty urban refugees looking for a quieter existence has created an interesting balance on the town's dusty streets.

Sights

Pucará RUINS
(admission incl Museo Arqueológico Argentines/Latin Americans/others AR$15/20/30, Mon free; ⏲9am-6pm) The reconstructed pre-Columbian fortification, the *pucará,* is 1km south of the center across an iron bridge. Its situation is undeniably strategic, commanding the river valley both ways and, though the site was undoubtedly used before, the ruins date from the 11th to 15th centuries. The 1950s reconstruction has taken liberties; worse yet is the earlier, ridiculous monument to pioneering archaeologists bang where the plaza would have been. Nevertheless, you can get a feel of what would have been a sizable fortified community. Most interesting is the 'church,' a building with a short paved walkway to an altar; note the niche in the wall alongside. The site itself has great views and, seemingly, a cardón cactus for every soul that lived and died here. For further succulent stimulation, there's a cactus garden by the entrance.

Museo Arqueológico MUSEUM
(Belgrano 445; admission included with pucará; ⏲9am-6pm) The well-presented Museo Arqueológico displays some artifacts from the *pucará,* and exhibits give an insight into the life of people living around that time. The room dedicated to ceremonial masks is particularly impressive. The museum is in a striking colonial house on Plaza Prado.

BOLIVIA VIA SALVADOR MAZZA

RN 34 continues past Calilegua to Argentina's northernmost settlement, Salvador Mazza (also known as Pocitos), a major frontier with Bolivia. Cross the **frontier** (⏲24hr), and take a shared taxi 5km to the larger Bolivian settlement of Yacuiba, which has weekly flights to La Paz, and buses to Tarija (12 hours) and Santa Cruz (15 hours). There's no Bolivian consulate, so get your visa in Jujuy or Salta if you need one. Salvador Mazza is served by numerous buses from Jujuy, Salta and other northern cities.

The Quebrada de Humahuaca

The tortured rockscapes and palette of mineral colors changing through the day makes this arid valley a highlight of the northwest. Exploring the indigenous villages and towns strung along it is a delight.

Tilcara

1 A range of excellent small hotels, stunning landscapes, excursions and the cactus-studded ruins of an indigenous fortress make this many travelers' favorite base in the Quebrada (p213).

Purmamarca

2 This small town is dominated by its surrounding crags, which feature some of the valley's most vibrant mineral colorings. The focus of things here is the great artisan market on the square (p212).

Uquía

3 This village has the region's standout church, a beautiful 17th-century structure whose interior famously features paintings of the main angels packing muzzle-loading weaponry (p219).

Humahuaca

4 The valley's largest town has an authentic feel and makes a good base for the region. Picturesque cobbled streets, fair-trade handcrafts and typical northwestern dishes, such as locro or llama stew are highlights (p219).

Iruya

5 A long, rickety drive over a spectacular mountain pass, this remote village preserves a traditional and indigenous feel. Surrounded by imposing cliffs and mountains, it's a place whose slow pace obliges you to step off the frenzied wheel for a day or three (p220).

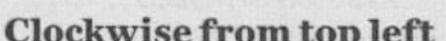

Clockwise from top left
1. Tilcara (p213) **2.** Cerro de los Siete Colores (p212), Purmamarca **3.** Church, Uquia (p19) **4.** Local fabrics

2

JODY/SHUTTERSTOCK ©

3

JAVIER ETCHEVERRY / ALAMY ©

Activities

Of several interesting walks around Tilcara, the most popular is the two-hour hike to **Garganta del Diablo**, a pretty canyon and waterfall. Head toward the *pucará,* but turn left along the river before crossing the bridge. The path to the Garganta leaves this road to the left just after a sign that says *'Cuide la flora y fauna.'* Swimming is best in the morning, when the sun is on the pool.

Tilcara Mountain Bike (☎0388-15-500-8570; tilcarabikes@hotmail.com; Belgrano s/n; ⏰9:30am-7pm) is a friendly setup just past the bus terminal that hires out well-maintained mountain bikes (AR$15/70 per hour/day) and provides a helpful map.

WORTH A TRIP

CALILEGUA AND BARITÚ NATIONAL PARKS

Jujuy province's eastern portion is Las Yungas, a humid and fertile subtropical zone where arid, treeless altiplano gives way to montane forest and, in places, dense cloud forest. Two national parks, with abundant, colorful birdlife and harder-to-spot mammals such as pumas, tapirs and jaguars, allow you to explore this ecosystem.

Parque Nacional Calilegua

This accessible park stretches up the Serranía de Calilegua range to peaks such as Cerro Hermoso, offering boundless views above the forest and across the Chaco to the east.

There are seven marked trails, from 20-minute strolls to tough four-hour hikes. The best places for bird and mammal watching are near the stream courses in the early morning or late afternoon.

From Valle Grande, beyond the park boundaries to the west, it's possible to hike in a week to Humahuaca along the Sierra de Zenta, or to Tilcara.

The park's **headquarters** (☎422046; calilegua@apn.gov.ar; ⏰7am-2pm Mon-Fri) is in Calilegua village, 5km north of Libertador General San Martín. The ranger at the **park entrance** (admission free; ⏰9am-6pm) in Aguas Negras has more information about trails and conditions. There's another ranger station at Mesada de las Colmenas, 13km past Aguas Negras and 600m higher.

The developed **campground** is some 300m from the ranger station at the entrance. It is free and has bathrooms and shower, but no shop.

Libertador General San Martín is a sizable sugarcane town; places to stay include **Hotel Los Lapachos** (☎03886-423790; ayresdelnortehotel@yahoo.com; Entre Ríos 400; s/d AR$80/100; ❄), which tries hard with its scalloped handbasins and wine-red carpets, a block from the plaza. Little Calilegua is more appealing, with a tumbledown tropical feel and a deafening chorus of cicadas. Near the park office, **Jardín Colonial** (☎03886-430334; San Lorenzo s/n; s/d without bathroom AR$40/80) is a lovely bungalow with rooms, a shady porch and a verdant, sculpture-filled garden.

Numerous buses between Jujuy/Salta and Salvador Mazza stop at Libertador General San Martín and Calilegua, and some will let you off at the junction for the park, 3km north of Libertador and 2km south of Calilegua. It's 8km from here to the ranger station at Aguas Negras; there's enough traffic to hitchhike. It's also easy to taxi it from either town.

Parque Nacional Baritú

Much more remote, **Baritú** (☎0387-15-507-4432; baritu@apn.gov.ar) can only be accessed by road through Bolivia (usually 4WD only). From RN 34, 90km beyond Calilegua, head for Orán then Aguas Blancas. Crossing into Bolivia, you hug the north bank of Río Bermejo, heading westward 113km, before crossing back into Argentina at La Mamora. A further 17km gets you to Los Toldos, and another 26km brings you to Lipeo, a hamlet at the northwest corner of the park. It has a ranger station and campsite but no other services, though locals will offer accommodation in their homes. There are various trails to tackle on foot or horseback. Los Toldos has accommodations, eateries and shops. Speak to rangers or the parks office in Salta before coming. If you read Spanish, www.baritupar-quenacional.blogspot.com is a good resource.

CHILE VIA SUSQUES

The paved road climbs doggedly from Purmamarca through spectacular bleak highland scenery to a 4150m pass, then crosses a plateau partly occupied by the Salinas Grandes. You hit civilization at **Susques**, 130km from Purmamarca, which has gas and an ATM.

Susques is well worth a stop for its terrific village **church** (admission by donation; ⏲8am-6pm). Dating from 1598, it has a thatched roof, cactus-wood ceiling and beaten-earth floor, as well as charismatic, naïve paintings of saints on the whitewashed adobe walls. There's a tourist office on the main road, and basic places to stay.

AndesBus runs Tuesday, Thursday, Saturday and Sunday from Jujuy to Susques (AR$42, four to five hours) via Purmamarca.

Beyond Susques, the road continues a further 154km (fuel up in Susques) to the Paso de Jama (4230m), a spectacular journey. This is the Chilean border, although Argentine **emigration** (⏲8am-midnight) is some way before it. No fruit, vegetables or coca leaves are allowed into Chile – they check. The paved road continues toward San Pedro de Atacama. Buses from Salta and Jujuy travel this route.

There are several places for horseback riding with or without a guide. You'll see phone numbers for *cabalgatas* (horseback rides) everywhere, and most accommodations can arrange it for you.

Tours

Several operators around town run trips up and down the Quebrada and to the Salinas Grandes.

Caravana de Llamas TREKKING
(☎495-5326; www.caravanadellamas.com; cnr Corte & Viltipico) A highly recommended llama-trekking operator running half-day excursions of varying difficulty (AR$160 to AR$240) around Tilcara, and in the Salinas Grandes, and multiday excursions, including a six-day marathon from Tilcara to the Las Yungas forested lowlands (AR$3600). The guide is personable and well informed about the area. Llamas are pack animals: you walk, they carry the bags. You can drop by to meet the llamas even if you're not planning a trip.

Festivals & Events

Tilcara celebrates several festivals during the year, the most notable of which is January's **Enero Tilcareño**, with sports, music and cultural activities. February's **Carnaval** is equally important as in other Quebrada de Humahuaca villages, as is April's **Semana Santa** (Holy Week). August's indigenous **Pachamama** (Mother Earth) festival is also worthwhile.

Sleeping

There's a huge variety, with numerous upmarket boutique hotels and dozens of simple hostels, guesthouses, and good-value rooms in private homes (the tourist office keeps a list of these).

Con los Ángeles LODGE $$
(☎495-5153; www.posadaconlosangeles.com.ar; Gorriti 156; s/d/superior d AR$280/320/395; @) The lovely, extensive grassy garden complete with sun loungers comes as a surprise coming from the street. Warmly run by a friendly young family, this features stylish common areas and thoughtfully decorated rooms arrayed along the lawn.

Posada de Luz LODGE $$
(☎495-5017; www.posadadeluz.com.ar; Ambrosetti 661; r AR$350-480; @) With a nouveau-rustic charm, this little place is a fantastic spot to unwind for a few days. More expensive rooms have sitting areas, but all feature pot-bellied stoves and individual terraces with deckchairs and views out over the valley. The excellent personal service is a real highlight.

Rincón de Fuego BOUTIQUE HOTEL $$
(☎427-1432; www.rincondefuego.com; Ambrosetti 445; s AR$348-436, d AR$436-545; @) Romantic and welcoming, this posada (inn) is tucked away at the top of town; it's a fine spot to retreat to with someone you love. Effective, artistic use of bare stone and adobe lends much atmosphere; the rooms are darkish but seductive, with woodstoves. Breakfast features bread baked in the patio's clay oven.

Malka GUESTHOUSE, HOSTEL $
(495-5197; www.malkahostel.com.ar; San Martín s/n, Barrio Malka; dm/s/d AR$70/170/260, cabin for 4 AR$500;) This rustic complex is a special place, both hotel and hostel. The welcoming owners, secluded, shady situation, thoughtfully different dorms, and smart stone-clad rooms with hammocks and deckchairs out front make it the sort of retreat you end up staying longer in than you expected. Good breakfast included and HI discount. Facing the church, head left for a block, then turn right and follow this road.

Cerro Chico CABINS $$
(0388-15-404-2612; www.cerrochico.com; d/q AR$300/400;) Two kilometers from town down a dirt road, this attractive complex of cabins climbs a hill with gorgeous Quebrada views and a remote, relaxing feel. The standard cabins are compact but handsome, and the pool area is a great little spot. Turn left straight after crossing the bridge into Tilcara and follow the signs.

Patio Alto HOTEL, HOSTEL $$
(495-5792; www.patioalto.com.ar; Torrico 675; dm/s/d AR$98/360/390; @) Great vistas from the coziness of your large bed are the highlight of the handsome modern rooms at this top-of-the-town hotel. There are also downstairs (but upmarket) dorms that are every bit as nice, with four single beds, cane lockers and kitchen use; the only thing missing is the view.

Aguacanto LODGE $$
(495-5817; www.aguacanto.com.ar; Corte 333; d/apt AR$240/470;) Spruce rooms and apartments surrounding a lawn featuring hammocks and one of Tilcara's most amazing views.

Club Hostel HOSTEL $
(0388-15-517-1234; www.clubhosteljujuy.com.ar; Jujuy 549; dm/d AR$60/200; @) Sociable hostel with a pleasant garden and decent, unadorned dorms. Privacy not the strong suit.

La Albahaca Hostel HOSTEL $
(0388-15-585-5994; www.albahacahostel.com.ar; Padilla s/n; dm/d AR$32/120;) Simple but very friendly, with comfortable private rooms and a sociable roof terrace.

Eating

El Patio ARGENTINE $$
(495-5044; Lavalle 352; mains AR$28-55; Wed-Mon) Tucked away between the plaza and the church, this has a lovely shaded patio and garden seating. It offers a wide range of tasty salads, inventive llama dishes and a far-from-the-madding-crowd atmosphere.

Los Puestos ARGENTINE $
(cnr Belgrano & Padilla; meals AR$25-50) Though a little touristy – we can't guarantee you won't be treated to a rendition of 'Sounds of Silence' on the panpipes at lunchtime – this makes up ground with its decor of local stone and chunky wood. Tasty regional specialties feature heavily – barbecued llama is one – but it's small touches, such as tiny bread rolls straight from the clay oven, that win friends.

Peña de Carlitos ARGENTINE $
(Lavalle 397; dishes AR$17-27) Hit the corner of the square for this cheery longstanding local restaurant, which offers live *folkloric* music with no cover charge every night, more of a mix of locals and visitors than in most places, and low-priced regional dishes.

El Nuevo Progreso ARGENTINE $$
(495-5237; Lavalle 351; mains AR$30-60) Sketchy service compensated for by an engaging atmosphere and delicious tourist-oriented cuisine, with imaginatively prepared llama dishes and great choose-your-own-ingredients house salads.

Information

There are several central internet places and call centers as well as a bank with ATM just off the plaza on Lavalle.

Tourist office (495-5135; Belgrano 366; 8am-1pm & 2-9pm Mon-Sat, 8am-noon Sun) Information on walks and has a list of accommodation prices.

Getting There & Away

The bus terminal is on the main street, Belgrano. There are services roughly every 45 minutes to Jujuy (AR$18, 1¾ hours), and north to Humahuaca (AR$4, 45 minutes) and La Quiaca (AR$41, 3½ hours). Several services daily hit Purmamarca (AR$4, 30 minutes) and Salta (AR$77, 3½ hours).

AROUND TILCARA

Maimará, 8km south, is a typical adobe valley settlement set beneath the spectacular and aptly named Paleta del Pintor (Painter's Palette) hill. Its hillside cemetery is a surprising sight with a picturesque backdrop.

Part of a chain that ran from Lima to Buenos Aires during viceregal times, **La Posta de Hornillos** (admission AR$3; 8am-6pm) is a beautifully restored staging post 11km south of Tilcara. The interesting exhibits include leather suitcases, some impressively fierce swords and a fine 19th-century carriage.

UQUÍA

03887 / POP 525 / ELEV 2818M

It's not often that you imagine the heavenly hosts armed with muzzle-loading weapons, but in this roadside village's fabulous 17th-century **church** (admission by donation; 10am-noon & 2-4pm) that's just what you see. A restored collection of Cuzco school paintings – the *ángeles arcabuceros* (arquebus-wielding angels) – features Gabriel, Uriel et al putting their trust in God but keeping their powder dry. There's also a gilt *retablo* (retable) with fine painted panels. By the church, **Hostal de Uquía** (490508; s/tw/d AR$110/160/175;) is a neat place with decent rooms and restaurant.

HUMAHUACA

03887 / POP 7985 / ELEV 2989M

The Quebrada's largest settlement is also its most handsome, with atmospheric cobblestoned streets, adobe houses and quaint plazas. You can feel the nearby puna here, with chilly nights, sparse air and a quiet Quechua-speaking population. Humahuaca is less altered by tourism than the towns further south, though there are good handicrafts shops, and folk musicians strum and sing in the restaurants.

Sights & Activities

Built in 1641, Humahuaca's **Iglesia de la Candelaria** (Buenos Aires) faces Plaza Gómez. Nearby, the lovably knobbly **cabildo** is famous for its clock tower, where a life-size figure of San Francisco Solano emerges at noon to deliver a benediction. From the plaza, a staircase climbs to rather vulgar **Monumento a la Independencia**.

Ask around for mountain guides for multiday treks to the Calilegua national park, with a stunning change in terrain as you descend into the subtropical forest systems.

Ser Andino (421659; www.serandino.com.ar; Jujuy 393) rents out bikes and offers excursions to places like the nearby ruins of Coctaca or the Salinas Grandes.

Festivals & Events

Besides **Carnaval**, which is celebrated throughout the Quebrada de Humahuaca in February, Humahuaca observes February 2 as the day of its patron, the **Virgen de Candelaria**.

Sleeping

The boutique hotel boom hasn't yet hit Humahuaca, which keeps it real with cheap family-run accommodations and a couple of midrange hotels. Prices given are for summer high season; they rise for Carnaval and drop for the rest of the year.

Hostal La Soñada GUESTHOUSE $
(421228; www.hostallasoniada.com; San Martín s/n; s/d AR$150/210;) Just across the tracks from the center, this is run by a kindly local couple and features spotless rooms with colorful bedspreads and good bathrooms. Breakfast is served in the attractive common area, and guests feel very welcome.

El Sol HOSTEL $
(421466; www.elsolhosteldehumahuaca.com; Barrio Milagrosa s/n; dm AR$45, d with/without bathroom AR$170/110;) In a peaceful location, signposted 800m across the river bridge, this curious, appealing adobe hostel has a variety of quirky dorm rooms with lockers, and pretty doubles under traditional cane ceilings. Some dorms are cramped, but this place is more than the sum of its parts.

TOREO DE LA VINCHA

You won't see bullfighting in Argentina – it was banned in the 19th century – but the unusual fiestas of **Casabindo** feature a *toro* (bull) as the central participant. This tiny and remote adobe puna village celebrates the Assumption on August 15 in style, and thousands make the journey to see the main event – man against beast in a duel of agility and wits.

The bull's horns are garlanded with a red sweatband that contains three silver coins. *Promesantes* (young men from the village) armed with only a red cloth then try to distract the animal's attention and rob it of its crown. The successful torero (matador) then offers the coins to the Virgin. The bull is unharmed. The festival has its origins in similar Spanish fiestas.

Casabindo is west of the Quebrada, accessible via a rough road beyond Purmamarca. Tour operators in Jujuy and Tilcara run trips to the festival.

Kitchen use and breakfast are included, there are HI discounts, and your third night is free.

Posada La Churita GUESTHOUSE $
(☎421055; http://posadalachurita.webege.com; Buenos Aires 456; r per person AR$45) Run by warm-hearted and motherly Olga, this is one of a few unheated cheapies on this street. In theory the rooms are dorms, but you may well get one to yourself. The shared bathrooms are clean and hot water reliable. Guests have use of the kitchen and a common area with tables.

Hostería Naty GUESTHOUSE $
(☎421022; www.hosterianaty.com.ar; Buenos Aires 488; s/d AR$100/140;) Right in the heart of town, this has friendly management, photos of nearby places you want to go to, and rooms of varying shapes and sizes at a fair price. The ones around the outside patio are quieter. Breakfast is included.

Eating & Drinking

Casa Vieja ARGENTINE $$
(cnr Buenos Aires & Salta; mains AR$30-60;) This warm and attractive corner restaurant is hung with basketry and large dreamcatchers. It serves various local dishes, overpriced, but including several appealing veggie options. Cozy El Portillo, nearby, offers the same menu.

K'Allapurca ARGENTINE $
(Belgrano 210; mains AR$24-38;) Tasty llama stews plus pizza, pasta and more at this oversized but welcoming main street restaurant.

Mikunayoc ARGENTINE
(cnr Corrientes & Tucumán; mains AR$20-45) Cordial service and a wide range of regionally-inspired dishes, including llama, make this a reliable choice.

Aisito BAR
(Arías s/n; 10pm-late) Head across the railway tracks from the bus terminal and turn right at the river to reach this unsigned bar. Locals gather in the attractive interior to bash out local music until rather late.

Shopping

The handicrafts market, near the defunct train station, has woolen goods, souvenirs and atmosphere. Near the plaza, **Manos Andinas** (Buenos Aires 401) sells fair-trade *artesanía*.

Information

There are several internet places around the center. The **tourist office** (Plaza Gómez s/n; 10am-9pm Mon-Fri) is in the *cabildo;* there's also an ATM on this plaza. The tourist office on the highway is usually shut, but young rascals outside sell pamphlets that the other office gives out free.

Getting There & Away

The **bus terminal** (cnr Belgrano & Entre Ríos) is three blocks south of the plaza. There are regular buses to Salta (AR$92, 4½ hours) and Jujuy (AR$21, 2¼ hours), and to La Quiaca (AR$32, three hours). There are two to three daily buses to Iruya (AR$28, three hours).

IRUYA

☎03887 / POP 1070 / ELEV 2780M

There's something magical about Iruya, a remote village just 50km from the main road but a world away in other respects. It makes a great destination to relax for a few days, and also allows proper appreciation of the Quebrada de Humahuaca region away from the busy barreling highway.

The journey is worth it in itself. Turning off RN 9, 26km north of Humahuaca, the *ripio* road ascends to a spectacular 4000m pass that marks the Jujuy–Salta provincial boundary. Here, there's a massive *apacheta* (travelers' cairn). The plastic bottles are from liquid offerings to Pachamama.

You then wind down into another valley and reache Iruya, with its pretty yellow-and-blue church, steep streets, adobe houses and spectacular mountainscapes (with soaring condors). It's an indigenous community with fairly traditional values, so respect is called for. Chatting with the friendly locals is the highlight here. You can also hike in the surrounding hills – ask for a local guide – or visit other communities in the valley. **Pablo Harvey** (☎0387-15-458-8417; pharvey_ar@yahoo.com.ar) runs unusual and recommended night walks with stargazing, music and Andean legends for AR$25 per person.

There's a bank with ATM in town and an internet place, both on San Martín.

Sleeping

The best way to contribute sustainably to the local community is staying in one of the many cheap accommodations in people's homes. We won't recommend any – spreading the wealth is best here – but can confirm that they are spotless and offer value for money (AR$30 to AR$45 per person in a private room).

Hostería Iruya HOTEL $$
(☎482002; www.hoteliruya.com; s/d AR$315/380, with view AR$375/435; 📶) At the top of the town, this place has light white rooms with wide beds, a spacious common area and a picturesque stone terrace with memorable views. It's worth the extra cash for the big-windowed rooms with valley vistas. There's a decent restaurant.

Federico III HOTEL $
(☎03887-15-629152; www.complejofedericoiii.com.ar; cnr San Martín & Salta; r per person AR$125) Just above the plaza at the bottom of town; this has pretty heated whitewashed rooms that surround a little courtyard. You can grab a room with a view; those without compensate with a TV. There's also a bar and restaurant.

Milmahuasi HOSTEL $
(☎0387-15-445-7994; www.milmahuasi.com; Salta s/n; dm/s/d AR$45/67/134; @📶) Clean and friendly hostel with comfortable rooms (the privates include breakfast) and an enticing roof terrace. HI discount.

Eating

Several simple *comedores* (basic cafeterias) serve local cuisine. At **Comedor Iruya** (cnr Lavalle & San Martín; dishes AR$15-35; ⏲10am-9pm) – don't confuse with nearby Iruyac – genial Juan and Tina serve delicious home-style meat and salad dishes in a cozy tin-roofed atmosphere.

Getting There & Away

Buses from Humahuaca (AR$28, three hours) leave two to three times daily; there is also a daily bus from Tilcara (AR$33, four hours).

The *ripio* road often becomes impassable in summer due to rain. You'll often see villagers hitchhiking – a good way to meet locals.

La Quiaca

☎03885 / POP 13,761 / ELEV 3442M

Truly the end of the line, La Quiaca is 5171km north of Ushuaia, and a major crossing point to Bolivia. It's a cold, windy place that has decent places to stay, but little to detain you.

After leaving the Quebrada de Humahuaca, paved RN 9 passes through **Abra Pampa**, a forlornly windy town 90km north of Humahuaca, and climbs through picturesque and typical altiplano landscapes. Look for the endangered vicuña off main routes.

La Quiaca is divided by its defunct train tracks; most services are west of them. North of town, a bridge across the river crosses to Villazón, Bolivia.

Sleeping & Eating

Hotel de Turismo HOTEL $
(☎422243; hotelmun@laquiaca.com.ar; cnr Árabe Siria & San Martín; s/d AR$108/153; @📶) Friendly and in gentle decline, this hotel offers handsome heated rooms with parquet floors and fine bathrooms. It's the best option in town.

Hostería Munay HOTEL $
(☎423924; www.munayhotel.com.ar; Belgrano 51; s/d AR$160/240) Set back from the pedestrian street (but you can still drive in and park), this is a decent option with heated rooms decorated with *artesanía*. It's substantially cheaper for walk-ins.

Copacabana Hostel GUESTHOUSE $
(☎423875; www.hostelcopacabana.com.ar; Pellegrini 141; r per person without bathroom AR$45; @📶) Across the tracks from the center, and a block up the street with the Banco de la Nación on the corner, this place offers small, rather sweet heated pink rooms with shared bathroom and amiable staff.

Eating options are simple. Hotel de Turismo is best; *bife de chorizo* (sirloin steak) with the works is AR$45, the set lunch AR$32. The hospitable **Frontera** (cnr Belgrano & Árabe Siria; mains AR$15-30) has meat plates, Spanish omelet and pasta, plus a set lunch for AR$24 and cheap unheated rooms.

Information

Change money on the Bolivian side of the border or at the bus terminal. Call centers and internet places abound.

Banco Macro (Árabe Siria 445) Has an ATM.

Information kiosk (⏲9:30am-1:30pm & 4-7pm) Run by a hostel, this offers decent information opposite the bus terminal.

Tourist office (☎422644; turismo@laquiaca.com.ar; ⏲7am-7pm) Branches at the border, and at the southern entrance to town.

Getting There & Away

The chaotic **bus terminal** (cnr Belgrano & España) has frequent connections to Jujuy (AR$58, four to five hours), Salta (AR$119, eight hours), and good-value services to Buenos Aires (AR$340, 27 hours). There is no transportation to Bolivia, but a few Argentine long-distance buses leave directly from Villazón's bus station.

Yavi

☎03887 / POP 207 / ELEV 3440M

Picturesque, indigenous Yavi, 16km east of La Quiaca via paved RP 5, is a great detour and lazy little hideaway, with the tumbledown romanticism of its adobe streets and two fascinating colonial-era buildings.

Yavi's intriguing **church** (admission by donation; ⊙10am-1pm & 2-6pm) preserves stunning altarpieces in sober baroque style, covered in gold leaf and adorned with excellent paintings and sculptures, mostly from the Cuzco school. The translucent onyx windows also stand out.

Opposite, the **Casa del Marqués Campero** was the house of the marquis who built the church in the late 17th century. Now a **museum** (admission AR$5; ⊙9am-1pm & 2-6:30pm Mon-Fri, 9am-6:30pm Sat & Sun), it displays beautifully restored furniture, exhibits on puna life and a lovable library.

As well as a good free campground by the river, there are several places to stay. **Hostal de Yavi** (☎421659; www.hostaldejavi.blogspot.com; Güemes 222; d/cabin for four AR$180/300) offers simple, comfortable rooms and an informal atmosphere with decent meals. **Hostería Pachamá** (☎03885-423235; www.pachamahosteria.net; cnr Pérez & Ruta 5; s/d AR$80/150) has rather charming rooms set around an adobe courtyard, and a pretty eating area, while likable **La Casona** (☎03885-422316; mccalizaya@hotmail.com; cnr Pérez & San Martín; dm AR$25, d with/without bathroom AR$80/60) has gnarled wooden floors and rustic rooms with stoves for winter nights.

> **BOLIVIA VIA VILLAZÓN**
>
> Crossing from La Quiaca to Villazón, Bolivia, walk, taxi or bus it to the bridge, then walk across, clearing immigration (open 24 hours). Bolivia is much nicer than Villazón promises, so head past the cut-price stalls and straight to the bus terminal or train station. Cheap but reliable accommodation options are by the bus terminal and the plaza if you need. Buses head to Tupiza (2¼ hours), La Paz (20 hours) and elsewhere. The train station is 1.5km north of the border crossing, with four weekly services to Tupiza (three hours), Uyuni (six hours) and Oruro (13 hours). Check www.fca.com.bo for schedules and prices. Bolivia is one hour behind northern Argentina.

Shared taxis and pickups (AR$10, 20 minutes) run to Yavi from La Quiaca's Mercado Municipal on Hipólito Yrigoyen; departures are much more frequent in the early morning. Otherwise, it's AR$40 in a taxi.

Salta

☎03873 / POP 535,303 / ELEV 1187M

Sophisticated Salta is a favorite of many travelers, smoothing ruffled psyches with its profusion of services, engaging active minds with its outstanding museums, and lighting romantic candles with its plaza-side cafes and the live *música folklórica* of its popular *peñas*. It offers the facilities of a large town, retains the comfortable vibe of a smaller place and preserves more colonial architecture than most places in Argentina.

Founded in 1582, it's now the most touristed spot in northwest Argentina, and has numerous accommodation options. The center bristles with travel and tour agents: this is the place to get things organized for onward travel.

Sights

Museo de Arqueología de Alta Montaña (MAAM) MUSEUM
(www.maam.org.ar; B Mitre 77; Argentines/foreigners AR$30/40, ⊙11am-7:30pm Tue-Sun) Perhaps the premier museum in northern Argentina, MAAM has a serious and informative exhibition focusing on Inca culture and, in particular, the child sacrifices the Inca left on some of the Andes' most imposing peaks (see boxed text, p223).

The centerpiece of the display is the mummified body of one of the three children (rotated every six months) discovered at the peak of Llullaillaco during the 1999 expedition. It was a controversial decision to display the bodies and it is a powerful experience to come face-to-face with them. The intricately plaited hair and clothes are perfectly preserved, and their faces reflect – who knows? – a distant past or a typical 21st-century Salta face; a peaceful passing or a tortured death. You decide.

The grave goods that accompanied the children impress by their immediacy, with colors as fresh as the day they were produced. The *illas* (small votive figurines of animals and humans) are of silver, gold, shell and onyx, and many are clothed in textiles. It's

THE CHILDREN GIVEN TO THE MOUNTAIN

The phrase 'human sacrifice' is sensationalist, but it is a fact that the Inca culture from time to time offered the lives of high-born children to please or appease their gods. The Inca saw this as an offering to ensure the continuing fertility of their people and the land. The high peaks of the Cordillera de los Andes were always considered sacred, and were chosen as sites for the sacrifices. The Inca felt that the children didn't die as such, but were reunited with their forefathers, who watched over the communities from the highest peaks.

The children, carefully selected for the role, were taken to the ceremonial capital of Cuzco, where they were the centerpieces of a large celebration – the *capacocha*. Ceremonial marriages between them helped to cement diplomatic links between tribes across the Inca empire. At the end of the fiesta, they were paraded twice around the plaza, and then had to return home in a straight line – an arduous journey that could take months. Once home, they were feted and welcomed, and then taken into the mountains. They were fed, and given quantities of *chicha* (an alcoholic drink made from fermented maize) to drink. When they passed out, they were taken up to the peak of the mountain and entombed, sometimes alive, presumably never to awaken, and sometimes having been strangled or killed with a blow to the head.

Three such children were found in 1999 near the peak of **Llullaillaco**, a 6739m volcano some 480km west of Salta, on the Chilean border. It's the highest known archaeological site in the world. The cold, low pressure and lack of oxygen and bacteria helped to preserve the bodies almost perfectly. The Doncella (Maiden) was about 15 at the time of death, and was perhaps an *aclla* (a 'virgin of the sun'), a prestigious role in Inca society. The other two, a boy and girl both aged six to seven (the girl damaged by a later lightning strike), had cranial deformations that indicated they came from high-ranking families. They were accompanied each by an *ajuar* (a selection of grave goods), which included textiles and small figurines of humanoids and camelids.

The mummies' transfer to Salta was controversial. Many felt they should have been left where they were discovered, but this, once the location was known, would have been impossible. Whatever your feelings on them, and the role of archaeology, they offer an undeniably fascinating glimpse of Inca religion and culture.

difficult to imagine that a more privileged look at pre-Columbian South American culture will ever be offered us. Also exhibited is the 'Reina del Cerro,' a mummy robbed from an Inca tomb in the 1920s that finally ended up here after a turbulent history. Some good videos give background information about the mummies and the expedition. There's a library as well as a good cafe-bar with terrace and wi-fi.

Pajcha – Museo de Arte Étnico Americano MUSEUM
(www.museopajchasalta.com.ar; 20 de Febrero 831; admission AR$20; ⏲10am-1pm & 4-8pm Mon-Sat) This eye-opening private museum is a must-see if you're interested in indigenous art and culture. Six exquisitely presented rooms present contemporary and recent artisanal work from all over Latin America. The quality of the pieces (which include amazing macaw-feather creations, religious sculpture from the Cuzco school, tools of the trade of Bolivian *kallawaya* healers and finely crafted Mapuche silver jewelry) is extraordinarily high, testament to decades of study and collection by the anthropologist founder. It's an exquisite dose of color and beauty, and run with great enthusiasm by the English-speaking management.

Museo Histórico del Norte MUSEUM
(Caseros 549; admission AR$5; ⏲9am-7pm Tue-Fri, 9am-1:30pm Sat & Sun) Set on the plaza in the *cabildo,* this lovely building has a collection that ranges from pre-Columbian ceramics through to colonial-era religious painting and sculpture (admire the fine pulpit from Salta's Jesuit church), and displays on Salta in the 19th and 20th centuries. The endless series of portraits of Salta's governors wouldn't be out of place in a beard-and-moustache museum, while the transportation collection includes an enormous 1911 Renault that puts any Hummer to shame.

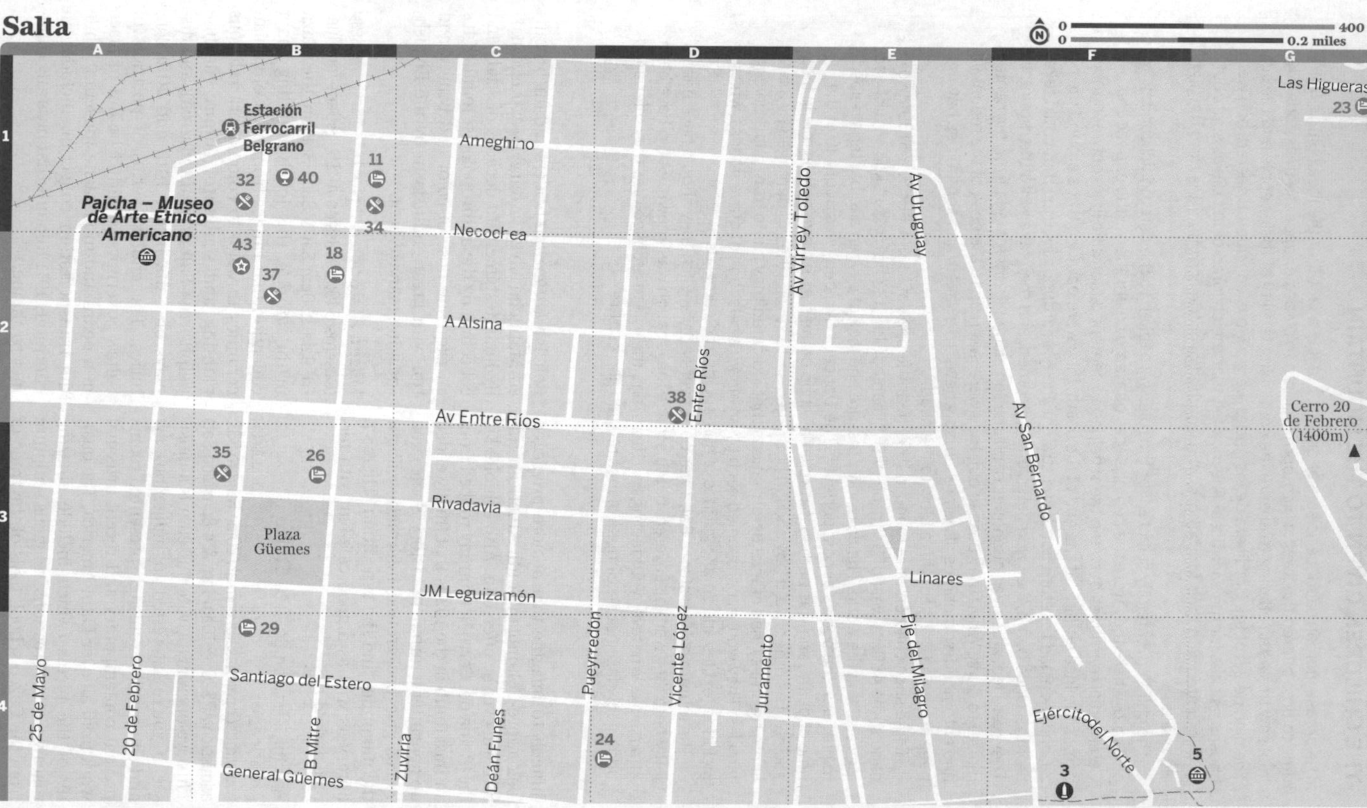
Salta
400 m
0.2 miles
Las Higueras
23
Estación Ferrocarril Belgrano
Ameghino
11
32
40
Pajcha – Museo de Arte Étnico Americano
34
Necochea
43
18
37
Av Virrey Toledo
Av Uruguay
A Alsina
38
Entre Ríos
Av Entre Ríos
Cerro 20 de Febrero (1400m)
Av San Bernardo
35
26
Rivadavia
Plaza Güemes
Linares
JM Leguizamón
29
Santiago del Estero
Pueyrredón
Vicente López
Juramento
Pje del Milagro
Ejército del Norte
25 de Mayo
20 de Febrero
B Mitre
Zuviría
Deán Funes
24
5
3
General Güemes

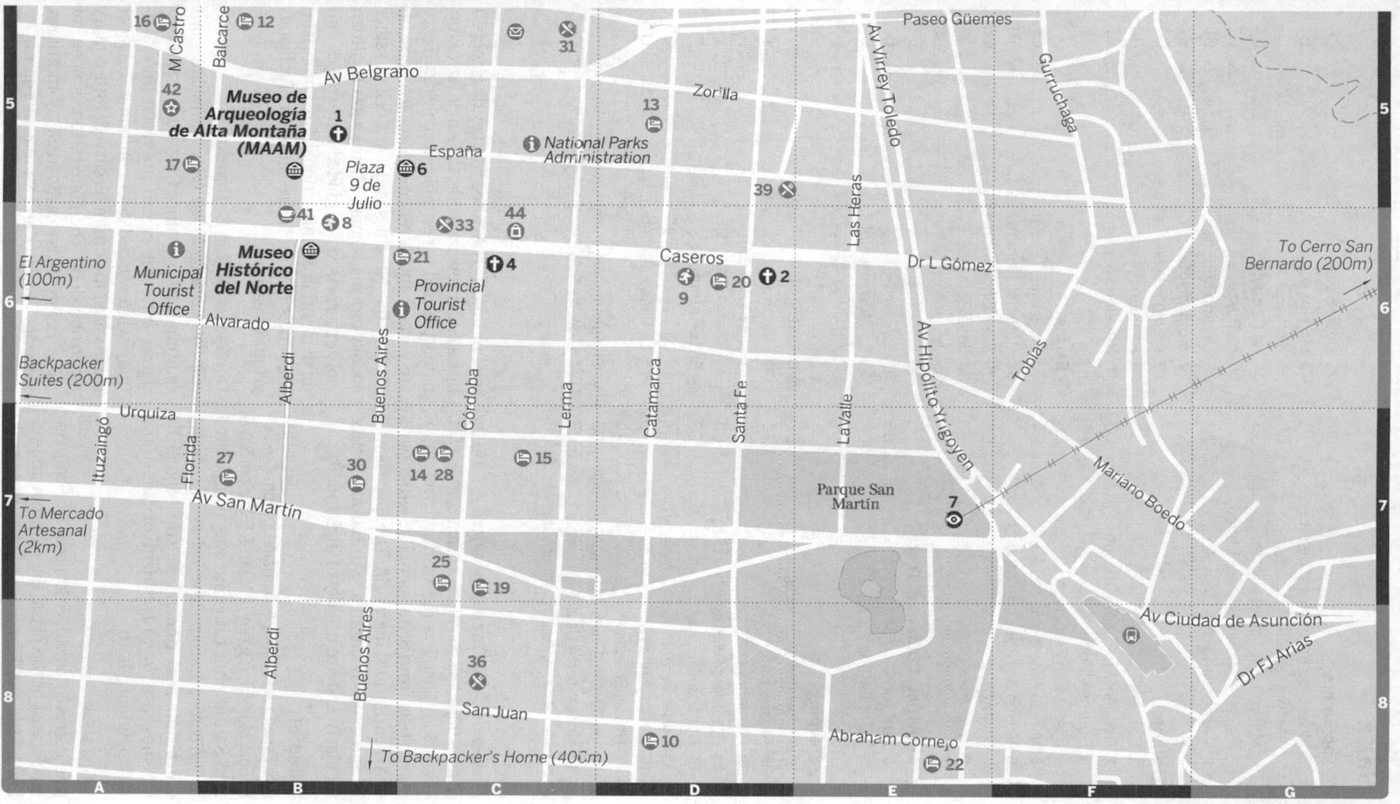
Paseo Güemes
Av Belgrano
Zorilla
Av Virrey Toledo
Gurruchaga
M Castro
Balcarce
Museo de Arqueología de Alta Montaña (MAAM)
España
National Parks Administration
Plaza 9 de Julio
Las Heras
Caseros
Dr L Gómez
To Cerro San Bernardo (200m)
El Argentino (100m)
Municipal Tourist Office
Museo Histórico del Norte
Provincial Tourist Office
Alvarado
Backpacker Suites (200m)
Urquiza
Alberdi
Buenos Aires
Córdoba
Lerma
Catamarca
Santa Fe
LaValle
Av Hipólito Yrigoyen
Tobías
Ituzaingó
Florida
Mariano Boedo
Parque San Martín
Av San Martín
To Mercado Artesanal (2km)
Av Ciudad de Asunción
Dr FJ Arias
San Juan
Abraham Cornejo
To Backpacker's Home (400m)
1
2
4
6
7
8
9
10
12
13
14
15
16
17
19
20
21
22
25
27
28
30
31
33
36
39
41
42
44
A
B
C
D
E
F
G
5
6
7
8

Salta

Top Sights

Museo de Arqueología de Alta Montaña (MAAM) B5
Museo Histórico del Norte B6
Pajcha – Museo de Arte Étnico Americano A2

Sights

1 Catedral B5
2 Convento de San Bernardo D6
3 Güemes Monument F4
4 Iglesia San Francisco C6
5 Museo Antropológico G4
6 Museo de Arte Contemporáneo (MAC) C5
7 Teleférico E7

Activities, Courses & Tours

8 Bus Turístico Salta B6
9 Salta Rafting D6

Sleeping

10 7 Duendes D8
11 Aldaba Hotel B1
12 Alejandro I B5
13 Bloomers B&B D5
14 Bonarda C7
15 Carpe Diem C7
16 Design Suites A5
17 Hostal El Alcázar A5
18 Hostal Prisamata B2
19 Hostel Terra Oculta C7
20 Hotel del Antiguo Convento D6
21 Hotel Salta C6
22 Inti Huasi E8
23 Kkala G1
24 La Candela D4
25 La Posta C7
26 Legado Mítico B3
27 Munay Hotel B7
28 Posada de las Farolas C7
29 Residencial Balcarce B4
30 Residencial Elena B7

Eating

31 Bio's Diet C5
32 Café del Tiempo B1
33 El Solar del Convento C6
34 José Balcarce B1
35 Jovi II B3
36 La Céfira C8
37 La Leñita B2
38 La Monumental D2
39 Ma Cuisine D5

Drinking

40 Macondo B1
41 New Time Café B6

Entertainment

42 La Casa de Güemes A5
43 La Vieja Estación B2

Shopping

44 Librería San Francisco C6

Museo de Arte Contemporáneo GALLERY
(Zuviría 90; admission AR$2; ⌚9am-8pm Tue-Sat, 4-8pm Sun) Displays the work of contemporary artists from Salta, as well as other parts of Argentina and the world. The space is well lit and expertly curated. Exhibitions change regularly and are usually of high quality.

Catedral CATHEDRAL
(cnr España & B Mitre; ⌚6:30am-12:15pm & 4:30-8:15pm Mon-Fri, 7:30am-12:15pm & 5-8:15pm Sat & Sun) Salta's pink cathedral was consecrated in 1878 and harbors the ashes of (among other notables) General Martín Miguel de Güemes, a *salteño* (resident of Salta) and independence hero.

Iglesia San Francisco CHURCH
(cnr Caseros & Córdoba; ⌚8am-noon & 5-9pm) Two blocks east of the plaza, the magenta-and-yellow Iglesia San Francisco is Salta's most striking landmark. The exuberant facade is topped by a slender tower; inside, the single nave is ornately painted to resemble stucco-work. There are several much-venerated images here, including the Niño Jesús de Aracoeli, a rather spooky crowned figure. There's a lovely garden cloister, accessed via guided tour (which run on demand in Spanish; donation appropriate) that takes in a mediocre museum of religious art and treasures.

Convento de San Bernardo CONVENT
(cnr Caseros & Santa Fe) Only Carmelite nuns may enter 16th-century Convento de San Bernardo, but visitors can approach the blindingly whitewashed adobe building (consider sunglasses) to admire its carved, 18th-century algarrobo door. The church, too, is open for visits before Mass early weekday mornings, Saturday evenings and Sunday mornings.

Cerro San Bernardo HILL

For outstanding views of Salta and its surroundings, take the **teleférico** (cable car; ☎431-0641; one way/roundtrip AR$15/30; ⏰10am-7pm) from Parque San Martín to the top of Cerro San Bernardo. A trail that takes you up the hill begins at the **Güemes monument** at the top of Paseo Güemes. Atop is a *confitería* (cafe offering light meals), whose terrace has the best views, a watercourse and *artesanía* shops.

Museo Antropológico MUSEUM

(www.antropologico.com.ar; cnr Ejército del Norte & Polo Sur; admission AR$5; ⏰8am-7pm Mon-Fri, 10am-6pm Sat) Just above the Güemes monument, on the lower slopes of Cerro San Bernardo, this welcoming museum has good representations of local ceramics, especially from the Tastil ruins (Argentina's largest pre-Inca town), and some well-designed displays in its attractive, purpose-built spaces.

Courses

Salta appeals as a spot for a Spanish course. **Bien Argentino** (☎475-0682; www.bien-argentino.com.ar) is one operator.

Tours

Salta is the base for a range of tours, offered by numerous agencies, particularly on Buenos Aires, between Caseros and Alvarado. Popular trips head to Cafayate (AR$195), Cachi (AR$220), San Antonio de los Cobres (the *Tren a las Nubes* route; AR$277), the same adding Salinas Grandes and Purmamarca (AR$435) and more. Several operators offer horseback riding, rafting and kayaking; paragliding, abseiling, climbing and hiking are also available.

Some operators:

Bus Turístico Salta BUS TOURS

(☎422-7798; www.busturisticosalta.com) Leaving from the plaza at regular intervals, this does a thorough circuit of the city (AR$50) in buses with English and Spanish commentary.

Clark Expediciones BIRDWATCHING

(☎497-1024; www.clarkexpediciones.com) Professional agency offering trips with highly competent English-speaking guides to the region's national parks and remote uplands. They're serious about bird-watching; trips include a half/full day in the Reserva del Huaico, a 60-hectare cloud forest reserve 8km west of Salta, two days to Parque Nacional El Rey and multiday tailored itineraries. Book well ahead.

Norte Trekking HIKING

(☎436-1844; www.nortetrekking.com) One of five agencies specifically approved for trips to Parque Nacional El Rey, it runs various multiday hikes, with some guaranteed departure dates listed on its website. They also do mountain treks.

Salta Rafting RAFTING, ZIPLINES

(☎421-3216; www.saltarafting.com; Caseros 177) Runs two-hour white-water rafting trips on the Class III Río Juramento, 100km from Salta (AR$170 including a barbecue lunch; transportation to/from Salta AR$80 extra). At the same location are spectacular 400m ziplines across a canyon (four-/nine-line trip AR$150/250).

Sayta HORSERIDING

(☎0387-15-683-6565; www.sayta.com.ar; Chicona) This *estancia* 40km from Salta runs excellent horseback-riding days, with optional *asado* (barbecue grill). It's also a place you can stay to experience a taste of Argentine gaucho life. A half-day with/without lunch costs AR$230/170, and full-board accommodation for a night is AR$350 (with a day's riding AR$450). Prices include transfers from Salta.

Sleeping

Carpe Diem B&B **$$**

(☎421-8736; www.carpediemsalta.com.ar; Urquiza 329; s/d AR$410/490; @ wifi) There's a real home-from-home feel about this B&B that's full of thoughtful touches, like home-baked bread at breakfast, enticing places to sit about with a book and a computer with internet connection in the attractive rooms. Singles with shared bathroom in the appealing grassy garden are small but a good deal at AR$200.

Aldaba Hotel HOTEL **$$**

(☎421-9455; www.aldabahotel.com; B Mitre 910; d standard/superior AR$374/418; ❄ @ wifi) A block away from the *peña* action of Calle Balcarce, this six-room place is nevertheless superbly quiet and tranquil. Run with a personal touch, it's decorated with restrained modern elegance, and boasts super-comfortable beds and friendly service. Superior rooms are slightly larger.

Bloomers B&B B&B **$$**

(☎422-7449; www.bloomers-salta.com.ar; Vicente López 129; s AR$300, d AR$350-450; ❄ @ wifi) Book ahead to grab one of the five rooms at this exquisitely stylish yet comfortable guesthouse. The second B here stands for brunch, served

MICHAEL TAYLOR/LONELY PLANET IMAGES ©

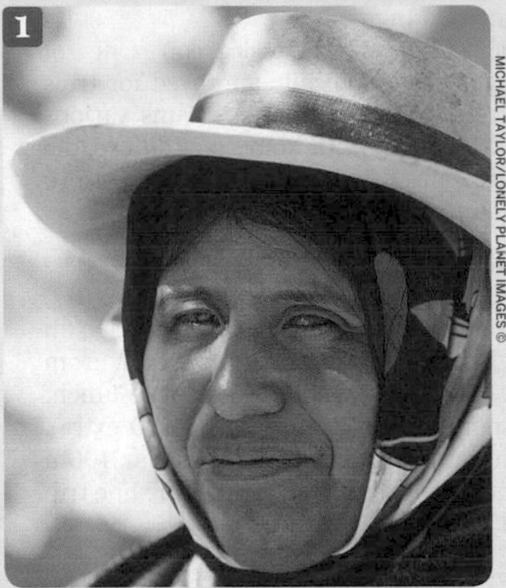

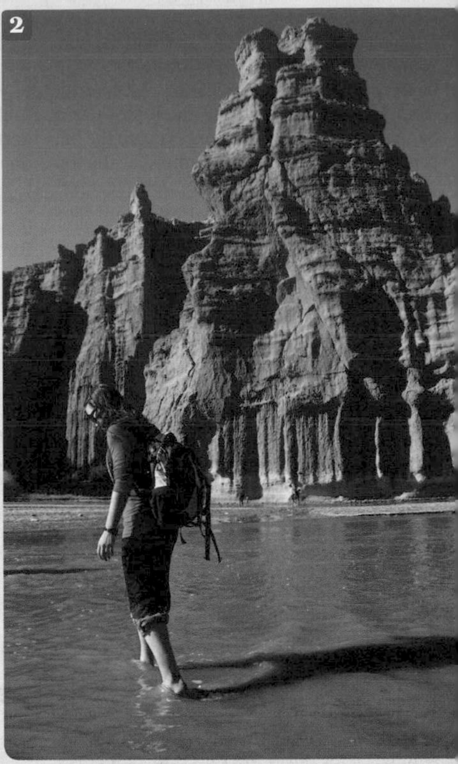

1. Quechua people
The Andean Northwest contains pockets of Quechua-speaking peoples.

2. Quebrada de Cafayate (p244)
A wild and spectacular landscape is carved out by the Río de las Conchas.

3. Iglesia San Francisco (p226)
Salta's most striking landmark is topped by a slender tower.

4. Purmamarca (p212)
A picturesque village watched over by a striking *cerro* (hill).

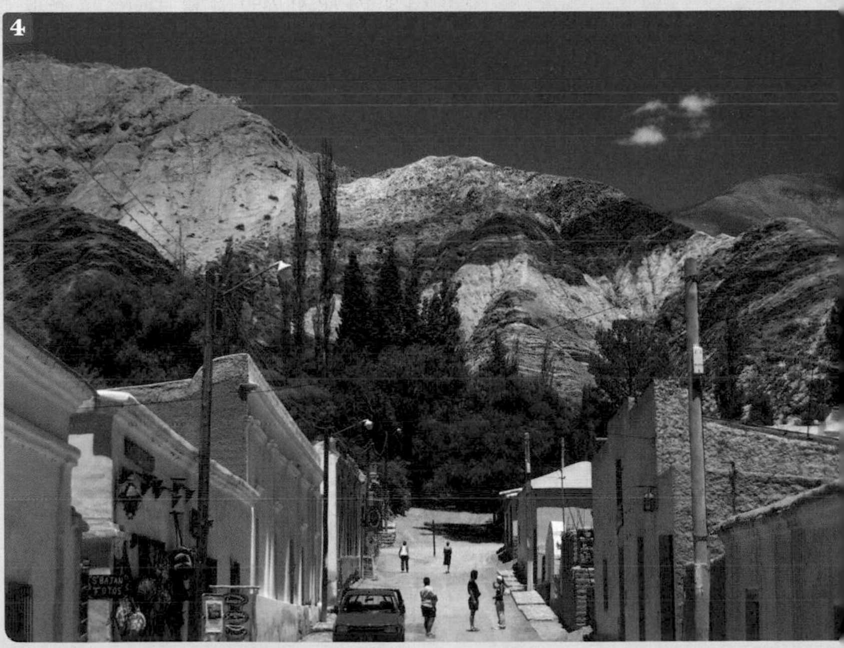

3

until noon. The color-themed rooms are all different and all delightful. It's like staying at a friend's – you can use the kitchen – but few of our friends have a place this pretty.

La Candela HOTEL **$$**
(☎422-4473; www.hotellacandela.com.ar; Pueyrredón 346; d AR$390-605; ❄@📶🏊) Decked out like a country villa with an L-shaped pool and grassy garden, this is nevertheless central and features excellent staff, good facilities and comfortable rooms, including a duplex apartment out the back. Different grades of room differ chiefly by size. The decor is one of easy elegance, with an eclectic range of art on the walls.

Salta por Siempre HOSTEL **$**
(☎423-3230; www.saltaporsiempre.com.ar; Tucumán 464; dm/s/d AR$50/100/200; @📶) It's eight blocks south of the plaza, but worth the trudge to this super-friendly hostel. The quiet and handsome building has glisteningly clean, colorful rooms with bathroom – some dorms have beds, others bunks – a proper kitchen and attractive shared spaces. Breakfast is included.

Inti Huasi HOSTEL **$**
(☎431-0167; www.intihuasihostel.com.ar; Abraham Cornejo 120; dm/d AR$45/120; @📶) A short stroll from the bus terminal, this hostel has an appealing atmosphere, with plenty of socializing in the good kitchen and grassy patio area. Dorms are spacious and comfortable, and you feel like you're crashing at a mate's place. Breakfast included.

Legado Mítico BOUTIQUE HOTEL **$$$**
(☎422-8786; www.legadomitico.com; B Mitre 647; r standard/superior/deluxe US$230/250/270; ❄@📶) The elegant rooms, some faithful to the style of this noble old Salta house, some with a lightly-worn indigenous theme, are reason enough to book in at this tranquil central retreat, particularly if you grab one of the downstairs ones with their own secluded bamboo-strewn patio. Courteous service and an atmosphere of refined relaxation are other high points. No under 12s.

Munay Hotel HOTEL **$**
(☎422-4936; www.munayhotel.com.ar; Av San Martín 656; s/d AR$160/240; 📶❄) With everything you could want in a budget hotel – a handy location, staff who are pleased to see you, well-furnished and clean bedrooms, shower curtains and breakfast – this is one to book ahead. Rooms with fan cost slightly less.

Kkala BOUTIQUE HOTEL **$$$**
(☎439-6590; www.hotelkkala.com.ar; Las Higueras 104; r US$200-270; ❄@📶🏊) Tucked away in the upmarket residential barrio of Tres Cerritos, this peaceful place makes relaxation easy. There are just six rooms surrounding a small garden with heated pool; the higher grades come with views and their own Jacuzzi. Decks with city vistas make perfect spots for a sundowner from the honesty bar. They normally don't take kids under 12.

Residencial Balcarce GUESTHOUSE **$**
(☎431-8135; www.residencialbalcarce.com.ar; Balcarce 460; s/d without bathroom AR$60/100, with bathroom AR$100/160; 📶) Just south of Plaza Güemes, a small entrance disguises a large interior at this value-packed place. In many ways, it's a standard *residencial,* with unadorned rooms with decent bathrooms, but the friendly service, grapevine-shaded patio and high hygiene levels make it a sound choice.

Design Suites HOTEL **$$$**
(☎011-5199-7465; www.designsuites.com; Belgrano 770; r/ste US$199/223; ❄@📶🏊) We're not 100% sure whether the look of this place – all exposed concrete and urban-trendy design – works in a colonial city such as Salta, but it's an undeniably attractive space. The excellent, quiet rooms have floor-to-ceiling windows, and the rooftop pool and Jacuzzi space offers memorable nighttime views of town. Service is willing.

Hostal El Alcázar GUESTHOUSE **$**
(☎422-3800; www.hostalelalcazar.com; Balcarce 81; s/d AR$150/200; @📶) Reliable and central, this place offers clean private rooms with bathroom but also has hostel-like facilities (eg a good kitchen) and a laid-back traveler-friendly attitude. It's a decent deal at Salta prices.

Residencial Elena GUESTHOUSE **$**
(☎421-1529; residencial.elena@gmail.com; Buenos Aires 256; s/d AR$140/200; 📶) Set in a neocolonial building with a charming interior patio, this has a choice location not far south of the plaza. Though it's on a busy central street, it's very quiet, and the Spanish longtime owners keep it shipshape.

Hotel del Antiguo Convento HOTEL **$$**
(☎422-7267; www.hoteldelconvento.com.ar; Caseros 113; r AR$325-450; ❄@📶🏊) Rooms are modern and sunny at this central hotel and there's a great little pool area out the back. A duplex apartment next to it sleeps four and goes for AR$460.

Backpacker's Home HOSTEL $
(☎423-5910; www.backpackerssalta.com; Buenos Aires 930; dm/d AR$100/255; @✈≋) Souvenir shops have given way to panelbeaters by the time you've walked the kilometer or so from the center, but this instant-social-life hostel appeals for the great backyard bar and pool area. Rates include breakfast and dinner. HI discounts apply and you can usually get it cheaper than we list here.

Hotel Salta HOTEL $$$
(☎426-7500; www.hotelsalta.com; Buenos Aires 1; s/d standard AR$400/590, s/d superior AR$560/720; ❄@✈≋) You pay extra for location here (but what a location) on a corner of the postcard-pretty central plaza, in a stately, traditional hotel. Facilities are good and service excellent, but the rooms are a tad disappointing. Try to grab one with a view of the church and Cerro San Bernardo. Superior rooms are bigger than the compact standards, and have bathtubs.

Alejandro I HOTEL $$$
(☎400-0000; www.alejandro1hotel.com.ar; Balcarce 252; r standard/superior/executive AR$760/825/950; ❄@✈≋) Salta's most upmarket big hotel is visible, for better or worse, from the whole city. The rooms are slick and modern, and get pricier and larger as you move higher up the building. There are all the five-star facilities, including a tour desk, and English-speaking service is efficient.

Hostel Terra Oculta HOSTEL $
(☎421-8769; www.terraoculta.com; Córdoba 361; dm/d AR$60/120; @✈) Handily located between the bus terminal and town center, this laid-back, labyrinthine spot is an upbeat hostel that sensibly has its light, comfortable dorms well separated from the excellent rooftop bar, where the action can go loud and late.

Camping Municipal Carlos Xamena CAMPGROUND $
(☎423-1341; Av Libano; per person/tent/car AR$5/10.25/10.25; ≋) One of Argentina's best campgrounds, this place has 500 tent sites and a huge pool (it takes a week to fill). It's typically loud in summer. Take bus 3B from Ituzaingó between San Martín and Mendoza. There's a supermarket near the campground.

La Posta GUESTHOUSE, HOSTEL $
(☎422-1985; www.laposta.todowebsalta.com.ar; Córdoba 368; dm/s/d AR$55/160/180; @✈) Upmarket guesthouse-hostel that's a class above your average Salta backpacker place. Lovely ensuite rooms, thoughtful decor, and a quiet, relaxing atmosphere.

Bonarda HOTEL $$
(☎421-5786; www.hotelbonarda.com; Urquiza 427; s/d AR$300/390; ❄✈) Some parts of this not-quite-convincing 'boutique' hotel are attractive; others feel like they've been done on the cheap. Large rooms open inward onto a spacious interior courtyard; some are airier than others.

Posada de las Farolas GUESTHOUSE $$
(☎421-3463; www.posadalasfarolas.com.ar; Córdoba 246; s/d AR$190/295; ❄✈) Good value for neat, clean air-con rooms in the center run by decent people.

El Argentino HOSTEL $
(☎422-0184; www.elargentinohostel.com.ar; Alvarado 1077; dm/d AR$35/120; @✈) Good for the price, with simple breakfast included, this has dark dorms – ensuite ones cost more – around a patio space in a friendly, traditional Salta house.

Backpacker Suites HOSTEL $
(☎431-8944; www.backpackerssalta.com; Urquiza 1045; dm/d AR$100/255; @✈) Suites? We think they mean ensuites, as the spacious modern dorms all have bathrooms. The brightly lit front area is a sociable zone, and breakfast and dinner are included. You can usually get it substantially cheaper, and there's HI discount.

Hostal Prisamata HOSTEL $
(☎438900; www.hostalprisamata.com; B Mitre 833; dm/d AR$45/150; @✈) Hammocks in the patio and a great location a street away from the Calle Balcarce action make this friendly hostel a top spot.

7 Duendes HOSTEL $
(☎421-4522; www.hostelsieteduendes.com.ar; San Juan 189; dm/d AR$40/90; @✈) Simple, slightly stuffy dorms open onto patio spaces at this cheap hostel. It's the good-natured staff and atmosphere that make it.

Eating

It's a toss-up between Salta and Tucumán for Argentina's best empanadas, but they're wickedly toothsome in both places. Locals debate the merits of fried (in an iron skillet – juicier) or baked (in a clay oven – tastier).

TOP CHOICE **José Balcarce** ARGENTINE **$$$**
(☎421-1628; cnr B Mitre & Necochea; mains AR$45-75; ⊙dinner Mon-Sat) Exposed stone walls, ambient music and solicitous service set the scene for a satisfying gourmet dining experience here. Starters like llama carpaccio could be followed by sea bass or other highland-type dishes involving lamb or trout. The wine list sees each grape variety described in human terms – merlot is a sensitive listener, with gay tendencies. Close to Salta's best.

Jovi II ARGENTINE **$$**
(Balcarce 601; mains AR$30-60) A long terrace overlooking the palms of Plaza Güemes is just one reason to like this popular local restaurant that does a huge range of dishes well, without frills and in generous portions. Several rabbit dishes, tasty fish and a succulent plate of the day are backed up by excellent service.

La Leñita PARRILLA **$$**
(cnr Balcarce & A Alsina; mains AR$45-73) This popular *parrilla* hits meaty heights on what is a hit-and-miss dining street. There's a wide range of tasty cuts, a central salad bar and solicitous service whether you're in a suit or singlet. The versatile staff serenade diners with Salta *folklore* halfway through dinner. The wine list is overpriced.

El Solar del Convento ARGENTINE **$$$**
(☎421-5124; Caseros 444; mains AR$50-75) Warmly decorated and popular, this reliable touristy choice offers solicitous service – the free apéritif wins points – and a varied menu. It specializes in *lomo* (sirloin) with tasty sauces, and also has fish dishes and *parrillada* (mixed grill) options. The wine list offers lots of (priced-up) provincial choices.

La Monumental PARRILLA **$**
(Entre Ríos 202; mains AR$20-45) The fluorescent lighting and phalanx of fans mark this out as a classic neighborhood grill. Generous quantities, including an impressive array of free nibbles, cheap house wine and decent meat seal the deal. There's a more upmarket restaurant with the same name across the road.

La Céfira PASTA **$**
(www.facebook.com/la.cefira; Córdoba 481; pasta AR$25-32; ⊙dinner Mon-Sat) This handsome dining room a few blocks south of the center is a cut far above the usual gnocchi-with-four-cheese-sauce joints. Delicious homemade pasta includes such temptations as squid-ink ravioli with crab, or spinach fettuccini with salmon and caper sauce.

Viejo Jack PARRILLA **$**
(Av Virrey Toledo 145; mains AR$50-70) Far enough out of the tourist zone to be authentic, but not so far it's a pain in the backside to get to, this is a down-to-earth spot very popular with locals for its *parrillada* and pasta. The serves are huge – designed for two to four – but you'll get a single portion (still enough for two) for 70% of the price.

Ma Cuisine FUSION **$$**
(☎421-4378; www.macuisineresto.com.ar; España 83; mains AR$38-56; ⊙lunch & dinner Tue-Sat, lunch Sun) The refreshingly crisp interior of this likeable little place sees a variety of changing dishes – pasta, fish and meat well-prepared and served with things like noodles or stir-fried vegetables – chalked up on the board. The friendly young couple that run it lived in France, so there's a certain Gallic influence at work.

Café del Tiempo ARGENTINE **$$**
(Balcarce 901; dishes AR$38-65; ⊙11am-4am Wed-Sun, 6pm-4am Mon & Tue) Decked out to resemble a Buenos Aires cafe, this has prices to match but offers a stylish terrace in the heart of the Balcarce zone; a top spot for a drink. There's some sort of performance or live music every night. The menu includes llama dishes and international offerings such as chop suey, and the *picadas* (shared appetizer plates) are great for a group.

Bio's Diet VEGETARIAN **$**
(Güemes 321; lunches AR$23; ⊙Mon-Sat; 🌿) A set menu that changes daily, plus tasty salads, soyburgers and options for special diets make this a welcome break from the steakhouse.

Drinking & Entertainment

See the boxed text (p233) for info on *peñas* – the classic Salta night-time experience. The two blocks of Balcarce north of Alsina, and the surrounding streets, are the main nightlife zone. Bars and clubs around here follow the typical boom-bust-reopen-with-new-name pattern, so just follow your nose.

Macondo BAR
(www.macondobar.com; Balcarce 980; ⊙8pm-late) After all the *folklórica* music on this street, the indie '90s-'00s mix in this trendy bar might come as a relief. Popular with locals and tourists, it keeps it lively until late and has a good streetside terrace.

New Time Café CAFE

(Caseros 602; ⏲8am-late; 📶) In the race for the accolade of Salta's best plaza cafe, this two-level corner spot wins by several lengths. It offers shady (in the afternoon) tables, great views of the *cabildo,* Cerro San Bernardo and cathedral, and wi-fi. Live music some nights.

Shopping

An artisan's market sets up every Sunday along Balcarce, stretching a couple of blocks south from the bus terminal.

Mercado Artesanal HANDICRAFTS

(Av San Martín 2555; ⏲8am-8:30pm) For souvenirs, this provincially sponsored market is the most noteworthy place. Articles include native handicrafts, such as hammocks, string bags, ceramics, basketry, leatherwork and the region's distinctive ponchos. To get here, take bus 2, 3 or 7 from downtown.

Librería San Francisco BOOKS

(Caseros 362) Decent selection of English books, mostly classics.

Information

There are lots of ATMs around the central streets, and call centers and internet places are plentiful.

Citibank (cnr España & Balcarce) Changes euros and US dollars, and has a high ATM withdrawal limit.

Hospital San Bernardo (☎432-0445; Tobías 69)

Municipal tourist office (☎437-3340; www.saltalalinda.gov.ar; Caseros 711; ⏲9am-9pm) Efficient multilingual staff.

National Parks Administration (APN; ☎431-2683; www.parquesnacionales.gov.ar; España 366; ⏲8:30am-2:30pm Mon-Fri) On the 3rd floor of the Aduana building, offers information and advice on the region's national parks. Contact before going to El Rey or Baritú.

Post office (Deán Funes 140)

Provincial tourist office (☎431-0950; www.turismosalta.gov.ar; Buenos Aires 93; ⏲8am-9pm Mon-Fri, 9am-8pm Sat & Sun) Top marks – friendly, efficient and multilingual. Ask staff about the condition of the roads if heading out in a rental car.

PEÑAS OF SALTA

Salta is famous Argentina-wide for its *folklore* (folk music), which is far more national in scope than tango. A *peña* is a bar or social club where people eat, drink and gather to play and listen, traditionally in the form of an impromptu jam session.

These days, the Salta *peña* is quite a touristy experience, with scheduled performances, CD sales and tour groups; nevertheless, it's a great deal of fun. Traditional fare is empanadas and red wine – delicious, but most places offer a wider menu.

Peña heartland is Calle Balcarce, between Alsina and the train station. There are several here, along with other restaurants, bars and *boliches* (nightclubs) – it's Salta's main nightlife zone.

Some *peñas* to get you started:

La Vieja Estación PEÑA **$$**

(☎421-7727; www.viejaestacion-salta.com.ar; Balcarce 885; show AR$15-25, mains AR$40-65; ⏲8pm-3am Tue-Sun) The best established of the Balcarce *peñas,* with a stage, wooden tables and three live shows per night. Top empanadas and other regional food.

La Casona del Molino PEÑA **$$**

(☎434-2835; Luis Burela 1; mains AR$28-50; ⏲lunch & 9pm-5am Tue-Sun) This former mansion, about 20 blocks west of Plaza 9 de Julio, is a Salta classic with several spacious rooms, each with different performers who work around the tables rather than on a stage.

La Casa de Güemes PEÑA **$$**

(España 730, mains AR$39-58; ⏲lunch & 9pm-late) This central historic house was once occupied by Güemes, a *salteño* (resident of Salta) independence hero who looms large in gaucho and *folklore* culture hereabouts. Decent, fairly priced food and good local music nightly, with no cover charge.

Getting There & Away

Air

Salta's **airport** is 9.5km southwest of town on RP 51. **Andes** (☎437-3514; www.andesonline.com; España 478) flies six times weekly to Buenos Aires and also services Córdoba and Jujuy. **Aerolíneas Argentinas** (☎431-1331; Caseros 475) flies four times daily to Buenos Aires and also flies to Puerto Iguazú and Mendoza. **LAN** (☎0810-999-9526; www.lan.com; Caseros 476) flies to Buenos Aires three times daily.

Aerosur (☎432-0043; www.aerosur.com; España 414) flies three times weekly to Santa Cruz, Bolivia.

Bus

Salta's **bus terminal** (Av Hipólito Yrigoyen) has frequent services around the country.

Three companies do the run to San Pedro de Atacama, Chile. Andesmar leave at around 7am on Monday, Wednesday and Friday. Geminis and Pullman do it at the same time on Tuesday, Thursday and Sunday. The services go via Jujuy and Purmamarca, take 9 to 10 hours and cost AR$200 to AR$220. They continue to Calama, Antofagasta, Iquique and Arica.

Ale Hermanos goes once or twice daily to San Antonio de los Cobres (AR$40, 5½ hours), while **Marcos Rueda** has daily Cachi (AR$40, 4½ hours) services, though it might be Flechabus on this route by the time you read this.

BUSES FROM SALTA

DESTINATION	COST (AR$)	DURATION (HR)
Bariloche	878	35
Buenos Aires	450-650	20
Cafayate	60	4
Córdoba	330	12
Jujuy	42	2
La Quiaca	119	8
La Rioja	250	10
Mendoza	480	18
Puerto Iguazú	457	24
Resistencia	285	10
Salvador Mazza	152	6
Santiago del Estero	155	6
Tucumán	101	4½

Car

Renting a car in Salta is a good option to see the surrounding highlands and valleys. There are many agencies; get several quotes, as there are frequent special offers. Typically, it's AR$270 to AR$300 per day for a week's hire, triple that for a 4WD. The stretches between San Antonio de los Cobres and La Poma (en route to Cachi), and north of Salinas Grandes toward Abra Pampa are usually 4WD only, but the *ripio* road between San Antonio and Salinas Grandes is normally passable in a standard car. Always check with the provincial tourist office for current conditions.

You can't take rental cars into Bolivia, but it is possible to take them into Chile paying a bit extra and giving a few days' notice.

Some companies:

AndarSalta (☎431-0720; www.andarsalta.com.ar; Buenos Aires 88)

Asís (☎431-1704; www.asisrentacar.com.ar; Buenos Aires 160)

Europcar (☎421-8848; Córdoba 20; www.europcar.com.ar)

Noa (☎431-7080; www.noarentacar.com; Buenos Aires 1)

Sixt (☎421-6064; Deán Funes 29; www.sixt.com.ar)

Getting Around

Buses 8A and 'Quijano' from San Martín near Buenos Aires run to the airport (AR$1.75), otherwise it's a AR$40 *remise* (taxi ride). There are also bookable shuttle buses that do hotel pickups (AR$38).

Local bus 5 (AR$1.75) connects the train station and downtown with the bus terminal.

Tren a las Nubes

The *Tren a las Nubes* (Train to the Clouds), Argentina's most famous railtrip, leaves Salta and heads down the Lerma Valley before ascending the multicolored Quebrada del Toro, continues past Tastil ruins and San Antonio de los Cobres, before reaching the trip's highlight – a stunning viaduct spanning a desert canyon at **La Polvorilla**, 4220m above sea level.

The trip is a touristy one, with *folklore* performances and multilingual commentary. It's a long day – leaving Salta at 7am, and not getting back until nearly midnight. The train runs on Thursdays and Saturdays from March to mid-December, and the return trip costs AR$695, which includes breakfast and snacks, but not lunch or dinner; you can eat in the dining car (set menus AR$75) – you're not meant to take food onboard.

Book tickets at the **office** (☎422-3033; www.trenalasnubes.com.ar) at Salta station or at travel agents in town. Look out for discount vouchers at tourist brochure racks.

Many tour operators in Salta run trips along the road that parallels the train's route, which is also a spectacular ascent; they include the viaduct and cost around AR$280.

San Antonio de los Cobres

☎03873 / POP 4274 / ELEV 3775M

This dusty little mining town is on the puna 168km west of Salta, and over 2600m above it. It's suffered greatly since the deterioration of the region's mining and associated railway, and relies heavily on tourism for income. It's a typical highland settlement, with adobe houses, near-deserted streets and a serious temperature drop when the sun goes down. It's worth stopping in to get the feel of this facet of Andean life. You can head north from here to the Quebrada de Humahuaca via the Salinas Grandes and Purmamarca, and, some of the year, south to Cachi (see p238).

Sights

There's little to see in town – though the sunsets are spectacular – but 16km to the west is the viaduct at La Polvorilla, the last stop of the *Tren a las Nubes*. You can climb up a zigzag path to the top of the viaduct and walk across it. *Remises* in San Antonio charge about AR$40 for the return journey.

Sleeping & Eating

Simple restaurants are dotted along Belgrano; these are good bets for empanadas, *milanesas* (breaded cutlets) and other local staples.

El Palenque GUESTHOUSE **$**
(☎490-9019; hostalelpalenque@hotmail.com; Belgrano s/n; d without bathroom AR$100, tr/q with bathroom AR$150/200) Welcoming and tidy, this is a fine choice a few blocks from the center, past the church. It looks closed from outside, but it's not. The rooms are insulated and (comparatively) warm; there's hot water and sound family ownership.

Hotel de las Nubes HOTEL **$$**
(☎490-9059; www.hoteldelasnubes.com; Caseros 441; s/d AR$290/370; Wi-Fi) The best place to stay and eat in town, this has attractively simple decoration in its comfortable rooms, which boast doubleglazing and heating. Book ahead. The restaurant (mains AR$25 to AR$45; open noon to 2pm and 7pm to 9.30pm) serves a short menu of local dishes; all are well prepared and nourishing.

Getting There & Away

There are daily buses from Salta (AR$40, 5½ hours) with Ale Hermanos. See also the *Tren a las Nubes*. There's precious little transportation running over the Paso de Sico to Chile these days; if you are trying to hitchhike, ask around town for trucks due to leave. From San Antonio, a good *ripio* road runs 97km north, skirting the Salinas Grandes to intersect with the paved RP52.

Salinas Grandes

Bring sunglasses for this spectacular **salt plain** in a remote part of the puna, at some 3350m above sea level. Once a lake that dried up in the Holocene, this is now a 525-sq-km crust of salt up to half a meter thick. On a clear day, the blinding contrast between the bright blue sky and the cracked and crusty expanse of white is spellbinding.

The *salinas* (salt plains) are in Salta province, but are most easily reached by heading west along the paved RP 52 from Purmamarca in Jujuy province. About 5km west of the intersection of RP52 and RN40 (the good *ripio* road that heads north 97km from San Antonio de los Cobres), there's a saltmining building; opposite, you can drive onto the salt pan to check out the rectangular basins from which the salt is periodically dug out. A few artisans sell decent stone carvings and llamas made from salt. A couple of places to buy drinks and food are on the road nearby.

The only way of reaching the *salinas* by public transportation is to jump off a Susques-bound bus from Jujuy or Purmamarca. Check the timetables carefully before doing this; on some days it's possible to catch a bus back to Purmamarca a couple of hours later, but on other days it's not. This road has enough traffic to hitchhike.

Otherwise, hire a car, grab a *remise* from Purmamarca, or take a tour from Jujuy or Salta. From the latter, it's a hellishly long day, unless you opt to overnight in Purmamarca.

The *salinas* are spectacular, but the otherworldly *salares* (salt flats) in southwestern Bolivia are even more so; if you're heading that way (or have already been), you might want to prioritize other attractions.

Valles Calchaquíes

The Valles Calchaquíes is one of Argentina's most seductive off-the-beaten-track zones: a winning combination of rugged landscapes, traditional workshops, strikingly attractive adobe villages and some of Argentina's best wines. Small but sophisticated Cafayate, with its wineries and paved highway, presents quite a contrast to more remote settlements such as Angastaco or Molinos, while Cachi, accessible from Salta via a spectacular road that crosses the Parque Nacional Los Cardones, is another peaceful and popular base. The vernacular architecture in these valleys merits special attention – even modest adobe houses might have neoclassical columns or Moorish arches.

In these valleys, indigenous Diaguita (Calchaquí) put up some of the stiffest resistance to Spanish rule. Military domination did not solve Spanish labor problems; their final solution was to relocate the Diaguita as far away as Buenos Aires, whose suburb of Quilmes bears the name of one group of these displaced people. The productive land that had sustained the Diaguita for centuries was formed by the Spaniards into large rural estates, the haciendas of the Andes.

PARQUE NACIONAL LOS CARDONES

Occupying some 650 sq km on both sides of the winding RP 33 from Salta to Cachi across the Cuesta del Obispo, Parque Nacional Los Cardones takes its name from the candelabra cactus known as the cardón, the park's most striking plant species.

In the treeless Andean foothills and puna, the cardón has long been an important source of timber for rafters, doors, window frames and similar uses. You see it often in vernacular buildings and the region's colonial churches.

Los Cardones is free to enter and still has no services – though a visitor center on the main road is gradually being renovated – but there is a **ranger office** (☎03868-496005; loscardones@apn.gov.ar; San Martín s/n) in Payogasta, 11km north of Cachi. Take plenty of water and protection from the sun. Buses between Salta and Cachi will stop for you, but verify times. Most people disembark at Valle Encantada, which is the most accessible, picturesque part of the park.

CACHI

☎03868 / POP 2200 / ELEV 2280M

The biggest place by some distance hereabouts – you'll hear locals refer to it as 'the city' – enchanting Cachi is nevertheless little more than a village, albeit one surrounded by stunning scenery. Overlooked by noble mountains, it boasts fresh highland air, sunny days and crisp nights. The cobblestones, adobe houses, tranquil plaza and opportunities to explore the surrounds mean that it's the sort of place that eats extra days out of your carefully planned itinerary.

Sights

Museo Arqueológico MUSEUM
(admission by AR$5 or AR$10 donation; ⏰10am-7pm Mon-Fri, 10am-6pm Sat, 10am-1pm Sun) On the plaza, this is a well-presented and professionally arranged account of the surrounding area's cultural evolution, with

WORTH A TRIP

PARQUE NACIONAL EL REY

East of Salta, this remote **national park** (elrey@apn.gov.ar) is at the southern end of the Yungas subtropical corridor and protects a habitat that is the most biologically diverse in the country.

There are various well-marked trails, some accessible by vehicle. **Laguna Los Patitos**, 2km from park headquarters, offers opportunities to observe waterbirds. Longer trails lead to moss-covered **Pozo Verde**, a three- to four-hour climb to an area teeming with birdlife. Other trails are of similar day-trip length and involve multiple river crossings.

There is free **camping** at the park's headquarters, with toilets, drinkable water, cold showers and evening power. There is no shop. Contact the APN office in Salta (see Information) for up-to-date info.

It's tough to get here. The last 46km are on rough *ripio* (gravel) road that's almost impassable if it's been raining. Last fuel is at General Güemes, 160km from the park, so consider taking extra gas. Without a 4WD, the easiest way to get here is via guided tour from Salta (p227). Public transportation reaches Lumbreras, 91km short of the park.

good background information on archaeological methods, all in Spanish. Don't miss the wall in the secondary patio, composed of stones with petroglyphs.

Next door, simple but attractive **Iglesia San José** (1796) has graceful arches and a barrel-vaulted ceiling of cardón wood. The confessional and other features are also made of cardón, while the holy water lives in a large *tinaja* (a big clay vessel for storing oil).

Todo lo Nuestro MUSEUM
(admission AR$10; ⌚9am-3pm) Two kilometers southwest of the center, on the edge of town, this is a labor of love that features replica buildings from several phases of the valley's history. It's a fascinating project; in some of the buildings it really feels as if the occupants have just stepped out for a minute. There's a rustically styled restaurant here, too.

Activities

A short walk from Cachi's plaza brings you to a **viewpoint** and then the picturesque hilltop **cemetery**; nearby is a rather unlikely airstrip. A longer walk (an hour and a bit) takes you to **Cachi Adentro**, a tiny village where there's not a great deal to do save swing on the seats in the demi-plaza or sip a soda from the only store. It's a particularly lovely walk in summer, when the streams and cascades are alive with water. From here, you could return a longer way (about 26km roundtrip): bear left past the church and then take a left down the road labelled Camino de las Carreras. This road winds around the valley and eventually crosses the river; shortly afterwards, turn left when you hit a bigger road (or right for 2km to the lovely Algarrobal campground); and this will lead you back to Cachi via the hamlet of La Aguada.

There's a handful of rather unremarkable **archaeological sites** dotted around the valley; these are signposted and also appear on the tourist office map of the area, and make destinations for picturesque hikes or drives.

For more strenuous hiking and mountaineering, **Santiago Casimiro** (☎03868-15-638545; san tiagocasimiro@hotmail.com; Barrio Cooperativa Casa 17) is a local guide. Many locals hire out **horses**; look for signs or ask in the tourist office.

Tours

Various operators offer excursions. **Urkupiña** (☎491317; uk_cachi@hotmail.com; Zorrilla s/n) runs cycling trips in the Cardones national park (AR$230), hiking and quad-bike excursions, trips to Cachi Adentro or nearby archaeological sites for around AR$50 to AR$60, and longer jaunts along Ruta 40 in both directions; this can be a good way to reach Cafayate (AR$190).

Sleeping

La Merced del Alto HOTEL $$$
(☎490020; www.lamerceddelalto.com; s/d AR$510/600; @ 🛜 🏊) Built of traditional whitewashed adobe with ceramic floors and cane ceilings, this hotel across the river from town is designed to look like an historic monastery. It offers excellent facilities and great peace and quiet, with cool, restrained rooms looking over either the hills beyond (slightly more expensive) or the interior patio. Public areas include a most inviting lounge, a good restaurant, and a rustic spa area. Service is multilingual and top-notch.

El Cortijo BOUTIQUE HOTEL $$
(☎491034; www.elcortijohotel.com; Av ACA s/n; s/d AR$330/415; ❄ 🛜) Opposite the ACA Hostería Cachi entrance, this stylish small hotel offers rooms that aren't large but are decorated with finesse, and some – particularly 'Los Padres', with its own private terrace with loungers (doubles AR$495) – have fabulous views of the sierra. There's also an on-site restaurant and helpful staff. Good value.

ACA Hostería Cachi HOTEL $$
(☎491105; www.soldelvalle.com.ar; Av ACA s/n; s/d AR$282/438; ❄ @ 🛜 🏊 👪) With its hilltop position, this family-friendly hotel has the best views in town, and there are worse ways to spend your day than relaxing poolside checking them out. Rooms are comfortable and unexciting but picturesquely surround a patio; there's even a little zoo.

Hotel Nevado de Cachi GUESTHOUSE $
(☎491912; s/d with bathroom AR$70/110, s without bathroom AR$40) Just off the plaza and by the bus stop, this is a decent budget choice with rooms around a patio. Beds are comfortable, and bathrooms – both shared and private – work well enough. Prices are a bit negotiable and vary slightly by room; try for the slightly dearer upstairs double round the back.

Camping Municipal CAMPGROUND $
(☎491902; oficinadeturismo.cachi@gmail.com; campsites AR$15-20; 🏊) On a hill southwest of the plaza, this offers shaded sites with barbecues surrounded by hedges; the municipal pool is here. There's also a hostel with dorms (AR$12) and a couple of cabins (AR$125); reserve at the tourist office.

Tampu HOTEL $$
(☎491092; www.tampucachi.com; Güemes s/n; d AR$420;) Nobly showing off its elegant lines and appealing garden and pool area, this historic villa should be a faultless place to stay. Rooms vary in size and shape, with original artworks on the walls and comfortable beds. There's a slight feeling that not everything gets mended when it should; the bathrooms aren't quite up to the overall package either, but it's got plenty of appeal nonetheless.

Hospedaje Don Arturo GUESTHOUSE $
(☎491087; http://hospedajedonarturo.blogspot.com; Bustamante s/n; s/d without bathroom AR$80/140, s/d AR$90/160) Rooms are cramped but spotless; the best feature is the lounge area and back deck looking over the riverbed.

Miraluna APARTMENTS $$
(☎0387-15-442-2371; www.miraluna.com.ar; Cachi Adentro; apt for 2/4 AR$480/580, large apt for 4 AR$650;) Seven kilometers from town, these artistically decorated cabins come in two sizes and have a fabulously peaceful setting.

La Mamama HOSTEL $
(☎491305; Suárez 590; dm/r without bathroom AR$30/60) A welcoming spot on the bus stop street, with simple rooms with saggy mattresses and a Cachi-casual feel.

Eating

For local dishes like *locro* and *humitas*, look for *confiterías* and *comedores* around the plaza and across from Hotel Nevado de Cachi. There are numerous tourist traps.

Ashpamanta ARGENTINE $$
(☎0387-15-451-4267; www.ashpamantarestaurante.com; Bustamante s/n; dishes AR$28-55) Compact and snug, this likable little place has a short but tasty menu of pasta, salads and a couple of more elaborate mains – quinoa risotto or panfried fillets with vegetables – that are prepared in an open kitchen behind the bar.

Oliver PIZZA $
(Ruíz de los Llanos 160; mains AR$22-55; ⏲8am-midnight;) On the plaza, this homey, multilevel, wooden-tabled restaurant is a reliable choice for tasty pizza, bruschetta and a couple of creative meaty mains. The terrace on the plaza is also a fine place for a sundowner.

Platos y Diseño ARGENTINE $
(Güemes s/n; dishes AR$15-40;) Uphill from the plaza, this has a relaxing dining area with local art and photos, slow but amiable service and decent for-the-tourists dishes.

Information

Tourist office (☎491902; oficinadeturismo.cachi@gmail.com; Güemes s/n; ⏲9am-8pm) On the plaza.

Getting There & Away

Marcos Rueda (☎491063) buses run between Salta and Cachi, though they might have been replaced by Flechabus by the time you read this. It's a spectacular ride, winding up to the Cuesta del Obispo pass, then traveling through the cactus-studded Parque Nacional Los Cardones. Buses to Salta (AR$40, 4½ hours) leave at 9.05am Monday to Saturday. There's a 3pm service on Monday, Thursday and Friday, and a 3.30pm service on Sunday. Seclantás is serviced daily and Molinos five times weekly, while three buses Monday through Saturday run to Cachi Adentro (AR$3, 30 minutes).

There are buses north to La Poma, an old hacienda town that, as far as public transport goes, is the end of the line. The road beyond, to San Antonio de los Cobres, is an arduous, spectacular ascent that criss-crosses a river and travels by lonely goat farms to a 4895m pass. It's only passable in a non-4WD at certain times (normally September to December); phone the **police** (☎0387-490-9051) for advice. Otherwise, approach San Antonio the long way round.

For Cafayate, you can get as far as Molinos, from where you can hitch or find a transport to Angastaco, which has bus service to Cafayate. Taking a tour from Cachi is an easier option.

SECLANTÁS

☎03868 / POP 300 / ELEV 2100M

Charming Seclantás is a quiet little place that's the spiritual home of the Salta poncho. There are many weavers' workshops in town, and north of here, along the road to Cachi, artisans' homes are marked with a sign indicating that you can drop in and peruse their wares; the stretch of road has been dubbed the **Route of the Artisans**. One of them, Señor Tero, wove a poncho worn by Pope John Paul II.

Places to stay in Seclantás are clustered around the plaza. Among them, **Hostería La Rueda** (☎498041; cnr Cornejo & Ferreyra; s/d with bathroom AR$90/120, without bathroom AR$70/100) is hospitable and spotless, featuring comfortable, pretty, common areas and decent rooms. The campground is just behind the church, and has a public pool as well as cabins.

There's a daily bus from Cachi to Seclantás (AR$17, 1¼ hours, two on Saturday); it continues to Molinos some days.

MOLINOS

☎03868 / POP 900 / ELEV 2020M

If you thought Cachi was laid-back, wait until you see Molinos, a lovely little backwater with a collection of striking adobe buildings in gentle decline; a stroll through the streets will reveal some real gems. Its picturesque appeal is augmented by shady streets and good accommodations. There's an ATM on the plaza.

Molinos takes its name from the still-operational flour mill on the Río Calchaquí. The town's restored **Iglesia de San Pedro de Nolasco**, in the Cuzco style, features twin bell towers and a cactus-wood ceiling. Nearby, the **Centro de Interpretación Molinos** (www.naturalezaparaelfuturo.org; Cornejo s/n; donation AR$10; ⊙8:30am-7pm) is a restored historic house with a good display on the region's culture and history in Spanish and English, tourist information and a craft shop.

About 1.5km west is the **Criadero Coquera**, where the government's agricultural research arm raises vicuñas: you can feed these beautiful creatures with straw. Here also is the **Casa de Entre Ríos**, where there's a fine artisans' market with spectacular ponchos and wallhangings woven from sheep, llama, and vicuña wool for sale. There are two simple rooms (AR$50 per person).

Los Cardones de Molinos (☎494061; cardonesmolinos@hotmail.com; cnr Sarmiento & San Martín; r per person with/without bathroom AR$80/60) is an excellent sleeping choice, with comfortable rooms with cactus furniture. You're treated as one of the family and can use the kitchen; the exceptionally welcoming and accommodating owner is a good source of local advice. Prices rise substantially in January.

Across from the church, adobe **Hacienda de Molinos** (☎494094; www.haciendademolinos.com.ar; Cornejo s/n; s/d standard US$100/120, r superior US$140-160; @🛜🏊) is also known as the Casa de Isasmendi, after Salta's last colonial governor, who was born, lived and died in this sprawling residence. It's been picturesquely restored, with sober, handsome rooms with inviting beds, antique furniture, cane ceilings and great bathrooms, set around lovely patio spaces. It's on the edge of the village and utterly peaceful. There's an overpriced but reasonable restaurant.

Also in town, a couple of down-home places do decent cheap meals.

There's a bus to Molinos from Cachi (AR$24, two hours) on Monday, Wednesday, Friday, Saturday and Sunday. It returns from Molinos at 7am Monday, Tuesday, Thursday and Saturday, and 2pm on Sunday. Shared *remises* run when there's demand to Salta via Cachi for the same price as the bus.

ANGASTACO

☎03868 / POP 900 / ELEV 1955M

Tiny Angastaco sits among some of the most dramatically tortuous rockscapes of the valley route. Forty kilometers south of Molinos and 54km north of San Carlos, it resembles other oasis settlements placed at regular intervals in the Valles Calchaquíes, with vineyards, fields of anise and cumin, and the ruins of an ancient *pucará*.

Angastaco has a gas station (with internet access) but no bank. There is a tourist office on the square, as well as an **archaeological museum** in the municipal building. Both are open irregular hours, but ask around in the *municipalidad* or police station and someone will help. **Horseback riding** is easily arranged via the Hostería Angastaco.

Hospedaje El Cardón (☎0387-15-459-0021; r per person with/without bathroom AR$40/30) is a decent budget choice. It's 50m to your right (the one with the fancy porch) if you're standing facing the church. **Hostería Angastaco** (☎491123; s/d AR$70/110; 🏊) feels a bit abandoned but offers excellent value for its rooms with artisanal throws on the beds and cardón chests. There's a restaurant and summer-only pool.

At research time, the only public transportation were buses heading south to San Carlos and Cafayate at 6am Monday to Saturday and 5pm Monday, Friday, and Sunday. Transport options to Molinos, 40km north, are limited. Transports (ask around) run the route for AR$200 to AR$250 total. They'll often meet the Cafayate bus, where you can share the fare with other passengers. Otherwise, it's a hitchhike; best done from the main road, where there's shade and a cafe to alleviate the likely long wait.

SAN CARLOS

☎03868 / POP 1900

A sizable traditional village, San Carlos, 22km north of Cafayate, is connected to it by paved road, a pleasant shock if you're arriving from the north. Most visitors push on through to Cafayate or Angastaco, but there's a special place to stay here in **La Casa de los Vientos** (☎03868-15-456525; www.casadelosvientos.com.ar; Barrio Cemitigre; s/d/f AR$150/220/300; @🏊👪), which is signposted off the main road at the Cachi end of

WORTH A TRIP

FINCA COLOMÉ

Fine wines are produced at this ecological **bodega** (☎03868-494044; www.bodegacolome.com; tasting AR$30-50; ⏰10:30am-6pm), which is set (as they say hereabouts) 'where the devil lost his poncho,' some 20km down a spectacular gravel road west from Molinos. The vineyards enjoy a stunning natural setting, surrounded by hills and mountains that seem to change color hourly. Forward thinking on environmental, social and cultural fronts is also in evidence: the complex is electrically self-sufficient, has funded substantial infrastructural improvements in the local community and boasts a stunning **museum** (admission free; ⏰2-6pm) designed by artist James Turrell, with a permanent exhibition of nine of his works. These are utterly memorable installations involving light and the strange frontiers of our own perception; it's a remarkable place. Both bodega and museum visits should be booked ahead by phone or email (museo@colomeargentina.com). The bodega also serves salads and baguettes for a light lunch.

Not far from Colomé, Bodega El Humanao is also worth a visit for its beautifully balanced cabernet-malbec blend, among others.

town. Built in the traditional manner of adobe, with terracotta tiles and cane ceilings, it incorporates some ingenious environmental innovations. The owners are potters, and the rooms (all different) are decorated with rustic flair and beauty. There's a heated indoor pool and very genuine welcome.

Cafayate

☎03868 / POP 11,785 / ELEV 1683M

Argentina's second center for quality wine production, Cafayate is a popular tourist destination but still has a tranquil small-town feel. It's a spectacularly scenic place, with the green of the vines backed by the soaring mountains beyond, and is one of northwest Argentina's most seductive destinations. It's easily reached from Salta via the tortured rockscapes of the Quebrada de Cafayate; it's also the southern terminus of the Valles Calchaquíes route. With a selection of excellent accommodations for every budget, and several wineries to visit in and around town, it invites laying up for a while to explore the surrounding area. Also, check out the excellent *artesanía*.

Cafayate is famous for its torrontés, a grape producing aromatic dry white wine, but the bodegas hereabouts also produce some fine reds from cabernet sauvignon, malbec and tannat.

Sights & Activities

Museo de la Vid y El Vino MUSEUM

(www.museodelavidyelvino.gov.ar; Av General Güemes; admission AR$30; ⏰10am-7.30pm Tue-Sun) This impressive new museum gives a good introduction to the area's wine industry. The atmospheric first section, which deals with the viticultural side – the life of the vines – through a series of poems and images, is particularly appealing. The second part covers the winemaking side, and there's a cafe where you can try and buy. English translations are good throughout.

Wine-Tasting WINERIES

There are several wineries offering tours and tastings in and around the town.

The visits (English and French available) are short and bright at **Bodega Nanni** (☎421527; www.bodegananni.com; Chavarría 151; tours free, tasting AR$10; ⏰9:30am-1pm & 2:30-6:30pm Mon-Sat, 11am-1pm & 2:30-6pm Sun), a small, central winery with a lovely grass patio. Its wines are organic, uncomplicated and drinkable.

Tiny **Salvador Figueroa** (☎421289; Pasaje 20 de Junio 25; tasting AR$5; ⏰9:30am-12:30pm & 3-7pm) is a friendly family winery in town that produces only 5000 bottles of torrontés and malbec per year with small hand-operated equipment. Nearby, **El Porvenir** (☎422007; www.bodegaselporvenir.com; Córdoba 32; ⏰10am-6pm Mon-Fri, 10am-1pm Sat) focuses on quality wine production. The tour is free, but tastings cost AR$30, AR$60 or AR$90 depending on which wines you want to try.

Bodega El Esteco (☎421283; www.elesteco.com.ar; tours AR$20; ⏰tours 10am, 11am, noon, 2:30pm, 3:30pm, 4.30pm & 5:30pm Mon-Fri, 10am, 11am & noon Sat), on the northern edge of town, is a smart and attractive winery producing some of the region's best wines. The tasting is a little spartan though.

Three kilometers south of town, **Bodega Etchart** (☎421310; www.bodegasetchart.com; RN 40; ⏲tours hourly 9:15am-4:15pm Mon-Fri, 9:15am-12:15pm Sat) offers a cheerful free tour including tasting. It produces some six million bottles of quality torrontés, cabernet and malbec per year.

Five kilometers west of town along the road to Río Colorado (it's signposted 'Mounier'), small, organic and friendly **Bodega de las Nubes** (☎422129; www.bodegamounier.com; ⏲9:30am-5:30pm Mon-Fri, 9am-2pm Sat, 9:30am-1pm Sun) has a fabulous position at the foot of the jagged hills. The short tour and tasting nominally costs AR$15, but if you buy wine it's not charged. It also does tasty *picadas*. Ring ahead to check it is open and if you want to eat.

Museo Arqueológico MUSEUM
(cnr Colón & Calchaquí; admission by donation; ⏲11:30am-9pm Mon-Fri, 11:30am-3pm Sat) This private museum's collection was left by enthusiastic archaeologist Rodolfo Bravo and merits a visit. Sourced mostly from grave sites in a 30km radius from Cafayate, the excellent array of ceramics, from the black and gray wares of the Candelaria and Aguada cultures to late Diaguita and Inca pottery, are well displayed across two rooms. While there's not much explanation, the material speaks for itself.

Río Colorado WALKING, SWIMMING
A 6km walk southwest of town leads you to the Río Colorado. Follow the river upstream for about 1½ hours to get to a 10m **waterfall**, where you can swim. There's a second waterfall further up. Look out for hidden **rock paintings** on the way (for about AR$10, local children will guide you). If you want to ride out to the trailhead, you can leave your bike at the nearby house for a few pesos. You could combine this walk with a visit to Bodega de las Nubes. Warning: if the river is high after rains in January and February, the route to the waterfall becomes strenuous and dangerous. Sudden torrents can come down quickly from the mountains at any time of year, so always keep an eye upstream while bathing.

Tours

The standard minibus tour of the Quebrada leaves in the afternoon, when the colors are more vivid, and costs around AR$70. Three- to four-hour treks in the Quebrada and Río Colorado are also popular. Day-long trips to Cachi (AR$250) are tiring, while Quilmes (AR$100) can be visited more cheaply in a taxi if you're two or more. Horseback rides range from a couple of hours (AR$150) to all day (AR$300). Many places around the plaza hire out bikes (around AR$60 for a full day). **Rentamotos** (☎0387-15-466-5522; rentamotosvcalchaquies@hotmail.com.ar; cnr Belgrano & Güemes) hires motorbikes for AR$180 a day.

Tour operators have offices on the plaza. Readers aren't usually blown away by the service offered – check with other travelers before choosing – but the Quebrada scenery speaks for itself.

Festivals & Events

La Serenata de Cafayate, in late February, is a very worthwhile three-day *folklore* festival. The **Fiesta de la Virgen del Rosario**, on October 4, is the town fiesta and gets lively.

Sleeping

Cafayate has numerous places to stay, with new boutique hotels popping up like mushrooms and simple *hospedajes* on every street.

TOP CHOICE **Killa** BOUTIQUE HOTEL $$
(☎422254; www.killacafayate.com.ar; Colón 47; s/d/ste AR$403/475/540; ❄@🛜🏊) Classy, comfortable and well run, this handsome and recommendable hotel has colonial style given warmth by its creative use of natural wood, stone and local *artesanía*. The gorgeous rooms – not a TV in sight – have great bathrooms, and the upstairs suites – worth the small extra investment – have cracking views and private balcony spaces. There's a pretty pool area and impeccable hospitality.

Villa Vicuña BOUTIQUE HOTEL $$
(☎422145; www.villavicuna.com.ar; Belgrano 76; s/d AR$360/490; ❄@🛜) Peacefully set around twin patios, this offers an intimate retreat with beautiful, spotless rooms with big beds and reproduction antique furniture. Service and breakfast are good, and you can lose hours deciphering the offbeat mural sculpture in the courtyard. Discount if you pay cash.

Patios de Cafayate HOTEL $$$
(☎422229; www.patiosdecafayate.com; RN40; r US$490-530; ❄@🛜🏊) Though just a short walk north of town, this secluded place is a seductive getaway. Set in a beautiful centenarian estancia, it's a classy, elegant spot with helpful

professional service. Rooms are classically colonial, with noble dark wood furniture and local *artesanía,* and look over either the surrounding vineyards or the garden area, which includes a great swimming pool. There's also a spa complex. Enter via El Esteco winery.

Hostal del Valle GUESTHOUSE $
(☎421039; www.welcomeargentina.com/hostaldel valle; San Martín 243; s/d AR$165/220; ❄📶) This enticing place offers myriad flowering pot plants, and pretty rooms with large, inviting beds and excellent bathrooms. There are a couple of smaller, darker rooms that are a little cheaper but still worthwhile. Breakfast is served in a rooftop conservatory with privileged views. Great for the price.

Portal del Santo HOTEL $$
(☎422400; www.portaldelsanto.com.ar; Chavarría 250; s/d AR$310/396; 📶❄🏊) Cool white elegance is the stock in trade of this hospitable hotel that resembles a colonial palace with its arched arcades. The lower rooms open onto the front porch and also the inviting back garden and pool area; the rooms on the top floor (double/suite AR$462/700) have mountain views and even more space. The suites sleep four.

Hotel Munay HOTEL $$
(☎0388-15-585-4718; www.munayhotel.com.ar; Chavarría 64; s/d AR$240/280; ❄📶🏊) The elegant simplicity and clean uncluttered lines of this hotel seem to reflect the surrounding sierra. Rooms are unadorned, attractive and spotless, with good bathrooms. Excellent value, helpful service and a hospitable atmosphere make this a sound choice.

Rusty-K Hostal HOSTEL $
(☎422031; www.rustykhostal.com.ar; Rivadavia 281; dm AR$50, d with/without bathroom AR$190/160; @📶) The peace of the vine-filled patio garden here is broken only by the occasional pock-pock of table tennis. Cute doubles and an excellent attitude make this Cafayate's budget gem. Book ahead.

Cafayate

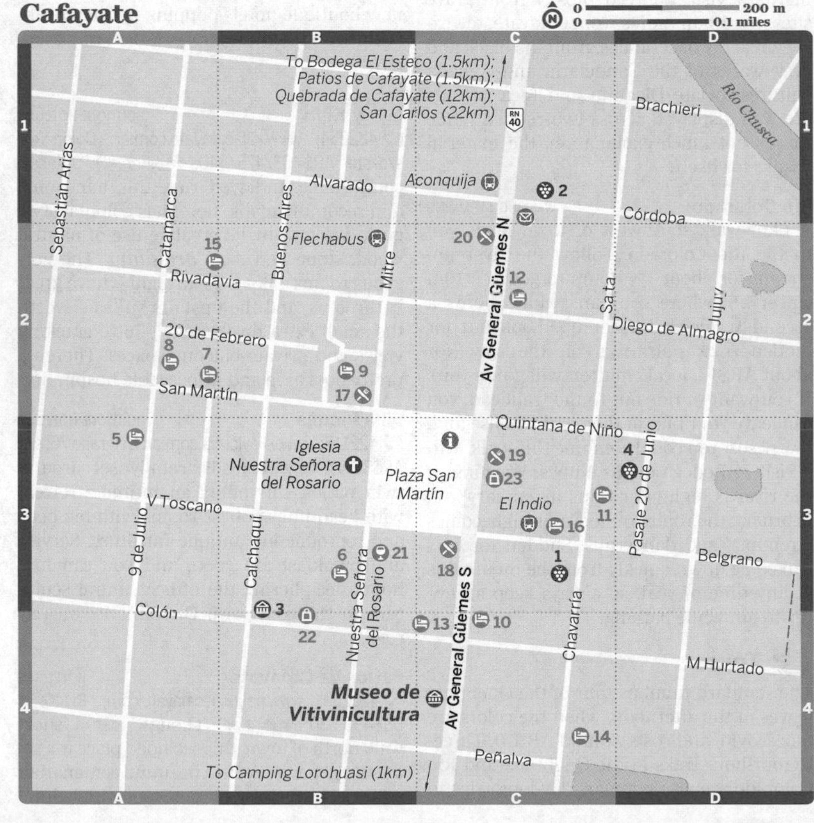

El Portal de las Viñas GUESTHOUSE **$$**
(☎421098; www.portalvinias.com.ar; Nuestra Señora del Rosario 155; d/q AR$250/400;) Just off the square, this is a comfortable non-luxury option with plenty of personality. Highlights are the courteous and genuine welcome from the interesting owner and the general tranquility. The rooms, with terracotta-tiled floors and spacious bathrooms, are set around a vine-shaded courtyard.

Hotel Tinkunaku HOTEL **$$**
(☎421148; Diego de Almagro 12; s/d AR$150/260;) There's plenty of value for your peso here at this warmly-run hotel which features good-sized modern rooms in a quiet, central location. The place has a relaxed atmosphere and a summer pool out back.

Cafayate

Hostel Ruta 40 HOSTEL **$**
(☎421689; www.hostel-ruta40.com; Av General Güemes 178; dm/d AR$45/180;) Dorms are darkish and can be a little stuffy, but facilities and atmosphere are good at this central hostel. Private rooms with bathroom are a decent deal, breakfast is included and there's a kitchen. HI discount applies.

Cabañas Luna y Sol APARTMENTS **$$**
(☎421852; www.lunaysol.fr; 9 de Julio 31; s/d/q AR$265/350/590;) An enticing option for families and couples, these cute apartments come with kitchenette and living area; the larger ones are duplex, with two sleeping areas. There's also a little pool.

Hostal Ñusta GUESTHOUSE **$$**
(☎421852; www.lunaysol.fr; Catamarca 15; d AR$240-300;) Small, generously-run guesthouse. Superior rooms have air-con and flatscreen TVs.

Hotel Emperador HOTEL **$**
(☎421268; Av Güemes 46; s/d AR$150/200;) Rooms don't nearly live up to the attractive lobby, but this is a friendly decent-value option with a great location on the square.

Hostel El Balcón HOSTEL **$**
(☎421739; www.elbalconhostel.com.ar; 20 de Febrero 110; dm AR$50-70, d AR$220;) Travelers either love or hate this place. The rooftop bar's a great spot, but the spacious dorms suffer from noise at weekends and there's a mercenary feel to the setup – staff sell its tours hard.

Camping Lorohuasi CAMPGROUND **$**
(☎422292; campsites per person AR$10;) This municipal campground 10 minutes' walk from the center along Av General Güemes can get dusty when the wind blows. Facilities are OK, and there's a small grocery store.

Eating

There are many similar options around the plaza, offering adequate local dishes backed by live *folkloric* music at weekends.

TOP CHOICE **Casa de las Empanadas** ARGENTINE **$**
(Mitre 24; dozen empanadas AR$30) Decorated with the scrawls of contented customers, this no-frills place has a wide selection of empanadas that are all absolutely delicious. Local wine in ceramic jugs and *humitas, locro* and *tamales* can round out the meal.

El Terruño ARGENTINE $$
(☎422460; www.terrunogourmet.com; Av General Güemes 30; mains AR$37-60; 📶) Plaza-side seating and polite service are backed up by the food at this restaurant, which curiously has two menus, one of which is less traditional, with dishes like salmon and avocado salad, and well-prepared mains, including plenty of fish dishes. A sax player seated in the doorway caters to both indoor and outdoor diners.

El Rancho ARGENTINE $
(www.elranchocafayate.com.ar; V Toscano 4; mains AR$25-48) A cut above the string of hit-and-miss places around the plaza, this has a short, simple menu of local dishes, including *locro* and some good chicken plates. It's owned by a bodega, so competition wines are overpriced. It appeals on winter nights, with a crackling fire, and the nights when a blind guitarist plays unobtrusive *folklórica*.

Heladería Miranda ICE CREAM $
(Av General Güemes; cones AR$7-16; ⏰10am-10pm) A frequent dilemma in Argentina is whether to go for a rich red cabernet or a dry white torrontés, but it doesn't usually occur in ice-cream parlors. It does here: the Miranda's wine ice creams are Cafayate's pride and joy.

Drinking

TOP CHOICE **Chato's Wine Bar** WINE BAR
(Nuestra Señora del Rosario 132; ⏰7pm-midnight) Run by a cordial English-speaking boss, this unusual place is decorated with warmth and style. It's the only proper wine bar in Cafayate, with a list of some 200 available by the glass, and a great place for a tasting session, a drink in friendly surroundings, or a chat about wine or anything else.

Shopping

There are numerous *artesanía* shops on and around the central plaza. The **Mercado Artesanal** (Av General Güemes; ⏰9am-10pm) cooperative features many locals' high-quality work at more-than-fair prices. For fine silver, check out the workshop of **Jorge Barraco** (Colón 157).

Information

There are banks with ATM on the plaza, as well as phone/internet places.

Tourist information kiosk (☎422442; Plaza San Martín; ⏰8am-8pm) On the northeast corner of the plaza.

Getting There & Away

Flechabus (Mitre s/n) runs five to six daily services to Salta (AR$60, four hours) and also runs once or twice daily to Angastaco (AR$22, two hours) via San Carlos. By the time you read this, there may also be a Cachi service. **Aconquija** (cnr Av General Güemes & Alvarado) leaves two to four times daily for Tucumán (AR$90 to AR$103, five to 6½ hours) via Amaicha del Valle and Tafí del Valle (AR$52 to AR$64, 2½ to four hours); some buses go via Santa María (AR$30, two hours). **El Indio** (Belgrano s/n) runs once daily to Salta, and also has services to Santa María.

Getting Around

Taxis congregate on the plaza opposite the cathedral and can be useful for reaching out-of-town bodegas and other destinations. If there's none around, call ☎422128. To Quilmes with waiting time costs around AR$200, to San Carlos one-way it's AR$40, to Angastaco AR$120.

Quebrada de Cafayate

North of Cafayate, the Salta road heads through the barren and spectacular Quebrada de Cafayate, a wild landscape of richly colored sandstone and unearthly rock formations. Carved out by the Río de las Conchas, the canyon's twisted sedimentary strata exhibit a stunning array of tones, from rich red ochre to ethereal green. While you get a visual feast from the road itself – it's one of the country's more memorable drives or rides – it's worth taking the time to explore parts of the canyon. The best time to appreciate the canyon is in the late afternoon, when the low sun brings out the most vivid colors.

A short way north of Cafayate, Los Médanos is an extensive dune field that gives way to the canyon proper, where a series of distinctive landforms are named and signposted from the road. Some, such as El Sapo (the Toad) are fairly underwhelming, but around the Km 47 mark, the adjacent Garganta del Diablo (Devil's Throat) and Anfiteatro (Amphitheatre) are much more impressive. Gashes in the rock wall let you enter and appreciate the tortured stone, whose clearly visible layers have been twisted by tectonic upheavals into extraordinary configurations.

These landmarks are heavily visited, and you may be followed by locals hoping for some pesos for a bit of 'guiding.' *Artesanía* sellers and musicians hover around these landmarks, but there's no reliable place to buy food or water.

Getting There & Away

There are several ways to see and explore the canyon. Tours from Salta are brief and regimented; it's much better to take a tour from closer Cafayate, where bikes are also easily hired. Bikes can be taken on board Cafayate-Salta buses, which will let you off and on anywhere in the Quebrada area.

You could also combine the bus with walking and maybe hitching. Be aware of the schedules between Salta and Cafayate, and carry food and plenty of water in this hot, dry environment. A good place to start your exploration is the Garganta del Diablo; several other attractions are within easy walking distance of here.

TUCUMÁN & AROUND

Though it's the country's second smallest province, Tucumán has played a significant role in Argentina's story. It was here that independence was first declared, and the massive sugar industry is of great economic importance.

The city of Tucumán is full of heat and energy, in complete contrast to the lung-cleansing air of Tafí del Valle, up in the hills to the west. Beyond, Argentina's most important pre-Columbian site is Quilmes, on the Cafayate road. South of Tucumán, Santiago del Estero province is a backwater with an enjoyably sleepy feel.

Tucumán

0381 / POP 738,479 / ELEV 420M

Baking hot, energetic and brash, (San Miguel de) Tucumán, the cradle of Argentine independence, is the nation's fifth-largest city and feels like it, with a metropolitan bustle that can come as quite a shock after the more genteel provincial capitals elsewhere in the northwest. You may not like it at first, but don't be put off. This isn't the usual patter: Tucumán really rewards time spent getting to know it. You may find you prefer it at night, when the fumes and heat of the day have lulled, and the cafes and bars come to life.

Tucumán's blue-collar feel and a down-to-earth quality is complemented by a lively cultural scene, and its cafe-bars, bookstores, art exhibitions and traditional *peñas* put it a step ahead of its serene neighbors. Less advanced is the courtship behavior of the average *tucumano* (inhabitant of Tucumán) – women can expect higher-than-usual numbers of *piropos* (flirtatious remarks) here.

History

Founded in 1565, Tucumán only distinguished itself from the rest of the region when it hosted the congress that declared Argentine independence in 1816. Unlike other colonial cities of the northwest, Tucumán successfully reoriented its economy after independence. At the southern end of the frost-free zone of sugarcane production, it was close enough to Buenos Aires to take advantage of the capital's growing market. By 1874 the railway reached the city, permitting easy transportation of sugar, and local and British capital contributed to the industry's growth. Economic crises have hit hard in the past but sugarcane's growing use as a fuel source means there's plenty of optimism about the future.

Sights

Casa de la Independencia (Casa Histórica) MUSEUM
(Congreso 151; admission adult/child AR$10/free; 10am-6pm) Unitarist lawyers and clerics (Federalists boycotted the meeting) declared Argentina's independence from Spain on July 9, 1816, in the dazzlingly whitewashed late colonial Casa de la Independencia. Portraits of the signatories line the walls of the room where the declaration was signed, the only actual original part of the structure – the rest has been rebuilt. There's plenty of information in Spanish on the lead-up to these seismic events, but you can also get a guided tour (free) in English.

There's a sound-and-light show nightly except Thursday at 8:30pm; entry is AR$10/5 per adult/child.

Next to the building are open areas with various *artesanía* stalls and stands selling traditional foods.

FREE **Museo Folclórico Manuel Belgrano** MUSEUM
(Av 24 de Septiembre 565; 9am-1pm & 3-8pm Tue-Sun) Occupying a colonial house, this pleasant museum features a good collection of traditional gaucho gear, indigenous musical instruments (check out the *charangos* made from an armadillo shell) and weavings, as well as some indigenous pottery.

FREE **Casa del Obispo Colombres** MUSEUM
(8am-1pm & 2-6:30pm Mon-Fri, 8am-6pm Sat & Sun) In the center of Parque 9 de Julio (formerly Bishop Colombres' El Bajo plantation), handsome 18th-century Casa del

Obispo Colombres is a museum dedicated to the sugar industry, which the active cleric (an important figure in the independence movement) effectively set up. The information panels are translated into English.

Tours

Any number of tour operators offer excursions from sedate city strolls to canoeing, challenging hikes and paragliding; the city has hosted the Paragliding World Cup. Most paragliding operators are based in San Javier in the hills to the northwest. The tourist office can supply a fuller list. One worthwhile hike is the beautiful, accessible, four-day trek from Tucumán to Tafí del Valle.

Some operators:

Montañas Tucumanas OUTDOOR ACTIVITIES
(☎0381-15-467-1860; www.montanastucumanas.com) A cordial and professional setup, this offers hiking, climbing, canyoning, rappelling and more, near Tucumán and further afield.

Tucumán Parapente PARAGLIDING
(☎0381-15-444-7508; www.tucumanparapente.com.ar) Excellent tandem paragliding flights over the Yungas forests, as well as instruction.

Turismo del Tucumán TOURS
(☎422-7636; www.turismodeltucuman.com; Crisóstomo Álvarez 435) Guided trips to spots of interest around the province, including Tafí del Valle and Quilmes.

Walter 'Paco' Castro PARAGLIDING
(pacoflight@hotmail.com) Reader-recommended hang-gliding instructor who offers tandem flights.

Festivals & Events

Celebrations of the **Día de la Independencia** (Argentina's Independence Day) on July 9 are vigorous in Tucumán, the cradle of the country's independence. *Tucumanos* also celebrate the **Batalla de Tucumán** (Battle of Tucumán) on September 24.

Tucumán

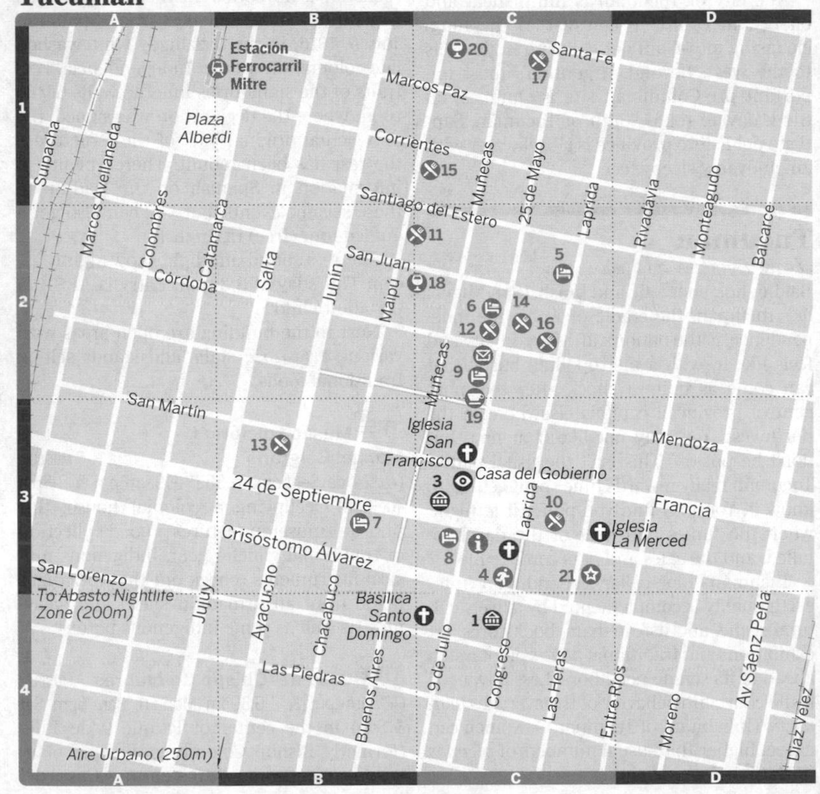

Sleeping

Most of Tucumán's hotels are overpriced, but you can negotiate substantial discounts, particularly if paying cash.

Tucumán Center HOTEL **$$$**
(☎452-5555; www.tucumancenterhotel.com.ar; 25 de Mayo 230; s/d AR$550/630; ❄@🛜≋) It's hard to fault this upmarket, business-class hotel bang in the center of town. Service and facilities – including a small gym and outdoor pool – are first-rate, and the huge beds are mighty comfortable. Suites come with space to spare and a bathtub with bubbles. It offers big discounts in summer; check the website for specials.

Aire Urbano BOUTIQUE HOTEL **$$$**
(☎424-2397; www.aireurbano.com; Ayacucho 681; d/superior d AR$550/615; ❄@🛜≋) A few blocks south of the center opposite a plaza, this small oasis is a welcome find. It feels like you're staying over at a friend's place, but it's one of those friends who has a pool, sauna and Jacuzzi in the grassy patio and a most tastefully decorated lounge area. Rooms are great; superiors are larger and also have their own Jacuzzi.

Casa Calchaquí GUESTHOUSE **$**
(☎425-6974; www.casacalchaqui.com; Lola Mora 92, Yerba Buena; s/d/q AR$160/220/310; ❄🛜≋👪) Six kilometers west of the center in the upmarket barrio of Yerba Buena, this is a welcome retreat. Comfortably rustic rooms surrounding a garden space with hammocks, bar service and a minipool make it a top spot to relax. Yerba Buena has good restaurants and nightlife. Grab a taxi (AR$30; make sure you specify it's in Yerba Buena) or bus 102 or 118 from opposite the bus terminal. The street is off Av Aconquija as the street numbers reach 1100. They also have bikes for hire.

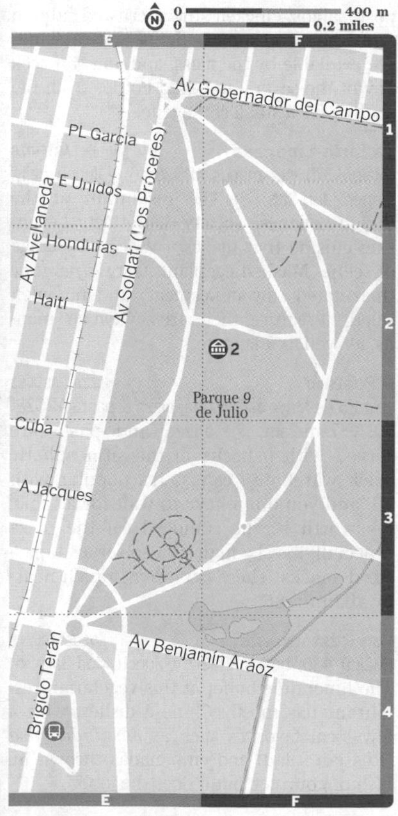

Tucumán

Sights

1 Casa de la Independencia (Casa Histórica) ... C4
2 Casa del Obispo Colombres ... F2
3 Museo Folclórico Manuel Belgrano ... C3

Activities, Courses & Tours

4 Turismo del Tucumán ... C3

Sleeping

5 Backpacker's Tucumán ... C2
6 Hotel Carlos V ... C2
7 King Hotel ... B3
8 Swiss Hotel Metropol ... C3
9 Tucumán Center ... C2

Eating

10 El Portal ... C3
11 Fon Restaurante ... C2
12 Il Postino ... C2
13 Il Postino 2 ... B3
14 La Leñita ... C2
15 La Sirio-Libanesa ... C1
16 Mí Nueva Estancia ... C2
17 Setimio ... C1

Drinking

18 Costumbres Argentinas ... C2
19 Filipo ... C3
20 Plaza de Almas ... C1

Entertainment

21 Peña El Cardón ... C3

Backpacker's Tucumán HOSTEL $
(☎430-2716; www.backpackerstucuman.com; Laprida 456; dm AR$55, s with/without bathroom AR$122/110, d with/without bathroom AR$174/164; @📶) This reliable and welcoming hostel is a short walk away from the lively 25 de Mayo eating scene, and has a relaxed, airy charm allied to plenty of facilities. Dorms are spacious, with fans and high ceilings. Noise echoes a little through the building. HI discount applies.

Swiss Hotel Metropol HOTEL $$$
(☎431-1180; www.swisshotelmetropol.com.ar; 24 de Septiembre 524; s/d AR$480/610; ❄@📶🏊) The modern rooms and spacious bathrooms on offer here are perhaps slightly offset by the tiny balconies (standing room only). The fantastic rooftop pool makes up for a lot though, as does the very central location. These are rack rates; actual prices are substantially lower.

Hotel Carlos V HOTEL $$
(☎431-1666; www.redcarlosv.com; 25 de Mayo 330; s/d AR$355/435; ❄@📶) There's something rather charming about the rooms here – it must be the parchment-colored walls and bright bedspreads, for they certainly aren't huge. Offering a fine central location and fairly classic ambience, as well as a busy café-restaurant, this is a decent Tucumán address.

King Hotel HOTEL $
(☎431-0211; Chacabuco 18; s/d AR$130/160; ❄📶) Traveling salespeople keep returning to this hotel because it's comfortable, clean and in the heart of things. Prices are very fair by Tucumán standards. It often fills up by mid-afternoon, so you might want to book ahead.

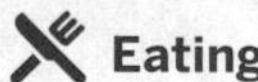

Eating

Tucumán is famous for its excellent eggy empanadas, which you'll find everywhere. Calle 25 de Mayo is eat street, studded with modern cafe-bars offering a variety of traditional and international cuisines.

If you want to blend in here, you'd better have an ice cream in your hand at all times; there are several ice-creameries around the plaza that can sort you out.

Mi Nueva Estancia PARRILLA $
(☎430-7049; Córdoba 401; mains AR$30-50) Delicious! That's the verdict on the cuts of meat at this popular grill restaurant, but the salad bar and other menu choices also win points. Value is great here for both quality and quantity, and service is friendly and efficient.

La Leñita PARRILLA $$
(☎422-9196; 25 de Mayo 377; mains AR$45-65) One of the best *parrilla* restaurants around in this part of the world, this wins few points for interior design (who thought the sports bar look was a good idea?), but stands out for service and the sheer quality of the meat. Try *picana* (rump steak) or the delicious *mollejitas* (sweetbreads). Sit strategically to avoid the air-con's arctic wind. Staff sing *folklore* music halfway through the night.

El Portal ARGENTINE $
(☎422-6024; Av 24 de Septiembre 351; dishes AR$4-42; ⏰10am-11pm) Half a block east of Plaza Independencia, this rustic indoor/outdoor eatery has a tiny but perfectly formed menu, based around empanadas, *locro* and the like. Delicious and authentic.

Setimio ARGENTINE $$
(☎431-2792; Santa Fe 512; dishes AR$35-65; ⏰7:30pm-1:30am Mon-Sat) Wall-to-wall bottles decorate this smart wine shop and restaurant, whose short menu features a pair of posh salads, chicken stirfry, crusted salmon and other toothsome delights. Several wines are available by the glass, and you can pick any of the several hundred bottles from the shelves for a small corkage fee.

La Sirio-Libanesa MIDDLE EASTERN $
(Maipú 575; set menus AR$25-46; ⏰lunch daily, dinner Mon-Sat; 🖉) The restaurant at the Syrian-Lebanese society offers tasty Levantine cuisine that makes a welcome change of scene. Mashed eggplant, tasty *kipe naye* (marinated raw mincemeat) and tabouleh salad all feature; there are several set menus, as well as à la carte.

Il Postino PIZZA, PASTA $$
(cnr 25 de Mayo & Córdoba; pizza & pasta AR$28-50; ⏰7am-2am; 🖉) Pizza and pasta are served with panache in this atmospheric brick warehouse eatery. It's popular with all, and you often have to wait for a table. It's worth it: the standard (of the pizza especially) is sky-high. It also serves tapas-sized snacks. There's another branch nearby at Junín 86.

Fon Restaurante VEGETARIAN $
(Maipú 435; buffet AR$30; ⏰lunch Mon-Sat; 🖉) The lunchtime buffet at this vegetarian restaurant has mostly Chinese dishes, with a few local favorites such as *ensalada rusa* (Russian salad) and empanadas thrown in. It's not gourmet, but it does the job.

Drinking & Entertainment

From Thursday to Saturday nights, most of the action is in the Abasto region, on Calle Lillo. Follow San Lorenzo west from the town center, and you'll hit the middle of the zone. There are dozens of bars and nightclubs – take your pick. Other popular *boliches* can be found in Yerba Buena, 6km west of the town center.

Filipo CAFE
(Mendoza 501; licuados AR$16; ⏲7am-1am) Glasses gleaming on the gantry, outdoor tables and bow-tied waiters make this a great cafe. Top espresso, prize-worthy apple *licuados* (blended fruit drinks), and beer served as if it were Bollinger are the highlights.

Plaza de Almas CAFE, BAR
(www.plazadealmas.com; Maipú 791; mains AR$20-40; ⏲8pm-late) This intimate and engaging multilevel place is popular with bohemian young *tucumanos* and is one of the best of Tucumán's many combination cafe-bar-restaurant-cultural centers. The short but interesting menu offers a range of kebabs and salads, among other choices.

Peña El Cardón TRADITIONAL MUSIC
(☎497-8235; Las Heras 50) This historical and traditional *peña* gives a good idea of what these places were like before they started putting on touristy shows. There are regular cultural events, a pretty patio and delicious empanadas. Live *folklore* music on Fridays and Saturdays starts about 10pm, goes very late and gets rowdy.

Costumbres Argentinas BAR
(San Juan 666; ⏲9:30pm-4am Wed-Sun) Though the address seems like a contradiction in terms, this unusual, popular and welcoming bar has an arty bohemian vibe and sometimes puts on live music. There's a big two-level beer garden out the back, which is the place to be on summer nights. Simple food is also available.

Information

Tucumán is bristling with internet cafes and call centers. Many downtown banks have ATMs.

El Ateneo (25 de Mayo 182) Excellent bookshop. Also maps, a small selection of airport novels in English, and a cafe.

Hospital Padilla (☎429-0969; Alberdi 550)

Tourist office (☎430-3644; www.tucumanturismo.gob.ar; 24 de Septiembre 484; ⏲8am-10pm Mon-Fri, 9am-9pm Sat & Sun) On the plaza, helpful and knowledgeable. There's another office in the shopping center at the bus terminal, open the same hours.

Getting There & Away

Air

Aerolíneas Argentinas (☎431-1030; 9 de Julio 110) has several daily flights to Buenos Aires. **LAN** (☎422-0606; Laprida 176) heads there one to two times daily, **Sol** (www.sol.com.ar) links Tucumán with Rosario and Córdoba several times weekly, and **Aerosur** (☎452-2300; Rivadavia 137) flies three times weekly to Santa Cruz in Bolivia.

Bus

Tucumán's **bus terminal** (Brígido Terán 350) is a major project with 60 platforms and plenty of shops and services. The bus **information booth** (☎430-6400) is outside, by the supermarket.

Train

Argentina's trains aren't what they used to be, but Tucumán is still connected to Buenos Aires (via Santiago del Estero and Rosario) twice a week from the beautiful **Estación Mitre** (☎430-9220; www.ferrocentralsa.com.ar) in the northwest of town. Services frequently take hours longer than advertised, but it's an old-fashioned experience that might appeal to those in no hurry or on a strict budget.

BUSES FROM TUCUMÁN

DESTINATION	COST (AR$)	DURATION (HR)
Buenos Aires	438	16
Cafayate	72	6½
Catamarca	80	4
Córdoba	185	7-9
Jujuy	113	5
La Quiaca	207	11
La Rioja	129	6
Mendoza	333	13
Posadas	408	17
Resistencia	247	11
Salta	101	4½
Salvador Mazza	204	10
San Juan	304	12
Santiago del Estero	43	2
Tafí del Valle	30	2½-3

At time of research, trains were leaving Buenos Aires' Retiro station at 9:55am on Monday and Friday for the 25-hour journey. From Tucumán, trains left at 5pm on Wednesday and 7.40pm on Saturday.

The trip costs AR$45/70/130 in *turista* (2nd class)/1st class/Pullman (reclinable seats) or AR$400 for two in a sleeper.

Getting Around

Aeropuerto Benjamín Matienzo is 8km east of downtown. The odd bus heads there from the terminal; a *remise* costs around AR$45 from the town center.

For getting around the city, local buses (AR$2.50) clearly mark their major destinations on the front.

There are several car-rental places. A reliable choice is **Móvil Renta** (☎431-0550; www.movilrenta.com.ar; San Lorenzo 370).

Tafí del Valle

☎03867 / POP 3300 / ELEV 2100M

The lovely hilltown of Tafí is where the folk of Tucumán traditionally head to take refuge from the summer heat. The journey from the city is a spectacular one: the narrow gorge of the Río de los Sosas – with its dense, verdant subtropical forest on all sides – opens onto a misty valley beneath the snowy peaks of the Sierra del Aconquija. The precipitous mountain road merits a window seat on the bus.

Tafí makes a fine spot to hang out for a few days, with crisp mountain air, many budget accommodations and a laid-back scene. There are also a couple of memorable historic ranches to stay at.

Tafí's center is a triangle of three streets. Av Miguel Critto is the main street running east to west. If you turn left out of the bus terminal, you soon join it. Off it, Av Perón is the center of activity, and Belgrano climbs from Perón past the church. Most public services are near the unusual semicircular plaza.

Sights & Activities

Several people around town hire out horses (look for *'alquilo caballos'* or *'cabalgatas'*) for rides in the valley.

Capilla La Banda CHURCH, MUSEUM

(Av José Frías Silva; admission AR$5; ⌚8am-6pm) This 18th-century Jesuit chapel, acquired by the Frías Silva family of Tucumán on the Jesuits' expulsion and then expanded in the 1830s, was restored to its original configuration in the 1970s. Note the escape tunnel under the altar. A small collection of funerary urns, religious art of the Cuzco school, ecclesiastical vestments and period furniture is on display.

The chapel is a short walk from downtown. Cross the river bridge and follow the road; you'll see it on your left after 750m.

Walks Around Tafí HIKING

Several nearby peaks and destinations make hiking in the mountains around Tafí del Valle an attractive prospect; try 3000m **Cerro El Matadero**, a four- to five-hour climb; 3600m **Cerro Pabellón** (six hours); and 4500m **Cerro El Negrito**, reached from the statue of Cristo Redentor on RN 307 to Acheral. The trails are badly marked, and no trail maps are available; you can hire guides: ask at the tourist office. An easier hike climbs **Cerro El Pelao** for views over the town. The path starts on the left as soon as you've crossed the bridge. It takes about 1¼ hours to climb, and less to come down. From the same trailhead you can walk a pleasant 10km to **El Mollar**, following the river and the reservoir, visit the menhir park (see p252) and get the bus back.

Tours

La Cumbre (☎421768; www.lacumbretafidelvalle.com; Perón 120) offers various two- to three-hour trips around the valley on 4WD tracks or taking in sights such as the menhir park near El Mollar and a traditional cheese factory (AR$100 per person). It also organizes more rigorous full-day trips and excursions to the Quilmes ruins.

Sleeping

There are many choices, including several budget places charging around AR$40 per person for simple dorm rooms. Prices rise about 25% in January, Easter and July when Tafí gets packed. Unheated rooms can get distinctly chilly at any time of year.

If you've got transport, there's also a handful of excellent *estancia* hotels along the road to Santa María.

TOP CHOICE **Estancia Los Cuartos** ESTANCIA $$

(☎0381-15-587-4230; www.estancialoscuartos.com; Critto s/n; s/d AR$250/290; 📶) Oozing character from every pore, this lovely spot with grazing llamas lies between the bus terminal and the town center. Two centuries old, it feels like a museum, with venerable books lining antique shelves, and authentic rooms redolent with the smell of aged wood and woolen blankets. There are rooms in a new annex that offer more comfortable beds but less history, although they remain true to the feel of the place. Traditional cheeses are also made here.

Las Tacanas ESTANCIA $$
(☎421821; www.estancialastacanas.com; Perón 372; s/d AR$420/450; @📶) Impeccably preserved and decorated, this fabulous historic complex was once a Jesuit *estancia* and is a most memorable place to stay. The adobe buildings, more than three centuries old, house a variety of tasteful, rustic rooms with noble furniture and beamed ceilings. Though it's in the center of town, it feels like you're in a country retreat, and there's a warm welcome from the family that has owned it for generations.

Hotel Tafí HOTEL $$
(☎421007; www.hoteltafiweb.com.ar; Belgrano 177; s/d AR$280/350; @) Despair not when you see it from the street, for things improve once you get inside, with a ski-lodge feel and helpful staff. The medium-sized rooms have gleaming bathrooms, wood-tile floors, mountain views and tiny TVs. There's a pleasant rocky garden, and the huge fireplace makes the comfortable lounge area the place to be on a chilly night.

Hostería Lunahuana HOTEL $$
(☎421330; www.lunahuana.com.ar; Av Miguel Critto 540; s/d AR$358/466; ❄@📶) This stylish and popular hotel has rooms decorated with flair – some have mezzanines accessed by spiral staircases. The whole place is decked out with interesting and tasteful decorations, and service is professional and friendly.

Hostel la Cumbre HOSTEL $
(☎421768; www.lacumbretafidelvalle.com; Perón 120; dm/d without bathroom AR$55/130) The happy orange and ochre color of the courtyard and views from the roof terrace make this a good choice. The rooms are cramped but clean, and there's a decent kitchen and welcoming staff.

Hospedaje Celia GUESTHOUSE $
(☎421170; Belgrano 443; r per person AR$50) Set back from the road 100m uphill from the church, this place offers bright, white and comfortable rooms with private bathroom. There are inconveniences – no sockets in the rooms, for example – but the price is right.

Los Palenques Hostel HOSTEL $
(☎421677; www.lospalenqueshostel.com.ar; Los Palenques s/n; dm AR$40; @) Friendly and rustic with simple dorms with bathroom surrounding a courtyard with sierra views. From the bus terminal, follow Critto past the tourist office and take the first left; the hostel's about 400m up this road.

Hotel Virgen del Valle HOTEL $$
(☎421016; Los Menhires s/n; virgendelvalle@tafidelvalle.com; d AR$250; @❄📶) Just off the main drag in the heart of town, this features spacious, comfortable rooms around a small courtyard. One of the only midrange options with wi-fi at time of research.

Nomade Hostel HOSTEL $
(☎0381-15-440-0656; www.nomadehostel.com.ar; Los Castaños s/n; dm AR$40; @📶) Relaxed and welcoming place a 10-minute walk from the bus terminal. Turn right, follow the tarmac road, and you'll see it signposted on the right. HI discount.

Camping Los Sauzales CAMPGROUND $
(☎421880; Los Palenques s/n; per person/tent AR$15/20, per car AR$10-20) Run-down but pleasant grassy campsite about 750m west of the plaza. Also has simple cabins and bungalows (AR$80 to AR$140).

DAY TRIPS FROM TUCUMÁN

The fertile, hilly area northwest of Tucumán is known as **Las Yungas**, and offers plenty of appealing day trips that get you out of the hot, busy city. The tourist offices offer good information on destinations, which include the reservoir of **El Cadillal** (Dique Celestino Gelsi) offering camping, swimming and windsurfing, or the **Parque Sierra de San Javier**, a university-operated reserve offering guided walks, including one to the small but pretty Río Noque waterfall. San Pedro (go to ticket booth No 69) runs regular buses from Tucumán's bus terminal to El Cadillal (AR$5.20, one hour), while San Javier (no ticket booth, leaves from platforms 57 to 58) runs to San Javier (where there are a few places to stay) and the reserve. Tucumán tour operators also run trips out here and this is the paragliding area.

Eating & Drinking

Don Pepito PARRILLA $
(www.donpepitodetafi.com.ar; Perón 193; mains AR$32-52) It looks touristy, the level of service varies, and it charges too much for extras, but the meat is truly excellent. Bypass the set *parrilladas* and order off the menu. Kidneys, *bife de chorizo* or *chivito* (goat) are all fine choices and are served in generous portions. There's often live entertainment (small surcharge).

El Rancho de Félix ARGENTINE $
(cnr Belgrano & Juan de Perón; mains AR$29-46;) This big, warm thatched barn of a place is incredibly popular for lunch. Regional specialties such as *locro* and *humitas* feature heavily on the menu, but *parrilla* and pasta are also on offer. It doesn't open evenings if things are quiet.

Kkechuwa BAR
(Perón s/n) Friendly place with an excellent range of artisanal beers and food options ranging from sandwiches to llama dishes.

Information

Several places offer phone calls and internet access.

Banco Tucumán (Av Miguel Critto) In the *municipalidad* building. Has an ATM.

Tourist office (Av Miguel Critto; 8am-9pm) At the junction of the pedestrian street.

Getting There & Away

Tafí's impressive **bus terminal** (Av Miguel Critto) is 400m east of the town center. Empresa Aconquija has six to nine buses a day to Tucumán (AR$30, three hours). Buses head the other way to Santa María (AR$34, two hours, four to six daily) and Cafayate (AR$52 to AR$64, 2½ to four hours) via Amaicha del Valle and the Quilmes ruins turnoff.

The road from Tucumán is beautiful, and the road to Santa María, Quilmes and Cafayate is spectacular, crossing the 3050m pass known as Abra del Infiernillo (Little Hell Pass).

Getting Around

Hourly in summer (every three hours in winter), local Aconquija buses do most of the circuit around Cerro El Pelado, in the middle of the valley. One goes on the north side, another on the south side, so it's possible to make a circuit of the valley by walking the link between them.

Around Tafí del Valle

There are several attractions in the valley around Tafí, including **Parque de los Menhires** (admission AR$3; 9am-7pm), a collection of more than 100 carved standing stones found in the surrounding area. They were produced by the Tafí culture some 2000 years ago, but they have been somehow stripped of dignity by being removed from their original locations. The site lies 12km south of Tafí, off the plaza in the village of El Mollar.

SANTA MARÍA

03838 / POP 10,800 / ELEV 1900M

This lies on the route between Tafí del Valle and Cafayate, and is a handy base for exploring the ruins at Quilmes. It actually sits within Catamarca province and makes a fine stopover.

The attractive plaza is the center of town, and lies nine blocks north of the bus terminal. A remarkably helpful **tourist office** (421083; www.munisantamaria.gov.ar/turismo; 7am-11pm Mon-Fri, 8am-10pm Sat & Sun), with heroic opening hours, is located under the trees in the square itself. On one corner of the plaza, the recommended **Museo Arqueológico Eric Boman** (cnr Belgrano & Sarmiento; 9am-8pm Mon-Fri, 10am-8pm Sat) has a worthwhile collection of ceramics and gold and silver grave jewelry from this important archaeological zone. Ask to see the back room, where a whole lot more elaborately decorated funerary urns are stored. Next door is an **artesanía cooperative**, selling woven goods and other handicrafts at more-than-fair prices.

There are many places to stay in town, including the welcoming **Residencial Pérez** (420257; hotelperez@hotmail.com; San Martín 94; s/d AR$70/100), with spotless rooms set around a viney courtyard behind a cafe near the plaza (no sign).

Eating options on the plaza include **El Colonial del Valle** (420897; cnr Esquiú & San Martín; mains AR$20-40), a traditional *confitería* that serves good coffee and tamales, a set lunch for AR$28 and reasonable fuller meals.

There are several buses daily to Tucumán (AR$60, five hours) via Tafí del Valle (AR$34, 1½ hours) and two daily to Cafayate (AR$30, two hours) via Quilmes. Three buses a week go to Belén (AR$40 to AR$60, five hours). *Remises* from the terminal to the center cost AR$5.

AMAICHA DEL VALLE

☎03892 / POP 3214

On the main road between Tafí del Valle and Cafayate, this dusty settlement has a notable indigenous feel and, indeed, is famous for its **Pachamama festival** in February, which includes music, dancing and a llama sacrifice to bless the harvest. On the main road, the ornate and unusual **Museo de Pachamama** (admission AR$20; ⊙8am-1pm & 2-6pm) is a picturesque if locally controversial collection of indigenous art and artifacts in a sizable indoor-outdoor setting.

Amaicha is useful for getting to the ruins at Quilmes, and has several places to stay, including hostels and campgrounds. Buses between Tafí (AR$28, 1½ hours) and Cafayate (AR$26, 1½ to 2½ hours) stop here.

QUILMES

☎03892

Dating from about AD 1000, **Quilmes** (Argentines/foreigners AR$5/10; ⊙8am-7pm) was a complex indigenous urban settlement that occupied about 30 hectares and housed as many as 5000 people. The inhabitants survived contact with the Inca, which occurred from about AD 1480 onward, but could not outlast the siege of the Spaniards, who in 1667 deported the remaining 2000 to Buenos Aires.

Quilmes' thick walls underscore its defensive purpose, but clearly this was more than just a *pucará*. Dense construction sprawls both north and south from the central nucleus, where the outlines of buildings, in a variety of shapes, are obvious even to the casual observer. For revealing views of the extent of the ruins, climb the trails up either flank of the nucleus. Be prepared for intense sun with no shade, and a large fly population keen on exploring your facial orifices.

In theory, there is a beautiful hotel and *confitería* at the site, as well as a museum. However, at the time of research, the government, local Diaguita community and concession holder were embroiled in a prolonged legal battle, so it was all closed. Friendly folk selling local ceramics sell cold drinks and will look after your bags; there's also a place at the main road junction that will do it, saving you lugging them.

Getting There & Away

Buses from Cafayate to Santa María or Tafí del Valle will drop passengers at the junction, but from there it's a 5km walk or hitchhike to the ruins. Otherwise, get off the bus at Amaicha del Valle, where a *remise* will charge around AR$70 one-way to the ruins, AR$160 return including waiting time. Often a few people are wanting to go, so you can share costs. Tours to Quilmes run from Cafayate and Tafí del Valle.

Santiago del Estero

☎0385 / POP 409,404

Placid Santiago del Estero enjoys the distinction of the title 'Madre de Ciudades' (Mother of Cities) for this, founded in 1553, was the first Spanish urban settlement in what is now Argentina. Sadly, it boasts no architectural heritage from that period, but still makes a pleasant stopover.

Santiagueños (residents of Santiago del Estero) enjoy a nationwide reputation for valuing rest and relaxation over work. Nevertheless, there's plenty of bustle around the town center, particularly in the evenings when life orbits around the pretty plaza and its adjoining pedestrian streets.

Sights

TOP CHOICE Centro Cultural del Bicentenario MUSEUMS, GALLERY

(CCB; www.ccbsantiago.gov.ar; Libertad s/n; admission AR$5; ⊙9am-9pm) This excellent cultural center on the plaza has given Santiago a real boost. It's an airy, modern space housing three museums, all imaginatively displayed; the highlight is the **anthropological collection**, with a stunning array of indigenous ceramics – mostly funerary urns used for secondary burial (remains were put in the pot after decomposition) – as well as jewelry, flutes and a large case filled with ornate loom weights. Fossils of mastodons and glyptodonts, an extinct family of creatures that somewhat resembled large armadillos, also impress.

The sparsely-labeled **historical museum** is attractively set around the patio of Santiago's noblest building and touches on slavery, the strife of the 19th century, and the role of women. The top floor **art gallery** features good temporary exhibitions. All info is in Spanish. There's a downstairs **cafe** that's a popular meeting place.

Parque Aguirre PARK, RIVERSIDE

Named for the city's founder and 10 blocks from Plaza Libertad, this enormous eucalypt- and casuarina-filled area has a small **zoo**, camping areas, a swimming pool and a **costanera** (riverside road). It's a fine place for a wander, with plenty to keep the kids entertained, and has a few *confiterías* and bars that get lively on weekend evenings.

Festivals & Events

Santiago's chaotic **Carnaval**, in February, resembles celebrations in the Quebrada de Humahuaca. During the entire last week of July, *santiagueños* celebrate the founding of the city. The centerpiece of this is the **Marcha de los Bombos**, a boisterous procession into the center of the city by some 2000 locals banging all manner of drums.

Sleeping

Hotel Savoy HOTEL $$
(☎421-1234; www.savoysantiago.com.ar; Tucumán 39; s/d AR$215/300; ❄📶) With a sumptuous entrance and gorgeous curving staircase, this place looks like a palace at first glance. Sadly, there are no four-poster beds or servants fanning you with ostrich feathers, but the smallish rooms are comfortable, with decent showers, and the service is attentive. It's also excellently located.

Hotel Carlos V HOTEL $$
(☎424-0303; www.carlosvhotel.com; Independencia 110; s/d standard AR$350/500, d superior AR$800; ❄@📶🏊) By far the most luxurious option in town, this has a great central location and rooms with business-level facilities, large comfortable beds and carpet that could do with a color change. Some rooms have a balcony to enjoy the city views. Superior rooms are larger with table and chairs. There's a gym and sauna as well as the indoor pool.

Hotel Avenida HOTEL $
(☎421-5887; avenidahotelsgo@yahoo.com.ar; Pedro León Gallo 405; s/d with bathroom AR$100/200, without bathroom AR$50/100; ❄📶) You have to feel for these people: they set up a welcoming little hotel, beautifully decorated with indigenous art and right opposite the bus terminal. Then the city moved the bus terminal to the other side of town. Nevertheless, it's well worth the short walk from the center. No breakfast.

Palace Hotel HOTEL $$
(☎421-2700; www.palacehotelsgo.com; Tucumán 19; s/d AR$200/310; ❄📶) Just off the plaza on a pedestrian mall, this has decent, darkish rooms. If you don't mind street noise, ask for one at the front for a dose of natural light. Discounts negotiable.

Residencial Emaus GUESTHOUSE $
(☎421-5893; Av Moreno Sur 675; s/d AR$90/150; 📶) Light and airy rooms with TV and benevolent management.

Campamento las Casuarinas CAMPGROUND $
(☎421-1390; Parque Aguirre; per person/tent AR$3/5) This cheap municipal campground is normally a pleasant, shady area, less than 1km from Plaza Libertad, but on Friday night a big party scene takes over for the weekend.

Eating & Drinking

Head to Roca between Salta and Libertad for a selection of popular cafes, bars and modish salon restaurants.

Mía Mamma ARGENTINE $$
(24 de Septiembre 15; mains AR$30-60) Set back from the plaza, this is a discreet and reliable restaurant with well-dressed waiters who see to your every need. There's a fine salad bar with plenty of vegetables (AR$28, or AR$18 with a main) and a wide choice of food that includes enormous *parrilla* options as well as a tasty *arroz a la valenciana* (paella).

Jockey Club ARGENTINE $$
(Independencia 68; mains AR$32-55) Strangely empty of pint-sized horse riders, the staid atmosphere of the Jockey Club belongs to another era but belies the quality and welcome variety of its cuisine. Elaborate and tasty creations with a Spanish touch are accompanied by cordially formal service.

Entertainment

El Patio del Indio Froilán TRADITIONAL MUSIC
(www.elindiofroilan.com.ar; Av Libertador Norte s/n, Barrio Boca del Tigre; ⏰Sun) For over 40 years now, local hero Froilán González has been making drums from the trunks of the ceibo tree. They are used by some of the biggest names in Latin music. On Sundays, locals and visitors gather at his workshop to eat empanadas, investigate drum-making and listen and dance to their music. It's a great scene.

La Casa del Folclorista TRADITIONAL MUSIC
(Parque Aguirre, Pozo de Vargas) On the way to the riverfront, this is a big barn of a *peña* that has live folk bands at weekends and cheap food. The music tends to kick off around 11pm.

Information

Several downtown banks have ATMs, and internet places are widespread. There's free wi-fi in the plaza.

Municipal tourist office (☎422-9800; Plaza Libertad s/n; ⏰8am-1pm & 5-8pm Mon-Fri, 9am-1pm & 5-8pm Sat) In a kiosk in the plaza itself.

Provincial tourist office (☎421-3253; www.turismosantiago.gov.ar; Av Libertad 417;

⏲7am-2pm & 3-8pm Mon-Fri, 10am-1pm & 5-8pm Sat & Sun) On the plaza. Displays work by local artists.

Getting There & Away

Aerolíneas Argentinas (☎422-4335; 24 de Septiembre 547) flies daily to Buenos Aires.

Bus

Santiago's shiny **bus terminal** (www.tosde.com.ar; cnr Perú & Chacabuco) is six blocks northwest of Plaza Libertad. For destinations like Salta and Catamarca, you may find quicker connections via Tucumán. There's no convenient local bus into town, but it's only AR$7 in a taxi.

Train

Santiago del Estero (actually, the adjacent twin town of La Banda) is on the Buenos Aires-Tucumán train line, which runs twice weekly. Trains run from La Banda **station** (☎427-3918) to Tucumán (4½ hours) and Buenos Aires' Retiro station (22 hours). See Tucumán for more

Santiago Del Estero

Top Sights

Centro Cultural del Bicentenario B3

Sights

1 Zoo D2

Sleeping

2 Campamento las Casuarinas D1
3 Hotel Carlos V B4
4 Hotel Savoy B3
5 Palace Hotel B3

Eating

6 Jockey Club B3
7 Mía Mamma B4

Entertainment

8 La Casa del Folclorista C2

BUSES FROM SANTIAGO DEL ESTERO

DESTINATION	COST (AR$)	DURATION (HR)
Buenos Aires	333	13
Catamarca	68	4½
Córdoba	138	6
Jujuy	166	7
La Rioja	171	7
Mendoza	390	17
Resistencia	207	8
Salta	155	6
Tucumán	47	2

details of this service. The station is located in the heart of La Banda; bus 17 does a circuit of Santiago's center before heading across the river to there.

Getting Around

Bus 15 (AR$1.75) goes to **Aeropuerto Mal Paso** (SDE; ☎434-3651; Av Madre de Ciudades), 6km northwest of downtown. A taxi from the city center costs AR$15.

CATAMARCA & LA RIOJA

Comparatively little visited by travelers, these provinces are wonderful fun to explore, and are rich in scenery and tradition. Both were home to several important pre-Columbian cultures, mostly maize cultivators who developed unique pottery techniques and styles, and subsequently the region contains many important archaeological sites.

Catamarca

☎0383 / POP 183,253 / ELEV 530M

Vibrant Catamarca has a completely different feel to the other towns of this size within the region.

San Fernando del Valle de Catamarca, to give the city its full name, has a lovely central plaza, Plaza 25 de Mayo, and noble buildings dot the streets. To the west of town, the huge eucalypts of Parque Navarro scent the air and are backed by the spectacular sierra beyond.

Sights

Sights outside of town easily accessible by bus include the grotto where the town's Virgin was found, a reservoir, indigenous ruins, and the picturesque foothills around Villa Las Pirquitas. The tourist office will explain them all and show you where to get the bus.

Museo Arqueológico Adán Quiroga MUSEUM

(Sarmiento 450; admission AR$7.50; ⏲7am-12:30pm & 3-8pm Mon-Fri, 9am-8pm Sat & Sun) This fine archaeological museum displays a superb collection of pre-Columbian ceramics from several different cultures and eras. Some – in particular the black Aguada ceramics with their incised, stylized animal decoration – is of truly remarkable quality. A couple of dehydrated mummies found at 5000m are also present, as well as a spooky shrunken head from the Amazon, and trays used to snort lines of *rape* (finely ground tobacco). There's also a colonial and religious section.

Catedral Basílica de Nuestra Señora del Valle CATHEDRAL

(Pl 25 de Mayo; ⏲6am-10pm) Dating from 1859, Catamarca's cathedral shelters the Virgen del Valle, who is the patron of Catamarca and one of northern Argentina's most venerated images since the 17th century. It overlooks Plaza 25 de Mayo, a truly beautiful square filled with robust jacaranda, araucaria, citrus and palm trees.

Festivals & Events

The **Fiesta de Nuestra Señora del Valle** takes place for two weeks after Easter. In an impressive manifestation of popular religion hordes of pilgrims come from the interior and from other Andean provinces to honor the Virgen del Valle. On her saint's day, December 8, she is similarly feted.

Sleeping

Most hotels offer discounted rates from those we list here, more so if you pay cash.

TOP CHOICE **Hotel Casino Catamarca** HOTEL $$

(☎443-2928; www.hotelcasinocatamarca.com; Esquiú 151; standard/superior r AR$450/550; ❄@🛜🏊) They've got space to spare at this peaceful but central hotel, which features handsome modern design and bags of facilities. The rooms are more than ample in size, with white sheets contrasting with wooden floors. Some have balconies; superiors add minibar, king-size beds and hydromassage tubs. There's a restaurant, decent gym, a small spa complex, and a cracking long pool and lawn area. And a casino, of course.

Residencial Tucumán GUESTHOUSE $
(☎442-2209; Tucumán 1040; s/d AR$120/180; ❄📶) This well-run, immaculately presented *residencial* has comfortable, spotless rooms, is excellent value and is about a one-minute walk from the bus terminal. For this reason you might want to book ahead.

Hotel Colonial HOTEL $
(☎442-3502; Av República 802; s/d AR$150/240; ❄📶) Cutely decorated in highland colonial style, with dimpled 'adobe' walls and cactus, this down-to-earth place represents value. The rooms are fairly ordinary, but there's space and everything works. Try to get one facing the rear for a bit more peace and quiet.

Hotel Pucará HOTEL $$
(☎443-0698; hotelpucara@hotmail.com; Caseros 501; s/d AR$180/255; ❄@📶) Style gurus need not apply. This peaceful hotel on the west side of town stands out for its gloriously kitschy faux-Chinese knickknacks and ruffled bedspreads. The china dog on the stairs appeals and appalls in equal measure, but the place is comfortable and well run.

Hotel Ancasti HOTEL $$
(☎443-5951; www.hotelancasti.com.ar; Sarmiento 520; s/d AR$360/454; ❄@📶) As ever, the handsome indigenous-art-inspired lobby of this upmarket central hotel is better than the rooms, which have been done up on the cheap but are comfortable enough. Bathrooms vary: some are tiny. There's cheerful service, mountain views from higher rooms, gym, sauna, and access to a nearby pool.

Residencial Avenida GUESTHOUSE $
(☎442-2139; Av Güemes 754; s without bathroom AR$60, d with/without bathroom AR$140/110) With plenty of rooms arranged around a central courtyard, the Avenida, meters from the bus terminal, is a fine place to rest your legs and your pesos. Most of the rooms are excellent value, although some are a little rickety.

San Pedro Hostel HOSTEL $
(☎445-4708; www.hostelsanpedro.com.ar; Sarmiento 341; dm AR$50; @📶🏊) This relaxed hostel feels like it's in gentle decline, but it's decent, with a big back garden that includes cactuses, a *parrilla* and a tiny pool. Dorms are OK (they pack plenty of bunks in) and they run another hostel around the corner.

Eating

There are eateries to the north of the plaza. Burger and *lomito* (steak sandwich) joints are on Güemes west of the bus terminal.

Salsa Criolla PARRILLA $$
(Av República 546; all-you-can-eat AR$79) On the plaza, this is a high-class all-you-can-eat *parrillada*. It doesn't try to stuff you with chorizo first like in some places – rather, it insists on tempting you with high-quality cuts long after you've insisted you don't want any more. There are à la carte options.

Los Hornitos BAKERY $
(Av Virgen del Valle 924; dozen empanadas AR$25; ⏲10am-10pm) The province's most legendary spot for empanadas – meat, cheese or chicken – this hole-in-the-wall cooks them on the street in two wood-fired clay ovens.

El Rincón de Lucho PARRILLA $$
(Av Presidente Castillo 65; dishes AR$17-44) This popular *parrilla* east of the center gets lively on weekend evenings when there's a live *folklore* show. Follow República eastwards then Av Puente Castillo curves northwards from it.

Drinking & Entertainment

There are a couple of weekend *boliches* along República west of the plaza, but the real pub action is in a zone north of the center on and around Av Gobernador Galindez.

Caravati CAFE
(Sarmiento 683; ⏲10am-midnight) The most inviting of the plaza's terraces, this is named after the Italian architect who designed much of central Catamarca, including the cathedral that stands alongside.

WORTH A TRIP

TERMAS DE RÍO HONDO

Halfway between Santiago del Estero and Tucumán, and served by regular buses between the two, this place is famous nationwide as a winter destination for its thermal water, and its nearly 200 hotels all have hot mineral baths. If you fancy a spa treatment, it's a good stop, though there's little else of interest beyond its famous chocolates and *alfajores* (filled sandwich cookies). You can get some great deals here with online hotel brokers, especially in the November to April off-season, when much of town shuts down.

Shopping

Catamarca is enthusiastic in promoting its fine natural products; the region is well known for wines, olive oil, walnuts, and various jams and conserves. There are several shops stocking these along Sarmiento and Rivadavia near the plaza.

Mercado Artesanal y Fábrica de Alfombras HANDICRAFTS
(Av Virgen del Valle 945; ⏲7am-1pm & 2-8pm Mon-Fri, 8am-8pm Sat, 8am-2pm Sun) For Catamarca's characteristic hand-tied rugs, visit this artisans' market. The market also sells ponchos, blankets, jewelry, red onyx sculptures, musical instruments and basketry.

Information

Banks with ATMs are around the plaza. There are numerous internet and phone places around the central streets.

Tourist office (☎443-7413; www.turismocatamarca.gov.ar; Sarmiento 683; ⏲8am-1pm, 5-9pm Mon-Fri, 8am-9:30pm Sat & Sun) Helpful place on the plaza. There's a desk in the bus terminal as well.

Getting There & Around

Air

Aerolíneas Argentinas (☎442-4460; Sarmiento 589) has three weekly flights to Buenos Aires and to La Rioja. A **minibus** (☎0383-15-468-5208; AR$35) runs from outside the Hotel Arenales on Sarmiento to **Aeropuerto Felipe Varela** (☎443-0080), some 22km east of town on RP33, to coincide with flights.

Bus

Catamarca's spruce **bus terminal** (☎442-3415; Av Güemes 850) includes a shopping complex and cinema. There are services around the province and across the country, including to Tucumán (AR$80, four hours), La Rioja (AR$51, two hours) and Buenos Aires (AR$378, 15 hours).

Catamarca

Top Sights

Belén

03835 / POP 27,829 / ELEV 1250M

Slow-paced Belén feels like, and is, a long way from anywhere, and will appeal to travelers who like things small-scale and friendly. It's one of the best places to buy woven goods, particularly ponchos. There are many *teleras* (textile workshops) around town, turning out their wares made from llama, sheep and alpaca wool. The nearby ruins of El Shincal are another reason to visit.

Sights

Museo Cóndor Huasi MUSEUM
(cnr Belgrano & San Martín; admission AR$2; 7am-1pm & 4-8pm Mon-Fri, 8am-1pm Sat) Upstairs at the end of a shopping arcade at a corner of the plaza, this museum has a good archaeological collection, including bronze axes, gold-leaf jewelry and an info panel (in Spanish) on hallucinogen use among the Diaguita people.

Sleeping & Eating

TOP CHOICE **Hotel Belén** HOTEL $$
(461501; www.belencat.com.ar; cnr Belgrano & Cubas; s/d AR$190/265;) A surprising presence in town, this stylish hotel has grotto-like rooms featuring exposed rock, inlaid-tile mosaics on the floors and wall, indigenous art and very comfortable beds. If you can ignore a few creaks and quirks – sound travels way too easily between bathrooms and not everything works all the time – it's a great place to stay at a good price.

Freddy Hostal GUESTHOUSE $
(461230; www.amarillasinternet.com/fredyhostal; Av Calchaquí 461; s/d AR$60/100;) One of a handful of cheap places on the main road through town, this is hospitable and features appealing rustic rooms around a patio with cactus garden. Air-con is 20 pesos extra.

1900 ARGENTINE $
(461100; Belgrano 391; mains AR$30-40) Beyond-the-call service is the key to this highly enjoyable restaurant a block down from the plaza. It's very popular, but it hates to turn people away, so a Tetris-like reshuffling of tables is a constant feature, bless 'em. Prices are more than fair, and there are a number of large platters designed to be shared. Well-mixed salads and juicy brochettes are highlights.

Shopping

There's a marquee off the plaza with a number of *artesanía* stalls selling ponchos, camelid-wool clothing and foot-trodden local wine. For more upmarket woven goods, **Cuna del Poncho** (461091; Roca 144) has reasonable prices, accepts major credit cards and arranges shipping.

Information

There's a bank at the corner of General Paz and Lavalle, near the tourist office.

Tourist office (461304; www.turismodebelen.com.ar; General Paz 180; 7am-1pm & 2-10pm Mon-Fri, 8am-10pm Sat, 9am-10pm Sun) Helpful. Also has a small mineral exhibition.

Getting There & Away

Belén's **bus terminal** (cnr Sarmiento & Rivadavia) is one block south and one block west of the plaza. Catamarca (AR$57, four to five hours) is the only long-distance destination served daily at a reasonable hour (1pm). There are night services to La Rioja and Córdoba, and several weekly buses to Santa María (AR$40 to AR$60, five hours) – a rickety service full of local character, and a spectacular journey.

The tourist office has better bus information than the terminal itself.

Around Belén

LONDRES & EL SHINCAL

Only 15km southwest of Belén, sleepy Londres (population 2134) is the province's oldest Spanish settlement. It dates from 1558, though it moved several times before returning here in 1612, and the inhabitants fled again during the Diaguita uprising of 1632. Its name (London) celebrated the marriage of the prince of Spain (and later King Philip II) to Mary Tudor, queen of England, in 1555.

Seven kilometers west are the Inca ruins of **El Shincal** (admission AR$5; ⌚8am-sunset). Founded in 1470, the town occupied a commanding position in the foothills of the mountains, surveying the vast valley to the south. The setting is spectacular, with fantastic views and great atmosphere. The site was pretty thoroughly ruined when excavations began in 1991, but the *ushno* (ceremonial platform) and *kallanka* (possibly a barracks) have been restored, and you can climb two hillocks on either side of the central square. Aligned to the rising and setting sun, they probably served as both lookouts and altars. Entrance usually includes a tour by one of the welcoming family that lives here and looks after the site.

There are five buses Monday to Saturday from Belén to Londres (AR$3), that continue to a spot a short walk from the ruins. A *remise* from Belén with waiting time is around AR$100. There's a campground between Londres and the ruins, and a cabin complex. Londres also has a couple of basic *residenciales*.

Beyond Londres, you can head on south to Chilecito, 200km away in La Rioja province along RN 40, if you have transportation. The drive is a spectacular one, with the imposing Sierra Famatina to the west and Sierra de Velasco to the east. The road is excellent.

La Rioja

☎0380 / POP 180,995 / ELEV 500M

Encircled by the graceful peaks of the Sierra de Velasco, La Rioja is quite a sight on a sunny day. And there are plenty of sunny days: summer temperatures rise sky-high in this quiet, out-of-the-way provincial capital. Even if you're on a short highlights tour, you might consider stopping off here – it's halfway between Mendoza and Salta – to take a tour to the Talampaya and Ischigualasto national parks.

Sights

Museo Folklórico MUSEUM

(Pelagio Luna 811; admission by donation; ⌚9am-1pm & 5-9pm Tue-Fri) The hugely worthwhile Museo Folklórico is set in a wonderful early-17th-century adobe building, and has fine displays on various aspects of the region's culture. Themes include *chaya* (local La Rioja music) and the Tinkunaco festival, weaving (with bright traditional wallhangings colored with plant extracts) and winemaking. The informative guided tour is excellent if your Spanish is up to it.

Landmark Buildings CHURCHES

La Rioja is a major devotional center, so most landmarks are ecclesiastical. Built in 1623 by the Diaguita under the direction of Dominican friars, the picturesque whitewashed **Convento de Santo Domingo** (cnr Pelagio Luna & Lamadrid; ⌚9:30am-12:30pm & 6-8pm Mon-Fri) is Argentina's oldest monastery. The date appears in the carved algarrobo doorframe, also the work of Diaguita artists.

The curious neo-Gothic **Convento de San Francisco** (cnr 25 de Mayo & Bazán y Bustos; ⌚7pm-9pm) houses the image of the Niño Alcalde, a Christ-child icon symbolically recognized as the city's mayor (see the boxed text p261).

The enormous and spectacular neo-Byzantine 1899 **catedral** (cnr Av San Nicolás de Bari & 25 de Mayo) contains the image of patron saint Nicolás de Bari.

Activities & Tours

Several operators run excursions around the province, including visits to the Parque Nacional Talampaya, which invariably includes the nearby Parque Provincial Ischigualasto ('Valle de la Luna') in San Juan province. These companies also offer excursions to high, remote parts of the Andes in the west of the province (see boxed text, p265, for more information on these destinations).

The La Rioja area has high drop-offs and thermals that make it a great zone for hang-gliding and paragliding; world records for long flights have been set here.

Corona del Inca TOUR

(☎442-2142; www.coronadelinca.com.ar; Pelagio Luna 914) Offers various excursions to highlights around the province.

EL TINKUNACO – CONFLICT RESOLUTION IN THE 16TH CENTURY

The fascinating and moving El Tinkunaco ceremony is a symbolic representation of the resolution of the clash of cultures that occurred at the birth of La Rioja. When Juan Ramírez de Velasco founded the city in 1591, he blithely ignored the fact that the land was owned and farmed by the Diaguita, who naturally took exception to their territory being carved up among Spanish settlers. They rebelled in 1593, and a bloody conflict was averted by the mediation of the friar Francisco Solano, later canonized for his efforts. The Diaguita trusted the cleric and listened to his message. They agreed to down their arms on two conditions: that the Spanish *alcalde* (mayor) resign; and that his replacement be the Christ child. The Spaniards agreed and peace was made. The new mayor became known as Niño Jesús Alcalde.

The Tinkunaco (the word means 'meeting' in Quechua) commemoration commenced not long afterwards. Every year at noon on December 31, two processions – one representing the Spaniards, one the Diaguita – cross town and meet at the Casa de Gobierno. The 'Spaniards' are dressed as religious penitents and *alféreces* (lieutenants) with uniform and flag. The 'Diaguita,' or *aillis*, wear headbands with mirrors and ponchos. The processions meet, and solemnly all fall to their knees before the image of the Niño Jesús Alcalde, then embrace. It's a powerful moment with its message about cultural differences and compromises.

Terra Riojana TOURS
(☎442-0423; www.terrariojana.com.ar) Does tours around the province.

Hugo Ávila HANG-GLIDING, PARAGLIDING
(☎445-1635, 0380-15-468-6949; www.vuelosaguilablanca.com.ar; Av Ramírez de Velasco, Km 7) Offers instruction and tandem flights.

Festivals & Events

La Chaya, the local variant of Carnaval, attracts people from throughout the country. Its name, derived from a Quechua word meaning 'to get someone wet,' should give you an idea of what to expect. The particular style of local music associated with the festival is also called chaya.

Taking place at noon December 31, the religious ritual of **El Tinkunaco** is one of Argentina's most interesting ceremonies (see the boxed text, above).

Sleeping

La Rioja's hotels often offer discounts if you pay cash and aren't afraid to bargain.

Naindo Park Hotel HOTEL $$$
(☎447-0700; www.naindoparkhotel.com; Av San Nicolás de Bari 475; s/d AR$620/714; ❄@☜≋) Just off the plaza, and dominating it assertively, La Rioja's finest hotel has an excellent level of service and comfort and prices to match. The rooms are good-sized, with original art on the walls and decent views.

Plaza Hotel HOTEL $$
(☎442-5215; www.plazahotel-larioja.com.ar; Av San Nicolás de Bari 502; s/d standard AR$345/396, s/d superior AR$422/450; ❄@☜≋) Right on the plaza, this hotel looks a great deal better from inside than out. Rooms overlooking the square are much nicer than those looking onto internal light wells. Superior rooms are also available; they have a newer feel and king-sized beds.

Gran Hotel Embajador HOTEL $
(☎443-8580; www.granhotelembajador.com.ar; San Martín 250; s/d AR$150/200; ❄☜) This cheery place is very tidy; the rooms upstairs are larger and sunnier – a good thing if dark-red color schemes oppress you – and some have balconies. It offers plenty of value, and is popular as a result; reservations are advised.

Hotel Talampaya HOTEL $$
(☎442-2005; www.hoteltalampaya.com.ar; Av JD Perón 1290; s/d AR$220/400; ❄@☜≋) A conversion from what was formerly a government hotel, this rather oversized, lugubrious building has rooms that are good at this price (especially the singles), and have excellent bathrooms and noisy balconies.

Residencial Anita GUESTHOUSE $
(☎442-4836; Coronel Lagos 476; s/d AR$80/95; ❄) Offering excellent value, the quiet and proper Anita is a few blocks away from the center in a residential district. Rooms are very clean, with spotless bathrooms, and

La Rioja

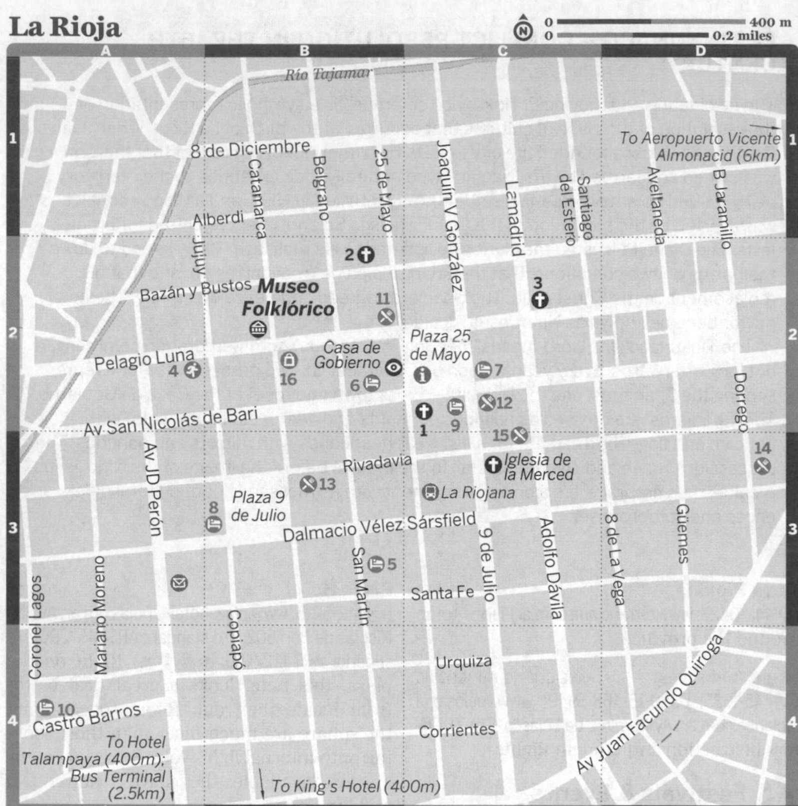

the plant- and saint-filled patio and plump pet dog are bonuses. It's not the sort of place that will appreciate you rolling in drunk at 4am.

Pensión 9 de Julio GUESTHOUSE $
(☎442-6955; cnr Copiapó & Dalmacio Vélez Sársfield; s/d AR$120/140; ❄@📶) Definitely a good deal, this place has clean and pleasant rooms in a central part of town. A shady, vine-covered patio overlooking the plaza of the same name is another bonus. The drawback is substantial traffic noise from exterior rooms.

King's Hotel HOTEL $$
(☎442-2122; www.k-hotellarioja.com.ar; Av Juan Facundo Quiroga 107; s/d AR$240/420; ❄@📶🏊) Though the King's has a few gray hairs appearing, it still has atmosphere. The rooms have space and are comfortable enough, but the big pluses are the service, buffet breakfast and the pool, sundeck and gym.

Hostel Apacheta HOSTEL $
(☎0380-15-444-5445; www.apachetahostel.com.ar; San Nicolás de Bari 669; dm AR$65; 📶) Wood has been put to imaginative uses in this central hostel. Furniture made from pallets and packing crates combines with antiques to make a pleasantly original design. It's a simple place; dorms feature a variety of beds and bunks, with plenty of room to move. You can rent bikes here.

Eating

Regional dishes to look for include *locro*, juicy empanadas, *chivito asado* (barbecued goat), *humitas*, *quesillo* (a cheese specialty) and olives. Cheap local wines are a good bargain in restaurants.

TOP CHOICE **La Vieja Casona** ARGENTINE $$
(☎442-5996; Rivadavia 457; mains AR$33-65) Cheerfully lit and decorated, this is a cracking place with a great range of regional spe-

La Rioja

Top Sights

Museo Folklórico....B2

Sights

1 Catedral....C2
2 Convento de San Francisco....B2
3 Convento de Santo Domingo....C2

Activities, Courses & Tours

4 Corona del Inca....A2

Sleeping

5 Gran Hotel Embajador....B3
6 Hostel Apacheta....B2
7 Naindo Park Hotel....C2
8 Pensión 9 de Julio....B3
9 Plaza Hotel....C2
10 Residencial Anita....A4

Eating

11 Café del Paseo....B2
12 El Marqués....C2
13 La Aldea de la Virgen de Luján....B3
14 La Stanza....D3
15 La Vieja Casona....C3

Shopping

16 Mercado Artesanal de La Rioja....B2

cialties, creative house choices and a menu of standard Argentine dishes – the *parrillada* here is of excellent standard. There's a fair selection of La Rioja wines, too, and wonderful smells from the busy kitchen.

La Stanza ITALIAN $$
(☎443-0809; Dorrego 1641; mains AR$32-62; ⏰Tue-Sun) One of the best places in town, this stylish restaurant serves imaginative pasta dishes that are a cut above most places, as well as other Italian favorites such as saltimbocca. The attractive interior is supplemented by an enticing courtyard terrace.

Café del Paseo CAFE $
(cnr Pelagio Luna & 25 de Mayo; light meals AR$15-33) This is your spot on the corner of the plaza to observe La Rioja life. Executives with Blackberries mingle with families and tables of older men chewing the fat over another slow-paced La Rioja day.

El Marqués ARGENTINE $
(Av San Nicolás de Bari 484; dishes AR$21-38; ⏰8am-midnight Mon-Sat) No surprises are on the menu here at this simple but effective local eatery. Pasta, pizza, omelets and grilled meats are well prepared and fairly priced. The fruit *licuados* are delicious.

La Aldea de la Virgen de Luján ARGENTINE $
(Rivadavia 756; lunches AR$25-30; ⏰7am-3pm & 7-11pm Mon-Sat, 10am-3pm Sun) Though serving good-value breakfasts and a fairly predictable range of dinner options, lunchtime is the place to be at this spot, when it offers daily regional specialties at a fair price.

Shopping

La Rioja is famous for both weavings and silverwork that combine indigenous techniques and skill with Spanish designs and color combinations. La Rioja crafts are exhibited and sold at the excellent **Mercado Artesanal de La Rioja** (Pelagio Luna 792; ⏰8am-noon & 4-8pm Tue-Fri, 9am-noon Sat & Sun).

Fittingly for a place named after Spain's most famous wine region, La Rioja wine has a national reputation.

Information

Tourist office (Plaza 25 de Mayo; ⏰8am-9:30pm) In a kiosk on the plaza itself. The provincial tourist office next to the bus terminal is more helpful.

Getting There & Away

Air

Aerolíneas Argentinas (☎442-6307; Belgrano 63) flies three times weekly to and from Buenos Aires.

Bus

La Rioja's **bus terminal** (Barrio Evita s/n) is an interesting building, picturesquely backed by

BUSES FROM LA RIOJA

DESTINATION	COST (AR$)	DURATION (HR)
Belén	57	5
Buenos Aires	380	17
Catamarca	51	2
Chilecito	30	3
Córdoba	147	6
Mendoza	230	8
Salta	250	10
San Juan	130	6
Santiago del Estero	171	7
Tucumán	129	6

the sierra. It's a long walk south from the center of town.

For Chilecito, **La Riojana** (☎443-5279; Buenos Aires 154) minibuses run three to four times a day. The trip costs AR$40 and takes 2½ hours, a little quicker than the bus.

Getting Around

Aeropuerto Vicente Almonacid (☎442-7239) is 7km east of town on RP 5. An airport taxi costs around AR$40. A taxi from the bus terminal to the city center costs about AR$15.

Chilecito

☎03825 / POP 49,432 / ELEV 1080M

With a gorgeous situation among low rocky hills and sizable snowcapped peaks, Chilecito, a stop on spectacular Ruta 40, has several interesting things to see, including an amazing abandoned cableway leading to a mine high in the sierra. With the intense heat, mining heritage and slopes around town dotted with cardón cactus, Chilecito has a Wild West feel and is definitely the most appealing place to spend a few quiet days in this part of the country. It's also a base for worthwhile excursions into the sierra.

Sights

Museo del Cablecarril MUSEUM

(suggested donation AR$5; ⌚8:30am-12:30pm & 2-6:30pm Mon-Fri, 8:30am-7pm Sat & Sun) This fascinating old cablecar station documents an extraordinary engineering project that gave birth to the town of Chilecito at the beginning of the 20th century. To enable the mining of gold, silver and copper from the Sierra de Famatina, a cablecar was constructed running from here, at the end of the railway line, to La Mejicana, at an altitude of 4603m, more than 3.5km above Chilecito and nearly 40km away. With nine stations, a tunnel and 262 towers, the project was completed in 1904. Men and supplies were carried to the mine, operated by a British firm, in four hours. WWI put an end to it and the line started to decay, although local miners continued using it until the 1930s.

The picturesque museum preserves photos, tools and documents from the cablecar and mine, as well as communications equipment, including an early cell phone. There's a detailed guided tour in Spanish, and you'll then be taken to the cablecar terminus itself – a rickety spiral staircase climbs to the platform, where ore carts now wait silently in line. It's worth going in the late afternoon, when the sun bathes the rusted metal and snowy sierras.

The museum is on the main road at the southern entrance to town, a block south of the bus terminal.

Museo Molino de San Francisco MUSEUM

(J Ocampo 63; admission AR$5; ⌚8am-noon & 2-7pm Mon-Fri, 8:30am-12:30pm & 2:30-7:30pm Sat & Sun) Chilecito founder Don Domingo de Castro y Bazán owned this colonial flour mill, which houses an eclectic assemblage of archaeological tools, antique arms, early colonial documents, minerals, traditional wood and leather crafts, banknotes, woodcuts, early cellphones and paintings. It's four blocks west of the plaza.

Samay Huasi MUSEUM

(admission AR$5; ⌚9am-7pm) Joaquín V González, writer and founder of the prestigious La Plata university in Buenos Aires, used this verdant ranch 2km from Chilecito as his country retreat. González' bedroom is preserved, as well as scrapbook material from his life. More interesting is a collection of paintings, mostly of the area. Below is a somewhat depressing natural sciences, archaeology and mineralogy collection.

To get there, head out from town past the Chirau-Mita cactus garden and follow the main road as it bends around to the right. Keep going and you'll see the *finca* on your right.

FREE **La Riojana** WINERY

(☎423150; www.lariojana.com.ar; La Plata 646; ⌚tours on the hour from noon-5pm Mon-Fri, 10am-noon Sat) La Riojana cooperative is the area's main wine producer, and a sizable concern. A good free tour (call or drop in to arrange a time; English is spoken) shows you through the bodega – think large cement fermentation tanks rather than rows of musty barrels – and culminates in a generous tasting. It's a block north and five west of the plaza.

Chirau-Mita GARDEN

This impressive cactus garden and handsome museum has irregular opening times, but it's worth dropping by just in case. In theory, it is open 9am to noon Monday to Friday, and costs AR$30 for the guided visit. Walk two blocks downhill from the plaza along El Maestro, then turn left; the garden is on your left just after crossing a stream.

Sleeping

A new five-star hotel and casino, Hotel Famatina, unsurprisingly owned by the local governor, was being built at 19 de Febrero 351 at time of research.

Hotel Chilecito HOTEL $
(Hotel ACA; ☎422201; www.aca.org.ar; T Gordillo 101; s/d AR$140/185, superior s/d AR$180/260;) With a quiet location near where the town ends among rocky hills, this ACA establishment offers fine value for money. There's space to burn here, with a garden and cavernous recreation room (pool table). The rooms are light, bright and pleasant, with tiled floors and gleaming bathrooms. There's also a decent restaurant.

Hotel Ruta 40 HOTEL $
(☎422804; www.hotelruta40.com.ar; Libertad 68; s/d with bathroom AR$100/160, without bathroom AR$70/100;) An excellent deal a couple of blocks from the plaza, this comfortable spot offers a variety of rooms with decent beds and clean, spacious bathrooms. Look at a few – some look over a vine-covered patio to the hills beyond.

Hostal Mary Pérez GUESTHOUSE $
(☎423156; hostal_mp@hotmail.com; Florencio Dávila 280; s/d AR$130/150;) A neat little *residencial* in the northeast of town that is more like a family-run hotel. The place is spotless – you may get high on the smell of cleaning products – and rooms come with TV and phone. They also offer apartments (2/4 people AR$170/250).

Hostel Paimán HOSTEL $
(☎429135; www.hotelruta40.com.ar; El Maestro 188; dm/s/d AR$50/80/140, s/d with bathroom AR$150/200;) With simple rooms opening onto a quiet courtyard, this is a friendly, relaxing place without frills. There's a kitchen and laundry; prices include very basic breakfast. You can also pitch a tent for AR$30 per person. Head down El Maestro from the plaza a couple of blocks.

Eating & Drinking

El Rancho de Ferrito ARGENTINE $
(Av Pelagio Luna 647; mains AR$24-48; Tue-Sun) A block west and seven north of the plaza, this inviting local restaurant is worth every step. You've seen the menu before – except for house specialties such as *cazuela de gallinu* (chicken stew: yum), and local wines – but the quality, price and atmosphere make it truly excellent.

La Posta ARGENTINE $$
(☎425988; cnr 19 de Febrero & Roque Lanús; mains AR$32-85; lunch & dinner) Warmly decorated and stylish, with shelves of deli products on sale, the cuisine and service here doesn't live up to the ambience or the prices but can provide a satisfying dinner nonetheless. Kid (*cabrito*) is a specialty here – try it stewed in torrontés wine. Follow 19 de Febrero four blocks north from the plaza.

Yops CAFE
(AE Dávila 70; 8am-2pm & 5pm-late Mon-Sat) Atmospheric and darkish, this bohemian spot

TRIPS AROUND CHILECITO

The western portion of La Rioja province is fascinating, with plenty of intriguing destinations in the sierras. Chilecito is a launch pad for a range of excellent excursions. Parque Nacional Talampaya is one appealing trip, which also takes in the Ischigualasto provincial park (p335) and crosses the picturesque Miranda pass. Northbound jaunts up RN 40 take in the ruins of El Shincal (p260) or the remote hot springs at Fiambalá, while for some serious 4WD mountain action, head up to the abandoned mine at La Mejicana (4603m), an ascent that takes in some amazing scenery and a broad palette of colors, including a striking yellow river. Deeper into the sierras by the Chilean border is sizable Laguna Brava, a flamingo-filled lake surrounded by awesomely bleak and beautiful Andean scenery. Higher still, at 5600m, is the sapphire-blue crater lake of Corona del Inca, only accessible in summer.

Operators in town such as **Salir del Cráter** (☎423854; www.salirdelcrater.com.ar), **Inka Ñan** (☎422418; www.inkanan.com.ar; 25 de Mayo 87), **Aventura Chilecito** (☎422989; www.hotelruta40.com.ar; Castro y Bazán 15) and **Cuesta Vieja** (☎424874; www.cuestavieja.com; Joaquín V González 467) run these trips, which cost around AR$250 to AR$550 per person depending on numbers. There's usually a minimum of two people, but it's always worth asking.

is comfortably Chilecito's best cafe, serving fine coffee and decent mixed drinks. Watch the locals' epic chess battles.

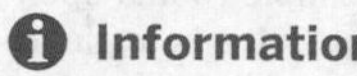

Information

The plaza has banks with ATMs and Internet/telephone places.

Tourist office (☎422688; info@emutur.com.ar; Castro y Bazán 52; ⏲8:30am-10pm) Enthusiastic staff and good material. Half a block off the plaza.

Getting There & Away

The bus terminal is 1.5km south of the center. There are regular services to La Rioja (AR$30, three hours), and beyond to Rosario, Buenos Aires and other cities. **La Riojana** (☎424710; Maestro 61) minibuses also do the La Rioja run for AR$10 more and in half an hour less. There are no buses north to Belén; to avoid the lengthy backtrack through La Rioja and Catamarca you could take a tour to Shinkal and stay in Belén.

Parque Nacional Talampaya

☎03825 / ELEV 1300M

The spectacular rock formations and canyons of this dusty desert national park are evidence of the erosive action of water that these days is hard to believe existed here. The sandstone cliffs are amazing, as are the distant surrounding mountainscapes. Talampaya is adjacent to fossil-rich Parque Provincial Ischigualasto in San Juan province (p335) and it's easy to combine the two if you have transport or visit with a tour.

Sights & Activities

The focus of most visits is the spectacular **Cañón de Talampaya**, a usually dry watercourse bounded by sheer sandstone cliffs. Condors soar on the thermals, and guanacos, rheas and maras can be seen in the shade of the several varieties of algarrobo tree along the sandy canyon floor.

A series of enigmatic **petroglyphs** carved into oxidized sandstone slabs are the first stop on the standard 2½-hour visit (AR$85), followed by, in the canyon itself, such highlights as the **Chimenea del Eco**, whose impressive echo effect is a guaranteed hit, the **Catedral** formation and the clerical figure of **El Monje**.

Longer 4½-hour excursions (AR$130) take in more remote sights. Trips are in comfortable minibuses and there's little walking involved; nevertheless, take water and protection from the fierce sun.

A newly-inaugurated 'Triassic' path takes you past life-size replicas of dinosaurs whose fossilized remains have been found in the Talampaya area.

Guided walks (AR$60 to AR$110) and trips on bicycles are also available; these can be more appealing if the heat's not too intense.

Sleeping & Eating

There are no accommodations in the park itself, but there's shadeless camping at the visitor center (AR$10 per person), which has decent toilets and showers. There's also a cafe here serving meals and cold drinks.

There are simple accommodations in Pagancillo, 29km north. A further 29km up the road, larger Villa Unión has several cabin and hotel options, some of them quite stylish.

Information

The park's **visitor center** (☎470356; www.talampaya.gov.ar; ⏲8am-6pm mid-Sep-Apr, 8:30am-5:30pm May-mid-Sep) is just off the RP 26; private vehicles are not allowed further into the park. Here you pay the AR$40 admission (AR$20 for Argentine citizens, free for under-16s), and arrange guided visits to the park.

Getting There & Away

Buses from La Rioja to Pagancillo and Villa Unión will leave you at the park entrance (AR$34, 3½ hours), from where it's only a 500m walk to the visitor center. The earliest bus leaves La Rioja at 7am, giving you plenty of time to make a day trip of it. There's a daily bus between Villa Unión, 58km up the road, and Chilecito (AR$40, three hours) over the spectacular Miranda pass. It leaves Villa Unión at 3pm; you can make it if you cadge a lift off someone in your tour group.

Córdoba & the Central Sierras

Includes »

Best Places to Eat

» La Nieta 'e La Pancha (p275)
» La Bordolesa (p284)
» Kasbah (p285)
» Morena (p290)
» El Paseo (p291)
» Tono (p293)

Best Places to Stay

» Hotel Azur (p274)
» Hostel La Cumbre (p285)
» Hospedaje Casa Rosita (p291)
» Estancia La Estanzuela (p298)

Why Go?

Argentina's second city is bursting with life. Home to not one but seven major universities, Córdoba has a young population that ensures an excellent nightlife and a healthy cultural scene. Córdoba also boasts a fascinating history, owing its architectural and cultural heritage to the Jesuits, who set up shop here when they first arrived in Argentina.

The rolling hill country out of town is dotted with places that could grab your attention for a day or a month, including five Jesuit missions that make for an easy day trip from the capital.

Adventure buffs also head to hills where the paragliding is excellent, or a couple of national parks offer excellent trekking opportunities.

Further to the southwest, the Valle de Conlara and Sierras Puntanas offer a real chance to get away from the crowds and into the heart of the countryside.

When to Go

Córdoba

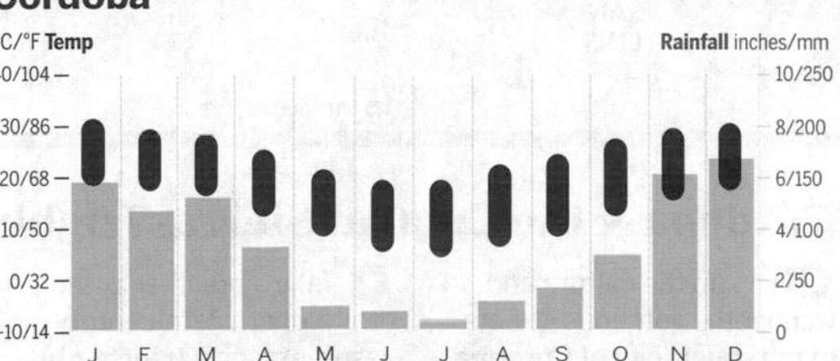

Nov–Feb During the day, cool off riverside in the Sierras. At night, hit Córdoba's sidewalk bars.

Jul–Sep Chances of snow at higher altitudes. Low rainfall makes for good trekking weather.

Rest of year Clear, cool days with occasional rain make these months ideal for outdoor activities.

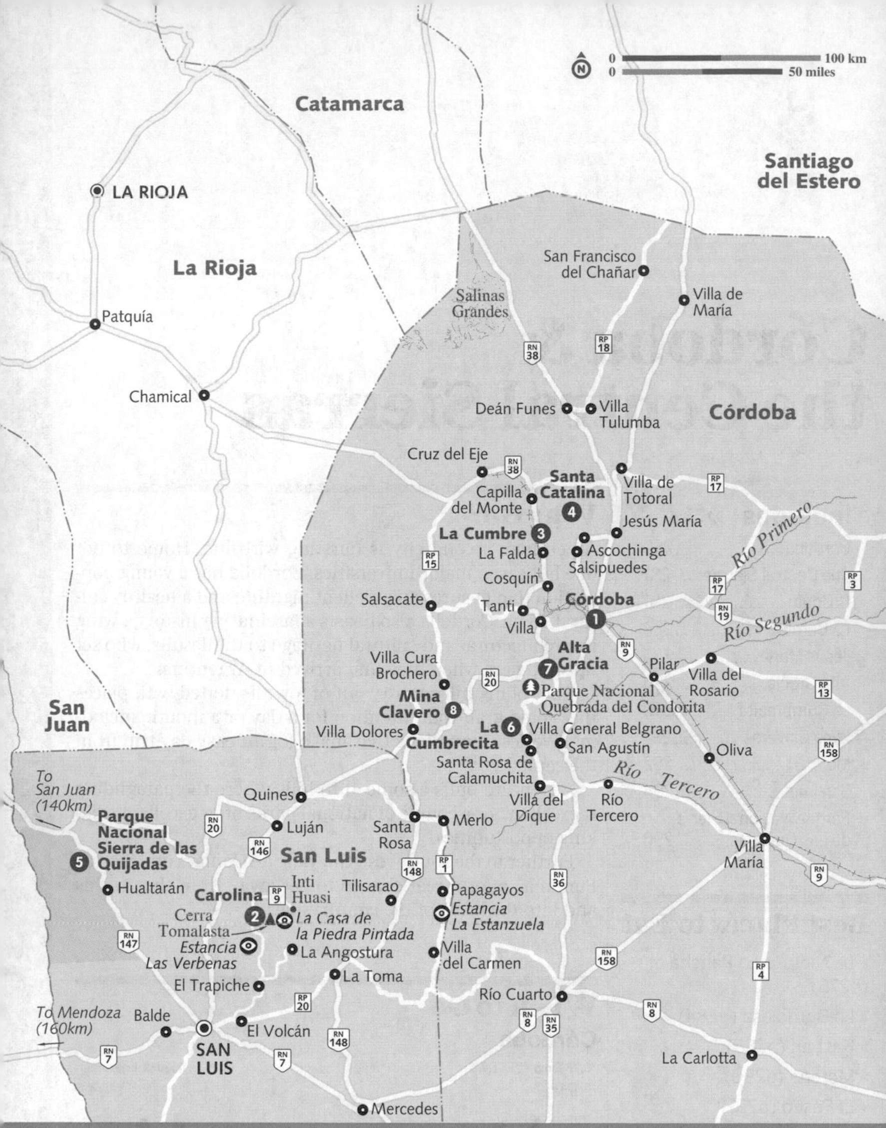

Córdoba & the Central Sierras Highlights

1. Lap up the culture and wander the gorgeous streets of the stately city of **Córdoba** (p269)
2. Check out ancient caves, rock art and stunning highland scenery around **Carolina** (p296)
3. Get high with the paragliding fanatics at **La Cumbre** (p284)
4. Take a breather at the atmospheric 17th-century Jesuit *estancia* (ranch) of **Santa Catalina** (p287)
5. Break in your hiking boots among the surreal rock formations of **Parque Nacional Sierra de las Quijadas** (p296)
6. Mellow out in the pedestrian-only mountain village of **La Cumbrecita** (p290)
7. Visit Che's house in **Alta Gracia** (p286)
8. Cool off riverside in the quaint resort town of **Mina Clavero** (p291)

National Parks

In San Luis province, the rarely visited Parque Nacional Sierra de las Quijadas (p296) is an excellent alternative to the better-known Parque Provincial Ischigualasto (p335) in San Juan province: getting there is far easier, and you'll often have the desert canyons and rock formations all to yourself. Parque Nacional Quebrada del Condorito (p291) is well worth a day trip from Córdoba to see the impressive Andean condors the park protects.

Getting There & Around

Córdoba makes an excellent stop if you're heading south or southwest toward Mendoza. The city has bus connections throughout the country.

The towns throughout the sierras are all easily accessible by public transportation, but many tiny, remote towns and Jesuit *estancias* (ranches) can only be reached with your own wheels. The sierras' dense network of roads, many well paved but others only gravel, make them good candidates for bicycle touring; Argentine drivers here seem a bit less ruthless than elsewhere in the country. A mountain bike is still the best choice.

CÓRDOBA

0351 / POP 1.526 MILLION / ELEV 400M

It's an old guidebook cliché, but Córdoba really *is* a fascinating mix of old and new. Where else will you find DJs spinning electro-tango in crowded student bars next to 17th-century Jesuit ruins?

Despite being a whopping 715km away from Buenos Aires, Córdoba is anything but a provincial backwater – in 2006 the city was awarded the hefty title of Cultural Capital of the Americas, and the title fitted like a glove. Four excellent municipal galleries – dedicated to emerging, contemporary, classical and fine art respectively – are within easy walking distance of each other and the city center.

Sights

There's plenty to see, so allow yourself at least a couple of days for wandering around. Most churches are open roughly from 9am to noon and from 5pm to 8pm. Museum opening hours change regularly depending on the season and the administration.

Most colonial sites lie within a few blocks of Plaza San Martín, the city's urban nucleus. The commercial center is just northwest of the plaza, where the main pedestrian malls – 25 de Mayo and Rivera Indarte – intersect. Obispo Trejo, just west of the plaza, has the finest concentration of colonial buildings. Just south of downtown, Parque Sarmiento offers relief from the bustling, densely built downtown.

East–west streets change names at San Martín/Independencia and north–south streets change at Deán Funes/Rosario de Santa Fe.

CENTRO

Downtown Córdoba is a treasure of colonial buildings and other historical monuments.

Iglesia Catedral CATHEDRAL

(cnr Independencia & 27 de Abril; guided visit AR$5; 9:30am-3:15pm) The construction of Córdoba's cathedral began in 1577 and dragged on for more than two centuries under several architects, including Jesuits and Franciscans, and though it lacks any sense of architectural unity, it's a beautiful structure. Crowned by a Romanesque dome, it overlooks Plaza San Martín. The lavish interior was painted by renowned *cordobés* (Córdoban) painter Emilio Caraffa. Guided visits of the belltower leave hourly between 9am and 3:15pm from Pasaje Santa Catalina 61, the entry on the north side of the cathedral.

Museo de la Memoria MUSEUM

(San Jerónimo s/n; admission free; 9am-6pm Tue-Fri) A chilling testament to the excesses of Argentina's military dictatorship, this museum occupies a space formerly used as a clandestine center for detention and torture. It was operated by the dreaded Department of Intelligence (D2), a special division created in Córdoba dedicated to the kidnap and torture of suspected political agitators and the 'reassignment' of their children to less politically suspect families.

The space itself is stark and unembellished, and the walls are covered with enlarged photographs of people who are still 'missing' after 30 years. There's not much joy here, but the museum stands as a vital reminder of an era that human-rights groups hope will never be forgotten.

Manzana Jesuítica NOTABLE BUILDING

Córdoba's beautiful Manzana Jesuítica (Jesuit Block), like that of Buenos Aires, is also known as the Manzana de las Luces (Block of Enlightenment), and was initially associated with the influential Jesuit order.

Designed by the Flemish Padre Philippe Lemaire, the **Iglesia de la Compañía de Jesús** (cnr Obispo Trejo & Caseros; admission free;

Córdoba

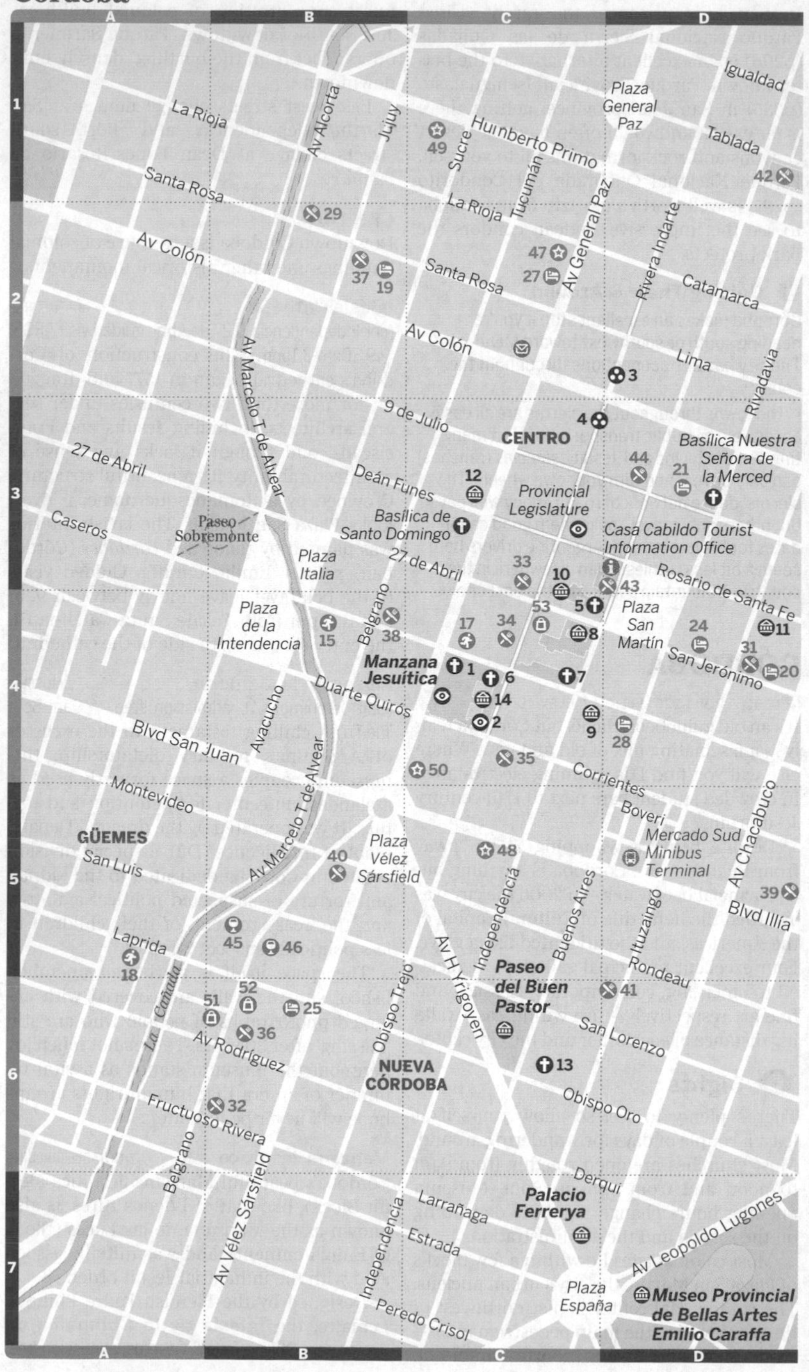

A
B
C
D
1
2
3
4
5
6
7
La Rioja
Av Alcorta
Jujuy
49
Sucre
Humberto Primo
Tucumán
Plaza
General
Paz
Igualdad
Tablada
42
Santa Rosa
La Rioja
Av General Paz
29
Av Colón
37
19
47
27
Santa Rosa
Rivera Indarte
Catamarca
Av Marcelo T de Alvear
Av Colón
Lima
Rivadavia
3
9 de Julio
4
CENTRO
Basílica Nuestra
Señora de
la Merced
27 de Abril
44
21
Deán Funes
12
Provincial
Legislature
Caseros
Paseo
Sobremonte
Basílica de
Santo Domingo
Casa Cabildo Tourist
Information Office
Plaza
Italia
27 de Abril
33
10
43
Rosario de Santa Fe
Plaza
de la
Intendencia
15
Belgrano
38
17
34
53
5
8
Plaza
San
Martín
24
11
31
20
San Jerónimo
Manzana
Jesuítica
1
6
7
Duarte Quirós
14
2
9
28
Avacucho
Blvd San Juan
50
35
Corrientes
Av Marcelo T de Alvear
Montevideo
Boveri
Mercado Sud
Minibus
Terminal
Av Chacabuco
GÜEMES
Plaza
Vélez
Sársfield
40
48
San Luis
39
Blvd Illía
Av H Yrigoyen
Independencia
Buenos Aires
Ituzaingó
45
46
Laprida
18
Paseo
del Buen
Pastor
Rondeau
52
51
La Cañada
25
41
36
Av Rodríguez
Obispo Trejo
San Lorenzo
NUEVA
CÓRDOBA
13
Obispo Oro
32
Fructuoso Rivera
Belgrano
Av Vélez Sársfield
Derqui
Palacio
Ferrerya
Larrañaga
Estrada
Independencia
Av Leopoldo Lugones
Plaza
España
Museo Provincial
de Bellas Artes
Emilio Caraffa
Peredo Crisol

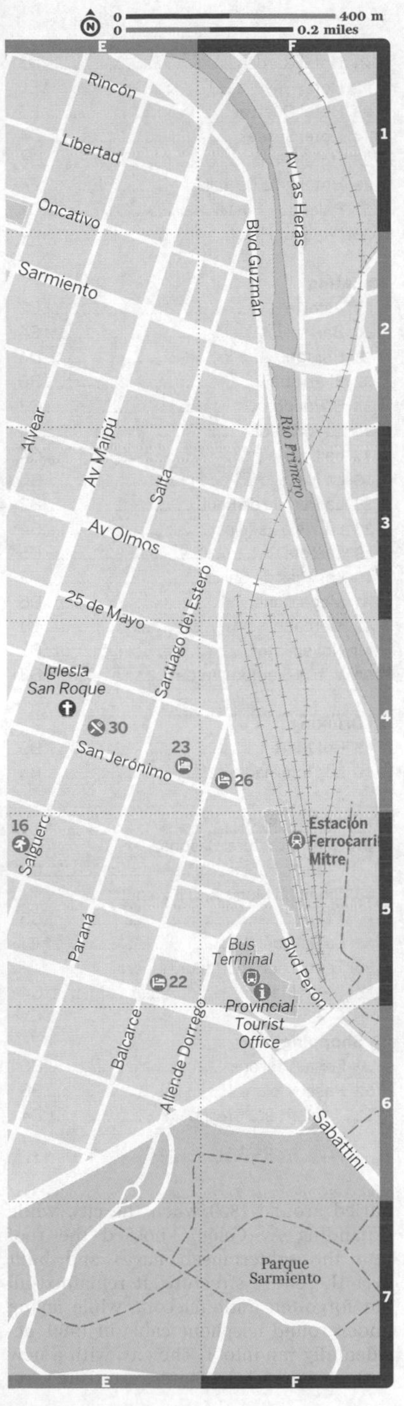

9am-1pm, 4-8pm) dates from 1645 but was not completed until 1671, with the successful execution of Lemaire's plan for a cedar roof in the form of an inverted ship's hull. Lemaire, unsurprisingly, was once a boat builder. Inside, the church's baroque altarpiece is made from carved Paraguayan cedar from Misiones province. The **Capilla Doméstica**, completed in 1644, sits on Caseros, directly behind the church. Its ornate ceiling was made with cowhide stretched over a skeleton of thick taguaro cane and painted with pigments composed partially of boiled bones.

In 1613 Fray Fernando de Trejo y Sanabria founded the Seminario Convictorio de San Javier, which, after being elevated to university status in 1622, became the **Universidad Nacional de Córdoba** (Obispo Trejo 242; 9am-1pm & 4-8pm). The university is the country's oldest and contains, among other national treasures, part of the Jesuits' Grand Library and the **Museo Histórico de la Universidad Nacional de Córdoba** (guided visits per person AR$10; 10am, 11am, 5pm & 6pm Tue-Sun). Guided visits are the only way to see the inside and are well worth taking. The guides let you wander through the Colegio and peek into the classrooms while students run around.

Next door, the **Colegio Nacional de Monserrat** (Obispo Trejo 294) dates from 1782, though the college itself was founded in 1687 and transferred after the Jesuit expulsion. Though the interior cloisters are original, the exterior was considerably modified in 1927 by restoring architect Jaime Roca, who gave the building its present baroque flare.

In 2000 Unesco declared the Manzana Jesuítica a World Heritage site, along with five Jesuit *estancias* throughout the province.

Museo Histórico Provincial Marqués de Sobremonte MUSEUM

(433-1661/71; Rosario de Santa Fe 218; admission AR$3; 9am-1pm Mon-Fri) It's worth dropping into this museum, one of the most important historical museums in the country, if only to see the colonial house it occupies: an 18th-century home that once belonged to Rafael Núñez, the colonial governor of Córdoba and later viceroy of the Río de la Plata. It has 26 rooms, seven interior patios, meter-thick walls and an impressive wrought-iron balcony supported by carved wooden brackets.

Córdoba

Top Sights
- Manzana Jesuítica C4
- Museo Provincial de Bellas Artes Emilio Caraffa D7
- Palacio Ferrerya C7
- Paseo del Buen Pastor C6

Sights
- Cabildo .... (see 43)
- 1 Capilla Doméstica C4
- 2 Colegio Nacional de Monserrat C4
- 3 Cripta Jesuítica D2
- 4 Cripta Jesuítica C3
- 5 Iglesia Catedral C4
- 6 Iglesia de la Compañía de Jesús C4
- 7 Iglesia de Santa Teresa y Convento de Carmelitas Descalzas de San José C4
- 8 Museo de Arte Religioso Juan de Tejeda C4
- 9 Museo de la Ciudad C4
- 10 Museo de la Memoria C3
- Museo Históricо de la Universidad Nacional de Córdoba .... (see 14)
- 11 Museo Histórico Provincial Marqués de Sobremonte D4
- Museo Iberoamericano de Artesanías .... (see 51)
- 12 Museo Municipal de Bellas Artes Dr Genaro Pérez C3
- 13 Parroquia Sagrado Corazón de Jesús de los Capuchinos C6
- 14 Universidad Nacional de Córdoba C4

Activities, Courses & Tours
- 15 Able Spanish School B4
- 16 Escuela Superior de Yoga E5
- 17 Facultad de Lenguas C4
- 18 Tsunami Tango A5

Sleeping
- 19 Aldea Hostel B2
- 20 Hotel Azur D4
- 21 Hotel Garden D3
- 22 Hotel Heydi E5
- 23 Hotel Quetzal E4
- 24 Hotel Sussex D4
- 25 Hotel Viena B6
- 26 Hotel Viña de Italia F4
- 27 Palenque Hostel C2
- 28 Windsor Hotel D4

Eating
- 29 Alcorta B2
- 30 Bar Yoly E4
- 31 Bursatil D4
- 32 El Arrabal B6
- 33 El Ruedo C3
- 34 La Alameda C4
- 35 La Candela C4
- 36 La Nieta 'e la Pancha B6
- 37 La Parrilla de Raul B2
- 38 La Vieja Esquina B4
- 39 La Zeta D5
- 40 Las Rías de Galicia B5
- 41 Mega Doner D6
- 42 Mercado Norte D1
- 43 Novecento D3
- 44 Verde Siempre Verde D3

Drinking
- 45 But Mitre B5
- 46 Los Infernadas B5

Entertainment
- 47 Centro Cultural Casona Municipal C2
- 48 Cineclub Municipal Hugo del Carril C5
- 49 La Sala del Rey C1
- 50 Teatro del Libertador General San Martín C4

Shopping
- 51 Feria Artesanal B6
- 52 Paseo Colonial B6
- 53 Talabartería Crespo C4

Cripta Jesuítica MUSEUM
(cnr Rivera Indarte & Av Colón; admission AR$2; 10am-3pm Mon-Fri) Built at the beginning of the 18th century by the Jesuits, the Cripta Jesuítica was originally designed as a novitiate and later converted to a crypt and crematorium. Abandoned after the Jesuit expulsion, it was demolished and buried around 1829 when the city, while expanding Av Colón, knocked the roof into the subterranean naves and built over the entire structure. It remained all but forgotten until Telecom, while laying underground telephone cable in 1989, accidentally ran into it. The city, with a new outlook on such treasures, exquisitely re-

stored the crypt and uses it regularly for musical and theatrical performances and art exhibits. Entrances lie on either side of Av Colón in the middle of the Rivera Indarte pedestrian mall.

FREE **Museo Municipal de Bellas Artes Dr Genaro Pérez** GALLERY
(Av General Paz 33; ⏲8am-8pm Tue-Sun) This art gallery is prized for its collection of paintings from the 19th and 20th centuries. Works, including those by Emilio Caraffa, Lucio Fontana, Lino Spilimbergo, Antonio Berni and Antonio Seguí, chronologically display the history of the *cordobés* school of painting, at the front of which stands Genaro Pérez himself. The museum is housed in Palacio Garzón, an unusual late-19th-century building named for its original owner; it also has outstanding changing contemporary art exhibits.

Plaza San Martín & Around PLAZA
Córdoba's lovely and lively central plaza dates from 1577. Its western side is dominated by the white arcade of the restored **Cabildo** (colonial town-council building), completed in 1785 and containing three interior patios, as well as basement cells. All are open to the public as part of the **Museo de la Ciudad** (Independencia 30; admission free; ⏲8am-8pm), a block to the south.

Occupying nearly half a city block, the **Iglesia de Santa Teresa y Convento de Carmelitas Descalzas de San José** (cnr Caseros & Independencia; ⏲6-8pm) was completed in 1628 and has functioned ever since as a closed-order convent for Carmelite nuns. Only the church itself is open to visitors. Once part of the convent, the **Museo de Arte Religioso Juan de Tejeda** (Independencia 122; ⏲9:30am-12:30pm Wed-Sat), next door, exhibits religious artifacts as well as paintings by *cordobés* masters, but was closed for renovations at time of research.

NUEVA CÓRDOBA & GÜEMES

Before the northwestern neighborhoods of Chateau Carreras and Cerro de las Rosas lured the city's elite to their peaceful hillsides, Nueva Córdoba was the neighborhood of the *cordobés* aristocracy. It's now popular with students, which explains the proliferation of brick high-rise apartment buildings. Still, a stroll past the stately old residences that line the wide Av H Yrigoyen reveals the area's aristocratic past.

Paseo del Buen Pastor CULTURAL CENTER
(Av H Yrigoyen 325; ⏲10am-8pm) This cultural center/performance space was built in 1901 as a combined chapel/monastery/women's prison. In mid-2007 it was re-inaugurated to showcase work by Córdoba's young and emerging artists. There are a couple of hip cafe-bars in the central patio area where you can kick back with an Appletini or two. The attached chapel (which has been desanctified) hosts regular live-music performances – stop by for a program, or check Thursday's edition of the local newspaper *La Voz del Interior* for details.

Parroquia Sagrado Corazón de Jesús de los Capuchinos CHURCH
(cnr Buenos Aires & Obispo Oro) While you're in the neighborhood, pop across the road to see this marvelous neo-Gothic church built between 1928 and 1934, whose glaring oddity is its missing steeple (omitted on purpose to symbolize human imperfection). Among the numerous sculptures that cover the church's facade are those of Atlases symbolically struggling to bare the spiritual weight of the religious figures above them (and sins and guilt of the rest of us).

Palacio Ferrerya GALLERY
(Av H Yrigoyen 551; admission AR$3; ⏲8am-8pm Tue-Sun) Nueva Córdoba's landmark building was built in 1914 and designed by Ernest Sanson in the Louis XVI style. The building itself is amazing, and has recently been converted into a fine-arts museum, featuring more than 400 works in 12 rooms spread over three floors. If you're into art or architecture, this place is a don't miss.

Museo Provincial de Bellas Artes Emilio Caraffa GALLERY
(Av H Yrigoyen 651; admission AR$3; ⏲10am-8pm Tue-Fri, 10:30am-7pm Sat-Sun) One of the city's best contemporary art museums stands ostentatiously on the eastern side of Plaza España. Architect Juan Kronfuss designed the neoclassical building as a museum and it was inaugurated in 1916. Exhibits change monthly. South of the museum the city unfolds into its largest open-space area, the **Parque Sarmiento**, designed by Charles Thays, the architect who designed Mendoza's Parque General San Martín.

Once a strictly working-class neighborhood, Güemes is now known for the eclectic **antique stores** and **artisan shops** that line the main drag of Belgrano, between

Rodríguez and Laprida. Its weekend *feria artisanal* (p277), one of the country's best, teems with antique vendors, arts and crafts and a healthy dose of Córdoba's hippies. It's within the same block as the **Museo Iberoamericano de Artesanías** (cnr Belgrano & Av Rodríguez; ⏲9am-3pm Mon-Fri), which houses beautiful crafts from throughout South America. A good way back to the city center is along **La Cañada**, an acacia-lined stone canal with arched bridges.

Courses

Córdoba is an excellent place to study Spanish; in many ways, being a student is what Córdoba is all about. Lessons cost about AR$50 per hour for one-on-one tuition or AR$450 to AR$800 per week in small classes.

Facultad de Lenguas SPANISH SCHOOL
(☎433-1073/5, ext 30; Av Vélez Sársfield 187) Part of the Universidad Nacional de Córdoba.

Able Spanish School SPANISH SCHOOL
(☎422-4692; www.ablespanish.com.ar; Caseros 45) Offers accommodation and afternoon activities at extra cost and discounts for extended study.

Tsunami Tango DANCE SCHOOL
(☎15-313-8746; www.tsunamitango.blogspot.com; Laprida 453) Tango classes and *milongas* (tango halls) Tuesday to Saturday. The website lists times.

Escuela Superior de Yoga YOGA
(☎427-0712; Salgüero 256) Offers yoga classes with monthly rates.

Tours

All of the city's hostels and most of the hotels can arrange tours within the city and around the province.

City Tours WALKING TOUR
(in Spanish/English AR$30/50) Absorb Córdoba's rich history by taking one of the guided walking tours that depart at 9:30am and 11:30am Monday to Friday from Casa Cabildo (p280). Reserve a day in advance if you want a tour in English. There are also free thematic tours on an irregular basis – ask at the tourist office to see the schedule.

Festivals & Events

During the first three weeks of April, the city puts on a large **crafts market** (locally called 'FICO') at the city fairgrounds, in the north near Chateau Carreras stadium. Bus 31 from Plaza San Martín goes there. Mid-September's **Feria del Libro** is a regional book fair.

Sleeping

Hotels on and around Plaza San Martín make exploring the center a cinch, but you'll have to walk several blocks for dinner and nightlife. Hotels along La Cañada and in Nueva Córdoba, on the other hand, mean going out to dinner and hitting the bars is a simple matter of walking down the street.

CENTRO

TOP CHOICE **Hotel Azur** BOUTIQUE HOTEL $$$
(☎424-7133; www.azurrealhotel.com; San Jerónimo 243; r AR$680-1200; P❄@🛜🏊) Surprisingly one of a kind here in Córdoba, the Azur mixes minimal chic with eclectic local and international furnishings to pull off a very stylish little boutique hotel. Rooms are all they should be and the common areas (including rooftop deck and pool area) are extremely inviting.

Palenque Hostel HOSTEL $
(☎423-7588; www.palenquehostel.com.ar; Av General Paz 371; dm from AR$50, d without bathroom AR$140; ❄@🛜) By far the prettiest hostel in Córdoba, the Palenque occupies a classic old house and retains much of its original charm. Facilities are extensive, including laundry area, air-con and nightly cooking classes. Dorms are large, with plenty of room to move.

Windsor Hotel HOTEL $$$
(☎422-4012; www.windsortower.com; Buenos Aires 214; r/ste AR$678/808; P❄🛜🏊) In a great downtown location, the Windsor is one of the few classic hotels in town with any real style. The lobby's all dark wood and brass, and the rooms have been tastefully renovated with modern fittings.

Hotel Quetzal HOTEL $$
(☎426-5117; www.hotelquetzal.com.ar; San Jerónimo 579; s/d AR$140/220; P❄@🛜) Spacious, minimalistic, modern rooms are what's on offer here. A surprisingly tranquil option in a busy neighborhood.

Aldea Hostel HOSTEL $
(☎426-1312; www.aldeahostel.com; Santa Rosa 447; dm from AR$55, r with/without bathroom AR$90/80 per person; @🛜) Plain but spacious rooms in a mildly inconvenient location. The patio, rooftop terrace and bar areas ooze atmosphere and the vibe is young and friendly.

Hotel Garden HOTEL $$
(☎421-4729; www.garden-hotel.com.ar; 25 de Mayo 35; r standard/deluxe AR$150/250; ❄📶) About as central as it gets. Standard rooms (fan, unrenovated) are OK value, but the deluxe ones (air-con, refurbished) are several steps up in quality and a reasonable deal.

Hotel Sussex HOTEL $$
(☎422-9070; www.hotelsussexcba.com.ar; San Jerónimo 125; s/d AR$250/320; ❄📶🏊) Another wonderful lobby (this one sporting vaulted ceilings, grand piano and fine art) leads on to more workaday rooms. At this price, you'd want to be getting plaza views.

Hotel Viña de Italia HOTEL $$
(☎425-1678; www.hotelvinadeitalia.com.ar; San Jerónimo 611; s/d AR$180/245; P❄📶) There's a bit of elegance left in this 150-room hotel, and the midsize rooms include TV, phone, air-con and heating. The rooms aren't nearly as graceful as the lobby, but they're still a good deal.

Hotel Heydi HOTEL $$
(☎422-2219; www.hotelheydi.com.ar; Blvd Illía 615; s/d AR$280/350; ❄) This is the best of the bunch near the bus terminal: a modern, immaculate place with friendly, professional staff.

NUEVA CÓRDOBA & LA CAÑADA

Tango Hostel HOSTEL $
(☎425-6023; www.tangohostelcordoba.com.ar; Riviera 70; dm AR$52, r with/without bathroom AR$145/130; @📶) A cozy little hostel tucked away in Nueva Córdoba, run by young travelers who know how a hostel should be.

Hotel Viena HOTEL $$
(☎460-0909; www.hotelviena.com.ar; Laprida 235; s/d AR$230/290; ❄@📶) This modern hotel in the heart of Nueva Córdoba offers bright, clean rooms and an excellent breakfast buffet. There are lots of nooks for sitting in the lobby area, and there's a restaurant on the premises. Good choice.

Eating

TOP CHOICE **La Nieta 'e La Pancha** FUSION $$
(☎468-1920; Belgrano 783; mains AR$50-90; ⏰dinner Tue-Fri, 4:30pm-1am Sat & Sun) The wonderful staff prepares and serves a changing menu of delectable regional specialties, creative pastas and house recipes. Be sure to save room for dessert. Check out the lovely upstairs terrace, which catches breezes and gives ample people-watching ops on the street below.

El Arrabal ARGENTINE $$
(☎460-2990; Belgrano 899; mains AR$40-80; ⏰lunch & dinner) One of the few old-style restaurants in Nueva Córdoba (OK, so it may be a reconstruction…), this place serves slightly pricey but imaginative regional and house specialties. It packs out for the dinner tango show (AR$20) at 11pm Thursday to Saturday. Make a reservation.

Verde Siempre Verde VEGETARIAN $
(9 de Julio 36; mains from AR$25; ⏰lunch & dinner; 🌿) Delicious vegetarian buffet that also serves set meals.

Mercado Norte MARKET $
(cnr Rivadavia & Oncativo; ⏰Mon-Sat) Córdoba's indoor market has delicious and inexpensive food, such as pizza, empanadas and seafood. Browsing the clean stalls selling every imaginable cut of meat, including whole *chivitos* (goat) and pigs, is a must.

Las Rías de Galicia SPANISH $$
(Montevideo 271; set lunch AR$35, mains AR$40-85; ⏰lunch & dinner) An upscale Spanish restaurant with the best-value set lunch in town. Going à la carte gets you all sorts of goodies, including some excellent seafood selections.

Bar Yoly PARRILLA $
(Plazoleta San Roque, Salguero & San Jerónimo; set meals AR$25; ⏰lunch & dinner) Neighborhood *parrillas* (steak restaurants) are fast disappearing in Córdoba, but the Yoly is one of the best, and still hanging in there. Get here reasonably early and beat the old guys out of a table on the small shady plaza.

Novecento INTERNATIONAL $$
(cnr Rosario de Santa Fe & Independencia; mains AR$40-70; ⏰lunch & dinner) There are few more atmospheric options for dining downtown than this cute little cafe-restaurant, set in the courtyard of the historic *cabildo* building. The menu ticks all the 'classic' boxes and throws in a few welcome surprises.

La Parrilla de Raul PARRILLA $
(Jujuy 278; mains AR$15-30; ⏰lunch & dinner) Of Córdoba's *parrillas,* this is probably one of the most famous. *Parrillada* (mixed grill) for two costs only AR$40, not including extras such as drinks or salad.

El Ruedo CAFE $
(cnr Obispo Trejo & 27 de Abril; mains around AR$30; ⏰8am-10pm) It doesn't stray too far from the steak, sandwich and pizza formula here, but

the plaza-side spot under big shady trees is a winner, as are the *limonadas con soda* (lemon juice with soda water) on a hot day.

La Zeta MIDDLE EASTERN **$$**
(cnr Corrientes & Salguero; mains AR$40-70; ⌚lunch & dinner) Excellent Middle Eastern food (with a couple of Mediterranean faves thrown in) provides a welcome dash of variety. There's not much to be said for the decor, but the flavors more than make up for that.

Bursatil CAFE **$**
(San Jerónimo & Ituzaingó; mains AR$35-60; ⌚breakfast, lunch & dinner) Stylish, modern cafes are starting to pop up in the old part of town, and Bursatil is one of the finest. There's a cool modern interior, good coffee and a small, Asian-inspired menu.

Mega Doner TURKISH **$**
(Ituzaingó 528; set meals AR$28-45; ⌚lunch & dinner) Conveniently located in Nueva Córdoba's bar district, this place specializes in real giro *doners*. Daily lunch specials are an excellent deal and there's outdoor seating.

Alcorta STEAKHOUSE **$$**
(☎424-7452; Av Alcorta 330; mains AR$45-80; ⌚lunch & dinner) This upmarket *parrilla*, esteemed for its grilled meats (many say they're the best in town), also serves delicious pasta and fish. Try the *mollejitas al sauvignon blanc* (sweetbreads in a white wine sauce).

Drinking

Córdoba's drink of choice is Fernet (a strong, medicinal-tasting herbed liquor from Italy), almost always mixed with Coke. If you don't mind a rough morning, start in on the stuff.

Nightlife in Córdoba basically divides itself into three areas. All the bright young things barhop in Nueva Córdoba – a walk along Rondeau between Avs H Yrigoyen and Chacabuco after midnight gives you a choice of dozens of bars, mostly playing laid-back (or ribcage-rattling) electronic music.

North of the center, there's a string of live-music venues on Blvd Guzmán near the corner of Av General Paz.

Across the river on Av Las Heras between Roque Sáenz Peña and Juan B Justo (the

LOVE BY THE HOUR

Every city in Argentina has *hoteles por hora* (hourly rate hotels), where people take their secret lovers for a romp in the good old proverbial hay. They vary from cheap, nondescript *residenciales* (cheap hotels) to deluxe love pads with black lights, wall-to-wall mirrors, nonstop sex-TV, Jacuzzis and room-service menus featuring every imaginable sex toy under the sun. These deluxe versions are a part of under-the-table Argentine culture that possibly shouldn't be missed (provided you're traveling with a partner who's game, of course).

Córdoba boasts four deluxe *hoteles por hora* on the road to the airport, and if you haven't experienced one of these Argentine institutions, now's your chance. Although they're geared toward folks with cars, you can go in a taxi (trust us, we know). Here's a quick primer on how they work.

First, it's all about anonymity. As you drive into the hotel a big number flashes on a sign; that's your room number. Drive to the garage door with your number on it, pull in and close the garage door; if you're in a taxi, the driver will drop you in the garage and leave. Close the garage door and enter the room.

In five minutes the phone will ring, and the attendant will ask you if you'd like a complimentary beverage, which he or she then delivers through a tiny sliding door in the wall so no one sees anybody. When the attendant knocks on the door, you open it, take your drinks and pay for the room (AR$80 for two hours is the going rate). Ten minutes before your time is up, the attendant will courteously ring again to tell you it's time to get your gear back on.

Of the four hotels on the airport road, the best is **Eros Hotel** (Camino al aeropuerto, Km 5.5). Rooms have Jacuzzis, bedside control panels, all the right TV channels and *all* the fun stuff. And it's impeccably clean.

A taxi costs about AR$30 each way from town. If you take one, call a *remise* (telephone taxi) from your hotel and have the driver pick you up later. They all know the drill – no pun intended.

area known locally as Abasto) are the discos and nightclubs. Go for a walk along here and you'll probably pick up free passes to some, if not all, of them.

Los Infernadas BAR
(Belgrano 631) A laid-back bar playing an eclectic range of music. Live music Thursday to Sundays and a big *patio cervecero* (beer garden) make this a standout.

But Mitre BAR
(www.butmitre.com; Av Marcelo T de Alvear 635) Extremely popular bar and dance club on La Cañada. Check it out, especially on Thursday night.

El Barranco BAR
(Av Las Heras 58; admission AR$6-12) In the busy Albasto scene, this live-music venue and disco is a good place to start, if only for the fact that it gets a crowd before 1am. Fridays are Latin dance parties; on Saturdays there are live bands.

☆ Entertainment

La Voz del Interior, Córdoba's main newspaper, has a reasonably comprehensive entertainment section every Thursday with show times and the like.

Cuarteto music (a Córdoba invention) is big here and played live in many venues. Unfortunately, it's also the gangsta rap of Argentine folk music and tends to attract undesirable crowds. **La Sala del Rey** (Humberto Primero 439) is a respectable venue and the best place to catch a *cuarteto* show.

Centro Cultural Casona Municipal CULTURAL CENTER
(cnr Av General Paz & La Rioja; ⏲8am-8pm Sun-Fri, 10am-10pm Sat) Shows contemporary and avante garde art, hosts concerts and offers month-long art and music courses.

Teatro del Libertador General San Martín THEATER
(☎433-2319; Av Vélez Sársfield 365; admission AR$30-170; ⏲box office 9am-9pm) It's well worth going to a performance here, if only to see the opulence of the country's most historic theater. The theater was completed in 1891, and the floor was designed to be mechanically raised and leveled to the stage, so seats could be removed, allowing for grand parties for the aristocracy of the early 1900s.

Cineclub Municipal Hugo del Carril CINEMA
(☎433-2463; www.cineclubmunicipal.org.ar; Blvd San Juan 49; admission AR$10; ⏲box office 9am-late) For a great night (or day) at the movies, pop into this municipal film house, which screens everything from art flicks to Latin American award winners and local films. Stop by for a program. There's also live music and theatrical performances here.

DON'T MISS

LOCAL FLAVOR

Looking to chow down with Córdoba's student crowd? Pull up a stool at any of the following, where the empanadas, beer and *locro* (spicy corn and meat stew) flow freely.

La Alameda (Obispo Trejo 170; empanadas AR$4, locro AR$22; ⏲lunch & dinner) Pull up a bench and wash down your homemade empanadas with some ice-cold beer. Then write some graffiti on the wall.

La Candela (Duarte Quirós 67; empanadas AR$4, locro AR$24; ⏲lunch & dinner) Rustic and wonderfully atmospheric, run by three cranky but adorable señoras.

La Vieja Esquina (cnr Belgrano & Caseros; empanadas AR$4, locro AR$28; ⏲lunch Mon-Sat) A cozy little lunch spot with stools and window seating. Order at the bar.

Shopping

Antique stores line Calle Belgrano in barrio Güemes, where there is also a **feria artisanal** (artisans' market; cnr Rodriguez & Belgrano; ⏲5-10pm Sat & Sun), one of the country's best. You'll find Argentine handicrafts at several stores downtown.

Paseo Colonial ACCESSORIES
(Belgrano 795; ⏲10am-9pm Mon-Sat, 5-10pm Sun) To find out what the city's hip young designers have been working on, slip into this little arcade, featuring a variety of small shops selling clothes, homewares and jewelry.

Talabartería Crespo SOUVENIRS
(☎421-5447; Obispo Trejo 141; ⏲Mon-Sat) Leather goods made from *carpincho* (a large rodent that makes a beautifully spotted leather) are the specialty here. Sweaters, knives and *mate* (tealike beverages) paraphernalia grace the shelves as well.

1

2

FLK/IMAGEBROKER ©

3

ARCO IMAGES GMBH/ALAMY ©

rque Nacional Sierra de uijadas (p296)
worldly rock formations make eat hiking opportunities.

2. Iglesia Catedral (p269)
Córdoba's beautiful church is crowned by a Romanesque dome.

3. Estancia Santa Catalina (p287)
This Jesuit *estancia* is one of the Sierra's most beautiful and is a Unesco World Heritage site.

Information

Internet Access

Internet cafes are tucked into *locutorios* (telephone kiosks) throughout the center, and they're everywhere in Nueva Córdoba.

Laundry

Trapitos (☎422-5877; Independencia 898; full service about AR$25)

Medical Services

Emergency hospital (☎421-0243; cnr Catamarca & Blvd Guzmán)

Money

Cambios (money-exchange offices) and ATMs are on Rivadavia north of the plaza; both are also at the main bus terminal and airport.

Cambio Barujel (cnr Rivadavia & 25 de Mayo) High commissions.

Maguitur (☎421-6200; 25 de Mayo 122) Charges 3% on traveler's checks.

Post

Main post office (Av General Paz 201)

Tourist Information

ACA (Automóvil Club Argentino; ☎421-4636; cnr Av General Paz & Humberto Primo) Argentina's auto club; good source for provincial road maps.

Casa Cabildo Tourist Information Office (☎434-1200; Independencia 30; 🕗8am-8pm) The provincial and municipal tourist boards occupy the same office in the historic Casa Cabildo.

Provincial tourist office airport (☎434-8390; Aeropuerto Pajas Blancas; 🕗8am-8pm); bus terminal (☎433-1982; 🕗8am-9pm)

Travel Agencies

Asatej (☎422-9453; www.asatej.com; Av Vélez Sársfield 361, Patio Olmos, Local 412) On the 3rd floor of Patio Olmos shopping center. Non-profit student travel agency with great staff. Open to all ages and nonstudents.

Getting There & Away

Air

Córdoba's international airport, **Ingeniero Ambrosio Taravella** (☎434-8390), charges an AR$116 departure tax on all international departures but this will most likely be included in your ticket.

Aerolíneas Argentinas/Austral (☎482-1025; Av Colón 520) has offices downtown and flies several times daily to Buenos Aires. **Lan** (☎452-3030; Av Alcorta 206) flies daily to Buenos Aires and Santiago, Chile. **Sol** (☎0810-122-7765; www.sol.com.ar) flies to Rosario, Tucumán and Mendoza. **Andes Líneas Aéreas** (☎426-5809; www.andesonline.com; Colón 532) flies to Salta and **Aero Chaco** (☎0810-345-2422; www.aerochaco.net) flies to Resistencia .

Bus

Córdoba's **bus terminal** (NETOC; ☎423-4199, 423-0532; Blvd Perón 300) is about a 15-minute walk from downtown. **Rede Ticket** (Obispo Trejo 327) sells tickets for all the major bus companies without charging commission. Its downtown location is handy for booking in advance.

On the top floor of the terminal several bus companies offer services to the same destinations as those offered by the minibus terminal. Be aware that those leaving from the terminal

BUSES FROM CÓRDOBA

DESTINATION	COST (AR$)	DURATION (HR)
Bahía Blanca	322	12
Bariloche	624	22
Buenos Aires	250	10
Catamarca	155	5-6
Corrientes	356	12
Esquel	691	25
Formosa	479	12
Jujuy	345	12
La Rioja	160	7
Mendoza	280	10
Merlo	88	5½
Montevideo (Uruguay)	463	15
Neuquén	486	17
Paraná	155	6
Puerto Iguazú	547	22
Puerto Madryn	549	18-20
Resistencia	308	13
Río Gallegos	2101	40
Rosario	143	6
Salta	377	12
San Juan	210	14
San Luis	180	6
San Martín de los Andes	485	21
Santiago del Estero	159	6
Tucumán	218	8

MINIBUSES FROM CÓRDOBA

DESTINATION	COST (AR$)	DURATION (HR)
Alta Gracia	11	1
Capilla del Monte	40	3
Cosquín	22	1¼
Jesús María	15	1
La Falda	27	3
La Cumbre	35	3
Mina Clavero	50	3
Villa Carlos Paz	10	1
Villa General Belgrano	32	2

stop everywhere, often adding an hour to the journey time.

Several companies offer service to Chilean destinations, including Santiago (AR$322, 16 hours), although some involve changing buses in Mendoza.

Minibus

Frequent minibuses leave from **Mercado Sud minibus terminal** (Blvd Illia, near Buenos Aires). Most go direct, while some stop at every little town along the way. It's worth asking, as this can shave an hour off your travel time.

In summer there may be direct buses to La Cumbrecita, but it will probably be quicker to go first to Villa General Belgrano.

Train

Trains leave Córdoba's **Estación Ferrocarril Mitre** (☎426-3565; Blvd Perón s/n) for Rosario (AR$22/30/54 in *turista/primera/*Pullman class, nine hours) and Buenos Aires' Retiro station (AR$30/50/90/300 in *turista/primera/*Pullman/*camarote*, 17 hours) at 2:40pm on Sundays and 7:30pm on Wednesdays. There is a dining car and bar on board. Tickets often sell out weeks in advance, especially in the *camarote* (two-person sleeping cabin), so book as soon as possible.

Trains to Cosquín (AR$6.50, two hours) leave from **Estación Rodriguez del Busto** (☎477-6195; Cardeñosa 3500) on the northwest outskirts of town at 9:10am and 11:20am daily, with an extra 12:20pm service on weekends. Buses A4 and A7 from the central plaza go to the station or it's an AR$25 taxi ride.

Getting Around

The airport is 15km north of town via Av Monseñor Pablo Cabrera. Intercórdoba goes to/from the airport from the main bus station (AR$5). A taxi into town shouldn't cost you more than AR$50.

Buses require rechargeable magnetic cards or *cospeles* (tokens), both of which are available from nearly every kiosk in town. Rides cost AR$2.50.

A car is very useful for visiting some of the nearby Jesuit *estancias* that cannot be reached by bus. Depending on seasonal demand, economy cars cost around AR$200 with 200km. Try the following:

Alamo (☎499-8436; Sheraton Hotel, Duarte Quirós 1300)

Europcar (☎422-4867, 481-7683; Entre Ríos 70) Inside I Iotel Dora.

THE CENTRAL SIERRAS

Nowhere near as visually spectacular as the nearby Andes, the Central Sierras more than make up for it by being way more hospitable. The area is dotted with little towns that are worth a quick visit or a longer stay, and is connected by an excellent road network with frequent bus services.

From the hippy chic of paragliding capital La Cumbre to the over-the-top kitsch of Villa Carlos Paz, you'd have to be one jaded traveler not to find something to your liking here. Kicking back is easily done – the riverside village of Mina Clavero is a favorite, as are the ex-Jesuit centers of Alta Gracia and Jesús María. Things get decidedly Germanic down south, and the pedestrian-only La Cumbrecita is not to be missed for *spaetzle* (German egg noodles), bush walks and swimming holes.

Cosquín

☎03541 / POP 39,840 / ELEV 720M

Cosquín is known throughout the country for its **Festival Nacional del Folklore** (www.aquicosquin.org), a nine-day national folk-music festival which has been held in the last week of January since 1961. The town gets packed for the festival, stays busy all summer and goes pleasantly dead the rest of the year. The slightly more hardcore **Cosquín Rock Festival** used to be held here, until the neighbors decided that teenagers with wallet chains, studded wristbands and piercings weren't really the tourist trade they were looking for.

Central Sierras

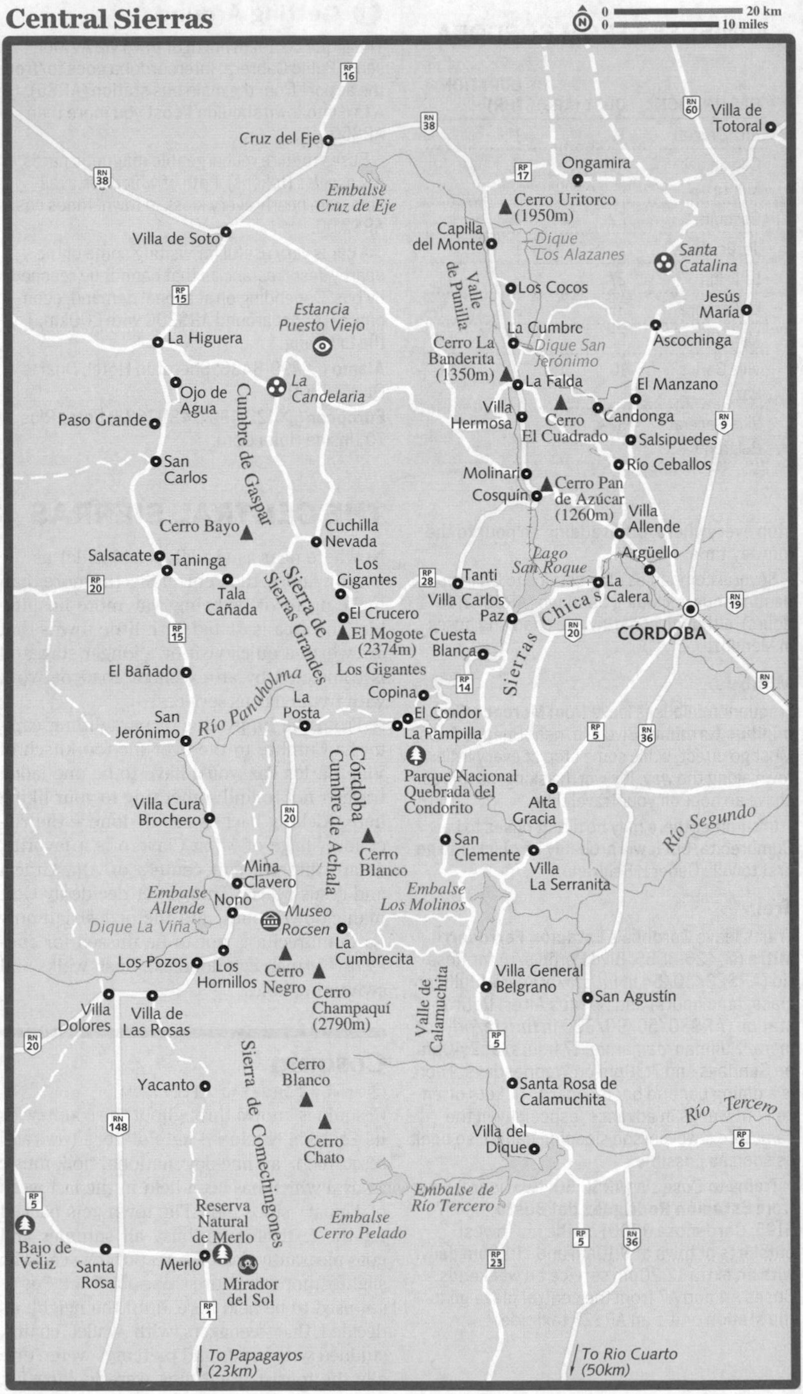

0 20 km
0 10 miles

Cruz del Eje
Embalse Cruz de Eje
Villa de Soto
Villa de Totoral
Ongamira
Cerro Uritorco (1950m)
Capilla del Monte
Dique Los Alazanes
Santa Catalina
Valle de Punilla
Los Cocos
Jesús María
Estancia Puesto Viejo
La Higuera
La Cumbre
Ascochinga
Cerro La Banderita (1350m)
Dique San Jerónimo
La Falda
El Manzano
Ojo de Agua
La Candelaria
Villa Hermosa
Cerro El Cuadrado
Candonga
Paso Grande
Cumbre de Gaspar
Salsipuedes
San Carlos
Río Ceballos
Molinari
Cerro Pan de Azúcar (1260m)
Cosquín
Villa Allende
Cerro Bayo
Cuchilla Nevada
Salsacate
Taninga
Los Gigantes
Lago San Roque
Argüello
Tala Cañada
Sierra de Sierras Grandes
Tanti
La Calera
Villa Carlos Paz
Sierras Chicas
El Crucero
El Mogote (2374m)
Cuesta Blanca
CÓRDOBA
Los Gigantes
El Bañado
Río Panaholma
Copina
La Posta
El Condor
San Jerónimo
La Pampilla
Parque Nacional Quebrada del Condorito
Córdoba Cumbre de Achala
Alta Gracia
Villa Cura Brochero
Río Segundo
San Clemente
Cerro Blanco
Villa La Serranita
Mina Clavero
Embalse Allende
Nono
Embalse Los Molinos
Museo Rocsen
Dique La Viña
La Cumbrecita
Los Pozos
Los Hornillos
Cerro Negro
Cerro Champaquí (2790m)
Villa General Belgrano
Valle de Calamuchita
San Agustín
Villa Dolores
Villa de Las Rosas
Sierra de Comechingones
Cerro Blanco
Yacanto
Santa Rosa de Calamuchita
Río Tercero
Cerro Chato
Villa del Dique
Embalse de Río Tercero
Embalse Cerro Pelado
Reserva Natural de Merlo
Bajo de Veliz
Santa Rosa
Merlo
Mirador del Sol
To Papagayos (23km)
To Rio Cuarto (50km)

RP 16, RN 38, RN 60, RP 17, RP 15, RP 28, RP 20, RN 9, RN 19, RN 20, RP 14, RP 5, RN 36, RN 148, RP 6, RP 23, RP 1

The festival relocated a few years ago to the banks of the nearby (and aptly named) Lago San Roque.

East of town, 1260m **Cerro Pan de Azúcar** offers good views of the sierras and, on a clear day, the city of Córdoba. An **aerosilla** (chairlift; return ticket AR$35; ⏲10am-5pm) runs to the summit regularly in summer – check with the tourist office in the off season. A taxi to the base should cost about AR$80, including waiting time.

Across the river from the center of town (turn left after the bridge), Av Belgrano forms 4km of waterfront promenade – a great place for a stroll on a summer's day, dotted with swimming holes that pack out when the temperature rises.

The **municipal tourist office** (☎453701; www.cosquin.gov.ar; San Martín 560; ⏲8am-9pm Mon-Fri, 9am-6pm Sat & Sun) has a good map of the town.

Sleeping & Eating

Hostería Siempreverde HOTEL $
(☎450093; www.hosteriasiempreverde.com; Santa Fe 525; s/d AR$140/190; 📶) This lovely old house has good-sized, modern rooms out back. There's a big, shady garden and the breakfast/lounge area is comfortable and stylish.

San Martín, between the plaza and the stadium, is lined with cafes, restaurants and *parrillas*.

Hospedaje Petit HOTEL $
(☎451311; petitcosquin@hotmail.com; A Sabattini 739; s/d AR$100/150) Steepled roofs and lovely antique floor tiles in the lobby give way to some fairly ordinary, modern rooms in the interior. It's decent value, though – clean, spacious and central.

La Casona STEAKHOUSE $$
(San Martín & Corrientes; mains AR$35-60; ⏲lunch & dinner) A frequently recommended *parrilla* set in an atmospheric old building and specializing in grilled *chivito* (goat).

Getting There & Away

There are many daily departures north to La Falda (AR$8, 45 minutes) and La Cumbre (AR$12, 1¼ hours); and south every 20 minutes to Villa Carlos Paz (AR$10, 40 minutes) and Córdoba (AR$22, 1¼ hours). There are a few departures daily for Buenos Aires (AR$280, 11 hours).

Trains depart for Córdoba's Estación Rodriguez del Busto (AR$6.50, 2½ hours) at 8am and 3:30pm daily with an extra 4:30pm service on weekends.

La Falda

☎03548 / POP 35,990 / ELEV 934M

A woodsy resort town, La Falda is busier than its Central Sierra neighbors and not quite as interesting. It's worth a day or two of your time, though, for walks in the hills and around the grounds of the defunct Hotel Eden.

La Falda's main **plaza** (cnr Sarmiento & Rivadavia) is a charming, tranquil affair, all the more so for being removed from the main drag. On weekends, and daily in summer, there's a **feria artisanal** (⏲daylight hours) here.

The **tourist office** (☎423007; www.lafalda.gov.ar; Av Eden 93; ⏲8am-8:30pm) is very helpful and has excellent maps of the area.

THERE'S SOMETHING WEIRD IN THEM THAR HILLS

For some reason, Córdoba's Sierras region is one of the quirkiest in Argentina, and the great thing about traveling in the region is that every once in a while you stumble upon something truly wonderful and unexpected. Here are a few of our favorites:

Capilla del Monte This otherwise sleepy little hill town is world-famous amongst UFO watchers who come here in the hope of communing with the extraterrestrials from on top of the mystical Cerro Uritorco (p286).

Villa General Belgrano (www.elsitiodelavilla.com/oktoberfest) The town's strong German heritage gives it a very European flavor, which really takes off as the beer starts flowing in Oktoberfest.

Carlos Paz (www.villacarlospaz.gov.ar/turismo) Like a mix between Vegas and Disneyland, this lakeside getaway is dotted with theme hotels (the Great Pyramids, the Kremlin) and centered around a massive cuckoo clock.

Museo Rocsen (www.museorocsen.org) Near the tiny town of Nono, outside of Mina Clavero, the 11,000-plus pieces on display form probably the most eclectic collection of trash/treasure you're ever likely to see.

ESTANCIAS IN THE CENTRAL SIERRAS

From rustic little getaways to sprawling, atmospheric ranches, the Central Sierras offer a small but excellent selection of *estancias*.

Estancia La Estanzuela (p298) Wonderfully preserved, set on lush grounds.

Estancia Las Verbenas (p296) Set in a beautiful glade, it's a truly rustic experience.

La Rancheria de Santa Catalina (p287) Spend the night in the old slave quarters.

Sights & Activities

A favorite **hiking** trail takes about two hours to the nearby summit of 1350m Cerro La Banderita. And since you're in town, take a guided tour of the once-extravagant, now-decaying **Hotel Eden** (admission by tour AR$20; ⏲10am-6pm), built in 1897, where the guest list included Albert Einstein, the duke of Savoy and several Argentine presidents. From the hotel, follow signs to **El Chorito**, a lookout with spectacular views out over the Sierras Chicas.

When the weather heats up, locals and tourists alike head for **7 Cascadas** (admission AR$10; ⏲daylight hr), which has three pools and a variety of swimming holes under waterfalls that were created when the local dam was built. It's a 3km walk or AR$20 *remise* ride from town.

Sleeping & Eating

Residencial Old Garden HOTEL **$$**
(☎422842; www.hoteloldgarden.com.ar; Capital Federal 28; s/d AR$120/200;) Definitely one of the better accommodation deals in the Sierras, this is a beautiful old house, lovingly maintained by the live-in owners.

Hotel Mediterraneo HOTEL **$**
(☎842-1246;www.hotel-mediterraneo.com.ar;Guëmes 149; r per person AR$80;) Nothing too flashy, but a good budget deal – clean and quiet, with a decent-sized swimming pool and good on site restaurant.

La Bordolesa STEAKHOUSE **$**
(cnr Sarmiento & Saavedra; mains from AR$35; ⏲lunch & dinner) A laid-back, modern *parrilla* with two grills going – one inside and one out. If the weather's good, grab a table on the lawn and a platter of *picadas* (finger food: AR$40 for two) – it's a fine way to while away a few hours.

Getting There & Away

The bus terminal sits on RN 38, just north of Av Eden. There are regular buses and minibuses south to Cosquín (AR$8, 45 minutes), Villa Carlos Paz (AR$15.50, 1¼ hours) and Córdoba (AR$27, two hours), and north to La Cumbre (AR$6.50, 30 minutes) and Capilla del Monte (AR$11, one hour). There are regular long-distance runs to Buenos Aires (from AR$281, 12 hours) and other destinations.

La Cumbre

☎03548 / POP 10,090 / ELEV 1141M

A favorite getaway for Córdoba dwellers and foreigners alike, La Cumbre packs a lot of character into a small space. It's an agreeable little town due to its wide streets and mild mountain climate, and there are plenty of adventures to be had in the surrounding hills. The town gained worldwide fame among paragliders when it hosted the 1994 World Paragliding Cup, and enthusiasts of the sport have made La Cumbre their home, giving the town an international feel. The launch site, 380m above the Río Pinto, provides a spectacular introduction to the sport and there are plenty of experienced instructors around, offering classes and tandem flights.

Sights & Activities

Head to the south side of town to the road known as **Camino de los Artesanos**, where more than two dozen homes sell homemade goodies, from jams and chutneys to wool, leather and silver crafts. Most homes open from 11am to sunset.

There are excellent views from the **Cristo Redentor**, a 7m statue of Christ on a 300m hilltop east of town; from the Plaza 25 de Mayo, cross the river and walk east on Córdoba toward the mountains – the trail begins after a quick jut to the left after crossing Cabrera.

Flying from the launch at Cuchi Corral (and hanging out by the Río Pinto afterward) is truly a memorable experience. The launch site (La Rampa) is about 10km west of town via a signed dirt road off the highway. **Toti López** (☎03548-15-636592) and **Carlos Vega** (☎491941) offer tandem flights and lessons. Everyone charges about the same. Tandem flights cost AR$400 for a half-hour; full courses cost AR$4000.

At the **Aeroclub La Cumbre** (☎452544; Camino a los Troncos s/n) you can arrange everything from tandem flights to ultralights. Ask for Andy Hediger (former paragliding world champion) or Hernán Pitocco (number four in the world in paragliding acrobatics). You can also test your nerves parachuting with **Nicolás López** (☎452544).

Hacer Cumbre (☎03548-15-638424; www.hacercumbre.com; Caraffa 270) offers pretty much everything else in the area, including treks, 4WD off-roading and horseback tours in the breathtaking countryside around Cerro Ongamina. Day trips, including transfers and food, start at AR$560 for two people and become significantly cheaper if you get a group together. They also rent quality mountain bikes for AR$60/80 per half-day/day.

Sleeping

The proprietors of the following places can arrange any activities available in La Cumbre.

TOP CHOICE Hostel La Cumbre HOSTEL $
(☎451368; www.hostellacumbre.com; San Martín 186; dm AR$60, per person r AR$100; @☎☒) A couple of blocks behind the bus terminal, this converted English mansion is one of the most impressive hostels in the Sierras. Views from the front balcony are superb.

Hostería Pastoral HOTEL $$
(☎452787; www.hosteriapastoral.com.ar; Moreno 480; s/d AR$300/350 without spa treatments, AR$350/400 with spa access; P@☎☒) A cozy ski-lodge atmosphere, homey lounge areas and a huge yard with swimming pool make up for somewhat outdated rooms. If not, the spa with Jacuzzi, sauna and massages may tip the scales.

Camping El Cristo CAMPGROUND $
(☎451893; Monseñor P Cabrera s/n; campsites AR$20) Below the Cristo Redentor east of town, La Cumbre's exceptional campgrounds are only a short tramp from the center.

Eating & Drinking

TOP CHOICE Kasbah ASIAN $
(Alberdi & Sarmiento; mains AR$30-50; ⊙lunch & dinner) You may not be expecting a good Thai curry out here, but this cute little triangular restaurant comes up with the goods. Also on offer is a range of Chinese and Indian dishes.

Casa Caraffa ARGENTINE $$
(cnr Caraffa & Rivadavia; mains AR$40-65; ⊙lunch & dinner) An excellent main-street restaurant serving up delicious homemade pastas and a divine *bife de chorizo* (sirloin steak) with Roquefort sauce (AR$45).

El Pungo PUB
(www.elpungopub.com.ar; Camino de los Artesanos s/n; cover from AR$20; ⊙noon-late Sat & Sun) This somewhat legendary watering hole attracts musicians from all over the country (Argentine folk musicians Charly Garcia and Fito Paez have played here).

Information

Banco de la Provincia de Córdoba (cnr López y Planes & 25 de Mayo) Has an ATM.

Tourist office (☎452966; www.lacumbre.gov.ar; Av Caraffa 300; ⊙8am-9pm Apr-Jun & Aug-Nov, to midnight Dec-Mar & Jul) Across from the bus terminal in the old train station. Friendly staff will supply a handy map of the town and surroundings.

Getting There & Away

Buses depart regularly from La Cumbre's convenient **bus terminal** (General Paz, near Caraffa), heading northward to Capilla del Monte (AR$7, 30 minutes) or south to La Falda (AR$6.50, 30 minutes), Cosquín (AR$12, 1¼ hours), Villa Carlos Paz (AR$20, 1½ hours) and Córdoba (AR$35, 2½ hours). Minibuses (which take about half an hour less) are the fastest way to Córdoba. There is also direct service to Buenos Aires (AR$326, 12½ hours).

Jesús María

☎03525 / POP 51,590

Sleepy little Jesús María earns its place on the map by being home to one of the most atmospheric Jesuit *estancias* in the region – the Unesco-listed **Museo Jesuítico Nacional de Jesús María** (☎420126; admission AR$10; ⊙8am-7pm Mon-Fri, 10am-noon & 2-6pm Sat & Sun). The church and convent were built in 1618 and are set on superbly landscaped grounds. The Jesuits, after losing their operating capital to pirates off the Brazilian coast, sold wine they made here to support their university in colonial Córdoba. The museum has good archaeological pieces from indigenous groups throughout Argentina, informative maps of the missionary trajectory and well-restored (though dubiously authentic) rooms.

Jesús María is also home to the annual **Fiesta Nacional de Doma y Folklore** (www.festivaljesusmaria.com.ar), a 10-day celebration of gaucho horsemanship and customs beginning the first weekend of January. The festival draws crowds from all over the country, and accusations of animal cruelty from animal-rights groups, who argue that whipping horses and making them perform acrobatics in front of noisy crowds under bright lights is tantamount to torture.

Most people do Jesús María as a day trip from Córdoba. Frequent minibuses (AR$15, one hour) leave Córdoba's Mercado Sud terminal and bus terminal daily.

Alta Gracia

03547 / POP 48,170 / ELEV 550M

Set around a 17th-century Jesuit reservoir, Alta Gracia is a tranquil little mountain town of winding streets and shady parks. The star attraction here is the 17th-century Jesuit *estancia*, whose exquisite church, nighttime lighting, and lovely location between a tiny reservoir and the central plaza make it one of the most impressive of Córdoba province's Unesco World Heritage sites. Revolutionary Che Guevara spent his adolescence in Alta Gracia and his former home is now a museum. Most visitors find a day enough and head back to Córdoba for the night.

CLOSE ENCOUNTERS

It's not just the freaks and hippies. Even normal-looking people in Capilla del Monte have stories about strange lights appearing in formation in the night skies over nearby Cerro Uritorco. The stories go way back, too. In 1935 Manuel Reina reported seeing a strange being dressed in a tight-fitting suit while he was out walking on a country road. In 1986 Gabriel and Esperanza Gómez saw a spaceship so big that its lights illuminated the surrounding countryside. The next day a burn mark measuring 122m by 64m was found at the point where it reportedly landed.

A couple of years later, 300 people witnessed another ship, which left a burn mark 42m in diameter. And in 1991, another burn mark was found. This one measured 12m in diameter, with a temperature of 340°C. Geologists were called in and they claimed that nearby rocks had recently been heated to a temperature of 3000°C.

Why all this activity around Capilla del Monte? This is where it gets really weird. One theory is that *Ovnis* (UFOs) visit the area because Cerro Uritorco is where the knight Parsifal brought the Holy Grail and the Templar Cross at the end of the 12th century. He did this to lay them beside the Cane of Order, which had been made 8000 years before by Lord Voltán of the Comechingones, the indigenous tribe that inhabited this region.

Another theory offers that they are drawn here because underneath Uritorco lies Erks, a subterranean city which, according to 'hermetic scientists' is where the future regeneration of the human species will take place. Inside you'll find the Esfera Temple and the three mirrors used to exchange data with other galaxies, and where you can see the details of the life of every human being.

The official explanation? Good ol' meteorological phenomena, caused by supercharged ion particles in the atmosphere, mixed in with a healthy touch of mass hysteria.

Whatever you believe, one thing's for sure – all this hype isn't hurting little Capilla del Monte's tourist industry one bit. Until recently, the only people climbing Uritorco were goatherds and a few interested townsfolk. These days, numbers can approach 1000 per day, all hoping to catch a glimpse of the mysterious lights.

If you want to climb Uritorco (1950m) you must start the climb before midday, and begin your descent by 3pm. The 5km hike to the top affords spectacular views. From Capilla del Monte, catch a taxi or walk the 3km to the base of the mountain.

Capilla del Monte is a comfortable enough place to base yourself – the town has plenty of restaurants and lodging – the **tourist office** (03548-481903; www.capilladelmonte.gov.ar; cnr Av Pueyrredón & Buenos Aires) in the old train station has mounds of information. For more info on UFOs in the area, drop in to the **Centro de Informes Ovni** (482485; www.ciouritorco.org; Juan Cabus 397; 10am-4pm). There is frequent bus service south to Córdoba (AR$23, three hours), stopping at all towns on the RN 38, and long-distance service to Buenos Aires.

WORTH A TRIP

ESTANCIA SANTA CATALINA

One of the most beautiful of the Sierra's Unesco World Heritage sites, the Jesuit *estancia* of **Santa Catalina** (☎03525-421600; www.santacatalina.info; admission AR$5-15; ⏰10am-1pm & 3-7pm Tue-Sun, closed Jan, Feb, Jul & Semana Santa), some 20km northwest of Jesús María, is a quiet, tiny place, where the village store occupies part of the *estancia*, and old-timers sit on the benches outside and watch the occasional gaucho ride past on a horse. Much of the *estancia* is off-limits to visitors, but guided **tours** (each site AR$5) are available, taking in the chapel, cloisters and novitiate, where unmarried slave girls were housed.

The grounds themselves, while a fraction of their former selves, are lovely and well maintained and you can easily while away an hour or two wandering around. Outside the *estancia*, around the back, is the original reservoir built by the Jesuits, now slowly being overtaken by tall-stemmed lilies.

Santa Catalina is the only Unesco World Heritage *estancia* still under private ownership. Part of the family owns and operates **La Ranchería de Santa Catalina** (☎03525-424467; s without bathroom AR$170, d AR$590;), a lovely inn, restaurant (meals around AR$45) and crafts store in the *ranchería*. It has only two rooms, which occupy the former slave quarters and, while small, are carefully decorated and retain their original stone walls. Three more rooms with bathrooms are being constructed, using traditional techniques. The place is run by a friendly couple who are more than willing to fill you in on the illustrious story of the *estancia*, from Jesuit times to the present.

A taxi out here from Jesús María costs about AR$100.

The **tourist office** (☎428128; www.altagracia.gov.ar; Reloj Público, cnr Av del Tajamar & Calle del Molino; ⏰7am-10:30pm summer, to 7pm winter) occupies an office in the clock tower.

Sights & Activities

Jesuit Estancia NOTABLE BUILDING

From 1643 to 1762, Jesuit fathers built the **Iglesia Parroquial Nuestra Señora de la Merced** (west side of Plaza Manuel Solares; admission free), the *estancia's* most impressive building. Directly south of the church, the colonial Jesuit workshops of **El Obraje** (1643) are now a public school. Beside the church is the **Museo Histórico Nacional del Virrey Liniers** (☎421303; www.museoliniers.org.ar; admission AR$5, Wed free; ⏰9am-1pm & 3-7pm Tue-Fri, 9:30am-12:30pm & 3:30-6:30pm Sat, Sun & holidays), named after former resident Virrey Liniers, one of the last officials to occupy the post of Viceroy of the River Plate. If you want to know every last historical detail, guided tours in English (AR$30 per person; held at 10am, 11:30am, 3:30pm and 5pm) are available and recommended – call to reserve one day in advance. If you just have a passing interest, each room has an information sheet in English, which gives you a fair understanding of what's going on.

Directly north of the museum, across Av Belgrano, the **Tajamar** (1659) is one of the city's several 17th-century dams, which together made up the complex system of field irrigation created by the Jesuits.

Museo Casa de Ernesto Che Guevara MUSEUM

(Avellaneda 501; admission AR$5; ⏰2-7pm Mon, 9am-7pm Tue-Sun) In the 1930s, the family of youthful Ernesto Guevara moved here because a doctor recommended the dry climate for his asthma. Though Che lived in several houses – including the house in Rosario, where he was born – the family's primary residence was Villa Beatriz, which was purchased by the city and restored as this museum. Its cozy interior is now adorned with a photographic display of Che's life, and a couple of huge photographs commemorating a recent visit from Fidel Castro and Hugo Chávez. If you think you've been on the road for a while, check out the map detailing Che's travels through Latin America – whatever you think of the man's politics, you have to admit he was well traveled. A small selection of Che paraphernalia (including cigars, of course) is on sale.

Sleeping & Eating

A number of cafe-bar-restaurants with sidewalk seating are scattered along Av Belgrano, in the three blocks downhill from the Jesuit museum.

The Legend of Che

One of Cuba's greatest revolutionary heroes, in some ways even eclipsing Fidel Castro himself, was an Argentine. Ernesto Guevara, known by the common Argentine interjection 'che,' was born in Rosario in 1928 and spent his first years in Buenos Aires. In 1932, after Guevara's doctor recommended a drier climate for his severe asthma, Guevara's parents moved to the mountain resort of Alta Gracia.

He later studied medicine in the capital and, in 1952, spent six months riding a motorcycle around South America, a journey that opened Guevara's eyes to the plight of South America's poor. The journal he kept during his trip hit bookstores around the world and inspired the movie *The Motorcycle Diaries*.

After his journey, Guevara traveled to Central America, finally landing in Mexico, where he met Fidel Castro and other exiles. The small group sailed to Cuba on a rickety old yacht and began the revolution that overthrew Cuban dictator Fulgencio Batista in 1959. Unfulfilled by the bureaucratic task of building Cuban socialism, Guevara tried, unsuccessfully, to spread revolution in the Congo, Argentina and finally Bolivia, where he was killed in 1967.

Today Che is known less for his eloquent writings and speeches than for his striking black-and-white portrait as the beret-wearing rebel – an image gracing everything from T-shirts to CD covers – taken by photojournalist Alberto Korda in 1960.

In 1997, on the 30th anniversary of Che's death, the Argentine government issued a postage stamp honoring Che's Argentine roots. You can take a look at the stamps and other Che memorabilia by visiting Alta Gracia's modest Museo Casa de Ernesto Che Guevara (see p287), inaugurated on June 14, 2001, on what would have been Che's 73rd birthday.

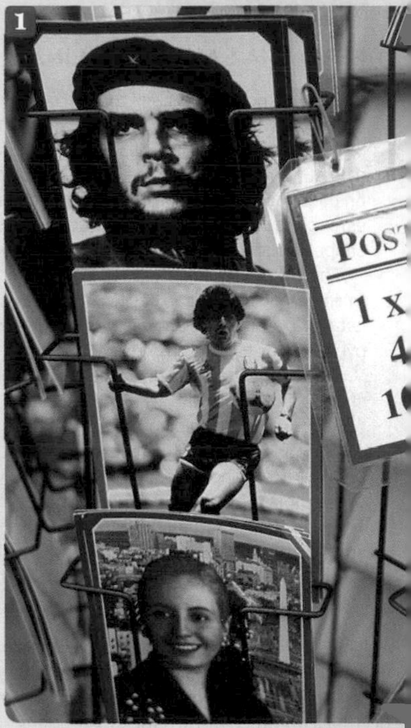

Clockwise from top left
1. Postcards **2.** Museo Casa de Ernesto Che Guevara (p287), Alta Gracia **3.** Mural, Plaza Dorrego (p54), San Telmo

2

FLK/IMAGEBROKER ©

TRAVEL INK/GETTY ©

Nuestra Señora de Altagracia HOTEL $$
(☎432213; www.altagraciaposada.com.ar; Avellaneda 346; s/d AR$410/450;) Bright and modern – if somewhat cramped – rooms in a lovely old house set on leafy grounds. The location just downhill from the Che museum is good for that, but is a bit removed from the rest of town.

Alta Gracia Hostel HOSTEL $
(☎428810; www.altagraciahostel.com.ar; Paraguay 218; dm AR$50, r AR$160) Five short blocks downhill from the Jesuit museum, Alta Gracia's hostel offers a fair deal. Dorms are roomy enough and the kitchen should meet your needs.

Morena FUSION $$
(Sarmiento 413; mains AR$40-70; ⊙lunch & dinner) Some of the best eats in town are on offer in the lovely dining salon of this upscale restaurant, a couple of blocks uphill from the reservoir.

Getting There & Away

Minibuses depart regularly for Córdoba (AR$11, one hour) a block uphill from the *estancia*. The **bus terminal** (Tacuarí at Perón) near the river also has departures for Córdoba and Buenos Aires (AR$321, 13 hours). Buses to Villa General Belgrano stop every hour on RP 5, about 20 blocks along Av San Martín from the center.

La Cumbrecita

☎03546 / POP 740 / ELEV 1300M

The pace of life slows waaaay down in this alpine-styled village, nestled in the forest in the Valle de Calamuchita. The tranquillity is largely thanks to the town's pedestrian-only policy. It's a great place to kick back for a few days and wander the forest trails leading to swimming holes, waterfalls and scenic lookouts.

Visitors must park their cars in the dirt parking lot (AR$30) before crossing the bridge over Río del Medio by foot.

The helpful **tourist office** (☎481088; www.lacumbrecita.gov.ar; ⊙8:30am-9pm summer, 10am-6pm winter) is on the left, just after you cross the bridge into town.

Sights & Activities

Hiking is the best reason to visit La Cumbrecita. Short trails are well marked and the tourist office can provide a crude but useful map of the area. A 25-minute stroll will take you to **La Cascada**, a waterfall tucked into the mountainside. **La Olla** is the closest swimming hole, surrounded by granite rocks (people jump where it's deep enough). **Cerro La Cumbrecita** (1400m) is the highest point in town, about a 20-minute walk from the bridge. Outside town, the highest mountain is the poetically named **Cerro Wank** (1715m); a hike to the top takes about 40 minutes.

For guided hikes further into the mountains, as well as horseback riding (AR$110 for four hours), trout fishing and mountain biking, contact **Viviendo Montañas** (☎481172; www.viviendomontanas.blogspot.com; Las Truchas s/n), which has an office on the main road in town. The company can also take you trekking to the top of **Cerro Champaquí** (2790m), the highest peak in the Sierras (a two-day trek), starting from AR$550 per person.

Sleeping & Eating

La Cumbrecita has more than 20 hotels and *cabañas* in the surrounding hills; the tourist office is a good resource. Make reservations in summer (January and February), during Easter and during Villa General Belgrano's Oktoberfest.

DON'T MISS

OKTOBERFEST IN VILLA GENERAL BELGRANO

If you're in the Sierras around the start of October, consider dropping in to Villa General Belgrano, a small, usually mellow town that celebrates its German heritage with the 10-day, nationally recognized Oktoberfest. While the beer runs as freely as it does at Oktoberfests all over the world, there are also parades, endless concerts and other cultural presentations. The festival also features so much delicious street food that you'll be loosening a couple of buttons on your Lederhosen, even if you're not a drinker.

Regular buses (AR$32, two hours) run to Villa General Belgrano from Córdoba's Mercado Sud minibus terminal.

Hospedaje Casa Rosita HOTEL $
(☎481003; Calle Principal s/n; s/d without bathroom AR$150/200) A humble little *hospedaje* (family home) set in a charming house by the river at the entrance to the village. If you can, go for room 1, which has a bay window overlooking the river.

Hotel La Cumbrecita HOTEL $$
(☎481052; www.hotelcumbrecita.com.ar; s/d AR$180/360; ❄🏊) Built on the site of the first house in La Cumbrecita, this rambling hotel has some excellent views out over the valley. Rooms aren't huge, but most have fantastic balconies. The extensive grounds include a gym and tennis courts.

Hostel Planeta HOSTEL $
(☎03546-15-409847; dm AR$70, r AR$100 per person) The best hostel in town is reached via a steep path next to the Hotel Las Verbenas tennis court. It's set in a lovely traditional house and has a good dining area and kitchen, reasonable dorms and killer views.

El Paseo PARRILLA $$
(mains AR$40-75; ⊙lunch & dinner Thu-Sun) Out by the La Olla swimming hole, this place serves up a good *parrilla*, plus all the Germanic standards. It's great for afternoon beer.

Restaurante Bar Suizo EUROPEAN $
(Calle Pública s/n; mains AR$30-50; ⊙breakfast, lunch & dinner) Pull up a wooden bench under the pine tree and try some of the excellent Swiss German options such as *spaetzle* with wild mushroom sauce.

Getting There & Away

From Villa General Belgrano, **Transportes Pajaro Blanco** (☎461709) has seven departures to La Cumbrecita (AR$27, one hour) from 7am to 7:30pm. The last bus back from La Cumbrecita leaves at 8:40pm. In summer there may be occasional minibuses from Córdoba's Mercado Sud terminal.

Parque Nacional Quebrada del Condorito

ELEV 1900-2300M

This national park protects 370 sq km of stunning rocky grasslands across the Pampa de Achala in the Sierras Grandes. The area, particularly the *quebrada* (gorge) itself, is an important condor nesting site and flight training ground for fledgling condors. A 9km, two- to three-hour hike from the park entrance at **La Pampilla** leads to the Balcón Norte (North Balcony), a clifftop over the gorge where you can view the massive birds circling on the thermals rising up the gorge. You can visit easily as a day trip from Córdoba or on your way to Mina Clavero.

Any bus from Córdoba to Mina Clavero will drop you at La Pampilla (AR$25, 1½ hours), where a trailhead leads to the gorge. To return to Córdoba (or on to Mina Clavero), flag a bus from the turnoff. Hostels in Córdoba arrange day tours to the park.

For more information on the park, contact **Intendencia del PN Quebrada del Condorito** (☎03541-433371; www.quebradacondorito.com.ar; Sabattini 33) in Villa Carlos Paz.

Mina Clavero

☎03544 / POP 15,690 / ELEV 915M

Really jumping in summertime, Mina Clavero pretty much empties out for the rest of the year, leaving visitors to explore the limpid streams, rocky waterfalls, numerous swimming holes and idyllic mountain landscapes at their own pace.

Mina Clavero is 170km southwest of Córdoba via RN 20, the splendid Nuevo Camino de las Altas Cumbres (Highway of the High Peaks). It sits at the confluence of Río de Los Sauces and Río Panaholma, in the Valle de Traslasierra.

The **tourist office** (☎470171; www.minaclavero.gov.ar; Av San Martín 1464; ⊙7am-midnight Dec-Mar, 9am-9pm Apr-Nov) has standard brochures and a useful map of town.

Sights & Activities

Mina Clavero's *balnearios* (swimming areas) get mobbed in summer, but are often empty the rest of the year. The boulder-strewn gorges of the Río Mina Clavero are easily explored. A lovely *costanera* (riverside road) has been constructed, running from the pedestrian bridge all the way to the **Nido de Aguila**, the best swimming hole around – this makes for a great afternoon stroll. From there head west along the Río de Los Sauces and you'll hit **Los Elefantes**, a *balneario* named for its elephant-like rock formations. A 3km walk south along the river will take you to **Villa Cura Brochero**, where you'll find black pottery that is characteristic of this region.

Traslasierra Aventura (☎470439; www.traslasierra.com/traslasierraaventura) offers tours of the nearby Comechingones mountains, condor spotting and horseback riding.

Sleeping

Many accommodations close around the end of March, when the town almost rolls up the sidewalks.

La Casa de Pipa HOTEL $$
(☎470480; www.lacasadepipa.com; Hernán Cortés at Colón; s/d AR$250/300; closed May & Jun;) This is a beautiful *hostería* (lodging house) set on mildly sloping grounds. There's plenty of shady spots, a good pool, a couple of barbecues and a lovely sunny breakfast room with views out over the mountains. It's about five blocks uphill from San Martín.

Andamundos Hostel HOSTEL $
(☎470249; www.andamundoshostel.com.ar; San Martín 554; dm/d AR$50/160;) A rustic little setup a couple of blocks from the center of town. The big yard backing on to the river is a bonus.

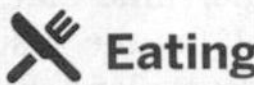

Eating

Most of Mina Clavero's restaurants are along San Martín. Head south over the river for more upscale *parrillas* and restaurants.

La Mamita PARRILLA $
(cnr San Martín & Recalde; mains AR$30-50; lunch & dinner) The most frequently recommended *parrilla* in town, serving up tasty empanadas and good-value set meals in front of the plaza.

Palenque INTERNATIONAL $$
(San Martín 1191; mains AR$40-80; lunch & dinner) Funky works of art on the walls and live music on the weekends make this a popular spot. It's a great place for drinks and the snacks and meals are a good deal, too.

Rincón Suizo CAFE $
(Champaqui 1200; mains AR$30-60; lunch & dinner) This comfy teahouse on the river prides itself on its homemade ice creams, delicious Swiss food (including fondue, raclette and ratatouille) and *torta selva negra*.

> **MINA CLAVERO SHORTCUT**
>
> The Río Mina Clavero splits the town in two. If you arrive at the bus terminal and are headed for Andamundos or La Casa de Pipa, take the pedestrian bridge across the river – from there it's only a couple of blocks to the former and a short taxi ride to the latter. Otherwise you have to go the long way around.

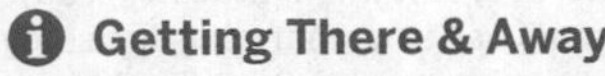

Getting There & Away

The **bus terminal** (Mitre 1191) is across the Río Mina Clavero from the town center. There are several daily buses to Córdoba (AR$45, three hours) and at least three a day to Merlo (AR$34, 2½ to three hours). Minibuses to Córdoba are faster (AR$35, 2½ hours). A couple of buses per day depart for Buenos Aires (AR$366, 13 hours). For destinations in San Juan and Mendoza provinces, go to nearby Villa Dolores (AR$15, one hour).

SAN LUIS & AROUND

The little-visited province of San Luis holds a surprising number of attractions, made all the better by the fact that you'll probably have them all to yourself.

The province is popularly known as La Puerta de Cuyo (the door to Cuyo), referring to the combined provinces of Mendoza, San Luis and San Juan (see also the boxed text, p301).

The regional superstar is without doubt the Parque Nacional Sierra de las Quijadas, but the mountain towns along the Valle de Conlara and Sierras Puntanas are well worth a visit if you're looking to get off the tourist trail.

Merlo

☎02652 / POP 18,300 / ELEV 890M

At the top of the Valle de Conlara, the mountain town of Merlo is a growing resort known for its gentle microclimate (the local tourist industry buzzword) in a relatively dry area. The town is located 200km northeast of San Luis, tucked into the northeast corner of San Luis province.

The **municipal tourist office** (☎476078; www.villademerlo.gov.ar; Coronel Mercau 605; 8am-8pm) has maps and information on hotels and campgrounds.

Sights & Activities

For a sweeping view of the town and valley, head up to the Mirador del Sol. Buses leave from the old bus terminal and cost AR$6 for the 40-minute ride. If you've got your walking shoes on (or better, have a private vehicle), you can continue on this road another 12km to the Mirador de los Condores, which is up on the mountain ridge, and gives views in both directions. There's a **confitería** (mains AR$20-40) up here and if the wind is

WORTH A TRIP

LOS GIGANTES

This spectacular group of rock formations, 80km west of Córdoba, is fast becoming Argentina's rock-climbing capital. The two highest peaks are the granite giants of Cerro de La Cruz (2185m) and El Mogote (2374m). There are numerous Andean condors – the park is only 30km from Parque Nacional Quebrada del Condorito, and the birds have slowly taken to this area as well. The area is home to the tabaquillo tree, with its papery peeling bark, which is endangered in Argentina and only found here and in Bolivia and Peru.

Getting here is complicated. **Sarmiento** (☎0351-433-2161) buses leave Córdoba's main bus terminal at 8am Wednesday to Monday and 6am on Tuesday (AR$35, two hours). The bus pretty much turns around and comes back again, meaning you have to spend the night. Schedules change frequently, so be sure to check.

Get off at El Crucero (tell the driver you're going to Los Gigantes). From there it's a 3km walk to La Rotonda, where there is a super-basic **hospedaje** (☎03541-498370; campsite per person AR$15, dm AR$45, per person kitchen use AR$15) and a small store (beer, soft drinks and snacks only), which is open on weekends.

At La Rotonda you can hire guides (AR$65) to show you around the cave complexes and take you to the top of Cerro de La Cruz. It's not a long hike, but there is some tricky rock scrambling involved. Guides are recommended because the maze of trails through the rocks can be hard to follow and if the fog comes down, you can easily get lost.

right, you can watch the parasailing maniacs taking off from the nearby launchpad.

Two kilometers from the center, in Rincon del Este, on the road to the Miradors, the **Reserva Natural de Merlo** (admission free; ⏰daylight hr) is a lovely spot for creekside walks up to a couple of swimming holes. The obligatory ziplines have been installed here and you can go whizzing through the canopy overhead for AR$40. **El Rincon del Paraiso** (set meals AR$35-60; ⏰breakfast & lunch), about 400m from the park entrance, is a beautiful, shady restaurant in the middle of the park – a great place for lunch or a couple of drinks.

Volando Bajo (☎476248; www.volandobajo turismo.tur.ar; Pringles 459) is the most established of the plethora of tour operators in town. It offers tours to the nearby archaeological/paleontological park at Bajo de Veliz (half-day AR$120), and a trip combining the nature reserve, and Miradors de Sol and de los Condores (half-day AR$90). Tandem parasailing flights cost around AR$350 and last 20 to 30 minutes, depending on wind conditions.

Sleeping

Hostería Cerro Azul HOTEL $$
(☎478648; www.hosteriacerroazul.com.ar; cnr Saturno & Jupiter; r AR$250; ❄) This bright, modern hotel just off the main drag offers big rooms with spacious bathrooms and tiny TVs. The lounge-dining area is gorgeous, with high cathedral ceilings.

Merlo Hostel HOSTEL $
(☎476928; www.merlohostel.com.ar; Av del Sol 1025; dm AR$55; @☎❄) A sweet little family home-turned-hostel. Dorms could be bigger, but there are good hangout areas, it's an excellent, central location and this is one of the few true budget options in town.

Eating & Drinking

Tono ARGENTINE $$
(Av del Sol 690; mains AR$40-70; ⏰lunch & dinner) Specializing in regional foods and using lots of local ingredients, this place is a good bet anytime, but Thursday to Saturday nights feature live *trova* (folk) bands, making it even better.

Cirano ITALIAN $
(Av del Sol 280; mains AR$25-40; ⏰lunch & dinner) Ignore the flashing fairy lights – there are some good-value eats on offer here, and an excellent set lunch or dinner for AR$25.

La Cerveceria BAR $
(Av del Sol 515; ⏰2pm-late) If you're looking for a beer, this is your spot – there's eight different types of microbrew on offer, plus the national and imported standbys, sidewalk seating and snacks.

BUSES FROM MERLO

DESTINATION	COST (AR$)	DURATION (HR)
Buenos Aires	283	12
Córdoba	88	6
Mendoza	154	8
Mina Clavero	34	3
San Luis	59	4

Getting There & Away

Long-distance buses leave from the **new bus terminal** (RN 1 at Calle de las Ovejas), about eight blocks south of the town center.

Getting Around

Local buses leave from the **old bus terminal** (492858; cnr Pringles & Los Almendres) in the center of town. There are departures for the Mirador del Sol (AR$6, 40 minutes), Piedra Blanca (AR$3, 20 minutes), Bajo de Veliz (AR$10, one hour), Papagayos (AR$5, one hour) and the nearby artisan village of Cerro de Oro (AR$2.50, 30 minutes).

San Luis

0266 / POP 215,850 / ELEV 700M

Even people from San Luis will tell you that the best the province has to offer lies outside of the capital. That said, it's not a bad little town – there are a few historic sights here and the central Plaza Pringles is one of the prettiest in the country. The town's main nightlife strip, Av Illia, with its concentration of bars, cafes and restaurants, makes for a fun night out.

On the north bank of the Río Chorrillos, San Luis is 260km from Mendoza via RN 7 and 456km from Córdoba via RN 148.

Sights

The center of town is the beautiful tree-filled Plaza Pringles, anchored on its eastern side by San Luis' handsome 19th-century **cathedral** (Rivadavia). Provincial hardwoods such as algarrobo (carob tree) were used for the cathedral's windows and frames, and local white marble for its steps and columns.

The commercial center is along the parallel streets of San Martín and Rivadavia between Plaza Pringles in the north and Plaza Independencia in the south.

On the north side of Plaza Independencia is the provincial **Casa de Gobierno** (Government House). On the south side of the plaza, the **Iglesia de Santo Domingo** (cnr 25 de Mayo & San Martín) and its convent date from the 1930s, but reproduce the Moorish style of the 17th-century building they replaced. Take a peek at the striking algarrobo doors of the attached **Archivo Histórico Provincial** around the corner on San Martín.

Dominican friars at the **mercado artesanal** (cnr 25 de Mayo & Rivadavia; 8am-1pm Mon-Fri), next to Iglesia de Santo Domingo, sell gorgeous handmade wool rugs as well as ceramics, onyx crafts and weavings from elsewhere in the province.

Also stroll over to the lovely former **train station** (Avs Illia & Lafinur) for a look at its green corrugated-metal roofs and decorative ironwork dating from 1884.

Sleeping

San Luis' better hotels cater to a business crowd, filling up quickly on weekdays and offering discounts on weekends.

Hotel Castelmonte HOTEL $$
(442-4963; hotelcastelmonte769@gmail.com; www.castelmontehotel.com.ar; Chacabuco 769; s/d AR$80/110;) An excellent-value midrange hotel. Its spacious rooms have wooden parquetry floors and good firm beds. While central, it's set back from the road, keeping things nice and quiet.

San Luis Hostel HOSTEL $
(442-4188; www.sanluishostel.com.ar; Falucho 646; dm/tw AR$55/140;) San Luis' best and most central hostel has it all, from pool table to DVD library, excellent kitchen and shady backyard with barbecue. The 16-person dorms (segregated for male and female) could be a bit more atmospheric, but apart from that it's pure gold.

Vista Suites & Spa BUSINESS HOTEL $$$
(442-5794; www.vistasuites.com.ar; Av Illia 526; ste from AR$660;) The latest addition to San Luis' seemingly saturated business hotel scene features way-slick design, a gourmet restaurant, day spa, indoor pool and all the other comforts you'd expect for the price.

Eating & Drinking

Traditional San Luis dishes include *empanadas de horno* (baked empanadas) and *cazuela de gallina* (chicken soup).

Los Robles PARRILLA **$$**
(Colón 684; mains AR$45-80; ⌚lunch & dinner) This upmarket *parrillas* has great atmosphere, attentive service and a menu that goes way beyond the usual offerings.

Aranjuez CAFE **$**
(cnr Pringles & Rivadavia; mains AR$25-50; ⌚breakfast, lunch & dinner) A fairly standard cafe/bar/restaurant on the plaza, this one gets a mention for the sidewalk tables out on the pedestrian thoroughfare which make it a great spot for drinks, snacks and people-watching.

There are numerous laid-back bars along Av Illia. As is the deal all over the country, they start late and end late. Go for a stroll and see which one you like.

Information

Several banks, mostly around Plaza Pringles, have ATMs.

ACA (Automóvil Club Argentino; ☎423188; Av Illia 401) Auto club; good source for provincial road maps.

Las Quijadas Turismo (☎443-1683; San Martín 874) Tours to Parque Nacional Sierra de las Quijadas, La Angostura and Inti Huasi.

Post office (cnr Av Illia & San Martín)

Regional hospital (☎442-2627; Av República Oriental del Uruguay 150) On the eastward extension of Bolívar.

Tourist office (☎442-3479; www.turismo.sanluis.gov.ar; intersection of Junín, San Martín & Av Illia; ⌚8am-9pm) The helpful staff can supply a good map of the town and its attractions plus offer good advice on regional attractions.

Getting There & Around

Air

San Luis airport (☎442-2427/57) is 3km northwest of the center; taxis cost around AR$15.

Aerolíneas Argentinas (☎442-5671, 443-7981; Av Illia 472) flies daily to Buenos Aires (AR$788).

Bus & Car

At the time of writing, San Luis was constructing a new **bus terminal** on the eastern edge of town. Until that's up and running, the **old terminal** (☎442-4021; España, btwn San Martín & Rivadavia) is about six blocks north of the main plaza. Provincial destinations, including Merlo (AR$26, four hours), El Volcán (AR$5, 30 minutes), Carolina (AR$13, two hours), Inti Huasi (AR$17, 2½ hours) and Balde (AR$7.50, 45 minutes), are served by local operators, whose ticket offices are in a separate building just in front of the main terminal complex.

There are long-distance departures daily to the destinations in the following table. For destinations such as Neuquén and Bariloche, you might have to head first to Mendoza or San Rafael.

Hertz (☎cell phone 15-455-9655; Av Illia 305) is the local car-rental agency.

BUSES FROM SAN LUIS

DESTINATION	COST (AR$)	DURATION (HR)
Buenos Aires	290	11
Córdoba	145	7
Mendoza	95	5
Rosario	200	9
San Juan	108	5
San Rafael	75	5
Santa Fe	230	12

Around San Luis

BALDE

☎0266

This small village, 35km west of San Luis, is remarkable only for its thermal baths. The municipal complex is a decidedly down-at-heel affair, while a new spa resort offers oodles of comfort in gorgeous surrounds.

Centro Termal Municipal (☎449-9319; Av Esteban Agüero s/n; 1hr baths per person AR$12, campsites AR$10, cabin for 2 people AR$180; ⌚baths 8am-6pm) offers small rooms with a bath and a bed to relax, rented by the hour. They're clean enough and decent value for a quick dip. Cabins (located across the road) are spacious for two.

Los Tamarindos (☎444-2220; www.jardinesdetamarindos.com; Av Esteban Agüero s/n; s/d AR$200/300, cabins s/d AR$230/350; ⌚baths 8am-6pm) is a wonderful thermal baths complex featuring a couple of public pools for day use – an outdoor one at 26°C (AR$20 per person) and a lovely, clean indoor one (AR$35 for both). The rooms here are standard, with small baths fed by hot spring water, but the cabins are a real treat – they're much more spacious and have a separate tub where you can get neck deep in the water.

Regular buses run to and from San Luis' bus terminal to the bus terminal at Balde (AR$7.50, 45 minutes), which is a short walk to either of the complexes.

Parque Nacional Sierra de las Quijadas

Fans of the *Road Runner* cartoon will feel oddly at home among the red sandstone rock formations in this rarely visited **national park** (admission AR$20). The park comprises 1500 sq km of canyons and dry lake beds among the Sierra de las Quijadas, whose peaks reach 1200m at Cerro Portillo. Recent paleontological excavations by the Universidad Nacional de San Luis and New York's Museum of Natural History unearthed dinosaur tracks and fossils from the Lower Cretaceous, 120 million years ago.

Despite the shortage of visitors here, access to the park is excellent: buses from San Luis to San Juan will drop visitors at the park entrance and ranger station (AR$30, 1½ hours) just beyond the village of Hualtarán, about 110km northwest of San Luis via RN 147 (San Juan is 210km to the northwest). At this point, a 6km dirt road leads west to a viewpoint overlooking the **Potrero de la Aguada**, a scenic depression beneath the peaks of the sierra that collects the runoff from much of the park and is a prime wildlife area. At the ranger station you can hire guides; two-hour, 3km treks to see the famous dinosaur footprints leave hourly between 9am and 4pm and cost AR$25 per person. Four-hour treks to a 150m-deep canyon in the park leave at 1:30pm and cost AR$50. A minimum group size of two people applies to both treks.

Other **hiking** possibilities in the park are excellent, but the complex canyons require a tremendous sense of direction or, preferably, the assistance of a local guide. Even experienced hikers should beware of summer rains and flash floods, which make the canyons extremely dangerous.

There's a shady **campground** (campsites free) near the overlook, and a small store with groceries and drinks, including very welcome ice-cold beer.

Buses from San Juan to San Luis pass every hour or so, but they don't always stop. It's sometimes possible to catch a lift from the park entrance to the overlook.

Valle de las Sierras Puntanas

From San Luis the RP 9 snakes its way northwards, following the course of the Río Grande. Along the way, small villages are slowly developing as tourist destinations while still retaining much of their original character. The picturesque mining town of Carolina and nearby Inti Huasi cave are highlights of the region, and the landscapes higher up in the valley, with their rolling meadows and stone fences, probably resemble the Scottish highlands more than anything you've seen in Argentina so far.

ESTANCIA LAS VERBENAS

Set in a gorgeous glade in the Valle de Pancanta, this **estancia** (☎02652-430918; RP 9, Km 68; per person incl full board AR$220; 📶) does rustic to the hilt, with plenty of hearty food served up among animal-skin decoration and rough-hewn furniture. Rooms are basic but comfortable. Two-hour horseback-riding tours (AR$40 per person) to a nearby waterfall are bound to be a highlight of your stay here. The signposted entrance to the property is just after the bridge on the highway, from where it's another 4km to the farmhouse. If you're coming by bus, call and staff will pick you up from the highway.

CAROLINA

☎02651 / POP 270 / ELEV 1610M

Nestled between the banks of the Río Grande and the foothills of Cerro Tomalasta (2020m), Carolina is a photogenic little village of stone houses and dirt roads. Take away the power lines and you could be stepping back in time 100 years. The region boomed in 1785 when the Spanish moved in to exploit local gold mines that had first been used by the Inca. Nobody uses street addresses in Carolina – the town is small enough to navigate without them.

Sights & Activities

One of the quirkier museums in the country, **Museo de Poesia** (admission free; ⏰10am-6pm Tue-Sat) honors San Luis' favorite son, poet Juan Crisóstomo Lafinur. The museum has a few artifacts from the poet's life, plus handwritten homages to the man by some of Argentina's leading poets.

Across the creek and up the hill from the poetry museum is a small **stone labyrinth**, set on the hilltop. It should provide an hour or so of entertainment (or, if your sense of direction is really bad, days of frustration).

Huellas Turismo (☎02652-490224; www.huellasturismo.com.ar) is the local tour operator – it can set you up with tours of the local gold mine (AR$40, two hours), rock climbing and rappelling trips on Cerro Tomalasta,

WORTH A TRIP

EL VOLCÁN

A small village nestled in the hills east of San Luis, El Volcán (there is no volcano here, by the way) is a laid-back summer getaway spot. The star attraction is the river that runs through the middle of town, where Balneario La Hoya, a series of natural rock pools, offers shady swimming spots and picnic areas.

El Volcán is close enough to San Luis to make it an easy day trip, but there are plenty of cabins for rent, especially during summer.

Hotel El Volcán (☎0266-449-4044; Banda Norte s/n; s/d AR$220/300; ❄≋) is the only real hotel in the village. It's a sprawling complex set on shady grounds that run down to the river. The hotel closes off-season – call to make sure it's open. **El Mantial** (Balneario La Hoya; mains AR$22-40; ⏲breakfast, lunch & dinner) has decent food and great views out over the river. Portions are big and service is quick, if somewhat impersonal.

Regular buses run to and from San Luis' main bus terminal (AR$5, 30 minutes).

and tours of Inti Huasi, La Casa de la Piedra Pintada and La Angostura.

Sleeping & Eating

Accommodation is improving in Carolina, but if you can't find a place, ask in the restaurants for a *casa de familia* (room in a private house with shared bathroom), which rents for around AR$40 per person.

La Posta del Caminante HOTEL $$
(☎490223; www.lapostadelcaminante.com.ar; RP 9 s/n; s/d AR$230/380; @☈≋) Carolina's one hotel is set in a gorgeous stone building on the edge of town. A lovely seminatural rock swimming pool out the back completes the picture. The hotel is open mainly in summer, so if you're set on staying here, call ahead.

Rincón del Oro Hostel HOSTEL $
(☎490212; Pringles s/n; dm AR$50) Set on a hilltop overlooking town, this great little hostel has a rustic, intimate feel despite its 57-bed capacity.

La Tomalasta CAFETERIA $
(mains AR$25-40; ⏲breakfast, lunch & dinner) Good-value home-cooked meals. If it looks like it's closed, go around the back to the general store and ask them to open up.

Getting There & Away

Regular buses run from Carolina to San Luis (AR$13, two hours), passing through El Volcán. Some continue on to Inti Huasi (AR$6, 30 minutes).

AROUND CAROLINA

INTI HUASI

This wide, shallow **cave** (admission free; ⏲daylight hr), whose name means 'house of the sun' in Quechua, makes an interesting stop, as much for the gorgeous surrounding countryside as the cave itself. Radiocarbon dating suggests that the cave was first inhabited by the Ayampitín some 8000 years ago. There are regular buses here from San Luis (AR$17, 2½ hours), passing through Carolina (AR$6, 30 minutes).

LA CASA DE LA PIEDRA PINTADA

Coming from Carolina, 3km before the Inti Huasi cave, a dirt track turns off to Paso de los Reyes. From the turnoff, it's an easy 5km signposted walk to **La Casa de la Piedra Pintada** (admission free), where more than 50 rock carvings are easily visible in the rock face. Follow the signs until you reach an open meadow at the base of Cerro Sololasta and you see the new cable-and-wood walkway up the cliff face that gives you access to the site. Once you're finished with the rock art, continue up the hill for spectacular views out over the Sierras Puntanas.

If you're unsure about getting here on your own, there's usually someone around at Inti Huasi who will guide you for a nominal fee.

LA ANGOSTURA

This site, 22km northeast of El Trapiche, holds one of the most extensive collections of indigenous rock art in the region. There's around 1000 examples here, painted and carved onto a shallow concave cliff face. Some are wonderfully preserved, while others fade with exposure to the weather. Keep an eye out for three mortar holes carved into the rock floor; they were most likely used to grind grain.

The site is tricky to access, even with a private vehicle. On the El Trapiche–Paso de los Reyes road, a signpost leads off to the right, through a closed (but not locked) gate. From there, it's 2.5km along a very bad dirt road to an abandoned stone farmhouse where the road ends.

The trail to the site is unmarked, but if you head uphill, veering right, you'll reach a stone bluff on the hilltop, giving excellent views over the valley. Descending on the right side of the bluff, you'll see the wire fence set up to protect the works of art.

Tour operators in Carolina (see p296) and San Luis (see p295), including the San Luis Hostel (p294) come out here, but it's not a popular excursion – get a group together, or expect to pay top dollar.

Valle de Conlara

Heading northeast to Merlo from San Luis, the landscape changes dramatically as the road climbs into the hills. Leaving San Luis the land is arid and desertlike, Papagayos has its own unique vistas, punctuated by palm trees, while Merlo is a lush mountain town.

ESTANCIA LA ESTANZUELA

Set on a Jesuit mission dating from 1750, this gorgeous **estancia** (☎02656-420559; www.estanzuela.com.ar; per person with full board AR$320;) has been left in near-original condition from the days when it was a working farm. Floors are wood or stone, walls are meter-thick adobe and many ceilings are constructed in the traditional gaucho style. The house is decorated like a museum, with antique furniture, paintings and family heirlooms galore. A small pond that the Jesuits built for irrigation serves for romantic rowboating outings and there is plenty of horseback riding and nature walking to be done. This is a very special – near-magical – place and the minimum three-night stay should not be hard to adhere to. Prices include meals, drinks and activities.

The property is located 2km off RP 1, between Villa del Carmen and Papagayos. The closest public transport is to Papagayos from Merlo. Reservations for rooms are essential and must be made at least two days in advance. If you don't have your own transport, ask about getting picked up in Papagayos or San Luis.

PAPAGAYOS

☎02656 / POP 430

Possibly the last thing you're expecting to see in this part of the world is a valley full of palm trees, but that's exactly where this small town is situated. The town is located on the banks of the Arroyo Papagayos and has huge Caranday palms surrounding it, giving the area a certain notoriety for handicrafts made from their trunks and branches.

Small stores (mostly attached to workshops) selling these *artesanias en palma* are scattered around town. **Rosa López** (in front of plaza) has the best range. The tourist office can provide a map showing all the store locations, along with other local attractions.

The *arroyo* (creek) is a good place to cool off – its length is dotted with swimming holes. For a more formal swimming environment, the Balneario Municipal offers swimming pools, picnic and barbecue areas.

For horseback riding and trekking to local waterfalls and swimming spots out of town, ask at the tourist office or Hostería Los Leños.

The **Oficina de Turismo** (☎480093; www.papagayos.gov.ar; RP 1 s/n; 8am-8pm) is useful for contacting guides and arranging tours, and has decent maps of the town.

Hostería Los Leños (☎481812; Av Comechingones 555; r AR$200;) is the best-looking hotel in town, featuring fresh new rooms with spacious bathrooms and a good-sized swimming pool. Also on offer are excellent home-cooked meals (mains AR$25 to AR$40) and staff can set you up with a picnic lunch if you're off on a day trip.

From Papagayos' main plaza there are regular buses to Merlo (AR$5, one hour).

Mendoza & the Central Andes

Includes »

Best Places to Eat

» Anna Bistro (p312)
» El Quincho de María (p325)
» Remolacha (p329)
» Café Tibet (p319)

Best Places to Stay

» Hotel Bohemia (p306)
» San Martín Hotel & Spa (p324)
» El Alemán (p331)
» Casa Antucura (p321)
» Microtel Inn (p325)
» 50 Nudos (p333)

Why Go?

A long, narrow sliver of desert landscape, the Mendoza region is home to two of Argentina's claims to fame – the Andes and wine. The city itself is lively and cosmopolitan and the surrounding area boasts hundreds of wineries offering tours – an educational (and occasionally intoxicating) way to spend an afternoon or a month.

If you can put your glass down for a minute, there's plenty more to keep you busy. Just down the road is Aconcagua, the Americas' highest peak and a favorite for mountain climbers the world over. A couple of ski resorts give you the chance to drop into fresh powder while Mendoza's tour operators offer up a bewildering array of rafting, mountain biking and paragliding options.

To the north, often-overlooked San Juan province is well worth a visit, as much for its small but important selection of wineries as for the surreal desert landscape of the Parque Provincial Ischigualasto.

When to Go

Mendoza

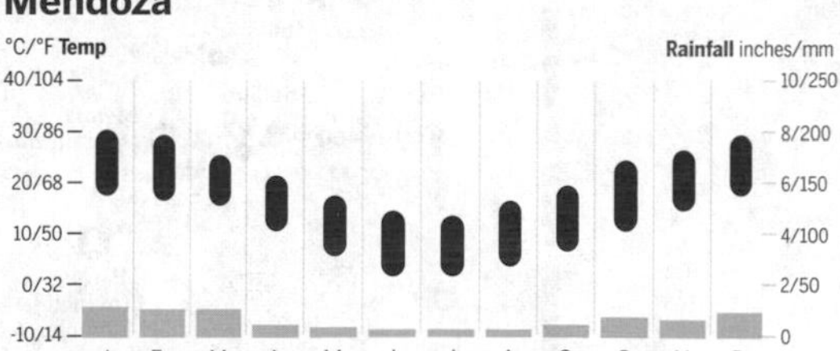

Dec–Mar Hot, dry weather makes this the perfect time to climb the region's highest peaks.

Apr–Jun Autumn is spectacular, thanks to the colors of Mendoza's trees and grapevines.

Jul–Sep Ski season paints the Andes white – a breathtaking sight, even for nonskiers.

Mendoza & the Central Andes Highlights

1. Carve tracks in fresh powder on the world-class slopes of **Las Leñas** (p326)
2. Grab some wheels and treat yourself to a tour of the wineries in **Maipú** (p318)
3. Get away from the crowds and into the stunning Valle de Calingasta in **Barreal** (p330)
4. Discover dinosaur fossils embedded in bizarre rock formations in **Parque Provincial Ischigualasto** (p335)
5. Make the scene in any number of hip bars on Av Arístides in **Mendoza** (p301)
6. Soak those aching traveling bones in the thermal complex at **Cacheuta** (p316)
7. Touch the roof of the Americas on **Cerro Aconcagua** (p320), the highest peak in the western hemisphere

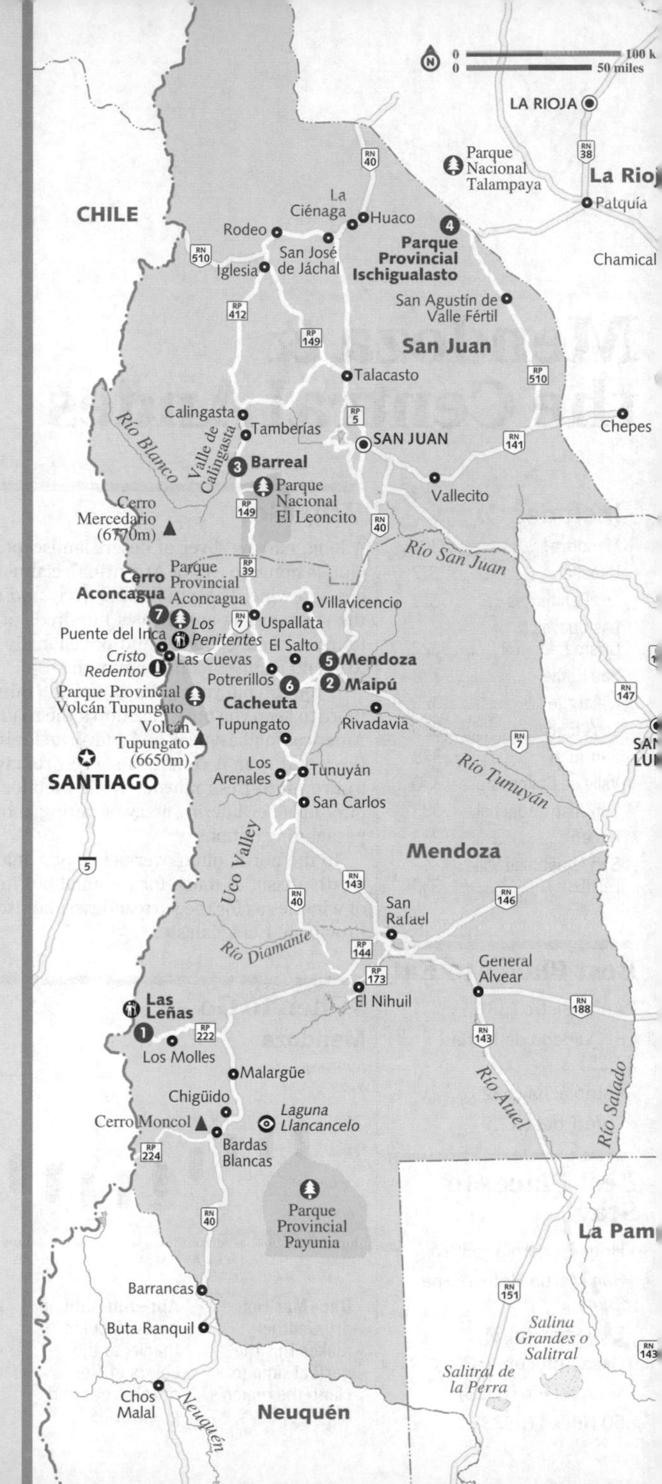

National & Provincial Parks

The region's most famous park is Parque Provincial Aconcagua (p320), home of 6962m Cerro Aconcagua, the highest peak outside the Himalayas. Nearby Parque Provincial Volcán Tupungato (p322) is another favorite climbing destination. For mind-blowing volcanic landscapes, visit the little-known Parque Provincial Payunia (p326) near Malargüe. In neighboring San Juan province Parque Provincial Ischigualasto (p335) is world famous for its dinosaur fossils as well as its spectacular desert rock formations.

Getting There & Away

With flights to/from nearby Santiago (Chile), Mendoza has the region's only international airport. There are regular flights to Mendoza, San Juan and San Luis from Buenos Aires. During ski season there are usually flights to Malargüe, near Las Leñas ski resort. Bus transportation is excellent throughout the province. If you're heading south to the Lake District, the fastest way can be to head to Neuquén city, but if you don't mind taking it slow, a seldom-explored section of RN 40 between Mendoza and Neuquén provinces can be a worthwhile detour.

Mendoza

0261 / POP 935,000 / ELEV 703M

A bustling city of wide, leafy avenues, atmospheric plazas and cosmopolitan cafes, Mendoza is a trap. Even if you've (foolishly) only given it a day or two on your itinerary, you're bound to end up hanging around, captivated by the laid-back pace while surrounded by every possible comfort.

Ostensibly it's a desert town, though you wouldn't know unless you were told – *acequias* (irrigation ditches) that run beside every main road and glorious fountains that adorn every main plaza mean you'll never be far from the burble of running water.

Lively during the day, the city really comes into its own at night, when the bars, restaurants and cafes along Av Arístides fill up and overflow onto the sidewalks with all the bright young things, out to see and be seen.

All over the country (and in much of the world), the name Mendoza is synonymous with wine, and this is the place to base yourself if you're up for touring the vineyards, taking a few dozen bottles home or just looking for a good vintage to accompany the evening's pizza.

The city's wide range of tour operators also makes it a great place to organize rafting, skiing and other adventures in the nearby Andes.

Mendoza is 1050km west of Buenos Aires via RN 7 and 340km northwest of Santiago (Chile) via the Los Libertadores border complex.

Strictly speaking, the provincial capital proper is a relatively small area with a population of only about 120,000, but the inclusion of the departments of Las Heras, Guaymallén and Godoy Cruz, along with nearby Maipú and Luján de Cuyo, swells the population of Gran Mendoza (Greater Mendoza) to nearly one million.

The city's five central plazas are arranged like the five-roll on a die, with Plaza Independencia in the middle and four smaller plazas lying two blocks from each of its corners. Be sure to see the beautifully tiled Plaza España.

Av San Martín is the main thoroughfare, crossing the city from north to south, and Av Las Heras is the principal commercial street.

A good place to orient yourself is the **Terraza Mirador** (free; 9am-1pm), which is the rooftop terrace at **City Hall** (9 de Julio 500), offering panoramic views of the city and the surrounding area.

Dangers & Annoyances

Mendoza has long been one of Argentina's safer destinations, but economic woes have caught up here, too, resulting in an increased number of street crimes. Tourists are rarely the target here and the city is still a safe place, but there are a few things to watch out for. Bag snatching and pickpocketing (particularly when the victim is wandering around with their hands full) are on

CUYO

The provinces of Mendoza, San Juan and, to some extent, neighboring San Luis (covered in the Córdoba & the Central Sierras chapter) are traditionally known as the Cuyo, a term which is derived from the indigenous Huarpe word *cuyum*, meaning 'sandy earth.' The Huarpes were the original practitioners of irrigated agriculture in the region, a legacy still highly visible throughout the region today. The term is one you'll encounter often, whether in the names of local bus companies, businesses and newspapers, or in everyday conversation.

the rise, as is the practice of snatching MP3 players from joggers in the park.

The areas around the bus terminal and on Cerro de la Gloria (in Parque General San Martín) now have an increased police presence, but are still considered dangerous at night. Increased caution is recommended during the early afternoon, too, as police tend to take the siesta along with everybody else. There have been several reports of people picking locks on hostel lockers – if you have something really valuable, leave it at your hostel's reception or, better yet, in its safe.

Mendoza

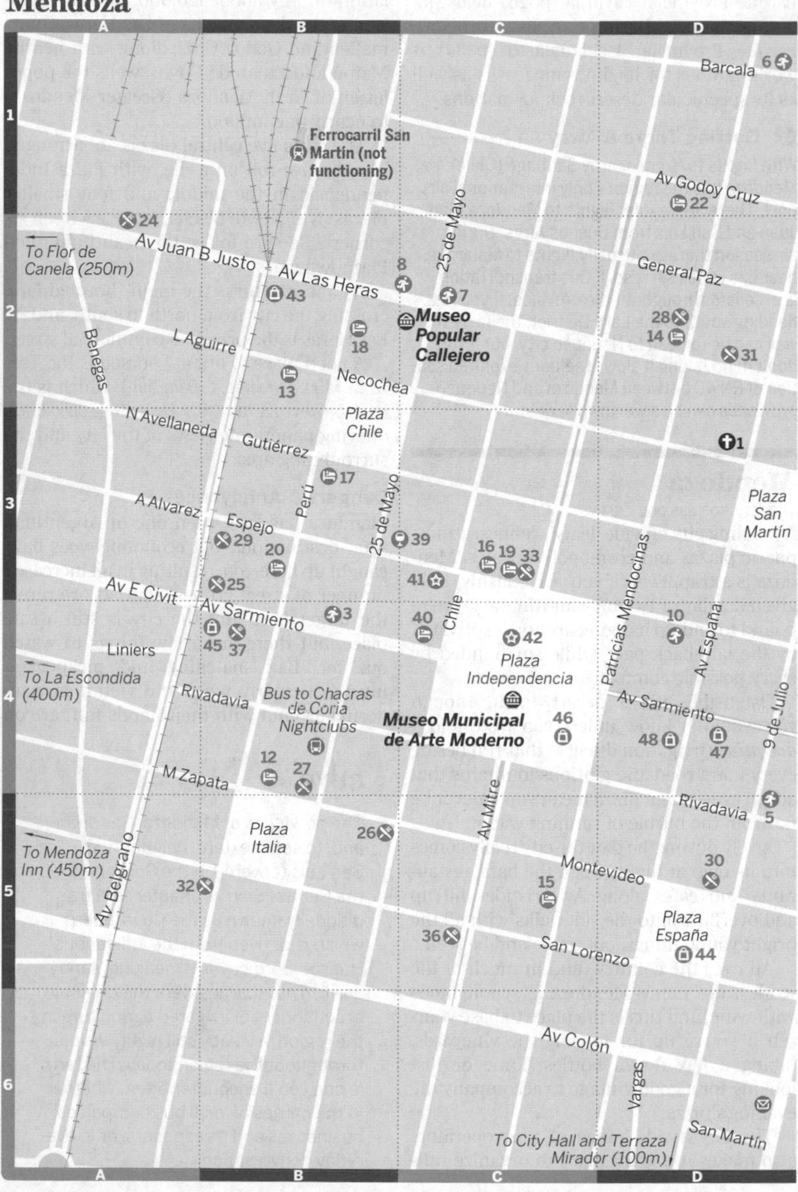

Sights

Museo Fundacional MUSEUM

(cnr Alberdi & Videla Castillo; admission AR$8; 8am-8pm) Mendoza's Museo Fundacional protects excavations of the colonial *cabildo* (town council), destroyed by an earthquake in 1861. At that time, the city's geographical focus shifted west and south to its present location. A series of small dioramas depicts Mendoza's history, working through all of human evolution as if the city of Mendoza were the climax (maybe it was).

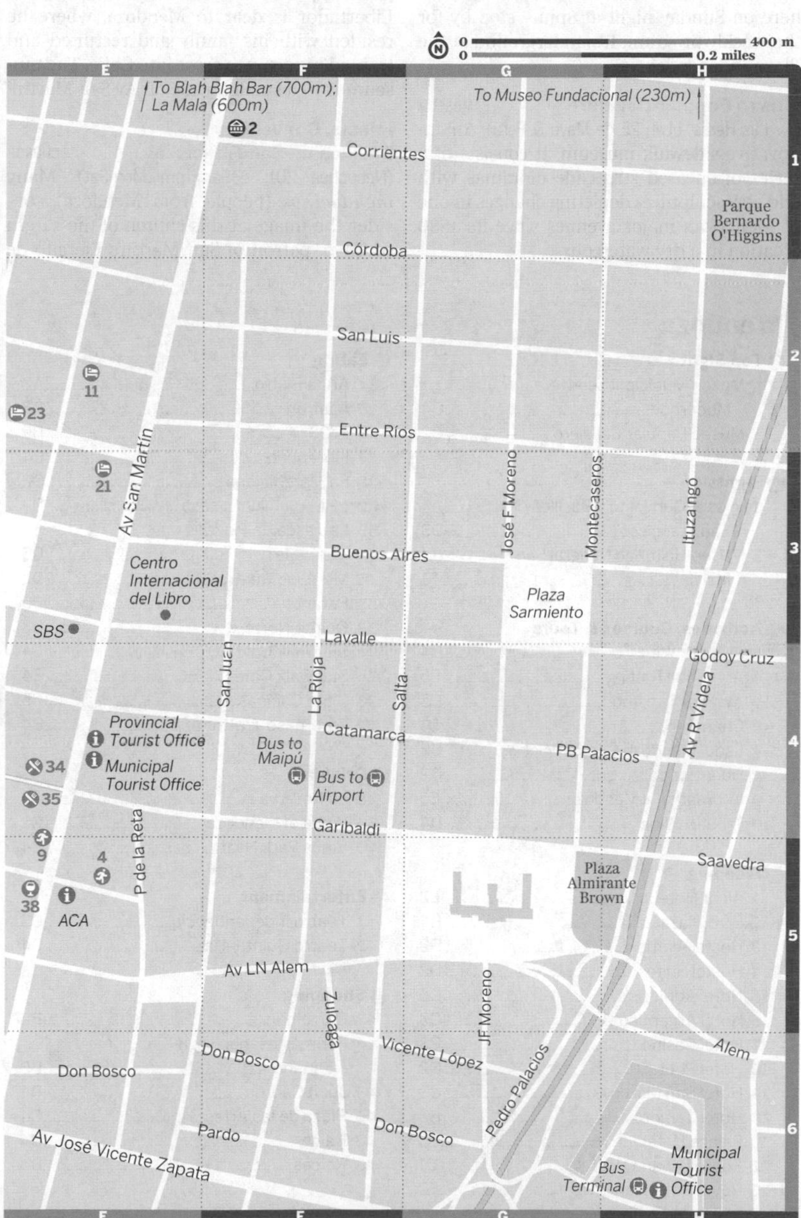

Museo Municipal de Arte Moderno MUSEUM
(Plaza Independencia; ⏲9am-8pm Tue-Sat, 4-8pm Sun & Mon) This is a relatively small but well-organized facility with modern and contemporary art exhibits. Free concerts and theatrical performances are usually held here on Sunday night at 8pm – stop by for the weekly program. It's underground at the Plaza Independencia,

Museo Popular Callejero MUSEUM
(Av Las Heras, btwn 25 de Mayo & Perú) An innovative sidewalk museum. It consists of a series of encased streetside dioramas with odd clay sculptures depicting changes in one of Mendoza's major avenues since its 1830 creation in a dry watercourse.

Museo Histórico General San Martín MUSEUM
(Remedios Escalada de San Martín 1843; admission AR$8; ⏲9am-1pm Mon-Fri) Honors José de San Martín, the general who liberated Argentina from the Spanish and whose name graces parks, squares and streets everywhere; the Libertador is dear to Mendoza, where he resided with his family and recruited and trained his army to cross into Chile. The museum is in a small arcade off Av San Martín.

Iglesia, Convento y Basílica de San Francisco CHURCH
(Necochea 201; ⏲9am-1pm Mon-Sat) Many *mendocinos* (people from Mendoza) consider the image at this church of the Virgin of Cuyo, patron of San Martín's Ejército de

Mendoza

Top Sights
Museo Municipal de Arte Moderno C4
Museo Popular Callejero C2

Sights
1 Iglesia, Convento y Basílica de San Francisco D3
2 Museo Histórico General San Martín F1

Activities, Courses & Tours
3 Ampora Wine Tours B4
4 Argentina Rafting E5
5 Aymará Turismo D5
6 Chamonix D1
7 Esquí Mendoza Competición C2
8 Huentata C2
9 International Mendoza E5
10 Trout & Wine D4

Sleeping
11 Alcor Hotel E2
12 B&B Plaza Italia B4
13 Hostel Alamo B2
14 Hostel Suites D2
15 Hotel Abril C5
16 Hotel Argentino C3
17 Hotel Casino B3
18 Hotel Petit B2
19 Hotel San Martín C3
20 Hotel Zamora B3
21 Palace Hotel E3
22 Punto Urbano Hostel D1
23 Royal Hotel Horcones E2

Eating
24 Anna Bistro A2
25 Azafrán B3
26 El 23 .... B5
27 Florentino B4
28 La Marchigiana D2
29 La Mira B3
30 La Tasca de Plaza España D5
31 Mercado Central D2
32 Patancha B5
33 Quinta Norte C3
34 Sidewalk Cafes E4
35 Sidewalk Cafes E4
36 Siete Cocinas C5
37 Tommaso Trattoria B4

Drinking
38 La Reserva E5
39 Vines of Mendoza C3
40 Vines Park Hyatt C4

Entertainment
41 Teatro Independencia C3
42 Teatro Quintanilla C4

Shopping
43 Carrefour B2
44 Feria Artesanal Plaza España D5
45 Juan Cedrón B4
46 Plaza de las Artes C4
47 Raices D4
48 Raices D4

los Andes (Army of the Andes), miraculous because it survived Mendoza's devastating 1968 earthquake. In the Virgin's semicircular chamber, visitors leave tributes to her and to San Martín. A mausoleum within the building holds the remains of San Martín's daughter, son-in-law and granddaughter, which were repatriated from France in 1951.

Parque General San Martín PARK

Walking along the lakeshore and snoozing in the shade of the rose garden in this beautiful 420-hectare park is a great way to enjoy one of the city's highlights. Walk along Sarmiento/Civit out to the park and admire some of Mendoza's finest houses on the way. Pick up a park map at the **Centro de Información** (☎420-5052, ext 22; cnr Avs Los Platanos & Libertador; ⏲9am-5pm), just inside the impressive entry gates, shipped over from England and originally forged for the Turkish Sultan Hamid II. The park was designed by Carlos (Charles) Thays in 1897, who also designed Parque Sarmiento in Córdoba. Its famous **Cerro de la Gloria** has a monument to San Martín's Ejército de los Andes for its liberation of Argentina, Chile and Peru from the Spaniards. On clear days, views of the valley make the climb especially rewarding.

Activities

Once you've sucked down enough fine wine and tramped around the city, get into the Andes, Mendoza's other claim to fame, for some of the most spectacular mountain scenery you'll ever see. Numerous agencies organize climbing and trekking expeditions, rafting trips, mule trips and cycling trips. For guides for Aconcagua, see p322.

Aymará Turismo ADVENTURE TOURS

(☎420-2064; www.aymaramendoza.com.ar; 9 de Julio 1023) Mule trips, trekking and rafting.

Argentina Rafting ADVENTURE TOURS

(☎429-6325; www.argentinarafting.com; Amigorena 86) Rafting, mountain biking, kayaking, paragliding and rock climbing, amongst other activities.

Cabaña La Guatana HORSE RIDING

(☎15-668-6801; www.criolloslaguatana.com.ar; Maza Sur 8001, Lulunta, Maipú) Horseback tours through the vineyards of Maipú.

Argentina Ski Tours SKIING

(☎630-0026; www.argentinaskitours.com; 2724 Benielli) Full-service ski tours and lessons in Spanish or English. Best quality ski-equipment rental in town. Also brokers a range of on-mountain accommodations.

CLIMBING & MOUNTAINEERING

Mendoza is famous for Cerro Aconcagua, the highest mountain in the Americas, but the majestic peak is only the tip of the iceberg when it comes to climbing and mountaineering here. The nearby Cordón del Plata boasts several peaks topping out between 5000m and 6000m, and there are three important rock-climbing areas in the province: Los Arenales (near Tunuyán), El Salto (near Mendoza) and Chigüido (near Malargüe).

Pick up a copy of Maricio Fernandez' full-color route guide (Spanish only), *Escaladas en Mendoza,* at **Inka Expediciones** (☎425-0871; www.inka.com.ar; Av Juan B Justo 345, Mendoza). For up-to-date information, contact the **Asociación Argentina de Guías de Montaña** (www.aagm.com.ar). See p322 for a list of the most experienced guides operating throughout the province.

For climbing and hiking equipment, both rental and purchase, visit **Chamonix** (☎425-7572; www.chamonix-outdoor.com.ar; Barcala 267).

SKIING & SNOWBOARDING

Los Penitentes (p319) has the best skiing near Mendoza, although further south, Las Leñas (p326) has arguably the best skiing in South America. For standard ski and snowboard equipment rental, try **Esquí Mendoza Competición** (☎429-7944; Av Las Heras 583) or any of the shops along Av Las Heras. In high season, all charge AR$80 to AR$125 per day for a skis-boots-poles package and about AR$125 per day for a snowboard with boots. Most rent gloves, jackets and tire chains, as well. If you're an intermediate or advanced skier, Argentina Ski Tours can set you up with much better equipment.

WHITE-WATER RAFTING

The major rivers are the Mendoza and the Diamante, near San Rafael. Most agencies offer trips ranging from one-hour runs (AR$145) to full-day descents (from AR$420) and multi-day expeditions. Transport costs AR$50 extra. Well-regarded Argentina Rafting operates a base in Potrerillos but you can book trips at its Mendoza office.

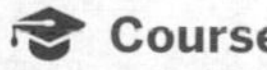

Courses

Fundación Brasilia SPANISH

(☎423-6917; www.fundacionbrasilia.org; Av Arístides Villanueva 251) Offers individual Spanish classes for AR$90 per hour as well as group classes.

Tours

Huentata GUIDED TOUR
(☎425-7444; www.huentata.com.ar; Av Las Heras 699) Conventional travel agency that organize trips in and around town. Possibilities include half-day tours of the city (AR$70), and day tours of the Cañon del Atuel (AR$190), Villavicencio (AR$90) or the high cordillera around Potrerillos, Vallecito and Uspallata (AR$150).

Internacional Mendoza BICYCLE RENTAL
(☎423-2103; www.internacionalmendoza.com; San Martín 1070, Local 3) Rents bikes for AR$40 for six hours, including a city map and MP3 player with audio bike tour of the city.

Wine Tours

For the casual sipper, a self-guided tour of Maipú (see p318) or any of the bodega tours offered by various travel agencies around town will likely satisfy. There are also a few companies operating out of Mendoza offering deluxe wine tours. They're not cheap, but small group sizes, English-speaking guides and access to exclusive vineyards are among the benefits. All those listed here also offer tours of the Valle de Uco (see p321), an important new wine-growing region 150km south of Mendoza that's near-impossible to explore by public transport and is only just starting to appear on tour-agency itineraries.

Trout & Wine TOURS
(☎425-5613; www.troutandwine.com; Espejo 266) Organizes custom-designed full-day tours of Luján de Cuyo (AR$710) and the Uco valley (AR$750) with a maximum group size of eight. From November to March it runs fly-fishing tours in the Valle de Uco for AR$1500, including all gear and a barbecue lunch out in the highlands accompanied by – you guessed it – some very fine wines.

Ampora Wine Tours TOURS
(☎429-2931; www.mendozawinetours.com; Av Sarmiento 647) A well-established operation that concentrates on midrange and top-end wines. It has tours leaving every day to Luján de Cuyo and Maipú (AR$700) and the Uco valley (AR$730). Tours focus more on tasting than winemaking techniques. Also offers four-hour cooking classes led by famous winery chefs from the region (AR$525).

Mendoza Wine Camp TOURS
(☎630-0026; www.mendozawinecamp.com) A young company offering tours aimed more at connoisseurs and industry professionals. Tours are led by experts and each winery visit focuses on one aspect of production (rather than covering them all at every winery you visit). Also offers horseback wine tours and a great *asado* (barbecue grill) cooking class day trip. Prices run about AR$770 per day.

Festivals & Events

Mendoza's biggest annual event, the **Fiesta Nacional de la Vendimia** (National Wine Harvest Festival), lasts about a week, from late February to early March. It features a parade on Av San Martín with floats from each department of the province, numerous concerts and *folklórico* events, and it all culminates in the coronation of the festival's queen in the Parque General San Martín amphitheater.

Sleeping

Note that hotel prices rise from January to March, most notably during the wine festival in early March. Some hostels in Mendoza will only rent you a bed if you buy one of their tours. None of these are listed below.

TOP CHOICE **Hotel Bohemia** BOUTIQUE HOTEL $$$
(☎420-0575; www.bohemiahotelboutique.com; Granaderos 954; s/d AR$360/425; ❄@🛜🏊) Somewhat out of place in Mendoza's otherwise workaday hotel scene, this repurposed family home features slick design, comfortable common areas and small but well-appointed rooms featuring minimalist decoration. It's about eight blocks west of the Plaza Independencia.

Hotel Argentino HOTEL $$
(☎405-6300; www.argentino-hotel.com; Espejo 455; s/d AR$374/400; ❄@🛜🏊) Right on the central plaza, this business-class hotel has some fine features, including large rooms and a decent-sized swimming pool. Pay extra for a balcony overlooking the plaza.

Hostel Alamo HOSTEL $
(☎429-5565; www.hostelalamo.com.ar; Necochea 740; dm AR$65, d with/without bathroom AR$190/145; @🛜🏊) An impeccable hostel in a great location, the Alamo offers roomy four-bed dorms, great hangout areas and a wonderful backyard with a small swimming pool.

B&B Plaza Italia B&B $$$
(☎423-4219; www.plazaitalia.net; Montevideo 685; r AR$400; ❄🛜) This six-room B&B is hard to beat when it comes to friendliness and delicious breakfasts. The house is lovely, the owners (who speak English) are divine, and

the living room is just right for reading. It's like being at home.

La Escondida HOTEL **$$**
(☎425-5202; www.laescondidabb.com; Julio A Roca 344; s/d AR$269/310; P❄@📶🏊) Set in a huge house in the quiet residential neighborhood known as La Quinta, rooms here aren't fancy but the place just feels right. Great value, run by a friendly family.

Alcor Hotel HOTEL **$$**
(☎438-1000; www.alcorhotel.com.ar; General Paz 86; s/d AR$250/295; ❄📶) One block from busy Av Las Heras, this is a recently renovated hotel that has maintained a few of its original charms. Rooms are big, light and well proportioned, with some comfy touches. Discounts apply for stays longer than three days.

Plan B Hostel HOSTEL **$**
(☎420-2869; www.hostelplanb.com; Olascoaga 1323; dm/d AR$68/160; @📶) Set in a quiet residential neighborhood just out of the center, this beautiful little hostel offers six-bed dorms with good mattresses, OK private rooms and a tranquil, friendly atmosphere.

Punto Urbano Hostel HOSTEL **$**
(☎429-5281; www.puntourbanohostel.com; Av Godoy Cruz 332; dm AR$60 d with/without bathroom AR$180/140; @📶) Just north of the city center, this hostel maintains an air of intimacy despite its grand proportions. The dorms are regular, but the doubles are extremely good value – spacious, with wide-screen TVs and tastefully decorated bathrooms. The large backyard – good for smoking, drinking, barbecuing and generally hanging out – is an added bonus.

Hotel Casino HOTEL **$**
(☎425-6666; www.nuevohotelcasino.com.ar; Gutiérrez 668; s/d AR$120/150; P❄📶) Facing on to Plaza Chile, the Hotel Casino offers some good, spacious rooms and some smallish, ordinary ones. They're all clean and comfortable, but have a look at a few before deciding.

Mendoza Inn HOSTEL **$**
(☎438-0818; www.mendozahostel.com; Av Arístides Villanueva 470; dm/d from AR$65/220; @📶🏊) With a great location and friendly, bilingual staff, this is one of the city's better hostels. Common areas are spacious and the big shady backyard and pool are definite pluses.

Hotel Zamora HOTEL **$**
(☎425-7537; Perú 1156; s/d AR$90/160; P❄📶) With a lot more style than most in this price range, this sweet little family-run hotel offers comfortable rooms, a buffet breakfast and a charming courtyard with tinkling fountain and Spanish tilework.

Hotel San Martín HOTEL **$$**
(☎438-0677; www.hsm-mza.com.ar; Espejo 435; s/d AR$235/265; ❄@📶) Fronting the plaza, this three-story brick hotel offers solid value. There's plenty of tasteful tile work and rooms are spacious and comfortable with modern bathrooms and big windows.

Hostel Suites HOSTEL **$**
(☎423-7018; www.hostelsuitesmendoza.com; Mendocinas 1532; dm/s/d AR$70/100/200; ❄@📶) A definite step above most other hostels in town, this one is well designed and well organized, offering a decent deal on dorms and extremely good-value singles. Free activities, tours, a good kitchen, rooftop terrace and a central location round out the picture.

Hotel Petit HOTEL **$$**
(☎423-2099; www.petit-hoteles.com.ar; Perú 1459; s/d AR$130/170; P❄📶) An excellent, central location, friendly welcome and big buffet breakfast make up for the slightly cramped rooms at this clean but ageing hotel.

Royal Hotel Horcones HOTEL **$$**
(☎425-0045; www.hotelhorcones.com; Av Las Heras 145; s/d AR$160/210; ❄@📶) A good deal on very central, spacious rooms. The wallpaper could do with a change, but the parquetry floors and sunny patio area are winners.

Palace Hotel HOTEL **$$**
(☎423-4200; www.hotelpalace.com.ar; Av Las Heras 70; s/d AR$200/250; P❄📶) The fading '70s charm of this large hotel is compensated for by its great, central location and a few classy decorations left over from the good ol' days. Rooms are generously sized and those at the front boast views out over the busy avenue.

Hotel Abril HOTEL **$$**
(☎429-0027; www.hotel-abril.com; Mendocinas 866; s/d from AR$210/235; P❄@📶) A modern hotel with touches of class, the Abril never really lives up to its 'boutique' claims, but is a pretty good deal for the price, amenities and location.

Eating

Some of Mendoza's best restaurants, often with outdoor seating and lively young crowds, are along Av Arístides Villanueva, the western extension of Av Colón. West of

(Continued on page 312)

Mendoza's Wine

From humble beginnings...

Since the Jesuits first planted vines in northern Argentina more than 500 years ago, Argentine wine has gone from strength to strength, and the country is now recognized as one of the leading international wine producers.

The first major improvement came with the arrival of European immigrants in the 19th century. These folks brought varieties from their home countries, replacing the Jesuit's criollo vines with 'noble' varieties such as merlot and cabernet sauvignon. The new grapes brought a minimal increase in quality, but even so, Argentine wine remained a very domestic product, often to be enjoyed with a big blast of soda to take the edge off.

Then, as if from nowhere, Argentine wines hit the world stage with a vengeance, and these days a Mendoza merlot has just as much (if not more) cachet than a comparably priced Chilean red.

While the wineries have definitely improved their marketing, in the end it all comes down to quality – Argentine wines are good and they just keep getting better. One of the keys to successful wine making is controlled irrigation. A big rain before a harvest can spoil an entire crop, something winemakers in the desertlike Mendoza region don't have to worry about. Nearly every drop of water is piped in, and comes as beautiful fresh snowmelt from the Andes.

Desert vineyards have another advantage – the huge variation between daytime and nighttime temperatures. Warm days encourage sugar production and help the grapes grow a nice thick skin. Cool nights ensure good acidity levels and low humidity means bugs and fungus aren't a problem.

Clockwise from top left
1. French oak barrels, Mendoza **2.** Catena Zapana winery (p316) **3.** Wine bottles, Mendoza

The techniques are improving, too – better hygiene standards, the further replacement of old 'criollo' vines with 'noble' varieties such as malbec, cabernet sauvignon, merlot and syrah, and the practice of ageing wines in smaller oak barrels (with a lifespan of a few years) rather than large barrels (which would be used for up to 70 years) have all had positive effects.

And you can't talk about Argentine wines without talking price-to-quality rat The country's economic crash in 2001 wa a boon for exporters as prices plummetec and overnight Argentine wine became a highly competitive product. Land here is (relatively) cheap and labor so inexpensiv that nearly every grape in the country is hand-picked, a claim that only top-end wines in other countries can make.

C.Sauvignon
2000
Weinert.

2

The Grape Escape

As Mendoza's wine industry grows so does its sister industry of wine tourism. These days it's not whether you can do a wine tour, but really which one and how.

There are options for every budget. If you're watching your pesos, biking around the Maipú region is an excellent value option. Wineries here are close together and their tour prices are low, so you can visit several in a day and taste some decent wines without breaking the bank. The area is also home to artisanal chocolate, olive oil and deli goods. Be aware that this is a very popular way to spend the day, and some wineries will herd you through like cattle to make space for the next group. For more on the Maipú region, see p318.

If you're not a cyclist but not ready to commit to a full-on wine tour either, a good middle option is the satellite town of Luján de Cuyo, 19km south of Mendoza. You can bus and taxi around the area wi a minimum of planning, hit three or four wineries (after which the tours tend to ge a little repetitive anyway) and be back in Mendoza before nightfall. For more on th Luján de Cuyo area, see p316.

Those who can afford a little more and are more interested in learning about techniques in a more relaxed setting should consider a tour with one of the outfits listed on p306. You'll avoid the crowds, and sometimes even get to meet the winemakers. The gourmet lunch and top-shelf tastings that come with these tours are additional draws. The gourmet lunch at one of the wineries and top-shel tastings that come with these tours may the scales, too. All the companies referre to above can organize custom tours for th serious connoisseur, designed to take in the specific wineries, regions or even win that you are particularly interested in.

But if you have the time and money, t best way to tour the region is strictly DIY Rent a car in Mendoza, buy one of the winery maps on sale at every newsstand and make your own itinerary. Make the

Below
Wine tasting, Mendoza

ost of your freedom by visiting the Valle Uco – home to some of the Mendoza ion's most cutting-edge wineries. about 150km south of the city, but rc arc plenty of wineries offering ommodations and even specialty Wine dges – you can stay out there and toodle und to your heart's content. Be warned, ugh, that Argentina has a zero-tolerance for driving under the influence – if ever were to get pulled over out on of those lonely country roads after a vy day in the tasting room you could in trouble. For more on the Valle de region, including wineries to visit and ces to stay, see p321.

ove
e-tasting cycling tour, Mendoza

MENDOZA SHOPPING LIST

Spoiled for choice? Here are our top picks:

Reds

» Cavagnaro Malbec (AR$75)
» Kaiken Cabernet Savignon (AR$107)
» Salentein Primus Malbec (AR$200)
» Carinae Prestige Blend (AR$244)

Whites

» Angelica Zapata Chardonnay Alta (AR$90)
» Terrazas de los Andes Tardio Petit (AR$95)
» Tapiz Single Vineyard Sauvignon Blanc (AR$55)
» Alta Vista Premium Torrontes (AR$50)

(Continued from page 307)

Plaza Independencia, Av Sarmiento is lined with the city's most traditional, albeit touristy, *parrillas* (steak restaurants), while east of the plaza along the Sarmiento *peatonal* (pedestrian street), you'll find numerous sidewalk cafes with outdoor seating. The Sarmiento cafes are required visiting for coffee. The renovated **Mercado Central** (cnr Av Las Heras & Patricias Mendocinas) is a good hunting ground for reasonably priced set meals.

TOP CHOICE Anna Bistro FUSION **$$**
(Av Juan B Justo 161; mains AR$50-80; ⏲lunch & dinner) One of Mendoza's best-looking restaurants offers a wonderful garden area, cool music and carefully prepared dishes.

La Flor de la Canela PERUVIAN **$**
(Av Juan B Justo 426; mains AR$30-40; ⏲lunch & dinner) Need something spicy? Check out this authentic, bare-bones Peruvian eatery a few blocks from the center. What it lacks in atmosphere it makes up for in flavor.

Patancha INTERNATIONAL **$$**
(Perú 778; mains AR$45-70; ⏲lunch & dinner) A cute little place serving up some great tapas alongside traditional favorites like humitas and the occasional surprise such as seafood stir-fry. The AR$38 set lunch is a bargain.

La Tasca de Plaza España SPANISH **$$**
(☎423-3466; Montevideo 117; mains AR$40-80; ⏲dinner) With excellent Mediterranean and Spanish tapas (mostly seafood), great wines, intimate atmosphere, good art and friendly service, La Tasca is one of Mendoza's best.

Florentino FUSION **$$**
(Montevideo 675; mains AR$50-80; ⏲dinner) One of the more innovative restaurants downtown, it specializes in lighter dishes combining flavors you're unlikely to find elsewhere. Vegetarian and celiac options available.

El Palenque ARGENTINE **$**
(Av Arístides Villanueva 287; mains AR$37-52; ⏲lunch & dinner Mon-Sat) Don't miss this superb, extremely popular restaurant styled after an old-time *pulpería* (tavern), where the house wine is served in traditional *pinguinos* (white ceramic penguin-shaped pitchers). The food and appetizers are outstanding, and the outside tables are always full and fun.

Siete Cocinas ARGENTINE **$$$**
(San Lorenzo & Mitre; mains AR$65-100; ⏲dinner) Promising a gastronomical tour of Argentina's seven regional cuisines, this place delivers handsomely with delicacies such as goat cheese ravioli, slow-cooked pork and Patagonian lamb-and-mushroom pie.

Tommaso Trattoria ITALIAN **$$**
(Av Sarmiento 762; mains AR$40-60; ⏲lunch & dinner) An excellent, trilingual (Italian, Spanish and English) menu featuring a good range of creative regional Italian dishes. The wine list is impressive and the tables out the front are the place to be on a balmy evening.

Cocina Poblana MIDDLE EASTERN **$**
(Av Arístides Villanueva 217; dishes AR$30-45; ⏲lunch & dinner Mon-Sat) The very tasty, inexpensive Middle Eastern food here (hummus, falafel, dolmas) comes as a welcome break from all that steak. The shish kebab served with tabouleh salad is a definite winner.

Quinta Norte ARGENTINE **$**
(Av Mitre & Espejo; set meals AR$25-40; ⏲lunch & dinner) Sidewalk dining right across from the plaza. The menu's not huge, but there are some good dishes and the AR$25 set lunches are some of the best in town. A great place to grab a coffee and recharge the batteries.

El 23 ARGENTINE **$$$**
(Montevideo & Chile; mains AR$50-100; ⏲lunch & dinner) With a great courtyard setting and some good seafood and steak dishes, this restaurant (with attached wine store) is a good bet anytime, but particularly on a sunny day. Set meals (AR$52) and wine by the glass are available.

La Marchigiana ITALIAN **$$**
(Patricias Mendocinas 1550; mains AR$40-60; ⏲lunch & dinner) Mendoza's most frequently recommended Italian restaurant. The decor may seem stark, but the service is warm and a few Argentine twists to the classic Italian menu keep things interesting.

La Mira FUSION **$$**
(Av Belgrano 1191; mains AR$45-60; ⏲lunch & dinner) Delicious, innovative dishes in a relaxed environment. Each dish comes as a full meal (some with side orders of vegetables) and there's a small but respectable wine list.

Azafrán FUSION **$$$**
(☎429-4200; Av Sarmiento 765; mains AR$70-100; ⏲lunch & dinner Mon-Sat) It's hard to figure out what's the bigger draw here – the rustic-chic decor, the small but creative menu or the extensive wine list. Who cares? Enjoy them all.

Drinking

For a great night on the town, walk down Av Arístides Villanueva, where it's bar after bar; in summer, entire blocks fill with tables and people enjoying the night. On the other side of town is the Tajamar, which is similar, but more laid-back and bohemian. This area is your best bet to hear live music.

Wine is available pretty much everywhere in Mendoza (right down to gas stations), but there are a few places that specialize.

Por Acá BAR

(☎420-0346; Av Arístides Villanueva 557) Purple and yellow outside and polka-dotted upstairs, this bar-lounge gets packed after 2am, and by the end of the night, dancing on the tables is not uncommon. Good retro dance music.

La Reserva GAY

(Rivadavia 34; admission free-AR$25) This small, nominally gay bar packs in a mixed crowd and has outrageous drag shows at midnight every night, with hard-core techno later.

Vines of Mendoza WINE BAR

(Espejo 567; ⏲3-10pm) This friendly, central wine bar (where everybody, down to the security guards, seems to speak English) offers flights (tastings of five selected wines) and top-shelf private tastings. It also offers wine-appreciation classes which give you an idea of how to taste wine – a great idea before hitting the bodegas.

Blah Blah Bar BAR

(Escalada 2307) A Tajamar favorite, Mendoza's version of a dive bar is hip but restrained, with a casual atmosphere and plenty of outdoor seating.

Vines Park Hyatt WINE BAR

(Chile 1124; ⏲11am-midnight) In the superformal surrounds of Mendoza's best-looking hotel, this is a relaxed and intimate wine bar offering wine by the glass, cheese platters and tapas.

☆ Entertainment

Check the tourist offices or museums for a copy of *La Guía,* a monthly publication with comprehensive entertainment listings. *Los Andes,* the daily rag, also has a good entertainment section.

Nightclubs

Finding a dance floor generally means abandoning downtown for one of two areas: the northwest suburb of El Challao, or Chacras de Coria, along the RP 82 in the southern outskirts. The former is reached by bus 115 from Av Sarmiento. Chacras de Coria is reached from the stop on La Rioja between Catamarca and Garibaldi by taking bus 10, *interno* (internal route number) 19, or from the corner of 25 de Mayo and Rivadavia by taking bus 10, *interno* 15. In both cases simply asking the driver for *los boliches* (the nightclubs) is enough to find the right stop. The nightclubs in both El Challao and Chacras de Coria are all right next to each other, and you can walk along to take your pick from the ever-changing array. **Alquimia** (Ruta Panamericana & Cerro Aconcagua, Chacras de Coria; admission AR$20-50; ⏲Wed-Sat) was the hot club out here at the time of research – with a bit of luck it may still be going by the time you arrive.

Many visitors to Mendoza (and *mendocinos* for that matter) find the effort involved getting to these places far outweighs the fun they have while there, often opting for the smaller bars along Av Arístides Villanueva. One exception is **La Mala** (Escalada 2233; admission AR$20-33), in the Tajamar nightlife precinct. It gets a good crowd and was the hottest club around at the time of writing.

Theater & Live Music

For everything from live music to avante-garde theater, check the program at the **Centro Cultural Tajamar** (Escalada 1921; admission free-AR$35) in the Tajamar district.

The main theaters in town are **Teatro Quintanilla** (☎423-2310; Plaza Independencia) and the nearby **Teatro Independencia** (☎438-0644; cnr Espejo & Chile).

Shopping

Av Las Heras is lined with souvenir shops, leather shops, chocolate stores and all sorts of places to pick up cheap Argentine trinkets. Items made of *carpincho* (spotted tanned hide of the capybara, a large rodent) are uniquely Argentine and sold in many of the stores.

Unless you are looking for a very obscure top-of-the-range bottle (or a sales assistant who knows what they're talking about), the best place to buy wine in town, in terms of price and variety, is the supermarket **Carrefour** (Avs Las Heras & Belgrano; ⏲8am-10pm). Specialty wine stores stock finer wines, have staff who speak at least a little English and can pack your bottles for shipping.

Plaza de las Artes MARKET
(Plaza Independencia; ⌚5-11pm Fri-Sun) Outdoor crafts market in the Plaza Independencia.

Raices HANDICRAFTS
(Av España 1092) High-quality weavings, *mates* (tealike beverages), jewelry and more. There is another location nearby on Av Sarmiento 162.

Juan Cedrón WINE
(Av Sarmiento 278) A small but well-chosen selection lines the walls. Doubles as a wine bar. Occasional tastings and sidewalk tables.

Centro Internacional del Libro BOOKSHOP
(☎420-1266; Lavalle 14) Small selection of classics and best-sellers in English.

SBS BOOKSHOP
(Gutiérrez 54) A large range of novels in English, Lonely Planet guidebooks, maps and wine-related literature. Also TOEFL resources and textbooks for Spanish students.

Information

Emergency

Servicio Coordinado de Emergencia (☎428-0000) Call for an ambulance.

Immigration

Immigration office (☎424-3512; Av San Martín 1859) In Godoy Cruz, south of the city center.

Internet Access

Internet cafes are ubiquitous throughout the center, and all charge about AR$5 per hour. There are several large ones along the Av Sarmiento *peatonal*.

Telefónica (cnr Avs Sarmiento & San Martín; per hr AR$5) Serves coffee and has phones, too.

Laundry

La Lavandería (☎429-4782; San Lorenzo 352; full service about AR$25)

Media

La Guía This free monthly events magazine is a must-have if you plan on keeping up with Mendoza's hectic cultural scene. Pick up a copy at any tourist office.

Wine Republic (www.wine-republic.com) An excellent English-language magazine focusing on wine but also featuring good reviews of up-and-coming restaurants, Mendoza gossip and a couple of entertaining articles. Pick up a copy at Vines of Mendoza or Trout & Wine.

Medical Services

Hospital (☎420-0600, 420-0063; cnr José F Moreno & Alem)

Money

There are many ATMs downtown. The following two banks are architectural landmarks; Banco Mendoza is massive.

Banco de la Nación (cnr Necochea & 9 de Julio)

Banco Mendoza (cnr Gutiérrez & San Martín)

Cambio Santiago (Av San Martín 1199) Charges 2% commission on traveler's checks.

Post

Post office (Av San Martín at Colón)

Tourist Information

ACA (Automóvil Club Argentina; ☎420-2900; cnr Av San Martín & Amigorena) Argentina's auto club; good source for provincial road maps.

Municipal tourist offices (www.turismo.mendoza.gov.ar) bus terminal (☎431-5000, 431-3001; ⌚9am-10pm); City Hall (☎413-2101; 9 de Julio 500; ⌚9am-9pm).

Provincial tourist office (☎420-2800; www.turismo.mendoza.gov.ar; Av San Martín 1143; ⌚8am-10pm Mon-Fri) Good maps; plenty of brochures.

Travel Agencies

Asatej (429-0029; mendoza@asatej.com.ar; Av Sarmiento 223) Recommended student and discount travel agency.

Isc Viajes (☎425-9259; www.iscviajes.com; Av España 1016) Travel agent and Amex representative.

Getting There & Away

Air

Aerolíneas Argentinas/Austral (☎420-4185; Av Sarmiento 82) Share offices; Aerolíneas flies several times daily to Buenos Aires (from AR$800).

Lan (☎425-7900; Rivadavia 135) Flies three times daily to Santiago, Chile, the only international flights from Mendoza.

Sol (☎0810-444-4765; www.sol.com.ar) Flies to Córdoba (AR$636) and Rosario (AR$1077).

Bus

Mendoza is a major transport hub so you can travel to just about anywhere in the country. Mendoza's **bus terminal** (☎431-5000, 431-3001; cnr Avs R Videla & Acceso Este, Guaymallén) has domestic and international departures. You can book tickets at no extra cost downtown at the **Terminal del Centro** (9 de Julio 1042).

DOMESTIC

Several companies send buses daily to Uspallata (AR$22, two hours) and Los Penitentes (AR$26, four hours), the latter for Aconcagua.

During the ski season several companies go directly to Las Leñas (about AR$95, seven hours).

A number of companies offer a morning bus service to the Difunta Correa Shrine (p334; AR$80 return, departs 7:30am) in San Juan province; the journey is three hours each way and the bus waits three hours before returning. Buses to Maipú leave from the stop on La Rioja between Garibaldi and Catamarca.

INTERNATIONAL

Numerous companies cross the Andes every day via RN 7 (Paso de Los Libertadores) to Santiago, Chile (AR$110, seven hours), Viña del Mar (AR$110, seven hours) and Valparaíso (AR$100, eight hours). The pass sometimes closes due to bad winter weather; be prepared to wait (sometimes days) if weather gets extreme.

Several carriers have connections to Lima, Perú (AR$1295, 60 to 70 hours), via Santiago, Chile, and there are at least two weekly departures to Montevideo, Uruguay (from AR$400, 25 hours), some with onward connections to Punta del Este and Brazil.

International buses depart from the main bus terminal. Companies are at the eastern end of the terminal.

Getting Around

To/From the Airport

Plumerillo International Airport (☎448-2603) is 6km north of downtown on RN 40. Bus 68 ('Aeropuerto') from Calle Salta goes straight to the terminal.

Bus

Mendoza's bus terminal is really just across the street from downtown. After arriving, walk under the Videla underpass and you'll be heading toward the center, about 15 minutes away.

BUSES FROM MENDOZA

There are daily departures from Mendoza's bus terminal to the destinations in the following table, and sometimes upwards of 10 to 20 per day to major cities. Prices reflect midseason fares.

DESTINATION	COST (AR$)	DURATION (HR)
Bahía Blanca	425	16
Bariloche	485	20
Buenos Aires	375	13-17
Catamarca	280	10
Chos Malal	255	13
Córdoba	255	10
Jujuy	486	22
Maipú	6	45 min
Malargüe	65	5
Mar del Plata	530	19
Neuquén	320	10-12
Resistencia	750	24
Río Gallegos	1370	41
Rosario	335	12
Salta	530	18
San Juan	61	2½
San Luis	95	3½
San Rafael	29	3
Santa Fe	430	14
Tucumán	415	14
Zapala	330	16

Otherwise, the 'Villa Nueva' trolley (actually a bus) connects the terminal with downtown.

Local buses cost AR$2.50 – more for longer distances – and require a magnetic Redbus card, which can be bought at most kiosks in denominations of AR$2 and AR$5. Most *lineas* (bus lines) also have *internos* (internal route numbers) posted in the window; for example, *linea* 200 might post *interno* 204 or 206; watch for both numbers. *Internos* indicate more precisely where the bus will take you.

Car

Rental-car agencies are at the airport and along Primitivo de la Reta.

Avis (☎447-0150; Primitivo de la Reta 914)

Localiza (☎429-6800; Primitivo de la Reta 936, Local 4)

National/Alamo (☎429-3111; Primitivo de la Reta 928)

Around Mendoza

Sites in this section are Mendoza's closest major attractions, but you could easily visit Puente del Inca and Las Cuevas (near the Chilean border; see p322) in a day.

WINERIES

Thanks to a complex and very old system of river-fed aqueducts, land that was once a desert now supports 70% of the country's wine production. Mendoza province is wine country, and many wineries near the capital offer tours and tasting. Countless tourist agencies offer day tours, hitting two or more wineries in a precisely planned day, but it's also easy enough to visit on your own. Hiring a *remise* (taxi) is also feasible. Some winery tours and tastings are free, though some push hard for sales at the end, and you never taste the *good* stuff without paying. Malbec, of course, is the definitive Argentine wine.

With a full day it's easy to hop on buses and hit several of the area's most appealing wineries in the outskirts of neighboring Maipú, only 16km away. See p318 for a self-guided tour. For a look at what the cutting-edge wineries are doing, consider renting a car or going on a tour of the Valle de Uco – see p321. Another option is the area of Luján de Cuyo, 19km south of Mendoza, which also has many important wineries. Buses to Maipú leave from La Rioja, between Garibaldi and Catamarca in central Mendoza; buses to wineries in Luján de Cuyo leave from Mendoza's bus terminal.

Mendoza's tourist office on Garibaldi near Av San Martín provides a basic but helpful map of the area and its wineries. Also look for the useful three-map set *Wine Map: Wine and Tasting Tours*.

Luigi Bosca (☎0261-498-1974; www.luigibosca.com.ar; San Martín 2044, Luján de Cuyo; guided visits AR$35; ⏲Mon-Sat by reservation only), which also produces Finca La Linda, is one of Mendoza's premier wineries. If you're into wine, don't miss it. Tours are available in Spanish and English. Take bus 380 (AR$3, one hour) from platform 53 in Mendoza's bus terminal.

The modern **Bodegas Chandon** (☎0261-490-9968; www.bodegaschandon.com.ar; RN 40, Km 29, Agrelo, Luján de Cuyo; guided visits AR$20; ⏲Mon-Sat by reservation only) is popular with tour groups and known for its sparkling wines (champagne). Tours are available in Spanish and English. Take bus 380 (AR$3, one hour) from platform 53 in Mendoza's bus terminal.

Catena Zapata (☎0261-413-1100; www.catenawines.com; Calle Cobos 5519, Agrelo, Luján de Cuyo; ⏲visits/tours by appointment 10am-6pm Mon-Sat) is one of Argentina's most esteemed wineries. Tours are fairly mundane but are conducted in English, German or Spanish. Tasting – if you put down the cash – can be educational indeed. Get there by taxi (cheaper if you catch a bus to Luján de Cuyo and grab one from there).

CACHEUTA

☎02624 / ELEV 1237M

About 40km southwest of Mendoza, in the department of Luján de Cuyo, Cacheuta is renowned for its medicinal thermal waters and agreeable microclimate.

Complejo Termal Cacheuta (☎429133; www.termascacheuta.com; RP 82, Km 41; admission AR$35; ⏲10am-6pm) This excellent, open-air thermal-baths complex is one of the best in the country, due to its variety of pools and dramatic setting on the side of a valley. Midweek is the best time to come as weekends get crowded with kids splashing around on the waterslide and in the wave pool, and the air runs thick with the smoke from a thousand *parrillas*.

There is lodging at the lovely **Hotel & Spa Cacheuta** (☎490152/3; www.termascacheuta.com; RP 82, Km 38; s/d with full board from AR$1115/1570;), where prices include a swimming pool, hot tubs and massage, in addition to optional recreation programs. Nonguests may use the baths for around AR$240 per person.

BUYING WINE

While it's illegal to post wine from Argentina, countries such as the USA and Canada have no restriction on how much you can bring home in your luggage, provided you pay duty. And duty can be as low as US$5 for 40 bottles for the US.

If you are planning on transporting wine, it's best to stop in at a specialty wine store where they can pack bottles to avoid breakage (remember that many airlines have restrictions on bottles in hand luggage). If you're just looking for a bottle to have with dinner, supermarkets around town have an excellent selection in the less-than-AR$100 range.

Campers can pitch a tent at **Camping Termas de Cacheuta** (482082; RN 7, Km 39; campsite per person AR$30).

Expreso Uspallata (in Mendoza 0261-438-1092) runs daily buses to Cacheuta (AR$32, 1½ hours).

POTRERILLOS

02624 / ELEV 1351M

Set above the newly built Potrerillos reservoir in beautiful Andean precordillera, Potrerillos is one of Mendoza's white-water hot spots, usually visited during a day's rafting trip from the capital.

Located about 1km uphill from the ACA campground, Argentina Rafting (see p305) offers rafting and kayaking on the Río Mendoza. Trips range from a 5km, one-hour Class II float to a 50km, five-hour Class III–IV descent over two days. Organize trips at the Mendoza office or at the base here in Potrerillos.

El Puesto Hostel (02624-15-655-9937; www.elpuestohostel.com.ar; Av Los Condores s/n; dm AR$55) This newish hostel has four- to six-bed dorms in a tranquil setting. Table tennis and darts are on hand to keep you entertained and hearty traditional meals are available (AR$35 to AR$55).

Camping del ACA (482013; RN 7, Km 50; campsites members/nonmembers AR$25/35) offers shady sites near the reservoir just below the new town.

VILLAVICENCIO

0261 / ELEV 1800M

If you've ordered mineral water from any restaurant or cafe in Argentina, odds are you've ended up with a bottle of Villavicencio on your table. These springs are the source, and their spectacular mountain setting once hosted the prestigious thermal baths resort of the **Gran Hotel de Villavicencio** (admission free; 8am-8pm). Popular with the Argentine elite during the middle of the 20th century, the resort has been closed for more than a decade; promises have floated around for years that it would 'soon' reopen.

Panoramic views from the hair-raising winding turns leading to Villavicencio make the journey an attraction in itself. There is free camping alongside the attractive **Hostería Villavicencio** (439-6487; meals AR$50-70), which has no accommodations but serves gourmet meals in charming surrounds.

There is no public transport to the valley. Nearly every tour operator in Mendoza offers half-day tours (AR$90) that take in the hotel grounds, the bottling plant and short walks in the surrounding countryside.

Uspallata

02624 / POP 4000 / ELEV 1751M

A humble little crossroads town on the way to the Chilean border, Uspallata is an oasis of poplar trees set in a desolate desert valley. The polychrome mountains surrounding the town so resemble highland Central Asia that director Jean-Jacques Annaud used it as the location for the epic film *Seven Years in Tibet*.

The town first gained fame as a low budget base for the nearby ski fields at Los Penitentes, but has recently been coming into its own with a few companies offering treks, horseback riding and fishing expeditions in the surrounding countryside.

There's a post office and a Banco de la Nación, which has an ATM. The tiny **tourist office** (420009; RN 7 s/n; 9am-8pm) is across from the YPF gas station. It has good information on local sights and activities and some very basic (but still useful) area maps.

Sights & Activities

A kilometer north of the highway junction in Uspallata, a signed lateral leads to ruins and a museum at the **Museo Las Bóvedas** (admission free; 10am-6pm), a smelting site since pre-Columbian times. An easy 8km walk north of town brings you to Cerro Tunduqueral, where you'll find sweeping views and Inca rock carvings.

Uspallata Aventura (☎ 15 598-8135) offers a range of outdoor activities, including horseback riding, mountain-bike tours, rock climbing, trekking and 4WD off-roading. Prices generally run at AR$80/150 for half-/full-day trips, depending on group size. It also rents mountain bikes for AR$8 per hour.

WORTH A TRIP

MAIPÚ: A GOURMET EXPERIENCE

The small town of Maipú, just out of Mendoza, is so packed with wineries, olive oil farms and other gourmet businesses that it's easy to hit five or six in a day. All offer tours and most finish proceedings with at least a small sampling of their produce.

Accordingly, a few companies in Maipú rent bikes and electric scooters, making a day tour of the area an excellent outing, and a lot more fun than the often rushed half-day wine tours on offer from Mendoza tour agencies.

To get to Maipú, catch the 173 bus from the bus stop on La Rioja in Mendoza and get off at the triangular roundabout. Bike-hire competition here is serious business (there have been fistfights in the street between operators) and the main companies are all within walking distance of each other. Go for a stroll and see who has the best wheels. Among operators are **Mr Hugo Bikes** (☎0261-497-4067; www.mrhugobikes.com; Urquiza 2228; bikes per day AR$60) and **Bikes & Wines** (☎0261-410-6686; www.bikesandwines.com; cnr Urquiza & Montecaseros; bikes per day AR$60). All will supply you with a (basic) map of the area and some may offer to take you in a van to your furthest point, meaning you only have to ride the 12km back to base.

All of the following are open 10am to 5pm Monday to Friday and 10am to 1pm Saturday. Reservations are not necessary at any.

Carinae (☎0261-499-0470; www.carinaevinos.com; Aranda 2899; tours AR$20) is the furthest south you really want to go – it's a small, French-owned winery producing a lovely rosé and some good reds. Tour fees are deducted from any wine purchases you make.

Across the road is **LAUR** (www.laursa.com.ar; Aranda 2850; tours AR$10), a 100-year-old olive farm. The 15-minute tour tells you everything you need to know about olive oil production and is followed by a yummy tasting session.

Heading back to Urquiza, go past the big roundabout and venture north. The first winery you come to is **Di Tomasso** (☎0261-499-0673; Urquiza 8136; tours AR$20), a beautiful, historical vineyard dating back to the 1830s. The tour includes a quick pass through the original cellar section.

Heading north again, take a right on Moreno to get to **Viña del Cerno** (☎0261-481-1567; www.elcerno.com.ar; Moreno 631; tours AR$10), a small, old-fashioned winery supervised by its two winemaker owners. The underground cellar complex is atmospheric, but tastings can be a little rushed.

Back out on Urquiza, it's a little under 3km to Zanichelli, where you turn left and travel another 1km to get to **Almacen del Sur** (Zanichelli 709; set meals AR$50-200; ⏲lunch). This working farm produces and exports gourmet deli goods that are grown and packed on the premises. Free tours of the production facilities are available. There's also an excellent restaurant here, serving delicious set lunches (the more expensive ones come accompanied by local wines) in a leafy garden setting.

Head back to Urquiza and continue north until you get to the big roundabout. Turn right and follow the signs to **Historia y Sabores** (Carril Gómez 3064). Seven families run this little chocolate- and liqueur-making operation. Tours are brief, but the lovely rustic surrounds and comfy bar (where you're offered a free shot of liqueur) make it a worthwhile stop.

Along Urquiza, keep heading north until you get to where you got off the bus, take a right on Montecaseros and continue for 500m to reach **Bodega La Rural** (☎0261-497-2013; www.bodegalarural.com.ar; Montecaseros 2625; ⏲9am-1pm & 2-5pm Mon-Fri). Winery tours here are fairly standard (and you probably have the idea by now) but the museum is fascinating – displaying a huge range of winemaking equipment from over the years, including a grape press made from an entire cowskin. Tours in Spanish leave on the hour. If you want one in English, call ahead, or you can simply walk around on your own.

Fototravesías 4x4 (☎420185; www.fototravesias4x4.com, in Spanish; day trips per person AR$90-200), near the main intersection, offers exciting 4WD tours in the surrounding mountains. The owner is a photographer and is especially amenable to ensuring travelers get good shots.

Sleeping & Eating

In the summer high season (when climbers from around the world descend on the area), reservations are wise.

Hostel Uspallata HOSTEL $
(☎in Mendoza 0261-15-466-7240; www.hosteluspallata.com.ar; RN 7 s/n; dm/d AR$55/180, cabins AR$350; @) Friendly hostel 7km east of town with plain but comfortable rooms. Dinner (AR$45 to AR$60) is available. There's good hiking from the hostel and you can rent bikes and horses here. Ask the bus driver to drop you at the front before you hit Uspallata.

Hotel Portico del Valle HOTEL $
(☎420103; Las Heras s/n; s/d AR$120/190) A recently constructed, vaguely modern hotel right on the crossroads. It's nothing fancy, but fine for a few days.

Hostería Los Cóndores HOTEL $$
(☎420002; www.loscondoreshotel.com.ar, in Spanish; Las Heras s/n; s/d AR$220/290) Close to the junction, this is the finest hotel in the center of town. There's plenty of space, modern furnishings, and a gut-busting breakfast buffet is included in the price.

Café Tibet CAFE $
(cnr RN 7 & Las Heras; mains AR$25-35; breakfast, lunch & dinner) No visit to Uspallata would be complete without at least a coffee in this little oddity. The food is nothing spectacular, but the decor, comprising leftover props from *Seven Years in Tibet*, is a must for fans of the surreal.

El Rancho PARRILLA $
(cnr RN7 & Cerro Chacay; mains AR$35-50; lunch & dinner) This is the coziest and most reliable *parrilla* in town, serving all the usual, plus a good roasted *chivo* (goat).

Getting There & Away

Expreso Uspallata (☎420045) runs several buses daily to and from Mendoza (AR$22, 2½ hours). Buses continue from Uspallata to Las Cuevas (AR$25, two hours), near the Chilean border, and stop en route at Los Penitentes, Puente del Inca and the turnoff to Laguna Los Horcones for Parque Provincial Aconcagua. They can be flagged from all of these locations on their return to Uspallata from Las Cuevas.

Andesmar has daily morning departures to Santiago (AR$110, six hours) and Valparaíso (AR$110, seven hours) in Chile.

At the time of writing a new bus service was being planned to connect Uspallata with Barreal in San Juan province – it should be operating by the time you read this.

All buses leave from the Expreso Uspallata office in the little strip mall near the junction.

Los Penitentes

☎02624

So named because the pinnacles resemble a line of monks, **Los Penitentes** (☎420229; www.lospenitentes.com) has both excellent scenery and snow cover (in winter). It's 165km west of Mendoza via RN 7, and offers downhill and cross-country skiing at an altitude of 2580m. Lifts (AR$130 to AR$205 per day) and accommodations are modern, and the vertical drop on some of its 21 runs is more than 700m. Services include a ski school (private lessons are around AR$170), equipment rentals (skis AR$95 per day, snowboards AR$125) and several restaurants and cafeterias. For transportation details, see Getting There & Away, left.

In high ski season (July and August) and during peak climbing season (December through to March), make reservations up to a month in advance for all of the following options.

Sleeping

Hotel & Hostería Ayelén HOTEL $$
(☎in Mendoza 0261-427-1123; www.ayelenpenitentes.com.ar; s/d from AR$300/600) A four-star resort hotel with comfortable accommodations in the main hotel and cheaper rooms in the *hostería* (lodging house) alongside. The lobby and restaurant are great, but the wallpaper in the rooms could use a change.

Hostel Los Penitentes HOSTEL $
(☎0261-425-5511; www.penitentes.com.ar; dm AR$130) A cozy converted cabin, owned by Mendoza's HI Campo Base, it accommodates 38 people in extremely close quarters, and has a kitchen, wood-burning stove and three shared bathrooms. It's all good fun with the right crowd. Lunch and dinners are available for AR$30 to AR$50 each.

Hostería Los Penitentes HOTEL $$
(☎in Mendoza 0261-438-0222; d with half-board AR$300) This modest *hostería* with plain, comfortable rooms has a restaurant and bar and offers full board with ski passes.

Refugio Aconcagua HOTEL $$
(☎in Mendoza 0261-424-1565; www.refugioaconcagua.com.ar; r with half-board per person AR$260) There's nothing fancy about the rooms at this place, but they're an OK size and considering you're in the middle of the resort, with a private bathroom and two meals a day, they're a good deal. The restaurant here serves up big, hearty set meals (AR$35 to AR$70) and is open year-round.

Parque Provincial Aconcagua

North of RN 7, nearly hugging the Chilean border, Parque Provincial Aconcagua protects 710 sq km of the wild high country surrounding the western hemisphere's highest summit, 6962m Cerro Aconcagua. Passing motorists (and those who can time their buses correctly) can stop to enjoy the view of the peak from **Laguna Los Horcones**, a 2km walk from the parking lot just north of the highway.

During trekking season there are rangers stationed at Laguna Los Horcones; the junction to Plaza Francia, about 5km north of Los Horcones; at Plaza de Mulas on the main route to the peak; at Refugio Las Leñas, on the Polish Glacier Route up the Río de las Vacas to the east; and at Plaza Argentina, the last major camping area along the Polish Glacier Route.

Only highly experienced climbers should consider climbing Aconcagua without the relative safety of an organized tour.

CERRO ACONCAGUA

Often called the 'roof of the Americas,' the volcanic summit of Aconcagua covers a base of uplifted marine sediments. The origin of the name is unclear; one possibility is the Quechua term Ackon-Cahuac, meaning 'stone sentinel,' while another is the Mapuche phrase Acon-Hue, signifying 'that which comes from the other side.'

Italian-Swiss climber Mathias Zurbriggen made the first recorded ascent in 1897. Since then, the peak has become a favorite destination for climbers from around the world, even though it is technically less challenging than other nearby peaks. In 1985 the Club Andinista Mendoza's discovery of an Incan mummy at 5300m on the mountain's southwest face proved that the high peaks were a pre-Columbian funerary site.

Reaching the summit requires a commitment of at least 13 to 15 days, including acclimatization time; some climbers prefer the longer but more scenic, less crowded and more technical Polish Glacier Route.

Potential climbers should acquire RJ Secor's climbing guide *Aconcagua* (Seattle, The Mountaineers, 1999). The website www.aconcagua.com.ar and Mendoza government's website, www.aconcagua.mendoza.gov.ar, are also helpful.

Nonclimbers can trek to **base camps** and **refugios** beneath the permanent snow line. On the Northwest Route there is also the relatively luxurious **Hotel Refugio Plaza de Mulas** (www.refugioplazademulas.com.ar), which was undergoing a change of ownership at time of research, but may have reopened by the time you read this.

Permits

From December to March permits are obligatory for both trekking and climbing in Parque Provincial Aconcagua; park rangers at Laguna Los Horcones will not permit visitors to proceed up the Quebrada de los Horcones without one. Fees vary according to the complex park-use seasons. Permits cost AR$410/800 for trekkers (three/seven days) and AR$3000 for climbers (20 days) during high season (December 15 through to January 31); AR$380/660 for trekkers and AR$2200 for climbers during midseason (December 1 to December 14 and February 1 through to February 20); and AR$380/660 (trekking) and AR$1200 (climbing) in low season (November 15 through to November 30 and February 21 through to March 15). Argentine nationals pay about 30% of overseas visitors' fees at all times. These fees climb (steeply) each year – check www.aconcagua.mendoza.gov.ar for the latest information.

Organized tours rarely, if ever, include the park entrance fee. Fees should be paid in Argentine pesos but can be paid in US dollars, and you must bring your original passport with you when you pay the fee. The permit start-date takes effect when you enter the park.

All permits are available only in Mendoza at the provincial tourist office (p314).

Routes

There are three main routes up Cerro Aconcagua. The most popular one, approached by a 40km trail from Los Horcones, is the **Ruta Noroeste** (Northwest Route) from Plaza de Mulas, 4230m above sea level. The **Pared Sur** (South Face), approached from the base camp at Plaza Francia via a 36km trail from Los Horcones, is a demanding technical climb.

From Punta de Vacas, 15km southeast of Puente del Inca, the longer but more scenic **Ruta Glaciar de los Polacos** (Polish Glacier Route) first ascends the Río de las Vacas to the base camp at Plaza Argentina, a distance of 76km. Climbers on this route must carry ropes, screws and ice axes, in addition to the usual tent, warm sleeping bag and clothing, and plastic boots. This route is more expensive because it requires the use of mules for a longer period.

Mules

The cost of renting cargo mules, which can carry about 60kg each, has gone through the roof: the standard fee among outfitters is AR$770 for the first mule from Puente del Inca to Plaza de Mulas, though two mules cost only AR$1157. A party of three should pay about AR$6170 to get their gear to the Polish Glacier Route base camp and back.

TOURING THE VALLE DE UCO

Seriously remote and woefully signposted, the Valle de Uco – home to some of Mendoza's top wineries – is best visited on a guided tour. If you've got the time and patience, though, you can easily rent a car in Mendoza to make the trip. Reservations are essential for touring any of the following 'must sees' in the region:

Pulenta Estate WINERY

(☎0261-420-0800; www.pulentaestate.com; RP 86) A boutique winery started by the ex-owners of the Trapiche label. Tours of the beautiful modern facility focus on tasting, not production.

Andeluna Estate WINERY

(☎02622-423226; RP 89, Km 11; ⊙tours 10:30am, 12:30pm & 3:30pm) Tastings of the wonderful wines produced here take place in a charming old-world-style tasting room. There are also great mountain views from the patio.

La Azul WINERY

(☎02622-423593; www.bodegalaazul.com.ar; RP 89 s/n) A small winery producing excellent malbecs. Tours are in Spanish only, but focus mainly on tasting – you're in and out in 20 minutes.

Salentein WINERY

(☎02622-429000; www.bodegasalentein.com; RP 89 s/n) A state-of-the-art, Dutch-owned winery that's distinctive for its on-site contemporary-art gallery and its method of moving grapes and juice by hand and gravity, rather than by machine.

Francois Lurton WINERY

(☎0261-441-1100; www.francoislurton.com; RP 94, Km 21) An ultramodern facility run by two French brothers from a famous winemaking family, producing one of the best Mendoza torrontés on the market. Excellent tours with impressive tasting areas and barrel room.

The valley is an easy day trip from Mendoza, but there are some wonderfully atmospheric places to stay out here, including **Tupungato Divino** (☎02622-448948; www.tupungatodivino.com.ar; cnr RP 89 & Calle los Europeos; r AR$640; ❄@), **Posada Salentein** (☎02622-429000; www.bodegasalentein.com; RP 89 s/n; s/d with full board AR$1630/1940; ❄@🛜≋) and **Casa Antucura** (☎in Buenos Aires 11-3481-6188; www.casaantucura.com; Barandica s/n, Tunuyán; s/d from AR$860/1500; ❄@≋).

If you're looking for a lunch stop, most of the above wineries offer gourmet meals. Otherwise, **Ilo** (cnr Cabral & Belgrano, Tupungato; mains AR$50-70; ⊙lunch & dinner) is generally considered the best in Tupungato – the good range of seafood dishes makes it a winemakers' favorite.

For mules, contact Rudy Parra at Aconcagua Trek or Fernando Grajales, following. If you're going up on an organized tour, the mule situation is, of course, covered.

Tours

Many of the adventure-travel agencies in and around Mendoza arrange excursions into the high mountains. It is also possible to arrange trips with some overseas-based operators.

The following are the area's most established and experienced operators.

Daniel Alessio Expediciones HIKING
(www.alessio.com.ar) Located in Mendoza; contact online.

Fernando Grajales HIKING
(www.grajales.net) Contact online.

Inka Expediciones HIKING
(0261-425-0871; www.inka.com.ar; Juan B Justo 345, Mendoza) Fixed and tailor-made expeditions. Airport to airport costs AR$13,600 to AR$15,700.

Rudy Parra's Aconcagua Trek HIKING
(in Mendoza 0261-429-2650; www.rudyparra.com; Barcala 484) Contact Rudy by telephone.

Several guides from the **Asociación Argentina de Guías de Montaña** (www.aagm.com.ar) lead two-week trips to Aconcagua, including **Pablo Reguera** (www.pabloreguera.com.ar) and **Mauricio Fernández** (www.summit-mza.com.ar).

All guides and organized trips are best set up online or by telephone *at least* a month in advance. Everything – guides, mules, hotels etc – must be booked far in advance during peak climbing months.

Getting There & Away

The two park entrances – Punta de Vacas and Laguna Los Horcones – are directly off RN 7 and are well signed. The Los Horcones turnoff is only 4km past Puente del Inca. If you're part of an organized tour, transport will be provided. To get here by bus, take an early morning Expreso Uspallata bus from Mendoza. Buses bound for Chile will stop at Puente del Inca, but often fill up with passengers going all the way through.

From Los Horcones, you can walk back along the RN 7 to Puente del Inca or time your buses and catch a Mendoza-bound bus back down.

Las Cuevas & Cristo Redentor

02624 / ELEV 3200M

Pounded by chilly but exhilarating winds, the rugged high Andes make a fitting backdrop for Cristo Redentor, the famous monument erected after a territorial dispute between Argentina and Chile was settled in 1902. The view is a must-see either with a tour or by private car (a tunnel has replaced the hairpin road to the top as the border crossing into Chile), but the first autumn snowfall closes the route. You can hike the 8km up to El Cristo via trails if you don't have a car.

Parque Provincial Volcán Tupungato

Tupungato (6650m) is an impressive volcano, partly covered by snowfields and glaciers, and serious climbers consider the mountain a far more challenging, interesting and technical climb than Aconcagua. The main approach is from the town of **Tunuyán**, 82km south of Mendoza via RN 40, where the **tourist office** (02622-488097, 02622-422193; República de Siria & Alem) can provide info. Many of the outfitters who arrange Parque Provincial Aconcagua treks can also deal with Tupungato.

San Rafael

0260 / POP 118,830 / ELEV 690M

Arriving by bus at San Rafael's scruffy terminal, you're bound to be underwhelmed. Persevere, though – a few blocks away lies a busy, modern town whose streets are lined with majestic old sycamores and open irrigation channels. It's not exactly Mendoza, but it's getting there.

There is nothing to do in town – part of its allure, really – except wander its shady streets and plazas or while the day away in a cafe. There are, however, several esteemed wineries within biking distance that are well worth a visit.

San Rafael is 230km southeast of the city of Mendoza via RN 40 and RN 143, and 189km northeast of Malargüe via RN 40. Most areas of interest in town are northwest of the Av H Yrigoyen and Av San Martín intersection.

San Rafael

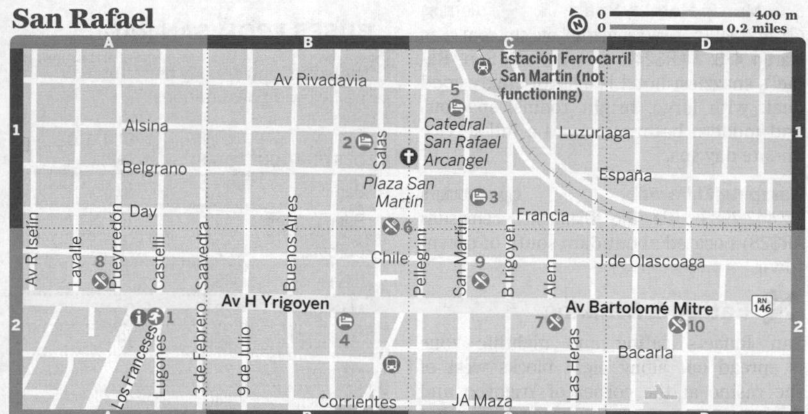

Sights & Activities

San Rafael is flat (hence the proliferation of bike riders here), and when in Rome…get a bike. Several places around town rent out clunkers, but if you're looking for a smooth ride, try **Ciclos Adelcor** (Av H Yrigoyen & Los Franceses; per hour AR$7).

There are a few wineries within walking or cycling distance of town offering free tours and tasting. Head west on RN 143, which has a welcome bike path along its side. The modern and highly regarded **Bianchi Champañera** (☎443-5600; www.vbianchi.com; cnr RN 143 & Valentín Bianchi; tours AR$15; ⏰9am-noon & 2-5pm Mon-Fri) is the furthest west, but still only 6km away. Tours are friendly, offering visitors a glimpse into the making of sparkling wine (champagne), and English is spoken.

A couple of kilometers out of town, **Suter** (☎442-1076; www.sutersa.com.ar; Av H Yrigoyen 2850; short tours free; ⏰9:30am-12:30pm & 2-5pm Mon-Fri) is a rather unromantic, modern affair, but a worthwhile stop for some discounted wine. For AR$220 you can set up a half-day tour, visiting the vineyards with an agronomist, tasting specialty wines and eating a big lunch in the vineyard.

For info about these and other wineries in the area, contact the tourist office.

San Rafael

Activities, Courses & Tours

1	Ciclos Adelcor	A2

Sleeping

2	Hostel Tierrasoles	B1
3	Hotel España	C1
4	Hotel Jardín	B2
5	San Martín Hotel & Spa	C1

Eating

6	El Restauro	B1
7	La Pagoda	C2
8	Malbec	A2
9	Nina	C2
10	Parrilla Listo El Pollo	D2

Sleeping

Hotel España HOTEL $
(☎442-1192; www.hotelespanasrl.com.ar; Av San Martín 270; s/d from AR$100/160) It may not scream 'Spain,' but the mod 1960s-ish interior is definitely unique. Rooms in the 'colonial' sector open onto a delightful patio area, making them more attractive (and a better deal) than the spacious rooms in the pricier 'celeste' sector.

Hostel Tierrasoles HOSTEL $
(☎443-3449; www.tierrasoles.com.ar; Alsina 245; dm/d AR$70/200; @📶) Simply the best-looking hostel in town has OK-sized dorms and a couple of good sitting areas. The inviting backyard (with barbecue for guest use) rounds out the picture.

Hotel Jardín HOTEL $$
(☎443-4621; www.hoteljardinhotel.com.ar; Av H Yrigoyen 283; s/d AR$200/300; ❄📶) There is indeed a garden here – or better said, a courtyard – filled with baroque touches such as fountains and sculptures of nude Greek figures. Rooms face onto it and are big and comfortable, if slightly soulless.

San Martín Hotel & Spa HOTEL $$
(☎442-0400; www.sanmartinhotelspa.com; San Martín 435; r AR$240; P❄@☎≋) San Rafael's snazziest hotel is a surprisingly good deal, with large, bright rooms, spacious and modern bathrooms and a full-service on-site day spa.

Camping El Parador CAMPGROUND $
(☎442-7983; Isla Río Diamante; campsites AR$28) Located about 6km south of downtown.

Eating & Drinking

San Rafael's eating and nightlife zone is spread out along eight blocks west of the casino at the corner of Yrigoyen and Pueyrredón. Go for a wander and see what grabs your fancy.

Malbec PARRILLA $$
(cnr Av H Yrigoyen & Pueyrredón; mains AR$50-70; ⏲lunch & dinner) San Rafael's most frequently recommended *parrilla* holds no surprises, but has a good range of pastas and salads and, yes, some big juicy steaks.

Nina PIZZERIA $
(Av San Martín & Olascoaga; mains AR$30-50; ⏲breakfast, lunch & dinner) The menu doesn't stretch much beyond pizzas and sandwiches, but this is a good coffee spot and becomes a happening bar with live music later.

La Pagoda BUFFET $$
(Av Bartolomé Mitre 188; tenedor libre AR$40; ⏲lunch & dinner) Anybody familiar with the all-you-can-eat scene in Argentina won't find too many surprises here, but the food (Argentine and Chinese) is fresh enough – get there early – and there's certainly plenty of it.

Parrilla Listo El Pollo PARRILLA $
(Av Bartolomé Mitre s/n; parrilla AR$35; ⏲lunch & dinner) The roadside *parrilla* is an Argentine classic and this one's a great example. Grab a sidewalk table (not that there's any choice) and knock elbows with taxi drivers while feasting on big cheap chunks of meat.

El Restauro INTERNATIONAL $$
(cnr Salas & Day; mains AR$60-90; ⏲dinner) The snootiest restaurant around has some excellent dishes on offer using local ingredients and regional recipes. A fair wine list features local heavy hitters such as Suter and Bianchi.

BUSES FROM SAN RAFAEL

There are regular daily departures to the following destinations.

DESTINATION	COST (AR$)	DURATION (HR)
Bariloche	425	16
Buenos Aires	445	14
Córdoba	273	11
Las Leñas	48	3
Malargüe	28	3
Mar del Plata	490	16
Mendoza	28	3
Neuquén	240	9
San Luis	120	4

Information

Banco de Galicia (Av H Yrigoyen 28) Several banks along Av H Yrigoyen have ATMs, including Banco de Galicia.
Cambio Santiago (Almafuerte 64) Charges 2.5% on traveler's checks.
Hospital Teodoro J Schestakow (☎442-4490; Emilio Civit 151)
Municipal tourist office (☎442-4217; www.sanrafael turismo.gov.ar; Av H Yrigoyen 745; ⏲8am-8pm) Helpful staff and useful brochures and maps.
Post office (cnr San Lorenzo & Barcala)

Getting There & Around

Aerolíneas Argentinas/Austral (☎443-8808; Av H Yrigoyen 395) flies daily except on Sunday to and from Buenos Aires (from AR$1037).

If you're headed to Patagonia, there's one minibus per day that leaves from the office of **Transportes Leader** (☎442-1851; Perú 65) for Buta Ranquil (AR$120, eight hours) in Neuquén province via Malargüe. It leaves at 6pm daily except on Saturday and seats sell out very quickly. It's recommended to book (and pay) a couple of days in advance to ensure a seat. Tramat runs regular buses on this route on Thursday and Sunday, terminating in Chos Malal (AR$185, 10 hours).

San Rafael's **bus terminal** (Suárez) is conveniently located downtown.

Renta Autos (☎442-4623; www.rentadeautos.com.ar; Av H Yrigoyen 818) offers the best deals on car rentals in town.

Malargüe

☎0260 / POP 20,540 / ELEV 1400M

Despite serving as a base for Las Leñas, one of Argentina's snazzier ski resorts, Malargüe is a mellow little town that even gets a little rough around the edges. For skiers it's a cheaper alternative to the luxury hotels on the mountain. The dry precordillera that surrounds the town is geologically distinct from the Andes proper, and two fauna reserves, Payén and Laguna Llancancelo, are close by. Caving is possible at Caverna de Las Brujas and Pozo de las Animas. The nearby Parque Provincial Payunia is a 4500-sq-km reserve with the highest concentration of volcanic cones in the world.

Due to Malargüe's remote location, it's a great spot for stargazing, and the newly opened **Planetarium** (☎447-2116; Villegas & Aldeo; tours AR$15; ⏲5-9pm) is an excellent, state-of-the-art complex featuring some freaky architecture and some reasonably entertaining audiovisual presentations.

Activities & Tours

Several companies offer excellent 4WD and horseback-riding excursions, and if you don't have a car, these are generally the best way to get into the surrounding mountains. Possible day trips include Caverna de Las Brujas (AR$140 per person, which includes AR$60 park entrance fee and obligatory guide), Los Molles and Las Leñas (AR$140) and the marvelous Laguna Llancancelo and Malacara volcano (AR$160 plus AR$65 entry fee). One of the most exciting drives you might ever undertake is the 12-hour 4WD tour through Parque Provincial Payunia (AR$360); be sure your tour stops at all the sites – those that combine the visit with Laguna Llancancelo only visit half the sites in Payunia.

Karen Travel (☎447-2226; www.karentravel.com.ar; Av San Martín 54) and **Payunia Travel** (☎447-2701; www.payuniatravel.com; Av San Martín 581) are amongst the well-established agencies in town offering the above tours.

Sleeping

Malargüe has abundant, reasonably priced accommodations. Prices quoted here are for ski season (June 15 through to September 15) and drop by up to 40% the rest of the year. Singles are nonexistent during ski season, when you'll likely be charged for however many beds are in the room.

Microtel Inn BOUTIQUE HOTEL **$$$**
(☎447-2300; www.microtelmalargue.com.ar; Ruta 40 s/n; s/d AR$400/500; P❄@🛜🏊) At the northern edge of town, the most luxurious hotel for miles around lays it all on – buffet breakfast, art gallery, indoor pool... Rooms are spacious and modern and come with hydromassage tubs which are a welcome sight after a hard day on the slopes.

Hotel El Cisne HOTEL **$$**
(☎447-1350; cnr Civit & Villegas; s/d AR$300/360; ❄🛜) A new, ultramodern hotel with a good central location. Rooms are big, with plenty of furnishings and attractive pine-lined ceilings.

Hostel La Caverna HOSTEL **$**
(☎442-7569; www.lacavernahostel.com.ar; Rodriguez 445; dm/d AR$60/180; P@🛜) In a case of last-man-standing, Malargüe's best downtown hostel is this one, a good party place with cramped but comfortable dorms.

Camping Municipal Malargüe CAMPGROUND **$**
(☎447-0691; Alfonso Capdevila s/n; campsites AR$40) At the northern end of town, 300m west of Av San Martín, this is the closest place to camp.

Hotel Bambi HOTEL **$$**
(☎447-1237; Av San Martín 410; s/d AR$280/340) Friendly hotel with clean but faded rooms with basic bathrooms. It's the most comfortable place downtown.

Hotel de Turismo HOTEL **$$**
(☎447-1042; Av San Martín 224; s/d AR$240/300) The Turismo's a good standby – there are plenty of rooms (which are nothing special) so it rarely fills up. Downstairs, the restaurant-cafe lifts the tone with a few charming touches.

Eating

TOP CHOICE **El Quincho de María** ARGENTINE **$**
(Av San Martín 440; mains AR$35-70; ⏲lunch & dinner) The finest dining in the center is at this cozy little *parrilla* where everything from the gnocchi to the empanadas is handmade. Don't miss the mouth-watering shish kebabs for AR$30.

La Posta PARRILLA **$$**
(☎447-1306; Av General Roca 374; mains AR$40-60; ⏲lunch & dinner) A friendly neighborhood *parrilla,* La Posta comes up with the goods in the juicy steak, wine list and televised football departments.

Information

Banco de la Nación (cnr Av San Martín & Inalicán) One of several banks downtown with ATMs.

Post office (cnr Adolfo Puebla & Saturnino Torres)

Tourist office (447-1659; www.malargue.gov.ar; RN 40, Parque del Ayer; 8am-11pm) Helpful tourist office with facilities at the northern end of town, on the highway.

Getting There & Around

From Malargüe's **bus terminal** (cnr Av General Roca & Aldao) there are several direct buses to Mendoza daily (AR$57, five hours), plus others requiring a change in San Rafael (AR$28, three hours). In summertime there's one departure daily for Los Molles (AR$15, one hour) and Las Leñas (AR$20, 1½ hours).

Transportes Leader (447-0519; Av San Martín 775) operating out of the Club Los Amigos pool hall has one minibus leaving for Buta Ranquil (AR$105, five hours) in Neuquén at 9pm Sunday to Friday. Seats sell out fast – it's recommended that you book (and pay) at least two days in advance. Tramat runs the same route, leaving from the bus terminal on Thursdays and Sundays to Chos Malal (AR$120, six hours).

For winter transportation to Los Molles and Las Leñas ski resorts, contact any of the travel agencies listed, p325. They offer a roundtrip shuttle service, including ski rentals, from AR$80-120 per person.

Around Malargüe

0260

Geologically distinct from the Andean mountains to the west, the volcanically formed landscapes surrounding Malargüe are some of the most mind-altering in Argentina and have only recently begun to receive tourist attention. Visiting the following places is impossible without your own transportation, though Malargüe's excellent travel agencies can arrange excursions to all of them.

Just over 200km south of Malargüe on the RN 40, the spectacular **Parque Provincial Payunia** is a 4500-sq-km reserve with a higher concentration of volcanic cones (over 800 of them) than anywhere else in the world. The scenery is breathtaking and shouldn't be missed. The 12-hour 4WD tours or three-day horseback trips offered by most of the agencies in Malargüe are well worth taking.

Lying within its namesake fauna reserve about 60km southeast of Malargüe, **Laguna Llancancelo** is a high mountain lake visited by more than 100 species of birds, including flamingos.

Caverna de Las Brujas is a magical limestone cave on Cerro Moncol, 72km south of Malargüe and 8km north of Bardas Blancas along RN 40. Its name means 'Cave of the Witches.' The cave complex stretches for 5km. Guided tours (admission and flashlights included in the price) take two to three hours. Tours depart with a minimum group size of two, although getting more people together will bring down the per-person cost. Check with tour operators in Malargüe for details.

LOS MOLLES

Before Las Leñas took over as the prime ski resort in the area, Los Molles was the only place around where you could grab a poma (ski lift). These days it's a dusty windswept village that would be slowly sinking into obscurity if not for its reasonably priced accommodation alternatives for those wishing to be near, but not in, Las Leñas, and its favored status for rock climbers, hikers and other rugged outdoor types. The village straddles RP 222, 55km northwest of Malargüe. Karen Travel in Malargüe offers a range of activities in the dramatic countryside that surrounds the village.

Hostel CAP (11-15-5726-3255; www.caphostel.com; dm AR$150-185) is one of the best set-up hostels in the country, offering heated pool, bar, 'digital playroom', heliskiing, free transfers to Las Leñas and extra-snuggly duck down duvets.

The most modern and best equipped of the hotels here, **Hotel Los Molles** (449-9712; www.losmolleshotel.com.ar; RP 222, Km 30; r per person AR$360) features big rooms with balconies facing out over the valley. A decent restaurant serves good-value set meals (AR$40).

Buses heading between Malargüe (AR$15, one hour) and Las Leñas (AR$5, 30 minutes) pass through the village.

Las Leñas

0260

Designed primarily to attract wealthy foreigners, **Las Leñas** (447-1281; www.laslenas.com; mid-Jun-late-Sep) is Argentina's most self-consciously prestigious ski resort. Since its opening in 1983 it has attracted an international clientele who spend their days on the slopes and nights partying until the sun comes up. Because of the dry climate, Las Leñas has incredibly dry powder.

Its 33 runs cover 33 sq km; the area has a base altitude of 2200m, but slopes reach 3430m for a maximum drop of 1230m. Outside the ski season Las Leñas is also attempting to attract summer visitors who enjoy weeklong packages, offering activities such as mountain biking, horseback riding and hiking.

Las Leñas is 445km south of Mendoza and 70km from Malargüe, all via RN 40 and RP 222.

Lift Tickets & Rentals

Prices for lift tickets vary considerably throughout the ski season. Children's tickets are discounted about 30%. One-day tickets range from AR$206 in low season to AR$315 in high season (week passes are AR$1096 to AR$1681). Also available are three-day, four-day, two-week and season passes.

Rental equipment is readily available and will set you back about AR$133 per day for skis or snowboards.

Sleeping & Eating

Las Leñas has a small village with five luxury hotels and a group of 'apart hotels', all under the same management. They are generally booked as part of a weeklong package, which includes lodging, unlimited skiing and two meals per day. Despite the country's economic troubles, rates for foreigners staying in Las Leñas have changed little. All bookings are done either online at www.laslenas.com or centrally through **Ski Leñas** (in Buenos Aires 011-4819-6000/60; ventas@laslenas.com; Cerrito 1186, 8th fl).

Hotel Acuario HOTEL $$$

(per person AR$10,100-14,300;) The most humble of the hotels here is still very comfortable, and, with 'only' 40 rooms, cozier than other options.

Hotel Escorpio HOTEL $$$

(per person AR$6900-13,300;) This 47-room hotel is nominally three stars, but still top-notch, with an excellent restaurant. Guests can use facilities at the Hotel Piscis.

Hotel Aries HOTEL $$$

(s AR$8211-12,300 d AR$10,300-15,400;) Aries is a four-star hotel with a sauna, gym facilities, a restaurant and luxuriously comfortable rooms.

Virgo Hotel & Spa HOTEL $$$

(per person AR$9000-14,000;) The newest hotel in the village, this one goes all out, with a heated outdoor swimming pool, sushi bar, whirlpool bath and cinema.

Hotel Piscis HOTEL $$$

(s AR$13,300-22,700, d AR$16,650-28,450;) The most extravagant of Las Leñas' lodgings is the five-star, 99-room Hotel Piscis. This prestigious hotel has wood-burning stoves, a gymnasium, sauna, an indoor swimming pool, the elegant Las Cuatro Estaciones restaurant, a bar, a casino and shops. Rates depend on time of the season, and are based on double occupancy.

Apart Hotel Gemenis (weekly per person AR$8000-15,000) and **Apart Hotel Delphos** (weekly per person AR$8000-15,000) offer similar packages without meals but do have well-equipped kitchenettes.

There are also small apartments with two to six beds and shared bathrooms, equipped for travelers to cook for themselves. Budget travelers can stay more economically at Los Molles, 20km down the road, or at Malargüe, 70km away.

Restaurants in the village run the comestible gamut, from cafes, sandwich shops and pizzerias to upscale hotel dining rooms. The finest restaurant of all is Las Cuatro Estaciones, in Hotel Piscis.

Getting There & Away

There is a bus service operating in season from Mendoza (AR$95, 6½ hours), San Rafael (AR$48, three hours) and Malargüe (AR$20, 1½ hours).

South Along the RN 40

From Malargüe the RN 40 winds its way through rugged desert landscapes and into Neuquén province. Despite what many will tell you, there *is* public transport along this route. Tramat runs regular buses between Mendoza and Zapala twice a week and Transportes Leader runs minibuses between San Rafael and Buta Ranquil Sunday to Friday. See the Mendoza, San Rafael and Malargüe transport sections for details. From Buta Ranquil there are connections to Neuquén and Chos Malal, but you may get stuck for the night. There's no real reason to be here, but there are a couple of cheap hotels, one nice accommodations option, and enough restaurants and cafes to keep you from starving.

JUST A LOAD OF HOT AIR

While traveling through San Juan, especially in autumn and winter, you may become acquainted – through hearsay if not through experience – with one of the region's meteorological marvels: *el zonda*. Much like the chinook of the Rockies or the foehn of the European Alps, the *zonda* is a dry, warm wind that can raise a cold day's temperature from freezing to nearly 20°C (68°F). The *zonda* originates with storms in the Pacific that blow eastward, hit the Andes, dump their moisture and come whipping down the eastern slopes, picking up heat as they go. The wind, which varies from mild to howling, can last several days; *sanjuaninos* (people from San Juan) can step outside and tell you when it will end – and that it will be cold when it does. It's a regular occurrence, giving the region – and the *sanjuaninos* – severe seasonal schizophrenia, especially during winter.

San Juan

☎0264 / POP 492,830 / ELEV 650M

Living in the shadow of a world-class destination like Mendoza can't be easy and, to its credit, San Juan doesn't even try to compete. Life in this provincial capital moves at its own pace, and the locals are both proud of and humble about their little town.

No slouch on the wine production front, San Juan's wineries are refreshingly low-key after the Mendoza bustle, and the province's other attractions are all within easy reach of the capital. Most come here en route to Parque Provincial Ischigualasto.

In 1944 a massive earthquake destroyed the city center, and Juan Perón's subsequent relief efforts are what first made him a national figure. The city goes dead in summer, especially on Sunday, when all of San Juan heads to the nearby shores of Dique Ullum for relief from the sun.

San Juan is 170km north of Mendoza via RN 40 and 1140km from Buenos Aires. Like most Argentine cities, San Juan's grid pattern makes orientation very easy; the addition of cardinal points – *norte* (north), *sur* (south), *este* (east) and *oeste* (west) – to street addresses helps even more. East-west Av San Martín and north-south Calle Mendoza divide the city into these quadrants. The functional center of town is south of Av San Martín, often referred to as Av Libertador.

Sights & Activities

If you need a little perspective on things, make your way up the **Lookout Tower** (cnr Mendoza & Rivadavia; admission AR$5; ⏲9am-1pm & 5-9pm) for a sweeping view out over the town and surrounding countryside.

Museum hours change often, so check with the tourist office for updated information.

Casa Natal de Sarmiento (Sarmiento 21 Sur; admission AR$5; ⏲9am-1pm & 2-5:30pm Mon-Fri, 9am-2pm Sat, 10am-1pm & 2-6pm Sun) is named for Domingo Faustino Sarmiento, whose prolific writing as a politician, diplomat, educator and journalist made him a public figure within and beyond Argentina. Sarmiento's *Recuerdos de Provincia* recounted his childhood in this house and his memories of his mother. It's now a museum.

Museo de Vino Santiago Graffigna (☎421-4227; www.graffignawines.com; Colón 1342 Norte; ⏲9am-5:30pm Mon-Fri, 10am-4pm Sat & Sun) is a wine museum well worth a visit. It also has a wine bar where you can taste many of San Juan's best wines. Take bus 12A from in front of the tourist office on Sarmiento (AR$2, 15 minutes) and ask the driver to tell you when to get off.

Tour operators in San Juan provide lots of options for taking in the sights.

Mario Agüero Turismo TOURS
(☎422-0840; General Acha 17 Norte) Offers organized tours including Parque Provincial Ischigualasto.

Triasico Turismo TOURS
(☎422-8566; www.triasico.com.ar; Sarmiento 42 Sur) Specializes in Ischigualasto tours (AR$420, minimum two people) – come here if you're struggling to get a group together.

Sleeping

San Juan Hostel HOSTEL $
(☎420-1835; www.sanjuanhostel.com; Av Córdoba 317 Este; dm AR$40-50, d with/without bathroom AR$155/110; @ 📶) An excellent little hostel with a variety of rooms placed conveniently between the bus terminal and downtown. Good info on tours and local attractions, and a rooftop Jacuzzi rounds out the picture.

Hotel Alhambra HOTEL $$
(☎421-4780; www.alhambrahotel.com.ar; General Acha 180 Sur; s/d AR$180/260; ❄ 📶) Cozy, car-

peted rooms with splashes of dark wood paneling, giving them a classy edge. Little touches such as leather chairs and gold ashtray stands in the hallways give it a kitschy appeal and the central location seals the deal.

Hotel del Bono Suite HOTEL **$$$**
(☎421-7600; www.hoteldelbono.com.ar; Mitre 75 Oeste; d/ste AR$340/600; ❄☜≋) With some slick design features taking the edge off the corporate blandness, this is a good deal for the price, and the well-stocked kitchenettes and rooftop pool are added bonuses.

Albertina Hotel HOTEL **$$**
(☎421-4222; www.hotelalbertina.com; Mitre 31 Este; r from AR$450; ❄@☜) A slick, business-class hotel on the plaza. The tiny rooms are a bit of a letdown, but the bathrooms are big.

Plaza Hotel HOTEL **$**
(☎422-5179; plazahotelsanjuan@hotmail.com; Sarmiento 344 Sur; s/d AR$160/220; ❄) There's no plaza in sight, but the large, unrenovated rooms here represent fair value. Check out a few for better ventilation and light.

Eating

Most restaurants are right downtown, and many of the city's hippest eateries are around the intersection of Rivadavia and Entre Ríos.

TOP CHOICE **Remolacha** PARRILLA **$$**
(cnr Av José Ignacio de la Roza & Sarmiento; mains AR$50-80; ⏲lunch & dinner) One of the biggest *parrillas* in town, the dining room is a bit ordinary, but eating in the garden is a lush experience. Get a table by the picture windows looking into the kitchen and you'll be able to see your meal being hacked off the carcass before getting thrown on the flames. Excellent salads, too.

Baró INTERNATIONAL **$**
(Rivadavia 55 Oeste; mains AR$30-60; ⏲breakfast, lunch & dinner) This popular main-street cafe/restaurant has the best variety of pasta dishes in town and a relaxed atmosphere that make it a good stop for coffee or drinks at any time.

de Sánchez FUSION **$$**
(Rivadavia 61 Oeste; mains AR$50-80; ⏲lunch & dinner) San Juan's snootiest restaurant is actually pretty good. It has a creative menu with a smattering of seafood dishes, an adequate wine list (featuring all the San Juan heavy hitters) and a hushed, tranquil atmosphere.

Soychú VEGETARIAN **$**
(Av José Ignacio de la Roza 223 Oeste; buffet AR$30; ⏲lunch & dinner Mon-Sat, lunch only Sun) Excellent vegetarian buffet attached to a health-food store selling all sorts of groceries and a range of teas. Arrive early for the best selection.

Shopping

The **Mercado Artesanal Tradicional** (Traditional Artisans Market; Centro de Difusión Cultural Eva Perón) is an excellent local handicrafts market with an assortment of items for sale including ponchos and the brightly colored *mantas* (shawls) of Jáchal.

Information

ACA (Automóvil Club Argentina; ☎422-3781; 9 de Julio 802) Argentina's auto club; good source for provincial road maps.

Banco de San Juan (cnr Rivadavia & Entre Ríos) Has an ATM.

Cambio Santiago (General Acha 52 Sur) Money exchange.

Cyber Neo (cnr Mitre & Entre Ríos; per hr AR$5) One of countless internet cafes in San Juan.

BUSES FROM SAN JUAN

Various companies serve the following destinations daily.

DESTINATION	COST (AR$)	DURATION (HR)
Barreal	55	4
Buenos Aires	450	14
Calingasta	50	3½
Catamarca	230	8
Córdoba	240	11
Huaco	45	3
Jujuy	451	20
La Rioja	163	7
Mendoza	61	3
Neuquén	430	15½
Rodeo	45	3½
Rosario	327	14
Salta	466	17
San Agustín de Valle Fértil	60	4½
San José de Jáchal	33	3
San Luis	123	5
Tucumán	360	13

Hospital Rawson (☎422-2272; cnr General Paz & Estados Unidos)

Laverap (Rivadavia 498 Oeste; full laundry service about AR$25)

Post office (Av José Ignacio de la Roza 259 Este)

Provincial tourist office (☎421-0004; www.turismo.sanjuan.gov.ar; Sarmiento 24 Sur; ⏰8am-8pm) Has a good map of the city and its surroundings plus useful information on the rest of the province, particularly Parque Provincial Ischigualasto.

Getting There & Away

Air

Aerolíneas Argentinas/Austral (☎421-4158; Av San Martín 215 Oeste) flies twice daily to Buenos Aires (AR$801) except Sunday (once only).

Bus

From San Juan's **bus terminal** (☎422-1604; Estados Unidos 492 Sur) there are international services to Santiago (AR$245, nine hours), Viña del Mar and Valparaíso, Chile. Some require a change of bus in Mendoza.

Except in summer, when there may be direct buses, service to Patagonian destinations south of Neuquén requires a change of bus in Mendoza, though through-tickets can be purchased in San Juan.

Getting Around

Las Chacritas Airport (☎425-4133) is located 13km southeast of town on RN 20. A taxi or *remise* costs AR$45. For car rental, try **Classic** (☎422-4622; Av San Martín 163 Oeste).

Valle de Calingasta

The Calingasta Valley is a vast smear of scenic butter cradled between the Andes and the rumpled, multicolored precordillera, and is one of the most beautiful regions in both San Juan and Mendoza provinces.

With the completion of two new reservoirs, the spectacular cliffside RP 12 is now closed. Most maps will show the old road, but drivers have to take RP 5 north to Talacasto, then the RP 149, which snakes around west and then south to Calingasta.

CALINGASTA

☎02648 / POP 2095 / ELEV 1430M

Calingasta is a small agricultural town shaded by álamos (poplars) on the shores of Río de los Patos. There's little to do, though a visit to the 17th-century adobe chapel **Capilla de Nuestra Señora del Carmen** makes a nice stop on the way to Barreal. Looming on the horizon 7km out of town is **Cerro El Calvario**, the site of an indigenous cemetery where several mummies have been found. One example can be seen in Calingasta's small **archaeological museum** (admission AR$5; ⏰10am-1pm & 4-8pm Tue-Sat), just off the main plaza.

The folks at Calingasta's **tourist information office** (☎441066; www.calingastaturismo.gov.ar; RP 12), at the entrance to town from San Juan, are helpful for sights and lodging in the area.

If you wish to spend the night, lay your head at the modest **Hospedaje Nora** (☎421027; cnr Cantoni & Sarmiento; s/d AR$120/140), featuring simple but spacious rooms in a family house. Those in the building out the back are a better deal. There's a **municipal campground** (campsites AR$23) down by the river. The meals at **Doña Gorda** (Calle Principal; mains AR$25-40) will stave off your hunger – on offer are tasty empanadas and good-value set meals.

Two buses a day roll through town, heading for San Juan (AR$50, 3½ hours) and Barreal (AR$7, 30 minutes).

BARREAL

☎02648 / POP 4530 / ELEV 1650M

Barreal's divine location makes it one of the most beautifully situated towns you'll likely ever come across. Sauces (weeping willows), álamos and eucalyptus trees drape lazily over the dirt roads that meander through town, and views of the Cordillera de Ansilta – a stretch of the Andes with seven majestic peaks ranging from 5130m to 5885m – are simply astonishing. Wandering along Barreal's back roads is an exercise in dreamy laziness.

Presidente Roca is the main drag through town, a continuation of RP 149 that leads from Calingasta to Barreal and on to Parque Nacional El Leoncito. Only a few streets have names; businesses listed without them simply require asking directions.

Sights & Activities

Wander down to the **Río de los Patos** and take in the sweeping views of the valley and the **Cordillera de Ansilta**, whose highest peak, **Ansilta**, tops out at 5885m. To the south, **Aconcagua** and **Tupungato** are both visible, as is the peak of **Cerro Mercedario** (6770m).

At the south end of Presidente Roca is a sort of triangular roundabout. Follow the road east (away from the Andes) until it leads into the hills; you'll see a small shrine and you can **hike** into the foothills for more stunning views. Follow this road for 3km and you'll come to a mining site (the gate should be open). Enter and continue for 1km to reach a **petrified forest**.

White-water rafting is excellent – more for the scenery than for the rapids themselves – and most trips start 50km upriver at **Las Hornillas**. Contact **Barreal Rafting** (☎0264-15-530-7764), the best-established rafting operator in town.

Las Hornillas (site of two *refugios* – rustic shelters – and a military outpost) also provides **climbing** access to the Cordón de la Rameda, which boasts five peaks over 6000m, including Cerro Mercedario. Climbing here is more technical than Aconcagua and many mountaineers prefer the area. Ramon Ossa, a Barreal native, is a highly recommended mountain guide and excursion operator who knows the cordillera intimately; contact him at **Cabañas Doña Pipa** (☎441004; www.fortunaviajes.com.ar). He can arrange trips to Cerro Mercedario and expeditions across the Andes in the footsteps of San Martín, including mules and equipment.

Explora Parques (☎ 0264-15-503-2008; www.exploraparques.com; Mariano Moreno s/n) offers tours of the nearby El Leoncito national park, fishing trips and 4WD treks.

Barreal is best known for **carrovelismo** (land sailing), an exhilarating sport practiced on a small cart with a sail attached. Fanatics come from miles away to whizz around out on the gusty, cracked lake bed at Pampa El Leoncito, about 20km from town and adjacent to the national park. **Rogelio Toro** (☎0264-15-671-7196; dontoro.barreal@gmail.com) hires the necessary equipment and also gives classes.

For access to the *refugio* at Las Hornillas, climbing information, guide services and **mountain bike** rental, visit Maxi at **Cabañas Kummel** (☎441206; Presidente Roca s/n).

Sleeping & Eating

El Alemán HOTEL **$$**
(☎0264-15-411-9913; www.elalemanbarreal.com; r for 2/4 people AR$250/300; ⊙breakfast, lunch & dinner) Down by the river, with sweeping views of the Andes, this German/Argentine-owned complex has some of the best-looking rooms in town. Rooms are cute and cozy and the lack of TVs adds to the overall tranquility of the place. There's an excellent restaurant (mains AR$40 to AR$60) on the premises, serving hearty dishes and superb breakfasts made from the freshest ingredients. Call ahead to get picked up from the town center.

THE MENDOZA SHOPPING LIST

Spoiled for choice? Here are our top picks...

Reds

» Cavagnaro Malbec (AR$75)

» Kaiken Cabernet Savignon (AR$107)

» Salentein Primus Malbec (AR$200)

» Carinae Prestige Blend (AR$244)

Whites

» Angelica Zapata Chardonnay Alta (AR$90)

» Terrazas de los Andes Tardio Petit (AR$95)

» Tapiz Single Vineyard Sauvignon Blanc (AR$55)

» Alta Vista Premium Torrontes (AR$50)

Posada Don Lisandro HOSTEL **$**
(☎0264-15-505-9122; www.donlisandro.com.ar; Av San Martín s/n; dm AR$50, s/d with shared bathroom AR$150/200) This newish *posada* (inn) is actually a 100-year-old house. The original cane-and-mud ceilings remain, as do a few sticks of room furniture. There's a kitchen for guest use and lovely, shady grounds to lounge around in.

Posada San Eduardo HOTEL **$$**
(☎441046; cnr San Martín & Los Enamorados; s/d AR$220/280;) This handsome adobe inn offers refreshing rooms with whitewashed walls set around a beautiful shady courtyard. Rooms have a quiet elegance, with natural poplar bed frames and chairs. Pay a little extra and you get your very own fireplace.

Pizzería Clif PIZZERIA **$**
(Presidente Roca s/n; mains AR$30-50; ⊙dinner) Won't be winning any decor design awards, but cooks up some decent pizzas and turns into a bar later on.

Restaurante Isidro ARGENTINE **$$**
(Presidente Roca s/n; mains AR$45-60; ⊙breakfast, lunch & dinner) Offers a fairly standard range of meats and pastas and some delicious meat empanadas. Also a good selection of wines from the San Juan region.

Information

Banco de la Nación (Presidente Roca s/n) Has an ATM.

IWS Comunicaciones (San Martín s/n; per hr AR$6) Internet access (slow).

Tourist office (441066; turismo@calingasta.gov.ar; Presidente Roca s/n; 8am-8pm) Located beside the main plaza; offers a list of excursion operators and accommodations.

Getting There & Away

Barreal's right at the end of the line, but there are two departures per day for San Juan (AR$55, four hours), which pass through Calingasta (AR$7, 30 minutes).

At the time of writing a new bus service was being planned to connect Barreal with Uspallata in Mendoza province – it should be operating by the time you read this.

RUTA DEL VINO DE SAN JUAN

San Juan's winery tourism industry isn't quite as developed as that of Mendoza, but in a lot of ways that's a good thing. There are no crowds for a start, and tours are occasionally conducted by the winemakers themselves. A few wineries have got together to promote the Ruta del Vino de San Juan (the San Juan Wine Route). The best way to do it, if you want to hit them all in one day, is to hire a car. Starting from downtown San Juan, it's about a 40km return stopping at all the places listed here. It is feasible to do it by public transport and taxi, too. None of the wineries listed below require reservations.

The first stop on the route should be **Las Marianas** (0264-423-1191; www.bodegalasmarianas.com.ar; Calle Nuevo s/n; 9am-8pm Mon-Sat). One of the prettiest wineries in the region, this one was built in 1922, abandoned in 1950 and reinstated in 1999. The main building is gorgeous, with thick adobe walls and a few examples of the original winemaking equipment lying around. The mountain views out over the vineyard are superb. If you're coming by bus, catch the 16 (AR$3, 40 minutes) near the corner of Santa Fe and Mendoza in San Juan. Get off at the corner of Calle Aberastain and Calle Nuevo, where you'll see a signpost to the winery (an 800m walk).

Making your way back to Calle Aberastain, turn right and follow the road south for 500m to **Viñas de Segisa** (0264-492-2000; www.saxsegisa.com.ar; Aberastain & Calle 15; 9am-7pm Mon-Sat). This stately old winery has more of a museum feel than others. The tour of the underground cellar complex is excellent and tastings are generous. This is one of the few wineries who actually admit to 'chipping' (adding oak chips to young wines to improve flavor).

If you're not up for a walk, now's the time to call a *remise* (taxi). If you are, make your way back north to Calle 14, turn right and continue for 5km until you hit RN 40. Turning left, after about 1km you'll come to **Fabril Alto Verde** (0264-421-2683; www.fabril-altoverde.com.ar; RN 40 btwn Calle 13 & 14; 9am-1pm & 2:30-6:30pm Mon-Fri), a big, state-of-the-art winery that sells 90% of its wine for export; tours here are in English or Spanish and come accompanied by a rather dreary promotional video. The award-winning organic brands Buenas Hondas and Touchstone are produced here.

Next, catch a 24 bus heading north on RN 40 up to Calle 11. Turning right down Calle 11 for 300m brings you to **Miguel Mas** (0264-422-5807; miguelmas@infovia.com.ar; Calle 11 s/n; 9am-5pm Mon-Fri). This small winery makes some of the country's only organic sparkling wine (champagne) and other wine. The whole process – apart from inserting the cork in bottles – is done by hand. Tours (in Spanish only) take you through every step of the process.

Making your way back out to RN 40, flag down a 24 bus, which will take you back to the bus terminal in San Juan.

If you've still got a thirst up when you get back to the bus terminal, consider hopping on bus 23 to check out one of South America's most curious wineries, **Cavas de Zonda** (0264-494-5144; www.cavasdezonda.com; Ruta 12 s/n, Zonda; 9am-5pm Mon-Fri, 11am-5pm Sat & Sun), in a cave about 16km west of San Juan, via the RP 12, near the town of Zonda. This champagne-maker boasts having the only wine cellar in South America whose 'roof is a mountain' and, true or not, its temperatures are perfect for cellaring its excellent sparkling wines. And hey...it's a darn good marketing tool. Bus 23 leaves the San Juan bus terminal from platform 20 six times daily (AR$4).

San José de Jáchal

☎02647 / POP 12,100

Founded in 1751 and surrounded by vineyards and olive groves, Jáchal is a charming village with a mix of older adobes and contemporary brick houses. *Jachalleros* (the local residents) are renowned for their fidelity to indigenous and gaucho craft traditions; in fact, Jáchal's reputation as the Cuna de la Tradición (Cradle of Tradition) is celebrated during November's **Fiesta de la Tradición**. Except during festival season, finding these crafts is easier in San Juan.

Across from the main plaza the **Iglesia San José**, a national monument, houses the **Cristo Negro** (Black Christ), or Señor de la Agonía (Lord of Agony), a grisly leather image with articulated head and limbs, brought from Potosí in colonial times.

Jáchal's accommodation scene isn't what you'd call thriving, but the **Hotel San Martín** (☎420431; www.jachalhotelsanmartin.com; Echegaray 387; s/d AR$75/100, with shared bathroom AR$40/60; ❄@), a few blocks from the plaza, does the job. It's not quite as contemporary as it looks from the outside, but rooms are big and comfortable and the bathrooms are modern.

La Taberna de Juan (San Martín s/n; mains AR$20-25; ⏰lunch & dinner) is a bright and cheery *parrilla* facing the plaza. Meat is the go here, but there's a range of pasta dishes and salads, too. Set lunches are particularly good value.

There are several daily buses to San Juan (AR$27, three hours) from Jáchal's **bus terminal** (cnr San Juan & Obispo Zapata).

Rodeo

☎02647 / ELEV 2010M

Rodeo is a small, ramshackle town with picturesque adobe houses typical of the region, 42km west of San José de Jáchal.

Rodeo has recently become famous – world famous – for **windsurfing** and **kitesurfing**. The town is only 3km away from one of the best windsurfing sites on the planet: **Dique Cuesta del Viento**, a reservoir where, between mid-October and early May, wind speeds reach 120km/h nearly every afternoon, drawing surfers from around the globe. Even if you don't take to the wind, it's worth spending a day or two wandering around Rodeo and hanging out on the beach absorbing the spectacular views and watching the insanity of airborne windsurfers.

Inside the town hall, the **tourist office** (municipalidad_iglesia@yahoo.com.ar; ⏰8am-8pm) provides a list of places to stay and information on local attractions.

On Playa Lamaral, on the shore of the reservoir, HI affiliate **Rancho Lamaral** (☎0264-15-660-1197; www.rancholamaral.com; dm/d AR$40/100) offers simple rooms in a refurbished adobe house. It also offers windsurfing classes (one/three classes AR$100/270) and kitesurfing courses, and rents all equipment.

TOP CHOICE **50 Nudos** (☎011-15-5759-0525; www.50nudos.com; Puque s/n; s/d AR$120/180) offers charming, rustic rooms. Follow the signs from the main street to these. Optional are larger rooms with sitting area and breakfast served in your room.

La Surfera (Santo Domingo s/n; mains AR$15-30; ⏰lunch & dinner) is on the main street in the center of town. This laid-back restaurant/cafe/reggae bar is HQ for Rodeo's surprisingly large hippy community. Vegetarian meals are predictably good; meat dishes could be better.

From San Juan's bus terminal, there are several departures daily for Rodeo (AR$30, 5½ hours).

San Agustín de Valle Fértil

☎02646 / POP 5180

Reached via comically undulating highways that cut through the desert landscape, San Agustín de Valle Fértil makes an excellent base for trips to the nearby Parque Provincial Ischigualasto. It's a measure of just how dry the countryside is that this semiarid valley gets called 'fertile.'

Apart from visiting the park, there's not much to do around these parts, but the ponderous pace of life here, where people sit on the sidewalks on summer evenings greeting passersby, has mesmerized more than one visitor.

San Agustín lies among the Sierra Pampeanas, gentle sedimentary mountains cut by impressive canyons, 247km northeast of San Juan via RN 141 and RP 510, which continues to Ischigualasto and La Rioja. San Agustín is small enough that locals pay little attention to street names, so you may need to ask for directions.

Sleeping & Eating

Eco Hostel HOSTEL $
(☎420147; www.ecohostel.com.ar; Mendoza 42; dm/d AR$35/120;) One of the better hostels in town, with a great location half a block from the plaza and a tiny above-ground pool. Can arrange good-value tours to local sights, including Parque Provincial Ischigualasto.

Hostería & Cabañas Valle Fértil HOTEL $$
(☎420015; www.alkazarhotel.com.ar; Rivadavia s/n; s/d in hostería AR$185/212, 4-person cabaña AR$300) This place has the wraps on lodging in town, with a well-sited *hostería* above the reservoir and fully equipped *cabañas* nearby. The *hostería* also has a good restaurant (mains AR$38 to AR$55) serving food from 6am to 11pm. Both are reached from Rivadavia on the way to the river. The *hostería* also owns the town's best campground, **Camping Valle Fértil** (Rivadavia s/n; sites AR$30). It's shaded by a monotone cover of eucalyptus trees, and gets very crowded during long weekends and holidays, but it's quiet enough off-season and midweek. If the *hostería* is too much of a walk for you, there are good, simple restaurants along Rivadavia, leading west from the plaza.

La Florencia PARRILLA
(cnr Mitre & Acha; mains AR$25-40; lunch & dinner) Has a good range of *parrilla* offerings, including *chivito* (baby goat – order two hours in advance) and a delicious *lomo al roquefort* (beef with roquefort cheese sauce; AR$32).

Information

Cámara de Turismo (Mitre, btwn Entre Ríos & Mendoza) A private tourist office that has an office in the bus terminal.

Municipal tourist office (General Acha; 7am-1pm & 5-10pm Mon-Fri, 8am-1pm Sat) Across from the plaza. Arranges car or mule excursions into the mountain canyons and backcountry. Also keeps an updated list of hotel prices.

Post office (cnr Laprida & Mendoza)

Turismo Vesa (☎420143; www.turismovesa.com; Mitre s/n) For tours to Parque Provincial Ischigualasto, Talampaya, El Chiflón and horseback riding.

Getting There & Away

From San Agustín's **bus terminal** (Mitre, btwn Entre Ríos & Mendoza) daily buses head to San Juan (AR$60, 4½ hours).

DIFUNTA CORREA

Legend has it that during the civil wars of the 1840s Deolinda Correa followed the movements of her sickly conscript husband's battalion on foot through the deserts of San Juan, carrying food, water and their baby son in her arms. When her meager supplies ran out, thirst, hunger and exhaustion killed her. But when passing muleteers found them, the infant was still nursing at the dead woman's breast. Commemorating this apparent miracle, her shrine at Vallecito is widely believed to be the site of her death.

Difunta literally means 'defunct,' and Correa is her surname. Technically she is not a saint but rather a 'soul,' a dead person who performs miracles and intercedes for people; the child's survival was the first of a series of miracles attributed to her. Since the 1940s her shrine, originally a simple hilltop cross, has grown into a small village with its own gas station, school, post office, police station and church. Devotees leave gifts at 17 chapels or exhibit rooms in exchange for supernatural favors. In addition, there are two hotels, several restaurants, a commercial gallery with souvenir shops, and offices for the nonprofit organization that administers the site.

Interestingly, truckers are especially devoted. From La Quiaca, on the Bolivian border, to Ushuaia in Tierra del Fuego, you will see roadside shrines with images of the Difunta Correa and the unmistakable bottles of water left to quench her thirst. At some sites there appear to be enough parts lying around to build a car from scratch!

Despite lack of government support and the Catholic Church's open antagonism, the shrine of Difunta Correa has grown as belief in her miraculous powers has become more widespread. People visit the shrine all year round, but at Easter, May 1 and Christmas, up to 200,000 pilgrims descend on Vallecito. Weekends are busier and more interesting than weekdays.

There are regular departures to Vallecito from San Juan and Mendoza.

Parque Provincial Ischigualasto

Also known fittingly as **Valle de la Luna** (Valley of the Moon; www.ischigualasto.org; admission AR$70), this park takes its name from the Diaguita word for 'land without life'. Visits here are a spectacular step – or drive, as the case may be – into a world of surreal rock formations, dinosaur remains and glowing red sunsets. The park is in some ways comparable to North American national parks such as Bryce Canyon or Zion, except that here, time and water have exposed a wealth of fossils (some 180 million years old, from the Triassic period).

The park's **museum** displays a variety of fossils, including the carnivorous dinosaur Herrerasaurus (not unlike Tyrannosaurus rex), the Eoraptor lunensis (the oldest-known predatory dinosaur) and good dioramas of the park's paleoenvironments.

The 630-sq-km park is a desert valley between two sedimentary mountain ranges, the Cerros Colorados in the east and Cerro Los Rastros in the west. Over millennia, at every meander in the canyon, the waters of the nearly dry Río Ischigualasto have carved distinctive shapes in the malleable red sandstone, monochrome clay and volcanic ash. Predictably, some of these forms have acquired popular names, including **Cancha de Bochas** (the ball court), **El Submarino** (the submarine) and **El Gusano** (the worm), among others. The desert flora of algarrobo trees, shrubs and cacti complement the eerie landforms.

From the visitor center, isolated 1748m **Cerro Morado** is a three- to four-hour walk, gaining nearly 800m in elevation and yielding outstanding views of the surrounding area. Take plenty of drinking water and high-energy snacks.

Tours

All visitors to the park must go accompanied by a ranger. The most popular tours run for three hours and leave on the hour (more or less), with cars forming a convoy and stopping at noteworthy points along the way, where the ranger explains (in Spanish only) exactly what it is you're looking at.

If you have no private vehicle, an organized tour is the only feasible way to visit the park. These are easily organized in San Agustín. Otherwise ask the tourist office there about hiring a car and driver. Tour rates (not including entry fees) are about AR$420 per person from San Juan (through any travel agency in town), or about AR$130 per person from San Agustín. Tours from San Juan generally depart at 5am and return well after dark.

A variety of other tours (around AR$40 per person) are available from the visitor center here. Options include spectacular full-moon tours (2½ hours) in the five days around the full moon, treks to the summit of Cerro Morado (three to four hours), and a 12km circuit of the park on mountain bikes.

Sleeping & Eating

There is camping at the **visitor center** (per person AR$10), which has a *confitería* (cafe) serving simple meals (breakfast and lunch) and cold drinks; dried fruits and bottled olives from the province are available. There are toilets and showers, but because water is trucked in, don't count on it. There's no shade.

Getting There & Away

Ischigualasto is about 80km north of San Agustín via RP 510 and a paved lateral road to the northwest. Given its size and isolation, the only practical way to visit the park is by private vehicle or organized tour. Note that the park roads are unpaved and some can be impassable after rain, necessitating an abbreviated trip.

Bariloche & the Lake District

Includes »

Best Places to Eat

- » La Nonna Francesa (p339)
- » El Mesón (p356)
- » Ñancú Lahuén (p358)
- » Tinto Bistro (p359)
- » La Trattoria de la Famiglia Bianchi (p365)

Best Places to Stay

- » Hostería La Escampada (p373)
- » Hostería la Balconada (p346)
- » Hostería Chimehuín (p348)
- » Bardas Hotel (p338)
- » Hostería La Masía (p353)

Why Go?

Home to some of the country's most spectacular scenery, the Lake District hosts thousands of visitors each year. People come to ski, fish, climb, trek and generally bask in the cool, fresh landscapes created by the huge forests and glacier-fed lakes.

The paleontological sites and outstanding wineries just out of the city of Neuquén are well worth stopping off for en route; and way, way south is the resort town of Bariloche, with its picture-postcard location on the banks of the Lago Nahuel Huapi.

Getting away from the crowds is easily done. The lakeside villages of Villa Traful and San Martín de los Andes fill up for a short time in summer and are blissfully quiet the rest of the year. To the north, Chos Malal makes an excellent base for exploring nearby volcanoes, lagoons and hot springs.

When to Go

Bariloche

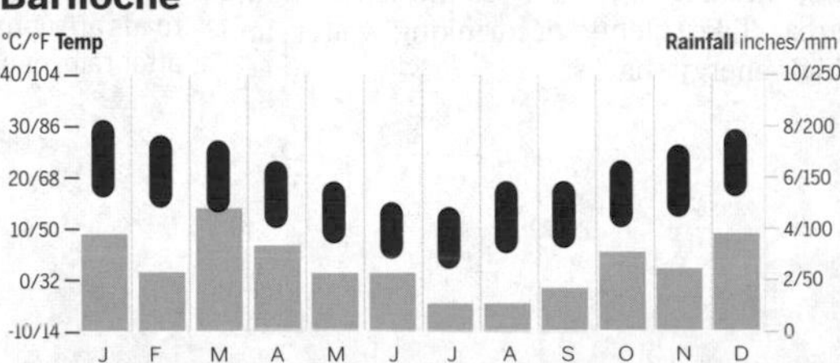

Mar-May Warm days, cool nights and autumn leaves make this a great time to visit.

Jun-Sep Snow season sees ski resorts open up and the mountain vistas turn even more spectacular.

Oct-Dec Moderate temperatures and blooming wildflowers, so put your trekking boots on.

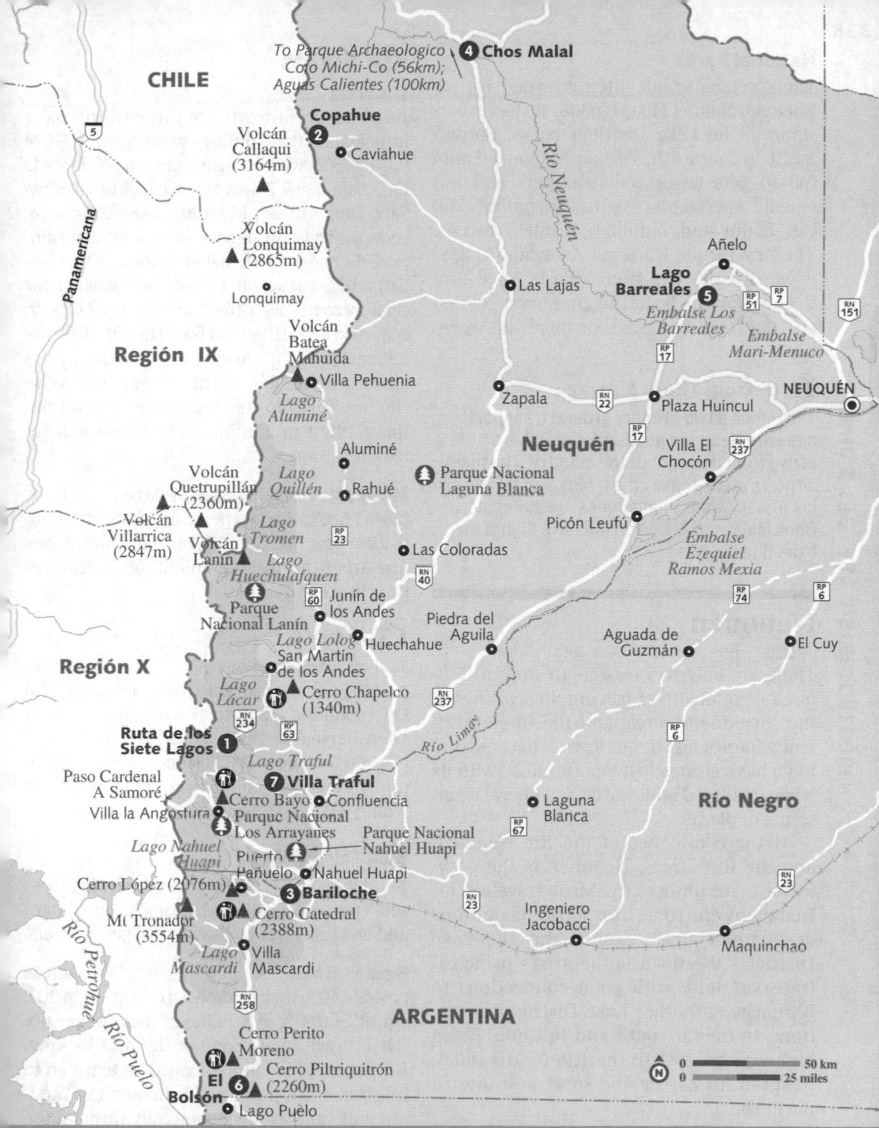

Bariloche & the Lake District Highlights

1. Drive the **Ruta de los Siete Lagos** (RN 234; p354), a breathtaking road winding between alpine lakes and pehuén forests
2. Soak your worries away in a bubbling mud bath in the thermal resort town of **Copahue** (p341).
3. Base yourself in **Bariloche** (p360) for some fun mountain adventures
4. Get off the tourist trail in **Chos Malal** (p342) and out into its spectacular surrounds
5. Follow in the footsteps of dinosaurs at **Lago Barreales** (p338)
6. Hit the hippie market in **El Bolsón** (p371) for fresh fruits and other yummies
7. Wind down for a few days surrounded by the gorgeous scenery of **Villa Traful** (p357)

National Parks

The spectacular but often crowded Parque Nacional Nahuel Huapi (p368) is the cornerstone of the Lake District's parks. Bordering it to the north, Parque Nacional Lanín (p349) gets fewer trail trampers and has equally spectacular sights, including Volcán Lanín and humbling pehuén forests. The tiny Parque Nacional Arrayanes (p358) is worth a day trip from Villa la Angostura to check out its beautiful cinnamon-colored arrayán trees. See p583 for more on Argentina's parks.

Getting There & Away

The region's two primary ground transport hubs are Neuquén and Bariloche, where buses arrive from throughout the country. The main airports are in these cities, plus San Martín de los Andes, while smaller ones are in Zapala, Chos Malal and El Bolsón. All have flights to/from Buenos Aires.

Neuquén

☎0299 / POP 264,600 / ELEV 265M

There are only two reasons to stop in Neuquén – the wealth of paleontological sites in the surrounding area, and the three excellent wineries just out of town. That said, the town has a strangely hypnotic effect, with its wide, tree-lined boulevards and liberal smattering of plazas.

At the confluence of the Río Neuquén and the Río Limay, Neuquén is the province's easternmost city. Most travelers hit Neuquén en route to more glamorous destinations in Patagonia and the Lake District – the town is the area's principal transport hub, with good connections to Bariloche and other Lake District destinations, to the far south and to Chile. Paved highways go east to the Río Negro valley, west toward Zapala and southwest toward Bariloche.

Known as Félix San Martín in town, the east–west RN 22 is the main thoroughfare, lying a few blocks south of downtown. Don't confuse it with Av San Martín (ie sans the 'Félix'), the obligatory homage to Argentina's national icon. The principal north–south street is Av Argentina, which becomes Av Olascoaga south of the old train station. Street names change on each side of Av Argentina and the old train station. Several diagonal streets bisect the conventional grid.

Sights

Wineries WINERY

Just outside of town are three of the most important Patagonian wineries – **NQN** (☎489-7500; www.bodeganqn.com.ar; RP 7, Picada 15; ⊙9am-1pm & 2-4pm Mon-Fri, 10:30am-4:30pm Sat & Sun), **Fin del Mundo** (☎485-5004; www.bodegadelfindelmundo.com; RP 8, Km9, San Patricio Del Chañar; ⊙10am-4pm Mon-Fri, 10am-5pm Sat) and **Schroeder** (☎508-6767; www.familiaschroeder.com; Calle 7 Nte, San Patricio del Chañar; admission AR$20; ⊙9am-5pm Mon-Fri, 10:30am-5:30pm Sat & Sun). Access to the vineyards is almost impossible without your own vehicle, but Turismo Arauquen can get you out there, often in combination with a paleontological tour.

Museo Nacional de Bellas Artes GALLERY

(☎443-6268; Bartolomé Mitre & Santa Cruz; ⊙10am-8pm Tue-Sat, 4-8pm Sun) Showcases fine arts from the region and often features traveling exhibitions.

Tours

Turismo Arauquen GUIDED TOURS

(☎442-6476; www.arauquen.com; H Yrigoyen 720) Offers guided visits to paleontology sites of Lago Barreales, Plaza Huincul and Villa El Chocón for about AR$190 per person (minimum four), which can be combined with winery visits (AR$250 per person).

Sleeping

Neuquén's hotels mainly cater to the business set. They are fairly unexciting in all ranges and less than great value for budget travelers.

Bardas Hotel HOTEL $$

(☎442-2403; www.bardashotel.com.ar; Roca 109; s/d AR$300/475; ❄📶) One of the smaller hotels in town is also one of the best looking. If it weren't in Neuquén you'd be tempted to call this a boutique hotel. Rooms are modern, but vary widely – generally those at the front are more spacious.

Punto Patagonico HOSTEL $

(☎447-9940; www.puntopatagonico.com; Periodistas Neuquinas 94; s/d AR$110/170, without bathroom AR$90/150; @📶) Neuquén's best hostel is a good deal – it's well set up with comfy dorms, spacious lounge and a good garden area.

Parque Hotel HOTEL $$

(☎442-5806; Av Olascoaga 271; s/d AR$165/250) There are a few charming touches in the spacious, tile-floored rooms here. Some are showing their age these days, but most have good views out over the busy street below.

Eating & Drinking

The many *confiterías* (cafes) along Av Argentina are all pleasant spots for breakfast and morning coffee. There are numerous bars and *confiterías* in the area north of Parque Central and around the meeting of the diagonals.

La Nonna Francesa INTERNATIONAL **$$**
(430-0930; 9 de Julio 56; mains AR$55-80; lunch & dinner) Some of Neuquén's finest dining can be found at this French-Italian trattoria – the pastas are all extremely good, but the trout dishes are the absolute standouts.

Confitería Donato CAFE **$**
(cnr JB Alberdi & Santa Fe; mains AR$30-50; breakfast, lunch & dinner) Plenty of dark wood paneling and brass fittings give this place an old-time feel and the wraparound seats may have you lounging around for hours on end. The menu runs the usual *confitería* gamut, with plenty of sandwiches, cakes and coffee on offer. There is live music Friday to Sunday nights and the occasional tango show – drop in for the schedule.

Olivetti INTERNATIONAL **$$$**
(Brown 168; mains AR$80-100; lunch & dinner) The fanciest restaurant in town has an impressive wine list and draws influences from French, Italian and Spanish cuisines. The set lunches (AR$60) are a worthy investment.

Shopping

Paseo de los Artesanos HANDICRAFTS
(Av Independencia, Parque Central; 10am-9pm Wed-Sun) Neuquén's largest selection of regional handicrafts is at this outlet, north of the old train station.

Artesanías Neuquinas HANDICRAFTS
(Brown 280) This provincially sponsored store offers a wide variety of high-quality Mapuche textiles and wood crafts.

Information

Neuquén's dozens of travel agencies are almost all located near downtown. Several banks along Av Argentina, between Parque Central and Roca, have ATMs.

ACA (Automóvil Club Argentino; 442-2325; Diagonal 25 de Mayo at Rivadavia) Argentina's auto club; good source for provincial road maps.

Banca Nazionale del Lavoro (cnr Av Argentina & Rivadavia)

Cambio Pullman (Ministro Alcorta 144) Money exchange.

Post office (Rivadavia & Santa Fe)

Provincial tourist office (442-4089; www.neuquentur.gov.ar; Félix San Martín 182; 8am-10pm) Great maps and brochures.

Regional hospital (443 1474; Buenos Aires 421)

Telecentro (Av Argentina at Ministro González; per hr AR$5; 24hr) Internet access.

Getting There & Away

Air

Neuquén's **airport** (444-0525) is west of town on RN 22. **Aerolíneas Argentina/Austral** (442-2409/10/11; Santa Fe 52) flies to Buenos Aires (from AR$800) four times daily Monday to Friday and twice daily on weekends. **American Jet** (444-1085; www.americanjet.com.ar; Aeropuerto Presidente Perón) is the regional carrier, with flights to Chos Malal (AR$262) and Chapelco (AR$308) – the nearest airport to San Martín del los Andes and Junín de los Andes.

Bus

Neuquén is a major hub for domestic and international bus services. Accordingly, its **bus terminal** (445-2300; cnr Solalique y Ruta 22), about 3.5km west of Parque Central, is well decked out, with restaurants, gift stores and even a luggage carousel! To get downtown take either a Pehueche bus (AR$2.50; buy a ticket at local 41) or a taxi (AR$28).

Several carriers offer service to Chile: **Plaza** (446-5975) goes to Temuco (AR$156, 11 hours) via Zapala and Paso Pino Hachado.

Neuquén is a jumping-off point for deep-south Patagonian destinations. Northern destinations such as Catamarca, San Juan, Tucumán, Salta and Jujuy may require a bus change in Mendoza, though the entire ticket can be purchased in Neuquén.

Getting Around

Neuquén is a good province to explore by automobile, but drivers should be aware that RN 22, both east along the Río Negro valley and west toward Zapala, is a rough road with heavy truck traffic. If you're looking for a rental car, **Turismo Arauquen** (442-6476; www.arauquen.com; H Yrigoyen 720) has the best rates in town.

BUSES FROM NEUQUÉN

The following table lists daily departures to nearly all long-distance destinations; provincial destinations are served numerous times daily.

DESTINATION	COST (AR$)	DURATION (HR)
Aluminé	86	6
Bahía Blanca	187	7½
Buenos Aires	423	17
Chos Malal	132	6
Córdoba	440	16
El Bolsón	182	7
Esquel	215	10
Junín de los Andes	130	6
Mendoza	320	13
Puerto Madryn	255	11
Río Gallegos	860	29
San Martín de los Andes	147	6
San Rafael	235	10
Viedma	110	8
Villa la Angostura	165	7
Zapala	80	3

Zapala

02942 / POP 35,400 / ELEV 1200M

Taking its name as an adaptation of the Mapuche word *chapadla* (dead swamp), Zapala got off to a bad start, image-wise. Not much has changed. This is a humble little place where the locals amuse themselves with walks up and down the main street, punctuated by lengthy pauses on street corners.

Sights & Activities

The main excuse for rolling through town is to visit the nearby Parque Nacional Laguna Blanca, with its awesome array of birdlife, or to take advantage of the town's bus connections for the rarely visited northern reaches of the Lake District.

Centro Cultural ARTS CENTER
(San Martín & Chaneton; 5-10pm) In front of the plaza, this hosts concerts and shows work by local artists and recently released Hollywood blockbusters.

Festivals

Zapala's **Feria de la Tradición**, held in the second week in November, showcases regional culture, with plenty of folk music, gaucho horse skill demonstrations, handicraft exhibits and regional food on sale.

Sleeping & Eating

Zapala has very limited accommodations.

Hotel Hue Melén HOTEL $$
(432109; www.hotelhuemelen.com; Almirante Brown 929; s/d AR$300/450;) You may be faintly surprised by the quiet stylishness of this hotel-casino complex. King-size beds, full bathtubs, contemporary art on the walls...it's wonderful what gambling money can buy you.

Hotel Pehuén HOTEL $
(423135; Etcheluz & Elena de la Vega; s/d AR$135/200;) Despite its (rather mysterious) two-star status, this is the best budget deal in town, conveniently near the bus terminal, with clean rooms, an attractive (classy, even) lobby and a good restaurant below.

Mayrouba ARGENTINE $$
(Monti & Etcheluz; mains AR$50-80; breakfast, lunch & dinner) The best-looking restaurant in town also serves up some of the tastiest fare. There are shades of Middle Eastern influence on the menu and Patagonian faves such as smoked trout (AR$55). If you're up

BUSES FROM ZAPALA

DESTINATION	COST (AR$)	DURATION (HR)
Aluminé	40	3½
Buenos Aires	473	18
Chos Malal	75	3
Caviahue	73	3
Junín de los Andes	68	3
Laguna Blanca	23	½
Neuquén	72	3
San Martín de los Andes	67	3½
Temuco (Chile)	190	6
Villa Pehuenia	80	4½

for a few drinks, it turns into a bar later on, with an impressive cocktail list.

El Chancho Rengo CAFE $
(☎422795; Av San Martín & Etcheluz; sandwiches AR$30-50; ⏲breakfast, lunch & dinner) It's likely half the town saunters in here for an espresso each day. Outdoor tables and good coffee and sandwiches make it great for a light bite.

Information

Banco de la Provincia del Neuquén (San Martín & Etcheluz) Bank with ATM.

Laguna Blanca national park office (☎431982; lagunablanca@apn.gov.ar; Av Ejercito Argentino 217; ⏲8am-3pm Mon-Fri) For information on Parque Nacional Laguna Blanca.

Tourist office (☎424296; RN 22, Km1398; ⏲7am-9pm) Located on the highway, 2km west of town center.

Getting There & Away

The **bus terminal** (☎421370; Etcheluz & Uriburu) is about four blocks from Av San Martín. Buses for Mendoza (AR$330, 16 hours) and points along the RN 40 leave on Friday and Sunday. During summer there are frequent departures for Copahue (AR$80, four hours).

Parque Nacional Laguna Blanca

At 1275m above sea level and surrounded by striking volcanic deserts, Laguna Blanca is only 10m deep, an interior drainage lake that formed when lava flows dammed two small streams. Only 30km southwest of Zapala, the lake is too alkaline for fish but hosts many bird species, including coots, ducks, grebes, upland geese, gulls and even a few flamingos. The 112.5-sq-km park primarily protects the habitat of the black-necked swan, a permanent resident.

Starting 10km south of Zapala, paved and well-marked RP 46 leads through the park toward the town of Aluminé. If you're catching a bus, ask the driver to drop you off at the information center. If you don't have your own transport, ask at the National Parks office in Zapala if you can get a ride out with the rangers in the morning. A taxi to the park should charge around AR$240, including two hours' waiting time.

There is a small improved campground with windbreaks, but bring all your own food. There's a **visitor center** (⏲9am-6pm Fri-Sun) with information displays and maps of walking trails, but there's no place to eat.

Copahue

☎02948 / ELEV 2030M

This small thermal springs resort stands on the northeastern side of its namesake volcano among steaming, sulfurous pools, including a bubbling hot-mud pool, the popular **Laguna del Chancho** (admission AR$20; ⏲8am-6pm). The setting, in a natural amphitheater formed by the mountain range, is spectacular, but the town isn't much to look at.

Copahue has been gaining in popularity, mainly with Argentine tourists, as the growth in tourist infrastructure shows. Due to snow cover, the village is only open from the start of December to the end of April.

The village centers on the large, modern **Complejo Termal Copahue** (☎299-442-4140; www.termasdecopahue.com; Ortiz Velez; baths AR$30, spa treatments from AR$40), which offers a wide range of curative bathing programs.

The best hotel in the village, **Hotel Termas** (☎495186; www.hoteltermascopahue.com.ar; Doucloux s/n; s/d from AR$302/448; wi-fi), features modern rooms, atmospheric common areas and an excellent restaurant serving traditional Argentine and regional foods.

Residencial Codihue (☎495151; codihue@futurtel.com.ar; Velez s/n; s/d AR$140/260) is the best budget option in town, with simple rooms just down the road from the thermal baths complex. Full board is available.

Parrillada Nito (Zambo Jara s/n; mains AR$50-70; lunch & dinner) is the most frequently recommended *parrilla* (steak house) in town.

In summer, one bus daily runs to Neuquén (AR$157, seven hours) via Zapala (AR$80, four hours). There are no scheduled departures for the rest of the year.

Caviahue

☎02948 / POP 470 / ELEV 1600M

On the western shore of Lago Caviahue, the ski village of Caviahue lies at the southeast foot of Volcán Copahue. A better-looking village than Copahue, this one is growing rapidly, too – construction noise fills the air during summer.

Activities

Walks WALKING

There are some good short walks from the village, including a popular day trek that goes up past the **Cascada Escondida** waterfall to **Laguna Escondida**. Another walk to the four waterfalls known as **Cascadas Agrio** starts from across the bridge at the entrance to town. The tourist office has an excellent map showing these and other walks around the area.

Caviahue Tours HIKING, ADVENTURE TOURS

(☎495138; www.caviahuetours.com; Av Bialous Centro Comercial local 11) If you have a taste for adventure, this company organizes treks, including to Laguna Termal and Volcán Copahue, rents mountain bikes in summer and offers dog-sledding trips in winter.

Hotel Caviahue SPA

If you fancy some pampering, this hotel has a day spa where you can enjoy a thermal bath (AR$30) and treatments (from AR$50).

Centro de Ski Cerro Caviahue SKIING

(☎495043; www.caviahue.com) A little under 2km west of Caviahue, this ski resort has seven chairlifts, and four pomas, which take skiers all the way up to the peak of Volcán Copahue (2953m). Equipment hire (skis/snowboard around AR$91 per day) is also available on the mountain or in the village. Adult day passes range from AR$134 to AR$248, depending on the season.

Sleeping & Eating

Hotel Caviahue HOTEL $$

(☎495044; hotelcaviahue@issn.gov.ar; 8 de Abril s/n; s/d AR$200/390) A rambling, older-style hotel set up the hill, with views out over the village, lake and mountains. It's the only hotel open in the village year-round. Rates drop around 30% off-season. Also on the premises is the only restaurant (mains AR$35 to AR$60) in town to stay open year-round.

Hebe's House HOSTEL $

(☎495238; www.hebeshouse.com.ar; Mapuche & Puesta del Sol; dm/d AR$100/280; Dec-Sep) With the only hostel for miles around, Hebe crams them in to cozy but cramped dorms. It's set in a cute alpine building and offers kitchen access, laundry facilities and plenty of tourist information. If you're coming in winter, book well ahead.

Information

Cyber Caviahue (Las Lengas s/n; per hr AR$6; 8am-1pm & 4-9pm) Internet access.

Oficina de Turismo (☎495036; www.caviahue-copahue.gov.ar; 8 de Abril s/n) In the *municpalidad* (city hall). Good maps and up-to-date info on local accommodations.

Getting There & Away

One bus daily runs to Neuquén (AR$130, 6½ hours) via Zapala (AR$73, 3½ hours). If you're headed for Chos Malal, you can shave a couple of hours off your travel time by getting off in Las Lajas (AR$55, 2½ hours) and waiting for a bus there. Check your connection times with the bus company **Cono Sur** (☎02942-432607) though – if you're going to get stranded, Zapala is the place to do it.

Chos Malal

☎02948 / POP 14,420 / ELEV 862M

Cruising through the stark, desertlike landscape north of Zapala doesn't really prepare you for arrival at this pretty little

oasis town. Set at the convergence of Río Neuquén and Río Curi Leuvú, the town boasts two main plazas, bearing the names of the two superheroes of Argentina – San Martín and Sarmiento. Around the former is the majority of the historic buildings, including the Fuerte IV Division fort (go around the back for sweeping views out over the river valley). Five blocks south is Plaza Sarmiento, where you'll find banks and businesses.

Activities

Tunduca TOURS, TREKS
(☎422829; www.tunduca.com.ar; Jujuy 60) The only tour operator in town offers everything from fly-fishing, horseback riding and rafting to day trips to the geysers and hot springs (p344) north of town and the rock carvings at Colo Michi-Co archaeological park. It can also arrange five-day treks to the summit of Volcán Domuyo (4710m), the highest volcanic peak in Patagonia.

LAGUNA TERMAL TREK

This day trip, which should be possible in around eight hours, is easy enough to do on your own, leaving from Copahue. Due to snow conditions, it's only possible from December to April unless you bring special equipment. If you'd like to take the side route to the peak of Volcán Copahue, it's recommended that you go with an experienced guide. Caviahue Tours (p342) is among the many tour operators offering guides on this route.

From the Hotel Valle del Volcán at the upper (southwest) edge of the village, cross the little footbridge and climb briefly past a life-size statue of the Virgin. The well-worn foot track leads across a sparsely vegetated plain towards the exploded cone of Volcán Copahue, dipping down to lush, green lawns by the northern shore of the Lagunas Las Mellizas' western 'twin.' Follow a path along the lake's north side past little black-sand beaches and gushing springs on its opposite shore, to reach the start of a steam pipeline, one to 1¼ hours from the village. The roaring of steam from the subterranean Copahue Geothermal Field entering the *vapoducto* and irregular explosive blasts of discharging steam can be heard along much of the trek. Cross the lake outlet – further downstream is a wide, easy ford – then cut up southwest over snowdrifts past a tarn to meet a 4WD track at the edge of a small waterlogged meadow. Turn right and follow this rough road up around left (or take a vague trail marked with white paint splashes to its right until you come back to the road on a rocky ridge below a wooden cross). The 4WD track continues westward up through a barren volcanic moonscape to end under a tiny glacier on the east flank of Volcán Copahue, 1¼ to 1½ hours from the pipeline.

Ascend southwest over bouldery ridges, crossing several small mineral-and-meltwater streams. To the northwest, in Chile, the ice-smothered Sierra Velluda and the near-perfect snowy cone of Volcán Antuco rise up majestically. From the third streamlet (with yellowy, sulfur-encrusted sides), cut along the slope below a hot spring then climb to the top of a prominent gray-pumice spur that lies on the international border. Ascend the spur until it becomes impossibly steep, then traverse up rightward over loose slopes into a gap to reach Laguna Termal, 1¼ to 1½ hours from the end of the 4WD track (3½ to 4¼ hours from Copahue).

Filling Volcán Copahue's eastern crater, this steaming hot lake feeds itself by melting the snout of a glacier that forms a massive rim of ice above its back wall. Sulfurous fumes often force trekkers to retreat from the lake, but these high slopes also grant a wonderful vista across the vast basin (where both villages are visible) between the horseshoe-shaped Lago Caviahue (Lago Agrio) and the elongated Lago Trolope to the northeast. From here, more experienced trekkers can continue up to the summit of Volcán Copahue.

To get back to Copahue, retrace your ascent route. If you have a decent map of the area, you can follow the Arroyo Caviahue (Río Agrio) and RN 26 back to town.

Warning

Particularly on windy days, acrid fumes rising from Laguna Termal can be overpowering due to sulfur dioxide gas (which attacks your airways). Approach the lake cautiously – don't even consider swimming in it. Less experienced trekkers are advised to go with an organized tour.

WORTH A TRIP

NORTH OF CHOS MALAL

Heading north from Chos Malal brings you to a couple of wonderful, rarely visited attractions. Public transportation is rare and often nonexistent, but if you have the time and patience you'll be well rewarded.

Parque Archaeologico Colo Michi-Co

This small archaeological site features one of the most important collections of Pehuenche rock art in Patagonia. There are over 600 examples here, carved with symbolic figures and abstract designs. Getting to the site without a private vehicle is tricky. Buses leave Chos Malal at 8am Friday for the village of Varvarco (AR$45, three hours). From there, it's 9km south on the RP 39 to the Escuela Colo Michi-Co (buses will drop you off), where you'll see a signpost leading to the park, an 8km walk away. Bring everything – there's nothing out here.

If all that walking doesn't excite you, contact **Señora La Gallega** (☎02948-421329) in Varvarco – there aren't any *remises* (radio taxis) there, but the señora should be able to hook you up with a car and driver, charging around AR$9 per kilometer, plus waiting time. Hitchhiking is common practice in the area, but be prepared for long waits.

Aguas Calientes

These excellent natural outdoor hot springs located at the foot of the Volcán Domuyo are spread over 20 sq km and feature three main sites. The main one at Villa Aguas Calientes is suitable for swimming; Las Olletas is a collection of bubbling mud pits and Los Tachos are geysers, spurting up to heights of 2m. The site is 40km north of Varvarco, where the last public transport terminates. If you don't have your own wheels, your best way of getting here is with Tunduca (p343) in Chos Malal. If you can get to Varvarco on your own, you can ask about hiring a driver with Señora La Gallega.

Sleeping & Eating

Most accommodations are located between the two plazas. People in Chos Malal eat a lot of goat, and you may find yourself doing the same while you're there.

Hostería Don Costa HOTEL $$
(☎421652; hostdoncosta@hotmail.com; s/d AR$180/260; ❄@📶) Attractive, modern rooms set well back from the road in case Chos Malal ever has a noisy night. Rooms are on the small side (like, door-bumping-bed small), but excellent value for the price. Get one upstairs for a balcony, sunlight and ventilation.

Residencial Kallfü Küyen HOTEL $
(☎421263; Jujuy 60; s/d AR$90/140, apt AR$200) The best budget deal in town has clean, spacious rooms half a block from Plaza Sarmiento.

Las Delicias de L'Traful BAKERY $
(Roca 80; pastries AR$8-10; ⏲breakfast, lunch & dinner) The best bakery/cafe in town serves up yummy, super-fresh baked goods and excellent coffee.

Canan ARGENTINE $$
(General Paz 560; mains AR$40-70; ⏲lunch & dinner) For a good meal in pleasant surrounds Chos Malal doesn't have a whole lot of options. This place is rightly popular, though, with good pizzas and *parrilla* and an OK wine list.

Information

Banco de la Nación (cnr Sarmiento & Urquiza) Has an ATM.

Hospital Zonal Gregorio Avárez (☎421400; cnr Entre Ríos & Flores) English speaker usually on-site.

Laco (Sarmiento 280; per hr AR$6; ⏲9am-8pm) Provides internet access.

Tourist Information (☎421991; turnorte@neuquen.gov.ar; 25 de Mayo 89; ⏲8am-8pm) Has good maps of the town and surrounds.

Getting There & Around

American Jet (☎299-444-1085; www.americanjet.com.ar) flies from Neuqúen to Chos Malal and back twice weekly.

Regular buses depart for Zapala (AR$75, three hours), Neuquén (AR$132, six hours) and Varvarco (AR$50, three hours). Three minibuses a day leave between 4:30pm and 5pm for Buta Ranquil (AR$25, two hours). Buses for Mendoza (AR$255, 13 hours) and points along the RN 40 leave on Monday and Friday.

North along the RN 40

Following the RN 40 north from Chos Malal gives you more wild desert scenery, tiny windswept towns and expansive, empty vistas. Despite what many will tell you, there *is* public transportation along this route. Tramat runs regular buses between Zapala and Mendoza twice a week. Failing that, **Transportes Leader** (☎in Buta Ranquil 02948-493268; cnr Malvinas & Jadull) runs minibuses between Buta Ranquil and San Rafael, Sunday to Friday. There's regular bus service from Neuquén and Chos Malal to Buta Ranquil, where you may get stuck for the night. There's no real reason to be here, but there are a couple of cheap hotels, one nice one, and enough restaurant-cafes to keep you from starving.

Aluminé

☎02942 / POP 4500 / ELEV 400M

Time seems to have stopped for Aluminé and, although it's an important tourist destination, it is less visited than destinations to the south. Situated 103km north of Junín de los Andes via RP 23, it's a popular fly-fishing destination and offers access to the less-visited northern sector of Parque Nacional Lanín. The Río Aluminé also offers excellent white-water rafting and kayaking.

Sights & Activities

Traditional Communities VILLAGES

The nearby Mapuche communities of **Aigo** and **Salazar**, on the 26km dirt road to **Lago Rucachoroi** (in Parque Nacional Lanín), sell traditional weavings, araucaria pine nuts and, in summer, *comidas tipicas* (traditional dishes). Salazar is an easy, signposted 12km walk or bike ride out of town – just follow the river. Aigo is another 14km along.

Aluminé Rafting OUTDOORS

(☎496322; www.interpatagonia.com/aluminerafting; Conrado Villegas 610)For rafting on the Río Aluminé (best in November), as well as kayaking, fly-fishing, trekking and rock climbing.

Mali Viajes BICYCLE RENTAL, TOURS

(☎496310) In front of the tourist office on the plaza, Mali Viajes rents out bikes for AR$20/80 per hour/day. During summer it offers scenic tours to Mapuche communities, circumnavigating Lago Ruca Choroi en route to Villa Pehuenia.

The tourist office keeps a list of available **fishing** guides and sells licenses (AR$75/250/350 per day/week/season).

Sleeping & Eating

If you're traveling in a group, ask the tourist office about its list of self-catering cabins – some just out of town – that offer good value for three or more people. High season coincides with the November-through-April fishing season.

Hotel de la Aldea HOTEL $$

(☎496340; www.hoteldelaaldea.com.ar; RP 23 & Crouzielles; s/d from AR$200/300;❄📶) A sprawling brick wonderland out on the highway (a two-minute walk from the center of town), the Aldea is comfortable enough with modern, slightly cramped rooms. It's definitely worth paying the extra AR$30 for the river views.

Nid Car HOTEL $

(☎496131; nidcaralumine@yahoo.com.ar; cnr Christian Joubert & Benigar; s/d AR$100/150) Very standard and slightly spacious rooms just uphill from the plaza. Cheapest in town and not a bad deal.

Los Araucarias PARRILLA $

(cnr Candelaria & C Joubert; mains AR$35-50; ⌚lunch & dinner) This standard *parrilla* restaurant offers a down-home atmosphere and an impressive wine list.

La Posta del Rey ARGENTINE $$

(C Joubert 336; mains AR$45-70; ⌚breakfast, lunch & dinner) Inside the Hostería Aluminé, this is the best eating option in town, serving up all the Argentine standards plus some good Patagonian favorites such as lamb, venison and trout.

Information

Banco del Provincia del Neuquén (cnr Conrado Villegas & Torcuato Mordarelli) Bank and ATM.

Nex Sur (☎496027; Av RIM 26 848; per hr AR$6) Internet access; uphill from plaza.

Tourist office (☎496001; info@alumine.gov.ar; Christian Joubert, Plaza San Martín; ⌚8am-8pm mid-Mar-Nov, 9am-9pm Dec-mid-Mar) For local info and maps, fishing permits, road conditions etc.

Getting There & Away

Aluminé's **bus terminal** (☎496048) is just downhill from the plaza, an easy walk to any of the hotels listed here. Aluminé Viajes and Albus go daily to/from Neuquén (AR$86, six hours), Zapala (AR$40, three to 3½ hours), Villa Pehuenia (AR$25, one hour) and San Martín de los Andes (AR$40, 4½ hours).

Villa Pehuenia

☎02942 / POP 366 / ELEV 1200M

Villa Pehuenia is an idyllic little lakeside village situated on the shores of Lago Aluminé, 102km north of Junín de los Andes (via RP 23 and Aluminé) and 120km west of Zapala, via RP 13. There are several Mapuche communities nearby, including Puel, located between Lago Aluminé and Lago Moquehue.

The village lies at the heart of the Pehuen region, named of course after the pehuén (araucaria) trees that are so marvelously present. If you have a car, the Circuito Pehuenia is a great drive; it's a four- to six-hour loop from Villa Pehuenia past Lago Moquehue, Lago Ñorquinco, Lago Pulmarí and back around Lago Aluminé. Mali Viajes in Aluminé offers scenic back-road tours along this route in summer, starting from Aluminé.

Sights & Activities

Volcán Batea Mahuida VOLCANO

From the top of here (2010m) you can see eight volcanoes (from Lanín to the south to Copahue to the north) in both Argentina and Chile. Inside Batea Mahuida is a small crater lake. You drive nearly to the top (summer only) and then it's an easy two-hour walk to the summit.

Batea Mahuida SKIING

(☎02942-15-661527; www.cerrobateamahuida.com.ar; day pass AR$75-95) Volcán Batea Mahuida is the location of this small Mapuche-operated ski park, which is little more than a few snowy slopes with a T-bar and a poma. If you're a Nordic skier, you're in better luck – a circuit goes around the park, taking in awesome views of the volcano and lakes.

Los Pehuenes ADVENTURE TOURS

(☎498029; www.pehuenes.com.ar; Centro Comercial) The local adventure-tourism operator offers rafting, trekking, horseback riding and 4WD off-roading trips.

Sleeping & Eating

Many businesses in Villa Pehuenia close down off season. Those listed here are open year-round. *Hosterías* (lodging houses) and *cabañas* are spread around the Peninsula de los Coihues.

Hostería la Balconada HOTEL $$$

(☎02942-15-473843; www.hosterialabalconada.com.ar; r AR$565-715; wifi) One of the finest, coziest accommodation options in town, this one sits out on a cliff on the peninsula. If you can, it's worth paying the extra for the lake views.

Hostería de las Cumbres HOTEL $$

(☎498097; r AR$300) Right down by the waterfront in the main part of town, this cozy little *hostería* has smallish rooms coming off waynarrow corridors. Lake views from the front rooms, however, make this one a winner.

Anhedonia INTERNATIONAL $$

(mains AR$45-80; ⊙lunch & dinner) Down by the waterfront, Anhedonia offers a good selection of fondues, meat and pasta dishes and has a great deck out front for catching a few rays.

Information

Banco de la Provincia del Neuquén (RP 13 s/n) Next to the police station; has an ATM.

Oficina de Turismo (☎498044; www.villapehuenia.gov.ar; RP 13 s/n) At the entrance to town; is extremely helpful and provides good maps of the region.

Getting There & Around

Exploring the area is tough without a car, though hitchhiking is definitely feasible in summer. **Destinos Patagonicos** (☎498067; Centro Comercial) is the representative for Albus, the only bus company currently serving the village. There are daily buses to Zapala (AR$80, 4½ hours), Neuquén (AR$155, seven hours) and Aluminé (AR$25, one hour).

Junín de los Andes

☎02972 / POP 13,590 / ELEV 800M

A much more humble affair than other Lake District towns, Junín's a favorite for fly fishers – the town deems itself the trout capital of Neuquén province and, to drive the point home, uses trout-shaped street signs. A couple of circuits leading out of town take in the scenic banks of the Lago Huechulafquen, where Mapuche settlements welcome visitors. Outside of peak season, these circuits are best done by private vehicle (or incredibly enthusiastic cyclists), but travel agents based here offer reasonably priced tours.

The center is between the highway and the river. Don't confuse Av San Martín, runs on the west side of Plaza San Martín, with Félix San Martín, two blocks west.

Sights & Activities

Junín's surroundings are more appealing than the town itself, but the museum is well worth seeing.

Museo Mapuche MUSEUM

(cnr Ginés Ponte & Joaquín Nogueira; ⌚10am-noon & 4-8pm Mon, Wed & Fri) The collection here includes Mapuche weavings and archaeological pieces.

Vía Cristi LANDMARK

Situated about 2km from the center of town, near the end of Av Antardida Argentina, Vía Cristi contains a collection of 22 sculptures, bas reliefs and mosaics winding its way up Cerro de la Cruz and vividly depicting the Conquest of the Desert, Mapuche Legends, Christian themes and indigenous history.

Trout Fishing FISHING

The area around Junín is prime country for trout-fishing, and the Río Aluminé, north of Junín, is an especially choice area. Catch-

THE MAPUCHE

The Lake District's most prevalent indigenous group, the Mapuche, originally came from Chilean territory. They resisted several attempts at subjugation by the Inca and fought against Spanish domination for nearly 300 years. Their move into Argentina began slowly. Chilean Mapuche were making frequent voyages across the Andes in search of trade as far back as the 17th century. Some chose to stay. In the 1880s the exodus became more pronounced as the Chilean government moved into Mapuche land, forcing them out.

Another theory for the widespread move is that, for the Mapuche, the *puelmapu* (eastern land) holds a special meaning, as it is believed that all good things (such as the sun) come from the east.

Apart from trade, the Mapuche (whose name means 'people of the land' in Mapudungun, their language) have traditionally survived as small-scale farmers and hunter-gatherers. There is no central government – each extended family has a *lonko* (chief) and in times of war families would unite to elect a *toqui* (axe-bearer) to lead them.

The role of *machi* (shaman) was and still is an important one in Mapuche society. It is usually filled by a woman, whose responsibilities included performing ceremonies for curing diseases, warding off evil, dreamwork, and influencing weather, harvests, social interactions. The *machi* was also well schooled in the use of medicinal herbs but, as Mapuche access to land and general biodiversity in the region has decreased, this knowledge is being lost.

Estimates of how many Mapuche live in Argentina vary according to the source. The official census puts the number at around 300,000, while the Mapuche claim that the real figure is closer to 500,000.

Both in Chile and Argentina, the Mapuche live in humble circumstances in rural settings, or leave the land to find work in big cities. It is estimated that there are still 200,000 fluent Mapudungun speakers in Chile, where nominal efforts are made to revive the language in the education system. No such official program has been instituted in Argentina and, while exact numbers are not known, it is feared that the language here may soon become extinct.

Apart from loss of language, the greatest threat to Mapuche culture is the loss of land, a process that has been under way ever since their lands were 'redistributed' after the Conquest of the Desert and many Mapuche were relocated to reserves – often the lowest-quality land, without any spiritual significance to them. As with many indigenous peoples, the Mapuche have a special spiritual relationship with the land, believing that certain rocks, mountains, lakes and so on have a particular spiritual meaning.

Despite a relatively well-organized land-rights campaign, the relocation continues today, as Mapuche lands are routinely reassigned to large commercial interests in the oil, cattle and forestry industries. Defiant to the end, the Mapuche don't look like fading away any time soon. They see their cultural survival as intrinsically linked to economic independence and Mapuche-owned and -operated businesses are scattered throughout the Lake District.

and-release is obligatory. Fishing permits (AR$75/250/350 per day/week/season) are available through the tourist office.

Ciclismo Mavi BICYCLE RENTAL
(Felix San Martín 415) Rents mountain bikes for AR$20/75 per hour/day.

Festivals & Events

In January the **Feria y Exposición Ganadera** displays the best of local cattle, horses, sheep, poultry and rabbits. There are also exhibitions of horsemanship, as well as local crafts exhibits, but this is the *estanciero's* (*estancia* owner's) show.

In July, the Mapuche celebrate their crafts skills in the **Semana de Artesanía Aborígen**.

The **National Trout Festival** takes place in November.

Sleeping

High season coincides with fishing season (November through April); during low season, prices are lower than those that are quoted here.

Hostería Chimehuín HOTEL $$
(491132; www.interpatagonia.com/hosteriachimehuin; cnr Coronel Suárez & 25 de Mayo; s/d AR$210/260;) This is a beautiful spot a few minutes from the center of town. Book early and you'll have a good chance of snagging a room with a balcony overlooking the creek. Either way, rooms are big, warm and comfortable and the whole place has a tranquil air to it.

Rüpú Calel HOTEL $$
(491569; Coronel Suárez 560; s/d AR$180/260) While they may look big and bare to some, the rooms here have a pleasing simplicity and are sparkling clean, as are the spacious bathrooms.

Camping Laura Vicuña CAMPGROUND $
(Ginés Ponte s/n; camp sites per person AR$25) You won't find a much more sublime location for an urban campground: perched on an island in between two burbling creeks, with all the facilities, plus fully equipped cabins (three-night minimum).

Tromen Hostel HOSTEL $
(491498; www.hosteltromen.com.ar; Lonquimay 195; dm/d AR$50/120) A cozy little hostel located upstairs in a family home. If the place ever fills up it could get quite cramped, but it's a good deal nonetheless.

Eating

Junín has fairly mediocre restaurants, though local specialties such as trout, wild boar and venison may be available.

Ruca Hueney PARRILLA $$
(491113; cnr Colonel Suárez & D Milanesio; mains AR$50-80; lunch & dinner) Ruca Hueney, Junín's oldest restaurant, is reliable and has the most extensive menu in town. Portions are large; service is abrupt. There's a cheaper take-out counter next door in case you were thinking about a picnic at the park across the street.

Turicentro CAFE $
(Domingo Milanesio 590; mains AR$25-40; breakfast, lunch & dinner) You could hardly think of a less appealing name, but this bright, comfortable cafe by the tourist office is a good place for coffee and a sandwich.

Information

Banco de la Provincia de Neuquén (Av San Martín, btwn Coronel Suárez & General Lamadrid) Opposite the plaza.

bits (Coronel Suárez 445 btwn Domingo Milanesio & Don Bosco; per hr AR$5) Internet access.

Club Andino Junín de los Andes (Félix San Martín 358) Provides information on the Volcán Tromen climb as well as other excursions within the Lanín national park.

Park office (491160; Domingo Milanesio at Coronel Suárez; 9am-8:30pm Mon-Fri, 2:30-8:30pm Sat & Sun) Next to the tourist office. Has information on Parque Nacional Lanín.

Picurú Turismo (492829; www.picuruturismo.com.ar; Coronel Suárez 371) Recommended tour operator for trips into Parque Nacional Lanín and tours of Mapuche communities.

Post office (cnr Coronel Suárez & Don Bosco)

Tourist office (491160, 492575; www.junindelosandes.gov.ar; cnr Domingo Milanesio & Coronel Suárez; 8am-11pm Nov-Feb, 8am-9pm Mar-Oct) Enthusiastically helpful staff. Fishing permits and a list of licensed fishing guides available.

Getting There & Away

Junín and San Martín de los Andes share Chapelco airport, which lies midway between the two towns. There are regularly scheduled flights to Buenos Aires and Neuquén. A *remise* (taxi) into town should run you about AR$45. Another option is walking the 1km out to the highway and flagging down a passing bus (AR$10, 25 minutes).

BUSES FROM JUNÍN DE LOS ANDES

DESTINATION	COST (AR$)	DURATION (HR)
Buenos Aires	622	22
Neuquén	133	6
San Martín de los Andes	15	1
Zapala	68	3

The **bus terminal** (☎492038; Olavarría & Félix San Martín) is three blocks from the main plaza. El Petróleo goes three times a week to Aluminé (AR$32, three hours). To Mendoza you must change buses in Neuquén or Zapala.

Parque Nacional Lanín

Dominating the view in all directions along the Chilean border, the snowcapped cone of 3776m Volcán Lanín is the centerpiece of this **national park** (www.parquenacionallanin.gov.ar), which extends 150km from Parque Nacional Nahuel Huapi in the south to Lago Ñorquinco in the north.

Protecting 3790 sq km of native Patagonian forest, Parque Nacional Lanín is home to many of the same species that characterize more southerly Patagonian forests, such as the southern beeches – lenga, ñire and coihue. The area does host some unique specimens, though, such as the extensive stands of the broadleaf, deciduous southern beech, raulí, and the curious pehuén (monkey puzzle tree; *Araucaria araucana),* a pinelike conifer whose nuts have long been a dietary staple for the Pehuenches and Mapuches. Note, though, that only indigenous people may gather *piñones* (pine nuts) from the pehuénes.

The towns of San Martín de los Andes, Junín de los Andes and Aluminé are the best bases for exploring Lanín, its glacial lakes and the backcountry.

LAGO TROMEN

This northern approach to **Volcán Lanín** (3776m), which straddles the Argentina-Chile border, is also the shortest and usually the earliest in the season to open for hikers and climbers. Before climbing Lanín, ask permission at the Lanín national park office in San Martín or, if necessary, of the *gendarmería* (border guards) in Junín. To prove that you are adequately equipped, it's obligatory to show equipment, including plastic tools, crampons, ice axe and clothing – including sunglasses, sunblock, gloves, hats and padded jackets.

From the trailhead at the Argentine border station, it's five to seven hours to the **CAJA refugio** (capacity 20 people), at 2600m on the Camino de Mulas route; above that point, snow equipment is necessary. There's a shorter but steeper route along the ridge known as the Espina del Pescado. Trekkers can cross the Sierra Mamuil Malal to Lago Huechulafquen via Arroyo Rucu Leufu (see p349).

Contact Andestrack (p352) or the park office in San Martín to organize guides for climbing Lanín. The hike usually takes two days: you leave early the first and stay at the RIM *refugio* (shelter), rise before dawn the following day, hike to the summit and walk down. If you want to go up in winter, Andestrack can set you up with guides to hike up and board or ski down.

LAGO QUILLÉN

Situated in the park's densest pehuén forests, this isolated lake is accessible by dirt road from Rahué, 17km south of Aluminé, and has many good **camp sites**. Other nearby lakes include **Lago Rucachoroi**, directly west of Aluminé, and **Lago Ñorquinco** on the park's northern border. There are Mapuche reservations at Rucachoroi and Quillén.

LAGO HUECHULAFQUEN

The park's largest lake is also one of its most central and accessible areas. Despite limited public transportation, it can be reached from San Martín and – more easily – Junín de los Andes. RP 61 climbs from a junction just north of Junín, west to Huechulafquen and the smaller Lago Paimún, offering outstanding views of Volcán Lanín and access to trailheads of several excellent hikes.

From the ranger station at **Puerto Canoa**, a good trail climbs to a viewpoint on Lanín's shoulder, where it's possible to hike across to Paso Tromen or continue climbing to either of two *refugios:* the **RIM refugio** belongs to the army's Regimiento de Infantería de Montaña, while the **CAJA refugio** belongs to the Club Andino Junín de los Andes (p348). Both are fairly rustic but well kept and can be bases for attempts on the summit. The initial segment follows an abandoned road, but after about 40 minutes it becomes a pleasant woodsy trail along the **Arroyo Rucu Leufu**, an attractive mountain stream. Halfway to

Parque Nacional Lanín

the *refugio* is an extensive **pehuén forest**, the southernmost in the park, which makes the walk worthwhile if you lack time for the entire route. The route to RIM's *refugio*, about 2450m above sea level, takes about seven hours one way, while the trail to CAJA's *refugio* takes a bit longer.

Another good backcountry hike circles **Lago Paimún**. This requires about two days from Puerto Canoa; you return to the north side of the lake by crossing a cable platform strung across the narrows between Huechulafquen and Paimún. A shorter alternative hike goes from the very attractive campground at **Piedra Mala** to **Cascada El Saltillo**, a nearby forest waterfall. If your car lacks 4WD, leave it at the logjam 'bridge' that crosses the creek and walk to Piedra Mala – the road, passable by any ordinary vehicle to this point, quickly worsens after a harsh winter. Horses are available for rent at Piedra Mala. Transportes Ko-Ko runs buses to Piedra Mala daily in summer from the San Martín bus terminal.

Campsites are abundant along the highway; travelers camping in the free sites in the narrow area between the lakes and the highway must dig a latrine and remove their own trash. If you camp at the organized sites (which, though not luxurious, are maintained), you'll support Mapuche concessionaires who at least derive some income from lands that were theirs before the state usurped them a century ago. Good campsites include **Camping Raquithue** (per person AR$35) and **Bahía Cañicul** (☎02972-490211; AR$35).

Noncampers should treat themselves to a stay at **Hostería Refugio Pescador** (☎02972-491756; www.patagon-fly-fishing.com; r per person incl full board AR$480) or the three-star **Hostería Paimún** (☎02972-491758; www.interpatagonia.com/hosteriapaimun; r per person incl full board AR$480); both cater to fishing parties.

LAGO LÁCAR & LAGO LOLOG

From San Martín, at the east end of Lago Lácar, there is bus service on RP 48, which runs along the lake to the Chilean border at Paso Hua Hum. You can get off the bus anywhere along the lake or get off at Hua Hum and hike to **Cascada Chachín**; bus drivers know the stop. From the highway, it's 3km down a dirt road and then another 20 minutes' walk along a trail to the waterfall. It's a great spot for a picnic.

About 15km north of San Martín de los Andes, Lago Lolog offers good fishing in a largely undeveloped area. You'll find free camping at **Camping Puerto Arturo**. Transportes Ko-Ko runs four buses daily in summer to Lago Lolog from San Martín (AR$8).

ℹ Information

The Lanín national park office in San Martín produces brochures on camping, hiking and climbing in the park. Scattered throughout the park proper are several ranger stations, but they usually lack printed materials. The national park's website (www.parquenacionallanin.gov.ar) is full of useful information.

ℹ Getting There & Away

Although the park is close to San Martín and Junín, public transportation is not extensive; see p356 and p351 for details. With some patience, hitchhiking is feasible in high season. Buses over the Hua Hum and Tromen passes, from San Martín and Junín to Chile, will carry passengers to intermediate destinations but are often full.

San Martín de los Andes

☎02972 / POP 31,500 / ELEV 645M

Like a mellower version of Bariloche, San Martín has two peak periods: winter for skiing at Cerro Chapelco and summer for trekking, climbing etc in nearby Parque Nacional Lanín. Brave souls also swim in the chilly waters of Lago Lácar on the western edge of town. Between these times it's a quiet little town with a spectacular setting that retains much of the charm and architectural unity that once attracted people to Bariloche. A boat ride on the lake is pretty much a must if you're passing through, and if the snow's cleared (anytime from November onwards) and you're heading south, you should seriously think about leaving town via the scenically neck-straining Ruta de los Siete Lagos (RN 234), which runs south to Villa la Angostura, Lago Nahuel Huapi and Bariloche.

Sights

Almost everything in San Martín de los Andes is within walking distance of the *centro cívico* (civic center), and the shady lakefront park and pier are a delightful place to spend an afternoon. Av San Martín is the main commercial street, running northeast from the lakefront toward the highway.

Museo Primeros Pobladores MUSEUM
(M Rosas; admission AR$3; ⏲2-7pm Mon-Fri) Regional archaeological and ethnographic items such as arrowheads, spear points, pottery and musical instruments are the focus of this museum, located two doors north of the tourist office, near Av Roca.

Activities

Ruta de los Siete Lagos DRIVING TOUR
From San Martín, RN 234 follows an eminently scenic but rough, narrow and dusty

EXCURSIONS TO PARQUE NACIONAL LANÍN

In summer, buses leave the terminal in Junín several times a day for destinations within the national park, allowing you to hit the trails and camp in some beautiful areas. The buses run three 'circuits' and charge AR$24.50 one way.

Lago Huechulafquen & Puerto Canoa (via RP 61)

From Puerto Canoa, on the north shore of the lake, there are three worthwhile hikes, including a 1½-hour roundtrip walk to the Cascada del Saltillo and a seven-hour roundtrip hike to **Cara Sur de Lanín** (south face of Volcán Lanín). For the latter, park rangers require you set out by 11am. Ranger stations are at the entrance to Huechulafquen and at Puerto Canoa. From Puerto Canoa, the boat **Jose Julian** (☎02972-429264, 428029; www.catamaranjosejulian.com.ar) offers boat trips on the lake. Buses depart Juniń's terminal twice in the morning (usually around 8am and 11am) and once in the afternoon (around 4pm). Be sure to catch the last bus back unless you plan to camp.

Circuito Tromen (via RN 23 & RP 60)

Buses depart twice daily to **Lago Tromen**, from where there is a 1½-hour roundtrip walk along the river, passing a fine araucaria forest and a lookout with fabulous views of the lake. Another 45-minute walk takes you to the base of **Volcán Lanín's Cara Norte** (north face). This is one departure point for the two- to three-day ascent of Lanín. Park rangers inspect equipment and test any climbers who plan to go without a guide. To hire a guide, contact the tourist office in Junín (p348). This is the access point for the CAJA *refugio* (shelter) and two military-owned *refugios*. Lago Tromen can also be reached by taking any bus that goes to Chile and getting off at Tromen.

Circuito Curruhué (via RP 62)

Buses depart once or twice daily for **Lago Curruhué** and **Lago Epulafquen**; near the latter is a trailhead that leads to the **Termas de Lahuen-Có** (☎424709; www.lahuenco.com), about one hour's walking from the head. Package tours out here – including transportation, lunch and spa treatments – cost around AR$536 and can be organized through the center or through tour operators in town. Luxurious **rooms** (from s/d AR$964/1240) are available, should you want to spend the night. You can also hike from here to the crater of Volcán Achen Niyeu.

San Martín de Los Andes

route past numerous alpine lakes to Villa la Angostura. It's known as the Ruta de los Siete Lagos (Seven Lakes Route) and its spectacular scenery has made the drive famous. Sections of the 110km route close every year due to heavy snowfalls – December to May is the best time to schedule this trip, but ask around for current conditions. Full-day tours from San Martín, Villa la Angostura and Bariloche regularly do this route, but there's also a scheduled bus service (p357) and, with a little forward planning, it's possible to drive/cycle it yourself.

HG Rodados BICYCLE RENTAL
(☎427345; Av San Martín 1061) Mountain biking is an excellent way to explore the surrounding area and a good way to travel the Ruta de los Siete Lagos. Rent bikes here for around AR$46 per day.

Mirador Bandurrias VIEWPOINT
(admission AR$3) A 2.5km steep, dusty hike ends with awesome views of Lago Lácar; be sure to take a snack or lunch. Tough cyclists can reach the *mirador* (viewing point) in about an hour via dirt roads.

Playa Catrite BEACH
Walk, bike or hitch to this protected rocky beach, 4km away down RN 234 (there's a bus three times daily in summer). It has a laid-back restaurant with a nice deck.

Lanín Turismo RAFTING
(☎425808; www.laninturismo.com; Av San Martín 431) With this outfit, rafting on the Río Meliquina, south of San Martín, or the Río Hua Hum to the west, costs about AR$180 for the day trip, including transfers. The river is spectacular and suitable for kids.

Andestrack OUTDOORS
(☎420588; www.andestrack.com.ar; Coronel Rhode 782) There are excellent opportunities for trekking and climbing in Parque Nacional Lanín. This is a young, enthusiastic company that has been highly recommended for mountain biking, canoeing, snowshoeing and dog sledding in the park.

Bumps SKIING
(☎428491; www.skienchapelco.com.ar; Villegas 459) Skiing and snowboarding at nearby Cerro Chapelco attracts enthusiastic winter crowds. In San Martín, rental equipment is available here and at many other places along San Martín. Ski gear and snowboards rent for AR$125 to AR$150 per day. You can also rent equipment on the mountain.

San Martín de Los Andes

Sights

1 Museo Primeros Pobladores C2

Activities, Courses & Tours

2 Andestrack B2
3 Bumps B3
4 HG Rodados D2
5 Lanín Turismo B2

Sleeping

6 Colonos del Sur B2
7 El Oso Andaluz Hostel D2
8 Hostería Hueney Ruca C3
9 Hostería La Masía C3
10 La Posta del Cazador A2
11 Turismo Hotel D1

Eating

12 Bamboo D3
13 Deli A3
14 El Mesón B3
15 El Regional D3
16 Ku D2
17 La Casona C3
18 Pizza Cala D2

Shopping

19 Artesanías Neuquinas C2
20 El Carpincho C2
21 Patalibro C2

Festivals & Events

San Martín celebrates its founding on February 4 with speeches, parades and other festivities; the **parade** itself is an entertainingly incongruous mix of military folks, firefighters, gauchos, polo players and foxhunters.

Sleeping

As a tourist center, San Martín is loaded with accommodations, but they're relatively costly in all categories, especially in summer high season (January to March) and peak ski season (mid-July and August), when reservations are a must. Quality, however, is mostly high. In low season, prices can drop by 40%.

Hostería La Masía HOTEL $$
(☎427688; www.hosterialamasia.com.ar; Obeid 811; s/d AR$240/360;) Taking the whole Edelweiss thing to the next level, La Masía offers plenty of dark-wood paneling, arched doorways and cast-iron light fittings. Rooms are big and comfortable and most have mountain views. Fireplaces warm the lobby, and the owners are usually around to make sure everyone feels at home. Superb.

La Posta del Cazador HOTEL $$
(☎427501; www.postadelcazador.com.ar; San Martín 175; s/d AR$280/350;) A large, rather somber lodge that's heavy on the dark woods and hunting paraphernalia. The location's good and the serious-sized breakfast should set you up for the day.

Hostería Hueney Ruca HOTEL $$
(☎421499; www.hosteriahueneyruca.com.ar; cnr Obeid & Coronel Pérez; s/d AR$180/260) The big terracotta-tiled rooms here look onto a cute, well-kept little backyard. Beds are big and firm and bathrooms spacious, with glass-walled shower stalls.

La Raclette HOTEL $$
(☎427664; www.laraclette.com.ar; Pérez; r AR$300;) Not suitable for claustrophobes, the narrow, low-ceilinged hallways here lead on to spacious, comfortable rooms. What really tips the scales are the downstairs common areas – a lounge-bar area and cozy little conversation pit centered around a big open fireplace.

El Oso Andaluz Hostel HOSTEL $
(☎427232; www.elosoandaluz.com.ar; Elordi 569; dm/d AR$55/150;) San Martín's coziest little downtown hostel has a good bed-to-bathroom ratio, atmospheric common areas and good value private rooms.

Turismo Hotel HOTEL $
(☎427592; www.interpatagonia.com/hotelturismo; Mascardi 517; s/d AR$165/210;) A classic '70s ski lodge, right down to the stuffed deer's head and old-school pool table in the lobby. Rooms are comfortable enough, but best avoided if you have problems with glaring yellow paint jobs.

Camping ACA CAMPGROUND $
(☎427332; Av Koessler 2640; camp sites with 2-person minimum per person AR$35) This is a spacious campground on the eastern outskirts of town. However, you should try to avoid sites near the highway.

Colonos del Sur HOTEL $$
(☎427106; www.colonosdelsur.com.ar; Rivadavia 686; r AR$260) A big, modern hotel pleasingly constructed in the alpine style. Rooms are spacious and bright, with large modern bathrooms, firm beds and faux wooden floorboards.

La Ruta de los Siete Lagos

One Day by Car or Three to Four Days by Bike

A spectacular road between towering, snow-capped mountains, crystal clear lakes and dense pine forests, this is a 110km Lake District classic. Bike it, drive it, tour it or bus it – don't miss it.

JOHN ELK III/LONELY PLANET IMAGES ©

» Leaving San Martín de los Andes you'll pass the Mapuche town of Curruhuinca before coming to the lookout at Arroyo Partido and the dark-blue Lago Machónico.

» Look for the turnoff to Lago Hermoso, which is surrounded by mixed ñire, pehuén and radale forests. Colored deer are common in this area.

» Next up is the Cascada Vullignanco, a 20m waterfall. About 2km beyond it, the road runs between Lago Villarino and Lago Falkner, which has a wide, sandy beach.

» Stop at the Lago Escondido, a beautiful blue-green lake hidden in the pine forests and take the side road to Lago Traful, a popular camping and fishing spot.

» After 30km look for the Villa Traful (see p357) turnoff – it's 27km from here to the Villa, down a good dirt road, passing scen lakeside bush campgrounds.

» Back on the main road, after 20km a turnoff leads to Lago Espejo, an emerald-green lake whose grassy banks make an excellent campground.

» Continuing south, you'll catch glimpses of Lago Espejo Grande on the right throug the trees.

» About 5km on, you'll see Lago Correnta From there it's another 25km to Villa la Angostura (p358).

Clockwise from top

1. Wildflowers, Siete Lagos (p351) **2.** Lago Espejo **3.** Desert landscape, Seven Lakes region **4.** San Martín de los Andes (p351)

2

JOHN ELK III/LONELY PLANET IMAGES ©

3

JOHN ELK III/LONELY PLANET IMAGES ©

Eating & Drinking

TOP CHOICE El Mesón INTERNATIONAL $$
(Rivadavia 888; mains AR$50-70; ⏲lunch & dinner) This cute little place has one of the most creative menus in town, with plenty of trout dishes, paella and a couple of vegetarian options.

Pizza Cala PIZZERIA $$
(Av San Martín 1111; mains AR$30-60; ⏲lunch & dinner) The local's choice for pizza is this cozy little setup. All the classics are here, plus some 'gourmet' options, eg smoked trout, spinach and eggplant.

Ku INTERNATIONAL $$$
(Av San Martín 1053; mains AR$50-80; ⏲lunch & dinner) The late-night favorite is this elegant restaurant, which serves a range of meats, homemade pastas and 'mountain food.'

Deli CAFE $
(cnr Villegas & Costanera MA Camino; mains AR$30-60; ⏲breakfast, lunch & dinner) Cheapest place on the lakeside with outdoor seating and reliable food. Good for afternoon beer and french fries. Very popular.

El Regional ARGENTINE $$$
(Villegas 953; mains AR$60-100; ⏲lunch & dinner) Specializing in *tablas* (sampler platters), this is a great place to try Patagonian classics such as boar, venison and trout in a variety of styles. Take advantage of the early-bird dinner discount by arriving before 8:30pm.

Bamboo PARRILLA $$$
(cnr Belgrano & Villegas; mains AR$60-90; ⏲lunch & dinner) One reader claims this upmarket *parrilla* serves 'the best meat in all of Argentina.' We haven't tried all the meat in Argentina (yet), so you be the judge.

La Casona ARGENTINE $$
(Villegas 744; mains AR$30-70; ⏲lunch & dinner) The cozy atmosphere belies the wide menu, with some good twists on regional favorites. Try the boar stew in black-beer sauce or the lamb and wild mushroom risotto.

Shopping

Many local shops sell regional products and handicrafts.

Artesanías Neuquinas HANDICRAFTS
(☎428396; M Rosas 790) A Mapuche cooperative with high-quality weavings and wood crafts on offer.

El Carpincho ACCESSORIES
(Capitán Drury 814) Gaucho regalia.

Patalibro BOOKSHOP
(☎421532; patalibro@yahoo.com.ar; Av San Martín 866) Good selection of books on Patagonia in Spanish; some Lonely Planet titles and novels in English. Carries the excellent *Sendas y Bosques* park trail maps (AR$45).

Information

The travel agencies listed in Activities, as well as many others along Av San Martín, Belgrano and Elordi, offer standard services as well as excursions.

ACA (Automóvil Club Argentino; ☎429430; Av Koessler 2175) Good source for provincial road maps.

Andina Internacional (☎427871; Capitán Drury 876) Money exchange, including traveler's checks.

Athos (☎429855; Av San Martín 808; per hr AR$5) Internet access in kiosk upstairs.

Banco de la Nación (Av San Martín 687) Has an ATM.

Cooperativa Telefónica (Capitán Drury 761) Offers internet access and telephone cabins.

Lanín national park office (Intendencia del Parque Nacional Lanín; ☎427233; www.parquenacionallanin.gov.ar; Emilio Frey 749; ⏲8am-2pm Mon-Fri) The office provides limited maps as well as brochures and information on road conditions on the Ruta de los Siete Lagos.

Nieves de Chapelco (☎427825; www.cerrochapelco.com; cnr M Moreno & Roca) Provides information and sells lift tickets for the Cerro Chapelco ski resort.

Post office (cnr Av Roca & Coronel Pérez)

Ramón Carrillo Hospital (☎427211; cnr Coronel Rohde & Av San Martín)

Tourist office (☎425500, 427347; www.smandes.gov.ar; cnr Av San Martín & M Rosas; ⏲8am-9pm Apr-Nov, to 10pm Dec-Mar) Provides surprisingly candid information on hotels and restaurants, plus excellent brochures and maps.

Getting There & Away

Air

Flights from **Chapelco airport** (☎428388; RN 234) to Buenos Aires cost about AR$1110 with **Aerolíneas Argentinas** (☎427003/04; Capitán Drury 876). **American Jet** (☎411300; www.americanjet.com.ar; San Martín 555 local 2) flies to Neuquén (AR$303).

Boat

Naviera (☎427380; naviera@smandes.com.ar) sails from the **passenger pier** (Muelle de Pasajeros; Costanera MA Camino) as far as Paso Hua Hum on the Chilean border, at 10am. A dock has been under construction for several years at Hua Hum – when it is completed, passengers will be able to disembark to cross the border. For now, you have to get off at Chachin, about an hour's walk from Hua Hum. Departure times change; call the ferry company or check with the tourist office. The fare is AR$130/250 one way/return.

Bus

The **bus terminal** (☎427044; cnr Villegas & Juez del Valle) is a block south of the highway and 3½ blocks southwest of Plaza San Martín.

La Araucana goes to Villa Traful daily during summer (AR$40, 2½ hours). If you're heading to Villa La Angostura or Bariloche in summer, Transportes Ko-Ko regularly takes the scenic Ruta de los Siete Lagos (RN 234) instead of the longer but smoother Rinconada route.

To get to Aluminé you must first change buses in Zapala or Junín de los Andes (where there are three departures per week).

Igi-Llaima takes RP 60 over Paso Tromen (also known as Mamuil Malal) to Temuco, Chile (AR$120, six hours), passing the majestic Volcán Lanín en route; sit on the left for views.

From San Martín there is direct service in summer via RN 231 over Paso Cardenal A Samoré (Puyehue) to Osorno and Puerto Montt in Chile.

Getting Around

Chapelco airport (☎428388; RN 234) is midway between San Martín and Junín. Any bus heading north out of San Martín can drop you at the entrance.

Transportation options slim down during low season. In summer Transportes Airen goes twice daily to Puerto Canoa on Lago Huechulafquen (AR$26) and will stop at campgrounds en route. Albus goes to the beach at Playa Catrite on Lago Lácar (AR$12) several times daily, while Transportes Ko-Ko runs four buses daily to Lago Lolog (AR$12) in summer only.

BUSES FROM SAN MARTÍN DE LOS ANDES

There are frequent daily departures to these destinations.

DESTINATION	COST (AR$)	DURATION (HR)
Bariloche	75	4½
Buenos Aires	585	20-23
Junín de los Andes	15	1
Neuquén	147	6
Villa la Angostura	42	4
Zapala	67	3½

San Martín has no lack of car-rental agencies.

Alamo (☎410811; Av San Martín 836, 2nd fl)

Sur (☎429028; Villegas 830)

Cerro Chapelco

Located 20km southeast of San Martín, **Cerro Chapelco** (☎02972-427845; www.cerrochapelco.com) is one of Argentina's principal winter-sports centers, with a mix of runs for beginners and experts, and a maximum elevation of 1920m. The **Fiesta Nacional del Montañés**, the annual ski festival, is held during the first half of August.

Lift-ticket prices vary, depending on when you go; full-day passes run from AR$170 to AR$285 for adults, AR$140 to AR$240 for children. The slopes are open from mid-June to early October. The low season is mid-June to early July and from August 28 to mid-October; high season is around the last two weeks of July. Rental equipment is available on-site as well as in San Martín.

Transportes Ko-Ko runs two buses each day (three in summer; AR$25 return) to the park from San Martín's bus terminal. Travel agencies in San Martín also offer packages with shuttle service, or shuttle service alone (AR$35); they pick you up at your hotel.

Villa Traful

☎0294 / POP 821 / ELEV 720M

This little village enjoys an almost achingly beautiful location surrounded by mountains on the southern banks of Lago Traful. The place really packs out in January, February and Easter, when booking accommodations three months in advance is advised. The rest of the year, you may just have it to yourself. Depending on what you're into, November, December, March and April are great times to be here.

Getting here is half the fun – Villa Traful is 80km north of Bariloche via unpaved RP 65.

Sights & Activities

Cascadas de Arroyo Blanco & Coa Có WATERFALL, VIEWPOINT

These two waterfalls are a moderately easy, two-hour roundtrip walk from town that can be done without a guide. Walk uphill on the street running beside the *guardaparque* (park ranger) office and follow the signs. From where the path forks at the open field it's 500m on the left to the 30m-high Coa Có. Return and take the other fork for 1km to the smaller Cascadas de los Arroyos Blancos. Far more spectacular than the actual waterfalls are the lookouts along the way, which give you a bird's-eye view of the forest, lake and mountains beyond.

Lagunas las Mellizas LAKE, VIEWPOINT
Starting with a boat ride across the lake, this trek of moderate difficulty begins with a 2½-hour climb through cypress forests before reaching a lookout with views of the Lagunas Azul and Verde (Blue and Green Lagoons). If you've still got the legs for it, fording a stream gets you to an area with a variety of well-preserved Tehuelche rock paintings, dated at around 600 years old.

Eco Traful TOURS
(447-9139; www.ecotraful.blogspot.com) A recommended agency that leads trips to Lagunas Las Mellizas (AR$180/240 per person walking/horseback) and Cerro Negro (AR$85 per person), and organizes boat rides and fishing trips.

Sleeping & Eating

There are only a few places to stay unless you rent a *cabaña* (the tourist office has a complete listing).

Albergue & Camping Vulcanche HOSTEL $
(447-9028; www.vulcanche.com; camp sites per person AR$20, dm AR$55) In a beautiful wooded area on the eastern edge of the village, this grassy campground and hostel has decent dorms and a good kitchen.

Hostería Villa Traful HOTEL $
(447-9005; cabanastraful@yahoo.com.ar; r AR$170) A pleasant little mom-and-pop-run operation on the western edge of town. Rooms are aging but comfortable, there's a good restaurant on the premises, and the owners organize boating and fishing trips.

TOP CHOICE **Ñancú Lahuén** ARGENTINE $$
(mains AR$40-65; lunch & dinner) A cute little log cabin set up in the center of the village. Trout dishes are the specialty (try 'em with the almond sauce), but the menu stretches to *parrilla* and a good range of salads as well.

There are also a couple of restaurants tucked into the trees and a general store.

Information

Banco de la Provincia de Neuquén In the middle of the village; has an ATM that accepts Visa and MasterCard.

Tourist office (447-9099; www.villatraful.gov.ar; daily Dec-Feb, Sat-Wed Mar-Jan) On the eastern side of the village.

Getting There & Away

Villa Traful has better bus connections in summertime (December to February). La Araucana has daily services to Villa la Angostura (AR$22, two hours) and summer services to San Martín de los Andes (AR$40, 2½ hours). There are services from Bariloche (AR$25, two hours) daily in summer and three in summer.

Villa la Angostura

0294 / POP 13,800 / ELEV 850M

An upmarket resort town on the northwestern shore of Lago Nahuel Huapi, Villa la Angostura provides accommodations and services for nearby Cerro Bayo, a small but popular winter-sports center.

It's worthwhile stopping by in summer, too, for lake cruises and walks in the small but incredibly diverse Parque Nacional Los Arrayanes (a small peninsula dangling some 12km into the lake), and because this is the southern starting point for the breathtaking trip along the Ruta de los Siete Lagos.

The village consists of two distinct areas: El Cruce, which is the commercial center along the highway, and La Villa, nestled against the lakeshore, 3km to the south. Though La Villa is more residential, it still has hotels, shops, services and, unlike El Cruce, lake access.

Sights & Activities

Several outfitters in town offer trekking, horseback riding and guided mountain-bike rides, and the tourist office provides information on each. Mountain biking is a great way to explore the surrounding area.

Parque Nacional Los Arrayanes PARK
(pedestrian/cyclist AR$25/35) This inconspicuous, often overlooked park, encompassing the entire Quetrihué peninsula, protects remaining stands of the cinnamon-barked arrayán, a member of the myrtle family. In Mapudungun (language of the Mapuche) the peninsula's name means 'place of the arrayánes.'

The park headquarters is at the southern end of the peninsula, near the largest concentration of arrayánes, in an area known as **El Bosque**. It's a three-hour, 12km hike to the tip of the peninsula, on an excellent

interpretive nature trail. You can also hike out and get the ferry back from the point (p360), or vice versa. There are two small lakes along the trail. Regulations require hikers to enter the park before midday and leave it by 4pm in winter and around 6pm to 7pm in summer.

From the park's northern entrance at La Villa, a very steep 20-minute hike leads to two **panoramic overlooks** of Lago Nahuel Huapi.

Cabalgatas Correntoso HORSE RIDING
(☎0294-15-451-0559; Cacique Antriao 1850) For horseback riding (half-day to multiday trips). Contact Tero Bogani, who brings the gaucho side of things to his trips. Prices start at AR$230 for a three-hour outing.

Centro de Ski Cerro Bayo SKIING
(☎449-4189; www.cerrobayoweb.com; full-day pass AR$165-185) From June to September, lifts carry skiers from the 1050m base up to 1700m at this 'boutique' (read small but expensive) winter resort, 9km northeast of El Cruce via RP 66. All facilities, including rental equipment (AR$90 to AR$138), are available on-site.

Cerro Belvedere HIKING
A 4km hiking trail starts from Av Siete Lagos, northwest of the tourist office, and leads to an **overlook** with good views of Lago Correntoso, Nahuel Huapi and the surrounding mountains. It then continues another 3km to the 1992m summit. After visiting the overlook, retrace your steps to a nearby junction that leads to **Cascada Inayacal**, a 50m waterfall. If you're coming out here, get a map at the tourist office as the trails can be confusing.

Cycling BICYCLE RENTAL
(cnr Arrayanes & Las Mutisias) Rents good quality bikes for AR$50/80 per half-/full day.

Vela Aventura BOAT TRIPS
(☎449-4834; www.vela-aventura.com.ar) Offers sailboat rides around the lake. A three-hour trip costs about AR$580 for up to four people.

Sleeping

Except for camping and Angostura's growing hostel scene, accommodations are pricey; in summer, single rooms are almost impossible to find – expect to pay for two people.

Verena's Haus HOTEL $$
(☎449-4467; www.verenashaus.com.ar; Los Taiques 268, El Cruce; s/d AR$180/280; Wi-Fi) With all the heart-shaped motifs and floral wallpaper, this one probably doesn't qualify as a hunting lodge, but it is a good deal for couples looking for a quiet, romantic spot. Rooms are big, spotless and packed with comfy features.

Italian Hostel HOSTEL $
(☎449-4376; www.italianhostel.com.ar; Los Marquis 215, El Cruce; dm AR$50; Wi-Fi) With plenty of space and all the comforts you'd expect, this is the town's standout hostel. The kitchen is well equipped, you can use the *parrilla* and the lounge is comfy in a rustic kinda way. The only drawback: the 10-bed dorm.

Hotel Angostura HOTEL $$
(☎449-4224; www.hotelangostura.com; Blvd Nahuel Huapi 1911, La Villa; s/d from AR$390/420, bungalow AR$600-950; Wi-Fi) Ignore the squishy rooms and the deer-antler light fittings – this is an awesome location. It's perched up on a clifftop overlooking the bay and the national park; your biggest problem here is going to be neck crick from checking out the view – no matter which way you're walking.

Camping Cullumche CAMPGROUND $
(☎449-4160; moyano@uncu.edu.ar; Blvd Quetrihué s/n; camp sites per person AR$24-30) Well signed from Blvd Nahuel Huapi, this secluded but large lakeside campground can get very busy in summer, but when it's quiet, it's lovely.

Residencial Río Bonito HOTEL $
(☎449-4110; riobonito@ciudad.com.ar; Topa Topa 260, El Cruce; r AR$160; Wi-Fi) Bright and cheery rooms in a converted family home a few blocks from the bus terminal. The big, comfortable dining-lounge area is a bonus, as are the friendly hosts and kitchen use for guests.

Eating

There are several restaurants and *confiterías* in El Cruce along Los Arrayanes and its cross streets.

Tinto Bistro FUSION $$$
(☎449-4924; Nahuel Huapi 34, El Cruce; mains AR$60-90; ⌚lunch & dinner) Besides the fact that the food (regional cuisine prepared with European flair) is excellent, the owner, Martín Zorreguieta, is the brother of Máxima, princess of the Netherlands. Feast on that.

La Encantada ARGENTINE $$
(☎449-5515; Cerro Belvedere 69, El Cruce; mains AR$45-90; ⌚lunch & dinner) A cute little cottage offering all of your Patagonian and Argentine favorites. The food is carefully prepared and beautifully presented, and the

atmosphere is warm and inviting. The *ojo de bife* (eye-fillet steak) for two is a definite winner if you are a couple of carnivores.

Los Troncos ARGENTINE $$
(Av Arrayanes 67, El Cruce; mains AR$40-70; ⏲breakfast, lunch & dinner) Specializing in 'mountain food,' this lovely little place serves up a range of tempting dishes, such as deer stew, trout with almond sauce and wild mushroom stew.

La Caballeriza PARRILLA $$$
(Av Arrayanes 44, El Cruce; mains AR$50-90; ⏲lunch & dinner) The most upmarket *parrilla* in town has a good range of dishes, an intimate atmosphere and surprisingly reasonable prices.

Gran Nevada ARGENTINE $
(Av Arrayanes 106, El Cruce; mains AR$30-50; ⏲lunch & dinner) With its big-screen TV (quite possibly showing a football game) and big, cheap set meals, this is a local favorite. Come hungry, leave happy.

Information

Banco de la Provincia (Calle Las Frambuesas btwn Cerro Belvedere & Nahuel Huapi, El Cruce) Has an ATM.

HoraCero (☎449-5055; Av Arrayanes 45, El Cruce; internet per hr AR$6) Pizzeria with internet in back.

Post office (Las Fucsias 40, lvl 3, El Cruce)

Tourist office (☎449-4124; www.villalaangostura.gov.ar; cnr Arrayanes & Av Siete Lagos, El Cruce; ⏲8:30am-9pm)

Getting There & Away

Villa la Angostura's **bus terminal** (cnr Av Siete Lagos & Av Arrayanes, El Cruce) is across the street from the tourist office in El Cruce. Some buses stop in El Cruce on runs between Bariloche and San Martín de los Andes.

For Chile, **Andesmar** (☎449-5217) goes over Paso Cardenal Samoré to Osorno (AR$120, 3½ hours).

There are numerous daily departures to Bariloche (AR$27, one hour) and two daily departures to Neuquén (AR$165, seven hours). Albus goes several times daily in summer to San Martín de los Andes (AR$42, four hours) by the scenic Ruta de los Siete Lagos. La Araucana has daily services to Villa Traful (AR$22, two hours).

Getting Around

BOAT Two companies run daily ferries from the dock (next to Hotel Angostura in La Villa) to the tip of Quetrihué peninsula, Parque Nacional Los Arrayanes (one way AR$82 to AR$93, return AR$164 to AR$196, plus AR$20 national park entrance). Purchase tickets at the dock before hiking out, to secure a space on the return. The ride takes 45 minutes and you can put a bicycle on the boat.

BUS Transportes 15 de Mayo runs hourly buses from the terminal to La Villa (AR$1.50, 15 minutes), up Av Siete Lagos to Lago Correntoso (AR$1.50, 15 minutes), and south down Av Arrayanes to Puerto Manzano on Lago Nahuel Huapi (AR$1.50, 15 minutes). From July through September, and December through March, 15 de Mayo runs six or seven daily buses to the ski resort at Cerro Bayo (AR$15, one hour).

TAXI Taxis are the best means of getting to the trailheads, although some are served by local buses. Both leave from the local bus terminal on Av Siete Lagos, just north of Av Arrayanes.

Bariloche

☎0294 / POP 102,020 / ELEV 770M

Strung out along the shoreline of Lago Nahuel Huapi, in the middle of the national park of the same name, Bariloche (formally San Carlos de Bariloche) has one of the most gorgeous settings imaginable. This, combined with a wealth of summer and winter activities in the surrounding countryside, has helped it become, for better or worse, the Lake District's principal destination.

The soaring peaks of Cerros Catedral, López, Nireco and Shaihuenque (to name just a few) – all well over 2000m high – ring the town, giving picture-postcard views in nearly every direction.

These mountains aren't just for gazing, though – excellent snow coverage (sometimes exceeding 2m at the *end* of the season) makes this a winter wonderland, and a magnet for skiers and snowboarders.

In summertime the nature buffs take over, hitting the hills to climb, hike trails, fish for trout and ride mountain bikes and horses.

There's so much fun to be had that this has become the destination for Argentine high school students' end of year celebrations. And if all this wasn't enough, Bariloche is also Argentina's chocolate capital and the only thing that approaches the amount of storefront window space dedicated to fresh chocolate is the infinite number of peculiar gnomes of all sizes and demeanors sold in nearly every shop downtown.

Officially founded in 1902, the city really began to attract visitors after the southern branch of the Ferrocarril Roca train line arrived in 1934 and architect Ezequiel Bustillo adapted Central European styles into a tasteful urban plan. Bariloche is now known for its alpine architecture, which is given a Patagonian twist through the use of local hardwoods and unique stone construction, as seen in the buildings of Bustillo's *centro cívico*.

The flip side of Bariloche's gain in popularity is uncontrolled growth: in the last two decades the town has suffered as its quaint neighborhoods have given way to high-rise apartments and time-shares. The silver lining is that many accommodations have remained reasonably priced.

Sights

The principal commercial area is along Av Bartolomé Mitre. Do not confuse VA O'Connor (also known as Vicealmirante O'Connor or Eduardo O'Connor) with similarly named John O'Connor, which cross each other near the lakefront.

Centro Cívico NEIGHBORHOOD

A stroll through Bariloche's center, with its beautiful log-and-stone buildings designed by architect Ezequiel Bustillo, is a must. Besides, posing for a photo with one of the barrel-toting Saint Bernards makes for a classic Argentine snapshot, and views over the lake are superb. The buildings house the municipal tourist office and the museum.

Museo de la Patagonia MUSEUM

(☎442-2309; Centro Cívico; admission by donation; ⏲10am-12:30pm & 2-5pm Tue-Fri, 10am-6pm Sat) The museum is filled with archaeological and ethnographic materials, lifelike stuffed animals and enlightening historical evaluations on such topics as Mapuche resistance to the Conquest of the Desert.

Activities

Bariloche and the Nahuel Huapi region are one of Argentina's major outdoor recreation areas, and numerous operators offer a variety of activities, particularly horseback riding, mountain biking and white-water rafting.

Mountaineering & Trekking

The national park office distributes a brochure with a simple map, adequate for initial planning, that rates hikes as easy, medium or difficult and suggests possible loops. Many of these hikes are detailed in Lonely Planet's *Trekking in the Patagonian Andes*.

Club Andino Bariloche (p366) provides loads of information (including on camping), and issues obligatory permits for trekking in Parque Nacional Nahuel Huapi. For AR$45, its *Mapa General de la Guía de Sendas y Picadas* is cartographically mediocre, but has good trail descriptions and is indispensable for planning. It sells three additional trekking maps, all of which include mountain-bike trails.

Skiing

Nahuel Huapi's ski resort, **Cerro Catedral** (☎440-9000; www.catedralaltapatagonia.com), was once South America's trendiest, and has been superseded only by Las Leñas (near Mendoza) and resorts in Chile. Las Leñas has far superior snow (dry powder), but it lacks Catedral's strong point: views. There's nothing like looking over the shimmering lakes of Nahuel Huapi from its snowy slopes.

Day passes run between AR$195 and AR$290, depending on the season. If you need lessons, stop into the ski schools at Cerro Catedral or Club Andino Bariloche. Two-hour private lessons run at about AR$400. For rental equipment, try **Baruzzi Deportes** (☎442-4922; Urquiza 250) or **Martín Pescador** (☎442-2275; martinpescador@bariloche.com.ar; Rolando 257). Equipment is also available on-site. Sets of skis, boots and poles rent for between AR$55 and AR$65, and snowboarding gear between AR$77 and AR$80 per day, depending on the season.

Mountain Biking

Bicycles are ideal for the Circuito Chico (though this 60km loop demands endurance; see p368) and other trips near Bariloche; most roads are paved and even the gravel roads are good. Mountain-bike rental, including gloves and helmet, costs around AR$70 per day at a number of places. Try **Bikeway** (☎445-6571; www.bikeway.com.ar; Perito Moreno 237).

Fishing

Fly-fishing draws visitors from around the world to Argentina's accessible Andean-Patagonian parks, from Lago Puelo and Los Alerces in the south to Lanín in the north.

On larger lakes, such as Nahuel Huapi, trolling is the preferred method, while fly-fishing is the rule on most rivers. The season runs mid-November to mid-April. For more information, contact the **Asociación de Pesca y Caza Nahuel Huapi** (Hunting & Fishing Club; ☎442-1515; www.apcnh.com; cnr Costanera 12 de Octubre & Onelli). For rental equipment and guide hire, try Baruzzi

Bariloche

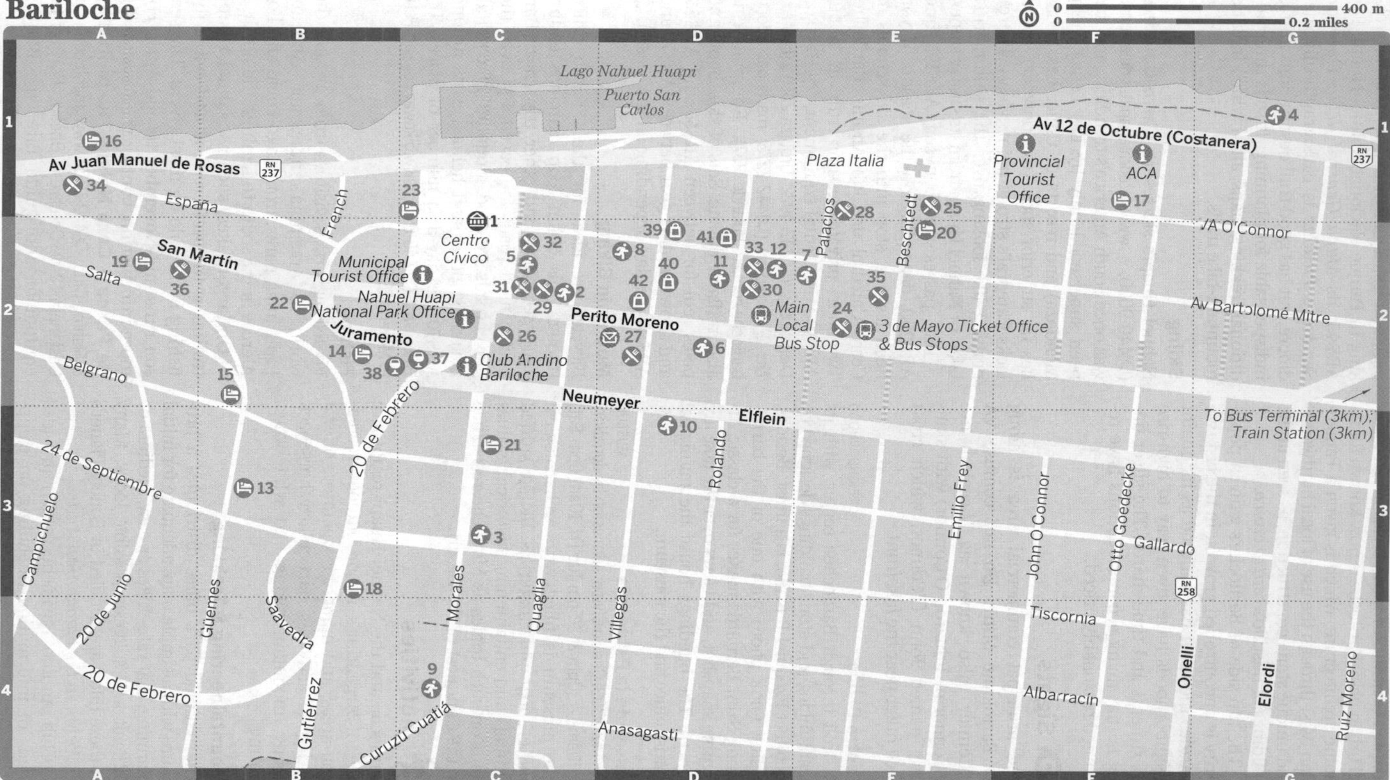
N
0
400 m
0
0.2 miles
A
B
C
D
E
F
G
1
2
3
4
Lago Nahuel Huapi
Puerto San Carlos
Av 12 de Octubre (Costanera)
Av Juan Manuel de Rosas
RN 237
Plaza Italia
Provincial Tourist Office
ACA
España
French
Centro Cívico
Municipal Tourist Office
Nahuel Huapi National Park Office
San Martín
Salta
Juramento
Perito Moreno
Club Andino Bariloche
Belgrano
Neumeyer
Elflein
/A O'Connor
Av Bartolomé Mitre
Palacios
Beschtedt
Main Local Bus Stop
3 de Mayo Ticket Office & Bus Stops
To Bus Terminal (3km); Train Station (3km)
20 de Febrero
24 de Septiembre
Rolando
Emilio Frey
John O Connor
Otto Goedecke
Gallardo
RN 258
Campichuelo
20 de Junio
Güemes
Saavedra
Gutiérrez
Morales
Quaglia
Villegas
Tiscornia
Onelli
Elordi
Ruiz Moreno
Albarracín
Anasagasti
Curuzú Cuatiá
1
2
3
4
5
6
7
8
9
10
11
12
13
14
15
16
17
18
19
20
21
22
23
24
25
26
27
28
29
30
31
32
33
34
35
36
37
38
39
40
41
42

Bariloche

Sights

1 Museo de la Patagonia C2

Activities, Courses & Tours

2 Adventure Center C2
3 Aguas Blancas C3
4 Asociación de Pesca y Caza Nahuel Huapi G1
5 Baruzzi Deportes C2
6 Bikeway D2
7 Catedral Turismo E2
8 Espacio D2
9 eXtremo Sur C4
10 La Montaña D3
11 Martín Pescador D2
12 Tom Wesley Viajes de Aventura D2

Sleeping

13 Hospedaje Wikter B3
14 Hostel 41 Below B2
15 Hostel El Gaucho B2
16 Hostel Patanuk A1
17 Hostería Adquintue F1
18 Hostería La Paleta del Pintor B3
19 Hostería La Sureña A2
20 Hostería Piuke E2
21 Hotel Carlos V C3
22 Hotel Edelweiss B2
23 Hotel Tirol C1

Eating

24 Cerros Nevados E2
25 Covita E1
26 Días de Zapata C2
27 El Boliche de Alberto D2
28 Familia Weiss E1
29 Helados Jauja C2
30 Huang Ji Zhong D2
31 La Esquina C2
32 La Marca C2
33 La Marmite D2
34 La Trattoria de la Famiglia Bianchi A1
35 Los Tehuelches E2
36 Rock Chicken A2

Drinking

37 Los Vikingos C2
38 South Bar B2

Shopping

39 Abuela Goya D2
40 Huitral-Hue D2
41 Mamuschka D2
42 Paseo de los Artesanos D2

Deportes or Martín Pescador (p361). Both offer guided fishing trips for about AR$1400 per day for one or two people (price is the same either way and includes all equipment, lunch, transport and guide). Fishing licenses (AR$120/360/480 per day/week/season) are required and available at these shops.

Horseback Riding

Most travel agencies along Av Bartolomé Mitre offer horseback-riding trips.

Cabalgatas Carol Jones HORSE RIDING
(☎442-6508; www.caroljones.com.ar) For something special, contact the amiable Carol Jones, who offers half-day horseback riding from her family *estancia* outside of town for AR$280 per person. The price includes transportation to/from town and an excellent *asado* (barbecue grill) outside. She also offers multiday pack trips by horse for AR$800 per person per day.

Tom Wesley Viajes de Aventura OUTDOORS
(☎443-5040; Av Bustillo, Km15.5) Offers horseback riding and mountain biking. This operator has been long in the business and has an excellent reputation.

Rafting & Kayaking

Rafting and kayaking on the Río Limay and the Río Manso have become increasingly popular in recent years. The best time to be on the rivers is November through February, though you can raft October through Easter.

eXtremo Sur RAFTING, KAYAKING
(☎442-7301; www.extremosur.com; Morales 765) In business since 1991, this outfit offers several trips on the Río Manso: the Manso Inferior (class II to III, AR$350 per person) is suitable for all ages; the Manso a la Frontera (class III to IV, AR$470 per person, ages 14 and up) is a fun and beautiful stretch of the river before the Chilean border. There's also a three-day Expedición Río Manso (class III to IV, around AR$2600), in which you camp riverside at excellent facilities.

Aguas Blancas RAFTING, KAYAKING
(☎443-2799; www.aguasblancas.com.ar; Morales 564) Like eXtremo Sur, this business also has an excellent reputation and offers similar trips.

Pura Vida Patagonia KAYAKING
(☎15-441-4053; www.puravidapatagonia.com) Offers kayaking trips on the Lago Nahuel Huapi, ranging from half-day stints to overnight camp-'n'-kayak trips, custom-designed to match your skill level.

Paragliding

The mountains around Bariloche make for spectacular paragliding. If you wish to take to the sky, it will cost you around AR$350 for a 20-minute to half-hour tandem flight with, among others, **Luis Rosenkjer** (☎442-7588) or **Parapente Bariloche** (☎15-455-2403; Cerro Otto base).

Courses

La Montaña LANGUAGE COURSE
(☎452-4212; www.lamontana.com; Elflein 251) This is a recommended Spanish school.

Tours

Countless tourist agencies along and near Av Bartolomé Mitre, such as Turisur (see boxed text, p371), run minibus tours to the national park and as far south as El Bolsón. Prices range from AR$70 for a half-day trip along the Circuito Chico to AR$180 to San Martín de los Andes via the scenic Ruta de los Siete Lagos.

Adventure Center DRIVING TOUR
(☎442-8368; www.adventurecenter.com.ar; Perito Moreno 30) Four-day trips down the fabled RN 40 as far as El Calafate are offered for AR$650 per person. Trips run from the end of September to April. Prices include accommodations, but national park entries and food are separate.

Bariloche Moto Tours MOTORBIKE TOURS
(☎446-2687; www.barilochemototours.com) Organizes custom-tailored motorbike tours to everywhere between southern Patagonia and northern Chile and beyond.

Espacio
(☎443-1372; www.islavictoriayarrayanes.com; Av Bartolomé Mitre 139) Espacio offers cruises on Nahuel Huapi lake in its 40ft catamaran *Cau Cau* during summer. Reserve your place two days in advance.

Festivals & Events

For 10 days in August, Bariloche holds its **Fiesta Nacional de la Nieve** (National Snow Festival).

In January and February the **Festival de Música de Verano** (Summer Music Festival) puts on several different events, including the **Festival de Música de Cámara** (Chamber Music Festival), the **Festival de Bronces** (Brass Festival) and the **Festival de Música Antigua** (Ancient Music Festival).

On May 3 is the **Fiesta Nacional de la Rosa Mosqueta**, celebrating the fruit of the wild shrub used in many regional delicacies.

Sleeping

From camping and private houses to five-star hotels, Bariloche's abundant accommodations make it possible to find good value even in high season, when reservations are a good idea. Prices peak during ski season (July and August), drop slightly during high season (January and February) and are lowest the rest of the year. The following are high-season prices.

Hostería La Paleta del Pintor HOTEL $$
(☎442-2220; 20 de Febrero 630; s/d AR$170/260) Everything about this place screams 'cute,' but the rooms are big and airy, with small but spotless bathrooms and big-screen TVs.

Hotel Carlos V HOTEL $$
(☎442-5474; www.carlosvpatagonia.com.ar; Morales 420; s/d AR$280/360; @ wi-fi) At first glance a fairly standard business hotel, the Carlos V has plenty of hidden charm. That, the central location and the good-sized rooms make it hard to beat.

Hostel 41 Below HOSTEL $
(☎443-6433; www.hostel41below.com; Juramento 94; dm/d without bathroom AR$55/180; @ wi-fi) An intimate, Kiwi-run hostel with clean dorms, fine doubles (with good views) and mellow vibe. The kitchen and common room are excellent and it also offers great rooms (AR$295) in a nearby apartment.

Hospedaje Wikter HOTEL $
(☎442-3248; www.hospedajewikter.com.ar; Güemes 566; s/d AR$110/130; wi-fi) Up the hill away from the center, this friendly little *hospedaje* offers spacious rooms in a bright, modern building. Bathrooms are bigger than most in this price range and some rooms have good views.

La Selva Negra CAMPGROUND $
(☎444-1013; campingselvanegra@speedy.com.ar; Av Bustillo, Km2.9; camp sites per person AR$40) Located 3km west of town on the road to Llao Llao, this is the nearest organized camping area. It has good facilities and, in the fall, you can step outside your tent to pick apples.

Hostel Patanuk HOSTEL $
(☎443-4991; www.patanuk.com; Av JM de Rosas 585; dm/d AR$55/190;) Bariloche's only lakefront hostel is a definite winner. Big picture windows put you right in front of the water and mountains. Hardwood floors, a spacious kitchen and comfy lounge round out the picture.

Hostería Katy HOTEL $$
(☎444-8023; www.gringospatagonia.com; Av Bustillo, Km24.3; s/d AR$155/310; @) One of the closest *hosterías* to the national park, this one's set in a charming family home. It's a family-run operation; the rooms are warm and comfortable, with big bathrooms and firm beds.

Hostería Piuke HOTEL $$
(☎442-3044; res.piuke@gmail.com; F Beschtedt 136; s/d AR$190/230) One of the better-value hotels down near the lakefront, this one has good-sized, comfortable rooms and some very hip retro '70s furnishings.

Hotel Edelweiss HOTEL $$$
(☎444-5500; www.edelweiss.com.ar; San Martín 202; r from AR$1120; @) One of the better business-class hotels in town, the Edelweiss manages to retain a warmth despite its size. All the facilities are here, including a fantastic 7th-floor day spa and swimming pool.

Hostel El Gaucho HOSTEL $
(☎452-2464; www.hostelgaucho.com; Belgrano 209; dm/d AR$50/150;) An extremely laid-back little hostel featuring four-bed dorms and OK kitchen and lounge areas. It's a short walk uphill from the center.

Hostería Adquintue HOTEL $$
(☎452-2229; www.hosteriaadquintue.com.ar; VA O'Connor 766; s/d AR$170/260) Spacious, if slightly plain, rooms on the edge of the busy downtown district. Good value for the location.

Hotel Tirol HOTEL $$
(☎442-6152; www.hosteriatirol.com.ar; Libertad 175; s/d AR$300/400; @) Right in the middle of town, this charming little lodge offers comfortable, spacious rooms. Those out the back have spectacular views out over the lake and to the mountain range beyond, as does the bright sitting/breakfast area.

Hosteria La Sureña HOTEL $$
(☎442-2013; www.hosterialasurena.com.ar; San Martín 432; s/d AR$230/280;) The lobby and facade are a lot more impressive than the rooms, but they're still OK – on the smallish side, but functional and clean.

Eating

Bariloche has some of Argentina's best food, and it would take several wallet-breaking, belt-bursting and intestinally challenging weeks to sample all of the worthwhile restaurants. Regional specialties, including *cordero* (lamb, cooked over an open flame), *jabalí* (wild boar), *ciervo* (venison) and *trucha* (trout), are especially worth trying.

TOP CHOICE **La Trattoria de la Famiglia Bianchi** ITALIAN $$
(☎442-1596; España 590; mains AR$40-60; lunch & dinner) Finally, an Italian restaurant that offers something different. Excellent, creative pastas, a good range of meat dishes and some wonderful risottos, with ingredients such as seafood and wild mushrooms.

Los Tehuelches PARRILLA $
(Beschtedt 281; mains AR$35-50; lunch & dinner) The best-value *parrilla* in town, this no-frills place attracts a lot more locals than tourists. The range of set meals is impressive and a *bife de chorizo* (sirloin) with salad for AR$40 is nothing to be sneered at in this town. The house red is not recommended, except for fans of the very rough hangover.

La Esquina CAFE $$
(Urquiza & Perito Moreno; mains AR$30-70; breakfast, lunch & dinner) The most atmospheric *confitería* in town has good coffee, reasonably priced sandwiches and burgers, and some good regional specialties.

Helados Jauja ICE CREAM $
(Perito Moreno 14; ice cream from AR$10) Ask anyone in town who serves the best ice cream in Bariloche and they'll reply with one word: 'Jauja.' Many say it's the best in the country.

Covita VEGETARIAN $
(VA O'Connor 511; set meals AR$40; lunch & dinner;) The best vegetarian restaurant for miles around has a small but varied menu with a couple of Asian-inspired dishes.

Familia Weiss ARGENTINE $$

(Palacios 167; mains AR$40-70; lunch & dinner) A popular family restaurant offering good-value regional specialties such as venison, trout and goulash. The picture menu is handy for the Spanish-challenged, there's a good atmosphere and nightly live music.

El Boliche de Alberto PARRILLA $$

(443-1433; Villegas 347; mains AR$50-70; lunch & dinner) It's worth dining at this esteemed *parrilla* simply to see the astonished look on tourists' faces when a slab of beef the size of a football lands on the table; it's the AR$70 *bife de chorizo* (the AR$60 portion is plenty).

Rock Chicken FAST FOOD $

(San Martín 234; mains AR$28-40; 10am-late) Late night munchies? Midday junk-food cravings? The beef, burgers and fried chicken here won't be winning any culinary awards, but they get the job done.

La Marca INTERNATIONAL $$

(Urquiza 240; mains AR$35-70; lunch & dinner) Upscale *parrilla* with reasonable (for Bariloche) prices. Choose from the impressive range of brochettes (shasliks) – beef, chicken, venison, lamb and salmon. On a sunny day, grab a garden table at the side.

Días de Zapata MEXICAN $$

(442-3128; Morales 362; mains AR$50-70; lunch & dinner) A warm and inviting little Mexican restaurant. Dishes tend more toward the Tex Mex than you would think (the owners hail from Mexico City) but the flavors are good and the servings generous.

Huang Ji Zhong CHINESE $

(Rolando 268; mains AR$30-50; lunch & dinner) There's exactly one Chinese restaurant in town, and it's not bad – all the usual suspects at decent prices.

La Marmite ARGENTINE $$

(442-3685; Av Bartolomé Mitre 329; mains AR$50-80; lunch & dinner) A trusty choice for Patagonian standards such as trout and venison. Also the place to come for chocolate fondue (AR$100 for two), in case you haven't eaten enough of the stuff cold.

Cerros Nevados BUFFET $$

(Perito Moreno 338; all you can eat AR$58; lunch & dinner) Every Argentine town has at least one gut-busting *tenedor libre* (all-you-can-eat restaurant); Bariloche's lays it on thick, with plenty of *parrilla* items, pastas, salads and *fiambres* (cold meats).

Drinking

Los Vikingos BAR

(cnr Juramento & 20 de Febrero) A laid-back little corner bar serving a good range of local microbrewery beers at excellent prices. The music's cool and the decor eclectic. DJs play on weekends.

South Bar BAR

(Juramento s/n) Mellow local pub where you can actually have a conversation while you drink your beer. Darts, too.

Shopping

Bariloche is renowned for its chocolates, and dozens of stores downtown, from national chains to mom-and-pop shops, sell chocolates of every style imaginable. Quality, of course, varies: don't get sick on the cheap stuff.

Mamuschka FOOD

(442-3294; Av Bartolomé Mitre 298) Quite simply, the best chocolate in town. Don't skip it. Seriously.

Abuela Goye FOOD

(443-3861; Av Bartolomé Mitre 258) Another of Bariloche's long-time chocolate makers. Still small and still worth trying.

Huitral-Hue CLOTHING

(442-6760; Villegas 250; Mon-Sat) Good selection of traditional ponchos, textiles and wool sweaters.

Paseo de los Artesanos HANDICRAFTS

(cnr Villegas & Perito Moreno) Local craftspeople display wares of wool, wood, leather, silver and other media here.

Information

Banks with ATMs are ubiquitous in the downtown area.

ACA (Automóvil Club Argentino; 442-3001; Av 12 de Octubre 785) Argentina's auto club has provincial road maps.

Cambio Sudamérica (Av Bartolomé Mitre 63) Change foreign cash and traveler's checks here.

Club Andino Bariloche (442-2266; www.activepatagonia.com.ar, www.clubandino.com.ar; 20 de Febrero 30; 9am-1pm & 4-8:30pm Dec-Mar, Mon-Fri only Apr-Nov) Best source of hiking information on Nahuel Huapi. Gives information on hikers' refuges in the park.

Hospital (442-6100; Perito Moreno 601) *Long* waits, no charge.

Municipal tourist office (442-9850; www.barilochepatagonia.info; Centro Cívico; 8am-9pm) It has many giveaways, including useful maps and the blatantly commercial but still useful *Guía Busch*, updated biannually and loaded with basic tourist information about Bariloche and the Lake District.

Nahuel Huapi national park office (Intendencia del Parque Nacional Nahuel Huapi; ☎423121; www.nahuelhuapi.gov.ar; San Martín 24; ⊙8am-4pm Mon-Fri, 9am-3pm Sat & Sun)

Post office (Perito Moreno 175)

Provincial tourist office (☎442-3188/89; secturrn@bariloche.com.ar; cnr Av 12 de Octubre & Emilio Frey) Has information on the province, including an excellent provincial map and useful brochures in English and Spanish.

Sanatorio San Carlos (☎442-9000/01/02, emergency 430000; Av Bustillo, Km1; consultations AR$75) Excellent medical clinic.

Telecom (Av Bartolomé Mitre 85; per hr AR$5) Upstairs; fast internet connection.

BARILOCHE BUS CARDS

Bariloche's local buses work with magnetic cards that can be purchased at the **3 de Mayo ticket office** (☎442-5648; Perito Moreno 480), downtown or at the bus terminal. You can also pick up handy *horarios* (schedules) for all destinations from these offices. Cards cost AR$14 (recharged with however much credit you want). You can also buy individual tickets, but for most routes a ticket will cost AR$6, while using the card costs AR$1.50. Some hostels, including 41 Below, loan cards to guests on payment of a deposit.

Getting There & Away

Air

Aerolíneas Argentinas (☎442-2425; Av Bartolomé Mitre 185) has flights to Buenos Aires (AR$1446) twice daily Monday through Wednesday and three times daily the rest of the week. In high season there are direct weekly flights to Córdoba and El Calafate and possibly Ushuaia.

LAN (☎443-1077; www.lan.com; Av Bartolomé Mitre 500) flies to Chile and Buenos Aires, and **LADE** (☎442-4812; www.lade.com.ar; J O'Connor 214) covers southern destinations.

Boat

It's possible to travel by boat and bus to Chile aboard the Cruce de Lagos tour. See p371.

Bus

Bariloche's **bus terminal** (☎443-2860) and train station are east of town across the Río Ñireco on RN 237. Shop around for the best deals, since fares vary and there are frequent promotions. During high season it's wise to buy tickets at least a day in advance. The bus terminal tourist office is helpful.

The principal route to Chile is over the Cardenal A Samoré (Puyehue) pass to Osorno (AR$120, five hours) and Puerto Montt (AR$140, six hours), which has onward connections to northern and southern Chilean destinations. Several companies make the run.

To San Martín de los Andes and Junín de los Andes, Albus, Transportes Ko-Ko and **Turismo Algarrobal** (☎442-7698) take the scenic (though often chokingly dusty) Ruta de los Siete Lagos (RN 234) during summer, and the longer, paved La Rinconada (RN 40) route during the rest of the year.

Train

The **Tren Patagonico** (www.trenpatagonico-sa.com.ar) leaves the **train station** (☎442-3172; 12 de Octubre 2400, downtown office at B Mitre 125 local 5), across the Río Ñireco next to the bus terminal. Departures for Viedma (16 hours) are 5pm Thursday and Sunday; fares range from AR$75.50 in *economica* to AR$304 in *camarote* (1st-class sleeper). Departure times change frequently so it's best to check with the tourist office beforehand.

Getting Around

To/From the Airport

Bariloche's **airport** (☎440-5016) is 15km east of town via RN 237 and RP 80. A *remise* costs about AR$70. Bus 72 (AR$6) leaves from the main bus stop on Perito Moreno.

Bus

At the main local bus stop, on Perito Moreno between Rolando and Palacios, **Codao del Sur** and **Ómnibus 3 de Mayo** run hourly buses to Cerro Catedral. Codao uses Av de los Pioneros, while 3 de Mayo takes Av Bustillo.

From 6am to midnight, municipal bus 20 leaves the main bus stop every 20 minutes for the attractive lakeside settlements of Llao Llao and Puerto Pañuelo. Bus 10 goes to Colonia Suiza 14 times daily. During summer three of these, at 8:05am, noon and 5:40pm, continue to Puerto Pañuelo, allowing you to do most of the Circuito Chico using public transport. Departure times from Puerto Pañuelo back to Bariloche via Colonia Suiza are 9:40am, 1:40pm and 6:40pm. You can also walk any section and flag down buses en route.

Ómnibus 3 de Mayo buses 50 and 51 go to Lago Gutiérrez every 30 minutes, while in summer the company's Línea Mascardi goes to

BUSES FROM BARILOCHE

The following services have at least three departures per day.

DESTINATION	COST (AR$)	DURATION (HR)
Bahía Blanca	398	12-14
Buenos Aires	667	20-23
Córdoba	538	22
El Bolsón	38	2
Esquel	80	4½
Junín de los Andes	60	3
Mendoza	485	19
Neuquén	162	7
Río Gallegos	594	28
San Martín de los Andes	75	4
San Rafael	425	15
Viedma	180	12
Villa la Angostura	27	1½

Villa Mascardi/Los Rápidos three times daily. Ómnibus 3 de Mayo's Línea El Manso goes twice on Friday to Río Villegas and El Manso, on the southwestern border of Parque Nacional Nahuel Huapi.

Buses 70, 71 and 83 stop at the main bus stop, connecting downtown with the bus terminal.

Car

Bariloche is loaded with the standard car-rental agencies and is one of the cheapest places to rent in the country. Prices vary greatly depending on season and demand, but usually come in around AR$250 per day with 200km.

Andes (☎443-1648; www.andesrentacar.com.ar; San Martín 162)

Budget (☎444-2482; www.budgetbariloche.com; B Mitre 717)

Hertz (☎442-3457; www.milletrentacar.com.ar; Quaglia 352)

Taxi

A taxi from the bus terminal to the center of town costs around AR$20. Taxis within town generally don't go over the AR$10 mark.

Parque Nacional Nahuel Huapi

☎02944

One of Argentina's most-visited national parks, Nahuel Huapi occupies 7500 sq km in mountainous southwestern Neuquén and western Río Negro provinces. The park's centerpiece is Lago Nahuel Huapi, a glacial remnant over 100km long that covers more than 500 sq km. To the west, a ridge of high peaks separates Argentina from Chile; the tallest is 3554m Monte Tronador, an extinct volcano that still lives up to its name (meaning 'Thunderer') when blocks of ice tumble from its glaciers. During the summer months, wildflowers blanket the alpine meadows.

Nahuel Huapi was created to preserve local flora and fauna, including its Andean-Patagonian forests and rare animals. The important animal species include the huemul (Andean deer) and the miniature deer known as pudú. Most visitors are unlikely to see either of these, but several species of introduced deer are common, as are native birds.

CIRCUITO CHICO

One of the area's most popular and scenic driving excursions, the Circuito Chico begins on Av Bustillo, on Bariloche's outskirts, and continues to the tranquil resort of **Llao Llao**. At **Cerro Campanario** (Av Bustillo, Km 18), the **Aerosilla Campanario** (☎427274) lifts passengers to a panoramic view of Lago Nahuel Huapi for AR$50.

Llao Llao's **Puerto Pañuelo** is the point of departure for the boat and bus excursion across the Andes to Chile, as well as to Parque Nacional Los Arrayanes on Península Quetrihué.

Parque Nacional Nahuel Haupi

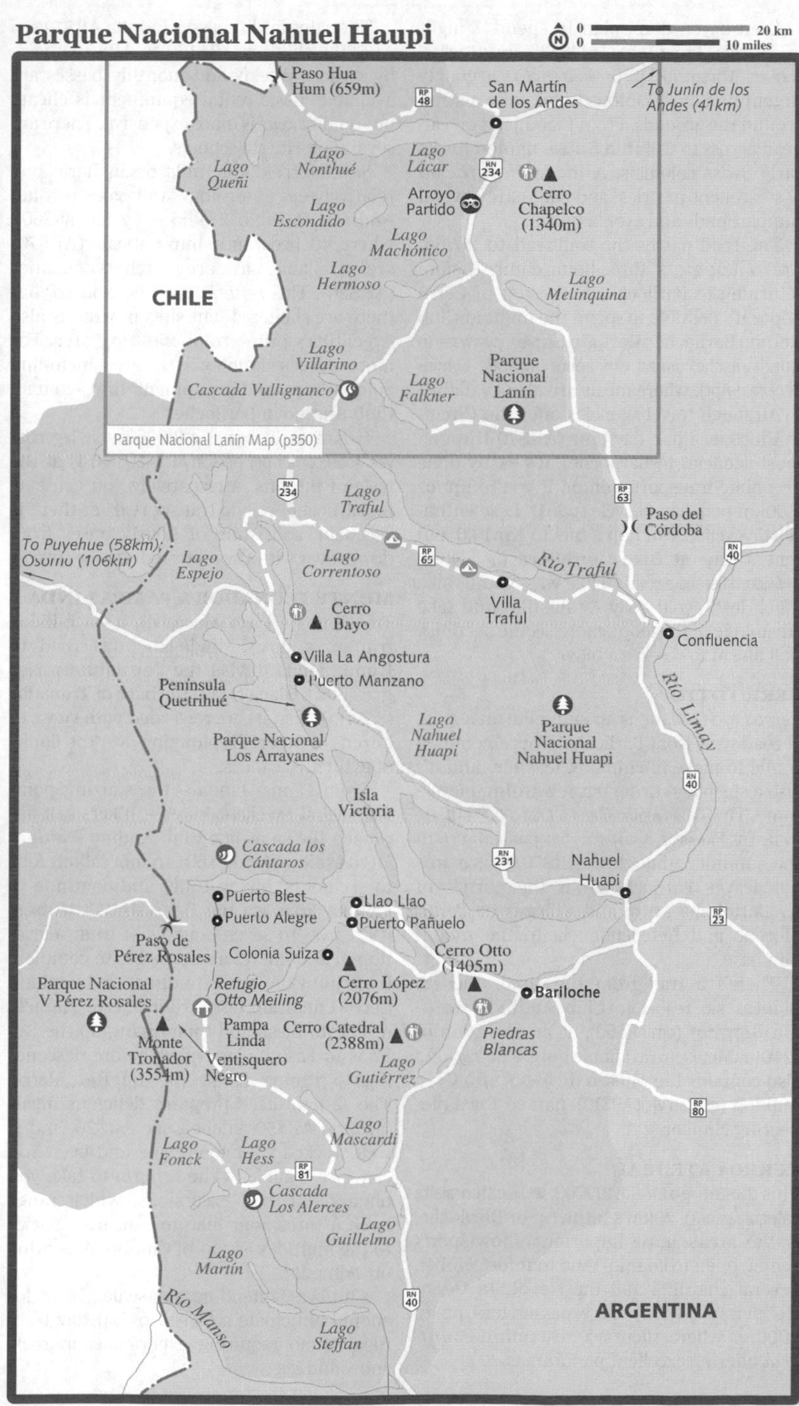

0 20 km
0 10 miles
Paso Hua Hum (659m)
RP 48
San Martín de los Andes
To Junín de los Andes (41km)
Lago Queñi
Lago Nonthué
Lago Lácar
RN 234
Arroyo Partido
Cerro Chapelco (1340m)
Lago Escondido
Lago Machónico
Lago Hermoso
Lago Melinquina
CHILE
Lago Villarino
Parque Nacional Lanín
Lago Falkner
Cascada Vullignanco
Parque Nacional Lanín Map (p350)
RN 234
Lago Traful
RP 63
Paso del Córdoba
To Puyehue (58km); Osorno (106km)
Lago Espejo
Lago Correntoso
RP 65
Río Traful
RN 40
Cerro Bayo
Villa Traful
Confluencia
Villa La Angostura
Puerto Manzano
Península Quetrihué
Río Limay
Parque Nacional Los Arrayanes
Lago Nahuel Huapi
Parque Nacional Nahuel Huapi
RN 40
Isla Victoria
Cascada los Cántaros
RN 231
Nahuel Huapi
Puerto Blest
Puerto Alegre
Llao Llao
Puerto Pañuelo
RP 23
Paso de Pérez Rosales
Colonia Suiza
Cerro Otto (1405m)
Parque Nacional V Pérez Rosales
Refugio Otto Meiling
Cerro López (2076m)
Bariloche
Pampa Linda
Cerro Catedral (2388m)
Piedras Blancas
Monte Tronador (3554m)
Ventisquero Negro
Lago Gutiérrez
RP 80
Lago Mascardi
Lago Fonck
Lago Hess
RP 81
Cascada Los Alerces
Lago Guillelmo
Lago Martín
RN 40
Río Manso
ARGENTINA
Lago Steffan

Even if you don't plan to spend a night in **Hotel Llao Llao** (448530; www.llaollao.com.ar; d from AR$1570;), arguably Argentina's most famous hotel, take a stroll around the grounds. From Llao Llao you can head across to **Colonia Suiza**, named for its early Swiss colonists. A modest *confitería* has excellent pastries, and there are several campgrounds and even a hostel.

The road passes the trailhead to 2076m **Cerro López**, a three-hour climb, before returning to Bariloche. At the top of Cerro López it's possible to spend the night at Club Andino Bariloche's **Refugio López** (www.cerrolopezbariloche.com.ar; dm about AR$50; mid-Dec–mid-Apr), where meals are also available.

Although travel agencies offer the Circuito Chico as a half-day tour (AR$70 through most agencies in Bariloche), it's easily done on public transportation or, if you're up for a 60km pedal, by bicycle (p361). Less enthusiastic cyclists can hop a bus to Km18.6 and rent a bike at **Bike Cordillera** (524828; www.cordillerabike.com). This way you'll bike much less, avoid busy Av Bustillo and take advantage of the loop's more scenic sections. Call ahead to reserve a bike.

CERRO OTTO

Cerro Otto (1405m) is an 8km hike on a gravel road west from Bariloche. There's enough traffic to make hitchhiking feasible, and it's also a steep and tiring but rewarding bicycle route. The **Teleférico Cerro Otto** (441035; Av de Los Pioneros, Km5) carries passengers to the summit (adult/child AR$70/40); a free bus leaves Bariloche from the corner of Av Bartolomé Mitre and Villegas or Perito Moreno and Independencia to the mountain base.

There's a trail from the small Piedras Blancas ski resort to Club Andino's **Refugio Berghof** (dm AR$60), at an elevation of 1240m. Meals are available here. The *refugio* also contains the **Museo de Montaña Otto Meiling** (guided visit AR$10), named for a pioneering climber.

CERRO CATEDRAL

This 2388m **peak** (409000; www.catedralaltapatagonia.com), 20km southwest of Bariloche, is the area's most important snow-sports center, open from mid-June to mid-October. Several chairlifts and the **Aerosilla Cerro Bellavista** (AR$95) carry passengers up to 2000m, where there's a restaurant-*confitería* offering excellent panoramas.

The rates for lift passes (adults AR$195 to AR$290, children AR$160 to AR$240) vary by season. Weekly and monthly passes are available. Basic rental equipment is cheap, but quality gear is more expensive. There are several on-site ski schools.

Several **trekking** trails begin here: one relatively easy four-hour walk goes to Club Andino's **Refugio Emilio Frey** (dm AR$60), where 40 beds and simple meals (AR$70) are available, as are kitchen facilities (AR$20). This *refugio* itself is exposed, but there are sheltered tent sites in what is also Argentina's prime **rock-climbing** area. For more on rock climbing in the area, including guided trips and equipment hire, contact Club Andino in Bariloche.

Hostería Knapp (460062; www.legendaryskihotel.com; r per person AR$420;) is at the base of the lifts. Alternatively you can stay in Bariloche; public transport from there is excellent, consisting of hourly buses from downtown with Ómnibus 3 de Mayo (p367).

MONTE TRONADOR & PAMPA LINDA

Traveling via Lago Mascardi, it's a full-day trip up a dusty, single-lane dirt road to Pampa Linda to visit the **Ventisquero Negro** (Black Glacier) and the base of Tronador (3554m). Visitors are rewarded with views of dozens of waterfalls plunging over the flanks of extinct volcanoes.

From Pampa Linda – the starting point for several excellent **hikes** – hikers can approach the snow-line Club Andino **Refugio Otto Meiling** (dm AR$60) on foot (about four to six hours' hiking time) and continue to Laguna Frías via the **Paso de las Nubes**; it's a five- to seven-hour walk to an elevation of 2000m. It's also possible to complete the trip in the opposite direction by taking Cerro Catedral's ferry from Puerto Pañuelo to Puerto Blest, and then hiking up the Río Frías to Paso de las Nubes before descending to Pampa Linda via the Río Alerce. The *refugio* itself prepares delicious meals (around AR$50, kitchen use AR$20) and is well stocked with good wine and beer. You can hire a guide at the *refugio* to take you on a number of excursions, which range from a three-hour hike to a nearby glacier to the multiday ascent of Cumbre Argentina on Tronador.

Climbers intending to scale Tronador should anticipate a three- to four-day technical climb requiring experience on rock, snow and ice.

The road to **Pampa Linda** passes **Los Rápidos**, after which it becomes extremely narrow. Traffic is therefore allowed up to Pampa Linda until 2pm. At 4pm cars are allowed to leave Pampa Linda for the return trip. For AR$60 one way, Club Andino Bariloche has summer transport (end of November to April) to Pampa Linda at 8:30am daily, returning around 5pm. Buses depart from in front of Club Andino, and the 90km ride takes about 2½ hours. Park entry fees (AR$50) must be paid en route at the ranger station at Villa Mascardi (the bus stops so you can do this).

Sleeping

In addition to the campgrounds in the Bariloche area, there are sites at Lago Gutiérrez, Lago Mascardi, Lago Guillelmo, Lago Los Moscos, Lago Roca and Pampa Linda. *Refugios* are mostly open from December to the end of April. Reservations are not accepted – beds are allocated on a first come, first served basis but a space will always be found (maybe on the floor) for whoever arrives.

Within the park are a number of hotels tending to the luxurious, though there is also the moderately priced **Hostería Pampa Linda** (☎490517; www.hosteriapampalinda.com.ar; s/d AR$400/580). For a real treat, stay at the secluded **Hotel Tronador** (☎441062; www.hoteltronador.com; s/d from AR$500/540; ⊙Nov–mid-Apr), at the northwest end of Lago Mascardi on the Pampa Linda road.

Information

A good source of information about the park is the Nahuel Huapi national park office in Bariloche.

For trekking maps and information about hiking in the region, see Lonely Planet's *Trekking in the Patagonian Andes* by Carolyn McCarthy or, if you read Spanish, the locally published *Las Montañas de Bariloche* by Toncek Arko and Raúl Izaguirre.

Getting There & Around

For transportation information from Bariloche, see p367. For road conditions in and around the national parks, call **Parque Nacional Estado de Rutas** (☎105) toll-free.

El Bolsón

☎0294 / POP 18,000 / ELEV 300M

It's not hard to see why the hippies started flocking to El Bolsón back in the '70s. It's a mellow little village for most of the year, nestled in between two mountain ranges. When summer comes, it packs out with Argentine tourists who drop big wads of cash and disappear quietly to whence they came.

THE CRUCE DE LAGOS

One of Argentina's classic journeys is the Cruce de Lagos, a scenic 12-hour bus-and-boat trip over the Andes to Puerto Montt, Chile. Operated exclusively by **Turisur** (☎426228; www.cruceandino.com; Mitre 219; per person AR$980), the trip begins around 8am in Bariloche (departure times vary) with a shuttle from Turisur's office to Puerto Panuelo near Hotel Llao Llao. The passenger ferry from Puerto Pañuelo leaves immediately after the shuttle arrives so, if you want to have tea at Llao Llao, get there ahead of time on your own (but make sure you bought your ticket in advance). Service is daily in the summer, Monday to Friday the rest of the year. In winter (mid-April to September) the trip takes two days and passengers are required to stay the night in Peulla, Chile, where you have the choice of **Hotel Natura Patagonica** (☎in Chile 65-212053; www.hotelnatura.cl; s/d AR$857/891; @📶) or the **Hotel Peulla** (☎in Chile 65-212053; www.hotelpeulla.cl; s/d AR$506/536; @📶). There used to be a more economical option at Puerto Blest, but it was closed at time of research. Ask about this option at Turisur.

Bicycles are allowed on the boats, and sometimes on the buses (provided you dismantle them), so cyclists may end up having to ride the stretches between Bariloche and Pañuelo (25km), Puerto Blest and Puerto Alegre (15km), Puerto Frías and Peulla (27km), and Petrohué and Puerto Montt (76km); the tourist office may have info about alternative transportation between Petrohué and Puerto Montt for cyclists hoping to avoid the ride.

In winter it's not possible to purchase tickets only for segments of the trip (except between Puerto Pañuelo and Puerto Blest; AR$246). In summer (December to April) it's possible to buy just the boat sections (AR$343). Either way, if you're cycling Turisur will cut your rate slightly since you won't be riding the buses. Though the trip rarely sells out, it's best to book it at least a day or two in advance.

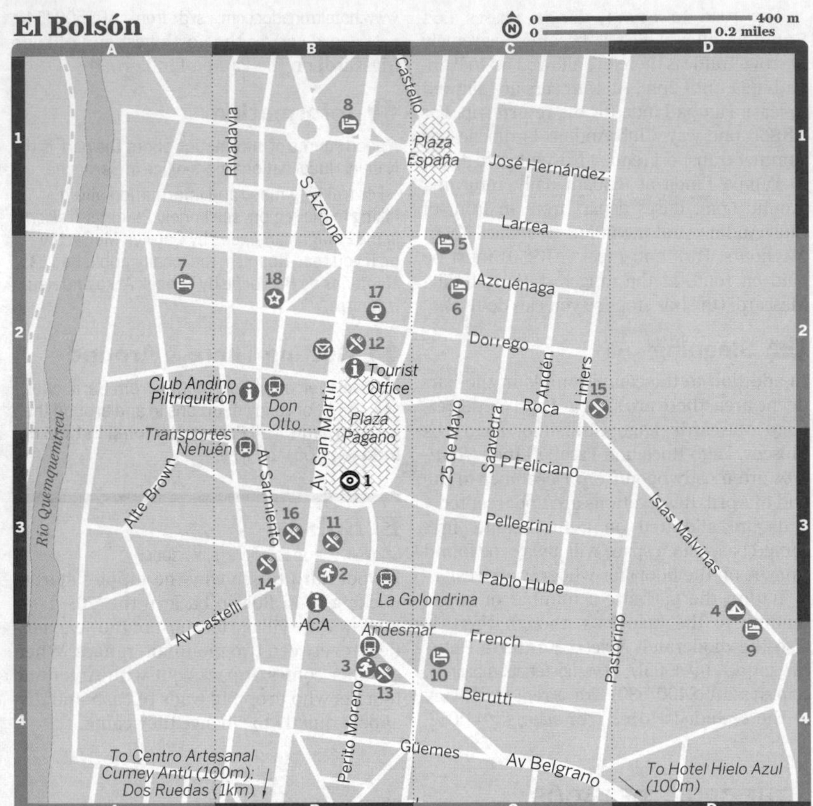

In the last 30-odd years El Bolsón has been declared both a non-nuclear zone and an 'ecological municipality' (are you getting the picture yet?). What's indisputable is that just out of town are some excellent, easily accessible hikes that take in some of the country's (if possibly not the world's) most gorgeous landscapes.

The town welcomes backpackers, who often find it a relief from Bariloche's commercialism and find themselves stuffing their bellies with natural and vegetarian foods and the excellent beer, sweets, jams and honey made from the local harvest.

Rows of poplars lend a Mediterranean appearance to the local *chacras* (farms), most of which are devoted to hops (El Bolsón produces nearly three-quarters of the country's hops) and fruits.

Motorists should note that El Bolsón is the northernmost spot to purchase gasoline at Patagonian discount prices.

Sights & Activities

Near the southwestern border of Río Negro province, El Bolsón lies in a basin surrounded by mountains, dominated by the longitudinal ridges of Cerro Piltriquitrón to the east and the Cordón Nevado to the west.

Feria Artesanal MARKET

(10am-4pm Tue, Thu & Sat) Local craftspeople sell their wares at this market, along the south end of Plaza Pagano, which boasts over 320 artists, who make and sell everything from wooden cutting boards and handcrafted *mate* gourds to jewelry, flutes and marionettes. With numerous food vendors (adhering to the regulation that everything sold in the market must be handmade), it's a chance to sample local delicacies. On sunny Sundays the *feria* operates about half-tilt.

Grado 42 OUTDOORS

(449-3124; www.grado42.com; Av Belgrano 406) For adventures in the surrounding country-

El Bolsón

Sights

1 Feria Artesanal B3

Activities, Courses & Tours

2 Grado 42 .... B3
3 Maputur B4

Sleeping

4 Camping Refugio Patagónico D3
5 Hostel El Bolsón C2
6 Hostería La Escampada C2
7 Hostería Luz de Luna A2
8 Hotel Cordillera B1
9 Refugio Patagónico D4
10 Residencial Valle Nuevo C4

Eating

11 Boulevarde B3
12 Jauja B2
13 La Salteníta B4
14 Las Brasas B3
15 Otto Tipp C2
16 Patio Venzano B3

Drinking

17 Bar 442 .... B2

Entertainment

18 Centro Cultural Eduardo Galeano B2

Shopping

Monte Viejo .... (see 2)

side, this company offers extensive trekking, mountain biking and other tours around El Bolsón, and rafting on the Río Manso. Trips on the Manso Inferior (class II to III) cost AR$285 per person (including lunch); on the Manso a la Frontera (class II to IV) trips cost AR$370 (including lunch and dinner).

Maputur OUTDOORS, BICYCLE RENTAL
(☎449-1440; Perito Moreno 2331) Similar trips to those offered by Grado 42. Rents mountain bikes for AR$45/60 per half-/full day.

Festivals & Events

Local beer gets headlines during the **Festival Nacional del Lúpulo** (National Hops Festival), over four days in mid-February. El Bolsón also hosts a weekend **jazz festival** (www.elbolsonjazz.com.ar) in December.

Sleeping

Budget travelers are more than welcome in El Bolsón, where reasonable prices are the rule rather than the exception.

TOP CHOICE **Hostería La Escampada** HOTEL $$
(☎448-3905; www.laescampada.com.ar; Azcuénaga 561; s/d AR$250/350; wi-fi) A refreshing break from El Bolsón's stale accommodation scene, the Escampada is all modern design with light, airy rooms and a relaxed atmosphere.

Hostel El Bolson HOSTEL $
(☎477-0176; www.hostelelbolson; Moreno 3038; dm/s/d from AR$60/100/120; @wi-fi) A great little hostel, with a couple of good private rooms, spacious dorms and excellent kitchen, living and outdoor areas.

Hostería Luz de Luna HOTEL $$
(☎449-1908; www.luzdelunaelbolson.com.ar; Dorrego 150; s/d AR$260; wi-fi) Although spacious, the rooms here manage to retain a pleasant, homelike feel. Individual decoration and spotless bathrooms add to the appeal. Go for one upstairs for better light and views.

Hotel Cordillera HOTEL $$
(☎449-2235; cordillerahotel@elbolson.com; Av San Martín 3210; s/d AR$320/373; wi-fi) The seemingly endless renovations continue at El Bolsón's top hotel – chances are it will be quite an impressive sight if it ever reopens. Get a room at the front for the views.

Refugio Patagónico HOSTEL $
(☎448-3628; www.refugiopatagonico.com; Islas Malvinas s/n; dm/d AR$55/180; wi-fi) A modern hostel on the outskirts of town (five minutes' walk from the plaza). Dorms have six beds and bathrooms, doubles are unheated.

Camping Refugio Patagónico CAMPGROUND $
(☎15-463-5463; Islas Malvinas s/n; camp sites per person AR$25) Not bad as far as campgrounds go – basically a bare field, but a pleasant stream burbles alongside it. Services are good, including *asados* and a modern toilet block.

Hotel Hielo Azul HOTEL $$
(☎449-3222; Ruta 40 s/n; s/d AR$160/280; wi-fi) A large, plain hotel on the southern outskirts of town, Hielo Azul offers large tiled rooms and a decent restaurant. A reasonable deal.

GRANT DIXON/LONELY PLANET IMAGES ©

1. Centro Cívico (p361)
Bariloche's civic center contains many log-and-stone buildings.

2. Nahuel Huapi (p361)
Skiing over the snowy slopes while looking down on the shimmering lakes is one of the area's best activities.

3. Araucaria
The monkey puzzle tree produces edible pine nuts.

4. Parque Nacional Nahuel Huapi (p368)
This national park was created to preserve local flora and fauna.

Residencial Valle Nuevo HOTEL **$**
(☎449-2087; 25 de Mayo 2345; s/d AR$100/160) With spotless bathrooms, big-screen TVs and rocking views out the back onto mountain peaks, these are some of the best budget rooms in town. If you're coming in summer, book well ahead.

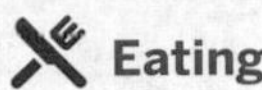

Eating

El Bolsón's restaurants lack Bariloche's variety, but food is consistently good value and often outstanding, thanks to fresh local ingredients and careful preparation. *Trucha arco iris* (rainbow trout) is the local specialty.

Feria artesanal MARKET **$**
(⏲10am-4pm Tue, Thu & Sat) The market is the best and most economical place to eat. Goodies here include fresh fruit, Belgian waffles with berries and cream, huge *empanadas* for AR$4, sandwiches, fritatas, *milanesa de soja* (soy patties), locally brewed beer and regional desserts.

La Salteñita FAST FOOD **$**
(Belgrano 515; empanadas AR$3-4; ⏲10am-9pm) For spicy northern *empanadas,* try this cheap rotisserie.

Jauja ARGENTINE **$$**
(Av San Martín 2867; mains AR$40-80; ⏲breakfast, lunch & dinner) The most dependable *confitería* in town serves up all your faves with some El Bolsón touches (such as homemade bread and strawberry juice) thrown in. The daily specials are always worth checking out – the risotto with lamb and wild mushrooms is divine. The attached ice-creamery is legendary – make sure you leave room for a kilo or two.

Otto Tipp ARGENTINE **$$**
(cnr Roca & Islas Malvinas; mains AR$50-80; ⏲lunch & dinner Dec-Feb, dinner Wed-Sat Mar-Jan) After a hard day of doing anything (or nothing) there are few better ways to unwind than by working your way through Mr Tipp's selection of microbrews. Guests are invited to a free sampling of the six varieties and there's a good selection of regional specialties, such as smoked trout and Patagonian lamb cooked in black beer.

Boulevarde PIZZERIA **$**
(cnr Av San Martín & Pablo Hube; pizzas from AR$40; ⏲lunch & dinner) Excellent thin-crust pizzas like you've probably been craving and a vaguely Irish-pub atmosphere. Around midnight the town's teen population rolls in and the party really starts.

Patio Venzano ARGENTINE **$$**
(cnr Sarmiento & Pablo Hube; mains AR$40-60; ⏲lunch & dinner) On sunny days you'll want to arrive a little early to guarantee an outside table. No surprises on the menu (pasta, *parrilla*), but the atmosphere's a winner.

Las Brasas PARRILLA **$$$**
(☎449-2923; cnr Av Sarmiento & Pablo Hube; mains AR$50-100; ⏲lunch & dinner) The finest dining option in town. Las Brasas' signature dish is Patagonian lamb, but it offers other *parrilla* favorites, plus a variety of trout dishes.

Drinking & Entertainment

Bar 442 BAR
(☎449-2313; Dorrego 442) This venue doubles as a disco on Friday nights and often has live music on Saturday nights.

Dos Ruedas BAR
(Av San Martín 2538) Laid-back pub with pool tables, sports on the big screen and a friendly atmosphere; south of the center.

Centro Cultural Eduardo Galeano THEATER
(☎449-1503; cnr Dorrego & Onelli) Small performance space featuring local (sometimes international) theater, music and dance. Stop by for a program or ask around town.

Shopping

El Bolsón is a craft-hunter's paradise. Besides the regular *feria artesanal* there are several other outlets for local arts and crafts.

Centro Artesanal Cumey Antú CLOTHING
(Av San Martín 2020) This outlet sells high-quality Mapuche clothing and weavings.

Monte Viejo HANDICRAFTS
(cnr Pablo Hube & Av San Martín) Quality ceramics, woodcrafts, silver and Mapuche textiles.

Information

ACA (Automóvil Club Argentino; ☎449-2260; cnr Avs Belgrano & San Martín) Auto club; has provincial road maps.

Banco de la Nación (cnr Av San Martín & Pellegrini) Has an ATM.

Club Andino Piltriquitrón (☎449-2600; www.capiltriquitron.com.ar; Sarmiento, btwn Roca & Feliciano; ⏲Dec-Mar) Visitors interested in exploring the surrounding mountains can contact this office for information on hiking conditions, which refuges are open and general trail queries. Occasionally open 6pm to 8pm off season.

Post office (Av San Martín 2806)

Rancho Net (Av San Martín at Av Belgrano; per hr AR$5) Internet access.

Tourist office (☎449-2604, 445-5336; www.elbolson.gov.ar; Av San Martín & Roca; ⏰9am-9pm, to 10pm in summer) At the north end of Plaza Pagano. It has a good town map and brochures, plus information on accommodations, food, tours and services. Maps of the surrounding area are crude but helpful. Superb staff.

Getting There & Away

El Bolsón has no central bus terminal, but most companies are on or near Av San Martín.

Andesmar (☎449-2178; Av Belgrano & Perito Moreno) goes to Bariloche (AR$35, two hours) and Esquel (AR$42, two to three hours), and to points north of there, usually with a change in Neuquén (AR$159, eight hours).

TAC (☎449-3124; cnr Av Belgrano & Av San Martín) goes to Bariloche (AR$35, two hours) and Neuquén (AR$159, nine hours); the company sells tickets to Mendoza, Córdoba and other northern destinations, though you'll have to change buses in Neuquén.

Don Otto (☎449-3910; Av Belgrano 406) goes to Bariloche and Comodoro Rivadavia (AR$255, 11 hours), with connections in Esquel for Trelew and Puerto Madryn.

Transportes Nehuén (☎449 1831; cnr Sarmiento & Padre Feliciano) goes to El Maitén, Bariloche and Los Alerces.

Getting Around

Bus

Local bus service to nearby sights is extensive during the busy summer months, but sporadic in fall and winter, when you'll have to hire a taxi or take a tour. The tourist office provides up-to-date information. Local buses cost AR$1.50.

Transportes Nehuén (☎449-1831; cnr Sarmiento & Padre Feliciano) has summer bus services to many local destinations.

La Golondrina (☎449-2557; Pablo Hube & Perito Moreno) goes to Cascada Mallín Ahogado, leaving from the south end of Plaza Pagano; and to Lago Puelo, leaving from the corner of Av San Martín and Dorrego.

Taxi

Remises are a reasonable mode of transportation to nearby trailheads and campgrounds. Companies include **Radio Taxi El Rusito** (☎449-1224), **Patagonia** (☎449-3907) and **Avenida** (☎449-3599); call for rides.

Around El Bolsón

The outskirts of El Bolsón offer numerous ridges, waterfalls and forests for hikers to explore. With lots of time, and food and water, some of the following places can be reached by foot from town, though buses and *remises* to trailheads are reasonable. Mountain biking is an excellent way to get out on your own; for rentals try Maputur in El Bolsón.

Popular destinations include **Cabeza del Indio**, a lookout 7km from town and **Cascada Mallín Ahogado**, a small waterfall 10km north of town that provides access to the Club Andino Piltriquitrón's **Refugio Perito Moreno** (☎in El Bolsón 449-2600; per night with/without sheets AR$40/25), a great base for several outstanding hikes. From here it's 2½ hours to the 2206m summit of **Cerro Perito Moreno** (☎493912; lift pass AR$66-100, ski or snowboard rental AR$70), a small ski resort with a base elevation of 1000m.

Serious hikers head for the 2260m **Cerro Piltriquitrón** a granite ridge yielding panoramic views across the valley of the Río Azul to the Andean crest along the Chilean border. Midway up is the **Bosque Tallado** (Sculpture Forest) and the Club Andino's **Refugio Piltriquitrón** (dm AR$35). Beds here are outstanding value, but bring your own sleeping bag. Moderately priced meals are available. From the *refugio* it's another two hours to the summit. Water is abundant along most of the summit route, but hikers should carry a canteen and bring lunch to enjoy at the top.

For more information on these and other hikes in the area and the various hikers' *refugios* operating, contact the Club Andino Piltriquitrón in El Bolsón.

In Chubut province, 15km south of El Bolsón, the **Parque Nacional Lago Puelo** protects a windy, azure lake suitable for swimming, fishing, boating, hiking and camping. By the waterfront the launch **Juana de Arco** (☎02944-498-946; www.interpatagonia.com/juanadearco) takes passengers across the lake to Argentina's Pacific Ocean outlet at the Chilean border (AR$150, three hours). Hardcore hikers can walk into Chile from here – a small tourist office at the dock has details.

Peuma Hue (☎499372; www.peuma-hue.com.ar; s/d from AR$180/280) is a comfortable lakeside resort complex nestled between two rivers with great views of the mighty Piltriquitrón mountain range. There are both free and fee campsites at the park entrance, including **Camping Lago Puelo** (☎499186; per person AR$25).

Regular buses go to Lago Puelo from El Bolsón in summer, but there's reduced service on Sunday and off-season.

Patagonia

Includes »

Best Places to Eat

» Pura Vida (p444)

» Patagonia Resto-Bar (p387)

» Afrigonia (p459)

» La Tablita (p444)

» El Muro (p433)

Best Places to Stay

» Bahía Bustamante (p428)

» Del Nomade Hostería Ecologica (p391)

» La Tosca (p386)

» Tierra Patagonia (p468)

» Nothofagus B&B (p431)

Why Go?

On South America's southern frontier, nature grows wild, barren and beautiful. Spaces are large, as are the silences that fill them. For the newly arrived, such emptiness can be as impressive as the sight of Patagonia's jagged peaks, pristine rivers and dusty backwater oases. In its enormous scale, Patagonia offers an innumerable wealth of potential experiences and landscapes.

Though no longer a dirt road, lonely Ruta Nacional 40 (RN 40) remains the iconic highway that stirred affection in personalities as disparate as Butch Cassidy and Bruce Chatwin. On the eastern seaboard, paved RN 3 shoots south, connecting oil boomtowns with ancient petrified forests, Welsh settlements and the incredible Península Valdés. Then there is the other, trendy Patagonia where faux-fur hoodies outnumber the guanacos. Don't miss the spectacular sights of El Calafate and El Chaltén, but remember that they're a world apart from the solitude of the steppe.

When to Go

El Calafate

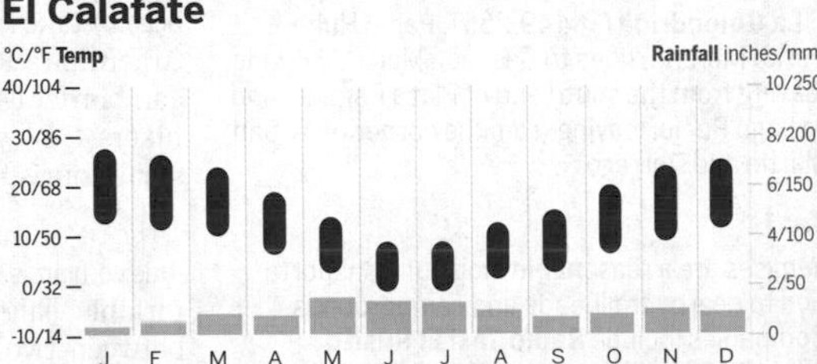

Nov–Mar Warmest months, ideal for *estancia* visits and driving Ruta 40.

Jun–mid-Dec Right whales migrate to Península Valdez.

mid-Sep–early Mar Coastal fauna, including penguins, marine birds and sea lions, abounds.

National Parks & Reserves

Patagonia's national parks boast diverse landscapes, solitude and incredible wildlife. There are the coastal treasures of Monte León (p410) and the newly designated Isla Pingüino (p407), the ancient forests of Los Alerces (p422), the raw beauty of Perito Moreno (p428), and the dazzling glaciers and peaks of Los Glaciares (p434). Noteworthy Chilean parks included here are Torres del Paine (p462), remote Bernardo O'Higgins (p461) and the paleolithic Pali Aike (p456). Among Patagonia's world-class natural reserves, Península Valdés (p389) ranks at the top. Whatever you do, don't leave this region without setting foot in at least a couple.

Getting There & Around

Patagonia is synonymous with unmaintained *ripio* (gravel) roads, missing transport links and interminable bus rides. Flights, though expensive, connect the highlights. Before skimping on your transport budget, bear in mind that the region comprises a third of the world's eighth-largest country.

If you're bussing it along the eastern seaboard, note that schedules are based on the demands of Buenos Aires, with arrivals and departures frequently occurring in the dead of night. Off-season transport options are greatly reduced. In high season demand is high – buy tickets as far in advance as possible. For information on transport with tour operators along RN 40, see p417

COASTAL PATAGONIA

Patagonia's cavorting right whales, penguin colonies and traditional Welsh settlements are all accessed by Argentina's coastal RN 3. While this paved road takes in some fascinating maritime history, it also travels long yawning stretches of landscape that blur the horizon like a never-ending blank slate. It's also a favored travel route for oversized trucks on long-haul trips.

Wildlife enthusiasts shouldn't miss the world-renowned Península Valdés, the continent's largest Magellanic penguin colonies at Área Natural Protegida Punta Tombo, and Ría Deseado's diverse seabird population. The quiet villages of Puerto San Julián and Camarones make for quiet seaside retreats, while Gaiman tells the story of Welsh settlement through a lazy afternoon of tea and cakes.

Viedma

☎02920 / POP 53,000

Sharing the lush Río Negro with sister city Carmen de Patagones, Viedma is comparatively bustling and prosperous. For travelers, the capital of Río Negro province is a less picturesque but more convenient base with good services and amenities, an attractive riverfront, upscale cafes and a jogging path close to downtown.

In 1779 Francisco de Viedma put ashore to found the city after his men started dying of fever and thirst at Península Valdés. In 1879 it became the residence of the governor of Patagonia and the political locus of the country's enormous southern territory. A century later, the radical Alfonsín administration proposed moving the federal capital here from Buenos Aires but was crushingly defeated.

Sights & Activities

Launch operators at the pier offer kayak rentals and river cruises on the Río Negro. The season for sport fishing runs from November to early July, with rainbow trout (catch and release), silverside and carp.

FREE **Museo Cardenal Cagliero** MUSEUM
(☎02920-15-308671; Rivadavia 34; ⏰8am-1pm Mon-Fri) This Salesian museum features incredible ceiling paintings and a neat fish-vertebrae cane (check out the cardinal's office). It's housed in the Centro Histórico Cultural Salesiano, the former Vicariato de la Patagonia, a massive 1890 brick structure on the corner of Colón.

FREE **Museo Gobernador Eugenio Tello** MUSEUM
(☎425900; San Martín 263; ⏰9am-4:30pm Mon-Fri, 4-6pm Sat) Displays on European settlement, Tehuelche tools, artifacts, deformed skulls and skeletons.

Festivals

Regata del Río Negro FESTIVAL
(www.regatadelrionegro.com.ar; ⏰mid-January) A week of events including the world's longest kayak race, a 500km paddle from Neuquén to Viedma.

Fiesta del Siete de Marzo FESTIVAL
(Carmen de Patagones; ⏰early March) Celebration marking the 1827 underdog triumph of Carmen de Patagones over better-equipped

Patagonia Highlights

1. Gaze upon the blue-hued **Glaciar Perito Moreno** (p446) as icebergs fall in thunderous booms
2. Get immersed in the millennial forests and clear lakes of lush **Parque Nacional Los Alerces** (p422)
3. Hike under the toothy **Fitz Roy Range** (p434) near El Chaltén, Argentina's trekking capital
4. See southern right whales cavort in the waters of **Reserva Faunística Península Valdés** (p389)
5. Ride the wide-open range and feast on slow-roasted lamb at an **estancia** (p428)
6. Blaze your own trail on the legendary **Ruta 40** (p417)

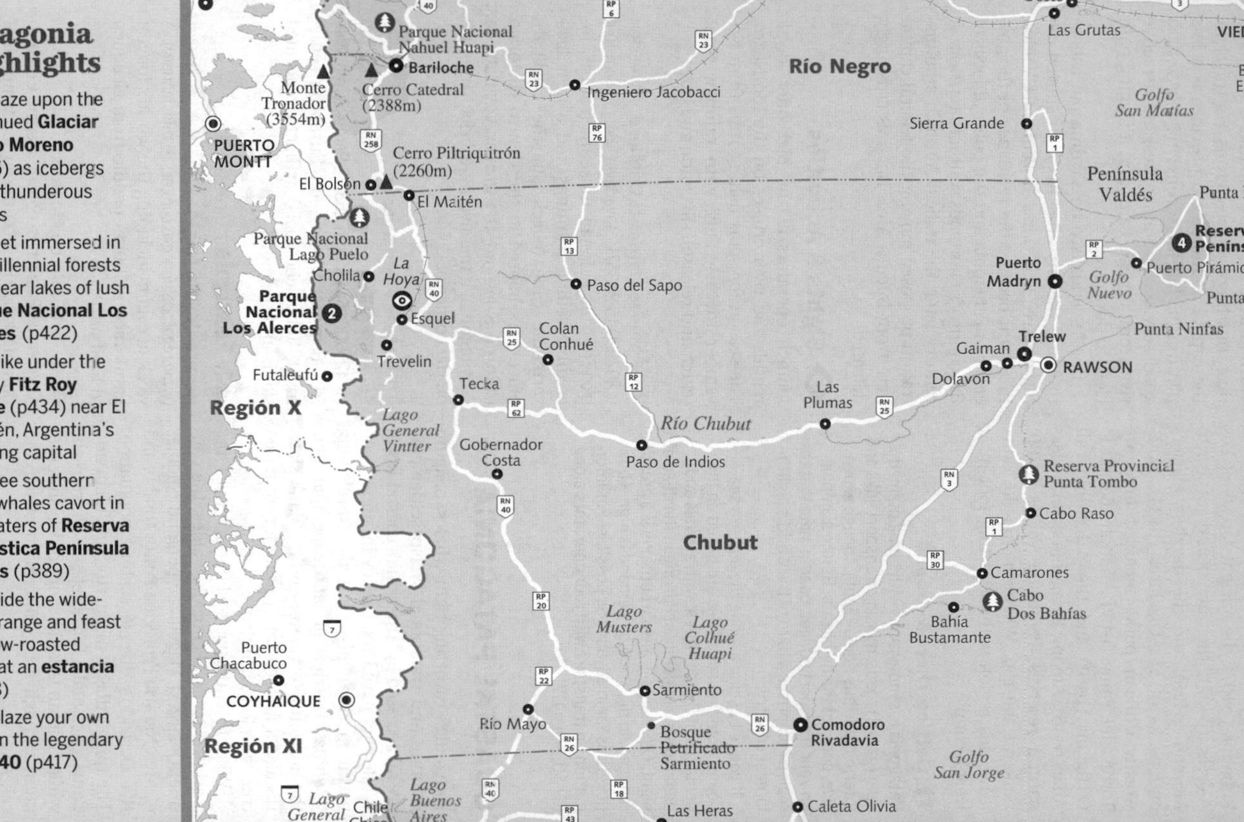

7 Detour to Chile to imbibe the raw beauty of **Torres del Paine** (p462)

invaders during the war with Brazil. Features 10 days of *música folklórica* (Argentine folk music), parades and traditional food and crafts.

Sleeping & Eating

Hotel Nijar HOTEL **$$**
(☎422833; www.hotelnijar.com; Mitre 490; s/d/tr AR$220/310/405; P@☎) A smart business hotel located four blocks from the river. Rooms are small but tidy and adequate, with cable TV. Those facing the street may be noisy.

Hotel Peumayén HOTEL **$**
(☎425222/234; www.hotelpeumayen.com.ar; Buenos Aires 334; s/d/tr AR$195/287/385; @) An old business hotel, dated but well kept, with canary-yellow walls and carpeted rooms. Each floor has a small kitchen.

La Ochava CAFE **$**
(cnr Alsina & 25 de Mayo; sandwiches AR$40; ⊙breakfast, lunch & dinner) This cafe-pub is housed in an antique corner building with high ceilings and original woodwork. Try the *cerveza artesanal* (craft beer) and a steak, burger or sandwich while soaking up the old-fashioned atmosphere.

Sal y Fuego ARGENTINE **$$**
(Av Villarino 55; mains AR$45-65) This hip riverfront hangout offers classic Argentine dishes with a few surprises, such as chicken in sweet-and-sour plum sauce. In the afternoon, you can have coffee under the shade of a weeping willow at the adjoining cafe.

Information

ATMs and internet cafes are in the center along Buenos Aires.

Direccion de Pesca de Río Negro (☎420326) For fishing information and licenses.

Hospital Artémides Zatti (☎422333; Rivadavia 351)

Informes Turisticos (☎427171; www.viedma.gov.ar, in Spanish; Av Francisco de Viedma 51) Offers local and regional information on the waterfront.

Post office (cnr 25 de Mayo & San Martín)

Tourist office (☎427171; bus terminal) Offers lodging and transportation details.

Tritón Turismo (☎431131; Ceferino Namuncurá 78) Changes traveler's checks, rents cars and runs tours.

DON'T MISS

HISTORIC CARMEN DE PATAGONES

Steep cobblestone streets and colonial stylings breathe a little romance into this languid river town, a jaunt across the Río Negro from Viedma. The eager **tourist office** ☎464819; www.patagones.gov.ar; Mitre 84; ⊙7am-7pm Mon-Fri, 10am-1pm & 6-9pm Sat & Sun Dec-Feb) offers maps and brochures.

Plaza 7 de Marzo commemorates an 1827 victory over invading Brazilians. Salesians built the **Templo Parroquial Nuestra Señora del Carmen** here in 1883. Its image of the Virgin, dating from 1780, is southern Argentina's oldest. Two of the original seven Brazilian flags captured in battle sit on the altar. Just west of the church, **Torre del Fuerte** is the last vestige of the 1780 fort that once occupied the entire block.

Below the tower, twin cannons that once guarded the Patagonian frontier flank the 1960s **Pasaje San José de Mayo** staircase leading to the riverside. At the base of the steps, **Rancho de Rial** (Mitre 94) is an 1820 adobe that belonged to the town's first elected mayor. Three blocks west, the **Cuevas Maragatas** (Maragatas Caves; Rivadavia s/n), excavated in the riverbank, sheltered the first Spanish families who arrived in 1779.

Two blocks east, the early-19th-century **Casa de la Cultura** (Mitre 27) was formerly a *tahona* (flour mill). Across the street, preserved frontier home (c 1800) **La Carlota** (cnr Bynon & Mitre) is decorated with typical 19th-century furnishings; ask about guided tours at the museum.

At **Parque Piedra Buena** a bust honors this naval officer responsible for saving countless shipwrecked sailors. A block west, **Museo Histórico Emma Nozzi** (☎462729; ⊙10am-noon & 7-9pm Mon-Fri, 7-9pm Sat) houses an impressive collection of artifacts from Argentina's southern frontier, including details on the town's former black slave population.

BUSES FROM VIEDMA

DESTINATION	COST (AR$)	DURATION (HR)
Bahía Blanca	110	3
Bariloche	360-510	14-15
Buenos Aires	325-465	13
Comodoro Rivadavia	358-412	10-13
Las Grutas	100	2½
Puerto Madryn	175-200	5-6
Trelew	200-230	8

Getting There & Around

Air

Aeropuerto Gobernador Castello is 15km southwest of town on RP 51; a taxi to the center costs AR$8. **Aerolíneas Argentinas** (☎423033) flies twice a week to Buenos Aires (AR$667 one-way). **LADE** (☎424420) lands here on Mondays and Fridays en route to Comodoro Rivadavia.

Boat

From the pier at the foot of 25 de Mayo, a frequent ferry service (AR$2) connects Viedma and Carmen de Patagones from 6:30am until 10pm.

Bus

Viedma's **bus terminal** is 13 blocks southwest of the plaza, a 20-minute walk.

To Puerto Madryn, **Don Otto** (☎425952) and **El Cóndor** (☎427003) offer the best service. To Bariloche, **Las Grutas S.A.** (☎420383) and **El Valle** (☎427501) also travel.

For Balneario El Cóndor (AR$6, 30 mins) and La Lobería (AR$12, one hour), **Ceferino** (☎424542) leaves from Plaza Alsina six times daily in summer.

Coastal Río Negro

La Ruta de los Acantilados occupies a beautiful stretch along Río Negro's 400km Atlantic coastline. Repeated wave action has worn the ancient cliff faces (three million to 13 million years old) to reveal a wealth of fossils. While the area teems with activity in the summer, it shuts down in the off-season.

Balneario El Cóndor, 31km southeast of Viedma at the mouth of the Río Negro, has the largest parrot colony in the world, with 35,000 nests in its cliff faces. Don't miss the century-old lighthouse, Patagonia's oldest.

Some 30km further south, there's a permanent southern sea-lion colony at **La Lobería** (Reserva Faunística de Punta Bermeja), on the north coast of Golfo San Matías. The population peaks during spring, when males come ashore to fight other males and establish harems of up to 10 females. The females give birth from December onward. Visitors will find the observation balcony, directly above the mating beaches, safe and unobtrusive. Buses from Viedma pass within 3km of the colony.

At the northwest edge of Golfo San Matías, 179km west of Viedma along RN 3, the crowded resort of **Las Grutas** (The Grottos; www.balneariolasgrutas.com, in Spanish) owes its name to its eroded sea caves. Thanks to an exceptional tidal range, the beaches can expand for hundreds of meters or shrink to just a few. The **tourist office** (☎02934-497470; Galería Antares, Primera Bajada) has tide schedules. Buses leave hourly to San Antonio Oeste, 16km northeast, with more lodging.

Besides free meals for bus drivers, **Sierra Grande**, 125km south of Las Grutas, only has one thing going for it: gasoline at subsidized *precios patagónicos* (Patagonian prices). Almost everyone fills up their tank, grabs an uninspired snack and carries on.

Puerto Madryn

☎0280 / POP 80,000

The gateway to Península Valdés, Puerto Madryn bustles with tourism and industry. It retains a few small-town touches: the radio announces lost dogs and locals are welcoming and unhurried. With summer temperatures matching those of Buenos Aires, Madryn holds its own as a modest beach destination, but from June to mid-December the visiting right whales take center stage. From July to September, these migrating whales come so close they can be viewed without taking a tour – either from the coast 20km north of town or from the town pier.

The sprawling city is the second-largest fishing port in the country and home to Aluar, Argentina's first aluminum plant, built in 1974. A sheltered port facing Golfo Nuevo, Puerto Madryn was founded by Welsh settlers in 1886. Statues of immigrants and Teheulche along the shoreline pay tribute to its history. The Universidad de la Patagonia is known for its marine biology department, and ecological centers promote conservation and education.

Puerto Madryn

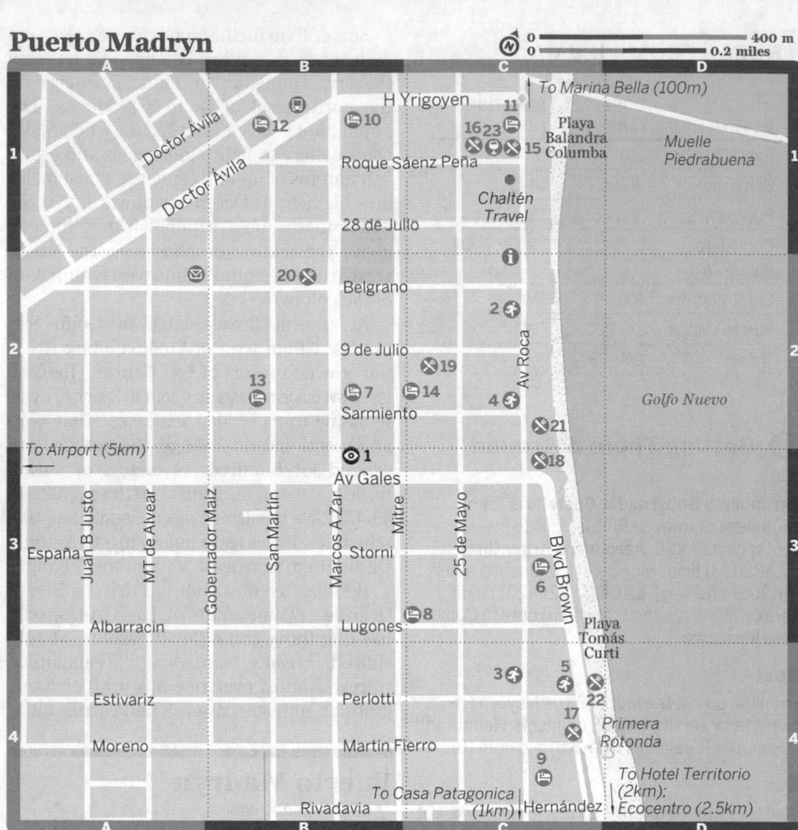

Sights

Puerto Madryn is just east of RN 3, 1371km south of Buenos Aires and about 65km north of Trelew. The action in town centers on the *costanera* and two main parallel avenues, Av Roca and 25 de Mayo. Bulevar Brown is the main drag alongside the beaches to the south.

EcoCentro MUSEUM

(☎445-7470; www.ecocentro.org.ar; J Verne 3784; admission AR$55; ⏰9am-noon & 3-7pm Mon-Fri) Celebrating the area's unique marine ecosystem, this masterpiece brings an artistic sensitivity to extensive scientific research. There are exhibits on the breeding habits of right whales, dolphin sounds and southern elephant-seal harems, a touch-friendly tide pool and more. The building includes a three-story tower and library, the top features glass walls and comfy couches for reading. Bring your binoculars: whales may be spotted from here.

It's an enjoyable 40-minute walk or 15-minute bike ride along the *costanera* to the Ecocentro. Shuttles run three times daily from the tourist office on Av Roca, or you can catch a Línea 2 bus to the last stop and walk 1km.

Museo Provincial de Ciencias Naturales y Oceanográfico MUSEUM

(☎445-1139; cnr Domecq García & José Menéndez; admission AR$6; ⏰9am-noon & 3-7pm Mon-Fri, 3-7pm Sat & Sun) Feeling up strands of seaweed and ogling a preserved octopus show a hands-on museum approach. The 1917 Chalet Pujol features marine and land mammal exhibits, preserved specimens, plus collections of Welsh wares. Explanations in Spanish are geared to youth science classes, but it's visually informative and creatively presented. Twist up to the cupola for views of the port.

Puerto Madryn

Sights

1 Fundación Patagonia Natural B3

Activities, Courses & Tours

2 Flamenco Tour C2
3 Lobo Larsen C4
4 Nievemar C2
5 Scuba Duba C4
Windsurf & Kayak Hire ....(see 22)

Sleeping

6 Chepatagonia Hostel C3
7 El Gualicho B2
8 El Retorno C3
9 Hi! Patagonia Hostel C4
10 Hostería Las Maras B1
11 Hotel Bahía Nueva C1
12 La Casa de Tounens B1
13 La Tosca B2
14 Posada del Catalejo C2

Eating

15 Ambigú C1
16 Estela C1
17 Heladería Mares C4
18 Lizzard Café C3
19 Mr Jones C2
20 Patagonia Resto Bar B2
21 Plácido C2
22 Vernadino Club de Mar C4

Drinking

23 Margarita Bar C1

Fundación Patagonia Natural CONSERVATION ORGANIZATION
(☎445-1920; www.patagonianatural.org, in Spanish; Marcos A Zar 760; ⏲9am-4pm Mon-Fri) A well-run nongovernmental organization, Fundación Patagonia Natural promotes conservation and monitors environmental issues. Volunteers here diligently nurse injured birds and marine mammals to health.

Activities

Diving & Snorkeling

With interesting shipwrecks and sea life nearby, Madryn and the Península Valdés have become Argentina's diving capitals. Dives start at around AR$290; some agencies also offer courses, night dives and multi-day excursions. Some of the above outfitters also offer the popular option of snorkeling with sea lions (per person AR$750) in Punto Lomas. The following are PADI-affiliated.

Lobo Larsen DIVING
(☎447-0277, 02965-15-516314; www.lobolarsen.com; Av Roca 885, Local 2) Reputable local outfitter; offers special baptism excursion for first-timers.

Scuba Duba DIVING
(☎445-2699; www.scubaduba.com.ar, in Spanish; Blvd Brown 893) Quality operator.

Madryn Buceo DIVING
(☎0280-15-456-4422; www.madrynbuceo.com) Offers dive baptisms, snorkeling with sea lions and regular outings, with hostel pick-up service.

Windsurfing & Kayaking

In high season, a hut next to Vernardino Club de Mar (p387) offers lessons and rents out regular and wide boards and kayaks by the hour. South of Muelle Piedrabuena, **Playa Tomás Curti** is a popular windsurfing spot.

Hiking & Biking

Most hostels rent bikes.

Costas de Patagonia ADVENTURE SPORTS
(☎447-1842; www.postasdepatagonia.com) Offers 4x4 combined with trekking, mountain biking, deep-sea fishing and kayak excursions in small groups with bilingual guides.

Tours

Countless agencies sell tours to Península Valdés; prices do not include the AR$70 park admission fee or whale watching (AR$250). Most hotels and hostels also offer tours; get recommendations from fellow travelers before choosing. Ask how large the bus was, if it came with an English-speaking guide, where they ate and what they saw where – different tour companies often visit different locations. Bringing your own binoculars is a good idea.

Tours to Punta Tombo (p401) from Puerto Madryn cost about the same as those offered from Trelew (p396), but they require more driving time and thus less time with the penguins.

Recommended tour companies:

Flamenco Tour GUIDED TOUR
(☎445-5505; www.flamencotour.com; Av Roca 331) Offerings range from the standard whale-watching and snorkeling trips to stargazing 4WD journeys along the coast (telescopes and bilingual instruction included).

DON'T MISS

CLIMB ABOARD THE PATAGONIAN TRAIN

Among the last of Argentina's great long-distance trains, **Tren Patagónico** (442-2130; www.trenpatagonico-sa.com.ar, in Spanish) offers service replete with dining and cinema cars. From the coastal Patagonian town of Viedma, It crosses the plains to Bariloche (economy/1st class/Pullman/bed AR$76/100/155/304, 17 hours) at 6pm on Saturdays; children five to 12 years pay half price. Trains depart from the station on the outskirts of town. Check the website for the current schedule, which changes often.

Nievemar GUIDED TOUR
(445-5544; www.nievemartours.com.ar; Av Roca 493) Amex representative. Excursions include whale watching and visits to sea-lion colonies and the petrified forest.

Sleeping

Book ahead, especially if you want a double room. Tourist offices offer a comprehensive lodging list with prices that include nearby *estancias* (ranches) and rental apartments.

All hostels have kitchens and many offer pickup from the bus terminal, but most are a short, flat walk away.

TOP CHOICE **Hi! Patagonia Hostel** HOSTEL $
(445-0155; www.hipatagonia.com, in Spanish; Av Roca 1040; dm/d AR$50/150; @) Reservations are essential at this sociable suburban-style house featuring both private rooms and dorm beds with down comforters, a cocktail bar in the grassy courtyard, bike rental, climbing wall and barbecues. Owner Gaston is a consummate host and amateur meteorologist (which helps when planning day trips).

La Tosca HOSTEL $
(445-6133; www.latoscahostel.com; Sarmiento 437; dm/tw/d/ste AR$70/170/200/250; @) A tie for the best hostel in town is this cozy guesthouse where the owners and staff greet you by name. The creation of a well-traveled couple, La Tosca is modern and comfy, with a grassy courtyard, good mattresses, varied breakfasts and the occasional homemade dinner. New double suites are a wonderful addition. There are also bike rentals.

Hotel Territorio BOUTIQUE HOTEL $$$
(447-1496; Av Roca 33; www.hotelterritorio.com.ar; d/tr AR$535/602, ste AR$1245; @) Set behind beautiful dunes with ocean views, this 36-room hotel is minimal chic – with polished concrete, plush modern furniture and an entire whale vertebrae gracing a yawning hall. Kids can use a spacious play room. The Punta Cuevas location is a trek from the center, but there's a cool cocktail bar and a contemporary spa.

La Casa de Tounens HOSTEL $
(447-2681; www.lacasadetounens.com; Pasaje 1ero de Marzo 432; dm/s/d without bathroom AR$55/140/170, s/d AR$170/220; @) A congenial nook near the bus station, run by a friendly Parisian-Argentine couple. With only six rooms, personal attention is assured. There's a cozy stone patio, homemade bread for breakfast and free use of bicycles.

El Gualicho HOSTEL $
(445-4163; www.elgualicho.com.ar, in Spanish; Marcos A Zar 480; dm/d/tr/q AR$55/220/246/265; @) After a slick, major renovation, this sleek, contempo hostel provides very stylish digs, though mattresses are mysteriously cheap. We love the ample common spaces, with billiards and hammocks, but being truly massive (with 120 beds) makes it somewhat impersonal. Rents bikes.

La Posada Hotel INN $$
(447-4087; www.la-posada.com.ar; Mathews 2951; d/superior AR$410/480; @) This modern inn amid rolling green lawns offers a quiet alternative to lodging in town. Its tidy, light-filled rooms with bright accents come with cable TV; in the garden there's a pool and barbecue grill. It's 2km south of the town center.

Casa Patagonica B&B $$
(445-1540; www.casa-patagonica.com.ar; Av Roca 2210; d/tr without bathroom AR$180/220, d/t AR$260/300; @) Warm and relaxed, with homemade cakes for breakfast and a *quincho* for cooking or barbecues. Lodgings are in a brick home with vaulted ceilings and impeccably kept rooms, five blocks from the beach and 1km south of the center.

Chepatagonia Hostel HOSTEL $
(445-5783; www.chepatagoniahostel.com.ar; Storni 16; dm/tw AR$60/175; @) Just a stone's throw from the beach, this well-run hostel is

owned by a friendly couple who book tours for guests and fire up the grill for barbecues twice a week. Adding to the appeal are comfortable beds and the possibility of glimpsing a breaching whale from the hostel balcony.

El Retorno HOSTEL **$**
(445-6044; www.elretornohostel.com.ar; Mitre 798; dm/tw AR$55/180; @) Run by the indefatigable Gladys, a den mother to travelers from all over. Besides dorms and snug doubles, there's a solarium, barbecue area, bike rental and table tennis.

Hostería Las Maras INN **$$**
(445-3215; www.hosterialasmaras.com.ar; Marcos A Zar 64; s/d AR$320/390, superior AR$390/430; @) Brick walls, exposed beams and wicker furniture create an intimate setting for couples – in the lobby anyway. Guest rooms are just small, prim and servicable – if design is important to you, upgrade to a superior room.

Posada del Catalejo HOSTEL **$**
(447-5224; www.posadadelcatalejo.com.ar; Mitre 46; dm/d without bathroom AR$60, d/tr AR$260/300; @) Located in an old-fashioned building that makes the place feel more like a budget B&B. The worn-out dorms beg for some love but doubles are nice. Guests get one free hour on the rental bikes.

Hotel Bahía Nueva HOTEL **$$**
(445-0045/145; www.bahianueva.com.ar; Av Roca 67; s/d AR$372/438; @) Stretching to resemble an English countryside retreat, the Bahía Nueva includes a foyer library and flouncy touches. Its 40 rooms are well groomed, but only a few have ocean views. Highlights include a bar with billiards and a TV (mostly to view movies and documentaries), and tour information.

Camping ACA CAMPGROUND **$**
(445-2952; info@acamadryn.com.ar; Camino al Indio; s/d campsites AR$25/30; closed May-Aug) These 800 gravel campsites are sheltered by trees to break the incessant wind. Although there are no cooking facilities, some snacks (and sometimes prepared meals) are available. From downtown, city bus 2 goes within 500m of the campground; get off at the last stop (La Universidad).

Eating & Drinking

TOP CHOICE **Patagonia Resto-Bar** SEAFOOD **$$$**
(Belgrano 323; mains AR$66; noon-3pm, 8pm-late, closed Mon) With circular leather booths and stark marine photos, this popular newcomer pleases with innovative cuisine carefully prepared and kindly priced. It's also a nice spot to hook up for drinks.

Mr Jones PUB **$**
(9 de Julio 116; mains AR$38; dinner) Serving a wealth of yummy stouts and reds, homemade pot pie, and fish and chips, this favorite local pub always delivers. Service is friendly but tends to be slow.

Ambigú ARGENTINE **$$**
(www.ambiguresto.com.ar; cnr Av Roca & Roque Sáenz Peña; mains AR$45-60) Locals gravitate toward this corner cafe with a focus on fresh ingredients. Ambigú masters a gamut of dishes, including seafood – try the *langostinos* (prawns) in sea salt – and pizza. The setting is an elegant renovation of a historic bank building, backlit by warm colors.

Plácido ARGENTINE **$$$**
(445-5991; www.placido.com.ar; Av Roca 506; mains AR$70; noon-3pm, 8pm-late) Chic and waterfront, this white-linen restaurant serves beautifully presented versions of traditional dishes such as shrimp in garlic and *cordero patagónico* (Patagonian lamb) in a minimalist setting. Try the shellfish sampler paired with a white from Bodega Fin del Mundo.

Vernardino Club de Mar SEAFOOD **$$$**
(447-4289; www.vernardinoclubdemar.com.ar; Blvd Brown 860; mains AR$40-80; breakfast, lunch & dinner) With unbeatable beachfront atmosphere, Vernadino is a hot spot for drinks and wok dishes. Take a seat on the patio in the early morning and you'll feel like you're having breakfast on the sand.

Estela PARRILLA **$$$**
(445-1573; Roque Sáenz Peña 27; mains AR$45-78; noon-2:30pm & 8pm-midnight Tue-Sun) The sweet smell of sautéeing garlic stops pedestrians in their tracks, this classic *parrilla* also does pasta and fish in an intimate, unpretentious setting. While it has a longstanding reputation, some customers have complained of uneven day-to-day quality.

Heladería Mares ICE CREAM **$**
(Martin Fierro 85; cone AR$20; 10am-midnight) A must stop for a creamy *dulce de leche* ice cream.

Lizzard Café CAFE **$**
(cnr Avs Roca & Gales; mains AR$38; 7am-2am) The 'burger pizza' hasn't caught on yet, but this corner cafe, which also serves decent salads, fills up since it's almost always open.

 Entertainment

Bars and dance clubs come and go, so ask locals what's *de moda* (in) now.

Margarita Bar BAR
(Roque Sáenz Peña; ⏲11am-4am) With a trendy edge, this low-lit brick haunt has a laundry list of cocktails, a friendly bar staff and decent food. On weekends there's dancing after 1:30am.

Marina Bella CLUB
(www.marinabella.com.ar; Av Rawson 115; cover AR$25) This up-all-night disco flytrap attracts all ages, with reggaeton, cumbia, and electronica on different dance floors, including an open-air tent in summer. Women go cover-free.

 Information

Call centers and internet cafes abound in the center. Some travel agencies accept traveler's checks as payment for tours.

Banco de la Nación (9 de Julio 127) Has an ATM and changes traveler's checks.

Dirección de Cultura (Av Roca 444; showers AR$3.50) Showers available downstairs, beneath the Museo de Arte Moderno.

Hospital Subzonal (☎4451999; R Gómez 383)

Post office (cnr Belgrano & Gobernador Maíz)

Recreo (cnr 28 de Julio & Av Roca) Stocks a good selection of regional books, maps and a few English-language novels and guidebooks. There is another branch on the corner of 25 de Mayo and Roque Sáenz Peña.

Thaler Cambio (☎445-5858; Av Roca 497; ⏲9:30am-1pm & 6-8pm Mon-Fri, 10am-1pm & 7-9pm Sat & Sun) Poorer rates for traveler's checks.

Tourist office (☎445-3504, 456067; www.madryn.gov.ar/turismo, in Spanish; Av Roca 223; ⏲7am-10pm Mon-Fri, 8am-11pm Sat & Sun Dec-Feb, reduced hours off-season) Helpful and efficient staff, and there's usually an English or French speaker on duty. Check the *libro de reclamos* (complaint book) for traveler tips. There's another helpful desk at the bus terminal.

 Getting There & Away

Due to limited connections, it pays to book in advance, especially for travel to the Andes.

Air

Though Puerto Madryn has its own modern airport 5km west of town, **Aeropuerto El Tehuelche**, most commercial flights still arrive in Trelew (see p398), 65km south.

Newcomer **Andes** (☎445-2355; www.andesonline.com; Av Roca 624) has flights to Buenos Aires' Aeroparque (AR$1177) several times a week. **Aerolíneas Argentinas** (☎445-1998; Av Roca 427) flies from Trelew but has a ticketing representative here.

Bus

Puerto Madryn's full-service **bus terminal** (Doctor Avila, btwn Independencia & Necochea), behind the historic 1889 Estación del Ferrocarril Patagónico, has an ATM and a helpful tourist information desk. Bus timetables are clearly posted and large luggage lockers are available for rent.

Bus companies include **Andesmar** (☎447-3764), **Don Otto** (☎445-1675), **28 de Julio** (☎447-2056), **Mar y Valle** (☎447-2056), **Que Bus** (☎445-5805), **Ruta Patagonia** (☎445-4572), **TAC** ☎447-4938) and **TUS** (☎445-1962). **Chaltén Travel** (☎445-4906; Av Roca 115) has buses to Esquel and offers connecting service north on RN40 (to Bariloche) or south (to Perito Moreno and El Chaltén).

BUSES FROM PUERTO MADRYN

DESTINATION	COST (AR$)	DURATION (HR)
Bariloche	381-433	14-15
Buenos Aires	437-481	18-20
Comodoro Rivadavia	130-150	6-8
Córdoba	501-575	18
Esquel	205-258	7-9
Mendoza	527-632	23-24
Neuquén	224-260	12
Río Gallegos	456-524	15-20
Trelew	16	1
Viedma	126-146	5-6

The bus to Puerto Pirámides, operated by Mar y Valle (AR$24, 1½ hours), leaves at 9:45am and returns to Madryn at 6pm. On Monday, Wednesday and Friday there are 6:30am and 4pm departures, returning at 8am and 1pm.

Getting Around

Rent a bicycle for travel in and around town.

To/From the Airport

Southbound 28 de Julio buses to Trelew, which run hourly Monday through Saturday between 6am and 10pm, will stop at Trelew's airport on request.

Radio taxis, including **La Nueva Patagonia** (447-6000), take travelers to and from Madryn's airport for about AR$18, while **Eben-Ezer** (447-2474) runs a service (AR$50) to Trelew's airport.

Car

A roundtrip to Península Valdés is a little over 300km. A group sharing expenses can make a car rental a relatively reasonable and more flexible alternative to taking a bus tour if you don't have to pay for extra kilometers – rent under clear terms.

Rates vary, depending on the mileage allowance and age and condition of the vehicle. The family-owned **Centauro** (0280-15-340400; www.centaurorentacar.com.ar; Av Roca 733) gets high marks as an attentive and competitively priced rental agency. Basic vehicles run AR$395 per day, with insurance and 400km included.

Around Puerto Madryn

Home to a permanent sea-lion colony and cormorant rookery, the **Reserva Faunística Punta Loma** (admission AR$25) is 17km southwest of Puerto Madryn via a good but winding gravel road. The overlook is about 15m from the animals, best seen during low tides. Many travel agencies organize two-hour tours (AR$100) according to the tide schedules; otherwise, check tide tables and hire a car or taxi, or make the trek via bicycle.

Twenty kilometers north of Puerto Madryn via RP 1 is **Punta Flecha** observatory, a recommended whale-watching spot.

Reserva Faunística Península Valdés

Home to sea lions, elephant seals, guanacos, rheas, Magellanic penguins and numerous seabirds, Unesco World Heritage site Península Valdés is one of South America's finest wildlife reserves. More than 80,000 visitors per year visit this sanctuary, which has a total area of 3600 sq km and more than 400km of coastline.

The wildlife viewing is truly exceptional, though the undisputed main attraction is the endangered *ballena franca austral* (southern right whale). The warmer, more enclosed waters along the Golfo Nuevo, Golfo San José and the coastline near Caleta Valdés from Punta Norte to Punta Hércules become prime breeding zones for right whales between June and mid-December. For details on the region's ocean wildlife, see p392.

One doesn't expect lambs alongside penguins, but sheep *estancias* occupy most of the peninsula's interior, which includes one of the world's lowest continental depressions, the salt flats of Salina Grande and Salina Chica, 42m below sea level. At the turn of the 20th century, Puerto Pirámides, the peninsula's only village, was the shipping port for the salt extracted from Salina Grande.

About 17km north of Puerto Madryn, paved RP 2 branches off RN 3 across the Istmo Carlos Ameghino to the entrance of the **reserve** (admission per day AR$70). The **Centro de Interpretación** (8am-8pm), 22km beyond the entrance, focuses on natural history, displays a full right whale skeleton and has material on the peninsula's colonization, from the area's first Spanish settlement at Fuerte San José to later mineral exploration. Don't miss the panoramic view from the observation tower.

If you are sleeping in Puerto Madryn but plan to visit the park on two consecutive days, ask a ranger to validate your pass so you can re-enter without charges.

PUERTO PIRÁMIDES

0280/ POP HUMANS 430, WHALES 400-1700

Set amid sandy cliffs on a bright blue sea, this sleepy old salt port now bustles with tour buses and visitors clad in orange life jackets. Whales mean whopping and ever-growing tourism here, but at the end of the day the tour buses split and life in this two-street town regains its cherished snail's pace.

Av de las Ballenas is the main drag, which runs perpendicular to Primera (1era) Bajada, the first road to the beach, stuffed with tour outfitters. A small **tourist office** (449-5048; www.puertopiramides.gov.ar; 1era Bajada) helps with travelers' needs. Visitors can access the internet at **Telefónica** (Av de las Ballenas) and take out cash from the ATM at **Banco de Chubut** (Av de las Ballenas).

Reserva Faunística Península Valdés

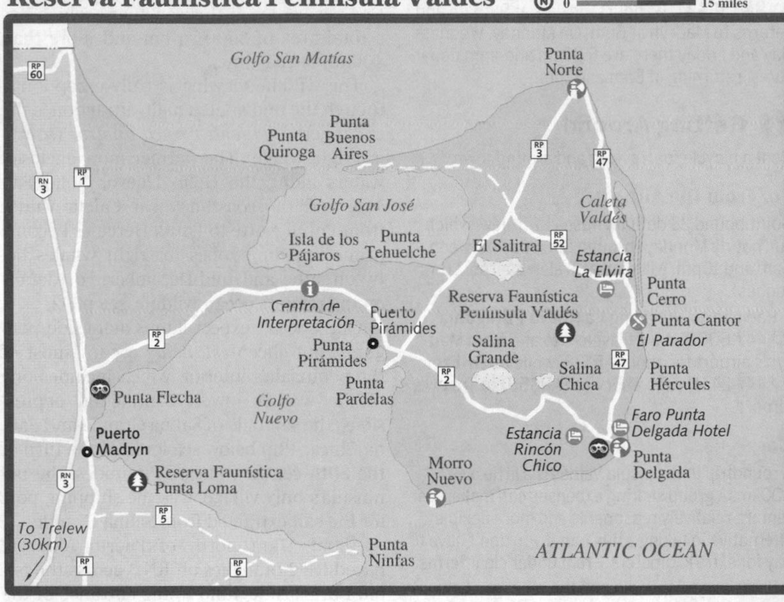

Activities

While most visitors focus on whale watching, adventure offerings continue to grow.

Area *estancias* offer **horseback riding**. But adventurers don't have to stray far just join the local kids at the **sandboarding** hill at the end of the second road down to the beach.

Visitors can walk to the **sea-lion colony** less than 5km from town (though mostly uphill). It is a magnificent spot to catch the sunset, occasional whale sightings and views across the Golfo Nuevo toward Puerto Madryn. Time your visit with the tides; high tides finds all the sea lions swimming out to sea.

Tours

TOP CHOICE **Patagonia Explorers** KAYAKING
(☎0280-15-434-0619; www.patagoniaexplorers.com; Av de las Ballenas) This band of brothers (and sister) offer top-notch guided hikes and sea-kayaking trips. A new three-day trip on the Golfo San José includes paddling with sea lions and lots of wildlife watching and wilderness camping. There's also full moon and sunset options. Check the website or drop by its office for more information.

Patagonia Scuba DIVING
(☎0280-15-435-4646; www.patagonia-scuba.com.ar, in Spanish; Av de las Ballenas s/n; dive AR$290) A reputable PADI-certified outfitter offering diving trips and snorkeling with sea lions. The best water visibility is in August. Find them on Facebook.

WHALE TOURS

This is the place to glimpse spy-hopping, breaching and tailing cetaceans on a **whale-watching excursion** (adult/child AR$260/130), arranged in Puerto Madryn or Puerto Pirámides. The standard trip lasts 1½ hours, but longer excursions are available.

When choosing a tour, ask other travelers about their experiences and check what kind of boat will be used: smaller, Zodiac-style inflatable rafts offer more intimacy but may be less comfortable. By law, outfitters are not allowed within 100m of whales without cutting the motor, nor allowed to pursue them.

Check your outfitter's policies. When the port is closed due to bad weather, tour bookings are usually honored the following day (although these days are more crowded). Outside of whale-watching season (June to December), boat trips aren't worthwhile unless you adore sea lions and shorebirds.

The following is a partial list of reputable outfitters:

Bottazzi WHALE WATCHING
(☎449-5050; www.titobottazzi.com; 1era Bajada) A recommended family business in its sec-

ond generation and the only company with its own boats. More personalized sunset cruises feature a smaller boat. Also has an office in Puerto Madryn.

Hydrosport WHALE WATCHING
(449-5065; www.hydrosport.com.ar; 1era Bajada) In addition to whale watching, runs dolphin-watching tours and has naturalists and submarine audio systems on board.

Whales Argentina WHALE WATCHING
(449-5015; www.whalesargentina.com.ar; 1era Bajada) Offers quality trips with a bilingual guide; also runs personalized excursions on a four-seater semi-rigid boat.

Sleeping

Staying over helps pack in more watching wildlife, though it's worth noting that there are few good-value lodgings here and little happening at night. Still, campers gloat about hearing whales' eerie cries and huffing blow holes in the night – an extraordinary experience.

You will have to get a voucher from your hotel if you plan to exit and re-enter the park, so as to not pay the park entry fee twice. Watch for signs advertising rooms, cabins and apartments for rent along the main drag.

Del Nomade Hostería Ecologica LODGE $$$
(449-5044; www.ecohosteria.com.ar; Av de las Ballenas s/n; d/t AR$760/840; @) Owned by a renowned Argentine nature photographer, this ecolodge comprises eight stylish rooms with homey, minimalist style and homemade breakfasts. Maximum effort has been put into making it green – using wood from fallen trees, enzymatic water treatment, solar panels, composting and natural cleaning agents. You can get in the wildlife mood browsing the stacks of National Geographics and onsite photography. Long-stay discounts are available.

La Casa de la Tía Alicia GUESTHOUSE $
(449-5046; http://lacasadelatiaalicia.blogspot.com; Av de las Ballenas s/n; per person AR$70) Aunt Alicia is all about *buena onda* (good vibes), and her petal-pink house is undoubtedly the best value in town. Rooms share two bathrooms; a three-person cabin is also available and there's a cute garden area.

La Posta APARTMENT $$
(449-5005; www.lapostapiramides.com.ar; 1era Bajada s/n; d/tr/q AR$270/320/350) Adorable cabin-style apartments that fit up to five. Right in the middle of the action, with cozy, clean interiors, exposed brick walls, simple wood furniture, cable TV and kitchenettes.

De Luna GUESTHOUSE $$
(449-5083; www.deluna.com.ar; Av de las Ballenas s/n; d/cabin AR$250/350) Bright and cheerful, choose from spacious and inviting rooms in the main house, or a crunched but lovely guest cabin, perched above the house with excellent views.

Motel ACA MOTEL $$
(449-5004; www.motelacapiramides.com.; Av Roca s/n; s/d AR$325/420;) One of the better bets in town, though the beach location can be noisy. The attached restaurant, open to the public, serves fresh seafood and offers bay views through huge glass windows.

Restingas Hotel LUXURY HOTEL $$$
(449-5101; www.lasrestingas.com; 1era Bajada; d garden/ocean view AR$717/844; @) A beachfront luxury hotel and spa with spacious rooms and an attractive glass-walled living room. While service appears lax, watching whales from your bedroom is a big plus. Guests do praise the abundant buffet breakfast; its gourmet restaurant is open to the public.

Paradise HOTEL $$
(449-5030; www.hosteriaparadise.com.ar; 2da Bajada; d AR$480; @) A dozen simple tile and brick-walled rooms, expansive and cool. Some have views and Jacuzzi tubs. Outside of the whale-watching season, rates are significantly lower.

Camping Municipal CAMPGROUND $
(15-469-9161; per person AR$25) Convenient, sheltered gravel camp sites with clean toilets, a store and hot pay showers, down the road behind the gas station. Come early in summer to stake your spot. Avoid camping on the beach: high tide is very high.

Hostel Bahía Ballenas HOSTEL $
(423-8766; www.bahiaballenas.com.ar; Av de las Ballenas s/n; dm AR$100; @) A bare-bones brick hostel with two enormous single-sex dorms; the 'Backpackers' sign will catch your eye. Rates include kitchen use and internet (spotty throughout town).

Eating & Drinking

Restaurants flank the beachfront, down the first street to the right as you enter town. Note that water here is desalinated: sensitive

Patagonian Wildlife

Thanks to deep ocean currents that bring nutrients and abundant food, the coast of southern Argentina plays host to bountiful marine life. To see them hunt, court, nest and raise their young renews one's sense of wonder along these lonely Atlantic shores.

Magellanic Penguin

1 Adorable and thoroughly modern, penguins co-parent after chicks hatch in mid-November. See the action at Punta Tombo (p401), Ría Deseado (p407) and Bahía Bustamante (p428).

Southern Right Whale

2 In spring, the shallow waters of Península Valdés (p389) attract thousands of these creatures to breed and bear young.

Commerson's Dolphin

3 These small dolphins often join boaters in play. See them all year at Playa Unión (p399), in Ría Deseado (p407) and Puerto San Julián (p408).

Southern Sea Lion

4 Found year-round along the southern coast of Argentina, these burly swimmers feed on squid and the odd penguin.

Killer Whale

5 To witness raw nature at work, visitors flock to Punta Norte (p394) on Península Valdés, where these powerful creatures almost beach themselves in the hunt for sea lions, from mid-February to mid-April.

Southern Elephant Seal

6 Consummate divers, these monsters spend most of the year at sea. In austral spring, spy on their breeding colony at Punta Delgada (p394) on Península Valdés. Watch for beachmasters – dominant males controlling harems of up to 100 females.

Clockwise from top left
1. Magellanic penguins **2.** Southern right whale **3.** Commerson's dolphin **4.** Southern sea lion

2

JUAN CARLOS MUNOZ/NATURE PICTURE LIBRARY ©

3

YANNIS EMMANUEL MAVROMATAKIS/ALAMY ©

stomachs should stick to the bottled stuff. If self-catering, it's best to haul your groceries from Puerto Madryn.

TOP CHOICE **La Estación** SEAFOOD $$
(Av de las Ballenas s/n; mains AR$45; ⊙noon-midnight, closed Tue) This funky, fresh eatery is the ideal spot to crack open a bottle of wine and savor it. Though the vibe is casual, dishes like *langostinos a la plancha* (grilled prawns), fresh scallops and lamb sorrrentinos are fit for kings. There's also breakfast.

El Viento Viene CAFE $
(1era Bajada; mains AR$25; ⊙9am-7:30pm) This little nook is a charming spot for coffee, sandwiches and homemade pie, also selling innovative arts and crafts.

Getting There & Around

During summer, the Mar y Valle bus service travels from Puerto Madryn to Puerto Pirámides (AR$24, 1½ hours) at 8:55am and returns to Madryn at 6pm, with fewer departures in off-season. Bus tours from Puerto Madryn may allow passengers to get off here.

AROUND PUERTO PIRÁMIDES

If you're driving around the peninsula, take it easy. Roads are *ripio* and washboard, with sandy spots that grab the wheels. If you're in a rental car, make sure you get all the details on the insurance policy. Hitchhiking here is nearly impossible and bike travel is long and unnervingly windy.

ISLA DE LOS PÁJAROS

In Golfo San José, 800m north of the isthmus, this bird sanctuary is off-limits to humans, but visible through a powerful telescope. It contains a replica of a chapel built at Fuerte San José. See the boxed text, p395, to find out how this small island figures into Antoine de St-Exupéry's *The Little Prince.*

PUNTA DELGADA

In the peninsula's southeast corner, 76km southeast of Puerto Pirámides, sea lions and, in spring, a huge colony of elephant seals are visible from the cliffs. Enter the public dirt road right of the hotel.

TOP CHOICE **Estancia Rincón Chico** INN $$$
(☎471733, 02965-15-688302; www.rinconchico.com.ar; d incl full board AR$2300; ⊙mid-Sept-Mar) With a prime location for wildlife watching, this refined and recommended inn hosts university marine biologists, student researchers and tourists. Lodging is in a modern, corrugated-tin ranch house with eight well-appointed doubles and a *quincho* (thatched-roof building) for barbecues. In addition to guided excursions, there are paths for cycling and walking on your own.

Faro Punta Delgada Hotel LUXURY HOTEL $$$
(☎458444, 02965-15-406304; www.puntadelgada.com; d incl half-/full board AR$1540/1920) A luxury hotel in a lighthouse complex that once belonged to the Argentine postal service. Horseback riding, 4WD tours and other activities are available. Nonguests can dine at the upscale restaurant serving *estancia* fare. Guided naturalist walks down to the beach leave frequently in high season.

PUNTA CANTOR & CALETA VALDÉS

In spring, elephant seals haul themselves onto the long gravel spit at this sheltered bay, 43km north of Punta Delgada. September has females giving birth to pups, while males fight it out defending their harem – a dramatic sight from the trails that wind down the hill. You may even see guanacos strolling the beach.

Tour groups fill up **El Parador** (☎474248; www.laelvira.com.ar; meals AR$120), a decent self-service restaurant offering a salad bar, coffee, drinks and rest rooms. It is part of **Estancia La Elvira** (☎474248; www.laelvira.com.ar; d incl half-/full board AR$950), a comfortable lodging with a modern construction that lacks the romance of a seasoned guesthouse. Activities include horseback riding, agrotourism and nature strolls. A few kilometers north of El Parador, there's a sizable colony of burrowing Magellanic penguins.

PUNTA NORTE

At the far end of the peninsula, solitary Punta Norte boasts an enormous mixed colony of sea lions and elephant seals. Its distance means it is rarely visited by tour groups. But the real thrill here is the orcas: from mid-February through mid-April these killer whales come to feast on the unsuspecting colonies of sea lions. The chances are you won't see a high-tide attack, but watching their dorsal fins carving through the water is enough to raise goose bumps.

There's a small but good **museum** that focuses on marine mammals, and has details on the Tehuelche and the area's sealing history.

THE LITTLE PRINCE

From an apartment in Manhattan in 1941, a French pilot and writer, in exile from the battlefields of Europe, scripted what would become one of the most-read children's fables, *The Little Prince*. Antoine St-Exupéry, then 40 years old, had spent the previous 20 years flying in the Sahara, the Pyrenees, Egypt and Patagonia – where he was director of Aeropostal Argentina from 1929 to 1931. Intertwined in the lines of *The Little Prince* and Asteroid B612 are images of Patagonia ingrained from flights over the windy, barren landscape.

Legend has it that the shape of Isla de los Pájaros, off the coast of Península Valdés, inspired the elephant-eating boa constrictor (or hat, as you may see it), while the perfectly conical volcanoes on the asteroid are modeled on those seen en route to Punta Arenas, Chile. The author's illustrations show the little prince on mountain peaks resembling the Fitz Roy Range (one such peak now bears his name). And, possibly, meeting two young daughters of a French immigrant after an emergency landing in Concordia, near Buenos Aires, helped mold the character of the prince.

St-Exupéry never witnessed the influence his young character would enjoy. In 1944, just after the first publication of *The Little Prince*, he disappeared during a flight to join French forces-in-exile stationed in Algiers. His Patagonia years also figure in two critically acclaimed novels, *Night Flight* and *Wind, Sand and Stars*, both worthwhile reads on long Patagonia trips.

Trelew

☎0290 / POP 100,000

Though steeped in Welsh heritage, Trelew isn't a postcard city. In fact, this uneventful midsized hub may be convenient to many attractions, but it's home to few. The region's commercial center, it's a convenient base for visiting the Welsh villages of Gaiman and Dolavon. Also worthwhile is the top-notch dinosaur museum.

Founded in 1886 as a railway junction, Trelew (tre-*ley*-ooh) owes its easily mispronounced name to the Welsh contraction of *tre* (town) and *lew* (after Lewis Jones, who promoted railway expansion). During the following 30 years, the railway reached Gaiman, the Welsh built their Salón San David (a replica of St David's Cathedral, Pembrokeshire), and Spanish and Italian immigrants settled in the area. In 1956 the federal government promoted Patagonian industrial development and Trelew's population skyrocketed.

Trelew is situated 65km south of Puerto Madryn via RN 3.

The center surrounds Plaza Independencia, with most services located on Calles 25 de Mayo and San Martín, and along recently renovated Av Fontana. East–west streets change names on either side of Av Fontana.

Sights

The tourist office sometimes has an informative walking-tour brochure, in Spanish and English, describing most of the city's historic buildings.

TOP CHOICE Museo Paleontológico Egidio Feruglio MUSEUM

(☎442-0012; www.mef.org.ar; Av Fontana 140; adult/child AR$35/25; ⏲10am-6pm) Showcasing the most important fossil finds in Patagonia, this natural-history museum offers outstanding life-sized dinosaur exhibits and more than 1700 fossil remains of plant and marine life. Nature sounds and a video accent the informative plaques, and tours are available in a number of languages. The collection includes local dinosaurs, such as the tehuelchesaurus, patagosaurus and titanosaurus. With an international team, museum researchers helped discover a new and unusual species called *Brachytrachelopan mesai*, a short-necked sauropod. Feruglio was an Italian paleontologist who came to Argentina in 1925 as a petroleum geologist for YPF.

Kids aged eight to 12 can check out the 'Explorers in Pyjamas' program, which invites kids to sleep over and explore the museum by flashlight. The museum also sponsors interesting group tours to **Geoparque Paleontológico Bryn Gwyn**, in the badlands along the Río Chubut (25km

Trelew

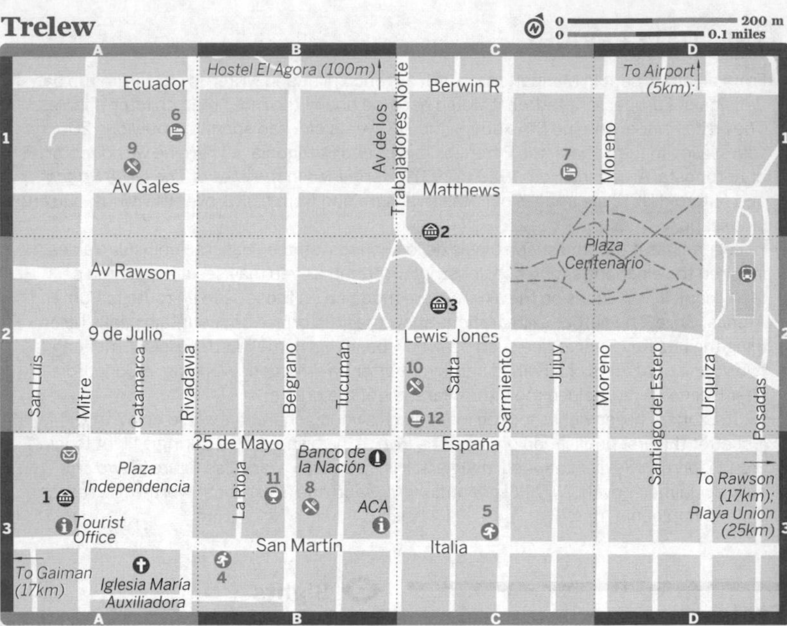

Trelew

Sights

1 Museo de Artes Visuales A3
2 Museo Paleontológico Egidio Feruglio C1
3 Museo Regional Pueblo de Luis C2

Activities, Courses & Tours

4 Alcamar Travel B3
5 Nievemar C3

Sleeping

6 Hotel Rivadavia A1
7 Patagonia Suites Apart C1

Eating

8 La Bodeguita B3
9 Majadero A1
10 Miguel Angel C2

Drinking

11 Boru Irish Pub & Restobar B3
12 Touring Club C2

from Trelew, or 8km south of Gaiman via RP 5). The three-hour guided visits are a walk through time, visiting exposed fossils dating as far back as the Tertiary, some 40 million years ago.

FREE **Museo de Artes Visuales** MUSEUM
(☎443-3774; Mitre 351; ⏰8am-8pm Mon-Fri, 2-8pm Sat & Sun) Adjoined to the tourist office, the small visual-arts museum features works on loan from the Museo Nacional de Bellas Artes in Buenos Aires, as well as polished relics from Welsh colonization.

Museo Regional Pueblo de Luis MUSEUM
(☎442-4062; cnr Av Fontana & Lewis Jones; admission AR$2; ⏰8am-1pm & 3-8pm Mon-Fri) In a former train station, displays historical photographs, clothing and period furnishings of Welsh settlers.

Tours

Several travel agencies run excursions to Área Natural Protegida Punta Tombo (AR$180, plus AR$35 admission), some passing by Puerto Rawson on the way back to see *toninas overas* (Commerson's dolphins) when conditions are agreeable. The actual time at Punta Tombo is only about 1½ hours. Full-day trips to Península Valdés are also on offer, but going to Puerto Madryn first is a better bet: there are more options, prices are similar and there's less driving time.

Local agencies worth checking out are Amex representative **Nievemar** (☎443-4114; www.nievemartours.com.ar, in Spanish; Italia 20), which accepts traveler's checks, and **Alcamar Travel** (☎442-1448; San Martín 146).

Festivals & Events

Gwyl y Glaniad FESTIVAL
On July 28 the landing of the first Welsh is celebrated by taking tea in one of the many chapels.

Eisteddfod de Chubut CULTURAL FESTIVAL
A Welsh literary and musical festival, held in late October. The tradition started in 1875.

Aniversario de la Ciudad FESTIVAL
October 20; commemorates the city's founding in 1886.

Sleeping

Trelew's accommodations are largely dated and geared toward the business traveler; in addition, spots fill up fast. Travelers can find more variety in nearby Puerto Madryn or Gaiman.

Hostel El Agora HOSTEL $
(☎442-6899; http://hostelagora.com.ar; Edwin Roberts 33; dm/s/d AR$60/75/150; wi-fi) A backpacker haven, this cute brick house is sparkling and ship-shape. Features include a tiny patio, book exchange and laundry. They also do guided bicycle tours. It's two blocks from Parque Centenario and four blocks from the bus terminal.

Patagonia Suites Apart APARTMENT $$
(☎442-1345,0280-453-7399;www.patagoniansuites.com; Matthews 186; studio/1-br/2-br AR$320/410/600; wi-fi) A foxy addition to town, these 13 modern apartments feature wood details, hairdryers and corduroy bedspreads. They also come with fully-equipped kitchens and cable TV. The complex faces Parque Centenario.

La Casona del Río B&B $$$
(☎443-8343; www.lacasonadelrio.com.ar; Chacra 105; s/d AR$464/528; @) Five km outside the city center, on the bank of the Chubut River, this English-style B&B is a thoroughly charming refuge. Guest rooms are smart and bright, other features include a library, tennis court, gazebo and rental bikes.

Hotel Rivadavia HOTEL $
(☎443-4472; www.cpatagonia.com/rivadavia, in Spanish; Rivadavia 55; s/d AR$145/190) Up on a hill, this small family-run hotel offers good value, though the rooms with gauzy curtains are somewhat faded. Breakfast costs extra.

Camping Patagonia CAMPGROUND $
(☎0280-15-440-6907, per person AR$20) Shady and spacious, this green campground has a small convenience store, electricity and hot showers, but limited public transport. It's 7km from town on RN 7, off the road to Rawson.

Eating

Majadero ARGENTINE $$$
(☎443-0548; Av Gales 250; mains AR$40-75; ⏲8pm-midnight Mon-Sat, noon-6pm Sun) Iron lamps and brickwork restore the romance to this 1914 flour mill – a must if you're in town. On weekends it's packed, with the main attraction, the wood-fired *parrilla,* grilling steaks and even vegetables to perfection.

Miguel Angel ITALIAN $$
(☎443-0403; Av Fontana 246; mains AR$30-75; ⏲closed Mon) This chic eatery, outfitted with sleek white booths, departs from the everyday with savory dishes such as gnocchi and wild mushrooms and pizza with bacon and basil on crisp, thin crust. The lunch menu (AR$45) proves satisfying.

WELSH LEGACY

The Welsh opened the door to settling Patagonia in 1865, though the newfound freedom cost them dearly. Few had farmed before and the arid steppe showed no resemblance to their verdant homeland. After nearly starving, they survived with the help of the Tehuelche, and eventually occupied the entire lower Chubut valley, founding the towns and teahouses of Rawson, Trelew, Puerto Madryn and Gaiman.

Today about 20% of Chubut's inhabitants have Welsh blood, but a revival of Welsh culture is dragging it back from the grave. According to Welsh historian Fernando Coronato, 'For the old principality of Wales, Patagonia meant its most daring venture.' This renewed bond means yearly British Council appointments of Welsh teachers and exchanges for Patagonian students. Curious Welsh tourists visit to time-travel in their own culture, thanks to Patagonia's longtime isolation.

La Bodeguita ARGENTINE $

(Belgrano 374; mains AR$25-38; ⏲Tue-Sun) A popular stop for meats, pasta and seafood, this restaurant boasts attentive service and a family atmosphere.

Drinking

TOP CHOICE Touring Club CAFE

(Av Fontana 240; snacks AR$12; ⏲6:30am-2am; @) Old lore exudes from the pores of this historic *confitería,* from the Butch Cassidy 'Wanted' poster to the embossed tile ceiling and antique bar back. Even the tuxedoed waitstaff appear to be plucked from another era. Service is weak and the sandwiches are only so-so, but the ambience is one of a kind.

Boru Irish Pub & Restobar PUB

(Belgrano 341) Hip and attractive, featuring a beautiful wood bar and a row of cozy red booths, Boru serves up icy beer and plates piled high with french fries.

Information

ATMs and *locutorios* with internet are plentiful downtown and around the plaza.

ACA (Automóvil Club Argentino; ☎435197; cnr Av Fontana & San Martín) Argentina's auto club; good source for provincial road maps.

Post office (cnr 25 de Mayo & Mitre)

Tourist office (☎442-6819; www.trelewpatagonia.gov.ar; Mitre 387; ⏲8am-8pm Mon-Fri, 9am-9pm Sat-Sun; wi-fi) Helpful and well stocked, with free wi-fi, city maps and some English-speaking staff.

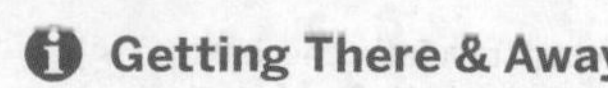

Getting There & Away

Air

Trelew's airport is 5km north of town off RN 3. Airport tax is AR$18.

Aerolíneas Argentinas (☎442-0210; 25 de Mayo 33) flies direct daily to Buenos Aires (AR$844) and several times a week to Esquel (AR$2110), Bariloche, Ushuaia (AR$2025) and El Calafate (AR$1633).

LADE (☎443-5740), at the bus terminal, flies to Comodoro Rivadavia (AR$343) on Fridays.

Bus

Trelew's full-service bus terminal is six blocks northeast of downtown.

For Gaiman (AR$5), **28 de Julio** (☎443-2429) has 18 services daily between 7am and 11pm (reduced weekend services), with most continuing to Dolavon (AR$10, 30 minutes). Buses to Rawson (AR$4, 15 minutes) leave every 15 minutes.

Mar y Valle (☎443-2429) and 28 de Julio run hourly buses to Puerto Madryn. Mar y Valle goes to Puerto Pirámides (AR$33, 2½ hours) daily at 8:15am, with additional service in summer. **El Ñandú** (☎442-7499) goes to Camarones (AR$66, four hours) at 8am on Monday, Wednesday and Friday.

Long-distance bus companies include **El Cóndor** (☎443-1675), **Que Bus** (☎442-2760), **Andesmar** (☎443-3535), **TAC** (☎443-1452), **TUS** (☎442-1343) and **Don Otto** (☎442-9496).

Of several departures daily for Buenos Aires, Don Otto has the most comfortable and most direct service. Only Don Otto goes to Mar del Plata, while TAC goes to La Plata. TAC and Andesmar service the most towns. For Comodoro Rivadavia there are a few daily departures with

BUSES FROM TRELEW

DESTINATION	COST (AR$)	DURATION (HR)
Bahía Blanca	220-240	12
Bariloche	210-242	13-16
Buenos Aires	375-415	18-21
Comodoro Rivadavia	82-102	5-6
Córdoba	364-416	19
Esquel	110-160	8-9
La Plata	331-415	19
Mar del Plata	288-328	17-21
Mendoza	476-572	24
Neuquén	215-258	10
Puerto Madryn	14	1
Río Gallegos	443-500	14-17
Viedma	170	8

TAC, Don Otto or Andesmar, all of which also continue to Río Gallegos.

Getting Around

From the airport, taxis charge AR$35 to downtown, AR$85 to Gaiman and AR$300 to Puerto Madryn. Car-rental agencies at the airport include **Hertz** (☎447-5247) and **Rent a Car Patagonia** (☎442-0898).

Around Trelew

Rawson, 17km east of Trelew, is Chubut's provincial capital, but nearby **Playa Unión**, the region's principal playground, has the capital attraction: *toninas overas* (Commerson's dolphins; see p392). Playa Unión is a long stretch of white-sand beach with blocks of summer homes. Dolphin tours depart **Puerto Rawson** from April to December. For reservations, contact **Toninas Adventure** (☎449-8372; toninasadventure@msn.com).

To reach the beach, get off at Rawson's plaza or bus terminal and hop on a green 'Bahía' bus, which heads to Puerto Rawson before turning around.

Gaiman

☎0280 / POP 10,000

Cream pie, dainty tea cakes, *torta negra* (a rich, dense fruit cake) and a hot pot of black tea – most visitors take an oral dose of culture when visiting this quintessential Welsh river-valley village. Locals proudly recount the day in 1995 when the late Diana, Princess of Wales, visited Gaiman to take tea (her teacup is still on display at Ty Te Caerdydd). Today, about one-third of the residents claim Welsh ancestry and teahouses persist in their afternoon tradition, even though their overselling sometimes rubs the charm a little thin.

The town's name, meaning Stony Point or Arrow Point, originated from the Tehuelche who once wintered in this valley. After the Welsh constructed their first house in 1874, the two groups peacefully coexisted for a time. Later immigrant groups of *criollos,* Germans and Anglos joined. Gaiman's homey digs provide great value for lodgers, but the town offers little in the way of diversion beyond quiet strolls past stone houses with rose gardens after a filling teahouse visit.

Tiny Gaiman is 17km west of Trelew via RN 25. Av Eugenio Tello is the main road, connecting the main town entrance to leafy Plaza Roca. Most of the teahouses and historic sites are within four blocks of the plaza. Across the river are fast-growing residential and industrial areas.

Sights

Gaiman is ideal for an informal walking tour, past homes with ivy trellises and drooping, oversized roses. Architecturally distinctive churches and chapels dot the town. **Primera Casa** (cnr Av Eugenio Tello & Evans; admission AR$5) is the first house, built in 1874 by David Roberts. Dating from 1906, the **Colegio Camwy** (cnr MD Jones & Rivadavia) is considered the first secondary school in Patagonia.

The old train station houses the **Museo Histórico Regional Gales** (cnr Sarmiento & 28 de Julio; admission AR$3; ⏲3-6pm Tue-Sun), a fine small museum holding the belongings and photographs of town pioneers.

The **Museo Antropológico** (cnr Bouchard & Jones; admission AR$5) offers humble homage to the indigenous cultures and history. Ask the tourist office for access. Nearby is the 300m **Túnel del Ferrocarril**, a brick tunnel through which the first trains to Dolavon passed in 1914.

Sleeping

TOP CHOICE **Yr Hen Ffordd** B&B $
(☎449-1394; www.yrhenffordd.com.ar; Jones 342; d AR$220; 📶) This charming B&B is run by a young couple who give you a set of keys to the front door so you can come and go as you please. Rooms are simple but cozy, with cable TV and private bathrooms with great showers. In the morning, work up an appetite for the divine homemade scones.

Hostería Gwesty Tywi B&B $
(☎449-1292; www.hosteria-gwestytywi.com.ar; Chacra 202; d AR$200; @) Diego and Brenda run this wonderful Welsh B&B with large gardens and snug, frilly rooms. Breakfast includes a selection of jams, cold meats and bread. They are glad to help with travel planning and occasionally fire up the barbecue, to the delight of guests. It's a bit far from the center.

Dyffryn Gwyrdd GUESTHOUSE $
(☎449-1777; patagongales@yahoo.com.ar; Av Eugenio Tello 103; s/d/tr AR$120/170/200; 📶) Open when the rest are not, this canary-yellow place features bright and simple carpeted

IN CHATWIN'S PATAGONIA

Over 30 years on, Bruce Chatwin's *In Patagonia*, a cubist rendering of this southern extreme, has become a pilgrim's guide to it. Who knew that his musings on errant wanderings would transform them into tourist attractions: hiking from Estancia Harberton to Viamonte (guided with snack breaks); taking tea in Gaiman (hundreds do it weekly); even the sacred milodon cave (marred with a life-sized replica of this prehistoric Chewbacca).

Not to worry. It's a big place. Patagonia's willful landscape and exiled eccentrics will long remain, and anyone with a good pair of boots and a willingness to break them in (as Chatwin did) can still find plenty to discover.

rooms with fans and throw pillows. The bathrooms are dated but spotless and there's a quiet bar and TV area.

Camping Bomberos Voluntarios CAMPGROUND $
(☎449-1117; cnr Av Yrigoyen & Moreno; adult/child AR$20/5) An agreeable campground with hot-water showers and fire pits

Eating

Tarten afal, tarten gwstard, cacen ffrwythau, spwnj jam and *bara brith* and a bottomless pot of tea – hungry yet? Afternoon tea is taken as a sacrament in Gaiman – though busloads of tourists get dump-trucked in teahouses without warning. The best bet is to look for places without buses in front, or wait for their departure. Tea services usually run from 2pm to 7pm.

Ty Nain TEAHOUSE $$$
(Yrigoyen 283; tea AR$60-80; ⏲closed May) It's been a decade since Ty Nain was written up in the *Washington Post* and *Los Angeles Times*, but the endorsements are still plastered on the front lawn. Inside an ivy-clad 1890 home, Ty Nain persists as one of the country's most traditional teahouses. The adjoining museum has some interesting Welsh artifacts.

Gwalia Lan ARGENTINE $$
(cnr Av Eugenio Tello & Jones; mains AR$50; ⏲12:30-3pm, 7:30pm-midnight Tue-Sat, 12:30-3pm Sun) Considered Gaiman's best restaurant, it serves homemade pasta and well-seasoned meat dishes that are consistently good. Service is attentive.

Ty Cymraeg TEAHOUSE $$$
(www.gaimantea.com; Matthews 74; tea AR$70) Teatime in this riverside house includes sumptuous pies and jams. The youngest member of the Welsh family that owns the place, an energetic twentysomething named Miguel, is happy to explain Welsh traditions from poetry competitions to the significance of carved wooden 'love spoons' – his knowledge adds significantly to the experience.

Plas y Coed TEAHOUSE $$
(www.plasycoed.com.ar; Jones 123; tea AR$65) Run by the original owner's great-granddaughter in a gorgeous brick mansion, Plas y Coed pleases the palette and senses, with friendly service, fresh cakes and serious crochet cozies for that steaming-hot pot. Rooms are also available for rent (doubles AR$280.)

Los Alamos CAFE $$
(Belgrano 211; mains AR$42-60; ⏲noon-3pm, 8pm-midnight) A modern brick cafe with riverstone bar and friendly waitstaff. Dishes like chicken stir-fry, salads and pastas make a refreshing departure from the ubiquitous cakes.

Information

There's one ATM on the plaza at Banco del Chubut, but it does not always work, so bring cash. *Locutorios* and internet can be found along the main drag.

Post office (cnr Evans & Yrigoyen) Just north of the river bridge.

Tourist office (Informes Turísticos; ☎449-1571; www.gaiman.gov.ar, in Spanish; Belgrano 574; ⏲9am-8pm Mon-Sat, 11am-8pm Sun) Ask for a map and guided tours of historic houses.

Getting There & Away

During the week, 28 de Julio buses depart for Trelew (AR$5) frequently from Plaza Roca, from 7am to 11pm (fewer services on weekends). Most buses to Dolavon (AR$5) use the highway, but some take the much longer gravel 'valley' route. *Remise* (taxi) services are cheaper in Gaiman than in Trelew; the trip to Trelew costs around AR$110 for up to four passengers.

Around Gaiman

To experience an authentic historic Welsh agricultural town, head to the distinctly nontouristy **Dolavon** (population 2500; www.dolavon.com.ar), 19km west of Gaiman via paved RN 25. Welsh for 'river meadow,' the town offers pastoral appeal, with wooden waterwheels lining the irrigation canal, framed by rows of swaying poplars. The historic center is full of brick buildings, including the 1880 **Molino Harinero** (☎0280-449-2290; romanogi@infovia.com.ar; Maipú 61) with still-functioning flour mill machinery. It also has a cafe-restaurant, **La Molienda** (meals AR$45), serving handmade breads and pasta with local wines and cheeses. Call owner Romano Giallatini for opening hours.

Área Natural Protegida Punta Tombo

Continental South America's largest penguin nesting ground, **Punta Tombo** (admission AR$35; ⌚9am-8pm Aug-Apr) has a colony of more than half a million Magellanic penguins and attracts many other birds, most notably king and rock cormorants, giant petrels, kelp gulls, flightless steamer ducks and black oystercatchers. A new management plan requires rangers to accompany visitors on rookery visits.

Trelew-based travel agencies run day-long tours but may cancel if bad weather makes the unpaved roads impassable. If possible, come in the early morning to beat the crowds. Most of the nesting areas in the 200-hectare reserve are fenced off: respect the limits and remember that penguins can inflict serious bites.

The new **Centro Tombo** (⌚8am-6pm) is an interpretive visitor's center. Guests and tours park here and take a shuttle to the rookery. Shuttle frequency depends on demand, but it's greater in the morning. There's a bar and *confitería* on-site, but it's best to bring a picnic lunch.

Punta Tombo is 110km south of Trelew and 180km south of Puerto Madryn via well-maintained gravel RP 1 and a short southeast lateral. Motorists can proceed south to Camarones via scenic but desolate Cabo Raso. If you can get a group together, it may be worth renting a car in Trelew or Puerto Madryn to come here.

Camarones

☎0297 / POP 1300

In the stiff competition for Patagonia's sleepiest coastal village, Camarones takes home the gold. Don't diss its languorous state: if you've ever needed to run away, this is one good option. Its empty beaches are conducive to strolling and townsfolk are masters of the art of shooting the breeze. It is also the closest hub to the lesser-known Cabo Dos Bahías nature reserve (p402), where you can visit 25,000 penguin couples and their fuzzy chicks.

Spanish explorer Don Simón de Alcazaba y Sotomayor anchored here in 1545, proclaiming it part of his attempted Provincia de Nueva León. When the wool industry took off, Camarones became the area's main port. The high quality of local wool didn't go unnoticed by justice of the peace Don Mario Tomás Perón, who operated the area's largest *estancia*, Porvenir, on which his son (and future president) Juanito would romp about. The port flourished, but after Comodoro Rivadavia finished its massive port, Camarones was all but deserted.

In 2009, the paving of RN 1 meant the start of direct bus services from Comodoro Rivadavia. To a moderate degree, tourism is increasing, so hurry to this coastal village now if you want to be able to say you knew Camarones way back when.

Festivals

Fiesta Nacional del Salmón FISHING

A weekend of deep-sea fishing competitions featuring a free Sunday seafood lunch and the crowning of Miss Salmoncito, celebrated in February.

Sleeping & Eating

TOP CHOICE **Camping Camarones** CAMPGROUND $

(☎0297-15148524; www.campingcamarones.com; San Martín; per person/vehicle AR$20/20; cabin per person AR$100) At the waterfront port, this peaceful campground is run by a friendly older couple. Sonia can cook up fresh shrimp, seafood and salmon for guests with advance notice. Hot showers and electricity are other perks.

Hotel Indalo Inn HOTEL $$

(☎496-3004; www.indaloinn.com.ar; cnr Sarmiento & Roca; d/cabin AR$270/370) Currently the only game in town, Indalo could just as well be called indolent – guests seem almost a nuisance to staff. Remodeled rooms are a bit of a squeeze, but feature good bedding and strong showers. The cabins run by the inn are more expensive but offer sea views.

Alma Patagonica CAFE $$

(cnr Sarmiento & Roca; pizzas AR$50; 11am-midnight) A gem, this restored century-old frontier bar is run by enthusiastic hipsters with an eye on preserving local tradition. Homemade fish empanadas are excellent, washed back with a massive cold beer. Plans are in the works to add lodgings.

Information

Tourist office (☎496-3040; Tomas Espora s/n; ⏲8am-9pm Dec-May) Very helpful, with maps, good tips on scenic outings and lodging information. Located oceanfront.

Patagonia Austral Expediciones (☎0297-156258180; patagoniaustralexpeditions@hotmail.com) Contact for fishing excursions and outings to see dolphins and nearby islands.

Getting There & Away

At a gas-station junction 180km south of Trelew, RP 30 splits off from RN 3 and heads 72km east to Camarones. Transportes Ñandú buses go to Trelew (AR$66, four hours) at 4pm on Monday, Wednesday and Friday. Transportes ETAP goes to Comodoro Rivadavia (AR$50, 3½ hours) on Tuesday and Thursday at 1pm.

Local taxis make the 30-minute ride to Cabo Dos Bahías.

Cabo Dos Bahías

Thirty rough kilometers southeast of Camarones, the isolated **Cabo Dos Bahías** (admission AR$20; ⏲year-round) rookery attracts far fewer visitors than Punta Tombo, making it an excellent alternative. You'll be rewarded with orcas, a huge colony of nesting penguins in spring and summer, whales in winter and a large concentration of guanacos and rheas. Sea birds, sea lions, foxes and fur seals are year-round residents.

You can pitch a tent for free at Cabo Dos Bahías Club Naútico or on any of the beaches en route from Camarones.

Comodoro Rivadavia

☎0297 / POP 180,000

Surrounded by dry hills of drilling rigs, oil tanks and wind-energy farms, tourism in the dusty port of Comodoro (as it's commonly known) usually means little more than a bus transfer. What this modern, hardworking city does provide is a gateway to nearby attractions with decent services. It sits at the eastern end of the Corredor Bioceánico highway that leads to Coyhaique, Chile.

Founded in 1901, Comodoro was once a transport hub linking ranches in nearby Sarmiento. In 1907 the town struck it rich when workers drilling for water struck oil instead. With the country's first major gusher, Comodoro became a state pet, gaining a large port, airport and paved roads. Today it is a powerhouse in the now-privatized oil industry. Although the recession hit hard in 2001, this boomtown rebounded with a flashy casino, elegant shops and hot rods on the streets. Now it holds the dubious status of the largest consumer of plasma TVs in Argentina.

Commerce centers on principal streets Av San Martín and Av Rivadavia. Between Mitre and Belgrano Av, San Martín has upscale boutiques and shops unknown to most of Patagonia.

Sights

Museo Nacional del Petróleo MUSEUM
(☎455-9558; admission AR$20; ⏲9am-5pm Tue-Fri, 3-6pm Sat) Intransigent petroleum fans should head to Museo Nacional del Petróleo for an insider look at the social and historical aspects of petroleum development. Don't expect balanced treatment of oil issues – the museum was built by the former state oil agency YPF (it is now managed by the Universidad Nacional de Patagonia). While its historical photos are interesting, the detailed models of tankers, refineries and the entire zone of exploitation are best left to the die hard. Guided tours are available.

The museum is in the suburb of General Mosconi, 3km north of downtown. Take a *remise* from downtown (AR$40) or bus 7 'Laprida' or 8 'Palazzo' (AR$1.75, 10 minutes); get off at La Anónima supermarket.

Museo Regional Patagónico MUSEUM
(☎477-7101; cnr Av Rivadavia & Chacabuco; admission free; ⏲9am-6pm Mon-Fri, 11am-6pm Sat & Sun) Decaying natural-history specimens overshadow some small yet entertaining archaeological and historical items, including well-crafted pottery, spear points and materials on early South African Boer immigrants.

Tours

Several agencies arrange trips to Bosque Petrificado Sarmiento (p408) and Cueva de las Manos (p427).

Ruta 40 (☎446-5337; www.ruta-40.com) organizes well-informed and personalized 4WD trips on RN 40 and in other parts of Patagonia. It's run by Mónica Jung and Pedro Mangini, a dynamic duo who speak English, German and Italian.

The urban train tour **Circuito Ferroportuario** (admission free) takes visitors on a circuit from the tourist office to visit containers, warehouses, historical installations and workshops on the port.

Sleeping

Catering mainly to business travelers and long-term laborers, lodging here fits two categories: the ritzy and the run-down. Brisk business means lodgings are overpriced and often full – book ahead.

Lucania Palazzo Hotel HOTEL **$$$**
(☎449-9300; www.lucania-palazzo.com, in Spanish; Moreno 676; s/d/ste AR$800/885/1045; @📶) Comodoro's answer to the Trump Towers, the sparkling Palazzo offers ocean views from every room and tasteful modern decor, although ventilation could be better. While overpriced, there's a decent restaurant and the eager staff offers helpful recommendations.

Hotel Victoria HOTEL **$$**
(☎446-0725; Belgrano 585; s/d/tr AR$290/360/420) If the aroma of baking pastries is any indication, the breakfast (AR$20) is worth the extra cost here, the friendliest hotel on the block. Soothing, good-sized rooms have firm twin beds, desks and cable TV.

Hospedaje Belgrano HOTEL **$$**
(☎447-8439; Belgrano 546; s/d without bathroom AR$90/170) This basic guesthouse may be the only budget option left in the city center: don't mind the stale smell of cigarettes in the hallways. Rooms are clean enough, but the space-saving shared bathrooms, with showerheads suspended over the toilets, leave something to be desired.

WORTH A TRIP

BAHÍA BUSTAMANTE

A number of coastal reserves feature Patagonia's diverse marine life, but few illuminate the exuberance of this ecosystem like this historic 80-hectare **estancia** (in Buenos Aires ☎11-47780125; 0297-4801000; www.bahiabustamante.com; s/d incl full board & activities AR$1519/1815), located between Trelew and Comodoro Rivadavia. Romantics will love the sprawling steppe, rolling grass dunes and pebble beaches that beg you to bask in the slow rhythms of life on this deserted coast. Excursions are thoughtfully guided by bilingual naturalists, and include sea kayaking, trekking the onsite 65-million year-old petrified forest and boat trips to see Magellanic penguins, sea lions and marine birds.

Another quirky footnote in Patagonian history, Bahía Bustamante was founded by an entrepreneurial Andalucian immigrant who used the abundant algae in the bay to manufacture agar agar, a natural food thickener. At one point hundreds of workers lived on the *estancia*, which became a kind of Wild West, complete with a police station and jail cell. In pre-settlement times, Tehuelches traveled the area, leaving behind their small tools and middens.

These days, the much-reduced algae harvests also include comestible seaweed which is mostly exported to Japan. An *estancia* tour explains the sheep farming operation, which is in the midst of transitioning to better ecological practices. Grazing rotation promotes soil and native plant recovery and recently-introduced Merino hybrids are better adapted to the ecosystem.

The *estancia* has the sleepy feel of a ghost village coming back to life. Its heart is the former general store, now converted to a rustic-chic living room and dining area where you might dine on local lamb or seaweed crepes with the grandsons of the founder, who now run the *estancia*. Lodgings are in comfortable seafront cabins with big red loungers recycled from shipping palettes. For a more economical approach, cabins facing the steppe (triples AR$507) offer an optional salad box with provisions from the onsite greenhouse, takeout from the restaurant, and a la carte excursions (per person AR$130). Look for a spa in the works.

Once you've come all this way, it's optimal to stay at least three days. The time to see fauna is between mid-September and early March, with January and February ideal to go swimming. Bird watching is best during November hatching but it's also cool to watch sea lions nurse new pups in January. Most visitors fly into Comodoro, but if you have a car, it's worthwhile to take the scenic coastal route from nearby Camarones.

Camping Municipal CAMPGROUND $
(☎445-2918; Rada Tilly; www.radatilly.com.ar/turismo-camping.html, in Spanish; per person AR$15) At the windy beach resort of Rada Tilly, situated 15km south of Comodoro, this campground has sites that contain handy windbreaking shrubs. The wide beach is one of Patagonia's longest and there's a sea-lion colony near the south end below Punta del Marqués.

Eating

The oil boom has bankrolled a taste for fine dining. Look for the free *Sabores del Sur* restaurant directory in hotels.

La Tradición PARILLA $$
(☎446-5800; Mitre 675; mains AR$38-80; ⏲closed Sun) A favorite of townsfolk, this elegant *parrilla* grills excellent beef and whole roast lamb in a setting of white linens and oil paintings (literally, since their subjects are oil rigs!).

Puerto Mitre PIZZERÍA $
(☎446-1201; 25 de Mayo & Ameghino; mains AR$30-55) The place for pizza and classic Argentine empanadas, staple traveler fare.

Chocolates ICE CREAM $
(Av San Martín 231; cones AR$8; 👪) Ice-cream junkies will appreciate this parlor's selection of velvety chocolate and rich *dulce de leche* flavors. If you're traveling with children, bring them here to ride the miniature carousel.

Drinking & Entertainment

Molly Malone CAFE
(☎447-8333; cnr 9 de Julio & Av San Martín 292; mains AR$25-45) Run by the Golden Oldies rugby club, this funky little resto-pub is a pleasant stop for breakfast, set lunch or an evening Quilmes. The food's just average but the atmosphere is fun and inviting.

La Nueva Cabaña PUB
(9 de Julio 821; ⏲8pm-6am Tue-Thu, 10pm-6am Fri & Sat) This rustic pub and dance spot attracts a young crowd for *musica electronica*, rock, folk and pop.

Cine Teatro Español CINEMA
(☎447-7700; www.cinecr.com.ar, in Spanish; Av San Martín 668; admission AR$15) A stately, old-fashioned cinema that offers a wide selection of Hollywood flicks.

Information

Locutorios abound around downtown.

ACA (Automóvil Club Argentino; ☎446-0876; cnr Dorrego & Alvear) Maps and road info.

Banco de la Nación (cnr Av San Martín & Güemes) Most of Comodoro's banks and ATMs, including this one, are along Av San Martín or Av Rivadavia.

Centro de Internet Comodoro (Rivadavia 245) Open till late.

Hospital Regional (☎444-2287; Av Hipólito Yrigoyen 950)

Post office (cnr Av San Martín & Moreno)

Thaler Cambio (Mitre 943) Changes traveler's checks.

Tourist office (☎447-4111; www.comodoro.gov.ar/turismo, in Spanish; Av Rivadavia 430; ⏲8am-3pm Mon-Fri) Friendly, well stocked and well organized. A desk at the bus terminal is, at least in theory, open from 8am to 9pm.

Getting There & Away

The Corredor Bioceánico – RN 26, RP 20 and RP 55 – is a straight highway link to Coyhaique, Chile, and its Pacific port, Puerto Chacabuco. Developers are promoting this commercial transport route as an alternative to the Panama Canal, since the pass is open year-round and it is the continent's shortest distance between ports on both oceans. Paved RN 26, RP 20 and RN 40 lead to Esquel and Bariloche.

Air

Aeropuerto General Mosconi (CRD; ☎454-8190) is 9km north of town.

Aerolíneas Argentinas (☎444-0050; Av Rivadavia 156) flies a couple of times daily to Buenos Aires (AR$857).

Comodoro is the hub for **LADE** (☎447-0585; Av Rivadavia 360), which wings it at least once a week to El Calafate (AR$426), Río Gallegos (AR$454), Trelew (AR$361), Ushuaia (AR$678) and Buenos Aires (AR$724) and points in between. Schedules and routes change as often as the winds. A taxi to the airport costs AR$50 from the center.

Bus

The chaotic **bus terminal** (Pellegrini 730) receives all buses plying RN 3. Stop at the helpful tourist desk to enquire about maps and travel assistance.

Most bus schedules are divided into northbound and southbound departures. **Andesmar** (☎446-8894) departs five times daily (between 1:15am and 3pm) for points north including Trelew, Rawson and Puerto Madryn.

TAC (☎444-3376) follows the same route and continues to Buenos Aires. **Etap** (☎447-4841)

BUSES FROM COMODORO RIVADAVIA

DESTINATION	COST (AR$)	DURATION (HR)
Bariloche	270	12
Buenos Aires	590-687	24
Coyhaique, Chile	180	11
Esquel	180-200	10
El Calafate	378	14
Los Antiguos	165	5
Puerto Deseado	125	4
Puerto Madryn	129-147	6
Río Gallegos	149-275	10-11
Río Mayo	65	3.5
Sarmiento	40	2
Trelew	105-125	5

runs to Esquel and Río Mayo daily, to Sarmiento four times daily and to Coyhaique, Chile at 8am on Wednesdays and Saturdays.

For Los Antiguos and connections to Chile Chico, via the town of Perito Moreno, **Empresa Robledo** (☎446-8187) has twice-daily services. **Taqsa** (☎447-0564) goes to Bariloche and El Calafate in the evening.

Schedules are in constant flux; upon arrival at the bus station, ask at each bus line's desk for information on departure times.

Getting Around

Bus 8 'Directo Palazzo' (AR$1.75) goes directly to the airport from outside the downtown bus terminal.

Expreso Rada Tilly links Comodoro's bus terminal to the nearby beach resort (AR$3) every 20 minutes on weekdays and every 30 minutes on weekends.

Rental cars are available from **Avis** (☎454-9471; at airport) and **Localiza** (☎446-3526; Av Rivadavia 535). **Dubrovnik** (☎444-1844; www.rentacardubrovnik.com; Moreno 941) rents 4WD vehicles.

Puerto Deseado

☎0297 / POP 13,300

Some 125km southeast of the RN 3 junction, RN 281 weaves through valleys of rippling pink rock, past guanacos in tufted grassland, to end at the serene and attractive deep-sea-fishing town of Puerto Deseado. While the town is ripe for revitalization, it is also apparent that change takes a glacial pace here: witness the vintage trucks rusting on the streets like beached cetaceans. But the draw of the historic center, plus the submerged estuary of Ría Deseado (p407), brimming with seabirds and marine wildlife, make Puerto Deseado a worthy detour.

In 1520 the estuary provided shelter to Hernando de Magallanes after a crippling storm waylaid his fleet; he dubbed the area 'Río de los Trabajos' (River of Labors).

In 1586 English privateer Cavendish explored the estuary and named it after his ship *Desire,* its name today. The port attracted fleets from around the world for whaling and seal hunting, compelling the Spanish crown to send a squadron of colonists under the command of Antonio de Viedma. After a harsh winter, more than 30 of them died of scurvy. Those who survived moved inland to form the short-lived colony of Floridablanca. In 1834 Darwin surveyed the estuary, as did Perito Moreno in 1876.

Puerto Deseado is two hours southeast of the RN 3 junction at Fitz Roy via dead-end RN 281. The center of activity is the axis formed by main streets San Martín and Almirante Brown.

Sights & Activities

Estación del Ferrocarril Patagónico HISTORIC SITE
(admission by donation; ⏲4-7pm Mon-Sat) Train fans can check out the imposing English-designed railway station off Av Oneto, built by Yugoslav stonecutters in 1908. Puerto Deseado was once the coastal terminus for a cargo and passenger route that hauled wool and

lead from Chilean mines from Pico Truncado and Las Heras, located 280km northwest.

Vagón Histórico LANDMARK
(cnr San Martín & Almirante Brown) In the center of town, this restored 1898 wagon is famous as the car from which rebel leader Facón Grande prepared the 'Patagonia Rebellion'. In 1979 the car was almost sold for scrap, but disgruntled townspeople blocked the roads to stop the sale. A few blocks west is the attractive **Sociedad Española** (San Martín 1176), c 1915.

FREE **Museo Regional Mario Brozoski** MUSEUM
(☎487-1358; cnr Colón & Belgrano; ⏲10am-5pm Mon-Fri, 3-7pm Sat) Displays relics of the English corvette *Swift,* sunk off the coast of Deseado in 1776. Divers continue to recover artifacts from this wreck, which was discovered in 1982.

Club Naútico WATER SPORTS
(☎0297-15-419-0468) Paddling and windsurfing can be enjoyed in summer. On the waterfront, rents boards and kayaks (summer only). Depending on current conditions, sport fishing can be an option; inquire at the pier.

City Tour WALKING TOUR
A self-guided tour is a good start to if you want to catch the vibes of Deseado. Pick up a *Guía Historica* map (in Spanish) from either tourist office.

Tours

Darwin Expediciones BOAT TOUR
(☎0297-15-624-7554; www.darwin-expeditions.com; Av España 2601) Offers sea-kayaking trips, wildlife observation, and multiday nature and archaeology tours with knowledgeable guides. Its best seller is the eco-safari tour of Reserva Natural Ría Deseado (AR$211).

Los Vikingos BOAT TOUR
(☎487-0020, 0297-15-624-5141/4283; www.losvikingos.com.ar; Estrada 1275) Trips on land and sea. Tours, some led by marine biologists, include Reserva Natural Ría Deseado and Monumento Natural Bosques Petrificados.

Sleeping

Ask at the tourist office about (relatively) nearby *estancias*.

Hotel Los Acantilados HOTEL $$
(☎487-2167; http://hotelosacantilados.com.ar, in Spanish; cnr Pueyrredón & Av España; s/d standard AR$240/276, s/d superior AR$408/504; @) More inspiring from outside than in, these clifftop digs do boast an extensive lounge with fireplace: the perfect chill spot. Superior rooms and the dining room look out on the waterfront, while standard rooms are plain with dated bathrooms.

Cabañas Las Nubes CABIN $$
(☎0297-15-403-2677; www.cabanaslasnubes.com.ar; Ameghino 1351; d/q cabins AR$380/510; wi-fi) The nicest digs in town are these deluxe two- and three-story hilltop cabins with fully equipped kitchens and some ocean views. Unfortunately, service lags.

Residencial Los Olmos HOTEL $
(☎487-0077; Gregores 849; d AR$220) A solid budget option kept spotless by a vigilant matron, this brick house has 19 small rooms with TV, ample heat and private bathrooms.

Camping Cañadón Giménez CAMPGROUND $
(☎0297-15-466-3815; RN 281; per tent AR$30, 4-person cabins AR$150; ⏲year-round) Four kilometers northwest of town, but only 50m from the Ría Deseado, this campground is sheltered by forest and high rocky walls. Bare-bones cabins sleep four; bring your own linens. Showers, hot water and simple provisions are available.

Eating

Puerto Deseado has chicken rotisseries all over town, good for a quick bite.

Puerto Cristal SEAFOOD $$
(Av España 1698; mains AR$42-70; ⏲noon-3pm & 8pm-midnight, closed Wed) Bridezilla décor aside, this popular seafood haunt satisfies with sturdy portions of grilled fish, fried calamari and an extensive wine selection.

La Cueva Pizza con Historia PIZZERIA $
(Ex-Estacion Ferrocarril; pizzas AR$32-50; ⏲4-7pm & 9pm-midnight, closed Fri) The ambiance couldn't be stranger, amidst relics from the railroad and a defunct doctor's office (those instruments!) in this converted train-station bar, where locals come for pitchers of frothy beer and gooey pizzas.

Puerto Darwin PUB $$
(www.darwin-expeditions.com; Av España 2581; mains AR$60; ⏲9am-2am; wi-fi) Featuring sandwiches, *picudas* and fish, this cafe run by Darwin Expediciones is easygoing and has views of the port. It's a hike from downtown and street numbers aren't labeled: keep walking along the water until you reach the other side of a fenced-in industrial area.

Drinking & Entertainment

Late-night spots include swanky disco **Jackaroe Boliche** (Mariano Moreno 663), housed in an unfortunate building.

Information

Banks, ATMs, *locutorios* and internet are all found along San Martín.

Banco de la Patagonia (San Martín & Almirante Brown)

CIS Tour (☎487-2864; www.cistours.com.ar; San Martin 916) Handles local tours and flight reservations.

Dirección Municipal de Turismo (☎487-0220; http://puertodeseado.tur.ar, in Spanish; San Martín 1525; ⏲9am-8pm daily) Helpful with maps; there's another English-speaking desk at the bus terminal, but its hours are limited.

Hospital Distrital (☎487-0200; España 991)

Post office (San Martín 1075)

Getting There & Around

The **bus terminal** (Sargento Cabral 1302) is on the northeast side of town, nine long blocks and slightly uphill from San Martín and Av Oneto. **Taxis** (☎487-2288; 487-0645) are metered.

There are five daily departures to Comodoro Rivadavia (AR$113, four hours) through **La Únion** (☎4870188) and **Sportman** (☎4870013), whose 7:15pm bus is timed to link with Sportman connections to El Calafate. Sportman also goes to Río Gallegos (AR$234) twice daily. Schedules change frequently; inquire at the bus terminal about departures.

If you're thinking of getting off at godforsaken Fitz Roy (where locals claim the only thing to see is the wind!) to make progress toward Comodoro or Río Gallegos, think again: buses arrive at a demonic hour and the only place to crash is the campground behind Multirubro La Illusion.

Reserva Natural Ría Deseado & Parque Interjurisdiccional Marino Isla Pingüino

Flanked by sandy cliffs, these aquamarine waters create sculpted seascapes you won't forget. Considered one of South America's most important marine preserves, Ría Deseado is the unique result of a river abandoning its bed, allowing the Atlantic to invade 40km inland and create a perfect shelter for marine life. The recent designation of Parque Interjurisdiccional Marino Isla Pingüino (a mouthful, but essentially a national park) will likely expand offerings for visitors.

The marine life is abundant. Several islands and other sites provide nesting habitats for seabirds, including Magellanic penguins, petrels, oystercatchers, herons, terns and five species of cormorant. Isla Chaffers is the main spot for the penguins, while Banco Cormorán offers protection to rock cormorants and the striking gray cormorant. Isla Pingüino has nesting rockhoppers (arriving mid-October) and elephant seals. Commerson's dolphins, sea lions, guanacos and ñandús (ostrichlike rheas) can also be seen while touring the estuary.

The best time to visit is from December to April. Darwin Expediciones (p406) runs circuits that take in viewing of Commerson's dolphins, Isla Chaffers, Banco Cormorán as well as a walk to a penguin colony. The main attraction of the all-day Isla Pingüinos excursion (AR$464) is the punked-out rockhopper penguins with spiky yellow and black head feathers, but the tour also includes wildlife watching, sailing and hiking. Tours have a four-person minimum. Los Vikingos (p406) makes similar excursions with bilingual guides and organizes overland trips.

Monumento Natural Bosques Petrificados

During Jurassic times, 150 million years ago, this area enjoyed a humid, temperate climate with flourishing forests, but intense volcanic activity buried them in ash. Erosion later exposed the mineralized *Proaraucaria* trees (ancestors of the modern *Araucaria*, unique to the southern hemisphere), up to 3m in diameter and 35m in length. Today, the 150-sq-km **Monumento Natural Bosques Petrificados** (Petrified Forests Natural Monument; admission free; ⏲9am-9pm year-round) has a small visitor center, English-language brochure and short interpretive trail, leading from park headquarters to the largest concentration of petrified trees. Until its legal protection in 1954, the area was plundered for some of its finest specimens; these days you're not allowed to take home souvenirs.

The park is 157km southwest of Caleta Olivia, accessed from the good gravel RP 49, leading 50km west from a turnoff at Km 2074 on RN 3. There's no public transport. Buses from Caleta Olivia leave visitors at the junction, but you may wait several hours for a lift into the park. Los Vikingos (p406) runs tours from Puerto Deseado.

WORTH A TRIP

BOSQUE PETRIFICADO SARMIENTO

Fallen giants scatter the pale sandstone landscape at this **petrified forest** (admission AR$20; ⏲dawn-dusk), 30km southeast of Sarmiento. The forest, brought here by strong river currents from the mountainous regions about 65 million years ago, has logs 100m in length and 1m wide. For travelers, this area is much more accessible than the Monumento Natural Bosques Petrificados (p407) further south.

Go with your own rental car, or ask at the tourist office in Sarmiento for *remise* rates for the 1½-hour roundtrip. Try to stay through sunset, when the striped bluffs of Cerro Abigarrado and the multihued hills turn brilliantly vivid.

Located 10km west of Sarmiento, working cherry farm **Chacra Labrador** (☎489-3329, 0297-15-404-3222; www.hosterialabrador.com.ar; d AR$390; P ᯤ) is a charming 1930s homestead offering bed and breakfast. Rooms are few but luxuriant, with big cozy beds, antique furniture, pots of tea and crackling fires.

The eager staff at Sarmiento's **tourist office** (☎0297-4898220; www.coloniasarmiento.gov.ar/turismo; cnr Infanteria 25 & Pietrobelli; ⏲8am-7pm Mon-Fri, 11am-5pm Sat & Sun) can provide *remise* rates and maps; the website has lodging information. Sarmiento is 148km west of Comodoro along RN 26 and RP 20. Etap buses run daily to Comodoro Rivadavia (AR$40, two hours). **Buses Etap** (☎0297-4893058) goes to Río Mayo (AR$40, 1½ hours) go at 9:30pm daily.

There's basic camping and provisions at **La Paloma**, 20km before park headquarters. Camping in the park is prohibited.

Puerto San Julián

☎02962 / POP 6143

The perfect desolate-yet-charismatic locale for an art film, this small town bakes in bright light and dust, in stark contrast to the startling blue of the bay. Considered the cradle of Patagonian history, the port of San Julián was first landed in 1520 by Magellan, whose encounter with local Tehuelches provided the region's mythical moniker (see the boxed text, p409). Viedma, Drake and Darwin followed. While its human history is proudly put forth, the landscape speaks of geologic revolutions, with its exposed, striated layers, rolling hills and golden cliffs.

Puerto San Julián's first non-native settlers came from the Falkland Islands (Islas Malvinas) with the late-19th-century wool boom. Scots followed with the San Julián Sheep Farming Company, which became the region's primary economic force for nearly a century. Recent growth has the city developing like never before with mining and seafood-processing industries, there's also a local university. For travelers, it is a relaxed and welcoming stop, as well as a great place to see Commerson's dolphins.

Sights & Activities

Banco Cormorán PENGUIN COLONY

The last census found 130,000 penguins inhabiting this stretch which you can visit by boat. The penguins stick around from September to April; when conditions permit, you'll be able to step off the boat and walk around an island where penguins swim, doze and guard their eggs. The tour also stops at Banco Justicia to see the cormorant rookeries and other seabirds. From December to March there's a good chance you'll see the Commerson's dolphin (p392), known as the world's smallest dolphin. Two-hour excursions on Bahía San Julián (AR$150 per person) are run by a marine biologist-led team at **Expediciones Pinocho** (☎454600; pinochoexcursiones.com.ar; cnr Mitre & 9 de Julio).

Circuito Costero DRIVING TOUR

Take a *remise* or your own poor, abused rental car on the incredibly scenic 30km drive following Bahía San Julián on a dirt road. A series of golden bluffs divide beautiful beaches with drastic tides. The area includes a sea-lion colony and the penitent attraction of Monte Cristo (with its stations of the cross).

Centro Artesenal Municipal ARTS & CRAFTS

(Moreno s/n; ⏲8am-8pm Mon-Fri) A cool cooperative selling handmade ceramics and woven goods.

Museo Nao Victoria MUSEUM
(admission AR$12; ⊙8am-9:30pm) Relive Magellan's landing at this museum and theme-park with life-sized figures cloaked in armor and shown celebrating Mass and battling mutiny, at the port on a reproduction.

Another option is trekking the coastline and checking out the abundant birdlife. If you have a friend (or make one), you can rent **tandem bicycles** (02962-15-532312) to explore. For more information on either activity, consult the tourist information kiosk.

Sleeping & Eating

Hostería Miramar GUESTHOUSE $$
(454626; hosteriamiramar@uvc.com.ar; San Martín 210; s/d AR$240/260; @) Natural light fills this cheerful waterfront option run by a local family. Eleven rooms, including a family-sized apartment, are super-clean with TVs, carpeted floors and somewhat dated mint-green decor.

Hotel Ocean HOTEL $
(452350; San Martín 959; s/d/tr AR$210/240/270; P) This remodeled brick building has attractive, well-scrubbed rooms with firm beds and a backdrop of tropical tones. Friendly staff are happy to assist travelers – when you're tired and hungry and the bus has dropped you off in town around midnight (as it probably will), they'll help you find an open restaurant.

Hotel Bahía HOTEL $$
(453144; www.hotelbahiasanjulian.com.ar, in Spanish; San Martín 1075; s/d/tr AR$250/280/450; @) This glass-front hotel feels decadent in a place like San Julián. Rooms are modern and beds firm, while TV and laundry service are perks. The cafe-bar is open to the public.

Costanera Hotel HOTEL $$
(452300; www.costanerahotel.com; 25 de Mayo 917; s/d AR$210/280; P) After major renovations, this waterfront mainstay feels new again. Rooms are standard but tidy, and the restaurant is good.

Camping Municipal CAMPGROUND $
(452806; Magallanes 650; per person AR$25) On the waterfront at the north end of Vélez Sarsfield, this full-service campground has hot showers, laundry and windbreaks.

Restaurante Costanera Hotel ARGENTINE $$
(25 de Mayo 917; mains AR$32-70; ⊙noon-3pm, 8-11pm) Slightly formal but a good value, this crisp hotel restaurant overcomes a bland setting with good wines and satisfying dishes like grandmother's potatoes, laced with cream and bacon.

La Rural PARRILLA $
(Ameghino 811; mains AR$22-30) Service is friendly but the hearty food mediocre. Still, the whole town seems to congregate at this unpretentious spot. Fare ranges from meat and potatoes to grilled fish and pasta.

Information

Banco Santa Cruz (cnr San Martín & Moreno) Has a Link ATM.

Dirección de Turismo (454396; www.sanjulian.gov.ar, in Spanish; Av San Martín 135; ⊙8am-2pm Mon-Fri)

Post office (cnr San Martín & Belgrano).

Getting There & Away

Bus

Most RN 3 buses visit San Julián's **bus terminal** (San Martín 1552) at insane hours. Before settling for a bus that will drop you off in the port at

BIG FEET, TALL TALES

Say 'Patagonia' and most think of fuzzy outdoor clothes, but the name that has come to symbolize the world's end still invites hot debate as to its origin.

One theory links the term 'Patagón' to a fictional monster in a best-selling 16th-century Spanish romance of the period, co-opted by Magellan's crew to describe the Tehuelche as they wintered in 1520 at Puerto San Julián. Crew member and Italian nobleman, Antonio Pigafetta, described one Tehuelche as 'so tall we reached only to his waist...He was dressed in the skins of animals skillfully sewn together...His feet were shod with the same kind of skins, which covered his feet in the manner of shoes...The captain-general [Magellan] called these people Patagoni.'

Another theory suggests that the name comes from the Spanish *pata*, meaning paw or foot. No evidence corroborates the claim that the Tehuelche boasted unusually big feet (it's possible that the skins they wore made their feet seem exceptionally large). But it's good fodder for the genre of travelers' tales, where first impressions loom larger than life.

4am, try **Don Otto** (☎452072), which delivers southbound travelers to San Julián at civilized evening hours. **Via Tac** (☎454049) goes to Puerto Madryn (AR$310, 12 hours). **Andesmar** (☎454403) goes to Comodoro Rivadavia (AR$132, six hours). **Taqsa** (☎454667) goes to Bariloche (AR$421) and Río Gallegos (AR$133, 4½ hours) at 4am, where travelers can make connections south.

There are slightly more expensive door-to-door service options, all operating Monday to Saturday in the early morning hours. **Cerro San Lorenzo** (☎452403; Berutti 970) serves Gobernador Gregores at 8am (AR$115, four hours).

Bus schedules may change, so always confirm departures ahead of time.

Parque Nacional Monte León

Inaugurated in 2004, this fine coastal national park protects over 600 sq km of striking headlands and archetypal Patagonian steppe, and 40km of dramatic coastline with bays, beaches and tidal flats. Once a hunting ground for nomads, and later frequented by the Tehuelche, this former *estancia* is home to abundant Magellanic penguins, sea lions, guanacos and pumas. Bring binoculars: the wildlife watching is prime.

Hiking along the coastline, with its unusual geographic features, is best when low tide exposes stretches of sandy and rocky beach. In October 2006 the park's signature landscape attraction, **La Olla** (a huge cavelike structure eroded by the ocean), collapsed from repeated tidal action. Accessible at low tide, **Isla Monte León** is a high offshore sea stack heavily mined for guano between 1933 and 1960. Now it has been recolonized by cormorants, Dominican gulls, skuas and other seabirds. Use caution and know the tide tables before setting out: the tidal range is great, exposed rocks are slippery and the water returns quickly.

Nature trails split off from the main road, leading to the coast. The **penguin trail** crosses the steppe, leading to an overlook of the rookery. It's forbidden to leave the trail, but seeing these 75,000 couples shouldn't be difficult. The roundtrip takes 1½ hours. Cars can reach the prominent cliff **Cabeza de León** (Lion's Head), where a 20-minute trail leads to the sea lion colony.

There is free camping on the beach, with access to picnic tables, but visitors must bring their own water. The other option is the charming **Hostería Monte León** (☎in Buenos Aires 011-4621-4784, in Ushuaia 02901-431851; www.monteleon-patagonia.com; s/d incl half-board AR$886/1646; ⌚Nov-Apr), a refurbished century-old *casco* (ranch house) of an 1895 *estancia*. The four-bedroom house retains the spartan style of the Patagonian farmhouse, with iron-rod beds, basic tasteful furnishings and an open kitchen with iron wood stove.

For boat excursions or fly-fishing for steelhead, consult with the **park office** (www.pnmonteleon.com.ar). The park entrance is 30km south of Comandante Luis Piedrabuena or 205km north of Río Gallegos, directly off RN 3. Watch for it carefully since signage is poor.

Río Gallegos

☎02966 / POP 110,000

Hardly a tourist destination, this coal shipping, oil-refining and wool-raising hub is a busy port with a few merits for travelers. Since the reign of the Kirchners, the capital city of their home province has been spruced up and spit polished. Outside of town, visitors can find some of the continent's best fly-fishing, traditional *estancias* and amazingly low tides (retreating 14m). Traveler services are good here but most zip through en route to El Calafate, Puerto Natales or Ushuaia.

Gallegos' economy revolves around nearby oilfields, with coal deposits shipped to ocean-going vessels at Punta Loyola. Home to a large military base, the city played an active role during the Falklands War. The main street, formerly Roca, was renamed Kirchner in honor of the former president.

Sights

FREE Museo Provincial Padre Jesús Molina MUSEUM

(☎423290; Av San Martín & Ramón y Cajal; ⌚9am-8pm Mon-Fri, 3-8pm Sat) Satiate your appetite for dinosaur dioramas and modern art at this museum offering exhibits on anthropology, paleontology, geology and fine arts. The Tehuelche ethnology exhibit includes fascinating photographs and local history.

FREE Museo de Arte Eduardo Minnicelli MUSEUM

(☎436323; Maipú 13; ⌚8:30am-7pm Tue-Fri, 2-6pm Sat & Sun) Shows rotating exhibits from larger museums and paintings by Santa Cruz artists, with a mission to educate through art. Also a good spot to get news on local cultural gatherings.

Río Gallegos

FREE **Museo Malvinas Argentinas** MUSEUM
(☎420128; cnr Pasteur & San Martín; ⊙8am-noon Mon & Thu, 1-5:30pm Tue & Fri, closed Wed) Perhaps a must-see for Brits, this museum gets inside the Argentine claim to the Islas Malvinas.

Plaza San Martín PLAZA
Pretty, with quiet benches in the shade of poplars and purple-blossom jacarandas.

FREE **Museo de los Pioneros** MUSEUM
(☎437763; cnr Elcano & Alberdi; ⊙10am-8pm) In a prefabricated 1890s metal-clad house shipped from England, this museum has good displays on early immigrant life.

Funda Cruz CULTURAL CENTER
(G Lista 60) Another attractive, imported, prefabricated wooden house. Once a customs office, it now hosts cultural activities as well as a *salón de té* (teahouse).

Río Gallegos

Sights

Sleeping

Eating

Tours

The large penguin rookery at Cabo Vírgenes, 140km southeast of Río Gallegos, can be visited from October to March. Excursions can be booked through **Al Sur Turismo** (436743; www.alsurturismo.com.ar; Errazuriz 194); an eight-hour trip costs AR$300 per person, with a minimum of three travelers (plus AR$15 park admission). Prices go up for smaller groups.

Sleeping

Since hotels cater mainly to business travelers, good-value budget accommodations are scarce.

TOP CHOICE Hotel Aire de Patagonia BOUTIQUE HOTEL $$
(02966-15569588; www.hotelairepatagonia.com.ar; Sarsfield 58; s/d AR$360/450;) Fresh and modern, this welcoming boutique hotel zings you up to your room in a hydraulic capsule elevator. Amenities include soft Egyptian cotton sheets, radiant floors and flatscreen TVs. The cute confitería is a good spot for a quiet espresso or board game.

Hostel Elcira HOSTEL $
(429856; www.elcira.com.ar; Zucarino 431; dm AR$70, d with bathroom AR$180;) An impeccable yet kitschy family home with friendly hosts. It's far from the center but just a 10-minute walk (or AR$20 taxi ride) from the bus terminal.

Hotel Sehuen HOTEL $$
(425683; www.hotelsehuen.com, in Spanish; Rawson 160; s/d/tr AR$220/295/276) Boasting national-level service awards, this cozy, light-filled hotel provides all-round good value. Wake up to the local newspaper in a the breakfast area with vaulted ceilings. Rooms are plain but well kept.

El Viejo Miramar HOTEL $$
(430401; hotelviejomiramar@yahoo.com.ar; Av Kirchner 1630; s/d AR$195/250) Snug carpeted rooms and spotless bathrooms make this affable choice a good one. Its personable owner makes guests feel at ease. Rates include breakfast (but not a second cup of coffee).

Hotel Covadonga HOTEL $
(420190; hotelcovadongargl@hotmail.com; Av Kirchner 1244; d with/without bathroom AR$225/195) Good value and grandmotherly, the tidy Covadonga has large rooms with creaky floors, and a sunny living room with worn leather sofas. Rooms with private bathrooms are worth the upgrade. Cash discounts are offered.

Eating & Drinking

TOP CHOICE Laguanacazul GOURMET $$$
(444114; cnr G Lista & Sarmiento; mains AR$80-115; noon-3pm, 8pm-midnight, closed Mon) Laguanacazul dares to take Patagonian cuisine to new places, with stir-fried trout and slow-cooked lamb with vegetables. The waterfront location is lovely and the interior quite stylish, but the service is practically snobbish; it's not advisable to come in here wearing grubby backpacker clothes.

Pizza Roma Express PIZZERIA $
(434400; Av San Martín 650; pizzas AR$16-34; 11am-late) Cheap and casual, with service that's friendlier than you'll find elsewhere in town, this is where students and families dine on burgers, gnocchi and salads, and older gents share big bottles of cold Quilmes beer.

RoCo ARGENTINE $$
(420203; Av Kirchner 1175; mains AR$35-65; 8am-midnight, closed Sun) On the main thoroughfare, this upscale eatery pleases with swift service and a varied menu. Start with lamb empanadas, main dishes include pasta, king crab and Patagonian lamb with fresh peas.

Information

Banks on Av Kirchner have ATMs. Internet is widely available in internet cafes and some restaurants.

ACA (Automóvil Club Argentino; 420477; Orkeke 10) Gas station, maps and traveler services.

Centro de Informes Turistico (422365; Av San Martín s/n; Oct-Apr) Useful info kiosk on median strip.

Hospital Regional (420289; José Ingenieros 98)

Immigration office (420205; Urquiza 144; 9am-3pm Mon-Fri)

Municipal tourist office (436920; www.riogallegos.gov.ar; cnr Av Kirchner & Córdoba; 9am-3pm Mon-Fri) A desk at the bus terminal keeps longer hours.

Post office (Av Kirchner 893)

Provincial tourist office (422702; www.santacruz.gov.ar, in Spanish; Av Kirchner 863; 9am-7pm Mon-Fri, 10am-1pm & 5-8pm Sat & Sun) Most helpful, with maps, bilingual staff and detailed info.

Thaler Cambio (Av San Martín 484; ⏲10am-3pm Mon-Fri, 10am-1pm Sat) Changes traveler's checks.

Tur Aike (☎422436; turaiketurismo@ciudad.com.ar; Zapiola 63) Helpful for airline bookings.

Getting There & Away

Air

Río Gallegos' airport is 7km northwest of town.

Aerolíneas Argentinas (☎422020/21; Av San Martín 545) flies daily to Buenos Aires (AR$920) and frequently to Ushuaia (AR$544). **LADE** (☎422316; Fagnano 53/57) flies several times a week to Buenos Aires (AR$931), Río Grande (AR$268), El Calafate (AR$278), Comodoro Rivadavia (AR$454) and Ushuaia (AR$544).

Bus

Río Gallegos' **bus terminal** (cnr RN 3 & Av Eva Perón) is about 3km southwest of the center. Companies include **El Pingüino** (☎442169), **Líder** (☎442160), **Bus Sur** (☎442687), **Andesmar** (☎442195), **Sportman** (☎442595) and also **TAC** (☎442042). Companies going to Chile include **Ghisoni** (☎442687), **Pacheco** (☎442765) and **Tecni-Austral** (☎442427). **Taqsa** (☎423130; www.taqsa.com.ar, in Spanish; Estrada 71) beelines straight from the airport to Puerto Natales and El Calafate.

Getting Around

It's easy to share metered taxis (AR$22) between downtown, the bus terminal and the airport. From Av Roca, buses marked 'B' or 'terminal' link the center and the bus terminal (AR$2).

Car rental is expensive due to the poor conditions of the roads to most places of interest. Despite exchange rates, rental deals are often better in Punta Arenas, Chile (see p456). For local rentals, try **Riestra Rent A Car** (☎421321; www.riestrarentacar.com; Av San Martín 1508).

BUSES FROM RÍO GALLEGOS

DESTINATION	COST (AR$)	DURATION (HR)
Buenos Aires	740	36-40
Comodoro Rivadavia	249	9-11
El Calafate	94	4-5
El Chaltén	140	9
Esquel	430	19
Puerto Madryn	454	15-20
Puerto Natales (Chile)	90	5-7
Puerto San Julián	117	4½
Punta Arenas (Chile)	65	5-6
Río Grande	265	7-8
Trelew	431	14-17
Ushuaia	360	12-14

Around Río Gallegos

Visiting a working *estancia* affords an intimate glimpse into the unique Patagonian lifestyle. These are not luxury hotels, but homes that have been converted into comfortable lodgings. Meals are often shared with the owners, and token participation in the daily working life is encouraged. For *estancias* in Santa Cruz province, contact the provincial tourist office in Río Gallegos (p412) or see www.estanciasdesantacruz.com.

Named for gold once found on the coast, **Estancia Monte Dinero** (☎02966-428922; www.montedinero.com.ar; day trip AR$345, per person incl full board AR$802; ⏲Oct-Apr) is a comfortable, old-world lodging with intricate hand-painted doors, billiards and well-appointed rooms. Dudes see the typical *estancia* activities – dog demos, shearing etc – and can also take trips to nearby **Cabo Vírgenes**, where Magellanic penguins nest September through March. The *estancia* museum displays an intriguing assortment of goods salvaged from shipwreck after the family Greenshyls sailed here from Ireland in 1886. Travel agencies in Río Gallegos offer day trips here starting in mid-November.

THE FALKLAND ISLANDS/ ISLAS MALVINAS

☎500 / POP 3140

Windswept, hilly, remote and difficult to access, the Falkland Islands nevertheless have much to offer the intrepid traveler. Bays, inlets, estuaries and beaches create a tortuous, attractive coastline flanked by abundant wildlife. Located 500km to the east of Argentina in the South Atlantic Ocean, these sea islands attract striated and crested caracaras, cormorants, oystercatchers and snowy sheathbills. A plethora of penguins – Magellanic, rockhopper, macaroni, gentoo and king – share top billing with elephant seals, sea lions, fur seals, five dolphin species and killer whales.

Falkland Islands/Islas Malvinas

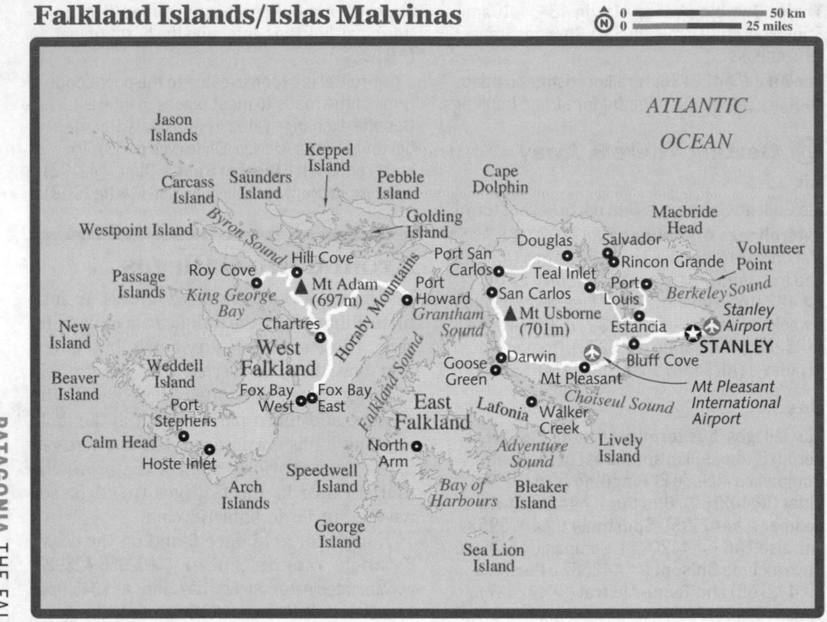

Stanley (population 2000), the islands' capital on East Falkland, is an assemblage of brightly painted metal-clad houses and a good place to throw down a few pints and listen to island lore. 'Camp' – as the rest of the islands are known – hosts settlements that began as company towns (hamlets where coastal shipping could collect wool) and now provide rustic backcountry lodging and a chance to experience pristine nature and wildlife. Even though there are 400km of roads, the islands have no street lights.

Planning

The best time to visit is from October to March, when migratory birds (including penguins) and marine mammals return to the beaches and headlands. Cruise ships to South Georgia and Antarctica run from November through March. The annual sports meetings, with horse racing, bull riding and sheepdog trials, take place in Stanley between Christmas and New Year, and on East and West Falkland at the end of the shearing season in late February. Summer never gets truly hot (the maximum high is 24°C or 75°F), but high winds bring chills. For more details, pick up Lonely Planet's *Antarctica* guide.

History

The sheep boom in Tierra del Fuego and Patagonia owes its origins to the cluster of islands known as the Falkland Islands to the British or Las Islas Malvinas to the Argentines. They had been explored, but never fully captured the interest of either country until Europe's mid-19th-century wool boom. After the Falkland Islands Company (FIC) became the islands' largest landholder, a population of stranded gauchos and mariners grew rapidly with the arrival of English and Scottish immigrants. In an unusual exchange, in 1853 the South American Missionary Society began transporting Yaghan Indians from Tierra del Fuego to Keppel Island to proselytize them.

Argentina's claim goes back to the 1820s, but it wasn't until 1982 that Argentine President Leopoldo Galtieri, then drowning in economic chaos and allegations of corruption, gambled that reclaiming the islands would unite his country. British Prime Minister Margaret Thatcher (also suffering in the polls) didn't hesitate in striking back, thoroughly humiliating Argentina in the Falklands War.

In 2010, Argentine President Cristina Fernández de Kirchner made statements which renewed Argentina's claim on the Falklands, diffusing the progress which had been made in the previous decade for increased cooperation between British, Falkland Islands and Argentine governments. Relations with Argentina remain cool, with most South American trade going via Chile.

Visas & Documents

Visitors from Britain and Commonwealth countries, the EU, North America, Mercosur countries and Chile don't need visas. If coming from another country, check with the British consulate. All nationalities must carry a valid passport, an onward ticket and proof of sufficient funds (credit cards are fine) and pre-arranged accommodations. In practice, arrivals who don't have prebooked accommodations are held in the arrivals area while rooms are found.

Money

There's no ATM on the Falklands and only one bank in Stanley, though credit and debit cards are widely accepted. Pounds sterling and US dollars in cash or traveler's checks are readily accepted, but the exchange rate for US currency is poor. Don't bother changing to Falkland pounds (FK£). In peak season, expect to spend US$150 to US$300 per day, not including airfare; less if camping or staying in self-catering cottages.

Information

Visit Stanley's **Jetty Visitors Centre** (☎22215; info@falklandislands.com), at the public jetty on Ross Rd. The *Visitor Accommodation Guide* lists lodgings and campgrounds. For trip planning, see the essential website **Falkland Islands Tourism** (www.visitorfalklands.com). In the UK, contact **Falkland House** (☎020 7222 2542; 14 Broadway, London SW1H 0BH).

Getting There & Away

From South America, **LanChile** (www.lan.com) flies to Mt Pleasant International Airport (MPA; near Stanley) every Saturday from Santiago, Chile, via Puerto Montt, Punta Arenas and – one Saturday each month – Río Gallegos, Argentina. Roundtrip fares are CH$530,000 from Punta Arenas with advance booking.

From **RAF Brize Norton** (www.raf.mod.uk/rafbrizenorton), in Oxfordshire, England, there are regular Royal Air Force flights to Mt Pleasant (18 hours, including a two-hour refueling stop on tiny Ascension Island in the South Atlantic). Roundtrip fares are UK£2244. Travelers continuing on to Chile can purchase one-way tickets for half the fare. Bookings from the UK can be made through the **Falkland Islands Government Office** (☎020-7222-2542; www.falklands.gov.fk; travel@falklands.gov.fk; Falkland House, 14 Broadway, Westminster, London SW1H 0BH). Payment by cash or personal or bank check; credit cards are not accepted.

Getting Around

From Stanley, **Figas** (☎27219; reservations@figas.gov.fk) serves outlying destinations in eight-seater aircraft.

Several Stanley operators run day trips to East Falkland settlements, including **Discovery Falklands** (☎21027; discovery@horizon.co.fk and dive outfitter **South Atlantic Marine Services** (☎21145; www.falklands-underwater.com). **Adventure Falklands** (☎21383; pwatts@horizon.co.fk) specializes in wildlife (featuring king, gentoo and Magellanic penguins) and historical tours.

Trekking and camping are feasible; however, there are no designated trails and getting lost is not unheard of. Always seek permission before entering private land.

INLAND PATAGONIA

Save for the travel hubs of El Calafate and El Chaltén, RN 40 and its offshoots are bit of a backwater. The ultimate road trip, 40 parallels the backbone of the Andes, where ñandús doodle through sagebrush, trucks kick up whirling dust and gas stations rise on the horizon like oases.

Now that more than half the 1228km stretch between Esquel and El Calafate is paved, travel is considerably easier, although the rough parts still remain pretty rough. For now, public transport stays limited to a few summer-only tourist shuttle services, and driving requires both preparation and patience.

RN 40 parallels the Andes from north of Bariloche to the border with Chile near Puerto Natales, then cuts east to the Atlantic Coast. Highlights include the Perito Moreno and Los Glaciares national parks, the rock art of Cueva de los Manos and remote *estancias*.

This section picks up the RN 40 in Esquel, from where it continues paved until south of Gobernador Costa, where it turns to gravel.

From there on down, it's gravel most of the way, with slowly increasing numbers of paved sections, mainly near population centers. At the time of writing, the last 130km before El Chaltén, the 120km further to El Calafate and 130km beyond it were paved.

Esquel

☎02945 / POP 40,000 / ELEV 570M

If you tire of the gnome-in-the-chocolate-shop ambience of Bariloche and other cutesy Lakes District destinations, regular old Esquel will feel like a breath of fresh air. Set in western Chubut's dramatic, hikeable foothills, Esquel is a hub for Parque Nacional Los Alerces and an easy-going, friendly base camp for abundant adventure activities – the perfect place to chill after hard travel on RN 40.

Founded at the turn of the 20th century, Esquel is the region's main livestock and commercial center. It's also the historic southern end of the line for *La Trochita*, the narrow-gauge steam train (see p418). The town takes its name from Mapundungun, meaning either 'bog' or 'place of the thistles.'

RN 259 zigzags through town to the junction with RN 40, which heads north to El Bolsón and south to Comodoro Rivadavia. South of town, RN 259 passes a junction for Parque Nacional Los Alerces en route to Trevelin.

Sights & Activities

Esquel's best attractions are of the outdoor variety, notably Parque Nacional Los Alerces and La Hoya. Esquel's nearby lakes and rivers offer excellent **fly fishing**, with the season running from November to April. You can purchase a license at the **YPF gas station** (cnr 25 de Mayo & Av Ameghino; ⏲daylight hrs) that houses the ACA. **Mountain biking** is a good way to get out of town and explore the surrounding hills and trails.

Cerro La Hoya SNOW SPORTS
Despite wide open bowls and some of Argentina's best powder skiing, this 1350m **resort** (☎02945-453018; www.cerrolahoya.com, in Spanish; lift ticket adult/child AR$160/125; ⏲Jun-Oct skiing) is just starting to become well-known. While cheaper and less crowded than Bariloche, it is smaller and comparatively tame, ideal for families. Summer activities include hiking, chairlift rides and horse riding. Equipment can be rented on-site or at sport shops in Esquel. Minibus transfers cost AR$50 round-trip; taxis may be a better deal for groups. It's 13km north of Esquel.

Museo de Culturas Originarias Patagónicas MUSEUM
(☎451929; Nahuel Pan; admission AR$5; ⏲2-5pm) Displays a modest collection of Mapuche artifacts; La Trochita stops here.

FREE **Museo del Tren** MUSEUM
(☎451403; www.latrochita.org.ar; cnr Roggero & Urquiza; ⏲8am-2pm Mon-Sat). Just outside town, this train museum is in the Roca train station where *La Trochita*, Argentina's famous narrow-gauge steam train, stops. In summer, several tour agencies sell tickets for roundtrip rides on the antique train.

Tours

Expediciones Patagonia Aventura ADVENTURE TOUR
(EPA; ☎457015; www.epaexpediciones.com, in Spanish; Av Fontana 482) Offers rafting, canyoning, horseback riding and trekking. Whitewater rafting trips (half day AR$270 with transport) go on the Río Corcovado (90km away). The EPA's riverside hostel is a good option if you want to overnight. Canopy tours, horseback riding and trekking use the mountain center, an attractive wooden lodge (full pension AR$380) based in Parque Nacional Los Alerces. Guests have access to kayaks, and camping is also available.

Circuito Lacuestre BOATING
Numerous travel agencies sell tickets for the Circuito Lacustre boat excursion in Parque Nacional Los Alerces (see p422); buying a ticket in Esquel assures a place on the often-crowded trip. Full-day excursions, including the lake cruise, cost AR$195 when sailing from Puerto Chucao or AR$250 from Puerto Limonao, including transfers to and from the park.

Coyote Bikes BICYCLE RENTAL
(☎455505; Rivadavia 887; ⏲9am-1pm, 3:30-8pm Mon-Fri, 9am-1pm Sat) For mountain bike rentals and trail details in summer

Festivals & Events

Semana de Esquel FESTIVAL
A weeklong February event that celebrates the city's 1906 founding.

Fiesta Nacional de Esquí SKI FESTIVAL
(National Skiing Festival) Takes place in mid-September at La Hoya.

Sleeping

Esquel has many accommodations; check with the tourist office for more listings, which include cabins and apartments geared for ski vacations.

SURVIVING RUTA NACIONAL 40

Patagonia's RN 40 is the quintessential road trip. No one gets anywhere fast here – the weather can be wily and the gravel loose. It can seem to go on forever. But it is also magical, when after rattling along for hours, the interminable flat line of steppe bursts open with views of glacial peaks and gem-colored lakes.

Be Prepared

Everyone should travel with necessary repair equipment. If renting a car, carry two full-sized *neumáticos* (spare tires) and make sure that the headlights work and that suspension, tires and brakes are in good shape. The gravel can puncture gas tanks, so be sure to have extra fuel on hand, as well as oil and generous supplies of food and water. Gas is subsidized in Patagonia, so fill up the tank at each opportunity.

Road Rules

The law requires seatbelts and headlights turned on during daylight hours. Respect speed limits: 65km/h to 80km/h is a safe maximum speed.

Sheep *always* have the right of way. While most will scurry out of the way, some are not so quick. Guanacos and ñandús are other potential hazards. Slow down, give them distance and watch out for unsigned *guardaganados* (cattle guards).

Driving Etiquette

Signal hello to oncoming drivers by flashing your headlights or raising an index finger with your hand on the steering wheel. An unwritten rule: stop to help anyone stranded on the side of the road. There's no 'roadside assistance' here and cell phones are without signal on many stretches. Along windy roads, toot your horn before barreling round blind curves.

Letting Someone Else Deal with It

Several travel agencies coordinate two- to five-day minivan transport along RN 40 from El Calafate to Bariloche, via El Chaltén, Perito Moreno and Los Antiguos. Service follows fair weather, from mid-October/November to early April, depending on demand and road conditions. Pricier guided tours stretch the trip over four or five days.

Recommended outfitter **Las Loicas** (☎02963-490272; www.lasloicas.com; Lago Posadas; per person AR$3165) offers a five-day trip between El Chaltén and Perito Moreno/Los Antiguos that includes a bilingual guide, meals, four nights' accommodations, and visits to Cueva de las Manos, Lago Posadas and Parque Nacional Perito Moreno.

If you're really up for a road trip, contact **Ruta 40** (☎0297-446-5337; www.ruta-40.com; Comodoro Rivadavia). The small, multilingual outfitter takes travelers on 10-day journeys on RN40 from Bariloche to El Calafate, with stops at Cueva de las Manos and several lovely *estancias*. Consult for current rates and departure dates.

Quicker, more straightforward travel along RN 40 can be arranged through **Chaltén Travel** (☎011-4326-7282; www.chaltentravel.com; Sarmiento 559, piso 8, Buenos Aires), which runs northbound two-day shuttles, leaving at 8am from El Calafate, with accommodation in Perito Moreno. Southbound three-day shuttles leave Bariloche at 6:45am on odd-numbered days, with accommodations in Perito Moreno and El Chaltén. Buses stop in Los Antiguos as well. It is usually available from November to March. For the one-way trip, prices start at AR$700 per person (not including accommodation or food). It's possible to hop on and off along the route, but space on the next shuttle is not reservable. Combinations to Puerto Madryn are also available for northbound travelers. Chaltén Travel has branches in **El Calafate** (☎02902-492212; Av Libertador 1174), **El Chaltén** (☎02962-493005; cnr Guemes & Lago del Desierto), **Puerto Madryn** (☎02965-454906; Av Roca 115) and **Bariloche** (☎02944-423809).

Though less organized and reliable than the tour options above, bus line **Taqsa** (☎0297-432675) offers high-season service north and south between El Calafate and Bariloche (AR$648, 31 hours, October to April), with stops in El Chaltén, Perito Moreno and Esquel.

TOP CHOICE **Sol Azul** HOSTEL $

(☎455193; www.hostelsolazul.com.ar; Rivadavia 2869; dm AR$60; P 📶) With the good looks of a mountain lodge, this welcoming new hostel ups the ante with a sauna and a fully decked-out kitchen with industrial stoves lined with spices. Dorms are in a house out back, with small but super-tidy bathrooms. When we visited, the dude factor was high, but it was also snowboarding season. It's a taxi ride to the center, on the northern edge of town.

Hostería Canela B&B B&B $$$

(☎453890; www.canelaesquel.com; cnr Los Notros & Los Radales, Villa Ayelén; d/tr AR$570/705, q apt AR$941; 📶) Veronica and Jorge's refined B&B, tucked away in a pine forest 2km outside the town center feels elegant and comfortable, an ideal match for mature guests. The English-speaking owners offer in-room tea service and the comfortable beds are topped with pristine white linens.

Hostería La Chacra B&B $$

(☎452802; www.lachacrapatagonia.com; RN 259, Km 5; d AR$300; @ 📶) If you want a shot of local culture, nothing is better than this country lodging in a 1970s home with ample bright rooms, generous gringo breakfasts and thick down bedding. Get here via shuttle, taxi or Trevelin bus – they pass hourly.

Planeta Hostel HOSTEL $

(☎456846; www.planetahostel.com; Av Alvear 2833; dm/d AR$80/200; @ 📶) This old but boldly painted downtown house features friendly service but cramped rooms. Down comforters, a spotless communal kitchen and a flat-screen TV lounge are a cut above the usual.

Altos del Faldeo APARTMENTS $$

(☎453108; www.altosdelfaldeo.com.ar, in Spanish; Desalojo del 37; d/q apt AR$300/400; P 📶) These quiet backyard apartments delight travelers with details like hydro-massage tubs, daily maid service and the bonus of breakfast and outdoor grills.

LA TROCHITA: THE OLD PATAGONIAN EXPRESS

Clearly an anachronism in the jet age, Ferrocarril Roca's **La Trochita** (☎in Esquel 02945-451403; www.patagoniaexpress.com/el_trochita.htm), Argentina's famous narrow-gauge steam train, averages less than 30km/h on its meandering journey between Esquel and El Maitén – if it runs at top speed. Despite the precarious economics of its operations, the project has survived even the most concerted efforts to shut it down. In its current incarnation, subsidized by the city of Esquel and the provincial governments, *La Trochita* – which Paul Theroux facetiously called *The Old Patagonian Express* – provides both a tourist attraction and a service for local citizens.

Like many state projects, completion of the line seemed an interminable process. In 1906 the federal government authorized the southern branch of the Roca line, between Puerto San Antonio on the Atlantic coast and Lago Nahuel Huapi. In 1922 Ferrocarriles del Estado began work on the narrow-gauge section; it didn't reach the halfway point of Ñorquinco until 1939. In 1941 the line made it to the workshops at El Maitén, and in 1945 it reached the end of the line at Esquel.

Since then, the line has suffered some of the oddest mishaps in railroad history. Three times within a decade, in the late 1950s and early 1960s, the train was derailed by high winds, and ice has caused other derailments. In 1979 a collision with a cow derailed the train at Km 243 south of El Maitén; the engine driver was the appropriately named Señor Bovino.

In full operation until 1993, *La Trochita*'s 402km route between Esquel and Ingeniero Jacobacci was probably the world's longest remaining steam-train line, with half a dozen stations and another nine *apeaderos* (whistle-stops). The Belgian Baldwin and German Henschel engines refilled their 4000L water tanks at strategically placed *parajes* (pumps) every 40km to 45km. Most of the passenger cars, heated by wood stoves, date from 1922, as do the freight cars.

During summer, the **Tren Turístico** (tickets AR$180; ⏲10am twice weekly, additional departures Jan-Feb) travels from Roca station in Esquel to Nahuel Pan, the first station down the line, 20km east. At Nahuel Pan, the train stops for photo ops and a small artisan market – make sure you pick up a few piping hot *tortas fritas* pastries made by local women. The trip takes 45 minutes one-way and space is tight: if you're squished between other tourists, escape to the cafe car for a hot chocolate.

Hostería Angelina INN $$
(☎452763; www.hosteriaangelina.com.ar; Av Alvear 758; s/d AR$300/350; @📶) Hospitable and polished, with a courtyard fountain, Angelina follows international standards with professional service and a good breakfast buffet.

Plaza Esquel Hostería & Spa HOTEL $$
(☎457002; www.patagoniaandesgroup.com.ar; Av Ameghino 713; s/d/apt AR$275/340/440; @📶) One of the newest hotels in Esquel, this attractive *hostería* in front of the plaza offers modern rooms with new fixtures.

Hostería Cumbres Blancas INN $$$
(☎455100; www.cumbresblancas.com.ar, in Spanish; Av Ameghino 1683; d AR$720; @📶) While this inn is shiny and lavish, Cumbres Blancas does not surpass its packaged feel. Sportsmen and -women will enjoy having their own fly-casting pond and putting green for a few days. Rooms are decked out in crisp colors and fresh-feeling linens.

Los Ñires de Esquel HOTEL $
(☎452559; www.rinconesdelsur.com.ar; San Martín 820; s/d AR$170/220; 📶) These basic rooms have the benefit of fresh paint and quaint décor, with private bathrooms and cable TV. They're well located near the leafy Plaza San Martín.

Eating

La Luna RESTO BAR $$
(Av Fontana 656; pizza AR$45; ⏲noon-4pm & 7pm-1am) This chic rock'n'roll restaurant-bar offers tasty spinach pizza and heaped portions of steak and fries. The evening crowd spills out of wooden booths and brick nooks, drinking Patagonia's artisan beers.

Don Chiquino ITALIAN $$
(Amhegino 1641; mains AR$50; ⏲lunch & dinner) Of course, pasta is no novelty in Argentina, but the owner-magician performing tricks while you wait for your meal is. The ambiance is happy-cluttered and dishes such as sorrentinos prove satisfying.

María Castaña CAFE $
(cnr 25 de Mayo & Rivadavia; snacks AR$25; ⏲9am-late) A favorite at this frilly cafe is waffles with *dulce de leche;* it's also good for breakfast, sandwiches and ice-cream sundaes. Grab an overstuffed chair in the back.

La Abuela ARGENTINE $
(Rivadavia 1109; mains AR$40; ⏲lunch & dinner) Shoehorn yourself into this family nook decked out in lace tablecloths, and enjoy cheap gnocchi and home-cooked classics like *puchero* (vegetable and meat stew) with a carafe of passable house wine.

Killarney's Irish Resto Pub PUB $
(☎457041; cnr Sarmiento & Av Alvear; mains AR$28-40; ⏲noon-late) Don't let the Irish-pub atmosphere fool you into thinking this is just another stock standard watering hole: Killarney's serves up good set lunches, too, and a range of hearty soups, salads and sandwiches with the Guinness, of course.

Drinking & Entertainment

Hotel Argentino BAR
(25 de Mayo 862; ⏲4pm-5am) This lanky and lowbrow Wild West saloon is much better suited to drinking than sleeping, but by all means stop by: the owner is friendly, the 1916 construction is stuffed with relics and sculptures, and the place gets more than a little lively on weekends.

Dirección Municipal de Cultura CULTURAL CENTER
(☎451929; Belgrano 330) Sponsors regular music, cinema, theater and dance.

Information

ACA (Automóvil Club Argentino; ☎452382; cnr 25 de Mayo & Av Ameghino) Inside YPF gas station; sells fishing licenses.

Banco de la Nación (cnr Av Alvear & General Roca) Has an ATM and changes traveler's checks.

Banco del Chubut (Av Alvear 1147) Has an ATM.

Hospital Regional (☎450009; 25 de Mayo 150)

Post office (cnr Avs Fontana & Alvear)

Tourist office (☎451927; www.esquel.gov.ar; cnr Av Alvear & Sarmiento; ⏲7am-11pm) Well organized, helpful and multilingual, with an impressive variety of detailed maps and brochures.

Getting There & Around

Air

When volcanic ash from Chile closes Bariloche's airport, flights are re-routed through Esquel with land transfers. Esquel's airport is 20km east of town off RN 40. Taxis will set you back around AR$35.

Aerolíneas Argentinas (☎453614; Av Fontana 406) flies to Buenos Aires (AR$1646) several times a week.

Bus

Esquel's full-service **bus terminal** (cnr Av Alvear & Brun) is close to the center.

Transportes Jacobsen (☎453528) goes to Futaleufú, Chile (AR$26, 1½ hours), at 8am and 6pm Monday and Friday. Buses go hourly to Trevelin (AR$5, 30 minutes), stopping near the corner of Av Alvear and 25 de Mayo on the way out of town.

In summer, **Transportes Esquel** (☎453529) goes through Parque Nacional Los Alerces (AR$20, 1¼ hours) to Lago Futalaufquen at 8am daily (and also at 2pm and 6pm in January). The first bus goes all the way to Lago Puelo (AR$50, six hours), stopping in Lago Verde (AR$30) at 10:30am and Cholila at noon. An open ticket allows passengers to make stops along the way between Esquel and Lago Puelo or vice-versa. Note that the service is reduced off-season.

Train

The narrow-gauge steam train *La Trochita* departs from the diminutive **Roca train station** (www.latrochita.org.ar; cnr Roggero & Urquiza; ⌚8am-2pm Mon-Sat). There's a frequent tourist-oriented service to Nahuel Pan (see the boxed text, p418). For the timeless *Old Patagonian Express* feeling, it's best to catch a bus to El Maitén for the less touristy excursion to Desvio Thomae, but this service is only available from time to time. Confirm schedules online or via the tourist office.

Car

Compact rentals start around AR$200 a day, including 100km and insurance. Try **Patagonia Travel Rent A Car** (☎455811, 02945-15-692174; www.patagoniatravelrentacar.com, in Spanish; Av Alvear 1041), which has a good range of vehicles.

BUSES TO ESQUEL

Buses go daily to the following destinations:

DESTINATION	COST (AR$)	DURATION (HR)
Bariloche	62-88	4¼
Buenos Aires	690	25
Comodoro Rivadavia	180	8
El Bolsón	32-52	2½
Neuquén	245	10
Puerto Madryn	205-258	7-9
Río Gallegos	430	18
Trelew	185-245	8-9

Trevelin

☎02945 / POP 10,000 / ELEV 735M

Historic Trevelin (treh-*veh*-lehn), from the Welsh for town *(tre)* and mill *(velin)*, is the only community in interior Chubut with a notable Welsh character. Easygoing and postcard pretty, this pastoral village makes a tranquil lodging alternative to the much busier Esquel (remember, everything is relative here), or an enjoyable day trip for tea. The surrounding countryside is ripe for exploration.

Just 22km south of Esquel via paved RN 259, Trevelin centers around the octagonal plaza Coronel Fontana. Eight streets radiate from it, including the principal thoroughfare, Av San Martín (also the southward extension of RN 259). RN 259 forks west 50km to the Chilean border and to Futaleufú, 12km beyond.

Sights

Museo Regional Molino Viejo MUSEUM
(☎02945-480189; cnr 25 de Mayo & Molino Viejo; admission AR$5) Occupies the restored remains of a 1922 grain mill. At the time of research it was closed for renovation. It's a couple of blocks east of the plaza, at the end of 25 de Mayo.

Festivals & Events

Mercado de Artisanos ARTISAN MARKET
Fills Plaza Coronel Fontana on Sundays in summer and on alternate Sundays the rest of the year.

Aniversario de Trevelin FESTIVAL
Commemorates the founding of the city on March 19.

Eisteddfod FESTIVAL
The biggest Welsh celebration of the year, this multilingual festival where bards compete in song and poetry takes place at the end of October.

Sleeping

TOP CHOICE **Casaverde Hostel** HOSTEL $
(☎480091; www.casaverdehostel.com.ar; Los Alerces s/n; dm/d/tr/q AR$70/230/280/320, 2-/4-/6-person cabin AR$350/460/550; @🛜) A convivial retreat perched above town, Casaverde is homey and helpful. Guests relax in the spacious rooms and sunny common areas, and wake up to breakfast (AR$20) with bottomless mugs of real cof-

WORTH A TRIP

ON BUTCH CASSIDY'S TRAIL IN CHOLILA

Butch Cassidy, the Sundance Kid, and Etta Place tried settling down and making an honest living near this quiet farming community outside the northeast entrance to Parque Nacional Los Alerces. The bandits' tale is recounted by Bruce Chatwin in the travel classic *In Patagonia*. Though the threesome's idyll only lasted a few years, their partially restored homestead still stands, just off RP 71 at Km 21, 8km north of Cholila. Cholila's enthusiastic **Casa de Informes** (☎02945-498040/131; www.turismocholila.gov.ar; RP 71, at RP 15; ⊙summer only) has a helpful regional map and will gladly point you in the right direction.

To overnight in this funky Patagonian outpost, check out the hospitable **Piuke Mapu Hostel** (☎02945-15-685608; www.piukemapu.com; Av Soberanía Argentina 200; dm AR$35), located three blocks from the plaza. Young owners Laura and Dario also run a community garden and mountain refuge and guide local trekking and Alpine excursions.

fee, homemade bread and jams. They also sell park and train tours and rent bikes (AR$15 per hour). It's a 10-minute walk from the plaza, off Av Fontana.

Hostería Casa de Piedra LODGE $$
(☎480357; www.casadepiedratrevelin.com, in Spanish; Brown 244; d/tr AR$250/290, 5-person apt AR$350, 6-person cabin AR$390; 📶) A haven for anglers, this elegant stone lodge boasts a huge fireplace and rustic touches. Buffet breakfast includes yogurt, homemade bread, cakes and fruit.

Cabañas Wilson CABINS $$
(☎480803; www.wilsonpatagonia.com.ar; RP 259 at RP 71; 4-/6-person cabins AR$450/480; 📶) Savor the serenity surrounding these wood-and-brick cabins on the edge of town. The cabins include daily cleaning service, extra covers and a barbecue deck. An abundant breakfast (AR$25) is optional.

Cabañas Oregon CABINS $$
(☎480408; www.oregontrevelin.com.ar, in Spanish; cnr Av San Martín & JM Thomas; 4-person cabin AR$350; 📶👪) Scattered around an apple orchard on the south side of town, these appealing log cabins come with handmade wooden furniture. Features include kitchen and TVs. Kid-friendly, there's also a swingset. The onsite grill restaurant (closed Tuesdays) is reputed as the best spot in town to eat meat, with good service.

Circulo Policial CAMPGROUND $
(☎480947; Costanera Río Percy & Holdich; campsites per person AR$25; ⊙closed winter) Fine, grassy campsites with shade. From Av San Martín 600 block, walk two blocks west on Coronel Holdich and turn left down the gravel road.

Eating

Just as visitors to Trelew flock to Gaiman, so visitors to Esquel head to Trevelin for Welsh tea. Teahouses are typically open from 3pm to 8pm. Often the portions are big enough to share – ask first if it's OK.

Nain Maggie TEAHOUSE $$$
(☎480232; www.casadetenainmaggie.com; Perito Moreno 179; tea service AR$70; ⊙10am-12:30pm & 3-8:30pm) Trevelin's oldest teahouse occupies a modern building but has high traditional standards. Along with a bottomless pot, there's cream pie, *torta negra* and scones.

La Mutisia TEAHOUSE $$
(☎480165; Av San Martín 170; tea service AR$55) The only other teahouse where everything is reliably homemade.

Information

Banco del Chubut (cnr Av San Martín & Brown) Just south of the plaza, with an ATM.

Gales al Sur (☎480427; www.galesalsur.com.ar; Patagonia 186) Esquel buses stop at this travel agency, which also arranges tours.

Post office (Av San Martín) Just south of the plaza.

Tourist office (☎480120; www.trevelin.org, in Spanish; Plaza Fontana; ⊙8am-9pm) Helpful, with a free town map, information on local hikes and English-speaking staff.

Getting There & Away

The **bus terminal** (cnr Roca & RN 40) faces the main plaza. Most services originate in Esquel. **Gales del Sur** (☎480427; RN 259) has hourly buses to Esquel (AR$5, 30 minutes). Buses cross the border to Chile's Futaleufú (AR$26, one hour) on Mondays and Fridays at 8:30am and 6pm, plus Wednesdays in summer.

Parque Nacional Los Alerces

02945

This collection of spry creeks, verdant mountains and mirror lakes resonates as unadulterated Andes. The real attraction, however, is the alerce tree *(Fitzroya cupressoides),* one of the longest-living species on the planet, with specimens that have survived up to 4000 years. Lured by the acclaim of well-known parks to the north and south, most hikers miss this gem, which makes your visit here all the more enjoyable.

Resembling California's giant sequoia, the alerce flourishes in middle Patagonia's temperate forests, growing only about 1cm every 20 years. Individual specimens of this beautiful tree can reach over 4m in diameter and exceed 60m in height. Like the giant sequoia, it has suffered overexploitation because of its valuable timber. West of Esquel, this 2630-sq-km park protects some of the largest alerce forests that still remain.

Because the Andes are relatively low here, westerly storms deposit nearly 3m of rain annually. The park's eastern sector, though, is much drier. Winter temperatures average 2°C, but can be much colder. The summer average high reaches 24°C, but evenings are usually cool.

While its wild backcountry supports the seldom-seen huemul (Andean deer) and other wildlife, Los Alerces functions primarily as a trove of botanical riches which characterize the dense Valdivian forest.

Activities

As well as sailing and hiking, travel agencies in Esquel do fishing, canoeing, mountain-biking, snorkeling and horseback-riding.

Sailing

Traditionally, **Circuito Lacustre** is Los Alerces' most popular excursion and involves

Parque Nacional Los Alerces

sailing from Puerto Limonao up Lago Futalaufquen and through the narrow channel of the Río Arrayanes to Lago Verde.

Low water makes it necessary to hike the short distance between Puerto Mermoud, at the north end of Lago Futalaufquen, and Puerto Chucao on Lago Menéndez. Launches from Puerto Chucao handle the second segment of the trip (1½ hours) to the northern nature trail **El Alerzal**, the most accessible stand of alerces. Another option (recommended) is to arrive at Puerto Chucao via a 1500m very scenic trail that crosses the bridge over Río Arrayanes.

The launch remains docked for over an hour at El Alerzal trailhead, sufficient for an unhurried hike around the loop trail that passes **Lago Cisne** and an attractive waterfall to end up at **El Abuelo** (Grandfather), a 57m-tall, 2600-year-old alerce.

From Puerto Limonao, the excursion costs AR$140; from Puerto Chucao it's AR$110. Departures are in the morning from Limonao and at midday from Chucao, returning to Chucao around 5pm and to Limonao at 7pm. In summer, purchase tickets in Esquel to ensure a seat.

Hiking

Hikers must sign in at the one of the ranger stations before heading out.

Day hikes can be undertaken from several interpretive trails located near **Lago Futalaufquen**. There is also a 25km trail from **Puerto Limonao** along the south shore of Futalaufquen to **Hostería Lago Krüger** (p423), which can be done in a long day, or broken up by camping at **Playa Blanca**. Boat excursions from Puerto Limonao to Lago Krüger cost AR$110 per person.

For longer hikes, see Lonely Planet's *Trekking in the Patagonian Andes*.

Sleeping & Eating

En route to the park, watch for roadside signs advertising ideal picnic goods: homemade bread, delicious Chubut cheese, fresh fruit and Welsh sweets. In Villa Futalaufquen there are a couple of basic grocery stores and a summer-only restaurant, but it's best to bring your own provisions.

Los Alerces has several full-service campgrounds, all of which have showers, grocery stores and restaurants on-site or nearby. Free (no services) and semi-organized campgrounds exist near most of these fee sites.

With a group, *cabañas* can be an affordable option.

TOP CHOICE **Hostería Futalaufquen** INN **$$$**
(☎470008; www.hosteriafutalaufquen.com; d incl half-board AR$1100, 4-/5-person apt AR$980/1080) Exclusive and elegant, this country inn is on the quieter western shore of the lake, 4.5km north of the Villa at the end of the road. It offers well-appointed doubles and log cabins (without kitchens). A range of activities – from kayaking to rappelling – can be arranged from here. Afterwards, collapse by the fire with a plate of dessert. Reservations can be made at Sarmiento 635 in Esquel.

Lago Verde Wilderness Resort CABINS **$$$**
(☎in Buenos Aires 011-4816-5348; www.hosteriaselaura.com; 2-/4-person cabins incl full board AR$2047/3249; Nov-April) Rustic yet ritzy, these raspy stone *cabañas* feature big cozy beds, panoramic forest views and earthy motifs. Anglers can rent motorized rafts to cast from the lake's every nook and cranny. A gourmet restaurant and teahouse cater to travelers and guests. It's 35km north of the Villa.

Cabañas Tejas Negras CABINS **$$$**
(☎471012, 471046, 02945-1541-7248; tejasnegras@infovia.com.ar; 4-/5-person cabins AR$550/750; ⏲year-round) With a lawn like a golf course and a handful of prim A-frames, Nilda and Hector have hosted guests for 40 years. Think retreat: there are no football matches on these greens where tranquility is savored. Note to parents – they only take kids who are well-behaved!

Camping & Hostería Lago Krüger CAMPGROUND **$$$**
(☎02945-15-4424-7964; www.lagokrugger.com.ar; campsites per person AR$60, refugio incl full board per person AR$550) This attractive and relatively isolated lakefront mountain refuge is accessible by the 25km trail that leaves from Hostería Futalaufquen (see p423), or by launch from Puerto Limonao (AR$140).

Traiguen CABINS **$$**
(☎02945-15-68-3606; 6-person cabins AR$350; ⏲year-round) You might need good clearance to make it up the dirt road, but these few, ample cabins have lovely lake views and their going rate is a steal. Run by the *simpatico* Graciela and her giant tomcats.

Hostería Quime Quipan INN **$$**
(☎471021; www.cpatagonia.com/quimequipan, in Spanish; d incl breakfast AR$350-380 ⏲Nov-Apr) In a breathtaking setting, this old-fashioned guesthouse offers pleasant but dated rooms – splurge for those with lake views. Non-

guests can dine at the cozy, sunlit restaurant (meals AR$80), an après-fishing pit stop.

Camping Río Arrayanes CAMPGROUND $
(☎454381; adult/child AR$30/15) A new campground, with showers, bathrooms and grills, located in one of the most scenic areas of the park.

Camping Lago Rivadavia CAMPGROUND $
(☎454381; adult/child AR$30/15) These idyllic spots at Lago Rivadavia's south end are sheltered in the trees with picnic tables and a boat launch. There's an electricity hookup, too. It's 42km north of the Villa.

Camping Lago Verde CAMPGROUND $
(☎454421; campsites per person AR$45, 4-person cabin AR$450) With deluxe remodeled cabins and full-service camping, this campground flanks the eastern shore of its namesake lake, 35km northwest of Villa Futalaufquen. Besides nearby Lago Verde Wilderness Resort, it's the only option on this tranquil lake.

Complejo Turístico Bahía Rosales CAMPGROUND $$
(☎471044; campsites per person AR$30, 4-person refugio AR$280) This sprawling complex has flat campsites by the water, other lodging options and sporting facilities. At the north end of Lago Futalaufquen, it is 1.5km from the main road via a dirt path.

Autocamping Los Maitenes CAMPGROUND $
(☎471006; per person AR$30) On a slip of grass between the main road and the lake, these spots have lovely water views. Campsites include shade, electricity hookup and fire pits, 200m from the Intendencia.

Information

During the high season (Christmas to Semana Santa) foreigners pay AR$50 admission. In Villa Futalaufquen you'll find the **Intendencia** (park office; ☎471015/20; ⏲8am-9pm summer, 9am-4pm rest of year), where rangers have details about hiking, camping and guided excursions. Get your fishing permits here. The headquarters also house the **Museo y Centro del Interpretación**, a natural-history museum. The visitor center at the northern end of the park is only open December through February.

Getting There & Away

For information on getting to/from the park, see p420.

Gobernador Costa

☎02945 / POP 2000

When you find a town where a child snaps the tourist's picture (and not the reverse), it's something of an anomaly. This rusted little cattle town abuts the yawning stretch of RN 40 between Esquel and Río Mayo, at the intersection of RP 20 for Sarmiento and Comodoro Rivadavia. Some 20km west of town, RP 19 leads to **Lago General Vintter** and several smaller blue-ribbon lakes near the Chilean border; camping is possible along the shores.

Traveler services are few but reasonable. **Banco Chubut** (cnr Sarmiento & San Martín) has an ATM machine. On the edge of fields, **Camping Municipal** (cnr 2 de Abril & Los Suecos; per person AR$20) has electricity and hot water. The newish motel-style **Hotel Roca** (☎491126; Av Roca s/n; d AR$190) has tidy brick rooms and a restaurant. If it's booked out, check **Residencial El Jair** (☎02945-15-547276; cnr San Martín & Sarmiento; per person AR$90), with basic rooms and special rates for families.

From the **bus terminal** (Av Roca s/n), buses go to Esquel and continue to Bariloche at 3:45am every day but Saturday. For Comodoro Rivadavia (AR$110, eight hours), buses leave twice daily. Both routes are paved.

Río Mayo

☎02903 / POP 3500 HUMANS, 800,000 SHEEP

The national capital of sheep shearing is a surprisingly humdrum place, save for the petroleum workers and waylaid gauchos practicing their wolf-whistles on female *turistas*. This barren pit stop is 200km south of Gobernador Costa and 135km north of Perito Moreno.

The **Casa de Cultura** (☎420400; Ejército Argentino s/n; ⏲9am-noon & 3-6pm) houses a tourist office, with information on local mountain-biking options. **Banco del Chubut** (cnr Yrigoyen & Argentina) has an ATM.

January's **Festival Nacional de la Esquila** features merino wool-quality competitions and guanaco shearing in anticipation for the main event: the long-anticipated crowning of the national sheep-shearing queen.

The following lodgings offer meals, otherwise the YPF is a good bet for a quick sandwich and coffee. The picture of eccentricity, **El Viejo Covadonga** (☎420020; San Martín 573; dm/s/d AR$60/120/180) features rooms with good down covers but varying in quality. Its coveted feature is the orange vinyl bar. **Hotel Akatá** (☎420054; San Martín 640; d incl breakfast AR$200; @) has internet but little else; its wood-panel rooms are dark and airless.

There are daily morning services from the **bus terminal** (☎420174; cnr Fontana & Irigoyen) to Comodoro Rivadavia (AR$70, 4½ hours), Sarmiento and Coyhaique (Chile). Schedules change regularly so check at the bus terminal. Heading south to Perito Moreno, the road is unpaved. The only regularly scheduled services on this rugged stretch of RN 40 are summer-only backpacker shuttles.

Perito Moreno

☎02963 / POP 4300

Don't confuse this dull town with the jaw-dropping national park of the same name or the glacier near El Calafate – the only tourist attraction here is cruising the strip on Saturday night. A brief stopover en route to the more inviting Andean oasis of Los Antiguos, Perito Moreno does have a good range of services for a town on RN40, though area mining means hotels are often booked. Attractions Cueva de las Manos and Parque Nacional Perito Moreno are not far off.

The town's glory came in 1898, when explorer Perito Moreno challenged Chile's border definition of *'divortum aquarum continental'* (which claimed the headwaters of Pacific-flowing rivers as Chilean territory) by rerouting the Río Fénix, which flows through town, to Atlantic-bound Río Deseado. The river and the area remained Argentine, and the town took his name. The main drag, San Martín, leads north to RP 43 and south to RN 40; it's 128km south to Bajo Caracoles and 135km north of Río Mayo.

Tours

The experienced **GuanaCondor Tours** (☎432303; jarinauta@yahoo.com.ar; Perito Moreno 1087; ⏲10am-noon & 4-8pm Mon-Wed & Sat, 5-8pm Sun) runs tours in summer to Cueva de las Manos (AR$250 per person), accessing the park via the former Estancia Los Toldos, with a challenging hike that adds considerably to the experience. Also ask about trips to Monte Zeballos, a high mesa with excellent views, and the overnight trip to Paso Tehuelche.

Hugo Campañoli (☎432336) is a local guide who takes groups of three or more to Cueva de las Manos on day trips.

Sleeping & Eating

Posada el Caminante GUESTHOUSE $$
(☎432204; Rivadavia 937; d AR$280) The best bet in town, Señora Ethiel's inn fills up fast. This welcoming hostess has four spotless rooms with comfy beds, heating and private, modern bathrooms. The abundant breakfast (extra) is worthwhile, especially during fruit season.

Hotel Americano HOTEL $$
(☎432074; www.hotelamericanoweb.com.ar; San Martín 1327; s/d/tr AR$195/300/360, superior s/d/tr AR$350/410/475; P 📶) Thriving Americano also has a decent grill and cafe that's busy in the evenings. Rooms vary widely – some lack windows, others can be quite cozy – so ask to see a few before deciding.

Hotel Belgrano HOTEL $
(☎432019; www.hotelbelgrano.guiapatagonia.net; San Martín 1001; dm/s/d AR$70/170/240) This big, boxy corner hotel has spacious concrete rooms with decent mattresses but not much ambience. Most folks shuffle in during the wee hours from Chaltén Travel shuttles.

Camping Municipal CAMPGROUND $
(Laguna de los Cisnes, off Mariano Moreno; per tent AR$20, plus AR$10 per person, vehicles AR$15-25, 4-person cabañas per person AR$120) The cheapest option for backpackers is this campground with rustic cabins on the south side of town. It's shaded by breezy poplars and has hot showers.

Salón Iturrioz CAFE $
(cnr Rivadavia & San Martín; sandwiches AR$30; ⏲8am-8pm; 📶) This charming brick corner cafe is the temporary home of antiques and photographs that will eventually be on display at the Museo Regional Cueva de las Manos (being built across the street). Check out the artifacts, including a gorgeous old silver cash register, while waiting for your hot chocolate.

There are a couple of well-stocked *panaderías* (bakeries) and supermarkets along San Martín.

Information

Banco de Santa Cruz (cnr San Martín & Rivadavia) Has an ATM and changes traveler's checks.

Hospital Distrital (☎432040; Colón 1237)

Post office (cnr JD Perón & Belgrano)

Tourist office (☎432732; peritomoreno@santacruzpatagonia.gob.ar; San Martín; ⏲7am-11:30pm Mon-Fri, 8am-3pm Sat & Sun) Helpful, with a surprising number of pamphlets and brochures. There is also a desk at the bus terminal.

Zoyen (☎432207; zoyenturismo@yahoo.com.ar; Peron 1008) Good local travel agency with trips to Cueva de las Manos in high season.

Getting There & Away

LADE (☎432055; San Martín 1065) flies to El Calafate, Río Gallegos, Río Grande and Ushuaia.

The bus terminal sits behind the YPF rotunda at the northern entrance to town. Taxis (AR$10) provide the only transport between here and the center, other than a flat 15-minute walk. Buses leave a few times daily for Los Antiguos (AR$35, 40 minutes), though departure times aren't reliable as they're usually scheduled to connect with incoming buses from RN 40, which are often delayed. In the afternoon, starting at 3:50pm, multiple buses also head for Comodoro Rivadavia (AR$147, five hours) via RN3.

Several shuttle services also offering excursions serve travelers on RN 40. From November to April, **Chaltén Travel** (☎ in El Calafate 2902-492212; www.chaltentravel.com) goes north to Bariloche (11 hours), departing from Hotel Belgrano in Perito Moreno at 8pm on even-numbered days. Shuttles leave Hotel Belgrano at 8am to head south to El Chaltén (11 hours) on odd-numbered days.

The bus company **Taqsa** (☎432675) now runs the entire stretch of RN 40 between El Calafate and Bariloche several times a week starting at the end of October, stopping at El Chaltén, Bajo Caracoles, Perito Moreno and Esquel along the way. For more Ruta 40 options, see the boxed text, p417.

Los Antiguos

☎02963 / POP 2900

Situated on the windy shores of Lago Buenos Aires, the agricultural oasis of Los Antiguos is home to *chacras* (small independent farms) of cherries, strawberries, apples, apricots and peaches. Before Europeans arrived, it was *I-Keu-khon* or 'Place of the Elders' to Tehuelches. It makes an attractive crossing to Chile and the stretch of road between Perito Moreno and Los Antiguos affords spectacular lake views.

Volcán Hudson's 1991 eruption covered the town in ash, but farms have bounced back. In summer **Lago Buenos Aires**, South America's second-biggest lake, is warm enough for a brisk swim. The stunning **Río Jeinemeni** is a favored spot for trout and salmon fishing.

Most services in the town are on or near east-west Av 11 de Julio, which heads west to the Chilean frontier at Chile Chico, the region's most convenient border crossing. Perito Moreno and RN 40 are 60km east.

Festivals & Events

Fiesta de la Cereza CHERRY FESTIVAL

Rodeos, live music and the crowning of the national Cherry Queen during the second weekend of January. Artisan goods are sold and *peñas folkloricas* (Argentine folk music concerts) at private farms go on all night long – see the tourist information office for more information.

Sleeping & Eating

Hostería Antigua Patagonia HOTEL $$

(☎491038; www.antiguapatagonia.com.ar, in Spanish; RP 43 Acceso Este; s/d AR$413/482, ste AR$525-585) In a stunning setting, this plush lakefront complex has a dose of rustic, with wooden trunks in rooms, four-poster beds and a stone fireplace that begs you to curl up like a cat. It's 2km east of town.

Cabañas Rincon de los Poetas CABINS $

(☎491051; Patagonia Argentina 226; d/tr/q AR$240/280/320) These snug wooden cabins equipped with kitchenettes are nothing fancy, but they prove good value for couples and families. It's located two blocks from the center.

Hotel Los Antiguos Cerezos HOTEL $$

(☎491132; hotel_losantiguoscerezos@hotmail.com; Av 11 de Julio 850; s/d AR$210/280) Modern rooms all feature private bathroom and TV, and hearty meals satisfy a regular crowd of farmers, gauchos and businessmen.

Albergue Padilla GUESTHOUSE $

(☎491140; San Martín 44; dm/d AR$80/280) Chaltén Travel shuttles deposit lodgers at this family-run institution after dark. The dorms share bathrooms (with plenty of hot water). You'll have to shell out a few extra pesos for sheets and towels. The staff have RN 40 shuttle tickets and the latest details on Chilean border crossing and ferries.

Camping Municipal CAMPGROUND $

(☎491265; RP 43; tent site/dm/cabin AR$15/100/150) Windbreaks help considerably at this lakeshore site 1.5km east of town. Dorms are in windowless cabins with hot showers are available in the evening; whole cabins sleep up to four.

TOP CHOICE **Viva El Viento** CAFE $

(☎491109; www.vivaelviento.com; Av 11 de Julio 447; mains AR$25-40; ⏰9am-9pm Oct-Apr) This stylish cafe and restaurant – boasting fresh salads, strong coffee, free wi-fi and warm service by the Dutch owner and his Argentine girlfriend – is a traveler's oasis. The menu offers gourmet versions of classic dishes like milanesas, burgers, grilled salmon and steak.

Information

Banco de Santa Cruz (Av 11 de Julio 531) Has a 24-hour ATM.

Locutorio (Alameda 436) Also has internet.

Post office (Gregores 19)

Tourist information office (491261; www.losantiguos.tur.ar, in Spanish; Av 11 de Julio 446; 8am-8pm) Helpful, with a map of town and farms selling fresh produce. The website has comprehensive lodging and transport information in multiple languages.

Getting There & Around

The gradual paving of RN 40 may alter transport options and times, so get current information.

Buses go several times daily to nearby Perito Moreno (AR$35, 40 minutes). Those in a rush to move on will find more transport links there to other parts of Patagonia. For Chile, **La Unión** (491078; cnr Perito Moreno & Patagonia Argentina) crosses the border to Chile Chico (AR$20) on weekdays at noon.

From mid-November to March, **Chaltén Travel** (www.chaltentravel.com) goes to El Chaltén on even-numbered days at 9am, stopping first in Perito Moreno. See the boxed text, p417 for northbound schedules.

Ferry **El Tehuelche** (in Chile 56-67-234240) crosses Lago General Carrera daily from Chile Chico to Puerto Ibañez (passengers/vehicles CH$2000/18,000, 2 hours) daily at 7:30am, but check for schedule changes. Larger vehicles must pay extra, according to size. Alternatively, it's possible to continue overland around the lake's southern shore to Carretera Austral and Coyhaique.

Leiva Remise (491228) taxi service is useful when it's pouring rain and you need a ride to your hotel.

Cueva de las Manos

Unesco World Heritage site **Cueva de las Manos** (Cave of the Hands; admission AR$50; 9am-7pm) features incredible rock art, a must-see if you pass through. Dating from about 7370 BC, these polychrome paintings cover recesses in the near-vertical walls with imprints of human hands, drawings of guanacos and, from a later period, abstract designs. Of around 800 images, more than 90% are of left hands; one has six fingers.

The approach is via rough but scenic provincial roads off RN 40, abutting Río de las Pinturas. Drive with caution: bounding guanacos are abundant. There are two points of access: a more direct route via Bajo Caracoles, 46km away on the south side of the river; and another from Hostería Cueva de las Manos, on the north side, via a footbridge. Guides in Perito Moreno organize day trips (around AR$250 per person plus park entrance fee). The trip from Perito Moreno is about 3½ hours (one way) over rocky roads. Once you arrive at the caves, free guided walks are given every hour by knowledgeable staff. There's an information center and a basic *confitería* at the reception house near the southern entrance, but it's best to bring your own food.

On the doorstep of Argentina's best deposit of rock art, **Hostería Cueva de las Manos** (in Buenos Aires 011-5237-4043; www.cuevadelasmanos.net; dm/d AR$127/485, cabin for 2/3/4/6 people AR$582/705/823/1013; Nov-Apr), formerly Estancia Los Toldos, sits a short distance off RN 40, 52km south of Perito Moreno. Guests can stay in cabins, the *hostería* or a 20-person dormitory. Rooms are plain but well appointed. Guests and tour groups can approach Cueva de los Manos via a scenic but challenging hiking trail (summer only) that starts from the *hostería*, descends the canyon and crosses Río de las Pinturas.

Rustic but welcoming **Estancia Casa de Piedra** (02963-432199; off RN 40; campsites per person AR$30, dm AR$100; Dec-Mar), a basic ranch 76km south of Perito Moreno, has plain rooms and allows camping. It's a good spot for trekkers to hunker down: there are nearby volcanoes and you can take a beautiful day-long hike to the Cueva de las Manos via Cañon de las Pinturas. From the *estancia*, it's 12km to the canyon, then another 6km to the cave – estimate about 10 hours round-trip. Hikers should get an early start and bring their own food; guides can be contracted here but the trail is clear enough to go without one.

Bajo Caracoles

Blink and you'll miss this dusty gas stop. Little has changed since Bruce Chatwin dubbed it 'a crossroads of insignificant importance with roads leading all directions apparently to nowhere' in *In Patagonia* in 1975. If you're headed south, fill the tank,

ESTANCIAS IN PATAGONIA

Most assume *estancias* are all about livestock, but these offbeat offerings prove otherwise.

A Wealth of Wildlife

» Meet the neighbors – that would be the penguins, seabirds and elephant seals – around Península Valdés' **Estancia Rincón Chico** (p394).

» Spot dozens of the namesake species of **Estancia El Cóndor** (p428) at this rugged mountain ranch north of El Chaltén.

» View the diverse fauna of Magellanic penguins, sea lions, guanacos and pumas at **Hostería Monte León** (p410).

Breathtaking Beauty

» Luxuriate among glaciers, lakes and the ragged Mt Fitz Roy in the exclusive **Hostería Estancia Helsingfors** (p449).

» Gallop the rugged splendor surrounding Parque Nacional Perito Moreno at the hospitable **Estancia Menelik** (p429).

» Explore the wonders of a petrified forest and sea islands inhabited solely by birds, penguins and sea lions at the magical **Bahía Bustamante** (p428).

Just Like Indiana Jones

» Trek to Unesco World Heritage site Cueva de las Manos from **Hostería Cueva de las Manos** (p427), via the serpentine red-rock canyon of Río de las Pinturas.

The Bargain Bin

» Grab your zzzs in a bunk bed and save some bucks: **Estancia Menelik** (p429) and **Estancia Casa de Piedra** (p429) all offer affordable *refugio* (rustic shelter) lodgings.

since it's the only reliable gas pump between Perito Moreno (128km north) and Tres Lagos (409km south). From here RP 39 heads west to Lago Posadas and the Paso Roballos to Chile.

Lodgers put on a brave face for **Hotel Bajo Caracoles** (☎02963-490100; d AR$280), with old gas heating units that require a watchful eye. It also stocks basic provisions, serves decent coffee and has the only private telephone in town.

Heading south, RN 40 takes a turn for the worse: it's 100km of gravel to Las Horquetas, a blip on the radar screen where RN 40, RP 27 and RP 37 intersect. From here it's another 128km southeast via RP 27 to Gobernador Gregores, the first half of which is currently paved.

Parque Nacional Perito Moreno

Wild and windblown, Parque Nacional Perito Moreno is an adventurer's dream. Approaching from the steppe, the massive snowcapped peaks of the Sierra Colorada rise like sentinels. Guanacos graze the tufted grasses, condors circle above, and wind blurs the surface of aquamarine and cobalt lakes. If you come here, you will be among 1200 yearly visitors – that is, mostly alone. Solitude reigns and, save for services offered by local *estancias,* you are entirely on your own.

Honoring the park system's founder, this remote but increasingly popular park encompasses 1150 sq km, 310km southwest of the town of Perito Moreno. Don't confuse this gem with Parque Nacional Los Glaciares (home to the Perito Moreno Glacier) further south.

The sedimentary Sierra Colorada is a palette of rusty hues. Beyond the park boundary, glacier-topped summits such as 3706m **Cerro San Lorenzo** (the highest peak in the area) tower over the landscape. The highest peak within the park is Cerro Mié (2254m).

As precipitation increases toward the west, the Patagonian steppe grasslands along the park's eastern border become sub-Antarctic forests of southern beech, lenga and coihue. Because the base altitude exceeds 900m, weather can be severe. Summer is usually comfortable, but warm clothing and proper gear are imperative in any season. The water is pure but you must bring all food and supplies.

Sights & Activities

Behind the information center, a one-hour interpretive trail leads to **Pinturas Rupestres**, a small number of cave paintings with interpretive signs in English. Consult park rangers for backpacking options and guided walks to the pictographs at **Casa de Piedra** on Lago Burmeister, and to **Playa de los Amonites** on Lago Belgrano, where there are fossils.

From Estancia La Oriental, it's a 2½-hour hike to the summit of 1434m **Cerro León** for a dazzling panorama. Immediately east of the summit, the volcanic outcrop of **Cerro de los Cóndores** is a nesting site. Pumas have also been spotted here and guanacos down below.

Sleeping & Eating

There are free campgrounds at the information center (barren and exposed; no fires allowed); at Lago Burmeister, 16km from the information center (more scenic and well sheltered among dense lenga forest; fires allowed); and at El Rincón, 15km away (no fires). None has showers, but there are pit toilets.

Estancia Menelik ESTANCIA $

(satellite phone 011-4152-5500, in Buenos Aires 011-4735-7704; www.cielospatagonicos.com; refugio per person AR$106, per person full board AR$633; Oct-Mar) With a panorama of Parque Nacional Perito Moreno, this working ranch built in 1920 is a prime destination for horseback riding. You won't find any Marlboro man wannabees here, it's the real deal. Highlights include overnight trips to the high camp of Veranada de Jones. Shoestring travelers can stay in a simple bunkhouse. Horse riding excursions run a reasonable AR$148 per day. Travelers should have their own vehicle.

Information

Visitors must register at the park's information center on the eastern boundary; it's stocked with informative maps and brochures. Rangers offer guided hikes; they can also be contacted via the national parks office in Gobernador Gregores, where it may be possible to arrange a ride.

Getting There & Away

Public-transport changes often; check with tourist offices in Perito Moreno, Los Antiguos and El Calafate for updates. Las Loicas (see the boxed text, p417) can take travelers here from Perito Moreno. In summer hitchhiking is possible from the RN 40 junction, but the park is so large that getting to trailheads presents difficulties. From April to November the road is impassable at times. If you're driving, carry spare gas and tires.

Gobernador Gregores

02962 / POP 2521

Sleepy Gobernador Gregores is one of the better stops on this route, with of hotels and shops offering a cheerful demeanor.

Gregores is 60km east of RN 40 on RP 25. It's the nearest town to Parque Nacional Perito Moreno (still 200km west) and an ideal spot to get supplies and arrange transportation. There's a **tourist office** (491259; gregoresturismo@yahoo.com.ar; San Martín 514; 8am-2pm Mon-Fri) and the **national parks administration office** (491477; San Martín 882; 9am-4pm Mon-Fri) can be helpful if you have plans to go to Parque Nacional Perito Moreno.

Seventy kilometers west of town via RP 29, the waters of **Lago Cardiel** are well loved by anglers for blue-ribbon salmon and rainbow trout fishing. From the junction to the lake it's another 116km to **Tres Lagos**, where a jovial couple run a 24-hour YPF station, then another 123km west to El Chaltén. At present, the route to Tres Lagos is the last unpaved section of RN 40 this far south.

Summer-only **Camping Nuestra Señora del Valle** (491398; gregoresturismo@yahoo.com.ar; cnr Roca & Chile; free campsites) has showers, hot water and stone grills. Hot meals (AR$60) and firm beds are at friendly **Cañadón León** (491082; Roca 397; s/d/tr AR$230/280/370;), with 11 rooms that are ample and spotless. Reserve ahead. It also rents cars and provides regional transfers.

Cerro San Lorenzo (cnr San Martín & Alberdi) buses leave for Puerto San Julián (AR$115, four hours) Monday to Saturday at 4pm or 6pm – ask at the office for exact departure times. **Taqsa** (Paralello 956) goes to Río Gallegos (AR$576, eight hours) daily.

El Chaltén

02962 / POP 600

An odd collection of chalets and shacks, this colorful village overlooks the stunning northern sector of Parque Nacional Los Glaciares.

Every summer, thousands of trekkers come to explore the world-class trails that start right here. Founded in 1985, in a rush to beat Chile to the land claim, El Chaltén is still a frontier town, albeit an offbeat one, featuring constant construction, hippie values and packs of roaming dogs. Every year more mainstream tourists come to see what the fuss is all about, but in winter months (May to September) most hotels and services board up and transportation links are few.

El Chaltén is named for Cerro Fitz Roy's Tehuelche name, meaning 'peak of fire' or 'smoking mountain' – an apt description of the cloud-enshrouded summit. Perito Moreno and Carlos Moyano later named it after the *Beagle's* Captain FitzRoy, who navigated Darwin's expedition up the Río Santa Cruz in 1834, coming within 50km of the cordillera.

Sights & Activities

The streets of El Chaltén are empty at midday when travelers are out hiking, rock climbing and horseback riding in the surrounding mountains. For more details on tours and excursions, see Activities, p434.

Reserva Los Huemules NATURE PRESERVE
(satellite phone 011-4152-5300; www.loshuemules.com; entry AR$50) This private 5500-hectare reserve has 25km of marked trails, a quiet alternative to the national park that's just abutting it. Stop by the visitor center first. It's 17km beyond El Chaltén, just after Río Eléctrico.

Capilla de los Escaladores CHAPEL
A simple chapel of Austrian design memorializes the many climbers who have lost their lives to the precarious peaks since 1953.

Festivals & Events

Fiesta del Pueblo FESTIVAL
Every October 12, on the wet heels of winter while streets are still mired in mud, El Chaltén celebrates the town anniversary, with dancing in the school gym, barbecues and live music.

El Chaltén

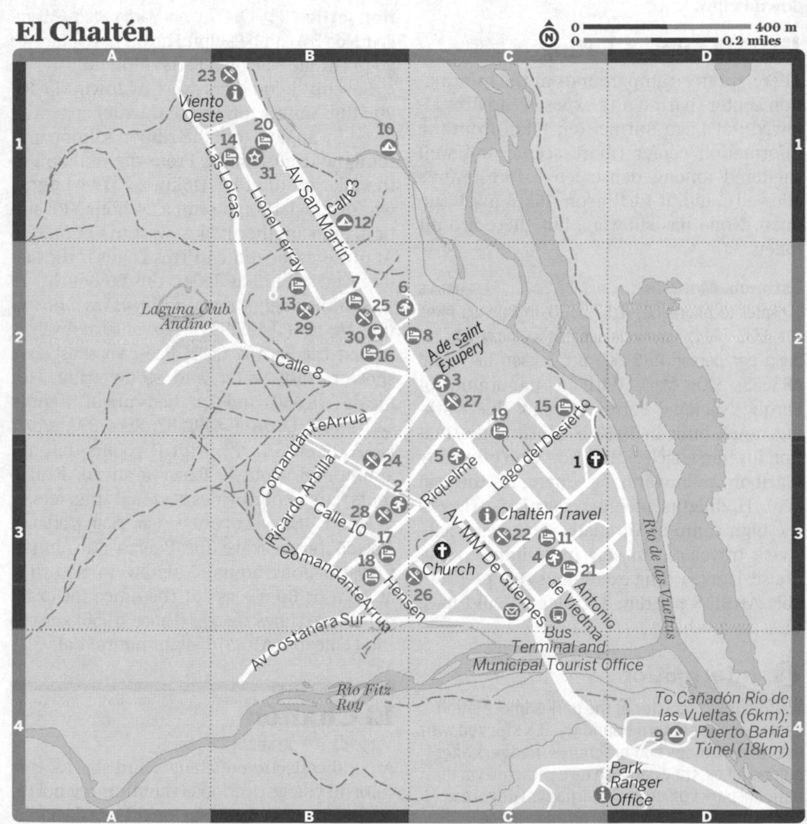

Fiesta Nacional de Trekking FESTIVAL

In the last week of February, this event brings a circus of outdoor freaks for rock climbing, bouldering and woodcutting competitions, as well as running and mountain-bike races.

Sleeping

Reservations should be made at least one month in advance for the January-February high season – demand here is that great. Plus it would be particularly depressing to arrive in the dark with the wind howling and no bed waiting. One solution is to bring a bombproof tent – there's always space in the campgrounds.

Dorm beds fill up fast in summer. Unless otherwise noted, thin walls, cramped dorms and insufficient shared facilities are the norm.

TOP CHOICE **Nothofagus B&B** B&B $$

(493087; www.nothofagusbb.com.ar; cnr Hensen & Riquelme, s/d/tr without bathroom AR$190/200/280, s/d/tr AR$280/290/340; Oct-Apr;) Attentive and adorable, this chalet-style inn offers a toasty retreat with hearty breakfast options. Green practices include separating organic waste and replacing towels only when asked. Wooden-beam rooms have carpet and some views, but most have bathrooms shared with one other room.

Anita's House CABINS $$

(493288; www.anitashouse.com.ar; Av San Martín 249; cabin for 2/3/4 people AR$380/400/450;) When the wind howls, these few modern cabins are a snug spot for groups, couples or families, smack in the center of town. Owner-run, the service is impeccable. Kitchens come fully equipped and there's room service and cable TV. Two-story cabins, with higher rates, are more spacious.

Posada Lunajuim INN $$$

(493047; www.posadalunajuim.com.ar; Trevisán 45; s/d/tr AR$574/701/838) Combining modern comfort with a touch of the off-beat, this welcoming inn gets good reviews from guests. The halls are lined with the owner's monochrome sculptures and textured paintings, and a stone fireplace and library provide a rainy-day escape. Nice touches include DIY box lunches and a buffet breakfast.

Albergue Patagonia GUESTHOUSE $

(493019; www.patagoniahostel.com.ar; Av San Martín 493; dm/d without bathroom AR$60/190, s/d/t AR$270/320/360; Sep-May) After a recent remodel, this already welcoming wooden farmhouse is gorgeous. Dorms in a separate building are spacious and modern, with good service and a humming atmosphere. They also rent bikes.

El Chaltén

Sights

1 Capilla de los Escaladores ... C3
Casa de Guías ... (see 30)
El Relincho ... (see 12)

Activities, Courses & Tours

2 Chaltén Fishing ... B3
3 El Chaltén Mountain Guides ... C2
Fitzroy Expediciones ... (see 5)
4 Las Lengas ... C3
5 Patagonia Aventura ... C3
6 Patagonia Mágica ... B2

Sleeping

7 Albergue Patagonia ... B2
8 Anita's House ... C2
9 Campamento Confluencia ... D4
10 Camping El Refugio ... B1
11 Condor de los Andes ... C3
12 El Relincho ... B1
13 Hostería El Puma ... B2
14 Hostería Koonek ... B1
15 Inlandsis ... C2
16 Los Cerros ... B2
17 Nothofagus B&B ... B3
18 Posada La Base ... B3
19 Posada Lunajuim ... C2
20 Rancho Grande Hostel ... B1
21 Senderos Hosteria ... C3

Eating

22 Domo Blanco ... C3
23 El Muro ... B1
24 Estepa ... B3
25 Fuegia Bistro ... B2
26 La Chocolatería ... C3
27 La Lucinda ... C2
28 La Tapera ... B3
Patagonicus ... (see 22)
29 Ruca Mahuida ... B2

Drinking

30 La Cervecería ... B2

Entertainment

31 Zafarrancho ... B1

WORTH A TRIP

ESTANCIA EL CÓNDOR

A burly slice of heaven, this remote **estancia** (☎satellite phone 011-4152-5400, in Buenos Aires 011-4735-7704; www.cielospatagonicos.com; per person incl full board AR$633; ⊙Oct-Mar) sits tucked into the shores of Lago San Martín. A private nature reserve, tawny steppe, mossy beech forest and frozen mountaintops comprise its 40,000 hectares.

Even for Patagonia this landscape seems oversized – from the massive turquoise lake (known as O'Higgins on its Chilean side) to the craggy cliffs where condors wheel on the wind. Riding enthusiasts could do a week on horseback without running out of fresh terrain; in addition, the adjoining mountain refuge of La Nana provides a basecamp even deeper in the wilderness. Trails are also apt for hiking, though river crossings should always be made with a guide. A daytrip to the *condorera* (where condors nest) is a highlight.

The *estancia* occupies a curious footnote in Patagonian history. Its *puesto* (homestead) La Nana was home to an infamous Brit named Jimmy Radburn, who kidnapped a Tehuelche woman named Juana (with her consent – she had already been sold off by her father to pay a gambling debt) and came to this ultra-remote spot at the turn of the 20th century to raise a family. Currently La Nana is only accessible by a day-long hike or ride from the main *casco*.

Lodgings are comfortable but not luxuriant. The *casco* has six rooms, each with a private bathroom, a large stone fireplace and a small collection of literature on the region. Sometimes an overflow of visitors may stay at a more rustic bunkhouse on site. Meals include fresh vegetables from the greenhouse and meat from the ranch.

Visitors need their own transportation. El Cóndor is located three hours from Tres Lagos, 118km off RN40, on the way to El Chaltén. Currently, there is no legal border crossing here.

Senderos Hostería B&B $$$
(☎493336; www.senderoshosteria.com.ar; Perito Moreno s/n; s/d AR$642/752) This contemporary, corrugated tin home offers wonderful amenities for trekkers with a little extra cash to spend on accommodations: a popular onsite wine bar and restaurant, smart rooms with soft white sheets and occasional Fitz Roy views.

Hostería El Puma LODGE $$$
(☎493095; www.hosteriaelpuma.com.ar; Lionel Terray 212; s/d AR$604/743; P📶) This luxury lodge with 12 comfortable rooms offers intimacy without pretension. The rock-climbing and summit photographs and maps lining the hall may inspire your next expedition, but lounging by the fireplace is the most savory way to end the day.

Posada La Base GUESTHOUSE $$
(☎493031; www.elchaltenpatagonia.com.ar; Calle 10, No 16; d/tr/q AR$320/360/400) A smart, sprawling house with spacious rooms that all face outside and have access to an immaculate kitchen. Large groups should book rooms 5 and 6, which share an inside kitchen with dining area. The reception area has a popular video loft with a multilingual collection.

Inlandsis GUESTHOUSE $
(☎493276; www.inlandsis.com.ar; Lago del Desierto 480; small/large d AR$210/280, cabin for 2/3/4/6 people AR$400/430/460/530; ⊙Oct-Apr) This small, relaxed brick house offers economical rooms with bunk beds (some are airless, check before booking) or larger, pricier doubles with two twin beds or a queen-sized bed. Inlandsis also has bilevel cabins with bathtubs, kitchens and DVD players.

Condor de Los Andes HOSTEL $
(☎493101; www.condordelosandes.com; cnr Río de las Vueltas & Halvor Halvorsen; dm/d AR$90/310; ⊙Oct-Apr) This homey hostel has the feel of a ski lodge, with worn bunks, warm rooms and a roaring fire. The guest kitchen is immaculate and there are comfortable lounge spaces.

Rancho Grande Hostel HOSTEL $
(☎493092; www.ranchograndehostel.com; Av San Martín 724; dm/d/tr AR$70/270/290; @) Serving as Chaltén's Grand Central Station (Chaltén Travel buses stop here), this bustling backpacker factory has something for everyone, from bus reservations to internet (extra) and cafe service. Clean four-bed rooms are stacked with blankets, and bathrooms sport rows of shower stalls. Doubles and triples come with private bathrooms.

Hostería Koonek GUESTHOUSE $$

(☎493304; www.hosteriakoonek.com.ar; Lionel Terray 415; d/tr AR$280/320; ⊙Oct-May) Tidy and welcoming, this guesthouse is built next to a bluff popular with rock climbers. Its eight rooms accommodate up to four guests each. All come with private bathrooms that are tiny but clean.

Los Cerros HOTEL $$$

(☎493182; www.loscerrosdelchalten.com; Av San Martín s/n; s/d AR$1174/1384; ⊙Nov-Apr; @📶) This chic, top-end *hostería* perched on a hill has sweeping views of the valley. The style is tribal-modern with thick woven wall hangings and natural fibers. The absence of TVs and phones in rooms is meant to bring you back to nature (but the gourmet meals and wine selections will surely zip you right back to civilization).

Hostel Pioneros del Valle HOSTEL $

(☎491368; www.caltur.com.ar/pioneros/hostel.html; Av San Martín 451; dm AR$80; 📶) New on the hostel scene, this untested behemoth has mixed six-bed dorms with in-room bathrooms, lockers and free wi-fi, in addition to a plasma TV. Run by a transport company, there's also travel & sleep packages.

Campamento Confluencia CAMPGROUND $

(campsites free) A zero-amenity campground across from the park ranger office and visitor center.

Camping El Refugio CAMPGROUND $

(☎493221; Calle 3 s/n; campsites per person AR$25, dm AR$50) This private campground is attached to a basic hostel – hot showers for campers are included in the fee. Sites are exposed and there is some sparse firewood (fires are OK).

El Relincho CAMPGROUND $

(☎493007; www.elrelinchopatagonia.com.ar; Av San Martín 505; campsites per person AR$35; vehicles AR$5-10) Another private campground, similarly wind-whipped.

Eating & Drinking

Groceries, especially produce, are limited and expensive. Bring what you can from El Calafate.

TOP CHOICE **El Muro** ARGENTINE $$

(Av San Martín 912; mains AR$35-60; ⊙dinner) For exquisite, ribsticking mountain food (think sweet and sour lamb chops or trout with crisp grilled veggies), head to this tiny outpost at the end of the road. Portions are abundant and desserts – such as warm apple pie or bread pudding – should practically be mandatory.

La Cervecería BREWPUB $

(Av San Martín 320; snacks AR$30; ⊙lunch & dinner till late) That aprés-hike pint usually evolves into a night out in this humming pub with *simpatico* staff and a feisty female beer master. Savor a stein of unfiltered blond pilsner or turbid bock with pasta or *locro* (a spicy stew of maize, beans, beef, pork and sausage).

Fuegia Bistro INTERNATIONAL $$

(Av San Martín 342; mains AR$35-60; ⊙dinner Mon-Sat) Favored for its warm ambience and savory mains, this upscale eatery boasts good veggie options and a reasonable wine list. Try the homemade pasta with ricotta, spinach and fresh mushrooms, or trout with lemon.

La Lucinda CAFE $

(Av San Martín 175; sandwiches AR$35; ⊙7am-midnight; 🖉) With homemade soups and stews, hot sandwiches (including good vegetarian options) and a selection of coffee, tea and wine. This artsy, sky-blue cafe is friendly and almost always open – a godsend when the weather is howling. Breakfast is served too.

La Tapera TAPAS $$

(cnr Antonio Rojo & Riquelme; mains AR$30-70; ⊙lunch & dinner) This ambient eatery specializes in tapas but wintry staples such as pumpkin soup and grilled steak are also good options. On cold days, you can sit so close to the open fireplace that you'll have to peel off a layer.

Estepa PATAGONIAN $$

(cnr Cerro Solo & Av Antonio Rojo; mains AR$35-80; ⊙noon-1am Tue-Sun) Local favorite Estepa cooks up consistent, flavorful dishes such as lamb with calafate sauce, trout ravioli or spinach crepes.

La Chocolatería CAFE $

(Lago del Desierto 105; snacks AR$15-30) This irresistible chocolate factory tells the story of local climbing legends on the walls. It makes for an intimate evening out, with options ranging from spirit-spiked hot cocoa to wine and fondue.

Ruca Mahuida GOURMET $$$

(Lionel Terray 55; mains AR$50-85; ⊙7-11pm) Smoked trout, squash soufflé and salmon ravioli are a welcome departure from typical fare at this stone house with sheepskin benches. Though we wish it were more consistent, it has gotten some rave reviews.

Patagonicus PIZZERIA $
(Av MM De Güemes 57; pizza AR$40; closed Wed & May-Sep) The best pizza in town, with 20 kinds of pie, salads and wine served at sturdy wood tables surrounded by huge picture windows. Cakes and coffee are also worth trying.

Domo Blanco ICE CREAM $
(Av MM De Güemes s/n; snack AR$12; 2pm-midnight) Homemade ice cream made with fruit harvested from a local *estancia* and calafate bushes in town.

Entertainment

Zafarrancho, behind Rancho Grande Hostel (p432), is a bar-cafe that has internet and screens movies.

Information

Technologically speaking, El Chaltén is a study in contrasts: there's no cell phone reception and one ATM (located in the bus station), but you're likely to pick up a good wi-fi signal in your hotel room and you won't have any problem finding a long-distance call center or gas station. Credit cards are almost useless, though some restaurants are starting to accept them, but traveler's checks, euros and US dollars are widely accepted. If you're coming from El Calafate, just take out the cash you'll need there and skip the possible complications in El Chaltén. Surf www.elchalten.com for a good overview of the town.

Chaltén Travel (493092; cnr Av MM De Güemes & Lago del Desierto) Books airline tickets and offers weather-dependent internet service.

Municipal tourist office (493370; comfom elchalten@yahoo.com.ar; Terminal de Omnibus; 8am-8pm) Friendly and extremely helpful, with lodging lists and good information on town and tours. English is spoken.

Park ranger office (493004/24; donations welcome; 9am-8pm) Many daytime buses stop for a short bilingual orientation at this visitor center, just before the bridge over the Río Fitz Roy. Park rangers distribute a map and town directory and do a good job of explaining the park's ecological issues. Climbing documentaries are shown at 3pm daily – great for rainy days.

Puesto Sanitario (493033; AM De Agostini 70) Provides basic health services.

Viento Oeste (493200; Av San Martín 898) Sells books, maps and souvenirs and rents a wide range of camping equipment, as do several other sundries shops around town.

Getting There & Away

El Chaltén is 220km from El Calafate via newly paved roads.

All buses go to the new **bus terminal**, located near the entrance to town. For El Calafate (AR$75, 3½ hours), **Chaltén Travel** (493005/92; Av San Martín 635) has daily departures at 7:30am and 6pm in summer. **Cal-tur** (493079; San Martín 520) and **Taqsa** (493068; Av Antonio Rojo 88) also make the trip, but neither company will take advance reservations. Service is less frequent off-season.

Las Lengas (493023; Antonio de Viedma 95) Shuttles directly to El Calafate Airport (AR$120) in high season. Also has minivans to Lago Desierto (AR$130), Hostería El Pilar (AR$50) and Río Eléctrico (AR$50).

Chalten Travel goes to Bariloche on odd days of the month in high season (AR$620, two days), with an overnight stop in Perito Moreno (meals and accommodation extra).

Parque Nacional Los Glaciares (North)

In the northern part of the park, the Fitz Roy Range – with its rugged wilderness and shark-tooth summits – is the de-facto trekking capital of Argentina. It also draws world-class climbers for whom Cerro Torre and Cerro Fitz Roy are milestone ascents notorious for brutal weather conditions. But you don't have to be extreme to enjoy the numerous well-marked trails for hiking and jaw-dropping scenery – that is, when the clouds clear.

Parque Nacional Los Glaciares is divided into geographically separate northern and southern sectors. El Chaltén is the gateway town for the northern part of the park, with all the operators for tours and activities mentioned in this section. El Calafate is the gateway town for the southern section of the park, which features the Perito Moreno Glacier.

Activities

Hiking

Before heading out, stop by the park ranger office for updated trail conditions. The most stable weather for hiking comes not in summer but in March and April, when there is less wind (and fewer people). During the winter months of June and July trails may be closed – check first with the park ranger office.

Experienced backpackers can register to hike in the remote areas, which require some route finding. A first-person ranger

Parque Nacional Los Glaciares (North)

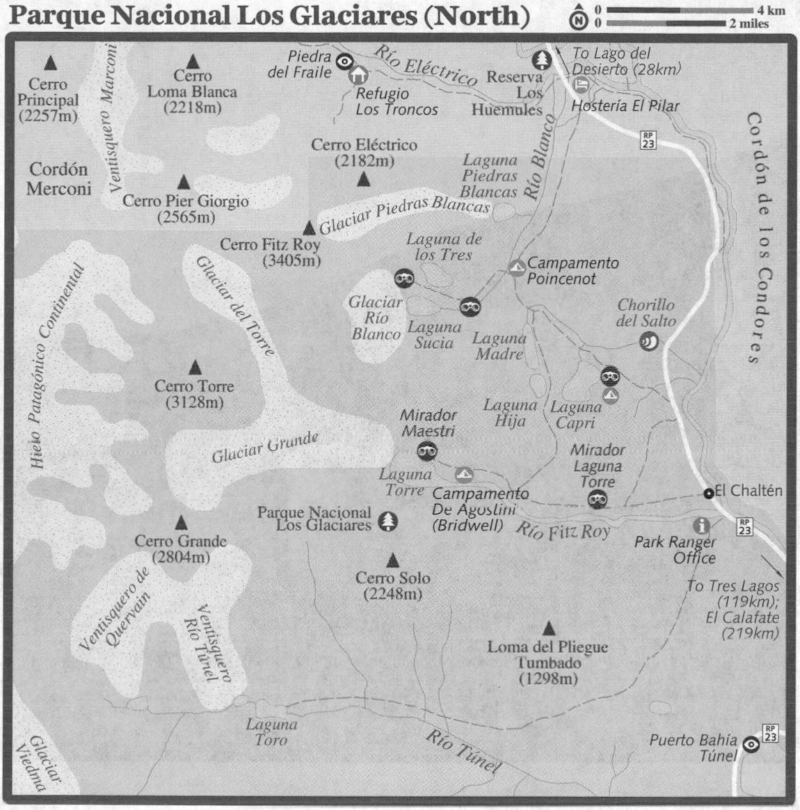

update is necessary for these hikes. For more information on hiking, read Lonely Planet's *Trekking in the Patagonian Andes*.

LAGUNA TORRE

If you have good weather – ie little wind – and clear skies, make this hike (three hours one way) a priority, since the toothy Cerro Torre is the most difficult local peak to see on normal blustery days.

There are two trail options which later merge. One starts at the northwestern edge of El Chaltén. From a signpost on Av San Martín, head west on Eduardo Brenner and then right to find the signposted start of the track. The Laguna Torre track winds up westwards around large boulders on slopes covered with typical Patagonian dry-land plants, then leads southwest past a wet meadow to a junction with a trail coming in from the left (see the following start) after 35 to 45 minutes.

Starting from the southern end of El Chaltén, follow Lago del Desierto west past the edge of town, then drop to the riverbed, passing a tiny hydroelectric installation. At a signpost the route climbs away from the river and leads on through scattered lenga and ñire woodland (a small, deciduous southern beech species), with the odd wire fence to step over, before merging with a more prominent (signposted) path coming in from the right.

Continue up past a rounded bluff to the **Mirador Laguna Torre**, a crest with the first clear view up the valley to the extraordinary 3128m rock spire of Cerro Torre, above a sprawling mass of intersecting glaciers.

The trail dips gently through stands of lenga, before cutting across open scrubby river flats and old revegetated moraines to reach a signposted junction with the Sendero Madre e Hija, a shortcut to Campamento Poincenot, 40 to 50 minutes on. Continuing

1

CHRISTOPHER GROENHOUT/LONELY PLANET IMAGES ©

4

NIGEL HICKS/ALAMY ©

2
ROLANDO GARIBOTTI/GETTY ©

Extreme Patagonia

Over 130 years ago, Lady Florence Dixie ditched high society to ride horses across the Patagonian steppe. Today, you can still fulfill a dream of scaling unnamed peaks, paddling beside sea lions or tracing a glacier's edge.

Horseback Riding

1 *Estancias* (ranches; p428) remind us how good it is to ride without fences, to feel the heat of a campfire and sleep under the stars.

Ice Climbing

2 Adrenaline, check. Near El Chaltén, eco-camps help you tackle the surreal frozen terrain in Parque Nacional Los Glaciares (p439), where good guiding services make it accessible even to amateurs.

Glacier Trekking

3 More than a hike, it's a full-immersion aesthetic experience. Strap on crampons and explore these living sculptures in Torres del Paine (p464) or Parque Nacional Los Glaciares (p439 and p448).

Diving

4 Clear waters, nearby shipwrecks and cool marine life make Península Valdés (p385) the diving capital of Argentina, with the best visibility in August.

Sea Kayaking

5 Paddle with penguins and Commerson's dolphins in Ría Deseado (p406) and Bahía Bustamante (p428), or play alongside sea lions near Península Valdés (p389).

Driving Ruta 40

6 Watch herds of dusky guanaco, or the slow approach of shimmering peaks. The sky was never bluer or bigger than on this remote road (p417) that flanks the Andes, an icon of slow travel.

3
CHRISTOPHER GROENHOUT/LONELY PLANET IMAGES ©

Clockwise from top left
1. Horseback riding, El Calafate (p440) **2.** Rock climbing, Cerro Fitz Roy (p438) **3.** Glaciar Perito Moreno (p448) **4.** Puerto Pirámides (p389)

up valley, bear left at another signposted fork and climb over a forested embankment to cross a small alluvial plain, following the fast-flowing glacial waters of the Río Fitz Roy. You'll arrive at **Campamento De Agostini** (formerly Bridwell) after a further 30 to 40 minutes. This free campground (with pit toilet) gets busy; it serves as a base camp for Cerro Torre climbers. The only other nearby camping is in a pleasant grove of riverside lengas below Cerro Solo.

Follow the trail along the lake's north side for about an hour to **Mirador Maestri** (no camping).

LAGUNA DE LOS TRES

This hike to a high alpine tarn is a bit more strenuous (four hours one way). The trail starts from a yellow-roofed pack station. After about an hour, there's a signed lateral to excellent free backcountry **campsites** at Laguna Capri. The main trail continues gently through windswept forests and past small lakes, meeting the Lagunas Madre and Hija trail. Carrying on through wind-worn ñire forest and along boggy terrain to **Río Blanco** (three hours) and the woodsy, mice-plagued **Campamento Poincenot**. The trail splits before Río Blanco to Río Eléctrico. Stay left to reach a climbers' base camp. Here the trail zigzags steeply up the tarn to the eerily still, glacial **Laguna de los Tres** in close view of 3405m Cerro Fitz Roy. Be prepared for high, potentially hazardous winds and allow extra time. Scurry down 200m left of the lookout for an exceptional view of the emerald-green **Laguna Sucia**.

PIEDRA DEL FRAILE

At Campamento Poincenot, the trail swings west to Laguna de los Tres or northeast along Río Blanco to Valle Eléctrico and Piedra del Fraile (eight hours from El Chaltén; five hours from the Río Blanco turnoff). From the turnoff, the latter trail leads to **Glaciar Piedras Blancas** (four hours), which ends with a scramble over massive granite boulders to a turquoise lake with dozens of floating icebergs. Pass through pastures and branches left up the valley along **Río Eléctrico**, enclosed by sheer cliffs, before reaching the private **Refugio Los Troncos** (campsites AR$50, refugio beds AR$110-180). Reservations are not possible since there are no phones – simply show up. The campground has a kiosk, restaurant and excellent services, and the owners can recommend trails.

Rather than backtrack, it's possible to head east, hopping over streams to RP 23, the route back to El Chaltén. You'll pass waterfall **Chorillo del Salto** on the way.

Buses to Lago del Desierto drop hikers at the Río Eléctrico bridge (AR$60).

LOMA DEL PLIEGUE TUMBADO & LAGUNA TORO

Heading southwest from the park ranger office, this trail (four to five hours one way) skirts the eastern face of Loma del Pliegue Tumbado going toward Río Túnel, then cuts west and heads to Laguna Toro. it's the only hike that allows views of both Cerros Torre and Fitz Roy at once. The hike is gentle, but prepare for strong winds and carry extra water.

LAGO DEL DESIERTO & CHILE

Some 37km north of El Chaltén is Lago del Desierto, near the Chilean border – a nice day-hike for rainy days with no visibility of the Fitz. A 500m trail leads to an overlook with fine lake and glacier views.

An increasingly popular way to get to Chile is crossing the border here with a one-to-three day trekking/ferry combination to Villa O'Higgins, the last stop on the Carretera Austral. The route is also popular with cyclists. Plans have started to put a road in here, but it may take decades.

For details, see the boxed text, p439.

☞ Tours

Las Lengas BUS TOUR
(☎493023; Viedma 95) Minibus service to Lago del Desierto (AR$130), leaving El Chaltén at 8:30am and 3pm daily. All-day trips (AR$150) stay at the lake for six hours. At the south end of the lake, travelers can dine in the inviting restaurant at **Hostería El Pilar** (☎493002; www.hosteriaelpilar.com.ar).

Patagonia Aventura BOAT TOUR
(☎493110; www.patagonia-aventura.com.ar; per person AR$130) Navigates Lago del Desierto. The alternative is a five-hour trek between the south end and the north end of the lake.

Hielo Sur BOAT TOUR
(☎56-067-431821; www.villaohiggins.com, in Spanish) This Chilean catamaran takes border-crossers from Candelario Mansilla to Glaciar O'Higgins (CH$65,000) on the Southern Ice Shelf, on its way to Villa O'Higgins, or goes to Villa O'Higgins (CH$40,000) more directly via Puerto Bahamondez. From Puerto Bahamondez, bus service to Villa O'Higgins is CH$2000.

Ice Climbing & Trekking

Many companies offer ice-climbing courses and ice treks, some including sleds pulled by Siberian huskies. Multiday guided hikes over the Hielo Patagónico Continental (Continental Ice Field) have the feel of polar expeditions. Catering to serious trekkers, this route involves technical climbing, including use of crampons and strenuous river crossings.

Fitzroy Expediciones MOUNTAINEERING
(Map p430; ☎493178; www.fitzroyexpediciones.com.ar; Av San Martín 56, El Chaltén) Runs glacier-trekking excursions on the south face of Cerro Torre. The trek usually begins at 7am, starting with a 2½-hour hike in (or camp out at Thorwood the previous night). Note that Fitzroy Expediciones does accept credit cards, unlike most businesses in town.

Casa de Guias MOUNTAINEERING
(Map p430; ☎493118; www.casadeguias.com.ar; Av San Martín 310, El Chaltén) Friendly and professional, with English-speaking guides certified by the Argentine Association of Mountain Guides (AAGM). They specialize in small groups. Offerings include mountain traverses, ascents for the very fit and rock-climbing classes.

Patagonia Aventura MOUNTAINEERING
(Map p430; ☎493110; www.patagonia-aventura.com.ar, in Spanish; Av San Martín 56, El Chaltén) Offers ice trekking (AR$440) and ice climbing (AR$550) on Glaciar Viedma. Trips include a six-hour hike with views of the glacier, a 2½-hour ice trek through truly awesome landscapes and all-day instruction in ice climbing.

El Chaltén Mountain Guides MOUNTAINEERING
(Map p430; ☎493267; www.ecmg.com.ar; Rio de las Vueltas 218, El Chaltén) Licensed guides do ice field traverse and ice-trekking day trips on Glaciar Torre. Rates decrease significantly with group size.

Fly-Fishing

Anglers should see **Chaltén Fishing** (Map p430; ☎493185; www.chaltenfishing.com.ar, in Spanish; Av Antonio Rojo 88, El Chaltén) for half-day trips to Lago del Desierto or on full-day excursions that include a few hours at Laguna Larga. Equipment is provided; call for current rates and information on fishing licenses.

WORTH A TRIP

HEADING INTO CHILE

Gonzo travelers can skirt the Southern Ice Field on foot to get from Argentina's Parque Nacional Los Glaciares and El Chaltén to Villa O'Higgins, the last stop on Chile's Carretera Austral. This one- to three-day trip can be completed between November and March. Bring all provisions, Chilean currency plus your passport and rain gear. Boat delays are not unheard of, so be prepared to stay overnight and pack enough food. Here's the nuts and bolts:

» Grab the shuttle bus from El Chaltén to the south shore of Lago del Desierto, 37km away (AR$130, one hour).

» Take the ferry to the north shore of Lago del Desierto (AR$130, 4½ hours). Another option is to hike the coast (15km, five hours). Pass through Argentine customs and immigration here. Camping is allowed.

» From the north shore of Lago del Desierto, trek or ride to Laguna Larga (1½ hours). Camping is not allowed.

» Trek or ride to Laguna Redonda (1½ hours). Camping is not allowed.

» Trek or ride to Candelario Mansilla (two hours). Candelario Mansilla has lodging in a family farmhouse, guided treks and horse rental (riding/pack horse CH$15,000/15,000 per day). Pass through Chilean customs and immigration here.

» Take the Hielo Sur catamaran (CH$40,000, four hours) at Candelario Mansilla on the south edge of Lago O'Higgins. It goes one to three times a week, most often on Saturdays with some Monday or Wednesday departures. Take the 8am bus from Puerto Bahamondez to Villa O'Higgins (CH$1500).

In Villa O'Higgins, **El Mosco** (☎54-067-431867; www.patagoniaelmosco.com; camping/dm per person CH$5000/11,000) has good lodging options. For Chilean ferry information, consult **Hielo Sur** (in Chile ☎067-431-821/822; www.villaohiggins.com) in O'Higgins.

Horseback Riding

Horses can be used to trot round town and to carry equipment with a guide (prices negotiable), but are not allowed unguided on national-park trails. Outfitter **El Relincho** (Map p430; ☎493007; www.elrelinchopatagonia.com.ar; San Martín 545, El Chaltén) takes riders to the pretty valley of Río de las Vueltas (AR$280, four hours) and also offers more challenging rides combined with a ranch barbecue. Cabin-style accommodations are also available (AR$480 for four people).

Kayak & Canoe Trips

As El Chaltén grows, so do the aquatic offerings. **Fitzroy Expediciones** (Map p430; ☎493178; www.fitzroyexpediciones.com.ar; Av San Martín 56, El Chaltén) has half-day guided kayaking trips on the Río de las Vueltas that stop for lunch at the company's adventure camp. (Overnight stays are also available in the timber lodge and eight cabins, 17km north of town – ask at the office in El Chaltén for more info.) You can also book two-day canoe and camping trips to Río La Leona.

Lake Cruises

Contact **Patagonia Aventura** (Map p430; ☎493110; www.patagonia-aventura.com.ar, in Spanish; Av San Martín 56, El Chaltén) about tourist launches from the Puerto Bahía Túnel on the north shore of Lago Viedma. The trip (per person AR$110, plus AR$60 transfer) takes in impressive views of the 40m Glaciar Viedma, grinding from Cerro Fitz Roy. Boat trips leave at 3:30pm and last 2½ hours.

Rock Climbing

Outfitters around town rent equipment; **Patagonia Mágica** (Map p430; ☎486261; www.patagoniamagica.com; Fonrouge s/n, El Chaltén) runs one-day rock-climbing workshops for beginners. Experienced climbers can go on the Glaciar Laguna Torre with certified guides.

Sleeping

Free backcountry campgrounds have one pit toilet. Some sites have dead wood for windbreaks but fires are prohibited. Water is pure as glacial melt; only wash downstream from the campground and pack out all trash.

Getting There & Away

The national park is just outside El Chaltén, which is convenient if you're driving your own car; otherwise, most excursions offer transfers in and out of the park for around AR$60. For details of transportation to El Chaltén, see Getting There & Away, p434.

El Calafate

☎02902 / POP 22,000

Named for the berry that, once eaten, guarantees your return to Patagonia, El Calafate hooks you with another irresistible attraction: Glaciar Perito Moreno, 80km away in Parque Nacional Los Glaciares. The glacier is a magnificent must-see, but its massive popularity has encouraged tumorous growth and rapid upscaling in once-quaint El Calafate. However, it's still a fun place to be with a range of traveler services. The strategic location between El Chaltén and Torres del Paine (Chile) makes it an inevitable stop for those in transit.

Located 320km northwest of Río Gallegos, and 32km west of RP 11's junction with northbound RN 40, El Calafate flanks the southern shore of Lago Argentino. The main strip, Av del Libertador General San Martín (typically abbreviated to Libertador), is dotted with cutesy knotted-pine souvenir shops, chocolate shops, restaurants and tour offices. Beyond the main street, pretensions melt away quickly: muddy roads lead to adhoc developments and open pastures.

January and February are the most popular (and costly) months to visit, but as shoulder-season visits grow steadily, both availability and prices stay a challenge.

Sights & Activities

TOP CHOICE Glaciarium MUSEUM

(☎497912; www.glaciarium.com; adult/child AR$80/55; ⏲9am-8pm Sep-May, 11am-8pm May-Aug) Unique and exciting, this gorgeous new museum illuminates the world of ice. Displays and bilingual films show how glaciers form, along with documentaries on continental ice expeditions and stark meditations on climate change. Adults can suit up in furry capes for the *bar de hielo* (AR$40 including drink), a blue-lit below-zero club serving vodka or fernet & Coke, of course, in glasses made of ice. The gift shop sells handmade and sustainable gifts crafted by Argentine artisans. They also host international cinema events. It's 6km from Calafate toward the national park. To get there, take the hourly transfer (roundtrip AR$25) from 1ero de Mayo between Av Libertador and Roca.

Reserva Natural Laguna Nimez BIRD-WATCHING

(binocular rental AR$20; ⏲daylight hours) Prime avian habitat alongside the lakeshore, north of town with a self-guided trail and staffed Casa Verde information hut. It's a great place to spot flamingos – but watching birds from El Calafate's shoreline on Lago Argentino can be just as good.

Centro de Interpretacíon Historico MUSEUM
(☎497799; www.museocalafate.com.ar; Av Brown & Bonarelli; admission AR$30; ⏰10am-8pm Sept-May, 11am-8pm June-Aug) Small but informative, with a skeleton mold of Austroraptor Cabazaii (found nearby) and Patagonian history displays. The friendly host invites museumgoers for a post-tour *mate*.

Tours

Some 40 travel agencies arrange excursions to the glacier and other local attractions, including fossil beds and stays at regional **estancias**, where you can hike, ride horses or relax. Tour prices for Glaciar Perito Moreno (around AR$150 per person) don't include the park entrance fee. Ask agents and other travelers about added benefits, such as extra stops, boat trips, binoculars or multilingual guides. For other boat and tour operators based in El Calafate, see p448.

Caltur TOUR
(☎491368; www.caltur.com.ar; Av Libertador 1080) Specializes in El Chaltén tours and lodging packages.

Chaltén Travel TOUR
(☎492212/480; www.chaltentravel.com; Av Libertador 1174) Recommended tours to the glacier, stopping for wildlife viewing (binoculars provided); also specializes in RN 40 trips. Outsources some excursions to **Always Glaciers** (www.alwaysglaciers.com, in Spanish).

Overland Patagonia TOUR
(☎491243, 492243; www.glaciar.com) Operates out of both Hostel del Glaciar Libertador and Hostel del Glaciar Pioneros; organizes the alternative glacier trip (AR$230), which includes hiking and navigating the lake.

Calafate Fishing FLY-FISHING
(☎496545; www.calafatefishing.com; Av Libertador 1826; ⏰10am-7pm Mon-Sat) Offers fun fly-fishing trips to Lago Roca (half day AR$690) and Lago Strobbel, where you can test rumors that the biggest rainbow trout in the world lives here.

Sleeping

Though lodgings are abundant, popular offerings may book well in advance. The core high season is January to February, although some places extend it from mid-October until April. Luxury hotels are being added at a quick clip, though not all offer the same standard. Look for deep discounts in low season.

The tourist office has a complete list of *cabañas* and apartment hotels, which are the best deals for groups and families. Most hostels offer pickup from the bus terminal.

TOP CHOICE **Lautaro** GUESTHOUSE $
(☎492698; www.hospedajelautaro.com.ar; Espora 237; dm/d without bathroom AR$65/180, s/d/tr/q 180/230/280/340; ⏰closed July; @📶) Chill and homey, this refurbished guesthouse reflects the playful efforts of young owners Dario and Belen. It's central, with pretty rooms in a bold palette. Guests can order box lunches made with fresh bread or dine-in on home-cooked meals that beat most local restaurants. There's also guest cooking facilities, free coffee, tea and trip planning.

Las Cabañitas CABINS $
(☎491118; www.lascabanitascalafate.com; Valentín Feilberg 218; 2-person cabin AR$250, dm/d without bathroom AR$80/220; ⏰closed Jul; 📶) A restful spot with snug storybook A-frames with spiral staircases leading to loft beds. The new, energetic owner Gerardo also cooks worthy meals and provides helpful information. Touches include English lavender in the garden, a barbecue area and guest cooking facilities.

I Keu Ken Hostel HOSTEL $$
(☎495175; www.patagoniaikeuken.com.ar; FM Pontoriero 171; dm/d/tr AR$80/360/400; @📶) Featuring helpful staff, artisan beer and a pet sheep, this quirky hostel has proven popular with travelers. Features include inviting common areas, a deck for lounging and first-rate barbecues (with amnesty for the pet sheep). Its location, near the top of a steep hill, offers views and a workout. Stay tuned – the owners are in the process of adding a second location.

Hostal Amancay INN $
(☎491113; www.hostalamancay.com; Gobernador Gregorio 1457; s/d/tr AR$180/230/290; 📶) Think small – this tin-front lodging masks a grassy courtyard surrounded by prim motel-style rooms. Owners Cecilia and park guide Marcelo provide warm service and lots of local knowledge. The breakfast room has self-service tea and a treasure trove of books, local guides and maps.

El Calafate

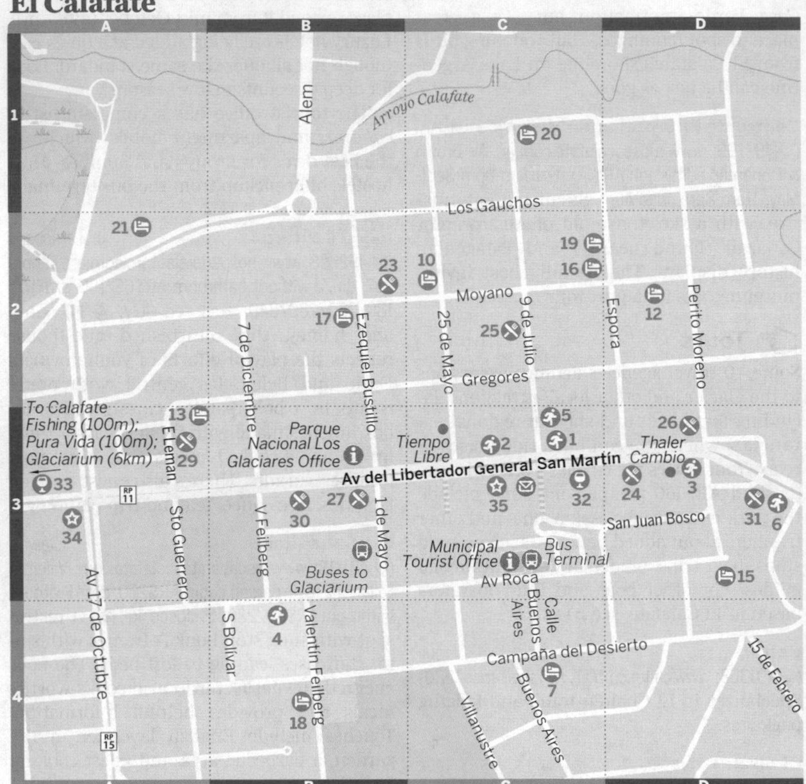

Hostel de las Manos HOSTEL $
(☎492996; www.hosteldelasmanos.com.ar; Feruglio 59; dm AR$65, d with bathroom AR$150; @) Immaculate and personable, this calm hostel alternative is across the footbridge from 9 de Julio. A wall of windows provides ample light. An expansion has produced some huge rooms with bright bedspreads and new fixtures.

Hostel del Glaciar Pioneros HOSTEL $
(☎491243; www.glaciar.com; Los Pioneros 251; dm/d AR$63/224; ⏲Nov-Mar; @) A 15-minute walk from town, recent renovations have improved this sprawling red house, one of the town's most longstanding hostels. Sociable, it includes comfortable common areas, small dorms and a small restaurant with homemade meals.

Hostel del Glaciar Libertador HOSTEL $$
(☎491792; www.glaciar.com; Av Libertador 587; dm/d AR$76/375; @) The best deals here are dorm bunks with thick covers. Behind a Victorian facade, modern facilities include a top-floor kitchen, radiant floor heating, new computers and a spacious common area with a plasma TV glued to sports channels.

America del Sur HOSTEL $$
(☎493525; www.americahostel.com.ar; Puerto Deseado 151; dm/d AR$80/420; @) This backpacker favorite has a stylish lodge setting with views. It's a social scene that boasts fun times, though the service seems a little smug. All-you-can-eat barbecues are regular.

Hotel La Loma INN $$
(☎491016; www.lalomahotel.com; Av Roca 849; dm/s/d AR$80/390/430; P ≋ @) Colonial furnishings and a lovely rock garden enhance this ranch-style retreat with opera on the Hi-fi (old radio). Superior rooms are spacious and bright, antiques fill the creaky hallways and reception boasts an open fire and plenty of books. Rates vary depending on the view.

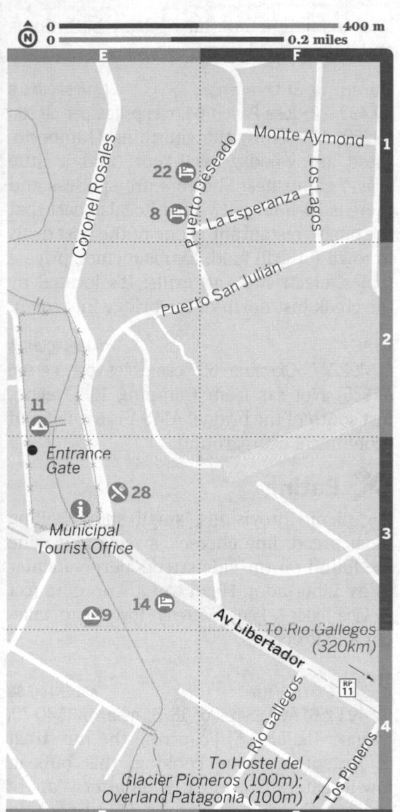

El Calafate

Activities, Courses & Tours

1 Cal-tur ... C3
2 Chaltén Travel ... C3
3 Hielo y Aventura ... D3
4 Leutz Turismo ... B4
5 Mar Patag ... C3
Overland Patagonia ... (see 14)
6 Solo Patagonia S.A. ... D3

Sleeping

7 Albergue Lago Argentino ... C4
8 America del Sur ... E1
9 AMSA ... E3
10 Calafate Hostel ... C2
11 Camping El Ovejero ... E2
12 Hospedaje Jorgito ... D2
13 Hostal Amancay ... A3
14 Hostel del Glaciar Libertador ... E3
15 Hotel La Loma ... D3
16 Hotel Michelangelo ... C2
17 Hotel Posada Los Álamos ... B2
18 Las Cabañitas ... B4
19 Lautaro ... C2
20 Los Dos Pinos ... C1
21 Los Sauces Casa Patagonica ... A2
22 Newenkelen ... E1

Eating

23 Cambalache ... B2
24 Casimiro Biguá ... D3
25 El Cucharón ... C2
26 La Anónima ... D3
27 La Lechuza ... B3
28 La Tablita ... E3
29 Los Amigos ... A3
30 Mirabile ... B3
31 Viva la Pepa ... D3

Drinking

el ba'r ... (see 5)
32 Librobar ... C3
33 Sholken ... A3

Entertainment

34 Don Diego de la Noche ... A3
35 La Tolderia ... C3

Posada Karut Josh B&B $$
(☎496444; www.posadakarutjosh.com.ar; Calle 12, No 1882, Barrio Bahía Redonda; d/tr AR$310/380) Run by an Italian-Argentine couple, this peaceful aluminum-sided B&B features big, bright rooms and a lovely garden with lake views. Breakfast is abundant and satisfying meals (AR$65) are also available.

Miyazato Inn B&B $$
(☎491953; www.interpatagonia.com/miyazatoinn; Egidio Feruglio 150, Las Chacras; d AR$369; P@) Resembling a simple Japanese inn, this elegant B&B wins points for personalized service. Breakfast include sweets and *medialunas* (croissants), and excursionists get a hot thermos of coffee or tea to go. It's a five-minute walk away from the center of town.

Newenkelen GUESTHOUSE $$
(☎493943; www.newenkelenposada.com.ar; Puerto Deseado 223; d AR$310; @) Perched on a hill above town, this intimate option features six immaculate brick rooms with tasteful bedding and mountain views.

Los Sauces Casa Patagónica LUXURY HOTEL $$$
(☎495854; www.casalossauces.com; Los Gauchos 1352/1370; d from AR$1182; @) With an award-winning restaurant, a full spa and spacious, immaculately manicured grounds where

exotic birds roam and staff members zip by in golf carts, Los Sauces feels less like a hotel and more like a luxury compound. The varied monochromatic interiors are gorgeous, with first-class beds, huge flat-screen TVs and stone bathrooms with Jacuzzis. Unfortunately, the reservation system is rather clumsy.

Casa de los Grillos B&B $$
(☎491160; www.casadegrillos.com.ar; Las Bandurrias s/n; d/apt AR$280/330) A quiet spot with fresh rooms, soft beds and attentive service. The backyard cabin offers shaggy bedspreads and all-new fixtures and appliances. There's self-service coffee, tea and spring water and a *quincho* (cook hut) provides ample cooking and recreation space.

Hotel Posada Los Álamos RESORT $$$
(☎491144; www.posadalosalamos.com; Moyano 1355; s/d/ste AR$591/620/924; @) Considering the amenities, prices are pretty reasonable at Calafate's original resort. There's lush rooms, overstuffed sofas, spectacular gardens, tennis courts, putting greens and a spa. It's enough to make you almost forget about seeing that glacier.

Hotel Michelangelo HOTEL $$
(☎491045; www.michelangelohotel.com.ar; Moyano 1020; s/d AR$420/480; @) Tour groups favor this Swiss chalet-style lodging in the center of town. Recently renovated, with a chic lobby and living area with stone fixtures and low lighting. Guest rooms have tasteful, muted colors, high ceilings and full amenities.

Hospedaje Jorgito GUESTHOUSE $
(☎491323; Moyano 943; per person with/without bathroom AR$80/65) The lovely Señora Virginia has received generations of travelers in her modest home, decorated with vintage Barbies, doilies and synthetic flowers. Rooms vary in size but are bright and well kept. Guests can use the large kitchen.

Calafate Hostel HOSTEL $$
(☎492450/2; www.hostels.org.ar; Moyano 1226; dm/s/d/tr AR$76/220/290/360; @) Best suited to large groups, this mammoth log cabin ends up feeling blander than the competition. Double-bunk dorms are cozy, while the new annex features tidy brick doubles.

Los Dos Pinos GUESTHOUSE $
(☎491271/632; www.losdospinos.com; 9 de Julio 358; campsites per person AR$25, dm/d/tr AR$50/280/350;) This labyrinthine lodging has a supermarket selection of rooms, all adequate though not charming. Dorms lack insulation but have clean bathrooms and kitchen facilities.

Camping El Ovejero CAMPGROUND $
(☎493422; José Pantín 64; campsites per person AR$20) Hosted by the charming Humberto, these are woodsy, well-kept (and a little noisy) campsites. Showers are spotless and there is 24-hour hot water. Locals boast that the onsite restaurant is one of the best deals in town for grill food. Extras include private tables, electricity and grills. It's located by the creek just north of the bridge into town.

AMSA CAMPGROUND $
(☎492247; Olavarria 65; campsites per person AR$25) Not far from Camping El Ovejero, just south of the bridge, AMSA is a quiet and economical campground.

Eating

For picnic provisions, small shops selling fresh bread, fine cheeses, sweets and wine are found on the side streets perpendicular to Av Libertador. Head to **La Anónima** (cnr Av Libertador & Perito Moreno) for cheap takeout and groceries.

TOP CHOICE **Pura Vida** ARGENTINE $$
(☎493356; Av Libertador 1876; mains AR$40-70; dinner Thu-Tue;) Featuring the rare treat of Argentine home cooking, this offbeat, low-lit eatery is a must. Even after years of success, the owners can be found cooking up buttery spiced chicken pot pies and filling wine glasses. For vegetarians, brown rice and wok veggies or various salads are satisfying, but don't skip the decadent chocolate brownie steeped in warm berry sauce and ice cream for dessert. Reserve ahead.

La Tablita PARRILLA $$
(Coronel Rosales 24; mains AR$40-80; lunch Thu-Tue, dinner daily) Steak and spit-roasted lamb are the stars at this satisfying parrilla, popular beyond measure for good reason. For average appetites a half-steak will do, rounded out with a good malbec, fresh salad or garlic fries.

El Cucharón ARGENTINE $$$
(9 de Julio 145; mains AR$40-84; lunch & dinner) This sophisticated eatery, tucked away in a small space a few blocks off the main street, is a relatively undiscovered gem and an excellent place to try the regional classic *cazuela de cordero*. The trout with lemon sauce and grilled vegetables is delicious, too.

Viva la Pepa CAFE $$
(Amado 833; mains AR$45; ⏰10am-midnight Fri-Wed) Decked out in children's drawings, this cheerful cafe specializes in crepes but also offers great sandwiches with homemade bread (try the chicken with apple and blue cheese), fresh juice and gourds of *mate*. Unfortunately, prices are somewhat inflated.

Casimiro Biguá ARGENTINE $$$
(www.casimirobigua.com; Av Libertador 963; mains AR$48-92; ⏰11am-1am) With warm copper accents and a hustling staff, this chic eatery and *vinoteca* (wine bar) offers an impressive list of 180 Argentine wines. The chef creates wonderful homemade pasta, risotto, lamb stew, and grilled trout and steak. Two new locations have popped up nearby to accommodate the masses: a trattoria and a *parrilla*.

Los Amigos SEAFOOD $$
(Ernesto Leman 40; mains AR$40-80; ⏰lunch & dinner) A real neighborhood restaurant run by a gregarious Uruguayan, Amigos specializes in seafood, but does standard Argentine fare too, with nice touches like marinated eggplant and peppers to spread on your bread.

Mirabile ITALIAN $$
(Av Libertador 1329; mains AR$40-60; ⏰11am-3pm, 7pm-11pm Tues-Sun) Locals favor this low-key restaurant with wooden tables for homemade pumpkin ravioli, lamb sorrentinos and panzottis served with king crab.

Cambalache CAFE $
(www.cambalacherestobar.com.ar; Moyano 1258; mains AR$35; ⏰noon-midnight) Housed in a restored tin house, this cheerful traveler's hub offers inexpensive wine and just average regional dishes like grilled steak and lamb stew.

La Lechuza PIZZERIA $$
(www.lalechuzapizzas.com.ar; cnr Av Libertador & 1 de Mayo; pizza AR$38-55; ⏰closed Sun) Serves a classic selection of empanadas, salads and pizza on round wooden plates – try the sheep cheese and olive pizza with a local microbrew.

Drinking

Sholken BREWERY
(Av Libertador 1630; mains AR$40; ⏰8pm-2am) After a day in the wind and sun, this snug brewpub is a godsend. Beer is brewed on-site and the tiny kitchen churns out heaping trays of meats and cheeses and spicy beef empanadas. For vegetarians, the endive salad with walnuts, blue cheese and passion-fruit dressing is excellent.

Librobar PUB
(☎491464; Av Libertador 1015; ⏰10am-3am, closed Tue; 📶) Upstairs in the gnome village, this hip book-bar serves coffee, bottled beers and pricey cocktails. It's a cozy atmosphere to peruse oversized photography books.

el ba'r CAFE
(9 de Julio s/n; mains AR$30; ⏰breakfast & lunch) This trendy patio cafe is the hot spot for you and your sweater-clad puppy to order espresso, *submarinos* (hot milk with melted chocolate bar), green tea or sandwiches.

Entertainment

La Toldería CLUB
(☎491443; www.facebook.com/LaTolderia; Av Libertador 1177) This petite storefront opens its doors to dancing and live acts at night, probably the best spot to try if you're feeling boisterous.

Don Diego de la Noche LIVE MUSIC
(Av Libertador 1603; ⏰until 5am) This perennial favorite serves dinner and features live music like tango, guitar and *folklórico* (Argentine folk music).

Information

Medical Services

Hospital Municipal Dr José Formenti (☎491001; Av Roca 1487)

Money

Withdraw your cash before the weekend rush – it isn't uncommon for ATMs to run out on Sundays. If you are headed to El Chaltén, consider getting extra cash here.

Banco Santa Cruz (Av Libertador 1285) Changes traveler's checks and has an ATM.

Thaler Cambio (Av Libertador 963; ⏰10am-1pm Mon-Fri, 5:30-7:30pm Sat & Sun) Usurious rates for traveler's checks, but open weekends.

Post

Post office (Av Libertador 1133)

Tourist information

ACA (Automóvil Club Argentino; ☎491004; cnr 1 de Mayo & Av Roca) Argentina's auto club; good source for provincial road maps.

Municipal tourist office (☎491090/466; www.elcalafate.gov.ar, in Spanish; cnr Rosales & Av Libertador; ⏰8am-8pm) With fairly apathetic service. There's also a kiosk at the bus terminal; both have some English-speaking staff.

Parque Nacional Los Glaciares office (491005/755; www.parquesnacionales.gov.ar; Av Libertador 1302; 8am-7pm Mon-Fri, 10am-8pm Sat & Sun) Offers brochures and a decent map of Parque Nacional Los Glaciares. It's better to get info here than at the park.

Travel Agencies

Most agents deal exclusively with nearby excursions and are unhelpful for other areas.

Tiempo Libre (491207; www.tiempolibreviajes.com.ar; 25 de Mayo 43) Books flights.

Getting There & Away

Air

The modern **Aeropuerto El Calafate** is 23km east of town off RP 11; the departure tax is AR$38.

Aerolíneas Argentinas (492814/16; Av del Libertador 1361) flies every day to Bariloche or Esquel (AR$1414), Ushuaia (AR$692), Trelew (AR$1633), and Aeroparque and Ezeiza in Buenos Aires (AR$1173).

LADE (491262; bus terminal) flies a few times a week to Río Gallegos (AR$260), Comodoro Rivadavia (AR$408), Ushuaia (AR$641) and Buenos Aires (AR$891). **Lan** (495-548; 9 de Julio 57) flies to Ushuaia weekly (round-trip AR$2465).

Bus

El Calafate's hilltop **bus terminal** (Av Roca s/n) is easily reached by a pedestrian staircase from the corner of Av Libertador and 9 de Julio. Book ahead in high season, as outbound seats can be in short supply.

For Río Gallegos, buses go four times daily; contact **Taqsa** (491843) or **Sportman** (492680). Connections to Bariloche and Ushuaia may require leaving in the middle of the night and a change of buses in Río Gallegos.

For El Chaltén, buses leave daily at 8am, 2pm and 6pm. Both **Caltur** (491368; www.caltur.com.ar; Av Libertador 1080) and **Chaltén Travel** (492212/480; www.chaltentravel.com; Av Libertador 1174) go to El Chaltén and drive RN 40 to Bariloche (AR$700) in summer, see p417.

BUSES FROM EL CALAFATE

DESTINATION	COST (AR$)	DURATION (HR)
El Chaltén	75	3½
Bariloche	650-700	31
Puerto Natales (Chile)	102	5
Río Gallegos	94-108	4

For Puerto Natales, **Cootra** (491444) and **Turismo Zahhj** (491631) depart at 8am and 8:30am daily, crossing the border at Cerro Castillo, where it may be possible to connect to Torres del Paine.

Getting Around

Airport shuttle **Ves Patagonia** (494355; www.vespatagonia.com) offers door-to-door service (one way/roundtrip AR$33/58). There are several car-rental agencies at the airport. **Localiza** (491398; www.localiza.com.ar; Av Libertador 687) and **Servi Car** (492541; www.servi4x4.com.ar; Av Libertador 695) offer car rentals from convenient downtown offices.

Renting a **bike** is an excellent way to get a feel for the area and cruise the dirt roads by the lake. Albergue Lago Argentino offers rentals.

Around El Calafate

From El Calafate, paved RN 40 cuts southeast across vast steppe for 95km, then jogs south at **El Cerrito** and turns to gravel. Staying on paved RP 5 means a slow-going, five-hour, 224km bore of a trip southeast to **Río Gallegos**. Halfway along RP 5, at Km 146, is the utilitarian **Hotel La Esperanza** (02902-499200; per person AR$100; year-round) and a gas-station diner with quick, friendly service. If you plan to stay, ask for a room in the newer cabin. From here, paved RP 7 connects back to RN 40 for the Chilean border crossing at Cerro Castillo–Cancha Carrera, Parque Nacional Torres del Paine and Puerto Natales.

Parque Nacional Los Glaciares (South)

Among Earth's most dynamic and accessible ice fields, **Glaciar Perito Moreno** is the stunning centerpiece of the southern sector of **Parque Nacional Los Glaciares** (adult/student AR$100/15). It's 30km long, 5km wide and 60m high, but what makes it exceptional in the world of ice is its constant advance – it creeps forward up to 2m per day, causing building-sized icebergs to calve from its face. Watching the glacier is a sedentary park experience that manages to be thrilling.

The glacier formed as a low gap in the Andes allowed moisture-laden Pacific storms to drop their loads east of the divide, where they accumulate as snow. Over millennia, under tremendous weight, this snow has recrystallized into ice and flowed slowly east-

Around El Calafate & PN Los Glaciares (South)

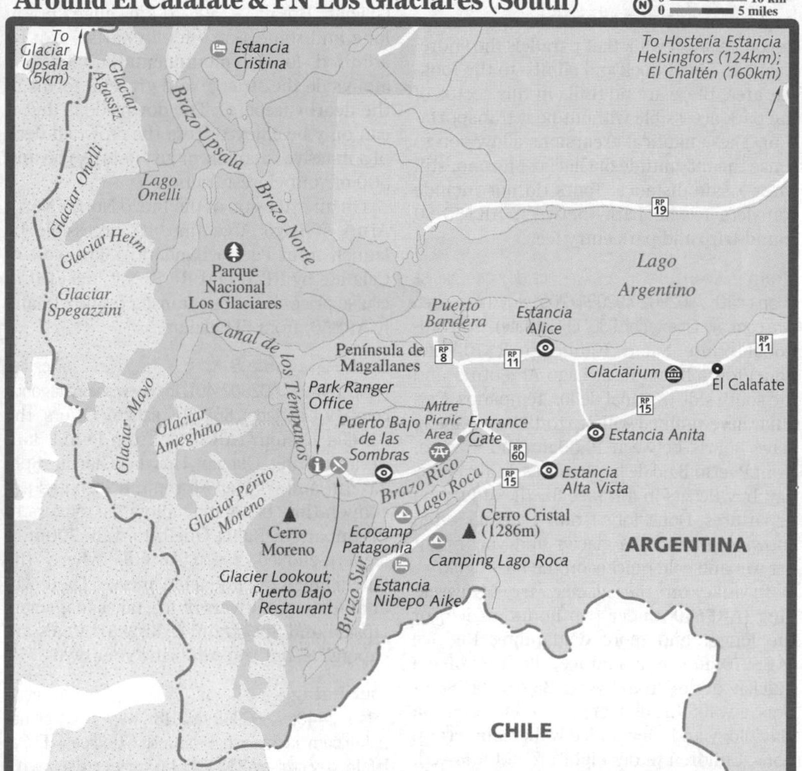

ward. The 1600-sq-km trough of **Lago Argentino**, the country's largest body of water, is evidence that glaciers were once far more extensive than today.

While most of the world's glaciers are receding, Glaciar Moreno is considered 'stable.' Regardless, 17 times between 1917 and 2006, as the glacier has advanced, it has dammed the Brazo Rico (Rico Arm) of Lago Argentino, causing the water to rise. Several times, the melting ice below has been unable to support the weight of the water behind it and the dam has collapsed in an explosion of water and ice. To be present when this spectacular cataclysm occurs is unforgettable.

Glaciar Moreno is as much an auditory as a visual experience when huge icebergs calve and collapse into the **Canal de los Témpanos** (Iceberg Channel). This natural-born tourist attraction at Península de Magallanes is close enough to guarantee great views, but far enough away to be safe. A series of steel catwalks (almost 4000m total) and vantage points allow visitors to see, hear and photograph the glacier. Sun hits its face in the morning and the glacier's appearance changes as the day progresses and shadows shift.

There is a free shuttle from the parking area to the catwalks. A closed *refugio* with glass walls allows for glacier viewing in bad weather, there's also a snack bar and two-story restaurant Nativos, serving cappuccino and sandwiches to sightseers. If you bring a picnic, remember that it is difficult and costly to remove trash from the area – please pack yours out.

For student rates, visitors must have a student ID. The main gateway town to the park's southern sector, El Calafate, is 80km east of the glacier by road. It's where you'll find all the operators for tours and activities mentioned in this section.

Activities

GLACIAR PERITO MORENO

Beyond a short walk that parallels the shoreline at the boat dock and climbs to the lookout area, there are no trails in this sector of the park accessible without boat transportation. These nautical excursions allow you to sense the magnitude of Glaciar Moreno, still from a safe distance. Tours do not include transfers to the park (between AR$50-80 round-trip) and park entry fee.

Hielo y Aventura ICE TREKKING, CRUISE

(Map p440; ☎02902-492094/205; www.hieloyaventura.com; Av Libertador 935, El Calafate) Conventional cruise Safari Nautico (AR$70, one hour) tours Brazo Rico, Lago Argentino and the south side of Canal de los Témpanos. Catamarans crammed with up to 130 passengers leave hourly between 10:30am and 4:30pm from Puerto Bajo de las Sombras. If it's a busy day, buy tickets in advance for the afternoon departures. Don't forget rain gear: it's often snowing around the glacier and you might get wet and cold quickly on the boat deck.

To hike on the glacier, try Minitrekking (AR$540, under two hours on ice) or the longer and more demanding Big Ice (AR$770, four hours on ice). Both involve a quick boat ride from Puerto Bajo de las Sombras, a walk through lenga forests, a chat on glaciology and then an ice walk using crampons. Children under eight are not allowed; reserve ahead and bring your own food.

GLACIAR UPSALA & LAGO ONELLI

Glaciar Upsala – 595-sq-km huge, 60km long and some 4km wide in parts – can be admired for its monumental dimensions alongside the strange and graceful forms of the nearby icebergs. The downside is that it can only be enjoyed from the crowded deck of a massive catamaran: just nature, you and 300 of your closest friends.

On an extension of the Brazo Norte (North Arm) of Lago Argentino, it's accessible by launch from Puerto Bandera, 45km west of Calafate by RP 11 and RP 8. Not included in cruise prices is the bus transfer (approximately AR$50) from El Calafate.

Solo Patagonia S.A. CRUISE

(Map p440; ☎02902-491115; www.solopatagonia.com; Av Libertador 867, El Calafate) Offers the All Glacier tour (AR$450) from Punta Bandera, visiting Glaciar Upsala, Glaciar Spegazzini and Glaciar Moreno. If icebergs are cooperating, boats may allow passengers to disembark at Bahía Onelli to walk 500m to iceberg-choked **Lago Onelli**, where the Onelli and Agassiz glaciers merge. Their other all-day tour, Rivers of Ice, takes in glaciers Upsala and Spegazzini (AR$295). Meals are expensive, but you can bring your own.

Mar Patag LUXURY CRUISE

(Map p440; ☎02902-492118; www.crucerosmarpatag.com, in Spanish; 9 de Julio 57, office 4, El Calafate; day cruise AR$1034) Luxury cruises with onboard chef serving gourmet meals. The

GLACIOLOGY 101

Ribbons of ice, stretched flat in sheets or sculpted by weather and fissured by pressure, glaciers have a raw magnificence that is mind-boggling to behold.

As snow falls on the accumulation area, it compacts to ice. The river of ice is slugged forward by gravity, which deforms its layers as it moves. When the glacier surges downhill, melted ice mixes with rock and soil on the bottom, grinding it into a lubricant that keeps pushing the glacier along. At the same time, debris from the crushed rock is forced to the sides of the glacier, creating features called moraines. Movement also causes cracks and deformities called crevasses.

The ablation area is where the glacier melts. When accumulation outpaces melting at the ablation area, the glacier advances; when there's more melting or evaporation, the glacier recedes. Since 1980, global warming has contributed greatly to widespread glacial retreat.

Another marvel of glaciers is their hue. What makes some blue? Wavelengths and air bubbles. The more compact the ice, the longer the path that light has to travel and the bluer the ice appears. Air bubbles in uncompacted areas absorb long wavelengths of white light so we see white. When glaciers calve into lakes, they dump a 'glacial flour' comprised of ground-up rock that gives the water a milky, grayish color. This same sediment remains unsettled in some lakes and diffracts the sun's light, creating a stunning palette of turquoise, pale mint and azure.

day trip leaves from the private port of La Soledad and takes in glaciers Upsala and Spegazzini. The three-day cruise also visits glaciers Mayo and Moreno.

LAGO ROCA

The serene south arm of Lago Argentino, with lakeshore forests and mountains, features good hikes and pleasant camping. *Estancia* accommodations occupy this section of the park, where most visitors rarely travel. No entrance fee is charged. For transportation, contact Caltur.

Cerro Cristal HIKING

A rugged but rewarding 3½-hour hike, with views of Glaciar Moreno and the Torres del Paine on clear days. The trail begins at the education camp at La Jerónima, just before the Camping Lago Roca entrance, 55km southwest of El Calafate along RP 15.

Cabalgatas del Glaciar HORSE RIDING

(☎495447; www.cabalgatasdelglaciar.com) Day and multi-day riding or trekking trips with glacier panoramas to Lago Rocas and Paso Zamora on the Chilean border. Also available through Caltur (p441).

Leutz Turismo HORSE RIDING

(Map p440; ☎02902-492316; www.leutzturismo.com.ar; EP Gómez 112, El Calafate) Offers day trips to Estancia Nibepo Aike (AR$155) from El Calafate. The morning or afternoon visits include tea, *mate* and fresh pastries, a sheep-shearing demonstration and an hour of horseback riding.

Sleeping & Eating

TOP CHOICE **Camping Lago Roca** CAMPGROUND $

(☎02902-499500; www.losglaciares.com/campinglagoroca; per person AR$44, cabin dm for 2/4 AR$190/290) This full-service campground with restaurant-bar, located a few kilometers past the education camp, makes an excellent adventure base. The clean concrete-walled dorms provide a snug alternative to camping. Hiking trails abound, and the center rents fishing equipment and bikes and coordinates horseback riding at the nearby *estancia*.

Hostería Estancia Helsingfors ESTANCIA $$$

(☎satellite phone 11-52770195; www.helsingfors.com.ar; per person full board AR$1287; ⊙Oct-Apr) The simply stunning location ogling Cerro Fitz Roy from Lago Viedma makes for lots of love-at-first-sight impressions. Intimate and welcoming, this former Finnish pioneer ranch is a highly regarded luxury destination, though it cultivates a relaxed, unpretentious ambience. Guests pass the time on scenic but demanding mountain treks, rides and visits to Glaciar Viedma. It's on Lago Viedma's southern shore, 170km from El Chaltén and 180km from El Calafate.

Estancia Cristina ESTANCIA $$$

(☎02902-491-133, in Buenos Aires 011-4803-7352; www.estanciacristina.com; s/d incl full board & activities AR$2553/4220; ⊙Oct-Apr) Locals in the know say the most outstanding trekking in the region is right here. Lodging is in bright, modern cabins with expansive views. A visit includes guided activities and boating to Glaciar Upsala. Accessible by boat, it's at Punta Bandera, off the northern arm of Lago Argentino.

Ecocamp Patagonia CAMPGROUND $$$

(☎11-5199-0401; www.ecocamp-patagonia.com; per person 3-day/2-night package AR$3904) An all-inclusive nature camp which features hikes and ice trekking on the glacier and overnights in luxury domes with comfortable beds, hot water showers and all meals (lunch boxes for day trips). Provides transfers.

Estancia Nibepo Aike ESTANCIA $$$

(☎02902-492797, in Buenos Aires 011-5272-0341; www.nibepoaike.com.ar; RP 15, Km 60; s/d incl full board AR$844/1688; ⊙Oct-Apr) This working sheep and cattle ranch offers the usual assortment of *estancia* highlights. In addition to horseback riding, guests have the option to explore the surroundings on two wheels from the bicycle stash.

Getting There & Away

Glaciar Perito Moreno is 80km west of El Calafate via paved RP 11, passing through the breathtaking scenery around Lago Argentino. Bus tours (AR$110 roundtrip, AR$80 for transport only) are frequent in summer – see p441, or simply stroll down El Calafate's Av Libertador. Buses leave El Calafate in the early morning and afternoon, returning around noon and 7pm.

CHILEAN PATAGONIA

Rugged seascapes rimmed with glacial peaks, the stunning massifs of Torres del Paine and howling steppe characterize the other side of the Andes. Once you come this far, it is well worth crossing the border. Chilean Patagonia consists of the isolated Aisén and Magallanes regions, separated by the southern continental ice field. This section covers Punta Arenas, Puerto Natales and Parque Nacional Torres del Paine. For in-depth coverage of Chile, pick up Lonely Planet's *Chile & Easter Island*.

Most nationals of countries that have diplomatic relations with Chile don't need a visa. Upon entering, customs officials issue a tourist card, valid for 90 days and renewable for another 90; authorities take it seriously, so guard it closely to avoid the hassle of replacing it. If arriving by air, US citizens must pay a one-time reciprocal entry fee of US$132, valid for the life of the passport; Canadians pay US$132 and Australians US$61.

Temperature-sensitive travelers will quickly notice a difference after leaving energy-rich Argentina: in public areas and budget accommodations central heating is rare; warmer clothing is the norm indoors.

US cash is not widely accepted. Prices here are given in Chilean pesos (CH$).

Punta Arenas

61 / POP 130,200

Today's Punta Arenas is a confluence of the ruddy and the grand, witnessed in the elaborate wool-boom mansions, the thriving petrochemical industry and its port status. Visitors will find it the most convenient base to travel around the remote Magallanes region, with good traveler services. Watch for more cruise-ship passengers and trekkers to replace the explorers, sealers and sailors of yesterday at the barstools – but save a spot for the old guard.

Founded in 1848 as a penal settlement and military garrison, Punta Arenas was conveniently situated for ships headed to Alta California during the gold rush. The economy took off only in the last quarter of the 19th century, after the territorial governor authorized the purchase of 300 purebred sheep from the Falkland Islands (Islas Malvinas). This experiment encouraged sheep farming and, by the turn of the century, nearly two million grazed the territory.

Sights & Activities

Museo Regional Braun-Menéndez MUSEUM

(244216; Magallanes 949; admission CH$1500, free Sun; 10:30am-5pm Mon-Sat, 10:30am-2pm Sun in summer, to 2pm daily in winter) This opulent mansion testifies to the wealth and power of pioneer sheep farmers in the late 19th century. The well-maintained interior houses a regional historical museum (ask for booklets in English) and original exquisite French-nouveau family furnishings, from intricate wooden inlaid floors to Chinese vases.

In former servants' quarters, a downstairs cafe is perfect for a pisco sour while soaking up the grandeur.

Plaza Muñoz Gamero PLAZA

A central plaza of magnificent conifers surrounded by opulent mansions. Facing the plaza's north side, The Casa Braun-Menéndez houses the private **Club de la Unión** (241489; admission CH$1000; 10:30am-1pm & 5-8:30pm Tue-Fri, 10:30am-1pm & 8-10pm Sat, 11am-2pm Sun), which also uses the tavern downstairs (open to the public). The nearby **monument** commemorating the 400th anniversary of Magellan's voyage was donated by wool baron José Menéndez in 1920. Just east is the former **Sociedad Menéndez Behety**, which now houses Turismo Comapa. The **cathedral** sits west.

Reserva Forestal Magallanes RESERVE

(daylight hrs) Great hiking and mountain biking through dense lenga and coihue, 8km from town.

Cementerio Municipal CEMETERY

(main entrance at Av Bulnes 949; 7:30am-8pm) Among South America's most fascinating cemeteries, with both humble immigrant graves and flashy tombs, like that of wool baron José Menéndez, a scale replica of Rome's Vittorio Emanuele monument, according to Bruce Chatwin. See the map inside the main entrance gate.

It's an easy 15-minute stroll northeast of the plaza, or catch any taxi *colectivo* (shared taxi with specific route) in front of the Museo Regional Braun-Menéndez on Magallanes.

Museo Naval y Marítimo MUSEUM

(205479; Pedro Montt 981; adult/child CH$1200/600; 9:30am-12:30pm & 2-5pm Tue-Sat) A naval and maritime museum with historical exhibits which include a fine account of the Chilean mission that rescued Sir Ernest Shackleton's crew from Antarctica. The most imaginative display is a replica ship complete with bridge, maps, charts and radio room.

Museo Regional Salesiano MUSEUM

(221001; Av Bulnes 336; admission CH$2000; 10am-12:30pm & 3-6pm Tue-Sun) Especially influential in settling the region, the Salesian order collected outstanding ethnographic artifacts, but their museum touts their role as peacemakers between the Yaghan and Ona and settlers.

Tours

Worthwhile day trips include tours to the **Seno Otway pingüinera** (penguin colony; p456), 48km to the north. Tours (from CH$15,000) leave at 4pm daily October through March, weather permitting.

Visits to the town's first settlements at **Fuerte Bulnes & Puerto Hambre** (admission CH$1000) leave at 10am. Both tours can be done in one day; by sharing a rental car and going at opposite times visitors can avoid the strings of tour groups. Most lodgings will help arrange tours – if they don't run their own operation.

Torres del Paine tours are abundant from Punta Arenas, but the distance makes for a very long day; it's best to organize transport from Puerto Natales.

If you have the time, a more atmospheric alternative to Seno Otway is the thriving Magellanic penguin colonies of **Monumento Natural Los Pingüinos** (p456) on Isla Magdalena. Five-hour ferry tours (adult/child CH$25,000/13,000) land for an hour at the island and depart the port on Tuesday, Thursday and Saturday, December through February. Confirm times in advance. Book tickets through **Turismo Comapa** (☎200200; www.comapa.com; Magallanes 990) and bring a picnic.

Tours also go to destinations such as Parque Nacional Pali Aike.

Recommended agencies:

Frieda Lange & Co TOUR
(☎613991; www.friedalange.com; Errazurriz 950; ⊙8am-6pm) Recommended innovative bilingual city tours and trips to Fuerte Bulnes.

Turismo Aonikenk TOUR
(☎228332; www.aonikenk.com; Magallanes 619) Recommended English-, German- and French-speaking guides. Offers Cabo Froward treks, visits to the king penguin colony in Tierra del Fuego, and cheaper open expeditions geared at experienced participants. Also has information on Estancia Yendegaia.

Inhóspita Patagonia HIKING
(☎224510; Lautaro Navarro 1013) Offers trekking trips to Cabo Froward, the southernmost point on mainland South America.

Turismo Pali Aike TOUR
(☎223301; www.turismopaliaike.com; Lautaro Navarro 1129)

Turismo Pehoé TOUR
(☎241373; www.pehoe.com; José Menéndez 918)

Turismo Yamana KAYAKING
(☎221130; www.yamana.cl; Errázuriz 932) Kayaking trips on Magellan Strait.

Sleeping

On the cruise-ship circuit, Punta Arenas has a plethora of hotels. Foreigners are not required to pay the additional 18% IVA charge if paying with US cash, traveler's checks or credit card. Off-season (mid-April to mid-October) prices drop. Rates include breakfast.

TOP CHOICE **Ilaia Hotel** BOUTIQUE HOTEL $$
(☎723100; www.ilaia.cl; Ignacio Carrera Pinto 351; d/tr CH$60,000/65,000) Playful and modern, this high-concept boutique hotel is run with family warmth. Sly messages are written to be read in mirrors, rooms are simple and chic and an incredible glass lookout room gazes out on the Strait. A yoga studio is in the works; in the meantime, there are various therapies available and healthy breakfasts that include chapati bread, homemade jam, avocados, yogurt and more. But you won't find a television.

Tragaluz B&B B&B $$
(☎613938; www.tragaluzpatagonia.cl; Mejicana 1194; s/d/tr CH$35,000/40,000/48,000, apt CH$50,000; @ 📶) Homey describes this classic aluminum two-story with mosaic mirrors and warm towel racks. The young American and Chilean hosts Dan and Lorena are super-friendly and knowledgeable about outdoor pursuits. While rooms are standard, the breakfast includes fruit, good coffee and treats like scrambled eggs with veggies or homemade waffles with palm honey. Watch for a greenhouse Jacuzzi in the works.

Imago Mundi HOSTEL $
(☎613115; www.imagomundipatagonia.cl; Mejicana 252; dm/d CH$10,000/25,000; @) Infused with wanderlust, this rambling house has snug bunks in electric colors and cozy spaces. Guests can chill in the onsite cafe, check out the climbing wall and the rotating cultural events (like arthouse movies and workshops) hosted here. Tables are crafted from old doors, and the hostel recycles and composts waste.

Hotel Patagonia Pionera INN $$$
(☎222045; www.hotelpatagoniapionera.cl; Arauco 786; s/d CH$57,000/68,300; P @ 📶) This immaculate restored brick mansion is an elegant and intimate alternative to the big downtown hotels. Expect crisp white duvets,

Punta Arenas

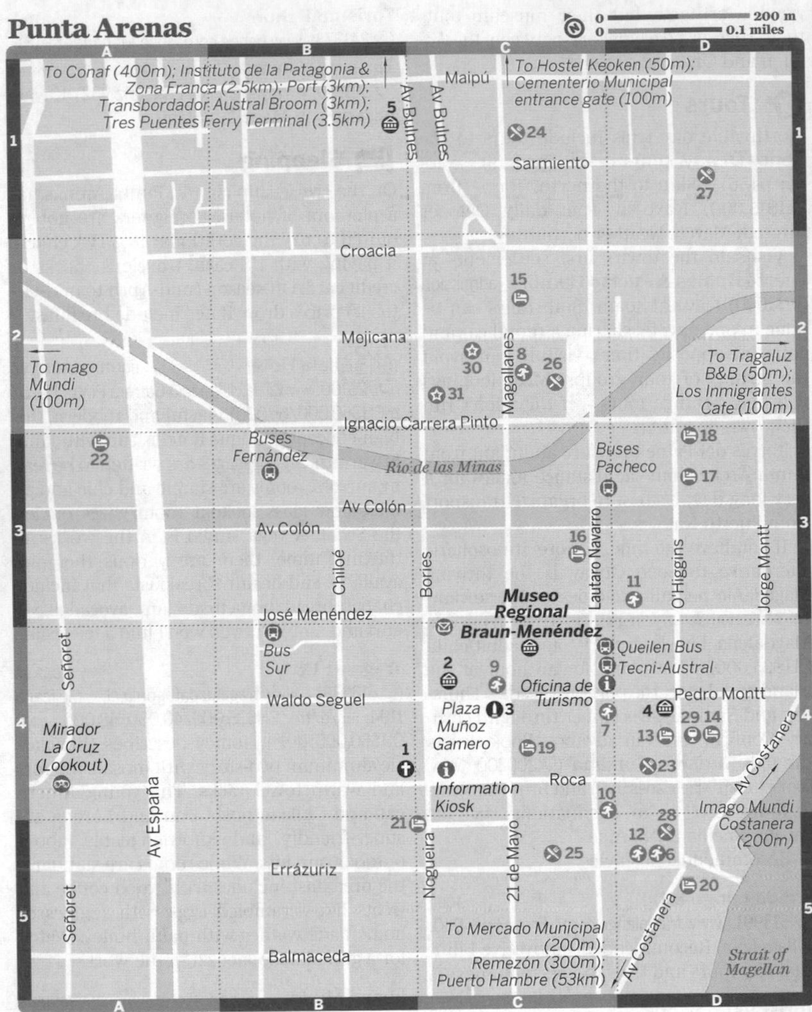

tangerine accents and hardwood floors. It's in a well-heeled residential neighborhood, only six blocks from the plaza.

Hospedaje Magellanes B&B $

(☎228616; www.aonikenk.com; Magellanes 570; s/d without bathroom CH$25,000/30,000; @☎) A great, inexpensive option run by a German-Chilean couple who are also Torres del Paine guides with an onsite travel agency. With just a few quiet rooms, there are often communal dinners or backyard barbecues by the climbing wall. Breakfast includes brown bread and strong coffee.

Hospedaje Independencia GUESTHOUSE $

(☎227572; www.chileaustral.com/independencia; Av Independencia 374; camping/dm CH$2000/5000; @) One of the last diehard backpacker haunts with cheap prices and bonhomie to match. Despite the chaos, rooms are reasonably clean and there are kitchen privileges, camping and bike rentals.

Hostal La Estancia GUESTHOUSE $

(☎249130; www.estancia.cl; O'Higgins 765; dm/s/d without bathroom CH$12,000/20,000/30,000, d CH$25,000; @☎) An old downtown house with big rooms, vaulted ceilings and tidy shared bathrooms. Longtime owners Alex

Punta Arenas

Top Sights

Museo Regional Braun-Menéndez C4

Sights

1 Cathedral B4
2 Club de la Unión C4
3 Monument to Magellan C4
4 Museo Naval y Marítimo D4
5 Museo Regional Salesiano B1
Sociedad Menéndez Behety .... (see 9)

Activities, Courses & Tours

6 Frieda Lange & Co D5
7 Inhóspita Patagonia C4
8 Turismo Aonikenk C2
9 Turismo Comapa C4
10 Turismo Pali Aike C4
11 Turismo Pehoé D3
12 Turismo Yamana D5

Sleeping

13 Al Fin del Mundo D4
14 El Conventillo D4
15 Hospedaje Magellanes C2
16 Hostal Fitz Roy C3
17 Hostal La Estancia D3
18 Hostal Terrasur D3
19 Hotel Cabo de Hornos C4
20 Hotel Dreams del Estrecho D5
21 Hotel Plaza C5
22 Ilaia Hotel A3

Eating

23 Café Almacen Tapiz D4
24 Damiana Elena C1
25 Fuente Hamburg C5
26 La Marmita C2
27 Secreto de la Patagonia D1
28 Sotito's D5

Drinking

29 Jekus D4
La Taberna .... (see 2)

Entertainment

30 Cine Estrella C2
31 Kamikaze C2

and Carmen are eager to help with travel plans. There's a book exchange, kitchen use, laundry and storage.

Hostal Fitz Roy GUESTHOUSE $
(☎240430; www.hostalfitzroy.com; Lautaro Navarro 850; dm/d without bathroom CH$8000/25,000, d CH$30,000, 5-person cabin CH$35,000; @) This country house in the city offers rambling, good-value rooms and an inviting, old-fashioned living room to pore over books or sea charts. Rooms have phones and TVs.

Hotel Dreams del Estrecho LUXURY HOTEL $$$
(☎600-6260000; www.mundodreams.com/detalle/dreams-punta-arenas; O'Higgins 1235; d/ste CH$97,000/117,000; P@) Parked at the water's edge, this glass oval high rise brings a little Vegas to the end of the world. It's a glittery atmosphere, with new rooms which are spacious and luxuriant, but the show-stopper is the swimming pool that appears to merge with the ocean. There's also a spa, casino and swank restaurant on site.

Hotel Cabo De Hornos BUSINESS HOTEL $$$
(☎242134; www.hoteles-australis.com; Plaza Muñoz Gamero 1025; d CH$109,000; @) This smart business hotel begins with a cool interior of slate and sharp angles, but rooms are relaxed and bright, with top-notch views. Service is good and the well-heeled bar just beckons you for a nightcap. The onsite restaurant is well-regarded too.

Hostal Terrasur INN $$
(☎243014; www.hostalterrasur.cl; O'Higgins 723; s/d CH$30,000/40,000; P@) The slightly upscale Terrasur nurtures a secret-garden atmosphere, from its rooms with flowing curtains and flower patterns to the miniature green courtyard.

El Conventillo HOSTEL $
(☎242311; www.hostalelconventillo.com; Pasaje Korner 1034; dm CH$8500; @) This cool brick hostel in the reviving waterfront district has remodeled carpeted dorms and clean row showers. Bright colors mask the fact that there is little interior light; rooms are windowless. Yogurt and cereal are part of a big breakfast.

Hostel Keoken GUESTHOUSE $
(☎244086; www.hostelkeoken.cl, in Spanish; Magallanes 209; s/d without bathroom CH$12000/24,000, with bathroom CH$17,000/30,000; @) Increasingly popular with backpackers, Hostel Keoken features comfortable beds topped with fluffy white down comforters and homemade pastries for breakfast. The center of town is a few minutes away on foot.

Al Fin del Mundo HOSTEL $

(☎710185; www.alfindelmundo.cl; O'Higgins 1026; dm/s/d without bathroom CH$10,000/15,000/20,000; @ 📶) On the 2nd and 3rd floors of a downtown building, these rooms are cheerful but due for updates. All share bathrooms with hot showers and a large kitchen, as well as a living area with a large TV, pool table and DVD library.

Hotel Plaza HOTEL $$$

(☎241300; www.hotelplaza.cl; Nogueira 1116; s/d CH$51,000/63,000; @) This converted mansion boasts vaulted ceilings, plaza views and historical photos lining the hall. Inconsistent with such grandeur, the country decor is unfortunate. But service is genteel and the location unbeatable.

Eating

Local seafood is an exquisite treat: go for *centolla* (king crab) between July and November or *erizos* (sea urchins) between November and July.

TOP CHOICE **La Marmita** CHILEAN $$

(Plaza Sampaio 678; mains CH$6000-10,000; ⊙lunch & dinner Mon-Sat) Recently revamped, this classic bistro enjoys wild popularity for its lovely, casual ambience and tasty fare. Besides fresh salads and hot bread, hearty dishes such as casseroles or seafood hark back to grandma's cooking, Chilean style. There's also a new take-out service.

Remezón GOURMET $$$

(www.patagoniasalvaje.cl, in Spanish; 21 de Mayo 1469; mains CH$10,000-15,000; ⊙lunch & dinner) An innovative mainstay with homey atmosphere. Garlic soup made with fragrant beef broth is a good starter, even shared. Game dishes are the house specialty, but the delicate *merluza negra* (black hake) shouldn't be missed, served with *chupe de espinaca* (spinach casserole). Chef Luis also offers group cooking workshops that include a trip to the local market.

Sotito's SEAFOOD $$$

(O'Higgins 1138; mains CH$5000-15,000; ⊙lunch & dinner) This seafood institution is popular with moneyed locals and cruise-ship travelers in search of a classy king crab feast. The decor may not be inspiring but the cuisine doesn't disappoint.

Café Almacen Tapiz CAFE $

(www.cafetapiz.cl; Roca 912; mains CH$5000; ⊙9am-9:30pm; 📶) Cloaked in alerce shingles, this lively cafe makes for an ambient coffee break. In addition to gorgeous layer cakes, there's salads and pita sandwiches with goat cheese, meats or roasted veggies.

Damiana Elena GOURMET $$$

(Magallanes 341; mains CH$7000-9000; ⊙dinner Mon-Sat) This elegant restaurant is in a romantic old house, off the beaten path in a residential neighborhood. The detour is worth it for the warm, sophisticated ambience and first-rate Chilean cuisine: highlights are salmon ceviche and grilled tilapia.

Fuente Hamburg CHILEAN $

(Errazurriz 856; mains CH$2500-4000; ⊙10:30am-8:30pm Mon-Fri, 10:30am-3pm Sat) Shiny barstools flank a massive grill churning out quickie bites. Grab a *churrasco* (thin-sliced beef) topped with tomatoes and green beans, served with fresh mayo on a soft bun.

Los Inmigrantes CAFE $

(www.inmigrante.cl; Quillota 559; mains AR$5000) In the historic Croatian neighborhood, this cafe serves generous oversized sandwiches of salmon, cured meats or veggies on all kinds of bread, as well as decadent cakes. On display are interesting relics from Dalmatian immigrants.

Mercado Municipal MARKET $

(21 de Mayo 1465) Fish and vegetable market with cheap second-floor *cocinerías* (eateries).

Secreto de la Patagonia SELF-CATERING $

(Sarmiento 1029) Locally-made artisan chocolates, goat cheese and preserved meats, worthy as gifts or park treats.

Imago Costanera CAFE $

(Costanera s/n; mains CH$3000; ⊙9am-9pm Mon-Fri, 10am-9pm Sat-Sun) A hip nook on the water, with loose-leaf teas, fair trade coffee and sandwiches. Flooding in 2012 affected this area; if closed there's cafe service in the Imago Mundi (p451) hostel.

Drinking

La Taberna PUB

(Sara Braun Mansion, Plaza Muñoz Gamero; ⊙7pm-2am, to 3am weekends) This dark and elegant subterranean bar, with polished wood fixtures and cozy nooks reminiscent of an old-fashioned ship, is a classic old-boys' club. The rooms fill with cigar smoke later in the evening, but the opportunity to sip pisco sours in the classy Sara Braun Mansion shouldn't be missed.

Jekus PUB
(O'Higgins 1021; ⌚6pm-3am) A restaurant that serves as a popular meeting spot for drinks, with happy hours, karaoke and soccer on the tube.

Entertainment

Kamikaze CLUB
(☎248744; Bories 655; cover incl 1 free drink CH$3000) Tiki torches warm up this most southerly dance club and, if you're lucky, there's occasional live rock band.

Cine Estrella CINEMA
(Mejicana 777) Shows first-run movies.

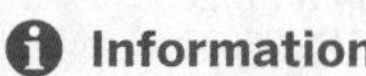

Information

Travel agencies in the city center, along Roca and Lautaro Navarro, change cash and traveler's checks. All are open weekdays and Saturday, with a few open on Sunday morning. Banks with ATMs dot the city center.

Conaf (☎223841; José Menéndez 1147) Has details on the nearby parks.

Hospital Regional (☎205000; cnr Arauco & Angamos)

Information kiosk (☎200610; Plaza Muñoz Gamero; ⌚8am-7pm Mon-Sat, 9am-7pm Sun) South side of the plaza.

Oficina de Turismo (☎241330; www.sernatur.cl; Lautaro Navarro 999; ⌚8am-6pm Mon-Fri) Has friendly, well-informed, multilingual staff, and lists of accommodations and transportation. Also has a list of recommended doctors.

Post office (Bories 911)

Sur Cambios (Lautaro Navarro 1001) Exchanges money.

Getting There & Away

The tourist offices distribute a useful brochure that details all forms of transport available.

Air

Punta Arenas' airport is located 21km north of town.

LanChile (☎241100, 600-526-2000; www.lan.com; Bories 884) flies several times daily to Santiago (CH$229,000) with a stop in Puerto Montt (CH$127,000), and on Saturday to the Falkland Islands (roundtrip CH$530,000). A new service goes direct to Ushuaia several times a week in summer. For national flights, book ahead online for the best deals. **Aerolineas Argentina** (☎0810-222-86527; www.aerolineas.com.ar) offers flights to various cities in Argentina.

Aerovías DAP (☎616100; www.aeroviasdap.cl; O'Higgins 891) From November to March, flies to Porvenir (CH$21,000) Monday through Saturday several times daily, and to Puerto Williams (CH$63,000) Monday through Saturday at 10am. Luggage is limited to 10kg per person.

Boat

Transbordador Austral Broom (☎580089; www.tabsa.cl) Operates three ferries to Tierra del Fuego. The car/passenger ferry *Crux Australis* to/from Porvenir (CH$5500/34,900 per person/vehicle, 2½ to four hours) usually leaves at 9am but has some afternoon departures; check the current online schedule. The faster Primera Angostura crossing (CH$1600/13,900 per person/vehicle, 20 minutes), northeast of Punta Arenas, sails every 90 minutes between 8:30am and 11:45pm. Broom sets sail for Isla Navarino's Puerto Williams (reclining seat/bunk CH$90,000/125,000 including meals, 34 hours) three or four times per month on Wednesday only, returning Saturday.

Cruceros Australis (☎in Santiago 02-442-3110; www.australis.com; ⌚Sep-May) Luxury four- and five-day cruises to Ushuaia and back (see p477). Turismo Comapa handles local bookings.

Bus

Buses depart from company offices, most situated within a block or two of Av Colón. Buy tickets several hours (if not days) in advance. The **Central de Pasajeros** (☎245811; cnr Magallanes & Av Colón) is the closest thing to a central booking office.

Companies and daily destinations include the following:

Bus Sur (☎614221; www.bus-sur.cl; José Menéndez 552) El Calafate, Puerto Natales, Río Gallegos, Ushuaia and Puerto Montt.

Buses Fernández/Buses Pingüino (☎221429/812; www.busesfernandez.com; Armando Sanhueza 745) Puerto Natales, Torres del Paine and Río Gallegos.

Buses Ghisoni (☎240646; www.busesbarria.cl; Av España 264) Comfortable buses to Río Gallegos, Río Grande and Ushuaia.

Buses Pacheco (☎242174; www.busespacheco.com; Av Colón 900) Puerto Natales, Río Gallegos and Ushuaia.

Tecni-Austral (☎222078; Lautaro Navarro 975) Río Grande.

Turíbus/Cruz del Sur (☎227970; www.busescruzdelsur.cl, in Spanish; Armando Sanhueza 745) Puerto Montt, Osorno and Chiloé.

Getting Around

To/From the Airport

Buses depart directly from the airport to Puerto Natales. **Transfer Austral** (☎282854) runs door-to-door shuttle services (CH$3000) to/from town to coincide with flights. Buses Fernández does regular airport transfers (CH$3000).

BUSES FROM PUNTA ARENAS

DESTINATION	COST (CH$)	DURATION (HR)
Puerto Montt	45,000	32
Puerto Natales	4000	3
Río Gallegos	10,000	5-8
Río Grande	20,000	7
Ushuaia	30,000	10

Bus & Taxi Colectivo

Taxi *colectivos*, with numbered routes, are only slightly more expensive than buses (about CH$800, or a bit more late at night and on Sundays); far more comfortable and much quicker.

Car

Cars are a good option for exploring Torres del Paine, but renting one in Chile to cross the border into Argentina can become prohibitively expensive due to international insurance requirements. If heading for El Calafate, it is best to rent your vehicle in Argentina. Purchasing a car to explore Patagonia has its drawbacks, as Chilean Patagonia has no through roads that link northern and southern Patagonia, so it is entirely dependent on the roads of Argentina or expensive ferry travel.

Punta Arenas has Chilean Patagonia's most economical rental rates, and locally owned agencies tend to provide better service. Recommended **Adel Rent a Car/Localiza** (☎235471/2, 09-882-7569; www.adel.cl; Pedro Montt 962) provides attentive service, competitive rates, airport pickup and good travel tips. Other choices include **Budget** (☎225983; O'Higgins 964), **Hertz** (☎248742; O'Higgins 987) and **Lubag** (☎710484; Magallanes 970).

Around Punta Arenas

PENGUIN COLONIES

There are two substantial Magellanic penguin colonies near Punta Arenas. Easier to reach is **Seno Otway** (Otway Sound; www.turisotway.cl; admission CH$5500; ⏲8am-6:30pm), with about 6000 breeding pairs, about an hour northwest of the city. The larger (50,000 breeding pairs) and more interesting **Monumento Natural Los Pingüinos** is accessible only by boat to Isla Magdalena in the Strait of Magellan (see p451).

Arrive via private vehicle or tour. If driving independently, pay attention as you head north on Ruta 9 (RN 9) – it's easy to miss the small sign indicating the turn-off to the penguin colony.

PARQUE NACIONAL PALI AIKE

Rugged volcanic steppe pocked with craters, caves and twisted formations, Pali Aike means 'devil's country' in Tehuelche. This desolate landscape is a 50-sq-km park along the Argentine border. Mineral content made lava rocks red, yellow or green-gray. Fauna includes abundant guanaco, ñandú, gray fox and armadillo. In the 1930s Junius Bird's excavations at 17m-deep **Pali Aike Cave** yielded the first artifacts associated with extinct New World fauna such as the milodón and the native horse *Onohippidium*.

The **park** (admission CH$1000) has several trails, including a 1.7km path through the rugged lava beds of the **Escorial del Diablo** to the impressive **Crater Morada del Diablo**; wear sturdy shoes or your feet could be shredded. There are hundreds of craters, some four stories high. A 9km trail from Cueva Pali Aike to **Laguna Ana** links a shorter trail to a site on the main road, 5km from the park entrance.

Parque Nacional Pali Aike is 200km northeast of Punta Arenas via Ch (rural road) 9, Ch 255 and a graveled secondary road from Cooperativa Villa O'Higgins, 11km north of Estancia Kimiri Aike. There's also access from the Chilean border post at Monte Aymond. There is no public transport, but Punta Arenas travel agencies offer full-day tours.

Puerto Natales

☎61 / POP 18,000

On the windswept shores of Seno Última Esperanza (Last Hope Sound), this formerly modest fishing village is now the well-trodden hub of the continent's number-one national park, Torres del Paine. Though tourism has transformed its rusted tin shop fronts into gleaming facades, Natales maintains its windswept charm, especially in the shoulder seasons.

The Navimag ferry through Chile's fjords ends and begins its trips here. Located 250km northwest of Punta Arenas via Ruta 9, Puerto Natales also offers frequent transport to El Calafate, Argentina.

Sleeping

Options abound, most with breakfast, laundry and lowered rates in off-season. Reserve ahead if arriving on the ferry. Hostels often rent equipment and arrange park transport.

Kau B&B $$
(☎414611; www.kaulodge.com; Pedro Montt 161; d CH$45,000;) With a mantra of simplicity, this aesthetic remake of a box hotel is cozy and cool. Thick woolen throws, picnic-table breakfast seating and well-worn, recycled wood lend casual intimacy. Rooms boast fjord views, central heating, bulk toiletries, and safe boxes. **The Coffee Maker** espresso bar boasts killer lattes and staff have tons of adventure information on tap.

Hotel IF Patagonia BOUTIQUE HOTEL $$$
(☎410312; www.hotelifpatagonia.com; Magellanes 73; d CH$70,000-90,000;) With brimming hospitality, IF (for Isabel and Fernando) is minimalist and lovely. Its bright, modern interior includes wool throws, down duvets and deck views of the fjord. Optional seafood dinners are prepared with the catch of the day. Watch for a spa in the works.

Amerindia B&B $$
(☎411945; www.hostelamerindia.com; Barros Arana 135; d with/without bathroom CH$40,000/30,000; 6-person apt CH$75,000; closed July; @) An earthy retreat with a woodstove, beautiful weavings and raw wood beams. Don't expect a hovering host; the atmosphere is chill. Guests wake up to cake, eggs and oatmeal in a cozy cafe open to the public, also selling organic chocolate and teas.

Hotel Indigo BOUTIQUE HOTEL $$$
(☎413609; www.indigopatagonia.com; Ladrilleros 105; d/ste CH$130,000/175,000; @) Hikers will head first to Indigo's rooftop Jacuzzis and glass-walled spa, but plush, restful rooms are stocked with apples and tea candles. Materials like eucalyptus, slate and iron overlap the modern with the natural to interesting effect. The star here is the fjord in front of you, which even captures your gaze in the shower.

Singular Hotel BOUTIQUE HOTEL $$$
(☎414040, bookings in Santiago 02-387-1500; www.the singular.com; Ruta 9, Km 1.5; d incl full board and excursions CH$580,000; @P) A notable newcomer, the Singular reclaims the space of a regional landmark, a former meatpacking and shipping facility on the sound. Heightened industrial design, like the chairs fashioned from old radiators in the lobby, is mixed with interesting vintage photos and antiques. The snug glass-walled rooms all have water views and the chic bar/restaurant (alongside the museum, open to the public) serves fresh local game. Guests can use the spa with pool and explore the surroundings by bike or kayak. It's located in Puerto Bories, 6km from the center.

Remota LODGE $$$
(☎414040, bookings in Santiago 02-387-1500; www.remota.cl; Ruta 9, Km 1.5; s/d 3 nights incl full board & excursions CH$1,110,000/1,548,000; @) Socialites beware – isolation is the idea here. Unlike most hotels, the exclusive remota draws your awareness to what's outside: silence broadcasts gusty winds, windows imitate old stock fences and a crooked passageway pays tribute to *estancia* sheep corridors. Though rooms are cozy, you'll probably want to spend all your time at 'the beach' – a glass-walled room with lounge futons that gape at the wild surroundings.

The Singing Lamb HOSTEL $
(☎410958; www.thesinginglamb.com; Arauco 779; dm CH$10,000) Sparkling clean and green (with compost, recycling, rainwater collection and linen shopping bags), this fresh hostel is run by a motherly Kiwi. The two long dorms feel a little institutional but thoughtful touches like central heating, a tasty breakfast (with eggs and homemade wheat toast), and sunroom compensate. To get here, follow Raimírez one block past Plaza O'Higgins.

Lili Patagonico's Hostal HOSTEL $
(☎414063; www.lilipatagonicos.com; Arturo Prat 479; dm/d without bathroom CH$8000/18,000, d CH$25,000; @) A sprawling house with a climbing wall, a variety of dorms and colorful doubles with brand-new bathrooms and down comforters.

Hostal Nancy HOSTEL $
(☎410022; www.nataleslodge.cl; Ramirez 543; dm/s/d CH$7000/9000/24,000; @) Nancy is *un amor*. Rooms in her house are hodgepodge, but also clean and comfortable, with down covers, good mattresses and central heating. Privates have their own bathrooms and there's a kitchen for cooking and new gear rentals.

Temauken Hotel B&B $$$
(☎411666; www.temauken.cl; Calle Ovejero 1123; s/d/tr/ste CH$55,000/75,000/90,000/110,000;) A cheerful and elegant choice well away from the center, this new three-story stilted home is plush and modern, with an ample, light-filled living room, panorama sea views and gourmet meals.

4Elementos GUESTHOUSE **$$**
(☎415751; www.4elementos.cl, in Spanish; Esmeralda 813; dm/s/d without bathroom CH$10,000/12,000/20,000, s/d CH$15,000/25,000) A pioneer of Patagonian recycling, the passionate mission of this spare guesthouse is educating people about proper waste disposal. Includes Scandanavian breakfasts. Guide service, park bookings and greenhouse tours are available.

Patagonia Aventura HOSTEL **$**
(☎411028; www.apatagonia.com; Tomás Rogers 179; dm/d CH$8000/20,000; ⊙mid-Sep–mid-May; @) On the plaza, this comfortable hostel has ambient dorms with down duvets and an attached tour agency also renting bikes. No kitchen facilities.

Erratic Rock II B&B **$$**
(☎414317; www.erraticrock2.com; Benjamin Zamora 732; d/tr CH$35,000/36,000; @ 📶) Billed as a 'hostel alternative for couples', this cozy home offers spacious doubles with throw pillows and tidy bathrooms. Breakfasts in the bright dining room are abundant.

Hostal Dos Lagunas GUESTHOUSE **$**
(☎415733; www.hostadoslagunas.com; cnr Barros Arana & Bories; dm/d CH$10,000/$25,000) Natales natives Alejandro and Andrea are

Puerto Natales

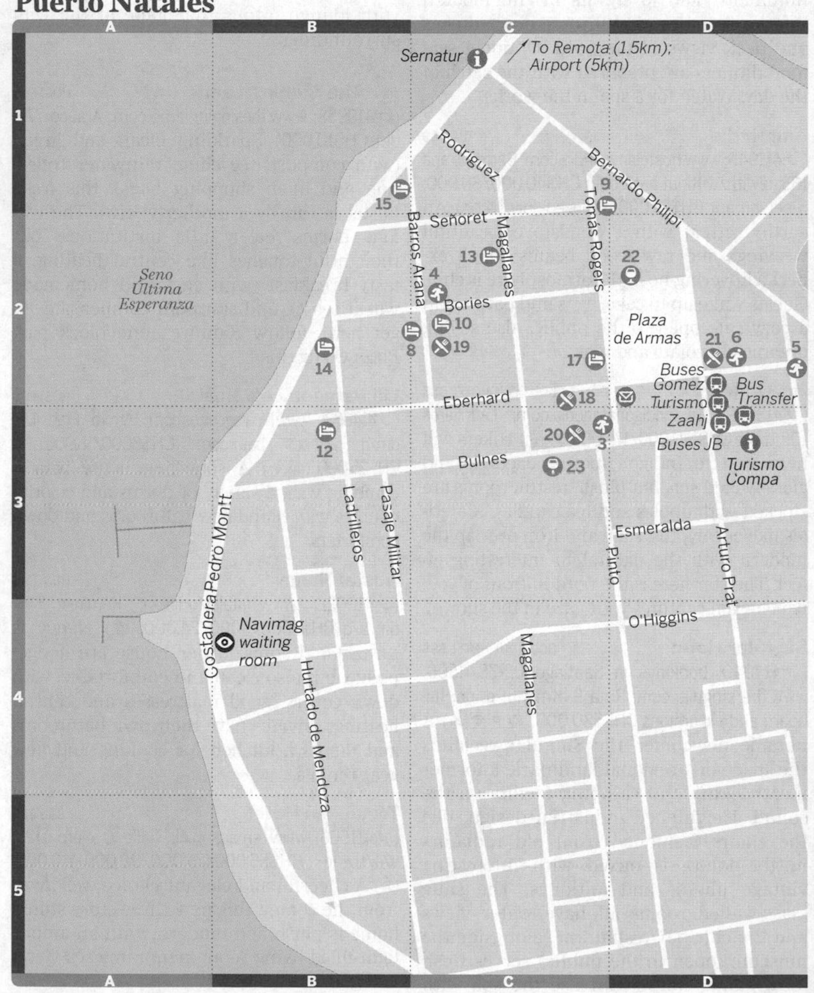

attentive hosts, spoiling guests with filling breakfasts, steady water pressure and travel tips.

Hostel Natales HOSTEL $
(☎414731; www.hostelnatales.cl; Ladrilleros 209; dm/d/tr CH$12,000/24,000/30,000; @) Tranquil and toasty, rooms here all have private bathroom. Generic, this spot doesn't have the energy of other hostels, but dorms are good value.

Casa Cecilia GUESTHOUSE $$
(☎613560; www.casaceciliahostal.com; Tomás Rogers 60; d with/without bathroom CH$38,000/25,000) Well kept and central, Cecilia is a reliable mainstay with good showers, highly-praised service and homemade wheat toast for breakfast. The only drawbacks are a small kitchen and cramped rooms.

Eating

TOP CHOICE Afrigonia FUSION $$
(Eberhard 343; mains CH$8000; ⏲lunch & dinner) Outstanding and wholly original, you won't find Afro-Chilean cuisine on any NYC menu. This romantic gem was dreamed up by a hardworking Zambian/Chilean couple. Fragrant rice, fresh ceviche and mint roasted lamb are prepared with succulent precision. Next door, a small takeout business of the same name sells wraps and salads which lack the flair of the restaurant.

La Mesita Grande PIZZERIA $$
(Arturo Prat 196; pizza CH$5500; ⏲lunch & dinner) Happy diners share one long, worn table for

Puerto Natales

Activities, Courses & Tours

	Antares	(see 15)
1	Baqueano Zamora	E4
2	Fantastico Sur	E3
3	Fortaleza Expediciones	C3
4	Indomita Big Foot	C2
5	Knudsen Tour	D2
6	Turismo 21 de Mayo	D2
	Vertice Patagonia	(see 12)

Sleeping

7	4Elementos	F3
8	Amerindia	C2
9	Casa Cecilia	C1
10	Hostal Dos Lagunas	C2
11	Hostal Nancy	F4
12	Hostel Natales	B3
13	Hotel IF Patagonia	C2
14	Hotel Indigo	B2
15	Kau	B1
16	Lili Patagonico's Hostal	E4
17	Patagonia Aventura	C2

Eating

18	Afrigonia	C2
19	La Aldea	C2
20	La Casa Magna	C3
21	La Mesita Grande	D2

Drinking

22	Baguales	D2
23	El Bar de Ruperto	C3
	The Coffee Maker	(see 15)

outstanding thin-crust pizza, quality pasta and organic salads.

Cangrejo Rojo CAFE $
(Santiago Bueras 782; mains CH$2000-4000; ⌚9am-1:30pm, 3-10:30pm, closed Mon) Unfathomably friendly and cheap, this cute corrugated tin cafe serves pies, ice cream, sandwiches and hot clay pot dishes like seafood casserole or lamb chops. To get here, follow Baquedano four blocks south of Plaza O'Higgins to Bueras.

La Casa Magna RESTAURANT $
(Bulnes 370; menu CH$3000; ⌚10:30am-midnight) Almost always open, this friendly no-frills eatery offers wonderful home cooking at bargain prices.

El Living CAFE $
(www.el-living.com; Arturo Prat 156; mains $5000; ⌚11am-11pm Nov-mid April; ✎) Indulge in the London lounge feel of this chill cafe. There's proper vegetarian fare, stacks of European glossies and a stream of eclectic tunes.

La Aldea MEDITERRANEAN $$
(Barros Arana 142; mains CH$7000; ⌚8pm-12am) Chef Pato changes the offerings daily, but the focus is fresh and Mediterranean. Think grilled clams, lamb tagine and quinoa dishes. Get here early, there's only eight tables.

Drinking

Baguales BREWERY
(www.cervezabaguales.cl; Bories 430; ⌚7pm-2am daily; weekends only in winter; ☎) Climber friends started this microbrewery as a noble quest for quality suds. They have succeeded. Gringo-style burgers and generous veggie tacos will whet your appetite. Get here early to grab a booth, supplied with its own metered tap and topo map to plan your route.

El Bar de Ruperto BAR
(cnr Bulnes & Magallanes; ☎) A typical bar with foosball, chess and other board games.

Information

Internet Resources

www.torresdelpaine.cl The best bilingual portal for the region.

Medical Services

Hospital (☎411582; Pinto 537)

Money

Most banks in town have ATMs.

Gasic (Bulnes 692) Decent rates on cash and traveler's checks.

Post

Post office (Eberhard 429)

Tourist Information

Conaf (☎411438; Baquedano 847) National parks service administrative office.

Municipal tourist office (☎614808; Plaza de Armas; ⌚8:30am-12:30pm & 2:30-6pm Tue-Sun) In the Museo Histórico, with attentive staff and region-wide lodgings listings.

Sernatur (☎412125; infonatales@sernatur.cl; Pedro Montt 19; ⌚9am-7pm Mon-Fri, 9:30am-6pm Sat-Sun) There's a second location with the municipal tourist office on the plaza.

Travel Agencies & Tours

Antares/Indomita Big Foot (☎414611; www.antarespatagonia.com; Pedro Montt 161) Guide service specializing in Torres del Paine, Antares can facilitate climbing permits and made-to-order trips. They also have the concession for ice hikes in the park. Indomita Big Foot runs kayak trips in the fjords and park.

Baqueano Zamora (☎613530; Baquedano 534) Runs horseback-riding trips in Torres del Paine.

Fantastico Sur (☎614184; www.fantasticosur.com; Esmeralda 661) Runs refugios Torres, El Chileno, Los Cuernos in Torres del Paine and offers park tours, guiding and trek planning services.

Fortaleza Expediciones (☎613395; www.fortaleza patagonia.cl; Tomás Rogers 235) Knowledgeable; rents camping gear.

Knudsen Tour (☎414747; knudsentour@yahoo.com; Blanco Encalada 284) Well regarded, with trips to El Calafate, Torres del Paine and alternative routes along Seno Último Esperanza.

Turismo 21 de Mayo (☎411978; www.turismo 21demayo.cl, in Spanish; Eberhard 560) Organizes day-trip cruises and treks to the Balmaceda and Serrano glaciers.

Turismo Comapa (☎414300; www.comapa.com; Bulnes 541; ⌚9am-1pm & 3-7pm Mon-Fri, 10am-2pm Sat) Navimag ferry and airline bookings.

Vertice Patagonia (☎412742; www.verticepatagonia.com; Ladrilleros 209) Runs Refugios Grey, Dickson and Paine Grande in Torres del Paine.

Getting There & Away

Air

Puerto Natales' small airport has frequent changes in service. Currently, only **Sky Airline** (toll-free in Chile ☎600-600-2828; www.skyairline.cl; Bulnes 682) flies to/from Punta Arenas once a week on Saturday (CH$33,000 round-trip), with connections to Puerto Montt and Santiago.

Boat

For many travelers, a journey through Chile's spectacular fjords aboard the **Navimag Ferry** (in

Santiago (☎56-2-442-3114; www.navimag.com) becomes a highlight of their trip. This four-day and three-night northbound voyage has become so popular it should be booked well in advance.

You can also try your luck. To confirm when the ferry is due, contact Turismo Comapa (p460) a couple of days before your estimated arrival date. The *Magallanes* transports cars and passengers. It leaves Natales early on Friday and stops in Puerto Edén (or the advancing Glaciar Pía XI on southbound sailings) en route to Puerto Montt. It usually arrives in Natales in the morning of the same day and departs either later that day or on the following day, but schedules vary according to weather conditions and tides. Disembarking passengers must stay on board while cargo is transported; those embarking have to spend the night on board.

High season is November to March, midseason is October and April and low season is May to September. Most folks end up in dorm-style, 22-bed berths, but often wish they had sprung for a private cabin. Fares vary according to view, cabin size and private or shared bathroom, and include all meals (including veggie options if requested while booking, but bring water, snacks and drinks anyway) and interpretive talks. Per-person fares range from CH$200,000 for a bunk berth in low season to CH$945,000 for a triple-A cabin in high season; students and seniors receive a 10% to 15% discount. Check online for current schedules and rates.

Bus

Puerto Natales has no central bus terminal. In high season book at least a day ahead, especially for early-morning departures. Services are greatly reduced in the off-season.

A second road has been opened to Torres del Paine and, although gravel, it is much more direct. Several tour operators use it. This alternative entrance goes alongside Lago del Toro to the Administración (park headquarters).

Buses leave for Torres del Paine two to three times daily at around 7am, 8am and 2:30pm. If you are headed to Mountain Lodge Paine Grande in the off-season, take the morning bus to meet the catamaran (one way CH$12,000, two hours). Tickets may also be used for transfers within the park, so save your stub. Schedules are in constant flux, so double-check them before heading out.

Companies and destinations include the following:

Bus Sur (☎614220; www.bus-sur.cl, in Spanish; Baquedano 668) Punta Arenas, Torres del Paine, Puerto Montt, El Calafate, Río Gallegos and Ushuaia.

Buses Fernández/El Pingüino (☎411111; www.busesfernandez.com; cnr Esmeralda & Ramírez) Torres del Paine and Punta Arenas. Also goes direct to Puerto Natales from the airport.

BUSES FROM PUERTO NATALES

DESTINATION	COST (CH$)	DURATION (HR)
El Calafate	12,000	5
Punta Arenas	4500	3
Torres del Paine	8000	2
Ushuaia	30,000	13

Buses Gomez (☎415700; www.busesgomez.com, in Spanish; Arturo Prat 234) Torres del Paine.

Buses JBA (☎410242; www.busesjb.cl; Arturo Prat 258) Torres del Paine.

Buses Pacheco (☎414800; www.busespacheco.com; Ramírez 224) Punta Arenas, Río Grande and Ushuaia.

Buses Transfer (☎412616; www.pumatour.cl; Bulnes 518) Torres del Paine, El Calafate and Ushuaia.

Cootra (☎412785; Baquedano 244) El Calafate daily at 8:30am.

Turismo Zaahj (☎412260/355; www.turismozaahj.co.cl, in Spanish; Arturo Prat 236/270) Torres del Paine and El Calafate.

Getting Around

Car rental is expensive and availability is limited; you'll get better rates in Punta Arenas or Argentina. Try **Emsa/Avis** (☎410775; Bulnes 632). Many hostels rent bikes.

Parque Nacional Bernardo O'Higgins

Virtually inaccessible, O'Higgins remains an elusive cache of glaciers. Only entered by boat, full-day excursions (CH$67,000 with lunch included) to the base of Glaciar Serrano are run by **Turismo 21 de Mayo** (☎061-411978; www.turismo21demayo.cl, in Spanish; Eberhard 560, Puerto Natales).

You can access Torres del Paine via boat to Glaciar Serrano. Passengers transfer to a Zodiac (a motorized raft), stop for lunch at Estancia Balmaceda and continue up Río Serrano, arriving at the southern border of the park by 5pm. The same tour can be done leaving the park, but may require camping near Río Serrano to catch the Zodiac at 9am. The trip, which includes park entry, costs CH$92,000 with Turismo 21 de Mayo.

CUEVA DEL MILODÓN

In the 1890s, Hermann Eberhard discovered the remains of an enormous ground sloth just 24km northwest of Puerto Natales. Nearly 4m tall, the herbivorous milodón survived on the succulent leaves of small trees and branches, but became extinct in the late Pleistocene. The 30m-high **cave** (admission CH$3000) pays homage to its former inhabitant with a life-size plastic replica of the animal. It's not exactly tasteful, but still worth a stop, whether to appreciate the grand setting and ruminate over its wild past or to take an easy walk up to a lookout point.

Camping (no fires) and picnicking are possible. Torres del Paine buses pass the entrance, 8km from the cave proper. There are infrequent tours from Puerto Natales; alternatively, you can hitchhike or share a taxi (CH$20,000). Outside of high season, bus services are infrequent.

Parque Nacional Torres del Paine

☎61

Soaring almost vertically to nearly 3000m above the Patagonian steppe, the Torres del Paine (Towers of Paine) are spectacular granite pillars that dominate the landscape of what just may be South America's finest **national park** (www.pntp.cl, in Spanish; high/low season in Chilean pesos only CH$15,000/8000).

Before its creation in 1959, the park was part of a large sheep *estancia*. Part of Unesco's Biosphere Reserve system since 1978, it shelters flocks of ostrich-like rheas (known locally as ñandús), Andean condors, flamingos and many other bird species. Conservation has been most successful with the guanaco *(Lama guanicoe)*, which grazes the open steppe where predatory pumas cannot approach undetected. Herds of guanacos don't even flinch when humans or vehicles approach.

Weather can be wildly changeable in this 1810-sq-km park. Expect four seasons in one day. Sudden rainstorms and knock-down gusts are just part of the adventure. Bring high-quality wet-weather gear, a synthetic sleeping bag and, if you are camping, a good tent.

Guided day trips from Puerto Natales are possible, but permit only a glimpse of what the park has to offer. Nature lovers should plan to spend anywhere from three to seven days.

In 2005 a hiker burned down 10% of the park using a portable stove in windy conditions. Be conscientious and tread lightly – you are one of more than 120,000 yearly guests.

Activities

Hiking

Torres del Paine's 2800m granite peaks inspire a mass pilgrimage of hikers from around the world. Most go for the circuit or the 'W' to soak in these classic panoramas, leaving other incredible routes deserted. The Paine Circuit (the 'W' plus the backside of the peaks) requires seven to nine days, while the 'W' (named for the rough approximation to the letter that it traces out on the map) takes four to five. Add another day or two for transportation connections.

Most trekkers start either route from **Laguna Amarga**. You can also hike from Administración or take the catamaran from Pudeto to Lago Pehoé and start from there; hiking roughly southwest to northeast along the 'W' presents more views of black sedimentary peaks known as Los Cuernos (2200m to 2600m). Trekking alone, especially on the backside of the circuit, is unadvisable. Tour operators in Puerto Natales offer guided treks, which include all meals and accommodations at *refugios* or hotels. Per person rates decrease significantly in groups.

THE 'W'

Most people trek the 'W' from right to left (east to west), starting at Laguna Amarga – accessible by a twice-daily 2½-hour bus ride from Puerto Natales. But hiking west to east – especially between Lago Pehoé and Valle Francés – provides superior views of Los Cuernos. To start the W from the west, catch the catamaran across Lago Pehoé, then head north along Lago Grey or Campamento Italiano, from which point excellent (and pack-free) day hikes are possible. The following segments are some of the W's most memorable.

In 2013, Camping Frances will open near the entrance to Valle Frances. Contact Fantastico Sur for details.

Refugio Las Torres to Mirador Las Torres HIKING

(Four hours one way) A moderate hike up Río Ascencio to a treeless tarn beneath the eastern face of the Torres del Paine for the closest view of the towers. The last hour is a knee-popping scramble up boulders (covered with knee- and waist-high snow in winter). There are camping and *refugios* at Las Torres and Chileno, with basic camping at Campamento Torres. In summer stay at Campamento Torres and head up at sunrise to beat the crowds.

Refugio Las Torres to Los Cuernos HIKING

(Seven hours one way) Hikers should keep to the lower trail as many get lost on the upper trail (unmarked on maps). There's camping and a *refugio*. Summer winds can be fierce.

Los Cuernos/Lago Pehoé to Valle Francés HIKING

(Five hours one way) In clear weather, the most beautiful stretch between 3050m Cerro Paine Grande to the west and the lower, still spectacular Torres del Paine and Los Cuernos to the east, with glaciers hugging the trail. Camp at Italiano and Británico, in the heart of the valley, or at the valley entrance at Campamento Frances, to open in 2013.

Mountain Lodge Paine Grande to Refugio Lago Grey HIKING

(Four hours one way from Lago Pehoé) A relatively easy trail with a few challenging downhill scampers. The glacier lookout is another half-hour's hike away. With camping and *refugios* at both ends.

Mountain Lodge Paine Grande to Administración HIKING

(Five hours) Up and around the side of Lago Pehoé, then through grassland along Río Grey. Not really part of the 'W,' but after the hike, cut out to the Administración to avoid backtracking to Laguna Amarga. Mountain Lodge Paine Grande can radio in and make sure that you can get a bus from Administración back to Puerto Natales. You can also enter the 'W' this way to hike it east to west.

PAINE CIRCUIT

This loop takes in the 'W' (described earlier), plus the backside between Refugio Grey and Refugio Las Torres. The landscape is desolate yet beautiful. Paso John Garner (the extreme part of the trek) sometimes has knee-deep mud and snow. There's a basic *refugio* at Los Perros or there's rustic camping.

Many hikers start the Paine Circuit by entering the park (by bus) at Laguna Amarga, then hike for a few hours to Refugio & Camping Chileno. From there, the circuit continues counter-clockwise, ending in Valle Frances and Los Cuernos. See the following for details on hikes within the Paine Circuit.

Refugio Lago Grey to Campamento Paso HIKING

(Four hours heading north, two hours going south) Hikers might want to go left to right (west to east), which means ascending the pass rather than slipping downhill.

Campamento Paso to Campamento Los Perros HIKING

(Four hours) This route has plenty of mud and sometimes snow. Don't be confused by what appears to be a campsite right after crossing the pass; keep going until you see a shack.

Campamento Los Perros to Campamento Dickson HIKING

(Around 4½ hours) A relatively easy but windy stretch.

Campamento Lago Dickson to Campamento Serón HIKING

(Six hours) As the trail wraps around Lago Paine, winds can get fierce and the trails vague; stay along the trail furthest away from the lake. On the way, Campamento Coiron has been closed since the 2005 fire.

Campamento Serón to Laguna Amarga HIKING

(Four to five hours) You can end the trek with a chill-out night and a decent meal at Refugio Las Torres.

DAY HIKES

Walk from Guardería Lago Pehoé, on the main park highway, to **Salto Grande**, a powerful waterfall between Lago Nordenskjöld and Lago Pehoé. Another easy hour's walk leads to **Mirador Nordenskjöld**, an overlook with superb views. Or try the more challenging but gorgeous four-hour trek to **Lago Paine**; its northern shore is accessible only from Laguna Azul, in the park's east.

Kayaking

A great way to get up close to glaciers, **Indomita Big Foot** (☎061-414611; www.indomita

Parque Nacional Torres del Paine

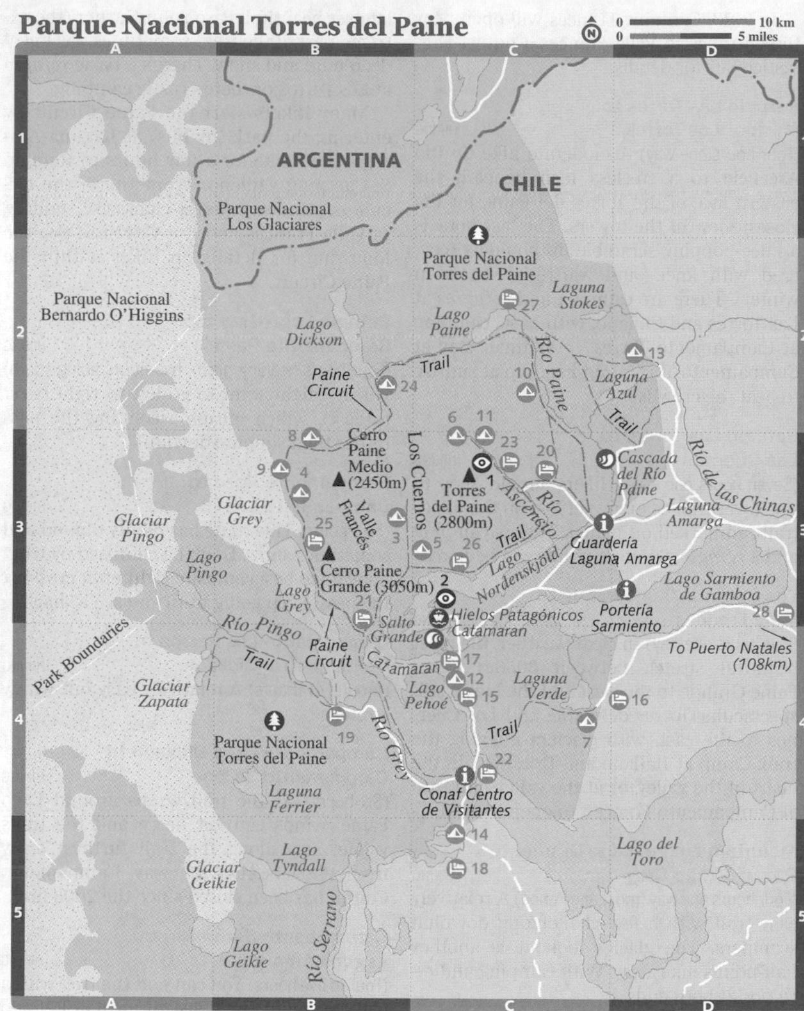

patagonia.com; Pedro Montt 161, Puerto Natales) leads three-hour tours of the iceberg-strewn Lago Grey from Hotel Grey (CH$45,000) or two-hour tours from the former Refugio Grey (CH$35,000), several times daily in summer. They also offer multi-day trips to Río Serrano.

Horseback Riding

The park is certainly a beautiful place to ride. Due to property divisions within the park, horses cannot cross between the western sections (Lagos Grey and Pehoé, Río Serrano) and the eastern part managed by Hostería Las Torres (Refugio Los Cuernos is the approximate cut-off). **Baqueano Zamora** (☎061-613530; www.baqueanozamora.com, in Spanish; Baquedano 534, Puerto Natales) runs excursions to Lagos Pingo, Paine and Azul, and Laguna Amarga (half-day CH$25,000).

Ice Trekking

A fun walk through a sculpted landscape of ice, and you don't need experience to go. **Antares** (☎414611; www.antarespatagonia.com; Pedro Montt 161, Puerto Natales) is the sole company with a park concession for ice hikes (CH$75,000) on Glacier Grey. Using the Conaf house (former Refugio Grey) as a base, the excursion includes a six-hour round-trip

Parque Nacional Torres del Paine

Sights

1 Mirador Las Torres C3
2 Mirador Nordenskjöld C3

Sleeping

3 Campamento Británico B3
4 Campamento Guardas B3
5 Campamento Italiano C3
6 Campamento Japonés C3
7 Campamento Laguna Verde C4
8 Campamento Los Perros B3
9 Campamento Paso B3
10 Campamento Serón C2
11 Campamento Torres C3
12 Camping Lago Pehoé C4
13 Camping Laguna Azul D2
14 Camping Río Serrano C5
Camping Serrano (see 18)
15 explora C4
16 Hostería Mirador del Payne D4
17 Hostería Pehoé C4
18 Hotel Cabañas del Paine C5
19 Hotel Lago Grey B4
20 Hotel Las Torres C3
21 Mountain Lodge Paine Grande B3
22 Posada Río Serrano C4
23 Refugio & Camping Chileno C3
24 Refugio & Camping Lago Dickson B2
25 Refugio & Camping Lago Grey B3
Refugio & Camping Las Torres (see 20)
26 Refugio & Camping Los Cuernos C3
27 Refugio Lago Paine C2
28 Tierra Patagonia D3

hike and three hours on the ice, available from October to May.

Rock Climbing

Expert guides have experience in many of the park's newer climbing areas; qualified climbers can join them for customized multiday trips, while beginners can get instruction and go on easier day climbs. Rock climbers of all levels should contact **Antares** (☎414611; www.antarespatagonia.com) or **Erratic Rock** (☎061-410355; www.erraticrock.com; Baquedano 719, Puerto Natales).

Sleeping

Make reservations! Arriving without them, especially in high season, limits you to camping. Travel agencies offer reservations, but it's best to deal directly with the various management companies (see Refugios, p465). Listings feature high-season rates.

Refugios

If you are hiking the 'W' or circuit, you will be staying in *refugios* (mountain huts) or campsites along the way. It is essential to reserve your spot and specify vegetarian meals in advance if required.

Refugio rooms have four to eight bunk beds each, kitchen privileges (for lodgers and during specific hours only), hot showers and meals. A bed costs CH$25,000 to CH$35,000, plus sleeping bag rental and meals CH$5500 to CH$10,000. Should a *refugio* be overbooked, staff provide all necessary camping equipment. Most *refugios* close by the end of April.

Refugios may require photo ID (ie a passport) upon check-in. Photocopy your tourist card and passport for all lodgings in advance to expedite check-in. Staff can radio ahead to confirm your next reservation. Given the huge volume of trekkers, snags are inevitable, so practice your Zen composure.

These listings match the 'W' hiking description direction. Rates listed are basic – if you want bed linens (vs your own sleeping bag), it's extra.

Refugio Las Torres LODGE **$$**
(☎in Puerto Natales 061-710050; www.fantasticosur.com; dm CH$21,500, incl full board CH$44,500; mid-Sept-April 30; @) An ample, attractive base camp with 60 beds and the added feature of a comfortable lounge, restaurant and bar. In high season, a nearby older building is put into use to handle the overflow, at discounted rates.

Refugio Chileno MOUNTAIN HUT **$$**
(☎in Puerto Natales 061-710050; www.fantasticosur.com; dm CH$19,500, incl full board CH$42,500; ⏲early Oct-mid-March) Nearest to the fabled towers, Chileno is one of the smallest refugios, with 32 beds and a small provisions kiosk. It's run on wind energy and toilets use composting biofilters.

Refugio Los Cuernos MOUNTAIN HUT **$$**
(☎in Puerto Natales 061-710050; www.fantasticosur.com; dm CH$19,500, incl full board CH$42,500;

The 'W'

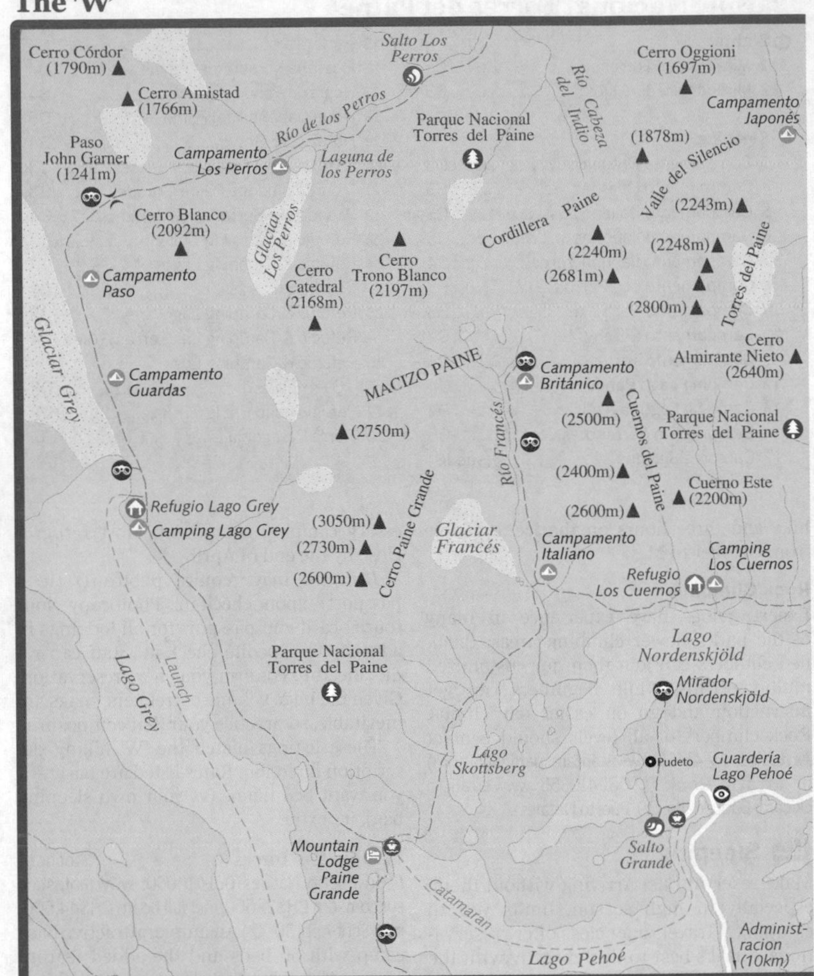

mid-Sept-April 30) Filling fast, this mid-W location tends to bottleneck with hikers going in either location. But with eight beds per room, this small lodge is more than cozy. New separate showers and bathrooms for campers relieve some of the stress. For a deluxe option, eight 2-person cabins with shared bath offer privacy, with skylights and access to a piping-hot wooden hot tub.

Mountain Lodge Paine Grande LODGE **$$**
(in Puerto Natales 061-412742; www.verticepatagonia.cl; dm CH$24,900, incl full board CH$44,500; year-round; @) Though gangly, this park installation on the W hiking circuit is nicer than most dorms, with sublime Los Cuernos views in all rooms. Its year-round presence is a godsend to cold, wet winter hikers, though meals are not available in winter (May to September). There's onsite camping, a kiosk with basic kitchen provisions and a more deluxe version of camping in domes.

Between Lago Grey and Valle Francés, it's a day hike from either and also accessible by ferry across Lago Pehoé.

Refugio Grey MOUNTAIN HUT **$$**
(in Puerto Natales 061-412742; www.verticepatagonia.cl; dm CH$15,000, incl full board

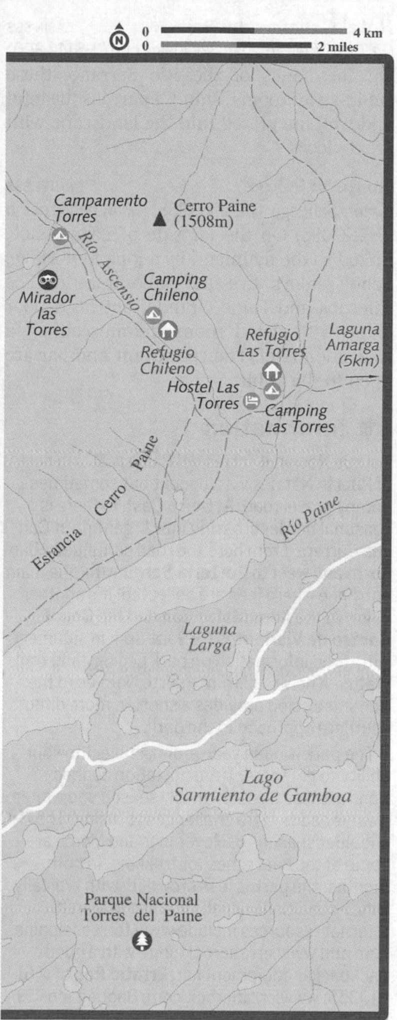

CH$35,500; year-round) Relocated inland from the lake, this deluxe new trekkers' lodge features a decked-out living area with leather sofas and bar, a restaurant-grade kitchen and snug bunkrooms that house 60, with plenty of room for backpacks. There's also a general store, and covered cooking space for campers. Prices may soon go up to match those of Mountain Lodge Paine Grande. Also runs in winter without meal service (May to September).

Refugio Dickson MOUNTAIN HUT **$$**
(in Puerto Natales 061-412742; www.verticepatagonia.cl; dm CH$15,000, incl full board CH$35,500; Nov-Mar) One of the oldest refugios and smallest, with 30 beds, in a stunning setting on the Paine circuit, near Glaciar Dickson.

Camping

The park has both fee camping and free camping. More services can be found at the former. For campground locations, see the Torres del Paine map (p464).

Camping at the *refugios* costs CH$4500 per site. *Refugios* rent equipment – tent (CH$7000 per night), sleeping bag (CH$5000) and mat (CH$1500) – but potential shortages in high season make it prudent to pack your own gear. Small kiosks sell expensive pasta, soup packets and butane gas, and cook shelters (at some campgrounds) prove useful in foul weather. Campgrounds generally operate from mid-October to mid-March, though those on the backside of the circuit may not open until November due to harsher weather. The decision is made by Conaf.

For bookings, **Vertice Patagonia** (061-412742; www.verticepatagonia.cl; Ladrilleros 209, Puerto Natales) looks after Camping Grey, Dickson, Perros and Paine Grande. **Fantastico Sur** (061-710050; www.fantasticosur.com; Esmeralda 661, Puerto Natales; 9am-1pm & 3-6pm Mon-Fri) owns camping Las Torres, Chileno and Seron.

Sites on the trekking routes administered by Conaf are free but basic. No rental equipment or showers. These are: Campamento Británico, Campamento Italiano, Campamento Paso, Campamento Serón, Campamento Torres and Camping Guardas.

Many campers have reported wildlife (in rodent form) lurking around campsites, so don't leave food in packs or in tents – hang it from a tree instead.

Hotels

When choosing lodgings, pay particular attention to location. Lodgings that adjoin the 'W' offer more independence and flexibility for hikers. Most offer multi-day packages.

Hotel Lago Grey HOTEL **$$$**
(712132; www.lagogrey.cl; booking address Lautaro Navarro 1061, Punta Arenas; d CH$154,000; @) Open year-round, this tasteful hotel has snug white cottages linked by raised boardwalks. The new deluxe rooms are lovely – with lake views and sleek modern style. The cafe (open to the public) overlooks the grandeur. Boat tours visit the glacier, stopping at the Conaf office on the other side of Lago Grey to pick up and drop off passengers.

explora DESIGN HOTEL **$$$**
(☎in Santiago 02-206-6060; www.explora.com; d per person 4 nights incl full board & transfers CH$1,390,000; @☒) Strutting with style, Torres del Paine's most sophisticated (and expensive) digs sit perched above the Salto Chico waterfall at the outlet of Lago Pehoé. Rates include airport transfers, full gourmet meals and a wide variety of excursions led by young, affable, bilingual guides. Views of the entire Paine massif pour forth from every inch of the hotel. But is it worth shelling out? Before you decide, check out the spa with heated lap pool, sauna, massage rooms and open-air Jacuzzi.

Hotel Las Torres HOTEL **$$$**
(☎617450; www.lastorres.com; booking address Magallanes 960, Punta Arenas; d from CH$145,000; ⊙closed June) A hospitable and well-run hotel with international standards, spa with Jacuzzi and good guided excursions. Most noteworthy, the hotel donates a portion of fees to nonprofit park-based environmental group AMA. The buffet serves organic vegetables from the greenhouse and organic meat raised on nearby ranches.

Tierra Patagonia DESIGN HOTEL **$$**
(☎in Santiago 02-263-0606; www.tierrapatagonia.com; d per person 4 nights incl full board & transfers CH$1,230,000; @☎☒) Sculpted into the sprawling steppe, this sleek newcomer is an inviting option. Think luxury lodge, with a lively living and circular bar focused on a grand fire pit and a beautiful oversized artist's rendition of a park map. Large, understated rooms enjoy panoramas of the Paine Massif. Located on Cerro Guido *estancia*, the hotel's ranch-focused activities are a strong asset. All-inclusive rates include airport transfer, daily excursions, use of spa, meals and drinks. It's on Lago Sarmiento, just outside the national park about 20km from Laguna Amarga.

Hostería Mirador del Payne INN **$$$**
(☎226930; www.miradordelpayne.com; booking address Fagnano 585, Punta Arenas; s/d CH$100,000/122,500) On the Estancia El Lazo in the seldom-seen Laguna Verde sector, this comfortable inn is known for its serenity, proximity to spectacular viewpoints and top-rate service – but not for easy park access. Activities include bird-watching, horseback riding and sport fishing. Call to arrange a ride from the road junction.

Hotel Cabañas del Paine CABIN **$$$**
(☎730177; www.cabanasdelpaine.cl; d CH$142,800) On the banks of the Río Serrano, these cabin-style rooms stand apart as tasteful and well integrated into the landscape with great views.

Hostería Pehoé HOTEL **$$$**
(☎in Santiago 02-296-1238; www.pehoe.cl; d CH$127,095) On the far side of Lago Pehoé, linked to the mainland by a long footbridge. Pehoé enjoys five-star panoramas of Los Cuernos and Paine Grande, but it's a poor value with dated rooms reminiscent of a roadside motel. The restaurant and bar are open to the public.

ℹ Information

Parque Nacional Torres del Paine is 112km north of Puerto Natales via a decent but sometimes bumpy gravel road. At Cerro Castillo there is a seasonal border crossing into Argentina at Cancha Carrera. From here the road continues 40km north and west to **Portería Sarmiento**, the main entrance where fees are collected. It's another 37km to the **Administración** and the **Conaf Centro de Visitantes** (⊙9am-8pm in summer), with good information on park ecology and trail status. A new road from Puerto Natales to the Administración provides a shorter, more direct southern approach to the park.

The park is open year-round, subject to your ability to get there. Transportation connections are less frequent in low season and winter weather adds extra challenges to hiking. The shoulder seasons of November and March are some of the best times for trekking. In both months, the park is less crowded, with typically windy conditions usually abating in March. Internet resources include www.torresdelpaine.com and www.erraticrock.com, with a good backpacker equipment list. **Erratic Rock** (☎61-410355; www.erraticrock.com; Baquedano 719, Puerto Natales) also holds an excellent information session every day at 3pm; go for solid advice on everything from trail conditions to camping. Travelers can also rent equipment onsite.

Books & Maps

The best trekking maps, by JLM and Luis Bertea Rojas, are widely available in Puerto Natales. For detailed trekking suggestions and maps, consult Lonely Planet's *Trekking in the Patagonian Andes*.

ℹ Getting There & Away

For details of transportation to the park, see p461. Going to El Calafate from the park on the same day requires joining a tour or careful advance planning, since there is no direct service. Your best bet is to return to Puerto Natales.

Getting Around

Shuttles (CH$2500) drop off and pick up passengers at Laguna Amarga, at the Hielos Patagónicos catamaran launch at Pudeto and at Administración.

The catamaran leaves Pudeto for Mountain Lodge Paine Grande (one way/round trip per person CH$12,000/19,000) at 9:30am, noon and 6pm December to mid-March, at noon and 6pm in late March and November, and at noon only in September, October and April. Another launch travels Lago Grey between Hotel Lago Grey and the beach near Refugio Lago Grey (CH$40,000, 1½ to two hours) a couple of times daily; contact the hotel for the current schedule.

Tierra del Fuego

Includes »

Best Places to Eat

- Kalma Resto (p480)
- Kaupé (p480)
- María Lola' Restó (p480)

Best Places to Stay

- Estancia Viamonte (p492)
- Galeazzi-Basily B&B (p478)
- Antarctica Hostel (p478)
- Cabañas del Beagle (p478)
- Hostería Yendegaia (p494)

Why Go?

The southernmost extreme of the Americas, this windswept archipelago is alluring as it is moody—at turns beautiful, ancient and strange. Travelers who first came for the ends-of-the-earth novelty discover a destination that's far more complex than these bragging rights. Intrigue still remains in a past storied with shipwrecks, native peoples and failed missions. In Tierra del Fuego, nature is writ bold and reckless, from the scoured plains, rusted peat bogs and mossy lenga forests to the snowy ranges above the Beagle Channel.

While distant and isolated, Tierra del Fuego is by no means cut off from the mainland, though the Argentine half is far more developed than its Chilean counterpart. Ports buzz with commerce and oil refineries prosper while adventure seekers descend in droves to fly-fish, hike and start Antarctic cruises. Shared with Chile, this archipelago features one large island, Isla Grande, Chile's Isla Navarino and many smaller uninhabited ones.

When to Go

Ushuaia

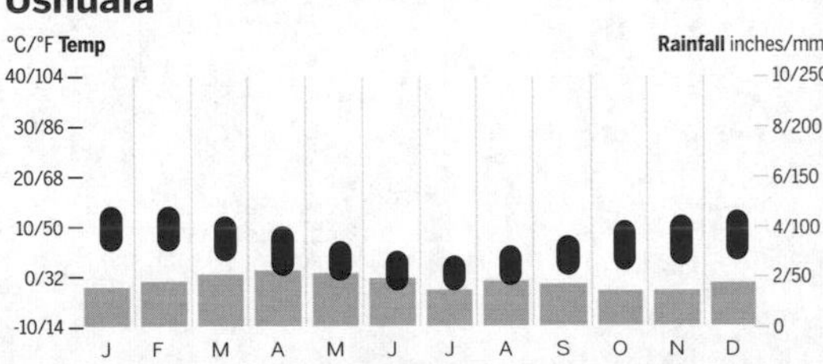

Nov-Mar Warmest months, best for hiking, penguin watching and estancia visits.

mid-Nov–mid-Apr Fly-fishing season.

Jul-Sep Optimal for skiing, snowboarding or dog sledding.

National Parks

Isla Grande is home to Parque Nacional Tierra del Fuego (p482), Argentina's first shoreline national park.

Getting There & Around

The most common overland route from Patagonia is via the ferry crossing at Punta Delgada (p455). Unlike the rest of Argentina, Tierra del Fuego has no designated provincial highways, but has secondary roads known as *rutas complementarias*, modified by a lowercase letter. References to such roads in this chapter are given as 'RC-a,' for example.

If renting a car in mainland Argentina, be aware that you must cross in and out of Chile a couple of times to reach Tierra del Fuego, and that this requires special documents and additional international insurance coverage. Most rental agencies can arrange this paperwork if given advance notice.

At the time of writing, Chile was building an alternate road to the southern end of the island. It currently links with Lago Fagnano, but a 4WD vehicle is required.

Visitors can fly into Río Grande or Ushuaia. Buses take the ferry from Chile's Punta Delgada; all pass through Río Grande before arriving in Ushuaia.

Ushuaia

02901 / POP 57,000

A busy port and adventure hub, Ushuaia is a sliver of steep streets and jumbled buildings below the snowcapped Martial Range. Here the Andes meet the southern ocean in a sharp skid, making way for the city before reaching a sea of lapping currents.

It's a location matched by few, and chest-beating Ushuaia takes full advantage of its end-of-the-world status as an increasing number of Antarctica-bound vessels call in to port. Its endless mercantile hustle knows no irony: the souvenir shop named for Jimmy Button (a native kidnapped for show in England), the ski center named for a destructive invasive species…you get the idea. That said, with a pint of the world's southernmost microbrew in hand, you can happily plot the dazzling outdoor options: hiking, sailing, skiing, kayaking and even scuba diving are just minutes from town.

Tierra del Fuego's comparatively high wages draw Argentines from all over to resettle here, and some locals lament the loss of small-town culture. Meanwhile, expansion means haphazard development advancing in the few directions the mad geography allows.

History

In 1870 the British-based South American Missionary Society set its sights on the Yahgan (or Yámana), a nomadic tribe whose members faced brutal weather conditions almost entirely naked – they didn't have any permanent shelter to keep clothing dry, and believed that the natural oil of their skin was better protection than soaking wet animal fur. Charles Darwin branded them 'the lowest form of humanity on earth.' Missionary Thomas Bridges didn't agree. After years among them, he created a Yahgan-English dictionary in the late 19th century, deeming their language complex and subtle.

The mission made Ushuaia its first permanent Fuegian outpost, but the Yahgan, who had survived 6000 years without contact, were vulnerable to foreign-brought illnesses and faced increasing infringement by sealers, settlers and gold prospectors. Four Yámana, including a teenager dubbed 'Jimmy Button,' were kidnapped by the naval captain Robert Fitz Roy and shipped back to England to be educated and paraded around as examples of gentrified savages. One died of disease, after months of public criticism, Fitz Roy agreed to return the rest to their homeland.

The tribe's legacy is now reduced to shell mounds, Thomas Bridges' famous dictionary and Jimmy Button souvenirs. At the time of writing, one elderly Yámana woman was still alive on Isla Navarino, the only native speaker of the language.

Between 1884 and 1947 the city became a penal colony, incarcerating many notorious criminals and political prisoners, both here and on remote Isla de los Estados. Since 1950 the town has been an important naval base.

Sights

Paralleling the Beagle Channel, Maipú becomes Malvinas Argentinas west of the cemetery, then turns into RN 3, continuing 12km to Parque Nacional Tierra del Fuego. To the east, public access ends at Yaganes, which heads north to meet RN 3 going north toward Lago Fagnano. Most visitor services are on or near San Martín, a block from the waterfront.

The tourist office distributes a free city-tour map with information on the historic houses around town. The 1894 **Legislatura Provincial** (Provincial Legislature; Maipú 465) was the governor's official residence. The century-old **Iglesia de la Merced** (cnr San Martín & Don Bosco) was built with convict

Tierra del Fuego Highlights

1. Explore the ancient Fuegian forests of **Parque Nacional Tierra del Fuego** (p482)
2. Speed through frozen valleys on a **dog sledding tour** (p476) near Ushuaia
3. Land the big one while fly-fishing at an **estancia** (p492) near Río Grande
4. Relive grim times in Ushuaia's infamous prison-turned-museum, **Museo Marítimo & Museo del Presidio** (p474)
5. Ski and snowboard with sublime views at the world's southernmost resort, **Cerro Castor** (p476)
6. Browse back in time in the quiet seaside village of **Porvenir** (p493)
7. Trek around the jagged peaks and sculpted landscapes on the five-day circuit of **Dientes de Navarino** (p489)

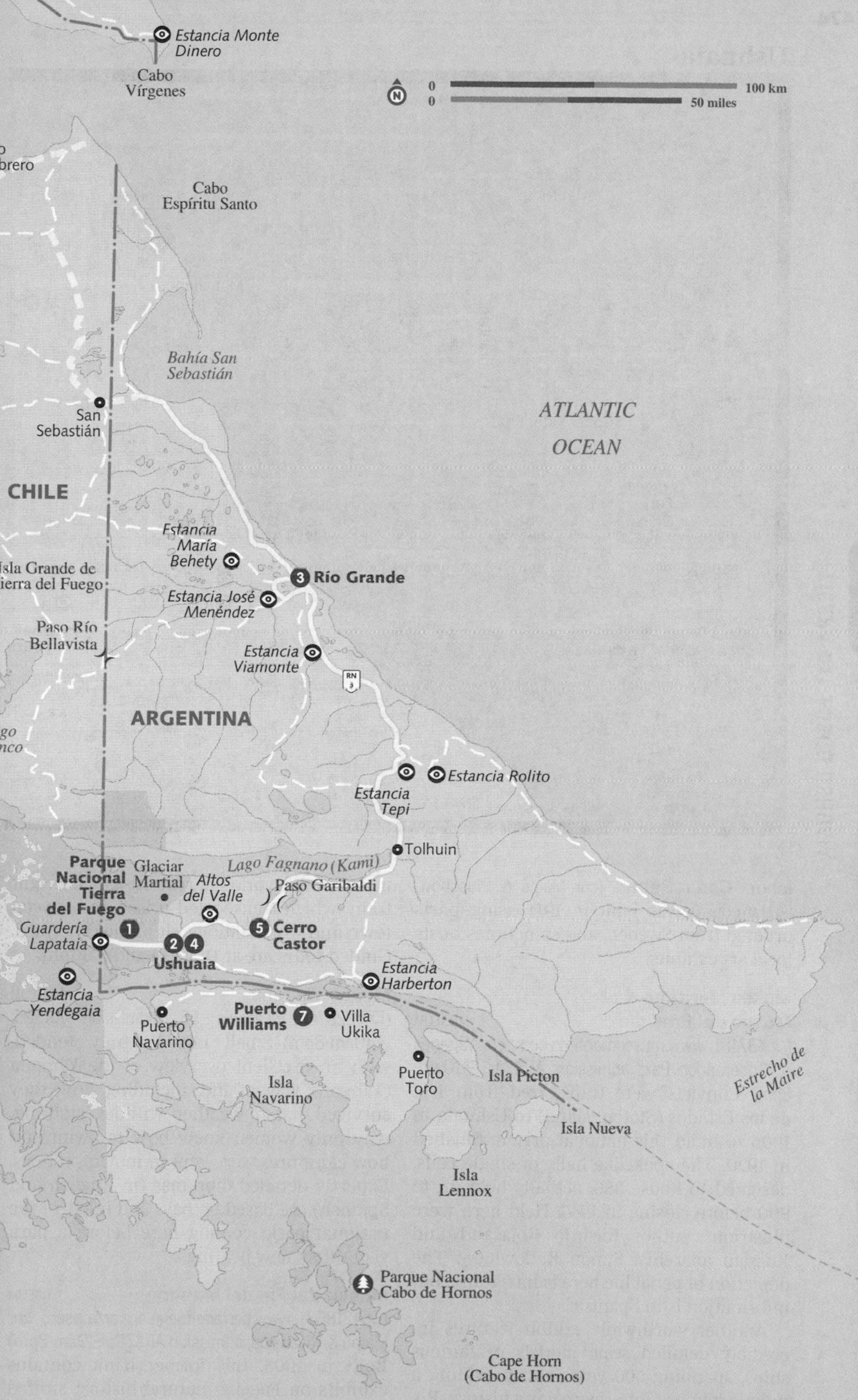

Estancia Monte Dinero
Cabo Vírgenes
0
100 km
0
50 miles
brero
Cabo Espíritu Santo
Bahía San Sebastián
San Sebastián
ATLANTIC OCEAN
CHILE
Estancia María Behety
Isla Grande de Tierra del Fuego
3 Río Grande
Estancia José Menéndez
Paso Río Bellavista
Estancia Viamonte
RN 3
ARGENTINA
Estancia Rolito
Estancia Tepi
Tolhuin
Lago Fagnano (Kami)
Parque Nacional Tierra del Fuego
Glaciar Martial
Altos del Valle
Paso Garibaldi
5 Cerro Castor
Guardería Lapataia
1
2 4
Ushuaia
Estancia Harberton
Estancia Yendegaia
Puerto Navarino
Puerto Williams 7
Villa Ukika
Puerto Toro
Isla Picton
Estrecho de la Maire
Isla Navarino
Isla Nueva
Isla Lennox
Parque Nacional Cabo de Hornos
Cape Horn (Cabo de Hornos)

Ushuaia

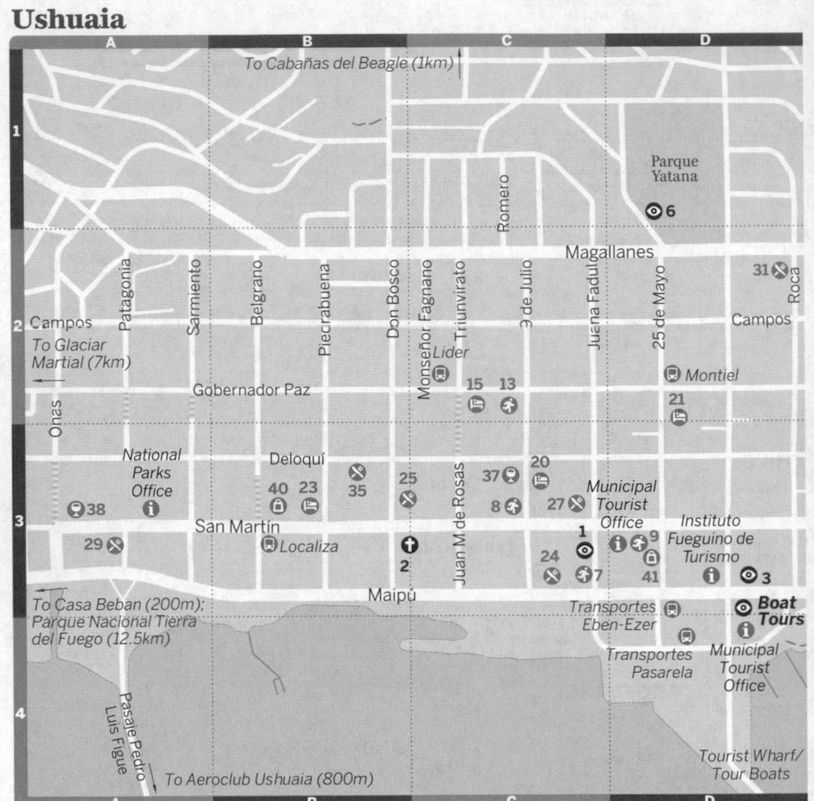

labor. **Casa Beban** (cnr Maipú & Plúschow; ⏲11am-6pm) was built in 1911 using parts ordered from Sweden, and sometimes hosts local art exhibits.

Museo Marítimo & Museo del Presidio MUSEUM
(☎437481; www.museomaritimo.com; cnr Yaganes & Gobernador Paz; admission AR$70; ⏲10am-8pm) Convicts were transferred from Isla de los Estados (Staten Island) to Ushuaia in 1906 to build this national prison, finished in 1920. The spokelike halls of single cells, designed to house 380, actually held up to 800 before closing in 1947. Held here were illustrious author Ricardo Rojasand and Russian anarchist Simón Radowitzky. The depiction of penal life here is intriguing, but information is in Spanish.

Another worthwhile exhibit features incredibly detailed scale models of famous ships, spanning 500 years and providing a unique glimpse into the region's history. Remains of the world's narrowest-gauge freight train, which transported prisoners between town and work stations, sit in the courtyard. Guided tours are at 11:30am and 6:30pm.

Museo Yámana MUSEUM
(☎422874; Rivadavia 56; admission AR$25; ⏲10am-8pm) Small but carefully tended, with an excellent overview of the Yámana (Yahgan) way of life, including how they survived harsh weather without clothing, why only women knew how to swim and how campfires were kept in moving canoes. Expertly detailed dioramas (in English and Spanish) are based on bays and inlets of the national park; coming here before a park visit offers new bearings.

Museo del Fin del Mundo MUSEUM
(☎421863; www.tierradelfuego.org.ar/museo; cnr Maipú & Rivadavia; admission AR$30; ⏲9am-8pm) Built in 1903, this former bank contains exhibits on Fuegian natural history, stuffed

birdlife, life of natives and early penal colonies, and replicas of moderate interest.

FREE **Parque Yatana** PARK
(Fundación Cultiva; ☎425212; cnr Magallanes & 25 de Mayo; ⊙3-6pm Wed-Fri) Part art project, part urban refuge, a city block of lenga forest preserved from encroaching development by one determined family.

Activities

Boating can be undertaken year-round. Hiking possibilities should not be limited to Parque Nacional Tierra del Fuego; the entire mountain range behind Ushuaia, with its lakes and rivers, is a hiker's high. However, many trails are poorly marked or not marked at all, and some hikers who have easily scurried uphill have gotten lost trying to find the trail back down. Club Andino Ushuaia (p481) has maps and good information. In an emergency, contact the **Civil Guard** (☎103, 22108).

Summer Activities

Cerro Martial & Glaciar Martial MOUNTAIN
(optional chairlift AR$55; ⊙10am-4pm) A hearty all-day hike from the city center leads up to Glaciar Martial, with fantastic panoramas of Ushuaia and the Beagle Channel. The views are more impressive than the actual glacier. Follow San Martín west and keep ascending as it zigzags. When you arrive at the ski run 7km northwest of town, either take the *aerosilla* (chairlift) or walk another two hours to make a full day of it. For the best views, hike an hour above the chairlift terminus. A cozy refuge offers coffee, desserts and beer at the *aerosilla* base. Weather is changeable so take warm, dry clothing and sturdy footwear.

Evening **canopy tours** (escuela@tierradelfuego.org.ar; Refugio de Montaña; AR$130; ⊙10am-5:15pm Oct-Jun) are run from the base of the *aerosilla* and offer an hour's worth of Tarzan time, zipping through the forest with 11 zip-line cables and two hanging bridges. The highest cable is 8m. It's by reservation only.

Catch a taxi up the hill or jump aboard one of the minivans (AR$35) that leave from the corner of Maipú and Juana Fadul every half-hour from 8:30am to 6:30pm to Cerro Martial.

Beagle Channel BOATING
Navigating the Beagle Channel's gunmetal-gray waters, with glaciers and rocky isles in the distance, offers a fresh perspective and decent wildlife watching. Operators are found on the tourist wharf Maipú between Lasserre and Roca. Harbor cruises are usually four-hour morning or afternoon excursions (AR$180 to AR$230) to sea lion and cormorant colonies. The number of passengers, extent of snacks and hiking options may vary between operators. A highlight is an island stop to hike and look at *conchales*, middens or shell mounds left by the native Yahgan.

Mago Del Sur SAILING
(☎02901-15-5148-6463; www.magodelsur.com.ar; charter per person per day channel/Antarctica AR$1266/1477) A recommended option for extended sailing trips, captained by Alejandro Da Milano, whose lifetime of experience ensures skill and safety at the helm.

Cruceros Australis CRUISE
(☎in Santiago 02-442-3110; www.australis.com; ⊙Sep-May) Luxurious four-day and five-day sightseeing cruises to Punta Arenas and back (starting from US$1498/1894 per person in low/high season), catering mostly to mature travelers. The Saturday

Ushuaia

Top Sights
Boat Tours ... D3
Museo Marítimo & Museo del Presidio ... F2

Sights
1 Club Andino Ushuaia ... C3
2 Iglesia de la Merced ... B3
3 Legislatura Provincial ... D3
4 Museo del Fin del Mundo ... E3
5 Museo Yámana ... E3
6 Parque Yatana ... D1

Activities, Courses & Tours
7 All Patagonia ... C3
8 Canal Fun ... C3
9 Compañía de Guías de Patagonia ... D3
10 Rumbo Sur ... E3
11 Tolkar ... E3
12 Turismo Comapa ... E3
13 Ushuaia Turismo ... C2

Sleeping
14 Antarctica Hostel ... E2
15 Freestyle ... C2
16 Galeazzi-Basily B&B ... E1
17 Hostel Cruz del Sur ... E3
18 La Casa de Tere B&B ... E1
19 La Maison de Ushuaia ... E1
20 Martín Fierro B&B ... C3
21 Mil 810 ... D2
22 Posada Fin del Mundo ... E1
23 Yakush ... B3

Eating
24 Almacen Ramos Generales ... C3
25 Bodegón Fueguino ... B3
26 Café Bar Tante Sara ... E3
27 Café-Bar Tante Sara ... C3
28 Chiko ... E3
29 El Turco ... A3
30 Kalma ... F3
31 Kaupé ... D2
32 La Anónima ... E2
33 La Estancia ... E3
34 Lomitos Martinica ... F3
35 María Lola Restó ... B3
36 Placeres Patagónicos ... E3

Drinking
37 Dublin Irish Pub ... C3
38 Macario 1910 ... A3

Entertainment
39 Cine Pakawaia ... F2

Shopping
40 Boutique del Libro ... B3
41 Boutique del Libro ... D3

departures from Ushuaia include the possibility of disembarking at Cape Horn. Low season is the first and last two months of the season. The cruise visits many otherwise inaccessible glaciers, but time alone and hiking opportunities are limited; the focus is more on nature talks and group excursions. Turismo Comapa (p477) handles local bookings.

Aeroclub Ushuaia SCENIC FLIGHTS
(☎421717, 421892; www.aeroclubushuaia.org.ar; flight 30min AR$443) Offers scenic rides over the channel.

Winter Activities

With the surrounding peaks loaded with powder, winter visitors should jump at the chance to explore the local ski resorts. Accessed from RN 3, resorts offer both downhill and cross-country options. The ski season runs from June to September, with July (winter vacation) the busiest month.

TOP CHOICE **Cerro Castor** SNOW SPORTS
(☎02901-15-605604/6; www.cerrocastor.com; full-day lift ticket adult/child AR$240/165; ⊙mid-Jun–mid-Oct) Fun and incredibly scenic, the largest resort is 26km from Ushuaia, with 15 runs spanning 400 hectares and a number of lodges with cafes and even a hip sushi bar. Rentals are available for skis, boards and cross-country skis. Multiday and shoulder-season tickets are discounted. Clear windbreaks are added to lifts on cold days. It's 26km from Ushuaia via RN3.

Nunatak Adventure SNOW SPORTS
(☎430329; www.nunatakadventure.com; RN 3, Km 3018; guided dog sledding AR$140) Snowshoe a beautiful alpine valley or dogsled with Siberian and Alaskan huskies bumping across Tierra Mayor. For a memorable night, combine either with an evening bonfire (AR$400). It also does guided snowcat rides. It's 19km from Ushuaia via RN3.

Altos del Valle SNOW SPORTS
(☎422234; www.gatocuruchet.com.ar) Gato Curuchet, the first South American in Alaska's Iditarod, teaches dog sledding at this winter resort,which is also the sponsor of popular annual dog-sled races at the end of August, where kids also compete. There's also good cross-country and snowshoeing areas, equipment rentals and full-moon trips. Extreme skiers can check out the snowcat skiing. It's 18km from Ushuaia via RN3.

Centro de Deportes Invernales Glaciar Martial SNOW SPORTS
(☎421423, 423340) About 7km northwest of town, this family-oriented area has downhill runs well suited for beginners; it also rents equipment.

Cerro Martial & Glaciar Martial SNOW SPORTS
(optional chairlift AR$55; ⏲10am-4pm) Ideal for families or a few hours of fun, this town winter sports center also rents ski equipment; ask about snowshoes to take a winter walk. For directions, see p475.

Tours

Many travel agencies sell tours around the region. You can go horseback riding, hiking, canoeing, visit Lagos Escondido and Fagnano, stay at an *estancia* (ranch) or spy on birds and beavers.

All Patagonia GUIDED TOUR
(☎433622; www.allpatagonia.com; Juana Fadul 60) Amex rep offering more conventional and luxurious trips.

Canal Fun ADVENTURE TOUR
(☎437395; www.canalfun.com; 9 de Julio 118) Run by hip young guys, these popular all-day outings include hiking and kayaking in Parque Nacional Tierra del Fuego (AR$425), the famous off-roading adventure around Lago Fagnano (AR$535), and a multisport outing around Estancia Harberton that includes kayaking around Estancia Harberton and a visit to the penguin colony (AR$785).

Compañía de Guías de Patagonia WALKING TOUR
(☎437753; www.companiadeguias.com.ar; San Martín 628) A reputable outfitter organizing excursions in the national park, full-day treks and ice-hiking on Glaciar Vinciguerra (AR$329), and recommended three-day treks to Valle Andorra and Paso la Oveja (AR$2026).

Nunatak Adventure ADVENTURE TOUR
(☎430329; www.nunatakadventure.com) Offers competitively priced adventure tours and has its own mountain base. Many travelers have enjoyed the off-roading day trip to Lago Fagnano with canoeing and a full barbecue (AR$460).

Patagonia Adventure Explorer HARBOR CRUISE
(☎02901-15-465842; www.patagoniaadvent.com.ar; tourist wharf) Comfortable boats with snacks and a short hike on Isla Bridges. For extra adventure, set sail in the 18ft sailboat. Full-day sail trips with wine and gourmet snacks or multiday trips are also available.

Piratour HARBOR CRUISE
(☎424834; www.piratour.com.ar; tourist wharf) Runs 20-person tours to Isla Martillo for trekking around Magellanic and Papúa penguins.

Rumbo Sur GUIDED TOUR
(☎422275; www.rumbosur.com.ar; San Martín 350) Ushuaia's longest-running agency specializes in more-conventional activities, plus a catamaran harbor cruise. It also handles bookings to Antarctica.

Tango y Che HARBOR CRUISE
(☎02901-15-517967; www.navegandoelbeagle.com; tourist wharf) With two 12-passenger boats, this owner-run tour includes a trek on Bridges Island and Beagle (what else?) beer on tap served for the cruise back to the harbor—very popular with the hostel crowd.

Tres Marías Excursiones HARBOR CRUISE
(☎436416; www.tresmariasweb.com; tourist wharf) The only outfitter with permission to land on Isla 'H' in the Isla Bridges natural reserve, which has shell mounds and a colony of rock cormorants. It takes only eight passengers.

Tolkar GUIDED TOUR
(☎431408/12; www.tolkarturismo.com.ar; Roca 157) Another helpful, popular, all-round agency, affiliated with Tecni-Austral buses.

Turismo Comapa BOATING
(☎430727; www.comapa.com; San Martín 245) Confirm Navimag and Cruceros Australis passages here.

Turismo de Campo GUIDED TOUR
(☎437351; www.turismodecampo.com, in Spanish; Fuegia Basquet 414) Organizes light trekking, Beagle Channel sailing trips and visits to Estancia Rolito near Río Grande. Also sells nine- to 12-night Antarctica passages.

Ushuaia Turismo GUIDED TOUR
(☎436003; www.ushuaiaturismoevt.com.ar; Gobernador Paz 865) Offers last-minute Antarctica cruise bookings.

Festivals & Events

Fin del Mundo Marathon RUNNING
(early Mar) A hugely popular international marathon on the southernmost course on the continent.

Longest Night FESTIVAL
(mid-Jun) The Festival Nacional de Noche Más Larga (the Longest Night) features two weeks of shows and music recitals (ranging from tango to jazz and popular music), with free events at locations throughout the city. For more information, contact the tourism office.

Marcha Blanca SNOW SPORTS
(www.marchablanca.com; mid-Aug) Running for a quarter of a century, Ushuaia's biggest ski event is the annual cross-country event which re-creates San Martín's historic August 17, 1817 crossing of the Andes. There's also a master class for ski enthusiasts, snow sculptures and a Nordic ski marathon.

Sleeping

Reserve ahead from January to early March. Check when booking for free arrival transfers. Winter rates drop a bit, some places close altogether. Most offer laundry service.

The municipal tourist office (p481) has lists of B&Bs and *cabañas* (cabins), and also posts a list of available lodgings outside after closing time.

Hostels abound, all with kitchens and most with internet access. Rates typically drop 25% in low season (April to October).

Antarctica Hostel HOSTEL $
(☎435774; www.antarcticahostel.com; Antártida Argentina 270; dm/d AR$70/125; @☜) This friendly backpacker hub delivers with a warm atmosphere and helpful staff. It turns out that an open floor plan and beer on tap are conducive to making friends. Guests lounge and play cards in the common room and cook in a cool balcony kitchen. Cement rooms are ample, with radiant floor heating.

Galeazzi-Basily B&B B&B $$
(☎423213; www.avesdelsur.com.ar; Valdéz 323; s/d with shared bath AR$190/280, d/tr/q cabin AR$390/450/520; @☜) The best feature of this elegant wooded residence is its warm and hospitable family who will make you feel right at home. Rooms are small but offer a personal touch. Since beds are twin-sized, couples may prefer a modern cabin out back. It's a peaceful spot, and where else can you practice your English, French, Italian and Portuguese?

Cabañas del Beagle CABIN $$$
(☎432785; www.cabanasdelbeagle.com; Las Aljabas 375; 2-person cabin AR$1055, 2-night minimum) Couples in search of a romantic hideaway delight in these rustic chic cabins with heated stone floors, crackling fireplaces and full kitchens stocked daily with fresh bread, coffee and other treats. The personable owner, Alejandro, wins high praise for his attentive service. It's 13 blocks uphill from the center and accessed via Av Leandro Alem.

Freestyle HOSTEL $
(☎432874; www.ushuaiafreestyle.com; Gobernador Paz 866/868; dm without/with bath AR$80/90; @☜) With an MTV vibe you'll love or not, this tricked-out hostel boasts modern dorms with cozy fleece blankets, a marble-countertop cooking area, and a sprawling living room with pool table, leatherette sofas and panoramic views. Brothers Emilio and Gabriel offer friendly tips and good tour connections.

La Posta HOSTEL $
(☎444650; www.laposta-ush.com.ar; Perón Sur 864; dm/d AR$85/135; @☜) This cozy hostel and guesthouse on the outskirts of town is hugely popular with young travelers thanks to warm service, homey decor and spotless open kitchens. The downside is that the place is far from the town center, but public buses and taxis are plentiful.

Los Cormoranes HOSTEL $
(☎423459; www.loscormoranes.com; Kamshen 788; dm/d/tr AR$70/280/330; @☜) More mellow than the competition, this friendly HI hostel is a 10-minute (uphill) walk north of the center. Good, warm, six-bed dorms face outdoor plank hallways – making that midnight bathroom dash bearable. Modern doubles have polished cement floors and bright down duvets – the best is room 10, with bay views. The abundant breakfast includes toast, coffee, do-it-yourself eggs and freshly squeezed orange juice.

La Casa de Tere B&B B&B $$
(☎422312; www.lacasadetere.com.ar; Rivadavia 620; s/d AR$211/253, d with bathroom AR$337) Tere showers guests with attention, but also gives them the run of the place in this beautiful

modern home with great views. Its three tidy rooms fill up fast. Guests can cook, and there's cable TV and a fireplace in the living room. It's a short but steep walk uphill from the center.

Posada Fin del Mundo B&B $$$
(437345; www.posadafindelmundo.com.ar; cnr Rivadavia & Valdéz; d without/with bath AR$422/527) A rambling family home which exudes character, starting with a snug living room with folk art and expansive water views. Eight fresh, tiled rooms tend toward the small side but beds are long. Pricey for its category, at least breakfast is abundant and there's also afternoon tea and cakes. Sometimes booked by entire ski teams in winter.

Cabañas Aldea Nevada CABIN $$$
(422851; www.aldeanevada.com.ar; Martial 1430; d AR$520, 2-night minimum; @) You expect the elves to arrive here any minute. This beautiful patch of lenga forest is discreetly dotted with 13 log cabins with outdoor grills and rough-hewn benches contemplatively placed by the ponds. Interiors are rustic but modern, with functional kitchens, wood stoves and hardwood details.

Cumbres del Martial INN $$$
(424779; www.cumbresdelmartial.com.ar; Martial 3560; d/cabin AR$1160/1667; @) This stylish place sits at the base of the Glaciar Martial. Standard rooms have a touch of the English cottage, while the two-story wooden cabins are simply stunners, with stone fireplaces, Jacuzzis and dazzling vaulted windows. Lush robes, optional massages (extra) and your country's newspaper delivered to your mailbox are some of the delicious details.

Los Cauquenes Resort & Spa RESORT $$$
(441300; www.loscauquenes.com; d incl breakfast AR$1223-1546, d/ste AR$1316/2772; @) A newer addition to Ushuaia, this sprawling wooden lodge sits directly on the Beagle Channel, in a private neighborhood with gravel-road access. Rooms are tasteful and well-appointed, special features include a play room stocked with kids' games and outdoor terraces with glass windbreaks and stunning views of the channel. Proof that Argentines will market anything, the spa features yerba maté scrubs and Andean peat masks. There's also a sauna and indoor-outdoor pool. Free shuttles to downtown leave every few hours. It's 4km west of the airport.

Familia Piatti B&B B&B $$
(437104; www.interpatagonia.com/familiapiatti, in Spanish; Bahía Paraíso 812, Bosque del Faldeo; s/d/tr AR$240/335/395; @) If idling in the forest sounds good, head for this friendly B&B with warm down duvets and native lenga-wood furniture. Hiking trails nearby lead up into the mountains. The friendly owners are multilingual (English, Italian, Spanish and Portuguese) and can arrange transport and guided excursions.

Martín Fierro B&B B&B $$
(430525; www.martinfierrobyb.com.ar; 9 de Julio 175; s/d with shared bath AR$250/350, s/d AR$350/500; Oct-Apr; P) Spending a night at this charming inn feels like staying at the cool mountain cabin of a worldly friend who makes strong coffee and has a great book collection. The owner, Javier, personally built the interiors with local wood and stone; these days he cultivates a friendly, laid-back atmosphere where travelers get into deep conversations at the breakfast table.

Yakush HOSTEL $
(435807; www.hostelyakush.com.ar; Piedrabuena 118; dm AR$85, d without/with bath AR$240/300; mid-Oct–mid-Apr;) Exuding warmth and skillfully adorned with whimsical drawings, this colorful hostel is well-kept and exceedingly friendly. Dorms have fresh sheets and good beds, and social spaces include an ample upstairs lounge with futons and slanted ceilings.

La Maison de Ushuaia B&B $$
(437414; www.lamaisondeushuaia.com; Bouchard 316; s/d AR$211/253, d/tr without bath AR$260/300; d AR$340; @) A matriarchal family, who spent years sailing the world, dug roots on this quiet side street. It's effervescent and welcoming, if a bit disorderly. The multilevel home features creative slatted woodwork, a loft bed (great for kids) and a prized master bedroom. Guests have kitchen use and French and English are spoken. It's uphill from the center.

Mil 810 HOTEL $$$
(437710; www.hotel1810.com; 25 de Mayo 245; d/tr incl breakfast AR$470/530; @) Billed as boutique, this is more like a small upscale hotel. The design is modern, with elements of nature, like a retention wall of river stones and a rock face trickling with water. Its 38 rooms feature brocade walls, rich tones, luxuriant textures and touches of abstract art. Rooms have flat-screen TVs and safes, and halls are monitored.

Hostel Cruz del Sur HOSTEL $
(☎434099; www.xdelsur.com.ar; Deloquí 242; dm AR$70-80, d AR$220; @) This easygoing hostel comprises two renovated houses (1920 and 1926), painted tangerine and joined by a passageway. Dorm prices are based on room capacity, the only disadvantage is your bathroom might be on another flight. There's a fine backyard patio, though indoor shared spaces are scant. Hosts do a fine job of rounding up groups to explore nearby areas.

Camping La Pista del Andino CAMPGROUND $
(☎435890; www.lapistadelandino.com.ar, in Spanish; Alem 2873; camp sites per person AR$22) A steep, uphill, 3km trek leads to this pleasant campground offering grassy or forested sites with views. While it's short on showers and toilets, perks include decent cooking facilities, a bar-restaurant, good common areas and bikes for rent (AR$25). It's at Club Andino Ushuaia's ski area. Call for free pickup from the airport or town center.

Camping Municipal CAMPGROUND $
(RN 3) About 10km west of town, en route to Parque Nacional Tierra del Fuego, this free campground boasts a lovely setting but minimal facilities.

Eating

TOP CHOICE **Kalma Resto** GOURMET $$$
(☎425786; www.kalmaresto.com.ar; Av Antartida 57; mains AR$55-105; ⊗8pm-midnight) Creating quite a stir, this tiny chef-owned gem presents Fuegian staples – like crab and octopus – in a giddy new context. Black sea bass, a rich deep-sea dweller, is combined with a tart tomato sauce for contrast, roast lamb stews with earthy pine mushrooms and the summer greens and edible flowers come fresh from the garden. Service is stellar, with young chef Jorge making the rounds of the few black linen tables. For dessert, splurge with a not-too-sweet deconstructed chocolate cake.

Kaupé INTERNATIONAL $$$
(☎422704; www.kaupe.com.ar; Roca 470; mains AR$80-120) For an out-of-body seafood experience, head to this candlelit house overlooking the bay. Chef Ernesto Vivian employs the freshest of everything and service is impeccable. The tasting menu (AR$360 with wine and champagne) features two starters, a main dish and dessert, with standouts such as king crab and spinach chowder or black sea bass in blackened butter.

Bodegón Fueguino PATAGONIAN $$
(☎431972; www.tierradehumos.com/bodegon; San Martín 859; mains AR$32-82; ⊗Tue-Sun) The spot to sample hearty home-style Patagonian fare or gather for wine and appetizers. This century-old Fuegian home is cozied up with sheepskin-clad benches, cedar barrels and ferns. A *picada* (shared appetizer plate) for two includes eggplant, lamb brochettes, crab and bacon-wrapped plums.

María Lola Restó ARGENTINE $$
(☎421185; Deloquí 1048; mains AR$45-70; ⊗noon-midnight Mon-Sat) 'Satisfying' defines the experience at this creative cafe-style restaurant overlooking the channel. Locals pack this silver house for homemade pasta with seafood or strip steak in rich mushroom sauce. Service is good and portions tend toward humongous: desserts can easily be split.

Chez Manu INTERNATIONAL $$$
(☎432253; www.chezmanu.com; Martial 2135; mains AR$55-90) If you are headed to Glaciar Martial, don't miss this gem on the way. Chef Emmanuel puts a French touch on fresh local ingredients, such as Fuegian lamb or mixed plates of cold *fruits de mer*. The three-course set lunch is the best deal. Views are a welcome bonus. It's 2km from town.

Chiko SEAFOOD $$
(☎432036; Av Antartida Argentina 182; mains AR$38-65; ⊗noon-3pm & 7:30-11:30pm Mon-Sat) Popular 2nd-floor restaurant with an odd assemblage of Chilean memorabilia that spells homesickness for the owners from Chiloe, but it's a clear boon to seafood lovers. King crab, *paila marina* (shellfish stew) and fish dishes are done so right that you might not mind the slow and sometimes clumsy service.

Almacen Ramos Generales CAFE $
(☎427317; www.ramosgeneralesushuaia.com; Maipú 749; mains AR$30-70; ⊗9am-midnight) The real draw of this ambient-rich general store are the croissants and crusty baguettes baked by the French pastry chef. But there's also local beer on tap, a wine list and light, if pricey, fare such as sandwiches, soups and quiche.

La Estancia STEAKHOUSE $$
(☎431241; Godoy & San Martín; mains AR$40-90) For authentic Argentine *asado*, it is hard to beat this reliable, well-priced grill. At night it's packed with locals and travelers alike, feasting on whole roast lamb, juicy steaks, sizzling ribs and heaping salads.

El Turco CAFE $

(☎424711; San Martín 1410; mains AR$22-55; ⊙noon-3pm & 8pm-midnight) Nothing fancy, this classic Argentine cafe nonetheless charms with reasonable prices and swift bow-tied waiters game to try out their French on tourists. Standards include *milanesa* (breaded meat), pizzas, crispy fries and roast chicken.

Placeres Patagónicos CAFE $$

(☎433798; www.patagonicosweb.com.ar; 289 Deloquí; mains AR$29-60) This stylish cafe-deli serves wooden cutting boards piled with homemade bread and mouth-watering local specialties: smoked trout and wild boar. Coffee arrives steaming in a bowl-sized mug.

Café-Bar Tante Sara CAFE $$

(☎433710; www.cafebartantesara.com.ar; cnr San Martín & Juana Fadul; mains AR$40-80) Popular for its ambiance, this corner bistro serves the usual suspects in a bubbly atmosphere. The sister branch near the intersection of San Martín and Rivadavia is often packed with locals having coffee and pastries.

Lomitos Martinica FAST FOOD $

(San Martín 68; mains AR$22-32; ⊙11:30am-3pm & 8:30pm-midnight) Cheap and cheerful, this greasy spoon with grillside seating serves enormous *milanesa* sandwiches and offers a cheap lunch special.

La Anónima SUPERMARKET $

(cnr Gobernador Paz & Rivadavia) A grocery store with cheap take-out.

Drinking

Geographically competitive drinkers should note that the southernmost bar in the world is not here but on a Ukrainian research station in Antarctica.

Dublin Irish Pub BAR

(☎430744; www.dublinushuaia.com; cnr 9 de Julio & Deloquí) Dublin doesn't feel so far away with the lively banter and free-flowing drinks at this dimly lit foreigners' favorite. Look for occasional live music and be sure to try at least one of its three local Beagle beers.

Macario 1910 PUB

(☎422757; www.macario1910.com; San Martín 1485; sandwiches AR$22; ⊙6pm-late) A welcoming pub with trans-Atlantic style of polished wood and leather booths. The tasty locally-made Beagle Beer flows on tap and the above-average pub fare includes fresh tuna sandwiches on homemade bread and plates stacked with shoestring fries made from scratch.

Küar Resto Bar PUB

(☎437396; www.kuar.com.ar; Av Perito Moreno 2232; ⊙6pm-late) This chic log-cabin-style bar welcomes the 'after-ski' crowd for cocktails, local beer and tapas. The interior is stylish but the highlight, especially at sunset, is the jaw-dropping views over the water. You'll have to catch a cab.

☆ Entertainment

Cine Pakawaia CINEMA

(☎436500; cnr Yaganes & Gobernador Paz; tickets AR$12) First-run movies are shown at the Presidio's fully restored hangar-style theater.

Casa de la Cultura PERFORMING ARTS

(☎422417; cnr Malvinas Argentinas & 12 de Octubre) Hidden behind a gym, this center hosts occasional live-music shows.

Shopping

Boutique del Libro BOOKS

(☎432117, 424750; 25 de Mayo 62; ⊙10am-9pm) Outstanding selection of Patagonia and Antarctica-themed material, with literature, guidebooks and pictorials (also in English); there's a branch at San Martín 1120.

Information

ACA (Automóvil Club Argentino; ☎421121; cnr Malvinas Argentinas & Onachaga) Argentina's auto club; good source for provincial road maps.

Administración de Parques Nacionales (National Parks office; ☎421315; San Martín 1395; ⊙9am-4pm Mon-Fri)

Cambio Thaler (San Martín 209; ⊙10am-1pm & 5-8pm Mon-Sat, 5-8pm Sun) Convenience equals slightly poorer exchange rates. Several banks on Maipú and San Martín have ATMs.

Club Andino Ushuaia (☎422335; www.clubandinoushuaia.com.ar, in Spanish; Juana Fadul 50; ⊙9am-1pm & 3-8pm Mon-Fri) Sells a map and bilingual trekking, mountaineering and mountain-biking guidebook. The club occasionally organizes hikes and can recommend guides. Unguided trekkers are strongly encouraged to register here or with the tourist office before hiking and after a safe return.

Hospital Regional (☎107, 423200; cnr Fitz Roy & 12 de Octubre)

Immigration office (☎422334; Beauvoir 1536; ⊙9am-noon Mon-Fri)

Instituto Fueguino de Turismo (Infuetur; ☎421423; www.tierradelfuego.org.ar; Maipú 505) On the ground floor of Hotel Albatros.

Municipal tourist office (☎432000, at airport 423970, outside of Tierra del Fuego 0800-333-1476; www.turismoushuaia.com, in Spanish; San Martín 674) Very helpful, with English- and

French-speaking staff, a message board and multilingual brochures, as well as good lodging, activities and transport info. Also at the airport and pier.

Post office (cnr San Martín & Godoy)

Getting There & Away

Air

LAN is the best bet for Buenos Aires; purchase tickets through local travel agencies. **Aerolíneas Argentinas** (☎421218; Maipú & 9 de Julio) jets to Buenos Aires (3½ hours) several times daily, sometimes stopping in El Calafate (70 minutes).

LADE (☎421123; San Martín 542) flies to Buenos Aires, El Calafate, Río Grande and may serve other destinations.

Boat

A few private yachts charter trips around the channel, to Cape Horn and Antarctica, see p475. These trips must be organized well in advance.

For Puerto Williams, **Ushuaia Boating** (☎02901-436193; www.ushuaiaboating.com.ar; Gobernador Paz 233; 1-way AR$528) goes daily in zodiac boats. Tickets include a 40-minute crossing plus an overland transfer from Puerto Navarino. Note: inclement weather often means cancellations. The more comfortable covered boat from **Fernandez Campbell** (☎433232; www.fernandezcampbell.com; tourist wharf; 1-way AR$528; ⏲10am & 3pm Fri-Sun) docks directly in Puerto Williams, with fewer winter departures.

Bus

Ushuaia has no bus terminal. Book outgoing bus tickets as much in advance as possible; many readers have complained about getting stuck here in high season. Depending on your luck, long waits at border crossings can be expected.

Bus Sur (☎430-727; San Martín 245) To Punta Arenas and Puerto Natales, Chile 3x weekly at 5:30am, connecting with Montiel.

Lider (☎436421; Gobernador Paz 921) Door-to-door minivans to Tolhuin and Río Grande six to eight times daily, with fewer departures on Sunday.

Montiel (☎421366; Gobernador Paz 605) Door-to-door minivans to Tolhuin and Río Grande with same frequency as Lider.

Tecni-Austral (☎431408/12; Roca 157) To Río Grande at 5am via Tolhuin; to Punta Arenas 3x weekly; to Río Gallegos daily at 5am.

Taqsa (☎435453; Godoy 41) To Río Grande at 5am via Tolhuin; to Punta Arenas and Puerto Natales, Chile 3x weekly at 5am; to Río Gallegos, El Calafate & Bariloche daily at 5am.

Transportes Pasarela (☎433712; cnr Maipú & 25 de Mayo) Roundtrip shuttles to Lago Esmeralda (AR$40), Lago Escondido (AR$90) and Lago Fagnano (AR$100), leaving around 10am and returning at 2pm and 6:30pm. Pay one way if you're planning to stay overnight and arrange for pickup.

For transport to Parque Nacional Tierra del Fuego, see p488.

BUSES FROM USHUAIA

DESTINATION	COST (AR$)	DURATION (HR)
Bariloche	774-844	36
Calafate	384	18
Punta Arenas, Chile	130-160	11
Río Gallegos	290-360	12
Río Grande	75-90	4
Tolhuin	50-60	2

Getting Around

Taxis to/from the modern airport (USH), 4km southwest of downtown, cost AR$25. Taxis can be chartered for around AR$140 per hour. There's a local bus service along Maipú.

Rental rates for compact cars, including insurance, start at around AR$464 per day; try **Localiza** (☎430739; Sarmiento 81). Some agencies may not charge for drop-off in other parts of Argentine Tierra del Fuego.

Hourly ski shuttles (AR$70 roundtrip) leave from the corner of Juana Fadul and Maipú to resorts along RN 3, from 9am to 2pm daily. Each resort also provides its own transportation from downtown Ushuaia.

Parque Nacional Tierra del Fuego

Banked against the channel, the hushed, fragrant southern forests of Tierra del Fuego are a stunning setting to explore. West of Ushuaia some 12km along RN 3, **Parque Nacional Tierra del Fuego** (admission AR$85) was Argentina's first coastal national park and extends 630 sq km from the Beagle Channel in the south to beyond Lago Fagnano in the north. For information, visit the **Centro de Visitantes Alakush** (⏲9am-7pm) with shorter hours in low season.

The public has access to only a couple of thousand hectares along the southern edge of the park, with short, easy trails designed more for day-tripping families than backpacking trekkers. The rest is protected as a *reserva natural estricta* (strictly off-limits

Parque Nacional Tierra del Fuego - Lapataia Sector

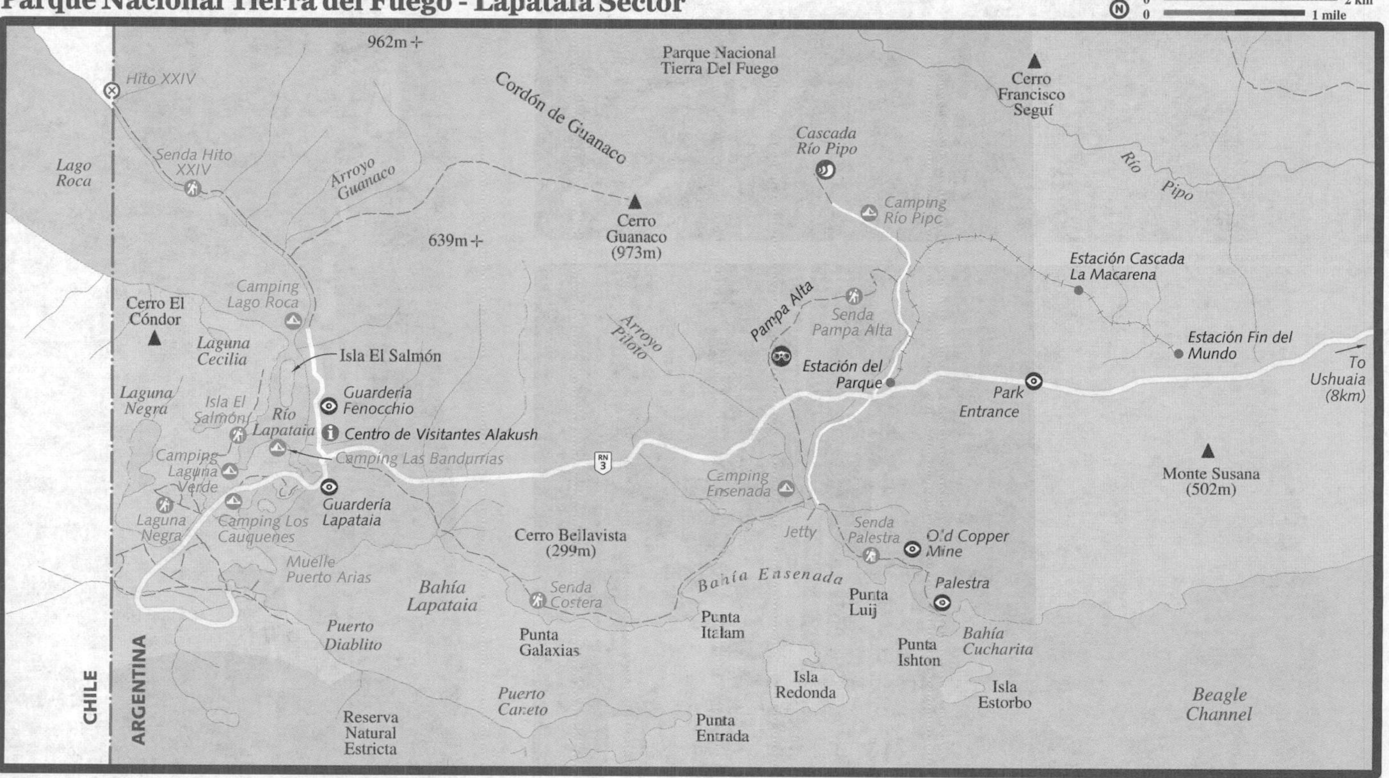

1

RALPH HOPKINS/LONELY PLANET IMAGES ©

2

4

GRANT DIXON/LONELY PLANET IMAGES ©

'shuaia (p471)
Andes meets the Southern Ocean in this
ing end-of-the-world port town.

arque Nacional Tierra del Fuego
82)
hillsides of this national park take on a
tacular glow of red during autumn.

aso de la Oveja (p477)
ee-day trek to this area is grueling, but
rding.

stancia Harberton (p488)
ided in 1886, this *estancia* is a bird-
her's paradise.

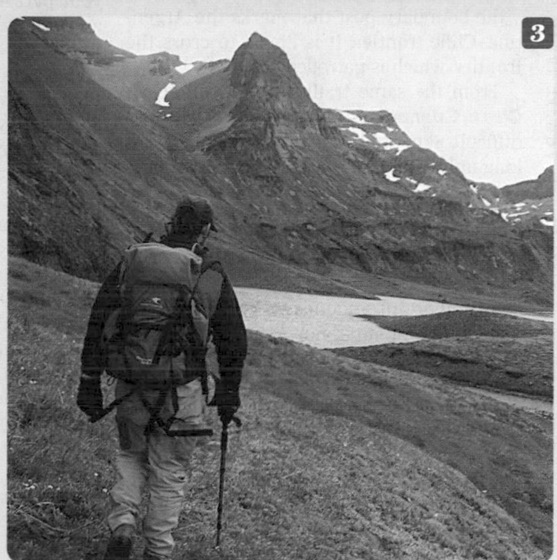

CAROLYN MCCARTHY ©

zone). Despite this, a few scenic hikes along the bays and rivers, or through dense native forests of evergreen coihue, canelo and deciduous lenga, are worthwhile. For spectacular color, come in autumn when hillsides of ñire glow red.

Birdlife is prolific, especially along the coastal zone. Keep an eye out for condors, albatross, cormorants, gulls, terns, oystercatchers, grebes, kelp geese and the comical, flightless, orange-billed steamer ducks. Common invasive species include the European rabbit and the North American beaver, both wreaking ecological havoc despite their cuteness. Gray and red foxes, enjoying the abundance of rabbits, may also be seen.

Hiking

After running 3242km from Buenos Aires, RN 3 reaches its terminus at the shores of Bahía Lapataia. From here, trails **Mirador Lapataia** (500m), with excellent views, and **Senda Del Turbal** (400m) lead through winding lenga forest further into the bay. Other short walks include the self-guided nature trail **Senda Laguna Negra** (950m), through peat bogs, and the **Senda Castorera** (400m), showcasing massive abandoned beaver dams on a few ponds.

SENDA HITO XXIV

From Camping Lago Roca, a flat 10km (four-hour) roundtrip trek leads around Lago Roca's forested northeast shore to Hito XXIV – that number is *veinticuatro* in Spanish – the boundary post that marks the Argentina–Chile frontier. It is illegal to cross the frontier, which is patrolled regularly.

From the same trailhead you can reach **Cerro Guanaco** (973m) via the steep and difficult 8km trail of the same name; it's a long uphill haul but the views are excellent.

SENDA COSTERA

This 8km (four-hour) trek leads west from Bahía Ensenada along the coastline. Keep an eye out for old *conchales* (archaeologically important mounds of shells left by Yahgan inhabitants), now covered in grass. The trail meets RN 3 a short way east of the park administration *(guardería)* center at Lapataia. From here it is 1.2km further to Senda Hito XXIV.

It might be tempting to roll up the cuffs and go clamming, but be aware that occasional red tides *(marea roja)* contaminate mollusks (such as clams and mussels) along the shore of the Beagle Channel.

SENDA PALESTRA

This 4km (three-hour) roundtrip trek from Bahía Ensenada follows a path eastward past an old copper mine to the popular rock-climbing wall of Palestra, near a *refugio* (rustic shelter) that is no longer in use.

SENDA PAMPA ALTA

The low heights of Pampa Alta (around 315m) grant long views across the Beagle Channel to Isla Navarino and Isla Hoste. RN 3 meets the trailhead 1.5km west of the Río Pipo and Bahía Ensenada road turnoffs (3km from the entrance gate). The 5km roundtrip trail first climbs a hill, passing a beaver dam along the way. Enjoy the impressive views at the lookout. A quick 300m further leads to a trail paralleling the Río Pipo and some waterfalls.

ISLA EL SALMÓN & LAGUNA NEGRA

From the road 2km southwest of Lapataia, a trail leads north along the western side of Río Lapataia to a fishing spot opposite Isla El Salmón. Laguna Negra, a lovely lake in the forest, is easily accessible via a 1km circuit loop signposted 200m past the trail to Isla El Salmón.

Sleeping & Eating

There is one *refugio* and various, mostly free, campgrounds. Most get crowded, which means sites can get unreasonably messy. Do your part to take your trash out of the park and follow a leave-no-trace ethic. Camping Ensenada is 16km from the park entrance and nearest the Costera trail; Camping Río Pipo is 6km from the entrance and easily accessed by either the road to Cañadon del Toro or the Pampa Alta trail. Camping Las Bandurrias, Camping Laguna Verde and Camping Los Cauquenes are on the islands in Río Lapataia.

The only fee-based campground and refugio is **Lago Roca** (camp sites per person/dm AR$9/40), 9km from the park entrance. The refugio dorm is available year-round except when weather prohibits transport to the park. Both offer hot showers, a good *confitería* (cafe offering light meals) and a tiny (expensive) grocery store. There is plenty of availability for camping at wild sites. Note that water at Lago Roca is not potable; boil it before using.

ANTARCTICA: THE ICE

For many travelers, a journey to Antarctica represents a once-in-a-lifetime adventure. Despite its high price tag, it is much more than just a continent to tick off your list. You will witness both land and ice shelves piled with hundreds of meters of undulating, untouched snow. Glaciers drop from mountainsides and icebergs form sculptures as tall as buildings. The wildlife is thrilling, with thousands of curious penguins and an extraordinary variety of flying birds, seals and whales.

More than 90% of Antarctic-bound boats pass through Ushuaia. In the 2010–11 season, that meant more than 36,000 tourists – a stunning contrast to the continent's population of 5000 (summer) or 1200 (winter) scientists and staff. But travel here is not without its costs. On November 23, 2007, the hull of the MV *Explorer* was gashed by ice but evacuated successfully before sinking. The circumstances were highly unusual, although the incident provoked further safety measures.

So long as you've got two or three weeks to spare, hopping on board a cruise ship is not out of the question. Some voyages take in the Islas Malvinas (Falkland Islands) and South Georgia (human population 10 to 20, estimated penguin population two to three million); some go just to the Antarctic Peninsula; others focus on retracing historic expeditions. A small but growing handful of visitors reach Antarctica aboard private vessels. All are sail-boats (equipped with auxiliary engines).

The season runs from mid-October to mid-March, depending on ice conditions. It used to be that peak-season voyages sold out; now most trips do. When shopping around, ask how many days you will actually spend in Antarctica, as crossing the Southern Ocean takes up to two days each way. And how many landings will there be? The smaller the ship, the more landings there are per passenger (always depending on the weather, of course). Tour companies charge anywhere from US$7000 to US$70,000, although some ships allow walk-ons, which can cost as little as US$5000.

Due to Ushuaia's proximity to the Antarctic Peninsula, most cruises leave from here. Last-minute bookings can be made through **Ushuaia Turismo** (☎02901-436003; www.ushuaiaturismoevt.com.ar; ushuaiaturismo@speedy.com.ar; Gobernador Paz 865). Other travel agencies offering packages include **Rumbo Sur** (☎02901-422275; www.rumbosur.com.ar; San Martín 350), **All Patagonia** (☎02901-433622; www.allpatagonia.com; Juana Fadul 60) and **Canal Fun** (☎02901-437395; www.canalfun.com; 9 de Julio 118), though there are many more.

Check that your company is a member of **IAATO** (www.iaato.org), which mandates strict guidelines for responsible travel to Antarctica. The following are just a few companies that go:

Adventure Associates CRUISE
(www.adventureassociates.com) Australia's first tour company to Antarctica, with many ships and destinations.

National Geographic Expeditions CRUISE
(www.nationalgeographicexpeditions.com) Highly recommended, with quality naturalists and experts, aboard the 148-passenger *National Geographic Explorer*.

Peregrine Adventures CRUISE
(www.peregrineadventures.com) Offers unique trips that include visiting the Antarctic Circle, with kayaking and camping options.

Quark Expeditions CRUISE
(www.quarkexpeditions.com) Three kinds of ships, from an icebreaker to a 48-passenger ship for close-knit groups.

WildWings Travel CRUISE
(www.wildwings.co.uk) UK-based company that focuses on bird-watching and wildlife in Antarctica.

For more information see Lonely Planet's *Antarctica* guidebook. Online, check out www.70south.com for up-to-date information and articles. In Ushuaia consult the very helpful **Oficina Antártica** (Antarctica tourist office; ☎02901-430015; antartida@tierradelfuego.org.ar) at the pier.

Getting There & Away

Buses leave from the corner of Maipú and Juana Fadul in Ushuaia every 40 minutes in high season from 9am to 6pm, returning between 8am and 8pm. Depending on your destination, a roundtrip fare is around ARS$70, and you need not return the same day. Private tour buses cost AR$100 for a roundtrip. Taxi fares shared between groups can be the same price as bus tickets.

The most touristy and, beyond jogging, the slowest way to the park, **El Tren del Fin de Mundo** (☎02901-431600; www.trendelfindemundo.com.ar; adult/child plus park entrance fee AR$155/50) originally carted prisoners to work camps. It departs (without the convicts) from the Estación del Fin de Mundo, 8km west of Ushuaia (taxis one way AR$30), three or four times daily in summer and once or twice daily in winter.

The one-hour, scenic narrow-gauge train ride comes with historical explanations in English and Spanish. Reserve in January and February, when cruise-ship tours take over. You can take it one way and return via minibus.

Hitchhiking is feasible, but many cars are already be full.

Puerto Williams (Chile)

☎61 / POP 2500

Forget Ushuaia: the end of the world starts where colts roam Main St and yachts rounding Cape Horn take refuge. Naval settlement Puerto Williams is the only town on Isla Navarino, the official port of entry for vessels en route to Cape Horn and Antarctica, and home to the last living Yahgan speaker.

Just outside Puerto Williams is some of the Southern Cone's most breathtaking scenery. With more than 150km of trails, Isla Navarino is a rugged, backpackers' paradise, with slate-colored lakes, mossy lenga forests and the ragged spires of the Dientes de Navarino. Trails lead past beaver dams, bunkers and army trenches as they climb steeply into the mountains and deeper into forests. Thousands of beavers, introduced from Canada in the 1940s, plague the island, though their numbers are diminishing due to an active eradication campaign (which means they're even on the menu, if you can find an open restaurant).

Mid-19th-century missionaries, followed by fortune-seekers during the 1890s gold rush, established a permanent European

DON'T MISS

ESTANCIA HARBERTON

Tierra del Fuego's first estancia, **Harberton** (Skype: estanciaharberton.turismo; www.estanciaharberton.com; tour & museum adult/child AR$45/free, half-board s/d/tr AR$802/1266/1772; ⏰10am-7pm Oct 15–Apr 15) was founded in 1886 by missionary Thomas Bridges and his family. The location earned fame from a stirring memoir written by Bridges' son Lucas, titled *Uttermost Part of the Earth*, about his coming of age among the now-extinct Selk'nam and Yahgan people. Available in English, the book is an excellent introduction to the history of the region and the ways of native peoples.

In a splendid location, the *estancia* is owned and run by Tomas Bridges' descendants. There's lodging and day visitors can attend guided tours (featuring the island's oldest house and a replica Yahgan dwelling), dine at the restaurant and visit the Reserva Yecapasela penguin colony. It's also a popular destination for bird watchers.

Onsite, the impressive **Museo Acatushún** (www.acatushun.com) houses a vast collection of mammal and bird specimens compiled by biologist Natalie Prosser Goodall. Emphasizing the region's marine mammals, the museum has inventoried thousands of mammal and bird specimens; among the rarest is a Hector's beaked whale. Much of this vast collection was found at Bahía San Sebastián, north of Río Grande, where a difference of up to 11km between high and low tide leaves animals stranded. Confirm the museum's opening hours with the *estancia*.

Reserve well in advance as there are no phones at the *estancia*, though Skyping may be possible. With advance permission, free primitive camping is allowed at Río Lasifashaj, Río Varela and Río Cambaceres. Harberton is 85km east of Ushuaia via RN 3 and rough RC-j, a 1½- to two-hour drive. In Ushuaia, shuttles leave from the base of 25 de Mayo at Av Maipú at 9am, returning around 3pm. Day-long catamaran tours are organized by local agencies.

presence here. The remaining mixed-race descendants of the Yahgan (Yámana) people are established in the small seaside village of Villa Ukika, a 15-minute walk east of town along the waterfront.

Sights & Activities

TOP CHOICE Dientes de Navarino HIKING
Gaining in popularity, this four- to five-day trekking circuit offers impossibly raw and windswept vistas under Navarino's toothy spires. Plans are underway to add a *refugio* and shelters in late 2012. For detailed trekking routes, refer to Lonely Planet's *Trekking in the Patagonian Andes*.

Museo Martín Gusinde MUSEUM
(621043; cnr Araguay & Gusinde; donation requested; 9am-1pm & 2:30-7pm Mon-Fri) An attractive museum honoring the German priest and ethnographer who worked among the Yahgans from 1918 to 1923. Focuses on ethnography and natural history.

Lago Windhond HIKING
This remote lake is a lesser known, but worthy, alternative to hiking the Dientes circuit, with sheltered hiking through forest and peat bogs. The four-day roundtrip is a better bet if there's high winds. For route details, ask at Turismo Shila or go with a guide.

Parque Etnobotanico Omora PARK
(www.omora.org) Latin America's southernmost ethnobotanical park has trails with plant names marked in Yahgan, Latin and Spanish. Take the road to the right of the Virgin altar, 4km (an hour's walk) toward Puerto Navarino. Donations accepted.

Kipa-Akar CULTURAL BUILDING
(Villa Ukika) A modest crafts shop that sells Yahgan language books, jewelry and knives made of scavenged whale bone. Ask a villager for help if it's closed.

Cerro Bandera HIKING
With expansive views of the Beagle Channel, this four-hour roundtrip starts at the Navarino Circuit. The trail ascends steeply through lenga to blustery stone-littered hillside planted with a Chilean flag. Self-supported backpackers can continue on the Dientes circuit.

Yelcho LANDMARK
Near the entrance to the military quarters is the original bow of the ship that rescued Ernest Shackleton's Antarctic expedition from Elephant Island in 1916.

Sleeping & Eating

Residencial Pusaki GUESTHOUSE $
(621116; pattypusaki@yahoo.es; Piloto Pardo 242; s/d CH$11,500/26,000) Run by a fun matriarch, this small home is well cared for. Patty also organizes group dinners, usually exquisitely prepared seafood caught fresh from the channel, also available to nonguests (mains CH$6000 to CH$10,000).

Refugio El Padrino HOSTEL $
(621136; Costanera 267; dm CH$10,000) Friendly and conducive to meeting others, this clean, self-service hostel offers small dorm rooms, located right on the channel.

Hotel Lakutaia HOTEL $$$
(621733; www.lakutaia.cl; d incl breakfast CH$65,000) About 3km east of town toward the airport, this modern full-service lodge will arrange transportation from Punta Arenas, and can organize day hikes to the Navarino Circuit and trips to Cape Horn. The library contains interesting history and nature references. Its only disadvantage is its isolation; you might leave without getting much of a feel for the quirky town. Lunch and dinner are also available.

La Picada del Castor SANDWICHES $
(Plaza de Ancla; mains CH$3500-5000; 10am-10pm Mon-Sat) The most likely to be open, serving huge sandwiches and platters of fries at low-lit booths.

La Trattoria de Mateo ITALIAN $$
(Plaza de Ancla; mains CH$4500-7000; noon-3:30pm & 6-10pm Tue-Sat, 12:30-4pm Sun) An Argentine-run cafe featuring homemade pastas with seafood options and pizzas.

Drinking

Club de Yates Micalvi BAR
(beer CH$2500; late Sep–May) As watering holes go, this may be like no other. A grounded German cargo boat, the *Micalvi* was declared a regional naval museum in 1976 but found infinitely better use as a floating bar, frequented by navy men and yachties.

Information

Near the main roundabout, the Centro Comercial contains the post office, internet access, Aerovías DAP and call centers. ATM, money exchange (US cash only, US$100 minimum) and Visa cash advances are possible at Banco de Chile.

Sernatur (621011; O'Higgins 165; 8am-1pm & 2-5pm Mon-Fri) Tourist information.

including printouts of a hiking map for Dientes de Navarino. It's located in the Municipalidad.

Turismo SIM (☎621150; www.simltd.com) Expert sailors with trekking and expedition possibilities south of the 54th parallel, including Cape Horn, the Cordillera Darwin, Isla Navarino, South Georgia Island and the Antarctic Peninsula.

Turismo Shila (☎78972005; www.turismoshila.cl; cnr O'Higgins & Pratt) Offers local guides, camping rentals and GPS maps. Also sells Fernandez Campbell (p482) boat tickets.

Getting There & Away

Puerto Williams is accessible by plane or boat. **Aerovías DAP** (☎621051; www.dap.cl; Plaza de Ancla s/n) flies to Punta Arenas (CH$65,000, 1¼ hours) at 11:30am Monday to Saturday from November to March, with fewer flights in winter. DAP flights to Antarctica may make a brief stopover here.

Using the new ferry *Patagonia*, **Transbordador Austral Broom** (www.tabsa.cl) sails from the Tres Puentes sector of Punta Arenas to Puerto Williams three or four times a month on Wednesdays, with departures from Puerto Williams back to Punta Arenas on Saturdays (reclining seat/bunk CH$88,000/105,000 including meals, 38 hours). Travelers rave about the trip: if the weather holds there are good views on deck and the possibility of spotting dolphins or whales.

For ferry options to Ushuaia, see p482.

Tolhuin & Lago Fagnano

☎02901

Named for the Selk'nam word meaning 'like a heart,' Tolhuin (population 2000) is a lake town nestled in the center of Tierra del Fuego, 132km south of Río Grande and 104km northeast of Ushuaia via smooth asphalt. This fast-growing frontier town of small plazas and sheltering evergreens fronts the eastern shore of Lago Fagnano, also known as Lago Kami. Tolhuin, with low-key horse riding, mountain biking, boating and fishing, is worth checking out as a tranquil lake spot.

Shared with Chile, the glacial-formed Lago Fagnano offers 117km of beaches, with most of its shoreline remote and roadless. Plans to create road access from Chile and put a catamaran here are developing.

Tolhuin's **tourist office** (☎492380, 492125; www.tierradelfuego.org.ar/tolhuin; Av de los Shelknam 80), behind the gas station, has information on hiking, horseback riding tours and gear rentals. Those coming from Ushuaia might get more-complete info from Ushuaia's tourist office (p481). **Banco de Tierra del Fuego** (Menkiol s/n) has an ATM.

Sleeping & Eating

Hostería Ruta Al Sur HOTEL $$
(☎492278; www.rutalsur.com.ar; Ruta 3, Km 2954; d/tr incl breakfast AR$270/295; @ 📶) A lovely new roadside lodge surrounded by old beech trees. Rooms are sparkling and there is a sprawling living room and restaurant. There are plans to add a swimming pool.

Camping Hain CAMPGROUND $
(☎02901-15-603606; Lago Fagnano; camp sites per person AR$10, 8-person refugios AR$130) Located on Lago Fagnano, with hot showers, grassy sites with wooden windbreaks, a huge barbecue pit and a *fogon* (sheltered fire pit and kitchen area).

Hostería Kaikén INN $$$
(☎492372; www.hosteriakaiken.com.ar; Lago Fagnano, Km 2942; d AR$470-540, 2-person cabin AR$350; @ 📶) This gorgeous lakeside inn is both refined and rustic, with beautiful colonial furniture, neutral tones and snug, down bedcovers. There's a stylish bar with panoramas of the lake and a dining room serving high-end cuisine.

Panadería La Unión BAKERY $
(☎492202; www.panaderialaunion.com.ar, in Spanish; Jeujepen 450, Tolhuin; snacks AR$3; ⏲24hr) First-rate *facturas* (pastries) and second-rate Nescafé cappuccinos keep this roadside attraction hopping. You may or may not recognize the Argentine celebrities gracing the walls (hint: the men are ageing rock stars, the women surgically enhanced). Buses break here to pick up passengers and hot water for *mate*.

Getting There & Away

Throughout the day, buses and minivans passing along RN 3 (often full in high season) stop at Panadería La Union en route to Ushuaia or Río Grande (AR$60).

Río Grande

☎02964 / POP 70,042

A monster trout sculpture at the entrance to town announces that you have come to the de facto fly-fishing capital of Tierra del Fuego, with some of the world's best blue-ribbon angling for colossal sea-run trout. But if you didn't come with rod in hand, the longest that you will likely stay in windswept Río Grande is a few hours, before hopping on a bus to Ushuaia, 230km southwest.

As wool baron José Menéndez' sheep stations developed, Río Grande became a growing makeshift service town. In 1893 the Salesian order, under the guidance of Monseñor Fagnano, set up a mission in an unsuccessful attempt to shelter the Selk'nam from the growing infringement.

As a petroleum service center, the town has an industrial feel: even the public art looks like giant, grim tinker toys. Geared at the business traveler, it's also pricey for visitors. Duty-free status, meant to foster local development, has brought in electronics manufacturing plants and wholesale appliance stores.

During the Falklands War the military played an important role here; memorials pay tribute to fallen soldiers.

Sleeping & Eating

Catering to suits and anglers, accommodations tends to be overpriced, not to mention sparse. There are a number of cheap but unsavory lodgings; others fill up fast. High-end places give a 10% discount for cash payments.

Posada de los Sauces HOTEL **$$**
(☎432895; www.posadadelossauces.com.ar; Elcano 839; s/d/tr AR$350/400/500; @ 📶) Catering mostly to the high-end anglers, this warm and professional hotel fosters a real lodge atmosphere, with fresh scents and woodsy accents. Deluxe rooms have Jacuzzis. The upstairs bar-restaurant, decked out in dark wood and forest green, is just waiting for stogies and tall tales to fill the air.

Hotel Villa HOTEL **$$**
(☎424998; hotelvillarg@hotmail.com; San Martín 281; d/tr incl breakfast AR$310/380; @ 📶 P) Opposite Casino Status, this refurbished place has a popular restaurant, a dozen spacious and stylish rooms outfitted with down duvets, and breakfast with *medialunas* (croissants).

Tante Sara CAFE **$$**
(Belgrano 402; mains AR$45-88) An upscale chain in Tierra del Fuego, this nonetheless cozy spot hosts both ladies having tea and cake, and boys at the varnished bar downing beer and burgers. Salads (such as romaine, egg, blue cheese and bacon) are surprisingly good, although the service can be quite sluggish.

Information

Most visitor services are along Avs San Martín and Belgrano.

Banco de la Nación (cnr San Martín & 9 de Julio) Has an ATM; there are also several others nearby.

Instituto Fueguino de Turismo (Infuetur; ☎426805; www.tierradelfuego.org.ar; Belgrano 319; ⌚9am-9pm) On the south side of the plaza.

Mariani Travel (☎426010; Rosales 281) Books flights and represents nearby *estancias*.

Municipal tourist kiosk (☎431324; turismo@riogrande.gob.ar; ⌚9am-8pm) Helpful kiosk on the plaza, with maps, *estancia* brochures and fishing details.

Post office (Rivadavia, btwn Moyano & Alberdi)

Thaler Cambio (☎421154; Rosales 259) Changes traveler's checks.

Getting There & Away

The **airport** (RGA; ☎420699) is off RN 3, a short taxi ride from town. **Aerolíneas Argentinas** (☎424467; San Martín 607) flies daily to Buenos Aires. **LADE** (☎422968; Lasserre 445) flies a couple of times weekly to Río Gallegos, El Calafate and Buenos Aires.

Lider (☎420003, 424-2000; www.lidertdf.com.ar; Moreno 635) Best option for Ushuaia and Tolhuin is this door-to-door minivan service, with several daily departures. Call to reserve.

Montiel (☎420997; 25 de Mayo 712) Ushuaia and Tolhuin.

At **Terminal Fuegina** (Finocchio 1194):

Buses Pacheco (☎421554) To Punta Arenas three times per week at 10am.

Taqsa (☎434316) To Ushuaia via Tolhuin.

Tecni-Austral (☎434316; ticket office Moyano 516) To Ushuaia via Tolhuin three times per week at 8:30am; to Río Gallegos and Punta Arenas three times per week.

Bus Sur (☎420997; www.bus-sur.cl; ticket office 25 de Mayo 712) To Ushuaia, Punta Arenas & Puerto Natales, Chile three times per week at 5:30am, connecting with Montiel.

BUSES FROM RÍO GRANDE

DESTINATION	COST (AR$)	DURATION (HR)
Punta Arenas, Chile	130-160	9
Río Gallegos	265	8
Tolhuin	50-60	2
Ushuaia	75-90	4

Estancias Around Río Grande

Much of Tierra del Fuego was once the sprawling backyard of wool baron José Menéndez. His first *estancia* – La Primera Argentina (1897), now known as **Estancia José Menéndez**, 20km southwest of Río Grande via RN 3 and RC-b – covered 1600 sq km, with more than 140,000 head of sheep. His second and most-treasured venture was La Segunda Argentina, totaling 1500 sq km. Later renamed **Estancia María Behety** (in Buenos Aires 011-4331-5061; www.maribety.com.ar, in Spanish) after his wife, it's still a working ranch, 17km west of Río Grande via RC-c. Besides boasting the world's largest shearing shed, it is considered a highly exclusive lodge, catering mainly to tour groups and elite anglers. Fishing lodge La Villa has six bedrooms and overlooks the Río Grande.

Several *estancias* have opened to small-scale tourism, offering a unique chance to learn about the region's history and enjoy its magic. Reserve as far in advance as possible.

The sons of early settler Thomas Bridges (see p488) established **Estancia Viamonte** (02964-430861, 02964-15-616813; www.estanciaviamonte.com; per person incl breakfast & dinner AR$760; Oct-Apr & by arrangement) in 1902 at the request of the Selk'nam, in part to protect the indigenous group. The Goodalls, descendents of the Bridges, now run it as a working ranch, with 22,000 head of sheep on 400 sq km. Guests stay in son Lucas' original dwelling, the Sea View, a comfortable English-style home within earshot of the crashing waves. Guided activity possibilities include horseback riding, hiking and fly-fishing the Río Ewan.

Founded by Tierra del Fuego's first rural doctor, the Basque-Provençal-style **Estancia Tepi** (02964-427245, 02964-15-504-2020; www.estanciatepi.com.ar, in Spanish; RC-a, Km 5; day trip/B&B/full board per person AR$464/760/886; Dec-Mar) is a working, 100-sq-km ranch. Horseback riding is offered for all levels, with traditional Patagonian mounts heaped with sheepskins. The property also boasts thermal baths, treks and tours. It's 80km from Río Grande and 150km from Ushuaia.

The rustic and charismatic **Estancia Rolito** (02901-437351, 02901-432419; www.tierradelfuego.org.ar/rolito, in Spanish; RC-a, Km 14; rper person half-/full board AR$608/920) is very Argentine and very inviting. Guests rave about the horseback-riding trips and hikes

THE TROUT ATLAS

You know a place takes fishing seriously when the tourism board posts a trout map online (www.tierradelfuego.org.ar/funcardio/trutamap.jpg). Hollywood stars, heads of state and former US presidents all flock to desolate stretches around Río Grande with dreams of the big one. Usually they are in luck.

Rivers around Río Grande were stocked in the 1930s with brown, rainbow and brook trout. It's now one of the world's best sea-run trout-fishing areas, with some local specimens weighing in at 15kg. Rainbow trout can reach 9kg.

Fishing excursions are mostly organized through outside agents, many in the USA. 'Public' fishing rivers, on which trips can be organized, include the Fuego, Menéndez, Candelaria, Ewan and MacLennan. Many of the more elite angling trips are lodged in *estancias* (ranches) with exclusive use of some of the best rivers.

There are two types of fishing licenses. License 1 is valid throughout the province, except in the national park. Contact **Asociación Caza y Pesca** (02901-423168; cazapescaush@infovia.com.ar; Maipú 822) in Ushuaia, or **Club de Pesca John Goodall** (02964-424324; Ricardo Rojas 606) in Río Grande. License 2 is valid for the national park and Patagonia. Contact the **National Parks office** (02901-421315; San Martín 1395) in Ushuaia or find more information on sport fishing in Argentina through the online portal **Pesca Argentina** (www.pescaargentina.com.ar, in Spanish). Other useful information:

Flies Rubber legs and woolly buggers.

License fees AR$100 per day or AR$420 per season, depending on where you fish.

Limit One fish per person per day, catch and release.

Methods Spinning and fly casting; no night fishing.

Season November 1 to April 15, with catch-and-release restrictions from April 1 to April 15.

FUEGIAN RITES OF PASSAGE

Part of traveling to Tierra del Fuego is searching for clues to its mystical, unknowable past. Souvenir shops sell a postcard of abstract intrigue: there's a naked man painted black. Fine horizontal white stripes cross his body from chest to foot. His face remains covered. So, what's this all about?

For people who lived exposed to the elements, dependent on their wits and courage, initiation ceremonies were a big deal. Those of the seafaring Yahgan (or Yámana) were surprisingly similar to those of the fierce northern neighbors they wanted little to do with, the nomadic hunters called Selk'nam (or Ona to the Yahgan). Both celebrated a male rite of passage that re-enacted a great upheaval when the men stole the women's secrets to gain power over them. In the Kina, Yahgan men interpreted the spirits by painting their bodies with black carbon and striped or dotted patterns that used the region's white and red clays. The Selk'nam undertook their Hain ceremony similarly adorned, taking young men into huts where they were attacked by spirits. In related ceremonies men showed their strength to women by fighting the spirits in theatrical displays, each acting with the characteristics of a specific spirit. These manly displays did not always achieve their desired effect of subjugation: one account tells of spirits dispatched to menace female camps that instead evoked hilarity.

With European encroachment, these ceremonies became more abbreviated and much of their detailed significance was lost. When the last Hain was celebrated in the early 20th century in the presence of missionaries, it had already crossed over from ritual to theater.

through ñire and lenga forest. Day trips from Ushuaia (with Turismo de Campo) stop by for lunch or dinner and guided horseback riding. Rolito is 100km from Río Grande and 150km from Ushuaia.

Porvenir (Chile)

61 / POP 5465

If you want a slice of home-baked Fuegian life, this is it. Most visitors come on a quick day trip from Punta Arenas tainted by seasickness. But spending a night in this rustic village of metal-clad Victorian houses affords you an opportunity to explore the nearby bays and countryside and absorb a little of the local life; bird watchers can admire the nearby king penguins, and lively populations of cormorants, geese and seabirds. While known for inaccessibility (there's no bus route here), the government is investing in completing roads through the southern extension of Chilean Tierra del Fuego, which will open up a whole untouched wilderness to visitors.

Porvenir experienced waves of immigration, many from Croatia, when gold was discovered in 1879. Sheep *estancias* provided more reliable work, attracting droves of Chileans from the island of Chiloé, who also came for fishing work. Today's population is a unique combination of the two.

Sights

On the plaza, the intriguing **Museo de Tierra del Fuego** (581800; www.museoporvenir.cl; Zavattaro 402; admission CH$500; 8am-5pm Mon-Thu, 8am-4pm Fri, 10:30am-1:30pm & 3-5pm Sat & Sun) has an interesting hodgepodge on display, including Selk'nam skulls and mummies, musical instruments used by the mission Selk'nams on Isla Dawson and an exhibit on early Chilean cinematography.

Activities & Tours

Though almost unknown as a wildlife-watching destination, Chilean Tierra del Fuego has abundant marine and bird life, which includes Peale's dolphins around Bahía Chilota and king penguins, found seasonally in Bahía Inútil. The recent discovery of this new king penguin colony has created quite a stir. As of yet, there's little procedure in place to protect the penguins from overvisitation. Please make your visit with a reputable agency, give the penguins ample berth and respect the nesting season.

Far South Expeditions (ecouve@fantasticosur.com; 4-passenger tours CH$60,000) offers transport to the king penguin colony or guided naturalist-run tours, with packages from Punta Arenas available. Gold-panning, horseback riding and 4WD tours can be arranged through the tourist office.

WORTH A TRIP

CHILEAN IN ROADS

South of Cameron, access to Chilean Tierra del Fuego once petered out into stark, roadless wilderness and the rugged Cordillera Darwin. But the Ministry of Public Works is working hard to create access to these southern points and develop future tourism destinations. Currently projects are underway to create a link to Ushuaia via Lago Fagnano. In the future, the same road will continue to Estancia Yendegaia.

For now, there's at least one worthy destination on the road. **Lodge Deseado** (☎91652564; www.lodgedeseado.cl; 2-/3-person cabin incl breakfast CH$135,000/160,000) marks a cozy spot to reel in wild trout, kick back in cool modern cabins and swap stories with the engaging owner Ricardo. It's located on Lago Deseado.

At the time of writing, the road to the western shore of Lago Fagnano was a rough five-plus hour journey in summer. A 4WD is required for this remote region (also see our tips for Ruta 40, p417). An earlier offshoot connects to the Argentine side via mountain pass Río Bellavista, which is only open December through March. Check with local police stations (known as *carabineros* in Chile) about the state of roads before leaving.

Sleeping & Eating

TOP CHOICE **Hosteriá Yendegaia** B&B $
(☎581919, 68256521; www.hosteriayendegaia.com; Croacia 702; s/d/tr incl breakfast CH$18,000/30,000/40,000; 📶P) Everything a B&B should be, with naturalist books (some authored by the owner) to browse, abundant breakfast, views of the strait and spacious rooms with thick down duvets. This historic Magellanic home (the first lodging in Porvenir) has been lovingly restored, and its family of hosts are helpful. Its tour agency, Far South Expeditions, runs naturalist-led trips.

Hotel Rosas GUESTHOUSE $
(☎580088; hotelrosas@chile.com; Philippi 296; s/d CH$20,000/28,000) Eleven clean and pleasant rooms offer heating and cable TV; some have wonderful views. Alberto, the owner, knows heaps about the region and arranges tours to Circuito del Loro, a historical mining site. The restaurant (*plato del día* CH$4600), serving fresh seafood and more, gets crowded for meals.

La Chispa CAFE $
(☎580054; Señoret 202; plato del día CH$4000) In an old aquamarine firehouse packed with locals for salmon dinners, lamb and mashed potatoes, and other home-cooked fare. It's a couple of blocks uphill from the water.

Club Croata SEAFOOD $$
(☎580053; Señoret 542; mains CH$4000-8000; ⏲11am-4pm & 7-10:30pm Tue-Sun) Formal to the verge of stuffy, this restaurant serves good seafood at reasonable prices, in addition to Croat specialties – pork chops with *chucrut* (sauerkraut). The pub is open to 3am.

Information

Banco de Estado (cnr Philippi & Croacia) Has a 24-hour ATM.

Hospital (☎580034; Wood, btwn Señoret & Guerrero)

Post office (Philippi 176) Faces the plaza.

Telefónica (Philippi 277) Next to the bank.

Tourist office (☎580094/8; www.muniporvenir.cl; Zavattaro 434; ⏲9am-5pm Mon-Fri, 11am-5pm Sat & Sun) Information is also available at the handicrafts shop on the *costanera* (seaside road) between Philippi and Schythe.

Getting There & Away

Aerovías DAP (☎616100; www.aeroviasdap.cl; O'Higgins 891) flies to Punta Arenas (15 minutes) Monday to Saturday from November to March, with fewer flights in the low season. For the airport, 6km north of town, DAP runs a door-to-door shuttle (CH$1800) and taxis charge CH$3500.

Transbordador Austral Broom (☎580089; www.tabsa.cl) operates the car/passenger ferry *Crux Australis* to/from Punta Arenas (per person/vehicle CH$5500/34,900, 2½ to four hours). It usually leaves at 9am but has some afternoon departures; check the current online schedule. The bus to the ferry terminal (CH$500), 5km away, departs from the waterfront kiosk an hour before the ferry's departure.

A good gravel road runs east along Bahía Inútil to the Argentine border at San Sebastián; allow about four hours. From San Sebastián (where there's gas and a motel), northbound motorists should avoid the heavily traveled and rutted truck route directly north and instead take the route from Onaisín to the petroleum company town of Cerro Sombrero, en route to the crossing of the Strait of Magellan at Punta Delgada-Puerto Espora.

Uruguay

Includes »

Best Places to Eat

» Picasso (p531)
» Mercado del Puerto (p507)
» Lo de Charlie (p538)
» Bodega y Granja Narbona (p522)
» La Silenciosa (p510)

Best Places to Stay

» Estancia La Sirena (p523)
» El Diablo Tranquilo (p545)
» Guardia del Monte (p544)
» Yvytu Itaty (p528)
» Termas San Nicanor (p526)

Why Go?

Wedged like a grape between Brazil's gargantuan thumb and Argentina's long forefinger, South America's smallest Spanish-speaking country has always been an underdog. Bypassed by the Spanish for its lack of mineral wealth, batted about like a ping-pong ball at the whim of its more powerful neighbors and neglected by many modern-day travelers, Uruguay remains a delightfully low-key, hospitable place where visitors can melt into the background – whether caught in a cow-and-gaucho traffic jam on a dirt road to nowhere or strolling with *mate*-toting locals along Montevideo's beachfront.

Short-term visitors will find plenty to keep them busy in cosmopolitan Montevideo, picturesque Colonia and party-till-you-drop Punta del Este. But if you've got time, dig a little deeper. Go wildlife-watching along the Atlantic coast, hot-spring-hopping up the Río Uruguay, or horseback riding under the big sky of Uruguay's vast interior, where fields spread out like oceans dotted with little cow and eucalyptus islands.

When to Go

Montevideo

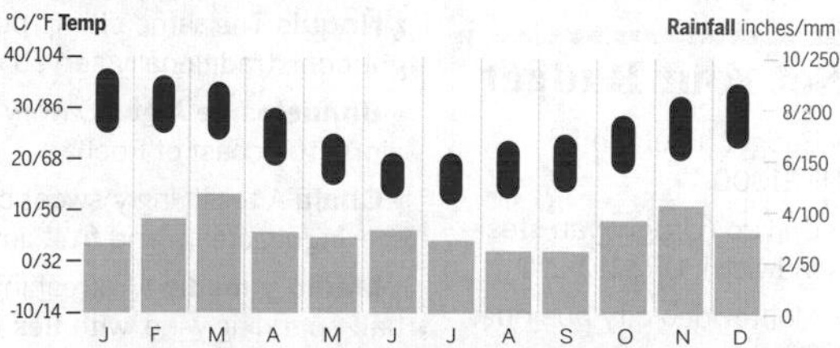

Feb Street theater and drumming consume Montevideo during Carnaval celebrations.

Mar Enjoy Tacuarembó's gaucho festival, plus warm water on Uruguay's beaches.

Oct Soak in a hot spring near Salto or channel Carlos Gardel at Montevideo's annual tango festival.

AT A GLANCE

- Currency: Uruguayan peso (UR$)
- Language: Spanish
- Money: ATMs widespread; credit cards widely accepted
- Visas: Not required for nationals of Western Europe, Australia, USA, Canada or New Zealand

Fast Facts

- Area: 176,215 sq km
- Population: 3.3 million
- Capital: Montevideo
- Emergency: ☎911
- Telephone country code: ☎598

Exchange Rates

Argentina	AR$1	UR$4.45
Australia	A$1	UR$20.14
Canada	C$1	UR$19.41
Chile	CH$100	UR$4.06
Euro zone	€1	UR$25.61
Japan	¥100	UR$24.47
New Zealand	NZ$1	UR$15.31
UK	UK£1	UR$30.59
USA	US$1	UR$19.80

Set Your Budget

- Budget hotel room: UR$1000
- *Chivito* (Uruguayan steak sandwich): UR$110-210
- Montevideo city bus ride: UR$18
- 1L bottle of local beer: UR$80
- Coffee: UR$35

Itineraries

Just popping over from Buenos Aires for a couple of days? Don't overdo it! Focus your energy on the easygoing, picturesque historical river port of Colonia or the urban attractions of Montevideo, both an easy ferry ride from the Argentine capital.

If you've got a week up your sleeve, continue north along the Atlantic coast and sample a few of Uruguay's best beaches: the 1930s-vintage resort of Piriápolis, glitzy Punta del Este, isolated Cabo Polonio, surfer-friendly La Paloma and La Pedrera or the relaxed beach-party town of Punta del Diablo. Alternatively, follow the Río Uruguay upstream towards Iguazú Falls via the wineries of Carmelo, the quirky industrial museum at Fray Bentos and the wonderful hot springs of Salto.

With a whole two weeks to spare, get out and explore Uruguay's interior, ride horses on a tourist *estancia* and settle into a slower-paced lifestyle under the wide open skies of Tacuarembó, Quebrada de los Cuervos or Villa Serrana.

GETTING THERE & AWAY

Most visitors cross by ferry from Buenos Aires, arriving in Colonia, Montevideo or Carmelo. A few airlines, including Pluna, Iberia and American, offer direct international flights to Montevideo; several others connect through Buenos Aires or São Paulo. Land links include three international bridges across the Río Uruguay to Argentina, and six main border crossings into Brazil.

Essential Food & Drink

- **Asado** Uruguay's national gastronomic obsession, a mixed grill cooked over a wood fire, featuring various cuts of beef and pork, chorizo, *morcilla* (blood sausage) and more
- **Chivito** A cholesterol bomb of a steak sandwich piled high with bacon, ham, fried or boiled egg, cheese, lettuce, tomato, olives, pickles, peppers and mayonnaise
- **Ñoquis** The same plump potato dumplings the Italians call *gnocchi*, traditionally served on the 29th of the month
- **Buñuelos de Algas** Savory seaweed fritters, a specialty along the coast of Rocha
- **Chajá** A terrifyingly sweet concoction of sponge cake, meringue, cream and fruit, invented in Paysandú
- **Medio y medio** A refreshing blend of half white wine, half sparkling wine, with ties to Montevideo's historic Café Roldós
- **Grappamiel** Strong Italian-style *grappa* (grape brandy), sweetened and mellowed with honey

MONTEVIDEO

POP 1.3 MILLION

Nation's capital and home to nearly half of Uruguay's population, Montevideo is a vibrant, eclectic place with a rich cultural life. Stretching 20km from east to west, the city wears many faces, from its industrial port to the exclusive beachside suburb of Carrasco near the airport. In the historic downtown business district, art deco and neoclassical buildings jostle for space alongside grimy, worn-out skyscrapers that appear airlifted from Havana or Ceauşescu's Romania, while to the southeast the shopping malls and modern high-rises of beach communities such as Punta Carretas and Pocitos bear more resemblance to Miami or Copacabana. Music, theater and the arts are alive and well here – from elegant older theaters and cozy little tango bars to modern beachfront discos – and there's a strong international flavor, thanks to the many foreign cultural centers and Montevideo's status as administrative headquarters for Mercosur, South America's leading trading bloc.

Montevideo lies almost directly across the Río de la Plata from Buenos Aires. For many visitors, the most intriguing area is the Ciudad Vieja, the formerly walled colonial grid straddling the western tip of a peninsula between the sheltered port and the wide-open river. Just east of the old town gate, the Centro (downtown) begins at Plaza Independencia, surrounded by historic buildings of the republican era. Av 18 de Julio, downtown Montevideo's commercial thoroughfare, runs east past Plaza del Entrevero, Plaza Cagancha and the Intendencia (town hall) towards Tres Cruces bus terminal, where it changes name to Av Italia and continues east towards Carrasco International Airport and the Interbalnearia.

Westward across the harbor, 132m Cerro de Montevideo (Map p500) was a landmark for early navigators and still offers outstanding views of the city. Eastward, the Rambla hugs Montevideo's scenic waterfront, snaking past attractive Parque Rodó (Map p500) and through a series of sprawling beach suburbs – Punta Carretas, Pocitos, Buceo and Carrasco – that are very popular with the capital's residents in summer and on weekends.

Sights

All sights are listed from west to east. Note that many Montevideo museums are known by their acronyms. Most exhibits are in Spanish only.

CIUDAD VIEJA

Museo del Carnaval MUSEUM

(Map p502; ☎2916-5493; www.museodelcarnaval.org; Rambla 25 de Agosto 218; admission UR$65; ⌚11am-5pm Tue-Sun) This museum houses a wonderful collection of costumes, drums, masks, recordings and photos documenting the 100-plus-year history of Montevideo's Carnaval. Behind the museum is the Carnaval-themed restaurant Tras Bambalinas and bleachers where spectators can view performances during the summer months.

Mercado del Puerto MARKET

(Map p502) No visitor should miss Montevideo's old port market building, at the foot of Pérez Castellano, whose impressive wrought-iron superstructure shelters a gaggle of reasonably priced *parrillas* (steak restaurants; see p507). On weekend afternoons in particular, it's a lively, colorful place where the city's artists, craftspeople and street musicians hang out.

Museo de Arte Precolombino e Indígena MUSEUM

(MAPI; Map p502; ☎2916-9360; 25 de Mayo 279; admission UR$60; ⌚1-6:30pm Mon-Fri, 10am-4pm Sat) This museum displays a permanent collection of artifacts and information about Uruguay's earliest inhabitants, along with rotating exhibits focused on native peoples of the Americas.

FREE **Museo de Artes Decorativas** MUSEUM

(Map p502; ☎2915-1101; 25 de Mayo 376; ⌚12:30-5:30pm Mon-Fri) The Palacio Taranco, a wealthy merchant's residence dating from 1910, is now home to this museum. The palatial building, designed by famous French architects Charles Girault and Jules Chifflot, is filled with ornate period furnishings, many brought over from Europe.

FREE **Museo Histórico Nacional** MUSEUM

The centerpiece of Uruguay's National Historical Museum is **Casa Rivera** (Map p502; ☎2915-1051; Rincón 437; ⌚11am-5pm Mon-Fri, 10am-3pm Sat), the former home of Uruguay's first president and founder of the Colorado Party, Fructuoso Rivera. The collection of paintings, documents, furniture and artifacts traces Uruguayan history from indigenous roots through to independence.

Plaza Constitución PLAZA

Also known as Plaza Matriz (Map p502), this was the heart of colonial Montevideo. On

Uruguay Highlights

1. Dance to a different drummer during Montevideo's month-long **Carnaval** (p506)
2. Catch a wave or a late-night beach party along the untamed shoreline at **Punta del Diablo** (p545)
3. Soak your weary traveling muscles in the thermal baths near **Salto** (p526)
4. Ride a horse, roast a cow and see how the gaucho-half live at **Estancia Yvytu Itaty** (p528) near Tacuarembó
5. Sunbathe on the 18th-century town wall, or bounce through the cobblestoned streets in a vintage car in picturesque **Colonia del Sacramento** (p516)
6. Lose yourself in the sand dunes and survey the sea lions from atop the lighthouse at **Cabo Polonio** (p543)
7. Ferry through the islands of the Paraná Delta to **Carmelo** (p521), then spend the afternoon wine-tasting at local Tannat vineyards

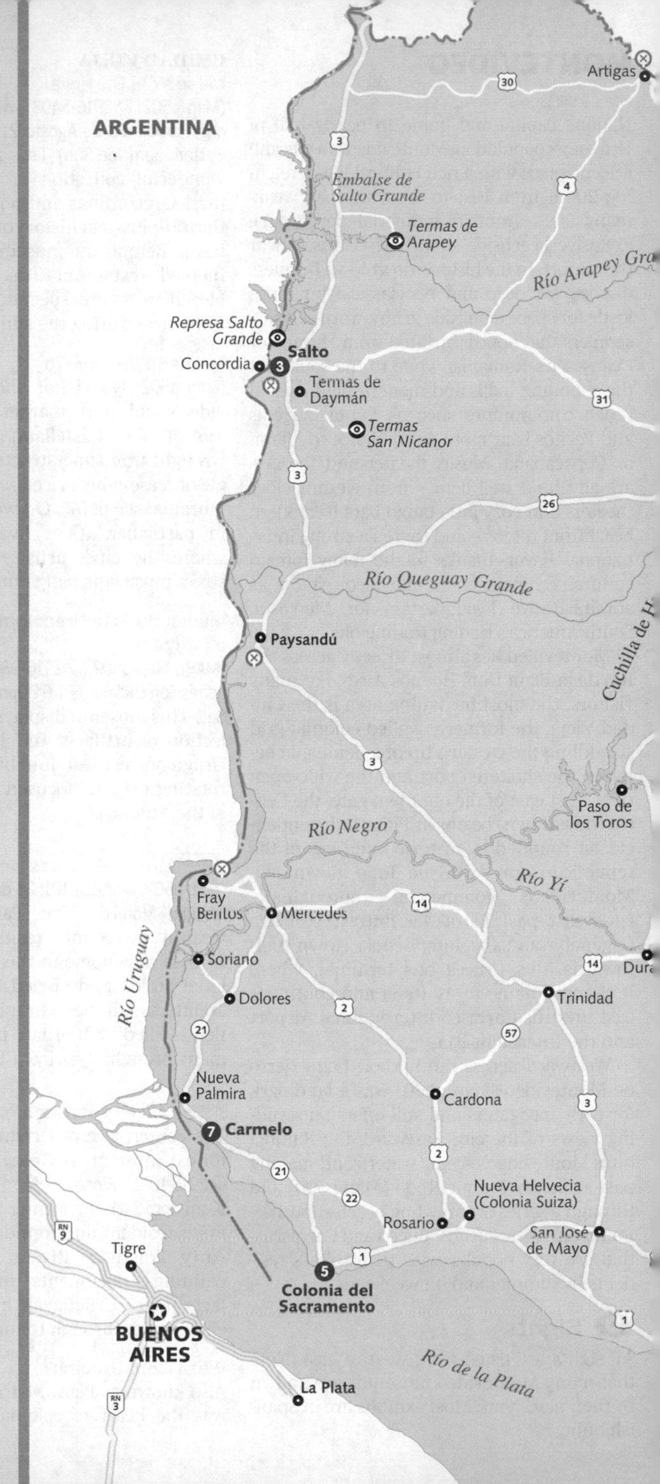

0 100 km
0 50 miles

BRAZIL

Santana do Livramento
Rivera
Valle de Lunarejo
Tranqueras
5
4 Tacuarembó
Valle Edén
59
26
Aceguá
8
Melo
26
San Gregorio de Polanco
Quebrada de los Cuervos
Jaguarão
Río Branco
18
7
Lago Artificial de Rincón del Bonete
Vergara
43
Laguna Merín
19
Cerro Chato
Carmen
Treinta
14
Cebollati
BR 471
14
19
José Batlle y Ordóñez
14
15
19
Lascano
Chuí
Chuy
Fuerte San Miguel
Barra del Chuy
Cerro Colorado
8
Parque Nacional Santa Teresa
Fortaleza de Santa Teresa
Cuchilla Grande
Florida
6
Laguna Negra
2 Punta del Diablo
13
7
Gruta Arequita
15
Laguna de Castillos
Villa Serrana
Sierra de Rocha
Minas
Monte de Ombúes
6 Cabo Polonio
Canelones
8
Parque Salus
39
Rocha
10
La Pedrera
Laguna de Rocha
Pan de Azúcar
La Paloma
ATLANTIC OCEAN
1
Atlántida
9
Faro José Ignacio
Piriápolis
1 MONTEVIDEO
Maldonado
La Barra (de Maldonado)
Punta del Este

Montevideo

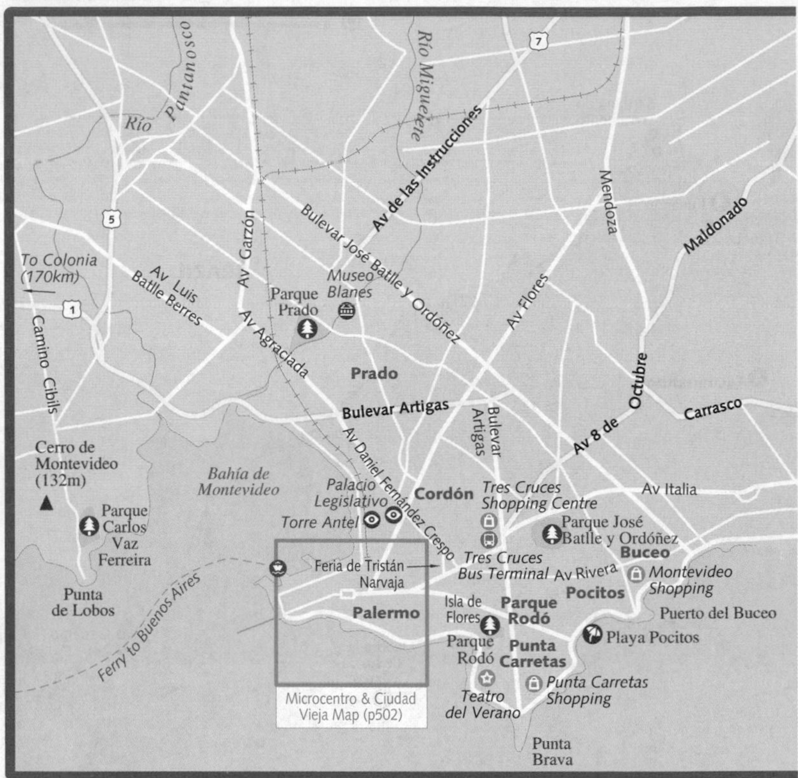

its east side stands the **Cabildo** (finished in 1812), a neoclassical stone structure that contains the **Museo y Archivo Histórico Municipal** (Municipal Archive & Historical Museum; ☎2915-9685; Juan Carlos Gómez 1362; ⏲12:30-5:30pm Tue-Sun). Opposite the Cabildo is the **Iglesia Matriz**, Montevideo's oldest public building. It was begun in 1784 and completed in 1799.

Museo Figari MUSEUM
(☎2915-7065; Juan Carlos Gómez 1427; admission UR$60; ⏲1-6pm Tue-Fri, 10am-2pm Sat) Ciudad Vieja's newest museum is devoted to Uruguayan painter Pedro Figari, whose landscapes and portraits masterfully convey a sense of Uruguayan life in the late 19th and early 20th centuries.

Museo Torres García MUSEUM
(Map p502; ☎2916-2663; Sarandí 683; admission UR$60; ⏲9:30am-7:30pm Mon-Fri, 10am-6pm Sat) This museum showcases the work of 20th-century Uruguayan painter Torres García, and has revolving exhibitions featuring other contemporary artists.

Teatro Solís THEATER
(Map p502; ☎2-1950-1856; www.teatrosolis.org.uy, in Spanish; Buenos Aires 678) Just off Plaza Independencia, elegant Teatro Solís is Montevideo's premier performance space (see p512 and p513). First opened in 1856, and completely renovated during the past decade, it has superb acoustics. Regularly scheduled tours (Tuesday through Sunday) provide an opportunity to see the actual performance space without attending a show. Spanish-language tours are free on Wednesdays, UR$20 other days; English- and Portuguese-language tours cost UR$40.

CENTRO

Plaza Independencia PLAZA
In the middle of this downtown plaza (Map p502) is the **Mausoleo de Artigas**, whose above-ground portion is a 17m, 30-ton statue

of the country's independence hero. Below street level, an honor guard keeps 24-hour vigil over Artigas' remains.

The 19th-century **Palacio Estévez**, on the south side of the plaza, was the Government House until 1985. On the east side of the plaza, the 26-story structure with the crazy beehive hairdo is **Palacio Salvo**, the continent's tallest building when it opened in 1927. At the plaza's west end is the **Puerta de la Ciudadela**, a stone gateway that is one of the only remnants of the colonial citadel demolished in 1833.

FREE Museo del Gaucho y de la Moneda MUSEUM

(Map p502; ☎2900-8764; Av 18 de Julio 998; ⊙10am-5pm Mon-Fri) Housed in the ornate Palacio Heber, this museum eloquently conveys the deep attachments between the gauchos, their animals and the land. The superb collection of historical artifacts includes horse gear, silver work, and *mates* and *bombillas* (metal straws with filters, used for drinking *mate*) in whimsical designs. Downstairs exhibits focus on banknotes, coins, and the Uruguayan economy's volatile history.

FREE Museo de Arte Contemporáneo MUSEUM

(MAC; Map p502; ☎2900-6662; Av 18 de Julio 965, 2nd fl; ⊙2-8pm Tue-Sun, 2-6:30pm Mon) This tiny museum displays continually rotating exhibits of modern Uruguayan painting and sculpture.

FREE Museo del Automóvil MUSEUM

(Map p502; ☎2902-4792; Colonia 1251, 6th fl; ⊙2-7pm Tue-Sun) The Automóvil Club del Uruguay's museum has a superb collection of vintage cars, including a mint 1910 Hupmobile.

FREE Museo de la Historia del Arte MUSEUM

(MuHAr; Map p502; ☎1950 ext 2191; Ejido 1326; ⊙noon-5:30pm Tue-Sun) In the basement of Montevideo's Palacio Municipal (town hall, also known as Intendencia), MuHAr features a wide-ranging collection of art – originals and reproductions of famous pieces – from Egypt, Mesopotamia, Persia, Greece, Rome and numerous Native American cultures.

FREE Centro Municipal de Fotografía MUSEUM

(CMDF; Map p502; ☎1950 ext 1219; San José 1360; ⊙10:30am-7pm Mon-Fri, 9:30am-2:30pm Sat) Rotating contemporary photo exhibits and a computerized archive of 100,000 historic photos can be seen here.

NORTH OF CENTRO

Torre Antel TOWER

(Map p500; ☎2928-4417; Guatemala 1075; admission free; ⊙tours 3:30-5pm Mon, Wed & Fri, 10:30am-noon Tue & Thu) For great views out across the city, take the elevator to the top of Montevideo's most dramatic modern skyscraper.

Palacio Legislativo HISTORIC BUILDING

(Map p500; ☎2924-1783; www.parlamento.gub.uy; Av Libertador General Lavalleja) Dating from 1908, and still playing host to Uruguay's Asamblea General (legislative branch), the 3-story neoclassical is also open for guided tours (UR$60) at 10:30am and 3pm Monday to Friday.

Microcentro & Ciudad Vieja

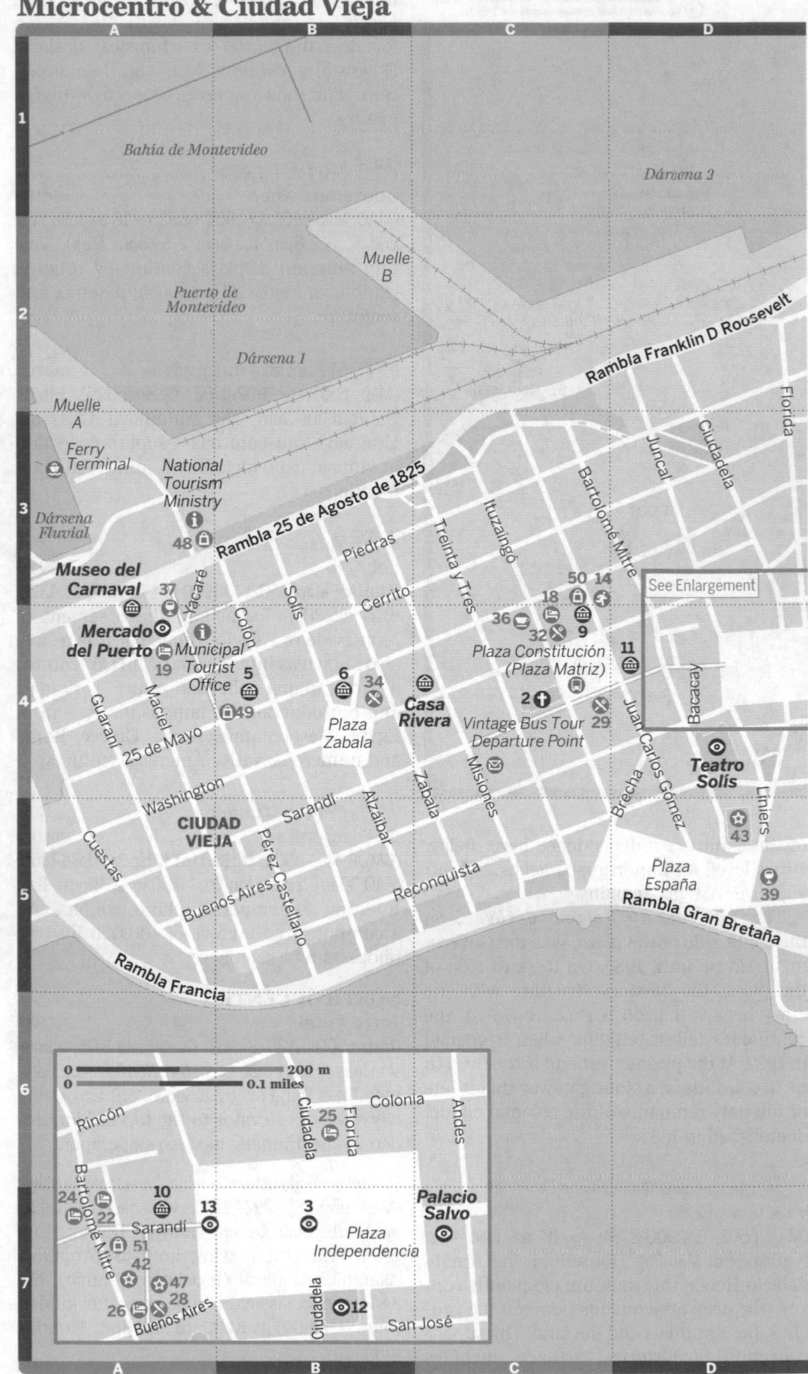

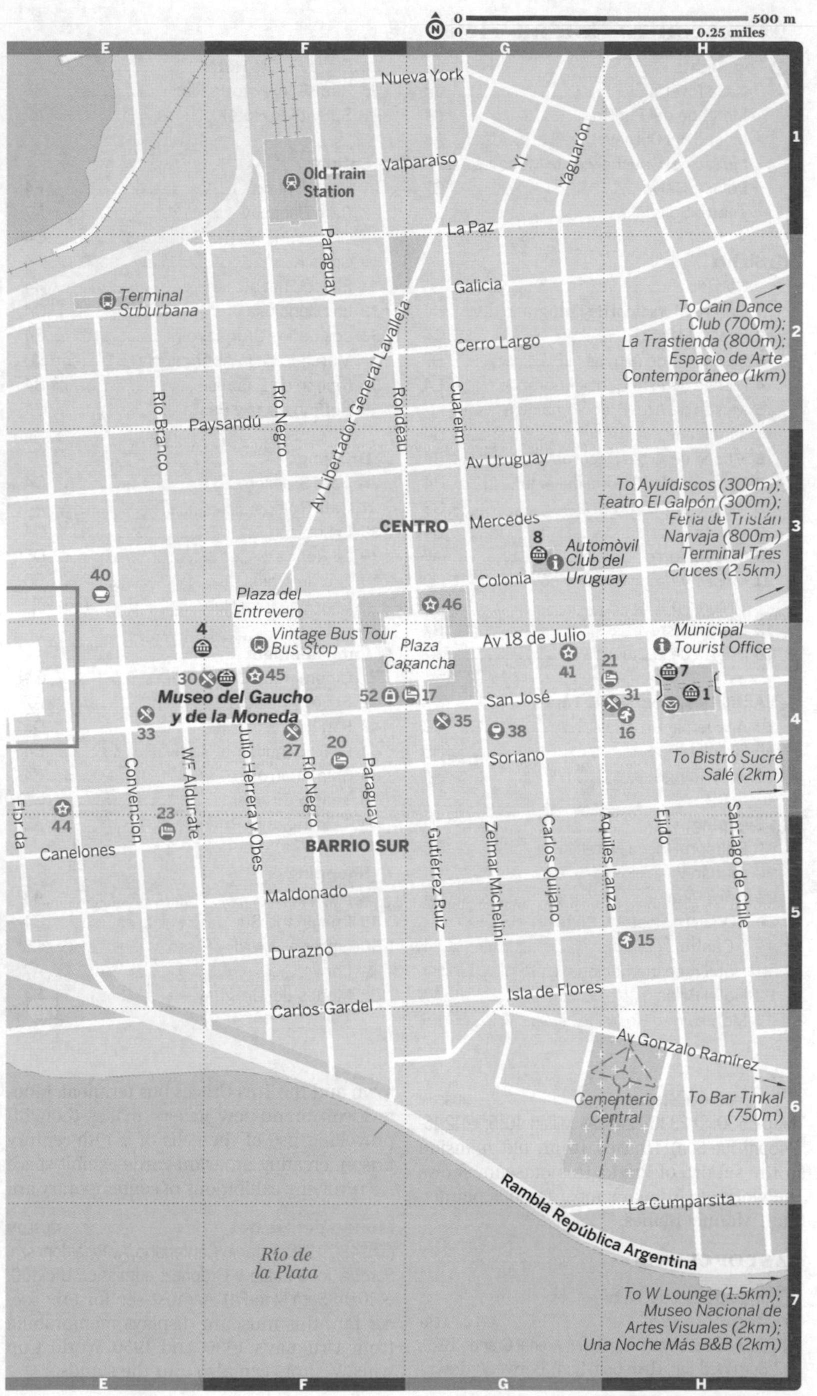

0 500 m
0 0.25 miles
Nueva York
Old Train Station
Valparaiso
Yí
Yaguarón
La Paz
Paraguay
Galicia
Terminal Suburbana
Av Libertador General Lavalleja
To Cain Dance Club (700m); La Trastienda (800m); Espacio de Arte Contemporáneo (1km)
Cerro Largo
Río Branco
Paysandú
Río Negro
Rondeau
Cuareim
Av Uruguay
To Ayuídiscos (300m); Teatro El Galpón (300m); Feria de Tristán Narvaja (800m); Terminal Tres Cruces (2.5km)
CENTRO
Mercedes
Automòvil Club del Uruguay
Colonia
Plaza del Entrevero
Vintage Bus Tour Bus Stop
Plaza Cagancha
Av 18 de Julio
Municipal Tourist Office
Museo del Gaucho y de la Moneda
San José
Soriano
To Bistró Sucré Salé (2km)
Convención
Julio Herrera y Obes
Paraguay
Canelones
BARRIO SUR
Gutiérrez Ruiz
Zelmar Michelini
Carlos Quijano
Aquiles Lanza
Ejido
Santiago de Chile
Maldonado
Durazno
Isla de Flores
Carlos Gardel
Av Gonzalo Ramírez
Cementerio Central
To Bar Tinkal (750m)
Rambla República Argentina
La Cumparsita
Río de la Plata
To W Lounge (1.5km); Museo Nacional de Artes Visuales (2km); Una Noche Más B&B (2km)
URUGUAY MONTEVIDEO

Microcentro Ciudad Vieja

Top Sights

- Casa Rivera ... C4
- Mercado del Puerto ... A4
- Museo del Carnaval ... A4
- Museo del Gaucho y de la Moneda ... F4
- Palacio Salvo ... C7
- Teatro Solís ... D4

Sights

- Cabildo ... (see 11)
- 1 Centro Municipal de Fotografía ... H4
- 2 Iglesia Matriz ... C4
- 3 Mausoleo de Artigas ... B7
- 4 Museo de Arte Contemporáneo ... E4
- 5 Museo de Arte Precolombino e Indígena ... B4
- 6 Museo de Artes Decorativas ... B4
- 7 Museo de la Historia del Arte ... H4
- 8 Museo del Automóvil ... G3
- 9 Museo Figari ... C4
- 10 Museo Torres García ... A7
- 11 Museo y Archivo Histórico Municipal ... D4
- 12 Palacio Estévez ... B7
- 13 Puerta de la Ciudadela ... A7

Activities, Courses & Tours

- 14 Academia Uruguay ... C3
- 15 Bicicleteria Sur ... H5
- 16 Joventango ... H4

Sleeping

- 17 Balmoral Plaza Hotel ... G4
- 18 Ciudad Vieja Hostel ... C4
- 19 Don Hotel ... A4
- 20 El Viajero Hostel & Suites Centro ... F4
- 21 Hotel Klee Inernacional ... H4
- 22 Hotel Palacio ... A7
- 23 Montevideo Hostel ... E5
- 24 Plaza Fuerte Hotel ... A7
- 25 Radisson Victoria Plaza ... B6
- 26 Spléndido Hotel ... A7

Eating

- 27 Bar Hispano ... F4
- 28 Café Bacacay ... A7
- 29 Cervecería Matriz ... C4
- 30 Comi.K ... F4
- 31 El Esquinazo ... H4
- 32 La Silenciosa ... C4
- 33 Los Leños Uruguayos ... E4
- Mercado de la Abundancia ... (see 31)
- 34 Rincón de Zabala ... B4
- 35 Ruffino Pizza y Pasta ... G4

Drinking

- 36 Café Brasilero ... C4
- 37 Café Roldós ... A4
- 38 El Lobizón ... G4
- 39 La Ronda ... D5
- 40 Oro del Rhin ... E3
- Shannon Irish Pub ... (see 42)

Entertainment

- 41 Cinemateca Uruguaya ... G4
- 42 El Pony Pisador ... A7
- 43 Fun Fun ... D5
- 44 La Bodeguita del Sur ... E4
- 45 Sala Zitarrosa ... F4
- 46 Teatro Circular ... G3
- 47 Teatro Sobre Ruedas ... A7

Shopping

- 48 Hecho Acá ... A3
- 49 Imaginario Sur ... B4
- 50 Librería Linardi y Risso ... C3
- 51 Louvre ... A7
- 52 Manos del Uruguay ... F4

FREE **Museo Blanes** MUSEUM
(Map p500; ☎2336-2248; Av Millán 4015; ⊙12:15-5:45pm Tue-Sun) Housed in an old mansion in the suburb of Prado, this museum shows the work of Uruguay's most famous painter, Juan Manuel Blanes.

EAST OF CENTRO

FREE **Espacio de Arte Contemporáneo** ART GALLERY
(☎2929-2066; www.eac.gub.uy; Arenal Grande 1929; ⊙2-8pm Wed-Sat, 11am-5pm Sun) Between downtown and the Tres Cruces bus terminal, Montevideo's brand-new gallery makes thought-provoking use of the cells of a 19th-century prison, creating an avant-garde exhibit space for revolving exhibitions of contemporary art.

Museo del Fútbol MUSEUM
(☎2480-1259; Estadio Centenario, Av Ricaldoni s/n, Parque José Batlle y Ordóñez; admission UR$100; ⊙10am-5pm Mon-Fri) A must-see for any soccer fan, this museum displays memorabilia from Uruguay's 1930 and 1950 World Cup wins. Visitors can also tour the stands.

FREE **Museo Nacional de Artes Visuales** MUSEUM
(MNAV; ☎2711-6124; www.mnav.gub.uy; cnr Av Herrera y Reissig & T Giribaldi; ⏲2-6:45pm Tue-Sun) Uruguay's largest collection of paintings is housed here in Parque Rodó. The large rooms are graced with works by Blanes, Cúneo, Figari and Torres García.

LA RAMBLA & EASTERN BEACHES

La Rambla, Montevideo's multi-kilometer coastal promenade, is one of the city's defining elements, connecting downtown to the eastern beach communities of Punta Carretas, Pocitos, Buceo and Carrasco. This is Montevideo's social hub on Sunday afternoons, when the place is packed with locals cradling thermoses of *mate* and socializing with friends.

Castillo Pittamiglio HISTORIC BUILDING
(☎2710-1089; www.castillopittamiglio.com; Rambla Gandhi 633) On the Rambla between Punta Carretas and Pocitos, is this eccentric legacy of local alchemist and architect, Humberto Pittamiglio. Its quirky facadc alone is worth a look. Spanish-language tours of the interior (UR$60) take place 5pm Tuesday and Thursday; weekend tours with variable hours are also offered – call for details.

Museo Naval MUSEUM
(☎2622-1084; cnr Rambla Costanera & LA de Herrera; admission UR$20; ⏲8:30am-noon & 2-6pm Fri-Wed) Along the eastern waterfront in Buceo, this museum traces the role of boats and ships in Uruguayan history, from the indigenous Charrúa's canoe culture to the dramatic sinking of the German *Graf Spee* offshore of Montevideo in 1939.

Activities

Rent a bike at **Bicicleteria Sur** (Map p502; ☎2901-0792; Aquiles Lanza 1100; per hr/day UR$20/180; ⏲9am-1pm & 3-7pm Mon-Fri, 10am-2pm Sat) and go cruising along the walking-jogging-cycling track that follows the riverfront Rambla. After about 2km you'll get to Playa Pocitos, which is best for **swimming** and where you should be able to jump in on a game of **beach volleyball**. A couple of bays further along at Puerto del Buceo you can get **windsurfing** lessons at the yacht club.

Buceo's **Yacht Harbor** is a picturesque spot for a stroll and a popular Sunday afternoon hangout.

Courses

The following Spanish and tango courses don't cater for the casual learner – you'd want to be staying at least a month to get your money's worth.

Academia Uruguay LANGUAGE COURSE
(Map p502; ☎2915-2496; www.academiauruguay.com; Juan Carlos Gómez 1408; group/individual classes per hr UR$220/500) One-on-one and group Spanish classes with a strong cultural focus. Also arranges homestays, private apartments and volunteer work.

Joventango TANGO COURSE
(Map p502; ☎2901-5561; www.joventango.org, in Spanish; Aquiles Lanza 1290) Tango classes for all levels, from beginner to expert.

Festivals & Events

Much livelier than its Buenos Aires counterpart, Montevideo's late-summer **Carnaval** is the cultural highlight of the year – see the boxed text, p506.

At Parque Prado, north of downtown, Semana Criolla festivities during **Semana Santa** (Holy Week) include displays of gaucho skills, *asados* and other such events.

In the last weekend of September or first weekend of October, Montevideo's museums, churches, and historic homes all open their doors free to the public during the **Días del Patrimonio** (National Heritage Days).

For 10 days in October, tango fills Montevideo's streets and performance halls during the **Festival del Tango**, organized by Joventango (p505).

Sleeping

Montevideo offers some appealing boutique hotels (including a noteworthy newcomer at the Mercado del Puerto), a thriving hosteling scene, and a host of dependable, if faded, mid-range hotels in the Centro.

CIUDAD VIEJA

TOP CHOICE **Don Hotel** BOUTIQUE HOTEL $$$
(Map p502; ☎2915-9999; www.donhotel.com.uy; Piedras 234; standard/superior r UR$3000/5000, ste UR$8000; ❄@🛜≋) Montevideo's newest hotel is a study in refined black, white, silver and gray, with Iberian wallpapers, linens and tiles throughout, plus Jacuzzis and remarkable full-on views of Mercado del Puerto's ornate rooftops from the superior rooms up front. A swimming pool, solarium and rooftop bar overlooking Montevideo's port and city skyline make this a classy choice. Meals at the

DON'T MISS

CARNAVAL IN MONTEVIDEO

If you thought Brazil was South America's only Carnaval capital, think again! *Montevideanos* cut loose in a big way every February, with music and dance filling the air for a solid month.

Not to be missed is the early February **Desfile de las Llamadas**, a two-night parade of *comparsas* (neighborhood Carnaval societies) through the streets of Palermo and Barrio Sur districts, just southeast of the Centro. *Comparsas* are made up of *negros* (persons of African descent) and *lubolos* (whites who paint their faces black for Carnaval, a long-standing Uruguayan tradition). Neighborhood rivalries play themselves out as wave after wave of dancers whirl to the electrifying rhythms of traditional Afro-Uruguayan *candombe* drumming, beaten on drums of three different pitches: the *chico* (soprano), *repique* (contralto) and *piano* (tenor). The heart of the parade route is Isla de Flores, between Salto and Gaboto. Spectators can pay for a chair on the sidewalk (UR$150) or try to snag a spot on one of the balconies overlooking the street.

Another key element of Montevideo's Carnaval are the *murgas*, organized groups of 15 to 17 gaudily dressed performers, including three percussionists, who perform original pieces of musical theater, often satirical and based on political themes. During the dictatorship in Uruguay, *murgas* were famous for their subversive commentary. All *murgas* use the same three instruments: the *bombo* (bass drum), *redoblante* (snare drum) and *platillos* (cymbals). *Murgas* play all over the city, and also compete throughout February in Parque Rodó at the **Teatro de Verano** (Map p500; admission from UR$70). The competition has three rounds, with judges determining who advances and who gets eliminated.

The fascinating history of Montevideo's Carnaval is well documented in the city's **Museo del Carnaval** (p497). Another great way to experience Carnaval out of season is by attending one of the informal *candombe* practice sessions that erupt in neighborhood streets throughout the year. One good place to find these is at the corner of Isla de Flores and Gaboto in Palermo. Drummers usually gather between 7pm and 7:30pm on Sunday nights.

well-regarded El Palenque restaurant, across the street in Mercado del Puerto, can be added directly to your room tab.

Hotel Palacio HOTEL $

(Map p502; ☎2916-3612; www.hotelpalacio.com.uy; Bartolomé Mitre 1364; r without/with balcony UR$900/1000; ❄📶) This ancient family-run hotel has sagging brass beds, antique furniture and a vintage elevator. Try for one of the two 6th-floor rooms with air-conditioning and superb views of the Ciudad Vieja from the large balconies. Downstairs rooms are fan-cooled and cost a bit less.

Ciudad Vieja Hostel HOSTEL $

(Map p502; ☎2915-6192; www.elviajeromontevideo.com; Ituzaingó 1436; dm UR$300-340, d UR$1100; @📶) Only a few steps away from the old city's abundant nightlife, this hostel has friendly staff, a homey, hip atmosphere, and an appealing layout on two upper floors of an older Ciudad Vieja building. There are separate kitchens and lounging areas on each level, a DVD library, roof deck, bikes for rent, city tours and a helpful bulletin board of cultural events.

Spléndido Hotel HOTEL $

(Map p502; ☎2916-4900; www.splendidohotel.com.uy; Bartolomé Mitre 1314; s with shared bathroom UR$440-760, d with shared/private bathroom from UR$900/1200; @📶) Faded, funky and friendly, the Spléndido offers excellent value for budget travelers preferring privacy over a hostel-style party vibe. Pricier rooms have 5m-high ceilings and French doors opening to balconies, some overlooking Teatro Solís. Bars on the street below get extremely noisy on weekends, and the Montevideo Philharmonic Orchestra rehearses next door some mornings (free concert anyone?).

Plaza Fuerte Hotel HOTEL $$$

(Map p502; ☎2915-6651; www.plazafuerte.com; Bartolomé Mitre 1361; d UR$2300, ste from UR$3300; ❄@📶) Housed in a stately building dating to 1913, the Plaza Fuerte has red-carpeted marble stairs, decorative tile floors and dramatic views from its 5th-floor bar and terrace. All rooms have 5m-high ceilings; the suites (some split over two levels, some with Jacuzzis) are especially elegant.

CENTRO

El Viajero Hostel & Suites Centro HOSTEL $

(Map p502; ☎2908-2913; www.elviajerodowntown.com; Soriano 1073; dm UR$300-360, d UR$1140-1330; @ 📶) Smack in the center of downtown, this newer hostel is attractively laid out in a historic building with a high-ceilinged, tile-walled pub area and a skylight roof that lets fresh air and light pour in on sunny days. Bike rentals (UR$250 per day) and excellent advice from the resident staff will get you out exploring; meals on the back patio five nights a week (from UR$150 to UR$300) may just lure you back.

Balmoral Plaza Hotel HOTEL $$$

(Map p502; ☎2902-2393; www.balmoral.com.uy; Plaza Cagancha 1126; s/d/ste from UR$2500/2700/3600; ❄ @ 📶) Central downtown location and bird's-eye views of leafy Plaza Cagancha are the big draws here. All rooms have minibars, safes, big TVs and double-glazed, soundproof windows. You'll also discover a garage, gym, sauna and business center.

Hotel Klee Internacional HOTEL $$

(Map p502; ☎2902-0606; www.klee.com.uy; San José 1303; s/d UR$1200/1500; ❄ @ 📶) With solid three-star amenities and a great location directly across from the Mercado de la Abundancia, the Klee is a good midtown option.

Radisson Victoria Plaza HOTEL $$$

(Map p502; ☎2902-0111; www.radisson.com/montevideouy; Plaza Independencia 759; r/ste UR$6000/7000; ❄ @ 📶 🏊) A five-star hotel towering over central Plaza Independencia, with luxurious rooms, a 25m swimming pool, and remarkable city views from the 25th-floor restaurant.

Montevideo Hostel HOSTEL $

(Map p502; ☎2908-1324; www.montevideohostel.com.uy, in Spanish; Canelones 935; dm per person HI member/nonmember UR$300/360; @ 📶) With musical instruments strewn everywhere, good internet facilities, a cellar bar, a nice fireplace and a spiral staircase connecting all three levels of the spacious central common area, this older hostel, managed by the same family for years, remains one of Montevideo's best budget options.

LA RAMBLA & EASTERN BEACHES

Cala di Volpe BOUTIQUE HOTEL $$$

(☎2710-2000; www.hotelcaladivolpe.com.uy; cnr Rambla Gandhi & Parva Domus, Punta Carretas; d/ste from UR$2400/3600; ❄ @ 📶 🏊) This classy place across from the beach abounds in boutique hotel features: comfy couches, writing desks, gleaming tile-and-marble bathrooms, and floor-to-ceiling picture windows with sweeping river views. There's a small rooftop pool and a nice restaurant.

Pocitos Hostel HOSTEL $

(☎2711-8780; www.pocitos-hostel.com; Sarmiento 2641, Pocitos; dm UR$380-400, s/d UR$900/1200; @ 📶) A few blocks from the Pocitos waterfront, this appealing hostel squeezes several four- to six-bed dorms and a couple of doubles into a converted old home with fireplace, high ceilings, guest kitchen, backyard barbecue and friendly staff.

Una Noche Más B&B HOMESTAY $$

(☎096-227406; www.unanochemas.com.uy; Patria 712, Apt 2, Punta Carretas; d UR$1120-1360; @ 📶) Near the beach in Punta Carretas, this is a great option for anyone seeking a 'homestay' experience in the big city. Friendly hosts Carla and Eduardo go out of their way to make guests feel welcome and also offer half- and full board upon request. There's a two-night minimum stay.

Pocitos Plaza Hotel HOTEL $$$

(☎2712-3939; www.pocitosplazahotel.com.uy; Benito Blanco 640, Pocitos; s/d standard UR$2200/2500, superior UR$2600/3000; ❄ @ 📶) This comfortable four-star is replete with services for the business traveler, although vacationers will also appreciate its sauna, sundeck and proximity to the beach. Superior rooms have sofas, whirlpool tubs and big closets.

Eating

Two of the most atmospheric places to eat are the converted market buildings. **Mercado del Puerto** (Pérez Castellano), on the Ciudad Vieja waterfront, is *the* classic place to eat in Montevideo. The densely packed *parrillas* here compete like rutting elk to show off their obscenely large racks – of roasted meat and veggies, that is! Weekends are the best time to savor the market's vibrant, crowded energy, but lunching executives and tourists keep the place buzzing on weekdays, too. The more affordable and less touristy **Mercado de la Abundancia** (cnr San José & Aquiles Lanza), in the heart of downtown, features three low-key eateries surrounding an open space where locals come every Saturday night to tango, salsa and more.

CHRISTOPHER GROENHOUT/LONELY PLANET IMAGES ©

1. Colonia del Sacramento (p516)
Only 50km from Buenos Aires by ferry, this picturesque town is a Unesco World Heritage site.

2. Punta del Este (p532)
One of South America's most-glamorous resorts, this seaside place positively buzzes.

3. Mercado del Puerto (p497)
Montevideo's old port market should not be missed, especially on weekends.

4. Playa El Emir (p532)
This Atlantic Ocean beach is a magnet for surfers.

JAVIER PIERINI/CORBIS ©

WAYNE WALTON/LONELY PLANET IMAGES ©

3

ALEXANDRE CAPPELLARI/ALAMY ©

CIUDAD VIEJA

TOP CHOICE La Silenciosa INTERNATIONAL $$$

(Map p502; ☎2915-9409; Ituzaingó 1426; dishes UR$280-480; ⊙lunch Mon-Sat, dinner Fri) With stone and brick walls, high ceilings and checkerboard marble floors, this restaurant has a fascinating history including stints as an 18th-century Jesuit seminary and as the tailor's shop where Carlos Gardel and other Uruguayan luminaries had their shirts made. The food is divine – from homemade pasta to scrumptious meat and fish dishes to desserts such as moist orange cake with green-tea ice cream. Three-course lunch menus including starter, main dish, dessert and a glass of wine is excellent value at UR$320.

Café Bacacay FUSION $$

(Map p502; Bacacay 1306; dishes UR$170-360; ⊙9am-late Mon-Sat) This chic little cafe across from Teatro Solís serves a variety of mouthwatering goodies: fish of the day with wasabi or *limoncello* (lemon liqueur) sauce, build-your-own salads with tasty ingredients such as grilled eggplant, spinach and smoked salmon, and a wide-ranging drinks menu. Desserts include chocolate cake, pear tart and lemon pie.

Rincón de Zabala CAFETERIA $

(Map p502; www.rdz.com.uy, in Spanish; Rincón 387; sandwiches UR$80-105, full meals incl dessert UR$160-200; ⊙9am-5pm Mon-Fri; wi-fi) This modern corner place serves up free wi-fi along with affordable breakfasts, sandwiches and cafeteria-style daily specials.

Cervecería Matriz BEER HALL $$

(Map p502; Sarandí 582; dishes UR$108-335; ⊙8am-1am Mon-Sat) Join the crowds enjoying beer and *chivitos* (Uruguay's classic steak sandwich) under the trees at this informal eatery on Ciudad Vieja's most picturesque square.

CENTRO

Los Leños Uruguayos PARRILLA $$

(Map p502; www.parrilla.com.uy; San José 909; dishes UR$180-395; ⊙11:30am-4pm & 7:30pm-midnight) This favorite haunt of Montevideo's business set has a nice salad bar and a big rack of meat always roasting on the fire up front. The lunchtime *menú ejecutivo* (fixed-price lunch menu; UR$240) and *sugerencias del chef* (chef's suggestions; UR$225) are both great deals, including *cubierto*, main dish, dessert and coffee.

Comi.K BRAZILIAN $$

(Map p502; Av 18 de Julio 994, 2nd fl; specials incl drink & dessert UR$220; ⊙8am-10pm Mon-Fri, 8am-4pm Sat) Inside the Brazilian cultural center, reasonably priced meals – including *feijoada* (Brazil's classic meat-and-black-bean stew) – are served in an elegant 2nd-floor salon with high ceilings and stained glass. There's live Brazilian music most Friday evenings.

El Esquinazo PARRILLA $$

(Map p502; Mercado de la Abundancia; pizza UR$60-200, mains UR$200-350; ⊙11am-midnight Mon-Sat) With its blazing fire and irresistible aroma of grilled meat, this popular *parrilla* epitomizes the Mercado de la Abundancia's cozy, relaxed ambience. Lunchtime prices are about half what you'd pay at the more touristy Mercado del Puerto – the *menu ejecutivo* includes a mixed grill and a glass of wine for UR$220. There's live jazz two Thursdays per month, plus tango or salsa on Saturday nights.

Bar Hispano CONFITERÍA $

(Map p502; San José 1050; meals UR$115-265; ⊙7am-2am) Old-school neighborhood *confiterías* (cafes offering light meals) like this are disappearing fast. The black-clad, gruffly efficient waiters can take pretty much any order you throw at them – a stiff drink to start the day, a full meal at 5pm or a chocolate binge in the early hours. The plethora of ever-changing *platos del día* includes options for almost every taste and budget.

Ruffino Pizza y Pasta ITALIAN $$

(Map p502; www.ruffino.com.uy; San José 1166; dishes UR$190-350; ⊙noon-3pm Sun-Fri, 8:30-midnight Mon-Sat) Extremely popular for Sunday lunch, Ruffino's is a good midrange Italian option. Try the Caruso (mushroom and cream) sauce, a uniquely Uruguayan specialty named for Italian tenor Enrico Caruso, who visited Montevideo in 1915.

Bosque Bambú VEGETARIAN $$

(www.comidavegetarianabambu.com; San José 1060; all-you-can-eat UR$240; ⊙noon-3pm Mon-Sat; vegetarian) One of the few truly veggie options in this meat-crazed country, this popular health food store offers food by the kilo or an all-you-can-eat lunch buffet; drinks cost extra.

EAST OF CENTRO

Bistró Sucré Salé FRENCH $$

(www.alliancefrancaise.edu.uy/bistrot.html, in Spanish; Blvd Artigas 1229, Parque Rodó; sandwiches

UR$80-120, dishes from UR$250; ⏲9:30am-8pm Mon-Fri) Wonderful European influences abound at this little cafe behind the Alianza Francesa: French music, brioches, tarts, Illy espresso, Van Gogh posters, plus a courtyard with fountain, iron gazebo and climbing roses.

LA RAMBLA & EASTERN BEACHES

La Pulpería PARRILLA **$$**
(cnr Lagunillas & Nuñez, Punta Carretas; mains UR$200-300; ⏲8am-12:30am Tue-Sat, noon-4pm Sun) The epitome of an intimate neighborhood *parrilla*, La Pulpería doesn't advertise its presence (drop by before 8pm and you won't even find a sign outside!); instead, it focuses its energy on grilling prime cuts of meat to perfection, and relies on word of mouth to do the rest.

Bar Tinkal CHIVITOS **$**
(cnr Frugoni & La Rambla; chivitos UR$150; ⏲8am-2am Mon-Sat) This corner bar has sunset views toward the river, but locals also rave about the *chivitos*, which stand out for their simplicity and quality. Rather than piling on an absurd number of ingredients, Tinkal focuses on basics: tender meat, fresh lettuce and a good roll to hold everything together.

Umaga INTERNATIONAL **$$$**
(☎2712-3141; cnr Luis de la Torre & Francisco Ros, Punta Carretas; dishes UR$350-490; ⏲8pm-midnight Tue-Sat) Umaga offers a concise menu of beautifully presented gourmet dishes in a comfortable old Punta Carretas home, done up in modern style. The innovative offerings range from grilled salmon with leeks and strawberries to desserts such as an apple-cinnamon-clove roll flambéed with grappa.

Drinking

Ciudad Vieja and Centro offer an intriguing mix of venerable old cafes and up-and-coming recent arrivals. Bars are concentrated on Bartolomé Mitre in Ciudad Vieja, and south of Plaza Independencia in the Centro.

TOP CHOICE **Café Brasilero** CAFE
(Map p502; Ituzaingó 1447, Ciudad Vieja; ⏲9am-8pm Mon-Fri) Reborn under new ownership in 2010, this old-fashioned 1877 cafe with small wooden tables and chairs, chandeliers, and historic photos gracing the walls, makes a delightful spot for morning coffee or afternoon tea. It's also an excellent lunch stop, with homemade bread, tasty pasta dishes and good-value *menus ejecutivos* (starter, main course, water and dessert for UR$235).

Café Roldós BAR-CAFE
(Map p502; Mercado del Puerto; ⏲9am-5pm) This historic bar-cafe in Mercado del Puerto is a perennial favorite. Since 1886 staff have been pouring their famous *medio y medio*, a refreshing concoction made from half wine, half sparkling wine (per bottle/glass UR$160/60). Throw in a few tasty sandwiches (UR$50 each), and you've got a meal!

Philomène TEAHOUSE
(Solano García 2455, Punta Carretas; ⏲9am-8:30pm Mon-Fri, 11am-8:30pm Sat) Big pots of tea, complete with tea cozies, are served alongside cookies and light meals in this pair of super-cozy, happily wallpapered, parlor-sized rooms in Punta Carretas.

La Ronda BAR
(Map p502; Ciudadela 1182, Centro; ⏲noon-late Mon-Sat, 7pm-late Sun) At this ultracool and usually jam-packed bar, patrons straddle the windowsills between the dark interior plastered with vintage album covers and the sidewalk tables cooled by breezes off the Rambla.

Shannon Irish Pub PUB
(Map p502; www.theshannon.com.uy; Bartolomé Mitre 1318, Ciudad Vieja; ⏲7pm-late) A perennial favorite, the Shannon pours a good pint and features live music every night, from rock to traditional Irish bands.

El Lobizón BAR
(Map p502; Zelmar Michelini 1264, Centro; ⏲8pm-3am) Lobizón's cellar-bar atmosphere, free-flowing pitchers of sangría and *clericó* (white wine mixed with fruit), and tasty snacks such as the famous *gramajo* (potatoes, ham and eggs) make it a very popular gathering place for young, artistic types.

Oro del Rhin CAFE, BAKERY
(Map p502; Convención 1403, Centro; ⏲8:30am-8pm Mon-Sat) With more than 75 years in business, you know they're doing something right! It's worth a visit just to ogle the gorgeous collection of cakes and pastries in the window.

Entertainment

Spanish-language websites with entertainment listings: www.lanochedemontevideo.com; www.espectador.com; www.cartelera.com.uy; and www.socioespectacular.com.uy.

Nightclubs

El Pony Pisador CLUB
(Map p502; www.elponypisador.com.uy); Ciudad Vieja (Bartolomé Mitre 1324; ⏲5pm-late Mon-

Fri, 8pm-late Sat & Sun); Pocitos (Iturriaga 3497; ⌚8pm-late Thu-Sat) This thriving bar and disco has multiple locations in Montevideo featuring live music nightly; depending on the evening and the location, you may find yourself dancing to blues, Brazilian, flamenco, oldies, soul, Latin or rock covers in English and Spanish. The Pocitos branch occasionally also hosts stand-up comics.

W Lounge CLUB
(cnr Rambla Wilson & Sarmiento, Parque Rodó; ⌚midnight-7am Thu-Sat) With two dance floors accommodating 3000 people, this nightclub in Parque Rodó is *the* place to shake your thang to rock, *cumbia* and techno beats. A taxi from the center should cost about UR$100.

Cain Dance Club GAY
(www.caindance.com; Cerro Largo 1833, Cordón; ⌚midnight-7am Sat & Sun) Montevideo's premier gay nightspot, Cain is a multilevel club with two dance floors playing everything from techno to Latin beats.

La Bodeguita del Sur DANCE
(Map p502; www.labodeguitadelsur.com.uy; Soriano 840, Centro; ⌚11pm-late Fri-Sun) For live salsa, hit this place on weekend nights.

Live Music & Dance

The legendary Carlos Gardel spent time in Montevideo, where the tango is no less popular than in Buenos Aires. Music and dance venues abound downtown.

TOP CHOICE Fun Fun LIVE MUSIC
(Map p502; ☎2915-8005; www.barfunfun.com; Ciudadela 1229, Mercado Central, Ciudad Vieja; ⌚9pm-late Wed-Sat) Since 1895 this intimate, informal venue in the Mercado Central has been serving its famous *uvita* (a sweet wine drink) while hosting tango and other live music on a tiny stage. The front deck is very pleasant.

Teatro Solís PERFORMING ARTS
(Map p502; ☎1950 ext 3323; www.teatrosolis.org.uy, in Spanish; Buenos Aires 678, Ciudad Vieja; admission from UR$200) The city's top venue is home to the Montevideo Philharmonic Orchestra and hosts formal concerts of classical, jazz, tango and other music, plus music festivals, ballet and opera.

Sala Zitarrosa PERFORMING ARTS
(Map p502; ☎2901-7303; www.salazitarrosa.com.uy; Av 18 de Julio 1012, Centro) Montevideo's best informal auditorium venue for big-name music and dance performances, including zarzuela, tango, rock, flamenco and reggae.

El Tartamudo Café LIVE MUSIC
(☎2480-4332; www.eltartamudo.com.uy, in Spanish; cnr 8 de Octubre & Presidente Berro, Tres Cruces; ⌚9pm-late Tue-Sun) Performances at this place just east of Tres Cruces bus terminal run the gamut from rock to tango to *candombe* to jazz.

La Trastienda LIVE MUSIC
(☎2402-6929; www.latrastienda.com.uy, in Spanish; Fernández Crespo 1763, Cordón; ⌚9pm-late Wed-Sat) This popular club hosts an eclectic mix of international musicians, playing everything from rock to reggae, jazz to folk, tango to electronica.

Cinema

Cinemateca Uruguaya CINEMA
(Map p502; ☎2900-9056; www.cinemateca.org.uy; Av 18 de Julio 1280; membership per month UR$255, plus 1-time sign-up fee UR$130) For art-

DON'T MISS

MONTEVIDEO WEEKEND HIGHLIGHTS

Weekends are the time to enjoy several of Montevideo's quintessential experiences.

Saturday morning Browse the antiques market on Plaza Matriz.

Saturday afternoon Discover your inner carnivore over lunch at Mercado del Puerto.

Saturday night Attend a performance at Teatro Solís or Sala Zitarrosa, sip *uvitas* and listen to live music at Baar Fun Fun, join locals dancing tango at Mercado de la Abundancia or party all night at clubs like El Pony Pisador.

Sunday morning Explore the labyrinth of market stalls at Mercado de Tristán Narvaja.

Sunday afternoon Join the parade of *mate*-toting locals strolling the 20km-long beachfront Rambla.

Sunday evening Catch a pre-Carnaval drumming rehearsal on the streets of Palermo.

house flicks, this film club charges a modest membership allowing unlimited viewing at its four cinemas. It hosts the two-week Festival Cinematográfico Internacional del Uruguay in March or April.

The rest of Montevideo's cinema scene is concentrated in the shopping malls east of downtown.

Theater

Montevideo's active theater community spans many worlds: from classical to commercial to avant-garde. Regular Spanish-language performances are staged at **Teatro Solís** (Map p502; ☎1950-3323; www.teatrosolis.org.uy, in Spanish; Buenos Aires 678, Ciudad Vieja), **Teatro El Galpón** (☎2408-3366; www.teatroelgalpon.org.uy, in Spanish; Av 18 de Julio 1618, Centro) and **Teatro Circular** (Map p502; ☎2901-5952; tcircular@adinet.com.uy; Rondeau 1388, Centro). Alternatively, **Teatro Sobre Ruedas** (Map p502; ☎2900-8618; www.barronegro.com, in Spanish; Bacacay 1318, Ciudad Vieja) stages interactive theater on a city bus whizzing through Montevideo's streets.

Spectator Sports

Football, a Uruguayan passion, inspires large and regular crowds. The main stadium, the **Estadio Centenario** (Map p500; Av Ricaldoni, Parque José Batlle y Ordóñez), opened in 1930 for the first World Cup, in which Uruguay defeated Argentina 4-2 in the final.

Shopping

Central Montevideo's traditional downtown shopping area is Av 18 de Julio. *Montevideanos* also flock to three major shopping malls east of downtown: Punta Carretas Shopping (Map p500), Tres Cruces Shopping (above the bus terminal; Map p500) and Montevideo Shopping (Map p500) in Pocitos/Buceo.

TOP CHOICE Feria de Tristán Narvaja MARKET
(Map p500; Tristán Narvaja, Cordón) This colorful Sunday-morning outdoor market is a decades-long tradition begun by Italian immigrants. It sprawls from Av 18 de Julio northwards along Calle Tristán Narvaja, spilling over onto several side streets. You can find used books, music, clothing, jewelry, live animals, antiques and souvenirs in its many makeshift stalls.

Saturday Flea Market MARKET
(Plaza Constitución, Ciudad Vieja) Every Saturday, vendors take over Ciudad Vieja's central square, selling antique door knockers, saddles, household goods and just about anything else you can imagine.

Manos del Uruguay WOOLENS
(Map p502; www.manos.com.uy; San José 1111) This national cooperative, a member of the World Fair Trade Organization, is famous for its quality woolen goods.

Imaginario Sur ARTS & CRAFTS
(Map p502; www.imaginariosur.com.uy; 25 de Mayo 265, Ciudad Vieja) This colorful, trendy shop features art, fashion and design work by dozens of Uruguayan artists.

Hecho Acá HANDICRAFTS
(Map p502; www.hechoaca.com.uy; cnr Rambla 25 de Agosto & Yacaré, Ciudad Vieja) Woolen goods and other handicrafts from around the country are nicely displayed here.

Ayuídiscos MUSIC
(www.tacuabe.com/ayui-discos; Av 18 de Julio 1618, Centro) This little store is an excellent source for Uruguayan music of all kinds.

Librería Linardi y Risso BOOKS
(Map p502; www.linardiyrisso.com; Juan Carlos Gómez 1435) Good source for photo essays on Montevideo and Uruguay, plus history, literature and out-of-print books.

Louvre ANTIQUES
(Map p502; www.louvreantiguedades.com.uy; Sarandí 652, Ciudad Vieja) The Louvre has three floors packed with antiques, including gaucho paraphernalia, paintings, furniture and jewelry.

Mercado de los Artesanos HANDICRAFTS
(Mercado de la Abundancia; ⊙10am-9pm Mon-Sat) A wide variety of artisans display their wares on the ground floor of Mercado de la Abundancia.

Information

Dangers & Annoyances

While Montevideo is pretty sedate by Latin American standards, you should exercise caution as in any large city. The Ciudad Vieja west of Plaza Matriz should be avoided at night, as wallet- and purse-snatchings are not uncommon. Montevideo's *policia turística* (tourist police) patrol the streets throughout Ciudad Vieja and the Centro and can help if you encounter any problems.

Emergency

Ambulance (☎105)
Fire (☎104)
Police (☎911)
Tourist Police (☎0800-8226)

Internet Access

Most accommodations have a guest computer in the lobby, free in-room wi-fi, or both.There are numerous internet cafes along San José and Av 18 de Julio, charging around UR$20 per hour.

Media

Montevideo's leading dailies are *El País* (www.elpais.com.uy), *El Observador* (www.elobservador.com.uy) and *Últimas Noticias* (www.ultimasnoticias.com.uy). The newsweekly *Búsqueda* (www.busqueda.com.uy) is also widely available at newsstands.

Medical Services

Hospital Británico (☎2487-1020; www.hospitalbritanico.com.uy; Av Italia 2420) Highly recommended private hospital with English-speaking doctors; 2.5km east of downtown.

Hospital Maciel (☎2915-3000; cnr 25 de Mayo & Maciel) The public hospital.

Money

Banks, exchange houses and ATMs are everywhere, including Av 18 de Julio and the bus terminal.

Banco Comercial (cnr Av 18 de Julio & Santiago de Chile) At eastern edge of downtown.

Banco de la Nación Argentina (Juan Carlos Gómez 1378) On Plaza Constitución.

Banco Santander (Av 18 de Julio 999) Opposite Plaza del Entrevero.

Indumex (Terminal Tres Cruces) Bus terminal currency exchange.

Post

Post office Centro (cnr Ejido & San José); Ciudad Vieja (Misiones 1328); Tres Cruces bus terminal (cnr Bulevar Artigas & Av Italia)

DIRECT INTERNATIONAL FLIGHTS FROM MONTEVIDEO

DESTINATION	AIRLINE
Asunción	Pluna, TAM
Buenos Aires	Pluna, Aerolineas Argentinas, Sol, BQB
Lima	Taca
Madrid	Iberia
Miami	American
Panama City	Copa
Porto Alegre, Brazil	Pluna, TAM, Gol
Rio de Janeiro	Pluna
Santiago	Pluna, LAN Chile
São Paulo	Pluna, TAM

Telephone

Antel Centro (cnr San José & Paraguay); Ciudad Vieja (Rincón 501); Tres Cruces bus terminal (cnr Bulevar Artigas & Av Italia)

Tourist Information

Municipal tourist office Centro (☎1950-2263; cnr Av 18 de Julio & Ejido; ⏲10am-4pm Mon-Fri); Ciudad Vieja (☎2916-8434; cnr Piedras & Pérez Castellanos; ⏲11am-5pm) City maps and general Montevideo information.

National Tourism Ministry Carrasco airport (☎2604-0386; ⏲8am-8pm); Port (☎2188-5111; Rambla 25 de Agosto; ⏲9am-6pm Mon-Fri); Tres Cruces bus terminal (☎2409-7399; ⏲9am-10pm) Info about Montevideo and destinations throughout Uruguay.

Getting There & Away

Air

Montevideo's stylishly redesigned **Carrasco international airport** (☎2604-0272; www.aeropuertodecarrasco.com.uy) is served by fewer airlines than Ezeiza in Buenos Aires.

One-stop service is available from London to Montevideo via Madrid, and from several other European and North American cities via Buenos Aires or São Paulo.

At the time of research, cut-rate airline BQB was initiating twice-weekly service from Montevideo to Salto, Uruguay's first regularly scheduled domestic flights in several years.

Boat

Buquebus (☎130; www.buquebus.com.uy) Centro (cnr Colonia & Florida); Ciudad Vieja (Terminal Puerto); Tres Cruces bus terminal (cnr Bulevar Artigas & Av Italia) runs daily high-speed ferries direct from Montevideo to Buenos Aires (three hours). Full *turista* class fares are UR$2005. Buquebus also offers less expensive bus-boat combinations to Buenos Aires via Colonia (slow boat UR$1047, 6¼ hours; fast boat UR$1352, 4¼ hours). Better fares for all services above are available with online advance purchase.

Even more affordable are the bus-boat combinations offered by **Colonia Express** (☎2400-3939; www.coloniaexpress.com; Tres Cruces bus terminal). Standard one-way fares for the 4¼-hour trip are UR$745 per person, but midweek rates drop as low as UR$595.

Cacciola Viajes (☎2401-9350; www.cacciolaviajes.com, in Spanish; Tres Cruces bus terminal) runs a scenic twice- to thrice-daily bus-launch service to Buenos Aires via the riverside town of Carmelo and the Argentine Delta suburb of Tigre. The eight-hour trip costs UR$899 one way.

Bus

Montevideo's modern **Tres Cruces bus terminal** (Map p500; ☎2401-8998; www.trescruces.com.

BUSES FROM MONTEVIDEO

DESTINATION	COST (UR$)	DURATION (HR)
INTERNATIONAL		
Asunción (Paraguay)	2640	21
Buenos Aires	880-980	10
Córdoba (Argentina)	1728-2075	15½
Florianópolis (Brazil)	2710	18
Porto Alegre (Brazil)	1779	12
Santiago de Chile	3257	28
São Paulo (Brazil)	3813	28
DOMESTIC		
Carmelo	297	3¼
Colonia	211	2¾
La Paloma	282	3½
La Pedrera	293	4
Mercedes	343	4
Paysandú	446	4½
Piriápolis	117	1½
Punta del Diablo	364	5
Punta del Este	170	2¼
Salto	602	6½
Tacuarembó	457	4½

uy; cnr Bulevar Artigas & Av Italia) is about 3km east of downtown. It has tourist information, clean toilets, a luggage check (UR$111 per 24 hours), public phones, ATMs and a shopping mall upstairs.

A taxi from the terminal to downtown costs UR$80 to UR$100. To save your pesos, take city bus CA1, which leaves Monday to Saturday from directly in front of the terminal (on the eastern side), traveling to Ciudad Vieja via Av Uruguay (UR$10, 15 minutes). On Sundays, take bus 21, 64, 187 or 330, all of which go to Plaza Independencia via Av 18 de Julio (UR$18, 15 minutes).

For the beach neighborhoods of Punta Carretas and Pocitos, take city buses 174 and 183, respectively, from in front of the terminal (UR$18). A taxi to either neighborhood costs around UR$100.

All destinations following are served daily (except as noted) and most several times a day. A small *tasa de embarque* (departure tax) is added to the ticket prices. Travel times are approximate.

EGA (☎2402-5164; www.ega.com.uy) provides the widest range of service to neighboring countries, running buses once weekly to Santiago, Chile (Monday) and São Paulo, Brazil (Sunday), twice weekly to Asunción, Paraguay (Wednesday and Saturday), and daily except Saturday to Porto Alegre, Brazil.

Service to Argentina is more frequent, with several competing companies offering multiple daily departures to Buenos Aires. Among other Argentine destinations, there are at least four weekly buses to Córdoba and Rosario, and one Friday departure to Paraná, Santa Fe and Mendoza.

Getting Around

To/From the Airport

From **Terminal Suburbana** (☎1975; cnr Río Branco & Galicia), five blocks north of Plaza del Entrevero, Copsa buses 700, 701, 704, 710 and 711 run to Carrasco airport (UR$32, 45 minutes). Coming from the airport, buses stop directly in front of the arrivals hall.

The 30- to 45-minute taxi ride to the airport from downtown Montevideo costs between UR$500 and UR$750, depending on time of day and place of depature. From the airport back into town, prices are higher (UR$800 to UR$1000).

Bus

Montevideo's city buses, operated by **Cutcsa** (☎2204-0000; www.cutcsa.com.uy), go almost everywhere for UR$18 per ride. For a clickable map showing which buses serve any given destination, visit www.montevideobus.com.uy (in Spanish).

Car

Most major international companies have counters at Carrasco airport. In downtown Montevideo, the following Uruguayan companies (with nationwide branches) offer good deals.

Multicar (☎2902-2555; www.redmulticar.com; Colonia 1227, Centro)

Punta Car (☎2900-2772; www.puntacar.com; Cerro Largo 1383, Centro)

Taxi

Montevideo's black-and-yellow taxis are all metered. It costs UR$25 to drop the flag (UR$30 at night and on Sunday) and roughly UR$1.50 per unit thereafter. Cabbies carry two official price tables, one effective on weekdays, the other (20% higher) used at night (between 10pm and 6am), Sundays and holidays. Even for a long ride, you'll rarely pay more than UR$150, unless you're headed to Carrasco airport.

WESTERN URUGUAY

From Colonia's tree-shaded cobblestone streets to the hot springs of Salto, the slow-paced river towns of western Uruguay have a universally relaxing appeal, with just enough urban attractions to keep things interesting. Here, the border with Argentina is defined by the Río de la Plata and the Río Uruguay, and the region is commonly referred to as *el litoral* (the shore).

Further inland you'll find the heart of what some consider the 'real' Uruguay – the gaucho country around Tacuarembó, with *estancias* sprinkled throughout the rural landscape and some beautiful, rarely visited nature preserves.

Colonia del Sacramento

POP 26,000

On the east bank of the Río de la Plata, 180km west of Montevideo, but only 50km from Buenos Aires by ferry, Colonia is an irresistibly picturesque town enshrined as a Unesco World Heritage site. Its Barrio Histórico, an irregular colonial-era nucleus of narrow cobbled streets, occupies a small peninsula jutting into the river. Pretty rows of sycamores offer protection from the summer heat, and the riverfront provides a venue for spectacular sunsets. Colonia's charm and its proximity to Buenos Aires draw thousands of Argentine visitors; on weekends, especially in summer, prices rise and it can be difficult to find a room.

Colonia was founded in 1680 by Manuel Lobo, the Portuguese governor of Rio de Janeiro, and occupied a strategic position almost exactly opposite Buenos Aires across the Río de la Plata. The town grew in importance as a source of smuggled trade items, undercutting Spain's jealously defended mercantile monopoly and provoking repeated sieges and battles between Spain and Portugal.

Although the two powers agreed over the cession of Colonia to Spain around 1750, it wasn't until 1777 that Spain took final control of the city. From this time, the city's commercial importance declined as foreign goods proceeded directly to Buenos Aires.

Sights & Activities

BARRIO HISTÓRICO

Colonia's Barrio Histórico is filled with visual delights. It's fun to just wander the streets and the waterfront. Historic Colonia's two main squares are the vast **Plaza Mayor 25 de Mayo** and the shady **Plaza de Armas**, also known as Plaza Manuel Lobo.

Portón de Campo HISTORIC SITE

(Manuel Lobo) The most dramatic way to enter Barrio Histórico is via the reconstructed 1745 city gate. From here, a thick fortified wall runs south along the Paseo de San Miguel to the river, its grassy slopes popular with sunbathers. Other famous streets include the narrow, roughly cobbled **Calle de los Suspiros** (Street of Sighs), lined with tile-and-stucco colonial houses, and the **Paseo de San Gabriel**, on the western riverfront.

Iglesia Matriz CHURCH

Plaza de Armas is the home to Uruguay's oldest church (begun in 1860), though it has been completely rebuilt twice. The plaza also holds the foundations of a house dating from Portuguese times.

Faro LIGHTHOUSE

(admission UR$15; ⌚1pm-sunset Mon-Fri, 11am-sunset Sat & Sun) One of the town's most prominent landmarks, Colonia's 19th-century lighthouse provides an excellent view of the old town. It stands within the ruins of the 17th-century **Convento de San Fran-**

cisco, just off the southwest corner of Plaza Mayor 25 de Mayo.

Puerto Viejo HISTORIC SITE
(Old Port) Colonia's yacht harbor makes for a very pleasant stroll. The nearby **Teatro Bastión del Carmen** (Rivadavia 223; admission free; ⏲10am-10pm) is a theater and gallery complex incorporating part of the city's ancient fortifications. It hosts rotating art exhibits and periodic concerts.

A single UR$50 ticket covers admission to Colonia's eight **historical museums** (☎4522-5609; museoscolonia@gmail.com; ⏲11:15am-4:45pm). All keep the same hours, but closing day varies by museum as noted following.

Museo Portugués MUSEUM
(Plaza Mayor 25 de Mayo 180; ⏲closed Wed) In this beautiful old house, you'll find Portuguese relics including porcelain, furniture, maps, Manuel Lobo's family tree and the old stone shield that once adorned the Portón de Campo.

Museo Municipal MUSEUM
(Plaza Mayor 25 de Mayo 77; ⏲closed Tue) Houses an eclectic collection of treasures including a whale skeleton, an enormous rudder from a shipwreck, historical timelines and a scale model of Colonia (c 1762).

Archivo Regional MUSEUM
(Misiones de los Tapes 115; ⏲closed Sat & Sun) On the northwest edge of the plaza, Archivo Regional contains historical documents along with pottery and glass excavated from the 18th-century Casa de los Gobernadores nearby.

Casa Nacarello MUSEUM
(Plaza Mayor 25 de Mayo 67; ⏲closed Tue) One of the prettiest colonial homes in town, with period furniture, thick whitewashed walls, wavy glass and original lintels (duck if you're tall!).

Museo Indígena MUSEUM
(Comercio s/n; ⏲closed Thu) Houses Roberto Banchero's personal collection of Charrúa stone tools, exhibits on indigenous history, and an amusing map upstairs showing how many European countries could fit inside Uruguay's borders (it's at least six!).

Museo del Azulejo MUSEUM
(cnr Misiones de los Tapes & Paseo de San Gabriel; ⏲closed Thu) This dinky 17th-century stone house has a sampling of French, Catalan and Neapolitan tilework.

Museo Español MUSEUM
(San José 164; ⏲closed Thu) Under renovation at the time of writing; has colonial pottery, clothing and maps.

REAL DE SAN CARLOS

At the turn of the 20th century, Argentine entrepreneur Nicolás Mihanovich spent US$1.5 million building an immense tourist complex 5km north of Colonia at Real de San Carlos. The complex included a 10,000-seat bullring, a 3000-seat *frontón* (court) for the Basque sport of jai alai, a hotel-casino and a racecourse.

Only the racecourse functions today, but the ruins of the remaining buildings make an interesting excursion, and the adjacent beach is popular with locals on Sundays.

Museo Paleontológico MUSEUM
(Real de San Carlos; ⏲Thu-Sun) This two-room museum displays glyptodon shells, bones and other locally excavated finds from the private collection of self-taught palaeontologist Armando Calcaterra.

Tours

The tourist office outside the old town gate organizes good **walking tours** led by local guides. Spanish-language tours (per person UR$100) leave at 11am and 3pm daily, with additional sunset tours at 7pm from November through Easter. For tours in other languages (per person UR$150), contact the tourist office or Colonia's **Asociación de Guías Profesionales** (☎099-379167; asociacionguiascolonia@gmail.com).

Gabriel Gaidano CAR TOUR
(☎099-806106; 1929vintage@gmail.com; per 15min/hr UR$200/600) Spins around town for up to four people in his 1929 Model A convertible. Look for him on Plaza de Armas.

Sleeping

Some hotels charge higher rates Friday through Sunday. Summer weekends are best avoided or booked well in advance.

Posada Plaza Mayor INN $$$
(☎4522-3193; www.posadaplazamayor.com; Comercio 111; d UR$2200-3000, ste UR$3400-3800; ❄@📶) Near the river in the heart of historic Colonia, the Playa Mayor comprises two colonial houses. The stone-walled, high-ceilinged 19th-century Spanish rooms surround a beautiful courtyard with a fountain; the adjoining 18th-century Portuguese structure houses several lovely common areas.

Colonia del Sacramento

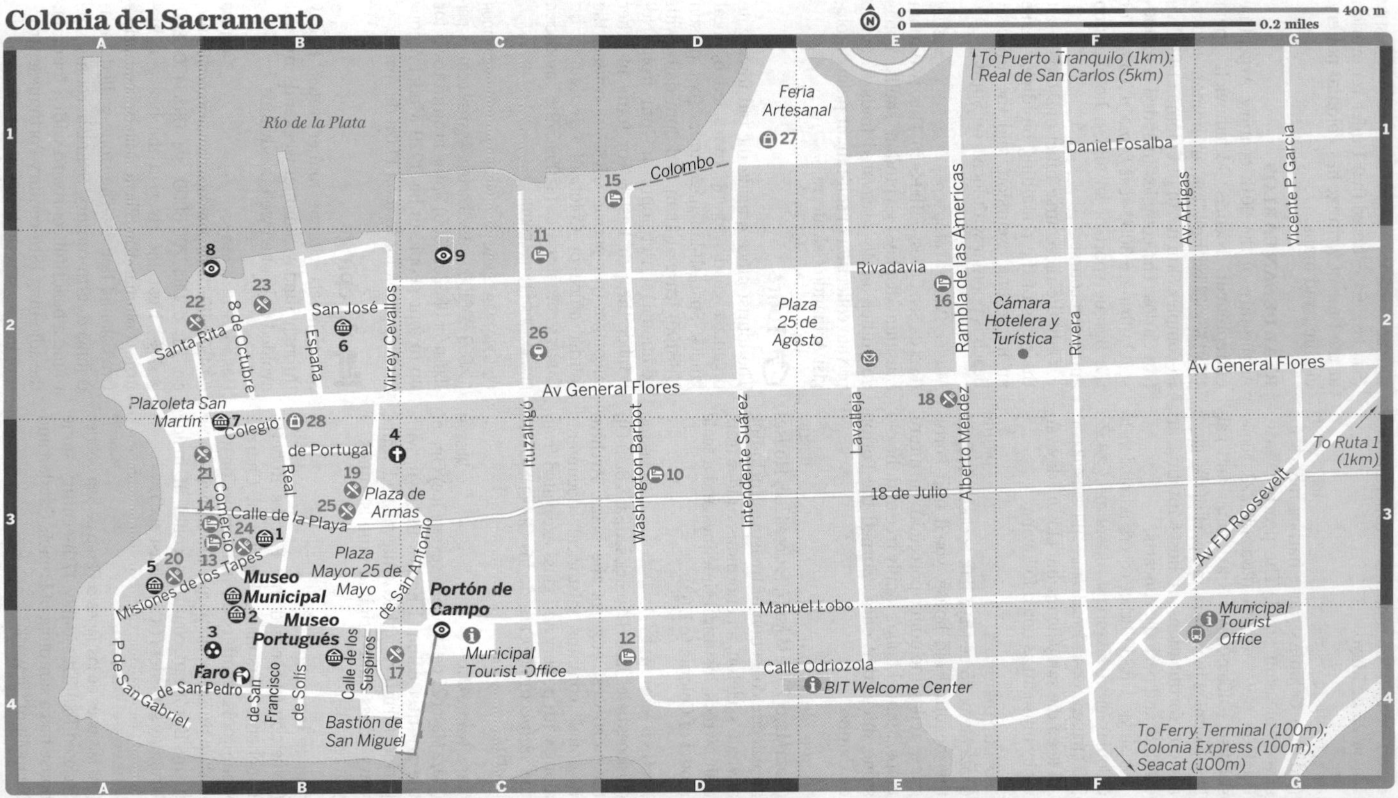

Colonia del Sacramento

Posada de la Flor HOTEL $$

(4523-0794; www.posada-delaflor.com; Ituzaingó 268; r with fan/air-con UR$1500/1900;) Serenely situated on a sycamore-lined street that ends at a small beach, the Flor's biggest draw is its upstairs terrace with lounge chairs overlooking the river.

El Viajero Hostel HOSTEL $

(4522-2683; www.coloniahostel.com; Washington Barbot 164; dm UR$340-380, d UR$1200-1600;) With bike rental, horseback excursions, a bar for guests and air-con in all rooms, this hostel is brighter, fancier and somewhat cozier than the competition, and the location two blocks east of Plaza de Armas couldn't be better.

Radisson Colonia Hotel LUXURY HOTEL $$$

(4523-0460; www.radissoncolonia.com; Washington Barbot 283; s/d weekends from UR$4100/5200, weekdays from UR$2700/3000;) If you value chain-hotel comforts over colonial charm, the Radisson has what you're looking for. This all-in-one facility features two pools and a spacious deck overlooking the river, plus sauna, gym, solarium, children's play area and garage. Visit during the week for much better rates.

Posada San Gabriel INN $$

(4522-3283; www.posadasangabriel.com.uy; Comercio 127; r downstairs/upstairs UR$1430/1540;) This simple six-room posada (inn) features stone walls, brass beds and a prime old town location. The two upstairs rooms with river views are well worth the extra pesos.

Posada del Ángel HOTEL $$

(4522-4602; www.posadadelangel.net; Washington Barbot 59; d standard/superior UR$1600/2400;) Cheerfully painted in yellow and periwinkle blue, this little hotel has amenities such as down comforters and a sauna for chilly nights and a swimming pool for the summer heat. Standard interior-facing rooms are dark; it's worth splurging on one with a view.

Sur Hostel HOSTEL $

(4522-0553; www.surhostel.com; Rivadavia 448; dm UR$340-400, s UR$700-1000, d UR$1000-1200;) The newest of Colonia's hostels, this place has a mix of private rooms and four- to eight-bed dorms, all with private bathrooms. There's a spacious guest kitchen and an upstairs sun terrace for clotheswashing and weekly barbecues (UR$150).

Eating & Drinking

Buen Suspiro PICADAS $$

(www.buensuspiro.com; San José 111; picadas from UR$170; 11am-midnight Thu-Tue) Duck your head as you pass under the wood beams in this cozy spot specializing in *picadas* (little snacks eaten with a toothpick). Sample local wines by the bottle or the glass, accompanied by spinach and leek tarts, ricotta-and-sesame balls, slices of local cheese and sausage, and more. Reserve ahead for a table by

WORTH A TRIP

ESTANCIA LIVING ON A LIMITED BUDGET

What do you get when you cross a tourist *estancia* and a hostel? Find out at the unique **Hostel Estancia El Galope** (☎099-105985; www.elgalope.com.uy; Cno Concordia; dm UR$500, d with shared/private bathroom UR$1400/1800) in the countryside 115km from Montevideo and 60km from Colonia. Experienced world travelers Mónica and Miguel offer guests a chance to settle into the relaxing rhythms of rural life, sharing stories by starlight late into the night. Optional activities include horseback rides (UR$600) and cycling (rental bikes provided). There's a sauna and a teeny-weeny pool to cool off in. Breakfast is included; other meals, from fondue to full-fledged *asados* (barbecues) are available for UR$180 to UR$280. Pickup from the bus stop in nearby Colonia Valdense is available upon request.

the fireplace in winter, or while away a summer afternoon on the intimate back patio.

La Bodeguita PIZZERIA **$$**
(www.labodeguita.net; Comercio 167; mini pizzas UR$80-95, dishes UR$270-350; ⏲dinner daily year-round, lunch Sat & Sun Apr-Nov) Nab a table out back on the sunny two-level deck and soak up the sweeping river views while drinking sangría (UR$195 per liter) or munching on La Bodeguita's mini pizzas, served on a cutting board.

El Rincón PARRILLA **$$**
(Misiones de los Tapes 41; dishes UR$200-320; ⏲lunch Thu-Tue, plus dinner Thu-Tue Dec-Easter) *Parrillada* (mixed grill) is king at El Rincón. It's best enjoyed on a sunny weekend afternoon, lounging out back under a big tree between stone and red-stucco walls, listening to Brazilian music or tango, and watching the riverfront scene as the outdoor grill exudes intoxicating smoky smells.

Puerto Tranquilo SEAFOOD **$$$**
(Rambla de las Américas s/n; dishes UR$280-400; ⏲11am-sunset) Specializing in freshly caught fish with wok-sautéed vegetables, this 'resto-bar' 1km north of town makes a great getaway from historic Colonia's touristy madness. Everything is served on the bamboo-shaded outdoor deck, where you can watch the sunset and get a picture-postcard view of locals splashing in the river or playing soccer and sunbathing on the sandy beach below. The restaurant also offers massages and other spa services.

Lentas Maravillas SANDWICHES, TEAHOUSE **$$**
(Santa Rita 61; sandwiches UR$200-270; ⏲2-7:30pm) Cozy as a friend's home, this is a dreamy spot to kick back with tea and cookies or a glass of wine and a sandwich between meals. Flip through an art book from owner Maggie Molnar's personal library and enjoy the incomparable river views, either from the upstairs fireplace room or the chairs on the grassy lawn below.

El Drugstore INTERNATIONAL **$$$**
(Portugal 174; tapas from UR$110, mains UR$175-490; ⏲noon-midnight) This funky corner place on Plaza de Armas is fun for a meal or a drink, with vividly colored, eclectically decorated walls, an open kitchen, fridges painted with clouds and elephants, and a vintage car on the cobblestones doubling as a romantic dining nook. Half of the 24-page menu is devoted to drinks; the other half to tapas and full meals, including a few vegetarian offerings. There's frequent live guitar music.

Pulpería de los Faroles SEAFOOD **$$**
(www.pulperiadelosfarolesrestaurant.com; Misiones de los Tapes 101; dishes UR$200-350; ⏲noon-midnight) Specializing in seafood and pasta, this eatery has a rainbow of colorful tablecloths in the artsy interior dining room, plus a sea of informal outdoor seating on Plaza Mayor 25 de Mayo. Half portions (UR$190) of several mains are available for light eaters and solo travelers.

Viejo Barrio ITALIAN **$$**
(Vasconcellos 169; dishes UR$220-300; ⏲lunch & dinner Thu-Mon, lunch Tue) Whether you're amused or annoyed by the eccentric waiter and his funny hats, Viejo Barrio remains a perennial old-town favorite thanks to its excellent homemade pasta and picturesque setting on historic Plaza de Armas.

Confitería La Pasiva CONFITERÍA **$**
(Av General Flores 444; dishes from UR$125; ⏲8am-1am) This bright, bustling chain *confitería* is dependable for breakfast, pizza or sandwiches any time of day.

Patrimonio BAR $$

(San José 111; dishes UR$190-270; ⏰noon-2am Thu-Tue) Colorful boards display the menu at this artsy resto-bar with its cavernous interior and tree- and umbrella-shaded riverfront terrace. Offerings include two-for-one drink specials, salads, burgers, homemade ravioli and reasonably priced *platos del día*.

Matamala Bar BAR

(Ituzaingó 222; ⏰9pm-late Thu-Sun) This little nightclub and bar with a fireplace makes a chic choice for tapas and drinks.

Shopping

Feria Artesanal HANDICRAFTS

(cnr Intendente Suárez & Daniel Fosalba; ⏰10am-7pm or 8pm) This handicrafts market, open daily, is on the northern waterfront.

Malvón WOOLENS

(☎4522-1793; Av General Flores 100; ⏰11am-7pm) Sells woolens from the national cooperative Manos del Uruguay, along with other Uruguayan handicrafts.

Information

Antel Barrio Histórico (Av General Flores 172); Centro (cnr Lavalleja & Rivadavia) Internet for UR$45 per hour.

BBVA (Av General Flores 299) One of several ATMs along General Flores.

BIT Welcome Center (☎4522-1072; www.bitcolonia.com; Odriozola 434; ⏰10am-7pm) Colonia's sparkling new welcome center, just across from the port, has tourist information, touch-screen information displays, a 'Welcome to Uruguay' video presentation and more.

Cámara Hotelera y Turística (☎4522-7302; cnr Av General Flores & Rivera; ⏰11am-6pm) Helps with hotel bookings.

Hospital Colonia (☎4522-2994; 18 de Julio 462)

Post office (Lavalleja 226)

Tourist offices (☎4522-3700; www.coloniaturismo.com) Barrio Histórico (Manuel Lobo 224; ⏰10am-6pm); Bus Terminal (Av Roosevelt; ⏰10am-6pm)

BUSES FROM COLONIA DEL SACRAMENTO

The following destinations are served at least twice daily.

DESTINATION	COST (UR$)	DURATION (HR)
Carmelo	94	1¼
Mercedes	211	3½
Montevideo	211	2¾
Paysandú	387	6
Salto	528	8

Getting There & Away

Boat

From the ferry terminal at the foot of Rivera, **Buquebus** (www.buquebus.com.uy; Av Roosevelt) runs two slow boats (UR$775, three hours) plus three or more fast boats (UR$1070, one hour) daily to Buenos Aires.

Colonia Express (www.coloniaexpress.com) and **Seacat** (www.seacatcolonia.com) run less frequent but more affordable high-speed ferry services. Each company offers two to three departures daily. Crossings take one hour, with day-of-departure fares ranging from UR$650 to UR$860.

All three companies offer child, senior and advance-purchase discounts.

Immigration for both countries is handled at the port before boarding.

Bus

Colonia's modern **bus terminal** (cnr Manuel Lobo & Av Roosevelt) is conveniently located near the port, within easy walking distance of the Barrio Histórico. It has tourist information, luggage storage (per day UR$100), money-changing and internet facilities.

Getting Around

Walking is enjoyable in compact Colonia, but motor scooters, bicycles and gas-powered buggies are popular alternatives. **Thrifty** (☎4522-2939; Av General Flores 172; bicycle/scooter/golf cart per hr UR$60/140/240, per 24hr UR$300/600/1000) rents everything from beater bikes to cars. Several other agencies rent cars (per day from UR$1000) and motorbikes near the bus and ferry terminals, including **Multicar/Moto Rent** (Manuel Lobo 505) and **Punta Car** (cnr 18 de Julio & Rivera).

Local buses go to the beaches and bullring at Real de San Carlos (UR$15) from along Av General Flores.

Carmelo

POP 18,000

Carmelo, dating from 1816, is a laid-back town of cobblestone streets and low old houses, a center for yachting, fishing and exploring the Paraná Delta. It straddles the Arroyo de las Vacas, a stream that widens into a sheltered harbor just below the Río Uruguay's confluence with the Río de la Plata. The town center, north of the arroyo (creek), is Plaza Independencia. South of the arroyo lies a large park with open space, camping, swimming and a huge casino.

Launches connect Carmelo to the Buenos Aires suburb of Tigre.

Sights & Activities

The arroyo, with large, rusty boats moored along it, makes for a great ramble, as does the 30-minute stroll to the beaches across the bridge.

Local wines have an excellent reputation. Just outside town (look for the gigantic wine bottle!), **Bodega Irurtia** (☎4542-2323; www.irurtia.com.uy; Av Paraguay, Km2.3) produces award-winning tannats and pinot noirs. Visitors can take a basic tour of the cellars (UR$60), a vineyard walk followed by wine, cheese and grappa tasting (UR$240) or a vintage car tour and top-shelf wine tasting with multilingual guide (UR$740).

Sleeping & Eating

TOP CHOICE **Bodega y Granja Narbona** ITALIAN $$$
(☎4540-4778; www.narbona.com.uy; Hwy 21, Km 267; dishes UR$300-460; ⏰9am-11pm) A refined rural retreat set amidst vineyards, orchards and verdant farm country 20km from Carmelo, this is a worthwhile detour for anyone with a car. The restored 1908 farmstead houses a simple restaurant with outdoor seating on a tiled terrace; the menu features homemade bread, gourmet pasta, vegetables from the adjoining organic garden and fabulous Tannat and *grappamiel* (grape brandy with honey) from Narbona's award-winning cellars. Inside you can browse shelves stacked floor to ceiling with locally produced olive oil, peach preserves and *dulce de leche* (milk caramel). There's a small posada (inn) out back, if you decide to stick around.

Camping Náutico Carmelo CAMPGROUND $
(☎4542-2058; dnhcarmelo@adinet.com.uy; Arroyo de las Vacas s/n; per tent UR$200) South of the arroyo, this pleasant tree-shaded campground with hot showers caters to yachties but accepts walk-ins too.

Hotel Rambla HOTEL $$
(☎4542-2390; www.ciudadcarmelo.com/rambla hotel; Uruguay 51; r UR$1200-1700; ❄📶) The blocky Rambla won't win any design awards, but it's conveniently close to the launch docks. The upstairs doubles with balconies facing the arroyo are cheerier than the interior rooms.

Piccolino URUGUAYAN $
(☎4542-4850; cnr 19 de Abril & Roosevelt; dishes UR$110-190; ⏰9am-midnight) This corner place has decent *chivitos* and views of the square.

BUSES FROM CARMELO

DESTINATION	COST (UR$)	DURATION (HR)
Colonia	94	1½
Mercedes	117	2
Montevideo	282	3½
Paysandú	282	5
Salto	422	7

Information

Antel (Barrios 329)

Banco Comercial (Uruguay 403) On Plaza Independencia.

Hospital (☎4542-2107; cnr Uruguay & Artigas)

Municipal tourist kiosks Playa Seré (⏰10am-10pm Jan-Mar, 10am-6pm Sat & Sun Apr-Dec) Plaza Independencia (⏰9am-6pm) On the main square and in the park near the campground.

New Generation Cyber Games (Uruguay 373; internet per hr UR$20; ⏰8am-midnight)

Post office (Uruguay 360)

Getting There & Away

Cacciola (☎4542-7551; www.cacciolaviajes.com; Wilson Ferreira 263; ⏰4:30-5:30am & 9am-7:30pm) runs twice-daily launches (thrice-daily in summer) to the Buenos Aires suburb of Tigre. The one-way 2½-hour trip costs UR$559, plus a UR$150 tax collected upon arrival in Tigre.

All bus companies are on or near Plaza Independencia. **Berrutti** (☎4542-2504; Uruguay 337) has the most frequent service to Colonia; **Chadre** (☎4542-2987) is the best bet for all other destinations.

Mercedes

POP 41,000

Capital of the department of Soriano, Mercedes is a livestock center with cobblestoned streets and a small pedestrian zone around the 18th-century cathedral on central Plaza

Independencia. The town's most appealing feature is its leafy waterfront along the south bank of the Río Negro.

Sights & Activities

Activities along the riverfront include boating, fishing and swimming along the sandy beaches, or simply strolling along the Rambla (especially popular on Sunday afternoons). The tourist office sells tickets for the **Catamaran Soriano I**, a cruise boat that began offering excursions on the Río Negro and Río San Salvador in summer 2011.

FREE Museo Paleontológico Alejandro Berro MUSEUM
(☎4532-3290; Parque Castillo Mauá; ⏰11am-5pm) In an old, white, castle-like building about 6km west of town, this museum displays a substantial fossil collection and an impressively well-preserved glyptodon shell discovered in a nearby riverbank in early 2010.

Sleeping & Eating

Camping del Hum CAMPGROUND $
(☎4532-2733; Isla del Puerto; sites per person/tent UR$20/40) Mercedes' spacious campground, one of the region's best, occupies half the Isla del Puerto in the Río Negro. Connected to the mainland by a bridge, it has swimming, fishing and sanitary facilities.

TOP CHOICE Estancia La Sirena ESTANCIA $$$
(☎4530-2271, 9910-2130; www.lasirena.com.uy, in Spanish; R 14, Km4.5; s incl breakfast/half-board/full board UR$1950/2600/3100, d UR$1950/4000/5200) Surrounded by rolling open country 15km upriver from Mercedes, this *estancia* is one of Uruguay's oldest and most beautiful. The spacious 1830 ranch house, with its cozy parlor and fireplaces, makes a perfect base for relaxation and excursions to the nearby river on foot or horseback. The isolated setting is perfect for stargazing, and the homemade food, often cooked on a giant outdoor grill, is delicious. Perfect hosts Rodney and Lucía Bruce speak English, French and Spanish.

Martín Fierro INTERNATIONAL $$
(☎4532-0877; Rambla Costanera s/n; dishes UR$90-210; ⏰lunch & dinner Tue-Sun) The riverfront setting at the foot of 18 de Julio is complemented by a varied menu featuring homemade pasta, grilled meat and fish, and wild cards such as the warm salad of wok-sauteed vegetables.

BUSES FROM MERCEDES

The following destinations are served at least once daily.

DESTINATION	COST (UR$)	DURATION (HR)
Buenos Aires	620	7
Carmelo	117	2
Colonia	211	3
Montevideo	338	3½-4½
Paysandú	148	2
Salto	327	4

Shopping

Lanas de Soriano WOOLENS
(☎4532-2158; www.lanasdesoriano.com, in Spanish; Colón 60; ⏰9am-noon Mon-Sat, 3-7pm Mon-Fri) A rainbow of beautiful handmade woolens is available in this shop, hidden away in a residential neighborhood near the waterfront.

Information

Antel (Roosevelt 681; internet per hr UR$19) Provides phone and internet service.

Banco Comercial (Giménez 719) ATM on Plaza Independencia.

Hospital Mercedes (☎4532-2177; cnr Sánchez & Rincón)

Municipal tourist office (☎4532-2733; turismo@soriano.gub.uy; Detomasi 415; ⏰8am-9pm) In a crumbling white building near the bridge to the campground.

Post office (cnr Rodó & 18 de Julio)

Getting There & Away

Mercedes' modern **bus terminal** (Plaza General Artigas) is about 10 blocks from Plaza Independencia, in a shopping center with ATMs, a post office, free public bathrooms, luggage storage and an emergency medical clinic. A local bus (UR$13) leaves hourly from just in front of the terminal, making a circuit around downtown.

Paysandú

POP 76,000

On the east bank of the Río Uruguay, connected to Colón, Argentina by the Puente Internacional General Artigas, Uruguay's third-largest city is just a stopover for most travelers en route to or from Argentina. The activity is on Plaza Constitución, six blocks north of the bus terminal.

WORTH A TRIP

THE LITTLE BEEF CUBE THAT CIRCLED THE GLOBE

In 1865, the Liebig Extract of Meat Company located its pioneer South American plant southwest of downtown Fray Bentos. It soon became Uruguay's most important industrial complex. British-run El Anglo took over operations in the 1920s and by WWII the factory employed 4000 people, slaughtering cattle at the astronomical rate of 2000 a day.

Looking at the abandoned factory today, you'd never guess that its signature product, the Oxo beef cube, once touched millions of lives on every continent. Oxo cubes sustained WWI soldiers in the trenches, Jules Verne sang their praises in his book *Around the Moon*, Stanley brought them on his search for Livingstone, Scott and Hillary took them to Antarctica and Everest. More than 25,000 people from more than 60 countries worked here, and at its peak the factory was exporting nearly 150 different products, using every part of the cow except its moo.

The former factory is now a museum – the **Museo de la Revolución Industrial** (☎4562-3690; admission UR$30, guided tour UR$50; ⏲9:30am-5pm Mar-Dec, 8am-8:30pm Jan & Feb). Guided tours (10am Monday to Saturday, 11am Sunday, plus 6pm daily in summer, 3pm daily rest of year) grant access to the intricate maze of passageways, corrals and abandoned slaughterhouses behind the museum.

Inside the factory dozens of colorful displays – ranging from the humorous to the poignant – bring this history vividly to life: a giant cattle scale where school groups are invited to weigh themselves; or the old company office upstairs, left exactly as it was when the factory closed in 1979, with grooves rubbed into the floor by the foot of an accountant who sat at the same desk for decades.

The adjacent town of Fray Bentos, with its pretty riverfront promenade, is the southernmost overland crossing over the Río Uruguay from Argentina. It's four hours by bus from Colonia or Buenos Aires, or 4½ hours from Montevideo.

Founded as a mid-18th-century outpost of cattle herders from the Jesuit mission at Yapeyú (in present-day Argentina), Paysandú gradually rose to prominence as a meat-processing center. Repeated sieges of the city during the 19th century (the last in 1864–65) earned it the local nickname 'the American Troy.'

Despite its turbulent history and its ongoing status as a major industrial center, modernday Paysandú is surprisingly sedate. To see the city's wilder side, visit during Carnaval or the annual week-long **beer festival** (held during Semana Santa).

Sights & Activities

FREE **Museo de la Tradición** MUSEUM
(☎4722-3125; Av de Los Iracundos 5; ⏲8am-4:45pm Mon-Sat, 1-6pm Sun) In parkland near the riverfront, this museum features a small but well-displayed selection of anthropological artifacts and gaucho gear.

FREE **Museo Histórico** MUSEUM
(☎4722-6220 ext 247; Av Zorrilla 874; ⏲8am-4:45pm Mon-Fri, 9am-1:45pm Sat) Displays evocative images from the multiple 19th-century sieges of Paysandú, including the bullet-riddled shell of the cathedral and women in exile watching the city's bombardment from an island offshore.

Teatro Florencio Sánchez THEATER
(☎4722-6220 ext 170; 19 de Abril 926) Uruguay's oldest theater (1876) outside of Montevideo, has many original features (including the curtain) and hosts occasional performances.

The latter two attractions were closed for renovation at the time of research but expected to reopen in 2012.

Sleeping

Hotel Casagrande HOTEL $$$
(☎4722-4994; www.hotelcasagrande.com.uy; Florida 1221; s/tw/d UR$1353/1974/2090; ❄@🛜) Homey and conveniently located, the Casagrande is Paysandú's nicest downtown hotel. Comfy armchairs, marble tabletops and big brass beds are among the boutique hotel amenities justifying the higher price tag.

Estancia La Paz ESTANCIA $$$
(☎4720-2272; www.estancialapaz.com.uy; Ruta 24, Km 86.5; r UR$2134; ❄@🛜🏊) The tennis courts, swimming pool and Muzak-filled common areas feel incongruous among the historic buildings and pristine natural set-

ting at this tourist *estancia* 30km southeast of Paysandú. Serious equestrians will appreciate the horseback-riding excursions, lasting from one day to a full week. Access is via a long dirt road: turn off at Km 86.5 on Ruta 24 or Km 336 on Ruta 3.

Hotel Rafaela HOTEL $
(☎4722-4216; 18 de Julio 1181; s/d with fan & shared bathroom UR$480/650, with air-con & private bathroom UR$700/950; ❄) Offering decent value just west of the main square; Rafaela's rooms are dark but large, and some have their own small patios.

Eating & Drinking

Pan Z URUGUAYAN $$
(☎4722-9551; cnr 18 de Julio & Setembrino Pereda; dishes UR$140 350; ⊙lunch & dinner) Popular 'Panceta' serves pizza, *chivitos* stacked high with every ingredient imaginable, and tasty desserts such as strawberry cake and tiramisu.

Los Tres Pinos PARRILLA $$
(www.lostrespinos.com.uy, in Spanish; Av España 1474; dishes UR$90-290; ⊙lunch & dinner) Carnivores will swoon over the excellent *parrilla* at this place five blocks east of Plaza Constitución, while budget travelers will appreciate the UR$90 *plato del día*.

Confitería Las Familias SWEETS $
(www.postrechaja.com, in Spanish; 18 de Julio 1152; chajá UR$50; ⊙9am-8pm) If you've got a sweet tooth (and we mean a *really* sweet tooth) pull up a stool at this ancient confectioner's shop and sample one of Uruguay's classic desserts: *chajá*, a dentist-friendly concoction of sugary meringue, fruit and cream invented here in 1927.

☆ Entertainment

Along the waterfront, Paysandú's intimate, tree-encircled **Teatro de Verano** is just across the street from the larger **Anfiteatro del Río Uruguay**, which seats up to 20,000 people and hosts major concerts during Paysandú's annual beer festival. Check with the tourist office for details of upcoming events at both venues.

Information

Antel (Montevideo 875)

Banco Santander (18 de Julio 1137) One of several ATMs along Paysandú's main street.

Hospital Escuela del Litoral (☎4722-4836; Montecaseros 520) South of the bus terminal.

Net One (Leandro Gómez 1193; internet per hr UR$12; ⊙24hr) Noisy with adolescent gamers, but open all night.

Post office (cnr 18 de Julio & Montevideo)

Tourist office Centro (☎4722-6220 ext 184; turismo@paysandu.gub.uy; 18 de Julio 1226; ⊙7am-8pm Mon-Fri, 10am-8pm Sat & Sun); Port (☎4722-9235; plandelacosta@paysandu.gub.uy; Av de Los Iracundos; ⊙noon-6pm Mon-Fri, 2-7pm Sat & Sun) First office is on Plaza Constitución; latter is next to Museo de la Tradición.

Getting There & Away

Paysandú's **bus terminal** (cnr Artigas & Av Zorrilla), six blocks due south of Plaza Constitución, is a hub for travel to and from Argentina.

BUSES FROM PAYSANDÚ

DESTINATION	COST (UR$)	DURATION (HR)	FREQUENCY
Asunción (Paraguay)	2640	17	5:30pm Wed & Sat
Buenos Aires	508-578	5½	12:40am nightly
Carmelo	282	5	twice daily
Colón (Argentina)	69	¾	frequent
Colonia	387	6	twice daily
Córdoba (Argentina)	1168	11	10:30pm Friday
Mercedes	144	2½	twice daily
Montevideo	452	4½	frequent
Paraná (Argentina)	617	4½	10:30pm Friday
Salto	144	2	frequent
Santa Fe (Argentina)	648	5½	10:30pm Friday
Tacuarembó	290	3½	twice daily

Salto

POP 103,000

Built near the falls where the Río Uruguay makes its 'big jump' (Salto Grande), Salto is Uruguay's second-largest city and the most northerly crossing point to Argentina. It's a relaxed place with some 19th-century architecture and a pretty riverfront. People come here for the nearby hot springs and the recreation area above the enormous Salto Grande hydroelectric dam.

Sights & Activities

Salto's **museums** (☎4732-9898) all close during January.

FREE **Museo de Bellas Artes y Artes Decorativas** MUSEUM
(Uruguay 1067; ⊙4-9pm Tue-Sat, 5-8pm Sun) Displays a nice collection of Uruguayan painting and sculpture in a historic two-story mansion with a grand staircase, stained glass and back garden.

FREE **Museo del Hombre y la Tecnología** MUSEUM
(cnr Av Brasil & Zorrilla; ⊙4-9pm) Housed in a historic market building and features excellent displays on local cultural development and history upstairs, and a small archaeological section downstairs.

Teatro Larrañaga THEATER
(Joaquín Suárez 39; ⊙4-9pm Mon-Sat) A red velvet- and chandelier-bedecked theater dating to 1882, it is open for visits and hosts occasional dance and theater performances.

Represa Salto Grande DAM
(☎4732-6131; ⊙8am-4pm) This massive hydroelectric dam, 14km north of town, provides 65% of Uruguay's electricity and is a symbol of national pride. Free hour-long guided tours visit both the Uruguayan and Argentine sides (no minimum group size, maximum wait 30 minutes). There's no public transport; a taxi from Salto costs about UR$700 roundtrip. En route, check out the stands selling freshly squeezed orange juice for UR$20 a liter!

Sleeping

Nearby hot springs also offer accommodations.

Gran Hotel Concordia HOTEL $$
(☎4733-2735; www.granhotelconcordia.com.uy, in Spanish; Uruguay 749; s/d UR$650/1200; ❄📶) This 1860s relic is a national historical monument and indisputably Salto's most atmos-

DON'T MISS

SALTO'S HOT SPRINGS

A whole slew of hot springs bubbles up around Salto.

Termas San Nicanor (☎4730-2209; www.sannicanor.com.uy, in Spanish; Ruta 3, Km 475; campsite/dm per person UR$200/410, d with shared/private bathroom UR$1350/1640; 📶🏊) Surrounded by a vast pastoral landscape, this is the most tranquil option. It has two gigantic outdoor thermal pools, a restaurant, and accommodations for every budget, including a high-ceilinged *estancia* house with large fireplaces and peacocks strolling the grounds. The 12km unpaved access road leaves Ruta 3 10km south of Salto. **Santa Lucia Bus** (☎099-732368) runs twice-daily shuttles (UR$50, one hour) from Salto.

Termas de Daymán (www.termasdedayman.com, in Spanish) About 8km south of Salto, Daymán is a heavily developed Disneyland of thermal baths complete with kids' water park. It's popular with Uruguayan and Argentine tourists who roam the town's block-long main street in bathrobes. For comfortable accommodations adjacent to the springs, try **La Posta del Daymán** (☎4736-9801; www.lapostadeldayman.com, in Spanish; campsite per person UR$100, r per person incl breakfast UR$700 1200; 📶🏊) Buses to the baths (UR$14) leave Salto's port via Av Brasil at 30 minutes past every hour (6:30am to 10:30pm), returning hourly from 7am to 11pm.

Termas de Arapey (www.termasarapey.com, in Spanish) About 90km northeast of Salto, Arapey offers multiple pools surrounded by gardens, fountains and paths to the Río Arapey Grande. Lodging is available at **Hotel Municipal** (☎4768-2441; www.hoteltermasdelarapey.com, in Spanish; s/d UR$1160/1590; ❄📶🏊). **Argentur** (☎4732-9931) runs one daily bus (two on Monday, Wednesday and Friday) from Salto (UR$125, 1½ hours).

pheric downtown hotel. A life-size wooden cutout of Carlos Gardel, who once stayed in room 32, greets you at the end of a marble corridor opening into a leafy courtyard filled with murals, sculptures and cats. Front rooms, with tall French-shuttered windows, overlook the courtyard. Back rooms flank a wrought-iron terrace, shaded by vines.

Salto Hostel HOSTEL $
(☎4733-7157; www.saltohostel.com; Uruguay 941; dm/d with shared bathroom UR$360/880; ⊙early-Mar–late Nov; @☜) In Salto's historic center, this comfortable hostel features spacious common areas, convenient computer facilities and helpful staff. Front dorms have tall windows overlooking the busy main street – great for light and air circulation, but it can get noisy at night.

Hotel Horacio Quiroga HOTEL $$$
(☎4733-4411; www.hotelhoracioquiroga.com; Parque del Lago, Salto Grande; s/d incl breakfast from UR$2200/3000, full board from UR$3200/5000; ❄@☜≋) On the lake above the dam, the luxurious Quiroga has its own thermal baths and spa facilities. Lakeview rooms are especially nice, with balconies overlooking the swimming pools and verdant grounds.

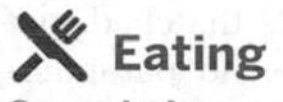

Eating

Casa de Lamas URUGUAYAN $$$
(☎4732-9376; Chiazzaro 20; dishes UR$120-345; ⊙dinner Wed, lunch & dinner Thu-Mon) This swank eatery is housed in a 19th-century building with pretty vaulted brickwork in the dining room. There's an excellent *menú de la casa* (set menu) for UR$315.

La Caldera PARRILLA $$
(Uruguay 221; dishes UR$100-240; ⊙lunch & dinner Tue-Sun) With fresh breezes blowing in off the river and sunny outdoor seating, this *parrilla* makes a great lunch stop; at dinnertime, the cozy interior dining room, with its view of the blazing fire, is equally atmospheric.

La Trattoria URUGUAYAN $$
(Uruguay 754; dishes UR$115-230; ⊙lunch & dinner) Locals flock to this high-ceilinged downtown eatery for fish, meat and pasta. Sit in the wood-paneled dining room or people-watch from a sidewalk table on busy Calle Uruguay.

Information

Antel (Grito de Asencio 33)

Banco Comercial (cnr Uruguay & Lavalleja) One of several banks at this intersection.

Cibertotal (Uruguay 635; per hr UR$20; ⊙9am-midnight) Downtown internet access.

Hospital Regional Salto (☎4733-3333; cnr 18 de Julio & Varela)

Post office (cnr Artigas & Treinta y Tres)

Tourist office (☎4733-4096; turismo@salto.gub.uy) bus terminal (⊙8am-11pm); Centro; (Uruguay 1052; ⊙8am-8pm Mon-Sat)

Getting There & Away

Air

From Salto's airport, 6km south of town, **BQB Lineas Aereas** (☎4733-8919; www.flybqb.com) offers thrice-weekly flights (Monday, Wednesday and Friday) to Montevideo's Carrasco airport.

Boat

Transporte Fluvial San Cristóbal (☎4733-2461; cnr Av Brasil & Costanera Norte) runs launches across the river to Concordia, Argentina (UR$100, 15 minutes) four times daily between 9:30am and 7:30pm, except Sunday.

Bus

Salto's **bus terminal** (Salto Shopping Center, cnr Ruta 3 & Av Batlle), 2km east of downtown,

BUSES FROM SALTO

DESTINATION	COST (UR$)	DURATION (HR)	FREQUENCY
Buenos Aires	668-738	7½	11pm nightly
Concordia (Argentina)	81	1	twice daily
Colonia	528	8	twice daily
Montevideo	587	6½	frequent
Paysandú	141	2	frequent
Tacuarembó	340	4	early am Mon, Wed & Fri

Connect in Concordia for additional Argentine destinations.

has ATMs, internet facilities, free public restrooms and a supermarket.

Tacuarembó

POP 54,000

In the rolling hills along the Cuchilla de Haedo, Tacuarembó is gaucho country. Not your 'we pose for pesos' types, but your real-deal 'we tuck our baggy pants into our boots and slap on a beret just to go to the local store' crew. It's also the alleged birthplace of tango legend Carlos Gardel.

Capital of its department, Tacuarembó has sycamore-lined streets and attractive plazas that make it one of Uruguay's most agreeable interior towns. The town center is Plaza 19 de Abril, linked by the main thoroughfares 25 de Mayo and 18 de Julio.

Sights

FREE Museo del Indio y del Gaucho MUSEUM
(cnr Flores & Artigas; ⏲8am-2pm Tue-Fri, 9am-1pm Sat) Paying romantic tribute to Uruguay's gauchos and indigenous peoples, this museum's collection includes stools made from leather and cow bones, elegantly worked silver spurs and other accessories of rural life.

Festivals & Events

Fiesta de la Patria Gaucha GAUCHO FESTIVAL
(www.patriagaucha.com.uy, in Spanish) In the first or second week of March, this colorful five-day festival attracts visitors from around the country to exhibitions of traditional gaucho skills, music and other activities. It takes place in Parque 25 de Agosto, north of town.

Sleeping & Eating

Yvytu Itaty ESTANCIA $$$
(☎4630-8421; www.vivituirsmorural.com ,in Spanish, yvytuitaty@hotmail.com; r per person incl full board, farm activities & horseback riding UR$1900, 2 or more people UR$1700) For a first-hand look at real gaucho life, this working *estancia* 50km southwest of Tacuarembó is warmly recommended. Since 2006, hosts Pedro and Nahir Clariget have been receiving overnight guests in their unpretentious ranch-style home and inviting them to participate in daily *estancia* routines. Pedro and his friendly cattle dogs delight in escorting guests around their 636-hectare domain on horseback, pausing en route to point out armadillos, ñandú nests and other local attractions. Back at the ranch, sip *mate* on the patio at sunset in anticipation of Nahir's tasty home cooking, which includes savory meat stews and traditional desserts such as *arroz con leche* (ride pudding). Call in advance for driving directions or to arrange pickup at Tacuarembó's bus station (UR$1200 roundtrip for a group of any size).

Hotel Plaza HOTEL $$
(☎4632-7988; hotelplaza@hotmail.com; 25 de Agosto 247; s/d UR$640/1050; ❄@📶) Painted a cheery yellow, with fish on the shower curtains and wireless internet in the rooms, the centrally located Plaza is Tacuarembó's most welcoming downtown hotel.

La Rueda PARRILLA $$
(W Beltrán 251; dishes UR$95-260; ⏲lunch & dinner Mon-Sat, lunch Sun) With its thatched roof and walls covered with gaucho paraphernalia, La Rueda is a friendly neighborhood *parrilla*.

BUSES FROM TACUAREMBÓ

DESTINATION	COST (UR$)	DURATION (HR)
Montevideo	457	4½
Paysandú	282	3½
Salto	340	4

Information

Antel (Sarandí 242)

Banco Santander (18 de Julio 258) One of several ATMs near Plaza Colón.

Tourist office (☎4632-7144; www.imtacuarembo.com, in Spanish; ⏲8am-7pm Mon-Fri, 9-11am Sat) Just outside the bus terminal.

Hospital Regional (☎4632-2955; cnr Treinta y Tres & Catalogne)

Post office (Ituzaingó 262)

Getting There & Around

The **bus terminal** (cnr Ruta 5 & Av Victorino Pereira) is 1km northeast of the center. A taxi into town costs about UR$50.

Valle Edén

Valle Edén, a lush valley 24km southwest of Tacuarembó, is home to the **Museo Carlos Gardel** (☎4632-3520 ext 30; admission UR$20; ⏲9:30am-5:30pm). Reached via a drive-through creek spanned by a wooden

ESTANCIA TOURISM IN URUGUAY

Estancias, the giant farms of Uruguay's interior, are a national cultural icon. The Uruguayan Ministry of Tourism has designated 'Estancia Turística' as a distinct lodging category, and dozens of such places have opened their doors to tourists, from traditional working farms to opportunistic wannabes. Typically, *estancias* organize daily activities with a heavy emphasis on horseback riding; many also provide overnight accommodations. Most are difficult to reach without a vehicle, although they'll often pick guests up with advance notice.

The granddaddy of Uruguayan tourist *estancias* is **San Pedro de Timote** (☎4310-8086; www.sanpedrodetimote.com; d Sun-Thu UR$4000-5600, Fri & Sat UR$5200-7600;). Its remarkable setting, 14km up a dirt road from the town of Cerro Colorado, amid 253 hectares of rolling cattle country, is greatly enhanced by the complex of historic structures, some dating to the mid-19th century: a gracious white chapel, a courtyard with soaring palm trees, a library with gorgeous tilework, and a circular stone corral. Common areas feature parquet wood floors, big fireplaces, comfy leather armchairs, two pools and a sauna. Prices include three meals, afternoon tea and two daily horseback-riding excursions (plus night rides during the full moon). Non-overnight guests can pay UR$1400 for lunch, afternoon tea and two horseback rides. Cerro Colorado is 160km northeast of Montevideo on Ruta 7.

Other tourist *estancias* covered in this book are listed under the city or town closest to them – our favorites include La Sirena, near Mercedes (see p523), Guardia del Monte (p544) and Yvytu Itaty (p528), near Tacuarembó.

In Montevideo, **Lares** (☎2901-9120; www.lares.com.uy; WF Aldunate 1320) and **Cecilia Regules Viajes** (☎2916-3012; www.ceciliaregulesviajes.com; Bacacay 1334, Local C) are travel agencies specializing in *estancia* tourism.

suspension footbridge, and housed in a former *pulpería* (the general store/bar that used to operate on many *estancias*), the museum documents Tacuarembó's claim as birthplace of the revered tango singer – a claim vigorously contested by Argentina and France!

Accommodations in Valle Edén are available at **Camping El Mago** (☎4632-7144; camp sites per tent/person UR$50/20). You can eat at the lovely historic mud-and-stone **Posada Valle Edén** (☎4630-2345; www.posadavalleeden.com.uy, in Spanish; dishes UR$190-260) or stay in one of their modern *cabañas* (UR$1560) across the street.

Empresa Calebus runs an 11:45am bus from Tacuarembó to Valle Edén, returning at 7:15pm (UR$38, 20 minutes).

EASTERN URUGUAY

The gorgeous 340km sweep of beaches, dunes, forests and lagoons stretching northeast from Montevideo to the Brazilian border is one of Uruguay's national treasures. Still largely unknown except to Uruguayans and their immediate neighbors, this region lies nearly dormant for 10 months of each year, then explodes with summer activity from Christmas to Carnaval, when it seems like every bus out of Montevideo is headed somewhere up the coast. For sheer fun-in-the-sun energy, there's nothing like the peak season, but if you can make it here slightly off-season, you'll experience all the same beauty for literally half the price.

Near the Brazilian border, amid the wide-open landscapes and untrammeled beaches of Rocha department, abandoned hilltop fortresses and shipwrecks offer mute testimony to the time when Spain and Portugal struggled for control of the new continent. Where lookouts once scanned the wide horizon for invading forces, a new wave of invaders has taken hold, from binocular-wielding whale-watchers in Cabo Polonio to camera-toting celebrity-watchers in Punta del Este.

Piriápolis

POP 8700

With its elegant old hotel and beachfront promenade backed by small mountains, Piriápolis is vaguely reminiscent of a Mediterranean beach town and is arguably Uruguay's most picturesque coastal resort. Less pretentious and more affordable than Punta del Este, it was developed for tourism in the 1930s by Argentine entrepreneur Francisco Piria, who built the imposing landmark Argentino Hotel and an eccentric hillside residence known as Castillo de Piria (Piria's Castle; p531).

Almost all the action happens in the 10-block stretch of beachfront between Av Artigas (the access road from Ruta 9) and Av Piria (where the coastline makes a broad curve southwards).

Streets back from the beach quickly become residential.

The surrounding countryside holds many interesting features, including two of Uruguay's highest summits.

Sights & Activities

Swimming and **sunbathing** are the most popular activities, and there's good **fishing** off the rocks at the end of the beach, where Rambla de los Argentinos becomes Rambla de los Ingleses.

For a great view of Piriápolis, take the **chairlift** (UR$100; 9am-sunset) to the summit of **Cerro San Antonio** at the east end of town.

Sleeping

Prices here are for high season. Low-season rates are up to 50% less.

Hotel Colón HOTEL **$$$**
(4432-2508; www.hotelcolonpiriapolis.com; Rambla 950; r without/with waterfront view UR$2100/2300;

URUGUAY'S OFF-THE-BEATEN-TRACK NATURE PRESERVES

Uruguay's interior, with its vast open spaces, is a naturalist's dream. The Uruguayan government has designated several natural areas for protection under its Sistema Nacional de Áreas Protegidas (SNAP) program. Funding remains minimal, and tourist infrastructure rudimentary, but intrepid travelers will be richly rewarded for seeking out these little-visited spots. Below are two preserves that best capture the spirit of Uruguay's wild gaucho country. Other SNAP preserves mentioned in this book include Cabo Polonio (p543), Cerro Verde (p546) and Laguna de Rocha (p540).

Valle del Lunarejo

This gorgeous valley, 95km north of Tacuarembó, is a place of marvelous peace and isolation, with birds and rushing water providing the only soundtrack.

Enchanting **Posada Lunarejo** (4650-6400; www.posadalunarejo.com, in Spanish; Ruta 30, Km 238; r incl breakfast/full board per person UR$1100/1800) occupies a restored 1880 building 2km off the main road, 3km from the river and a few steps from a *garza* (crane) colony. Further up the road, local guide **Mario Padern** (099-450653; Ruta 30, Km 230; walking tour depending on group size UR$600-1000) leads hikes from the canyon's edge down to a series of natural pools near the river's headwaters.

CUT (www.cutcorporacion.com.uy) offers the most convenient schedule to Valle del Lunarejo on its daily Montevideo–Tacuarembó–Artigas bus (leaving Montevideo at noon, UR$551, six hours; leaving Tacuarembó at 4:50pm, UR$94, 1½ hours). Posada Lunarejo can meet your bus if you call ahead.

Quebrada de los Cuervos

This hidden little canyon cuts through the rolling hill country 40km northwest of Treinta y Tres (325km northeast of Montevideo), providing an unexpectedly moist and cool habitat for a variety of plants and birds. There's a nature trail looping through the park (two hours roundtrip).

A perfect base for exploring this region is **Cañada del Brujo** (4452-2837; www.pleka.com/delbrujo; dm UR$480, meals UR$200-280), an ultrarustic hostel in an old schoolhouse 12km from the park. Hostel owner Pablo Rado can take you hiking or horseback riding to nearby waterfalls and introduce you to the joys of gaucho life: living by candlelight, drinking *mate*, sleeping under a wool poncho, eating simple meals cooked on the wood stove and watching spectacular sunsets under the big sky. With advance notice, he'll meet you in Treinta y Tres and drive you to the hostel in his old VW bug (per person UR$300).

Buses travel to Treinta y Tres nine times daily from Montevideo (UR$340, 4¼ hours).

❄@📶🏊) Built in 1910 by Francisco Piria for his son, this faux-Tudor mansion by the waterfront boasts fine views, gorgeous art nouveau details and an old-fashioned sitting room with fireplace. Wi-fi is in common areas only.

Argentino Hotel LUXURY HOTEL **$$$**
(☎4432-2791; www.argentinohotel.com.uy; Rambla de los Argentinos s/n; s/d incl breakfast from UR$2600/4000, half board UR$3100/5000, full board UR$3600/6000; ❄@📶🏊) Even if you don't stay here, you should visit this elegant 350-room European-style spa with two heated river-water pools, a casino, ice-skating rink and other luxuries.

Hostel Piriápolis HOSTEL **$**
(☎4432-0394; www.hostelpiriapolis.com; Simón del Pino 1136; dm/tw/d incl breakfast UR$330/780/850, nonmember surcharge per person UR$100; @📶) This 240-bed hostel, one of South America's largest, has several four-bed dorms, dozens of doubles and a guest kitchen. It's desolate as an airplane hangar when empty, but full of life (and often booked solid) in January and February.

Bungalows Margariteñas BUNGALOW **$$**
(☎4432-2245; www.margaritenias.com; cnr Zufriategui & Piedras; d/tr/q UR$1400/1500/1600; @📶) Near the bus terminal, this place has well equipped, individually decorated bungalows that sleep two to four. Affable owner Corina speaks English and meets guests at the bus station upon request.

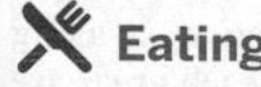

Eating

Most restaurants in Piriápolis are within a block of the Rambla.

TOP CHOICE **Café Picasso** SEAFOOD **$$**
(☎4432-2597; cnr Rojas & Caseros; dishes UR$140-300; ⏲lunch & dinner Dec-Mar, lunch daily, dinner Fri & Sat Apr-Nov) Hidden down a residential backstreet several blocks from the beach, chef-owner Carlos has converted his carport and front room into an informal, colorfully decorated restaurant with open-air grill. Locals chat astride plastic chairs and listen to tango recordings while Carlos cooks up some of the best fish anywhere on Uruguay's Atlantic coast, along with paella on Sundays. All mains come with mashed potatoes, mashed pumpkin, French fries or salad.

La Corniche PIZZERIA, SEAFOOD **$$**
(Manuel Freire s/n; dishes UR$160-290; ⏲lunch & dinner) This newly opened place specializes in pizza from the wood-fired oven and seafood from the blazing grill. Its sister cafe around the corner on La Rambla serves good espresso and pastries as well as lighter fare such as sandwiches on ciabatta bread.

HOSTEL-HOPPING UP THE COAST

Summer Bus (summerbus.com) is a new hop-on, hop-off bus service allowing travelers flexibility in traveling between hostels up and down Uruguay's Atlantic coast. With a single UR$1500 ticket, you can start your journey at the hostel of your choice and visit all 12 destinations, from Montevideo to Punta del Diablo.

Information

Antel (cnr Barrios & Buenos Aires; internet per hr UR$19; ⏲9am-9pm Mon-Sat)

Banco de la República (Rambla de los Argentinos, btwn Sierra & Sanabria) Convenient ATM.

Centro de Hoteles y Restaurantes (☎4432-2218; www.piriapolis.org.uy, in Spanish; ⏲9am-midnight Dec-Mar, 10am-6pm Apr-Nov) Adjacent to the tourist office; provides local hotel information and booking assistance.

Post office (Av Piria s/n)

Tourist office (☎4432-5055; www.turismopiriapolis.com; Rambla de los Argentinos; ⏲9am-midnight Dec-Mar, 10am-6pm Apr-Nov) Helpful staff and public toilets, on the waterfront near Argentino Hotel.

Getting There & Away

The **bus terminal** (cnr Misiones & Niza) is a few blocks back from the beach. COT and COPSA run frequent buses to Montevideo (UR$124, 1½ hours) and Punta del Este (UR$77, 50 minutes).

Around Piriápolis

North of town is **Castillo de Piria** (☎4432-3268; Ruta 37, Km 4; admission free; ⏲10am-5pm Tue-Sun), Francisco Piria's outlandishly opulent residence. At the time of research the interior was closed for renovations, but grounds remained open to the public. About 1km further inland, hikers can climb Uruguay's fourth-highest 'peak,' **Cerro Pan de Azúcar** (389m). The trail (three hours roundtrip) starts from the parking lot of the **Reserva de Fauna Autóctona** (Ruta 37, Km 5), narrowing from a gradual dirt road into a steep path marked with red arrows.

The privately operated **Sierra de las Ánimas** (☎094-419891; www.sierradelasanimas.com; Ruta 9, Km 86; ⊙Sat & Sun, plus Carnaval & Easter weeks) is just off the Interbalnearia (coastal highway), 25km toward Montevideo from Piriápolis. There are two good hiking trails, each three to four hours roundtrip: one leads to the 501m summit (Uruguay's second-highest), the other to the **Cañadón de los Espejos**, a series of waterfalls and natural swimming holes that are especially impressive after good rainfall. Other activities include mountain biking and camping. Coming from Montevideo by bus, get off at Parador Los Cardos restaurant and cross the highway. In cold or rainy weather, call ahead to verify it's open.

SOS Rescate de Fauna Marina (☎094-330795; sosfaunamarina@gmail.com; admission UR$50; ⊙by appointment), 10km south of Piriápolis, is Uruguay's premier marine-animal rescue and rehabilitation center. Run entirely by volunteers, its emphasis is on educating schoolchildren, who can assist with daily feedings and observe penguins, sea lions, turtles and other rescued wildlife. Visitors are asked to reserve ahead and support the center's mission with a small donation.

Punta del Este

POP 8900

OK, here's the plan: tan it, wax it, buff it at the gym, then plonk it on the beach at 'Punta.' Once you're done there, go out and shake it at one of the town's famous clubs.

Punta del Este – with its many beaches, elegant seaside homes, yacht harbor, high-rise apartment buildings, pricey hotels and glitzy restaurants – is one of South America's most glamorous resorts and easily the most expensive place in Uruguay. Extremely popular with Argentines and Brazilians, Punta suffered a period of decline during the Uruguayan and Argentine recessions, but has come back with a vengeance.

Celebrity-watchers have a full-time job here. Punta is teeming with big names, and local gossipmongers keep regular tabs on who's been sighted where. Surrounding towns caught up in the whole Punta mystique include the famed club zone of La Barra to the east and Punta Ballena to the west.

Punta itself is relatively small, confined to a narrow peninsula that officially divides the Río de la Plata from the Atlantic Ocean. The town has two separate grids: north of a constricted isthmus, just east of the yacht harbor, is the high-rise hotel zone; the southern area is largely residential. Street signs bear both names and numbers, though locals refer to most streets only by their number. An exception is Av Juan Gorlero (Calle 22), the main commercial street, universally referred to as just 'Gorlero' (not to be confused with Calle 19, *Comodoro* Gorlero).

Rambla Claudio Williman and Rambla Lorenzo Batlle Pacheco are coastal thoroughfares that converge at the top of the isthmus from northwest and northeast, respectively. Locations along the Ramblas are usually identified by numbered *paradas* (bus stops).

Sights

Beaches & Islands

Beaches are the big daytime draw in sunny Punta and there are plenty to choose from. On the west side of town, Rambla Gral Artigas snakes along the calm **Playa Mansa** on the Río de la Plata, then passes the busy **yacht harbor**, overflowing with boats, restaurants, nightclubs and beautiful people, before circling around the peninsula to the open Atlantic Ocean.

On the eastern side of the peninsula the water is rougher, as reflected in the name **Playa Brava** (Fierce Beach); the waves and currents here have claimed several lives. Also on the Atlantic side, you'll find surfer-friendly beaches such as **Playa de los Ingleses** and **Playa El Emir**.

From Playa Mansa, heading west along Rambla Williman, the main beach areas are La Pastora, Marconi, Cantegril, Las Delicias, Pinares, La Gruta at Punta Ballena, and Portezuelo. Eastward, along Rambla Lorenzo Batlle Pacheco, the prime beaches are La Chiverta, San Rafael, La Draga and Punta de la Barra. In summer, all have *paradores* (small restaurants) with beach service.

Punta's most famous landmark is **La Mano en la Arena**, a monster-sized sculpted hand protruding from the sands of Playa Brava (see p538).

Boats leave every half-hour or so (daily in season, weekends in off-season) from Punta del Este's yacht harbor for the 15-minute trip to **Isla Gorriti**, which has excellent sandy beaches, a couple of restaurants and the ruins of **Baterías de Santa Ana**, an 18th-century fortification.

About 10km offshore, **Isla de Lobos** is home to the world's second-largest southern sea-lion colony (200,000 at last count), as

WORTH A TRIP

VILLA SERRANA

Those seeking an off-the-beaten-track retreat will love the serenity of this little village nestled in hills above a small lake, 170km northeast of Montevideo. Nearby attractions include **Salto del Penitente**, a 60m waterfall.

Picturesquely perched above the valley, **La Calaguala** (☎4440-2955; www.lacalaguala.com, in Spanish; Ruta 8, Km 145; camp sites per person/tent UR$150/300, r per person incl breakfast/half-board/full board from UR$900/1200/1650) is a friendly family-run posada with attached restaurant; horseback riding, cycling and hiking excursions can be arranged. The slightly more expensive room with whirlpool tub and fireplace is extremely cozy on chilly nights.

To get here, take a bus from Montevideo to Minas (UR$141, two hours), then transfer to a **COSU** (☎4442-2256) bus to Villa Serrana (UR$50, 30 minutes, 9am and 5:30pm Tuesday and Thursday). Alternatively, any bus traveling northbound from Minas along Ruta 8 can drop you at Km 145, from where it's a stiff 4km uphill walk into town.

well as South America's tallest lighthouse. The island is protected and can only be visited on an organized tour (see p533).

Other Sights

Casapueblo GALLERY
(☎4257-8041; admission UR$120; ⏲10am-sunset) At Punta Ballena, a jutting headland 15km west of Punta del Este, Casapueblo is Uruguayan artist Carlos Páez Vilaró's exuberantly whimsical villa and art gallery. Gleaming white in the sun and cascading nine stories down a cliffside, it's one of Uruguay's most unique attractions. Visitors can tour five rooms, view a film on the artist's life and travels, and eat up the spectacular views at the upstairs cafeteria-bar. There's a hotel and restaurant, too. It's a 2km walk from the junction where Codesa's Línea 8 bus drops you.

FREE **Museo Ralli** MUSEUM
(☎4248-3476; www.museoralli.org; Los Arrayanes s/n; ⏲5-9pm Tue-Sun Jan & Feb, 2-6pm Sat & Sun Mar-May & Oct-Dec) In the suburb called Beverly Hills, it displays a wide-ranging collection of works by contemporary Latin American artists.

Activities

In summer, **parasailing**, **waterskiing** and **jet skiing** are possible on Playa Mansa. Operators set up on the beach along Rambla Claudio Williman between Paradas 2 and 20.

Sunvalleysurf SURFING
(☎4248-1388; www.sunvalleysurf.com, in Spanish; Parada 3½, Playa Brava) Wetsuits, surfboards, bodyboards and just about anything else you could want can be rented from its original shop on Playa Brava, plus branches on Playa El Emir and in La Barra. It also offers surfing and bodyboard lessons.

Tours

Calypso Charters & Excursiones BOAT TOUR
(☎4244-6152; www.calypso.com.uy, in Spanish; cnr Rambla Artigas & Calle 21; tours adult/child UR$1400/700) One of several companies offering two-hour tours to Isla de Lobos.

Sleeping

In summer Punta is jammed with people, and prices are astronomical; even hostels double their prices in January. In winter it's a ghost town, and places that stay open lower their prices considerably. Prices listed here are for high season, when even places classified as midrange tend to charge top-end rates. Off-season visitors will find prices more in keeping with the standard ranges defined on p549.

Las Cumbres BOUTIQUE HOTEL $$$
(☎4257-8689; www.cumbres.com.uy; Ruta 12, Km 3.9, Laguna del Sauce; d UR$3900-6800, ste UR$7200-14,300; ❄@🛜🏊) Near Punta Ballena, this understatedly luxurious hilltop paradise is eclectically decorated with treasures from the owners' world travels. Rooms abound with special features, such as writing desks, fireplaces and outdoor whirlpool tubs. Guests have access to spa treatments, beach chairs and umbrellas, and free mountain bikes, and the tearoom terrace (open to the public) has magnificent sunset views.

La Lomita del Chingolo GUESTHOUSE $$
(☎4248-6980; www.lalomitadelchingolo.com; Las Acacias btwn Los Eucaliptus & Le Mans; dm

Punta del Este

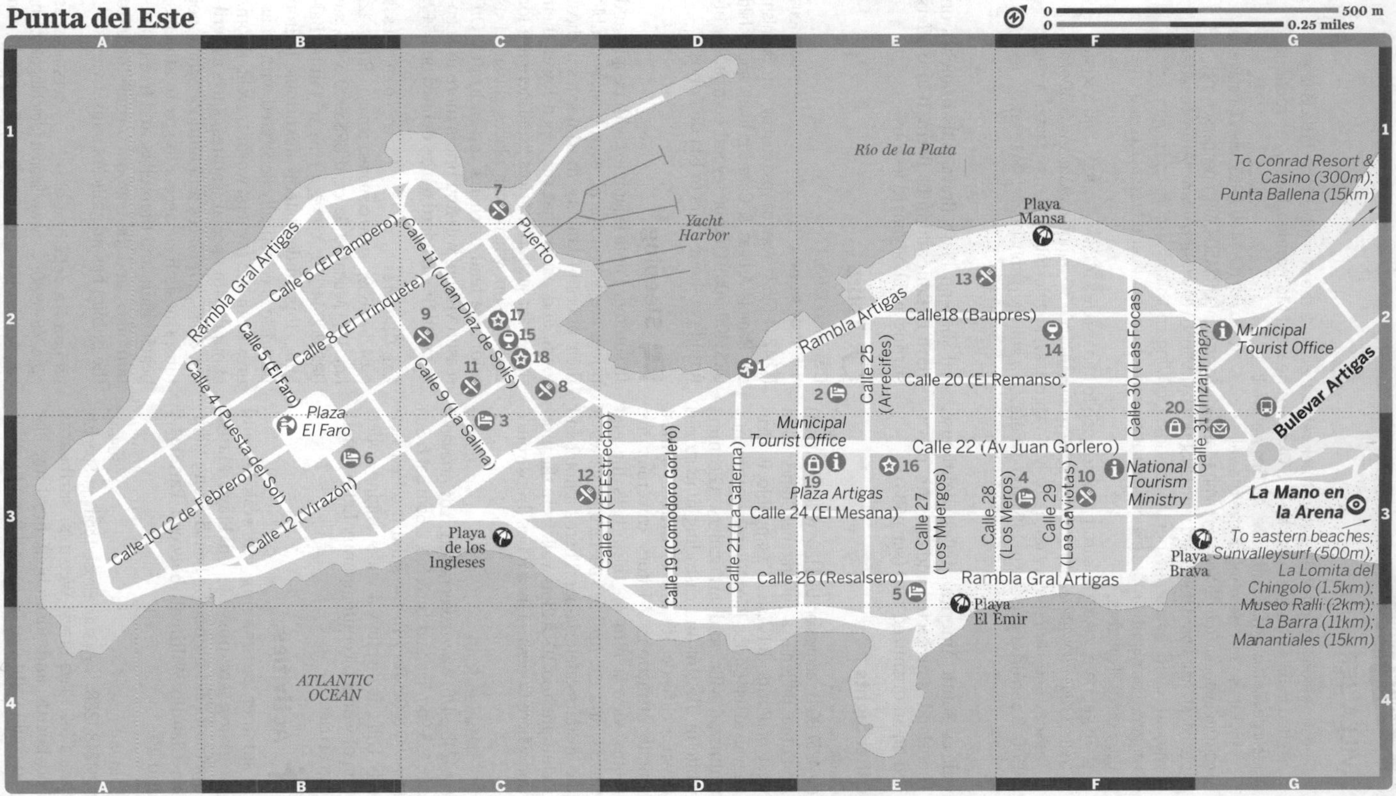

0 — 500 m
0 — 0.25 miles

Río de la Plata
Yacht Harbor
Puerto
ATLANTIC OCEAN
Playa Mansa
Playa de los Ingleses
Playa El Emir
Playa Brava
Plaza El Faro
Plaza Artigas
Municipal Tourist Office
National Tourism Ministry
La Mano en la Arena
Rambla Gral Artigas
Rambla Artigas
Bulevar Artigas
Calle 4 (Puesta del Sol)
Calle 5 (El Faro)
Calle 6 (El Pampero)
Calle 8 (El Trinquete)
Calle 9 (La Salina)
Calle 10 (2 de Febrero)
Calle 11 (Juan Díaz de Solís)
Calle 12 (Virazón)
Calle 17 (El Estrecho)
Calle 19 (Comodoro Gorlero)
Calle 21 (La Galerna)
Calle 24 (El Mesana)
Calle 25 (Arrecifes)
Calle 26 (Resalsero)
Calle 27 (Los Muergos)
Calle 28 (Los Meros)
Calle 29 (Las Gaviotas)
Calle 30 (Las Focas)
Calle 31 (Inzaurraga)
Calle18 (Baupres)
Calle 20 (El Remanso)
Calle 22 (Av Juan Gorlero)
To Conrad Resort & Casino (300m); Punta Ballena (15km)
To eastern beaches; Sunvalleysurf (500m); La Lomita del Chingolo (1.5km); Museo Ralli (2km); La Barra (11km); Manantiales (15km)

1 2 3 4 5 6 7 8 9 10 11 12 13 14 15 16 17 18 19 20

Punta del Este

Top Sights

La Mano en la Arena ... G3

Activities, Courses & Tours

1 Calypso Charters & Excursiones ... D2

Sleeping

2 Bonne Étoile ... E2
3 Hotel Concorde ... C3
4 Tas D' Viaje Hostel ... F3
5 Tas D' Viaje Hostel - Beach Annex ... E3
6 The Smalleast Hotel ... B3

Eating

7 Artico ... C1
8 Chiviteria Marcos ... C2
9 Il Baretto ... C2
10 La Fonda del Pesca ... F3
11 Lo de Charlie ... C2
12 Supermercado Disco ... C3
13 Virazón ... E2

Drinking

14 Company Bar ... F2
15 Moby Dick ... C2

Entertainment

16 Cine Libertador ... E3
17 Mambo Club ... C2
18 Soho ... C2

Shopping

19 Feria Artesanal ... E3
20 Manos del Uruguay ... F3

UR$700-1200, d UR$2400-3600; @) With one six-person dorm and five private rooms, this relaxed place is in a residential neighborhood north of the center. Hospitable owners Rodrigo and Alejandra welcome guests with internet and kitchen facilities, tasty breakfasts, impromptu backyard barbecues and plenty of information about the local area.

Tas D' Viaje Hostel HOSTEL $
(4244-8789; www.tasdviaje.com; Calle 24 btwn Calles 28 & 29; dm UR$400-1100, d UR$1600-2800; Aug-May; @) This newish hostel in an older downtown home wins lots of points for its friendly reception, unbeatable central location and inviting common areas. During the summer months, it also opens a sister **hostel** (Calle 26 btwn Calles 25 & 27; Dec-Feb), half a block from the beach at Playa El Emir.

La Posta del Cangrejo HOTEL $$$
(4277-0021; www.lapostadelcangrejo.com; La Barra; d UR$3800-9200, ste UR$5800-13,000; @) This beachside hotel in the heart of La Barra has whitewashed adobe walls, an award-winning French restaurant and a poolside terrace within earshot of the ocean. The upstairs suites have fireplaces, Jacuzzis, 29in TVs and nice sound systems.

El Viajero Brava Beach Hostel HOSTEL $
(4248-0331; www.elviajerobravabeach.com; cnr Charrúa & Av Francia; dm UR$300-875, d UR$1100-2600; @) This hostel's noisy, trafficky street corner location is rather dreary, but it's conveniently close to the bus station and Playa Brava, with perks including air-con in all rooms, laundry facilities, bike and surfboard rentals, surfing lessons, music-filled common areas and a lively 24-hour bar.

The Smalleast Hotel HOTEL $$
(4244-4992; www.thesmalleasthotel.com; Plaza El Faro; d UR$1400-2900, q apt UR$2400-3900; @) Despite the rather sullen reception, this newly remodeled small hotel offers some perks, including free beach towels and umbrellas, 32in LCD televisions and a pleasant location in the quiet residential district south of the port. Three rooms face the plaza, with fine views of Punta's lighthouse. Rates are slashed in half from March through Christmas.

Manantiales Hostel HOSTEL $
(4277-4427; www.elviajeropuntadeleste.com; Ruta 10, Km 164; dm UR$290-700, d UR$900-2400; Nov-Easter; @) If you're here to surf or just chill out, this hostel 12km east of Punta, with its swimming pool, surfboard rentals and backstreet location 15 minutes on foot from Bikini Beach, is a great bet. Private rooms and some dorms have air-con.

Bonne Étoile HOTEL $$
(4244-0301; www.hotelbonneetoile.com; Calle 20, btwn Calles 23 & 25; s UR$1400-3100, d UR$1600-3300; @) In a 1940s beach house adjoining a more modern six-story tower, Bonne Étoile has clean, spacious rooms, some with river views. The location between Gorlero and the port is hard to beat.

Hotel Concorde HOTEL $$$
(4244-4800; www.hotelconcorde.com.uy; Calle 9 btwn Calles 12 & 14; d UR$2300-3700, with kitchenette UR$3700-5200; @) Recently remodeled, this comfortable three-star offers a mix of rooms, including some with kitchenettes.

Uruguay's Beaches

Stretching from Montevideo to Brazil, 300km of beaches hug the Río de la Plata and the Atlantic Ocean. Choose the style that suits: from Punta del Este's glitz to Cabo Polonio's rusticity.

Punta del Diablo

1 Punta del Diablo (p545) is the end of the line. A few steps down the beach and you're in Brazil, but most folks stay put, seduced by waves, seafood shacks, beach bonfires and the national park.

Cabo Polonio

2 Its lighthouse beckoning from a lonely point dotted with makeshift houses, Cabo Polonio (p543) is a nature-lover's dream. Getting here, on a pitching truck ride through the dunes, is half the fun.

Punta del Este

3 The dividing line between the wild Atlantic and the Río de la Plata, Punta del Este's (p532) tidy peninsula full of highrises and perfect beaches morphs annually from sleepy beach town to summer playground for South America's 'see-and-be-seen' party set.

Piriápolis

4 A throwback to the 1930s, Piriápolis (p529) is about strolling the beachfront promenade past the grand hotel, or surveying the calm waters from the top of the chairlift.

La Paloma

5 Grab an ice-cream and head for the waves. Family-friendly La Paloma (p540), tucked behind a wall of sand dunes, is the very picture of unadorned beachside fun.

La Pedrera

6 No view on Uruguay's entire Atlantic coast matches the wide-angle perspective from La Pedrera's (p542) cliffs. Join the surfers up top and contemplate your beach options for the day.

Clockwise from top left
1. Punta del Diablo (p545) **2.** Cabo Polonio (p543)
3. Playa Brava (p532), Punta del Este

2

KRZYSZTOF DYDYNSKI/LONELY PLANET IMAGES ©

KRZYSZTOF DYDYNSKI/LONELY PLANET IMAGES ©

THE HAND IN THE SAND

La Mano en la Arena (Hand in the Sand), sculpted in iron and cement by Chilean artist Mario Irarrázabal, won first prize in a monumental art contest in 1982 and has been a Punta fixture ever since. The hand exerts a magnetic attraction over visitors to Punta, who climb and jump off its digits and pose for thousands of photos with it every year.

Up close, the hand is starting to show its age. There's graffiti scrawled all over it, and its ungraceful cement base often gets exposed by shifting sands. But watch out – the hand's still likely to reach out and grab you!

The comfortable common areas include big-screen computers with free wi-fi, some loud and fancy couches, a pool and a small bar.

Conrad Resort & Casino LUXURY HOTEL **$$$**
(4249-1111; www.conradhotels.com; Parada 4, Playa Mansa; d UR$5400-14,000;) For five-star amenities in downtown Punta, the high-rise, ultramodern Conrad is the obvious choice. Better rooms have terraces with sea views, the pool and spa complex is fabulous, and the casino offers entertainment extravaganzas.

Camping San Rafael CAMPGROUND **$**
(4248-6715; www.campingsanrafael.com.uy, in Spanish; camp sites per person UR$170-250, per vehicle UR$40; Nov-Easter) This campground, near the bridge to La Barra, has well-kept facilities on woodsy grounds, complete with store, restaurant, laundry, 24-hour hot water and other amenities.

Eating

TOP CHOICE **Lo de Charlie** MEDITERRANEAN **$$$**
(4244-4183; Calle 12, No 819; dishes UR$352-615; lunch & dinner Dec-Mar, dinner Wed-Mon, lunch Fri-Sun Apr-Nov) Owned by a fishing buddy of local artist Carlos Páez Vilaró and decorated with some of his work, this is one of Punta's premier restaurants. The endless culinary delights include gazpacho, risotto, homemade pasta, fish and shellfish.

Il Baretto ITALIAN **$$$**
(4244-5565; www.ilbarettopunta.com; cnr Calles 9 & 10; pizza UR$210-350, dishes UR$390-620; dinner daily mid-Dec–Carnaval, Thu-Sun rest of year) Candlelit garden seating on plush chairs and couches provides a romantic setting for feasting on Baretto's homemade pasta and desserts. It's also a pleasant place for 'after-beach' drinks, starting at 6pm on summer afternoons.

La Fonda del Pesca SEAFOOD **$$**
(Calle 29, btwn Gorlero & Calle 24; dishes UR$200-300; noon-11pm) A vividly painted hole-in-the-wall specializing in fish, La Fonda also serves up plenty of local color. Owner-chef Pesca makes personal appearances at diners' tables to make sure they're enjoying themselves.

Chivitería Marcos CHIVITOS **$$**
(Rambla Artigas, btwn Calles 12 & 14; chivitos UR$210; 11am-4am Dec-Mar, 11am-4pm & 8pm-late Apr-Nov) Montevideo-based Marcos earned its fame building mega-sandwiches to order. Choose from the 11 toppings and seven sauces, then try to balance the thing back to your table.

Virazón SEAFOOD **$$$**
(4244-3924; www.virazon.com.uy; cnr Rambla Artigas & Calle 28; dishes UR$275-625; lunch & dinner) Virazón serves great seafood. Grab a spot on the beachside deck and have fun watching the waiters try to look dignified as they cross the street with loaded trays.

Baby Gouda Deli Café CAFE **$$**
(4277-1874; Ruta 10, Km 161, La Barra; dishes from UR$250; noon-1am) An ultracool deli-cafe with an inviting outdoor deck, on the main drag in La Barra, a couple of blocks up from the beach.

Artico SEAFOOD **$$**
(Calle 8 No 1181; dishes UR$185-290; lunch & dinner) This port-side fish wholesaler does a brisk business in grilled seafood and paella, with lower prices that reflect its cafeteria-style service. There's also a salad bar (per 100g UR$60). It's one of the few places in Punta where you can eat by the water without spending a fortune.

Supermercado Disco SUPERMARKET **$**
(Calle 17, btwn Gorlero & Calle 24; 8am-11pm) For shelter from Punta's high prices, shop for groceries or grab a snack from the *rotisería* (delicatessen) here.

Drinking & Entertainment

A cluster of clubs in Punta's port area stays open all year (weekends only in low season). During the super-peak season from Christmas through January, an additional slew of beach clubs with ever-changing names open along Playa Brava, on the beach road to La Barra.

Bear in mind that it's social suicide to turn up at a nightclub before 2am here. In general, Punta's bars stay open as long as there's a crowd and sometimes have live music on weekends.

Moby Dick PUB
(www.mobydick.com.uy; Calle 13, btwn Calles 10 & 12) This classic pub near the yacht harbor is where Punta's dynamic social scene kicks off every evening.

Company Bar BAR
(☎4244-0130; Calle 29, btwn Calles 18 & 20) In downtown Punta, this place is open all year for dinner and drinks, with an international mix of live music from 10pm onwards.

Mambo Club CLUB
(☎448956; cnr Calle 13 & Calle 10) A popular dance spot featuring Latin grooves.

Soho DJ
(www.sohopuntadeleste.com, in Spanish; Calle 13, btwn Calles 10 & 12) Another dependable year-round dance spot featuring an ever-changing cast of international DJs.

Medio y Medio JAZZ
(www.medioymedio.com, in Spanish; Camino Lussich s/n, Punta Ballena) This jazz club and restaurant near the beach in Punta Ballena brings in performers from Uruguay, Argentina and Brazil.

Cine Libertador CINEMA
(Gorlero 796) Open year-round with movies on two screens.

Shopping

Manos del Uruguay WOOLENS
(www.manos.com.uy; Gorlero, btwn Calles 30 & 31) The local branch of Uruguay's national cooperative, selling fine woolens.

Feria Artesanal HANDICRAFTS
(Plaza Artigas) Artisans' fair on Punta's central square.

Information

Internet Access

High-priced internet places pop up like mushrooms each summer, but most close in the off-season. There's paid internet (per hour UR$60) year-round at the bus station. Many hotels and restaurants offer free wi-fi, and there's free municipal wi-fi on Plaza Artigas.

Money

Punta's many banks, ATMs and exchange offices are concentrated along Gorlero.

Banco de la República Oriental (cnr Gorlero & Calle 25)

Cambio Gales (cnr Gorlero & Calle 29) Currency exchange.

HSBC (cnr Gorlero & Calle 28)

Post

Post office (Gorlero 1035)

Telephone

Antel (cnr Calles 25 & 24; ⌚9am-5pm Mon-Sat) Another dependable option for internet (per hour UR$45) in the low season.

Tourist Information

Centro de Hoteles y Restaurantes (☎4244-0512; www.puntadelestehoteles.com; Plaza Artigas; ⌚8am-midnight Dec-Mar, 10am-6pm Mon-Sat Apr-Nov) Helps with hotel bookings.

Municipal tourist office (☎4244-6510; www.maldonado.gub.uy; Plaza Artigas; ⌚8am-midnight Dec 15-Mar 1, 8am-6pm rest of year) Maintains additional branches at bus station and at the corner of Calle 31 and the Rambla.

National Tourism Ministry (☎4244-1218; puntadeleste@mintur.gub.uy; Gorlero 942; ⌚10am-5pm)

Getting There & Away

Air

Aeropuerto Internacional de Punta del Este (PDP; www.puntadeleste.aero) is at Laguna del Sauce, 20km west of Punta del Este. All airlines following fly direct to Buenos Aires' Aeroparque:

Aerolíneas Argentinas (www.aerolineas.com.ar; Edificio Santos Dumont, Gorlero, btwn Calles 30 & 31)

BQB (www.flybqb.com) New cut-rate carrier, planning to expand to other destinations.

BUSES FROM PUNTA DEL ESTE

DESTINATION	COST (UR$)	DURATION (HR)
Montevideo	170	2¼
Carrasco Airport (MVD)	170	1¾
Piriápolis	70	1
Punta del Diablo	235	3
Rocha	117	1½

Pluna (www.flypluna.com) Also flies to São Paulo, Brazil.

Sol (www.sol.com.ar) Also flies to Rosario, Argentina.

Bus

From Punta's **bus terminal** (☎4249-4042; cnr Calle 32 & Bulevar Artigas), dozens of daily buses ply the coastal route to Montevideo. COT also has two daily northeast-bound buses to Rocha, the transfer point for La Paloma, La Pedrera and Cabo Polonio.

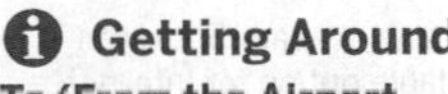

Getting Around

To/From the Airport

COT runs direct minivans from the bus station to Punta del Este's airport (UR$100, 20 minutes), leaving 1½ hours before each flight.

Bus

Minibuses leave every 20 minutes in summer from platform 8 at Punta's bus terminal and serve the eastern beaches en route to La Barra (UR$26, 20 minutes); others run to points west, including Punta Ballena.

Car

Car-rental outlets are ubiquitous near the bus terminal and along Gorlero. Some of the better deals include **Punta Car** (Bulevar Artigas 101), **Multicar** (Gorlero 860) and **Dollar** (Gorlero 961).

La Paloma

POP 3500

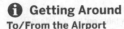

In the pretty rural department of Rocha, on a small peninsula 225km east of Montevideo, placid La Paloma is less developed, less expensive and much less crowded than Punta del Este. The town itself is rather bland and sprawling, but it has attractive sandy beaches and great surfing. Streets radiating diagonally from Av Nicolás Solari (the main street) are named after classical deities, making for funny-sounding intersections such as Eros and Adonis. On summer weekends the town often hosts free concerts on the beach, making accommodations bookings essential.

Sights & Activities

El Faro del Cabo Santa María LIGHTHOUSE

(admission UR$15; ⏲9am-1pm & 2:30pm-sunset) The 1874 completion of this local lighthouse, marked La Paloma's genesis as a summer beach resort. The unfinished first attempt collapsed in a violent storm, killing 17 French and Italian workers who are buried nearby. Outside is a solar clock using shadows cast by the lighthouse.

Peteco Surf Shop SURFING

(Av Nicolás Solari, btwn Av El Sirio & Av deNavío; rental shortboard/longboard/kayak/bodyboard/sandboard/wetsuit per day UR$400/600/800/400/400/400) The best surfing beaches are Los Botes, Solari and Anaconda southwest of town, and La Aguada and La Pedrera to the north. This very friendly surf shop rents all the necessary equipment and can hook you up with good local surfing instructors.

Laguna de Rocha RESERVE

An ecological reserve protected under Uruguay's SNAP program (see p530), is a vast wetland 10km west of La Paloma with populations of black-necked swans, storks, spoonbills and other waterfowl.

Sleeping

Hotel Bahía HOTEL **$$$**

(☎4479-6029; www.elbahia.com.uy; cnr Av del Navío & del Sol; d UR$1500-2400, with air-con UR$2200-3000; ❄📶) For its central location and overall comfort, Bahía is hard to beat. Rooms are clean and bright, with firm mattresses and bedside reading lights.

> WORTH A TRIP
>
> **FARO JOSÉ IGNACIO**
>
> The rich and famous flock to this highly fashionable little beachside town with its pretty lighthouse 30km east of Punta. Staying here is not for the faint of wallet; US$1000-a-night accommodations are the rule, such as the oceanfront **Playa Vik** (☎094-605212; www.playavik.com; Calle Los Cisnes; ❄@📶🏊), recently opened by billionaire Scandinavian businessman and art patron Alex Vik. To soak up José Ignacio's rarefied atmosphere without breaking the bank, head for the delightful beachside eatery **Parador La Huella** (☎4486-2279; www.paradorlahuella.com; Playa Brava; ⏲lunch & dinner Dec-Mar, lunch Fri-Sun, dinner Fri & Sat May-Nov), which specializes in sushi, grilled fish and clay-oven-fired pizza. Two buses daily make the 45-minute trip from Punta (UR$59), stopping in the main square near the **tourist office** (☎4486-2409; www.ligadejoseignacio.org; ⏲9am-2pm Fri-Mon).

La Paloma

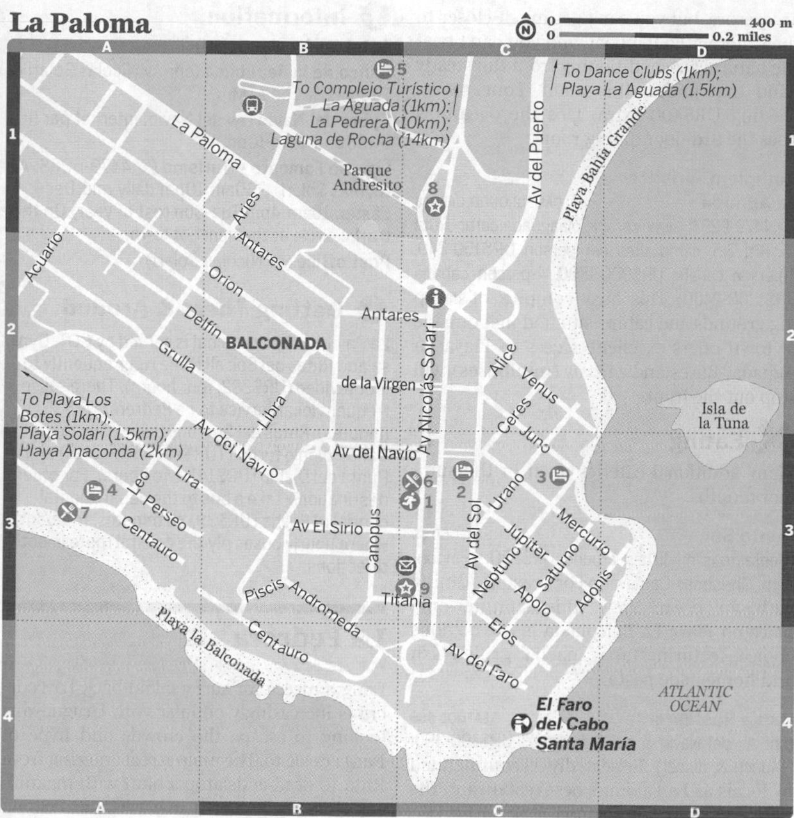

La Paloma Hostel HOSTEL $
(☎4479-6396; www.lapalomahostel.com; Parque Andresito; HI member UR$280-400, nonmember UR$340-480; ⊙closed variably in winter) Just north of town, this thatched-roofed hostel in shady Parque Andresito has large dorms with sleeping lofts, an indoor-outdoor kitchen and a lounge area with fireplace.

La Balconada Hostel HOSTEL $
(☎4479-6273; www.labalconadahostel.com.uy; Centauro s/n; dm UR$480-800, d with shared/private bathroom from UR$1600/2200; 📶) This surfer-friendly hostel has an enviable location a stone's throw from La Balconada beach, about 1km southwest of the center. Take a taxi from the bus station and the hostel will pick up the tab.

Hotel La Tuna HOTEL $$
(☎4479-6083; hoteleslatunaycribe.com; cnr Neptuno & Juno; s/d/tr from UR$950/1400/1950, 4-person apt UR$2300; @📶) The building is

La Paloma

Top Sights
El Faro del Cabo Santa María............ C4

Activities, Courses & Tours
1 Peteco Surf Shop............ C3

Sleeping
2 Hotel Bahía............ C3
3 Hotel La Tuna............ C3
4 La Balconada Hostel............ A3
5 La Paloma Hostel............ B1

Eating
Bahía Restaurante............ (see 2)
6 Heladería Popi............ C3
7 Punto Sur............ A3

Entertainment
8 Centro Cultural La Paloma............ C1
9 Cine La Paloma............ C3
Peteco Resto-Pub............ (see 1)

an eyesore, but you can't get much closer to the water without a boat, and you can't beat the natural air-conditioning from the steady wind that buffets this point. Four rooms (costing UR$400 extra) face the ocean, as does the 3rd-floor dining room.

Complejo Turístico La Aguada CAMPGROUND, CABIN $
(☎4479-9293; www.complejolaaguada.com; Ruta 15, Km 2.5; camp sites per person UR$150-240, 2-person cabaña UR$900-1800, 4-person cabaña UR$1200-2400) This busy complex of camping grounds and cabins situated just outside of town offers excellent access to Playa La Aguada. Buses and *micros* (minibuses) will stop out the front.

Eating

Many additional eateries open in the summer months.

Punto Sur SEAFOOD $$
(Centauro s/n; dishes around UR$250; ⊙noon-2am Christmas-Carnaval) For casual dining with an ocean view, this summer-only place on Playa La Balconada is the obvious choice, featuring tapas, paella, grilled fish and homemade pasta.

Bahía Restaurante SEAFOOD $$$
(cnr Av del Navío & del Sol; dishes UR$190-390; ⊙lunch & dinner) Repeatedly recommended by locals as La Paloma's best restaurant, the Bahía specializes in seafood.

Heladería Popi ICE CREAM $
(Av Nicolás Solari s/n; ice cream UR$50-80; ⊙noon-midnight) La Paloma's favorite ice cream shop.

Entertainment

In summer, take a midnight stroll out toward Playa La Aguada and follow your ears to La Paloma's string of **dance clubs**, lined up in a row like the thatched-roofed houses of the *Three Little Pigs*. Other entertainment options include:

Peteco Resto-Pub PUB
(Av Nicolás Solari) Behind Peteco Surf Shop, this patio bar hosts live music nightly in summer.

Cine La Paloma CINEMA
(Av Nicolás Solari) Has twin screens showing movies throughout the summer.

Centro Cultural La Paloma CULTURAL CENTER
(Parque Andresito) Shows occasional movies and hosts other cultural events year-round.

Information

Antel (Av Nicolás Solari)

Banco de la República (cnr Av Nicolás Solari & Titania) Has an ATM.

Cyber del Navío (Av del Navío; internet per hr UR$30; ⊙9am-10pm)

Liga de Fomento y Turismo (☎4479-6088; Av Nicolás Solari; ⊙10am-10pm daily mid-Dec–Easter, 10am-4pm Tue-Sun rest of year) On the traffic circle at the heart of town.

Post office (Av Nicolás Solari)

Getting There & Around

La Paloma's bus terminal is served by COT, Cynsa and Rutas del Sol; all three run frequently to Montevideo (UR$282, four hours). There's also frequent local service to La Pedrera (UR$35, 15 minutes). Rutas del Sol runs twice daily to the Cabo Polonio turnoff (UR$70, 45 minutes) and Punta del Diablo (UR$141, two hours). For other destinations, take a bus to the departmental capital of Rocha (UR$39, 30 minutes, frequent), where hourly buses ply the coastal route in both directions.

La Pedrera

POP 225

Long a mecca for surfers, laid-back La Pedrera is increasingly popular with Uruguayans looking to escape the crowds and hype of Punta del Este. The main street entering from Ruta 10 dead-ends atop a bluff with magnificent long views north toward Cabo Polonio and south toward La Paloma. Outside the summer months, tourist services are limited.

Sleeping & Eating

Rates drop dramatically in the off-season.

La Casa de la Luna HOSTEL $
(☎4470-2857; www.lacasadelaluna.com.uy; Ruta 10, Km 230; camp sites per person UR$400, dm UR$550-600, d UR$1800; @ 🛜) This small, homey hostel north of town offers camping, dorms and three upstairs doubles with distant ocean views. There's a guest laundry and a comfy common area with internet, DVD player and fireplace. Owner Paula has been instrumental in developing a two-hour nature trail exploring the surrounding *cárcavas* (badlands) ecosystem.

El Viajero La Pedrera Hostel HOSTEL $
(☎4479-2252; www.elviajerolapedrera.com; cnr Calles 3 & 11; dm without bathroom UR$340-550, d with bathroom UR$1200-2200; ⊙Nov-Easter; @ 🛜) Part of Uruguay's largest hostel chain,

WORTH A TRIP

HORSING AROUND IN THE HILLS

An hour inland from La Pedrera, the Sierra de Rocha is a lovely landscape of grey rocky crags interspersed with rolling rangeland. **Caballos de Luz** (☎099-400446; www.caballosdeluz.com; r per person incl full board & horseback rides UR$2000), run by the multilingual Austrian-Uruguayan couple Lucie and Santiago, offers hill-country horse treks lasting from two hours to a week, complete with three delicious vegetarian meals daily and overnight accommodation in a pair of comfortable thatched guest houses. They'll meet you at the bus station in Rocha, or you can drive there yourself (it's about 30 minutes off Hwy 9).

this place is tucked down a side street, within a five-minute walk of the bus stop and only 500m from La Pedrera's beach. The front deck, fire ring, and outdoor barbecue all invite mingling with other travelers.

Brisas de la Pedrera BOUTIQUE HOTEL **$$$**
(☎4479-2265; www.brisasdelapedrera.com; d UR$2600-5600; ⊙Oct-Easter; ❄📶) Sunny, spacious rooms and spectacular ocean views are the big draws at this recently renovated hotel in the heart of town.

Posada del Barco HOTEL **$$$**
(☎4479-2028; posadadelbarco@adinet.com.uy; Playa del Barco; d UR$1700-3100; ❄📶) This classy and comfortable place has sweeping views of La Pedrera's southern beach. Its annual Easter Week jazz festival attracts performers from Argentina, Brazil and Cuba.

Perillán SEAFOOD **$$$**
(cnr Av Principal & Rambla; dishes UR$360-420; ⊙lunch & dinner Nov-Easter) Candlelit and cozy, with colorfully decorated wooden tables, excellent seafood, a good wine list and an outdoor deck with a front-row seat on the crashing waves across the street, this is the perfect spot for a romantic dinner. Specialties include *gambas al ajillo* (garlic shrimp) and *cazuela de mariscos* (seafood stew with shrimp, squid, octopus and potatoes in a rich tomato broth).

Costa Brava SEAFOOD **$$$**
(dishes UR$250-400; ⊙lunch & dinner daily Dec-Mar, dinner Fri & Sat, lunch Sat & Sun Apr-Nov) Perched atop the bluffs overlooking the Atlantic, Costa Brava is all about seafood accompanied by an unbeatable view.

Information

La Pedrera's **tourist office** (⊙Dec-Easter) is in a tiny wooden kiosk on Calle Principal, a few blocks in from the beach. The closest ATMs are in La Paloma. Most accommodations in town offer free wi-fi and/or guest computers.

Getting There & Away

Buses southbound to Montevideo (UR$293) and northbound to the Cabo Polonio turnoff (UR$40) stop at the gigantic OSE tower (La Pedrera's tallest landmark) on the main street, a few blocks in from the waterfront. Schedules vary seasonally; a list is posted at the tourist office, across from the bus stop. There are also frequent buses to Rocha, where you can make connections north and south.

Cabo Polonio

POP 95

Northeast of La Paloma at Km 264.5 on Ruta 10 lies the turnoff to Cabo Polonio, one of Uruguay's wildest areas and home to its second-biggest sea-lion colony, near a tiny fishing village nestled in sand dunes. In 2009 the region was declared a national park, under the protective jurisdiction of Uruguay's SNAP program (see boxed text, p530). Despite a growing influx of tourists, Cabo Polonio remains one of Uruguay's most rustic coastal villages. There are no banking services, and the town's limited electricity is derived from generators, solar and wind power.

Sights & Activities

Faro Cabo Polonio LIGHTHOUSE
(admission UR$15; ⊙8:30am-sunset) Cabo Polonio's striking lighthouse provides a fabulous perspective on the point itself, the sea-lion colony, and the surrounding dunes and islands.

Wildlife viewing is excellent year-round. Below the lighthouse, southern sea lions *(Otaria flavescens)* and South American fur seals *(Arctocephalus australis)* frolic on the rocks every month except February. You can also spot southern right whales from late August to early October, penguins on the beach in July, and the odd southern elephant seal *(Mirounga leonina)* between January and March on nearby Isla de la Raza.

Surfing classes (per hour UR$250) are available in high season along with sandboard, skimboard and surfboard rentals (per hour UR$100). Inquire at the shop with the crazy surfing penguin logo, in the square where trucks from Ruta 10 drop you off.

Local accommodations can arrange **horseback rides** (per hour UR$200 to UR$250) along the beach and into the surrounding dunes.

Sleeping & Eating

Places listed here are open year-round. Many locals also rent rooms and houses. The hardest time to find accommodation is during the first two weeks of January. Off-season, prices drop dramatically.

Cabo Polonio Hostel HOSTEL **$**
(☎099-445943; www.cabopoloniohostel.com; dm/d UR$600/1050) Lit by candlelight and limited solar power, this hostel has hammocks overlooking the beach and a wood stove for cooking and staying cozy on stormy nights. Recommended for anyone wanting to appreciate Cabo's rustic simplicity.

Posada y Parador La Cañada GUESTHOUSE **$$**
(☎099-550595; posadalacaniada@gmail.com; dm/d UR$600/1500) Near the far end of Cabo Polonio's southern beach, this rustic posada mixes dorms and private rooms in a two-story house with spacious decks overlooking the dunes and ocean. Amenities include fishing gear, surfboards and meals cooked in the clay oven using fresh seafood and organic produce from the owners' garden. Solar and wind power provide all the electricity.

Pancho Hostal del Cabo HOSTEL **$**
(☎095-412633; www.hostaldelcabo.com; dm UR$500) Providing bare-bones dorms on two levels, Pancho's popular hostel is impossible to miss – you'll see the yellow corrugated roof, labeled with giant red letters, from the truck as you enter town.

La Perla del Cabo HOTEL-RESTAURANT **$$$**
(☎4470-5125; www.laperladelcabo.com, in Spanish; r UR$2000-4000) The unexceptional rooms at this beachfront hotel feel way overpriced in summer, but its prime location near the lighthouse makes it worth considering in the off-season. The attached restaurant (mains UR$215 to UR$295) has nice views of the ocean and is one of Cabo's few dependable year-round eateries.

Getting There & Away

Rutas del Sol runs two to five buses daily from Montevideo to the Cabo Polonio turnoff (UR$317, 4½ hours), where waiting 4WD trucks offer rides across the dunes into town (UR$150 roundtrip, 30 minutes).

Laguna de Castillos

Northwest of Cabo Polonio is the Laguna de Castillos, a vast coastal lagoon that shelters Uruguay's largest concentration of ombúes, graceful treelike plants whose anarchic growth pattern results in some rather fantastic shapes. In other parts of Uruguay the ombú is a solitary plant, but specimens here – some of them centuries old – grow in clusters, insulated by the lagoon from the bovine trampling that has spelled their doom elsewhere.

At **Monte de Ombúes** (☎099-295177), on the lagoon's western shore (near Km 267 on Ruta 10), brothers Marcos and Juan Carlos Olivera, whose family received this land from the Portuguese crown in 1793, lead two- to three-hour excursions (per person, five-person minimum UR$300). Tours begin with a 20-minute boat ride through a wetland teeming with cormorants, ibis, cranes and black swans, followed by a hike through the ombú forest. Departures are frequent in summer (pretty well anytime five people show up); other times of year, phone ahead for reservations.

TOP CHOICE **Guardia del Monte** (☎099-872588, 4475-9064; www.guardiadelmonte.com; Ruta 9, Km 261.5, Laguna de Castillos; r per person incl breakfast/half-board/full board UR$1700/2100/2500), overlooking the lagoon's northern shore, is at the end of a 10km dead-end road. This now-tranquil hideaway was established in the 18th century as a Spanish guard post to protect the Camino Real and the coastal frontier from pirates and Portuguese marauders. The lovely *estancia* house still oozes history, from the parlor displaying 18th-century maps and bird drawings to the kitchen's Danish woodstove salvaged from an 1884 shipwreck. All rates include optional afternoon tea, plus walking and horseback excursions along the lakeshore and into the surrounding ombú forest. Tasty meals are served on the ancient brick patio or in the cozy dining room, where a roaring fire beckons on chilly nights. Access to Guardia del Monte is from Ruta 9, a few kilometers south of the town of Castillos.

Punta del Diablo

POP 820

Once a sleepy fishing village, Punta del Diablo has long since become a prime summer getaway for Uruguayans and Argentines, and the epicenter of Uruguay's backpacker beach scene. Waves of seemingly uncontrolled development have pushed further inland and along the coast in recent years, but the stunning shoreline and laid-back lifestyle still exert their age-old appeal. To avoid the crowds, come outside the Christmas to February peak season; in particular, avoid the first half of January, when as many as 30,000 visitors inundate the town.

From the town's traditional center, a sandy 'plaza' just inland from the ocean, small dirt roads fan out in all directions. To get to the marina and the hostels listed following, head downhill 200m to the waterfront and continue northeast along the shoreline.

Sights & Activities

During the day you can rent surfboards or horses along the town's main beach, or trek an hour north to Parque Nacional Santa Teresa. In the evening there are sunsets to watch, spontaneous bonfires and drum sessions to drop in on...you get the idea.

Sleeping

The town's hostel scene has taken off dramatically in recent years, and there are several offerings beyond those listed here. *Cabañas* are the other accommodations of choice; this term applies to everything from rustic-to-a-fault shacks to custom-built designer condos with all modern conveniences. Most *cabañas* have kitchens and require you to bring your own bedding. For help finding something, ask at the supermarket in town, or check online at www.portaldeldiablo.com.uy. Rates skyrocket between Christmas and February.

TOP CHOICE El Diablo Tranquilo HOSTEL $$
(☎4477-2519; www.eldiablotranquilo.com; dm UR$720-960, tw UR$2000-2200, d UR$2200-3300; @☎) One of South America's most appealing hostels, this exceptionally well-designed place is the brainchild of expat American Brian Meissner. Follow the devilish red glow through the entryway, past the animated crowd on the circular fireside couch, and you'll find a mix of dorms and cushy doubles with endless perks. Along with wi-fi, high-speed computers, hammocks, a guest kitchen and laundry service, there are Paypal cash advances, bike and surfboard rentals, yoga and language classes and horseback excursions. Unsurprisingly, the average guest stay is nearly a week, and things can book up even in winter.

Two blocks downhill, right beside the beach, is EDT Playa Suites, Diablo Tranquilo's even cushier sister hostel. The best rooms upstairs have fireplaces, full-on ocean views and great sound systems, while the raucous bar-restaurant downstairs offers reasonably priced food (UR$160 to UR$220), beach service, and a party scene lasting late into the night. Undecided about what to drink? Spin the wheel of fate, and hope you don't land on the 'bartender's choice' – it's been the genesis of some pretty scary concoctions.

Del Norte Vengo y En El Sur Me Quedo CABAÑA $$
(☎099-878357; jasypo2876@yahoo.com; d UR$1600-2400, q UR$1600-2800) Two blocks north of the plaza, these colorful two-level *cabañas* have upstairs decks, ocean views, and satiny curtains and bedspreads. The young owners have lived in the US and speak excellent English.

La Casa de las Boyas HOSTEL $
(☎4477-2074; www.lacasadelasboyas.com; Playa del Rivero; dm UR$300-800, apt UR$2000-3200; @☎≋) A stone's throw from the beach and a 10-minute walk north of the bus stop, this hostel offers a pool, a guest kitchen, dorms of varying sizes and two kitchen-equipped apartments.

Eating

In high season, simply stroll the beachfront for your pick of seafood eateries and snack shacks by the dozen. Places listed here are among the few that remain open in winter. Another dependable year-round choice is the bar-restaurant at El Diablo Tranquilo.

El Viejo y El Mar SEAFOOD $$$
(full meals incl wine UR$360-400) At the dunes' edge, south of the town center, 'old man' Ernesto has just re-opened this delightfully ramshackle restaurant, suffused with a rustic-hip atmosphere. The candlelit walls are adorned with fishing nets, wine bottles, lanterns and guitars, and you're offered

whatever he's serving that night; the fixed-price menu usually includes fish, wine and dessert.

Cero Stress INTERNATIONAL $$
(mains UR$210-340; ⌚lunch & dinner) With a rustic interior dining room, an open kitchen and outdoor terraces with lovely ocean views, this laid-back eatery serves an eclectic menu featuring *rabas* (fried squid), *chivitos*, shrimp tacos, seafood stew and grilled fish with rice and vegetables. It also makes a mean *caipirinha* (Brazilian cocktail with sugar-cane alcohol).

Lo de Olga SEAFOOD $$
(mains UR$150-285; ⌚lunch & dinner) For delicious home-cooked fish and puffy-as-a-cloud *buñuelos de algas* (seaweed fritters), don't miss this sweet family-run restaurant on the way down to the port.

Information

Punta del Diablo has no ATMs except for the temporary ones set up briefly each summer. Bring cash with you, as few businesses accept credit cards and the nearest banks are an hour away in Castillos (40km southwest) or Chuy (45km north).

Getting There & Away

Rutas del Sol, COT and Cynsa all offer service to Punta del Diablo's new bus terminal, 2.5km west of town, which opened in early 2012. Between Christmas and Carnaval, all buses terminate here, leaving you with a five- to 10-minute shuttle (UR$25) or taxi (UR$100) ride into town. During the rest of the year, buses continue from the terminal to the town plaza near the waterfront.

Several direct buses run daily to Montevideo and Chuy on the Brazilian border; for other coastal destinations, you'll need to change buses in Castillos or Rocha.

BUSES FROM PUNTA DEL DIABLO

DESTINATION	COST (UR$)	DURATION (HR)
Castillos	59	1
Chuy	59	1
Montevideo	364	5
Rocha	117	1½

Parque Nacional Santa Teresa

This **national park** (☎4477-2101; www.ejercito.mil.uy/cal/sepae/sta_teresa.htm, in Spanish), 35km south of the Brazilian border, is administered by the army and attracts many Uruguayan and Brazilian visitors to its relatively uncrowded beaches. It offers 2000 dispersed camp sites in eucalyptus and pine groves, a very small zoo and a plant conservatory. There are also various grades of *cabañas* for rent; in January, prices range from UR$1400 for a basic A-frame to UR$3700 for a fancier oceanfront unit; between March and November these rates get slashed in half.

Buses from Punta del Diablo (UR$35, 15 minutes) will drop you off at Km 302 on Hwy 9; from here, you will need to walk or take a shuttle 1km to the Capatacía (park headquarters), where there's a phone, post office, market, bakery and **restaurant** (dishes UR$90-240; ⌚9am-10pm).

The park's star attraction, 4km further north on Ruta 9, is the impressive hilltop **Fortaleza de Santa Teresa** (admission UR$15; ⌚10am-7pm daily Dec-Mar, 10am-6pm Thu-Sun Apr-Nov), begun by the Portuguese in 1762 and finished by the Spaniards after its capture in 1793. At the park's northeastern corner is **Cerro Verde**, a coastal bluff protected under Uruguay's SNAP program (see the boxed text, p530).

UNDERSTAND URUGUAY

Uruguay Today

Recent years have seen a radical development in Uruguayan politics. After nearly two centuries of back-and-forth rule between the two traditional parties, Blancos and Colorados, Uruguayans elected the leftist Frente Amplio to power in 2005 and again in 2009. Over that span, the Frente Amplio government has presided over numerous social changes, including the banning of smoking in public, the legalization of abortion and civil unions between same-sex partners, and an ambitious program called Plan Ceibal that has distributed internet-ready laptops to every student in the country.

The current president, José Mujica, is noteworthy for having survived 13 years of imprisonment and torture during Uruguay's period of military rule (including two years imprisoned in the bottom of a well). Even so, in the same election that brought Mujica to power, Uruguayans voted down a referendum that would have opened the doors to prosecuting human rights abuses perpetrated during the 1973–1985 military dictatorship. The issue continues to divide the country, as evidenced by a May 2011 Congressional vote which nearly overturned these amnesty provisions (despite Mujica's own urgings to let sleeping dogs lie).

Mujica is well known for his grandfatherly style and humility. He famously donates over two-thirds of his salary to charities, refuses to live in the presidential palace, and for most of his political career he has eschewed suits and ties in favor of sweaters.

History

Uruguay's aboriginal inhabitants were the Charrúa along the coast and the Guaraní north of the Río Negro. The hunting-and-gathering Charrúa discouraged European settlement for more than a century by killing Spanish explorer Juan de Solís and most of his party in 1516. In any event there was little to attract the Spanish, who valued these lowlands along the Río de la Plata only as an access route to gold and other quick riches further inland.

The first Europeans to settle on the Banda Oriental (Eastern Shore) were Jesuit missionaries near present-day Soriano, on the Río Uruguay. Next came the Portuguese, who established present-day Colonia in 1680 as a beachhead for smuggling goods into Buenos Aires. Spain responded by building its own citadel at Montevideo in 1726. The following century saw an ongoing struggle between Spain and Portugal for control of these lands along the eastern bank of the Río de la Plata.

Napoleon's invasion of the Iberian peninsula in the early 19th century precipitated a weakening of Spanish and Portuguese power and the emergence of strong independence movements throughout the region. Uruguay's homegrown national hero, José Gervasio Artigas, originally sought to form an alliance with several states in present-day Argentina and southern Brazil against the European powers, but he was ultimately forced to flee to Paraguay. There he regrouped and organized the famous '33 Orientales,' a feisty band of Uruguayan patriots under General Juan Lavalleja who, with Argentine support, crossed the Río Uruguay on April 19, 1825, and launched a campaign to liberate modern-day Uruguay from Brazilian control. In 1828, after three years' struggle, a British-mediated treaty established Uruguay as a small independent buffer between the emerging continental powers.

For several decades, Uruguay's independence remained fragile. There was civil war between Uruguay's two nascent political parties, the Colorados and the Blancos (named, respectively, for the red and white bands they wore); Argentina besieged Montevideo from 1838 to 1851; and Brazil was an ever-present threat. Things finally settled down in the second half of the 19th century, with region-wide recognition of Uruguay's independence and the emergence of a strong national economy based on beef and wool production.

In the early 20th century, visionary president José Batlle y Ordóñez introduced such innovations as pensions, farm credits, unemployment compensation and the eight-hour work day. State intervention led to the nationalization of many industries, the creation of others and a new era of general prosperity. However, Batlle's reforms were largely financed through taxing the livestock sector, and when exports faltered mid-century, the welfare state crumbled. A period of military dictatorship began in the early 1970s, during which torture became routine, and more than 60,000 citizens were arbitrarily detained, but the 1980s brought a return to democratic traditions.

Culture

The one thing that Uruguayans will tell you that they're *not* is anything like their *porteño* cousins across the water. In many ways they're right. Where Argentines can be brassy and sometimes arrogant, Uruguayans tend to be more humble and relaxed. Where the former have always been a regional superpower, the latter have always lived in the shadow of one. Those jokes about Punta del Este being a suburb of Buenos Aires don't go down so well on this side of the border. There are plenty of similarities, though: the near-universal appreciation for the arts, the Italian influence and the gaucho heritage. Indeed, the rugged individualism and disdain that many Uruguayans hold for *el neoliberalismo* (neoliberalism) can be traced directly back to those romantic cowboy figures.

Uruguayans like to take it easy and pride themselves on being the opposite of the hot-headed Latino type. Sunday's the day for family and friends, to throw half a cow on the *parrilla* (grill), sit back and sip some *mate.* The population is well educated. The gap between rich and poor is much less pronounced than in most other Latin American countries, although the economic crises of the early 21st century have put a strain on the middle class.

Population

With 3.3 million people, Uruguay is South America's smallest Spanish-speaking country. The population is predominately white (88%) with 8% mestizo (people with mixed Spanish and indigenous blood) and 4% black. Indigenous peoples are practically nonexistent. The average life expectancy (just over 76 years) is one of Latin America's highest. The literacy rate is also high, at 98%, while population growth is a slow 0.5%. Population density is 19.8 people per sq km.

Religion

Forty-seven percent of Uruguayans are Roman Catholic. About one-third are from other Christian denominations. There's a small Jewish minority, numbering around 18,000. Uruguay has more self-professed atheists per capita than any other Latin American country. According to a 2008 American Religious Identification Survey, only slightly more than half of Uruguayans consider themselves religious.

Sports

Uruguayans, like just about all Latin Americans, are crazy about *fútbol* (soccer). Uruguay has won the World Cup twice, including the first tournament, played in Montevideo in 1930. The most notable teams are Montevideo-based Nacional and Peñarol. If you go to a match between these two, sit on the sidelines, not behind the goal, unless you're up for some serious rowdiness.

Asociación Uruguayo de Fútbol (☎02-400-7101; Guayabo 1531) in Montevideo can provide information on matches and venues.

Arts

Despite its small population, Uruguay has an impressive literary and artistic tradition. The country's most famous philosopher and essayist is José Enrique Rodó, whose 1900 essay *Ariel,* contrasting North American and Latin American civilizations, is a classic of the country's literature. Major contemporary writers include Juan Carlos Onetti, Mario Benedetti and Eduardo Galeano.

The most famous Uruguay-related film is Costa-Gavras' engrossing *State of Siege* (1973), filmed in Allende's Chile, which deals with the Tupamaro guerrillas' kidnapping and execution of suspected American CIA officer Dan Mitrione. Among the best movies to come out of Uruguay recently are César Charlone's award-winning *El Baño del Papa* (2007), based on Pope John Paul II's 1988 visit to Uruguay, and *3 Millones* (2011), in which father-son team Jaime and Yamandú Roos document their experiences accompanying Uruguay's football team to the 2010 South Africa World Cup.

Theater is popular and playwrights like Mauricio Rosencof are prominent. The most renowned painters are the late Juan Manuel Blanes, Pedro Figari and Joaquín Torres García. Sculptors include José Belloni.

Tango is big in Montevideo – Uruguayans claim tango legend Carlos Gardel as a native son, and one of the best-known tangos, *'La Cumparsita,'* was composed by Uruguayan Gerardo Matos Rodríguez. During Carnaval, Montevideo's streets reverberate to the energetic drumbeats of *candombe,* an African-derived rhythm brought to Uruguay by slaves from 1750 onwards. On the contemporary scene, several Uruguayan rock bands have won a following on both sides of the Río de la Plata, including Buitres, La Vela Puerca and No Te Va Gustar.

Food & Drink

Uruguayan cuisine revolves around grilled meat. *Parrilladas* (restaurants with big racks of meat roasting over a wood fire) are everywhere, and weekend *asados* (barbecues) are a national tradition. *Chivitos* are hugely popular, as are *chivitos al plato* (served with fried potatoes instead of bread). Vegetarians often have to content themselves with the ubiquitous pizza and pasta, although there are a few veggie restaurants lurking about. Seafood is excellent on the coast. Desserts are a dream of meringue, *dulce de leche* (milk caramel), burnt sugar and custard.

Tap water is OK to drink in most places. Uruguayan wines (especially tannats) are excellent, and local beers (Patricia, Pilsen and Zillertal) are passable.

Uruguayans consume even more *mate* than Argentines. If you get the chance, try to acquire the taste – there's nothing like whiling away an afternoon with new-found friends passing around the *mate*.

In major tourist destinations such as Punta del Este and Colonia, restaurants charge *cubiertos* (cover charges of UR$20 or more). Theoretically these pay for the basket of bread offered before your meal.

Environment

Though one of South America's smallest countries, Uruguay is not so small by European standards. Its area of 176,220 sq km is greater than England and Wales combined, or slightly bigger than the US state of Florida.

Uruguay's two main ranges of interior hills are the Cuchilla de Haedo, west of Tacuarembó, and the Cuchilla Grande, south of Melo; neither exceeds 500m in height. West of Montevideo the terrain is more level. The Río Negro flowing through the center of the country forms a natural dividing line between north and south. The Atlantic coast has impressive beaches, dunes, headlands and lagoons. Uruguay's grasslands and forests resemble those of Argentina's pampas or southern Brazil, and patches of palm savanna persist in the east, along the Brazilian border.

The country is rich in birdlife, especially in the coastal lagoons of Rocha department. Most large land animals have disappeared, but the occasional ñandú (rhea) still races across northwestern Uruguay's grasslands. Whales, fur seals and sea lions are common along the coast.

SURVIVAL GUIDE

Directory A-Z

Accommodations

Uruguay has an excellent network of hostels and campgrounds, especially along the Atlantic coast. Other low-end options include *hospedajes* (family homes) and *residenciales* (budget hotels).

Posadas (inns) are available in all price ranges and tend to be homier than hotels. Hotels are ranked from one to five stars, according to amenities.

PRICE RANGES

The following price ranges, used in Sleeping listings throughout this chapter, refer to a double room with bathroom in high season. Unless otherwise stated, breakfast is included in the price.

$	less than UR$1000
$$	UR$1000-2000
$$$	more than UR$2000

Country *estancias turísticas* (marked with blue National Tourism Ministry signs) provide lodging on farms (see the boxed text, p529).

Activities

Punta del Diablo, La Paloma, La Pedrera and Punta del Este all get excellent surfing waves, while Cabo Polonio and the coastal lagoons of Rocha department are great for whale and bird watching, respectively. Punta del Este's beach scene is more upmarket, with activities such as parasailing, windsurfing and jet skiing.

Horseback riding is very popular in the interior and can be arranged on most tourist *estancias* (see p529).

Business Hours

Opening times for individual businesses in this guide are only spelled out when they deviate from the standard hours outlined below.

Banks 1-6pm Mon-Fri. Exchange offices usually keep longer hours.

Bars, Pubs & Clubs 6pm-late. Things don't get seriously shaking until after midnight.

Restaurants noon-3pm & 9pm-midnight or later. If serving breakfast, open around 8am.

Shops 8:30am-1pm & 3-7pm Mon-Sat. In larger cities, department stores and supermarkets stay open at lunchtime and/or Sundays.

Electricity

Uruguay uses the same electrical plug as Argentina. See p590 for details.

Embassies & Consulates

All listings are in Montevideo:

Argentina (☎2902-8166; cmdeo.mrecic.gov.ar; Cuareim 1470)

Australia (☎2901-0743; www.dfat.gov.au/missions/countries/uy.html; Cerro Largo 1000)

Brazil (☎2707-2119; montevideu.itamaraty.gov.br; Artigas 1394)

Canada (☎2902-2030; www.canadainternational.gc.ca/uruguay; Plaza Independencia 749, Oficina 102)

France (☎2-1705-0000; www.ambafranceuruguay.org; Av Uruguay 853)

Germany (☎2902-5222; www.montevideo.diplo.de; La Cumparsita 1435)

Netherlands (☎2711-2956; www.holanda.org.uy; Leyenda Patria 2880, 2nd fl)

New Zealand (☎2622-1543; Miguel Grau 3789)

UK (☎2622-3630; ukinuruguay.fco.gov.uk; Marco Bruto 1073)

USA (☎2-1770-2000; uruguay.usembassy.gov; Lauro Muller 1776)

Festivals & Events

Uruguay's Carnaval (see p506) lasts for more than a month and is livelier than Argentina's. Semana Santa (Holy Week) has become known as Semana Turismo – many Uruguayans travel out of town and finding accommodations is tricky during this time. Other noteworthy events include the beer festival in Paysandú (p523) and Tacuarembó's Fiesta de la Patria Gaucha (p528).

Food

For information about Uruguayan cuisine, see p548 and p496.

Gay & Lesbian Travelers

Uruguay has gotten more GLBT-friendly in recent years. In January 2008 it became the first Latin American country to recognize same-sex civil unions nationwide.

In Montevideo, look for the pocket-sized **Friendly Map** (www.friendlymap.com.uy) listing GLBT-friendly businesses throughout Uruguay.

PRICE RANGES

The following price ranges, used in Eating listings throughout this chapter, refer to a standard main course.

$ less than UR$175

$$ UR$175-300

$$$ more than UR$300

Health

No vaccinations are required for Uruguayan travel. Uruguay has a good public-health system, and tap water is generally safe to drink. In this book, hospitals are listed under the Information heading for each city.

Insurance

Worldwide travel insurance is available at www.lonelyplanet.com/travel_services. You can buy, extend and claim online anytime – even if you're already on the road.

Internet Access

Internet cafes are commonplace in cities and larger towns; access costs about UR$20 per hour. Many Antel (state telephone company) offices also provide internet for UR$19 to UR$45 per hour.

Legal Matters

Illegal drugs are freely available in Uruguay, but getting caught with them is about as much fun as anywhere else in the world, and Uruguayan police and officials are not as bribe-hungry as many of their South American counterparts.

Maps

ITMB (shop.itmb.ca) publishes a useful map depicting Montevideo on one side and Uruguay on the other. Other good map sources in Uruguay include Ancap service stations, the **Automóvil Club del Uruguay** (www.acu.com.uy) and **Servicio Geográfico Militar** (www.sgm.gub.uy).

Money

Prices in this chapter are in *pesos uruguayos* (UR$), the official Uruguayan currency. Banknote values are 20, 50, 100, 200, 500 and 1000. There are coins of one, two, five and 10 pesos. For exchange rates, see p496.

US dollars are commonly accepted in major tourist hubs, where top-end hotels and even some budget accommodations quote US$ prices. However, beware of poor exchange rates at hotel desks. In many cases, you'll still come out ahead paying in pesos. Away from the touristed areas, dollars are of limited use.

ATMS

In all but the smallest interior towns, getting cash with your ATM card is easy. Machines marked with the green Banred or blue Redbrou logo serve all major international banking networks.

ATMs dispense bills in multiples of 100 pesos. To avoid getting stuck with large bills, don't request multiples of UR$1000 (ie take out UR$900 rather than UR$1000, UR$1900 rather than UR$2000 etc).

Many ATMs dispense US dollars, designated as U$S, but only in multiples of US$100.

CREDIT CARDS

Most upmarket hotels, restaurants and shops accept credit cards.

MONEYCHANGERS

There are *casas de cambio* in Montevideo, Colonia, the Atlantic beach resorts and border towns such as Chuy. They keep longer hours than banks but often offer lower rates.

TIPPING

Restaurants 10%

Taxis Round up a few pesos

Post

Postal rates are reasonable, though service can be slow. If something is truly important, send it by registered mail or private courier.

Public Holidays

Año Nuevo (New Year's Day) January 1

Día de los Reyes (Epiphany) January 6

Viernes Santo/Pascua (Good Friday/ Easter) March/April (dates vary)

Desembarco de los 33 (Return of the 33 Exiles) April 19; honors the exiles who returned to Uruguay in 1825 to liberate the country from Brazil with Argentine support

Día del Trabajador (Labor Day) May 1

Batalla de Las Piedras (Battle of Las Piedras) May 18; commemorates a major battle of the fight for independence

Natalicio de Artigas (Artigas' Birthday) June 19

Jura de la Constitución (Constitution Day) July 18

Día de la Independencia (Independence Day) August 25

Día de la Raza (Columbus Day) October 12

Día de los Muertos (All Souls' Day) November 2

Navidad (Christmas Day) December 25

Telephone

Uruguay's country code is ☎598. Antel is the state telephone company, with offices in every town. There are also private *locutorios* (telephone offices) everywhere.

As of 2010, all Uruguayan landline numbers are eight digits long, beginning with 2 for Montevideo or 4 for elsewhere in the country. Cell phone numbers consist of a three-digit prefix (most commonly 099) followed by a six-digit number. If dialing internationally, drop the leading zero.

Public phones require prepaid cards, sold in values of 25, 50, 100, 200 and 500 pesos, available at Antel offices or newspaper kiosks.

Many internet cafes have headphone-microphone setups and Skype installed on their computers.

CELL (MOBILE) PHONES

Rather than use expensive roaming plans, many travelers bring an unlocked cell phone (or buy a cheap one here) and simply insert a local SIM card. These are readily available at most kiosks, as are prepaid cards to recharge your credit.

Note that it's best to unlock your phone in your home country, since reliable providers of this service are hard to find in Uruguay.

Time

Uruguay Standard Time is three hours behind GMT and one hour ahead of Argentina. Daylight-saving time, when clocks are moved forward one hour, starts on the first Sunday in October. Clocks are put back an hour on the second Sunday in March.

Tourist Information

The **National Tourism Ministry** (www.turismo.gub.uy) operates 13 offices around the country. It distributes excellent free maps for each of Uruguay's 19 departments, along with specialized brochures on *estancia* tourism, Carnaval, surfing and other subjects of interest to travelers. Most towns also have a muncipal tourist office on the plaza or at the bus terminal.

Travelers with Disabilities

Uruguay is slowly beginning to plan for travelers with special needs. In Montevideo you'll find newly constructed ramps and dedicated bathrooms in high-profile destinations such as Plaza Independencia and Teatro Solis, and disabled access on the CA1 bus line. However, there's still a long way to go. Many budget hotels have at least one set of stairs and no elevator. On the bright side, taxis are cheap and locals are glad to help however they can.

Visas

Nationals of Western Europe, Australia, the USA, Canada and New Zealand automatically receive a 90-day tourist card, renewable for another 90 days. Other nationals may require visas. For extensions, visit the **Dirección Nacional de la Migración** (☎2916-0471; Misiones 1513) in Montevideo, or local offices in border towns.

Volunteering

All Uruguayan organizations accepting volunteers require a minimum commitment of one month, and many require at least basic Spanish proficiency. Following are some Montevideo-based groups:

Academia Uruguay (www.academiauruguay.com) Language school offering volunteer opportunities in Montevideo.

Karumbé (www.karumbe.org) Sea turtle conservation.

Women Travelers

Uruguayans are no slouches when it comes to *machismo*, but women are generally treated with respect, and traveling alone is safer here than in many other Latin American countries.

Getting There & Away

Flights and tours can be booked online at lonelyplanet.com/bookings.

Entering the Country

Uruguay requires passports of all foreigners, except those from neighboring countries (who need only national identification cards).

Passports are necessary for many simple, everyday transactions, such as checking into hotels.

Air

Airports & Airlines

Montevideo's **Carrasco International Airport** (MVD; aeropuertodecarrasco.com.uy) is the main port of entry, although a few direct flights from Argentina and Brazil serve **Punta del Este International Airport** (PDP; www.puntadeleste.aero). For specific information on flights that serve each airport, see p539.

Pluna, the Uruguayan national carrier, has an excellent safety record.

Airlines with direct flights to Uruguay:

Aerolíneas Argentinas (www.aerolineas.com.ar)

American Airlines (www.aa.com)

BQB (www.flybqb.com)

Copa (www.copaair.com)

Gol (www.voegol.com.br)

Iberia (www.iberia.com)

LAN (www.lan.com)

Pluna (www.flypluna.com)

Sol (www.sol.com.ar)

TACA (www.taca.com)

TAM (www.tam.com.br)

Land & Sea

Uruguay shares borders with the Argentine province of Entre Ríos and the southern Brazilian state of Rio Grande do Sul. Major highways and bus services are generally good, although buses from Montevideo to Buenos Aires are slower and less convenient than the ferries across the Río de la Plata. For Iguazú Falls, traveling via Argentina is faster and more straightforward than traveling through Brazil.

Getting Around

Bus

Buses are comfortable, fares are reasonable and distances are short. Most companies distribute free timetables. In the few cities that lack terminals, all companies are within easy walking distance of each other, usually around the main plaza.

Reservations are unnecessary except during holiday periods. On peak travel dates a

URUGUAYAN BORDER CROSSINGS

FROM	TO	ROAD NUMBER/DESCRIPTION
ARGENTINA		
Buenos Aires	Montevideo	Boat (Buquebus)
Buenos Aires	Colonia	Boat (Buquebus, Colonia Express, Seacat)
Tigre	Carmelo	Boat (Cacciola)
Gualeguaychú	Fray Bentos	Represa de Salto Grande (dam)
Colón	Paysandú	Puente General Artigas (bridge)
Concordia	Salto	Puente General San Martín (bridge)
Concordia	Salto	Boat (Transporte Fluvial San Cristóbal)
BRAZIL		
Chuí	Chuy	Hwy BR-471/UR-9
Jaguarão	Río Branco	Hwy BR-116/UR-26
Aceguá	Aceguá	Hwy RS-153/UR-8
Santana do Livramento	Rivera	Hwy BR-293/UR-5
Quaraí	Artigas	Hwy RS-060/UY-30
Barra do Quaraí	Bella Unión	Hwy BR-472/UY-3

single company may run multiple departures at the same hour, in which case they'll mark a bus number on your ticket; check with the driver to make sure you're boarding the right bus, or you may find yourself in the 'right' seat on the wrong bus!

Most towns with central bus terminals have a fee-based left-luggage facility.

Car & Motorcycle

Visitors to Uruguay who are staying less than 90 days need only bring a valid driver's license from their home country. Uruguayan drivers are extremely considerate, and even bustling Montevideo is quite sedate compared with Buenos Aires.

Uruguay imports all its oil. Unleaded gasoline cost UR$35.60 a liter at the time of research.

The **Automóvil Club del Uruguay** (www.acu.com.uy) has good maps and information.

HIRE

Economy cars rent for upwards of UR$1000 a day in the high season, with tax and insurance included. Online bookings are often cheaper than in-country rentals. Most credit-card companies' automatic LDW (loss-damage-waiver) insurance covers rentals in Uruguay.

ROAD RULES & HAZARDS

Drivers are expected to turn on their headlights during the daytime on all highways. In most towns, alternating one-way streets are the rule, with an arrow marking the allowed direction of travel.

Outside Montevideo, most intersections have neither a stop sign nor a traffic light; right of way is determined by who reaches the corner first. This can be nerve-wracking for the uninitiated! Arbitrary police stops and searches are rare.

Outside the capital and coastal tourist areas, traffic is minimal and poses few problems. Roads are generally in reasonable shape, but some interior roads can be rough. Keep an eye out for livestock and wildlife. Even in Montevideo's busy downtown, horse-drawn carts still operate, hauling trash or freight.

Hitchhiking

It's not uncommon to see locals hitchhiking in rural areas, as gas is expensive and relatively few people own cars. Safety is not as serious a concern as in most other countries, although foreigners looking to hitch a ride may encounter some raised eyebrows.

Local Transportation

Taxis, *remises* (radio-dispatched taxis) and local buses are similar to those in Argentina. Taxis are metered, and drivers calculate fares using meter readings and a photocopied chart. Between 10pm and 6am, and on weekends and holidays, fares are 20% higher. There's a small additional charge for luggage, and passengers generally tip the driver by rounding fares up to the next multiple of five or ten pesos. City bus service is excellent in Montevideo and other urban areas, while *micros* (minibuses) form the backbone of the local transit network in smaller coastal towns such as La Paloma.

Understand Argentina

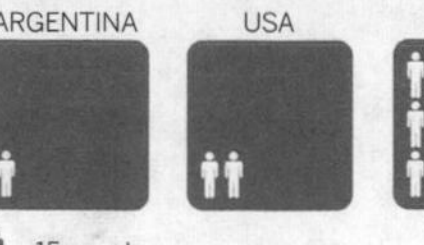

Argentina Today

Cristina's Reign

Cristina Kirchner was re-elected Argentina's president by a landslide majority of 54%. She ran on a platform that appealed to the populist vote, promising to raise incomes, restore industry and maintain Argentina's economic boom. Her approach worked like a charm.

Kirchner has often been compared to Evita for her fight against poverty and her administration of generous social programs – but both have also shown authoritarian tendencies, such as trying to censor the media and rule by decree.

Kirchner dismissed the Central Bank president for not allowing her to use currency reserves to pay off future debts, and strong-armed business into price-control agreements. Her government has also been accused of manipulating economic numbers; in March 2011, the *Economist* magazine stated that it no longer trusted inflation figures coming out of Argentina and would cease to publish them in favor of figures from a US-based analyst. The Falkland Islands are another hot topic, with Kirchner once again seriously challenging the island's sovereignty – just in time for the 30th anniversary of the Falklands War.

Despite her many detractors, this *presidenta* has made admirable strides – she's addressed the abuses of the military dictatorship, championed same-sex marriage laws and, over all, supported the blue-collar classes. And her people love her for it, just like they did Evita.

- » Area: 2.8 million sq km
- » Population: 40,120,000
- » Capital: Buenos Aires
- » Primary language: Spanish
- » Time: GMT minus three hours (depending on daylight savings time)
- » GDP per capita (PPP): US$16,000
- » Unemployment rate: 7.3%

Economic Woes

Argentina's currency devaluation in 2002 caused a demand for its suddenly cheap agricultural products. Helped along by skyrocketing government spending and growth in Brazil and China, this economic boom lasted through 2007 and revved up again in 2010. But now high inflation, a

Top Books

» Uttermost Part of the Earth (E. Lucas Bridges, 1947) Classic book about Tierra del Fuego's now extinct *indígenas*.

» In Patagonia (Bruce Chatwin, 1977) Evocative writing on Patagonia's history and mystique.

» The Motorcycle Diaries (1993, Ernesto Che Guevara et al) Based on the travel diary of the Argentine born revolutionist.

» And the Money Kept Rolling In (and Out) (Paul Blustein, 2005) How the IMF helped bankrupt Argentina.

Top Films

» La historia oficial (The Official Story, 1985) Oscar-winning film on the Dirty War.

» Historias mínimas (Intimate Stories, 2002) Three separate people traveling in Patagonia.

ethnicity

(% of population)

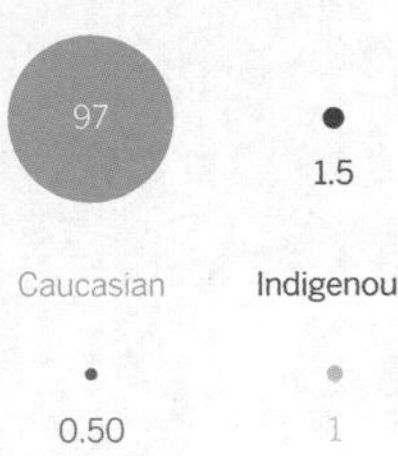

if Argentina were 100 people

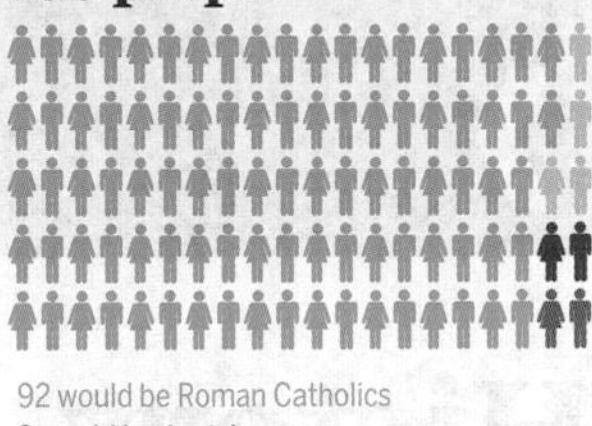

92 would be Roman Catholics
2 would be Jewish
2 would be Protestant
4 would be other

stronger peso and lower commodity prices are stalling the economy. The government is cutting back on its utility and transportation subsidies, so the public will be paying a truer price for these services. And in October 2011, in an effort to curb capital from heading overseas, the government required Argentines to substantiate their purchases of US dollars.

Cristina Kirchner will need to control inflation, unofficially hovering at around 25% ('official' estimates are less than half, 11%). She'll have to control spending to maintain cash reserves and equalize the trade balance. Government policies need to become more transparent to encourage both domestic and foreign investment. It's a tall order and devaluation is an increasing risk, but who knows – maybe another crash is just what Argentina needs to get on top again.

Sporting Success

One of the big shocks in the sporting world was in June 2011, when the famous *fútbol* club River Plate was demoted to second division. This was the first time it had happened in the club's 110-year existence, and it caused riots in Buenos Aires. The famous *Superclásico* matches against Boca have had to be put on hold until River Plate regains top-tier status.

Meanwhile, it was another great year for Rosario-born Lionel Messi, who won FIFA's Player of the Year award in 2009 and the equivalent Ballon d'Or award in 2010 and 2011. He currently plays in Spain for FC Barcelona, but captains the Argentine national team.

In other 2011 sporting news, the Dakar Rally was once again held in Argentina (and Chile). Argentina's tennis team made it to the Davis Cup final in Seville (but lost yet again to Spain). And the FIBA Championship basketball tournament (and Olympic qualifier) was held in Mar del Plata, in which Argentina won the final against Brazil.

» **Un novio para mi mujer** (A Boyfriend for My Wife; 2008) Comedy about a husband plotting his divorce.

» **El secreto de sus ojos** (The Secret in Their Eyes; 2009) Thriller that won the 2010 Oscar for best foreign-language film.

Greetings

» Say *buenos dias* or *buenas tardes* (good morning/good afternoon) when you walk into a room.

» *Adios* or *hasta luego* means goodbye.

» *Ciao* or *chau* is a casual goodbye to friends.

» *Che* is a casual word that means 'Hey!' Use it with friends.

» *Che boludo* is a phrase that should only be used with either a *very* good friend – or someone you want to tell off.

» Accept and give *besos* (kisses) on the cheek.

History

Like all Latin American countries, Argentina has a tumultuous history, one tainted by periods of despotic rule, corruption and hard times. The Dirty War was an especially brutal era that occurred not so long ago, and still lives in the memory of many Argentines. Wild rollercoaster economic woes are another hardship that Argentines have had to deal with over the decades. But Argentina's history is also illustrious, the story of a country that fought off colonial rule from Spain and was once one of the world's economic powerhouses. It's about a country that gave birth to the tango, and to international icons such as the gaucho, Evita Perón and Che Guevara. Understanding Argentina's past is paramount to understanding its present and, most importantly, to understanding Argentines themselves.

The following is just a brief introduction to the history of Argentina. If you'd like to read more, see p561 for some recommended titles.

Native Peoples

Many different native peoples ranged throughout what became Argentina. On the pampas lived the hunter-gather Querandí, and in the north the Guaraní were semisedentary agriculturalists and fishermen. In the Lake District and Patagonia, the Pehuenches and Puelches gathered the pine nuts of the araucaria, while the Mapuche entered the region from the west as the Spanish pushed south. Today there are several Mapuche reservations, especially in the area around Junín de los Andes.

Until they were wiped out by Europeans, there were indigenous inhabitants as far south as Tierra del Fuego ('Land of Fire'), where the Selk'nam, Haush, Yaghan and Alacaluf peoples lived as mobile hunters and gatherers. Despite frequently inclement weather they wore little or no clothing, but constant fires kept them warm and gave the region its name.

Of all of Argentina, the northwest was the most developed. Several indigenous groups, notably the Diaguita, practiced irrigated agriculture in the valleys of the eastern Andean foothills. Inhabitants were influenced

TIMELINE

10,000 BC

Humans, having crossed the Bering Strait approximately 20,000 years earlier, finally reach the area of modern-day Argentina. The close of one of the world's greatest human migrations nears.

7370 BC

Toldense culture makes its first paintings of hands inside Patagonia's famous Cueva de las Manos. The paintings prove humans inhabited the region this far back.

4000 BC

The indigenous Yaghan, later referred to as Fuegians by the English-speaking world, begin populating the southernmost islands of Tierra del Fuego. Humans could migrate no further south.

by the Tiahanaco empire of Bolivia and by the great Inca empire, which expanded south from Peru from the early 1480s. In Salta province the ruined city of Quilmes is one of the best-preserved pre-Incan sites.

Enter the Spanish

Just over a decade after Christopher Columbus accidentally encountered the Americas, other European explorers began probing the Río de la Plata estuary. Most early explorations of the area were motivated by rumors of vast quantities of silver. Spaniard Sebastian Cabot optimistically named the river the Río de la Plata (River of Silver), and to drive the rumors home, part of the new territory was even given the Latin name for silver *(argentum)*. But the mineral riches that the Spanish found in the Inca empire of Peru never panned out in this misnamed land.

The first real attempt at establishing a permanent settlement on the estuary was made by Spanish aristocrat Pedro de Mendoza in 1536. He landed at present-day Buenos Aires, but after the colonists tried pilfering food from the indigenous Querandí, the natives turned on them violently. Within four years Mendoza fled back to Spain without a lick of silver, and the detachment of troops he left behind beat it upriver to the gentler environs of Asunción, present-day capital of Paraguay.

Northwest Supremacy

Although Spanish forces reestablished Buenos Aires by 1580, it remained a backwater in comparison to Andean settlements founded by a separate and more successful Spanish contingency moving south from Alto Perú (now Bolivia). With ties to the colonial stronghold of Lima and financed by the bonanza silver mine at Potosí, the Spanish founded some two dozen cities as far south as Mendoza (1561) during the latter half of the 16th century.

The two most important centers were Tucumán (founded in 1565) and Córdoba (1573). Tucumán lay in the heart of a rich agricultural region and supplied Alto Perú with grains, cotton and livestock. Córdoba became an important educational center, and Jesuit missionaries established *estancias* (ranches) in the sierras to supply Alto Perú with mules, foodstuffs and wine. Córdoba's Manzana Jesuítica (Jesuit Block) is now the finest preserved group of colonial buildings in the country, and several Jesuit *estancias* in the Central Sierras are also preserved. These sites, along with the central plazas of Salta (founded in 1582) and Tucumán, boast the finest colonial architecture. For more on the Jesuits, see p184.

Buenos Aires: Bootlegger To Boomtown

As the northwest prospered, Buenos Aires suffered the Crown's harsh restrictions on trade for nearly 200 years. But because the port was ideal for trade, frustrated merchants turned to smuggling, and contraband

THE MISSION

The Mission (1986), starring Robert De Niro and Jeremy Irons, is an epic film about the Jesuit missions and missionaries in 18th-century South America. It's the perfect kickoff for a trip to northern Argentina's missions.

AD 1480s

The Inca empire expands into present-day Argentina's Andean northwest. At the time, the region was inhabited by Argentina's most advanced indigenous cultures, including the Diaguita and Tafí.

1536

Pedro de Mendoza establishes Puerto Nuestra Señora Santa María del Buen Aire on the Río de la Plata. But the Spaniards anger the indigenous Querandí, who soon drive the settlers out.

1553

Francisco de Aguirre establishes Santiago del Estero, furthering Spain's expansion into present-day Argentina from Alto Perú. Today the city is the country's oldest permanent settlement.

1561

The city of Mendoza is founded by Spaniards during their push to establish access to the Río de la Plata, where Spanish ships could deliver more troops and supplies.

trade with Portuguese Brazil and nonpeninsular European powers flourished. The wealth passing through the city fueled its initial growth.

With the decline of silver mining at Potosí in the late 18th century, the Spanish Crown was forced to recognize Buenos Aires' importance for direct transatlantic trade. Relaxing its restrictions, Spain made Buenos Aires the capital of the new viceroyalty of the Río de la Plata – which included Paraguay, Uruguay and the mines at Potosí – in 1776.

Argentina's national beer, Quilmes, is named after the now decimated indigenous group of northwest Argentina. It's also the name of a city in the province of Buenos Aires.

The new viceroyalty had internal squabbles over trade and control issues, but when the British raided the city in 1806 and again in 1807 (in an attempt to seize control of Spanish colonies during the Napoleonic Wars), the response was unified. Locals rallied against the invaders without Spanish help and chased them out of town.

The late 18th century also saw the emergence of the gauchos of the pampas (see p114). The South American counterpart to North America's cowboys, they hunted wild cattle and broke in wild horses that had multiplied after being left behind by expeditions on the Río de la Plata.

Independence & Infighting

Toward the end of the 18th century, criollos (Argentine-born colonists) became increasingly dissatisfied and impatient with Spanish authority. The expulsion of British troops from Buenos Aires gave the people of the Río de la Plata new confidence in their ability to stand alone. After Napoleon invaded Spain in 1808, Buenos Aires finally declared its independence on May 25, 1810.

One of the best-known contemporary accounts of postindependence Argentina is Domingo Faustino Sarmiento's *Life in the Argentine Republic in the Days of the Tyrants* (1868). Also superb is his seminal classic, *Facundo, Or Civilization & Barbarism* (1845).

Independence movements throughout South America soon united to expel Spain from the continent by the 1820s. Under the leadership of General José de San Martín and others, the United Provinces of the Río de la Plata (the direct forerunner of the Argentine Republic) declared formal independence at Tucumán on July 9, 1816.

Despite achieving independence, the provinces were united in name only. With a lack of any effective central authority, regional disparities within Argentina – formerly obscured by Spanish rule – became more obvious. This resulted in the rise of the caudillos (local strongmen), who resisted Buenos Aires as strongly as Buenos Aires had resisted Spain.

Argentine politics was divided between the Federalists of the interior, who advocated provincial autonomy, and the Unitarists of Buenos Aires, who upheld the city's central authority. For nearly 20 years bloody conflicts between the two factions left the country nearly exhausted.

The Reign of Rosas

In the first half of the 19th century Juan Manuel de Rosas came to prominence as a caudillo in Buenos Aires province, representing the interests of rural elites and landowners. He became governor of the province in

1565

Diego de Villarroel founds the city of San Miguel de Tucumán (referred to today simply as Tucumán), Argentina's third-oldest. The city was relocated further east 120 years later.

1573

The city of Córdoba is founded by Tucumán Governor Jerónimo Luis de Cabrera, establishing an important link on the trade routes between Chile and Alto Perú.

1580

Buenos Aires is re-established by Spanish forces, but the city remains a backwater for years, in comparison with the growing strongholds of Mendoza, Tucumán and Santiago del Estero.

1609

Jesuits begin building missions in northeast Argentina, including San Ignacio Miní (1610), Loreto (1632) and Santa Ana (1633), concentrating the indigenous Guaraní into settlements known as *reducciones*.

1829 and, while he championed the Federalist cause, he also helped centralize political power in Buenos Aires and proclaimed that all international trade be funneled through the capital. His reign lasted more than 20 years (to 1852), and he set ominous precedents in Argentine political life, creating the infamous *mazorca* (his ruthless political police force) and institutionalizing torture.

Under Rosas, Buenos Aires continued to dominate the new country, but his extremism turned many against him, including some of his strongest allies. Finally, in 1852, a rival caudillo named Justo José de Urquiza (once a staunch supporter of Rosas) organized a powerful army and forced Rosas from power. Urquiza's first task was to draw up a constitution, which was formalized by a convention in Santa Fe on May 1, 1853.

The Fleeting Golden Age

Elected the Republic of Argentina's first official president in 1862, Bartolomé Mitre was concerned with building the nation and establishing infrastructure. His goals, however, were subsumed by the War of the Triple Alliance (or Paraguayan War), which lasted from 1864 to 1870. Not

MORE HISTORICAL READS

The most comprehensive, though not necessarily most readable, book on Argentine history is David Rock's *Argentina 1516-1987: From Spanish Colonization to Alfonsín* (1987). It's worth the grunt.

Gargantuan in size and vast in scope, *The Argentina Reader* (2002), edited by Gabriella Nouzeilles and Graciela Montaldo, is a thorough compilation of some of the most important essays, excerpts and stories from Argentine history and culture.

For an interpretation of the gaucho's role in Argentine history, check out Richard W Slatta's book *Gauchos and the Vanishing Frontier* (1983).

Take a more personalized look into Argentina's past with Monica Szurmuk's *Women in Argentina* (2001), a collection of travel narratives by women – both Argentine and foreign – who traveled here between 1850 and 1930.

Journalist Horacio Verbitsky's book *The Flight: Confessions of an Argentine Dirty Warrior* (1996) was based on interviews with former Navy Captain Adolfo Scilingo, who acknowledged throwing political prisoners into the Atlantic. In 2005 Scilingo was found guilty of numerous counts of human-rights abuses.

Argentine writer Uki Goñi's *The Real Odessa* (2002) is the best and probably most meticulously researched book about Argentina's harboring of Nazi war criminals during the Perón administration.

Jacobo Timerman, an Argentine publisher and journalist who was outwardly critical of the 1976–83 military regime, was arrested and tortured by the military. He details the experience in his esteemed memoir *Prisoner Without a Name, Cell Without a Number* (1981).

1767

The Spanish Crown expels the Jesuits from all of New Spain, and the mission communities decline rapidly.

1776

Spain names Buenos Aires the capital of the new viceroyalty of the Río de la Plata. The territory includes the areas of present-day Paraguay, Uruguay and the mines at Potosí (Bolivia).

1806–07

Attempting to seize control of Spanish colonies, British forces raid Buenos Aires in 1806 and in 1807. Buenos Aires militias defeat British troops without Spain's help, which kindles ideas of independence.

May 25 1810

Buenos Aires declares its independence from Spain on May 25, although actual independence is still several years off. The city names the Plaza de Mayo in honor of the event.

until Domingo Faustino Sarmiento, an educator and journalist from San Juan, became president did progress in Argentina really kick in.

Buenos Aires' economy boomed and immigrants poured in from Spain, Italy, Germany and Eastern Europe. The new residents worked in the port area, lived tightly in the tenement buildings and developed Buenos Aires' famous dance – the tango – in the brothels and smoky nightclubs of the port (see p576). Elsewhere in the country, Basque and Irish refugees became the first shepherds, as both sheep numbers and wool exports increased nearly tenfold between 1850 and 1880.

Still, much of the southern pampas and Patagonia were inaccessible for settlers because of resistance from indigenous Mapuche and Tehuelche. In 1878, General Julio Argentino Roca carried out an extermination campaign on the indigenous people in what is known as the Conquista del Desierto (Conquest of the Desert). The campaign doubled the area under state control and opened Patagonia to settlement and sheep.

By the turn of the 20th century Argentina had a highly developed rail network (financed largely by British capital), fanning out from Buenos Aires in all directions. Still, the dark cloud of a vulnerable economy loomed. Industry could not absorb all the immigration, labor unrest grew and imports surpassed exports. Finally, with the onset of the world-wide Great Depression, the military took power under conditions of considerable social unrest. An obscure but oddly visionary colonel, Juan Domingo Perón, was the first leader to try to come to grips with the country's economic crisis.

PERÓN

A fascinating, fictionalized version of the life of ex-president Juan Perón, culminating in his return to Buenos Aires in 1973, is Tomás Eloy Martínez' *The Perón Novel* (1998).

Juan Perón

Juan Perón emerged in the 1940s to become Argentina's most revered, as well as most despised, political figure. He first came to national prominence as head of the National Department of Labor, after a 1943 military coup toppled civilian rule. With the help of Eva Duarte ('Evita'), his second wife (see p563), he ran for and won the presidency in 1946.

During previous sojourns in fascist Italy and Nazi Germany, Perón had grasped the importance of spectacle in public life and also developed his own brand of watered-down Mussolini-style fascism. He held massive rallies from the balcony of the Casa Rosada, with the equally charismatic Evita at his side. Although they ruled by decree rather than consent, the Peróns legitimized the trade-union movement, extended political rights to working-class people, secured voting rights for women and made university education available to any capable individual. Of course, many of these social policies made him disliked by conservatives and the rich classes.

Economic hardship and inflation undermined Juan Perón's second presidency in 1952, and Evita's death the same year dealt the country a blow and the president's popularity. In 1955 a military coup sent him into exile in Spain and begun nearly 30 years of catastrophic military rule.

July 9 1816

After successful independence movements throughout South America, the United Provinces of the Río de la Plata (Argentina's forerunner) declares formal independence from Spain at Tucumán.

THE ART ARCHIVE/ALAMY ©

» Congress of Tucumán

1829

Federalist caudillo Juan Manuel de Rosas becomes governor of Buenos Aires province and de facto ruler of the Argentine Confederation. He rules with an iron fist for more than 20 years.

1852

Federalist and former Rosas ally Justo José de Urquiza defeats Rosas at the Battle of Caseros and, in 1853, draws up Argentina's first constitution.

EVITA, LADY OF HOPE

'I will come again, and I will be millions.'

Eva Perón, 1952

From her humble origins in the pampas, to her rise to power beside President Juan Perón, María Eva Duarte de Perón is one of the most revered political figures on the planet. Known affectionately to all as Evita, she is Argentina's beloved First Lady, in some ways even eclipsing the legacy of her husband, who governed Argentina from 1946 to 1955.

At the age of 15 Eva Duarte left her hometown of Junín for Buenos Aires, looking for work as an actor, but eventually landing a job in radio. Her big chance came in 1944, when she attended a benefit at Buenos Aires' Luna Park. Here Duarte met Colonel Juan Perón, who fell in love with her; they were married in 1945.

Shortly after Perón won the presidency in 1946, Evita went to work in the office of the Department of Labor and Welfare. During Perón's two terms, Evita empowered her husband both through her charisma and by reaching out to the nation's poor, who came to love her dearly. She built housing for the poor, created programs for children and distributed clothing and food items to needy families. She campaigned for the aged, offered health services to the poor and advocated for a law extending suffrage to women.

Perón won his second term in 1952, but that same year Evita – at age 33 and the height of her popularity – died of cancer. It was a blow to Argentina and her husband's presidency.

Although remembered for extending social justice to those she called the country's *descamisados* (shirtless ones), the Evita and her husband ruled with an iron fist. They jailed opposition leaders and newspapers, and banned *Time* magazine when it referred to her as an 'illegitimate child'. However, there is no denying the extent to which she empowered women at all levels of Argentine society and helped the country's poor.

Today Evita enjoys near-saint status. Get to know her at Museo Evita (p62), or visit her tomb in the Recoleta cemetery (p59). You can also read her ghostwritten autobiography *La razón de mi vida* (My Mission in Life; 1951).

During his exile, Perón plotted his return to Argentina. In the late 1960s increasing economic problems, strikes, political kidnappings and guerrilla warfare marked Argentine political life. In the midst of these events, Perón returned to Argentina and was voted president again in 1973; however, after an 18-year exile, there was no substance to his rule. Chronically ill, Perón died in mid-1974, leaving a fragmented country to his ill-qualified third wife, Isabel.

The Dirty War & the Disappeared

In the late 1960s and early '70s, antigovernment feeling was rife, and street protests often exploded into all-out riots. Armed guerrilla organizations emerged as radical opponents of the military, the oligarchies and

1862

Bartolomé Mitre is elected president of the newly titled Republic of Argentina and strives to modernize the country by expanding the railway network, creating a national army and postal system, and more.

1865

More than 150 Welsh immigrants, traveling aboard the clipper *Mimosa*, land in Patagonia and establish Argentina's first Welsh colony in the province of Chubut.

1865–70

The War of the Triple Alliance is fought between Paraguay and the allied countries of Argentina, Brazil and Uruguay. Paraguay is defeated and loses territory.

1868

Domingo Faustino Sarmiento, an educator and journalist from San Juan, is elected president. He encourages immigration to Argentina, ramps up public education and pushes to Europeanize the country.

US influence in Latin America. With increasing official corruption exacerbating Isabel's incompetence, Argentina found itself plunged into chaos.

On March 24, 1976, a military coup led by army general Jorge Rafael Videla took control of the Argentine state apparatus and ushered in a period of terror and brutality. Videla's sworn aim was to crush the guerrilla movements and restore social order. During what the regime euphemistically labeled the Process of National Reorganization (known as El Proceso), security forces went about the country arresting, torturing and killing anyone on their hit list of suspected leftists.

Hectór Olivera's 1983 film *Funny Dirty Little War* is an unsettling but excellent black comedy set in a fictitious town just before the 1976 military coup.

During the period between 1976 and 1983, often referred to as the Guerra Sucia or Dirty War, human-rights groups estimate that anywhere from 10,000 to 30,000 people 'disappeared.' Ironically, the Dirty War ended only when the Argentine military attempted a real military operation: liberating the Falkland Islands (Islas Malvinas) from British rule.

LAS MADRES DE LA PLAZA DE MAYO

In 1977, after a year of brutal human-rights violations under the leadership of General Jorge Rafael Videla, 14 mothers marched into the Plaza de Mayo in Buenos Aires. They did this despite the military government's ban on public gatherings and despite its reputation for torturing and killing anyone it considered dissident. The mothers, wearing their now-iconic white head scarves, demanded information about their missing children, who had 'disappeared' as part of the government's efforts to quash political opposition.

The group, which took on the name Las Madres de la Plaza de Mayo (The Mothers of Plaza de Mayo), developed into a powerful social movement and was the only political organization that overtly challenged the military government. Las Madres were particularly effective as they carried out their struggle under the banner of motherhood, which made them relatively unassailable in Argentine culture. Their movement showed the power of women – at least in a traditional role – in Argentine culture, and they are generally credited with helping to kick start the reestablishment of the country's civil society.

After Argentina's return to civilian rule in 1983, thousands of Argentines were still unaccounted for, and Las Madres continued their marches and their demands for information and retribution. In 1986 Las Madres split into two factions. One group, known as the Línea Fundadora (Founding Line), dedicated itself to recovering the remains of the disappeared and to bringing military perpetrators to justice. The other, known as the Asociación Madres de Plaza de Mayo held its last yearly protest in January 2006, saying it no longer had an enemy in the presidential seat. Both groups, however, still hold silent vigils every Thursday afternoon in remembrance of the disappeared – and to protest other social causes.

For more information see www.madres.org.ar and www.abuelas.org.ar.

1869–95
The Argentine economy booms, immigration skyrockets as Italian and Spanish immigrants flood in, and Buenos Aires' population grows from 90,000 to 670,000. The tango emerges in Buenos Aires.

1872–79
José Hernández publishes his epic poem, 'El Gaucho Martín Fierro,' in two parts: 'El Gaucho Martín Fierro' (1872) and 'La Vuelta de Martín Fierro' (1879).

1926
Novelist and poet Ricardo Güiraldes publishes Don Segundo Sombra, a classic work of gaucho literature evoking the spirit of the gaucho and its impact on Argentine society.

1946
Juan Perón is elected president and makes changes to the Argentine political structure. Evita embarks on her social-assistance programs to help lower-class women and children.

The Falklands/Malvinas War

In late 1981 General Leopoldo Galtieri assumed the role of president. To stay in power amid a faltering economy and mass social unrest, Galtieri played the nationalist card and launched an invasion in April 1982 to dislodge the British from the Falkland Islands, which had been claimed by Argentina as its own Islas Malvinas for nearly a century and a half.

However, Galtieri underestimated the determined response of British Prime Minister Margaret Thatcher. After only 74 days Argentina's ill-trained, poorly motivated and mostly teenaged forces surrendered ignominiously. The military regime collapsed, and in 1983 Argentines elected civilian Raúl Alfonsín to the presidency.

The Falklands War is still a somewhat touchy subject in Argentina. If the subject comes up, try to call them 'Malvinas' instead of 'Falklands,' as many Argentines have been taught from a young age that these islands have always belonged to Argentina.

Aftermath of the Dirty War

In his successful 1983 presidential campaign, Alfonsín pledged to prosecute military officers responsible for human-rights violations during the Dirty War. He convicted high-ranking junta officials for kidnapping, torture and homicide, but when the government attempted to try junior officers, these officers responded with uprisings in several different parts of the country. The timid administration succumbed to military demands and produced the Ley de la Obediencia Debida (Law of Due Obedience), allowing lower-ranking officers to use the defense that they were following orders, as well as the Ley de Punto Final (Full Stop Law), declaring dates beyond which no criminal or civil prosecutions could take place. At the time, these measures eliminated prosecutions of notorious individuals; in 2003, however, they were repealed. Dirty War crime cases have since been reopened, and in recent years several officers have been convicted for Dirty War crimes. Despite these arrests, however, many of the leaders of El Proceso remain free, both in Argentina and abroad.

Nunca Más (Never Again; 1984), the official report of the National Commission on the Disappeared, systematically details military abuses from 1976 to 1983 – during Argentina's Dirty War.

The Menem Years

Carlos Saúl Menem was elected president in 1989, and quickly embarked on a period of radical free-market reform. In pegging the peso to the US dollar, he effectively created a period of false economic stability, one that would create a great deal of upward mobility among Argentina's middle class. However, his policies are widely blamed for Argentina's economic collapse in 2002, when the overvalued peso was considerably devalued.

Menem's presidency was characterized by the privatization of state-owned companies – and a few scandals. In 2001 he was charged with illegally dealing arms to Croatia and Ecuador and placed under house arrest. After five months of judicial investigation, the charges were

1952

Eva Perón dies of cancer on July 26 at age 33, one year into her husband's second term as president. Her death would severely weaken the political might of her husband.

1955

After the economy slides into recession President Perón loses further political clout and is finally thrown from the presidency and exiled to Spain after another military coup.

1976–83

Under the leadership of General Jorge Videla, a military junta takes control of Argentina, launching the country into the Dirty War. In eight years an estimated 30,000 people 'disappear.'

1982

With the economy on the brink of collapse once again, General Leopoldo Galtieri invades the Falkland Islands/Islas Malvinas, unleashing a wave of nationalism and distracting the country from its problems.

dropped; the following day he announced he would run again for president. In 2003 he did, only to withdraw after the first round. A failed 2007 bid for governor of his home province of La Rioja has pretty much written him off politics.

A bit of trivia: Carlos Menem's Syrian ancestry earned him the nickname 'El Turco' (The Turk). And in 2001 he married Cecilia Bolocco, a former Miss Universe who was 35 years his junior; they're now separated.

'La Crisis'

Fernando de la Rua succeeded Menem in the 1999 elections, inheriting an unstable economy and US$114 billion in foreign debt. With the Argentine peso pegged to the US dollar, Argentina was unable to compete on the international market and exports slumped. A further decline in international prices of agricultural products pummeled the Argentine economy, which depended heavily on farm-product exports.

By 2001 the Argentine economy teetered on the brink of collapse, and the administration, with Minister of Economy Domingo Cavallo at the wheel, took measures to end deficit spending and slash state spending. After attempted debt swaps and talk of devaluing the peso, middle-class Argentines began emptying their bank accounts. Cavallo responded by placing a cap of US$250 per week on withdrawals, but it was the beginning of the end.

By mid-December unemployment hit 18.3% and unions began a nationwide strike. Things came to a head on December 20 when middle-class Argentines took to the streets in protest of De la Rua's handling of the economic situation. Rioting spread throughout the country and President de la Rua resigned. Three interim presidents had resigned by the time Eduardo Duhalde took office in January 2002, becoming the fifth president in two weeks. Duhalde devalued the peso and announced that Argentina would default on US$140 billion in foreign debt, the biggest default in world history.

At least two terms came about due to Argentina's economic crisis: *el corralito* (a small enclosure) refers to the cap placed on cash withdrawals from bank accounts during 'La Crisis', while *cacerolazo* (from the word *cacerola*, meaning pan) is the street protest where angry people bang pots and pans.

Néstor Kirchner

Duhalde's Minister of Economy, Roberto Lavagna, negotiated a deal with the IMF in which Argentina would pay only the interest on its debts. Simultaneously, devaluation of the peso meant that Argentina's products were suddenly affordable on the world market, and by 2003 exports were booming. The surge was great for the country's GNP, but prices at home skyrocketed, plunging more of Argentina's already shaken middle class into poverty.

A presidential election was finally held in April 2003, and Santa Cruz Governor Néstor Kirchner emerged victoriously after his opponent, former president Carlos Menem, bowed out of the election.

By the end of his term in 2007, Kirchner had become one of Argentina's most popular presidents. He reversed amnesty laws that protected members of the 1976–83 junta against being charged for

1983

After the failure of the Falklands War and with an economy on the skids, Raúl Alfonsín is elected the first civilian leader of the country since 1976.

CARLOS CARRION/SYGMA/CORBIS ©

» Raúl Alfonsín

1999–2000

Fernando de la Rua succeeds Menem as president, inheriting a failing economy. Agricultural exports slump and strikes begin throughout the country. The IMF grants Argentina US$40 million in aid.

2002

Interim president Eduardo Duhalde devalues the peso, and Argentina defaults on a US$140 billion international debt (US$800 million owed to the World Bank), the largest default in history.

atrocities committed during the Dirty War. He took a heavy stance against government corruption and steered the economy away from strict alignment with the US (realigning it with that of Argentina's South American neighbors). And in 2005 he paid off Argentina's entire debt to the IMF in a single payment. By the end of Kirchner's presidency in 2007, unemployment had fallen to just under 9% – from a high of nearly 25% in 2002.

When the presidential seat went up for grabs in 2007, Argentines expressed their satisfaction with Kirchner's policies by electing his wife, well-known Senator Cristina Fernández de Kirchner, as president. Cristina won the presidency with a whopping 22% margin over her nearest challenger and became Argentina's first elected female president.

'La Presidenta'

When Cristina became 'la Presidenta', she faced two major challenges: tackling poverty and curbing inflation. Unlike her husband Néstor's successful tenure, however, hers has been rocky one peppered with scandals, tax bungles and rollercoaster approval ratings.

During her first days as president, a Venezuelan-American entering Argentina from Venezuela was found with almost US$800,000 cash in his suitcase. *Time* magazine wrote that US attorneys claimed this was Hugo Chavez' way of aiding Kirchner's election campaign, an allegation the Venezuelan president denied.

In March 2008 Kirchner significantly raised the export tax on soybeans, infuriating farmers who soon went on strike and blockaded highways; the tax was later rescinded. Then in June 2009, her power base was shattered when her ruling party lost its majority in both houses of Congress in the mid-term elections.

And in October 2010, Cristina was dealt a personal blow – her husband Néstor died suddenly of a heart attack. The country rallied around her, however, and sympathy towards her (along with a growing economy) helped her easily win the presidential re-election in October 2011.

For more recent news on Cristina and Argentina, see p556.

CRISTINA

Cristina Kirchner chooses Argentina's economy minister, Amado Boudou, as a running mate; the rugged Boudou drives a Harley-Davidson and jams with famous musicians on his Fender Telecaster guitar.

2003

Nestor Kirchner is elected president of Argentina after Carlos Menem bows out of the presidential race, despite winning more votes in the first round of elections.

2007

Former First Lady Cristina Fernández de Kirchner is elected president.

2010

Néstor Kirchner dies suddenly, dealing a serious blow to the Kirchner dynasty. Many thought he would run for president in 2011, and very likely win.

2011

Cristina Kirchner wins the presidential re-election race; a few months later she undergoes successful surgery after a cancer scare.

Life in Argentina

Throughout Latin America, Argentines endure a reputation for being cocky. 'How does an Argentine commit suicide?' goes the old joke. 'By jumping off his ego.'

Traveling to Argentina, you'll find a nugget of truth in this stereotype. But you'll also realize that a warm and gregarious social nature more accurately defines the Argentine psyche. Argentines are some of the most welcoming and endearing folks on the planet.

Argentina's workforce is more than 40% female, and women currently occupy over a third of Argentina's congressional seats.

Opinionated, brash and passionate, they're quick to engage in conversation and will talk after dinner or over coffee until the wee hours of the morning. Argentina's most visible customs are entirely social in nature. Look no further than the ritual of drinking *mate*, and their famous *asado* (barbecue).

While Argentines are friendly and passionate they also have a subtle broodiness to their nature, especially *porteños* (residents of Buenos Aires). This stems from a pessimism Argentines have acquired watching their country, one of the world's economic powerhouses during the late 19th and early 20th centuries, descend into a morass of international debt. They've endured military coups and severe government repression – while witnessing their beloved Argentina plundered by corrupt politicians.

But the broodiness is just a part of the picture. Add everything together and you get a people who are fun, fiery, opinionated and proud. And you'll come to love them for it.

Lifestyle

Although Buenos Aires holds more than one-third of the country's population, it's surprisingly unlike the rest of Argentina or, for that matter, much of Latin America. As is the case throughout the country, one's lifestyle in the capital depends mostly on money. A modern flat rented by a young advertising creative in Buenos Aires' Las Cañitas neighborhood differs greatly from a family home in one of the city's impoverished *villas* (shantytowns), where electricity and clean water are luxuries.

Argentines almost always exchange a kiss on the cheek in greeting – even among men. In formal and business situations, though, it is better to go with a handshake.

Geography and ethnicity also play important roles. Both of these Buenos Aires homes have little in common with that of an indigenous family living in an adobe house in a desolate valley of the Andean Northwest, where life is eked out through subsistence agriculture and earth goddess Pachamama outshines Evita as a cultural icon. In regions such as the pampas, Mendoza province and Patagonia, a provincial friendliness surrounds a robust, outdoor lifestyle.

Argentina has a relatively large middle class, though it's been shrinking significantly in recent years, and poverty has grown. On the other side of the spectrum, wealthy city dwellers have moved into *countries,* (gated communities) in surprising numbers.

One thing that all Argentines have in common is their devotion to family. The Buenos Aires advertising exec joins family for weekend dinners,

SOCIAL DOS & DON'TS

When it comes to social etiquette in Argentina, knowing a few intricacies will keep you on the right track.

Dos

» Greet people you encounter with *buenos días* (good morning), *buenas tardes* (good afternoon) or *buenas noches* (good evening).

» In small villages, greet people on the street and when walking into a shop.

» Accept and give *besos* (kisses) on the cheek.

» Use *usted* (the formal term for 'you') when addressing elders and in formal situations.

» Dress for the occasion; only tourists and athletes wear shorts in Buenos Aires.

Don'ts

» Don't refer to the Islas Malvinas as the Falkland Islands, and don't talk to strangers about the Dirty War.

» Don't suggest that Brazil is better than Argentina at *fútbol*, or that Pelé is better than Maradona. And don't refer to *fútbol* as soccer.

» Don't show up at bars before midnight, or nightclubs before 3am, or dinner parties right on time (be fashionably late).

» Don't refer to people from the United States as Americans or *americanos*; use the term estadounidenses instead. Some Latin Americans consider themselves 'American' (literally from America, whether it be North, Central or South).

and the cafe owner in San Juan meets friends out at the family *estancia* (ranch) for a Sunday *asado*. Children commonly live with their parents until they're married, especially within poorer households.

The Sporting Life

Fútbol (soccer) is an integral part of Argentines' lives, and on game day you'll know it by the cheers and yells emanating out of shops and cafes. The national team has been to the World Cup final four times and has triumphed twice, in 1978 and 1986. The Argentine team also won Olympic gold twice, at the 2004 and 2008 games. The most popular teams are Boca Juniors and River Plate (there are around two-dozen professional teams in Buenos Aires alone) and the fanatical behavior of the country's *barra brava* (hooligans) rivals that of their European counterparts. Among the best-known *fútbol* players are Diego Maradona, Gabriel Batistuta and Lionel Messi.

Rugby's popularity has increased in Argentina ever since Los Pumas, their national team, beat France in the first game of the 2007 Rugby World Cup and *again* in the play-off for third place. As an indicator of just how popular the sport has become, the *Superclásico* (the famed soccer match between Boca and River Plate) was rescheduled so it wouldn't conflict with Los Pumas' quarter-final match.

Horse racing, tennis, basketball, golf and boxing are also popular. Argentina has the top polo horses and players in the world, and the Dakar Rally has been taking place partly or mostly in Argentina since 2009.

Pato is Argentina's traditional sport, played on horseback and mixing elements from both polo and basketball. It was originally played with a duck (a 'pato') but now, thankfully, uses a ball encased in leather handles. Despite its long history and tradition, however, relatively few people follow it.

Jimmy Burns' *The Hand of God* (1997) is the definitive book about football legend Diego Maradona and makes a great read – even if you're not a soccer fanatic.

MARADONA

Argentine Cuisine

Argentines love eating. Most of their social and political life involves a table, be it for a leisurely coffee, an informal meal or an elegant banquet. While sophistication is not a national feature – beef and pasta are the two pillars upon which the national menu is based – it does exist. In Buenos Aires and other large cities, you'll find slick international restaurants including Japanese, Middle Eastern, Mexican, Southeast Asian, Brazilian and more, that serve intricately prepared dishes. But traditional Argentine food, which is rooted in Italian and Spanish cooking, is more modest.

Argentina has also established a reputation for fine wine. The number of wineries and vineyards is skyrocketing, not just in Mendoza province but in northwest Argentina and even northern Patagonia. And despite rising inflation, sampling fine wine remains an affordable luxury.

For cooking courses in Buenos Aires, see p68.

Staples & Specialties

Beef

When the first Spaniards came to Argentina, they brought cattle. But efforts at establishing a colony proved unfruitful, and the herds were abandoned in the pampas. Here, the cows found the bovine equivalent of heaven: plenty of lush, fertile grasses on which to feed, with few natural predators (aside from some gauchos) to limit their numbers. Then the Europeans recolonized and captured the cattle for their own use, intermixing them with other bovine breeds.

Traditionally, free-range Argentine cows ate nutritious pampas grass and were rasied without antibiotics and growth hormones. This made for a leaner and more natural-tasting meat. But, things are changing; see p123.

Average beef consumption in Argentina is around 60kg per person per year – though in the past, they ate even more.

BEEF

When it comes to national cuisine, Argentines produce what is arguably the world's best beef – and have mastered the art of grilling it. For the lowdown on beef, see boxed text.

Italian

Thanks to Argentina's Italian heritage, the national cuisine has been highly influenced by Italian immigrants who entered the country during the late 19th century. Along with an animated set of speaking gestures, they brought their love of pasta, pizza, gelato and more.

Many restaurants make their own pasta – look for *pasta casera* (handmade pasta). Some of the varieties of pasta you'll encounter are *ravioles*, *sorrentinos* (large, round pasta parcels similar to ravioli), *ñoquis* (gnocchi) and *tallerines* (fettuccine). Standard sauces include *tuco* (tomato sauce), *estofado* (beef stew, popular with ravioli) and *salsa blanca* (béchamel). Be aware that occasionally the sauce is *not* included in the price of the pasta – you choose and pay for it separately.

Pizza is sold at *pizzerías* throughout the country, though many regular restaurants offer it as well. It's generally excellent, so go ahead and order a slice or two.

Spanish

Spanish cooking is less popular than Italian, but forms another bedrock of Argentine food. In the country's Spanish restaurants you'll find paella, as well as other typically Spanish seafood preparations. Most of the country's *guisos* and *pucheros* (types of stew) are descendants of Spain.

Empanadas – small, stuffed turnovers ubiquitous in Argentina – are prepared differently throughout the country (for example, you'll find spicy ground-beef empanadas in the Andean Northwest, and in Patagonia, lamb is a common filling). They make for a tasty, quick meal and are especially good for bus travel.

Regional Flavors

Although *comida típica* can refer to any of Argentina's regional dishes, it often refers to food from the Andean Northwest. Food from this region, which has roots in pre-Columbian times, has more in common with the cuisines of Bolivia and Peru than with the Europeanized food of the rest of Argentina. It's frequently spicy and hard to find elsewhere (most Argentines can't tolerate anything spicier than a pinch of black pepper). Typical dishes can include everything from *locro* (a hearty corn or mixed-grain stew with meat), to tamales, *humitas* (sweet tamales) and fried empanadas.

In Patagonia, lamb almost wipes beef off the map. Along the coast, seafood is a popular choice and includes fish, oysters and king crab. In the Lake District, game meats such as venison, wild boar and trout are popular. In the west, the provinces of Mendoza, San Juan and La Rioja pride themselves on *chivito* (young goat). River fish, such as the dorado, pacú (a relative of the piranha) and surubí (a type of catfish), are staples in the northeast.

ALFAJORES

Alfajores are round, cookie-type sandwiches layered with *dulce de leche* or fruit preserves. Get them at *kioskos* (kiosks, or small street shops) – they're delicious and Argentina's answer to the candy bar.

THE BEEF ON BEEF

You walk into a traditional *parrilla* (steak house), breeze past the sizzling grill at the entrance and sit down feeling hungry, knife and fork in hand. You don't know a word of Spanish and you've never had to choose between more than two or three cuts of steak in your life – but the menu has at least 10 choices. What to do?

At a steakhouse, the *parrillada* (mixed grill) is a little bit of everything, often including *chorizo* (beef or pork sausage), *pollo* (chicken), *costillas* (ribs) and *carne* (beef). It can also come with more exotic items like *chinchulines* (small intestines), *molleja* (sweetbreads) and *morcilla* (blood sausage). You can order a *parrillada* for as many people as you want; the steakhouse adjusts its servings according to the party's size.

Prime beef cuts include the following:

Bife de chorizo Sirloin; a thick and juicy cut.

Bife de costilla T-bone; a cut close to the bone.

Bife de lomo Tenderloin; a thinly cut, more tender piece.

Cuadril Rump steak; often a thin cut.

Ojo de bife Rib eye; a choice smaller morsel.

Tira de asado Short ribs; thin strips of ribs.

Vacío Flank steak; textured, chewy and tasty.

Very important: if you don't specify, your steak will be cooked *a punto* (medium to well done). Getting a steak medium rare or rare is more difficult than you'd imagine. If you want some pink in the center, order it *jugoso*; if you like it truly rare, try *vuelta y vuelta*. Don't miss *chimichurri,* a tasty sauce often made of olive oil, garlic and parsley.

And if you're lucky enough to be invited to an *asado* (family or friends' barbecue), do attend – here the art of grilling beef has been perfected, and the social bonding is priceless.

A Taste of Argentina

Argentines take barbecuing to heights you cannot imagine. Their pizzas vie with those of New York and Naples. They make fabulous wines. *Mate*, that iconic tea, doubles as a social bond between family and friends. And your taste buds will sing as they sample Argentina's delectable ice cream.

Mate

1 Although most first-time *mate* drinkers can barely choke the stuff down, this strong green tea, sipped communally from a gourd with a filtering metal straw, is a cultural delight and social bonding experience.

Beef

2 Argentines have perfected the grilling of their flavorful beef. At its best you'll slice through the crispy, smoky and salted outer layers to uncover the tender and tasty meat within – and your mouth will love you.

Ice Cream

3 Step into one of Argentina's ice creameries and your hardest task will be choosing from dozens of flavors. The luscious treat will be swirled into a peaked mountain with a spoon stuck in the side – prepare for a sweet adventure!

Wine

4 Exploring Argentina by the glass will take you (and your palate) from the malbecs and cabernets of Mendoza to the crisp torrontés of Cafayate, and to the succulent syrahs of San Juan. A bottle a day – make that your motto.

Italian Food

5 You'll find pizza and pasta everywhere in Argentina and it'll make you wonder how the locals can consume so much of the stuff. When it's this consistently good, however, you'll understand.

1

4

Clockwise from top left
1. *Mate* (p574) **2.** Beef (p571) **3.** Ice cream (p574) **4.** Wine bottles, Mendoza (p301)

2

GABRIELDOM/DREAMSTIME ©

3

KRZYSZTOF DYDYNSKI/LONELY PLANET IMAGES ©

DULCE
DE LECHE

CREMA
VAINILL

Drinks

Mendoza is Argentina's premier wine region, but other provinces also produce excellent wines. For more on a couple of off-the-beaten-path Argentine wine destinations, see p321 and p332.

If Argentina has a national beer, it's Quilmes. Order a *porrón* and you'll get a half-liter bottle, or a *chopp* and you'll get a frosty mug of draft.

Argentines love their *café con leche* (coffee with milk). An espresso with a drop of milk is a *café cortado,* while a *lágrima* is mostly milk with a drop or two of coffee. Black and herbal teas are also available, and there's always *mate.*

Even in big cities such as Buenos Aires, the *agua de canilla* (tap water) is drinkable. In restaurants, however, most people order bottled mineral water – ask for *agua con gas* (with bubbles) or *agua sin gas* (without). In older, more traditional restaurants, carbonated water in a spritzer bottle *(un sifón de soda)* is great for drinking, though Argentines often mix it with cheap wine.

Ice cream is one of Argentina's greatest treats, more akin to Italian gelato than its creamy counterparts in France and the US. For a list of ice-cream shops in Buenos Aires, see p82.

Where to Eat & Drink

Argentines love to dine out, and there is no lack of places to find a bite to eat.

For the best meats, head to a *parrilla* (steak restaurant). *Confiterías* and cafes are open all day and much of the night, and often have a long list of both food and drinks. Bars or pubs usually have a more limited range of snacks and meals available, though some can offer full meals. A *tenedor libre* (literally, 'free fork') is an all-you-can-eat restaurant; quality

MATE & ITS RITUAL

The preparation and consumption of *mate* (pronounced *mah*-tay) is perhaps the only cultural practice that truly transcends the barriers of ethnicity, class and occupation in Argentina. More than a simple drink, *mate* is an elaborate ritual, shared among family, friends and co-workers.

Yerba mate is the dried, chopped leaf of *Ilex paraguayensis,* a relative of the common holly. Argentina is the world's largest producer and consumer of the stuff; Argentines consume an average of 5kg per person per year, more than four times their average intake of coffee.

Preparing and drinking *mate* is a ritual in itself. One person, the *cebador* (server), fills the *mate* gourd almost to the top with *yerba*, and then slowly pours hot water as he or she fills the gourd. The cebador then passes the *mate* to each drinker, who sips the liquid through the *bombilla,* a silver straw with a bulbous filter at its lower end. Each participant drinks the gourd dry each time. Remember it's bad form to touch the *bombilla*, and don't hold the *mate* too long before passing it on! A simple 'gracias' will tell the server to pass you by.

An invitation to partake in *mate* is a cultural treat and not to be missed, although the drink is an acquired taste and novices will find it very hot and bitter at first (adding sugar can be an option).

Because drinking *mate* is a fairly complex process, it is rarely served in restaurants or cafes. The simple solution is to do what traveling Argentines do: buy a thermos, a *mate* gourd, a *bombilla* and a bag of herb – stores often have a *mate* section. Cure your gourd by filling it with hot water and *yerba* and letting it soak for 24 hours. Nearly all restaurants, cafes and hotels are used to filling thermoses, sometimes charging a small amount. Simply whip out your thermos and ask: *'¿Podía calentar agua para mate?'* ('Would you mind heating water for *mate*?').

If you'd like to find out more about *mate*, visit a *mate* museum – there's one in Tigre (p104) and another in Posadas (p175).

is usually decent, but a minimum-drink purchase is often mandatory and costs extra.

Typical restaurants tend to be open only at meal times (1pm to 3:30pm for lunch and 9pm to 1am for dinner).

Note that Argentines eat little for breakfast – usually just a coffee with *medialunas* (croissants – either *dulce*, sweet, or *salada*, plain). *Tostadas* (toast) with *manteca* (butter) or *mermelada* (jam) is an alternative, as are *facturas* (pastries). Some higher-end hotels offer breakfast buffets, however.

Restaurant reservations are taken but are really only necessary on weekends at better restaurants (or during high season at Mar del Plata or Bariloche, for example). Ask for your bill by saying, *'la cuenta, por favor'* ('the bill, please') or making the 'writing in air' gesture. Most restaurants accept credit cards, but some (usually smaller ones) only take cash.

To save a few bucks, especially for lunch, opt for the *menú del día* or *menú ejecutivo*. These 'set menus' usually include a main dish, dessert and drink, all for a reasonable price.

The *choripán* is a classic snack-sandwich available at cheap take-out eateries or street stalls. It's made with two ingredients: *chorizo* (spicy sausage) and *pan* (bread). Top it with *chimichurri* sauce, and you've got a tasty and very cheap meal.

Vegetarians & Vegans

Health foods, organic products and vegetarian restaurants are available in Argentina's biggest cities, but outside of them you'll have to search harder.

Most restaurant menus include a few vegetarian choices, and pastas are a nearly ubiquitous option. *Pizzerías* and *empanaderías* (empanada shops) are good bets – look for empanadas made with *acelga* (chard) and *choclo* (corn). If you're stuck at a *parrilla*, your choices will be salads, baked potatoes, *provoleta* (a thick slice of grilled provolone cheese) and roasted vegetables.

Sin carne means 'without meat,' and the words *soy vegetariano/a* ('I'm a vegetarian') will come in handy when explaining to an Argentine why you don't eat their nation's renowned steaks.

Vegans will have a much harder time in Argentina; there isn't a word for 'vegan'. Make sure homemade pasta doesn't include egg, and that fried vegetables aren't cooked in lard (*grasa*; *manteca* means butter in Argentina). You'll need to be creative to survive here. One tip: look for accommodations with a kitchen, so you can shop for and cook your own food. Good luck.

For tips on where to eat *sin carne* in Buenos Aires, see p83.

At many finer Argentine restaurants, you'll be charged a per-person *cubierto*; this is a small 'fee' for bread and the use of utensils. It's not the tip, which is up to 10% and should be paid separately.

The Sounds of Argentina

Music and dance are unavoidable in Argentina, and none is more famous than the tango. But the country also grooves to different sounds, be it *chamamé* in Corrientes, *cuarteto* in Córdoba or *cumbia villera* in the poor neighborhoods of Buenos Aires.

Murga is a form of athletic musical theater composed of actors and percussionists. Primarily performed in Uruguay, *murga* in Argentina is more heavily focused on dancing than singing. You're most likely to see this exciting musical art form at Carnaval celebrations.

Tango

There's no better place to dive into tango than through the music of the genre's most legendary performer, singer Carlos Gardel (1887–1935). Violinist Juan D'Arienzo's *orquesta* (orchestra) reigned over tango throughout the 1930s and into the 1940s. Osvaldo Pugliese and Héctor Varela are important bandleaders from the 1940s, but the real giant of the era was *bandoneón* (small type of accordion) player Aníbal Troilo.

Modern tango is largely dominated by the work of *bandoneón* maestro Astor Piazzolla who moved the genre from the dance halls into the concert halls – *tango nuevo,* as it was called, was now for the ear. Piazzolla paved the way for the tango fusion, which emerged in the 1970s and continues to this day with *tango electrónica* (or neo tango) groups such as Gotan Project, Bajofondo Tango Club and Tanghetto.

While in Buenos Aires, keep an eye out for Orquesta Típica Fernández Fierro, who put a new twist on traditional tango songs, but also perform their own new creations. Another young orchestra to watch out for is Orquesta Típica Imperial.

Influential contemporary tango singers include Susana Rinaldi, Daniel Melingo and Adriana Varela. For more on the tango dance itself, see p88.

Cumbia villera is a relatively recent musical phenomenon: a fusion of *cumbia* and gangsta posturing with a punk edge and reggae overtones. Born of Buenos Aires' shantytowns, its aggressive lyrics deal with marginalization, poverty, drugs, sex and the Argentine economic crisis.

Folk Music

Traditional music is known as *folklore* or *folklórico.* It's an umbrella genre that captures numerous styles and there are popular contemporary branches (such as *chamamé, chacarera* and *zamba*).

One of Argentina's greatest contemporary *folklórico* musicians is accordionist Chango Spasiuk, a virtuoso of Corrientes' *chamamé* music. Horacio Guarany is a contemporary *folklórico* singer whose 2004 album *Cantor de Cantores* was nominated for a Latin Grammy in the Best Folk Album category. Eduardo Falú, Víctor Heredia, León Gieco and Soledad Pastorutti are other big names in *folklórico.*

Atahualpa Yupanqui (1908–92) is Argentina's most important *folklórico* musician of the 20th century. Yupanqui's music emerged with the *nueva canción* ('new song') movement that swept Latin America in the 1960s. *Nueva canción* was rooted in folk music and its lyrics often dealt with social and political themes. The genre's grande dame was Argentina's Mercedes Sosa (1935–2009), one of the best-known Argentine folk singers outside South America and winner of several Latin Grammy awards.

GARDEL & THE TANGO

In June 1935 a Cuban woman committed suicide in Havana; meanwhile, in New York and in Puerto Rico two other women tried to poison themselves. It was all over the same man: tango singer Carlos Gardel, who had just died in a plane crash in Colombia.

Gardel was born in France (a claim contested by both Argentina and Uruguay), and when he was three his destitute single mother brought him to Buenos Aires. In his youth he entertained neighbors with his rapturous singing, then went on to establish a successful performing career.

Gardel played an enormous role in creating the tango *canción* (song) and almost single-handedly took the style out of Buenos Aires' tenements and brought it to Paris and New York. His crooning voice, suaveness and overall charisma made him an immediate success in Latin American countries, a rising star during tango's golden years of the 1920s and 1930s. Unfortunately, Gardel's later film career was tragically cut short by that fatal plane crash.

His devoted followers cannot pass a day without listening to him; they say 'Gardel sings better every day.'

Rock & Pop

Musicians such as Charly García, Fito Páez and Luis Alberto Spinetta are *rock nacional* (Argentine rock) icons. Soda Stereo, Sumo, Los Fabulosos Cadillacs and Los Pericos rocked Argentina throughout the 1980s and maintain wild popularity. Bersuit Vergarabat endures as one of Argentina's best rock bands, with a musical complexity that is arguably without peer. R&B-influenced Ratones Paranoicos opened for the Rolling Stones in 1995, while La Portuaria – who fuse Latin beats with jazz and R&B – collaborated with David Byrne in 2006.

Other popular national groups include the offbeat Babasónicos; punk rockers Attaque 77; rockers Los Piojos, Los Redonditos de Ricota, Los Divididos, Catupecu Machu and Gazpacho; and metal-meets-hip-hop Illya Kuryaki and the Valderramas. Catchy Miranda! has an electro-pop style, while eclectic Kevin Johansen sings in both English and Spanish.

Born in Córdoba in the early 1940s, *cuarteto* is Argentina's original pop music: despised by the middle and upper classes for its arresting rhythm and offbeat musical pattern (called the *tunga-tunga*), as well as its working-class lyrics, it is definitely music from the margins. Although definitively *cordobés* (from Córdoba), it's played in working-class bars, dance halls and stadiums throughout the country.

CHARLY GARCÍA

Charly García's version of the Argentine national anthem does what Jimi Hendrix did for 'The Star-Spangled Banner,' but it earned García a court appearance for 'lacking respect for national symbols.'

Electrónica

Electrónica, or dance music, exploded in Argentina in the 1990s and has taken on various forms in popular music. Hybrid *bandas electrónicas* (electronic bands) are led by the likes of Intima, Mujik and Adicta, while Juana Molina's ambient-electronic music has been compared to Björk's.

DJ-based club and dance music is increasingly popular. Argentina's heavyweights include Aldo Haydar (a veteran of progressive house), Bad Boy Orange (the reigning king of Argentine drum 'n' bass), Diego Ro-K (also known as the Maradona of Argentine DJs) and Gustavo Lamas (who blends ambient pop and electro house). And award-winning Hernán Cattáneo, probably the best-known Argentine DJ, has played with Paul Oakenfold and at Burning Man.

One of Buenos Aires' most interesting music spectacles is La Bomba del Tiempo, a collective of percussionists whose explosive performances are improvisational, tribal and even simulate electronic dance music. Check them out at Ciudad Cultural Konex (see p96) on Monday evenings.

Literature & Cinema

Artistically, Argentina is one of Latin America's most compelling countries, containing a rich literary heritage and a vibrant and evolving film industry.

Literature

Journalist, poet and politician José Hernández (1831–86) gave rise to the *gauchesco* literary tradition with his epic poem *Martín Fierro* (1872), which acknowledged the role of the gauchos in Argentina's development. Argentine writing only reached an international audience during the 1960s and 1970s, when the stories of Jorge Luis Borges, Julio Cortázar, Ernesto Sábato, Adolfo Bioy Casares and Silvina Ocampo, among many others, were widely translated for the first time.

Victoria Ocampo (1890–1979) was a famous writer, publisher and intellectual who founded *Sur*, a renowned cultural magazine of the 1930s. For more on her, see the boxed text, p132. You can also visit her mansion near Buenos Aires (p103).

Despite being discovered and influenced by Borges in the 1940s, the writing of Julio Cortázar (1914–84) was considerably different. His short stories and novels are more anthropological and concern people living seemingly normal lives in a world where the surreal becomes commonplace. Cortázar's most famous book is *Hopscotch*.

Another great writer is Ernesto Sábato (1911–2011), whose complex and uncompromising novels have been extremely influential on later Argentine literature. *The Tunnel* (1948) is Sábato's engrossing existentialist novella about an obsessed painter and his distorted personal take on reality.

Adolfo Bioy Casares' (1914–99) sci-fi novella *The Invention of Morel* (1940) not only gave Alain Resnais the plot for his classic film *Last Year at Marienbad*, but also introduced the idea of the holodeck decades before *Star Trek* existed.

The contemporary, post-boom generation of Argentine writers is more reality-based, often reflecting the influence of popular culture and directly confronting the political angles of 1970s authoritarian Argentina. One of the most famous post-boom Argentine writers is Manuel Puig (1932–90, author of *Kiss of the Spider Woman*). In the Argentine tradition, Puig did much of his writing in exile, fleeing Argentina during the Perón years and ultimately settling in Mexico.

Argentines are pretty well-read – their literacy rate is over 97%. And in 2011, Buenos Aires was voted Unesco World Book Capital.

Osvaldo Soriano (1943–97), perhaps Argentina's most popular contemporary novelist, wrote *A Funny Dirty Little War* (1986) and *Winter Quarters* (1989). Juan José Saer (1937–2005) penned short stories and complex crime novels, while Rodrigo Fresán (1963–), the youngster of the post-boom generation, wrote the international bestseller *The History of Argentina*.

Other notable contemporary writers include Federico Andahazi, Ricardo Piglia and Tomás Eloy Martínez.

JORGE LUIS BORGES

Jorge Luis Borges (1899–1986), the brightest light of Argentine literature, is best known for the complex labyrinthine worlds and sophisticated mind teasers constructing his stories. As a half-Jewish, half-English Argentine who was educated in Europe, Borges was influenced by everything from Jewish cabalists to HG Wells, Cervantes and Kafka.

Borges' dry, ironic wit is paired with a succinct, precise style. His paradoxical *Ficciones* (1944) blurs the line between myth and truth, underscoring the concept that reality is only a matter of perception and that an infinite number of worlds can exist simultaneously. Another theme that Borges explored was the nature of memory and dreams.

His early stories such as *Death and the Compass* and *Streetcorner Man* offer a metaphysical twist on Argentine themes, and his later works, including *The Lottery in Babylon*, *The Circular Ruins* and *Garden of the Forking Paths* are works of fantasy. *Collected Fictions* (1999) is a complete set of his stories.

Borges went blind towards the end of his life, but kept publishing books. Though he received numerous honors in his lifetime – including the Cervantes Prize, the Legion of Honor and an OBE – Borges was never conferred the Nobel.

Cinema

One of Argentina's major contributions to cinema is Luis Puenzo's *The Official Story* (1985), which deals with the Dirty War. Another well-known international movie is Héctor Babenco's *Kiss of the Spider Woman* (1985), based on Argentine-born Manuel Puig's novel. Both movies won Oscars.

New Argentine Cinema developed in the 1990s, brought about by economic and political unrest. Films that spearheaded this movement include Martín Rejtman's *Rapado* (1992) and *Pizza, birra, faso* (Pizza, Beer, Cigarettes, 1998) by Adrián Caetano and Bruno Stagnaro.

Pablo Trapero is one of Argentina's foremost filmmakers. Among his works are award-winning *Mundo grúa* (Crane World, 1999), the ensemble road movie *Familia rodante* (Rolling Family, 2004) and *Nacido y criado* (Born and Bred, 2006), a stark story about a Patagonian man's fall from grace. His 2010 noir film *Carancho* played at Cannes Film Festival.

Daniel Burman's films include *Esperando al mesíah* (Waiting for the Messiah, 2000), *El abrazo partido* (Lost Embrace, 2004) and *Derecho de familia* (Family Law, 2006). His most recent effort, *Dos hermanos* (Brother and Sister, 2010) is the story of aging siblings who've recently lost their mother. The late Fabián Bielinsky's works include award-winning *Nueve reinas* (Nine Queens, 2000) and the 2005 neo-noir flick *El Aura*.

Lucrecia Martel's 2001 debut *La ciénaga* (The Swamp) and *La niña santa* (The Holy Girl, 2004) deal with the themes of social decay, Argentine bourgeois and sexuality in the face of Catholic guilt. Her powerful *La mujer sin cabeza* (The Headless Woman, 2008) was showcased at Cannes. Another acclaimed director, Carlos Sorin, takes us to the deep south of Argentina in *Historias mínimas* (Minimal Stories, 2002) and *Bombón el perro* (Bombón the Dog, 2004).

Juan José Campanella's *El hijo de la novia* (Son of the Bride) received an Oscar nomination for best foreign-language film in 2001, while *Luna de avellaneda* (Moon of Avellaneda, 2004) is a clever story about a social club and those who try to save it. In 2010 he won the Oscar for best foreign-language film with *El secreto de sus ojos* (The Secret in Their Eyes).

Other noteworthy films include Lucía Puenzo's *XXY* (2007), the tale of a 15-year-old hermaphrodite, and Juan Diego Solanas' *Nordeste* (Northeast, 2005), which tackles difficult social issues such as child trafficking; both were screened at Cannes. Finally, *El hombre de al lado* (The Man Next Door, 2009), by Mariano Cohn and Gastón Duprat, is a moral drama that won a prize at Sundance Film Festival.

FESTIVAL

Argentina's biggest film event is the Buenos Aires International Festival of Independent Film, held in April. Check out www.bafici.gov.ar for more information.

Natural World

The Land

Argentina. For anyone raised on *National Geographic* and adventure stories, the name is loaded with images: the Magellanic penguins of the Atlantic coast, the windswept mysteries of Patagonia and Tierra del Fuego, the vast grasslands of the pampas, the towering Andes and raging Iguazú Falls. Spanning from the subtropics to the edge of Antarctica, the country is simply unmatched in natural wonders.

At its mouth, the Río de la Plata is an amazing 200km wide, making it the widest river in the world – though some consider it more like a river estuary.

So it makes sense that Argentina is big – *really* big. With a total land area of about 2.8 million sq km, Argentina is the world's eighth-largest country – only slightly smaller than India. It stretches from La Quiaca on the Bolivian border, where summers can be brutally hot, to Ushuaia in Tierra del Fuego, where winters are experienced only by seasoned locals and the nuttiest of travelers. It's a distance of nearly 3500km, an expanse that encompasses a vast array of environments and terrain.

The Central & Northern Andes

In the extreme north, the Andes are basically the southern extension of the Bolivian *altiplano*, a thinly populated high plain between 3000m and 4000m in altitude, punctuated by even higher volcanic peaks. Although days can be surprisingly hot (sunburn is a serious hazard at high altitude), frosts occur almost nightly. The Andean Northwest is also known as the *puna*.

Further south, in the arid provinces of San Juan and Mendoza, the Andes climb to their highest altitudes, with 6962m Cerro Aconcagua topping out as the highest point in the western hemisphere. Here, their highest peaks lie covered in snow through the winter. Although rainfall on the eastern slopes is inadequate for crops, perennial streams descend from the Andes and provide irrigation water, which has brought prosperity to the wine-producing Cuyo region (the provinces of Mendoza, San Juan and San Luis). Winter in San Juan province is the season of the *zonda*, a hot, dry wind descending from the Andes that causes dramatic temperature increases (see p328).

The largest dinosaur ever discovered is *Argentinosaurus huinculensis*, uncovered in Neuquén province; the herbivore measured a massive 40m long and 18m high.

The Chaco

East of the Andes and the Andean foothills, much of northern Argentina consists of subtropical lowlands. This arid area, known as the Argentine Chaco, is part of the much larger Gran Chaco, an extremely rugged, largely uninhabited region that extends into Bolivia, Paraguay and Brazil. The Argentine Chaco encompasses the provinces of Chaco, Formosa and Santiago del Estero, the western reaches of Jujuy, Catamarca and Salta provinces, and the northernmost parts of Santa Fe and Córdoba.

The Chaco has a well-defined winter dry season, and summer everywhere in the Chaco is brutally hot. Rainfall decreases as you move east to west. The wet Chaco, which encompasses the eastern parts of Chaco and Formosa provinces and northeast Santa Fe, receives more rain than the dry Chaco, which covers central and western Chaco and Formosa provinces, most of Santiago del Estero and parts of Salta.

Mesopotamia

Also referred to as the Litoral (as in littoral), Mesopotamia is the name for the region of northeast Argentina between the Río Paraná and Río Uruguay. It's a region defined, as its names suggest, by its rivers, both a dominant part of the landscape. Here, the climate is mild, and rainfall is heavy in the provinces of Entre Ríos and Corrientes, which make up most of Mesopotamia. Hot and humid Misiones province, a politically important province surrounded on three sides by Brazil and Paraguay, contains part of Iguazú Falls, which descend from southern Brazil's Paraná Plateau. Shallow summer flooding is common throughout Mesopotamia and into the eastern Chaco, but only the immediate river floodplains become inundated in the west. Mesopotamia's rainfall is evenly distributed throughout the year.

Iguazú Falls consists of more than 275 individual falls that tumble from heights as great as 80m. They stretch for nearly 3km and are arguably the most amazing waterfalls on earth.

The Pampas & Atlantic Coast

Bordered by the Atlantic Ocean and Patagonia and stretching nearly to Córdoba and the Central Sierras, the pampas are Argentina's agricultural heartland. Geographically, this region covers the provinces of Buenos Aires and La Pampa, as well as southern chunks of Santa Fe and Córdoba.

This area can be subdivided into the humid pampas, along the Litoral, and the arid pampas of the western interior and the south. More than a third of the country's population lives in and around Buenos Aires, where the humid climate resembles Sydney's or New York City's in the spring, summer and autumn. Annual rainfall exceeds 900mm, but several hundred kilometers westward it's less than half that. Buenos Aires' winters are relatively mild.

Argentina is the world's third-highest producer of soybeans, after the USA and Brazil, but interestingly, Argentines don't really eat soy. Much of the country's soybeans are exported.

SOYBEANS

The pampas are an almost completely level plain of wind-borne loess (a fine-grained silt or clay) and river-deposited sediments. The absence of nearly any rises in the land makes the area vulnerable to flooding from the relatively few, small rivers that cross it. Only the granitic Sierra de Tandil (484m) and the Sierra de la Ventana (1273m), in southwestern Buenos Aires province, and the Sierra de Lihué Calel disrupt the otherwise monotonous terrain.

Moving south along the Atlantic coast from the Argentine capital, the province of Buenos Aires features the sandy, often dune-backed beaches that attracted the development of seaside resorts such as Mar del Plata and Necochea. Inland it's mostly the grasslands of the pampas. South of Viedma, cliffs begin to appear but the landscape remains otherwise desolate for its entire stretch south through Patagonia.

Patagonia & the Lake District

Ever-alluring Patagonia is the region of Argentina south of the Río Colorado, which flows southeast from the Andes and passes just north of the city of Neuquén. The Lake District is a subregion of Patagonia. Province-wise, Patagonia consists of Neuquén, Río Negro, Chubut and Santa Cruz. It's separated from Chilean Patagonia by the Andes.

The Andean cordillera is high enough that Pacific storms drop most of their rain and snow on the Chilean side. In the extreme southern reaches of Patagonia, however, enough snow and ice still accumulate to form the largest southern hemisphere glaciers outside of Antarctica.

East of the Andean foothills, the cool, arid Patagonian steppes support huge flocks of sheep, much of whose wool is exported to Europe. For such a southerly location, temperatures are relatively mild, even in winter, when more uniform atmospheric pressure moderates the strong gales that blow most of the year.

1

3

MIKE THEISS/ULTIMATE CHASE/CORBIS ©

2

PRISMA BILDAGENTUR AG/ALAMY ©

Argentina's National Parks

Argentina's national and provincial parks offer a huge variety, from the sweltering tropics of Parque Nacional Iguazú to the crashing glaciers of Parque Nacional Los Glaciares to the animal-rich coastal waters of Reserva Faunística Península Valdés.

Parque Nacional Los Glaciares

1 The shining jewel of this park (p434) is Perito Moreno Glacier. Constantly calving, you're practically guaranteed to hear the crack of huge ice chunks sheering off and crashing into the water.

Reserva Provincial Esteros del Iberá

2 Animal lovers shouldn't miss this relatively unspoiled reserve (p163), which teems with exotic creatures like capybaras, black caimans, howler monkeys and countless species of birds.

Parque Nacional Nahuel Huapi

3 One of Argentina's largest and most popular parks (p368) with scenic views, gorgeous lakes, excellent hiking and world-class skiing.

Parque Nacional Iguazú

4 Hundreds of thundering waterfalls combine into an unbelievable sheet of water stretching nearly 3km long, and falling up to 80m in gorgeous terraces (p186).

Reserva Faunística Península Valdés

5 Right whales, Commerson's dolphins, elephant seals and Magellanic penguins all congregate in great numbers along the shores of this protected reserve (p389).

Clockwise from top left

1. Glaciar Perito Moreno (p448) **2.** Capybara (p585) **3.** Parque Nacional Nahuel Huapi (p368)

Except for urban centers such as Comodoro Rivadavia (the center of coastal Patagonia's petroleum industry) and Río Gallegos (the hub for wool and meatpacking), Patagonia is thinly populated. Tidal ranges along the Atlantic coast are too great for major port facilities. In the valley of the Río Negro and at the outlet of the Río Chubut (near the town of Trelew), people farm and cultivate fruit orchards.

Tierra del Fuego

The world's southernmost permanently inhabited territory, Tierra del Fuego ('Land of Fire') consists of one large island (Isla Grande), unequally divided between Chile and Argentina, and many smaller ones, some of which have been the source of longtime contention between the two countries. When Europeans first passed through the Strait of Magellan (which separates Isla Grande from the Patagonian mainland), the fires that gave this land its name stemmed from the activities of the now endangered Yaghan people.

The northern half of Isla Grande, resembling the Patagonian steppes, is devoted to sheep grazing, while its southern half is mountainous and partly covered by forests and glaciers. As in Patagonia, winter conditions are rarely extreme, although hiking and outdoor camping are not advisable except for experienced mountaineers. For most visitors, though, the brief daylight hours during this season may be a greater deterrent than the weather.

Wildlife

With such variances in terrain and such great distances, it's no wonder Argentina boasts a wide range of flora and fauna. Subtropical rainforests, palm savannas, high-altitude deserts and steppes, humid-temperate grasslands, alpine and sub-Antarctic forests and rich coastal areas all support their own special life forms. The most exciting part is that visitors – especially those from the northern hemisphere – will find many of Argentina's plants and animals unfamiliar. Take the capybara, for instance, the world's largest rodent, or the araucaria (pehuén), a conifer appropriately deemed the 'monkey puzzle tree' in English. To protect these environments, Argentina has created an extensive system of national and provincial parks, which are often the best places to experience the country's unique wildlife.

ORCAS

Península Valdés is one of the few places on earth where killer whales (orcas) have been known to hunt sea lions by beaching themselves. You'd be *very* lucky to witness this phenomenon, however.

Animals

Northeast Argentina boasts the country's most diverse animal life. One of the best areas on the continent to enjoy wildlife is the swampy Esteros del Iberá, in Corrientes province, where animals such as swamp deer, capybara and caiman, along with many large migratory birds, are common. It's comparable – arguably even better – than Brazil's more famous Pantanal.

In the drier northwest the most conspicuous animal is the domestic llama, but its wild cousins, the guanaco and vicuña, can also be seen. Your odds of seeing them are excellent if you travel by road through Parque Nacional Los Cardones to Salta. Their yellow fur is often an extraordinary puff of color against the cactus-studded backdrop. Many migratory birds, including flamingos, inhabit the high saline lakes of the Andean Northwest.

In less densely settled areas, including the arid pampas of La Pampa province, guanacos and foxes are not unusual sights. Many bodies of water, both permanent and seasonal, provide migratory bird habitats.

Most notable in Patagonia and Tierra del Fuego is the wealth of coastal wildlife, ranging from Magellanic penguins, cormorants and gulls to sea lions, fur seals, elephant seals, orcas and whales. Several coastal reserves, from Río Negro province south to Tierra del Fuego, are home to

CAPYBARAS *Andy Symington*

Treading, with its webbed feet, a very fine line between cute and ugly, the capybara is a sizable semiaquatic beast that you're bound to encounter in the Iberá area. Weighing in at up to 75kg, the carpincho, as it's known in Spanish, is the world's largest rodent.

Very much at home both on land and in the water, the gentle and vaguely comical creature eats aquatic plants and grasses in great quantity. They form small herds, with a dominant male living it up with four to six females. The male can be recognized by a protrusion on its forehead that emits a territory-marking scent. The lovably roly-poly babies are born in spring.

Though protected in the Iberá area, the capybara is farmed and hunted elsewhere for its skin, which makes a soft, flexible leather. The meat is also considered a delicacy in traditional communities.

enormous concentrations of wildlife that are one of the region's greatest visitor attractions. Inland on the Patagonian steppe, as in the northwest, the guanaco is the most conspicuous mammal, but the flightless rhea, resembling the ostrich, runs in flocks across the plains.

For more on Patagonia's marine wildlife, see p392.

Plants

When it comes to plant life, the country's most diverse regions are in northeast Argentina, the Lake District, the Patagonian Andes and the subtropical forests of northwest Argentina.

The high northern Andes are dry and often barren, and vegetation is limited to ichu (sparse bunch grasses) and low, widely spaced shrubs, known collectively as tola. In Jujuy and La Rioja provinces, however, huge, vertically branched cardón cacti add a rugged beauty to an otherwise empty landscape. In the Andean *precordillera*, between the Chaco and the Andes proper, lies a strip of dense, subtropical montane cloud forest known as the Yungas. Spanning parts of Salta, Jujuy and Tucumán provinces, the Yungas are kept lush by heavy summertime rains, and are one of the most biologically diverse regions in the country.

The wet Chaco is home to grasslands and gallery forests with numerous tree species, including the quebracho colorado and caranday palm. The dry Chaco, although extremely parched, is still thick with vegetation. Its taller trees include the quebracho colorado, quebracho blanco, algarrobo, palo santo, and a dense understory of low-growing spiny trees and shrubs. Both quebracho and algarrobo trees produce highly valued hard woods that have lead to widespread deforestation throughout both regions of the Chaco.

The funny-looking *araucaria araucana* (monkey puzzle tree) grows in the Chilean and Argentine Lake Districts. It has long scaly branches and produces edible pine nuts.

In Mesopotamia rainfall is sufficient to support swampy lowland forests and upland savanna. Misiones' native vegetation is dense subtropical forest, though its upper elevations are studded with araucaria pines.

The once lush native grasses of the Argentine pampas have suffered under grazing pressure and the proliferation of grain farms that produce cash crops such as soy beans. Today very little native vegetation remains, except along watercourses like the Río Paraná.

Most of Patagonia lies in the rain shadow of the Chilean Andes, so the vast steppes of southeastern Argentina resemble the sparse grasslands of the arid Andean highlands. Closer to the border there are pockets of dense Nothofagus (southern beech) and coniferous woodlands that owe their existence to the winter storms that sneak over the cordillera. Northern Tierra del Fuego is a grassy extension of the Patagonian steppe, but the heavy rainfall of the mountainous southern half supports verdant southern beech forests.

Environmental Issues

Although Argentina boasts one of South America's largest systems of parks and reserves, much of those areas – not to mention the extremely sensitive regions around and between them – face serious threat. Deforestation is a major issue in the Chaco, where cultivation of genetically modified soy, sunflower crops and lumber are impacting on the health of the forests. It's equally troubling in the Yungas and the subtropical rainforests of Misiones province, where tea plantations and timber companies continue to destroy some of Argentina's most biologically diverse areas. The result is that many of the country's protected areas, especially those in the Gran Chaco and Mesopotamia, are virtual islands in a sea of environmental degradation. To complicate matters, genetically modified, herbicide-resistant soy has become Argentina's single most important cash crop – leading to accelerated deforestation and high levels of pesticides and herbicide in agricultural soils.

Most of Patagonia's glaciers are shrinking at an alarming rate, but the active Perito Moreno Glacier is considered 'stable' – it's advancing at roughly the same pace as it calves ice.

The good news is that 2007 saw the passing of the Ley de Bosques (National Forest Law), which levied a one-year nationwide moratorium on the clearing of native forests until proper management regulations could be established. However, Cristina Kirchner delayed putting the law into effect for over a year but in February 2009 was finally spurred on to implement it by activists who demanded action.

For other environmental issues, see p556.

Survival Guide

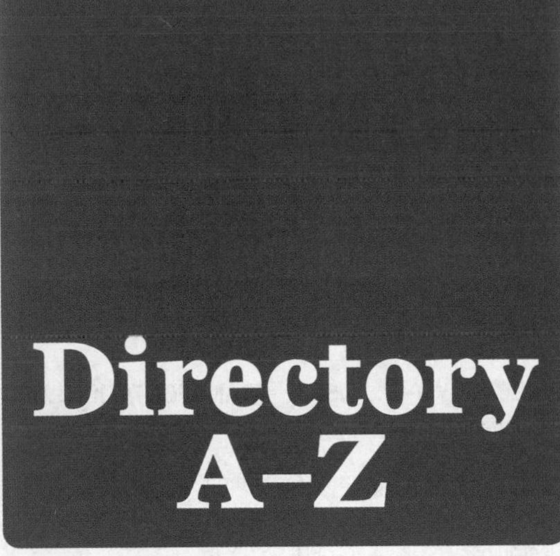

Directory A–Z

Accommodations

Accommodations in Argentina range from campgrounds to five-star luxury hotels. At the tourist-oriented hotels staff members will speak some English, though at more provincial accommodations you'll be practicing your *Español*.

All but the cheapest hotels have private bathrooms, and most accommodations include breakfast – usually *medialunas* (croissants) and weak coffee or tea. Note that many hotels offer discounted rates for extended stays, usually a week or more; negotiate this *before* you begin your stay.

PRICE RANGES

Inflation in Argentina is rampant, running (unofficially) at around 25%. To avoid getting price shock, check current prices.

Accommodation prices in this guidebook include tax and are general high-season rates (although not peak seasons like Christmas or Easter). Budget and midrange hotels almost always include taxes when quoting their prices, but top-end hotels usually do not – and it's 21%. Payment in cash (also at mid- to top-end hotels) sometimes incurs a 10% discount.

High season is generally January and February (when Argentines take their summer breaks), Semana Santa (Easter week) and July and August (except in Patagonia). Reserve ahead during these times. Outside these times, prices can drop anywhere from 20% to 50%.

The following are typical prices in high season:

$ less than AR$250 for a double room; AR$50 to AR$70 for a dorm bed

$$ from AR$250 to AR$500 per double room

$$$ more than AR$500 per double room

Cabañas

Some tourist destinations, especially at the beach or in the country, have cabañas for rent. These are usually standalone cabin-type accommodations, and nearly always have a stocked kitchen. They are a great deal for groups or families (as they often have several rooms), though sometimes their off-the-beaten-track location means you'll need a vehicle to reach them. The destination's tourist office is a good place to find a list of local cabañas.

Camping & Refugios

Camping can be a splendid way to experience Argentina, particularly the Lake District and Patagonia, where there are many good campgrounds. Nearly every Argentine city or town has a fairly central municipal campground, but these are hit-and-miss – sometimes delightfully woodsy, sometimes crowded and ugly.

Private campgrounds usually have good facilities: hot showers, toilets, laundry, barbecue for grilling, restaurant or *confitería* (cafe) and small grocery store. Free campgrounds are often excellent, especially in the Lake District, although they lack facilities. Municipal campgrounds are cheap, but can become party central on weekends.

Argentine camping equipment is often more expensive and inferior than you may be used to. Camp stoves take locally available butane cartridges (which should *not* be taken on airplanes). There are definitely mosquitoes in Argentina, but mosquito repellent is widely available.

Backpacking and backcountry camping opportunities abound in and around the national parks, especially those in the Lakes District and the south. Some parks have free or cheap *refugios* (basic shelters), which have cooking facilities and rustic bunks.

Estancias

Few experiences feel more typically Argentine than staying at an *estancia* (a traditional ranch, often called *fincas* in the northwest). *Estancias* are a wonderful way to spend time in remote areas of the country – and wine, horses and *asados* (traditional barbecues) are almost always involved. *Estancias* are especially common in the area around Buenos Aires, near Esteros del Iberá and throughout the Lake District and Patagonia. In the latter, they're often geared toward anglers. They're not cheap, but the rates generally include room, board and some activities. To easily locate many of the *estancias* covered in this book, see the photo feature on p116; in Uruguay, see p529).

Hospedajes, Pensiones & Residenciales

Aside from hostels, these are Argentina's cheapest accommodations, and the differences among them are sometimes ambiguous.

A *hospedaje* is usually a large family home with a few extra bedrooms (and, generally, a shared bathroom). Similarly, a *pensión* offers short-term accommodations in a family home, but may also have permanent lodgers. *Residenciales* generally occupy buildings designed for short-stay accommodations, although some (known euphemistically as *albergues transitorios)* cater to clientele who intend only *very* short stays – of two hours maximum. These are mostly used by young Argentine couples.

Rooms and furnishings at these accommodations are modest, often basic and usually clean, and rooms with shared bathrooms are the cheapest.

Hostels

Hostels are common in Argentina, and range from basic no-frill deals to beautiful, multi-perk offerings more luxurious than your basic hotel. Most fall in between, but all have common kitchens, living areas, shared bathrooms and dorm rooms. Most have a few private rooms with or without bathroom. It's crucial to remember that Argentines are night owls and hostelers tend to follow suit, so earplugs can be handy indeed.

Hostelling International (HI; www.hihostels.com) members get discounts at HI facilities. Other hostel networks include **minihostels** (www.minihostels.com) and **HoLa** (www.holahostels.com).

Hotels

Argentine hotels vary from depressing, utilitarian one-star places to luxurious five-star hotels with all the usual top-tier services. Oddly enough, many one- and two-star hotels can prove better value than three- and four-star lodgings. In general, hotels provide a room with private bathroom, often a telephone and usually a TV with cable. Sometimes they have a *confitería* or restaurant and almost always include breakfast, whether it be a few *medialunas* with coffee or full American-style buffet.

Rentals & Homestays

House and apartment rentals often save you money if you're staying in one place for an extended period. This can be an especially good deal during high season at resort locations, such as Bariloche or beach cities along the Atlantic coast (just book way ahead) – especially for groups. Tourist offices are good sources for listings.

During the tourist season, mostly in the interior, families rent rooms to visitors. Often these are excellent bargains,

PRACTICALITIES

- **Addresses** In Argentine addresses, the word *local* refers to a suite or office. If an address has 's/n' – short for *sin numero* (without number) – the address has no street number.
- **Laundry** Affordable *lavanderías* are widely available in Argentina.
- **Newspapers** Argentina's biggest papers are centrist *Clarín* (www.clarin.com), conservative *La Nación* (www.lanacion.com.ar) and lefty *Página 12* (www.pagina12.com.ar). The English-language daily is *Buenos Aires Herald* (www.buenosairesherald.com). *The Argentina Independent* (www.argentinaindependent.com) is an excellent English-language online newspaper.
- **Photography** Many photo stores can affordably transfer images from your digital camera to CD; you can also get them printed out. Old-fashioned print and slide film are available, as is developing.
- **Radio** In Buenos Aires tune into FM 92.7 for 24-hour tango, FM 98.3 for Argentine rock, FM 88.7 (www.fmlatribu.com) for alternative viewpoints. FM 100.1 (www.lacolifata.org) is presented by psychiatric asylum patients.
- **Smoking** Smoking bans differ by province. In Buenos Aires smoking is banned in most enclosed public spaces, including the majority of bars and restaurants.
- **Weights & Measures** Metric

BOOK YOUR STAY ONLINE

For more accommodations reviews by Lonely Planet authors, check out http://hotels.lonelyplanet.com. You'll find independent reviews, as well as recommendations on the best places to stay. Best of all, you can book online.

permitting access to cooking and laundry facilities while encouraging contact with Argentines. Generally we do not cover homestays in this book, since they change regularly. Tourist offices in many smaller towns or cities often maintain lists of such accommodations, so ask.

Courses

Argentina is a hot destination in which to learn Spanish. Most opportunities for Spanish-language instruction are based in Buenos Aires, though larger cities such as Mendoza and Córdoba are also excellent.

Tango classes are hugely popular in Buenos Aires, where cooking classes – both for Argentine and international cuisine – are also available.

Customs Regulations

Argentine officials are generally courteous and reasonable toward tourists. Electronic items, including laptops, cameras and cell (mobile) phones, can be brought into the country duty free, provided they are not intended for resale. If you're over 18 and entering from non-neighboring countries, you may bring up to 2L of alcohol, 400 cigarettes and 50 cigars.

If you're entering Argentina from a neighboring country, officials focus on different things. Travelers southbound from the central Andean countries may be searched for drugs, while those from bordering countries will have fruits and vegetables confiscated. Carrying illegal drugs will pretty much get you into trouble no matter which country you're coming from.

Discount Cards

The International Student Identity Card (ISIC) is available through www.isic.org; in Buenos Aires head to the student and discount travel agency **Asatej** (www.asatej.net), with several offices. It can help travelers obtain discounts on public transportation and admissions to museums. Any official-looking university identification may (or may not) be accepted as a substitute.

An HI card, available at any HI hostel (www.hostels.org.ar), will get you discounts on your stay at any HI facility. The **minihostel** (www.minihostels.com) and **HoLa** (www.holahostels.com) cards work in a similar way for a different network of hostels.

Travelers over the age of 60 can sometimes obtain senior-citizen discounts on museum admissions and the like. Usually a passport with date of birth is sufficient evidence of age.

Electricity

Argentina's electric current operates on 220V, 50 Hertz. Adapters are readily available from almost any *ferretería* (hardware store).

Most electronic equipment (such as cameras, pdas, telephones and computers) are dual/multi-voltage, but if you're bringing something that's not (such as a hairdryer), use a voltage converter or you might short out your device.

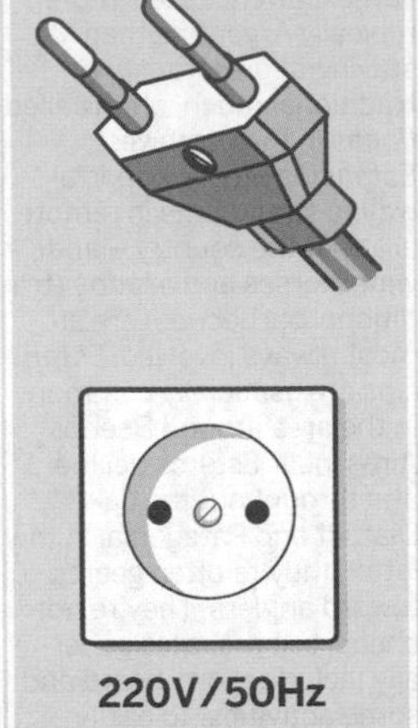

Embassies & Consulates

Following is a basic list of embassies and consulates in Buenos Aires. Some other cities around Argentina (especially near the borders) also have consulates to certain countries.

Australia (☎011-4779-3500; www.argentina.embassy.gov.au; Villanueva 1400)

Bolivia (☎011-4394-1463; www.embajadadebolivia.com.ar; Corrientes 545, 2nd fl)

Brazil (☎011-4515-2400; www.brasil.org.ar; Cerrito 1350)

Canada (☎011-4808-1000; www.canadainternational.gc.ca; Tagle 2828)

Chile (☎011-4808-8601; www.embajadadechile.com.ar; Tagle 2762)

France (☎011-4515-2930; www.embafrancia-argentina.org; Cerrito 1399)

Germany (☎011-4778-2500; www.buenos-aires.diplo.de; Villanueva 1055)

Italy (☎011-4114-4800; www.consbuenosaires.esteri.it; Reconquista 572)

Ireland (☎011-5787-0801; www.embassyofireland.ru/home/index.aspx?id=34777; Av del Libertador 1068, 6th fl)

Japan (☎011-4318-8200; www.ar.emb-japan.go.jp; Bouchard 547, 17th fl)

Netherlands (☎011-4338-0050; www.embajadaholanda.int.ar; Olga Cossettini 831, 3rd fl)

New Zealand (☎011-4328-0747; www.nzembassy.com/argentina; Carlos Pellegrini 1427, 5th fl)

Paraguay (☎011-4814-4803; Viamonte 1851)

Peru (☎011-4802-2000; Av del Libertador 1720)

Spain (☎011-4809-4900; www.embajadaenargentina.es; Av Figueroa Alcorta 3102)

UK (☎011-4808-2200; www.ukinargentina.fco.gov.uk; Dr Luis Agote 2412)

Uruguay (☎011-4807-3040; www.embajadadeluruguay.com.ar; Av Las Heras 1907)

USA (☎011-5777-4533; www.argentina.usembassy.gov; Colombia 4300)

Food

In this book, the following price indicators apply (for a main meal):

$ less than AR$45

$$ AR$45 to AR$65

$$$ more than AR$65

Gay & Lesbian Travelers

Argentina has become increasingly gay-friendly over recent years. Buenos Aires is one of the world's top gay destinations – with dedicated hotels and B&Bs; bars, nightclubs and restaurants; and even gay cruises calling at the port. The capital is home to South America's largest annual gay pride parade and has numerous gay and lesbian organizations and clubs. In 2002 Buenos Aires became the first Latin American city to legalize same-sex civil unions, and in July 2010 Argentina became the first Latin American country to legalize same-sex marriage.

Although Buenos Aires (and, to a lesser extent, Argentina's other large cities) is becoming increasingly tolerant, most of the rest of Argentina still feels uncomfortable with homosexuality. Homophobia rarely takes the form of physical violence, however; instead it manifests through inappropriate jokes and chatty disapproval any time the subject comes up. That said, gay people regularly travel throughout the country to return home with nothing but praise.

When it comes to public affection, Argentine men are more physically demonstrative than their North American and European counterparts. Behaviors such as kissing on the cheek in greeting or a vigorous embrace are innocuous even to those who express unease with homosexuality. Lesbians walking hand in hand should attract little attention, since heterosexual Argentine women frequently do so, but this would be very conspicuous behavior for men. When in doubt, it's best to be discreet.

For more on what's gay in Buenos Aires, see the boxed text, p95.

Health

Argentina is a modern country with good health and dental services. Sanitation and hygiene at restaurants is relatively high, and tap water is generally safe to drink throughout the country. If you want to make sure, ask '*¿Se puede tomar el agua de la canilla*?' (Is the tap water drinkable?).

Public health care in Argentina is reasonably good and free, even if you're a foreigner. Waits can be long, however, and quality inconsistent. Those who can afford it usually opt for the superior private-care system, and

TWO-TIER PRICING

Over the last decade, Argentina's popularity as a tourism destination has birthed an annoying two-tier pricing system: some businesses in certain areas (mostly in Buenos Aires, but also in Patagonia and parts of the Lake District) charge Argentines one price and 'nonresidents' a higher price. While you won't find this everywhere, you will encounter it at some tango shows, *estancias*, national parks, the national airline (Aerolíneas Argentinas) and upmarket hotels throughout the country.

Many accommodations also quote prices in US dollars rather than pesos. This doesn't necessarily mean you're getting charged more than Argentines; the peso is just so unstable that places prefer to use a currency that isn't always fluctuating.

here most doctors and hospitals will expect payment in cash. Many medical personnel speak English.

If you develop a life-threatening medical problem you may want to be evacuated to your home country. Since this may cost thousands of dollars, be sure to have the appropriate insurance before you depart. Your embassy can also recommended medical services.

A signed and dated note from your doctor, describing your medical conditions and medications (with their generic or scientific names) is a good idea. It's also a good idea to bring medications in their clearly labeled, original containers. Most pharmacies in Argentina are well supplied.

For more specific information on vaccinations to get before traveling to Argentina, see wwwnc.cdc.gov/travel/destinations/argentina.htm.

Dengue Fever

Dengue fever is a viral infection found throughout South America. It is transmitted by Aedes mosquitoes, which prefer to bite during the daytime and breed primarily in artificial water containers, such as cans, cisterns, plastic containers and discarded tires. As a result, dengue is especially common in densely populated, urban environments.

In 2009, several thousand cases of dengue were reported in the northern provinces of Argentina, with Chaco and Catamarca being hit the worst. There were even a few dozen cases in Buenos Aires. Fortunately, relatively few deaths resulted. Dengue usually causes flu-like symptoms, including fever, muscle aches, joint pains, headaches, nausea and vomiting, often followed by a rash. The body aches may be quite uncomfortable, but most cases resolve uneventfully in a few days.

Malaria

Malaria is transmitted by mosquito bites, usually between dusk and dawn. The main symptom is high spiking fevers, which may be accompanied by chills, sweats, headache, body aches, weakness, vomiting or diarrhea. Severe cases may involve the central nervous system and lead to seizures, confusion, coma and death.

Taking malaria pills is recommended for travel to rural areas along the borders with Bolivia (lowlands of Salta and Jujuy provinces) and Paraguay (lowlands of Misiones and Corrientes provinces).

Yellow Fever

Yellow fever is a life-threatening viral infection transmitted by mosquitoes in forested areas. The illness begins with flu-like symptoms, which may include fever, chills, headache, muscle aches, backache, loss of appetite, nausea and vomiting. These symptoms usually subside in a few days, but one person in six enters a second, toxic phase characterized by recurrent fever, vomiting, listlessness, jaundice, kidney failure and hemorrhage, leading to death in up to half of the cases. There is no treatment except for supportive care.

The yellow fever vaccine is recommended for all travelers greater than nine months of age who visit the northeastern forest areas near the border with Brazil and Paraguay.

Insurance

A travel insurance policy to cover theft, loss, medical problems and trip cancellation or delays is a good idea. Some policies specifically exclude dangerous activities such as scuba diving, skiing, rock climbing and even trekking; read the fine print. Check that the policy covers ambulances or an emergency flight home.

Keep all your paperwork in case you have to file a claim later. Paying for your flight with a credit card often provides limited travel insurance – ask your credit card company what it is prepared to cover. Worldwide travel insurance is available at www.lonelyplanet.com/travel_services. You can buy,

STANDARD HOURS

We've only listed business hours where they differ from the following standards:

Businesses in big cities 9am to 6pm Monday to Friday

Businesses in provinces 9am to 1pm, 3pm or 4pm to 9pm Monday to Friday

Restaurants noon to 3:30pm, 8pm to midnight or 1am (later on weekends)

Bars 8pm or 9pm to between 4am to 6am nightly

Cafes 6am to midnight or much later daily

Nightclubs 1am or 2am to between 6am and 8am Friday and Saturday

Post offices 8am to 6pm Monday to Friday and 9am to 1pm Saturday (regional variations)

Stores 9am or 10am to 8pm or 9pm Monday to Saturday

extend and claim online anytime – even if you're already on the road.

Internet Access

Wi-fi is increasingly available at many (if not most) hotels and cafes, restaurants and airports, and it's generally free. Hotels offering wi-fi are indicated throughout this book with a icon. If they have a public computer terminal the icon is @.

Internet cafes and *locutorios* (telephone centers) with very affordable internet access can be found in practically all Argentine towns and cities. To find the @ *(arroba)* symbol, try holding down the Alt key and typing 64. Or ask the attendant *'¿Cómo se hace la arroba?'* ('How do you make the @ sign?').

Legal Matters

Police can demand identification at any moment and for whatever reason. Always carry a photo ID or a copy of your passport, and – most importantly – *always* be courteous and cooperative.

The legal drinking age is 18. Marijuana, cocaine and most other substances that are illegal in the USA and many European countries are also illegal here. If arrested, you have the constitutional right to a lawyer, a telephone call and to remain silent (beyond giving your name, nationality, age and passport number). Don't sign anything until you speak to a lawyer. If you don't speak Spanish, a translator should be provided for you.

Maps

Tourist offices throughout the country provide free city maps that are good enough for tooling around town.

With offices in nearly every Argentine city, the **Automóvil Club Argentino** (ACA; www.aca.org.ar) publishes excellent maps of provinces and cities that are particularly good for driving. Card-carrying members of foreign automobile clubs can get discounts.

Geography nerds will adore the topographic maps available from the **Instituto Geográfico Nacional** (Map p64; ☎011-4576-5576; www.ign.gob.ar) in Buenos Aires.

Money

The Argentine unit of currency is the peso (AR$). Prices in this book are quoted in Argentine pesos unless otherwise noted.

Carrying cash and an ATM card is the way to go in Argentina.

ATMs

Cajeros automáticos (ATMs) are found in nearly every city and town in Argentina and can also be used for cash advances on major credit cards. They're the best way to get money, and nearly all have instructions in English. Depending on your home bank there are varying upper limits per withdrawal, and a small fee is charged on ATM transactions by the local bank (not including charges by your home bank). You can withdraw several times per day, but beware these charges – which are per transaction.

Cash

Paper money comes in denominations of two, five, 10, 20, 50 and 100 pesos. One peso equals 100 *centavos;* coins come in denominations of five, 10, 25 and 50 *centavos,* as well as one and two pesos. At present, US dollars are accepted by many tourist-oriented businesses, but you should always carry some pesos.

Don't be dismayed if you receive dirty and hopelessly tattered banknotes; they'll be accepted everywhere. Some places refuse torn or marked foreign banknotes, however, so make sure you arrive in Argentina with pristine bills.

> **CHANGING PESOS BACK TO DOLLARS**
>
> In October 2011 the government passed a law severely limiting the buying of dollars with Argentine pesos. For travelers this means that if you have leftover pesos after your trip to Argentina, it is unlikely you'll be able to change them back into dollars (or possibly any other hard currency). This might be the case even if you have a *cajero* (ATM) or *cambio* (exchange house) receipts! Your best bet is to simply use up all your pesos before you leave the country.

Counterfeiting, of both local and US bills, has become a problem in recent years, and merchants are very careful when accepting large denominations. You should be too; look for a clear watermark or running thread on the largest bills, and get familiar with the local currency *before* you arrive in Argentina. See www.santelmoloft.com/2011/07/22/fake-money-in-argentina. Being aware of fake bills is especially important in nightclubs or taxis (dark places where you should avoid using large bills in the first place).

Changing large denomination bills is a problem throughout the country. Use them at large supermarkets and restaurants. Taxi drivers, kiosks and small stores rarely change them, and you could easily find yourself without a means of paying.

Credit Cards

The most widely accepted credit cards are Visa and MasterCard, though American Express and a few others are valid in many establishments. Before you leave home, warn your credit-card

SPARE SOME CHANGE...?

You will quickly notice that small bills and coins are somewhat precious in Argentina, and especially in Buenos Aires. Some vendors won't sell a small item if you pay with a large bill, and even for larger purchases you might hear groans if you hand over a 100-peso note. So start thinking strategically when spending money.

Break large bills when making big transactions, like at restaurants or supermarkets. Save up a stash of small bills and coins for small purchases, and resist giving up coins unless you're begged to – and you will be. In Buenos Aires, obtaining a SUBE card (see p102) and charging it up means you can pre-pay for many bus or *subte* rides at once – and not have to sacrifice your small change. And when you withdraw money from an ATM, punch in an amount, such as 690 or 790 – so you'll get a few non-100 peso bills.

At least there's one silver lining – you're unlikely to be weighed down with too much change in Argentina.

company that you'll be using it abroad.

Some businesses add a *recargo* (surcharge) of 5% to 10% toward credit-card purchases. Also, the actual amount you'll eventually pay depends upon the exchange rate not at the time of sale, but when the purchase is posted to an overseas account, sometimes weeks later.

If you use a credit card to pay for restaurant bills, be aware that tips can't usually be added to the bill. Many lower-end hotels and private tour companies will not accept credit cards. Holders of MasterCard and Visa can get cash advances at banks and most ATMs – for a fee.

Moneychangers

US dollars are by far the preferred foreign currency, although Chilean and Uruguayan pesos can be readily exchanged at the borders. Cash dollars and euros can be changed at banks and *cambios* (exchange houses) in most larger cities, but other currencies can be difficult to change outside Buenos Aires. You'll need your passport to change money; avoid any sort of street-tout moneychanger.

Taxes & Refunds

Under limited circumstances, foreign visitors may obtain refunds of VAT (value-added tax) on purchases of Argentine products upon their departure from the country. A 'Tax Free' (in English) window decal identifies merchants participating in this program. You'll need to spend a total of AR$70 or more. When making purchases, present your passport to the merchant, who will make out an invoice/refund check for you. On leaving the country keep your invoices and the purchased items in your carry-on bag. Upon leaving the country show your purchases and paperwork to a customs official, who'll stamp it and tell you where to obtain your refund. Enjoy getting some tax money back, but just remember to leave yourself extra time at the airport to get this done.

Tipping & Bargaining

Note that restaurant tips can't be added to a credit card bill. And an interesting note: when your server is taking your bill with payment away, saying 'gracias' usually implies that the server should keep the change as tip. If you want change back, don't say 'gracias' – say 'cambio, por favor' instead.

Unlike many other South American countries, bargaining is generally not the norm in Argentina.

Bartenders they don't expect a tip, but some people give two pesos per drink

Delivery persons two to five pesos per delivery

Hotel cleaning staff 10 pesos per day (only at fine, upscale hotels)

Hotel porter two pesos per bag

Restaurant servers 10%; 15% for fine restaurants with great service

Spas 15%

Taxi drivers no tip unless they help with luggage; many people round up to nearest peso

Tour guides 10% to 15%

Traveler's Checks

Very high commissions are levied on traveler's checks, which are difficult to cash anywhere and specifically *not* recommended for travel in Argentina. Stores will *not* accept traveler's checks, and outside Buenos Aires it's even harder to change them.

Post

The more-or-less reliable **Correo Argentino** (www.correoargentino.com.ar) is the government postal service. Essential overseas mail should be sent *certificado* (registered). You can send packages less than 2kg from any post office, but anything heavier needs to go through *aduana* (a customs office). In Buenos Aires, this office is near Retiro bus terminal and is called Correo Internacional. Take your passport and keep the package open as you'll have to show its contents to a customs official.

Domestic couriers, such as **Andreani** (www.andreani.com.ar) and **OCA** (www.oca.com.ar), and international couriers like DHL and FedEx are far more dependable than the post office. But they're also far more expensive. The last two have offices only in the largest cities, while the first two usually serve as their connections to the interior of the country.

If a package is being sent to you, expect to wait awhile before receiving notification of its arrival. Nearly all parcels sent to Buenos Aires go to the international Retiro office, near the Buquebus terminal. To collect the package you'll have to wait (sometimes hours) first to get it and then to have it checked by customs. There's also a processing fee. Don't expect any valuables to make it through.

Public Holidays

Government offices and businesses are closed on Argentina's numerous public holidays. If the holiday falls on a midweek day or weekend day, it's often bumped to the nearest Monday; if it falls on a Tuesday or Thursday, then the in-between days of Monday and Friday are taken as holidays. Long-distance buses and hotels can fill up, so reserve ahead.

The following list does not include provincial holidays, which may vary considerably.

January 1 Año Nuevo, New Year's Day

February/March Carnaval. Dates vary from year to year, but celebrations always fall on a Monday and Tuesday become holidays

March 24 Día de la Memoria; Memorial Day. Anniversary of the day that started the 1976 dictatorship and subsequent Dirty War

March/April Semana Santa; Easter week. Dates vary; most businesses close on 'Good Thursday' and Good Friday; major travel week

April 2 Día de las Malvinas; honors the fallen Argentine soldiers from the Islas Malvinas (Falkland Islands) war in 1982

May 1 Día del Trabajador; Labor Day

May 25 Revolución de Mayo; commemorates the 1810 revolution against Spain

June 20 Día de la Bandera; Flag Day. Anniversary of death of Manuel Belgrano, creator of Argentina's flag and military leader

July 9 Día de la Independencia; Independence Day

August (third Monday in August) Día del Libertador San Martín; marks the anniversary of José de San Martín's death (1778–1850).

October 12 (second Monday in October) Día del Respeto a la Diversidad Cultural; a day to respect cultural diversity

November 20 (fourth Monday in November) Día de la Soberanía Nacional; Day of National Sovereignty

December 8 Día de la Concepción Inmaculada; celebrates the immaculate conception of the Virgin Mary

December 25 Navidad; Christmas Day

Relocating to Argentina

After the devaluation of the peso in 2002, foreigners began moving to Argentina in huge numbers. Although prices for just about everything (including food, apartments and transportation) has skyrocketed since then, Argentina remains a popular destination for expats.

Many folks simply rent an apartment in Buenos Aires and leave the country every three months to renew their visa. Others go the full route, purchasing property and jumping through hoops to obtain legal residency. Whatever you decide to do, don't expect to easily find work in Argentina, unless you're going to be employed by a foreign company or become an entrepreneur.

For those considering long-term relocation, do your homework. Here are some resources to help you along:

Argentina Residency & Citizenship Advisors (ARCA; www.argentinaresidency.com) Helps foreigners obtain legal residency and citizenship.

Buenos Aires Expatriates Group (www.baexpats.org) Popular expat website.

Craigslist (www. buenosaires.en.craigslist.org) Find a job, an apartment, a lover…

Expatargentina (www.expatargentina.wordpress.com) One expat's eclectic musings about living in BA.

Expat Connection (www.expat-connection.com) Runs events for both expats and locals.

Just Landed (www.justlanded.com) Good expat resources.

LandingPadBA (www.landingpadba.com) Insider info for expats and travelers alike.

South American Explorers (www.saexplorers.org/clubhouses/buenosaires) Member-based resource club.

Safe Travel

For tourists, Argentina is one of the safest countries in Latin America. This isn't to say you should skip down the street drunk with your money belt strapped to your head, but with a little common sense you can visit Argentina's big cities as safely as you could London, Paris or New York. That said, crime has been on the rise.

Petty Crime

The economic crisis of 1999–2001 plunged a lot of people into poverty, and street crime (pickpocketing, bag-snatching and armed robbery) has subsequently risen, especially in Buenos Aires. Still, most people feel perfectly safe in the big cities. In the small towns of the provinces you'd have to *search* for a crook to rob you.

Bus terminals are common places where tourists become separated from their possessions. For the most part bus terminals are safe, as they're usually full of families traveling and saying goodbyes, but they can also be prime grounds for bag-snatchers. Always keep an eagle eye on your goods. This is especially true in Buenos Aires' Retiro station.

At sidewalk cafe or restaurant tables, always have your bag close to you, preferably touching your body. You can also place the strap around your leg or tied around the furniture. Be careful showing off expensive electronics like laptops, iPods or iPads. Other places to be wary are tourist destinations and on crowded public transportation.

In Buenos Aires the **Tourist Police** (Comisaría del Turista; ☎011-4346-5748, ☎0800-999-5000; Av Corrientes 436; ⏲24hr) provides interpreters and helps victims of robberies and rip-offs. For more on safety in BA, see p99.

Pickets & Protests

Street protests have become part of daily life in Argentina, especially in Buenos Aires' Plaza de Mayo area. Generally these have little effect on tourists other than blocking traffic or making it difficult to see Buenos Aires' Plaza de Mayo and the Casa Rosada. The country has many *gremios* or *sindicatos* (trade unions), and it seems that one of them is always on strike. Transportation unions sometimes go on strike, which can affect travelers directly by delaying domestic flights and bus services. It's always a good idea to keep your eye on the news before traveling.

Drivers

Being a pedestrian in Argentina is perhaps one of the country's more-difficult ventures. Many Argentine drivers jump the gun when the traffic signal is about to change to green, drive extremely fast and change lanes unpredictably. Even though pedestrians at corners and crosswalks have legal right of way, very few drivers respect this and will hardly slow down when you are crossing. Be especially careful of buses, which can be reckless and, because of their large size, particularly dangerous.

Police & Military

The police and military have a reputation for being corrupt or irresponsible, but both are generally helpful and courteous to tourists. If you feel you're being patted down for a bribe (most often if you're driving), you can respond by tactfully paying up or asking the officer to accompany you to the police station to take care of it. The latter will likely cause the officer to drop it – though it could also lead you in to the labyrinthine bureaucracy of the Argentine police system. Pretending you don't understand Spanish may also frustrate a potential bribe.

Smoking

Many Argentines are heavy smokers, and you can't help but be exposed to it on the street. The good news for nonsmokers is that Argentina bans smoking in most restaurants, cafes, internet cafes, bars and other public places. Regulations and enforcement differ throughout the country. Smoking is prohibited on buses and all domestic flights.

Telephone

Two companies, Telecom and Telefónica, split the country's telephone services.

The easiest way to make a local phone call is to find a *locutorio*, which has private cabins where you make your calls, and then pay all at once at the register. *Locutorios* can be found on practically every other block. They cost about the same as street phones, are much quieter and you won't run out of coins. Most *locutorios* are supplied with phone books.

To use street phones, you'll pay with regular coins or *tarjetas telefónicas* (magnetic phone cards available at many kiosks). You'll only be able to speak for a limited time before you get cut off, so carry enough credit.

Toll free numbers begin with ☎0800; these calls can only be made within Argentina. Numbers that start with ☎0810 are charged on at a local rate only, no matter where (in Argentina) you are calling from.

The cheapest way to make an international call is to use an online service (such as Skype or Google Voice) or use a phone card. International calls can be made at *locutorios*, but they're more expensive this way. When dialing abroad, dial '00,' followed by the code of the country you're calling, then the area code and number.

Faxes are cheap and widely available throughout Argentina.

Medical emergency ☎107
Police ☎101 (or ☎911 in some larger cities)

ELECTRONICS WARNING

Note that buying a smart phone, and especially an iPhone, is extremely expensive in Argentina due to import restrictions – and they are not widely available. If you do bring your smart phone, don't flash it around unnecessarily or leave it unprotected somewhere. This goes for tablet computers and laptop computers, too.

CALLING TO ARGENTINA

To call a number in Argentina from another country, dial your international exit code, then the country code for Argentina, then the area code (without the zero) and number. For example, if you're calling a Buenos Aires landline number from the United States, you'd dial:

011-54-11-xxxx-xxxx

011 is the United States' international exit code

54 is Argentina's country code

11 is Buenos Aires' city code without the beginning zero

xxxx-xxxx is your local Buenos Aires phone number, usually eight digits

When dialing an Argentine cell phone from another country, dial your international exit code, then ☎54, then ☎9, then the area code without the 0, then the number – leaving out the ☎15 (which most Argentine cell phone numbers start with). For example, if you're calling a Buenos Aires cell phone number from the United States, you'd dial:

011-54-9-11-xxxx-xxxx

Fire ☎100
Directory assistance ☎110
Tourist Police ☎011-4346-5748, ☎0800-999-5000

CELL PHONES

It's best to bring your own unlocked tri- or quad-band GSM cell phone to Argentina, then buy an inexpensive SIM chip (you'll get a local number) and credits (or *carga virtual*) as needed. Both SIM chips and credits can be bought at many kiosks or *locutorios;* look for the *'recarga facil'* signs. Many Argentines use this system with their cell phones. Phone unlocking services are available; ask around.

You can also buy cell phones that use SIM chips; these usually include some credits for your first batch of calls. Be careful renting phones as they're not usually a better deal than outright buying a cell phone.

If you plan to travel with an iPhone or other G3 smart phone, prepare yourself – you may need to purchase an international plan to avoid being hit by a huge bill for roaming costs. On the other hand, it's possible to call internationally for free or very cheap, using a VoIP (Voice over Internet Protocol) system such as Skype. This is a constantly changing field, so do some research before you travel.

Cell phone numbers in Argentina are always preceded by '15.' If you're calling a cellular phone number from a landline, you'll have to dial 15 first. But if you're calling a cell phone from another cell phone, you don't need to dial 15 (at least within the same area code).

PHONECARDS

Telephone calling cards are sold at nearly all kiosks and make domestic and international calls far cheaper than calling direct. However, they must be used from a fixed line such as a home or hotel telephone (provided you can dial outside the hotel). They cannot be used at most pay phones. Some *locutorios* allow you to use them, and although they levy a surcharge, the call is still cheaper than dialing direct. When purchasing one, tell the clerk the country you will call so they give you the right card.

Time

Argentina is three hours behind GMT and generally does not observe daylight saving time (though this situation can easily change). When it's noon in Argentina, it's 10am in New York, 7am in San Francisco, 3pm in London and 1pm the next day in Sydney (add one hour to these destinations during their daylight saving times). Argentina uses the 24-hour clock in written communications, but both the 12- and 24-hour clocks can be used conversationally.

Toilets

Public toilets in Argentina are better than in most of South America, but there are certainly exceptions. For the truly squeamish, the better restaurants and cafes are good alternatives. Large shopping malls often have public bathrooms, as do international fast-food chains. Always carry your own toilet paper, since it often runs out in public restrooms, and don't expect luxuries such as soap, hot water and paper towels either. In smaller towns, some public toilets charge a small fee for entry.

Bidets are always available in hotel rooms and private homes, but not in public restrooms.

Tourist Information

Argentina's national tourist board is the Secretaría de Turismo de la Nación; its main office is in Buenos Aires. Almost every city or town has a tourist office, usually on or near the main plaza or at the bus terminal. Each Argentine province also has its own representation in Buenos Aires. Most of these are well organized, often offering a computerized database of tourist information, and can be worth a visit before heading for the provinces.

Travelers with Disabilities

Travelers with disabilities will find things somewhat difficult in Argentina. Those in wheelchairs in particular will quickly realize that many cities' narrow, busy and uneven sidewalks are difficult to negotiate. Crossing streets is also a problem, since not every corner has ramps (which are often in need of repair) and Argentine drivers don't have much patience for slower pedestrians, disabled or not.

Nevertheless, Argentines with disabilities do get around. In Buenos Aires there a few buses described as *piso bajo* – which lower to provide wheelchair lifts – and the Subte (subway) has a few accessible stations, especially the newer ones.

Except at four- and five-star properties, hotels usually do not have wheelchair-accessible rooms, meaning doors are narrow and there is little space to move around inside the room. Bathrooms at midrange and budget hotels are sometimes notoriously small, making it difficult for anyone (disabled or not) to get around in. For truly accessible rooms, you'll have better luck in pricier hotels. Call ahead and ask specific questions – even if a hotel defines a room as wheelchair-accessible, it may not be up to standards to which you're accustomed.

Other than the use of Braille on ATMs, little effort has been dedicated to bettering accessibility for the blind. Stoplights are rarely equipped with sound alerts. The **Biblioteca Argentina Para Ciegos** (Argentine Library for the Blind, BAC; ☎011-4981-0137; www.bac.org.ar) in Buenos Aires maintains a Braille collection of books in Spanish, as well as other resources.

In Buenos Aires, **QRV Transportes Especiales** (☎011-4306-6635, 011-15-6863-9555; www.qrvtransportes.com.ar) offers private transport and city tours in vans fully equipped for wheelchair users.

Also check out the following international organizations:

Accessible Journeys www.disabilitytravel.com

Flying Wheels Travel www.flyingwheelstravel.com

Mobility International USA www.miusa.org

Society for Accessible Travel & Hospitality www.sath.org

Visas

Nationals of the USA, Canada, most Western European countries, Australia and New Zealand do not need a visa to visit Argentina. Upon arrival, most visitors get a 90-day stamp in their passport. Those from the USA, Canada and Australia, however, must pay a significant 'reciprocity fee' upon arrival; see the boxed text, p602.

Dependent children traveling without *both* parents theoretically need a notarized document certifying that both parents agree to the child's travel. Parents may also wish to bring a copy of the custody form; however, there's a good chance they won't be asked for either document.

Depending on your nationality, very short visits to neighboring countries sometimes do not require visas. For instance, you might not need a Brazilian visa to cross from the Argentine town of Puerto Iguazú to Foz do Iguaçu and/or Ciudad del Este, Paraguay, as long as you return the same day. For more information on entering Brazil, see the boxed text (p189).

The same is true at the Bolivian border town of Villazón, near La Quiaca (see the boxed text, p222). Officials at Paraguayan crossings can charge a fine from crossers who don't have a Paraguayan visa (see the boxed text, p177).

Visa Extensions

For a 90-day extension on your tourist visa, get ready for bureaucracy and visit Buenos Aires' immigration office **Dirección Nacional de Migraciones** (☎011-4317-0234; www.migraciones.gov.ar/accesibleingles/?categorias; Antártida Argentina 1355; ⏲8am-2pm Mon-Fri). The fee is AR$300 – interestingly enough, the same charge as overstaying your visa.

Another option if you're staying more than three months is to cross into Colonia or Montevideo (both in Uruguay) or into Chile for a day or two before your visa expires, then return with a new 90-day visa. However, this only works if you don't need a visa to enter the other country.

Volunteering

There are many opportunities for volunteering in Argentina, from food banks to *villas miserias* to organic farms to working with monkeys. Some ask for just your time, or a modest fee – and some charge hundreds of dollars (with likely a low percentage of money going directly to those in need). Before choosing an organization, it's good to talk to other volunteers about their experiences.

Organizations include:

Centro Conviven (www.conviven.org.ar) Helps kids in Buenos Aires' *villas*.

Conservación Patagonica (www.patagonialandtrust.org/makeadifference_v.htm) Help to create a national park.

Eco Yoga Park (www.ecoyogapark.com/homeingles.html) One of a kind.

Fundación Banco de Alimentos (www.bancodealimentos.org.ar) Short-term work at a food bank.

Habitat for Humanity Argentina (www.hpha.org.ar) Building communities.

L.I.F.E. (www.lifeargentina.org) More help for kids in Argentine *villas*.

Parque Nacional Los Glaciares (☎02962-430004) Summer work with park rangers in El Chaltén. Spanish-language skills preferred.

Refugio del Caraya (www.volunteer-with-howler-monkeys.org)

Unión de los Pibes (www.uniondelospibes.blogspot.com) Buenos Aires' kids in need.

Voluntario Global (www.voluntarioglobal.org.ar) Community volunteering.

Referral services:

Anda Responsible Travel (www.andatravel.com.ar/en/volunteering)

Foundation for Sustainable Development (www.fsdinternational.org)

La Montaña (www.lamontana.com/volunteer-work) Volunteer in Bariloche.

Patagonia Volunteer (www.patagoniavolunteer.org) Opportunities in Patagonia.

South American Explorers (www.saexplorers.org/volunteer/home)

Volunteer South America (www.volunteersouthamerica.net) List of NGOs.

WWOOF Argentina (www.wwoofargentina.com) Organic farming in Argentina.

Voluntario Global (www.voluntarioglobal.org.ar) Community volunteering.

Writers can consider penning articles for the **Argentina Independent** (www.argentinaindependent.com), or interning at the **Buenos Aires Herald** (www.buenosaireshelald.com).

Women Travelers

Being a woman traveling in Argentina is a challenge, especially if you are young, alone and/or maintaining an inflexible liberal attitude. In some ways Argentina is a safer place for a woman than Europe, the USA and most other Latin American countries, but dealing with its machismo culture can be a real pain in the ass.

Some males brimming with testosterone feel the need to comment on a woman's attractiveness. This often happens when the woman is alone and walking by on the street; it occasionally happens to two or more women walking together, but never to a heterosexual couple. Verbal comments include crude language, hisses, whistles and *piropos* (flirtatious comments), which are often vulgar – although some can be eloquent.

The best thing to do is completely ignore the comments. After all, many Argentine women enjoy getting these 'compliments' and most men don't necessarily mean to be insulting; they're just doing what males in their culture are brought up to do.

On the plus side of machismo, expect men to hold a door open for you and let you enter first, including getting on buses; this gives you a better chance at grabbing an empty seat, so get in there quick.

Work

Unless you have a special skill, business, and/or speak Spanish, it's hard to find paid work in Argentina other than teaching English – or perhaps putting time in at a hostel or expat bar. And it's good to realize that you're not likely to get rich doing these things.

Working out of an institute in Buenos Aires, native English-speakers can earn around AR$40 per hour (and you aren't paid for prep time or travel time, which can add another hour or two for each hour of teaching). Twenty hours a week of actual teaching is about enough for most people. Frustrations include dealing with unpleasant institutes, time spent cashing checks at the bank, classes being spread throughout the day and cancelled classes. Institute turn-over is high and most people don't teach for more than a year.

A TEFL certification can certainly help but isn't mandatory for all jobs (check out www.teflbuenosaires.com). You'll make more money teaching private students, but it takes time to gain a client base. And you should take into account slow periods, such as December through February, when many locals leave town on summer vacation.

To find a job, call up the institutes or visit expat bars and start networking. March is when institutes are ramping up their courses, so it's the best time to find work. Many teachers work on tourist visas (which is not a big deal), heading over to Uruguay every three months for a new visa or visiting the immigration office for a visa extension.

For job postings, check out www.buenosaires.en.craigslist.org and the classified section of www.justlanded.com. You could also try posting on expat website forums, such as www.baexpats.org.

Transportation

GETTING THERE & AWAY

Flights, tours and rail tickets can be booked online at lonelyplanet.com/bookings.

Entering Argentina

Entering Argentina is straightforward; immigration officials at airports are generally quick to the point, while those at border crossings may take more time scrutinizing your passport. Once you're in the country, police can still demand identification any time. Carry at least a photocopy of your passport around at all times.

Air

Argentina has direct flights between North America, the UK, Europe, Australia, New Zealand, and South Africa, and from nearly all South American countries. You can fly to a neighboring country, such as Brazil, and continue overland to Argentina.

Airports

Aerolíneas Argentinas is the national carrier and has a decent international reputation. Most international flights arrive at Buenos Aires' **Aeropuerto Internacional Ministro Pistarini** (Ezeiza; ☎011-5480-6111), which is a 40- to 60-minute shuttle bus or taxi ride out of town. For information on how to get into town from Ezeiza, see p101.

Close to downtown Buenos Aires is **Aeroparque Internacional Jorge Newbery** (☎011-5480-6111), which handles mostly domestic flights but also a few international ones from neighboring countries.

Basic information on most Argentine airports can be found online at **Aeropuertos Argentina 2000** (www.aa2000.com.ar).

Land

Border Crossings

There are numerous border crossings from neighboring Chile, Bolivia, Paraguay, Brazil and Uruguay; the following lists are only the principal crossings. Generally, border formalities are straightforward as long as all your documents are in order.

BOLIVIA

La Quiaca to Villazón Many buses go from Jujuy and Salta to La Quiaca, where you must walk across a bridge to the Bolivian border.

Aguas Blancas to Bermejo From Orán, reached by bus from Salta or Jujuy, take a bus to Aguas Blancas and then Bermejo, where you can catch a bus to Tarija.

Salvador Mazza (Pocitos) to Yacuiba Buses from Jujuy or Salta go to Salvador Mazza at the Bolivian border, where you cross and grab a shared taxi to Yacuiba.

BRAZIL

The most common crossing is from Puerto Iguazú to Foz do Iguaçu. Check both cities for more information on the peculiarities of this border crossing, especially if you're crossing the border into Brazil only to see the other side of Iguazú Falls. For specifics, see p189. There is also a border crossing from Paso de los Libres to Uruguaiana (Brazil).

CHILE

There are numerous crossings between Argentina and Chile. Except in far southern Patagonia, every land crossing involves crossing the Andes. Due to weather, some high-altitude passes close in winter; even the busy Mendoza–Santiago route over RN 7 can close for several days (sometimes longer) during a severe storm. Always check road conditions, especially if you have a flight scheduled on the other side of the mountains. The following are the most commonly used crossings:

Bariloche to Puerto Montt This border crossing over the Andes to Chile is usually no fuss; an optional 'tour' is the famous, scenic 12-hour bus-boat combination. It takes two days in winter. See p371.

El Calafate to Puerto Natales and Parque Nacional Torres del Paine Probably the most beaten route down here, heading from the Glaciar Perito Moreno (near El Calafate) to Parque Nacional Torres del Paine (near Puerto Natales). Several buses per day in summer; one to two daily in the off-season.

Los Antiguos to Chile Chico Those entering Argentina from Chile can access the rugged RN 40 from here and head down to El Chaltén and El Calafate. Best in summer, when there's actually public transport available.

Mendoza to Santiago The most popular crossing between the two countries, passing 6962m Aconcagua en route.

Salta to San Pedro de Atacama (via Jujuy, Purmamarca and Susques) A 10-hour bus ride through the altiplano with stunningly beautiful scenery (see p217).

Ushuaia to Punta Arenas Daily buses in summer, fewer in winter, on this 10- to 12-hour trip (depending on weather conditions), which includes a ferry crossing at either Porvenir or Punta Delgada/Primera Angostura.

URUGUAY & PARAGUAY

There are two direct border crossings between Argentina and Paraguay: Clorinda to Asunción, and Posadas to Encarnación. From Puerto Iguazú, Argentina, you can also cross through Brazil into Ciudad del Este, Paraguay.

Border crossings from Argentine cities to Uruguayan cities include Gualeguaychú to Fray Bentos; Colón to Paysandú; and Concordia to Salto. All involve crossing bridges. Buses from Buenos Aires to Montevideo and other waterfront cities, however, are slower and less convenient than the ferries (or ferry-bus combinations) across the Río de la Plata.

Bus

Travelers can bus to Argentina from most bordering countries. Buses are usually comfortable, modern and fairly clean. Crossing over does not involve too many hassles; just make sure that you have any proper visas beforehand.

Train

A new train service between Argentina and Uruguay began in September 2011, linking Pilar in Argentina with Paso de los Toros in Uruguay. It's not currently very practical for travelers, but the hope is to eventually link Buenos Aires and Montevideo by rail.

River

There are several river crossings between Uruguay and Buenos Aires that involve ferry or hydrofoil, and often require combinations with buses.

Buenos Aires to Colonia Daily ferries (one to three hours) head to Colonia, with bus connections to Montevideo (additional three hours).

Buenos Aires to Montevideo High-speed ferries carry passengers from downtown Buenos Aires to the Uruguayan capital in only 2¾ hours.

Tigre to Carmelo Regular passenger launches speed from the Buenos Aires suburb of Tigre to Carmelo in 2½ hours (services also go to Montevideo from Tigre).

GETTING AROUND

Air

Airlines in Argentina

The national carrier, **Aerolíneas Argentinas** (☎0810-222-86527; www.aerolineas.com), offers the most domestic flights, but it's not necessarily better than its competitors. Other airlines with domestic flights include **LAN** (LAN; ☎0810-999-9526; www.lan.com) and **Líneas Aéreas del Estado** (LADE; ☎0810-810-5233; www.lade.com.ar), the air force's passenger service. The latter has some of the least expensive air tickets and specializes in Patagonia; the airline has very few flights, however, and most are short hops.

Some domestic airlines operate on a two-tier system, where foreigners pay more than locals for the same ticket. If you fly to Argentina with Aerolíneas Argentinas, however, you can get discounted domestic tickets. The catch is that you must purchase these outside Argentina, usually when you purchase your international flight.

Nearly all domestic flights land at **Aeroparque Internacional Jorge Newbery** (☎011-5480-6111;

IS THAT A BANANA IN YOUR BACKPACK?

You've been warned: don't bring any fresh produce, dairy products or meat when crossing from Argentina into Chile (either overland or by air). There will likely be an inspection of all baggage at the border or airport, possibly with cute Chilean sniffer dogs, and if you're found with any 'contraband' you could be fined up to US$300. Even dried or dehydrated food – and especially trail mix – might not be allowed.

So finish up that sandwich (quickly) and bring some water to help with all that the chewing. Don't expect such a thorough check when crossing back, however – good or bad, Argentina doesn't seem to care nearly as much about inspecting fruit-munching travelers.

EZEIZA ARRIVAL TIPS

Citizens from several countries have to pay a 'reciprocity fee' *(tasa de reciprocidad)* when they land in Ezeiza. This is equal to what Argentines are charged for visas to visit those countries. These fees include US$140 to US$150 for US citizens (good for five to 10 years), US$75 to US$150 for Canadians (good one to five years) and US$100 for Australians (good for one year). The fee is payable in cash, credit card or traveler's check. It's currently charged at Ezeiza only, but in the future might be collected at all immigration checkpoints.

To change money at Ezeiza, be careful with *cambios* (exchange houses). Their rates are generally bad and rarely they've been known to pass fake bills. For better rates, pass the rows of transport booths, go outside the doors into the reception hall and veer sharply to the right to find Banco de la Nación's small office; it's open 24 hours and has an ATM (there's another ATM nearby, next to Farmacity, and yet another way beyond, at the airline counters).

Ezeiza is about 35km from Buenos Aires' center. For shuttle buses and taxis from Ezeiza to the center, see p101. There's a helpful **tourist information booth** (5480-6111, 24hr) just beyond the city's taxi stand.

If you need a hotel near the airport, try the pleasant **Posada de las Aguilas** (4480-9637; www.posadadelasaguilas.com.ar; José Hernández 128; s/d AR$340/380;); it's just a few minutes from Ezeiza and it provides transfers.

www.aa2000.com.ar), a short distance north of downtown Buenos Aires.

Demand for flights around the country can be heavy, especially during some holidays (such as Christmas or Easter) and the vacation months of January, February and July. Seats are often booked out well in advance so reserve as far ahead as possible.

Bicycle

If you dig cycling your way around a country, Argentina has potential. You'll see the landscape in greater detail, have far more freedom than you would if beholden to public transportation, and likely meet more locals.

Road bikes are suitable for many paved roads, but byways are often narrow and surfaces can be rough. A *todo terreno* (mountain bike) is often safer and more convenient, allowing you to use the unpaved shoulder and the very extensive network of gravel roads throughout the country. Argentine bicycles are improving in quality, but are still far from equal to their counterparts in Europe or the USA.

There are two major drawbacks to long-distance bicycling in Argentina. One is the wind, which in Patagonia can slow your progress to a crawl. The other is Argentine motorists: on many of the country's straight, narrow, two-lane highways, they can be a serious hazard to cyclists. Make yourself as visible as possible, and wear a helmet.

Bring an adequate repair kit and extra parts (and the know-how to use them) and stock up on good maps, which is usually easier to do once you're in Argentina. Always confirm directions and inquire about conditions locally; maps can be unreliable and conditions change regularly. In Patagonia, a windbreaker and warm clothing are essential. Don't expect much traffic on some back roads.

For some good places around the country in which to spin your wheels, see p32.

Rental

Bicycle rentals (mostly mountain bikes) are available in many popular tourist destinations, such as along the Atlantic Coast, Mendoza, Bariloche and other towns throughout the Lake District and Córdoba's Central Sierras. Prices are by the hour or day, and are affordable.

Purchase

Many towns have bike shops, but high-quality bikes are expensive, and repair parts can be hard to come by. If you do decide to buy while you're here, you're best off doing so in Buenos Aires – selection in other major cities is pretty slim. Prices for an imported bike (which you'll want if you're doing serious cycling) are much higher than in their country of origin.

Boat

Opportunities for boat or river travel in and around Argentina are limited, though there are regular international services to/from Uruguay and to/from Chile via the Lake District. Further south, from Ushuaia, operators offer boat trips on the Beagle Channel in Tierra del Fuego.

Otherwise, if you must be on the water, head to the Buenos Aires suburb of Tigre, where there are numerous boat excursions around the delta of the Río de la Plata.

Bus

If you're doing any serious traveling around Argentina, you'll become very familiar with the country's excellent bus network, which reaches almost everywhere. Long-distance buses (known as *micros*) are fast, surprisingly comfortable and can be a rather luxurious experience. It's the way most Argentines get around. Larger luggage is stowed in the hold below, security is generally good (especially on the 1st-class buses) and attendants tag your bags. If you have a long way to go – say, Buenos Aires to Mendoza – overnight buses are the way to go, saving you a night's accommodations and the daylight hours for fun.

Hundreds of bus companies serve different regions but a few bigger lines (listed here) dominate the long-haul business:

Andesmar (☎0261-429-9501, 011-6385-0883; www.andesmar.com) Serves the entire country.

Chevallier (☎011-4000-5255; www.nuevachevallier.com) Routes from Bariloche to Salta.

El Rápido International (☎0261-429-9501, 011-6385-0883; www.elrapidoint.com.ar) Buenos Aires, Mendoza, Córdoba and Rosario. International service to Santiago and Viña del Mar (Chile) and Lima (Peru).

Via Bariloche (☎0810-333-7575; www.viabariloche.com.ar) Serves most destinations in La Pampa province, the Lake District and Patagonia.

Most cities and towns have a central bus terminal where each company has its own ticket window. Some companies post schedules prominently, and the ticket price and departure time is always on the ticket you buy. Expect restrooms, left luggage, fast-food stalls, kiosks and newspaper vendors inside or near almost every large terminal. In tourist destination cities they'll often have a tourist information office. There are generally few if any hotel touts or other traveler-hassling types at terminals; El Calafate is one notable exception.

One well-run Buenos Aires company where you can buy practically any long-distance bus ticket online (and without commission) is **Omnilíneas** (☎011-4326-3924; www.omnilineas.com). Its excellent website has bus travel tips and more.

Classes & Costs

Better bus lines such as Chevallier and Andesmar have modern coaches with spacious, comfortable seats, large windows, air-conditioning, TVs, toilets (though don't expect luxury here – and bring toilet paper) and sometimes an attendant serving coffee and snacks.

On overnight trips it's well worth the extra pesos to go *coche cama* (sleeper class), though the cheaper *semi-cama* (semisleeper) is definitely manageable. In *coche cama* seats are wider, recline almost flat and are far more comfortable. For even more luxury there's *ejecutivo* (executive) which is available on a few popular runs. If pinching pesos, *común* (common) is the cheapest class. For trips less than about five hours, there's usually no choice and buses are *común* or *semi-cama,* which are both usually just fine.

Bus fares vary widely depending on season, class and company. Patagonia runs tend to be the most expensive. Many companies accept credit cards.

Reservations

Often you don't need to buy bus tickets beforehand unless you're traveling on a Friday between major cities, when overnight *coche cama* services sell out fast. During holiday stretches, such as late December through February, July and August, tickets sell quickly so buy ahead of time. As soon as you arrive somewhere, especially if it's a town with limited services, find out which companies go to your next destination and when, and plan your trip.

When the bus terminal is on the outskirts of a big town or city, there are often downtown agencies selling tickets without commission. Ask at your hotel.

Seasonal Services

In the Lake District and northern Patagonia, bus services are good during summer (November through March), when there are many microbus routes to campgrounds, along lake circuits, to trail heads and to other destinations popular with tourists. Outside summer, however, these services slow way down.

In Patagonia the famed stretch of RN 40, or Ruta Nacional Cuarenta (Route 40), is infrequently traveled and rough, though it's slowly being paved. There's little public transport, and it's mostly via expensive, summertime microbus 'tours.' For more details, see p417.

Car & Motorcycle

Because Argentina is so large, many parts are accessible only by private vehicle, despite the country's extensive public transport system. This is especially true in Patagonia, where distances are great and buses can be infrequent.

Automobile Associations

Whenever driving in Argentina, it's worth being a member of the **Automóvil Club Argentino** (ACA; www.aca.org.ar), which has offices, gas stations and garages throughout the country and offers road service and towing in and around major destinations. ACA recognizes members of most overseas auto clubs and grants them privileges including road service and discounts on maps and accommodations. Bring your card.

Bring Your Own Vehicle

Chile is probably the best country on the continent for shipping a vehicle from overseas, though Argentina is feasible. Getting the vehicle out of customs typically involves routine but time-consuming paperwork.

Driver's License & Documents

Technically you're supposed to have an International Driving Permit to supplement your national or state driver's license (though you can rent a car without one). If you are stopped, police will inspect your automobile registration and insurance and tax documents, all of which must be up to date.

Drivers of Argentine vehicles must carry their title document (*tarjeta verde* or 'green card'); if it's a rental, make sure it's in the glove box. For foreign vehicles, customs permission is the acceptable substitute. Liability insurance is obligatory, and police often ask to see proof of insurance at checkpoints.

Fuel

Nafta (gas) prices are roughly similar to the US. Avoid *común* (regular) as it's usually low quality. Super and premium are better choices. In Patagonia gas prices are about a third what they are elsewhere. *Estaciones de servicio* (gas stations) are fairly common, but outside the cities keep an eye on your gas gauge. In Patagonia it's a good idea to carry extra fuel.

Rental

To rent a car, you must be at least 21 years of age and have a valid driver's license and a credit card. Agencies rarely ask for an International Driving Permit.

When you rent a vehicle find out how many kilometers are included. Unlimited-kilometer deals exist but are usually much more expensive, depending on the destination. Reserving a car with one of the major international agencies in your home country sometimes gets you lower rates.

One of the cheapest places to rent a car is Bariloche; if you're heading to Patagonia for example, this is a good place to rent. Taking a rental car out of Argentina is not usually allowed.

For motorcycle rentals, be at least 25 years of age and head to **Motocare** (☎4761-2696, www.motocare.com.ar/rental) located in Buenos Aires or Neuquén. Honda Transalps 700 are available; bring your own helmet and riding gear. For driving outside big cities only.

Purchase

Purchasing a vehicle in Argentina can be complicated for foreigners. This usually involves having a permanent local address, obtaining a CDI (a tax ID number) and paying for the vehicle in cash. To buy a used vehicle, you must transfer the title at a title transfer office, with the current owner and all his/her proper papers present. Make sure all licenses, unpaid tickets and taxes have been paid.

Speaking Spanish helps. Getting insurance without a DNI (national document) can be difficult but not impossible. As a foreigner without a DNI you may own a vehicle in Argentina; however, you theoretically cannot take it out of the country without a notarized authorization, which can be difficult to obtain.

It's wise to supplement this information with your own current research.

Insurance

Liability insurance is obligatory in Argentina, and police ask to see proof of insurance at checkpoints. If you plan on taking the car to neighboring countries, make sure it will remain covered (you'll have to pay extra). Among reputable insurers in Argentina are **Mapfre** (www.mapfre.com.ar) and **ACA** (www.aca.org.ar).

Road Rules & Hazards

Anyone considering driving in Argentina should know that Argentine drivers are aggressive and commonly ignore speed limits, road signs and even traffic signals. Night driving is not recommended; in many regions animals hang out on the road for warmth.

Have on hand some emergency reflectors *(balizas)* and a fire extinguisher *(matafuego)*. Headrests are required for the driver and passengers, and seatbelts are obligatory (though few wear them). Motorcycle helmets are also obligatory, although this law is rarely enforced.

You won't often see police patrolling the highways, but might meet them at major intersections and roadside checkpoints where they conduct meticulous document and equipment checks. Sometimes these checks are pretexts for graft. If you are uncertain about your rights, politely state your intention to contact your embassy or consulate. If you *do* want

NOW WE'RE GETTING SOMEWHERE

A very handy website for those driving around Argentina is www.ruta0.com. Among other things, you can punch in two destinations and get the recommended routes (and whether they're paved or not), distances (in kilometers), driving times and even how much it will cost in gas consumption. Now if it could only warn you where to avoid those crazy Argentine drivers.

to pay a bribe for the sake of expediency, ask *¿Puedo pagar la multa ahora?* ('Can I pay the fine now?').

Hitchhiking

Hitchhiking *(hacer dedo)* is never entirely safe in any country in the world. Travelers who decide to hitch should understand that they are taking a small but potentially serious risk. People who do choose to hitch will be safer if they travel in pairs and let someone know where they are planning to go.

Along with Chile, Argentina is probably the best country for hitching in all of South America. The major drawback is that Argentine vehicles are often stuffed full with families and children, but truckers will sometimes pick up backpackers. A good place to ask is at *estaciones de servicio* (gas stations) at the outskirts of large Argentine cities, where truckers gas up their vehicles.

Women can and do hitchhike alone, but should exercise caution and especially avoid getting into a car with more than one man. In Patagonia, where distances are great and vehicles few, hitchers should expect long waits and carry warm, windproof clothing and refreshments.

Having a sign will improve your chances for a pickup, especially if it says something like *visitando Argentina de Canada* (visiting Argentina from Canada), rather than just a destination. Argentines are fascinated by foreigners.

For good information (in Spanish) see www.autostopargentina.com.ar, or try www.wander-argentina.com/hitchhiking-in-argentina.

Local Transportation

Bus

Local Argentine buses, called *colectivos,* are notorious for charging down the street and spewing clouds of black smoke while traveling at breakneck speeds. Riding on them is a good way to see the cities and get around, providing you can sort out the often complex bus systems. Buses are clearly numbered and usually carry a placard indicating their final destination. Sometimes, identically numbered buses serve slightly different routes (especially in big cities), so pay attention to the placards. To ask 'Does this bus go (to the town center)?' say *'¿Va este colectivo (al centro)?'*

Most city buses operate on coins; you pay as you board. In some cities, such as Mendoza or Mar del Plata, you must buy prepaid bus cards or – in the case of Córdoba – *cospeles* (tokens) as well. In both cases, they can be bought at any kiosk.

Subway

Buenos Aires is the only Argentine city with a subway system (known as the Subte), and it's the quickest and cheapest way of getting around the city center.

Taxi & Remise

The people of Buenos Aires make frequent use of taxis, which are digitally metered and cheap by US and European standards. Outside the capital, meters are common but not universal, and you'll need to agree on a fare in advance. For more on taking taxis in BA, see p102.

Where public transportation is scarce, it's possible to hire a taxi with a driver for the day. If you bargain, this can be cheaper than a rental car, but always negotiate the fee in advance.

Remises are unmarked radio taxis without meters that have fixed fares (comparable to taxis) within a given zone. Any business will phone one for you if you ask.

Train

For many years there were major reductions in long-distance train service in Argentina, but recent years have seen some rail lines being progressively reopened. A good source for information is www.seat61.com/southamerica.htm.

Trains continue to serve most of Buenos Aires and some surrounding provinces. During the holiday periods, such as Christmas or national holidays, buy tickets in advance. Train fares tend to be lower than comparable bus fares, but trains are slower and there are fewer departure times and destinations. Long-distance trains have sleepers.

Train buffs will want to take the narrow-gauge *La Trochita* (see p418), which runs 20km between Esquel and Nahuel Pan. Another legendary ride is Salta's touristy but spectacular *Tren a las Nubes* (Train to the Clouds; p234), which at one point spans a desert canyon at the altitude of 4220m. And finally, a scenic stretch of track (and luxurious service aboard the Tren Patagónico, see p386) connects the Lake District hub of Bariloche to Viedma, on the Atlantic coast of Patagonia.

WANT MORE?

For in-depth language information and handy phrases, check out Lonely Planet's *Latin American Spanish Phrasebook*. You'll find it at **shop.lonelyplanet.com**, or you can buy Lonely Planet's iPhone phrasebooks at the Apple App Store.

Latin American Spanish pronunciation is easy, as most sounds have equivalents in English. Read our coloured pronunciation guides as if they were English, and you'll be understood. Note that kh is a throaty sound (like the 'ch' in the Scottish *loch*), v and b are like a soft English 'v' (between a 'v' and a 'b'), and r is strongly rolled. Also note that the letters *ll* (pronounced ly or simplified to y in most parts of Latin America) and *y* are pronounced like the 's' in 'measure' or the 'sh' in 'shut' in Argentina, which gives the language its very own local flavor. In this chapter, we've used the symbol sh to represent this sound. You'll get used to this idiosyncracy very quickly listening to and taking your cues from the locals.

The stressed syllables are indicated with an acute accent in written Spanish (eg *días*) and with italics in our pronunciation guides.

The polite form is used in this chapter; where both polite and informal options are given, they are indicated by the abbreviations 'pol' and 'inf'. Where necessary, both masculine and feminine forms of words are included, separated by a slash and with the masculine form first, eg *perdido/a* (m/f).

BASICS

Hello.	*Hola.*	o·la
Goodbye.	*Adiós./Chau.*	a·*dyos*/chow
How are you?	*¿Qué tal?*	ke tal
Fine, thanks.	*Bien, gracias.*	byen *gra*·syas
Excuse me.	*Perdón.*	per·*don*
Sorry.	*Lo siento.*	lo *syen*·to
Please.	*Por favor.*	por fa·*vor*
Thank you.	*Gracias.*	*gra*·syas
You're welcome.	*De nada.*	de *na*·da
Yes./No.	*Sí./No.*	see/no

My name is ...
Me llamo ... — me *sha*·mo ...

What's your name?
¿Cómo se llama Usted? — *ko*·mo se *sha*·ma oo·*ste* (pol)
¿Cómo te llamas? — *ko*·mo te *sha*·mas (inf)

Do you speak English?
¿Habla inglés? — *a*·bla een·*gles* (pol)
¿Hablas inglés? — *a*·blas een·*gles* (inf)

I don't understand.
Yo no entiendo. — yo no en·*tyen*·do

ACCOMMODATIONS

I'd like a ... room.	*Quisiera una habitación ...*	kee·*sye*·ra *oo*·na a·bee·ta·*syon* ...
single	*individual*	een·dee·vee·*dwal*
double	*doble*	*do*·ble

Signs

Abierto	Open
Cerrado	Closed
Entrada	Entrance
Hombres/Varones	Men
Mujeres/Damas	Women
Prohibido	Prohibited
Salida	Exit
Servicios/Baños	Toilets

LUNFARDO

Below are are some of the spicier *lunfardo* (slang) terms you may hear on your travels in Argentina.

boliche – disco or nightclub
boludo – jerk, asshole, idiot; often used in a friendly fashion, but a deep insult to a stranger
bondi – bus
buena onda – good vibes
carajo – asshole, prick; bloody hell
chabón/chabona – kid, guy/girl (term of endearment)
che – hey
diez puntos – OK, cool, fine (literally '10 points')
fiaca – laziness
guita – money
laburo – job
macanudo – great, fabulous
mango – one peso
masa – a great, cool thing
mina – woman
morfar – eat
pendejo – idiot
piba/pibe – cool young guy/girl
piola – cool, clever
pucho – cigarette
re – very, eg *re interestante* (very interesting)
trucho – fake , imitation , bad quality

¡Ponete las pilas! Get on with it! (literally 'Put in the batteries!')

Me mataste. – I don't know; I have no idea. (literally 'You've killed me')

Le faltan un par de jugadores. – He's not playing with a full deck. (literally 'He's a couple of players short')

che boludo – The most *porteño* phrase on earth. Ask a friendly local youth to explain.

How much is it per night/person?
¿Cuánto cuesta por noche/persona? — kwan·to kwes·ta por no·che/per·so·na

Does it include breakfast?
¿Incluye el desayuno? — een·*kloo*·she el de·sa·*shoo*·no

campsite	*terreno de cámping*	te·re·no de *kam*·peeng
hotel	*hotel*	o·*tel*
guesthouse	*hostería*	os·te·*ree*·a
youth hostel	*albergue juvenil*	al·*ber*·ge khoo·ve·*neel*
air-con	*aire acondicionado*	*ai*·re a·kon·dee·syo·*na*·do
bathroom	*baño*	*ba*·nyo
bed	*cama*	*ka*·ma
window	*ventana*	ven·*ta*·na

DIRECTIONS

Where's ...?
¿Dónde está ...? — *don*·de es·*ta* ...

What's the address?
¿Cuál es la dirección? — kwal es la dee·rek·*syon*

Could you please write it down?
¿Puede escribirlo, por favor? — *pwe*·de es·kree·*beer*·lo por fa·*vor*

Can you show me (on the map)?
¿Me lo puede indicar (en el mapa)? — me lo *pwe*·de een·dee·*kar* (en el *ma*·pa)

at the corner	*en la esquina*	en la es·*kee*·na
at the traffic lights	*en el semáforo*	en el se·*ma*·fo·ro
behind ...	*detrás de ...*	de·*tras* de ...
far	*lejos*	*le*·khos
in front of ...	*enfrente de ...*	en·*fren*·te de ...
left	*izquierda*	ees·*kyer*·da
near	*cerca*	*ser*·ka
next to ...	*al lado de ...*	al *la*·do de ...
opposite ...	*frente a ...*	*fren*·te a ...
right	*derecha*	de·*re*·cha
straight ahead	*todo recto*	*to*·do *rek*·to

EATING & DRINKING

Can I see the menu, please?
¿Puedo ver el menú, por favor? — *pwe*·do ver el me·*noo* por fa·*vor*

What would you recommend?
¿Qué me recomienda? — ke me re·ko·*myen*·da

Do you have vegetarian food?
¿Tienen comida vegetariana? — *tye*·nen ko·*mee*·da ve·khe·ta·*rya*·na

I don't eat (red meat).
No como (carne roja). — no *ko*·mo (*kar*·ne *ro*·kha)

That was delicious!
¡Estaba buenísimo! — es·*ta*·ba bwe·*nee*·see·mo

Cheers!
¡Salud! — sa·*loo*

The bill, please.
La cuenta, por favor. — la *kwen*·ta por fa·*vor*

I'd like a table for ...	*Quisiera una mesa para ...*	kee·*sye*·ra oo·na *me*·sa *pa*·ra ...
(eight) o'clock	*las (ocho)*	las (*o*·cho)
(two) people	*(dos) personas*	(dos) per·*so*·nas

Key Words

appetisers	*aperitivos*	a·pe·ree·*tee*·vos
bottle	*botella*	bo·*te*·sha
bowl	*bol*	bol
breakfast	*desayuno*	de·sa·*shoo*·no
children's menu	*menú infantil*	me·*noo* een·fan·*teel*
(too) cold	*(muy) frío*	(mooy) *free*·o
dinner	*cena*	*se*·na
food	*comida*	ko·*mee*·da
fork	*tenedor*	te·ne·*dor*
glass	*vaso*	*va*·so
hot (warm)	*caliente*	ka·*lyen*·te
knife	*cuchillo*	koo·*chee*·yo
lunch	*almuerzo*	al·*mwer*·so
main course	*plato principal*	*pla*·to preen·see·*pal*
plate	*plato*	*pla*·to
restaurant	*restaurante*	res·tow·*ran*·te
spoon	*cuchara*	koo·*cha*·ra
with/without	*con/sin*	kon/seen

Meat & Fish

beef	*carne de vaca*	*kar*·ne de *va*·ka
chicken	*pollo*	*po*·sho
duck	*pato*	*pa*·to
fish	*pescado*	pes·*ka*·do
lamb	*cordero*	kor·*de*·ro
pork	*cerdo*	*ser*·do
turkey	*pavo*	*pa*·vo
veal	*ternera*	ter·*ne*·ra

Fruit & Vegetables

apple	*manzana*	man·*sa*·na
apricot	*damasco*	da·*mas*·ko
artichoke	*alcaucil*	al·*kow*·seel
asparagus	*espárragos*	es·*pa*·ra·gos
banana	*banana*	ba·*na*·na
beans	*chauchas*	*chow*·chas
beetroot	*remolacha*	re·mo·*la*·cha
cabbage	*repollo*	re·*po*·sho
carrot	*zanahoria*	sa·na·o·rya
celery	*apio*	*a*·pyo
cherry	*cereza*	se·*re*·sa
corn	*choclo*	*cho*·klo
cucumber	*pepino*	pe·*pee*·no
fruit	*fruta*	*froo*·ta
grape	*uvas*	*oo*·vas
lemon	*limón*	lee·*mon*
lentils	*lentejas*	len·*te*·khas
lettuce	*lechuga*	le·*choo*·ga
mushroom	*champiñón*	cham·pee·*nyon*
nuts	*nueces*	*nwe*·ses
onion	*cebolla*	se·*bo*·sha
orange	*naranja*	na·*ran*·kha
peach	*durazno*	doo·*ras*·no
peas	*arvejas*	ar·*ve*·khas
(red/green) pepper	*pimiento (rojo/verde)*	pee·*myen*·to (*ro*·kho/*ver*·de)
pineapple	*ananá*	a·na·*na*
plum	*ciruela*	seer·*we*·la
potato	*papa*	*pa*·pa
pumpkin	*zapallo*	sa·*pa*·sho
spinach	*espinacas*	es·pee·*na*·kas

EL VOSEO

Spanish in the Río de la Plata region differs from that of Spain and the rest of the Americas, most notably in the use of the informal form of 'you'. Instead of *tuteo* (the use of *tú*), Argentines commonly speak with *voseo* (the use of *vos*), a relic from 16th-century Spanish requiring slightly different grammar. All verbs change in spelling, stress and pronunciation. Examples of verbs ending in *-ar*, *-er* and *-ir* are given below – the *tú* forms are included to illustrate the contrast. Imperative forms (commands) also differ, but negative imperatives are identical in *tuteo* and *voseo*.

The Spanish phrases in this chapter use the *vos* form. An Argentine inviting a foreigner to address him or her informally will say *Me podés tutear* (literally 'You can address me with *tú*'), even though they'll use the *vos* forms in subsequent conversation.

Verb	Tuteo	Voseo
hablar (speak): You speak./Speak!	*Tú hablas./¡Habla!*	*Vos hablás./¡Hablá!*
comer (eat): You eat./Eat!	*Tú comes./¡Come!*	*Vos comés./¡Comé!*
venir (come): You come./Come!	*Tú vienes./¡Ven!*	*Vos venís./¡Vení!*

strawberry	*frutilla*	froo·tee·sha
tomato	*tomate*	to·*ma*·te
vegetable	*verdura*	ver·*doo*·ra
watermelon	*sandía*	san·*dee*·a

Other

bread	*pan*	pan
butter	*manteca*	man·*te*·ka
cheese	*queso*	*ke*·so
egg	*huevo*	*we*·vo
honey	*miel*	myel
jam	*mermelada*	mer·me·*la*·da
oil	*aceite*	a·*sey*·te
pasta	*pasta*	*pas*·ta
pepper	*pimienta*	pee·*myen*·ta
rice	*arroz*	a·*ros*
salt	*sal*	sal
sugar	*azúcar*	a·*soo*·kar
vinegar	*vinagre*	vee·*na*·gre

Drinks

beer	*cerveza*	ser·*ve*·sa
coffee	*café*	ka·*fe*
(orange) juice	*jugo (de naranja)*	*khoo*·go (de na·*ran*·kha)
milk	*leche*	*le*·che
tea	*té*	te
(mineral) water	*agua (mineral)*	*a*·gwa (mee·ne·*ral*)
(red/white) wine	*vino (tinto/ blanco)*	*vee*·no (*teen*·to/ *blan*·ko)

EMERGENCIES

Help!	*¡Socorro!*	so·*ko*·ro
Go away!	*¡Vete!*	*ve*·te

Call ...!	*¡Llame a ...!*	*sha*·me a ...
a doctor	*un médico*	oon *me*·dee·ko
the police	*la policía*	la po·lee·*see*·a

Question Words

How?	*¿Cómo?*	*ko*·mo
What?	*¿Qué?*	ke
When?	*¿Cuándo?*	*kwan*·do
Where?	*¿Dónde?*	*don*·de
Who?	*¿Quién?*	kyen
Why?	*¿Por qué?*	por ke

I'm lost.
Estoy perdido/a. — es·*toy* per·*dee*·do/a (m/f)

I'm ill.
Estoy enfermo/a. — es·*toy* en·*fer*·mo/a (m/f)

I'm allergic to (antibiotics).
Soy alérgico/a a (los antibióticos). — soy a·*ler*·khee·ko/a a (los an·tee·*byo*·tee·kos) (m/f)

Where are the toilets?
¿Dónde están los baños? — *don*·de es·*tan* los *ba*·nyos

SHOPPING & SERVICES

I'd like to buy ...
Quisiera comprar ... — kee·*sye*·ra kom·*prar* ...

I'm just looking.
Sólo estoy mirando. — *so*·lo es·*toy* mee·*ran*·do

Can I look at it?
¿Puedo verlo? — *pwe*·do *ver*·lo

I don't like it.
No me gusta. — no me *goos*·ta

How much is it?
¿Cuánto cuesta? — *kwan*·to *kwes*·ta

That's too expensive.
Es muy caro. — es mooy *ka*·ro

Can you lower the price?
¿Podría bajar un poco el precio? — po·*dree*·a ba·*khar* oon *po*·ko el *pre*·syo

There's a mistake in the bill.
Hay un error en la cuenta. — ai oon e·*ror* en la *kwen*·ta

ATM	*cajero automático*	ka·*khe*·ro ow·to·*ma*·tee·ko
credit card	*tarjeta de crédito*	tar·*khe*·ta de *kre*·dee·to
internet cafe	*cibercafé*	see·ber·ka·*fe*
market	*mercado*	mer·*ka*·do
post office	*correos*	ko·*re*·os
tourist office	*oficina de turismo*	o·fee·*see*·na de too·*rees*·mo

TIME & DATES

What time is it?	*¿Qué hora es?*	ke *o*·ra es
It's (10) o'clock.	*Son (las diez).*	son (las dyes)
It's half past (one).	*Es (la una) y media.*	es (la *oo*·na) ee *me*·dya

morning	*mañana*	ma·*nya*·na
afternoon	*tarde*	*tar*·de
evening	*noche*	*no*·che

yesterday	*ayer*	a·*sher*
today	*hoy*	oy
tomorrow	*mañana*	ma·*nya*·na

Monday	*lunes*	*loo*·nes
Tuesday	*martes*	*mar*·tes
Wednesday	*miércoles*	*myer*·ko·les
Thursday	*jueves*	*khwe*·ves
Friday	*viernes*	*vyer*·nes
Saturday	*sábado*	*sa*·ba·do
Sunday	*domingo*	do·*meen*·go

TRANSPORTATION

boat	*barco*	*bar*·ko
bus	*colectivo/ micro*	ko·lek·*tee*·vo/ *mee*·kro
plane	*avión*	a·*vyon*
train	*tren*	tren

first	*primero*	pree·*me*·ro
last	*último*	*ool*·tee·mo
next	*próximo*	*prok*·see·mo

A ... ticket, please.	*Un boleto de ..., por favor.*	oon bo·*lee*·to de ... por fa·*vor*
1st-class	*primera clase*	pree·*me*·ra *kla*·se
2nd-class	*segunda clase*	se·*goon*·da *kla*·se
one-way	*ida*	*ee*·da
return	*ida y vuelta*	*ee*·da ee *vwel*·ta

I want to go to ...
Quisiera ir a ... — kee·*sye*·ra eer a ...

Does it stop at ...?
¿Para en ...? — *pa*·ra en ...

What stop is this?
¿Cuál es esta parada? — kwal es *es*·ta pa·*ra*·da

What time does it arrive/leave?
¿A qué hora llega/ sale? — a ke *o*·ra *she*·ga/ *sa*·le

Please tell me when we get to ...
¿Puede avisarme cuando lleguemos a ...? — *pwe*·de a·vee·*sar*·me *kwan*·do she·*ge*·mos a ...

I want to get off here.
Quiero bajarme aquí. — *kye*·ro ba·*khar*·me a·*kee*

airport	*aeropuerto*	a·e·ro·*pwer*·to
bus stop	*parada de colectivo*	pa·*ra*·da de ko·lek·*tee*·vo
platform	*plataforma*	pla·ta·*for*·ma
ticket office	*taquilla*	ta·*kee*·sha
timetable	*horario*	o·*ra*·ryo
train station	*estación de trenes*	es·ta·*syon* de *tre*·nes

Numbers

1	*uno*	*oo*·no
2	*dos*	dos
3	*tres*	tres
4	*cuatro*	*kwa*·tro
5	*cinco*	*seen*·ko
6	*seis*	seys
7	*siete*	*sye*·te
8	*ocho*	*o*·cho
9	*nueve*	*nwe*·ve
10	*diez*	dyes
20	*veinte*	*veyn*·te
30	*treinta*	*treyn*·ta
40	*cuarenta*	kwa·*ren*·ta
50	*cincuenta*	seen·*kwen*·ta
60	*sesenta*	se·*sen*·ta
70	*setenta*	se·*ten*·ta
80	*ochenta*	o·*chen*·ta
90	*noventa*	no·*ven*·ta
100	*cien*	syen
1000	*mil*	meel

I'd like to hire a ...	*Quisiera alquilar ...*	kee·*sye*·ra al·kee·*lar* ...
4WD	*un todo-terreno*	oon to·do·te·*re*·no
bicycle	*una bicicleta*	*oo*·na bee·see·*kle*·ta
car	*un coche/ auto*	oon *ko*·che/ *aw*·to
motorcycle	*una moto*	*oo*·na *mo*·to

helmet	*casco*	*kas*·ko
hitchhike	*hacer dedo*	a·*ser de*·do
mechanic	*mecánico*	me·*ka*·nee·ko
petrol/gas	*nafta*	*naf*·ta
service station	*estación de servicio*	es·ta·*syon* de ser·*vee*·syo
truck	*camion*	ka·*myon*

Is this the road to ...?
¿Se va a ... por esta carretera? — se va a ... por *es*·ta ka·re·*te*·ra

Can I park here?
¿Puedo estacionar acá? — *pwe*·do e·sta·syo·*nar* a·*ka*

The car has broken down.
El coche se ha averiado. — el *ko*·che se a a·ve·*rya*·do

I've run out of petrol.
Me he quedado sin nafta. — me e ke·*da*·do seen *naf*·ta

I have a flat tyre.
Tengo una goma pinchada. — *ten*·go *oo*·na *go*·ma peen·*cha*·da

GLOSSARY

abuelos – grandparents
ACA – Automóvil Club Argentino, which provides maps, road service, insurance and other services, and operates hotels and campgrounds throughout the country
acequia – irrigation canal
aerosilla – chairlift
alcalde – mayor
alfajor – round, cookietype sandwiches layered with dulce de leche or fruit preserves
alerce – large coniferous tree, resembling a California redwood, from which Argentina's Parque Nacional Los Alerces takes its name
arrayán – tree of the myrtle family, from which Argentina's Parque Nacional Los Arrayanes takes its name
arroyo – creek, stream
arte rupestre – cave paintings
asado – the famous Argentine barbecue
autopista – freeway or motorway

baliza – emergency reflector
balneario – any swimming or bathing area, including beach resorts, river beaches and swimming holes
bandoneón – an accordion-like instrument used in tango music
barra brava – fervent soccer fan; the Argentine equivalent of Britain's 'football hooligan'
bicho – any small creature, from insect to mammal; also used to refer to an ugly person
boleadoras – weighted, leather-covered balls attached to a length of thin rope, historically used as a hunting weapon by gauchos and some of Argentina's indigenous peoples; thrown at a guanaco or rhea's legs, they entangle the animal and bring it down
boliche – nightclub or disco
bombachas – a gaucho's baggy pants; can also mean women's underwear
bombilla – metal straw with filter for drinking *mate*
buena onda – good vibes

cabildo – colonial town council; also, the building that housed the council
cacerolazo – a form of street protest; it first occurred in December 2001 when people took to their balconies in Buenos Aires banging pots and pans *(cacerolas)* to show their discontent; the banging moved to the streets, then to cities throughout Argentina, and culminated in the resignation of President de la Rua
cajero automático – ATM
caldén – a tree characteristic of the dry pampas
camarote – 1st-class sleeper
cambio – money-exchange office; also *casa de cambio*
campo – the countryside; alternately, a field or paddock
característica – telephone area code
carnavalito – traditional folk dance
carpincho – capybara, a large (but cute) aquatic rodent that inhabits the Paraná and other subtropical rivers
cartelera – an office selling discount tickets
casa de cambio – money-exchange office, often shortened to *cambio*
casa de familia – family accommodations
casa de gobierno – literally 'government house,' a building now often converted to a museum, offices etc
castellano – the term used in much of South America for the Spanish language spoken throughout Latin America; literally refers to Castilian Spanish
catarata – waterfall
caudillo – in 19th-century Argentine politics, a provincial strongman whose power rested more on personal loyalty than political ideals or party affiliation
centro cívico – civic center
cerro – hill, mountain
certificado – certified mail
chacarera – traditional folk dance
chacra – small, independent farm
chamamé – folk music of Corrientes
chimichurri – sauce made of olive oil, garlic and parsley
coche cama – sleeper class
coima – a bribe; one who solicits a bribe is a *coimero*
colectivo – local bus
combi – long-distance bus
comedor – basic cafeteria
común – common class
Conaf – Corporación Nacional Forestal, Chilean state agency in charge of forestry and conservation, including management of national parks like Torres del Paine
confitería – cafe serving light meals
conjunto – a musical band
Conquista del Desierto – Conquest of the Desert, a euphemism for General Julio Argentino Roca's late-19th-century war of extermination against the Mapuche of northern Patagonia
contrabajo – double bass
cortado – coffee with milk
correo – post office
corriente – current
costanera – seaside, riverside or lakeside road or walkway
criollo – in colonial period, an American-born Spaniard, but now used for any Latin American of European descent; the term also describes the feral cattle and horses of the pampas
cruce – crossroads

día de campo – 'day in the country,' spent at an *estancia;* typically includes an *asado,* horseback riding and use of the property's facilities
desaparecidos (los) – the disappeared; the victims (estimated at up to 30,000) of Argentina's *Guerra Sucia* who were never found
dique – a dam; the resultant reservoir is often used for recreational purposes; can also refer to a drydock
Dirty War – see *Guerra Sucia*
dorado – large river fish in the Paraná drainage, known among fishing enthusiasts as the 'Tiger of the Paraná' for its fighting spirit

edificio – a building
ejecutivo – executive class
empanadas – meat or vegetable turnovers
encomienda – colonial labor system, under which Indian communities were required to provide laborers for Spaniards *(encomenderos),* and the Spaniards were to provide religious and language instruction; in practice, the system benefited Spaniards far more than native peoples
epa – an exclamation meaning 'Hey! Wow! Look out!'
ERP – Ejército Revolucionario del Pueblo, a revolutionary leftist group in the sugar-growing areas of Tucumán province in the 1970s that modeled itself after the Cuban revolution; it was wiped out by the Argentine army during the *Guerra Sucia*
esquina – street corner
estación de servicio – gas station
estancia – extensive ranch for cattle or sheep, with an owner or manager *(estanciero)* and dependent resident labor force; many are now open to tourists for recreational activities such as riding, tennis and swimming, either for weekend escapes or extended stays
este – east

facturas – pastries
facón – a knife used by gauchos that is traditionally worn in the small of the back behind the belt
folklore – Argentine folk music; also known as folklórico
fútbol – soccer

gasolero – motor vehicle that uses diesel fuel, which is much cheaper than ordinary gasoline in Argentina
guardaganado – cattle guard (on a road or highway)
guardia – watchman
Guerra Sucia – the Dirty War of the 1970s, of the Argentine military against left-wing revolutionaries and anyone suspected of sympathizing with them; also referred to as the 'military period'
guitarrón – an oversized guitar used for playing bass lines

horario – schedule

ichu – bunch grass of the Andean altiplano
ida – one-way
ida y vuelta – roundtrip
iglesia – church
interno – internal bus-route number; also a telephone extension number
IVA – *impuesto al valor agregado;* value-added tax, often added to restaurant or hotel bills in Argentina

jejenes – annoying biting insects
jineteada – rodeo

libro de reclamos – complaint book
locutorio – private long-distance telephone office; usually offers fax and internet services as well
lunfardo – street slang

manta – a shawl or bedspread
manzana – literally, 'apple'; also used to define one square block of a city
mate – tea made from *yerba mate* leaves; Argentina is the world's largest producer and consumer of *mate* and preparing and drinking the beverage is an important social ritual; the word also refers to the *mate* gourd the tea is prepared in
mazorca – political police of 19th-century Argentine dictator Juan Manuel de Rosas
medialuna – croissant
mercado artesanal – handicraft market
meseta – interior steppe of eastern Patagonia
mestizo – a person of mixed Indian and Spanish descent
milanesa – breaded cutlets
milonga – in tango, refers to a song, a dance or the dance salon itself
minutas – snacks or short orders
mirador – scenic viewpoint, usually on a hill but often in a building
monte – scrub forest; the term is often applied to any densely vegetated area
Montoneros – left-wing faction of the Peronist party that became an underground urban guerrilla movement in 1970s
mozo – waiter
municipalidad – city hall

nafta – gasoline or petrol
neumático – spare tire
norte – north

oeste – west
Ovnis – UFOs

parada – a bus stop
paraje – pump
parrilla – mixed grill or steak house; also *parrillada*
paseo – an outing, such as a walk in the park or downtown
pato – duck; also a gaucho sport where players on horseback wrestle for a ball encased in a leather harness with handles
peatonal – pedestrian mall, usually in the downtown area of major Argentine cities

pehuén – araucaria, or 'monkey puzzle' tree of southern Patagonia
peña – club that hosts informal folk-music gatherings
percha – perch, also means coathanger
picada – in rural areas, a trail, especially through dense woods or mountains; in the context of food, hors d'oeuvres or snacks
pingüinera – penguin colony
piqueteros – picketers
piropo – a flirtatious remark
piso – floor
porteño/a – inhabitant of Buenos Aires, a 'resident of the port'
precordillera – foothills of the Andes
primera – 1st class on a train
Proceso – short for El Proceso de Reorganización Nacional, the military's euphemism for its brutal attempt to remake Argentina's political and economic culture between 1976 and 1983
propina – a tip, for example, in a restaurant or cinema
pucará – in the Andean northwest, a pre-Columbian fortification, generally on high ground commanding an unobstructed view in several directions
pulpería – a country store or tavern
puna – Andean highlands, usually above 3000m
quebracho – literally, 'axbreaker'; tree common to the Chaco that's a natural source of tannin for the leather industry

quebrada – a canyon
quincho – thatch-roof hut, now often used to refer to a building at the back of a house used for parties

rambla – boardwalk
rancho – a rural house, generally of adobe, with a thatched roof
recargo – additional charge, usually 10%, that many Argentine businesses add to credit-card transactions
reducción – an Indian settlement created by Spanish missionaries during the colonial period; the most famous are the Jesuit missions in the triple-border area of Argentina, Paraguay and Brazil
refugio – a usually rustic shelter in a national park or remote area
remise – radio taxi without a meter that generally offers fixed fares within a given zone; also *remís*
riacho – stream
ripio – gravel
rotisería – take-out shop
rotonda – traffic circle, roundabout
RN – Ruta Nacional; a national highway
RP – Ruta Provincial; a provincial highway
ruta – highway

s/n -*sin número,* indicating a street address without a number
sábalo – popular river fish in the Paraná drainage
salar – salt lake or salt pan, usually in the high Andes or Argentine Patagonia
samba – traditional folk dance
semáforo – traffic light
semi-cama – semisleeper class
sendero – a trail in the woods
servicentro – gas station
siesta – lengthy afternoon break for lunch and, sometimes, a nap
Subte – the Buenos Aires subway system
sur – south
surubí – popular river fish frequently served in restaurants

tapir – large hoofed mammal of subtropical forests in northern Argentina and Paraguay; a distant relative of the horse
tarjeta magnética – magnetic bus card
tarjeta telefónica – telephone card
tarjeta verde – 'green card'; title document for Argentine vehicles that drivers must carry
teleférico gondola cable-car
tenedor libre – all you can eat
tola – high-altitude shrubs in the altiplano of northwestern Argentina
torrontés – an Argentine white grape and wine
trapiche – sugar mill
turista – 2nd class on a train, usually not very comfortable

vereda – pathway
vicuña – wild relative of domestic llama and alpaca, found in Argentina's Andean northwest only at high altitudes
vino tinto – red wine
vinoteca – wine bar

yacaré – South American caiman, found in humid, subtropical areas
yungas – in northwestern Argentina, transitional subtropical lowland forest

zapateo – folkloric tap dance
zona franca – duty-free zone
zonda – a hot, dry wind descending from the Andes

behind the scenes

SEND US YOUR FEEDBACK

We love to hear from travelers – your comments keep us on our toes and help make our books better. Our well-traveled team reads every word on what you loved or loathed about this book. Although we cannot reply individually to postal submissions, we always guarantee that your feedback goes straight to the appropriate authors, in time for the next edition. Each person who sends us information is thanked in the next edition – the most useful submissions are rewarded with a selection of digital PDF chapters.

Visit **lonelyplanet.com/contact** to submit your updates and suggestions or to ask for help. Our award-winning website also features inspirational travel stories, news and discussions.

Note: We may edit, reproduce and incorporate your comments in Lonely Planet products such as guidebooks, websites and digital products, so let us know if you don't want your comments reproduced or your name acknowledged. For a copy of our privacy policy visit lonelyplanet.com/privacy.

OUR READERS

Many thanks to the travelers who used the last edition and wrote to us with helpful hints, useful advice and interesting anecdotes:

Leif Ahlgren, Steve Ariantaj, Valerie Ballester, Stefaan Baumont, Joerg Bongartz, Diana Brandt, Bernd Breugem, Chiara Brivio, Shiloh Burrows, Victor Cabot, Brad Cantrell, Susanne Christau, Dawn Clarke, Nicolas Combremont, Leontine Crisson, Obed Dominguez, William K Elbring, Wilma Ezekowitz, Sandrine Fecker, Bill Fellows, Marta Fernandes, Sara Francis, Adrian Frey, Carlos Garcia, Brad Gardiner, Ramrio Gonzalez, Susann Gremler, Elisabeth Haase, Chris Hastings, Daniel Hatfield, Marjolein Hettinga, Stefan Hey, Kälin Nardin Josef, Eric Jensen, Marlene Kadikowski, Angela Kaufmann, Christoph Kessel, Marcin Konczykowski, Olivia Lamont, Lone & Ronald Larsen, Sergio & Anita Macgillavry, Marta Macias, Veronika Huber & Robert Marschinski, Noa Matzliach, Lea Mayer, Chris McMahon, Alejandra Moreno, Chiara Motta, Kristin Murpf, Alec Nacamuli, Stefan Nienstedt, Jorgelina Rodriguez Otero, Christien Oudshoorn, Astrid Padberg, Christophe Poggioli, Johannes Pöhlandt, Diederik Ravesloot, Philippe Rivoal, Marcelo Rizzi, Ewa Robertson, John Rocburgh, Sander Ruitenbeek, Alan Patrick Seabright, Josephine Steininger, Paul Stoffele, Trevor Sze, Guilherme Beyer Tho, Linda Thomson, Jan Willem van Hofwegen, Olivier Verhelst, Martin Walters, Ray & Marilyn Winter, J Ronald Wolff, Sylvia M Zapiola, Abby Zeveloff

AUTHOR THANKS

Sandra Bao

I'm grateful for the support of my veteran co-authors, along with commissioning editor Kathleen Munnelly. This book wouldn't be the fine thing it is without the help from Katie Alley, Jeff Barry, Sally Blake, Michael Cando, Miriam Cutler, Gustavo Ferrari, Judy Hutton, Madi Lang, Elizabeth Lovelace, Lucas Markowiecki, Maya May, Jimena Moses, Frances Ren (and Duff), Kristie Robinson, Jed Rothenburg and Sylvia Zapiola. Thanks especially to my godmother Elsa, and lots of love to my husband and house-watcher Ben Greensfelder.

Gregor Clark

Muchísimas gracias to the dozens of Uruguayans and resident expatriates who shared Uruguay's beauty with me, especially Miguel and Monica at El Galope, Lucia and Rodney at La Sirena, Nahir, Pedro and María Rosa at Yvytu Itaty, Rodrigo and Alejandra in Punta del Este, Brian in Punta del Diablo, Alain, Florencia, Delfina, François and Danilo in Montevideo and Gloria in Colonia. Back home, *abrazos* to Gaen, Meigan and Chloe, whose love and support sustained me through 3000km of Uruguayan wanderings.

Carolyn B McCarthy

Many people make a journey. Deep gratitude goes out to those whose help and support was instrumental along the way, especially Sandra Bao, Marcelo and Cecilia, Rafael Smart, Pedro Aquino, Alejandro, Astrid and Matias. In Ushuaia, Frances Basily concocted the world's best omelet. Expert tips came from Gaston, Hernan and Anita. Finally, hats off to Nicolas Rouviere for his skillful driving, truck maintenance and overall assuring presence. And to Andres Fernandez for saving the Hilux one last time.

Andy Symington

Many helpful and friendly people offered advice, information, and assistance along the way. These include the tourist offices of Posadas, Tucumán, Chilecito and Jujuy, and numerous taxi and remise drivers always keen to impart local knowledge. Specific thanks to Sebastián Clerico, Paola Carenzo, Graciela Chávez, to my family for their support, to Kathleen Munnelly and the Lonely Planet team, to Sandra Bao and all my fellow authors. Most importantly, *mil gracias, amor* to Elena Vázquez Rodríguez for accompanying me everywhere despite the Atlantic between.

Lucas Vidgen

Thanks first and foremost to the Argentines in general for making a country that's such a joy to travel and work in. In Mendoza, Charlie O'Malley was once again a great source of information and general gossip and in Córdoba, Ana Navarta provided some invaluable insights. Diego Rossi, Facundo Carrizo and Ofelia Ledesma helped fill in some serious blanks. And as always, thanks to América, Sofía and Teresa for being there, and for being there when I got back.

ACKNOWLEDGMENTS

Climate map data adapted from Peel MC, Finlayson BL & McMahon TA (2007) 'Updated World Map of the Köppen-Geiger Climate Classification', *Hydrology and Earth System Sciences*, 11, 163344.

.Cover photograph: Guanacos in the Fitz Roy Range, Grafissimo/Getty Images. Many of the images in this guide are available for licensing from Lonely Planet Images: www.lonelyplanetimages.com.

This Book

This 8th edition of Lonely Planet's *Argentina* guidebook was researched and written by Sandra Bao, Gregor Clark, Carolyn McCarthy, Andy Symington and Lucas Vidgen. Sandra, Gregor, Andy and Lucas also worked on the previous edition, along with Bridget Gleeson. This guidebook was commissioned in Lonely Planet's Oakland office, and produced by the following:

Commissioning Editor Kathleen Munnelly

Coordinating Editor Justin Flynn

Coordinating Cartographer Valeska Cañas

Coordinating Layout Designer Virginia Moreno

Managing Editors Anna Metcalfe, Bruce Evans, Martine Power, Dianne Schallmeiner

Managing Cartographer Alison Lyall

Managing Layout Designer Jane Hart

Assisting Editors Janice Bird, Jessica Crouch, Paul Harding, Kellie Langdon, Kate Mathews, Charles Rawlings-Way

Assisting Cartographers Jane Chapman

Cover Research Naomi Parker

Internal Image Research Nicholas Colicchia

Language Content Branislava Vladisavljevic

Thanks to Melanie Dankel, Ryan Evans, Larissa Frost, Briohny Hooper, Charlotte Orr, Trent Paton, Raphael Richards, Gabbi Stefanos, Gerard Walker, Simon Williamson

A

000 Map pages
000 Photo pages

B

M

N

O

000 Map pages
000 Photo pages

P

Q

R

S

000 Map pages
000 Photo pages

T

U

how to use this book

These symbols will help you find the listings you want:

- Sights
- Beaches
- Activities
- Courses
- Tours
- Festivals & Events
- Sleeping
- Eating
- Drinking
- Entertainment
- Shopping
- Information/ Transport

These symbols give you the vital information for each listing:

- Telephone Numbers
- Opening Hours
- Parking
- Nonsmoking
- Air-Conditioning
- Internet Access
- Wi-Fi Access
- Swimming Pool
- Vegetarian Selection
- English-Language Menu
- Family-Friendly
- Pet-Friendly
- Bus
- Ferry
- Metro
- Subway
- Tram
- Train

Reviews are organised by author preference.

Look out for these Icons:

- TOP CHOICE Our author's recommendation
- FREE No payment required
- A green or sustainable option

Our authors have nominated these places as demonstrating a strong commitment to sustainability – for example by supporting local communities and producers, operating in an environmentally friendly way, or supporting conservation projects.

Map Legend

Sights
- Beach
- Buddhist
- Castle
- Christian
- Hindu
- Islamic
- Jewish
- Monument
- Museum/Gallery
- Ruin
- Winery/Vineyard
- Zoo
- Other Sight

Activities, Courses & Tours
- Diving/Snorkelling
- Canoeing/Kayaking
- Skiing
- Surfing
- Swimming/Pool
- Walking
- Windsurfing
- Other Activity/ Course/Tour

Sleeping
- Sleeping
- Camping

Eating
- Eating

Drinking
- Drinking
- Cafe

Entertainment
- Entertainment

Shopping
- Shopping

Information
- Post Office
- Tourist Information

Transport
- Airport
- Border Crossing
- Bus
- Cable Car/ Funicular
- Cycling
- Ferry
- Metro
- Monorail
- Parking
- S-Bahn
- Taxi
- Train/Railway
- Tram
- Tube Station
- U-Bahn
- Other Transport

Routes
- Tollway
- Freeway
- Primary
- Secondary
- Tertiary
- Lane
- Unsealed Road
- Plaza/Mall
- Steps
- Tunnel
- Pedestrian Overpass
- Walking Tour
- Walking Tour Detour
- Path

Boundaries
- International
- State/Province
- Disputed
- Regional/Suburb
- Marine Park
- Cliff
- Wall

Population
- Capital (National)
- Capital (State/Province)
- City/Large Town
- Town/Village

Geographic
- Hut/Shelter
- Lighthouse
- Lookout
- Mountain/Volcano
- Oasis
- Park
- Pass
- Picnic Area
- Waterfall

Hydrography
- River/Creek
- Intermittent River
- Swamp/Mangrove
- Reef
- Canal
- Water
- Dry/Salt/ Intermittent Lake
- Glacier

Areas
- Beach/Desert
- Cemetery (Christian)
- Cemetery (Other)
- Park/Forest
- Sportsground
- Sight (Building)
- Top Sight (Building)

Andy Symington
Iguazú Falls & the Northeast; Salta & the Andean Northwest Andy's relationship with Argentina is a story of four generations: his grandmother lived here in the 1920s, and her father had a *mate* plantation in Corrientes province. Andy first visited the country with his own father, the start of a long love affair that has involved many trips all around the continent, a spell living and working in Buenos Aires, and a deep-rooted respect for provincial Argentina. Andy hails from Australia, lives in northern Spain, and has contributed to many Lonely Planet guidebooks.

Lucas Vidgen
Córdoba & the Central Sierras; Mendoza & the Central Andes; Bariloche & the Lake District Lucas first visited Argentina in 2001, and was captivated by the country's wide open spaces and cosmopolitan cities. The huge amounts of quality beef and wine didn't go unnoticed, either. Lucas has contributed to a variety of Latin American Lonely Planet titles including various editions of the *Argentina* and *South America* books. He currently lives in Quetzaltenango, Guatemala where he publishes – and occasionally works on – the city's leading nightlife and culture magazine, XelaWho (www.xelawho.com).

OUR STORY

A beat-up old car, a few dollars in the pocket and a sense of adventure. In 1972 that's all Tony and Maureen Wheeler needed for the trip of a lifetime – across Europe and Asia overland to Australia. It took several months, and at the end – broke but inspired – they sat at their kitchen table writing and stapling together their first travel guide, *Across Asia on the Cheap*. Within a week they'd sold 1500 copies. Lonely Planet was born.

Today, Lonely Planet has offices in Melbourne, London and Oakland, with more than 600 staff and writers. We share Tony's belief that 'a great guidebook should do three things: inform, educate and amuse'.

OUR WRITERS

Sandra Bao

Coordinating author; Buenos Aires; The Pampas & the Atlantic Coast Sandra is a Chinese-American born in Argentina, and this fact has confused many Chinese, Americans and Argentines she's met. Perpetually peripatetic, she's traveled to around 60 countries and has lived on three continents, but now calls the beautiful Pacific Northwest home. Sandra is proud to be a *porteña* and regularly returns to Argentina to investigate what the wildly fluctuating peso – which keeps her fully employed as a guidebook researcher – is doing. As well as writing many of the chapters of this book, over the last decade Sandra has contributed to a couple of dozen Lonely Planet titles on four continents.

Read more about Sandra at:
lonelyplanet.com/members/sandrabao

Gregor Clark

Uruguay Over the past 20 years, Gregor has traveled South America from tip to tail, developing a special fondness for Uruguay while researching the last three editions of this book. Favorite memories this time around include surveying Uruguay's Atlantic coast from atop Sierra de las Ánimas, riding horses through the rocky landscape of Sierra de Rocha and searching nationwide for the perfect *chivito*. He has contributed to a dozen other Lonely Planet titles, including *Brazil* and *South America on a Shoestring*.

Read more about Gregor at:
lonelyplanet.com/members/gregorclark

Carolyn McCarthy

Patagonia, Tierra del Fuego Author Carolyn McCarthy traveled overland over 5000km in winter to make this trip, visiting hundreds of attractions and three auto mechanics along the way. When not writing about her favorite destination of Patagonia, she tries to visit tropical nations. In the last seven years she has contributed to over a dozen Lonely Planet titles. She has also written for *National Geographic*, *Outside* and *Lonely Planet Magazine*, among other publications. You can follow her Americas blog at www.carolynswildblueyonder.blogspot.com.

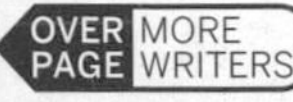

Published by Lonely Planet Publications Pty Ltd
ABN 36 005 607 983
8th edition – August 2012
ISBN 978 1 74220 015 6

10 9 8 7 6 5 4 3 2
Printed in China

Bestselling guide to Argentina – source: Nielsen BookScan, Australia, UK and USA, May 2011 to April 2012